THE DUBLIN REGION IN THE MIDDLE AGES

A

The Dublin Region in the Middle Ages

Settlement, Land-use and Economy

Margaret Murphy & Michael Potterton

MEDIEVAL RURAL SETTLEMENT PROJECT

Niall Brady, Director

B

A Discovery Programme Monograph

FOUR COURTS PRESS

Typeset in 11 pt on 15 pt Garamond by
Carrigboy Typesetting Services for
FOUR COURTS PRESS LTD
7 Malpas Street, Dublin 8, Ireland
www.fourcourtspress.ie
and in North America for
FOUR COURTS PRESS
c/o ISBS, 920 NE 58th Avenue, Suite 300, Portland, OR 97213.

A catalogue record for this title is available
from the British Library.

ISBN 978–1–84682–266–7

The Discovery Programme is grateful for the ongoing financial
support of the Heritage Council for all of its research projects.

The Discovery Programme also gratefully acknowledges
the generous financial contribution made by
Fingal County Council towards this publication.

Printed in Spain by Grafo, S.A.

Contents

Illustrations and tables

Tables

Preface

In commissioning a study of the landscape that surrounds Ireland's principal city in the medieval period, the Discovery Programme has taken a suitably bold and innovative step in Irish medieval settlement studies. It has done so within the context of the Medieval Rural Settlement Project (MRSP), which began in 2002 following a scoping study completed by Kieran O'Conor and published by the Programme in 1998. O'Conor identified that the greatest area of neglect by modern scholars was the study of the predominantly Gaelic settled areas. He also recognised that our understanding of life within the Anglo-Norman colony was vague. The MRSP is pursuing a series of modules that explore aspects of these observations. In addressing the question of Gaelic landholding, the O'Conor lordship in north Roscommon is being studied in detail by a process of intensive aerial reconnaissance which supports field-walking, environmental sampling, geophysical survey, investigation and excavation. Aspects of this module have been published and the detailed studies are due to appear in a series of monographs. The Project has also examined the documents that survive for the manor of Forth, Co. Carlow, which was held by the Bigod family in the late thirteenth century, and has conducted earthwork surveys, geophysical surveys and field-walking across the corresponding landscape at Castlemore, Co. Carlow, to present a detailed picture of an Anglo-Norman manor centre. The present volume, which is the first monograph to be published from the Project, considers a much larger landscape area, extending more than 30km around Dublin city. It is a desktop study only and assesses what insight can be achieved from the body of knowledge that exists already. The module is influenced by a research initiative of the Centre for Metropolitan History at the Institute of Historical Research, University of London that ran from 1988 to 1996 and studied the hinterland of medieval London. 'Feeding the City' was developed by a team of economic and social historians and historical geographers, whose study of documentary sources from a wide area around London has transformed the way in which medievalists study the socio-economic structure and dynamic of the later medieval countryside. The MRSP's approach is to add a new dimension by including archaeological data as the essential driving force of the present study. Archaeology in Ireland has experienced unprecedented growth in recent years, and there is considerable interest in exploring the new information that arises from such work. The Project has led Irish archaeology by initiating the first large-scale study of the excavation data, and the present volume is the first big synthesis to be published.

The authors of the volume have been its primary researchers and they were chosen for their proven expertise. Historian Dr Margaret Murphy was one of the team of scholars behind the London study. Dr Michael Potterton has published a detailed archaeological and historical study of Trim, Co. Meath. What started as a proposal to assess the viability of studying the archaeological and the historical sources evolved into the present synthesis. The volume represents the first detailed statement to be made in recent years on the development of the Dublin region and goes much further than earlier studies. It treats of secular lands as well as church lands; it considers how the land was worked; and it examines the evidence for the economic dynamic that tied the many and diverse elements together. The volume sets the scene by charting the nature of landholding on the eve of the Anglo-Norman invasion in 1169. It then develops a narrative that explores many facets of rural life throughout the high and late medieval periods to *c*.1650. What emerges is a clear sense of the richness of the sources. Margaret Murphy has been able to extract a great deal from a collection of written sources that are perhaps too often regarded as being patchy and of varied usefulness. The same sources are typical of such documents from medieval Ireland in general, and readers are afforded an inspiring insight to what can be expected with careful study from other parts of the country. In many respects, the range of sources from Ireland is more typical of those from Scotland and Wales and also from the Continent for the same period; all of these places contrast with England, where larger numbers and more continuous runs of documents survive. The Irish study may consequently be most useful as a comparator for non-English places. The archaeological data which underpins the project is merged as seamlessly as possible with the documentary material to produce a full narrative. The objective and factual insights which site assemblages can provide reveal the lives of ordinary people in ways that the written sources cannot easily achieve. This is revealed in terms of diet, trade and exchange, and also in industrial activities. The study establishes important baseline narratives while being conscious of discussions that are of interest to archaeologists and historians today. Invariably, there are areas that could be explored in further detail. As we are beginning to understand the complexity of cultural identity in medieval Ireland, future studies can now appreciate more easily the problems associated with trying to distinguish Gael from Gall; ecclesiastical from secular; rural from urban. Many details of the working manor and rural homestead remain poorly understood at present, but insights can be provided most usefully through archaeology with considered investigation strategies. The present volume lays a foundation for future research and exploration of this remarkable landscape.

The project team has relied heavily on the generosity of private sector consultancies and archaeologists who have been very happy to contribute information ahead of publication. We are also indebted to the new research that is being conducted in Irish universities by faculty and postgraduates in archaeology, history and related fields. The team appreciates the discussions that took place with the Project Committee at an early stage, and in particular we wish to thank Professor Bruce Campbell of Queen's University, Belfast, and Professor Terry Barry of Trinity College Dublin, for their support and constructive criticism. Professor Martin Carver, editor of *Antiquity*, Dr Brian Lacey, CEO of the Discovery Programme, and Raghnall Ó Floinn of the National Museum of Ireland, have been unfaltering in their encouragement. Dr Kieran O'Conor of the National University of Ireland, Galway, cast a critical eye over the manuscript in the later stages of its production, while the maps and plans have benefited greatly from the cartographic skills of Robert Shaw and Anthony Corns of the Discovery Programme. I had every intention of being more involved with this volume from the start, but the attention required of the other project modules has dictated that my own contributions have been more restricted. I am delighted to see in the present volume a realisation of an idea that occurred to me when first considering the wider Dublin area in 2002, and which was more fully forged in discussions with Terry Barry and Bruce Campbell. Margaret and Michael have accomplished a great achievement.

NIALL BRADY, FSA
Project Director
Medieval Rural Settlement Project

Editorial conventions

The conventions of *A new history of Ireland* have been followed with regard to personal names; place-names are usually given in their current English form (as used by the Ordnance Survey of Ireland), unless they are obscure or unidentifiable. Personal names of pre-1170 date are usually given in their Irish form, with later names standardised in English.

Acknowledgments

This book presents the results of a research module on the Dublin region that was undertaken as part of the Medieval Rural Settlement Project. The project was based in the Discovery Programme, Dublin, from 2002 to 2010 and was funded by the Heritage Council. The 'Dublin Module' was initiated by Dr Niall Brady, Director of the Medieval Rural Settlement Project, who first recognised the potential for a study of the rural region around the medieval capital using both archaeological and documentary sources. We are extremely grateful to Dr Brady for his role in establishing the project, for his practical support and guidance and for his contributions to this book.

Throughout the course of the research and writing, we were supported by our colleagues on the MRSP team, Anne Connon, Brian Shanahan and Rory McNeary. We are grateful to them and to our other Discovery Programme colleagues, particularly Brian Lacey, Kathleen O'Sullivan, Aoife Kane, Annaba Kilfeather, Ingelise Stuijts and Katherine Daly, for their willingness to share information and for their collegiality. Members of the DP Directorate, chaired by Michael Ryan, gave useful advice and encouragement and set us regular deadlines to keep the work on track.

The Project benefitted from a strong steering committee, and we are especially grateful for the sound advice and assistance provided by Bruce Campbell, Terry Barry, Raghnall Ó Floinn, Kieran O'Conor and Martin Carver. We received additional counsel from Umberto Albarella, Michael Ann Bevivino, Edel Bhreathnach, John Bradley, Howard Clarke, Linda Doran, Chris Dyer, Jim Galloway, Finbar McCormick, Mick Monk, Aidan O'Sullivan, Brendan Smith, Charlie Smyth and Bernadette Williams.

We would like to thank the librarians and archivists in the National Archives (London), the National Archives of Ireland, Trinity College Dublin, the National Library of Ireland, the Royal Irish Academy, the Royal Society of Antiquaries of Ireland, Hatfield House and King's Inns, who facilitated the research for this book. We are most grateful to Paul Dryburgh, who alerted us to the existence of several medieval documents in TNA and very generously allowed us to see his transcripts of Irish extents before they were published.

Robert Shaw and Anthony Corns spent hundreds of hours designing and refining maps and drawings, digitising plans and improving photographs. Without their skill and dedication, the illustrations in this book would be of much poorer quality. At an early stage, Denise Cronin digitised a series of Down Survey maps and her work is much appreciated. We are grateful to the individuals and institutions that helped us to source and allowed us to reproduce illustrations: the National Library of Ireland (especially Honora Faul, Catherine Lovett, Sandra McDermott and Colette O'Flaherty); the National Museum of Ireland (Mary Cahill, Andy Halpin, Ned Kelly, Aoife McBride, Raghnall Ó Floinn and Maeve Sikora); the Representative Church Body (Raymond Refaussé); the Royal Irish Academy (Sarah Gearty, Dave McKeon and Petra Schnabel); the Department of the Environment, Heritage and Local Government (Con Brogan, Tony Roche and Patricia Keenan); the Cambridge University Collection of Aerial Photographs (Alun Martin and Patsy Wilson-Smith); the Royal Society of Antiquaries of Ireland (Colette Ellison and Donal Fenlon); the National Archives of the UK (Paul Johnson); Lambeth Palace Library (Clare Brown); King's Inns (Jonathan Armstrong); the British Library (Auste Mickunaite);

Waterford Museum of Treasures (Rosemary Ryan); Hatfield House (Victoria Perry) and individual independent photographers (Terry Barry, Niall Brady, Michael Connaughton, Chris Corlett, Liam Coyle, Seamus Cullen, Margaret Eustice, Ronald Eustice, Karina Holton, Hugh Kavanagh, Tony Kavanagh, John Kenny, Matin Kuhn, Paddy Martin, Philip McCaffrey, Shawn McFarlane, Jason Moore, Noel Murphy, Tadhg O'Keeffe, Fionnuala Parnell, Hauke Steinberg and John Sunderland). Additional help with sourcing images was provided by Christine Baker, Chris Bolton, Patrick Bombaert, Sandra Browne, Roland Budd, Kurt Buhagiar, Catherine Bushe, Olga Caprotti, Bernat Casero Gumbau, Allister Clarke, Richard Clutterbuck, Mary Deevy, Simon Dick, Ian Doyle, Grace Fegan, Joanne Gaffrey, Vicky Ginn, Ginny Griffin, Margaret Gowen, Jim Keenan, Maria Lear, Susan Lyons, Steve Mandal, Conleth Manning, Julie Ann Matkin, Clare McCutcheon, Erika McGann, Kunak McGann, Donald Murphy, Suzanne Ní hAodha, Kevin O'Brien, Emmett O'Byrne, Fin O'Carroll, Aidan O'Connell, Edmond O'Donovan, Mike O'Neill, Aidan O'Sullivan, Colin Rynne, Linzi Simpson, Matthew Stout, David Sweetman, Claire Walsh and Heidi Ward.

A major component of this volume is formed by results from archaeological excavations across the Dublin region, and we are thankful to the consultancies, site directors and field archaeologists who gave us permission to use their work, to consult unpublished reports and surveys, and to reproduce plans and drawings. We are especially grateful to the following for their help in relation to excavations and monuments: Christine Baker, Ed Bourke, Emmet Byrnes, Laura Claffey, Rose Cleary, Richard Clutterbuck, Seamus Cullen, Niamh Doyle, Donal Fallon, Grace Fegan, Bill Frazer, Rob Goodbody, Kieron Goucher, Margaret Gowen, Eoin Grogan, Eoin Halpin, Alan Hayden, Madeleine Hill, Ruth Johnson, Annaba Kilfeather, Eoghan Kieran, Jonathan Kinsella, Ed Lyne, Conleth Manning, Melanie McQuade, Bernice Molloy, Rachel Moss, Donald Murphy, Franc Myles, Elizabeth O'Brien, Tomás Ó Carragáin, Ellen O'Carroll, Colmán Ó Clabaigh, Aidan O'Connell, David O'Connor, Edmond O'Donovan, Tadhg O'Keeffe, John Ó Néill, Hilary Opie, Emer Purcell, Sinéad Quirke, Caroline Rock, Rob Sands, Linzi Simpson, Geraldine Stout, Redmond Tobin, Claire Walsh and Angela Wallace.

To detail the ways in which each individual cooperated and assisted in the preparation of this book would necessitate a second volume, but it will at least be clear from the number of people mentioned in these acknowledgments that we received help from many quarters on a wide range of subjects. Among the others who provided us with assistance and advice over the course of the last seven years are Gillian Barrett, Fiona Beglane, Jason Bolton, Karl Brady, Thaddeus Breen, Vincent Butler, Judith Carroll, Beth Cassidy, Linda Clarke, Rose Cleary, Steve Davis, Gary Devlin, Liam Downey, Séan Duffy, Steven Ellis, George Eogan, James Eogan, Thomas Finan, Elizabeth FitzPatrick, Angela Gallagher, Eoin Grogan, Loreto Guinan, Valerie Hall, Sheila Hamilton-Dyer, Peter Harbison, Stephen Harrison, Mark Hennessy, Thomas Herron, Arlene Hogan, Karina Holton, Aideen Ireland, Stephen Johnson, Penny Johnston, Valerie Keeley, John Langdon, Jim Lydon, James Lyttleton, Ailbhe MacShamhráin, Ken McAllister, Conor McDermott, Tom McNeill, Rosanne Meenan, Michael Moore, Stephen Moorhouse, Karena Morton, Deirdre Murphy, Donald Murphy, Emily Murray, Ben Murtagh, Christopher Newman, Ken Nicholls, Emmett O'Byrne, Dáire O'Rourke, Cliona Papazian, Oliver Rackham, Raymond Refaussé, Gerry Rice, Matthew Seaver, Anngret Simms, John Soderberg, Andrew Tierney, John Vanek, Arnaud de Volder, Fintan Walsh and Joanna Wren. It is a pleasure to thank the publishers, Four Courts Press, and in particular Martin Fanning, Martin Healy, Meghan Donaldson and Anthony Tierney.

An earlier draft of this book was read in its entirety by Terry Barry, Michael Ann Bevivino, Niall Brady, Jim Galloway, Brian Lacey, Kieran O'Conor and an anonymous reviewer. We are deeply grateful to these scholars for their constructive criticism, helpful suggestions and sound advice.

MARGARET MURPHY & MICHAEL POTTERTON

Foreword

It is a very great pleasure to welcome this book. Although it deals with the hinterland of the medieval city of Dublin, this is the first major outcome from the Discovery Programme's Medieval Rural Settlement Project (MRSP). Other monographs are in preparation. This study has been greatly strengthened by its interdisciplinary nature and I want to congratulate warmly its two main authors – Dr Margaret Murphy and Dr Michael Potterton – for the way they seamlessly integrated their specialisms in history and archaeology, resulting in a richer and deeper understanding of the agricultural and maritime resources which underpinned the life of the urban population. The book is also an important exposition of the potential of archaeology to enhance the understanding of an historic period. I wish to thank all those who worked on or helped the project in their various ways. Special thanks, of course, must go to Dr Niall Brady, the Director of the MRSP, who was the first to conceive of this niche study within the project's wider scope. The study was pioneering also in that, avoiding major fieldwork itself, it sought to build on the vast amount of data already collected in the course of the development-associated archaeological excavations over the past thirty years or so. That approach has now been replicated in a number of areas of Irish archaeology – not least in other work being carried out by Dr Potterton – resulting in our much greater understanding of the disparate evidence accumulated during those years. Finally, I must repeat our thanks to the Heritage Council, which consistently supports our work, not only through its annual allocation of our core funding but in many other ways besides.

MICHAEL RYAN
Chairman, Discovery Programme

PART I

INTRODUCTION

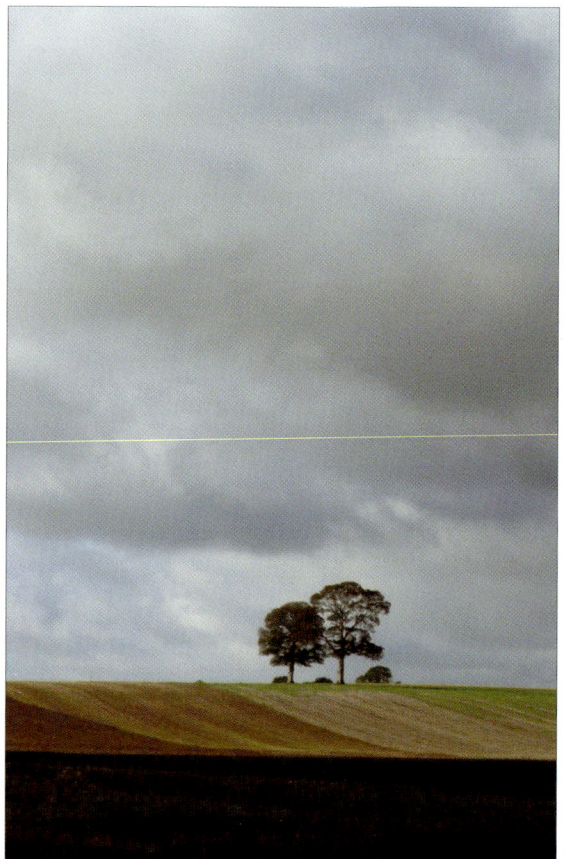

Figure 1.1 Landscapes of the Dublin region. (a) pastures near Rathdrum, Co. Wicklow (image courtesy of John Kenny); (b) the coast at Howth, Co. Dublin (image courtesy of Liam Coyle); (c) arable field near Swords, Co. Dublin (image courtesy of Fionnuala Parnell); (d) recently sown fields at Rathcoffey, Co. Kildare. The Dublin region encompasses a wide variety of terrain and ecosystems, from the wooded mountains of Wicklow to the rolling arable fields of north Dublin and Meath, and from the rich pastures of Kildare to the sometimes rugged shores and islands on the east coast. Throughout the Middle Ages, each part of this multifaceted hinterland developed a relationship with the city of Dublin, supplying it with food, raw materials and resources, generating revenue and acting as a buffer between the city and its enemies.

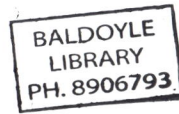

Introduction

Objectives

This is a study of the medieval region that contained and was defined by the presence of Dublin, Ireland's largest nucleated settlement. The overriding aim is to construct a picture of the medieval landscape and settlement features of the area using a wide range of archaeological and documentary sources.[1] It is primarily a study of the countryside rather than of the city, but rural-urban interaction is nevertheless an important theme. The city, then as now, profoundly affected its surrounding area, not least by its demands for food, fuel, raw materials and human resources. Although this is not a provisioning study, consideration is given to the ways in which resources may have been developed to service the city and how this affected the landscape and settlement features of the region.

In undertaking such a study, the Medieval Rural Settlement Project is breaking new ground in Ireland and is responding to a recognised need for research on urban hinterlands.[2] It is hoped that the study will lay foundations both for future work on the relationship between capital and countryside, and for studies of other urban hinterlands in Ireland that would enable the hinterland of Dublin to be compared with the hinterlands of other Irish towns, and urban centres elsewhere.

National and international contexts

The field of urban-rural relations in medieval Ireland is beginning to attract more attention from archaeologists and historians. John Bradley's important study of Scandinavian settlement appeared in 1988 and, drawing on a growing body of archaeological evidence, it depicted pre-Anglo-Norman Dublin as an urban hub within a wider rural landscape, rather than merely as a stronghold or colonial way-station.[3] Following on from Bradley's work, Mary Valante defined an 'agricultural hinterland' under the direct political control of the Viking town as well as a wider 'periphery zone' within which the inhabitants of Dublin raided and traded for the items they needed, 'establishing a web of economic activity which had the town at its centre'.[4] Valante also considered the possibility that demands from Dublin may have stimulated agricultural production in its hinterland.[5] In a more recent

---

1 Niall Brady, *Exploring Irish medieval landscapes* (Dublin, 2003), p. 30. **2** George Lambrick and Klara Spandl, *Urban archaeological practice in Ireland* (Kilkenny, 2000), pp 53–4; Gina Johnson, *Review of urban archaeology research* (Kilkenny, 2000), p. 43. **3** John Bradley, 'The interpretation of Scandinavian settlement in Ireland' in Bradley (ed.), *Settlement and society* (1988), pp 49–78; John Bradley, 'Some reflections on the problem of Scandinavian settlement in the hinterland of Dublin during the ninth century' in Bradley, Fletcher and Simms (eds), *Dublin in the medieval world* (2009), pp 39–62; see also P.F. Wallace, 'The economy and commerce of Viking-Age Dublin' in Düwel, Jankuhn, Siems and Timpe (eds), *Untersuchungen* (1987), pp 200–45. **4** Mary Valante, 'Dublin's economic relations with hinterland and periphery in the later Viking Age' in Duffy (ed.), *Medieval Dublin I* (2000), pp 69–83. **5** Ibid., pp 77–8.

Figure 1.2 Ireland, the Irish Sea, Dublin and the study area (shaded) that is the focus of this book. Dublin's location, half way down Ireland's east coast in the sheltered Liffey Estuary, allowed it to become one of the busiest ports in the Irish Sea region in the Middle Ages. It developed important trade-links with ports across the sea at Bristol and Chester, as well as many other commercial centres along the coastal fringes of northern and western Europe. As it evolved, Dublin's reliance on, and influence over, its own hinterland intensified and became more complex.

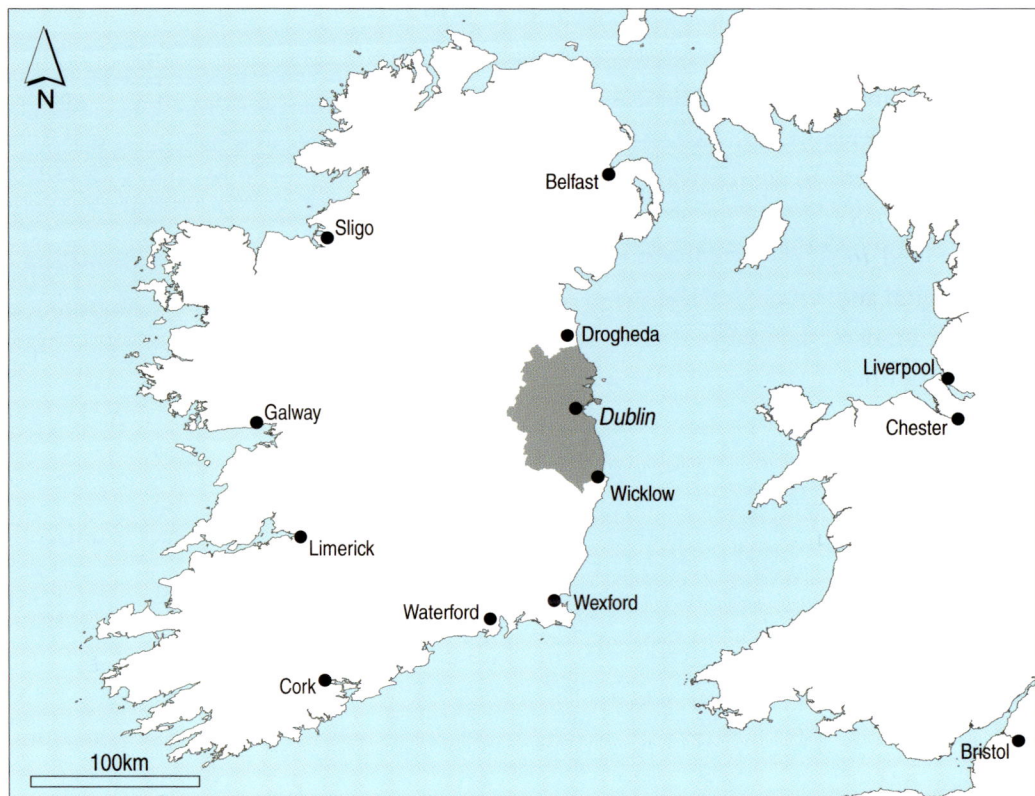

Figure 1.2 Ireland, the Irish Sea, Dublin and the study area (shaded) that is the focus of this book. Dublin's location, half way down Ireland's east coast in the sheltered Liffey Estuary, allowed it to become one of the busiest ports in the Irish Sea region in the Middle Ages. It developed important trade-links with ports across the sea at Bristol and Chester, as well as many other commercial centres along the coastal fringes of northern and western Europe. As it evolved, Dublin's reliance on, and influence over, its own hinterland intensified and became more complex.

study, the same author has proposed that Viking Waterford and Limerick were similarly at the centre of trade and provisioning hinterlands, although their spheres of activity were more restricted than that of Dublin.[6]

There has been growing awareness among archaeologists of the possibilities of using urban evidence to explore rural environments and the ways in which townspeople exploited the countryside of the immediate hinterland to provide food and shelter. This research has been driven by the increase in expertise in palaeo-environmental investigation and the expanding body of data regarding diet, fuel, crop-processing and local environment, much of which comes from the evidence of plant microfossils, insect remains and charred residues. Two separate studies published in 1990 demonstrate the potential for palaeo-environmental research to contribute to an understanding of early land-use and agricultural activity in Ireland.[7] In the same way, it is now widely acknowledged that 'archaeological timbers provide a unique archive for the reconstruction of contemporary rural woodlands',[8] and that 'insect evidence is extremely important in indicating not just woodland presence, but the nature of that woodland'.[9]

Siobhán Geraghty's 1996 analysis of botanical evidence from Viking Dublin recognised that urban plant remains reveal much about hinterland conditions.[10] This work included a discussion of the managed countryside surrounding Dublin and put forward estimates of

---

6 Mary Valante, *The Vikings in Ireland: settlement, trade and urbanization* (Dublin, 2008), pp 140–4, 163.   **7** Valerie Hall, 'Ancient agricultural activity at Slieve Gullion, Co. Armagh: the palynological and documentary evidence', *PRIA*, 90C5 (1990), 123–34; Valerie Hall, 'The documentary and pollen analytical records of the vegetational history of the Irish landscape, AD200–1650', *Peritia*, 14 (2000), 342–71; Michael O'Connell, 'Early land-use in north-east County Mayo: the palaeoecological evidence', *PRIA*, 90C9 (1990), 259–79.   **8** Aidan O'Sullivan, 'The wooden waterfronts: a study of their construction, carpentry and use of trees and woodlands' in Halpin, *The port of medieval Dublin* (2000), pp 62–92; Damian Goodburn, 'Waterlogged wood and timber as archives of ancient landscapes' in Coles and Goodburn (eds), *Wet site excavation and survey* (1991), pp 51–3; Damian Goodburn, 'Trees underground: new insights into trees and woodmanship in south-east England, *c*.AD800–1300', *BJS*, 46 (1994), 658–62.   **9** Eileen Reilly, 'The contribution of insect remains to an understanding of the environment of Viking-Age and medieval Dublin' in Duffy (ed.), *Medieval Dublin IV* (2003), pp 40–62 at p. 56.   **10** Siobhán Geraghty, *Viking Dublin: botanical evidence from Fishamble Street* (Dublin, 1996), pp 57–71.

the scale of the city's requirements and the effect of these demands on the hinterland area. By using data relating to the density of settlement within the excavated area of Dublin, Geraghty estimated that the town *c.*1050–1100 had a population of 4,500 and she went on to postulate the requirements of Dublin in terms of building wood and bread grains and to suggest the hinterland areas needed to supply these products.[11] In much the same way, Aidan O'Sullivan's 1998 study of the ways in which woodlands in the Dublin region were managed and exploited to supply the building and fuel requirements of the city illustrated how archaeological and palaeo-botanical evidence can be integrated with documentary material.[12]

Publications arising out of excavations carried out in Waterford in the 1980s and 1990s and in Cork from 1942 to 2000 appeared in 1997 and 2003.[13] Both books included specialist chapters on faunal and plant remains that discussed the provenance of urban supplies and the relationships between these towns and their agricultural hinterlands in the medieval period. Finbar McCormick's analysis of the large sample of animal bones from Waterford allowed him to chart change over time in the relative importance of species and to link this with changing patterns of agrarian exploitation of the surrounding countryside.[14] There is growing awareness of the importance of animal-bone assemblages and the potential they have to provide information about agricultural practices, breeding and processing.[15] The heightened awareness of the significance of archaeo-zoological remains means that there is now sufficient material for comparative analyses to be carried out, and some work of this kind has recently been completed for Dublin.[16] The rapidly increasing number of excavations, the rise in the number of specialists in areas such as osteo-archaeology and palaeo-botany, and the improved accessibility of a burgeoning corpus of data means that the time has never been better for studies of this type.[17]

Similar work is being undertaken in Britain and Europe, where among archaeologists, the themes of urban-rural relations and the functioning of towns within their regions were identified relatively recently as topics requiring investigation and research.[18] The potential of archaeological data in this regard has begun to be realised, particularly through the work of projects such as the Urban Hinterlands Project, the York Environs Project and the Wroxeter Hinterland Project, and the work on Novgorod and its hinterland.[19] In a number of

11 Geraghty, *Viking Dublin*, pp 57–71.   **12** Aidan O'Sullivan, 'Woodmanship and the supply of underwood and timber to Anglo-Norman Dublin' in Manning (ed.), *Dublin and beyond the Pale* (1998), pp 59–70.   **13** M.F. Hurley and O.M.B. Scully, with S.W.J. McCutcheon, *Late Viking-Age and medieval Waterford: excavations 1986–1992* (Waterford, 1997); R.M. Cleary and Maurice Hurley (eds), *Cork City excavations, 1984–2000* (Cork, 2003).   **14** Finbar McCormick, 'The animal bones' in Hurley et al., *Late Viking-Age and medieval Waterford* (1997), pp 819–53.   **15** Finbar McCormick and Emily Murray, *Knowth and the zooarchaeology of Early Christian Ireland* (Dublin, 2007); Dominic Perring, *Town and country in England: frameworks for archaeological research* (CBA Research Report, 134, 2002), pp 34–42; I.W. Cornwall, *Bones for the archaeologist* (London, 1956); S.J.M. Davis, *The archaeology of animals* (New Haven, 1987); Annie Grant, 'The use of tooth-wear as a guide to the age of domestic ungulates' in Bob Wilson, Caroline Grigson and Sebastian Payne (eds), *Ageing and sexing animal bones from archaeological sites* (BAR British Series, 109, 1982), pp 91–108; T.P. O'Connor, 'What shall we have for dinner? Food remains from urban sites' in Serjeantson and Waldron (eds), *Diet and crafts in towns* (1989), pp 13–23; Dale Serjeantson and Tony Waldron (eds), *Diet and crafts in towns: the evidence of animal remains from the Roman to the post-medieval period* (BAR British Series, 199, 1989); Jennifer Bourdillon, 'Countryside and town: the animal resources of Saxon Southampton' in Della Hooke (ed.), *Anglo-Saxon settlements* (Oxford and New York, 1988), pp 177–95.   **16** S.J. Turrell, 'The archaeozoology of medieval Dublin and Ireland' (MSc, QUB, 2003); Ciara MacManus, 'A study of excavated animal bones from thirteenth- to eighteenth-century Dublin' (BSc, QUB, 1995).   **17** For a discussion of this material and its potential for archaeological and historical research, see Margaret Murphy and Michael Potterton, 'Investigating living standards in medieval Dublin and its region' in Duffy (ed.), *Medieval Dublin VI* (2005), pp 224–56.   **18** John Schofield and Alan Vince, *Medieval towns* (Leicester, 1994), esp. ch. 8, 'Unfinished business and further questions', pp 204–14.   **19** Perring, 'Town and country in England'; Kate Giles and Christopher Dyer (eds), *Town and country in the Middle Ages: contrasts, contacts and interconnections, 1100–1500* (Leeds, 2005); P.V. Addyman, 'York in its archaeological setting' in P.V. Addyman and V.E. Black (eds), *Archaeological papers from York presented to M.W. Barley* (York, 1984), pp 7–21; J. Chartrand, J.D. Richards and B.E. Vyner, 'Bridging the urban-rural gap: GIS and the York Environs Project' in Jens Andersen, Irwin Scollar and Torsten Madsen (eds), *CAA92: computer applications and quantitative methods in archaeology* (Aarhus, 1993), pp 159–66; Vincent Gaffney, R.H. White and S.T.E. Buteux, 'Wroxeter, the Cornovii and the urban process: final report on the work of the Wroxeter Hinterland Project and Wroxeter Hinterlands Survey, 1994–1999' (forthcoming); Mark Brisbane and

countries, archaeological research is being used increasingly in studies of provisioning networks and trade hinterlands.[20]

British and European historians have been researching urban regions for some time, although there has been a recent increase in emphasis on this type of study. Many important works on English urban history have focused on the economic relationship between towns and their regions.[21] Recent publications illustrate the wide range of studies being conducted throughout Europe, and further afield, frequently in the context of research projects.[22] There has also been a significant escalation in the level of interest displayed in the role of urban centres as promoters of rural development and general economic growth.[23] Research on urban provisioning is also increasing.[24] The first book-length study of the grain supply of a medieval city was produced in 1993 by the 'Feeding the City' research project based in London.[25] This has been followed by papers on London's fuel supply and the changing nature of the grain supply in the post-Black Death period.[26] A recent study of the food and fuel supply of late medieval Cambridge (c.1450–1560) has explicitly applied the Feeding the City approach to a smaller urban centre in England, while in continental Europe, several towns have been the subject of provisioning studies.[27] Medieval Dublin was, of course, considerably smaller in size and population than medieval London – perhaps seven or eight times smaller according to one recent commentator.[28] Nonetheless, the same writer argues that in many other respects Dublin bore more similarity to London than to some of the larger provincial cities of medieval England, such as Bristol and Norwich, with which it had more in common in terms of size.

David Gaimster (eds), *Novgorod: the archaeology of a Russian medieval city and its hinterland* (British Museum Occasional Paper, 141, London, 2001); Mark Brisbane (ed.), *The archaeology of Novgorod, Russia: recent results from the town and its hinterland* (Society for Medieval Archaeology monograph series, 13, Lincoln, 1992). **20** Umberto Albarella, 'Meat production and consumption in town and country' in Giles and Dyer (eds), *Town and country in the Middle Ages* (2005), pp 131–48; Maureen Mellor, 'Making and using pottery in town and country' in Giles and Dyer (eds), *Town and country in the Middle Ages* (2005), pp 149–64; Jennifer Bourdillon, 'The animal provisioning of Saxon Southampton' in D.J. Rackham (ed.), *Environment and economy in Anglo-Saxon England* (CBA Research Report, 89, 1994), pp 120–5; O'Connor, 'What shall we have for dinner?'. **21** R.H. Britnell, *Growth and decline in Colchester, 1300–1525* (Cambridge, 1986); D.J. Keene, *Survey of medieval Winchester*, Winchester Studies, 2 (Oxford, 1985); D.J. Keene, 'Medieval London and its region', *London Journal*, 14 (1989), 99–111; Maryanne Kowaleski, *Local markets and regional trade in medieval Exeter* (Cambridge, 1995); Richard Holt, 'Gloucester in the century after the Black Death' in Holt and Rosser (eds), *The English medieval town* (1990), pp 141–59; Giles and Dyer (eds), *Town and country in the Middle Ages*; N.J. Higham, 'Changing spaces: towns and their hinterlands in the north-west, AD900–1500' in Gardiner and Rippon (eds), *Medieval landscapes* (2007), pp 57–70. **22** See, for example, S.R. Epstein (ed.), *Town and country in Europe* (Cambridge, 2001); J.A. Galloway (ed.), *Trade, urban hinterlands and market integration, c.1300–1600* (Centre for Metropolitan History Working Papers, 3, 2000); Michael Limberger, *Sixteenth-century Antwerp and its rural surroundings: social and economic changes in the hinterland of a commercial metropolis* (ca.1450–ca.1570) (Studies in European Urban History, 14 (1100–1800), Turnhout, Belgium, 2008); John Bintliff, Phil Howard and Anthony Snodgrass, *Testing the hinterland: the work of the Boeotia Survey (1989–1991) in the southern approaches to the city of Thespiai* (Cambridge, 2007); Alan Kolata, 'Tiwanaku and its hinterland', *Archaeology*, 40:1 (Jan./Feb. 1987), 36–41; Alan Kolata, *Tiwanaku and its hinterland: agroecology vol. 1: archaeology and palaeoecology of an Andean civilization* (Washington DC, 1996); Alan Kolata, *Tiwanaku and its hinterland: urban and rural archaeology vol. 2: archaeology and paleoecology of an Andean civilization* (Washington DC, 2003); Neville Morley, *Metropolis and hinterland: the city of Rome and the Italian economy, c.200BC–AD200* (Cambridge, 1996). See also the regional surveys by various authors in D.M. Palliser (ed.), *The Cambridge Urban History of Britain, Volume I, 600–1540* (Cambridge, 2000). **23** R.H. Britnell, *The commercialisation of English society, 1100–1500* (Cambridge, 1993); Jim Masschaele, *Peasants, merchants, and markets: inland trade in medieval England, 1150–1350* (New York, 1997). **24** For a summary, see Margaret Murphy, 'Feeding medieval cities: some historical approaches' in Carlin and Rosenthal (eds), *Food and eating in medieval Europe* (1998), pp 117–31. **25** B.M.S. Campbell, J.A. Galloway, D.J. Keene and Margaret Murphy, *A medieval capital and its grain supply: agrarian production and distribution in the London region, c.1300* (Historical Geography Research Series, 30, 1993). **26** J.A. Galloway, D.J. Keene and Margaret Murphy, 'Fuelling the city: production and distribution of firewood and fuel in London's region, 1290–1400', *EcHR*, 49:3 (1996), 447–72; J.A. Galloway, 'London's grain supply: changes in production, distribution and consumption during the fourteenth century', *Franco-British Studies*, 20 (1995), 23–34. **27** J.S. Lee, 'Feeding the colleges: Cambridge's food and fuel supplies, 1450–1560', *Economic History Review*, 41:2 (2003), 243–64; See Anon, *L'approvisionnement des villes de l'Europe occidentale au moyen âge et aux temps modernes* (Cinquièmes journées internationales d'histoire, 1985; Auch, Centre culturel de l'abbaye de Flaran). **28** H.B. Clarke, 'London and Dublin' in Francesca Bocchi (ed.), *Medieval metropolises: proceedings of the Congress of the Atlas Working Group, International Commission for the History of Towns* (Bologna, 1998), pp 103–25 at p. 122. For a discussion of Dublin's medieval population, see below, pp 30–1.

In Ireland, there has been a significant increase in work on and interest in medieval towns, and medieval Dublin in particular.[29] To date, however, documentary studies have tended to concentrate on Dublin's political relationship with its region in the medieval period and only the historians of the sixteenth and seventeenth centuries engaged with the themes of economic interaction and relations between town and country.[30] There has, of course, been significant research on the various forms of settlement in the Dublin area, even if it has not dealt specifically with this theme. In 1838, John D'Alton published one of the first detailed local histories produced in Ireland.[31] D'Alton was especially interested in family histories and antiquities, and his 1,000-page *History of Dublin* goes through the county, barony-by-barony, providing topographical, economic and cultural information on every town, village and location of note. Written a century ago, Elrington Ball's six-volume history of Co. Dublin gives detailed and scholarly accounts of the history of the county's parishes from their earliest records down to the start of the twentieth century.[32] Ball was also one of the contributors (along with T.J. Westropp, R.L. Praeger and others) to the *Handbook to the city of Dublin and the surrounding district*, first published in 1908.[33] This important book on Dublin and its wider region begins with a discussion of the local geology and contains a lengthy section on the archaeology and history of the region – including sections on Meath and Wicklow. Written over a hundred years ago, the book was already lamenting the fact that 'owing to its extension during the last century, Dublin has lost some of its more immediate rural environment'.[34] In assessing the medieval sources for the region, its authors concluded that 'until more progress is made in the examination of Irish manuscripts, it is not possible to write with authority on that portion [medieval] of the county's history'.[35]

A more recent publication on the settlement landscape of the Dublin area is Anngret Simms' and Patricia Fagan's study of the origins, forms and functions of villages in Co. Dublin.[36] There have been several other studies of medieval settlement, agriculture and land-use relating specifically to the Dublin area or drawing considerably on sources concerning this region.[37] Some manors in or near Co. Dublin have been the subject of individual research.[38] A recent study of the environmental history of medieval Co. Dublin was based on evidence relating to the archiepiscopal manors in the county.[39] To date, however, the only study that includes an analysis of agriculture in the region based on the evidence of several manors remains unpublished.[40]

Other recent works cover aspects of settlement in Dublin and surrounding counties; such as the evolution of fortifications, the foundation of boroughs and the distribution of

29 See the selected bibliography in H.B. Clarke, *IHTA: Dublin, part 1, to 1610* (Dublin, 2002), pp 33–6. **30** Colm Lennon, *The lords of Dublin in the age of reformation* (Dublin, 1989), ch. 1; Raymond Gillespie, 'Dublin 1600–1700: a city and its hinterlands' in Clark and Lepetit (eds), *Capital cities and their hinterlands* (1996), pp 84–104. **31** John D'Alton, *The history of the county of Dublin* (Dublin, 1838; 2nd ed., Cork, 1976). **32** F.E. Ball, *A history of the county of Dublin* (6 vols, Dublin, 1902–20). **33** G.A.J. Cole and R.L. Praeger (eds), *Handbook to the city of Dublin and the surrounding district* (Dublin, 1908). **34** Ibid., pp 223–4. **35** Ibid., p. 225. **36** Anngret Simms and Patricia Fagan, 'Villages in Co. Dublin: their origins and inheritance' in Aalen and Whelan (eds), *Dublin city and county* (1992), pp 79–119. **37** Kevin Down, 'Colonial society and economy' in Cosgrove (ed.), *A new history of Ireland: II* (1993), pp 439–91; Helmut Jäger, 'Land-use in medieval Ireland: a review of the documentary evidence', *IESH*, 10 (1983), 51–65; James Mills, 'Tenants and agriculture near Dublin in the fifteenth century', *JRSAI*, 21 (1891), 54–63; A.J. Otway-Ruthven, 'The organisation of Anglo-Irish agriculture in the Middle Ages', *JRSAI*, 81 (1951), 1–13. **38** Anngret Simms, 'Rural settlement in medieval Ireland: the example of the royal manors of Newcastle Lyons and Esker in south County Dublin' in B.K. Roberts and R.E. Glasscock (eds), *Villages, fields and frontiers: studies in European rural settlement in the medieval and early modern periods* (BAR International Series, 185, 1983), pp 133–52; D.N. Hall, Mark Hennessy and Tadhg O'Keeffe, 'Medieval agriculture and settlement in Oughterard and Castlewarden, Co. Kildare', *IG*, 18 (1985), 16–25; J.J. O'Loan, 'The manor of Cloncurry, Co. Kildare, and the feudal system of land tenure in Ireland', *Department of Agriculture Journal*, 18 (1961), 14–36; Karina Holton, 'Cloncurry, County Kildare' in Connell, Cronin and Ó Dálaigh (eds), *Irish townlands* (1998), pp 43–68; Anngret Simms and John Bradley, 'The geography of Irish manors: the example of the Llanthony cells of Duleek and Colp in Co. Meath' in Bradley (ed.), *Settlement and society* (1988), pp 291–326. **39** Teresa Bolger, 'An analysis of the environmental history of medieval County Dublin based on Archbishop Alen's register, *c*.1172–1534' in Duffy (ed.), *Medieval Dublin VIII* (2008), pp 287–317. **40** M.C. Lyons, 'Manorial administration and the manorial economy in Ireland, *c*.1200–*c*.1377' (PhD, TCD, 1984).

parish churches.[41] Closer to the city, an important study of Dublin's suburbs highlighted their extent and the varying ways in which they were used by their inhabitants and exploited by the city.[42] This has provided the impetus for further studies of land-use in areas close to the city such as Oxmantown and the western suburb.[43]

The reluctance of historians to address the topic of medieval Dublin's relationship with its hinterland is surprising, given the impetus provided by the inclusion of Dublin along with Ghent and London as one of the 'North Sea Regions' in Russell's 1972 work on medieval cities and regions.[44] Scholars in Ireland appear to have been reluctant to engage with this research, but this may be due to the fact that much of it, particularly the population estimates, has subsequently been criticised if not derided.[45]

Discussion of the relationship between medieval Dublin and its hinterland must necessarily address the question of the probable size of the city as well as the population density in the rural areas surrounding it. Most commentators would agree that the population of the city reached its medieval peak between the years 1250 and 1300, but whether that figure was as low as 10,000 or as high as 20,000 is a matter of debate. In the 1960s, Thomas Hollingsworth used the roll recording the names of people admitted to the Dublin guild of merchants to produce a population estimate of about 20,000 for 1246.[46] Little certitude can be attached to this figure as it involved estimates of numbers of guild members and of family size. Furthermore, it is generally acknowledged that membership of the merchants' guild did not necessarily imply long-term residence in the city, and this is certainly suggested by many of the surnames listed in the guild merchant roll. J.C. Russell posited a population figure of 11,000 for late thirteenth-century Dublin but, while this figure is frequently cited, it has little sound historical basis.[47] The Black Death of 1348 undoubtedly had a severe impact on population levels and it has recently been estimated that Dublin and its region suffered a 40 per cent reduction of population through a combination of mortality and emigration.[48] If the report of the Franciscan chronicler John Clyn that 14,000 people died in Dublin between August and Christmas 1348 was in any way accurate, then the population of the city must have been well over 20,000 in the mid-fourteenth century.[49] It seems likely that the city did not recover its pre-plague levels until the seventeenth century. Gearóid Mac Niocaill has used the early sixteenth-century tithe figures supplied by the

41 Tadhg O'Keeffe, 'Medieval frontiers and fortifications: the Pale and its evolution' in Aalen and Whelan (eds), *Dublin city and county* (1992), pp 57–78; John Bradley, 'The medieval boroughs of Co. Dublin' in Manning (ed.), *Dublin and beyond the Pale* (1998), pp 129–44; Linzi Simpson, 'Anglo-Norman settlement in Uí Briuin Cualann' in Hannigan and Nolan (eds), *Wicklow: history and society* (1994), pp 191–236; B.J. Graham, 'Anglo-Norman settlement in County Meath', *PRIA*, 125CII (1975), 223–48; B.J. Graham, 'The evolution of the settlement pattern of Anglo-Norman Eastmeath' in Buchanan, Butlin and McCourt (eds), *Fields, farms and settlement in Europe* (1976), pp 38–47; A.J. Otway-Ruthven, 'The medieval county of Kildare', *IHS*, 11:43 (1958–9), 181–99; Elizabeth O'Brien, 'Churches of south-east County Dublin, seventh to twelfth century' in Mac Niocaill and Wallace (eds), *Keimelia* (1988), pp 504–24; Mairín Ní Mharcaigh, 'The medieval parish churches of south-west Dublin', *PRIA*, 97C5 (1997), 245–96; Ailbhe MacShamhráin, 'The *Monasticon Hibernicum* project: the diocese of Dublin' in Duffy (ed.), *Medieval Dublin VI* (2005), pp 114–43; Michael O'Neill, 'The medieval parish churches of County Kildare' in Nolan and McGrath (eds), *Kildare: history and society* (2006), pp 153–93; Michael O'Neill, 'The medieval parish churches of County Kildare', *JCKAHS*, 19:3 (2004–5), 406–46; Michael O'Neill, 'The medieval parish churches in County Meath', *JRSAI*, 132 (2002), 1–56. **42** H.B. Clarke, '*Urbs et suburbium*: beyond the walls of medieval Dublin' in Manning (ed.), *Dublin and beyond the Pale* (1998), pp 45–58.   **43** Emer Purcell, 'Land-use in medieval Oxmantown' in Duffy (ed.), *Medieval Dublin IV* (2003), pp 193–228; Emer Purcell, 'The city and the suburb: medieval Dublin and Oxmantown' in Duffy (ed.), *Medieval Dublin VI* (2005), pp 188–223; Cathal Duddy, 'The western suburb of medieval Dublin: its first century', *IG*, 34:2 (2001), 157–75.   **44** J.C. Russell, *Medieval regions and their cities* (Newton Abbot, 1972).   **45** Gearóid Mac Niocaill, 'Socio-economic problems of the late medieval town' in Harkness and O'Dowd (eds), *The town in Ireland* (1981), pp 7–21 at p. 18; Clarke, 'London and Dublin', p. 107.   **46** T.H. Hollingsworth, *Historical demography* (London, 1969), pp 268–70. The roll recording admissions is printed in Philomena Connolly and Geoffrey Martin (eds), *The Dublin guild merchant roll, c.1190–1265* (Dublin, 1992), referred to hereafter as *DGMR*.   **47** J.C. Russell, 'Late thirteenth-century Ireland as a region', *Demography*, 3 (1966), 500–12.   **48** Maria Kelly, *The great dying: the Black Death in Dublin* (Stroud, Gloucestershire, 2003), pp 84–92.   **49** Bernadette Williams (ed.), *The annals of Ireland by Friar John Clyn* (Dublin, 2007), pp 246–7.

monastic extents to postulate (with many caveats!) a population of 8,000 for Dublin in 1540, and even as late as 1650, only 20,000 are estimated to have been living in Dublin.[50] A further complicating factor is the inclusion or exclusion of the suburban area in these calculations. Howard Clarke has proposed that, at the beginning of the fourteenth century, somewhere in the order of 80 per cent of the population of Dublin may have been living outside the city walls.[51]

Estimating the population size of any medieval city or region is problematic, but the case of Dublin, which lacks any quantifiable benchmark such as the 1377 poll-tax provides for English towns or the lists of inhabitants that survive for some continental cities, is immeasurably more difficult. A recent study that acknowledges the lack of population evidence for Ireland has suggested using the numerical count of parishes *c*.1300 to provide crude average densities at a national level. This undoubtedly will provide grounds for future research and debate.[52]

While there is uncertainty regarding the numbers living in or near Dublin at various points in the Middle Ages, it is clear, even at the most conservative population estimates, that the medieval city was sufficiently large for its demands to influence a substantial hinterland. Evidence of this impact can be found in the archaeological and documentary records.

Spatial limits

This monograph is the result of a four-year research project. It focuses on a spatially defined area in which systematic and intensive research was carried out. In order to encompass a study area that was large enough to identify patterns of development across the medieval hinterland, it was decided to select a 30km orbital zone around the city as the primary geographical focus. This does not imply a belief that urban regions were geometrically delineated or that they remained static over time. They were moulded by physical features and expanded and contracted in line with population changes. In medieval Ireland, endogenous dynamics, such as growing political instability, and exogenous factors, such as the requisitioning of resources to sustain overseas military campaigns, distorted the nature of provisioning networks considerably. The rationale for defining such a study area is also influenced by research on urban regions in other countries. These studies have shown that towns of widely varying population tended to have quite similarly sized local trade hinterlands. These zones can be related to the limits of direct provisioning in pre-industrial societies, which rarely exceeded 30 or 40km.[53] Comparative studies, such as that of medieval Bordeaux, also highlight the need to be flexible with respect to the perimeters of the study area.[54] While the core study area for the Dublin module comprises the 30km zone, a broader area has been defined to include fully each barony that is intersected by the 30km 'buffer'.[55] The extended area allows flexibility to include those sites and records that lie beyond the limit but nonetheless remain important to the study (Figures 1.2, 1.3).

50 Mac Niocaill, 'Socio-economic problems', p. 19.   **51** Clarke, '*Urbs et suburbium*', p. 48.   **52** H.B. Clarke, 'Population' in Duffy (ed.), *Medieval Ireland: an encyclopedia* (2005), pp 383–4.   **53** J.A. Galloway, 'Town and country in England, 1300–1570' in Epstein (ed.), *Town and country in Europe* (2001), pp 106–31 at p. 112; G.W. Grantham, 'Espaces privilégiés: productivité agraire et zones d'approvisionnement des villes dans l'Europe préindustrielle', *Annales*, 52 (1997), 695–726; S.H. Rigby, *Medieval Grimsby: growth and decline* (Hull, 1993), passim; P.J. Goodman, *The Roman city and its periphery: from Rome to Gaul* (London and New York, 2007), pp 20–1.   **54** Michel Bochaca, 'L'aire d'influence et l'espace de relations économiques de Bordeaux vers 1475' in Noël Coulet and Olivier Guyotjeannin (eds), *La ville au moyen âge* (Paris, 1998), pp 279–92.   **55** It is not possible to perfectly trace the exact boundaries of the medieval baronies, but the post-medieval borders used for the purposes of this study are likely to closely mirror their antecedents. Upper Duleek, Lower Talbotstown and Ballinacor North are included, but Lower Duleek, Upper Talbotstown and Ballinacor South, which lie entirely outside the 30km buffer, are not.

The study area incorporates Co. Dublin and parts of Cos. Kildare, Meath and Wicklow. Southwards, it includes the settlements of Dalkey, Bray, Greystones, Kilcoole, Newtown-mountkennedy and Roundwood, with Wicklow town just beyond its most southerly coastal extent. It reaches south-west past Blessington, Naas and Ballymore Eustace, as far as Dunlavin. Due west of Dublin lie Leixlip, Maynooth and Kilcock, and beyond these, Cloncurry is at the western edge of the study area. Dunshaughlin, Ashbourne, Swords and Skerries are all comfortably within the northern part of the area, while Duleek, Navan and Trim fall just outside it. Drogheda, a town with which Dublin had many important links throughout the Middle Ages, also lies outside the study area, being some 45km north of Dublin. The total study area comprises 2,827km^2 and contains approximately 282,743 hectares (698,686 acres).

Figure 1.4 Primary physical features of the landscape surrounding Dublin, showing a low-lying river basin of well-drained land in the central area and to the north, with the contrasting uplands of the Wickow Mountains to the south.

Physical characteristics (by Niall Brady)

The landscape of the study area is dominated by the broad, low-lying floodplain of the River Liffey, which empties into the Irish Sea at Dublin, and extends westwards through north Co. Kildare before turning south to its point of origin in the Wicklow Mountains (Figure 1.4). To the north, the same rolling flatland occurs, and if the study area was extended in this direction it would encounter the river valley and floodplain of the Boyne. The rich floodplain context provides an ideal environment for agrarian enterprise, and this potential is enhanced by the nature of the underlying soils. In contrast, the northern extent of the Wicklow Mountains in the south of the study area presents a different topographical environment, while the coastal zone adds a third ecosystem to the region. The area selected for study is therefore not a uniform landscape (Figure 1.1), and this presents a challenge to

Figure 1.5 Primary
geological zones in the
Dublin region, showing
the predominance of
limestones (upper
Paleozoic rocks) over
much of the study area,
with the distinctive
granites that distinguish
buildings in the south-
east of the county.

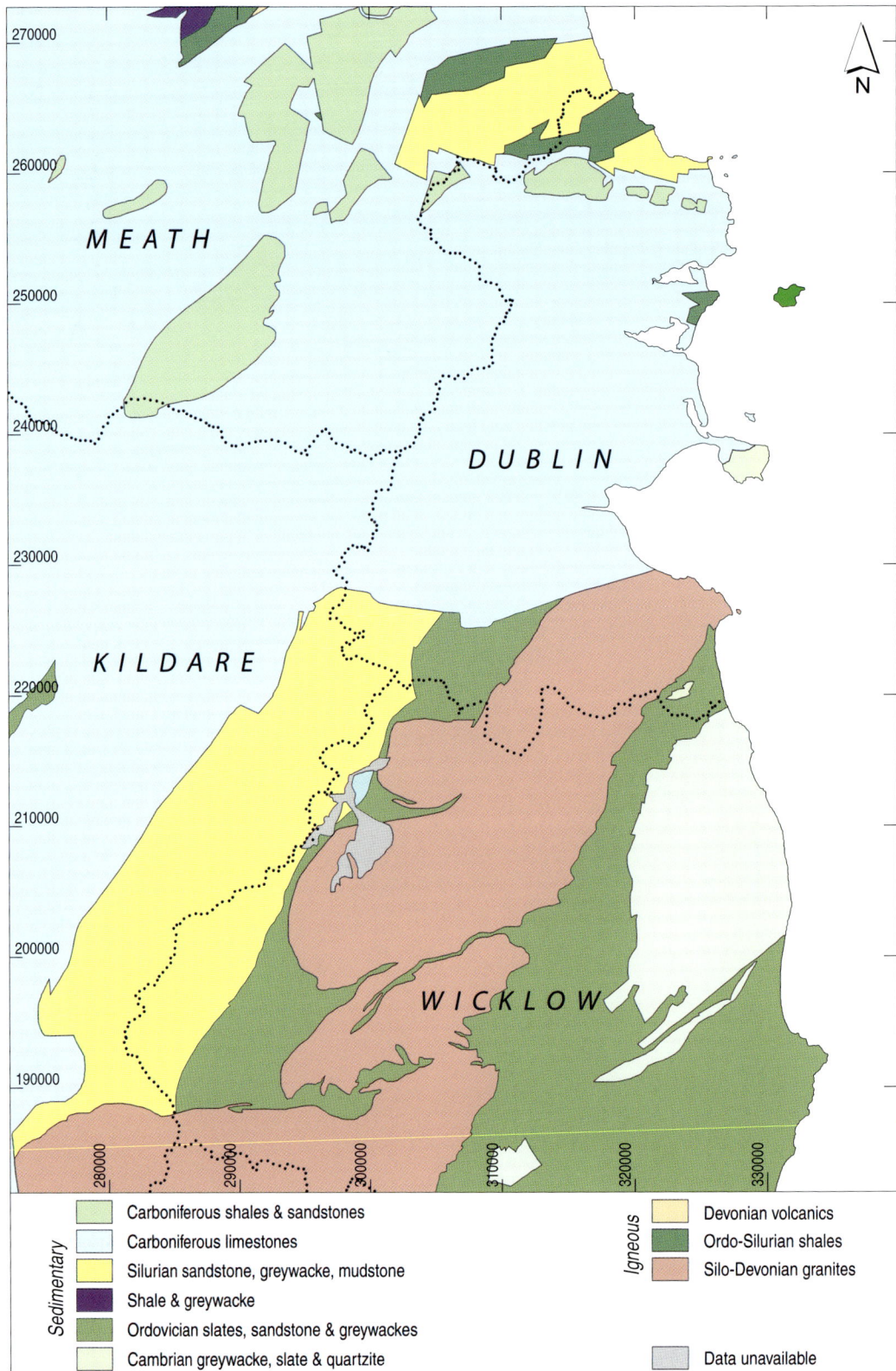

the project to understand how settlement patterns and land-use may reflect responses to the
various physical environments in the later medieval period.

   The underlying geology creates an essential point of departure in any landscape analysis
(Figure 1.5). Limestone is the predominant rock-type within the main floodplain areas of the
Liffey and the lesser river systems to the north. This is intermixed with shales and shale/
sandstone complexes in the area to the north of Dublin. Basalt is present only on Lambay.
There is a large area of quartz deposits around Balbriggan, and also to the south in a band

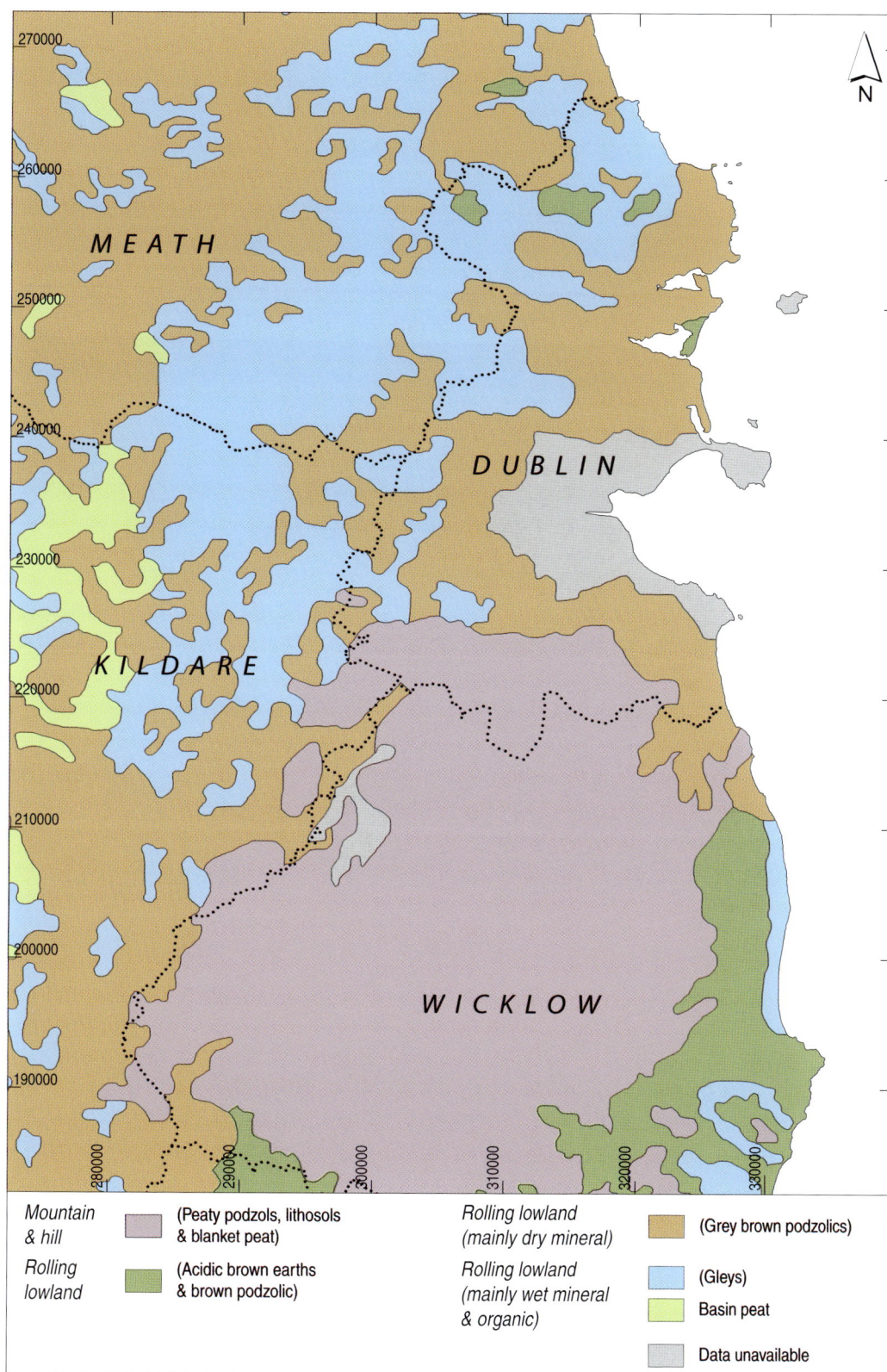

Figure 1.6 Primary soil types in the Dublin region. The grey-brown podzolic soils are suited to arable cultivation. The gleys and brown podzols sustain good pasture, while the peats, bog and peaty podzols are most suitable for rough grazing (source: Ireland, General Soil Map, 2nd ed., OSI, 1980, 1:575,000).

that extends south and south-west of Bray along the coast. Granite, for which the Wicklow Mountains are famous, exists in a single band that reaches south-west from Dalkey/Dún Laoghaire across the mountains and beyond the study area in the direction of Baltinglass, Rathvilly and Tullow, Co. Carlow. It was usually the case, with the exception of decorative stonework, that medieval construction exploited materials that were immediately to hand.[56]

56 L.F. Salzman, *Building in England down to 1540* (Oxford, 1952), p. 119; David Parsons, 'Stone' in Blair and Ramsay (eds), *English medieval industries* (1991), pp 1–27 at p. 22; Roger Stalley, 'Irish Gothic and English fashion' in Lydon (ed.), *The English in medieval Ireland* (1984), pp 65–86.

The cost of transporting stone was prohibitive and builders generally quarried outcrops at or immediately adjacent to the building site. Anyone who has visited the churches and castles across the south of Co. Dublin will know that the locally quarried coarse granite was the preferred building stone here throughout the Middle Ages (Chapter 16).

The underlying stone formations can throw light on building practice, while soil cover provides a necessary starting point to any analysis of agrarian production (Figure 1.6). Soil-types reflect the underlying rock formations that created them, and they are also influenced by external processes that may alter their character. In the Dublin region, much of the soil is classified as a glacial till derivative. The gleys and the grey brown podzolic soils that lie over most of the study area are derived from till that originated in the Irish Sea area before being dumped onto the rolling lowlands and coastal strip. There is a distinct pattern to these tills, in which the wet gleys, which are inferior soils for agricultural purposes, occupy an outer ring that straddles the 30km 'ring' around Dublin. Within this band, and the main river basin for the Liffey and the other rivers that empty into Dublin Bay, lie the more fertile and mainly dry grey-brown podzolic soils. The podzolics occupy much of the coastal strip from Skerries in the north to Greystones in the south, and reach inland to Maynooth, Leixlip and Tallaght. These are a superior type of agricultural soil to the gleys, and it is possible that their better fertility is a result of their position in the lower floodplain areas, where minerals would be regularly deposited as the fresh water made its way to the sea. The Wicklow Mountains present a different picture, where the soils are thin and low in minerals, perhaps since the last glaciation, when much of the original cover was eroded away.

The physical environment has also been moulded by drainage, and Figure 1.4 indicates the principal river catchments within the Dublin region. The rivers are not large by international standards, and most are quite narrow. Nevertheless, even the small water-courses could produce substantial estuaries in the right circumstances. Besides the Liffey, there is a plethora of lesser rivers and streams running towards the coast, including the Nanny, Delvin, Broad Meadow, Ward and Tolka Rivers north of the Liffey, and the Poddle, Dodder, Dargle and Vartry to the south. There is little direct influence from river systems that drain either further north, such as the Boyne, or to the west and south, such as the Barrow or the Slaney. This is a region where the drainage is aligned towards the east coast, with the main outlets at the Malahide and Rogerstown Estuaries in the north, Dublin Bay in the centre, and Killiney Bay and Wicklow Head in the south. The outpouring of rivers in the northern half of the study area and in Dublin created broad tidal floodplains, and it is here that rabbit warrens were established, as is witnessed in the seventeenth-century Down and Civil Surveys, on the sand dunes in Malahide and Portraine on either side of the Broad Meadow and Ward Estuaries. To the south, the proximity of the mountains to the sea has precluded the development of large estuaries and expanses of marshland.

The coastal zone provided safe havens for sea-going vessels. Dublin Bay occupies the central area where it is defined by Howth Head to the north and Dalkey to the south, and offers a broad shoreline that was largely secure from the prevailing south-westerly winds and all but the most severe easterlies. A major impediment to navigation within the Bay were the tidal mudflats, whose origins lie in the estuarine deposits of the Rivers Liffey, Dodder and Tolka, as well as the range of lesser streams that drain into the central and northern parts of the bay. The mudflats provided ideal locations for the setting-up of tidal fish-traps and other shore-based operations, but they were a hazard to shipping and restricted the points at which vessels could land at or close to shore safely. While shallow-drafted clinker ships and small boats, including dugout canoes, continued in use throughout the Middle Ages, larger vessels, such as carracks and other sailing ships, carried wine and merchandise across the Irish Sea. Dublin was unable to accommodate the larger vessels because the estuary was heavily silted by the early fourteenth century.[57] Deepwater access was possible at Dalkey, presumably using the facilities of Dalkey Sound and the Muglins to the east. The situation provided an economic opportunity for the haven to develop into the city's primary port for a time. The north-western shore of Lambay enjoyed a similar advantage. It was not until the fifteenth/sixteenth century that Ringsend took over as the deep-water port, where the pools at Clontarf and Poolbeg were used for berthing on the north and south sides of the Liffey Estuary. Access upriver to the city remained problematic until 1707, when the Ballast Office initiated a large-scale programme of land reclamation and dredging of the Liffey mouth to improve navigation.

Further south, and outside the study area, the tidal lagoon in Wicklow may have presented one of the few safe havens along this shingle coastline. The small headlands of Greystones and Bray would have offered small anchorages. In contrast, the Malahide Estuary to the north, and the rocky inlets associated with Rush, Skerries and Balbriggan, were natural local harbours in their own right.

The sub-surface topography of Dublin Bay, with its offshore banks such as the Burford Bank and the Kish Bank, presented its own impediments to sea-going communications during the Middle Ages. The observation of shipwreck material and artefactual debris that may be retrieved in fishing nets and during marine dredging projects echoes the concerns associated with navigating these shallows that are indicated on the surviving sea charts.[58]

The Dublin area is a physically diverse environment that would have presented a wide range of different economic opportunities to its inhabitants. The variety of ways in which this landscape and seascape were exploited during the later medieval period forms one of the primary themes of the present study.

Chronological limits

In very general terms, the word 'medieval' can be used to describe Ireland for the entire period from *c*.AD400 to *c*.1600 (in many cases, the terms 'medieval' and 'Middle Ages' are interchangeable). Increasing contact between Ireland and other parts of Europe in the twelfth century resulted in major church reform, the appearance of Romanesque architecture in the 1120s and 1130s, the coming of Continental religious orders in the 1140s and 1150s and the arrival of the Anglo-Normans in the 1160s and 1170s. These developments marked a great watershed in the history of Ireland, and it has become standard practice to apply the term 'early medieval' to the period up to about the middle of the twelfth century or a little later,[59] and the term 'late(r) medieval' (or more often simply 'medieval')[60] to the period after it.[61] The arrival of the Anglo-Normans in 1169 is usually seen as the fulcrum at the centre.[62] Some

57 Timothy O'Neill, *Merchants and mariners in medieval Ireland* (Dublin, 1987), p. 152.   **58** The potential for undisclosed wreckage sites to be found is indicated in Karl Brady, *Shipwreck inventory of Ireland: Louth, Meath, Dublin and Wicklow* (Dublin, 2008).   **59** See, for example, Dáibhí Ó Cróinín, *Early medieval Ireland, 400–1200* (London and New York, 1995); Nancy Edwards, *The archaeology of early medieval Ireland* (London, 2000); Nancy Edwards, 'The archaeology of early medieval Ireland, *c*.400–1169: settlement and economy' in Ó Cróinín (ed.), *A new history of Ireland: I* (2005), pp 235–300. The term 'Early Christian' as also used for this period – see, for example, Máire de Paor and Liam de Paor, *Early Christian Ireland* (London, 1958); Harold Mytum, *The origins of Early Christian Ireland* (London and New York, 1992).   **60** See, for example, A.J. Otway-Ruthven, *A history of medieval Ireland* (New York, 1968, 1980); Cosgrove (ed.), *A new history of Ireland: II* (1993); T.B. Barry, *The archaeology of medieval Ireland* (London, 1987); K.D. O'Conor, *The archaeology of medieval rural settlement in Ireland* (Dublin, 1998); Tadhg O'Keeffe, *Medieval Ireland: an archaeology* (Stroud, Gloucestershire, 2000); J.F. Lydon, *The lordship of Ireland in the Middle Ages* (Dublin, 1972; repr. 2003); K.W. Nicholls, *Gaelic and Gaelicized Ireland in the Middle Ages* (Dublin, 2003).   **61** See, for example, James Lydon (ed.), *England and Ireland in the later Middle Ages: essays in honour of Jocelyn Otway-Ruthven* (Dublin, 1981); Brendan Smith (ed.), *Ireland and the English world in the late Middle Ages: essays in honour of Robin Frame* (London, 2009).   **62** F.J. Byrne, 'The trembling sod: Ireland in 1169' in Cosgrove (ed.), *A new history of Ireland: II* (1993), pp 1–42.

commentators further subdivide the Middle Ages, referring to the period from *c.*1100 to *c.*1350 as 'high medieval', and the post-1350 period as 'late medieval'.[63] Settling on a date for the end of the Middle Ages is a more difficult matter.[64] Political historians usually take 1534 (and the death of the earl of Kildare) as marking the end of the medieval period in Ireland, and the beginning of the 'post-medieval' or 'early modern' period.[65] The 1530s also witnessed another major watershed in Irish history – the Dissolution of the Monasteries. Despite the closure of many religious houses, however, from an archaeological perspective at least, insufficient change is evident to justify drawing a line under the Middle Ages in the mid-sixteenth century.[66] On present archaeological evidence, the medieval period stretches right into the seventeenth century.[67]

In the current book, the term 'early medieval' is taken to mean *c.*500–1170 (that is, pre-Anglo-Norman), while the term 'medieval' refers to the period from 1170 to *c.*1650. The Viking Age is consequently a part of the early medieval period, just as the high Middle Ages are a part of the medieval period.

This book deals with a period of almost five hundred years, beginning in 1170 and concluding in 1660. This period witnessed a variety of political, economic and demographic changes. Major 'watershed' events, as well as the survival of valuable source material, helped to define the temporal limits. The early date marks the initial establishment of Anglo-Norman control in the region, with the capture of Dublin by Strongbow. The origins of many of the post-invasion landholding and settlement patterns lay in the pre-Anglo-Norman period, and discussion of this earlier period is included where appropriate. The terminal date of 1660 allows for the inclusion of the Civil and Down Surveys, the earliest detailed accounts of landscape and settlement in the Dublin region. The period between 1550 and 1650 does not, however, form part of the main focus of the study.

As will be clear from the descriptions of the principal archaeological and documentary sources outlined in the next chapter, the nature and quantity of relevant source material varies greatly within the period covered by the book. The archaeological evidence is frequently only datable to within a century or two. The documentary sources, in contrast, are fairly precisely dated but tend to occur in clusters, with some periods extensively covered and others relatively blank. There is a particular concentration of documentary material for the period 1250–1350, for example, partly due to the vagaries of survival and partly because this was a period characterised by direct management of estates and direct government at central and local levels. Of necessity, a disproportionate number of illustrations and examples relate to this period. The following one hundred years, however, is characterised by the poor survival of sources of all types, while useful but different sources are available for the sixteenth and early seventeenth centuries. It is therefore difficult to follow a considered chronological progression with relation to many of the themes presented in this book.

Themes

The book is divided into five parts (including I: Introduction; and V: Conclusions). The three core parts are entitled 'Settlement and Society', 'Exploitation of Resources' and

---

63 See, for example, B.D. Lyon (ed.), *The high Middle Ages, 1000–1300* (New York and London, 1964); Rolf Toman (ed.), *The high Middle Ages in Germany, 1000–1300* (Cologne, 1990); Art Cosgrove, *Late medieval Ireland, 1370–1541* (Dublin, 1981).   **64** O'Conor, *Medieval rural settlement in Ireland*, p. xi.   **65** See, for example, T.W. Moody, F.X. Martin and F.J. Byrne (eds), *A new history of Ireland, III: Early modern Ireland, 1534–1691* (Oxford, 3rd ed., 1989).   **66** E.M. Jope, H.M. Jope and E.A. Johnson, *An archaeological survey of County Down* (Belfast, 1966), preface; O'Conor, *Medieval rural settlement in Ireland*, p. xi.   **67** T.E. McNeill, 'Where should we place the boundary between the medieval and the post-medieval periods in Ireland?' in Audrey Horning, Ruairí Ó Baoill, Colm Donnelly and Paul Logue (eds), *The post-medieval archaeology of Ireland, 1550–1850* (Bray, 2007), pp 7–13.

'Processing and Distribution'. Each part is subdivided into chapters. Part II considers the ownership and occupation of land in the Dublin region, and a major theme is the extent to which different factors influenced the spatial and chronological patterns of settlement features that emerged across the region. Several recent studies have emphasised the ways in which existing patterns of landholding, territorial divisions and the placement of monuments moulded the settlement landscape that evolved after the coming of the Anglo-Normans in 1169.[68] No study has yet examined the relative importance of continuity and change in the hinterland of Dublin from a settlement perspective. Chapter 3 considers the political and economic control of the Dublin region before the arrival of the Anglo-Normans. This enables an assessment of the extent to which pre-existing factors determined subsequent patterns of landholding and the siting of important defensive monuments.

The relationship between lordship and land must take into account the different types of lord and their varying objectives. A significant portion of Part II is given over to analysis of the patchwork of lordship across the region, and this leads to a consideration of the principal monument-types – earthwork and masonry castles – associated with the first phase of Anglo-Norman control and the top layer of the lordship hierarchy (Chapter 5). This chapter charts the development of castle-building in the Dublin region from the twelfth to the seventeenth century, looking at location, form and function. It is evident that there were more earthwork castles in the region than is generally realised, and there is a clear association between early castles and churches. Over time, patterns of landholding across the region underwent change, as did the form of monument associated with lordship. The building, distribution and function of tower houses and fortified houses are also examined here. The tower houses of the Pale form a distinct architectural group with a number of unifying features. Tower houses are scarce in Wicklow, however, indicating that the Gaelic Irish in this part of the country – unlike many other places – did not take to building this type of castle.

Having characterised the top layer of the lordship hierarchy and its associated monuments, Part II moves on to a consideration of subinfeudation and the establishment of manor centres, granges, parishes, boroughs and associated settlements. The manor was the most important institution and settlement type introduced into Ireland by the Anglo-Normans, but much remains to be understood about its form and function. The Dublin region contained some of the largest and best documented manors in Ireland and therefore offers an opportunity to explore a variety of themes such as the make-up of the manorial centre and organisation of agricultural buildings, the chronology of tenant settlement, the balance between different types of manorial tenant and the relative importance of dispersed versus nucleated rural settlement forms. The church was a very significant landholder in the Dublin region and played a major role in settlement organisation. The consolidation of the parochial structure went hand-in-hand with manorial organisation and the Dublin region offers an excellent case-study for this process.

Having considered how the land was owned and divided and the components and organisation of rural settlements, Part III (Exploitation of Resources) explores how the resources of the region were managed and exploited to produce food, fuel and raw materials for both town and country. Agriculture was of course the key land-use, and assessing the balance between arable and pastoral husbandry at a regional level is a fundamental objective of this study. Good land quality allowed for the cultivation of a variety of crops, and documentary sources in conjunction with palaeo-environmental evidence permit an

---

68 See, for example, Graham, 'The evolution of the settlement pattern of Anglo-Norman Eastmeath'; M.-T. Flanagan, 'Anglo-Norman change and continuity: the castle of Telach Cail in Delbna', *IHS*, 28:112 (1993), 385–9; Edel Bhreathnach, 'Authority and supremacy in Tara and its hinterland, *c*.950–1200', *DPR*, 5 (1999), 1–23.

examination of the relative importance of different grains and their varying uses. Similarly, an analysis of the balance between different types of livestock and their functions as providers of traction, meat or other products, can reveal patterns in arable and pastoral regimes. This part also considers the evidence for horticulture, silviculture and the exploitation of natural resources, as well as the use that was made of rivers, the sea and the foreshore.

Part IV (Processing and Distribution) considers how the products of the land were processed in preparation for human consumption, and how these products were distributed across the region and further afield. Much of the evidence that is presented is concerned with the ways in which cereals were dried, milled and transformed into food and drink. Consideration is also given to how wool, fleeces and hides were prepared; how clay was used for pottery and how and where iron ore was smelted.

The next logical step is to move beyond production and processing towards consumption, and Part IV also considers the demands, principally for foodstuffs, that were generated within and beyond the region. Dublin's hinterland managed (most of the time) to successfully feed its rural dwellers, sustain Ireland's biggest urban population and generate a surplus for export overseas. The combined sources contain information relating to the foundation and functioning of markets and fairs and the location of market-places and other commercial foci. There is further data concerning trade, exchange and coinage. Evidence survives for the transport of goods by land and water and the ways in which Dublin-based religious and secular households obtained provisions from their rural estates.

This book is a synthesis of information on a wide range of subjects. It aims to contribute to debates on themes such as settlement landscapes, the role of lordship, the productivity of agriculture and interaction between town and countryside. Some topics and questions reappear throughout the various chapters below, and these core themes are identified and assessed in the closing chapter. It is hoped that this book will serve as a reference tool for archaeologists, historians and others working on specific sites or areas within the Dublin region, as well as for people engaged in research on wider aspects of national, or even international, medieval history and archaeology.

CHAPTER 2

Sources

Assembling the data

The archaeological sources

The archaeological research element of this study did not involve any new excavations or large-scale fieldwork campaigns. It has been essentially a desktop study, the aim of which has been to assemble, prioritise and synthesise a body of data deriving from a range of published and unpublished sources. In addition to the published catalogues, reports and studies, information was accessed in the files and databases of state repositories (especially the Department of the Environment, Heritage and Local Government [DEHLG] and the National Museum of Ireland [NMI]), through formal contact with the directors of excavations and through a small number of site visits.

Much of the work in identifying, mapping and describing the monuments of Ireland has been carried out under the auspices of the organisations formerly known as the Office of Public Works and Dúchas: the Heritage Service (Sites and Monuments Record; Record of Monuments and Places; Register of Historic Monuments; Archaeological Inventories; Archaeological Surveys). In addition to features that are still prominent in the landscape, other monuments have been identified over the years as a result of field-walking, geophysical research, aerial photography, satellite imagery, archaeological excavation and accidental discovery. Most of these have been incorporated into the Dúchas files (currently subsumed within the DEHLG), which are most complete for the pre-AD1700 period. These lists were used to establish a database of over 1,000 sites and monuments generally accepted as being broadly medieval in date (Figure 2.1). From this database, a series of maps has been produced that illustrate various distribution patterns, and that facilitate the comparison of the archaeological record with the documentary evidence.

The nature of infrastructural development and associated archaeological excavation recently witnessed in Ireland, particularly in the Dublin region, means that the existing corpus of knowledge is expanding at an unprecedented rate. Nonetheless, the time-consuming nature of post-excavation analysis means that it is rare for the findings of archaeological excavations to be published promptly and in detail. A core feature of the current study has been accessing the corpus of unpublished information generated by licensed archaeological excavations.

The last fifteen years has witnessed exponential growth in the number of archaeological projects undertaken in Ireland. Some sixty-three excavations took place in 1987, but by 2002 the annual figure had increased thirty-two-fold to 2,023. By 1 January 2003, a total of 1,632 licensed excavations had taken place within the Dublin study area alone (Figure 2.2).[1] Given

---

1 This information is derived from *Excavations bulletins*, Dúchas/DEHLG files, National Museum of Ireland files and a questionnaire designed specifically for this module.

Figure 2.1 Distribution of recorded medieval monuments in the Dublin region, broken down into broad categories, based on function. The categories are further subdivided in the following parts of this book.

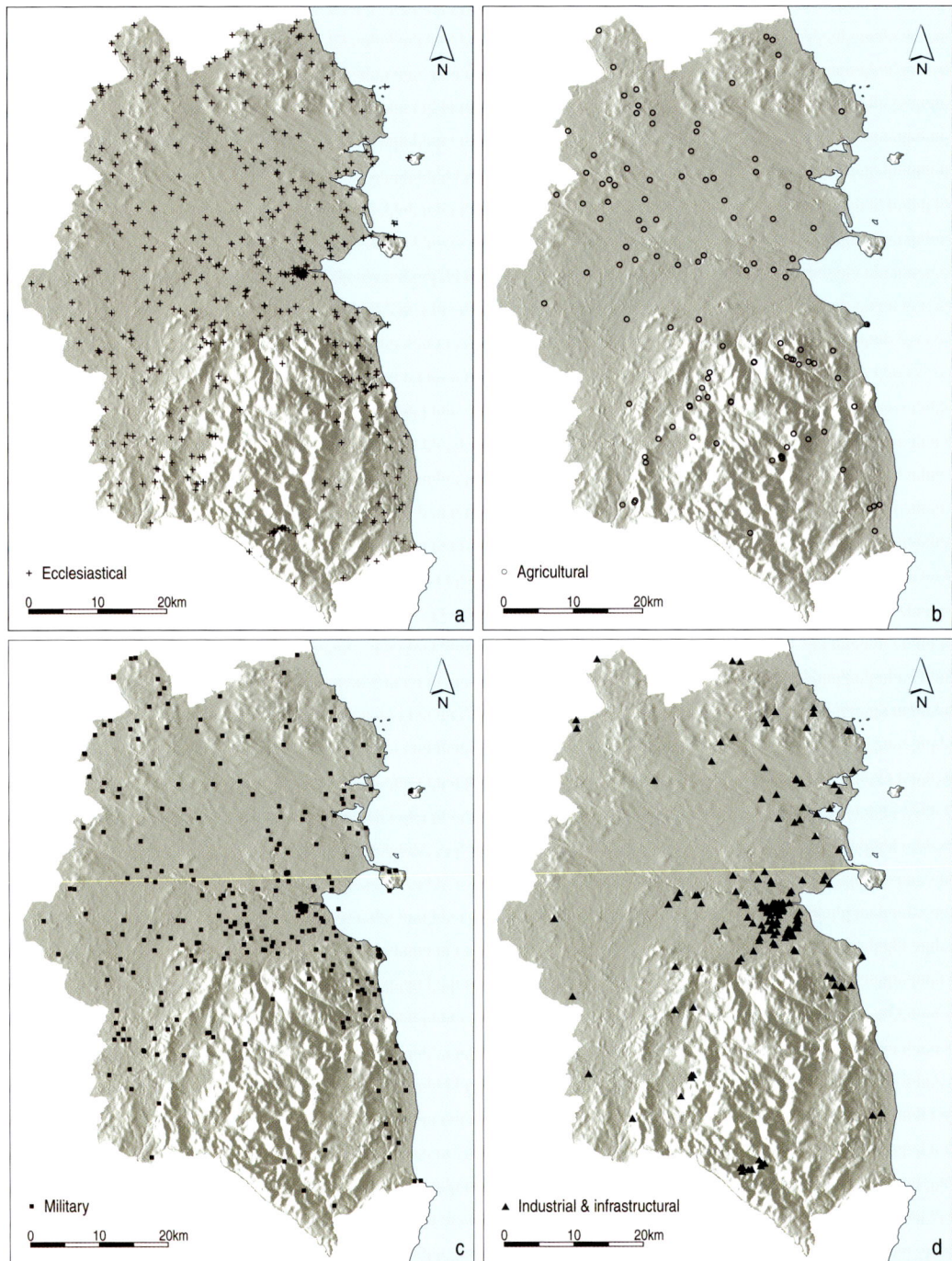

that so much of the increase has been driven by construction and infrastructural developments, there is little surprise at the distribution of archaeological activity across the region (Figure 2.3). The major concentration is in Dublin city, and over 600 sites have been investigated within a 5km radius of the city centre. Smaller groups can be identified at other lesser urban centres such as Dalkey, Dunshaughlin, Naas and Swords. Further concentrations appear along the lines of the major road construction projects radiating from the city – the M1, M3 (Figure 2.4), M4 and M50 for example – with a particularly large number of excavations taking place along the Southern Cross Route. On the other hand, there are some large tracts of unexcavated landscape, most noticeably across the Dublin/Wicklow Mountains, but also in the fertile and well-drained agricultural areas of south-east Co. Meath and north-west Co. Dublin.

A preliminary review of the excavation material was undertaken and an individual questionnaire was sent to each of the project directors concerning each site for which s/he

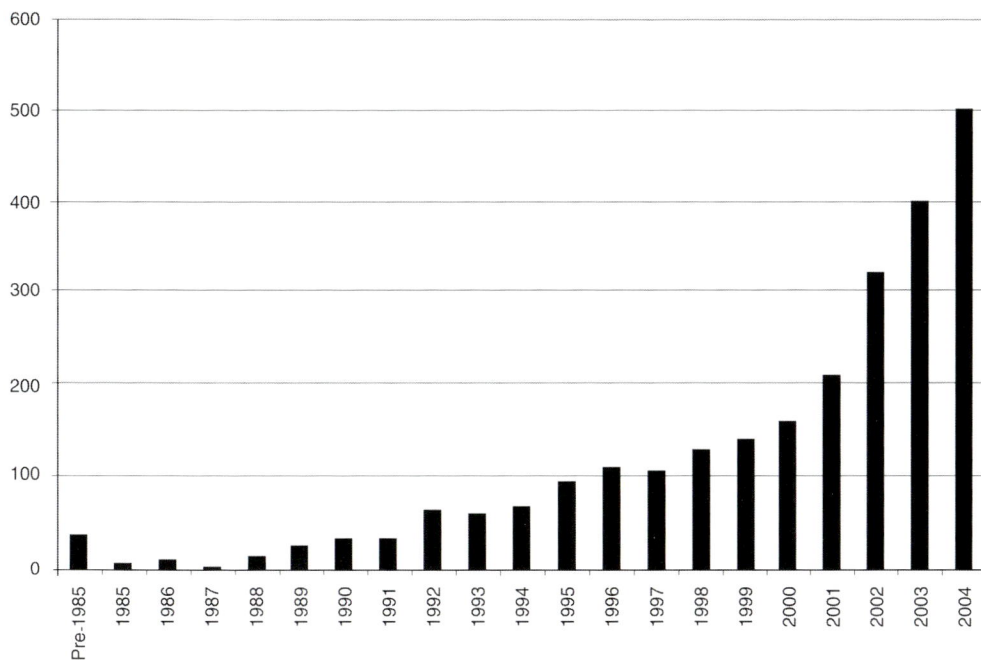

was responsible. The questionnaire enabled the project to identify material of particular significance and to focus research in these areas. By combining the results of the survey with an analysis of the summary accounts published in the *Excavations bulletin* and files on excavations held by the DEHLG and the NMI, a clear overview was formed of the nature of the work carried out and a list of reports of potential significance to the project was drawn up. Of the original list of 1,632 sites of potential interest to the project, only 430 contained recorded material of medieval date. In many instances this material amounted to no more than a few sherds of pottery or a 'possible medieval deposit'. While these finds are not insignificant in their own right, they must be viewed in the context of the much more significant discoveries of complex stratigraphical sequences containing a range of diagnostic artefacts and/or structural remains. In general, the most extensive excavations on which sampling strategies and the services of a range of specialists were employed were the most informative for the present study.

The preliminary survey of all archaeological excavations indicated that about one hundred reports merited further detailed analysis, and these have formed a core of archaeological source material for this project. A handful of these excavation reports have appeared as monographs, and a slightly larger number have been published as papers in academic journals or edited volumes. About one quarter of the excavations identified as being of interest to this project have been published in one of these ways. For the other 75 per cent, the mandatory reports lodged with the DEHLG and the NMI are the primary sources of information. These 'stratigraphical' reports are generally technical documents that include the background and methodology to the excavation, together with a presentation of the findings, usually including lists of features and finds, giving dimensions and outlining relationships. There will normally be some discussion of the findings, and a range of maps, plans, drawings and photographs. In addition, there may be supplementary reports contributed by specialists in various fields (see below). The combined 'strat. reports', as they are often called, are the key component of an excavation archive, but it is usually a significant, challenging and lengthy task to advance them to publication standard.

Given the nature of the present study, the specialist contributions sometimes appended to an excavation report were in many ways more fruitful than the core report itself. The

Figure 2.3 Distribution
of licensed excavations
in the Dublin study area,
to 2004. Recently
constructed major
roads and ongoing
large-scale projects are
also shown.

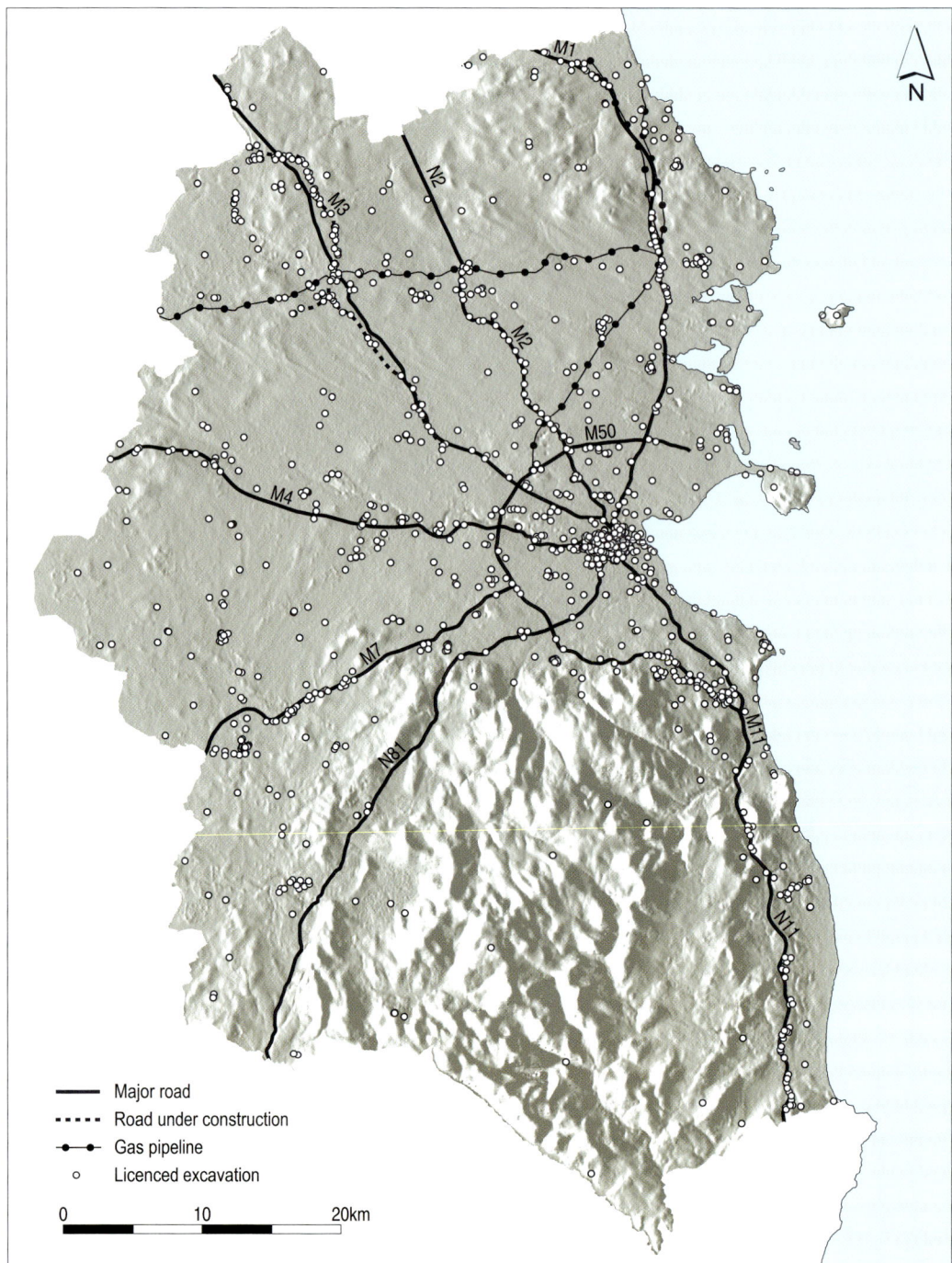

Figure 2.3 Distribution of licensed excavations in the Dublin study area, to 2004. Recently constructed major roads and ongoing large-scale projects are also shown.

survey identified that 60 per cent of all reports on excavations yielding medieval material contained no specialist report (Figure 2.6). Thirty-three per cent included a separate report on pottery, and this was followed in frequency by animal bones (20 per cent), palaeo-environmental remains (16 per cent), human remains (13 per cent) and coins (9 per cent) (Figure 2.6). A small number of reports contained contributions on other subjects such as glass, leather, textiles and other artefact types. In this project, particular emphasis was placed on palaeo-environmental and archaeo-zoological assemblages. While the corpus of data is relatively small, it contains some highly important information for the reconstruction of land-use and settlement patterns in the hinterland of medieval Dublin.

The documentary sources

Unlike the archaeological sources, which are increasing exponentially year on year, the body of documentary source material relating to the medieval Dublin region has undergone little

Figure 2.4 Recently completed archaeological excavations on the route of the M3 motorway at Dowdstown, Co. Meath (April 2007). Outside Co. Dublin, Meath is the only county on the island to be traversed by four motorways – the M1, M2, M3 and M4 – and the archaeological investigation that preceded the construction of the M3 yielded new information about human activity in the area from earliest times to the nineteenth century.

substantial change since the disastrous losses of June 1922, when the record store in the Public Record Office of Ireland in the Four Courts and its contents were destroyed by fire.[2] The surviving corpus of material for the Dublin region is rich in comparison with much of the rest of Ireland; nonetheless, a serious lacuna in the sources for social, economic and agrarian history results from the lack or poor survival of systematic collections of the type of documents required for the quantitative investigation of population size, wealth, land-use and productivity. The sources that have provided the material and the focus for many recent studies of medieval England are either completely lacking or survive in much smaller numbers for Ireland, as they do for Scotland and Wales.[3] The picture of land-use around medieval London and the spatial pattern of grain production there, for example, were reconstructed from thousands of inquisitions *post mortem* extents and hundreds of demesne account rolls.[4] A recent study of manorial agriculture across the whole of England in the period 1250–1450 has used some 1,100 demesne accounts, over a hundred of them for the county of Norfolk alone.[5] By comparison, only a tiny number of demesne accounts have survived for the whole of Ireland and unfortunately none of these relates to manors within the Dublin study area.[6] Whether these documents were ever produced in great numbers for manors in medieval Ireland is open to debate. The survival in the central account roll of the priory of Holy Trinity, Dublin (later known as Christ Church) of two 'haggard accounts' for

2 Only a handful of original medieval records survived the fire. They are listed in *RDKPRI*, 55, pp 97–8. Some excellent guides to surviving sources and substitute material have appeared in recent years: Philomena Connolly, *Medieval record sources* (Dublin, 2002); Judith Carroll, *Dublin city: sources for archaeologists* (Dublin, 2003); Paul Dryburgh and Brendan Smith (eds), *Handbook and select calendar of sources of medieval Ireland* (Dublin, 2004); Katharine Simms, *Medieval Gaelic sources* (Dublin, 2009).   3 For a discussion of the disparity in the amount of surviving material across Britain and Ireland, see R.H. Britnell, *Britain and Ireland, 1050–1530: economy and society* (Oxford, 2004), pp 1–2 and chs 13 and 23.   4 Campbell, Galloway, Keene and Murphy, *A medieval capital*, pp 16–23.   5 B.M.S. Campbell, *English seigniorial agriculture, 1250–1450* (Cambridge, 2000), pp 34–5.   6 The surviving accounts relate to manors held by Roger Bigod, earl of Norfolk, in the lordship of Carlow. They date from the later thirteenth century. The nearest manor to the Dublin study area is Ballysax, Co. Kildare, approximately 50km from Dublin. The National Archives, UK (hereafter TNA): PRO SC6/1237/1–6. M.C. Lyons, 'The manor of Ballysax, 1280–1288', *Retrospect*, 1 (1981), 40–50.

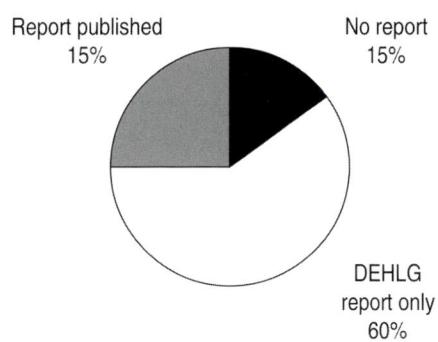

Report published
15%

No report
15%

DEHLG
report only
60%

the manors of Grangegorman and Clonkeen in Co. Dublin for 1343–4, as well as the account of the bailiff of Clonkeen for 1344–5 suggest that this ecclesiastical landlord, at least, produced similar documents for its directly managed estates.[7]

The situation with regard to manorial extents is relatively better and the collection of extent material assembled for the Dublin region offers the best opportunity for undertaking systematic analysis. The source is therefore described here in some detail. The essential function of the extent was to provide information on the value of manorial resources.[8] As a result, extents are one of the principal sources for land-use, buildings, resources, and tenurial obligations.[9] A typical extent itemised the principal types of land-use on the demesne (arable, meadow, pasture and wood) and any other resources (mills, dovecots, warrens, fishponds etc.; see Figure 2.7). A monetary valuation was normally attached to each resource, which represented the estimated annual rental value of each resource, rather than a capital or asset value.

The largest collection of extents for English manors is attached to inquisitions *post mortem* – the records of enquiry made by the crown on the death of the king's tenants-in-chief. In Ireland, *post mortem* enquiries were set up in response to a royal writ sent to the escheator, the official in the central government of the lordship with responsibility for administering lands in the king's hands.[10] The records emanating from inquisitions of this type held in Ireland would have been kept in the Irish chancery, but when the deceased held lands in both England and Ireland, copies of the inquisitions on the Irish lands were sent to the English chancery.

At least forty-eight inquisitions *post mortem* now in the National Archives PRO class C132–5 contain information on lands in Ireland.[11] The earliest extents for Ireland date from

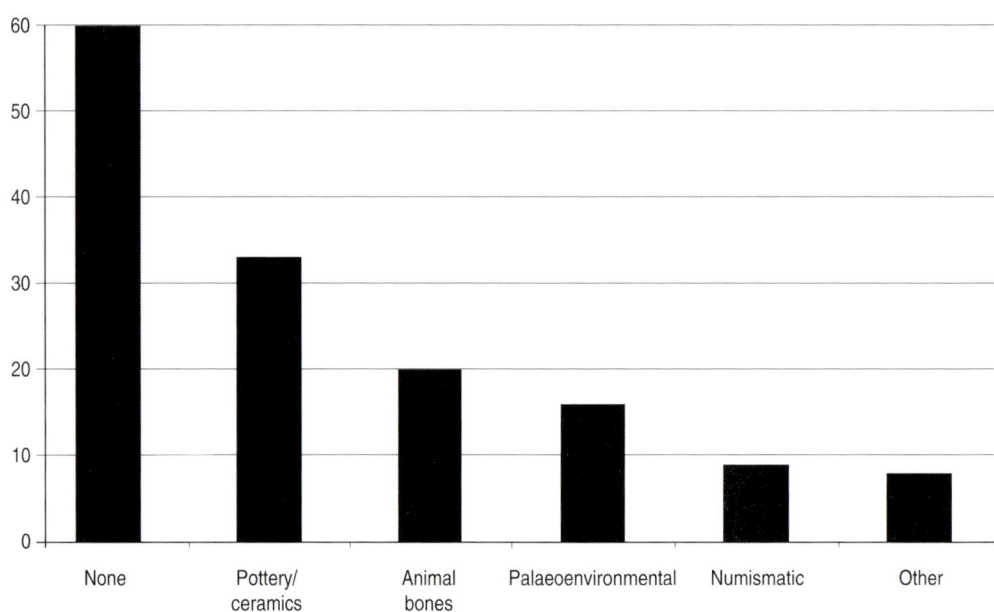

7 James Mills (ed.), *Account roll of the priory of the Holy Trinity, Dublin, 1337–1346* (Dublin, 1891; new ed., Dublin, 1996). **8** R.V. Lennard, 'What is an extent?', *EHR*, 44 (1929), 256–62. **9** Mark Bailey, *The English manor, c.1200–c.1500* (Manchester, 2002). **10** TNA:PRO C133/63. **11** These inquisitions were edited and published in 2007 (Paul Dryburgh and Brendan Smith (eds), *Inquisitions and extents of medieval Ireland* (London, 2007)). As this edition was not available when research for the present book was being carried out, the original documents were used and are

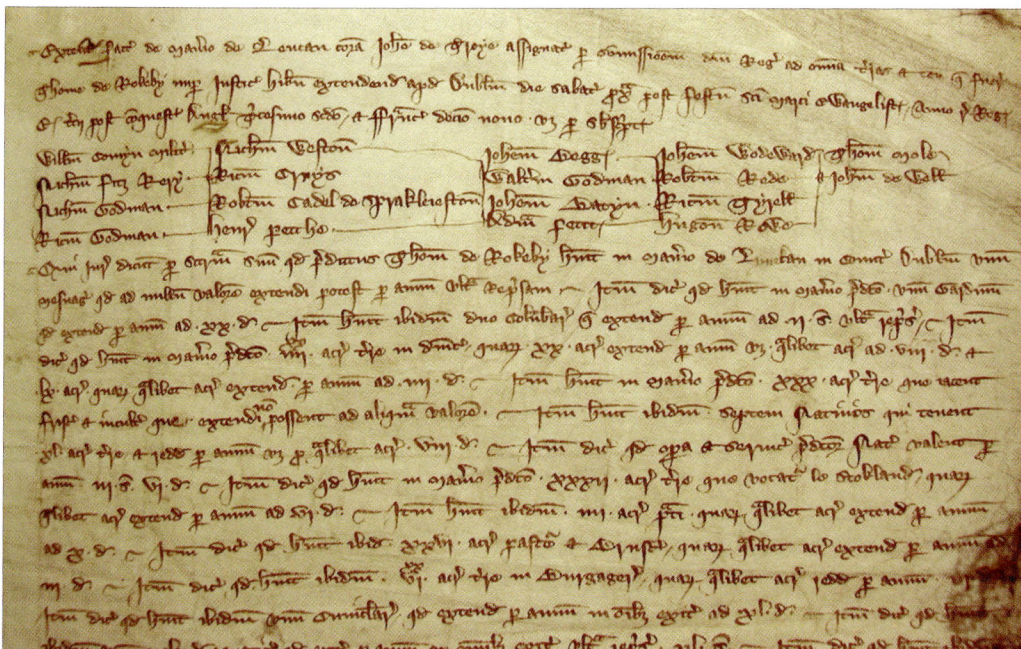

Figure 2.7 Extent for
the manor of Lucan,
Co. Dublin, 1358. This
document mentions
medieval monuments
such as fishponds and
dovecots as well as
describing local land-use
(image reproduced
courtesy of the
National Archives of the
UK, ref: TNA: PRO
C47/10/22/15).

1243 and relate to the lands of Richard de Burgh.[12] From then up to 1400 the extents provide information for approximately 240 'principal places', that is, manors, substantial land-holdings and boroughs, throughout Ireland.

A second class of executive extents are those which were drawn up in response to a royal writ known as *ad quod damnum.* This was issued when the king wished to be informed if the granting or transfer of any lands in which he had an involvement might be expected to damage his interests in any way.[13] Again, many such extents and other miscellaneous documents relating to Irish lands were enrolled in the records of the English exchequer. For the Dublin region, a total of twelve such extents have been located.

Extents can also be found in other sources. Perhaps the best known series for the Dublin area are those for the manors of the archbishop of Dublin which were drawn up in 1326 following the sequestration of the lands of Alexander de Bicknor, archbishop of Dublin (1317–49) and disgraced treasurer of Ireland (1308–14).[14] Occasionally, non-executive extents were commissioned by the owners of manors themselves and the resulting documents may contain substantially more detail than those drawn up by royal officials. Several such extents have survived for manors within or close to the Dublin region relating to the lands of the earls of Ormond and Kildare.

By combining the extents from these disparate collections, it has been possible to assemble a body of fairly systematic data relating to some forty manors or parcels of manors within the Dublin study area.[15] The earliest extent, for Balrothery, dates to 1253; the latest, for Lucan, was drawn up in 1358. The bulk of the extents date to the first decades of the fourteenth century (Figure 2.8). This chronology mirrors that found in England, where extents begin to become plentiful in the 1280s and tail off after the 1350s.[16] The reign of Edward I (1272–1307) was a peak period for the systematic collection of data by the English crown as it sought to maximise information about potential sources of income.[17] It was also

referenced.   **12** TNA:PRO C132/1/19; see Mark Hennessy, 'Manorial organisation in early thirteenth-century Tipperary', *IG*, 29:2 (1996), 116–25.   **13** These extents and other miscellaneous examples can be found in TNA:PRO classes C43 and C143, and most are calendared in *Calendar of inquisitions miscellaneous.*   **14** Charles McNeill (ed.), *Calendar of Archbishop Alen's register, c.1172–1534* (Dublin, 1950), pp 169–97. These very detailed extents cover the manors of Ballymore (Co. Kildare), Clondalkin, Colonia/St Sepulchre, Finglas, Rathcoole, Shankill (with Dalkey and Rathmichael), Swords (with Lusk and Clonmethan) and Tallaght.   **15** These extents are listed in Appendix 1, below. **16** Campbell, *Seigniorial agriculture*, p. 38.   **17** Britnell, *Britain and Ireland*, p. 270; Bailey, *The English Manor*, p. 38.

Figure 2.8 Dublin region
extents: numbers per
decade, 1250–1360.

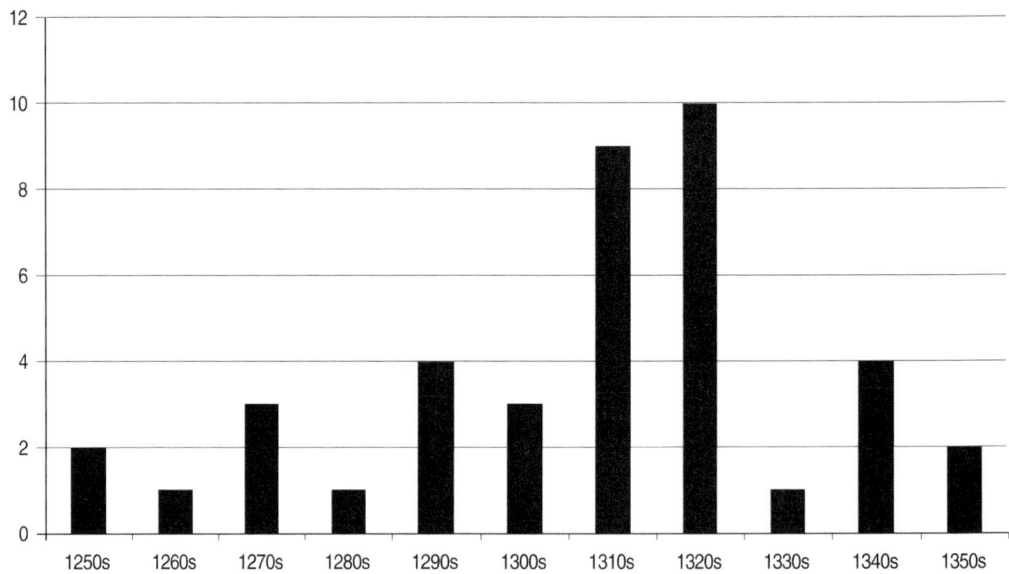

a time of intense interest in the management of manors when profits from agriculture and rents were at a high level. Inevitably, this encouraged the drawing up of extents and surveys to provide lords with details of expected issues and income.

The extents for the Dublin area relate to a number of different ownership categories and the holdings vary in size. They contain information concerning the large archiepiscopal manors, but some extents of the holdings of sub-tenants of the archbishop also survive. These date from the 1270s when the archiepiscopal lands were in the king's hand and information was required on the holdings of deceased tenants. There are also extents for the royal manors of Newcastle Lyons and Chapelizod (Dublin), Leixlip and Castlewarden (Kildare) and Bray (Wicklow), the Ormond manors of Bohernabreena, Corduff and Turvey (Dublin), Bray (Wicklow), Cloncurry (Kildare) and the earldom of Kildare lands in Maynooth (Figure 2.9). The distribution of extent information across the study area is by no means uniform, although it should be noted that the points on the map represent manorial caputs, while the manors themselves frequently covered extensive areas. There are clusters of data in the immediate environs of Dublin and also in the north and north-west of the region. Few records survive relating to non-manorialised Gaelic regions such as the Wicklow uplands and the marginal lands of north-east Kildare at the fringes of the study area. Further gaps in the coverage are in areas where the lands were owned by religious houses and were not subject to the type of royal investigative procedures that produced the extents.

Despite their less-than-perfect coverage, the extents represent a substantial collection of fairly systematic data on land-use and value. They also supply illuminating data relating to manorial buildings and associated resources such as mills, dovecots and warrens. An additional type of information contained in some of the extents relates to the holdings of the manorial tenants and their dues, both as money rents and as labour services. This information is extremely valuable for research into settlement, shedding light on the internal organisation of manors and also on the ethnic diversity that existed within the communities that made their living on the manors of Dublin's hinterland. Lists of manorial tenants and the monetary and/or labour services owed by them are also found in several other sources. These lists or rentals range in date from the mid-thirteenth century (for the archiepiscopal manors of Swords, Ballymore and Castlekevin) to the mid-fifteenth century (Rathmore, Co.

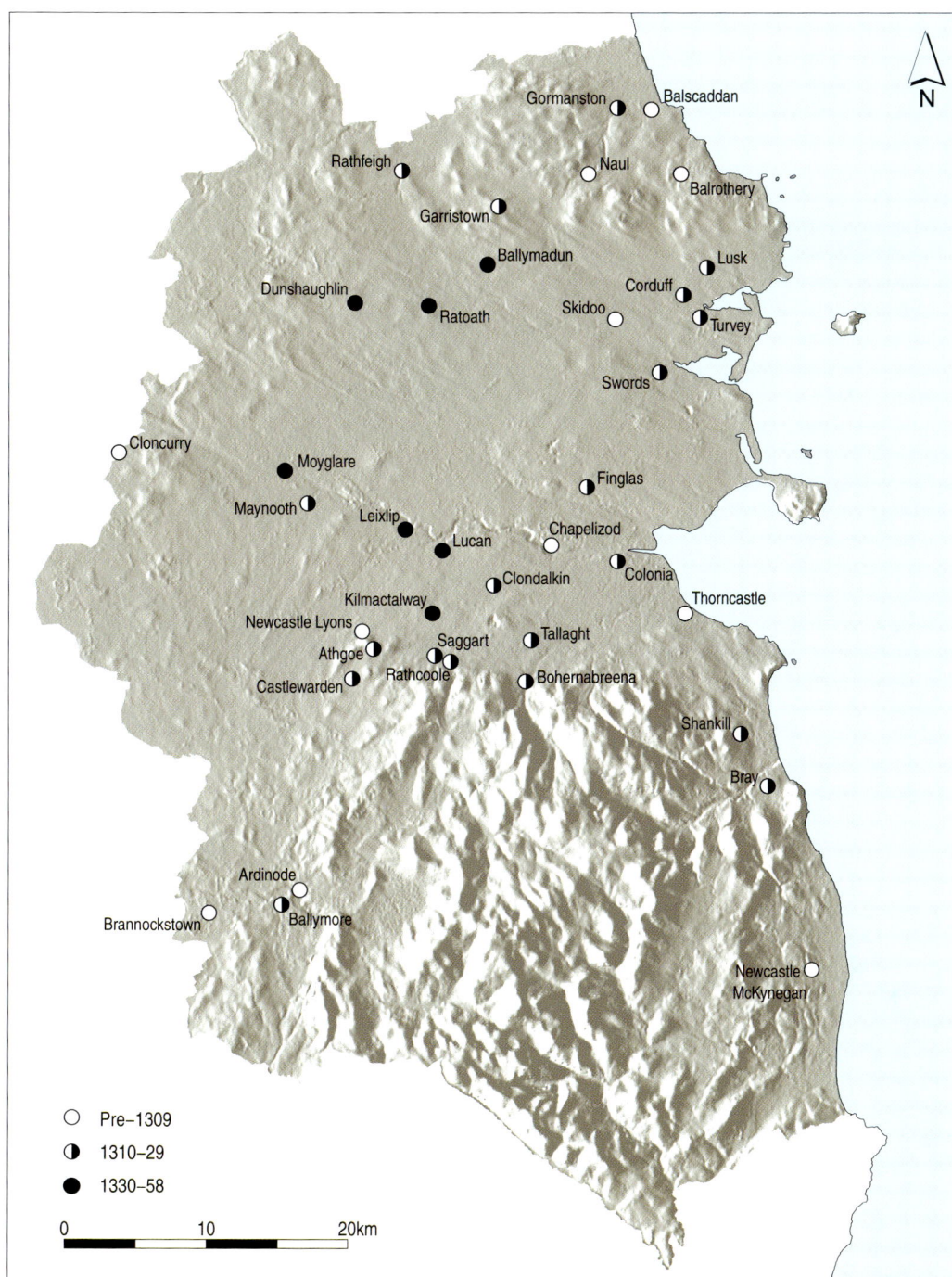

Figure 2.9 Dublin region extents: distribution.

Kildare). There are also fourteenth-century examples for the manors of Balscadden, Clonkeen, Coolock, Grangegorman and Maynooth.[18]

Alongside the extents and rentals, and assembled for the purposes of this study, is a collection of disparate information gleaned from a wide range of other sources relating to agriculture, land-use, buildings, resources and general economic topics. These sources include records of the Irish exchequer such as the pipe rolls, which contain the audited accounts of sheriffs of counties and seneschals of liberties, collectors of customs and subsidies, officials of cities and towns, provosts of royal manors, custodians of lands in the king's hands, purveyors, clerks of wages and keepers of works.[19] Of particular importance

18 McNeill (ed.), *Alen's Register*, pp 118–24 (Swords, Ballymore and Castlekevin); Dryburgh and Smith (eds), *Handbook*, pp 266–7, 271–4 (Coolock and Rathmore); Mills (ed.), *Account Roll*, pp 189–200 (Grangegorman, Clonkeen and Balscadden); *RBK*, pp 121–2 (Maynooth).   **19** All surviving rolls in this series were destroyed in 1922, but some valuable

for the Dublin region are the data relating to the administration of the royal manors as well as the accounts of the keepers of the lands of the archbishopric of Dublin while they were in the king's hands at various dates in the thirteenth century.

Further material relating to the administration of the royal manors can be found in the memoranda rolls.[20] These contain much additional material of economic interest including inventories or lists of household and personal goods, crops, livestock and agricultural equipment in which the king, for a variety of reasons, had an interest (these inventories are somewhat similar to those attached to medieval wills, of which we have individual examples in various Dublin sources and a register for the fifteenth century).[21] The potential of the memoranda rolls to shed light on aspects of social and economic history has been very little exploited.[22]

Although the original issue rolls of the Irish exchequer do not survive, audited copies of some rolls dating between the late thirteenth and the mid-fifteenth century are preserved in the records of the English exchequer. These have been edited and published by Philomena Connolly.[23] A wide variety of transactions are recorded, including payments for the purchase of stock for royal manors, details relating to the repair of mills and the purveyance of grain and other foodstuffs. Accounts of expenditure on military campaigns shed light on the condition of the countryside, on the maintenance of bridges and roads and on the construction of fortifications on manors.

The details of cases heard in the justiciar's court, which perambulated around Ireland, can shed light on a wide range of economic and social aspects of life in medieval Ireland.[24] Pleas held by the justiciar in small towns and boroughs throughout the lordship go some way to compensating for the almost complete absence of surviving manorial or hundred court rolls.[25] They are an important source of commodity prices, references to markets and fairs, descriptions of buildings, the nature of settlements, family structure, occupations etc. Distraints levied on those found guilty of offences or who failed to answer summonses were often in the form of agricultural produce or equipment while correspondence relating to legal cases and judgments can occasionally contain important information relating to the layout and appearance of settlements.

While this book is a study of the countryside around medieval Dublin rather than of the city itself, those sources which deal specifically with the city of Dublin cannot be

material has survived. The pipe roll for 1211–12 had been copied and it provides the earliest information on the organisation of the manorial economy in the colony: Oliver Davies and D.B. Quinn (eds), 'The Irish pipe roll of 14 John, 1211–12', *UJA*, 3rd ser., vol. 4, supplement (1941). There is a catalogue or summary in English of pipe rolls from 1229 to 1348 made by the PROI before the rolls were destroyed, as well as an unpublished calendar for 1356–7 (*Report of the deputy keeper of the public records in Ireland* (*RDKPRI*), 35–9 (1903–7); 42–5 (1911–13); 47 (1915); 53 (1926); 54 (1927); the unpublished calendar is NAI 999/184/18. There is a full transcript of the pipe roll for 1261–2 and most of 1262–3 as well as various extracts from rolls from the thirteenth and fourteenth centuries: RIA MSS 12D9 and 12D10. **20** Two original rolls survive for 1309–10 and 1319–20, along with a calendar that covers the first three quarters of the fourteenth century, with scattered material for the late fourteenth and fifteenth centuries. There are also some comprehensive extracts from the late thirteenth and early fourteenth centuries. For a full listing of surviving memoranda roll material, see J.F. Lydon, 'Survey of the memoranda rolls of the Irish exchequer 1295–1509', *Analecta Hibernia*, 23 (1966), 49–134. **21** The late fifteenth-century wills have been edited in H.F. Berry (ed.), *Register of wills and inventories of the diocese of Dublin, 1457–1483* (Dublin, 1898). For a listing of other medieval wills relating to Dublin, see Margaret Murphy, 'The high cost of dying: an analysis of *pro anima* bequests in medieval Dublin' in W.J. Sheils and Diana Wood (eds), *The church and wealth: studies in church history*, 25 (Oxford, 1987), pp 111–22 at p. 111. Additional wills can be found in Colm Lennon and James Murray (eds), *The Dublin city franchise roll, 1468–1512* (Dublin, 1998) (hereafter *DCFR*), passim. **22** Philomena Connolly, 'The Irish memoranda rolls: some unexplored aspects', *IESH*, 3 (1976), 66–74. **23** Philomena Connolly (ed.), *Irish exchequer payments, 1270–1476* (Dublin, 1998), referred to hereafter as *IEP*. **24** Three justiciary rolls (for 1312–13, 1317–18 and 1330–1) and four common bench rolls (for 1289–90, 1413–14, 1466–7 and 1479–80) have survived, as well as some detached fragments for 1330, 1335 and 1407. These are NAI KB1/1, KB1/2; British Library Additional Charters 13598–13600; see Connolly, *Medieval record sources*, pp 25–6. In addition, there exist calendars of the justiciary rolls from the period 1295–1318, and calendars of the itinerant justices' rolls from 1252 to 1306 for Cos. Dublin and Meath: James Mills (ed.), *Calendar of justiciary rolls, 1295–1303* (Dublin, 1905), referred to hereafter as *CJR, 1295–1303*; James Mills (ed.), *Calendar of justiciary rolls, 1305–7* (Dublin, 1914), referred to hereafter as *CJR, 1305–7*; Margaret Griffith (ed.), *Calendar of justiciary rolls, 1308–14* (Dublin, 1956), referred to hereafter as *CJR, 1308–14*. **25** There are just two short series of manorial court

ignored, particularly as most of the municipal records are accessible in edited collections.[26] Many of these records document the concern of the urban authorities with the sale, location and price of foodstuffs and fuel and they contain important information relating to the source of foodstuffs coming into the city. The location of market places is often an indication of the provenance of particular products. The migration hinterlands of the city can be reconstructed from the evidence contained in the thirteenth-century guild merchant roll and the fifteenth-century franchise roll and can therefore shed light on the trading contacts of medieval Dublin.[27]

It has already been noted that the church held almost half of the land in what is now the modern county of Dublin. The best documented single estate in the Dublin region was that of the archbishops of Dublin, whose manors covered large tracts of land both north and south of the Liffey.[28] The priory of Holy Trinity was second in importance among the ecclesiastical landholders. The priory account roll, mentioned above, was just one element in the huge collection of Christ Church deeds that survived in their original form up to 1922 and are now available in calendared form. Many of the deeds in this collection and in the two surviving volumes from Holy Trinity – the *Liber albus* and *Liber niger* – concern the priory's property and include charters, leases and rentals.[29] Cartularies and registers for some of the other religious houses that held land in the Dublin area survive. These include the abbeys of St Mary and St Thomas, the priory of All Hallows and the hospitals of Kilmainham and of St John outside the New Gate of Dublin.[30] There is also a surviving early sixteenth-century register for Dublin's second cathedral, St Patrick's, and this contains copies of deeds and other documents from the twelfth century onwards.[31] The extents, or descriptions of monastic possessions drawn up in 1540–1, when the monasteries were being dissolved, provide vital details about the layout of individual religious houses and granges, as well as the location and extent of ecclesiastical land.[32] Similar surveys were conducted into the Irish lands of English- and Welsh-based monasteries, and these have been edited in conjunction with records investigating the extent of the possessions of the earldom of Kildare, which were confiscated by the crown at the same time.[33]

Comparable material exists in the records of private landowners. The best collections of private deeds are those of the Butler earls of Ormond. Many of these documents concern lands in Cos. Dublin, Wicklow and Kildare and they date back to 1172 and extend throughout the medieval period. The Red Book of Ormond, compiled in the middle of the fourteenth century, is the oldest Irish family register extant and it contains much of interest including land grants, surveys and extents. The Red Book of Kildare was begun in 1503 but contains grants and deeds from the thirteenth and fourteenth centuries especially, and covers parts of Kildare which fall into the Dublin study area. The Gormanston Register, compiled

rolls relating to the Dublin region. These are for the manors of Lucan (1442–4) and Maynooth (1453–4): TNA:PRO SC2/227/74A and B. We are indebted to Dr Paul Dryburgh for information regarding these documents. **26** J.T. Gilbert (ed.), *Calendar of ancient records of Dublin* (19 vols, Dublin, 1889–1944), referred to hereafter as *CARD*; J.T. Gilbert (ed.), *Historic and municipal documents of Ireland, 1172–1320* (London, 1870), referred to hereafter as *HMDI*; see Mary Clark, 'People, places and parchment: the medieval archives of Dublin city' in Duffy (ed.), *Medieval Dublin III* (2002), pp 140–50. **27** *DGMR*; *DCFR*. **28** The register called *Crede Mihi* was compiled in the late thirteenth century and contains mostly deeds: J.T. Gilbert (ed.), *Crede Mihi: the most ancient register book of the archbishops of Dublin before the reformation* (Dublin, 1897). The *Liber niger Alani* was compiled for Archbishop John Alen (1529–34) and contains material from the twelfth century onwards: McNeill (ed.), *Alen's register.* **29** M.J. McEnery and Raymond Refaussé (eds), *Christ Church deeds* (Dublin, 2001), referred to hereafter as *CCCD*. **30** J.T. Gilbert (ed.), *Chartularies of St Mary's Abbey, Dublin* (2 vols, London, 1884), referred to hereafter as *CSMA*; J.T. Gilbert (ed.), *Register of the Abbey of St Thomas, Dublin* (London, 1889), referred to hereafter as *RAST*; Richard Butler (ed.), *Registrum prioratus omnium sanctorum juxta Dublin* (Dublin, 1845); Charles McNeill (ed.), *Registrum de Kilmainham* (Dublin, 1932), referred to hereafter as *Reg. Kilmainham*; Eric St John Brooks (ed.), *Register of the hospital of St John the Baptist without the New Gate of Dublin* (Dublin, 1936), referred to hereafter as *RHJB*. **31** N.B. White (ed.), *The 'Dignitas Decani' of St Patrick's Cathedral, Dublin* (Dublin, 1957). **32** N.B. White (ed.), *Extents of Irish monastic possessions, 1540–1541* (Dublin, 1943) (hereafter *EIMP*). **33** Gearóid Mac Niocaill (ed.), *Crown surveys of lands, 1540–41, with the*

at the end of the fourteenth century, documents lands in Cos. Dublin, Meath and Kildare while some of the deeds assembled in the Pembroke collection are also of interest.[34]

'Dublin-centred' histories of medieval Ireland, with their reliance on documentary sources produced by the colonial administration, have been justifiably criticised for their exclusion of the Irish.[35] This study, however, is focused on the region that surrounded the capital of the English lordship in Ireland and saw the most intensive settlement by the English. It therefore makes no apology for its reliance on the records of English administration, church and lordship. It is true that a substantial Gaelic population remained in the region following the arrival of the Anglo-Normans at the end of the twelfth century. They are sporadically revealed in the administrative, judicial and manorial sources, identified by their names and frequently by their status as betaghs (unfree manorial tenants) or *hibernici* (Irish). They have left no known sources that speak specifically of their lives, settlements or economy.

Over the course of the centuries, those parts of the study region that lay in east-Wicklow came increasingly under the control of Gaelic lords, while the communities that lived in the border areas between Dublin and Wicklow became partly Gaelicised. As a recent study has illustrated, it is possible to study the military and political history of the Leinster Irish in the late medieval period by using a combination of sources including fragmentary annals, genealogies, English chronicles and government accounts.[36] These sources reveal less about the topics of primary interest to this study such as habitations, agriculture and resources, but, where possible, such material was located and used.

Integrating the sources and addressing the research questions

It is clear from the above discussion that each body of source material has its strengths and weaknesses. A problem common to both archaeological and documentary material is the differential survival of the evidence and the varying degrees of its preservation, something which must be borne in mind constantly when interpreting and analysing evidence distributions. The archaeological research is dependent on reports that display wide variations in sampling policies, definitions, methodologies and systems of classification. Many of the original documentary sources survive only in transcribed or calendared versions where the interests and/or agenda of the individual copyist dictated the range of material recited and the detail in which it was copied.

The challenge of this study is to focus on areas of research to which these disparate and imperfect sources can be applied successfully. The research involved, on the one hand, reconciling precisely datable data from written records with archaeologically derived information that may only be generally datable to within a century or two. On the other hand, archaeological information pertaining to a precise location must be reconciled with written sources for an unidentified locale somewhere in a wider region. Furthermore, there is the challenge of fitting constantly evolving archaeological datasets into an established historical framework.

Kildare rental begun in 1518 (Dublin, 1992).   **34** Edmund Curtis (ed.), *Calendar of Ormond deeds* (6 vols, Dublin, 1932–43), referred to hereafter as *COD*; N.B. White (ed.), *The Red Book of Ormond* (Dublin, 1932), referred to hereafter as *RBO*; Gearóid Mac Niocaill (ed.), *The Red Book of the earls of Kildare* (Dublin, 1964), referred to hereafter as *RBK*; James Mills and M.J. McEnery (eds), *Calendar of the Gormanston register* (Dublin, 1916), referred to hereafter as *CGR*; NAI 2011/1; Anon, *Calendar of ancient deeds and muniments preserved in the Pembroke estate office, Dublin* (Dublin, 1891). **35** Duffy, *Ireland in the Middle Ages*, p. 3.   **36** Emmett O'Byrne, *War, politics and the Irish of Leinster, 1156–1606* (Dublin, 2003).

Throughout the book, the objective is to develop an integrated approach to the many overlapping bodies of data, while ensuring not to neglect areas where one source-type provides the lion's share of information. Of course, it cannot be expected that all of the various strands of evidence will agree and come together seamlessly. In extracting as much as possible from the available sources, one of the challenges of the project is to identify and interrogate the areas where the disparate sources coincide and best inform each other, but it is equally important to highlight conflicting evidence, to explain and to attempt to reconcile these discrepancies. 'Archaeological and historical evidence regarding any given topic should not be expected to fit neatly together or even complement each other. The complexity of society probably militates against such perfect solutions and the divergence between archaeological and historical data undoubtedly reflects that complexity'.[37]

37 Edel Bhreathnach, 'Medieval Irish history at the end of the twentieth century: unfinished work', *IHS*, 32:126 (2000), 260–71 at 266.

PART II

SETTLEMENT AND SOCIETY

CHAPTER 3

The Dublin region before 1170

'sicut … antiquitus fuisse in tempore Hiberniensium'[1]
'just as it was in the time of the Irish'

Introduction

The occupation of the region by the Anglo-Normans in 1170–1 and its subsequent settlement resulted in profound social, economic and political changes. There were, however, significant elements of continuity and overlap with existing settlement patterns. As the Normans had done in England and Wales, the Anglo-Normans in Ireland tended to step into the shoes of the previous rulers and landholders.[2]

The opening quotation comes from a document relating to the settlement of a boundary dispute in Glencullen, Co. Dublin, between 1212 and 1228 and it illustrates the frequent references that can be found in Anglo-Norman charters to territorial divisions that were already in existence before their arrival. Writing in 1894, James Mills stressed these elements of continuity, and this has also been done by more recent commentators such as Marie Therese Flanagan and Edel Bhreathnach.[3] In her study of south Brega, Bhreathnach argued persuasively that the changes in the post-Anglo-Norman period were not to the political boundaries but to the people in control. Observing a striking similarity between the most important sites in the pre-Anglo-Norman period and those later noted as sites of Anglo-Norman settlements, she concluded that the newcomers did not ignore the existing polity of the region but moulded it according to their own administrative, economic and military structures.[4] In order to explain and understand patterns of land-division and settlement after the arrival of the Anglo-Normans, a discussion of the existing political and ecclesiastical structures is clearly necessary.

Political and economic control in the pre-Anglo-Norman period

The site of Dublin lay at various political, ecclesiastical, cultural and economic interfaces in medieval Ireland. This is reflected in a communications network with Dublin as the focal point of four highways, where it stood at the eastern terminus of the Slige Mór.[5] This 'east-west highway … not only crossed the middle of the country at its narrowest point, but also symbolically divided it into two roughly equal halves, Leth Conn and Leth Moga'.[6] One of the first entries in the Annals of Ulster, reportedly from 4120BC, states that 'Eriu was divided in two from one Áth Cliath to the other', that is between Dublin and Galway.[7]

1 *CSMA*, I, p. 388.   **2** Robin Frame, *Colonial Ireland, 1169–1369* (Dublin, 1981), p. 71.   **3** James Mills, 'The Norman settlement in Leinster: the cantreds near Dublin', *JRSAI*, 24 (1894), 161–75 at 174; M.T. Flanagan, *Irish society, Anglo-Norman settlers, Angevin kingship: interactions in Ireland in the late twelfth century* (Oxford, 1989), p. 1; Bhreathnach, 'Authority and supremacy', 1.   **4** Bhreathnach, 'Authority and supremacy', 16–17.   **5** Colm O'Lochlainn, 'Roadways in ancient Ireland' in John Ryan (ed.), *Feilsgribhinn Eoin Mhic Neill* (Dublin, 1940), pp 465–74.   **6** H.B. Clarke, 'Conversion, church and cathedral: the diocese of Dublin to 1152' in Kelly and Keogh (eds), *History of the Catholic diocese of Dublin* (2000), pp 1–50 at pp 21–3.   **7** *AU*, *s.a.* 4120, pp 8–9. See Matthew Stout, 'Early medieval boundaries'

By the later twelfth century, Dublin had already been in existence for some 300 years and had become by far the most important urban settlement in Ireland and one of the richest ports in Western Europe.[8] It had also become a considerable focus of interest for the political ambitions of Irish kings, with candidates for high-kingship viewing control of Dublin as a necessary objective to achieving their goals.[9] The ecclesiastical importance of the town was increasing as well, and at the reforming ecclesiastical synod of Kells, held in 1152, Dublin was chosen as the centre of one of four ecclesiastical provinces.[10] Over the course of time, the town had come to exercise political, economic and ecclesiastical control over a significant hinterland territory. This territory was either directly controlled by the rulers of Dublin and held as their 'demesne', or was indirectly controlled through subject kings who were both Scandinavian and Irish.

In 1170, when Richard de Clare (Strongbow) defeated Ascall Mac Turcaill, the Hiberno-Norse king of Dublin, and took control of the town, he would naturally have laid claim to this territory as well.[11] The following year, Strongbow met with Henry II at Newnham in Gloucestershire and renewed his oath of fealty, 'surrendering to the king the chief town of the kingdom, Dublin, *along with the adjoining cantreds*'.[12] The precise bounds and limits of these cantreds were not defined in any contemporary documents, but they are believed by many commentators to equate broadly with the area that developed into the county of Dublin and which had its origin in the territory controlled by the rulers of Dublin and their subject kings.[13]

The emergence of the Dublin hinterland

The political and economic control of an extensive rural area by Scandinavian Dublin has been widely accepted since the publication of John Bradley's influential analysis in 1988.[14] The nature and chronology of the settlement within this area, however, is the subject of considerable debate.[15] Bradley proposed that the territory was largely inhabited and farmed by the Norse or Hiberno-Norse, to the extent that the Irish were forced into the Wicklow Mountains. Other commentators have been less sure of the extent of Scandinavian rural settlement, and have suggested that Dublin was able to exploit a hinterland area occupied and farmed by a 'sympathetic' Irish population with whom they had reached a commercial accommodation.[16] It has been argued, for instance, that there is a lack of archaeological evidence to support widespread Norse settlement and the displacement of Irish inhabitants.[17] Bradley pointed, however, to the similarity between the material culture of Dublin and that of rural Irish settlement sites, and the fact that this makes it virtually impossible to distinguish archaeologically between a rural Scandinavian settlement site and a rural Irish one of tenth- to twelfth-century date.[18]

in Condit and Corlett (eds), *Above and beyond* (2005), pp 139–48 at p. 140. **8** P.F. Wallace, 'Archaeology and the emergence of Dublin as the principal town of Ireland' in Bradley (ed.), *Settlement and society* (1988), pp 123–60. **9** Byrne, 'The trembling sod', p. 26; M.T. Flanagan, 'High-kings with opposition, 1072–1166' in Ó Cróinín (ed.), *A new history of Ireland: I* (2005), pp 899–933. **10** Ailbhe MacShamhráin, 'The emergence of the metropolitan see: Dublin, 1111–1216' in Kelly and Keogh (eds), *History of the Catholic diocese of Dublin* (2000), pp 51–71 at pp 56–8. **11** See Seán Duffy, 'Ireland's Hastings: the Anglo-Norman conquest of Dublin', *Anglo-Norman Studies*, 20 (1998), 69–86. **12** Gerald of Wales: *Expugnatio Hibernica, the conquest of Ireland: by Giraldus Cambrensis*, ed. A.B. Scott and F.X. Martin (Dublin, 1978), p. 89. **13** A.P. Smyth, *Celtic Leinster: towards an historical geography of early Irish civilisation, AD500–1600* (Dublin, 1982), pl. ix; K.W. Nicholls, 'The land of the Leinstermen', *Peritia*, 3 (1984), 535–58. See also Clare Downham, 'Fine Gall' in Seán Duffy (ed.), *Medieval Ireland: an encyclopedia* (New York, 2005), pp 170–1. **14** Bradley, 'The interpretation of Scandinavian settlement'. See also John Bradley, 'Scandinavian rural settlement in Ireland', *AI*, 9.3 (1995), 10–12. **15** Bradley revisits the evidence for ninth-century Scandinavian settlement in the hinterland of Dublin in a recent publication: Bradley, 'Some reflections'. **16** Wallace, 'Economy and commerce', p. 204; Simms and Fagan, 'Villages in Co. Dublin', p. 89. **17** Mark Clinton, 'The souterrains of Co. Dublin' in Manning (ed.), *Dublin and beyond the Pale* (1998), pp 117–28; Mark Clinton, 'Settlement patterns in the kingdom of Leinster (7th to mid-12th centuries)' in Smyth (ed.), *Seanchas* (2000), pp 275–98. **18** Bradley, 'The interpretation of Scandinavian settlement', p. 60.

Figure 3.1 Ninth-century oval brooch from Finglas, Co. Dublin (overall length 8.2cm). This is one of two brooches found in association with a burial on Church Street in 2004 (image courtesy of the National Museum of Ireland).

Figure 3.2 Collection of artefacts found at Cherrywood, Co. Dublin, including a ninth-century whale-bone plaque. This carved and decorated object was found within an enclosed cemetery, 1.6km to the south-east of Tully Church in 1998 (image courtesy of John Ó Néill).

The first phase of Scandinavian Dublin's existence lasted from 841 to 902, and has been called the '*longphort*' phase.[19] The settlement focused on a defended harbour, whose location remains debateable, but there is also evidence that an area within a 10km radius of this settlement came under Scandinavian control.[20] The possibility of a ninth-century Viking settlement at or near Clondalkin, 10km to the west of Dublin, is suggested by an annalistic reference to the death of one hundred Vikings there in 867.[21] The entry in the annals refers to Clondalkin as Dún Amlaíb, thereby linking it with Óláfr (Amlaíb) the White, king of Dublin from 853 to 873. The early monastery at Clondalkin was plundered by the Vikings in 833 and in the years following the establishment of the Dublin *longphort*, a satellite settlement or fort was set up in its vicinity.[22] There may have been similar satellite settlements at Donnybrook and Finglas, where ninth-century Viking burials have been found (Figure 3.1).[23] The discovery of a ninth-century whale-bone plaque of classic Norwegian style at Cherrywood, 14km south of Dublin, may point to early Scandinavian settlement at this location also (Figure 3.2).[24] Bradley has recently characterised ninth-

19 Howard Clarke, 'The bloodied eagle: the Vikings and the development of Dublin', *Irish Sword*, 18 (1991), 91–119. **20** See Bradley, 'Some reflections', pp 48–9. **21** *AU2, s.a.* 867.8. **22** Charles Doherty, 'Cluain Dolcáin: a brief note' in Smyth (ed.), *Seanchas* (2000), pp 182–8 at pp 184–5; Ruth Johnson, *Viking-Age Dublin* (Dublin, 2004), p. 67; Bradley and King, 'UAS 8:4: County Dublin', pp 215–16. **23** R.A. Hall, 'A Viking-Age grave at Donnybrook, Co. Dublin', *Med. Arch.*, 22 (1978), 64–83; P.F. Wallace, 'A woman of importance in ninth-century Finglas', *AI*, 18:3 (2004), 7; John Kavanagh, 'Excavation at Church Street, Finglas, Dublin', Unpublished excavation report submitted to the DEHLG, 2005; John Kavanagh, '4–8 Church Street, Finglas' in *Excavations 2004*, pp 139–40; Maeve Sikora, 'The Finglas burial: archaeology and ethnicity in Viking-Age Dublin' in Sheehan and Ó Corráin (eds), *The Viking Age: Ireland and the West* (2010), pp 402–17. **24** John Ó Néill, 'Excavation of pre-Norman structures on the site of an enclosed Early Christian cemetery at Cherrywood, County Dublin' in Duffy (ed.), *Medieval Dublin VII* (2006), pp 66–88; Bradley, 'Some

century Scandinavian settlement in Dublin and its region as a 'central *longphort* with a series of dependent forts from which the territory was governed'.[25] Within these areas, native settlement continued, with tributes being paid to the military elites. Along the coast, Scandinavian settlement extended further, from close to Lusk in the north, down to Dalkey in the south, while islands off the coast were also colonised at an early stage.

Scandinavian control of these areas ceased in 902 when an Irish coalition of Leinster and Brega captured Dublin and expelled the foreigners.[26] Some settlers may have remained, though, and may have facilitated the rapid reoccupation of territory that occurred when Dublin was 'refounded' in 917.[27] As the planned Hiberno-Norse town developed over the tenth century, so too did the hinterland area begin to take shape. The written sources start to refer to the *crích gall*, the 'territory of the foreigners'. When the high king Máel Sechnaill II sacked Dublin in 980, he proclaimed all Irish slaves in the *crích gall* to be free.[28] This territory, later called *Fine Gall* by the Irish and *Dyflinarskiri* in Scandinavian sources, seems by the eleventh century to have stretched from Dublin north to Skerries and west to Leixlip.[29] Much of Dyflinarskiri was, however, subject to periodic control by Irish kings, whether local or provincial, and the situation changed constantly. The principal political border was between Leinster to the south and Brega to the north.[30] During the tenth century, the Norse of Dublin, especially under their king Amlaíb Cuarán (952–80), exercised considerable control over the region around Dublin and appear to have been extending their interests northwards. In the 960s, Amlaíb married Dúnlaith, the sister of Domnall ua Néill, king of Tara, a move that has been linked with his patronage of the church at Skreen, beside Tara.[31] His subsequent marriage to Gormflaith, daughter of Murchad mac Finn, of the Uí Fáeláin branch of the Uí Dúnlainge, king of Leinster (966–72), may have similarly facilitated the expansion of Dublin's interests southwards into the Rathdown area.[32]

A poem written in praise of Amlaíb alludes to the ambitions of this king to rule over the whole kingdom of Brega, and this may indeed have been his intention when he came into conflict with Máel Sechnaill mac Domnaill at Tara in 980.[33] Amlaíb was defeated at the battle of Tara and retired to Iona, where he died the following year. His death put an end to Dublin's expansion northwards and it is likely that Dyflinarskiri then contracted. The increasing interest of Irish kings in Dublin must have affected the ability of the Norse to control independent estates within Dyflinarskiri and even Fine Gall. Up to and including the twelfth century, however, the Dublin Norse continued in their ambitions to control the area between the Liffey and the Boyne.[34] There is sufficient historical data to indicate that in the mid-eleventh century the Scandinavian orbit extended northwards to Swords. According to the Annals of Ulster, the attack by the king of Meath on Swords in 1035 was

reflections', pp 48–9.   **25** Bradley, 'Some reflections', p. 55.   **26** *AU, s.a.* 901.   **27** Bradley, 'Some reflections', p. 49. Excavations at Temple Bar West in Dublin, directed by Linzi Simpson, revealed the remains of late ninth- and tenth-century settlement, with 'no break in occupancy on the site, despite the period of "expulsion" between AD902 and 917. Thus, although the Viking warriors were expelled in 902, we must presume that this was confined to the ruling elite and that life at Dublin went on as usual, albeit with a reduced population' (see Linzi Simpson, 'The first phase of Viking activity in Ireland: archaeological evidence from Dublin' in Sheehan and Ó Corráin (eds), *The Viking Age: Ireland and the West* (2010), pp 418–29.   **28** *ATig.*, 2, p. 233; *CS, s.a.* 978; *AFM, s.a.* 979.   **29** David Greene, 'The evidence of place-names in Ireland' in Thorsten Andersson and Karl Inge Sandred (eds), *The Vikings* (Stockholm, 1978), pp 119–23.   **30** Within the Dublin study area shown in Figure 1.3, the baronies of Rathdown Upper and Lower, Newcastle, Ballinacor North, Lower Talbotstown, South and North Naas, Clane, Ikeathy, South and North Salt, Newcastle and Uppercross lay in the kingdom of Leinster, while the baronies of Coolock, Castleknock, Nethercross, Dunboyne, Upper Deece, Lower Deece, Skreen, Upper Duleek, Balrothery West and Balrothery East lay in the territory of Brega.   **31** Edel Bhreathnach, 'The documentary evidence for pre-Norman Skreen, County Meath', *RnM*, 9:2 (1996), 37–45 at 40–1.   **32** Bradley, 'Some reflections', p. 50.   **33** Charles Doherty, 'The Vikings in Ireland: a review' in Clarke, Ní Mhaonaigh and Ó Floinn (eds), *Ireland and Scandinavia* (1998), pp 288–330 at pp 297–8. See also Alex Woolf, 'Amlaíb Cuarán and the Gael, 941–81' in Duffy (ed.), *Medieval Dublin III* (2002), pp 34–43.   **34** Seán Duffy, 'Irishmen and Islesmen in the kingdoms of Dublin and Man, 1052–1171', *Ériu*, 43 (1992), 93–133 at 119, fn 125.

Athlumney

Skerries
Holmpatrick
Lusk
Lambay
Oldtown
Swords
Feltrim Hill
Cloghran   Kinsaley
St Doolagh's
Ireland's Eye
Finglas
Baldoyle
Glasnevin
Howth
Leixlip
Dollymount
Barnhall
Oxmantown
Kilmainham-Islandbridge
Clondalkin
Donnybrook
Brownsbarn
Balally
Dalkey   Dalkey Island
Laughanstown
Cherrywood
Rathmichael
Kilmalin
Curtlestown   Stagonnil
Windgate
Coolagad
Ballygunnar   Delgany
Rathturtle
Cooladoyle
Ballymore
Trudder
Ballymanus   Wicklow

N

● Place-name
◑ Archaeology
○ Documentary

0   10   20km

in retaliation for a raid carried out by the Dublin Norse on Ardbraccan, Co. Meath.[35] This indicates that Swords was regarded as part of the kingdom of Dublin at that time.[36] Later in the century, Gruffudd, subsequently prince of Gwynedd, and a great-grandson of King Sitric Silkbeard of Dublin, was raised at Cloghran, near Swords, and was fostered by an Ostman family who may have been tenants on the monastic lands.[37]

As Dublin grew, its dependency on the products of the surrounding countryside increased exponentially. The population of the town in the late eleventh to early twelfth century has been estimated at 4,500, and a settlement of this size would not have been able

35 *AU, s.a.* 1035, pp 474–5: 'Ard mBrecáin was plundered by Sitruic son of Amlaíb. Sord Coluim Chille was plundered and burned by Concobur ua Mael Sechlainn in revenge for it'.   **36** Bradley, 'The medieval boroughs of Co. Dublin', p. 138.   **37** Doherty, 'The Vikings in Ireland', p. 300; Edmund Curtis, 'Norse Dublin', *DHR*, 4 (1942), 96–108; repr. in Clarke (ed.), *Medieval Dublin: the making of a metropolis* (1990), pp 98–109 at p. 103; Seán Duffy, 'Ostmen, Irish and Welsh in the eleventh century', *Peritia*, 9 (1995), 378–96.

to survive without the produce of an extensive agricultural hinterland.[38] Everyday necessities – cereal crops in particular – were produced close to the town. The massive amounts of animal bones found during excavations in Dublin city, coupled with the evidence for large-scale leather-working, point to sizeable meat consumption on the part of the citizens. While pigs were reared within the town itself, cattle were supplied from its hinterland.[39] Timber, wattles, straw and other building materials were also required, while the raw materials for craft industries, including bone, antler, lead and copper, also originated in the countryside.[40] Siobhán Geraghty has identified a large variety of organic materials brought into Dublin from within Ireland, probably from the city's immediate hinterland.[41] She hypothesises an area of at least 10,000 acres needed to supply Dublin with wheat c.1100, while John Tierney has estimated that Hiberno-Scandinavian Dublin must have had consistent access to about a hundred acres of managed hazel coppice to build and renew its housing stock.[42] In addition to exploiting the hinterland to sustain the town, there is some evidence that Dublin was involved in the export of agricultural products to settlements such as Chester. The only specific commodity known to have been exported to Chester before 1066 was marten furs. Later evidence, however, suggests that hides, fish and agricultural produce also formed part of an extensive trade between these two settlements.[43]

Onomastic evidence can also be used to track the extent of Scandinavian settlement across the region (Figure 3.3). W.J. Smyth pointed out that about 15 per cent of the parish names in Co. Dublin are hybrid in character, being a mixture of Irish, Scandinavian and Anglo-Norman origin.[44] Viking influence is reflected, for instance, in parish names of Scandinavian origin, such as Dalkey (*Deilginis*, 'thorn island'), Howth (*Hofuth*, 'headland') and Leixlip (*Laxhlaup*, 'salmon leap').[45] Other place-names with a Norse derivation include Holmpatrick, Lambay and Skerries.[46] As one might expect, Scandinavian influence in the region diminishes with distance from Dublin, but there is nonetheless a significant concentration of potentially Viking-related place-names to the south of the city both in coastal zones and further inland (Figure 3.3).

In Co. Wicklow in particular, possible Hiberno-Norse influence can be detected in a range of place-names. Of these, Arklow and Wicklow are perhaps the best known, but Colmán Etchingham also noted that Killahurler, c.10km west of Arklow, may incorporate a Norse name like *Thoraldr* or *Thorhallr*, and that Coolagad, Priest's Gate and Windgate possibly include the Norse word *gata*, meaning a path or road.[47] The *gata* referred to in Coolagad and Windgate, both in the north-east of Co. Wicklow, may well be the ancient roadway joining Bray and Delgany. It is also possible, however, that the 'gate' element of these names derives from Old English *geat*, 'a gap'. Price believed that Stagonnil, a name associated with the church site in Powerscourt Demesne, may derive from the Norse *Gunhildarstaðir*, meaning 'Gunhild's house'.[48] Etchingham was reluctant to accept the *Sta* element as Norse, but he did agree that Stagonnil possibly incorporates the Norse woman's name, *Gunnhildr*.[49]

38 Geraghty, *Viking Dublin*; See also Valante, 'Dublin's economic relations'.   **39** Wallace, 'Economy and commerce', p. 203.   **40** P.F. Wallace, 'The archaeology of Ireland's Viking-Age towns' in Ó Cróinín (ed.), *A new history of Ireland: I* (2005), pp 814–41 at p. 834.   **41** Geraghty, *Viking Dublin*, pp 35–71.   **42** John Tierney, 'Woods and woodlands in early medieval Munster' in Michael Monk and John Sheehan (eds), *Early medieval Munster: archaeology, history and society* (Cork, 1998), pp 53–8.   **43** Alan Thacker (ed.), *Victoria county history of Cheshire, vol. 5, pt 1: the city of Chester* (London, 2003), p. 29.   **44** W.J. Smyth, 'Exploring the social and cultural topographies of sixteenth- and seventeenth-century county Dublin' in Aalen and Whelan (eds), *Dublin city and county* (1992), pp 121–79 at p. 150.   **45** Magne Oftedal, 'Scandinavian place-names in Ireland' in Almqvist and Greene (eds), *Proceedings of the seventh Viking Congress* (1976), pp 125–33 at p. 131.   **46** Simms and Fagan, 'Villages in Co. Dublin', p. 89.   **47** Colmán Etchingham, 'Evidence of Scandinavian settlement in Wicklow' in Hannigan and Nolan (eds), *Wicklow: history and society* (1994), pp 113–38 at pp 124, 127, 131; Liam Price, *The place-names of Co. Wicklow: barony of Rathdown* (Dublin, 1957), pp 319–20. **48** Price, *Place-names: Rathdown*, pp 296–8.   **49** Etchingham, 'Evidence of Scandinavian settlement in Wicklow', p. 131. Bradley has recently rejected both Windgate and Stagonil as possible Scandinavian place-names: Bradley, 'Some

Kilmalin is referred to in various medieval documents, from *c*.1280 onwards, as Stamolin (or variations of this) and, as with his explanation of Stagonnil, Price suggested that the sta-prefix may be derived from the Old Norse word *staðir*, which had the same meaning as the Irish *baile* or *teach* – 'place', 'dwelling', 'stead'.[50] In this case, however, Etchingham was reluctant to accept the suggestion made by Price.[51]

Place-names containing personal name elements are relatively common, and several Norse names appear to be preserved in north Co. Wicklow. Ballygunnar contains the Norse name *Gunnarr*, while Rathturtle and Curtlestown both preserve a version of the name of the Dublin Norse family of Mac Turcaill. Price noted that a variant name for Kilruddery ('Baliurodrach') may contain the Norse name *Rothrekr*.[52] Other Wicklow place-names mentioned by Etchingham that possibly contain Norse elements include the townlands of Ballymanus Upper, Ballymanus Lower, Cooladoyle and Trudder.[53] There is also some indication, in the form of personal names recorded in documentary sources, for the presence in and around Arklow and Wicklow of Hiberno-Norse inhabitants.[54] Similar evidence is known for the area around Rathturtle.[55] The identification in mid-thirteenth-century documentary sources of individuals described as 'Ostmen' or whose personal names indicate Scandinavian origin on many of the archiepiscopal manors in the Dublin region provides further proof of the breadth and persistence of Norse rural settlement.[56]

The archaeological evidence for Scandinavian rural settlement is most persuasive for Co. Dublin and the extreme north of Co. Wicklow. The excavated remains at Cherrywood of a possible rural Norse settlement constitute the only unambiguous evidence for habitation.[57] The site lies within a circular enclosure measuring 38m by 42m in diameter, which served as a cemetery in the sixth and seventh centuries. By the eighth century, however, the enclosed space was used for settlement, and radiocarbon determinations have helped to identify a sequence of structures ranging in date from AD680–980 to AD1020–1230. The associated artefacts and a corn-drying kiln would sit comfortably in any ringfort context for the most part, but the recovery of a ninth-century decorated whale-bone plaque from a pit (Figure 3.2) and, to a lesser degree, that of a silver ingot found outside the site, indicate a Scandinavian presence. Other finds typical of the material culture of ninth- and tenth-century Dublin included bone-comb fragments, blue glass and an amber bead. The possibility of this being a Scandinavian rural settlement is further endorsed by the remains of three bow-shaped and rectilinear buildings within the enclosed space. Such buildings are not traditionally associated with ringfort settlements. As the excavator has noted, the design for these buildings is more akin to structures excavated at Hedeby and on the Shetland Islands, where the Scandinavian context is clear.[58] The intermixture of Irish and Scandinavian cultural traits at Cherrywood is obvious, and suggests the level of integration that was experienced in this part of the Dublin region.

To date, excavated evidence for Scandinavian rural settlement in the Dublin hinterland remains sparse. The distribution of certain burial sites, however, and the distinctive granite grave-markers known as 'Rathdown Slabs' provides additional evidence of the extent of Scandinavian activity (Figure 3.6c).[59] Rathdown Slabs, which belong to the period from the

reflections', pp 50–1.   **50** Stamoling (*c*.1280, Gilbert (ed.), *Crede Mihi*, p. 142); Stamaleyn (1326, McNeill (ed.), *Alen's register*, p. 196), Stamolin (1530, McNeill (ed.), *Alen's register*, p. 196); Price, *Place-names: Rathdown*, p. 291. **51** Etchingham, 'Evidence of Scandinavian settlement in Wicklow', p. 131.   **52** Price, *Place-names: Rathdown*, p. 332. **53** Etchingham, 'Evidence of Scandinavian settlement in Wicklow', pp 126, 131.   **54** Ibid., pp 124–5.   **55** Ibid., p. 128. **56** See below, pp 93–4, 181–2.   **57** John Ó Néill, 'Cherrywood Science and Technology Park, Cherrywood' in *Excavations 1999*, pp 54–6; John Ó Néill, 'A Norse settlement in rural County Dublin', *AI*, 13:4 (winter 1999), 8–10; Ó Néill, 'Excavation of pre-Norman structures'; John Ó Néill and Jennie Coughlan, 'An enclosed early medieval cemetery at Cherrywood, Co. Dublin' in Corlett and Potterton (eds), *Death and burial in early medieval Ireland* (2010), pp 239–50. **58** Ó Néill, 'Excavation of pre-Norman structures', pp 84–5.   **59** Hall, 'A Viking-Age grave at Donnybrook'; William Frazer,

Figure 3.4 Three
'Rathdown Slabs'
now displayed on
the church wall at
Rathmichael,
Co. Dublin
(© Department
of the Environment,
Heritage and Local
Government).

tenth to the twelfth century, display a range of stylistic features, the most common motifs being herringbone patterns and cup-marks, often surrounded by concentric circles (Figure 3.4).[60] It has been suggested that these designs are comparable with the decorated bone and antler work retrieved from Viking levels in Dublin city.[61] It is generally agreed that the slabs were used to mark the graves of Christians of Viking descent. Outside Ireland, the closest parallels are to be found in the Viking-settled areas of Scotland and northern England.[62] Ó hÉailidhe drew particular attention to the similarity to slabs in Northumbria, adding that 'the relationship between Dublin and Northumbria is most significant as they were for many years ruled by the same dynasty and often by the same monarch'.[63] In Ireland, the slabs are exclusively associated with early churches in the former territory of Rathdown – situated in north-east Wicklow and south-east Dublin. This suggests that the Vikings had settled a considerable part of that area and that they played an important part in the development of churches there.

Viking burials discovered at Kilmainham and Islandbridge were part of a primary cemetery area associated with the settlement in Dublin.[64] Viking grave-goods and isolated

'Description of a great sepulchral mound at Aylesbury Road, near Donnybrook, in the county of Dublin ...', *PRIA*, 16C (1879), 29–55; William Frazer, 'The Aylesbury Road sepulchral mound ...', *PRIA*, 16C (1882), 116–18; Haakon Shetelig (ed.), *Viking antiquities in Great Britain and Ireland, part III: Norse antiquities in Ireland* (Oslo, 1940), pp 66–7; Raghnall Ó Floinn, 'Two Viking burials from Wicklow', *Wicklow Archaeology and History*, 1 (1998), 29–35; Kavanagh, 'Excavation at Church Street, Finglas'; Kavanagh, '4–8 Church Street, Finglas'. **60** P[adraig] Ó hÉailidhe, 'The Rathdown Slabs', *JRSAI*, 87 (1957), 75–88; P[adraig] Ó hÉailidhe, 'Early Christian grave-slabs in the Dublin region', *JRSAI*, 103 (1973), 51–64; Chris Corlett, 'The Rathdown Slabs: Vikings and Christianity', *AI*, 17:4 (winter 2003), 28–30; Christiaan Corlett, *Antiquities of old Rathdown: the archaeology of south County Dublin and north County Wicklow* (Bray, 1999), p. 45; Christiaan Corlett, 'Two recently discovered Rathdown Slabs from Taney graveyard, Dundrum, Co. Dublin', *JRSAI*, 132 (2002), 139–43; T.C. Breen, 'A pre-Norman grave-slab at Rathfarnham, County Dublin', *JRSAI*, 111 (1981), 120–3; Mary Harkin, 'St Nathi's church and graveyard, Dundrum, Co. Dublin' in Condit and Corlett (eds), *Above and beyond* (2005), pp 171–86 at pp 178–81; O'Brien, 'Churches of south-east County Dublin', pp 508–12; Clarke, 'Conversion, church and cathedral', pp 36–7. **61** Ó hÉailidhe, 'Early Christian grave-slabs', 58–9. **62** Ibid., 58–9; J.R. Allen and Joseph Anderson, *The Early Christian monuments of Scotland* (Edinburgh, 1903), pp 429–31; W.G. Collingwood, *Northumbrian crosses of the pre-Norman age* (London, 1927), p. 45. **63** Ó hÉailidhe, 'Early Christian grave-slabs', 59. **64** For instance, see Shetelig (ed.), *Viking antiquities*, pp 11–65; Elizabeth O'Brien, 'The location and context of Viking burials at Kilmainham and Islandbridge, Dublin' in Clarke, Ní Mhaonaigh and Ó Floinn (eds),

Figure 3.5 Silver 'thistle' brooch from Celbridge, Co. Kildare. This brooch-type is found in Ireland, Scotland and England, and was probably made in the late ninth or early tenth century. It is almost certainly of Irish manufacture, being of a type that evolved from pre-Viking penannular brooches. The silver may have been traded through Hiberno-Scandinavian Dublin into the hands of native craftsmen (image courtesy of the National Museum of Ireland).

Norse antiquities have also been discovered at over a dozen locations across the Dublin region, in Cos. Meath, Kildare and Wicklow (Figure 3.3).[65] The distribution extends beyond that of the Rathdown Slabs, and occupies the broad floodplain of the Liffey, as well as locations adjacent to the coast, such as Lusk. In a way that isolated finds and object hoards cannot attest, the presence of burials associated with particular traditions implies the association of settlement groups of the same cultural identity, and as such these remains reflect Scandinavian settlement in different parts of the Dublin region. The absence of large cemeteries further indicates the small-scale nature of that settlement, an interpretation that is supported by the Cherrywood farmstead.

The discovery of Viking-Age hoards adds further evidence of Scandinavian activity across the Dublin region, with coin hoards being particularly prevalent in the countryside

Ireland and Scandinavia (1998), pp 203–21; Elizabeth O'Brien, 'A tale of two cemeteries', *AI*, 9:3 (autumn 1995), 13–15; Elizabeth O'Brien, 'A reconsideration of the location and context of Viking burials at Kilmainham/Islandbridge, Dublin' in Manning (ed.), *Dublin and beyond the Pale* (1998), pp 35–44; W.R. Wilde, 'On the Scandinavian antiquities lately discovered at Islandbridge, near Dublin', *PRIA*, 10 (1866–9), 13–22; George Coffey and E.C.R. Armstrong, 'Scandinavian objects found at Islandbridge and Kilmainham', *PRIA*, 28C (1910), 107–22.   **65** George Coffey, 'A pair of brooches and chains of the Viking period, recently found in Ireland', *JRSAI*, 32 (1902), 71–3; Shetelig, *Viking antiquities*, pp 73, 76, 82–5, 90, 129; Raghnall Ó Floinn, 'The archaeology of the early Viking Age in Ireland' in Clarke, Ní Mhaonaigh and Ó Floinn (eds), *Ireland and Scandinavia* (1998), pp 131–65 at pp 144–5, 148; Ó Floinn, 'Two Viking burials from County Wicklow'; James Graham-Campbell, 'The Viking-Age silver hoards of Ireland' in Almqvist and Greene (eds), *Proceedings of the seventh Viking Congress* (1976), pp 39–74 at p. 60; J.C. Walker, *An historical essay on the dress of the ancient and Modern Irish* (Dublin, 1788), pl. xiii and p. 173; W.R. Wilde, *The beauties of the Boyne and its tributary, the Blackwater* (2nd ed., Dublin, 1850), pp 134–5; W.R. Wilde, *A descriptive catalogue of the antiquities of animal materials and bronze in the museum of the Royal Irish Academy* (Dublin, 1861), pp 573–4; P.J. Hartnett and George Eogan, 'Feltrim Hill, Co. Dublin: a Neolithic and Early Christian site', *JRSAI*, 94 (1964), 1–37 at 29, 30, 33; H.O'N.

to the south of the city.[66] However, the hoards and artefacts do not necessarily infer Scandinavian settlement. As Bradley has argued, such pieces are perhaps more usefully regarded as evidence for the nature and extent of trade and economic endeavour between the port town and its wider hinterland (Figure 3.5). Taken together with the historical, onomastic and other archaeological evidence, they contribute to a picture of significant Viking and Hiberno-Scandinavian interaction in the region around Dublin from the ninth to the twelfth century.

The emergence of the Dublin diocese

The early history of the diocese of Dublin has been traced by Howard Clarke, who asserts that the early medieval or pre-Viking diocese extended 'broadly speaking' from the Liffey-Camac to the Dodder.[67] It appears likely that there was an episcopal centre connected with the early monastic site of Duiblinn (Dubhlinn) in the vicinity of which the activities of abbots and bishops are frequently recorded. Duiblinn lay in the area controlled by the Uí Fergusa in the pre-Viking period and it was probably the location of their main church. Other important churches in this area included Kilmainham, Clondalkin and Donnybrook.

Outside the petty kingdom of the Uí Fergusa, there was a concentration of important church sites, many of them found in association with secular power centres.[68] In the territory of Uí Briúin Cualann, close to an Iron-Age hill fort, another diocesan centre probably existed at Tully (*Tulach na nEpscop*), while the important church at Newcastle Lyons was situated close to the Uí Dúnchada power centre at Lyons Hill (*Liamain*). The territory north-east of the Liffey came under the control of the Síl nÁedo Sláine lineage and contained important foundations at Finglas, Glasnevin, Kilmartin, Lusk and Swords.

Following the establishment of the Viking settlement in 841, episcopal functions for Duiblinn were transferred elsewhere, perhaps to Tully, in Laughanstown, near Cabinteely. Most of the monasteries in the surrounding area appear to have survived and many of the smaller churches probably did also. Clarke argues for a continuation of Christian practices in the region, fostered by widespread inter-marriage with the Scandinavians. Continuity of Christian burial practices in areas close to Norse Dublin is witnessed by the burials at Cabinteely and Castleknock, which ranged from the early medieval through to the high medieval period.[69] That most, if not all, of the major church sites in the Dublin region continued in use after the establishment of the *longphort* in 841 is evidenced by the annalistic record.[70] The move to re-establish Dublin as a bishopric came towards the end of the reign of Sitric Silkbeard, son of Amlaíb Cuarán, who was deposed as king of Dublin in 1036.[71] It was particularly associated with the foundation of Christ Church, which took place *c*.1030 or a little later.[72] An examination of the early endowments of the cathedral sheds light on landholding patterns in the hinterland region. These are contained in a charter of King John

Hencken, 'Lagore crannog: an Irish royal residence of the 7th to 10th centuries AD', *PRIA*, 53C (1953), 1–247 at 97–8 and fig. 31d; Thomas Fanning, *Viking-Age ringed pins from Dublin* (Dublin, 1994), pp 49–50; Mary Dunlevy, 'A classification of early Irish combs', *PRIA*, 88C (1988), 341–422 at 363–4.   **66** Michael Kenny, 'The geographical distribution of Irish Viking-Age coin hoards', *PRIA*, 87C (1987), 507–25; John Sheehan, 'Early Viking-Age silver hoards from Ireland' in Clarke, Ní Mhaonaigh and Ó Floinn (eds), *Ireland and Scandinavia* (1998), pp 166–202, esp. fig. 6.4, p. 174; Howard Clarke, 'The Vikings in Ireland: a historian's perspective', *AI*, 9:3 (autumn 1995), 7–9; Edwards, *The archaeology of early medieval Ireland*, pp 174–9.   **67** Clarke, 'Conversion, church and cathedral', pp 28–9.   **68** The most comprehensive listing to date of early medieval ecclesiastical sites in Co. Dublin can be found in MacShamhráin, 'The *Monasticon Hibernicum* project'.   **69** Clarke, 'Conversion, church and cathedral', p. 33; Malachy Conway, *Director's first findings from excavations in Cabinteely* (Dublin, 2000); E.P. Mc Loughlin, *Report on the anatomical investigation of the skeletal remains unearthed at Castleknock in the excavation of an early Christian cemetery in the summer of 1938* (Dublin, 1950), pp iii, iv, 71.   **70** Bradley, 'Some reflections', p. 53.   **71** Aubrey Gwynn, 'The origins of the see of Dublin' in Gerard O'Brien (ed.), *The Irish church in the eleventh and twelfth centuries* (Dublin, 1992), pp 50–67. **72** Clarke, 'Conversion, church and cathedral', p. 35.

dated to the first decade of the thirteenth century, which confirmed the lands of the cathedral and listed the donors.[73] The founder, Sitric Silkbeard, granted to the church its site in the town and lands north of the River Liffey at Grangegorman. Lambay and its access point from the mainland – Portraine – were subsequently granted by Murchad son of Diarmait mac Máel na mBó, who held the kingship of Dublin from 1052 to 1070. While Lambay had probably been in Scandinavian control for some time, Portraine was in southern Brega and Diarmait's granting of it to Christ Church can perhaps be seen as a deliberate statement of proprietorship over land north of the Liffey.[74] Most of the places that can be identified as early endowments of Christ Church, however, lay south of the river (Figure 3.6b). These included Clonkeen, Ballyogan (donated by Paul, son of Thorkell, and by Dormlagh, son of Paul), Tully, part of Cabinteely, part of Kiltiernan, another part of Kill of the Grange and *Tech na Breatan* near Kilgobbin. Both Bradley and Clarke have highlighted the correlation between the distribution of Rathdown Slabs with the early grants of land to Christ Church Cathedral (Figures 3.6b, 3.6c).[75]

The pre-Anglo-Norman endowments of another Dublin religious house, St Mary's Abbey, founded in 1139 as a Savigniac house but becoming Cistercian in 1147, are similarly illuminating.[76] The possessions of the abbey were listed in 1173–4 by William Fitz Audelin, and this list was included in Henry II's charter of confirmation to the abbey in 1174.[77] Colmcille Ó Conbhuí and Jocelyn Otway-Ruthven both concluded that the bulk of the lands mentioned in this charter came to the abbey in the period between its foundation and the coming of the Anglo-Normans.[78] These lands included Clonliffe, Raheny, Portmarnock, Bullock, Monkstown and Cnochroid in the neighbourhood of Glencullen, Balimacheilmer in Kilmahuddrick and Kilmactalway (Figure 3.6a). A large proportion of the lands south of Dublin lay in the territory of the family of Mac Gilla Mo Cholmóc, leading to a tradition that this family founded St Mary's.[79] At some time before the arrival of the Anglo-Normans, the Mac Gilla Mo Cholmócs became the chief grouping within the Irish dynasty of the Uí Dúnchada. They held territory in Uí Dúnchada, a district that lay south of the River Liffey in modern Co. Dublin and north-east Wicklow. They also held lands in the vicinity of Lyons Hill and had property and interests in Dublin city.[80]

The transfer of St Mary's from Savigniac to Cistercian affiliation, however, may have been the work of Diarmait Mac Murchada, king of Leinster, as it occurred during a period when he exercised control over Dublin.[81] During this same period of influence, Mac Murchada founded the abbey of St Mary de Hogges for Augustinian nuns. This was situated on the south side of Hoggen Green in close proximity to the former Viking assembly place, the Thingmount.[82] Mac Murchada's patronage of the new religious orders also saw him founding St Saviour's Augustinian priory at Glendalough, where he installed Laurence O'Toole as its first abbot.[83]

Territorial dioceses were established for the whole of Ireland at the synod of Ráith Bressail in 1111. Dublin was completely ignored in the diocesan organisational plan, however,

73 McNeill (ed.), *Alen's register*, p. 28; *RDKPRI*, 20, no. 364(c). Otway-Ruthven gives the date as 1203–9, while Clarke follows McNeill's date of 1202. A.J. Otway-Ruthven, 'The medieval church lands of County Dublin' in J.A. Watt, J.B. Morrall and F.X. Martin (eds), *Medieval studies presented to Aubrey Gwynn, SJ* (Dublin, 1961), pp 54–73 at p. 60; Clarke, 'Conversion, church and cathedral', p. 35. 74 Clarke, 'Conversion, church and cathedral', p. 35. 75 Ibid., fig. 3; Bradley, 'Scandinavian rural settlement', 12. 76 Aubrey Gwynn, 'The origins of St Mary's Abbey', *JRSAI*, 19 (1949), 110–25. 77 *CSMA*, I, p. 138. 78 Colmcille Ó Conbhuí, 'The lands of St Mary's Abbey, Dublin', *PRIA*, 62C3 (1962), 21–84 at 23 and map; Otway-Ruthven, 'Medieval church lands', p. 63. 79 Otway-Ruthven, 'Medieval church lands', p. 64. 80 See below, pp 86–9. 81 MacShamhráin, 'The emergence of the metropolitan see', p. 56. 82 Clarke, 'Conversion, church and cathedral', p. 49. 83 *MRHI*, p. 177; A.S. MacShamhráin, '*Prosopographica Glindelachensis*: the monastic church of Glendalough and its community, sixth to thirteenth centuries', *JRSAI*, 119 (1989), 79–97 at 86.

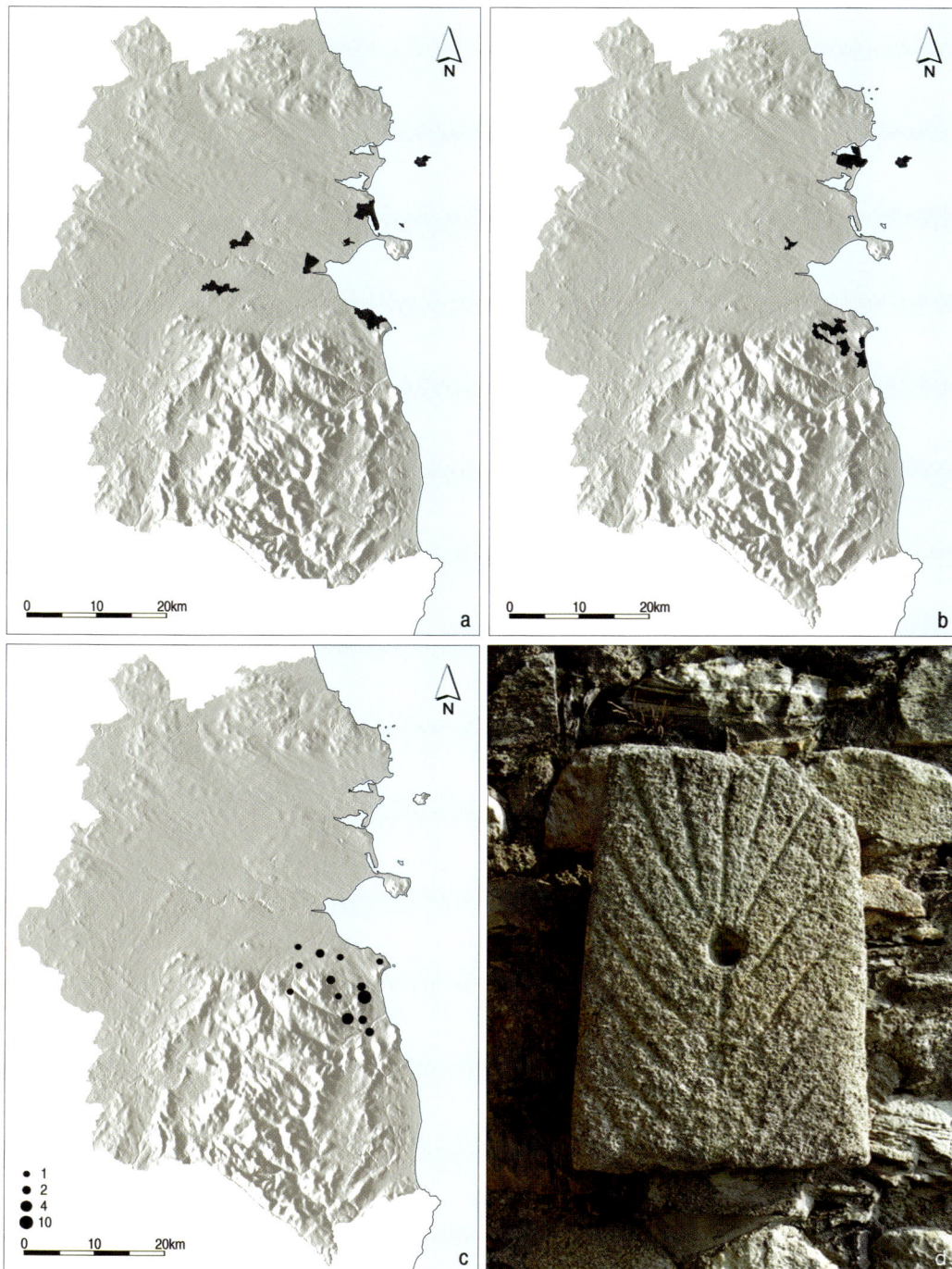

Figure 3.6 (a) lands held by St Mary's Abbey pre-1170; (b) lands held by Christ Church Cathedral pre-1170; (c) distribution of Rathdown Slabs; (d) Rathdown Slab attached to wall of Rathmichael Church, Co. Dublin (© Department of the Environment, Heritage and Local Government).

and its lands were incorporated into the diocese of Glendalough.[84] Prior to this, the diocese of Dublin had established a pattern of having its bishops consecrated at Canterbury, and the attempts by the ecclesiastical and secular promoters of Irish church reform to sever these links were probably the main reason behind its exclusion at Ráith Bressail. The limits of the Glendalough diocese were defined as being *ó Grianóc go Becc Ériú ocus ó Nás go Reachru*. These places have been identified as Greenoge townland to the north, Lambay to the east, Naas to the west and Killapeckure, just south of Arklow, to the south.[85] It suggests that the northern boundary of the earlier Dublin diocese, and by extension the territory under control of the Hiberno-Scandinavian town, was essentially the Broad Meadow River.[86] To

84 MacShamhráin, 'The emergence of the metropolitan see', pp 51–2. 85 Ibid., pp 51–2. 86 See map in T.W. Moody, F.X. Martin and F.J. Byrne (eds), *A new history of Ireland, IX: maps, genealogies, lists: a companion to Irish history, II* (Oxford, 1984), p. 26, no. 24.

the north of Glendalough/Dublin was the diocese of Duleek, to the west was Clonard and
to the south-west lay Kildare.

There was obviously a close connection between dynastic and diocesan interests. 'It
seems reasonable that a unitary Glendalough-Dublin diocese was created to serve Ua Briain
interests – combining as it did the Hiberno-Scandinavian kingdom and the Uí Muiredaig
realm'.[87] Dublin's increasing importance in secular Irish politics made it inevitable that
efforts would be made to reassert its position within the diocesan framework. In 1148, St
Malachy convened a synod at St Patrick's Island, Skerries, which, significantly, was situated
within the bounds of the Hiberno-Scandinavian kingdom and bishopric. In 1152, at the
synod of Kells, Dublin was not only reinstated but was elevated as the centre of a new
ecclesiastical province.[88] The ecclesiastical boundaries, as ever, closely reflected the political
situation and just as the diocese of Dublin coincided with the Hiberno-Scandinavian city
state, so the newly defined province of Dublin coincided with the provincial kingdom of
Diarmait Mac Murchada, king of Leinster.[89] The lands held directly by the see of Dublin,
which were to remain attached to the archbishopric throughout the medieval period, were
probably confirmed at the synod of Kells. It appears that a large proportion had been the
property of the major monasteries in the Dublin region. The earliest list of the lands of the
church of Dublin, which occurs in a bull of Pope Alexander III, includes Clondalkin,
Finglas, Lusk, Swords and Tallaght.[90] The date at which these monasteries ceased to exist and
their lands passed into episcopal ownership is uncertain. Lands in Wicklow are also listed in
the papal bull and, while these are not easy to identify, they include Kilcoole (*Cellcomgaill*),
Killadreenan (*Cell-achaich-Driegnig*) and an area in the vicinity of Djouce Mountain (*Digis*).
In Wicklow, the territorial holdings of the bishopric and abbey of Glendalough were
extensive, and much of these came into the possession of the Dublin see in the early
thirteenth century.[91]

In 1162, Diarmait Mac Murchada's brother-in-law, Laurence O'Toole, who had been
abbot of Glendalough for almost a decade, was consecrated as archbishop of Dublin and in
the same year Dublin recognised Mac Murchada as full overlord of their city state.[92] One of
Diarmait's first moves was to found All Hallows priory just west of the city walls. His
subsequent grant of Baldoyle to the priory demonstrates that he was not only overlord of
Dublin, but also of its hinterland.[93] Baldoyle (*Baile Dubgail* = 'the baile of the dark
foreigners') was in Fine Gall, some 11km north-east of Dublin. The charter describes it as a
terra and a *villa* whose boundaries did not require expounding, and included with the grant
of land were the men who lived there, named as Máel Isu Macfeilecan with his sons and
grandsons. This charter reveals important details concerning the relationship between
Dublin and its rural hinterland in the twelfth century. The place-name testifies to
Scandinavian connections, while the name of the chief tenant is clearly Irish. Diarmait
further granted that the land would be free from military service and rights to billet troops,
thus explicitly claiming these rights for himself as king of Dublin.

87 MacShamhráin, 'The emergence of the metropolitan see', p. 53. **88** *RDKPRI*, 20, p. 39; McNeill (ed.), *Alen's
register*, p. 38. According to statements made early in the thirteenth century, Cardinal Papiron, the legate, 'found a
bishop in Dublin, and another church in the mountains called a city and having a *chore-episcopus*, and considering that
Dublin should be metropolitan, gave a pall to the bishop there, and divided the diocese so that one part should belong
to the metropolis and the other to him who ruled in the mountains'. **89** MacShamhráin, 'The emergence of the
metropolitan see', p. 57. **90** McNeill (ed.), *Alen's register*, p. 3. **91** Ailbhe MacShamhráin, *Church and polity in pre-
Norman Ireland: the case of Glendalough* (Maynooth, 1996), pp 192–9. **92** F.X. Martin, 'Diarmait Mac Murchada and
the coming of the Anglo-Normans' in Cosgrove (ed.), *A new history of Ireland: II* (1993), pp 43–66 at p. 62. **93** For
the text of this charter and a discussion of its historical context, see M.T. Flanagan, *Irish royal charters: texts and contexts*
(Oxford, 2005), pp 64ff.

Chapter summary

The foregoing examination of the documentary, archaeological and onomastic evidence for political, economic and ecclesiastical control indicates that by the time of the Anglo-Norman arrival, the Dublin Norsemen were masters of a mainland territorial kingdom of considerable size, incorporating all of the modern county of Dublin and parts of Wicklow and Kildare.[94]

The Dublin region started to take shape from the foundation of the original *longphort* in 841. It began as a series of dispersed settlements, possibly military forts. The aim of these forts was to control important access routes and to facilitate both raiding into the interior and the management of agricultural land needed for provisioning the main settlement at Dublin. There was probably limited settlement outside these rural satellites, and inter-marriage with the local Irish may well have been underway. With the refoundation of Dublin in 917 and its rapid evolution into a trading town with house plots, streets and earthen defences, a more defined provisioning hinterland emerged. This territory, which initially may have stretched some 10 to 15km from the town, grew along with the urban centre until it encompassed an area similar to that of the modern county of Dublin. While some of the Scandinavian kings of Dublin, Amlaíb Cuarán in particular, developed ambitions to extend the town's control over a wider area, they were ultimately unsuccessful in this objective. Nonetheless, the kingship of Dublin was immeasurably enhanced by the fact that it brought with it control of such an extensive and fertile royal demesne.

Dublin's economic and topographical evolution was mirrored by ecclesiastical development, which saw its rapid progress from a constituent part of the Glendalough diocese in 1111 to an independent archdiocese in 1152. On the eve of the arrival of the Anglo-Normans, the city had a cathedral with an attached chapter of Augustinian canons, two further Augustinian houses in its eastern suburb and a Cistercian house just across the river. These religious houses had acquired substantial holdings north and south of the river which, when added to the sizeable landed property of the archbishop, were already creating a distinctive pattern of landholding in the hinterland.

An important question for which there is currently no clear answer is the extent to which the rural area was inhabited by Scandinavians. There is no shortage of evidence to show that the kings of Dublin exercised lordship over an extensive area, but did they plant tenants of their own kind to farm the land or did the existing Irish occupants remain, deciding that it was better to operate under Scandinavian control than be subjected to raiding and possible capture into slavery? The answer probably lies somewhere between the two extremes, and a hinterland that contained some Scandinavian, some native and many ethnically mixed settlements might be imagined. There is plenty of evidence that the material culture of Dublin was replicated in rural settlements in the hinterland, but this is to be expected given the economic and social ties that developed between town and countryside. Along with their artefacts, motifs and coinage, the Scandinavians may have diffused knowledge of agricultural practices into the countryside although evidence for this, apart from linguistic borrowing, is hard to find.[95] The countryside around Dublin was frequently raided by those who sought to punish the town for the actions of its political leaders, but it can be argued that the economic benefits of being within the urban provisioning zone outweighed the disadvantages.

---

94 They also sought to control a significant maritime hinterland, for a discussion of which, see Duffy, 'Irishmen and Islesmen'.   **95** For example, Fergus Kelly points out that the Irish word for 'sheaf of corn', *punnann*, is generally taken to be a Norse loan-word, and he proposes that the practice of cutting corn-stalks close to the ground and binding them into sheaves was associated with Scandinavian farming techniques (Fergus Kelly, *Early Irish farming* (Dublin, 2000), pp 238–9).

In the decades leading up to the arrival of the Anglo-Normans, the importance of Dublin in Irish national politics reached a peak. The Mac Turcaill kings switched the allegiance of the town and most importantly the fire-power of its army and fleet between various contenders for the high-kingship of Ireland. The Annals of Ulster record that in 1162 Diarmait Mac Murchada achieved unprecedented control over the foreigners of Dublin.[96] Four years later, however, another king, Ruaidrí Ua Conchobair of Connacht, was crowned in Dublin, and the town withdrew its allegiance from Mac Murchada. Even worse, the men of Dublin accompanied firstly Ua Conchobair and subsequently Ua Ruairc of Bréifne on the hostings that led to Mac Murchada's banishment across the sea to Bristol. When Diarmait next arrived in Dublin along with Strongbow and his Anglo-Norman allies, he showed little mercy to the Ostmen. In a remarkably short space of time, Scandinavian influence on Dublin came to an end, and the town became an Anglo-Norman city and centre of government. The Dublin region, which had taken shape over the previous three centuries, was now more permanent however. In many ways, it retained its identity over the subsequent centuries, and the silhouette of Dyflinarskiri reappeared in the later boundaries of county and Pale.

---

96 Duffy, 'Irishmen and Islesmen', 124–5.

CHAPTER 4

Land ownership after 1170

A considerable amount of land in the Dublin region changed hands in the decades following the arrival of the Anglo-Normans in 1170. There was clearly a large degree of continuity in the ownership of ecclesiastical lands and there is some limited evidence for the retention of lands by Gaelic and Hiberno-Scandinavian lords.[1] In general, however, while the pre-existing territorial framework was substantially adopted by the newcomers and established settlement foci were enthusiastically re-used, the people in control of the land changed radically. There was a very rapid redistribution of the holdings confiscated from defeated Irish and Ostman lords. Three figures were responsible for the initial apportioning of land in the Dublin region: Richard de Clare (Strongbow), Henry II and Hugh de Lacy.

In 1170, Diarmait Mac Murchada, accompanied by Strongbow and his Anglo-Norman allies, advanced on Dublin, where their arrival was awaited by Ruaidrí Ua Conchobair and the armies of his allies.[2] While negotiations were going on between the two sides, the Anglo-Normans breached the walls of Dublin and over-ran the city, killing many of the inhabitants and seizing their cattle and goods.[3] Ascall Mac Turcaill, the Scandinavian king of Dublin, fled to the Isles, Ua Conchobair withdrew, and Strongbow formally took possession of the city. The Scandinavians made an effort to retake the city following Diarmait Mac Murchada's death in May 1171, but they were defeated.[4] Ua Conchobair returned to lay siege once again to Dublin in August 1171, but this led to his defeat and humiliation. Despite his military success, Strongbow held Dublin for a brief period only; in August 1171, as part of his reconciliation deal with Henry II, he relinquished Dublin and its neighbouring cantreds to the king along with Waterford and Wexford.[5] The precise extent of these 'neighbouring cantreds' is unclear, but it is generally believed that they corresponded with the kingdom of the Scandinavian town as defined above.[6] Strongbow retained control over the rest of Leinster, in return for the service of one hundred knights. Henry II lost no time in visiting his new acquisitions and by the autumn of 1171 was handing over 'my city of Dublin' to the citizens of Bristol.[7] One of the main beneficiaries of the Anglo-Norman invasion of Ireland was therefore the port town of Bristol, which gained possession of a city that was at least as large as its own and was also its chief trading rival.[8]

Henry II was accompanied to Ireland by Hugh de Lacy, head of the Herefordshire branch of the de Lacy family. Before he left in April 1172, the king had appointed de Lacy

---

1 For example, the Mac Gilla Mo Cholmócs. See below, pp 86–9.   **2** *AFM*, *s.a.* 1170.   **3** *AFM*, *s.a.* 1170; Duffy, 'Ireland's Hastings'.   **4** Gerald of Wales: *Expugnatio Hibernica*, pp 68–9.   **5** Gerald of Wales: *Expugnatio Hibernica*, p. 89: 'Dubliniam … cum cantaredis adiacentibus'. G.H. Orpen, *Ireland under the Normans, 1169–1333* (Dublin, 2005), p. 92; Flanagan, *Irish society*, ch. 4.   **6** An alternative interpretation holds that this kingdom was already included under the grant of Dublin and that the neighbouring cantreds represented additional lands contiguous to this kingdom, including all or part of the kingdom of Uí Fáeláin. See M.T. Flanagan, 'Henry II and the kingdom of Uí Fáeláin' in Bradley (ed.), *Settlement and society* (1988), pp 229–39.   **7** Gearóid Mac Niocaill, *Na buirgéisí XII–XV aois* (2 vols, Dublin, 1964), I, pp 75–6.   **8** John Bradley, 'A tale of three cities: Bristol, Chester, Dublin and "the coming of the

Figure 4.1 Liberty of
the city of Dublin as
defined *c.*1171 (after
Clarke, Dent and
Johnson, *Dublinia*, p. 58).

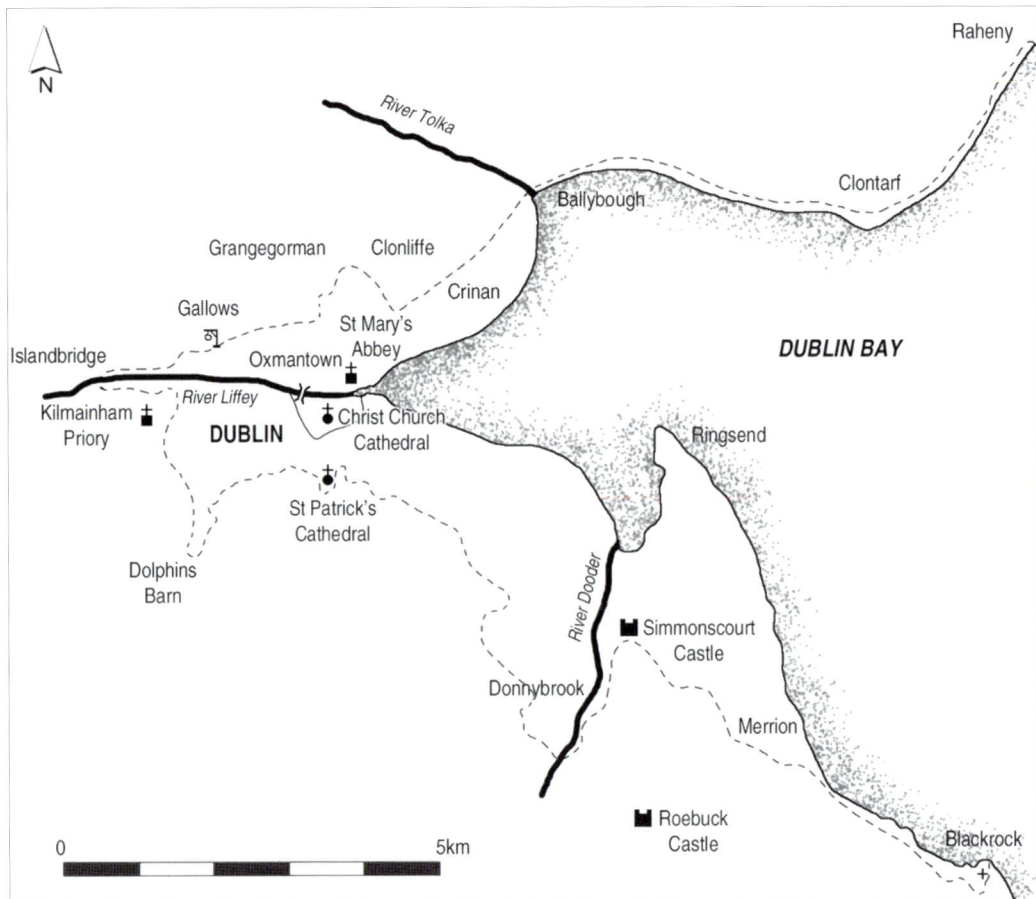

bailiff of Dublin and had granted him the kingdom of Meath 'as Murchada Ua Máel Sechlainn held it'.[9] By the time of Strongbow's death in 1176, he and de Lacy had accomplished the primary distribution of land in the Dublin region.

The immediate environs of the city

Despite Strongbow's short reign as lord of Dublin, it is clear that some land in the vicinity of the town had already been apportioned before Henry II arrived in October 1171. A pressing concern must have been to ensure the provisioning of the substantial military garrison needed to withstand attempts by the Irish and the dispossessed Hiberno-Norse to drive the invaders out of Dublin. Lands belonging to citizens who had fled or been killed were seized, and there is evidence for the agricultural exploitation of the hinterland by the Anglo-Normans almost immediately. In the autumn of 1171, for instance, when Dublin was under siege, 'the cavalry of the men of Bréifne and Uriel went to cut down the Englishmen's corn (*arba Saxanach*)'.[10] This implies that the newcomers had already taken possession of agricultural land and may even have been cultivating it themselves.

   Duffy has proposed that Dublin in 1171 was inhabited by 'the leaderless remainder of its pre-conquest population … the garrison installed by Strongbow and perhaps some recently arrived English entrepreneurs'.[11] Henry II made arrangements for the re-population of Dublin by loyal Englishmen when he granted the city to his men of Bristol to inhabit.[12] It

Normans"' in H.B. Clarke and J.R.S. Phillips (eds), *Ireland, England and the Continent in the Middle Ages and beyond: essays in memory of a turbulent friar, F.X. Martin, OSA* (Dublin, 2006), pp 51–66 at p. 60.   **9** *CGR*, pp 6, 177; G.H. Orpen (ed.), *The song of Dermot and the earl* (Oxford, 1892), ll 2725–32; Evelyn Mullally (ed.), *The deeds of the Normans in Ireland: a new edition of the chronicle formerly known as The song of Dermot and the Earl* (Dublin, 2002), ll 2723–30.   **10** *ATig., s.a.* 1171, p. 282.   **11** Seán Duffy, 'Town and crown: the kings of England and their city of Dublin', *Thirteenth-Century England*, 10 (2003), 95–117 at 102.

may have been representatives of Bristol, in Henry's entourage, who requested that there be at this stage a perambulation and recording of the boundaries of the territory that belonged to the citizens of Dublin. This important event appears to have occurred during the king's sojourn in the city. While the earliest surviving recitation of these boundaries is contained in the 1192 charter granted to Dublin by Henry's son John, the wording suggests that they had been fixed and confirmed by Henry in 1171–2.[13]

The place-names in this document are in some instances very corrupt and difficult to identify, but later perambulations of the bounds of the city allow the identification of the extent of the area. It amounted to some fifteen-and-a-half square kilometres (six square miles), and included important areas of common pasture as well as the coastal fringe as far as Raheny in the north and Blackrock in the south (Figure 4.1).[14]

The citizens of Dublin were successful in securing early confirmation of the lands around Dublin that pertained to the town. In the immediate post-conquest period, there must have been a good deal of confusion as to which lands were up for grabs and which had already been taken. There is evidence that the newcomers who settled in the town were, initially at least, able to assume possession over the landholdings of their vanquished predecessors both inside and outside the walls of the city.[15] The existing religious houses moved quickly to obtain confirmations of their holdings from Henry II in 1171, although the only charter that has survived is the royal grant to the priory of All Hallows confirming the lands that they held before Henry's coming to Ireland.[16] In 1174, however, Henry issued a charter to St Mary's Abbey confirming all the possessions 'which were given to it before and after Earl Richard arrived in Ireland'.[17]

The Anglo-Normans added considerably to the landed holdings of the existing Dublin monasteries and by 1190 had founded four new religious houses around the city. By 1200, the liberty of Dublin was ringed on all sides by ecclesiastical holdings (Figure 4.3). On the north side, Christ Church retained its holdings at Grangegorman and Glasnevin.[18] St Mary's Abbey similarly retained its large grange of Clonliffe with the adjacent lands of Ballybough, and by 1172–3 had also acquired Raheny.[19] Another pre-invasion foundation, the priory of All Hallows, held Donnycarney and Clonturk, which were confirmed to them by Henry II in 1171.

The role of the military orders in the settlement and defence of newly conquered lands was appreciated by the Anglo-Normans. In 1172, Henry II founded a preceptory for the Knights Templars at Clontarf granting them land there amounting to 1,190 acres.[20] West of the city, the preceptory of Knights Hospitallers at Kilmainham was founded by Strongbow c.1174 and endowed by him with lands that stretched for over 3km along the southern bank of the Liffey as far as Palmerston in the west.[21] On the northern side of the Liffey, the hospital held Kilmehauok, an area that contained about 500 acres, now mostly situated in the Phoenix Park.[22] These lands were granted to Kilmainham by Hugh Tyrell, who had acquired Castleknock from Hugh de Lacy (see below, pp 93, 129–30).

12 Mac Niocaill, *Na buirgéisí*, I, pp 75–6.   13 Mac Niocaill, *Na buirgéisí*, I, pp 78–81; see Duffy, 'Town and crown', 96–7; James Lydon, 'Dublin in transition: from Ostman town to English borough' in Duffy (ed.), *Medieval Dublin II* (2001), pp 128–41 at p. 140.   14 Clarke, '*Urbs et suburbium*', pp 44–7.   15 Duffy, 'Town and crown', 103–4, citing grants of lands to the church described as '*de conquestu meo*'.   16 Butler (ed.), *Registrum prioritas omnium sanctorum*, pp 11–20.   17 *CSMA*, I, p. 81.   18 McNeill (ed.), *Alen's register*, p. 3. The earliest statement of the lands of Christ Church occurs in a papal bull dated 20 April 1179.   19 These lands are included in Fitz Audelin's listing of 1172–3 and Henry II's subsequent confirmation of 1174: *CSMA*, I, pp 81, 138. Raheny was held from the monks by the de Curson family: see Ó Conbhuí, 'The lands of St Mary's Abbey', 46.   20 *CDI, 1285–92*, no. 666; p. 329; Orpen, *Ireland under the Normans*, p. 101; Otway-Ruthven, 'Medieval church lands', p. 66.   21 *HMDI*, pp 495–501; Charles McNeill, 'The Hospitallers at Kilmainham and their guests', *JRSAI*, 54 (1924), 15–30 at 17.   22 Mullally (ed.), *The deeds of the Normans*, p. 133; McNeill, 'Hospitallers', 17.

South-west of the town, the Augustinian abbey of St Thomas, founded in 1177, held the land of Donore and Thomas Court.[23] This amounted to some 327 acres of land, part of which developed into a suburban area of Dublin and the rest was retained as woodland and arable land to service the needs of the religious house.[24] East of Donore was the archiepiscopal manor of Colonia/St Sepulchre.[25] The lands of the manor comprised some 3,000 acres and formed a continuous block spreading southwards over seven different parishes.[26] Finally, the priory of All Hallows owned a small amount of land in Donnybrook, granted to them by Walter de Ridelesford.[27]

Virtually all the land in every direction within 4–5km of the liberty of Dublin was in ecclesiastical ownership. The maintenance of the citizen's rights to their common areas for pasture and recreational pursuits was consequently of prime importance. There were three common pasture lands reserved for the freemen of the city: St Stephen's Green, Hoggen Green and Oxmantown Green. The grazing of animals appears to have been the principal use to which this land was put, although certain parts of Oxmantown Green were maintained and harvested for hay.[28] There was also an area of common land close to St Kevin's Church in the southern suburb. This might be the land that the citizens of Dublin ploughed up in 1215 when the archbishop of Dublin was away attending the Lateran Council.[29]

The wider region: archiepiscopal and other ecclesiastical holdings

At a further remove from the city, the preponderance of ecclesiastical land ownership remained. The largest individual landowner across the region was the archbishop of Dublin. As has been seen above, in 1179 the archbishop's holdings comprised lands previously held by the monastic houses of Lusk, Swords, Finglas, Clondalkin and Tallaght, as well as lands in east Wicklow.[30] In 1190, Pope Clement III issued a confirmation to John Cumin, the first Anglo-Norman archbishop of Dublin. This included the Dublin manors mentioned above and the lands in east Wicklow, but also Ballymore (Ballymore Eustace, Co. Kildare) and 'half the cantred of St Kevin nearest Ballymore', which had been granted to the archbishop by Prince John.[31] At some date between 1190 and 1199, Prince John granted the archbishop the land of Coillacht, an area that joined up the holdings of Tallaght and Ballymore.[32] Coillacht was to be held by the archbishop in return for the services of one knight, and is therefore a rare example of the church holding property by military tenure in medieval Ireland.[33] In 1192, John further granted the archbishop that he and his successors should have the lands of the bishopric of Glendalough when that see was next vacant. In 1216, this arrangement was formally confirmed by Pope Innocent III, and the archbishop's holdings in Co. Wicklow were significantly augmented.[34]

Geographically, therefore, the archiepiscopal lands fell into three main groups (Figure 4.2). North of the Liffey lay Clonmethan, Finglas, Lusk, Portraine, Swords and Ireland's Eye. Of these, the largest manor was Swords, reckoned to contain some 9,000 acres.[35] These manors

23 *CPI*, p. 2.   **24** Clarke, '*Urbs et suburbium*', p. 51; Duddy, 'The western suburb of medieval Dublin'.   **25** Colonia was a subordinate to St Sepulchre. It appears in the fourteenth century under the name of Colon, and has been identified with a place called *Nova Colonia*, where, in the thirteenth century, the archbishop of Dublin had a residence. Archbishop Luke signed a decree there in 1253 and, in 1290, Archbishop John de Sandford received a deputation from the merchants of Dublin. It included the wooded area known as Cullenswood, the site of a slaughter of Dubliners by the Irish.   **26** Crumlin, Donnybrook, St Catherine's, St Nicholas Without, St Peter's and Taney: Otway-Ruthven, 'Medieval church lands', p. 72.   **27** Butler (ed.), *Registrum prioritas omnium sanctorum*, pp 67–9.   **28** *CARD*, i, p. 87; Purcell, 'Land-use in medieval Oxmantown', p. 226.   **29** McNeill (ed.), *Alen's register*, pp 44, 233.   **30** Ibid., p. 3. **31** Ibid., p. 17.   **32** Ibid., pp 24–5.   **33** *CDI, 1171–1251*, no. 475, p. 77; A.J. Otway-Ruthven, 'Knight service in Ireland', *JRSAI*, 89 (1959), 1–15 at 2.   **34** McNeill (ed.), *Alen's register*, p. 38.   **35** Otway-Ruthven, 'Medieval church lands', p. 57. Otway-Ruthven mapped a total of 55 townlands – mostly in the parish of Swords, with two in St Margaret's and one in Killossery.

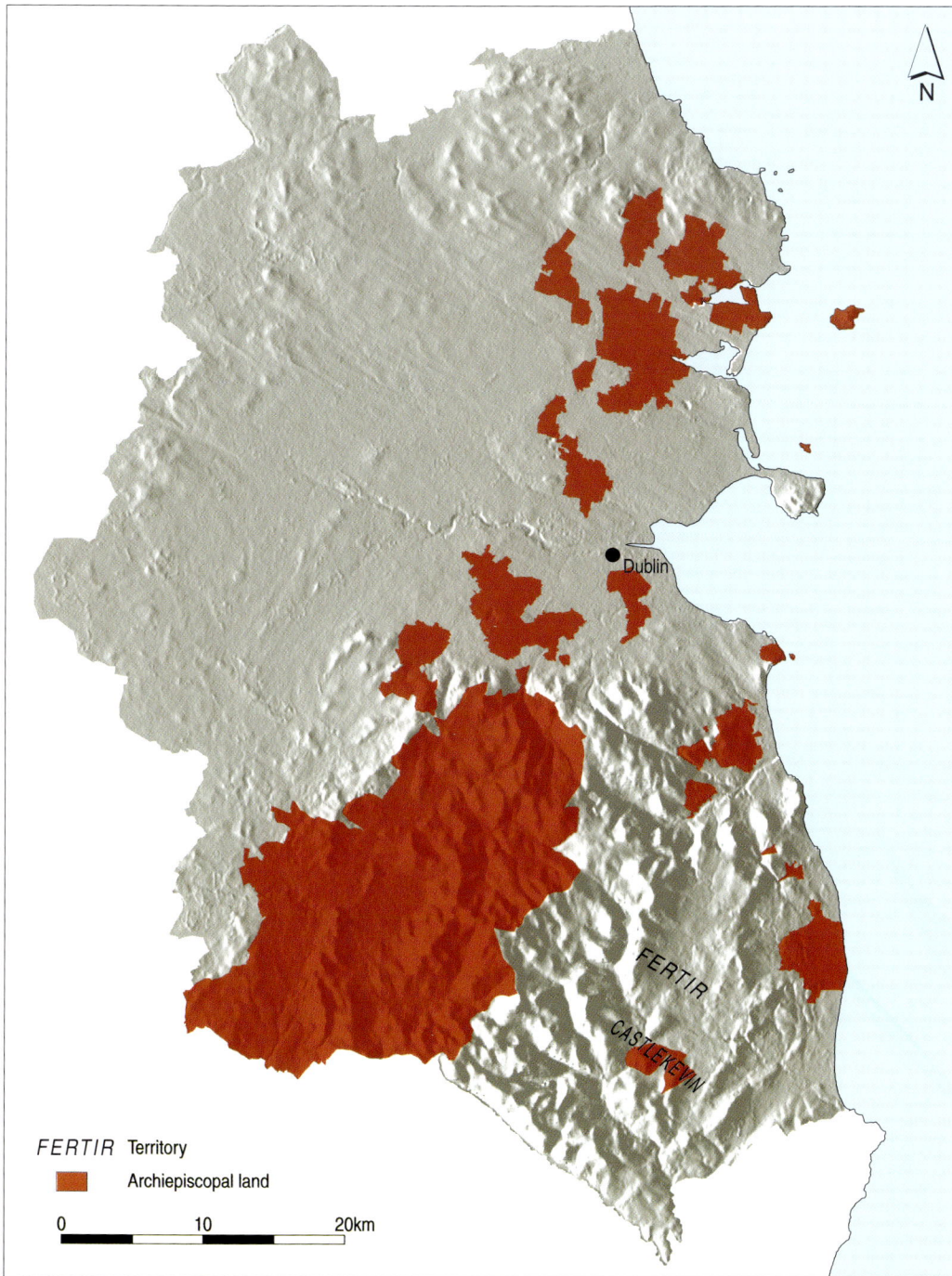

Figure 4.2 Archiepiscopal lands in the Dublin region. The boundaries of the archbishop's holdings in east Wicklow are particularly difficult to reconstruct. Their location is indicated here by the placement of the territorial names Fertir and Castlekevin.

FERTIR Territory

Archiepiscopal land

0   10   20km

appear to have equated closely with parishes of the same name. South of the Liffey, the archiepiscopal lands comprised Clondalkin, Rathcoole, Shankill, Colonia/St Sepulchre and Tallaght. The lands of Tallaght, another huge manor comprising over 14,000 acres, Clondalkin and Rathcoole were also largely contained within the parishes of the same name. Rathcoole did have as a member the land of Newtown, which formed a detached part of the parish of Saggart. In the cases of St Sepulchre and Shankill, however, there was less correspondence between manor and parish boundary. The lands of the manor of St Sepulchre, as mentioned above, were spread over seven different parishes. The manor of Shankill, which may not have been completely formed until the 1220s or 1230s, included Dalkey, Shankill itself and Rathmichael close by, all in Co. Dublin, together with Stagonnil (now Powerscourt) and Kilmacberne (near the Glen of the Downs) in north Wicklow. The north Wicklow properties may only have become part of the manor following the unification of the dioceses of Dublin and Glendalough in 1216. Stagonnil was mentioned in the charter of protection granted by Pope Alexander III to Bishop Malchus of Glendalough in 1179, and appears at that time to have belonged to Glendalough.[36] Kilmacberne was similarly mentioned in connection with the abbey of Glendalough in a charter of Strongbow dated to c.1173.[37]

A third assemblage of archiepiscopal lands was situated in the Kildare-Wicklow-Dublin borders, both east and west of the Wicklow uplands. There were manorial centres at Ballymore, Brittas, Castlekevin, Hollywood and Kilmasantan, but their lands are difficult to locate precisely, and manorial boundaries are uncertain in most cases.[38] In 1229, Henry III granted the newly appointed Archbishop Luke of Dublin a charter of disafforestation for his lands in south Dublin and Wicklow.[39] These lands were described as 'Saint Kevin's land, the land called Fertyr and the land called Coillacht' (Castlekevin, Vartry and Coillacht). It is specifically stated that these lands became part of the 'domain of the see of Dublin', having previously been part of the see of Glendalough and the abbey of Glendalough. The lands were bounded on the east by the royal manors of Othee and Obrun, and on the south by the Butler lands at Arklow, the baron of Naas' lands at Wicklow, and Omayle held by Philip son of Resius. On the west, they bounded with the lands of the baron of Naas and Maurice Fitz Gerald's manor of Rathmore. On the north, they were bounded by the king's lands at Saggart, de Ridelesford's land at Ballymaice, Richard de St Michael's land at Cruagh and 'thence by the brow of the hill to Shankill the archbishop's own land'.

The caput of the manor of Castlekevin was at Annamoe, close to Glendalough, and its lands included those formerly held by the abbey of Glendalough.[40] In the mid-thirteenth century, some of this property can be identified as being along the coastal strip, for example at Killiskey and at Killadreenan.[41] Most of the land, however, was mountainous and it adjoined other archiepiscopal holdings in the territory described as Fertir, which lay in and around the Vartry River (Figures 4.2, 4.4).[42] The records of a mid-thirteenth-century inquisition that was held at Castlekevin mention David the clerk's land at *Likin* and *Myneglas* (identified by McNeill as Lickeen and Moneystown, townlands adjacent to Castlekevin).[43] There are references to drownings occurring at *Inuerchell* [Ennereilly] and *Cestricronin* [?], which were also parts of the manor. The churches of *Kilmoholmoc* and *Dergory* are also mentioned [?Kilcommon, Arklow barony, and ?Delgany]. Identifiable lands named in a mid-thirteenth-century list of feoffees by deed at Castlekevin include Lickeen and Moneystown, the mountains and woods of Glasdrey, and Killadreenan.[44]

Coillacht was a forest that covered most of the barony of Lower Talbotstown, Co. Wicklow, but which also included some lands in the mountains of south-west Dublin. According to a note made by Archbishop Alen in his register, 'the four chief parts of the whole of Cowlagh seem to be beyond Bretas [Brittas]; their names are now changed thus: they call the first Clelagh [Elelagh R.] between Rathmor and Burgage; the second Stranemoke near Downisfford; the third, Carrike a cloke (previously in the possession of Holy Trinity), coterminous with the fee of the prior of Kilmainham and a continuation of the lands of Kilhele; the fourth Glanbrede nearer to Balimor'.[45]

Ballymore was a very large manor with a subsidiary demesne at Ballybough. One of the earliest references to its being in the ownership of the archbishop dates to c.1191 when John Cumin, archbishop of Dublin, granted the tithes 'of his manor of Ballymore' towards the

36 McNeill (ed.), *Alen's register*, p. 5, where it appears as *Thehugonaill*.   37 Ibid., p. 2: 'Cellmaccabuirinn in the land of Macgillamochalmoc'.   38 *RDKPRI*, 36, p. 41.   39 McNeill (ed.), *Alen's register*, p. 62.   40 Liam Price, *Place-names of Co. Wicklow: Barony of Ballinacor North* (Dublin, 1945), pp 31–2.   41 McNeill (ed.), *Alen's register*, pp 123–4. 42 *RDKPRI*, 36, p. 36; McNeill (ed.), *Alen's register*, pp 123–4. A church identified by Price as being in the present townland of Ashtown or Ballinafunshoge (Parish of Derrylossary) was said to be in *le Fertir* (Price, *Placenames: Ballinacor North*, p. 27).   43 McNeill (ed.), *Alen's register*, p. 111.   44 Ibid., p. 123.   45 Ibid., p. 25.

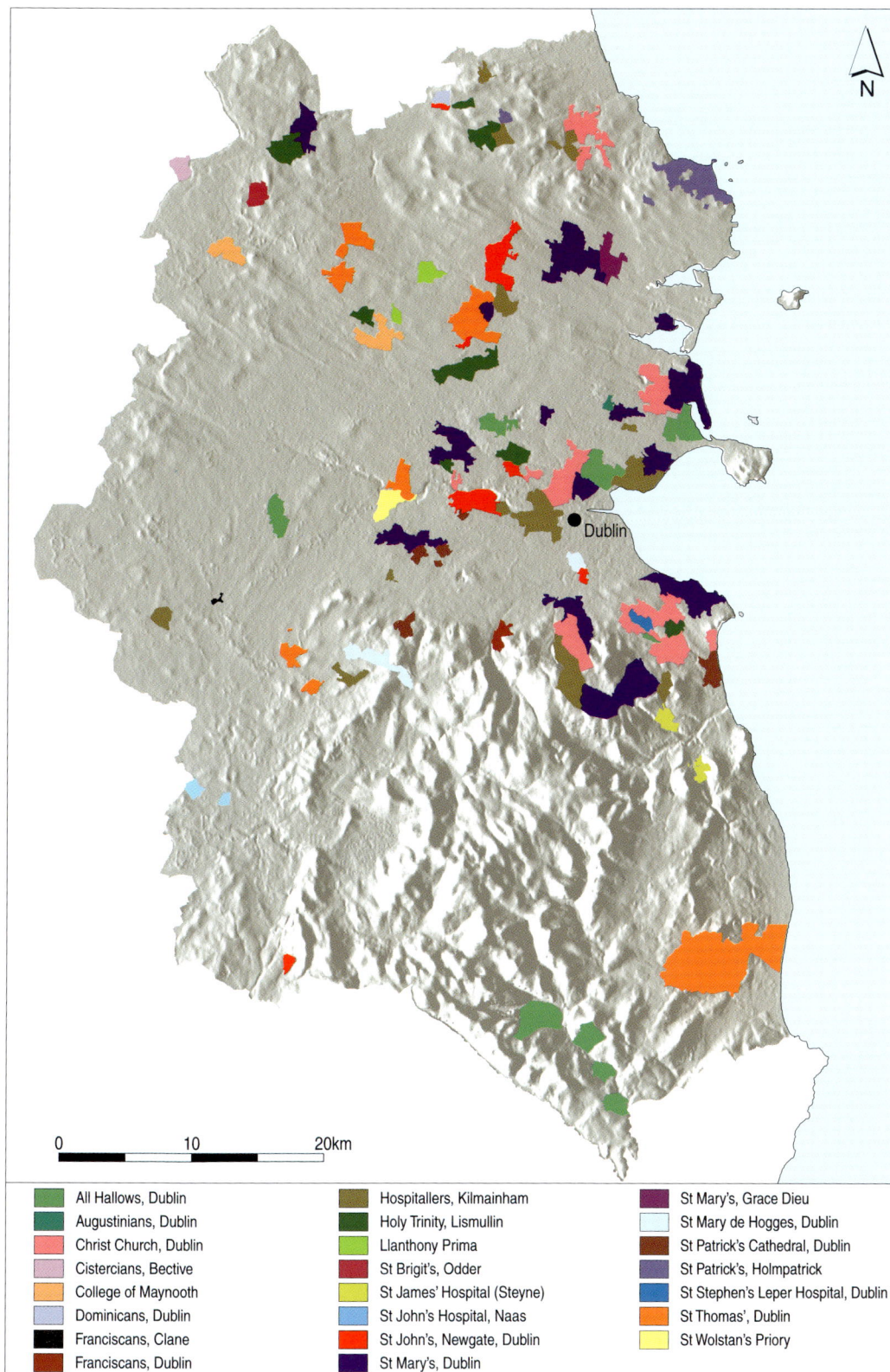

Figure 4.3 Lands in the wider Dublin region held by religious houses. Data on ecclesiastical holdings in Co. Dublin are drawn largely from Otway-Ruthven, 'Medieval church lands', while those for the rest of the region are from the 1540–1 extents of monastic property and various medieval cartularies and registers.

All Hallows, Dublin
Augustinians, Dublin
Christ Church, Dublin
Cistercians, Bective
College of Maynooth
Dominicans, Dublin
Franciscans, Clane
Franciscans, Dublin

Hospitallers, Kilmainham
Holy Trinity, Lismullin
Llanthony Prima
St Brigit's, Odder
St James' Hospital (Steyne)
St John's Hospital, Naas
St John's, Newgate, Dublin
St Mary's, Dublin

St Mary's, Grace Dieu
St Mary de Hogges, Dublin
St Patrick's Cathedral, Dublin
St Patrick's, Holmpatrick
St Stephen's Leper Hospital, Dublin
St Thomas', Dublin
St Wolstan's Priory

common fund of the newly instituted collegiate church of St Patrick.[46] A formal agreement of *c.*1200 between the same archbishop and William, lord of Naas, as to the boundaries of lands near Ballymore, gives some indication of the location and extent of the manor.[47] 'The dividing line was to be the public street that came from Radmor [Rathmore] near the castle

46 Ibid., p. 19.   47 Ibid., p. 28.

of Du'na^ud [Donode] to the River Liffey; all land to the south to be the archbishop's, all to the north to be William's'.[48]

The inquisition into the archbishop's exercise of jurisdiction, taken at Ballymore c.1260, reveals a manor populated by an ethnic mix of English, Welsh and Irish. Places within the manor include Baliodaly [Ballydallagh, Co. Kildare], Anhemelache [Burgage],[49] Ballylomane [Lemonstown, Co. Wicklow], Hollywood, Dunbokes [Dunboyke, Co. Wicklow] and Dunlavin. There is a very detailed list of feoffees by deed in the tenement of Ballymore dated 1256–66.[50] This includes holdings in the boroughs of Ballymore, Burgage and Hollywood. There is a collective entry for 'the men of Dunlavin' who held in excess of four carucates in that vill. Other groups held 360 acres in Cryhelp and common pasture between Cryhelp and Tobber. One Resericus, son of Resericus and Matilda his wife, had 'the whole custody of the tenement of Coxlach' [identified by Alen as Harroldstown with Threecastles], while the prior of Connell held the church of Carnalway from the archbishop for one pound of wax.[51]

Otway-Ruthven calculated that at the time of the Dissolution the cathedrals and religious houses of Dublin city and county held approximately 50,800 acres of land in Co. Dublin.[52] This corresponded to about 23 per cent of the acreage of the county and, when combined with the archiepiscopal holdings, it meant that almost half of the land in Co. Dublin was held by the church, a much higher proportion than occurred elsewhere in the country.

Figure 4.3 shows the lands in the wider Dublin region that were held by religious houses. The data for Co. Dublin is drawn from Otway-Ruthven's study and it has been extended for the whole study region chiefly by an examination of the extents of monastic property made in 1540–1. As can be seen, religious houses were particularly well-endowed in south-east Co. Dublin. Christ Church held the manor of Clonkeen in the parishes of Kill and Tully and Killiney before the Anglo-Normans arrived, while St Mary's Abbey held Carrickbrennan (Monkstown; Figure 7.62). By 1200, St Mary's had acquired Whitechurch (Haroldsgrange) and Glencullen, and in 1277 it received Kiltiernan from Gilbert Cruise.[53] In the course of the thirteenth century, Christ Church increased its holdings in south-east Co. Dublin when it was granted Ballyardor (Kilmashogue).[54] The Knights Hospitallers of Kilmainham had large holdings in the parishes of Cruagh (Tibradden and Glendoo), and following the Suppression of the Templars, they acquired lands in the parishes of Rathmichael and Oldconnaught.[55]

In the south-west of the county, landholding was dominated by the large estates of the archbishop and the king, and religious houses owned less land here. St Mary's Abbey had several townlands in the parish of Kilmactalway, while the nuns of St Mary de Hogges held Calliaghstown, which was a separate parish into the seventeenth century.[56]

In what is now Co. Wicklow, some Dublin religious houses received lands that had previously been held by the bishopric and priory of Glendalough. Shortly after the formal union of the dioceses of Dublin and Glendalough, Archbishop Henry of London granted the Augustinian priory of St Saviour at Glendalough along with its possessions and appurtenances to the Augustinian house of All Hallows, Dublin.[57] An inquisition of 1604 found that All Hallows held several messuages with 1,000 acres of arable land, 700 of pasture, 100 of wood and 200 of moor 'in cella silve … Salvatoris et Glenlorcan in Glandelagh'

---

48 The castle at Donode was a motte and bailey situated on a natural gravel crest (see Figure 5.7).   49 Burgage can be identified with Domhnach Imleach, a pre-Anglo-Norman ecclesiastical site which formed part of the diocesan see lands of the bishops of Glendalough in the twelfth century (Bradley and King, 'UAS 9: Wicklow', p. 20).   50 McNeill (ed.), *Alen's register*, pp 120–1.   51 Ibid., p. 125.   52 Otway-Ruthven, 'Medieval church lands', p. 56.   53 *CSMA*, 1, pp 88–9, 122–3, 107–8.   54 *CCCD*, nos. 60–3.   55 Otway-Ruthven, 'Medieval church lands', p. 66.   56 Ibid., pp 63, 69.   57 Butler (ed.), *Registrum prioritas omnium sanctorum*, pp 100–1.

and in the vills of Ballygardegowle, Ballylisk and Ballinluge. Glenlorcan appears as an alternative name for St Saviour's Priory, while Ballylisk and Ballinluge can be identified as Ballylusk and Ballylug in Knockrath parish. All Hallows also held land in the parish of Rathdrum (townlands of Ballygannon, Ballyhad and Rathdrum), which presumably they acquired as part of the same grant.[58]

Under the terms of the unification of the dioceses of Dublin and Glendalough, Pope Innocent III required that some of the possessions of the see of Glendalough be used to found a religious house or hospital. In compliance with this, Archbishop Henry of London founded the hospital of St James 'at the seashore called Steine outside of Dublin'.[59] The hospital was to serve the poor and pilgrims, particularly those embarking on pilgrimage to Compostella in Spain, and it was given for its support the lands of *Kilmachburnn* and *Kylmahennoth*, identified by McNeill as Monastery (parish of Powerscourt) and Kilmacanogue (parish of Kilmacanogue). The same archbishop gave to St Thomas' Abbey, Dublin, the land of Killiskey, a large parish in south-east Wicklow.[60] The mid-thirteenth-century rental of Castlekevin records that the abbot and convent of St Thomas, Dublin, 'have in perpetual alms all the land of Killwisk'.[61]

The priory of Llanthony Secunda in Gloucester had interests in the south-east of the region, which included the tithes of Glendalough and the church of Killoughter (parish of Rathnew), granted to it by Meiler Fitz Henry along with the church of Wicklow. It is not clear, however, if any lands were owned by the priory in this location.[62]

Llanthony Secunda and its mother house Llanthony Prima in Wales held the advowsons of several churches in north Co. Dublin but, again, their landed possessions were not extensive and may have comprised only the 60 acres at Newtown and Darndale in the barony of Coolock, which they are recorded as holding in 1541.[63] Hugh Tyrell similarly granted lands to a religious house based overseas when he gave the land of Clonsilla to the priory of Little Malvern, Worcester.[64] St Mary's purchased the land from Little Malvern in the fifteenth century, and it then formed a continuous bloc with Coolmine, which had been acquired much earlier. The Cistercian house had two further large holdings in north Co. Dublin, at Portmarnock and Ballyboghil. Other significant holdings of religious houses in this area included Holy Trinity's lands at Glasnevin, Kinsaley and Balscadden, All Hallows' granges at Clonturk, Donnycarny, Baldoyle and Ballycoolen (in the parishes of Cloghran and Castleknock) and the hospital of St John the Baptist's land in Palmerstown (barony of Balrothery West).[65] Two religious houses situated in north Co. Dublin held lands in their immediate environs: the priory of Holmpatrick held the parish of Holmpatrick, while the nuns of Gracedieu held over a thousand acres in Gracedieu itself, which was an independent parish at the time of the Dissolution.[66] The nunnery of Lismullin, Co. Meath, also owned lands in Castleknock and Clonsilla.[67]

The Dublin monasteries of St Mary's Abbey and St Thomas' Abbey acquired large holdings in Co. Meath due to the patronage of Hugh de Lacy and his followers. The de Feypos granted territory in the neighbourhood of Skreen to St Mary's, including the land later known as Monktown, and Ernold Brun granted Brownstown in the same area.[68] One of the largest ecclesiastical holdings in the barony of Ratoath was the grange of Dunshaughlin, granted to St Thomas' by Hugh de Lacy. This probably represented the lands of the pre-

58 Price, *Place-names: Ballinacor North*, pp 10–11, 14.   59 McNeill (ed.), *Alen's register*, p. 55.   60 *RAST*, pp 287–8.   61 McNeill (ed.), *Alen's register*, p. 124.   62 Eric St John Brooks (ed.), *The Irish cartularies of Llanthony Prima and Secunda* (Dublin, 1953), pp 254–8. See also Arlene Hogan, *The priory of Llanthony Prima and Secunda in Ireland, 1172–1541: lands, patronage and politics* (Dublin, 2008), pp 64, 167, 226.   63 Hogan, *Priory of Llanthony*, passim, p. 197.   64 *CSMA*, 2, pp xxii, 17–18.   65 Otway-Ruthven, 'Medieval church lands', passim.   66 Ibid., pp 68, 71.   67 Ibid., p. 70.   68 *CSMA*, 1, pp 68, 96–8, 228–9; 2, pp 78–9.

Anglo-Norman monastery and it lay between Dunshaughlin and the townlands of Lagore Big and Lagore Little.[69] It was later stated that the canons of St Thomas agreed that the men of Dunshaughlin should have access with their animals through their grange to the lake called Lagore.[70] This may reflect a traditional agreement dating from the pre-Anglo-Norman period and relating to the land of the early monastery, which presumably became the grange of St Thomas'. At the time of the Dissolution, this holding was described as the manor of Grangend, comprising the vills (townlands) of Grangend and Thomastown.[71] Immediately to the north lay the grange of Trevet, also held by St Thomas', along with the townland of Hallstown.

Elsewhere in the barony, St Thomas' owned the grange of Donaghmore by Greenoge, granted to them by Richard de Escotot and his son Walter (the same family that endowed St Thomas' with Trevet).[72] According to a 1333 extent of the manor of Ratoath, the abbey held ten carucates of land in 'Fleneston', which probably equated with the modern townlands of Fleenstown Great and Fleenstown Little.[73] St Thomas' had been granted the rectory of the church of Donaghmore before 1190 and, in addition, Richard de Escotot gave them the mill of Donaghmore with the land around the church, 'from the street as far as the great stream which the canons Gerard and Gilbert held along with an acre of land useful and necessary for said mill'.[74] The canons had permission to move the mill, if they saw fit. In a grant of c.1214, Walter de Escotot leased additional land in Donaghmore to St Thomas' for five silver marks per annum. The document was issued in Bristol, as the family held lands in the Severn Valley, and the payment by St Thomas' was to be made each year in the church of St Augustine, Bristol.[75]

The holdings of the Augustinian house of Llanthony Prima in Ratoath comprised the grange of Greater Ballybin in the parish of Cookstown and the lands known as Lesser Ballybin in the parish of Ratoath. The grant of Greater Ballybin was made before 1186 by Roger Lyche and was later confirmed by Prince John and Walter de Lacy.[76] In the middle of the thirteenth century, William Cook granted Llanthony a further twenty acres in Ballybin (in Cookstown).[77] According to an early fifteenth-century rental of Greater Ballybin, a total of 345 acres was divided between eleven tenants.[78] In 1540, the Irish lands of Llanthony priory were extended as part of the crown surveys. It was reported that the manor of Ballybin comprised a capital messuage and six cottages along with 220 acres of arable land and 20 acres of meadow.[79]

The hospital of St John the Baptist, Dublin, was granted a carucate of land in Baliokedin in the parish of Kilbrew and the tithes of a mill there by Robert Smith c.1190.[80] By the time of the Dissolution, however, their sole holding in the barony amounted to a vacant plot of ground in Greenoge, leased out for 6d.[81] The nunnery of Gracedieu based near Portraine, Co. Dublin, also held a small plot of land in Greenoge, while the Knights Hospitallers of Kilmainham had a large holding consisting of a messuage and 120 acres of arable and pasture.[82] Following its foundation in 1518, the secular college of the Blessed Virgin Mary at Maynooth was endowed with the manor of Rathbeggan in the barony of Ratoath. In 1540, Rathbeggan was valued at £11 17s. 2d. and a dozen tenants had holdings made up of between 24 and 43 acres of arable and 1–3 acres of meadow.[83]

69 CDI, 1285–92, no. 839, p. 381.   70 RAST, pp 26–7.   71 EIMP, pp 32–6.   72 RAST, pp 9–10, 12–13, 15–20, 22–4, 48, 261–2.   73 TNA: PRO C135/36.   74 RAST, pp 18–19.   75 RAST, pp 15–17; for the family, see Robert Bartlett, 'Colonial aristocracies of the high Middle Ages' in Robert Bartlett and Angus MacKay (eds), Medieval frontier societies (Oxford, 1989), pp 38–9.   76 Irish Cartul. Llanthony, pp 79–80, 84.   77 Ibid., p. 111.   78 Irish Cartul. Llanthony, pp 191–2.   79 Crown surveys, 1540–1, pp 45–6.   80 RHJB, p. 173.   81 EIMP, p. 60.   82 EIMP, pp 76, 115. 83 EIMP, p. 175.

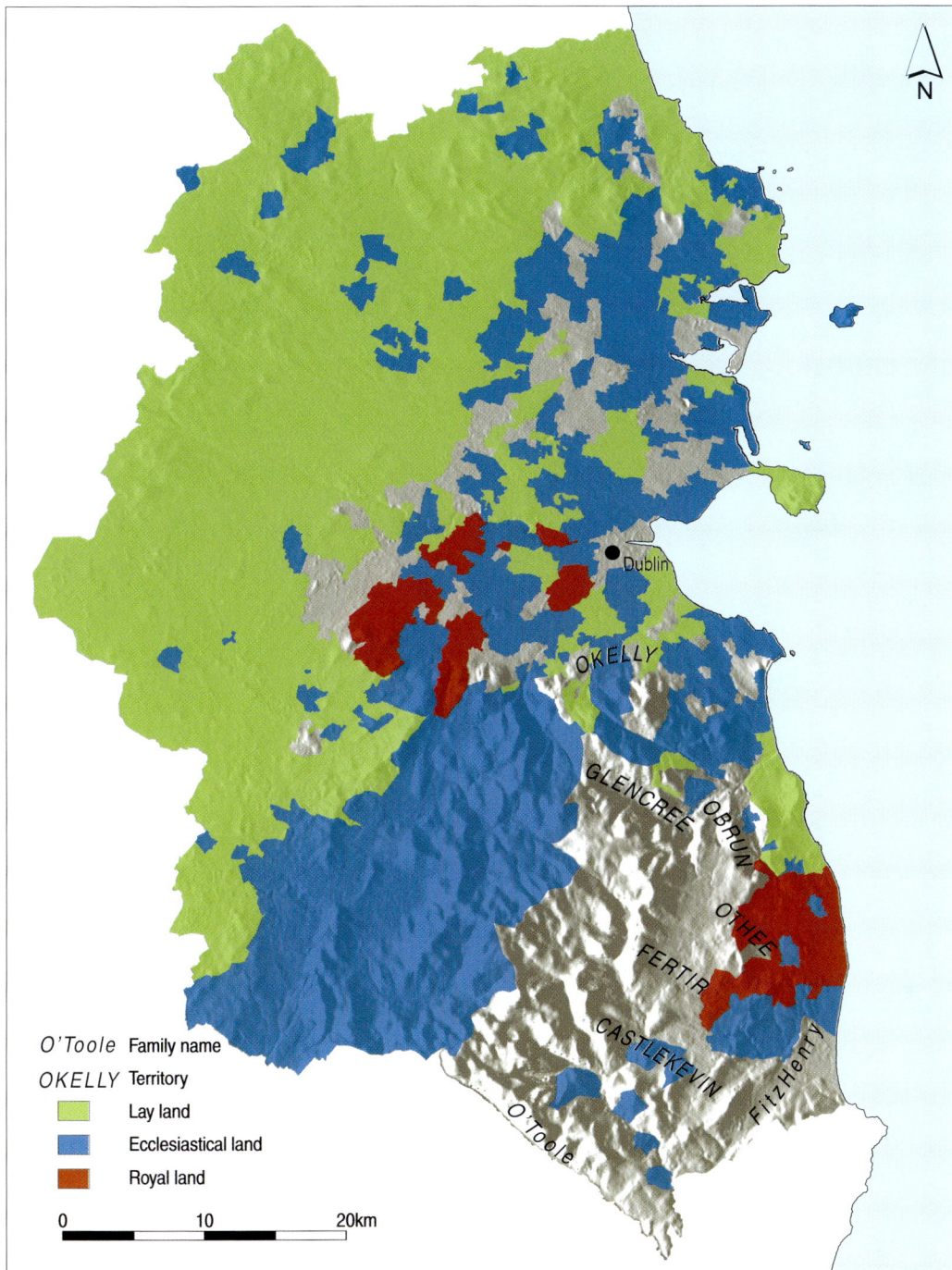

Figure 4.4 Land ownership in the Dublin region: general patterns. This map uses the broad categories of ecclesiastical, lay and royal to show the overall pattern of land ownership across the region.

In the barony of Skreen, the hospital of St John the Baptist, Dublin, was granted a carucate and five acres at Danestown by Robert de Aveinio in *c*.1190.[84] A further holding in the region comprised half a carucate that William Pippard granted them in Duleek in about 1260.[85] Another monastery that held land in the parish of Duleek was the priory of Holmpatrick.[86] The hospital of St John of Jerusalem, Kilmainham, had property in the parish of Naul, which formed part of their manor of Reynoldstown, most of which was in Co. Meath. The nunnery of Lismullin in Meath, founded in the middle of the thirteenth century, held the substantial manors of Lismullin and Belgree in Co. Meath, along with Garristown in the parish of Ardcath. Another house of nuns, that of St Brigit of Odder, held lands at Odder, Co. Meath.

84 *RHJB*, pp 250–1.   **85** *RHJB*, p. 228.   **86** *EIMP*, p. 51.

In Kildare, St Thomas' Abbey received land from various members of the de Hereford family and their retainers.[87] One of their largest holdings was the manor of Kill, which at the time of the Dissolution comprised several hundred acres of arable, meadow and pasture.[88] In addition, the abbey acquired lands at Leixlip and east Kildare in 1327 when it annexed the priory of St Catherine in Lucan.[89] Nearby, St Wolstan's Priory, founded c.1205, was reported to have a demesne of 185 acres and an additional holding of 1,000 acres in 1536.[90] The priory of All Hallows was granted Taghadoe by Maurice FitzGerald c.1240 and post-Dissolution inquisitions reveal that the priory held lands at Taghadoe and Windgates close by.[91] The Knights Hospitallers had preceptories at Kilteel and Killybegs in east Kildare, which in 1539 had holdings of about a hundred acres attached.[92] The hospital of St John, Naas, held over 200 acres of land, mostly arable, in the townland of Johnstown beside the precinct, as well as some smaller scattered holdings.[93]

The predominance of ecclesiastical landholding across the region and especially across the county of Dublin had important consequences for land-use and settlement organisation. A primary function of lands held by religious houses was to provision the house itself either directly with supplies or more indirectly with cash. The demands placed on the archiepiscopal lands were more episodic, reflecting the peripathetic nature of episcopal office. These lands were also regularly taken into the king's hand during vacancies, and came under the influence of a different set of management strategies.

The wider region: royal landholding

The lands retained by the crown as part of the royal demesne were all situated in the south of the region (Figure 4.4). In the early days, the intention seems to have been to keep a good deal of land permanently in demesne, and initially Henry II chose to retain all of north and south Dublin and the littoral as far as Arklow.[94] This in effect corresponded with the territory previously defined as the kingdom of Scandinavian Dublin.[95] The practicalities of administering such an extensive area appear to have rendered the plan unworkable, however, and by the start of the thirteenth century the royal holdings comprised five demesne manors in Co. Dublin: Chapelizod, Crumlin, Esker, Newcastle Lyons and Saggart. In Co. Wicklow, the crown held the manor of Newcastle McKynegan as well as lands known as Othee, Obrun and Okelly. Newcastle Lyons and Saggart were the largest manors, totalling about 4,000 acres. Each was virtually identical to the parish of the same name. The manors of Chapelizod, Crumlin and Esker were smaller and again appear to have been largely contiguous with the parishes of the same name.

The royal holdings in Co. Wicklow are less easy to define. In the south-east of the county, the crown retained the strategic area of Ballymackinegan, around modern Newcastle McKynegan, as well as the nearby lands of the Uí Theig.[96] An extent of the early fourteenth century reveals that there was a substantial demesne attached to the manor of Newcastle McKynegan as well as a number of large tenant holdings. It is not possible to identify the place-names in the extent, but they were presumably located close to the village of Newcastle and the castle.[97] According to a note made by Archbishop Alen in his register, the land of Kilcoole was also part of the king's manor of Newcastle.[98] The manor also contained a royal forest with timber works.[99]

---

87 *RAST*, pp 80–3, 300.   **88** *EIMP*, pp 39–40.   **89** Otway-Ruthven, 'Medieval church lands', pp 70–1.   **90** *MRHI*, p. 193.   **91** Butler (ed.), *Registrum prioritas omnium sanctorum*, p. 16.   **92** *Reg. Kilmainham*, pp 164–5; *EIMP*, pp 91–2.   **93** *EIMP*, pp 155–6.   **94** Otway-Ruthven, *A history of medieval Ireland*, p. 122.   **95** Smyth, *Celtic Leinster*, p. 45.   **96** Brian Shanahan, 'The manor in east County Wicklow' in Lyttleton and O'Keeffe (eds), *The manor in medieval and early modern Ireland* (2005), pp 132–59 at p. 137.   **97** *CDI, 1302–7*, no. 335, p. 115.   **98** McNeill (ed.), *Alen's register*, p. 25.   **99** *CDI, 1285–92*, no. 796, p. 363, no. 1151, p. 519.

It is even more difficult to assign territorial boundaries to the royal lands known as Othee, Obrun and Okelly, which do not appear to have had demesnes or administrative caputs but which were often accounted for together with Newcastle McKynegan. At the beginning of the thirteenth century, all three were farmed by Irish tenants or betaghs, and this probably remained the position throughout.[100] Othee included lands west and south of Newcastle McKynegan. By 1290, it was described as being in the marches of 'Glindelury', although it included lands as far north as Glencap.[101] To the north of Newcastle McKynegan, the holding of Obrun comprised scattered lands in Uí Briúin Cualann, not necessarily grouped together topographically.[102] It included Cork, near Bray, Ballycorus, parts of Kilmacanogue, Ballytenned (Powerscourt) and Carricgolyn, near Shankill. Obrun also incorporated the royal forest of Garfloun, somewhere between Powerscourt and Kilmacanogue. Another royal forest covered the entire valley of Glencree to the west of the archbishop's holding at Powerscourt.

James Mills placed the district of Okelly 'south of Tallaght, along the southern slopes of the hills, and stretching across the opening of Glenasmole'.[103] It included Killininny, Ballycullane and Kilmaceth (probably the present Kilmashogue). Kenneth Nicholls agreed with Mills, but added that Okelly extended considerably further east, to take in the present Balally and Ballinteer in the parish of Taney.[104] The pipe roll of 1235 includes an entry for the render of £18 3s. 4d. from the betaghs of Okelly with Ballyoculan, Kilmacheoth (Kilmashogue) and the land of Hamon Hohavelgan (identified by Nicholls as the modern Edmondstown in Whitechurch parish).[105] By the end of the thirteenth century, the manor of Okelly under that name had disappeared from the records.

The wider region: lay landholding

As distinct from grants to the church, which were inspired by piety and the wish to secure prayers and desirable burial sites, grants to laymen were motivated by the need to reward followers and secure future military service. Many of the men named as Strongbow's companions during the siege of Dublin in 1171 are later found as recipients of land grants in Leinster: Robert de Quency, Walter de Ridelesford, Maurice de Prendergast, Miles de Cogan, Meiler Fitz Henry, Miles son of David Fitz Gerald, Raymond le Gros and Maurice Fitz Gerald.[106] By and large, these men received lands in south Dublin, north-east Kildare and Wicklow, although Strongbow did make some grants north of the Liffey.[107] Hugh de Lacy established his followers in Meath but also granted land in north Co. Dublin to several of the same men.[108] This was partly done by de Lacy under the terms of the charter granted to him by Henry II in 1172, by which he was allowed to augment his grant of the kingdom of Meath by acquiring additional fees around Dublin during the period when he held the position of royal bailiff.[109] In addition, however, some confusion may have arisen over the precise boundary between Meath and those lands which formed part of the kingdom of Scandinavian Dublin that Henry II had reserved to himself. Some of the grants made by de

100 Davies and Quinn, 'Irish pipe roll of 14 John', 10; *RDKPRI*, 36, p. 59; *RDKPRI*, 37, p. 26; *RDKPRI*, 38, p. 55; *CDI, 1252–84*, no. 2329, pp 548–9.   101 *CDI, 1285–92*, no. 622, p. 313: 'petition of John de Ufford. Othey is a land of the king in Ireland in the marches of Glindelury which the Irish inhabit and hold of the k. at 2d. an acre. As the Irish often misapply and retain the king's rent, John asks the k. to enfeoff him of the land, rendering the above rent, customs and services – Let the justiciar be directed to turn the land to the king's profit by giving it to John or another as he may think fit …'; *CDI, 1252–84*, no. 2199, p. 510: (AD1284) 'grant to Wm Burnell three-and-a-half carucates and 10 acres of land in Glencappy, Ireland for 10 marks a year, with housebote and haybote in the wood of Baleconyn'.   102 Simpson, 'Anglo-Norman settlement in Uí Briuin Cualann', p. 107.   103 Mills, 'Norman settlement in Leinster', 170.   104 K.W. Nicholls, 'Three topographical notes', *Peritia*, 5 (1986), 409–15 at 411.   105 Mills, 'Norman settlement in Leinster', 173.   106 Orpen, *Ireland under the Normans*, p. 83.   107 *CSMA*, I, p. 258.   108 Otway-Ruthven, *A history of medieval Ireland*, p. 65.   109 *CGR*, p. 177.

Lacy in 'Ocadhesi' – that is, north-western Dublin – were later revoked by Philip of Worcester (who was sent to Ireland to replace de Lacy in 1184) and the lands were restored as royal mensal lands.[110] By the time Henry's son John was sent to govern the lordship of Ireland in 1185, the lands occupied by the Anglo-Normans around Dublin had been more or less thoroughly subinfeudated, and the process of manorial arrangement was already in its formative stages.[111]

The usual unit of land granted to a lay recipient was a knight's fee, originally calculated as the quantity of land necessary to allow the owner to be able to supply an armed knight to perform service for his overlord. The extent of a knight's fee varied depending on, among other things, the relative safety of its location. In Co. Meath, for instance, knight's fee sizes varied from twenty carucates in peaceful areas, to thirty in the marches.[112] Each carucate equated to about 120 medieval acres of arable land, with a medieval acre probably being between two and two-and-a-half statute acres.[113] The organisation of knight's fees into manors frequently displayed a close similarity with the organisation of medieval parishes (see below, pp 209–14). This correlation, together with the fact that in many areas parish boundaries changed little between the thirteenth and the seventeenth centuries, make it easier to trace the distribution and extent of the various medieval landholding units, especially manors.[114]

In virtually all cases, the recipients of lands to be held from the king in return for rendering military services were newcomers. In the Dublin region, however, there was an exceptional grant to a native king allowing him to retain his land as a military tenant. Domnall Mac Gilla Mo Cholmóc was one of the leading sub-kings of the provincial king of Leinster and was married to a daughter of Diarmait Mac Murchada at the time of the arrival of the Anglo-Normans.[115] The Mac Gilla Mo Cholmócs were the principal family of the Irish dynasty the Uí Dúnchada, and their holdings before the arrival of the Anglo-Normans were extensive. According to Nicholls, the territory of the Mac Gilla Mo Cholmócs consisted of Uí Dúnchada, Fir Cualann and Uí Gabla; this last he proposes, comprising an area now in north-west Wicklow.[116] The family endowed a number of ecclesiastical establishments including St Mary's Abbey, Dublin, and the abbey of Glendalough. In a charter of 1192, some of the possessions of the latter are described as being 'in the lands of Macgilleholmoche': these included Killegar, Ballyman, Delgany, Kilmacberne and Ballydonagh.[117]

The estates that the Mac Gilla Mo Cholmóc family were allowed to keep under their new masters centred on Lyons Hill and Rathdown, adjacent to Greystones and south of Bray in north-east Wicklow. Lymerhim (in the neighbourhood of Newcastle Lyons), with fifteen carucates, was confirmed to Domnall Mac Gilla Mo Cholmóc by King John.[118] Subsequently, he and his heirs are found dealing as owners with Rathdown and Kilruddery, Co. Wicklow, Glencullen, Ballyofrin (perhaps Balally), near Kilgobbin, with land in the parish of Clondalkin, Co. Dublin, and many other places that cannot be identified with certainty. He gave some of these lands to the religious houses of Irish foundations in Dublin – St Mary's Abbey and All Hallows Priory – as well as the new Anglo-Norman foundation of St Thomas. He held these lands as a military tenant, rendering a nominal rent of two otter-skins.[119] The family were dispossessed of their lands at Lymerhim (which was taken

110 Gerald of Wales: *Expugnatio Hibernica*, pp 359–60.   111 Otway-Ruthven, *A history of medieval Ireland*, p. 64.   112 A.J. Otway-Ruthven, 'Knight service in Ireland', *JRSAI*, 89 (1959), 1–15 at 11.   113 James Mills calculated that in the Dublin area the medieval acre was equivalent to about two-and-one-eighth statute acres: Mills, 'Tenants and agriculture', 58. Otway-Ruthven uses a multiplier of 2.5 to convert medieval acres to statute acres: Otway-Ruthven, *A history of medieval Ireland*, p. 117.   114 P.J. Duffy, 'The shape of the parish' in FitzPatrick and Gillespie (eds), *The parish in medieval and early modern Ireland* (2006), pp 33–61, esp. p. 41.   115 Mills, 'Norman settlement in Leinster'; J.T. Gilbert, *A history of the city of Dublin* (3 vols, Dublin, 1854–9), 1, pp 230–5.   116 Nicholls, 'The land of the Leinstermen', 538.   117 McNeill (ed.), *Alen's register*, p. 21.   118 Mills, 'Norman settlement in Leinster', 162; the confirmation of Lymerhim is in *CDI, 1171–1251*, no. 356, p. 53.   119 *RDKPRI*, 47, p. 17.

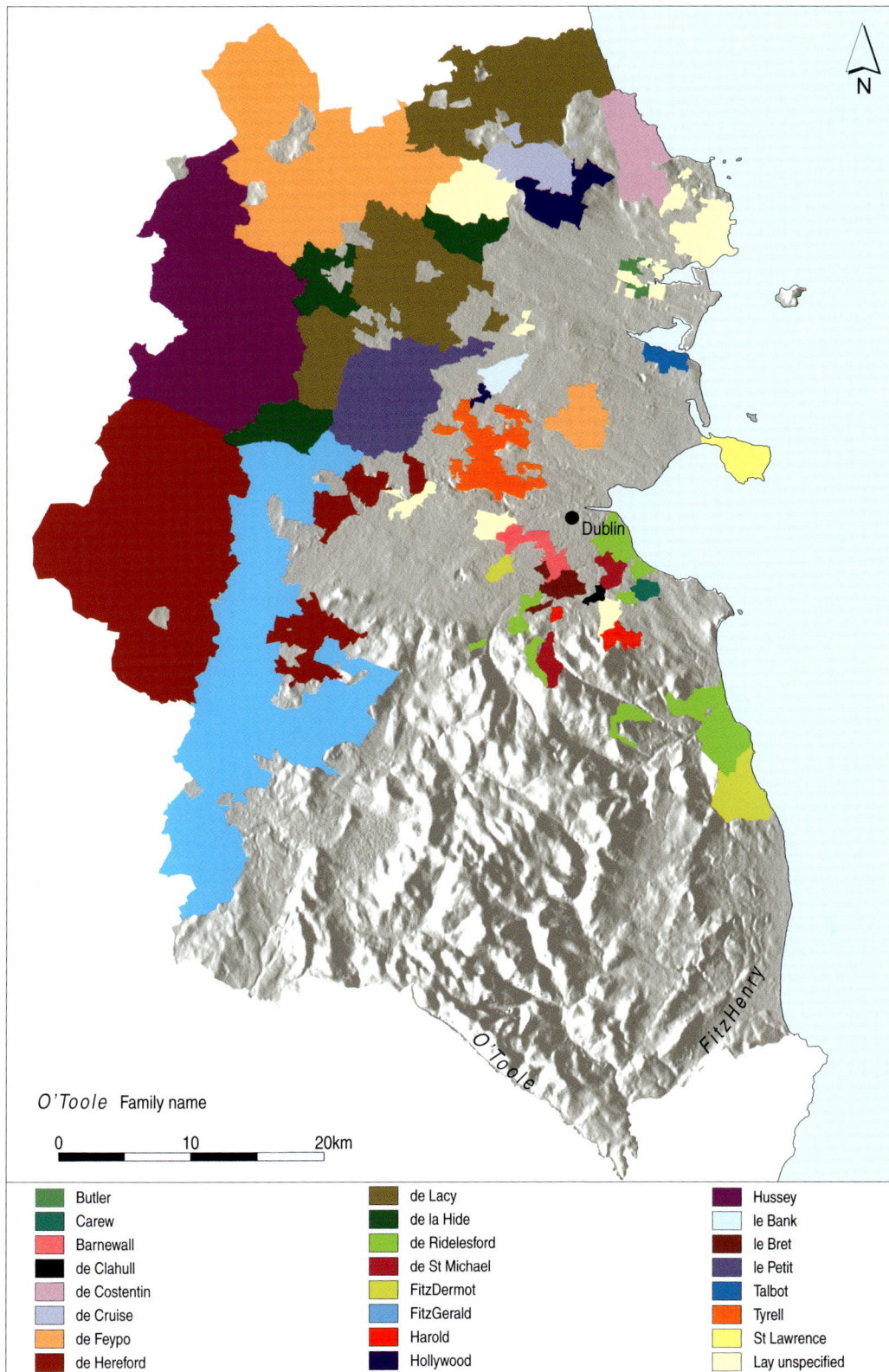

Figure 4.5 Map of lay lands in the Dublin region *c.*1250. This map uses charter and chronicle evidence from 1170–*c.*1250 to identify the primary lay grantees of land in the Dublin region.

O'Toole Family name

0   10   20km

Butler	de Lacy	Hussey
Carew	de la Hide	le Bank
Barnewall	de Ridelesford	le Bret
de Clahull	de St Michael	le Petit
de Costentin	FitzDermot	Talbot
de Cruise	FitzGerald	Tyrell
de Feypo	Harold	St Lawrence
de Hereford	Hollywood	Lay unspecified

back for the improvement of the royal manor of Newcastle Lyons), but continued to hold extensive lands (up to eight carucates) in the Rathdown area.[120] In the thirteenth century, the manor of Rathdown, which included all of Delgany parish, was held from the king by John, son of Diarmait, grandson of Domnall Mac Gilla Mo Cholmóc. John's father, Diarmait, also owned Kilruddery. The family, re-named the FitzDermots, continued as landowners in the

120 *CDI, 1171–1251*, no. 569, p. 88.

district for nearly a century-and-a-half after the arrival of the Anglo-Normans, although their wealth and importance steadily diminished. They retained a seat at Rathdown until at least 1301, when the area was attacked and burnt by the Irish and in 1305 they finally sold off their lands there to Nigel le Brun.[121] They also held land in the far south-east of the region, where a fortified manor house at Kilnamanagh in Glenealy parish is called MacDermot's Castle.[122] The family possibly retained another seat in the neighbourhood of Esker, Co. Dublin. The Uí Dúnchada were therefore one of the few Irish dynasties to do a deal with the Anglo-Normans and survive.[123]

The Mac Turcaill dynasty, which controlled Dublin in the twelfth century, was treated much less favourably than their sometime sub-kings, the Mac Gilla Mo Cholmócs. The Mac Turcaills held lands both north and south of Dublin and lost virtually everything after they were ousted from Dublin. In Uí Briúin Cualann, their lands had extended southwards from Tully to the Dargle River at Bray, and in addition they held lands in Glencullen and near Powerscourt.[124] In north Dublin, their lands in Portraine, Malahide, Portmarnock and Kilbarrack were forfeited, but Strongbow, on behalf of the king, confirmed Kinsaley and adjacent lands to Hamund Mac Turcaill c.1174.[125] These lands, which 'were held by him before the arrival of the English in Ireland', were now to be held from the king in return for an annual payment of two marks to supply lights before the holy cross in Holy Trinity Church.

Some of the land held by the Mac Turcaills in the south Dublin/north-east Wicklow district was given to Walter de Ridelesford. Strongbow had already given de Ridelesford the barony of Kilkea in the south of Co. Kildare and, in 1173, while acting as the king's deputy, he further rewarded his follower with lands in the south Dublin and north Wicklow area.[126] The grant comprised six carucates in Donnybrook and Ballymagreue identified by Brooks as lying in the Merrion/Booterstown district and a further four carucates that lay in the valley of the River Dodder and included Ballymaice and Knocklyon in the parish of Tallaght. The largest area granted, however, consisted of six knights' fees described as 'Brien and the land of the sons of Turchil'. It is not easy to say what de Ridelesford acquired under this part of the grant. The description was certainly not intended to include either the whole of the ancient Irish territory Uí Briúin Cualann or the whole of the lands that were held there by members of the Mac Turcaill family. Price suggested that the intention of the 1173 charter was to make a grant of the land that was then actually occupied by the remnants of the sept of Uí Briúin Cualann, and the land in their former territory that members of the Mac Turcaill family had taken and still held.[127]

The Uí Briúin appear to have occupied the coastal district south of the River Liffey at a very early date, perhaps before AD500, and to have gradually extended their territory further to the south. At one period or another, Dalkey, Rathmichael, Tully, Glenmunder/ Ballyman, Bray and Teach Conaill (near Powerscourt) were named as being in Uí Briúin Cualann; as was Delgany, according to an entry in the Annals of the Four Masters for the year 1021.[128] Walter de Ridelesford certainly held Bray, where he built a castle; it was presumably part of the land that the charter calls 'Brien'.

The townland of Curtlestown, west of Powerscourt, must also have formed part of 'the land of the sons of Turchil'. The de Ridelesfords owned a place called Ballibedan – part of

121 O'Byrne, *War, politics and the Irish of Leinster*, p. 24.   **122** Liam Price, *Placenames, VII: the baronies of Newcastle and Arklow* (Dublin, 1967), p. xxxv.   **123** Smyth, *Celtic Leinster*, p. 44. For the Mac Gilla Mo Cholmocs' transformation from Irish kings to Anglo-Norman noblemen, see Byrne, *War, politics and the Irish of Leinster*, pp 20–4. **124** Etchingham, 'Evidence of Scandinavian settlement in Wicklow', pp 121–2, 129–30.   **125** *CCCD*, no. 1.   **126** Eric St John Brooks, 'The de Ridelesfords', *JRSAI*, 81 (1951), 115–38 at 117–18.   **127** Liam Price, 'The grant to Walter de Ridelesford of Brien and the land of the sons of Turchil', *JRSAI*, 84 (1954), 72–7.   **128** *AFM, s.a.* 1021, pp 798–9.

this can be identified with the townland of Ballybrew, 3km to the north-west of Curtlestown. Price identifies the northern boundary of the five knights' fees as falling below Shankill, Rathmichael and Tully, which were held by the archbishop and Christ Church respectively. Kiltiernan to the west had been granted to St Mary's Abbey. Glencullen, or part of it, appears to have been claimed by de Ridelesford, while Glencree, as seen above, was a royal forest. On the south, the territory does not seem to have extended much beyond Bray. Although Delgany was apparently in Uí Briúin Cualann, in the thirteenth century the manor of Rathdown, which included all of Delgany parish, was held, as seen above, by the Mac Gilla Mo Cholmócs.

If Strongbow's original grant to de Ridelesford did encompass the extensive territory of Uí Briúin Cualann, it would have made him the dominant landholder in the region and it appears that this was perceived as a threat by Prince John when he became lord of Ireland. John confirmed Strongbow's grant c.1185x9 but the total quantity of land appears much constrained and when Walter's son attempted to get confirmation of his lands on his father's death c.1200, he was refused 'because the king suspects Walter's charter'.[129]

The de Ridelesfords did manage to retain a sizeable holding in the area, including the important coastal settlement of Bray, which had been named in the original grant. The crown did not regain control of Bray until the late thirteenth century.[130] During the early decades of the thirteenth century, de Ridelesford granted to the nunnery of Graney several rectories in the Bray area as well as the tithes of his mill there.[131] He also granted lands at Ballibedan (Ballybrew) and Glencullen to Richard de Cogan, who married his daughter Basilia.[132]

According to Gerald of Wales, Henry II granted the castle at Wicklow (*castello Guikingelonensi*) to Strongbow in 1173.[133] Strongbow subsequently allocated the cantred of Wicklow to Maurice Fitz Gerald. These lands were subsequently granted by Fitz Gerald to Meiler Fitz Henry. Although most of the lands lay to the south and west of Wicklow town, some lay within the study area (Figure 4.5). Fitz Henry granted the church of Killoughter (parish of Rathnew) to the priory of Llanthony.[134] Liam Price suggested that the moat at Ballymoat (parish of Glenealy) may have been the centre of Meiler's fief and also that the moated site at Ballinapark (parish of Rathnew) was associated with a tenant of Meiler.[135] By 1229, the lands had reverted to the barons of Naas, the FitzGeralds.[136]

In south Co. Dublin, a considerable lay grantee in the area referred to as the 'vale of Dublin' was Milo le Bret, whose lands centred on Rathfarnham and included parts of Kimmage and Templeogue.[137] Le Bret also held lands in Meath, some of which he gave to St Mary's Abbey about 1185.[138] In 1207, he agreed to exchange six carucates of his land in the vale of Dublin for lands 'without the king's demesne'.[139] The family remained as proprietors of the manor of Rathfarnham and at the end of the thirteenth century were rendering military service worth 68s. to the crown.[140] In 1284, Geoffrey le Bret was described as keeper of the king's peace in the valley of Dublin.[141]

John de Clahull, who was Strongbow's marshall and was granted extensive lands in the Laois/Carlow area, also was enfeoffed in Co. Dublin.[142] He was granted Dundrum, Ballycorus

129 *CDI, 1171–1251*, no. 143, p. 24. **130** *CDI, 1252–84*, no. 1798, p. 377, when Christina de Marisco, grand-daughter of de Ridelesford, exchanged the lands for lands in England. **131** Simpson, 'Anglo-Norman settlement in Uí Briuin Cualann', p. 196. **132** *CSMA*, I, no. 387. **133** Gerald of Wales: *Expugnatio Hibernica*, p. 121; Michael Clarke, 'The Black Castle, Wicklow', *JRSAI*, 74 (1944), 1–22 at 1; Eoin Grogan and Tom Hillery, *A guide to the archaeology of County Wicklow* (Greystones, 1993), p. 36; Simpson, 'Anglo-Norman settlement in Uí Briuin Cualann', pp 212–14. **134** Brooks (ed.), *The Irish cartularies*, pp 254–8. **135** Price, *Placenames: Newcastle and Arklow*, pp xxix–xxx. **136** McNeill (ed.), *Alen's register*, p. 62. **137** *CDI, 1171–1251*, no. 100, pp 15–16; Mills, 'Norman settlement in Leinster', 165. **138** *CSMA*, I, pp 125–7. **139** *CDI, 1171–1251*, no. 361, p. 54. **140** *CDI, 1285–92*, no. 1149, p. 517. **141** *CDI, 1252–84*, no. 2241, p. 518. **142** Eric St John Brooks (ed.), *Knights' fees in Counties Wexford, Carlow and Kilkenny* (Dublin,

and Taney, although the latter was gifted to Christ Church.[143] His brother Hugh was the first prior of Kilmainham, founded by Strongbow c.1174.[144] Another follower of Strongbow, Richard de St Michael, was granted the extensive territory of Reban in Co. Kildare, but the family are also found as owners of Cruagh, Roebuck and Clonskeagh in south Co. Dublin.[145] The Barnewall family, which in time became one of the principal landholding families in the region, are recorded in connection with Drimnagh, Terenure and part of Kimmage in the early thirteenth century.[146]

Some lay families appear as tenants of the large ecclesiastical estates in south-east Co. Dublin, including the Harolds, Howells and Walshes. The Harolds appear in connection with Whitechurch and Haroldsgrange, while the Walshes and Howells held land in Carrickbrennan and Brennanstown.[147] It has been suggested that these families may have formed part of a Welsh community living under Ostman control in this area before 1169.[148] If true, this would provide further evidence for continuity in landholding patterns in parts of the region.

A good deal of land in the strategically important south-west of Co. Dublin was retained as royal demesne, as seen above. The land of Lucan, however, appears to have been held in the 1190s by Alard Fitz William, who accompanied Prince John to Ireland in 1185 as his chamberlain.[149] Sometime before 1204, Fitz William granted Lucan to Werrys or Gwerris Peche, who paid King John forty marks and a palfrey for confirming the grant.[150]

Further to the west of Dublin, in 1171–2, Henry II divided the kingdom of Uí Fáeláin into three cantreds that he granted to Maurice Fitz Gerald, Robert Fitz Stephen and Meiler Fitz Henry.[151] After 1173, the king ceded the cantreds to Strongbow, who confirmed the grants to Fitz Gerald and Fitz Henry, but overturned Fitz Stephen's in favour of his own supporters, the de Hereford brothers, Adam, John and Richard.[152] Adam retained Leixlip along with Cloncurry and Oughterard. John was apportioned Kill, Celbridge, Clonshanbo and Mainham, including Rathcoffey. Adam was also granted the barony of Clane (formerly Otymy), but he passed it on to Richard.[153] The middle cantred of Uí Fáeláin, which included Naas, was granted to Maurice Fitz Gerald, along with the cantred of Wicklow, as seen above. The granting of these two blocks of land to Maurice Fitz Gerald resulted in the situation that pertained for the rest of the medieval period, whereby the county of Kildare included a portion of east Wicklow, separated from the main body of the county by the barrier of the Wicklow Mountains.[154] This grant was confirmed by John as lord of Ireland in 1185 to Maurice's son William, whose heirs bore the title of barons of Naas.[155] Another son of Maurice Fitz Gerald, called Gerald, the ancestor of the earls of Kildare, was confirmed in the lands of Laraghbryan, Maynooth, Rathmore, Straffan and Taghadoe, which he held from his brother, William.[156] These grants resulted in an extensive and almost uninterrupted expanse of lay-held lands in north-east Kildare.

The Irish dynasties of Kildare, the MacFáeláins of Uí Fáeláin and the Uí Thuathail of Uí Muiredaig, found that resistance to the concerted programme of conquest and settlement was futile. Although they lost most of their lands, they were not, as traditionally thought,

1950), pp 56–60. **143** McNeill (ed.), *Alen's register*, pp 8, 69–71. **144** Orpen, *Ireland under the Normans*, pp 137–8. **145** Ibid., p. 145; Ball, *A history of the county of Dublin*, vol. 3, p. 50. **146** *CDI, 1171–1251*, no. 726, p. 111, no. 2416, p. 361; Ball, *A history of the county of Dublin*, vol. 2, p. 147. **147** Emmett O'Byrne, 'A much disputed land: Carrickmines and the Dublin Marches' in Duffy (ed.), *Medieval Dublin IV* (2003), pp 229–52; Ball, *A history of the county of Dublin*, vol. 1, pp 99, 104–5, vol. 3, pp 55–7. **148** O'Byrne, 'A much disputed land', pp 231–2. **149** Orpen, *Ireland under the Normans*, p. 188. **150** *CDI, 1171–1251*, nos. 192, 197, p. 30. **151** Emmett O'Byrne, 'Conflict and change: the Irish of Kildare, 1000–1269' in Nolan and McGrath (eds), *Kildare: history and society* (2006), pp 129–52 at p. 143. **152** Gerald of Wales: *Expugnatio Hibernica*, p. 143; Orpen, *Ireland under the Normans*, pp 143–4; *RAST*, pp 102–4; Paul MacCotter, *Medieval Ireland: territorial, political and economic divisions* (Dublin, 2008), pp 17, 174–5, 183. **153** Orpen, *Ireland under the Normans*, p. 143. **154** Otway-Ruthven, 'The medieval county of Kildare', 182–3. **155** *CPI*, p. 5. **156** *RBK*,

Figure 4.6 Glenmalure, Co. Wicklow, which became a stronghold of the O'Tooles and later the O'Byrnes and was the scene of many defeats for the English (image courtesy of Aerofilms).

evicted wholesale. O'Byrne has marshalled convincing evidence that branches of both families made efforts to find a place within the new feudal settlement.[157] Those who were unsuccessful did flee, and some settled in the Wicklow uplands on the lands of the bishopric of Glendalough and around Glenmalure (Figure 4.6). The grant by Archbishop Laurence O'Toole of land around Glenmalure to the local priory of the Desert of St Coemgen has been interpreted as the creation of a sanctuary for his dispossessed O'Toole kinsmen.[158] Between 1256 and 1271, Archbishop Fulk de Sandford of Dublin confirmed to Moriertagh O'Toole 'the land of Glendeluri as assigned and perambulated by my bailiffs'.[159] By this time, the O'Tooles had spread into the district called Fertir and were holding lands in the archiepiscopal manor of Castlekevin.[160]

It is less clear where the O'Byrnes initially settled in the Wicklow Mountains, but Price suggested that it may have been in the Glenlurkin district, near Rosahane in the parish of Ballinacor (outside the study area).[161] From here, they spread north-east to Rathdrum and later they displaced the O'Tooles in parts of Glenmalure. Like the O'Tooles, this family was initially drawn into the Anglo-Norman manorial system, but in later centuries they came to dominate a large part of east Wicklow and to threaten the shrinking lands of the colonists.

Many of the lay lords who were established in north Co. Dublin owed their fiefs to Hugh de Lacy, but Strongbow did make some grants north of Dublin. He gave the land of Raheny to Vivien de Cursun and may also have granted Howth to Almeric de St Lawrence.[162] John, while earl of Mortain, confirmed to Almeric de St Lawrence II, the 'land of Houede (Howth) as his father held the same'.[163] The St Lawrences became one of the established families of north Co. Dublin, as did the Talbots of Malahide, who owed their land of Malahide to King Henry II.[164]

pp 14–15. **157** O'Byrne, 'Conflict and change: the Irish of Kildare', pp 145–9. **158** McNeill (ed.), *Alen's register*, p. 8; O'Byrne, *War, politics and the Irish of Leinster*, pp 17, 25; Price, *Placenames: Newcastle and Arklow*, p. xl. **159** McNeill (ed.), *Alen's register*, p. 136. **160** Ibid., pp 81–2, 110–11. **161** Price, *Placenames: Newcastle and Arklow*, p. xlii; O'Byrne, *War, politics and the Irish of Leinster*, pp 66–9. **162** *CSMA*, 1, p. 258. **163** *RPCH*, p. 2. Ball, *A history of the county of Dublin*, vol. 5. **164** D'Alton, *History of the county of Dublin*, p. 199.

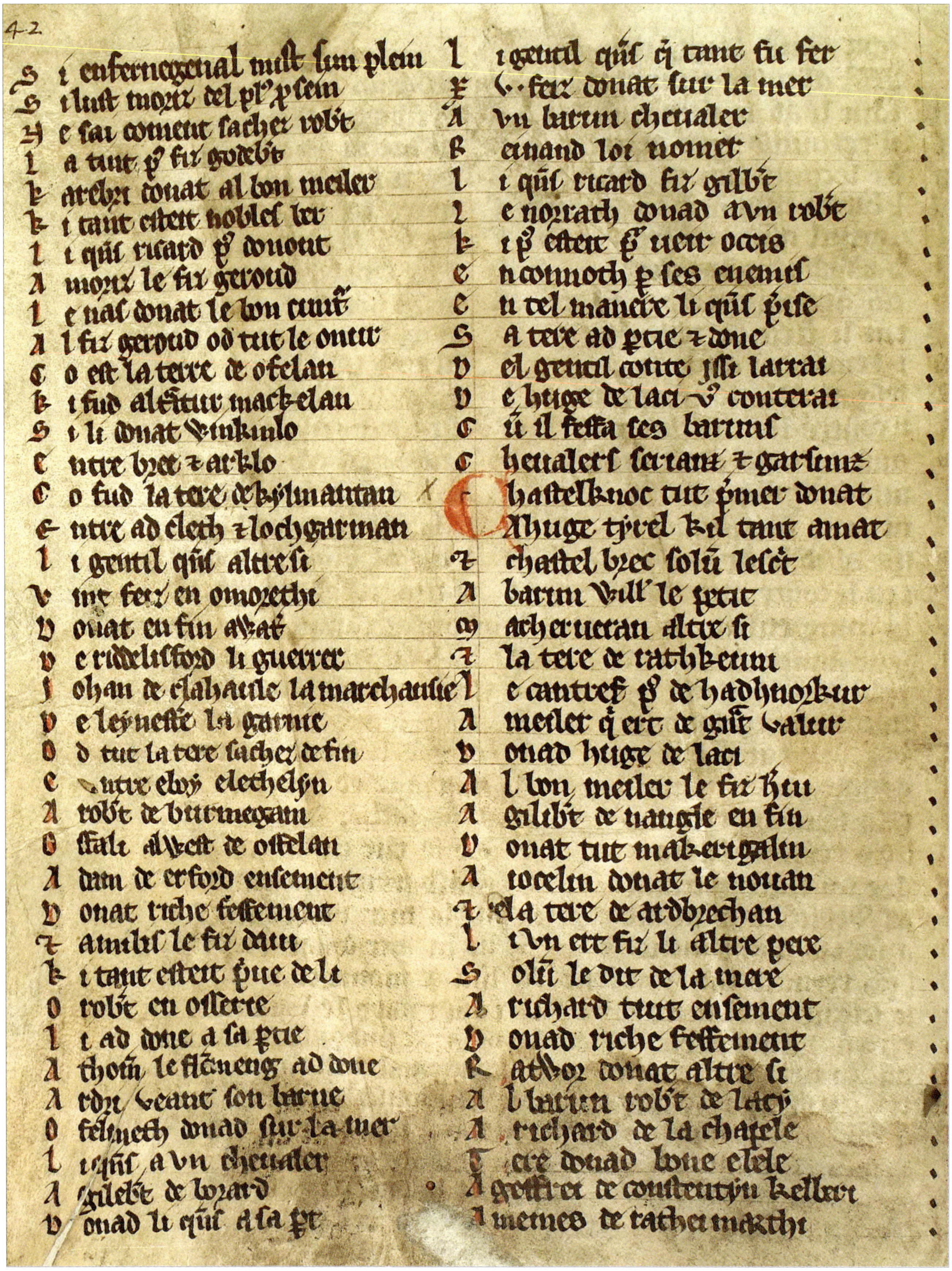

4.2.

Si enfernegenal mist sun plein
Si lust mort del pl' p'sein
Ne sai coment sacher robt
La tut p' fiz godebt
Karbry donat al bon meiler
Kil tant esteit nobles ber
Li quns ricard p' donout
A morz le fiz gerond
Le nas donat le bon cunt
Al fiz gerond od tut le onur
Co est la terre de ofelan
Kil fud al entur machelan
Si li donat vikinlo
Entre bree e arklo
Co fud la tere de bylmatan
Entre ad eleth e lochgarman
Li gentil quns altre si
Vint fert en omorethi
Donat en fin a walat
De riddelisford li guerreier
Iohan de clahaule la marchaucie
De le ynestie la garnie
Od tut la tere sacher de fin
Entre eloy e lethelyn
A robt de birmegam
Offali al west de offelan
Adam de erford ensement
Donat riche feffement
E amlis le fiz daui
Kil tant esteit p'ue de li
A robt en ossorie
Li ad done a sa ptie
A thom le flemeng ad done
Ardri veant son barne
Ofelmeth donad sur la mer
Li quns a vn cheualer
A gilebt de borard
Donad li quns a sa pt

Li gentil quns que tant fu fer
Fert donat sur la mer
A vn barun cheualer
Remand loi nomet
Li quns ricard fiz gilbt
Le norrath donad a vn robt
Li p' esteit p' uein occis
En connoth p ses enemis
En tel manere li quns p'ise
La tere ad ptie e done
Del gentil conte issi larrai
De huge de laci v' conterai
Cu il fessa ses baruns
Cheualers seriantz e garsuns
Chastelknoc tut p'mer donat
A huge tyrel kel tant amat
E chastel brec solu lesct
A barun will' le petit
Macheruetan altre si
La tere de rathkeum
E cantref p' de hadnoskur
A meiler q' ert de grant valur
Donad huge de laci
Al bon meiler le fiz henri
A gilebt de nangle en fin
Donat tut makerigalin
A iocelin donat le nouan
E la tere de ardbrechan
Li vn ert fiz li altre pere
Si cum le dit de la matere
A richard tuit ensement
Donad riche feffement
A adam donat altre si
A baron robt de laci
A richard de la chapele
Tere donad bone e bele
A geffrei de constentyn kellari
Remenes de tathermakthi

Figure 4.7 Extract from 'The Song of Dermot and the Earl', giving details of Hugh de Lacy's grants of lands to his barons (Carew MS 596, fo. 42r; image courtesy of the Trustees of Lambeth Palace Library).

Hugh de Lacy, under the terms of his 1172 grant from Henry II, was permitted to make grants around Dublin.[165] Castleknock, which was the largest lay holding in Co. Dublin, was granted by de Lacy to Hugh Tyrell, one of de Lacy's senior and most powerful supporters, 'whom he loved greatly'.[166] A knight's fee of ten ploughlands seems to have been the average in Co. Dublin,[167] but the Tyrells held sixty ploughlands for the service of three knights. De Lacy also established the de Feypo family at Santry and the Cruise family at Naul.

The territory of east Meath that is included in the Dublin region was very rapidly distributed by Hugh de Lacy to his followers following the 1172 grant of 'the land of Meath with all its appurtenances', to hold for the service of fifty knights.[168] In the charter, the kingdom of Meath was defined 'as Murchada Ua Máel Sechlainn held it', which referred to a period some twenty years earlier and ignored the more recent tenurial history of the kingdom, which had been characterised by division and counter-claim. This appears to have been a deliberate attempt on the part of Henry II to introduce de Lacy as an independent overlord and overlook both the rights of pre-Anglo-Norman proprietors and the possible claims of other Anglo-Normans, specifically Strongbow.[169] A further consideration was of course the need to insulate the royal demesne town of Dublin and the rich agricultural lands of its hinterland against Irish attack from the north.[170]

The 'land of Meath' granted to de Lacy did not exactly correspond to any single existing political unit; however it did contain an established pattern of territorial divisions related to focal points of settlement.[171] These divisions and settlements formed the basis for the process that de Lacy then initiated. This process, known as the subinfeudation of Meath, saw the subdivision of de Lacy's liberty into a number of smaller areas that he granted to his principal sub-tenants. Only three charter-texts of enfeoffment survive, but, fortunately, 'The Song of Dermot and the Earl' gives an account of the principal recipients of de Lacy's grants.[172]

Within the Dublin region, the barony of Dunboyne was granted to William le Petit, Skreen to Adam de Feypo and Deece to Hugh Hussey. Ratoath was retained by de Lacy as a demesne manor, but an extent of 1333 shows that this large baronial manor was organised into a number of sub-manors in the proprietorship of various free tenants.[173] Most of the parish names in the barony occur as centres of large holdings. Walter de la Hide held Dunshaughlin (along with his manors of Moyglare and Ballymadun) and Matthew Cruise had lands at Ballymaglassan.[174] Holdings of five carucates (600 medieval acres – perhaps 15,000 statute acres) were common; Jordan Derdiz held five carucates in Kilbrew, Philip de [?]orkeford held the same amount at Crickstown and Edmund Wafre at Killegland. Philip Fitz William held three carucates in Cookstown. De Lacy appears to have retained much of Duleek as part of his own demesne and this land passed into the hands of the de Verduns.[175]

By the middle of the thirteenth century, a distinctive pattern of landholding had emerged across the Dublin region (Figures 4.4–4.5). The rewarding of the followers of Strongbow and de Lacy resulted in a series of large baronial manors covering north-east Kildare and south-east Meath. Closer to Dublin, ecclesiastical landholding predominated, apart from in the south-west of Co. Dublin, where the royal manors were situated. Continuities between pre- and post-invasion periods were greatest in south-east Co. Dublin and north-east Wicklow, where religious houses such as Holy Trinity Priory and St Mary's

165 *CGR*, p. 177.   **166** Mullally (ed.), *The deeds of the Normans*, p. 133.   **167** Otway-Ruthven, 'Knight service in Ireland', 10.   **168** *CGR*, p. 177.   **169** For a discussion of Henry's motives in granting Meath to de Lacy, see Michael Potterton, *Medieval Trim: history and archaeology* (Dublin, 2005), pp 67–9.   **170** C.T. Veach, 'Henry II's grant of Meath to Hugh de Lacy in 1172: a reassessment', *RnM*, 18 (2007), 67–94 at 68.   **171** Bhreathnach, 'Authority and supremacy', 16–17.   **172** Mullally (ed.), *The deeds of the Normans*, pp 133–5, 162.   **173** TNA:PRO C135/36. **174** The Cruise family held land in Ballymaglassan since at least 1288: *CDI, 1285–92*, no. 412, p. 183, no. 457, p. 201, no. 476, p. 226.   **175** Orpen, *Ireland under the Normans*, p. 181.

Abbey retained their pre-invasion possessions, and existing tenants of Ostman, Irish and perhaps Welsh origin persisted. The archbishop of Dublin held most of north-west Wicklow and, along with the crown, asserted control over much of the area east of the mountains. On the southern fringes of the region, the O'Tooles and the O'Byrnes had started to carve out their later territories.

Landholding patterns in the later medieval period

For the first century after the conquest, the settlement organisation of the Anglo-Normans continued virtually un-checked. The pace of colonisation in certain areas was extremely rapid and this is obvious in parts of the Dublin region. The pipe roll of the fourteenth year of King John clearly shows the degree of settlement and agricultural exploitation present on the manors of east Meath in 1212, forty years after the arrival of the newcomers.[176] The mid-thirteenth-century inquisitions on the archiepiscopal manors of Dublin, Wicklow and Kildare (see pp 181–2) further testify to the presence of a significant level of manorial administration and a well-populated rural landscape. Agriculture, particularly arable agriculture, was profitable. This is clear from the earliest surviving extent for the Dublin region, which in 1260 valued the arable lands of Walter de Ridelesford in the vale of Dublin at 10*d.* per acre.[177] This figure, which represented the estimated annual rental value of an acre of land, was high – in both an Irish and an English context (see pp 290–1). Land in Dublin's hinterland was in demand, particularly by those well fixed to turn a profit, and individuals involved in trade and marketing of agricultural produce were keen to acquire their own holdings. In 1273, Theobald Butler leased out his four Co. Dublin manors of Turvey, Corduff, Rush and Balscadden to Fulk Mesoner, a merchant, for close to one hundred pounds.[178] Henry le Marshal, citizen and merchant of Dublin, held lands in the royal manor of Newcastle Lyons at the end of the thirteenth century and William Tailleburgh, another Dublin merchant, owned lands in Dardistown, Co. Meath, in 1306.[179]

In many parts of the study area, particularly in north Co. Dublin and east Meath, the stability and economic prosperity that had characterised the first century of Anglo-Norman control continued, fairly unimpeded, into the fourteenth century. Those parts of south Co. Dublin which bordered the Wicklow uplands, however, began to experience difficulties from the 1270s onwards. Periodic raids by the Irish who were based in the mountains necessitated expenditure on defence, and this lessened profits and weakened the ability of rural communities to withstand the environmental challenges that were a feature of the next century. The situation was much more serious for the manors in parts of north-east Wicklow and east Kildare, and the ability of the English to maintain control and ensure the stability necessary for farming and settlement was challenged, compromised and eventually destroyed.

The archiepiscopal lands in Wicklow were the first to experience these challenges. In July 1270, the Irish justiciar received an order from England instructing him to help the archbishop of Dublin deal with those who were rebelling against his authority.[180] This is often seen as marking the start of what O'Byrne has termed the 'seismic shift in attitude among the Irish in east Leinster towards the English'.[181] In the same year, the archiepiscopal manor of Castlekevin was described as being 'on the frontier of the whole march' and between 1271 and 1277 there was a full-scale war in the Wicklow Mountains.[182] Trouble had apparently been brewing in this area for some time, partly because of feuding among the

176 Davies and Quinn, 'Irish pipe roll of 14 John', passim.   177 TNA:PRO C132/46/18.   178 *COD*, 1, p. 183.
179 *CDI, 1285–92*, no. 953, p. 421; *CJR, 1305–7*, p. 261.   180 *HMDI*, p. 183.   181 O'Byrne, *War, politics and the Irish of Leinster*, p. 58.   182 NAI RC8/41: Memoranda roll, p. 368. Quoted by Lydon, 'Medieval Wicklow', fn 34.

English, but the initial rebellion by the O'Byrnes and O'Tooles may have been sparked by food shortages caused by bad weather and famine.[183] A long vacancy in the archbishopric of Dublin in this period exacerbated the situation, as royal officials took over the administration of Castlekevin and disturbed the fragile *status quo* that had existed between native and newcomer.[184]

Geoffrey de Geneville, the justiciar, led an expedition into the mountains in 1274 and was heavily defeated at Glenmalure. The Mac Murchada family assumed leadership of the rebels and inflicted other humiliating defeats on de Geneville in 1275 and 1276.[185] In 1277, Robert de Ufford, the new justiciar, managed to drive the Irish out of Glenmalure and secure an uneasy peace. He wrote to the king that 'the thieves who were in Glendelory have departed, many of them to another strong place', but urged that action should be taken on the issue of extending English law to the Irish.[186] Ufford also embarked on a programme of fortifying the royal and archiepiscopal manor centres, possibly including Castlekevin and other sites in Leinster.[187] The failure of the administration to deal with the underlying grievances of the Irish, however, ensured that trouble would inevitably arise again.

The effect of the 1270s war on the profitability of the archiepiscopal lands in Wicklow was immediate. In 1281, the royal administrator returned 'nothing for the manors of Castlekevin, Kilmacberne and Kilmasantan, which were waste and nobody cared to take them on because of the war with the Irish'.[188] In the same year, the keeper of the royal manor of Newcastle McKynegan was able to account for over £51 from manorial receipts including sales of corn, cows and cowhides, but his expenses, which included the wages of 'watchers' and armed men, came to £48.[189] In addition, over £74 was expended on fortifying the castle by building a tower (see pp 120–1, 130, 137, and Figures 5.8, 5.9).

The murder of the Mac Murchada brothers in 1282 did temporarily bring peace to the area, but it was short-lived. In 1294, the manors of Saggart and Newcastle Lyons had to be guarded 'against the Irish of the mountains' and in the spring of 1295 the Dublin chronicle reported that the Irish had 'wasted Leinster and burnt Newcastle [McKynegan] and other vills'.[190] Again, it appears that bad weather and famine played a part, but the feuding between two of the leading magnates in Ireland, the earl of Ulster and John Fitz Thomas, may also have inspired the Irish of the mountains to take up arms.[191] Rents at Castlekevin dwindled to £3 and the keeper of Newcastle McKynegan reported that two-and-a-half carucates (300 acres) of the demesne was untilled.[192]

Meanwhile, in parts of the region insulated from the warfare in Leinster, agriculture continued uninterrupted, and massive supplies of grain were accumulated for the provisioning of royal armies in Gascony and Scotland.[193] In 1295, the keeper of Swords accounted for issues of £94 5s. from this manor in a five-month period.[194] As the fourteenth century began, however, any anticipation of continued expansion proved to be short-lived. Circumstances and events ensured that in fact the Anglo-Norman colony declined in both area and profitability, that the population decreased, and that instability spread. Trends whose origins can perhaps be identified in the last quarter of the thirteenth century were accelerated by deteriorating weather conditions, poor harvests and famine in the first quarter

183 Lydon, 'Medieval Wicklow', p. 158. The famine appears to have been widespread: the *Annals of Inisfallen*, p. 371, reported that 'multitudes of poor people died of cold and hunger'. See also M.C. Lyons, 'Weather, famine, pestilence and plague in Ireland, 900–1500' in E.M. Crawford (ed.), *Famine: the Irish experience, 900–1900: subsistence crises and famines in Ireland* (Edinburgh, 1989), pp 31–74.   **184** Simpson, 'Anglo-Norman settlement in Uí Briuin Cualann', p. 208.   **185** O'Byrne, *War, politics and the Irish of Leinster*, pp 60–1.   **186** *CDI, 1252–84*, no. 1400, p. 263.   **187** *CDI, 1252–84*, no. 1412, pp 266–7; Kieran O'Conor, 'The later construction and use of motte and bailey castles in Ireland: new evidence from Leinster', *JCKAHS*, 17 (1987–91 [1993]), 13–29, esp. 24.   **188** *RDKPRI*, 36, p. 60.   **189** Ibid., p. 59.   **190** *CDI, 1293–1301*, no. 183, p. 83; *CSMA*, 2, p. 324.   **191** Lydon, 'Medieval Wicklow', p. 162.   **192** *RDKPRI*, 38, p. 47.   **193** Ibid., pp 32, 44–5, 49–52.   **194** Ibid., p. 46.

of the fourteenth century. The presence of the Bruces in Ireland in 1315–18 worsened the already precarious situation. In 1317, the Bruces and their army were deep in the heart of Co. Dublin; they had taken Castleknock and were threatening the city.[195] Dublin escaped, but it is clear that the resulting turmoil had a significant impact on its hinterland. Meadows, woods and orchards around the city and in Finglas and Clondalkin were damaged by the forces, which had been mustered to fight against the Scots.[196] Furthermore, the Wicklow Irish took the opportunity afforded by the diversion of troops to attack manors along the coast. Hugh Lawless, who was holding the manor of Bray from the king, claimed that the advent of the Scots had encouraged the Irish of the Leinster Mountains to go to war and they had with malice 'invaded, burned and altogether destroyed' his lands at Bray, along with 'all other lands and tenements of divers faithful of the king in those parts'.[197]

The arrival of the Black Death thirty years later devastated any lingering chances of full recovery. The population declined to such an extent that some manors, and even some of the smaller rural boroughs, were deserted entirely. In addition, the nature of the bubonic plague was such that its effects were greater in the more populous, urbanised areas than in the more dispersed settlements of the Gaelic Irish.[198] This altered the demographic considerably, and accentuated an already notable Gaelic resurgence. Legislation – such as the 'Statute of Kilkenny' (1366) – sought to curb the Gaelicisation of the English colony, where the Irish language, Irish personal names, Irish customs, Irish law and other Irish practices were becoming commonplace.

It would be a gross simplification to think that the population was made up of only two groups; the Irish and the English. Even before the beginning of the 1300s, it is also clear that there were significant differences between the descendants of the Anglo-Normans in Ireland and the English. The distinction was reflected in the contemporary ethnic terms of 'English by blood' and 'English by birth'. In retrospect, the Gaelicisation of the latter group, which was frowned upon by the former, was perhaps inevitable. As John Watt put it, the individuality of the group was produced 'when a transplanted society was conditioned at once by its cultural, political and psychological attachments to the mother country and by the consistent pressure of coexistence with a generally hostile indigenous population of significantly different culture'.[199] Society in the Dublin region in the fourteenth century and later was made up of a mixture of elements, including descendants of the first Anglo-Norman settlers, Gaelic Irish families and newly arrived residents from England and elsewhere.

It has been calculated that the average revenue of the Irish exchequer in 1278–99 was £6,300, but that it had plummeted to £2,512 by 1368–84.[200] Evidence suggests that government income continued to fall through the end of the fourteenth century and that the fifteenth century was even worse. The decreasing revenues had consequences for the defence of the colony. There were regular complaints back to England that lands once held by the crown had fallen into Irish hands, and warnings in the 1360s and 1390s especially that the colony was on the verge of breaking point. Two visits by Richard II in the 1390s did little to remedy the situation.

In addition to the cultural mix of groups in the Dublin region in the fourteenth century and later, marriages between the various groups were becoming increasingly common. Power and land continued to be held by the crown, the church and the upper echelons of the laity. The crown was represented in Ireland by an administration based, for the most part, in

195 Orpen, *Ireland under the Normans*, p. 529.   196 *HMDI*, p. 371.   197 *HMDI*, pp 456–8.   198 Kelly, *The great dying*, ch. 4, passim.   199 J.A. Watt, 'The Anglo-Irish colony under strain, 1327–99' in Cosgrove (ed.), *A new history of Ireland: II* (1993), pp 352–96 at p. 352.   200 Ibid., p. 366.

Dublin, and while some of the lay-lords were resident in Ireland, many of them were mostly absent. There was remarkable continuity in lands held by the church, so that the institutions that held estates in the late twelfth century generally retained those properties throughout most of the Middle Ages.

While there was also some continuity in landholding among the laity, this was somewhat complicated by marriage alliances, forfeiture and family lines dying out. What G.H. Orpen called 'the evils of feudal succession' frequently led to the division of large holdings to the point of weakness and the devolution of land to absentee lords.[201] Many of these lords were only interested in the profits that could come from their Irish lands and when these profits began to decrease, their interest similarly declined. One of the positive developments of the fourteenth century was the emergence of a distinctive colonial nobility made up of families whose interest lay squarely in Ireland.[202] During and after the Bruce invasion, King Edward II made many grants to lords who had remained faithful to the crown, and this had an impact on landholding patterns within some parts of the Dublin region. One of the most influential men in fourteenth-century Ireland was John fitz Thomas FitzGerald, fifth lord of Offaly, who was created earl of Kildare and thus acquired great estates in the county to add to his holdings of Rathmore, Maynooth and Laraghbryan.[203] He was head of one of the five great Anglo-Irish dynasties in the fourteenth century – the other earldoms being Ormond, Desmond, Louth and Ulster. The Hereford lands in Kildare had descended to the baronial family of Pippard by the 1260s and, in 1302, Sir Ralph Pippard granted all his manors including Cloncurry, Leixlip, Castlewarden and Oughterard to the king.[204] The Butlers ended up in possession of Cloncurry, Castlewarden and Oughterard, while Leixlip was leased out to the Hospitallers of Kilmainham.[205] Another long-established Anglo-Irish family in Kildare were the Londons. William of London was lord of Naas in the 1370s, and his daughter married Christopher Preston, a member of the influential Drogheda merchant family, through which alliance the London estates passed to the Prestons on William's death in 1386. Other landed families in north-east Kildare included the Eustaces at Castlemartin, the Aylmers at Lyons, the Flattisburys at Johnstown, the Kerdiffs at Kerdiffstown and the Wogans at Rathcoffey. Despite the solid nature of Anglo-Irish lordship in north-east Kildare, some of the manors were coming under increased pressure from Irish raiding. In 1414, the seneschal of the Butlers at Castlewarden appealed for, and received, money to hire archers to protect the manor.[206]

Most of Meath was controlled by a succession of very powerful and influential magnates. East Meath, or the liberty of Trim, passed from the de Lacys to Geoffrey de Geneville and then, in 1308, to Roger Mortimer. Mortimer was heir to Wigmore and other estates in the Welsh marches and was later to become the first earl of March. He was appointed king's lieutenant in Ireland in November 1316.[207] In March 1319, he was justiciar.[208] The Mortimer family continued to hold the lordship of Trim up to 1425, although there were several periods when the lands were under royal control due to minorities and other reasons.[209] When the crown was in control, the profits of the lordship were diverted into the

201 Orpen, *Ireland under the Normans*, p. 318. 202 Frame, *Colonial Ireland*, pp 119–20. 203 Otway-Ruthven, 'Medieval county of Kildare', pp 197–9. 204 Brooks, *Knights' fees*, pp 202–9; *CDI, 1302–7*, no. 149, pp 57–9. 205 Otway-Ruthven, 'Medieval county of Kildare', p. 198. 206 *COD*, 3, no. 8, pp 7–8. 207 *CPR, 1313–17*, p. 563; Thomas Rymer (ed.), *Foedera, conventiones, litterae et cujuscunque generis acta publica inter reges Angliae et alios quosuis imperatores, reges, pontifices, principes, vel communitates (1101–1654)* (20 vols, London, 1704–35), 2:1 (1312–46), pp 103–4; Moody, Martin and Byrne (eds), *A new history of Ireland: IX*, p. 472. Mortimer's appointment seems to have been made in order that he might deal with the critical state of affairs in Ireland – it appears strange then that he did not take up the position until a further five months had elapsed. 208 *CPR, 1317–21*, pp 317, 558; Richard Butler, *Jacobi Grace, Kilkeniensis: Annales Hiberniae* (Dublin, 1842), pp 96–7; Moody, Martin and Byrne (eds), *A new history of Ireland: IX*, p. 472. 209 Potterton, *Medieval Trim*, pp 92–112.

Figure 4.8 Effigy of a knight, from Ratoath, Co. Meath. This stone effigy, of an unidentified knight, is of late thirteenth- or early fourteenth-century date. A damaged inscription on it reads ORATE .PANIUM (?) … ALME(?) FILI FABRI … (taken from Hunt, *Medieval figure sculpture*, 1, p. 213; 2, pl. 10).

Irish exchequer providing a much-needed boost to the dwindling resources of the government. In the period 1322–7, revenue from Trim totalled approximately £300 a year and accounted for about 12 per cent of the total annual receipts recorded by the Irish treasurer.[210] It is clear that the revenue generated by the liberty of Trim continued to be significant into the second half of the century. In 1360–1, the first year of the minority of Edmund Mortimer, the king's custodians gathered £364 from Trim.[211] This figure accounted for 26 per cent of total exchequer revenue, underlining both the increasing importance of the city's hinterland in terms of its value to the Dublin administration and the concomitant diminishing returns of the rest of the colony.

The security of the lands of east Meath was put at risk both by the diversion of funds to Dublin and by the increasing tendency for the Mortimer family to live in England rather than Ireland. As the fourteenth century began, the vulnerability of the area to attacks from the north, west and south-west became ever more apparent. In 1309, men from Carbury invaded parts of the lordship of Trim, 'committing manslaughter, destroying by fire and [causing] other damages'.[212] In 1315, the county had to contend with the invasion of Edward Bruce on top of one of the worst famines of the medieval period. Bruce was joined by many of the gentry of Meath, including the de Lacys of Rathwire, descendants of the original Hugh and Walter – who saw the opportunity to regain the lordship for themselves – as well as Irish families such as the O'Melaghlins. Together, they defeated Roger Mortimer at Kells in December 1315 and although Trim was held for Mortimer, Bruce's army went on to waste and burn Westmeath.[213] In 1317, the Scots (this time with Robert Bruce at their head) marched down through Meath, stopping at Slane, Skreen and Ratoath, where they were ambushed by the earl of Ulster.

Some of the repercussions of the Bruce invasion were seen in Meath during the next century. The loyalty of many of the colonists had been shaken, and internal rivalry tended to weaken their solidarity'.[214] Meanwhile, the Irish grew in power and potency and the O'Melaghlins, Mageoghegans, O'Conors, O'Farrells and O'Reillys were continuously menacing the northern and western frontiers. Westmeath was particularly affected by the revival of Irish power and also the 'Gaelicisation' of some of the local Anglo-Norman lords like the Daltons, Dillons and Delameres. Eastmeath, despite its status as one of the four

210 TNA:PRO E 101/238/3, 7, 10, 16, 21, 27; E 101/239/3; Frame, 'Power and society in Ireland, 1272–1377', *Past and Present*, 76 (1977), 17–18 at 16. The value of Trim in the 1320s was comparable to many lesser Welsh marcher lordships: R.R. Davies, *Lordship and society in the March of Wales, 1282–1400* (Oxford, 1978), p. 196. **211** TNA:PRO E 101/244/3. **212** Quoted in Potterton, *Medieval Trim*, p. 92. **213** Otway-Ruthven, *A history of medieval Ireland*, p. 228. **214** John Brady, 'Anglo-Norman Meath', *RnM*, 2:3 (1961), 38–45 at 41.

obedient shires, was also coming under pressure. Before 1360, Irish troops were being employed to guard the tenants of the manor of Trim against 'the hostile incursions of the malefactors of Carbury and Offaly'.[215] In 1393, the English privy council granted Roger Mortimer £1,000 in consideration of the devastation of his Irish estates by the 'native rebels'.[216]

When in September 1394 Richard II became the first English king to visit Ireland since John in 1210, he was accompanied by the young Roger Mortimer and together they made diplomatic negotiations throughout the country, receiving submissions from several of the Irish chieftains.[217] Mortimer then remained in Ireland and was appointed king's lieutenant in 1395.[218] When he died in battle on 10 June 1398, his son and heir, Edmund, was only seven years of age and the lands once more reverted to the crown.[219] In 1400, following the deposition of Richard II and the accession of Henry Bolingbrook as Henry IV, custody of Trim was granted to Janico Dartas.[220] By his marriage to Joan Taaffe, a member of a distinguished Meath family, Dartas, who first came to prominence in Ireland in 1394, became a tenant under Edmund Mortimer.[221] In addition to Trim, Dartas had the custody of properties in Dublin, Kildare and elsewhere in Meath (including Ardbraccan, Ardmulchan and the priory of Fore).[222]

The Taaffes were one of several landholding families in fourteenth-century Meath. Among the others were the Husseys, the Nugents, the Cruises, the Nangles, the le Petits, the Tuyts and the Delahides. The Kerdiffs established themselves at Ratoath, Co. Meath, in the fourteenth century, with a secondary branch centred at Kerdiffstown near Naas, Co. Kildare.[223] John Darcy (d. 1347) established a dynasty in Co. Meath by marrying Joanna de Burgh, dowager countess of Kildare, in 1329. He had acted as constable of Trim Castle in the 1320s and held the position of justiciar on several occasions in the 1320s, 1330s and 1340s. He later served as an official of Edward III. The le Petit family continued to hold the manor of Dunboyne until 1320, when it passed into the hands of Thomas Butler, who had married Sinolda, daughter and heir of William le Petit.[224] Thereafter, Dunboyne became the caput of a cadet branch of the influential Butler family and remained so for the rest of the medieval period.

In 1425, Edmund Mortimer died of plague while at Trim Castle.[225] His estates passed to his nephew, Richard, duke of York, who was his most senior male relative. When York was killed at Wakefield on 30 December 1460, the lands and liberty of Trim passed into the hands of the crown, who held it for the rest of the Middle Ages. The liberty appears to have been suppressed.[226] In 1468, however, a statute was passed clearing the way for the appointment of a seneschal *pur la conseruacion de bone & pollitique reule del Counte de Mith* ('to maintain good and politic rule in the county of Meath').[227] This system proved

215 Potterton, *Medieval Trim*, p. 104.   **216** *DNB*, Mortimer, p. 145.   **217** Séamus Ó hInnse (ed.), *Miscellaneous Irish annals (AD1114–1437)* (Dublin, 1947), pp 152–3; J.A. Watt, 'John Colton, justiciar of Ireland (1382) and archbishop of Armagh (1383–1404)' in Lydon (ed.), *England and Ireland in the later Middle Ages* (1981), pp 196–213 at pp 203–4. **218** Moody, Martin and Byrne (eds), *A new history of Ireland: IX*, p. 475.   **219** R.R. Davies, 'Mortimer, Roger (VII), fourth earl of March and sixth earl of Ulster (1374–1398)' in *ODNB*; GEC, *Peerage*, 8, pp 449–50; Anthony Tuck, 'Anglo-Irish relations, 1382–1393', *PRIA*, 69C2 (1970), 15–31 at 19; Otway-Ruthven, *A history of medieval Ireland*, p. 336; *CPR, 1399–1401*, p. 468).   **220** *RPCH*, p. 171, no. 87.   **221** Edmund Curtis, 'Janico Dartas, Richard the Second's 'Gascon Squire': his career in Ireland, 1394–1426', *JRSAI*, 63 (1933), 182–205 at 194; Simon Walker, 'Janico Dartasso: chivalry, nationality and the man-at-arms', *History*, 84:273 (Jan. 1999), 31–51.   **222** *RPCH*, p. 154b, no. 52, p. 180, no. 1, p. 220, no. 80; Curtis, 'Janico Dartas', passim.   **223** Mary Ann Lyons, *Church and society in County Kildare, c.1470–1547* (Dublin, 2000), pp 174–5.   **224** T. Blake Butler, 'The barony of Dunboyne', *Irish Genealogist*, 2 (1943–55), 66–81, 107–21, 130–6, 162–4.   **225** *AConn, s.a.* 1424.2; Otway-Ruthven, *A history of medieval Ireland*, p. 269; GEC, *Peerage*, 8, p. 453; R.A. Griffiths, 'Mortimer, Edmund (V), fifth earl of March and seventh earl of Ulster (1391–1425)' in *ODNB*. **226** S.G. Ellis, 'The destruction of the liberties: some further evidence', *Bulletin of the Institute of Historical Research*, 54 (1981), 150–61 at 153. King's bench spent Easter term of 1461 and a year from Hilary term of 1467 at least, in Trim. **227** *Stat. Ire. 1–12 Edw. IV*, pp 466–7; William Betham, *Dignities feudal and parliamentary and the constitutional*

Figure 4.9 Landed
families in Meath
c. 1500. Landholding in
south-east Meath was
dominated by the
upwardly mobile
families of Barnewalls,
Plunketts and Prestons
(after Abraham,
'Upward mobility in
later medieval Meath').

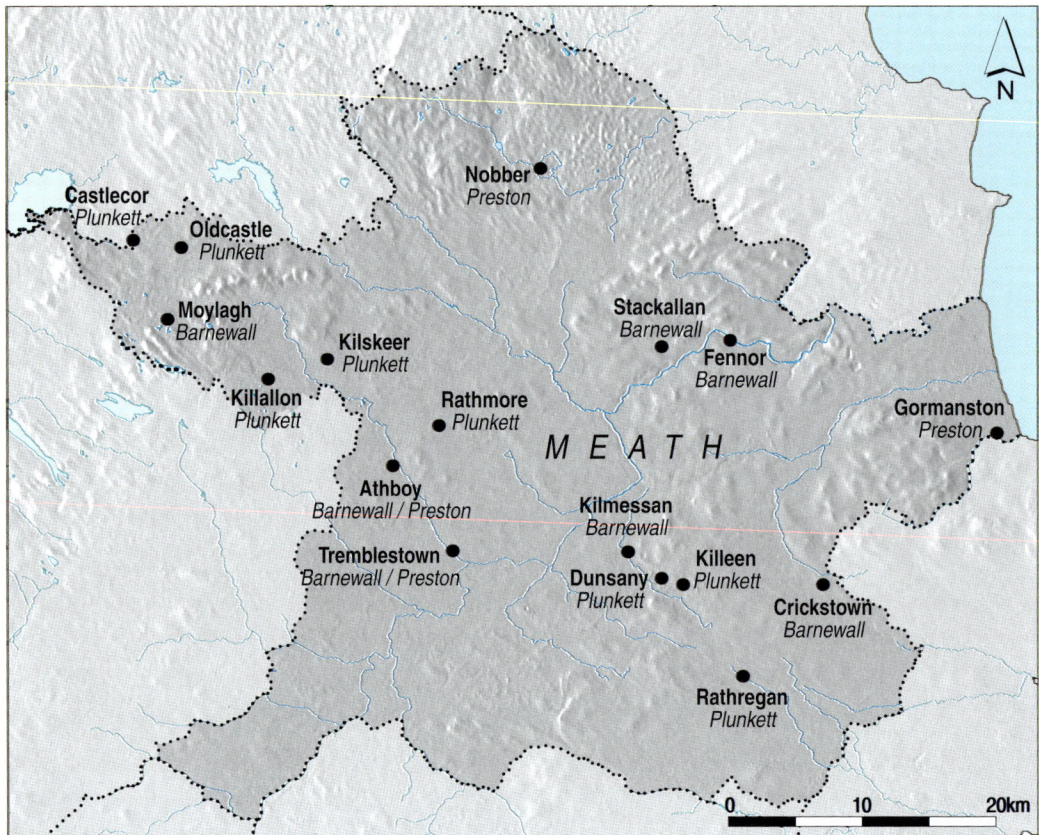

unsatisfactory, and in 1472 the king ordered that the liberty was to be restored.[228] This move was popular with the gentry of Meath but was opposed by the government and by the earl of Kildare.[229]

The later medieval period saw the creation of new wealth and upward mobility in parts of Meath.[230] Many Meath landholders were strongly involved in local government, supplying the personnel for various local offices, including the shrievalty, seneschalry of the liberty of Trim, and commissions of the peace. In the fifteenth century, members of the Meath gentry were found occupying influential posts in the chancery and exchequer of the central government, and also staffing the judiciary.

The available evidence suggests general stability in landed society in Meath, particularly among the baronial families of Anglo-Norman descent. As well as continuing to hold the estates that they received from Hugh de Lacy in the twelfth century, a number of these families succeeded in enhancing their landed wealth while maintaining and developing their activities in local and central government. Other families managed to establish themselves in the Meath aristocracy through land acquisition and marriage, and included, for example, the Plunketts, Barnewalls and Prestons (Figure 4.9).

Landholders in Meath, particularly the newcomers to the territorial elite, needed to display their status, association and cohesion with other families. Many upwardly mobile families chose to build architecturally ambitious tower-houses with more emphasis on display than defence, and parish churches to help express their leading role in society, and to commemorate their achievements. Consequently, some of the characteristics of late medieval Irish society that have been traditionally seen as detrimental to the overall health

legislature of the United Kingdom (Dublin, 1830), 1, p. 376.   **228** Betham, *Dignities*, pp 764–5.   **229** D.B. Quinn,
'Aristocratic autonomy, 1460–94' in Cosgrove (ed.), *A new history of Ireland: II* (1993), pp 591–618 at p. 603.
230 Kennedy Abraham, 'Upward mobility in later medieval Meath', *History Ireland*, 5:4 (1997), 15–20; Linda Clare, *On
the edge of the Pale: the rise and decline of an Anglo-Irish community in County Meath, 1170–1530* (Dublin, 2006).

of the colony – warfare, ineffectual central government in border areas, and the break up of aristocratic estates – led to the creation of new wealth and opportunities for advancement.[231]

The trend that had emerged in the thirteenth century of Dublin citizens and merchants acquiring property in south-east Meath continued into the later medieval period. Peter Highley, a well-off Dublin citizen who made his will in 1474, held forty acres of land near Killeigh, Co. Meath, from the baron of Skreen.[232] In the early sixteenth century, the dean and chapter of Christ Church, Dublin, leased land in Clonee to Robert Gossan, a Dublin glover.[233] A certain Robert de Bree was seneschal of Meath c.1310.[234] He was a Dublin merchant and property owner who had become mayor of the city in the late thirteenth century.[235] Bree was a Gaelic Irishman, and wrote to the king asking to be treated in the same way as an Englishman before the courts. Against the odds, some other Gaelic families came to prominence in the Dublin region. The Neills of Clondalkin, for example, were a prosperous commercial and farming family by the fifteenth century. William Neill had a farm and a tannery when he died in 1471, and another member of the family owned shops and land in Dublin.[236] In a court case of 1355, Simon Neill accused a man of breaking into his Clondalkin close.[237] The accused claimed that he did not have to answer the charges as Neill was a Gaelic Irishman. He may have been Irish, but Neill was a descendant of the O'Neills of Ulster and as such he was accorded English status and his complaint was upheld. As Watt points out, this case is a reminder that 'the Gaelic Irish living among the colonists were still, in the fourteenth century, disadvantaged at English law'.[238]

The county of Dublin, apart from its southern flanks on the edge of the mountains, remained firmly under the control of the English administration. Up to the Reformation, the archbishop continued to hold close to one quarter of the land in the county, with religious houses holding close to another quarter.[239] Much of this land was leased out to free-holders who paid a chief rent in return. The other half of the county's land was dominated by long-established medieval families such as the St Lawrences of Howth, the Talbots of Malahide and Garristown, the Barnewalls of Castleknock and Drimnagh, the Plunketts of Dunsoghly and Portmarnock, and the FitzWilliams at various points in the south of the county.[240]

Some of the smaller gentry families who were scattered throughout Co. Dublin had originated in the mercantile and legal worlds of Dublin. These included the Seagraves of Finglas, the Ushers of Donnybrook, the Fagans of Feltrim and the Bathes of Drumcondra.[241] Dublin's merchants and aldermen leased land from the monasteries and the archbishop and also from the king. In 1435, Archbishop Richard Talbot leased several parcels of land in Clondalkin to the aptly named Thomas Sanguyne, citizen and butcher of Dublin. The royal manors in south-west Dublin were also popular places for Dubliners to lease lands. In 1598, when a list of 'men of name' was constructed from Co. Dublin, about 10 per cent lived on the royal manors while others, such as Lord FitzWilliam of Merrion, had tenancies there.[242] Dublin merchant William Talbot held land in Saggart as well as Rathcoole and Templeogue at the end of the fifteenth century, while Nicholas Handcock, merchant and one time mayor

231 Abraham, 'Upward mobility', 20.   232 Berry (ed.), *Register of wills and inventories*, pp 128–33.   233 *CCCD*, no. 1224, p. 246.   234 RIA MS 12D12, p. 104.   235 J.A. Watt, 'Approaches to the history of fourteenth-century Ireland' in Cosgrove (ed.), *A new history of Ireland: II* (1993), pp 303–13 at p. 308.   236 Berry (ed.), *Register of wills and inventories*, pp 94–9, 200.   237 J.S. Brewer and William Bullen (eds), *Calendar of the Carew manuscripts preserved in the archiepiscopal library at Lambeth* (6 vols, London, 1867–73), 5, p. 452; John Barry (intr.), *Sir John Davies, The discovery of the true causes why Ireland was never entirely subdued, 1612* (repr. Shannon, 1969), pp 103–4.   238 Watt, 'Approaches to the history of fourteenth-century Ireland', p. 394.   239 Otway-Ruthven, 'Medieval church lands'. 240 Smyth, 'Exploring the social and cultural topographies', p. 132.   241 Ibid., p. 132.   242 Raymond Gillespie, 'Small worlds: settlement and society in the royal manors of sixteenth-century Dublin' in Clarke, Prunty and Hennessy (eds), *Surveying Ireland's past* (2004), pp 197–217 at p. 199.

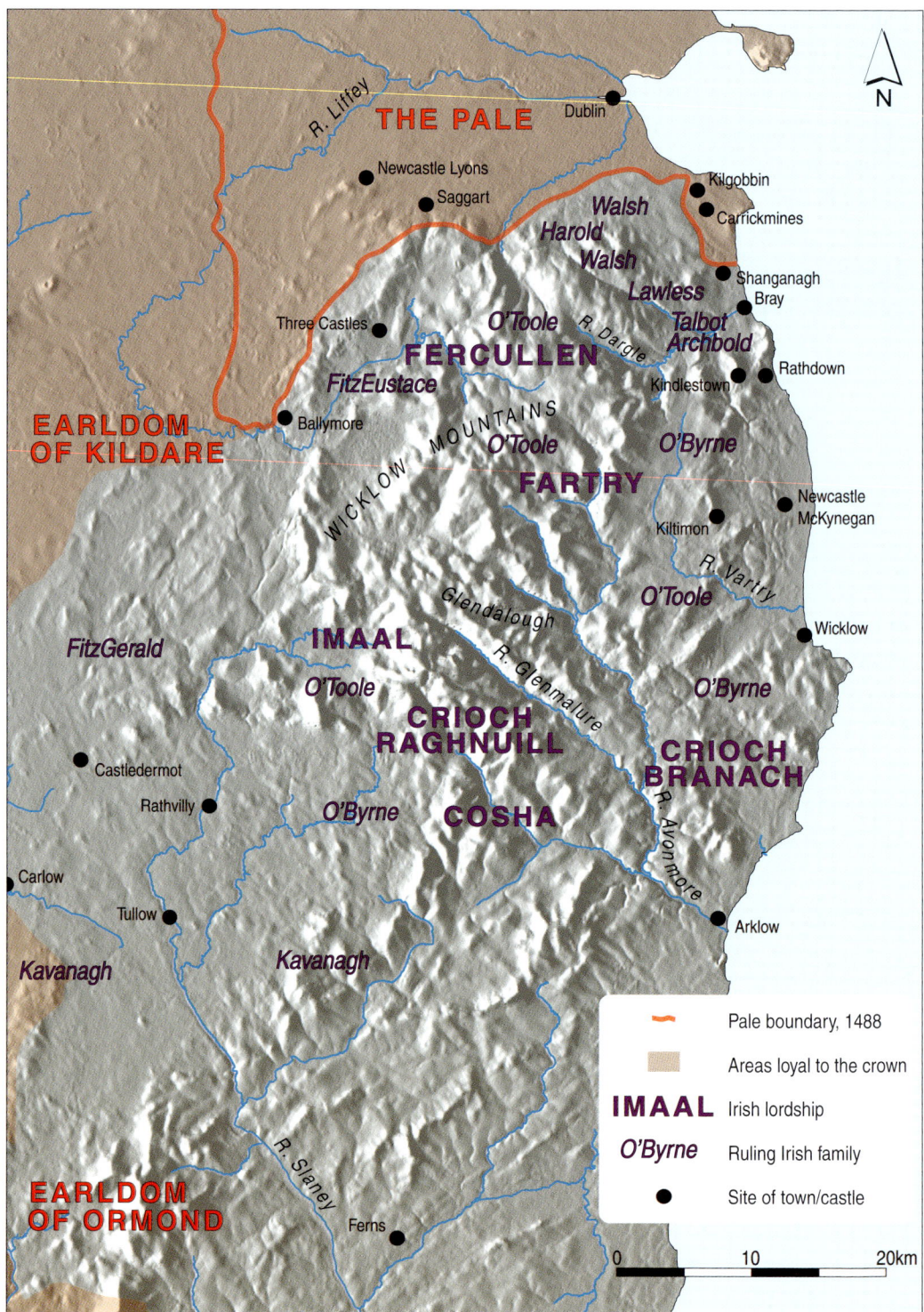

Figure 4.10 The region south of Dublin in the late fifteenth century. The O'Byrnes and O'Tooles were in control of the Dublin-Wicklow uplands, while 'marcher families' such as the Walshes, Archbolds and Harolds held sway in south-east Co. Dublin (map based on information supplied by Emmett O'Byrne and Sarah Gearty).

of Dublin, held lands on the royal manors of Crumlin and Saggart as well as in Swords and Straffan, Co. Kildare, when he died in 1547.[243]

Also in the south, the 'marcher families' such as the Harolds, Howells, Archbolds and Walshes, continued to occupy key positions at the interface of Dublin and Wicklow (Figure 4.10). These families were characterised by a clan structure, and the Dublin government dealt with them as they dealt with their Irish neighbours, by taking hostages and trying to enforce a sense of collective responsibility on the clan leader.[244] Some of these

243 J.G. Smyly, 'Old Latin deeds in the library of Trinity College 6', *Hermathena*, 73 (1948), 115–20 at 115, 119; J.G. Smyly, 'Old Latin deeds in the library of Trinity College 7', *Hermathena*, 74 (1949), 60–8 at 60, 63, 64, 67; Gillespie, 'Small worlds', pp 202–3, 215.   **244** Robin Frame, *English lordship in Ireland, 1318–1361* (Oxford, 1982), pp 28–9.

families, such as the Archbolds and Walshes, had in any case become increasingly Gaelicised. In 1468, it was claimed that Henry Walsh of Carrickmines spoke Irish, wore Irish dress and was reputed to use Irish law whenever it suited him.[245]

In south Dublin and north Wicklow, there was continual tension that regularly broke out into open warfare in the fourteenth and fifteenth centuries. The O'Tooles had been tenants of Anglo-Norman lords and the archbishops of Dublin through the thirteenth century, but after *c.*1300 they frequently became outright enemies of the crown and their supposed overlords. The situation was fluid, however, and at times the Irish lords chose to ally with the Anglo-Irish settlers before returning to attack them shortly afterwards. This has been aptly described as 'the merry-go-round of march politics'.[246] Through the fourteenth century, the Mac Murchadas were also involved in regular disturbances in Leinster, and in the fifteenth century they continued to levy black-rents on the Dublin exchequer. In 1374, the O'Byrnes captured and destroyed the castles of Newcastle and Wicklow, although both were promptly recovered and rebuilt, before Newcastle finally fell to the O'Byrnes in 1405.[247] Wicklow Castle seems to have remained in crown hands throughout the fifteenth century, but the town and harbour appear to have formed part of the O'Byrne territory.

In 1542, the O'Byrnes surrendered and were regranted their territory, but this arrangement was abandoned in 1566, from which time the territory was subject to the rule of a seneschal. The O'Tooles regained territories and expanded eastwards around Powerscourt. In 1542, Turlough O'Toole of Powerscourt and his brother, Art Óg of Castlekevin, gained official control of their lands through the government policy of surrender and regrant.

In Kildare, the FitzGeralds were especially powerful in the period 1470–1534, in political, economic and ecclesiastical affairs. They had been sub-tenants in the thirteenth century, gaining political importance in the fourteenth century, before losing territory to the Gaelic Irish. In the latter part of the fifteenth century, however, they regained most of these and also managed to recover lands lost to the Ormonds – including Oughterany, Oughterard, Castlewarden and Clintonscourt, as well as securing Lucan, Leixlip and several other manors – through marriage alliances, royal grants, legal settlements and purchase.[248] They expropriated Gaelic landowners and replaced them with their own tenants. It seems that most of these tenants were also Gaelic, however, as by 1550 the majority of the inhabitants of most parts of Meath and Kildare were Gaelic.[249]

The main FitzGerald seat was at Maynooth, and in the early sixteenth century there were about sixty cottages in the village.[250] Most of the tenants were Irish, but some had English names. The tenants worked in the village, at the castle and on the earl's manor, growing crops and keeping chickens. In 1518, Irishman Thomas Miagh, the village carpenter, was the ninth earl's master miller. He was assisted by an under-miller and also oversaw the operation of the mill at Rathmore.[251] After Maynooth, Leixlip was the most important and profitable of all the FitzGerald manors in Kildare. Although the names of some Irish tenants appear at Leixlip, there seems to have been a greater proportion of English tenants here than at Maynooth and Celbridge.[252] Mary Ann Lyons made the important observation that 'the proportion of customary tenants with Gaelic names employed on manors in the maghery (heartland) of Dublin and Meath numbered between a quarter and a half of the total

245 Emmett O'Byrne, 'One world: the communities of the southern Dublin marches', *History Ireland*, 13:3 (2005), 17–21 at 19.   246 Ibid., 18.   247 O'Byrne, *War, politics and the Irish of Leinster*, pp 106, 114–15.   248 Lyons, *Church and society*, p. 39.   249 S.G. Ellis, *Tudor Ireland: crown, community and the conflict of cultures, 1470–1603* (London and New York, 1985), p. 35.   250 *Crown surveys, 1540–1*, pp 133–4, 279–82.   251 Lyons, *Church and society*, pp 18, 23.   252 *Crown surveys, 1540–1*, pp 203–4.

recorded. In the case of Kildare, especially in the marches, that proportion rose to almost two-thirds'.[253]

Maynooth Castle was the hub of FitzGerald power and it was extended in 1426, soon becoming 'one of the richest earl's houses under the crown of England'.[254] There was a famous library in the castle, and in 1515 a college was built 'in a most beautiful form'. Cadet branches of the FitzGeralds resided at locations all across Kildare including, in the north-east of the county, at Blackhall (Clane), Osberstown (north of Naas), Cloncurry, Leixlip and Castletown (which they had held since the fourteenth century). The FitzGeralds were dominant in Lyons, Oughterard, Castlewarden, Donaghcumper, Stacumny, Kill and Rathmore, but other families were also influential in these areas, especially the Aylmers of Lyons. The manor of Rathmore was extensive, stretching into west Wicklow, while the town of Rathmore had burgesses and portreeves.[255] It was leased to the Husseys of Mulhussey in Meath in 1518, but by 1540 it was in the hands of the Eustace family. After the execution of James FitzGerald in 1537, the family lost control of Leixlip, Donadea and Kilcock. They also lost Maynooth, but nonetheless remained the most powerful family in the sixteenth century.

Fifteenth- and sixteenth-century Kildare 'had a solid lesser aristocracy and gentry establishment, with families such as the Wogans, the Eustaces and the Aylmers originally being of Anglo-Norman stock'.[256] The Kerdiffs, Flattisburys and Sherlocks were smaller families, owning relatively modest holdings and having limited influence politically.[257] By the sixteenth century, the Eustaces had become second to the FitzGeralds, in terms of influence and property ownership in Kildare. They had established themselves at Castlemartin Castle in the fourteenth century and had expanded from there. Most of their lands were in the southern half of the county, but by the early sixteenth century they also held lands at Confey in the north-east of the county, as well as across the county border into Dublin and Wicklow. They held castles at Blackhall (near Punchestown), Confey, Clongowes Wood, Donadea (Figure 5.45), Harristown and Kilashee, and these formed a strategic cordon of protection against the raiding Irish.

The Eustaces had made important links by marrying into the Plunketts of Dunsany, Co. Meath, the Aylmers of Donadea, Co. Kildare, the Butlers of Dunboyne, the Talbots of Malahide, the Travers of Monkstown, and the FitzGeralds of Osberstown, as well as a whole series of other lesser gentry families of the Pale, and some Gaelic families to boot.[258] Several members of the Eustace family married multiple times. Their principal seat was at Ballymore Eustace, which was situated at an important crossing point on the River Liffey, on the southern fringes of the Pale. Its location made it strategically important, and its castle was manned by the Eustaces in the fifteenth and early sixteenth centuries (Figure 4.11). This far south, the Gaelic Irish were in a large majority and Ballymore became increasingly hard to hold on to. It was targeted by the O'Byrnes and the O'Tooles and came under further attack during the Geraldine revolt, but it was still occupied by the Eustaces in the 1540s.[259]

In 1541, Henry VIII rewarded Sir Thomas Eustace, baron of Kilcullen, with the title of Viscount Baltinglass for his services against Kildare in the 1534 revolt. Despite their position as loyal Old English, the family – particularly its collateral branches – continued to interact with Gaelic culture and to marry into Gaelic families.[260] The second viscount's sisters were married to members of the O'Tooles and O'Byrnes respectively, and Gaelic scribes compiled genealogies tracing the families connections with Brian Bóruma. This did not, however, prevent the O'Tooles from raiding and exacting black rents from Ballymore Eustace.

253 Lyons, *Church and society*, p. 17.   254 Arnold Horner, *IHTA: Maynooth* (Dublin, 1995), p. 1.   255 Lyons, *Church and society*, p. 22.   256 Ibid., p. 13.   257 Ibid., p. 13.   258 Ibid., p. 153.   259 Ibid., pp 23–4.   260 Christopher Maginn, *'Civilizing' Gaelic Leinster: the extension of Tudor rule in the O'Byrne and O'Toole lordships* (Dublin, 2004), p. 153.

Figure 4.11 Ballymore Eustace Castle, Co. Kildare, by Gabriel Beranger, 1773. This was the principal seat of the Eustace family in the sixteenth century (image reproduced courtesy of the National Library of Ireland).

The Aylmers of Lyons also ranked among the most influential families of Co. Kildare in the early sixteenth century.[261] They had settled in Kildare soon after their arrival in Ireland in 1169 and established their primary seat at Lyons in 1300.[262] In the fifteenth century, they emerged as local and central government officials and consolidated these roles in the sixteenth century, while also expending their estates into Meath and Dublin. Like the Eustaces, the Aylmers advanced their fortunes considerably through astute marriage alliances. Donadea emerged as one of their secondary holdings in the sixteenth century, while they also came to possess Dollardstown (Bathe) and Macetown (Cheevers) in Co. Meath. The Aylmers, like the Barnewalls in Meath, remained Catholic throughout the sixteenth century.

The Wogans were also of Anglo-Norman origin and had their principal Irish seat at Rathcoffey, with properties in Ikeathy and Oughterany baronies.[263] Over the years, they intermarried with the FitzGeralds, the Eustaces, the Flattisburys and the Suttons, among others. While some gentry families experienced a growth in their wealth and influence through the Middle Ages, the Wogans are an example of one whose fortunes and standing decreased through the fifteenth and sixteenth centuries – even if various members of the family held posts such as viceroy, chancellor and high sheriff. In addition to Rathcoffey, they also had estates at Downings, Blackhall and Newhall in 1600.

The Flattisbury family were associated with Kildare from the thirteenth century, establishing a seat at Johnstown.[264] By the mid-fifteenth century, they held a third of the barony of Naas. Philip Flattisbury, 'a diligent antiquarian',[265] was employed by the eighth earl of Kildare to compile the Red Book of Kildare, begun in 1503, and later leased property

261 Lyons, *Church and society*, p. 164.   **262** Ibid., p. 164; H.H. Aylmer, 'The Aylmer family', *JCKAHS*, 1 (1891–5), 295–307; Fenton Aylmer, 'Sir Gerald Aylmer, knight and baronet', *JCKAHS*, 11 (1930–3), 267–385.   **263** Michael Devitt, 'Rathcoffey', *JCKAHS*, 3 (1899–1902), 79–98.   **264** Lyons, *Church and society*, p. 175; Arthur Vicars, 'The family of Flatesbury of Ballnasculloge and Johnstown, County Kildare', *JCKAHS*, 4 (1903–5), 87–94.   **265** According to Richard Stanihurst (quoted in Vicars, 'The family of Flatesbury', 89).

from the Kildares in Clane, Sallins, Baronrath, Whitechurch and Baronswood. By the late sixteenth century, they had established a second seat, at Palmerstown in west Dublin. Centred at Sherlockstown, the Sherlocks were another of north-east Kildare's minor gentry families but, like the Kerdiffs, they were a secondary branch of a more influential family – in this case the Sherlocks of Wexford.[266] The Kerdiffs were nonetheless involved in local politics and law in the fifteenth to seventeenth centuries. In the late sixteenth century, James Sherlock owned in Naas two castles, a stone house, thirty-five messuages, 132 acres of arable land, a garden and a watermill.[267]

The Sutton family held lands in Kildare at Clane, Kilcock, Naas, Richardstown, Tully, Castletown and Tipper. Edward Sutton held the manor and rectory of Killybegs, which was owned by the hospital of St John of Jerusalem. The Wellesleys were associated with Kildare from the late thirteenth century. In 1422, one branch of the family settled at Dangan in Co. Meath, but most of the Wellesley lands were in south Kildare. Members of the family served as senior ecclesiastics, but their active role in local and central government was minimal.

Manorial fortunes: the case of Saggart

The manor of Saggart provides a good example of the fortunes of a settlement on the fringes of the area that was to become known as the Pale.[268] It occupied a position of great strategic importance as a gateway into the heavily colonised hinterland of Dublin, functioning as a bridgehead between the unruly pastoral landscape of the Dublin/Wicklow Mountains and the ordered farmlands of the vale of Dublin. It was situated in an area crossed by two major overland routes – the highway from Dublin to Naas, and the route to Ballymore (Eustace) (Figure 4.12).

For almost a century from its establishment as a royal manor in the 1170s, Saggart's revenues steadily increased and it enjoyed remarkable prosperity. The potential for profitable farming and exchange was great, and it was one that the crown and the Irish exchequer managed to take advantage of with remarkable success for most of the thirteenth century. After almost a hundred years of lucrative agricultural exploitation, however, the area began to suffer from a combination of setbacks, but most particularly from regular attacks by the Leinster Irish. From the 1270s, parts of the area were described as lying 'in the march'. The southern part of the manor had always been environmentally challenging, but it became increasingly politically challenging as the rebellious Wicklow Irish gained control of the upland areas and used their position to penetrate into the manors and farms of lowland areas, advancing towards Dublin. Famine and an inability to meet rents acted as catalysts in a volatile environment. Saggart suffered a number of destructive raids during the 1270s. Its burgesses and farmers claimed that in one of these raids that occurred in summer while they were working in the fields, their stock had been driven off by Irish thieves and forty of their men had been killed and others taken prisoner while pursuing the raiders.[269]

The justiciar and his forces were heavily defeated at Glenmalure in 1274, and again in 1275 and 1276.[270] Between 1274 and 1278, the Dublin exchequer paid out almost fifty pounds to various individuals engaged in the protection of Saggart.[271] In the early 1280s, the tenants of the manor – both English and Irish – appealed directly to the king for lenience with regard to their rental arrears.[272] They described how they had been forced out of their homes

266 Lyons, *Church and society*, p. 175.   **267** Ibid., p. 175; J.F.M. Ffrench, 'Notes on the family of Sherlock: chiefly gathered from the state papers and other official documents', *JCKAHS*, 2 (1896–9), 39–47 at 46.   **268** A more detailed discussion of the fortunes of Saggart in the Middle Ages can be found in Margaret Murphy, 'The "key of the county": Saggart and the manorial economy of the Dublin March, *c*.1200–1540' in Clare Downham, Jenifer Ní Gradaigh and Emmett O'Byrne (eds), *The march in the medieval west* (forthcoming).   **269** Otway-Ruthven, *A history of medieval Ireland*, p. 201.   **270** O'Byrne, *War, politics and the Irish of Leinster*, pp 60–1.   **271** *IEP*, pp 12, 17–18, 22.   **272** G.O.

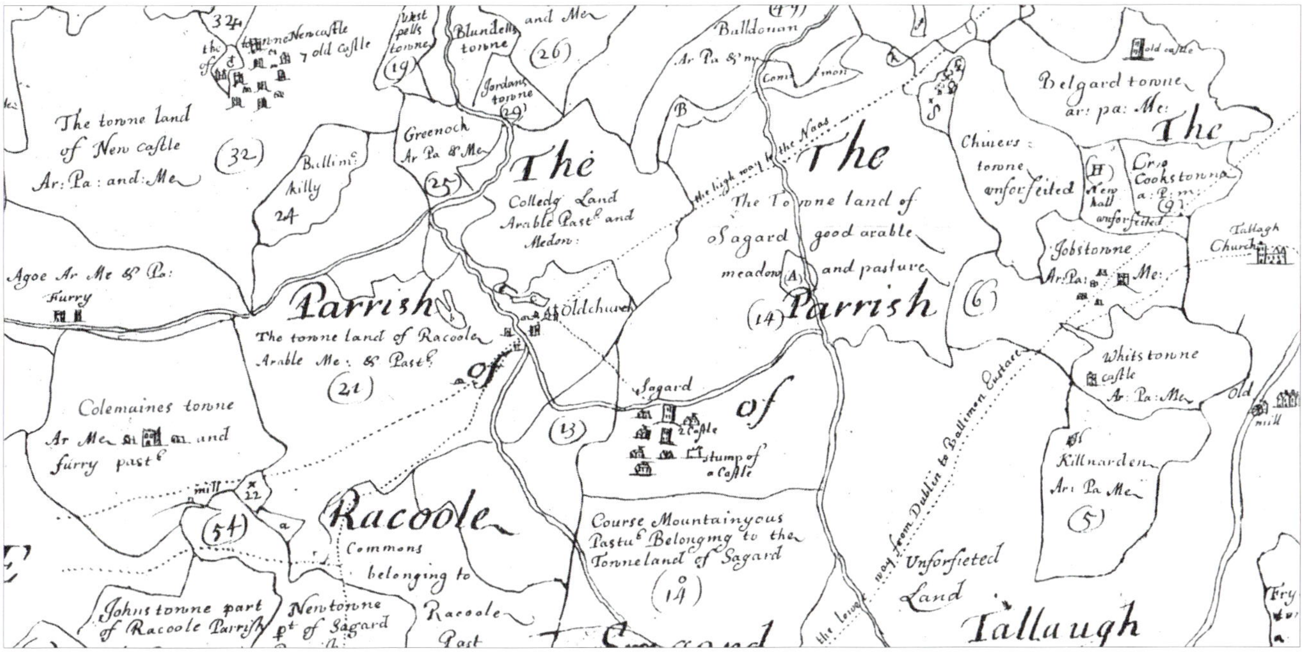

Figure 4.12 Extract
from the Down Survey
map of the barony of
Newcastle and
Uppercross, Co. Dublin,
showing a range of
settlements, including
Saggart (centre), with
two castles in addition
to the 'stump of a castle',
Newcastle, with its
'7 old castles' (top left),
and other castles at
Colmanstown, Belgard
and Whitestown. Two
mills are depicted, as
well as the church at
Tallaght and two roads
– 'the highway to the
Naas' and 'the lower
way from Dublin to
Ballimore Eustace'.

and how their relatives had been killed. Conditions deteriorated through the following years, so that by the first decade of the fourteenth century the cumulative effects of raiding, worsening climatic conditions and poor harvests led to the abandonment of several holdings in Saggart.[273]

The Annals of Ireland reported that Saggart and Rathcoole were again invaded by the O'Byrnes and the O'Tooles in June 1311.[274] Despite these and other attacks, however, some individuals were prepared to take the risk of farming on the frontier. In 1312, for instance, the justiciar was asked to hold an inquisition to enquire whether the king should grant a farm of forty acres in Saggart to William Douce.[275] The inquisition found that the grant would be to the king's advantage and to the advantage of all the inhabitants of that part of the country, as William already held adjoining land on which he had built a stone fortalice for the defence of the country against the Irish enemies of the Leinster Mountains.[276] If allowed to acquire these lands, the jurors stated that he would be better able to maintain and repair this fortalice for the greater defence and security of the country. It is unclear what the outcome of Douze's investment was, but in the following years Saggart was to suffer greatly from raids by both the Irish and the Scots and by famine caused by crop failure and animal murrains. Tenants from Saggart were involved in action against the followers of the Bruces when they were in the neighbourhood early in 1317.[277] By the 1320s, many tenants had left Saggart, and lands were abandoned and uncultivated. In the 1260s, Saggart yielded an annual profit of over £112; by 1332, this figure had dropped to less than £49.[278]

There is no direct evidence of the immediate effect of the Black Death of 1348–9 on the manor, and it is possible that mortality did not reach crisis proportions until the 1360s in the wake of the second major plague outbreak in 1361.[279] In July 1362, the seneschal of the royal demesne was ordered to lease lands vacated by the plague in Crumlin, Saggart and

Sayles, *Documents on the affairs of Ireland before the king's council* (Dublin, 1979), no. 41, p. 32.   **273** *IEP*, p. 122; Williams (ed.), *The Annals of Ireland by Friar John Clyn*, pp 154–5; Dryburgh and Smith (eds), *Handbook*, pp 79, 83–5, 93, 107, 109, 119; James Lydon, 'A land of war' in Cosgrove (ed.), *A new history of Ireland: II* (1993), pp 240–74 at p. 262.   **274** *CSMA*, 2, p. 339.   **275** TNA:PRO C143/91.   **276** *Fortalices* have been identified as an early form of tower house, although there is some question as to whether they were built of stone or timber: see Terry Barry, 'The last frontier: defence and settlement in late medieval Ireland' in T.B. Barry, Robin Frame and Katharine Simms (eds), *Colony and frontier in medieval Ireland: essays presented to J.F. Lydon* (London, 1995), pp 217–28 at pp 224–5; see also below, pp 145–57.   **277** *IEP*, p. 264.   **278** *RDKPRI*, 43, p. 61.   **279** Lyons, 'Weather, famine, pestilence and plague',

Newcastle Lyons to anyone who would be willing to hold them.[280] Not surprisingly, there was not a great take up of this offer and it is found repeated in later years. The manor had suffered more damaging raids in the late 1350s, when the O'Byrnes and O'Tooles were said to have 'taken a large prey' from Saggart.[281]

From the late fourteenth century, it becomes common to find grants to individuals of custody of the combined assets of Esker, Newcastle Lyons and Saggart, as the crown sought to recoup some profit from the manors by their use as rewards to individuals who had performed services on its behalf. In 1388, the three properties were valued at £132 when they were granted to Geoffrey de Vale to hold for the term of his life.[282] Twenty years later, the value of the same manors had fallen to 100 marks (£66 6s. 8d.).[283] By 1473, when custody of Newcastle Lyons and Saggart was granted to Roland FitzEustace, treasurer of Ireland, they were stated to be worth £60. It is doubtful if this was indeed the case, as the 1470s was a particularly bad decade for the area, with the Wicklow Irish and their allies threatening to eradicate any government control over the Dublin marches.[284] The community of Saggart were paying a black-rent to Edmund O'Toole in an attempt to protect themselves from attack, an agreement which a parliamentary decree of 1470 sought to force them to abandon.[285] Compliance with the decree brought swift retribution from the Irish, and Saggart was sacked in 1471–2, forcing many to abandon it.[286] Not long afterwards, an order was issued to enclose Saggart by defences: 'That whereas the town of Saggart is situate on the frontier of the March of the county of Dublin, and is a great defence of said county and if the said town were wasted or destroyed it would be a principal cause of the destruction of much of the said county'.[287]

At the beginning of the sixteenth century, the king's lands in Co. Dublin were stated to be of all others the worst and most wasted.[288] The extent for Saggart drawn up in 1540 underlines the contraction of the manor both in size and value.[289] There were sixty-three messuages in the central borough with five more in the subsidiary nucleus at *Balycher*. These holdings were in the hands of a small group of individuals with one – Robert Preston – holding sixteen. Two-hundred-and-ninety-nine acres were said to lie in the external fields. The total value of the manor was given as £21 7s.

The fiscal evidence for Saggart for the twelfth to the sixteenth century illustrates the stark reality of declining profitability in frontier zones. The trends in the agrarian economy, with the boom period of the thirteenth century giving way to sharp decline in the fourteenth century and stagnation in the fifteenth, were not confined to the march, however, and they were equally evident in parts of the country not directly affected by Irish raids and further afield. A recent analysis, which placed the Irish agrarian economic experience in the wider European context, found very similar patterns occurring from Scotland to southern Italy.[290] While some Anglo-Norman settlements did suffer greatly from Irish raiding activity and from events such as the Bruce invasion, their inability to recover can often be explained in terms of the general European experience of falling population and declining economies.

The sixteenth century

W.J. Smyth has identified the principal features that characterised the changing geography of landownership in Co. Dublin over the period 1541–1641 as growing secularisation,

p. 46.   **280** NAI RC8/28: Memoranda roll, pp 157–8.   **281** *IEP*, pp 472, 487, 494, 501–2; *RPCH*, p. 66.   **282** *RPCH*, p. 139.   **283** *RPCH*, p. 187.   **284** Emmett O'Byrne, 'A much disputed land: Carrickmines and the Dublin Marches' in Duffy (ed.), *Medieval Dublin IV* (2003), pp 229–52 at pp 245–6.   **285** *Stat. Ire. 1–12 Edw. IV*, p. 665.   **286** O'Byrne, 'A much disputed land', p. 246.   **287** *Stat. Ire. 1–12 Edw. IV*, p. 809.   **288** *State papers, King Henry VIII, vol. 2, pt. III: correspondence between the governments of England and Ireland, 1515–38* (London, 1834), p. 279.   **289** *Crown surveys, 1540–1*, pp 95–9.   **290** Britnell, *Britain and Ireland*, pp 43–4.

insertion of New English settler families and consolidation of the leading gentry families of the Pale.[291] The most important causative factor was the Dissolution of Dublin's monasteries and the redistribution of their extensive lands. It has been estimated, for example, that a single religious house, St Mary's Abbey, Dublin, accounted for some 17,000 statute acres in Co. Dublin and a further 3,700 acres in Co. Meath.[292] Much of this land had already been leased by lay landholders, but following the Dissolution it passed via the king into permanent secular ownership.

A small number of religious houses were suppressed in 1535–8, but the full-scale campaign of dissolution of the religious orders in the Pale took place in 1539–40.[293] Dublin Corporation acquired All Hallows Augustinian house, while the Dublin citizenry successfully appealed for the conserving of the cathedral church of Holy Trinity, the religious community being changed into a secular chapter.[294] Among the main beneficiaries of the monastic dissolutions in the Dublin area were old established families like the St Lawrences of Howth, who acquired lands in Baldoyle and Raheny, and the Barnewalls of Turvey, who acquired the lands of the nunnery of Gracedieu.[295] The Luttrells of Luttrellstown, connected by marriage to both Barnewalls and St Lawrences, acquired monastic lands in Tallaght and Coolmine. The FitzWilliam family, long established in south Dublin, also benefitted from post-Reformation land relocation and, over the course of the seventeenth century, they became the great landowners of south Co. Dublin. Many of the Dublin mercantile families who had acquired country estates in the later medieval period also augmented their holdings substantially. For example, the Fagans of Feltrim picked up pieces of church land from all over the county, especially in Lusk and Swords. Some of the monastic land was used to reward crown officials who were in favour with the king – men like John Travers, master of the king's ordnance in Ireland, who was granted a twenty-one-year lease of St Mary's grange of Carrickbrennan.[296] He left the property to his daughter, who married a Eustace, and thus this well-established family acquired Monkstown.

In Co. Meath, the Barnewalls, Plunketts and Prestons joined the ranks of the prominent families who benefitted from the redistribution of monastic land. Royal officials also profited, such as the vice-treasurer, Sir William Brabazon, who was granted the former lands of Llanthony Priory.[297] In Co. Kildare, the coincidence of the FitzGerald defeat and the monastic dissolution gave the crown an unrivalled opportunity to reward loyal subjects and shore up weaknesses in the Pale's defences. Those who benefitted were local loyalist families such as the Eustaces, Suttons and Aylmers, who enjoyed 'a relatively exceptional degree of aggrandisement through their acquisition of particularly lucrative dissolved monastic property'.[298] Dublin-based administrators such as John Alen, the lord chancellor, acquired choice properties and, along with his brother Thomas, became an important member of the Kildare gentry while continuing to live in Dublin. Thomas Alen was granted the property of St John's Hospital in Naas, the manor of St Thomas' Abbey, Dublin, at Kill, and the preceptory of the Hospitallers at Kilteel.[299] John Alen made an early and pre-emptive strike for St Wolstan's priory and its lands, and converted the monastic buildings into an unfortified mansion house at the core of his new estates.[300]

291 Smyth, 'Exploring the social and cultural topographies', p. 134. 292 Ó Conbhuí, 'The lands of St Mary's Abbey', 26. 293 Extents Ir. mon. possessions, p. iii; see Brendan Bradshaw, The Dissolution of the religious orders in Ireland under Henry VIII (Cambridge, 1974). 294 Bradshaw, Dissolution of religious orders, pp 110ff. 295 Smyth, 'Exploring the social and cultural topographies', p. 135. 296 Ó Conbhuí, 'The lands of St Mary's Abbey', 57–8. 297 Colm Lennon, Sixteenth-century Ireland: the incomplete conquest (Dublin, 1994), p. 148. 298 Lyons, Church and society, p. 176. 299 Ibid., p. 179. 300 William Nolan, 'Kildare from the documents of conquest: the monastic extents and the Civil Survey, 1654–1656' in Nolan and McGrath (eds), Kildare: history and society (2006), pp 233–71 at p. 250.

The Alens are early examples of the first phase in the introduction of English-born gentlemen and officials into the countryside around Dublin, a trend that was to become much more marked in the coming century. The Old English families of the Pale were the greatest beneficiaries of the redistribution of monastic land, but their success was in many cases to be short-lived.

Chapter summary

This chapter has tracked general landholding patterns across the region from the arrival of the Anglo-Normans to the beginning of the seventeenth century. For much of that period, there was considerable continuity of landholding in virtually all of the county of Dublin, along with adjoining baronies in east Meath and north-east Kildare. The preponderance of ecclesiastically held lands – both episcopal and monastic – played a significant role in fostering continuity. The solidity of many of the baronial families established by Strongbow and de Lacy in the decades following the conquest of Dublin in 1170 must also be stressed, although the families established by these men themselves died out in a relatively short time.

The church already held a lot of land before the Anglo-Normans arrived, but in virtually all cases their holdings were extended and new orders were endowed so that Dublin was ringed on all sides by ecclesiastical holdings. Some religious houses outside the country, like Llanthony and Little Malvern, were also granted lands. In general, however, the Dublin houses were large and prestigious enough to ensure that the new nobility did not feel the need to revert to religious houses in their homelands. The largest single landholder in the region was the archbishop of Dublin, whose considerable holdings in Co. Dublin were augmented by the acquisition at the beginning of the thirteenth century of the lands of the bishopric and abbey of Glendalough.

The Dublin region differed from other parts of Ireland, not just in terms of the large quantity of lands held by the church, but also in the scale of royal demesne holdings. The most stable of these were concentrated in the south-west of the region and here the manors generated income for the king and also formed a bastion of loyal settlers in an area that over time became a frontier between the land of peace and the land of war. The crown may originally have had the same aspirations for its holdings in Wicklow, but by the fourteenth century it was reduced to desperate and expensive attempts to hold onto its strongholds in the face of damaging Irish raids.

Granting land was a way of rewarding followers, and this was true whether it was of the magnitude of Henry II giving Meath to de Lacy, de Lacy enfeoffing Dunboyne to le Petit, or le Petit granting a couple of carucates to one of his retainers. The settlement pattern that emerged in south-east Meath and north-east Kildare, characterised by large baronial manors, was a direct result of the actions of Strongbow and de Lacy. The fact that these lands reverted to the king when heirs ran out gave the crown renewed opportunities to reward trusted servants, marry off wealthy heiresses and set up counter-balances to men who were growing too powerful.

What emerges most strongly from this study of landholding patterns across the region is the part played by Dublin in shaping the social geography of its hinterland. This was manifested in the estates held by the Dublin archbishop and religious houses, the lands administered by the central administration and increasingly by the acquisition of property by members of Dublin mercantile and legal families.

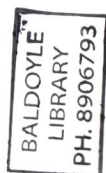

CHAPTER 5

Defence and fortification

Introduction

One of the first tasks carried out by the new land-holders in the region was to erect castles at locations chosen to serve as the caputs of their new fiefs.[1] For the Anglo-Normans, the construction of these fortifications was a primary stage in the establishment of settlement nodes, and their siting was highly strategic. Locations that were already focal points were sought out, particularly churches and monasteries, as well as crossroads, fording points and places where several routeways converged (Figure 5.1). The local physical environment was also a fundamental criterion – natural hillocks, ridges, eskers and other glacial features were preferred, while those in close proximity to rivers were favoured particularly. 'The new lords had a preference for established sites with an existing infrastructure, that is to say sites which were adequately connected by road and well supplied by water and with some political significance'.[2]

Some of the earliest fortifications were earthwork and timber castles – ringworks and mottes – but others were built of stone, right from the outset (such as Carrickfergus, Co. Antrim). In some cases, timber castles were quickly replaced by masonry structures (as at Trim, Co. Meath, and Maynooth, Co. Kildare), but elsewhere they continued to be used into the late fourteenth century, when they began to be replaced by tower houses.[3] There is some debate as to whether the Gaelic Irish were building masonry castles before the arrival of the Anglo-Normans.[4] What evidence there exists is mainly confined to Connacht and Ulster, however, and there is no sign of pre-Anglo-Norman castle-building in the Dublin region. The main period of stone castle building in Ireland was c.1170–1320, and this was followed by a lull until tower houses began to appear around 1400. Some of the earliest stone castles in Ireland had great towers or donjons, surrounded by defensive curtain walls, but the focus of others was a great hall located against the curtain wall. Through the thirteenth century, there was a move away from centrally placed keeps to a design where many of the main buildings and functions of the castle were incorporated into the curtain walls, towers and gates. Also in the thirteenth century, smaller castles known as hall-houses were built; Kindlestown Castle, Co. Wicklow, being one of the best examples. Later in the thirteenth century, or perhaps in the first years of the fourteenth, polygonal enclosure castles were built, and Ballyvolan, Co. Wicklow, is the best surviving example of this castle type.

---

[1] For a recent review of all aspects of castle studies in Ireland, see Terry Barry, 'The study of medieval Irish castles: a bibliographical survey', *PRIA*, 108C (2008), 115–36. [2] Simms and Fagan, 'Villages in Co. Dublin', p. 91. [3] See, for example, O'Conor, 'The later construction and use of motte and bailey castles in Ireland'; Kieran O'Conor, 'Motte castles in Ireland: permanent fortresses, residences and manorial centres', *Château Gaillard*, 20 (2002), 173–82 at 173–5. [4] See, for example, O'Keeffe, *Medieval Ireland*, pp 22–9.

Castles were first built by the crown and powerful magnates, but as merchant families increased their wealth, and consequently their need to protect it, they too began to build stone castles. The fifteenth and sixteenth centuries witnessed a proliferation of tall castles – tower houses – across Ireland. This was the first type of castle to be built in large numbers by the Gaelic Irish as well as the Anglo-Normans and their descendants. A series of semi-defended residences known as 'fortified houses' were built in Ireland in the sixteenth and seventeenth centuries, and these can be seen as the last generation of medieval castles.[5]

Earth-and-timber castles

Ringworks

One of the castle-types associated with early phases of Anglo-Norman settlement in Ireland is the earth-and-timber ringwork.[6] This reflects the pattern in England, where the first castles erected by the Normans in the eleventh century were also ringworks.[7] The earthen part of these castles consists of a roughly circular or oval area, enclosed by a bank and ditch. This would have been surmounted by a palisade, a residential area and (in some cases) a series of other structures. Approximately sixty-three ringworks have been tentatively identified in Ireland to date, but this figure is likely to be a long way short of the true number.[8] Writing in 1997, Tom McNeill commented that 'ringworks in Ireland are … impossible to define or identify',[9] and there are obvious difficulties in distinguishing between these early earthwork

5 David Sweetman, *Medieval castles of Ireland* (Cork, 1999), pp 175–98; O'Conor, *Medieval rural settlement in Ireland*, p. 25.   6 T.B. Barry, 'Anglo-Norman ringwork castles: some evidence' in Reeves-Smith and Hamond (eds), *Landscape archaeology in Ireland* (1983), pp 295–314; D.C. Twohig, 'Anglo-Norman ringwork castles', *Bulletin of the Group for the Study of Irish Historic Settlement*, 5 (1978), 7–9; T.E. McNeill, *Castles in Ireland: feudal power in a Gaelic world* (London, 1997), pp 60–3; O'Keeffe, *Medieval Ireland*, pp 29–33.   7 B.K. Davison, 'The origins of the castle in England', *Archaeological Journal*, 124 (1967), 202–11; D.J.C. King and Leslie Alcock, 'Ringworks of England and Wales', *Chateau Gaillard*, 3 (1969), 90–127; Kieran O'Conor, 'The earthwork castles of medieval Leinster' (PhD, University of Wales, College of Cardiff; 3 vols, 1993), 1, pp 68–73.   8 K.D. O'Conor, 'Irish earthwork castles', *Fortress*, 12 (1992), 1–12 at 3; Barry, *The archaeology of medieval Ireland*, pp 45–53. But see also McNeill, *Castles in Ireland*, pp 60–3; O'Keeffe, *Medieval Ireland*, pp 29–33.   9 McNeill, *Castles in Ireland*, p. 63.

fortifications and ringforts or other unclassified earthwork enclosures.[10] The problems of identification are exacerbated by the fact that some ringworks appear to have been created through the remodelling of existing ringforts, as for example at Rathangan, Co. Kildare.[11] This lack of clarity may at least in part account for the fact that the Department of the Environment, Heritage and Local Government (DEHLG) files do not record a single ringwork for the Dublin region. Over the past few years, however, a small number of possible examples have been identified tentatively. Though generally considered to be mottes, for example, the first castles at Castlekevin and Newcastle McKynegan may have been ringworks.[12] Excavations at a number of masonry keeps around the country have revealed the presence of ringwork structures beneath the stone buildings, including at Maynooth, Co. Kildare, and at Trim, Co. Meath.[13] It has also become clear that a number of the large multivallate sites recorded by the Archaeological Survey of Ireland as ringforts are in fact ringworks.[14]

There is a very large trivallate, or triple-banked ringwork at Rodanstown, Co. Meath, on high ground overlooking a stream and in close proximity to a medieval church (Figure 5.2).[15] This ringwork, almost certainly built by the Husseys (Mulhussey is less than

10 See, for instance, T.E. McNeill, 'Early castles in Leinster', *JIA*, 5 (1989/90), 57–64 at 58; Barry, *The archaeology of medieval Ireland*, p. 45; Sweetman, *Medieval castles of Ireland*, p. 4; O'Keeffe, *Medieval Ireland*, p. 30; P.D. Sweetman, 'Some ringwork castles in County Meath' in Condit and Corlett (eds), *Above and beyond* (2005), pp 393–8; O'Conor, 'Motte castles in Ireland', 173.   **11** O'Conor, 'The later construction and use of motte and bailey castles in Ireland', 15; O'Conor, *Medieval rural settlement in Ireland*, pp 22, 35.   **12** G.H. Orpen, '*Castrum Keyvini*: Castlekevin', *JRSAI*, 38 (1908), 17–27; Eoin Grogan and Annaba Kilfeather (comp.), *Archaeological inventory of County Wicklow* (Dublin, 1997), pp 176–7, 180; Sweetman, *Medieval castles of Ireland*, p. 14 (fig. 6); M.V. Ronan, 'Killadreenan and Newcastle', *JRSAI*, 63 (1933), 172–81; G.H. Orpen, '*Novum Castrum McKynegan*, Newcastle, County Wicklow', *JRSAI*, 38 (1908), 126–40; Twohig, 'Anglo-Norman ringwork castles'.   **13** Barry, 'Anglo-Norman ringwork castles', p. 307; Barry, *The archaeology of medieval Ireland*, p. 49; Ben Murtagh, 'The Kilkenny Castle archaeological project, 1990–1993: interim report', *Old Kilkenny Review*, 45 (1993), 101–17; P.D. Sweetman, 'Archaeological excavations at Ferns Castle, Co. Wexford', *PRIA*, 79C (1979), 217–45; Sweetman, *Medieval castles of Ireland*, pp 4–6; K.D. O'Conor, 'The origins of Carlow Castle', *AI*, 11:3 (autumn 1997), 13–16; Alan Hayden, pers. comm; Alan Hayden, 'Trim Castle, Co. Meath: excavations, 1995–8' (forthcoming), pp 57–78.   **14** Sweetman, *Medieval castles of Ireland*, p. 6.   **15** Sweetman, 'Some ringwork castles',

Figure 5.3 Aerial photograph showing Danestown ringwork (north) and church (south). Faint earthworks can be made out in the fields surrounding the monuments. The road running through the trees to the north of the site marks the barony boundary and the northern edge of the study area.

2km to the north-east), is likely to have been constructed on top of an earlier settlement site, perhaps a ringfort. About 8km to the north-east of Rodanstown, the raised circular earthwork beside the medieval church at Rathregan is listed by the county inventory and the SMR as a ringfort, but it is referred to as a ringwork by Gerald Rice.[16] The manor of Rathregan was granted by Hugh de Lacy to the le Blund family, and they may have built a fortification here. Further north in Co. Meath, at Danestown, a large ringwork is situated in a prominent position *c*.100m from a medieval church (Figures 5.3, 5.4).[17] The clear pattern of association between castle and church is also evident at Ballyvolan, less than 3km to the south of Newcastle, Co. Wicklow, where the possible ringwork is close to the medieval church at Kilmartin.[18]

The majority of the ringworks or potential ringwork sites in the Dublin region are located next to rivers or streams and are sited on relatively high ground, sometimes overlooking strategic crossing points. On the border between Cos. Kildare and Wicklow, for instance, the causewayed ringwork at Rathturtle is situated on naturally elevated ground overlooking the River Douglas (Figure 5.5).[19] David Sweetman has posited an association

pp 394–5; Gerard Rice, *Norman Kilcloon, 1171–1700* (Kilcloon, Co. Meath, 2001), pp i, 19, 24, 111; M.J. Moore, *Archaeological inventory of County Meath* (Dublin, 1987), pp 89, 90.   **16** Moore, *Archaeological inventory of County Meath*, pp 88; Rice, *Norman Kilcloon*, pp viii, 19, 24, 41.   **17** Sweetman, 'Some ringwork castles', pp 394–5. **18** Grogan and Kilfeather, *Archaeological inventory of County Wicklow*, p. 176.   **19** Ibid., pp 177, 179 (fig. 51); Sweetman, *Medieval castles of Ireland*, p. 16 (fig. 7).

Figure 5.4 The ringwork at Danestown, Co. Meath, from the south. This large flat-topped mound is surrounded by a fosse and outer bank. It was built on land that may have been held by Robert de Aveinio in the late twelfth century (see p. 83, above) (© Department of the Environment, Heritage and Local Government).

between ringwork castles or smaller mottes and the sub-division of the manor, suggesting that these residences belonged to sub-tenants.[20] Ringworks were certainly not constructed solely for this class, however, as witnessed by the sites at Maynooth and Trim, which were built for two of the most powerful families in medieval Ireland – the FitzGeralds and the de Lacys, respectively. Sweetman's hypothesis may hold true for other parts of the country, but in the Dublin region at least, it appears that the small number of ringworks were constructed by people of varying status.

Mottes

A motte is an earthen mound, either completely or partly man-made, built to support a timber or stone fortified structure. Some were constructed with an associated bailey – an enclosed area at the base of the mound that probably contained halls, kitchens, storage areas and, in some cases, accommodation for a lord's retinue. The often simple appearance of bare mottes in the landscape today belies the complexity and sophistication of their former defences and other components. It has been convincingly argued that some earthwork castles were at least as defensible and as complex as their masonry cousins.[21]

Mottes were constructed in Normandy from the first half of the eleventh century, and in England and Wales after the Norman conquest of 1066.[22] In many places in Europe, they continued to be built and occupied into the fourteenth century.[23] There has been some discussion about the dating of mottes in Ireland.[24] Kieran O'Conor believes that they had a later floruit than many people might expect, and that while many may have been built in the late twelfth century, some were not constructed until the late thirteenth and early

20 Sweetman, *Medieval castles of Ireland*, p. 22.   21 R.A. Higham and Philip Barker, *Timber castles* (London, 1992), pp 114–352; R.A. Higham, 'Timber castles in Great Britain' in Hartmut Hofricher (ed.), *Holz in der Burgearchitektur* (Braubach, 2004), pp 199–204 at p. 199.   22 Johnny de Meulemeester and Kieran O'Conor, 'Fortifications' in James Graham-Campbell with Magdalena Valor (eds), *The archaeology of medieval Europe, vol. 1: eighth to twelfth centuries AD* (Aarhus, 2007), pp 316–41 at pp 330–1.   23 Ibid., pp 325–31.   24 O'Conor, 'The later construction and use of motte and bailey castles in Ireland'; Kieran O'Conor, 'Castle studies in Ireland: the way forward', *Château Gaillard*, 23 (2008), 329–39.

Figure 5.5 The ringwork at Rathturtle, Co. Wicklow, situated on naturally elevated ground overlooking the River Douglas (image courtesy of David Sweetman and © Department of the Environment, Heritage and Local Government).

fourteenth century, with some remaining in use as fortifications until as late as *c*.1500.[25] There is little excavated evidence to test this suggestion, but the documentary sources tend to support O'Conor's view. Many of the mottes that were erected in Leinster and Meath in the last quarter of the twelfth century were built as permanent fortifications that may have continued in use until they were replaced by tower houses over 200 years later. At Athlumney, beside Navan, for instance, there is a motte overlooking the Boyne, and just 200m away is a tower house with a sixteenth-century stone house attached (Figures 5.40, 5.41). These structures surely represent three phases of lordly residence at the site, and yet there is no evidence for an intervening building between the motte and the tower house. The sequence is repeated at Scurlockstown and elsewhere.

Estimates vary as to the number of mottes built in Ireland,[26] but ongoing field-work and analysis suggest that the figure may be as high as 500. The DEHLG has records for almost 400 examples, but it is impossible to ascertain an exact figure without carrying out a detailed analysis of each file and visiting each recorded site. Whatever the precise numbers may be, the vast majority of mottes in Ireland were built in the (modern) province of Leinster and in east Ulster, and most were situated on lands that were under Anglo-Norman control before 1200. Underlying limestone is generally not conducive to the construction of mottes, as it dissolves easily, leaving little parent material for the generation of soils.[27] In much of Leinster, however, the bedrock is generally covered in a deep layer of drift soil, which is a perfect substitute.

While mottes and ringworks clearly had an important military role, they also functioned as administrative centres, and contributed to the stable conditions under which new

25 O'Conor, 'The later construction and use of motte and bailey castles in Ireland', 28.   **26** O'Conor, 'Castle studies in Ireland: the way forward', 329; O'Conor, 'Irish earthwork castles', 3; O'Conor, *Medieval rural settlement in Ireland*, p. 18; McNeill, *Castles in Ireland*, p. 63; O'Keeffe, *Medieval Ireland*, p. 16; Sweetman, *Medieval castles of Ireland*, pp 17, 19. See also Kieran O'Conor, 'Anglo-Norman castles in Co. Laois' in P.G. Lane and William Nolan (eds), *Laois: history and society* (Dublin, 1999), pp 183–212 at pp 190–6.   **27** Stuart Prior, *A few well-positioned castles: the Norman art of war* (Stroud, Gloucestershire, 2006), p. 187.

Figure 5.6 Distribution of mottes, baileys and ringworks in the Dublin region. While mottes are less common in Dublin than in neighbouring counties, the examples in Dublin more often have an associated bailey.

agricultural systems could be put into operation.[28] Mottes, in particular, rapidly became focal points for new communities and almost every one of the primary medieval settlement locations in the Dublin region developed in close proximity to a motte. For a time at least, important market and urban centres flourished in the shadows of some of the largest examples (as was the case in Meath for instance, at the boroughs of Dunboyne, Greenoge, Ratoath and Skreen). The importance of the motte is reflected, in some instances, in the name of the townland or area in which it is situated (for example, Ballymoat, Castlekevin, Castleknock, Castlewarden, Ladycastle, Moat Commons, Newcastle Lyons and Newcastle McKynegan).

It has been pointed out that medieval manor and parish boundaries in Ireland were often coterminous. It comes as little surprise then to note that of the 233 parishes in the

---

28 O'Conor, 'Motte castles in Ireland'; O'Conor, *Medieval rural settlement in Ireland*, pp 26–38.

Dublin region, only three have a second motte, and in two of these cases the second one is listed only as a 'possible' in the Sites and Monuments Record (SMR).[29] It may also be significant that no parish contains both a motte *and* a ringwork. The motte was the focal point of the manor, administratively and defensively, and in the majority of cases, it was situated in the most important townland in the parish – that is to say, the townland that gave the parish its name. This is in part related to the fact that many seigneurial manors were centred at locations that were (or had been) early monasteries or important churches.[30] Mottes were sometimes built close to these sites (as in Meath at Clonard, Dunshaughlin and Skreen).[31] In most such cases, the church site continued to develop, in association with the adjacent secular settlement. In a number of instances, mottes were built on top of earlier ringforts (as at Rathmore, Co. Kildare; Figure 5.14) – a practice that took advantage of an existing mound, accessible building materials and a proven location. The burial of pre-Anglo-Norman homesteads (even if these had already been abandoned) under larger mottes, representative of the 'new order', was certainly symbolic, but it is impossible to know for sure if this was a major consideration in the selection of sites for the new fortifications. Sweetman was more confident that the construction of ringworks on top of previously important sites (such as at Knowth and Loughcrew) was done in order to 'make a political statement'.[32]

Tadhg O'Keeffe has discussed the distribution of mottes and ringworks in the Dublin region in terms of the organised defence of a frontier.[33] In particular, he saw the regular arrangement of mottes around Dublin as representative of a formal protective cordon

29 In Co. Meath, the parish of Galtrim contains two mottes (at Galtrim and Clonymeath, with the latter being listed as a 'possible' only in the SMR). In Co. Wicklow, Powerscourt has two possible examples (at Knocksink and at Powerscourt), while in Co. Dublin, the parish of St Margaret's contains a motte at Newtown and another at Dunsoghly. **30** Flanagan, 'Anglo-Norman change and continuity', 389; Bhreathnach, 'Authority and supremacy', 15; Graham, 'The evolution of the settlement pattern of Anglo-Norman Eastmeath', p. 42. **31** See Prior, *A few well-positioned castles*, p. 206, fig. 67. Prior identified an early Anglo-Norman castle at thirteen of twenty-eight known early ecclesiastical centres in Meath. **32** Sweetman, 'Some ringwork castles', p. 393. **33** O'Keeffe, 'Medieval frontiers and fortifications', pp 59–61.

Figure 5.8 The church and motte at Newcastle McKynegan. The broad summit of this earthwork would have accommodated a range of timber buildings. The stone structure evident there now is a later gate-house (CUCAP Cambridge University Collection of Aerial Photographs).

encircling the city, and he considered the position of the stone castles at Maynooth and Trim as significant in relation to the surrounding earth-and-timber fortifications. In his analysis of early castles in Meath, Stuart Prior noted that the Anglo-Normans constructed castles at twenty-three of the thirty militarily important 'pivotal' points in the county.[34] Additionally, Donaghpatrick and Ratoath castles were each within 2.5km of a pivotal point, leaving only five strategically or tactically significant locations in Meath without a castle nearby. Prior concluded from this that 'many of the Anglo-Norman castles founded in Meath were sited in the landscape predominantly with military considerations in mind'.[35] The majority of mottes in Meath were built on high ground (*c.*60–120m above sea level), but there were none on the highest ground in the county (over 120m) – most likely because these places were too far from running water to easily sustain habitation (such as a garrison) for any length of time. Most of the mottes were close to rivers, and almost half were sited at crossing points. This implies that these castles overlooked roads as well as rivers, even if these roads can no longer be identified. A document of *c.*1200 mentions a 'public street' in Co. Kildare that ran from Rathmore (Figure 5.14), where there was a large motte and bailey, to the Liffey, via the large motte and bailey at Donode (Figure 5.7).[36]

Sixty-three motte sites are known in the Dublin region, of which sixteen (25 per cent) have evidence for baileys (Figure 5.6).[37] The number of baileys is relatively low, given that something approaching half of all mottes in Ireland have an associated bailey.[38] The size of the mottes varies considerably across the region, with the larger ones being among the most massive ever built in Europe. A study of mottes in Meath has shown that their scale appears to be related to the social rank of those for whom they were built.[39] This is also likely to be

34 Prior, *A few well-positioned castles*, pp 186, 188.   **35** Ibid., p. 187.   **36** McNeill (ed.), *Alen's register*, p. 28.   **37** These figures include both definite and possible examples, upstanding and demolished.   **38** Sweetman, *Medieval castles of Ireland*, pp 19, 22.   **39** Brian Graham, 'The mottes of the Norman liberty of Meath' in Harman Murtagh (ed.), *Irish midland studies: essays in commemoration of N.W. English* (Athlone, 1980), pp 39–56. The correlation between the size of a motte in Meath and the status of its owner has been discussed recently by Prior, albeit inconclusively (*A few well-positioned castles*, esp. p. 210).

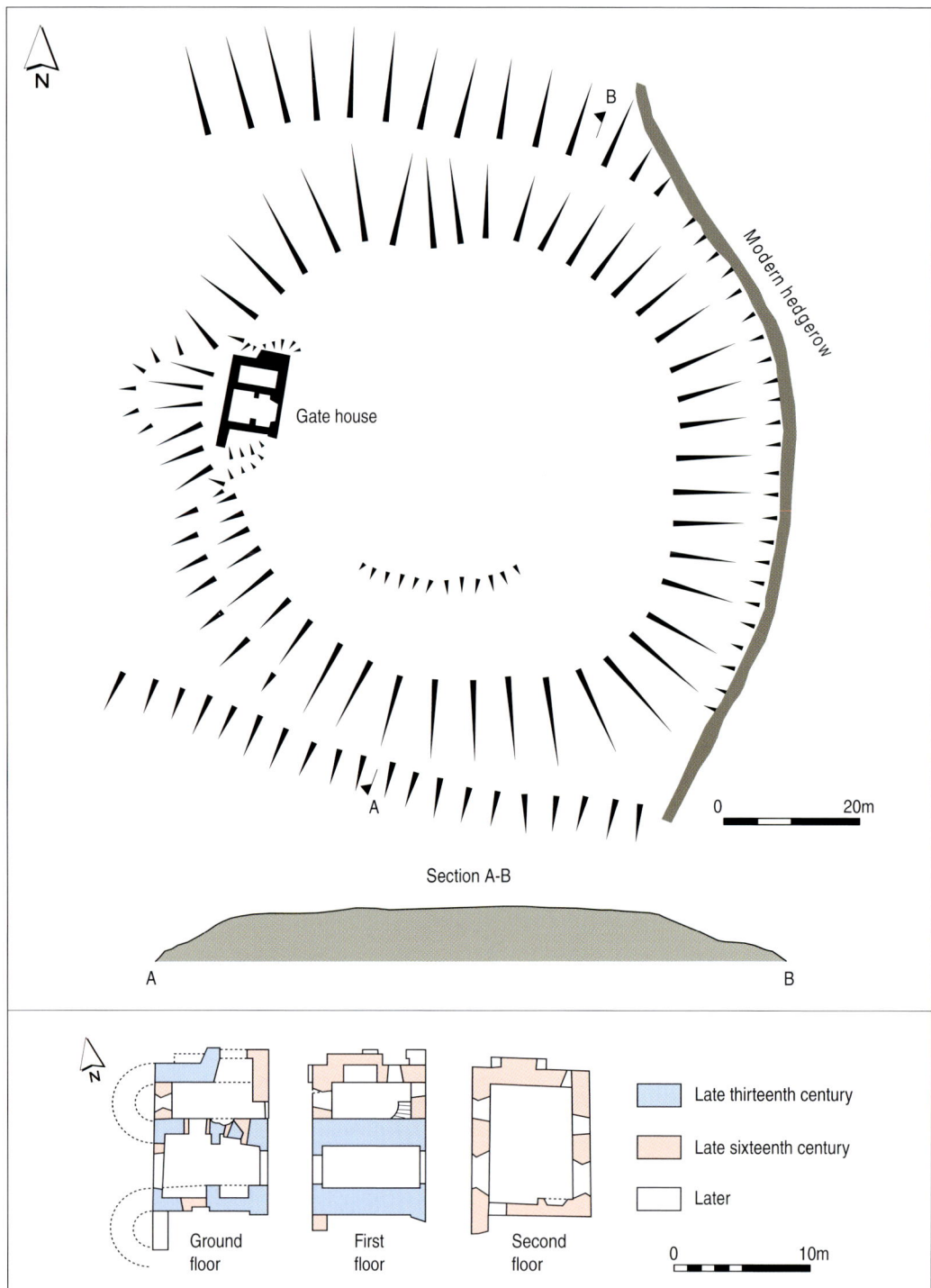

Section A-B

Late thirteenth century

Late sixteenth century

Later

Ground floor · First floor · Second floor

the case elsewhere, but detailed analysis of the type carried out by Brian Graham in Meath, which has more mottes than any other county in Ireland, has yet to be published for the rest of the country, and the data necessary for such analysis is not yet available for some parts of the Dublin region. Baileys are more likely to be connected with larger mottes, and in most cases these are associated with higher ranking lords and more prosperous manors, such as Castleknock, Ratoath and Skreen. Baileys *are* known, however, from a few smaller mottes, and other mottes without baileys may have had different, more ephemeral enclosures that served a similar purpose. It is also noteworthy that six of the seven mottes closest to Dublin city have evidence for an associated bailey.[40] On the other hand, not all mottes associated with high-ranking lords were provided with a bailey, and O'Conor's research in Leinster

40 These are Brazil, Castleknock, Dunsoghly, Killester, Newtown and Saint Helens.

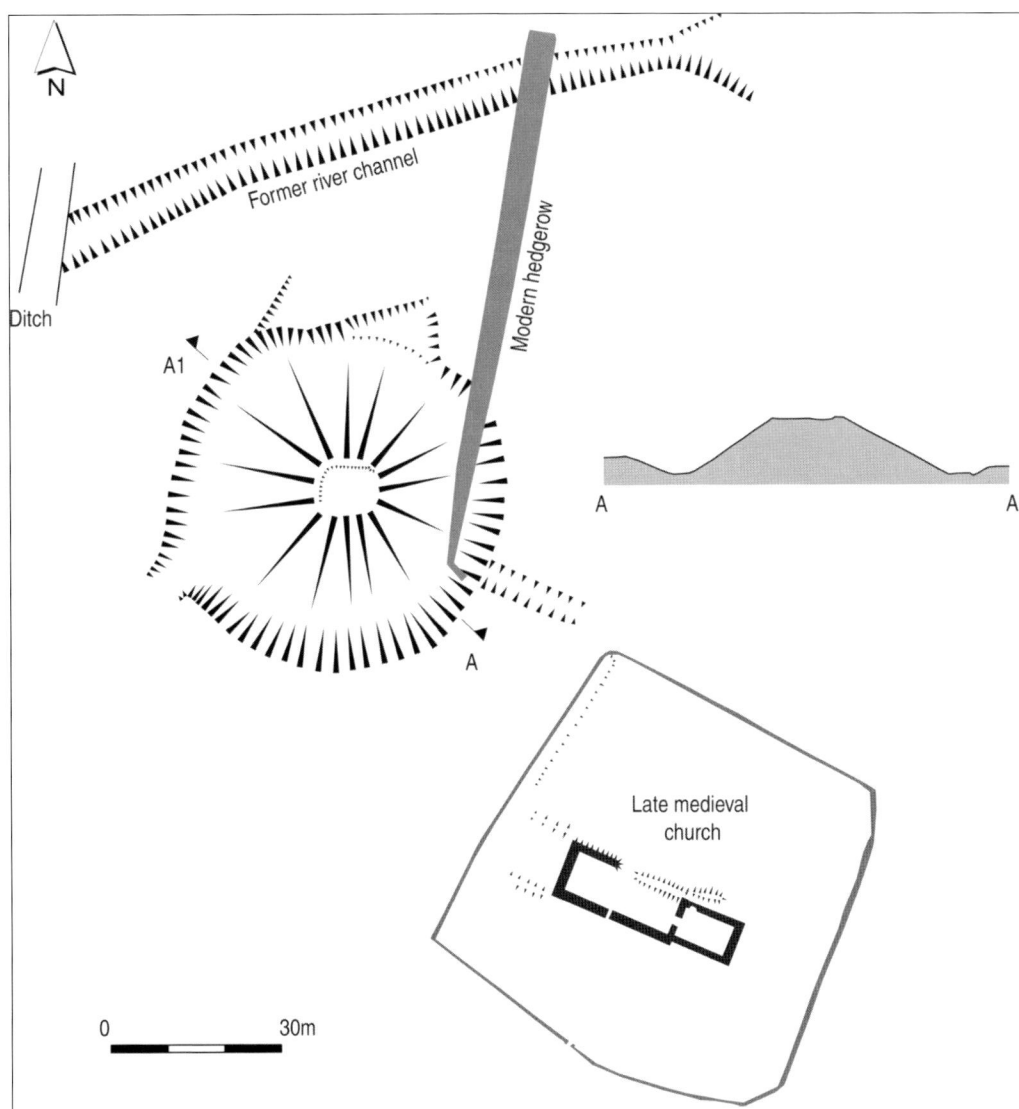

Figure 5.10 The motte and church at Cloncurry, Co. Kildare (after O'Conor, *Medieval rural settlement*, p. 30, fig. 9).

indicates that some were instead characterised by broad summits, as at Newcastle McKynegan, Co. Wicklow, where 'the huge motte summit … is more than large enough to take a plethora of buildings' (Figure 5.8).[41] Mottes with large summit areas are a characteristic of the periphery of the Wicklow Mountains, and it has been shown that these sites were ranked alongside important masonry castles.[42] It is likely that complex wooden structures afforded them strong security and extensive living quarters and other facilities.

Within the Dublin region, the density of mottes is far less to the south of the River Liffey than to the north. One of the reasons posited for this is the relatively peaceful nature of the settlement of the southern hinterland and the continuity of settlement in Uí Briúin Cualann, where the church and the family of Mac Gilla Mo Cholmóc retained much of their pre-invasion lands.[43] 'The benevolence of the English to the MacGiollamocholmoc dynasty greatly facilitated the bedding-down of the feudal settlement south of Dublin'.[44] As with most medieval monument types in Co. Wicklow, mottes are largely absent from the central mountainous area, and the majority are to be found within 10km of the coast (Figure 5.6).[45] This band of coastal land stretching south from Dublin was secured and subdivided relatively quickly after the Anglo-Norman arrival. The rapid subdivision and the

41 O'Conor, 'The earthwork castles of medieval Leinster', 1, pp 308–15, esp. p. 311.   **42** Ibid., p. 315.   **43** Linzi Simpson, 'Dublin's southern frontier under siege: Kindlestown Castle, Delgany, County Wicklow' in Duffy (ed.), *Medieval Dublin IV* (2003), pp 279–368 at pp 288–9.   **44** O'Byrne, *War, politics and the Irish of Leinster*, p. 23.
45 Simpson, 'Anglo-Norman settlement in Uí Briuin Cualann', p. 195.

Figure 5.11 The motte
at Mainham, Co. Kildare,
is situated in pasture
land close to the
medieval church.

importance attached to this narrow strip of land are reflected in the fact that nine of Co. Wicklow's fourteen mottes are located here, quite densely packed together. As elsewhere, the general pattern is one of larger numbers of mottes in the areas most densely settled by the Anglo-Normans.

While the medieval liberty of Meath had the highest concentration of mottes in Ireland, a large number of these were located close to the northern and western frontiers of the liberty, with fewer being built towards the more politically and socially stable lands closer to Dublin. Nonetheless, there are twenty-two mottes in the Meath portion of the study area (including six listed in the county inventory as 'possible').[46] Only four have a definite bailey (Agher, Galtrim (Figure 5.16), Ratoath and Skreen), although two others have some evidence for the former existence of one (Athlumney and Rathfeigh). Some of the destroyed mottes, such as Dunboyne, may have had baileys too. The majority of Meath's mottes with baileys occur in the north, towards the frontier with Bréifne, and this may reflect the fact that extra security, in the form of an enclosure, was needed in this area as protection against incursions from the Gaelic Irish. It is also possible that the baileys were used to station garrisons.

Fourteen mottes are known for Co. Dublin, including relatively simple ones like Mallahow as well as examples situated on naturally high ground at Ballymadrough, Corrstown (or Freedagh) and Kilshane. Three kilometres to the west of Swords Castle, the motte at Brazil is on the north bank of the River Ward, at a crossing point just 1km from the church at Killeek. Corrstown motte is 4km to the west of Brazil. The motte at Ballymadrough, which is 3km to the north-east of Swords, is 600m from the church at Kilcrea and 800m from Malahide Estuary.

The cultural geography of earth-and-timber castles in the Dublin region

The majority of mottes and ringworks in the Dublin region were built on the lands of lay lords. In north-east Kildare, the de Hereford family initiated an important campaign of

---

46 The 'possibles' are at Clonymeath, Culmullin, Donaghmore, Dunshaughlin, Knockudder and Scurlockstown (see Moore, *Archaeological inventory of County Meath*, pp 156–61).

Figure 5.12 The motte at Clane, Co. Kildare. This tree-covered earthwork castle is now surrounded by a housing estate.

motte construction. Overlooking the Ballycorron River, the earthwork castle at Cloncurry (Figures 5.1, 5.10) was referred to as a *mota* in 1304, and was described at that time as having a single-roomed wooden-roofed building on top of it.[47] This motte was built near the highest point of a natural ridge, and had commanding views to the south, east and west. Significantly, the highest part of the ridge is occupied by a graveyard, suggesting that the church and graveyard were in use *before* the motte was built (Figure 5.10).[48] Indeed, this is probably the site of the early church foundation traditionally associated with St Ninian (Figure 7.36).[49]

At Mainham, the motte and semi-circular bailey, which are beside the Gollymochy River, are located on a low ridge just to the south of the medieval church (Figure 5.11).[50] They were probably built for John de Hereford, while his brother Adam was responsible for the construction of the possible double-ditched motte and bailey at Castlewarden.[51] Adam held the barony of Clane (formerly Otymy) for a time, but subsequently gave it to his brother Richard.[52] It was almost certainly one of these who built the motte near the River Liffey at Clane (Figure 5.12).[53] Bulldozer interference in 1970 revealed that this motte, situated near a well called Sunday's Well in the townland of 'Moat Commons', was constructed of layers of stone and earth.[54] More recently, excavations beside the motte revealed some animal bones and one human inhumation in association with medieval pottery.[55] It is not clear how these finds relate to the construction or occupation of the motte. Fourteen kilometres downriver from Clane, the earliest castle at Leixlip, which was built before 1212, was situated on high

47 *RBO*, p. 27; Karina Holton, 'Medieval Cloncurry', *RnM*, 9:3 (1997), 73–88 at 80.   48 Bradley, Halpin and King, 'UAS 7:2: Kildare', p. 172.   49 Ibid., pp 167–79; O'Conor, *Medieval rural settlement in Ireland*, p. 30, fig. 9.   50 Lord Killanin and Michael Duignan, *The Shell guide to Ireland* (London, 1967), p. 162.   51 A.J. Otway-Ruthven, 'Knight's fees in Kildare, Leix and Offaly', *JRSAI*, 91:2 (1961), 163–81 at 166; Killanin and Duignan, *The Shell guide to Ireland*, p. 329. This enigmatic site is sometimes classified as a motte and bailey, and sometimes as a moated site. McNeill ('Early castles in Leinster', 63) remarks that this site is 'hardly clearly defined or large enough to be described as a motte with the enclosure as a bailey, but hardly classifiable as a straightforward moated site either'.   52 Orpen, *Ireland under the Normans*, p. 143.   53 Bradley, Halpin and King, 'UAS 7:2: Kildare', pp 149, 153.   54 Ibid., pp 153, 161.   55 Carmel Duffy, 'Moat Commons, Clane' in *Excavations 2003*, pp 237–8.

Figure 5.13 The ditch surrounding the motte at Kill, Co. Kildare, is fed with water by the Kill River. A document of 1540 refers to the motte as 'a small mountain surrounded by a dry ditch' (© Department of the Environment, Heritage and Local Government).

ground overlooking the junction of the Rye Water and the River Liffey, and John Bradley et al. surmised that this was probably a motte.[56] It too was almost certainly constructed by the de Herefords.

John de Hereford was granted the manor of Kill, and although there are no early documentary references to the caput, it was probably he who erected the motte and bailey there (Figure 5.13).[57] The name Kill (from *Cell*, 'church'),[58] indicates the early ecclesiastical significance of the site, and it is likely that de Hereford selected it at least partly on the basis that it was already an important location. The presence of the Kill River, which flows through the ditch of the motte, would also have been an influencing factor in the selection of a site for the fortification. In 1540, the motte was described as 'a small mountain surrounded by a dry ditch', and at that time the manorial court was still being held there periodically.[59]

The middle cantred of Uí Fáeláin, which included Naas, was granted to Maurice Fitz Gerald, along with the cantred of Wicklow. This grant was confirmed by John as lord of Ireland in 1185 to Maurice's son William, whose heirs bore the title of barons of Naas.[60] The motte at Naas, known as the 'North Motte', has faint traces of a bailey and was built by Maurice Fitz Gerald or his son William. It is on the highest point of a gravel ridge and may have been built on top of the earlier dun or fort.[61] It overlooks St David's Church, which was probably also built on the site of a pre-Anglo-Norman foundation. An Augustinian priory was established next to the motte in the late twelfth century.[62]

---

56 *RAST*, pp 142–3; Bradley, Halpin and King, 'UAS 7:3: Kildare', p. 309. **57** Gerald of Wales: *Expugnatio Hibernica*, p. 143; Orpen, *Ireland under the Normans*, pp 143–4; *RAST*, pp 102–4; Bradley, Halpin and King, 'UAS 7:3: Kildare', pp 295–6. **58** P.W. Joyce, *The origin and history of Irish names of places* (3 vols, Dublin, 1873–1913), 3, p. 406. **59** *EIMP*, p. 39; O'Conor, 'The later construction and use of motte and bailey castles in Ireland', 26. **60** *CPI*, p. 5. **61** Bradley, Halpin and King, 'UAS 7:4: Kildare', p. 354. Excavations close to the motte in 1979 uncovered two thirteenth-/fourteenth-century pits and eleven sherds of Leinster Cooking Ware (Kieran Campbell, 'Naas (Black Castle)' in *Excavations 1977–9*, pp 73–4). Elsewhere in the region, similar pottery has been recovered close to the mottes at Rathmore and Dunsoghly. **62** *MRHI*, p. 189.

The motte at Rathmore, which is one of the finest in Ireland, formed the core of the caput of the FitzGerald manor of the same name (Figure 5.14).[63] As this name suggests, it had been a site of some importance prior to the arrival of the Anglo-Normans, and it is possible that the motte was erected directly on top of the eponymous *rath mór*, or 'large fort'.[64] The motte, which is just 100m from the Hartwell River, is exceptionally large and has a very steep incline. Adjacent to the earthwork, the nineteenth-century church was built on the site of the medieval parish church. There are some faint traces of other banks in the surrounding fields and these may indicate the site of the deserted medieval borough. Just 4km downriver from Clane, the large, steep-sided motte at Straffan (Ladycastle) overlooks the Liffey to the north.[65]

A reference in 1422 to the 'Mote de Henryestown' suggests the presence of a motte at Harristown, 2.5km to the east of Kilcullen, but there is no other evidence for this, and no indication as to who the eponymous Henry may have been.[66] References to the castle of Harristown from the 1470s onwards, however, may relate to a structure on the site of the earlier earthwork (Figure 5.15).[67] This castle was on a prominent hill with clear views in all directions. Early Ordnance Survey maps mark the site of 'Harristown Castle (in ruins)',

Figure 5.14 At Rathmore, Co. Kildare, the motte, which may have been built on top of a ringfort, is less than 200m from the present Church of Ireland church, which was built on the site of its medieval precursor (CUCAP API6 image courtesy of Cambridge University Collection of Aerial Photographs).

63 Bradley, Halpin and King, 'UAS 7:4: Kildare', pp 422–35, esp. p. 433.   64 Ibid., pp 422, 429.   65 Excavations have taken place in close proximity to the motte at Ladycastle Lower, see below.   66 *RPCH*, p. 222, no. 1 (c).   67 Bradley, Halpin and King, 'UAS 7:2: Kildare', p. 191.

beside an area named the 'Deer Park'. The adjacent earthworks are probably the remains of the late seventeenth-century borough.[68]

The motte recorded by the SMR at Longtown Demesne is 1km to the east of the church at Killybegs Demesne. It was used as an ice-house, and McNeill wondered if this was indeed its original function, being unconvinced by its characterisation as a motte.[69] Otway-Ruthven noted that the 'Mote of Kilbeg … seems to be represented by an earthwork in the old churchyard in Killybegs Demesne'.[70] This motte was held by John de St Michael, and Otway-Ruthven suggested that it may earlier have been a sub-fee of the de Hereford barony of Otymy (Clane). There is some confusion as to whether there were one or two mottes at Longtown and Killybegs (if indeed there were any at all).

In Meath, Hugh de Lacy built a castle at Ratoath – probably the large motte and bailey that sits close to the Broad Meadow River at the very centre of the barony.[71] Elsewhere in the barony, which was part of de Lacy's own demesne, smaller mottes were built at Donaghmore, Greenoge, Rathbeggan and Dunshaughlin.[72]

The principal sub-tenants established by de Lacy in Skreen, Deece and probably Dunboyne followed de Lacy's example by establishing large mottes with baileys at, or close to, the centre of the estates they retained, while smaller mottes (generally without baileys) were built by their sub-tenants in more peripheral areas. De Feypo's motte at Skreen was constructed away from the summit of the Hill of Skreen at the centre of the barony.[73] The apex of the hill was already occupied by a church dedicated to St Colmcille (Figure 7.2), and it is possible that the builders of the motte chose to build on top of a pre-existing mound.[74]

68 Ibid., pp 189–95.   **69** McNeill, 'Early castles in Leinster', 63.   **70** Otway-Ruthven, 'Knight's fees', 169.   **71** Orpen, *Ireland under the Normans*, p. 180. For a tabulated summary of who (probably) built each of the early castles in Meath, see Prior, *A few well-positioned castles*, pp 182–5.   **72** Greenoge 'Mound', next to a church overlooking the Broad Meadow River, is recorded as a 'tumulus' in the county inventory (Moore, *Archaeological inventory of County Meath*, p. 30).   **73** Gerald of Wales: *Expugnatio Hibernica*, p. 195; Orpen, *Ireland under the Normans*, p. 184; Moore, *Archaeological inventory of County Meath*, p. 161.   **74** Elizabeth Hickey, *Skryne and the early Normans: papers concerning the medieval manors of the Feypo family in Ireland in the 12th and early 13th centuries* ([Navan], 1994), pp 34–7.

Figure 5.16 The large, flat-topped motte at Galtrim, Co. Meath, was probably built by Hugh Hussey in the early 1170s, but appears to have been abandoned by 1176.

The remains of a deserted settlement are present to the north of the site. On the very edges of the barony of Skreen, mottes were built at Ardmulchan, Athlumney and Dunsany, while the motte at Rathfeigh is slightly more central and may also have had a bailey. The large ringwork at Danestown, which is situated in a prominent position c.100m from a medieval church, is on the border between the baronies of Skreen and Duleek (Figures 5.3, 5.4).[75] Gerald of Wales claimed that it was Hugh de Lacy himself who had castles built for his barons in Meath at many places including Clonard, Delvin, Killare and Skreen.[76] That de Lacy was involved in the construction of castles on lands outside those that he retained for himself suggests that he had an overall plan for the arrangement of fortifications across his lordship.

Dunboyne was granted to William le Petit, and John Brady believed that a motte was constructed here between 1182 and 1187.[77] The earliest documentary reference to the castle comes in a charter, which can be dated to c.1205–10, in which le Petit granted the church of Dunboyne to the religious house of Llanthony Prima.[78] In return for the grant of the parish church of Dunboyne, le Petit required that one of the canons appointed by Llanthony should be available to celebrate mass in the chapel of his castle should the lord, lady or any other important magnate be in residence.[79] Recent excavations at Dunboyne Castle investigated part of the medieval ditch.[80] It was found to be U-shaped in section with steep sides, and measured a maximum of 8m wide by 4.5m deep. Refuse in the ditch included animal bones, oyster shells, timbers, pottery fragments and parts of at least two wooden bowls. Twelfth- to thirteenth-century cooking wares dominated the small pottery assemblage. Despite the excavations and other investigative work, it 'remains unclear whether the site was a motte, a ringwork or some other class of enclosure'. It appears that the ditch went out

75 Sweetman, 'Some ringwork castles', pp 394–5.   76 Gerald of Wales: *Expugnatio Hibernica*, p. 195.   77 Brady, 'Anglo-Norman Meath', 40.   78 Brooks (ed.), *The Irish cartularies*, pp 174–5.   79 For a full translation of this charter, see Hogan, *Priory of Llanthony Prima and Secunda in Ireland*, pp 259–60.   80 Claire Cotter, 'Dunboyne Castle, Castlefarm, Dunboyne' in *Excavations 2004*, pp 308–9.

Figure 5.17 This view of
Howth, Co. Dublin, was
drawn by Gabriel
Beranger in 1775, a
generation before the
earthen mound on the
right was levelled to
make way for the
Martello Tower.
Beranger described the
mound as 'the karne or
ancient burying place of
the pagan Irish kings and
nobility'. It is likely that
this mound was a motte
castle (image courtesy
of the Royal Irish
Academy, © RIA).

of use in the thirteenth century. Finds recovered by metal detector included stick-pins, nails,
keys, woodworking tools, mounts and three ring brooches. Most of these finds are thirteenth
century in date and appear to have been associated with the earthwork castle. Dunboyne is
close to the centre of the barony, and it is possible that mottes were built at the southern
(Knockudder) and northern (Priest Town) limits of the barony. Early editions of the
Ordnance Survey maps include a hachured feature at Priest Town, marked 'Kilbride Moat'.[81]

At Galtrim, Hugh Hussey's very large motte and possible bailey are close to an early
nineteenth-century church that incorporates a small number of medieval features that
probably belong to an earlier foundation at the same location.[82] This motte was abandoned
in 1176, however, along with the neighbouring one at Derrypatrick.[83] There is a dense
concentration of mottes along the rivers and streams of the northern half of the barony of
Deece, and five of these are within 8km of Galtrim. Typical of these is the small motte at
Scurlockstown, situated on the south bank of the River Boyne, less than 200m north of the
medieval church and graveyard. The motte and bailey at Agher, in the south-west of the
barony, are set within a complex of medieval remains that includes a deserted settlement, a
field system of at least fifteen acres, and a church site (now occupied by a nineteenth-century
church).[84] In contrast to the northern half of Deece, the motte at Agher is the only one in
the southern half of the barony. The multi-vallate ringwork at Rodanstown was almost
certainly built by the Husseys, and may have been built by them on top of an earlier ringfort
(Figure 5.2).[85] Our understanding of this large monument would surely benefit from a
campaign of geophysical survey at the site.

There is one possible example of a motte on church lands in Co. Dublin. A substantial
part of a motte and bailey is said to have survived at Killester into the 1920s.[86] Shortly after

81 This possible motte is recorded as an 'earthwork (site)' in the county inventory (Moore, *Archaeological inventory of
County Meath*, p. 112).   **82** Moore, *Archaeological inventory of County Meath*, pp 135–6, 159.   **83** Orpen, *Ireland under
the Normans*, p. 184; *AU, s.a.* 1176.   **84** Moore, *Archaeological inventory of County Meath*, pp 120, 127, 156, 164.
85 Sweetman, 'Some ringwork castles', pp 394–5; Rice, *Norman Kilcloon*, pp i, 19, 24, 111; Moore, *Archaeological
inventory of County Meath*, pp 89, 90.   **86** Liam Howlett, 'The Killester charter', *DHR*, 32 (1979), 69–71 at 71, referring

Figure 5.18 Castleknock Castle (1767), by Gabriel Beranger. The castle survived repeated requests by the king to have it demolished in the early thirteenth century, but over five hundred years later there was little left to see (image reproduced courtesy of the National Library of Ireland).

the conquest, Killester was granted by Holy Trinity priory to William Brun for an annual rent of half an ounce of gold and a pair of boots for the prior. The arrangement was made clear in a confirmation given by Archbishop Laurence O'Toole.[87] It is possible that the Brun family built the motte that has since been destroyed and whose exact location is a matter of speculation. Similarly, at Howth, nothing remains of the large flat-topped mound with an outer ring and a fosse drawn by the Huguenot artist Gabriel Beranger in 1775 (Figure 5.17), but Thomas Westropp believed that this 'mote-castle', subsequently levelled to make way for the Martello tower, was erected by Almeric de St Lawrence, the original grantee.[88]

The biggest lay holding in Co. Dublin, at Castleknock, was fortified by Hugh Tyrell with a large motte and bailey close to the River Liffey (Figure 5.18).[89] The 'Castle of Knock' is mentioned in 1200, but it was clearly a cause of some concern to the crown and, in 1214, mandates were issued to enquire how the castle had come to be in the hands of Richard Tyrell and to have it demolished.[90] Four years later, further orders were made to have the castle levelled, as it was 'a nuisance to the king's city of Dublin' and its demolition would be in the interests of 'the safety and security of the king's land of Ireland'.[91] The following year, the castle was still standing, and Tyrell was given permission to leave it so, on condition that he guarantee (by handing over hostages) that it would not be a cause of harm to the king or his city and that he would cede the castle to the justiciar in the event of war.[92] In 1222, the king ordered Tyrell to hand over the castle and vill of Knock to the justiciar, as part of a fair exchange.[93] Tyrell appears to have handed over his son, Hugh, as a hostage and the king called for him to be sent to England.[94] After the death of his father, Hugh agreed to give possession of the castle to the king or justiciar when requested, so that it could be used

to James Kenny, *A short history of Coolock parish* (Dublin, 1934).   **87** Printed in Howlett, 'The Killester charter', 69–70.   **88** Peter Harbison (ed.), *Beranger's views of Ireland* (Dublin, 1991), pp 24–5; Mike Salter, *Castles and stronghouses of Ireland* (Worcester, 1993), p. 64; T.J. Westropp, 'The promontory forts and adjoining remains in Leinster: part I, Co. Dublin', *JRSAI*, 52 (1922), 52–76 at 63–4.   **89** Orpen, *Ireland under the Normans*, p. 183.   **90** *CDI, 1171–1251*, no. 121, p. 18; no. 515, p. 81.   **91** Ibid., no. 841, p. 125.   **92** Ibid., no. 875, p. 130.   **93** Ibid., nos. 1046–7, p. 161.   **94** Ibid., no. 1139, p. 173.

as a garrison for the king's troops.[95] The strategic importance of Castleknock was evident in 1317 when Edward Bruce took the castle and imprisoned Hugh Tyrell and his wife before his brief siege of Dublin.[96]

There was only one motte on the royal holdings in Co. Dublin. This was located at Newcastle Lyons. This small motte (measuring 5m in height) is the only definite example in south Co. Dublin and it appears not to have had a bailey (Figure 5.19).[97] Edwards, Hamond and Simms saw this as an indication that in the initial stages of Anglo-Norman settlement in the district not much attention needed to be paid to security.[98] This need not be the case, however, as only a minority of mottes across the region seem to have had baileys – even in areas where security was a priority. Bradley noted that the mound that survives beside the church at Newcastle Lyons is presumably all that remains of the castle from which the settlement takes its name.[99]

One of the most important castles in Wicklow was built at the centre of the royal manor of Newcastle McKynegan before 1190.[100] Like so many of the earthwork castles in the region, it was built on the top of a natural rise, taking full advantage of the local topography. Just 5km to the north-west of Newcastle McKynegan, the motte at Newtownmountkennedy, which appears to incorporate a naturally circular mound, was also built on crown lands.

95 Ibid., no. 1253, p. 190.   **96** Orpen, *Ireland under the Normans*, p. 529.   **97** There may have been a second motte in south Co. Dublin – on his 1762 map of Co. Dublin, Rocque identifies a place called 'Moat Field', *c*.1.5km due west of Bray, and immediately east of this is the word 'Moat'. The 'Moat Field' is clearly shown on Taylor's 1816 map of the Environs of Dublin and a mound to the south of this is marked 'Moat'. It is marked as 'Toole's Moat' on early Ordnance Survey maps. This feature appears not to be listed in the SMR, and may be shown as a 'cairn' on the Ordnance Survey of Ireland Discovery Series 1:50,000 Sheet 56. Excavations in 1989 close to the motte revealed nothing of medieval date (V.J. Keeley, '"Toole's Moat", Old Connaught' in *Excavations 1989*, p. 20; see also W.F. Wakeman, 'On a recently discovered pagan sepulchral mound in the grounds of Old Connaught, near Bray, County Dublin', *JRSAI*, 24 (1894), 54–64). Mark Clinton has suggested that the earliest phase of the fortifications at Carrickmines, Co. Dublin, was 'possibly an irregularly shaped ringwork castle' ('Carrickmines Great' in *Excavations 2001*, pp 85–7).   **98** K.J. Edwards, F.W. Hamond and Anngret Simms, 'The medieval settlement of Newcastle Lyons, County Dublin: an interdisciplinary approach', *PRIA*, 83C14 (1983), 351–76 at 358; Tadhg O'Keeffe, 'Medieval architecture and the village of Newcastle Lyons' in Peter O'Sullivan (ed.), *Newcastle Lyons: a parish of the Pale* (Dublin, 1986), pp 45–61.   **99** Bradley, 'The medieval boroughs of Co. Dublin', p. 136.   **100** Ronan, 'Killadreenan and Newcastle'; Orpen, '*Novum Castrum McKynegan*'; Twohig, 'Anglo-Norman ringwork castles'; Grogan

Close to the medieval church at Kilmartin, and less than 3km to the south of Newcastle, lies the possible ringwork at Ballyvolan.[101] These early fortifications, which were all close to important north-south transport routes, formed a defensive cordon along the fertile lowlands between the mountains and the sea.[102]

There were several other mottes in Co. Wicklow, although which lord was responsible for their initial construction is not always clear. Situated in gently undulating terrain, the motte at Powerscourt Demesne is the largest in Wicklow, and if the royal Obrun manor had an administrative caput, this may have been it – although it could also have been built for Walter de Ridelesford, who was granted lands in this area. Unusually, there are two mottes within 900m of each other, and this may be a reflection of the extraordinary tenurial situation, in which lands in this area were held by a combination of the crown, the archbishop of Dublin and de Ridelesford himself. All three of these landholders are known to have had mottes constructed elsewhere in the county. Making the most of the local terrain close to Enniskerry, the possible motte at Knocksink was built on a naturally steep-sided rocky knoll beside the Glencullen River.

A possible motte was located at Ballydonagh, just west of Hollyfield House near Greystones, adjacent to a spring in a field called 'the Mount Field'.[103] As in so many other cases, a natural hill of gravel, sand and stones was shaped to make this possible motte. Eugene O'Curry recorded the site as a 'fine moate' in the nineteenth century, but in 1994 Simpson reported that gravel quarrying had reduced it to a small mound 6.5m high with a flat summit.[104] In May of 1192, Ballydonagh was described as lying 'in the lands of Macgilleholmoche', which family had granted it to the abbey of Glendalough.[105] It subsequently became attached to the archiepiscopal manor of Shankill and, in 1326, sixty acres were held there by Jordan Walrant.[106]

At nearby Killegar, a steep-sided 4m-high mound was identified by Liam Price as a possible motte.[107] Nothing remains of the site now and it is impossible to be sure of what it was originally. Killegar was one of the places mentioned as being among the possessions of the abbey of Glendalough in 1192, but by 1219–20 the church had been assigned to St Patrick's Cathedral, Dublin.[108] As Linzi Simpson points out, there may have been a small nucleated settlement around the motte and church.[109] O'Curry noted that there had been a 'moate' at Glenealy, but that it was cleared away by local people.[110] Simpson suggests that this may have been a motte built by Meiler Fitz Henry after he was granted Wicklow by Maurice Fitz Gerald.[111] The initial fortification at Wicklow town is usually ascribed to the Vikings, but Simpson suggests that it is more likely to have been an Anglo-Norman motte.[112] Gerald of Wales mentions that Wicklow Castle was granted to Strongbow in 1173, and it is possible that this was the prominently located earthwork known locally as 'Roundmount'.[113] It is likely that de Ridelesford's first castle at Bray was a motte, and the Down Survey maps depict a castle on the top of a large mound.[114] The later stone castle was built on high ground overlooking the River Dargle at the north-west end of the town, and this may be where the earth-and-timber fortification stood.

and Kilfeather, *Archaeological inventory of County Wicklow*, p. 180.　**101** Grogan and Kilfeather, *Archaeological inventory of County Wicklow*, p. 176.　**102** Also within this zone, and on the southern edge of the barony of Newcastle, the townland of Ballymoat, near Ballinaclough, is likely to derive its name from the presence of a motte, although there is no clear sign of one there now. Joyce translates *Baile-an-mhóta* as 'the town of the moat or mound' (*Irish names of places*, 1, pp 290–1; 3, p. 107).　**103** Christiaan Corlett and Mairéad Weaver (eds), *The Liam Price notebooks: the placenames, antiquities and topography of County Wicklow* (2 vols, Bray, 2002), 1, p. 60.　**104** Simpson, 'Anglo-Norman settlement in Uí Briuin Cualann', p. 200.　**105** McNeill (ed.), *Alen's register*, p. 21.　**106** Ibid., p. 196.　**107** Simpson, 'Anglo-Norman settlement in Uí Briuin Cualann', p. 200.　**108** McNeill (ed.), *Alen's register*, pp 21, 42.　**109** Simpson, 'Anglo-Norman settlement in Uí Briuin Cualann', p. 200.　**110** Ibid.　**111** Ibid.　**112** Ibid.　**113** Gerald of Wales: *Expugnatio Hibernica*, pp 120–1.　**114** G.D. Scott, *The stones of Bray* (Dublin, 1913; repr. Bray, 1984), p. 215; K.M. Davies, *IHTA: Bray* (Dublin, 1998), pp 1, 11; Mary Davies, *That favourite resort: the story of Bray, Co. Wicklow* (Bray, 2007), pp 29–33; Down Survey (1654–6), parish and barony maps, m. 2506, fo. 55, NLI MS.

Figure 5.20 The earthwork castle at Castlekevin, Co. Wicklow, was probably the hub of archiepiscopal manorial administration in the area. It is set in rich agricultural land. Despite its unusual square shape, it was probably a motte castle (© Department of the Environment, Heritage and Local Government).

Castlekevin Castle (Figures 5.20, 5.21) was constructed on archiepiscopal lands and may have been built for Archbishop Henry of London (1212–28).[115] It was evidently given the name of *Castrum Keyvin* because it was built on the lands of *Sámhadh Caoimhghin*.[116] It was the centre of archiepiscopal manorial administration in the mountains, with its main tenants being the O'Byrnes and the O'Tooles. The large earthworks visible at Castlekevin appear to be the remains of a square motte, and therefore may be late thirteenth- or fourteenth-century in date.[117] O'Conor has suggested that this possible remodelling of the defences at Castlekevin relates to the recorded expenditure of almost £350 in 1276–7 to provision and fortify the site against 'the Irish of the mountains'.[118]

On the other side of the mountains, Donard motte, also known as 'Ball Moat', may have been built by Jordan de Marisco, who was granted this manor by Archbishop Cumin before 1190.[119] The mottes at Donard, Knockroe and Mullycagh were all built at the foot of the Wicklow Mountains and were clearly intended as a defensive barrier in this frontier territory.[120] The motte at Knockroe (which has a bailey and linking causeway), near Hollywood, takes advantage of a naturally steep-sided ridge in a narrow valley. Pre-existing topographical features were also exploited for the construction of the mottes at Donard and, further to north in the barony, at Athdown. The motte at Athdown was located close to a ford over the River Liffey, but it is no longer extant.

There are indications from other parts of Ireland that some Gaelic Irish lords built mottes.[121] There is little evidence for this in the Dublin region, however, although it has been

115 Orpen, '*Castrum Keyvini*'; Grogan and Kilfeather, *Archaeological inventory of County Wicklow*, pp 176–7. **116** Price, *Place-names: Ballinacor North*, p. 32. **117** O'Conor, 'The later construction and use of motte and bailey castles in Ireland', 24. **118** Ibid. **119** McNeill (ed.), *Alen's register*, p. 287; *RHJB*, pp 211–12; Corlett and Weaver (eds), *The Liam Price notebooks*, 1, p. 295. **120** In 1943, Liam Price recorded that there was a 'big grass-covered tumulus' in a field called 'the Moat Field' in the townland of Mullycagh Upper (Corlett and Weaver (eds), *The Liam Price notebooks*, 2, pp 378–80). Overlooking Hollywood Glen, this feature is recorded as a 'tumulus' in the county inventory (Grogan and Kilfeather, *Archaeological inventory of County Wicklow*, pp 25–6), and Price appears to have thought that it was prehistoric. **121** O'Conor, *Medieval rural settlement in Ireland*, p. 76; Kieran O'Conor, 'Gaelic lordly settlement in the 13th and 14th century in Ireland' in Ingunn Holm, Sonja Innselset and Ingvild Øye (eds), *'Utmark': the outfield as*

suggested that the motte and manor at Cloncurry, Co. Kildare (Figures 5.1, 5.10), was a later MacFáeláin residence.[122] The source of this information is not clear. It is possible that future research will reveal evidence for Gaelic-built (or at least Gaelic-occupied) mottes, but even the strongly Gaelic areas of Wicklow seem to have been devoid of earth-and-timber castles throughout the Middle Ages. It may be that some of the mottes in the foothills of the mountains were built by the Irish to protect themselves from the Anglo-Normans.

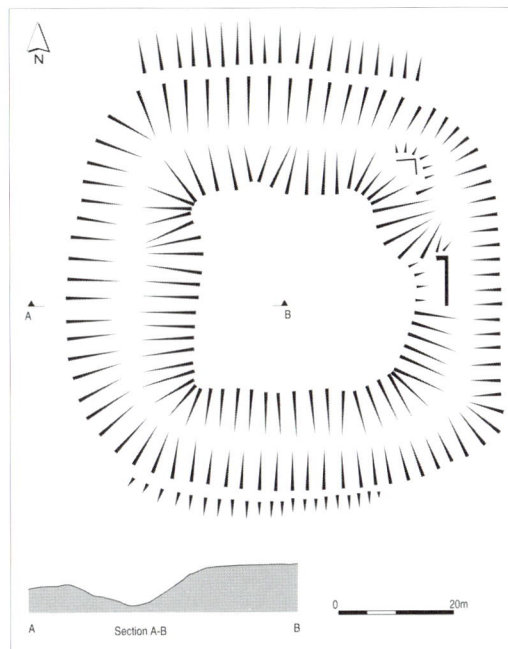

Figure 5.21 Plan of Castlekevin Castle, Co. Wicklow. Several sections of masonry defences survive at the site (after McNeill, *Castles in Ireland*, p. 144, fig. 92).

Masonry castles

Major stone fortresses, to c.1320

Somewhere in the region of 100 to 150 masonry castles of various sorts were built in Ireland between the last quarter of the twelfth century and the first years of the fourteenth.[123] In a small number of cases, stone castles were built on the sites of earlier mottes and ringworks. This appears to have been the case at Maynooth, for instance, where the keep that stands today was erected on top of the earlier earthwork structure.[124] Most of the early stone castles were situated on high ground with commanding views, and almost all were close to running water. Even some of the very earliest Anglo-Norman castles in Ireland were massive, with the de Lacy castle at Trim being the largest of them all. Other large castles were built in the late twelfth and thirteenth centuries at Carlingford, Carrickfergus, Castleroche, Dublin, Dunamase, Limerick, Rindoon and Roscommon, for example. Many of the earlier castles were characterised by a centrally located keep and enclosing curtain walls, but there appears to have been quite a rapid move away from this design to one in which the core buildings and functions of the castle were transferred to the surrounding walls, particularly the entrance gateway.

Of the ninety-four 'castles' recorded in the SMR for the Dublin region, probably fewer than a dozen had been built by the turn of the fourteenth century, and the vast majority of the region's fortifications, *c.*1300, were still of earth and timber.[125] The most notable early stone fortresses in the region (Figure 5.22) were Castleknock (Figures 5.18, 5.29), Dublin (Figures 5.23, 5.24), Dundrum (Figure 5.28), Kindlestown (Figures 5.33, 5.34), Maynooth (Figure 5.25), Newcastle McKynegan (Figures 5.8, 5.9) and Swords (Figures 5.25, 5.26). Early stone castles may also have been built at Ballymore, Bray, Castlekevin, Dunsany, Killegland, Leixlip and Rathcoffey.

Anglo-Norman Ireland was administered from Dublin, and the castle there was both functional and symbolic of royal authority. It is likely that the first castle became inadequate as a royal *capita* after *c.*1200, and it was soon replaced by a more substantial complex of

industry and ideology in the Iron Age and the Middle Ages (Bergen, 2005), pp 209–21 at p. 215; McNeill, *Castles in Ireland*, pp 73, 158; T.E. McNeill, 'The archaeology of Gaelic lordship east and west of the Foyle' in Duffy, Edwards and FitzPatrick (eds), *Gaelic Ireland* (2001), pp 346–56 at pp 346–8.   **122** O'Byrne, 'Conflict and change: the Irish of Kildare', p. 146.   **123** O'Conor, *Medieval rural settlement in Ireland*, p. 17.   **124** Sweetman, *Medieval castles of Ireland*, p. 37.   **125** O'Conor, *Medieval rural settlement in Ireland*, p. 17; O'Conor, 'The later construction and use of motte and bailey castles in Ireland'; O'Conor, 'Motte castles in Ireland'; O'Keeffe, 'Medieval frontiers and fortifications', pp 61–2; Moody, Martin and Byrne (eds), *A new history of Ireland: IX*, p. 34 (map 36, by Robin Glasscock, 'stone castles

Figure 5.22 Distribution
of clearly attested
masonry castles in the
Dublin region, to c.1320.

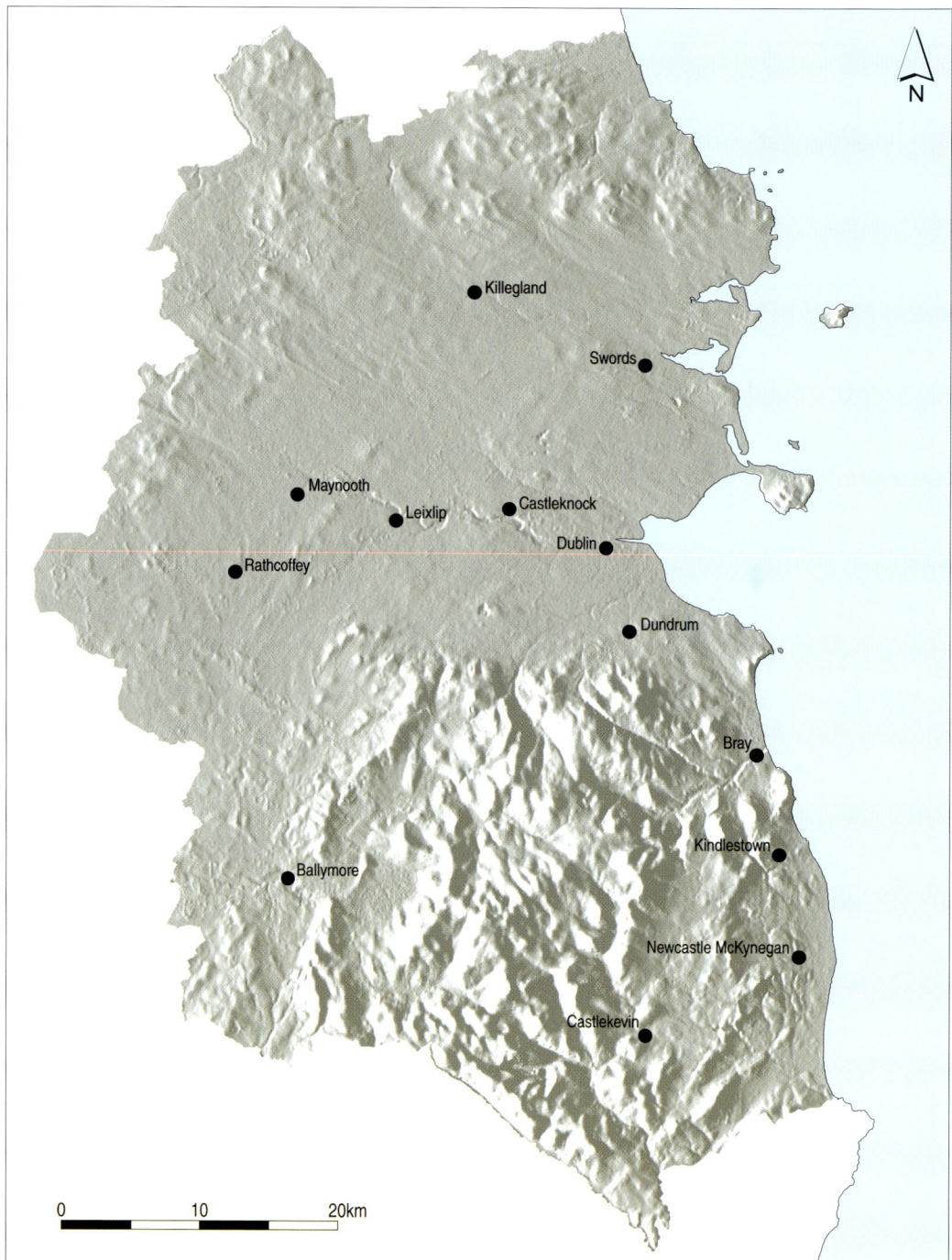

buildings.[126] O'Conor has argued that the earliest Anglo-Norman fortification at Dublin is likely to have been a stone castle, and that it was already in existence by April 1172.[127] Contemporary sources refer variously to its bridge, gates and ditch,[128] but the construction of the thirteenth-century replacement, and later works at the site have apparently obliterated

of Norman type before *c.*1320').   **126** McNeill, *Castles in Ireland*, p. 44; Orpen, *Ireland under the Normans*, pp 272–3; Mullally (ed.), *The deeds of the Normans*, p. 122, ll 2711–14; J.B. Maguire, 'Seventeenth-century plans of Dublin Castle' in Clarke (ed.), *Medieval Dublin: the making of a metropolis* (1990), pp 193–201; Ann Lynch and Conleth Manning, 'Dublin Castle: the archaeological project', *AI*, 4:2 (summer 1990), 65–8; Conleth Manning, 'Dublin Castle: the building of a royal castle in Ireland', *Chateau Gaillard*, 18 (1990), 119–22; Ann Lynch and Conleth Manning, 'Excavations at Dublin Castle, 1985–7' in Duffy (ed.), *Medieval Dublin II* (2001), pp 169–204; Conleth Manning, 'The Record Tower, Dublin Castle' in Kenyon and O'Conor (eds), *The medieval castle in Ireland and Wales* (2003), pp 72–95; J.F. Lydon, 'Dublin Castle in the Middle Ages' in Duffy (ed.), *Medieval Dublin III* (2002), pp 115–27.   **127** O'Conor, 'The earthwork castles of medieval Leinster', I, pp 109–13.   **128** *RAST*, pp 369–71; Mullally (ed.), *The deeds of the Normans*, ll 2711–14; William Stubbs (ed.), *Gesta regis Henrici Secundi* (2 vols, London, 1867), I, p. 30; *CDI, 1171–1251*, no. 116, pp 17–18.

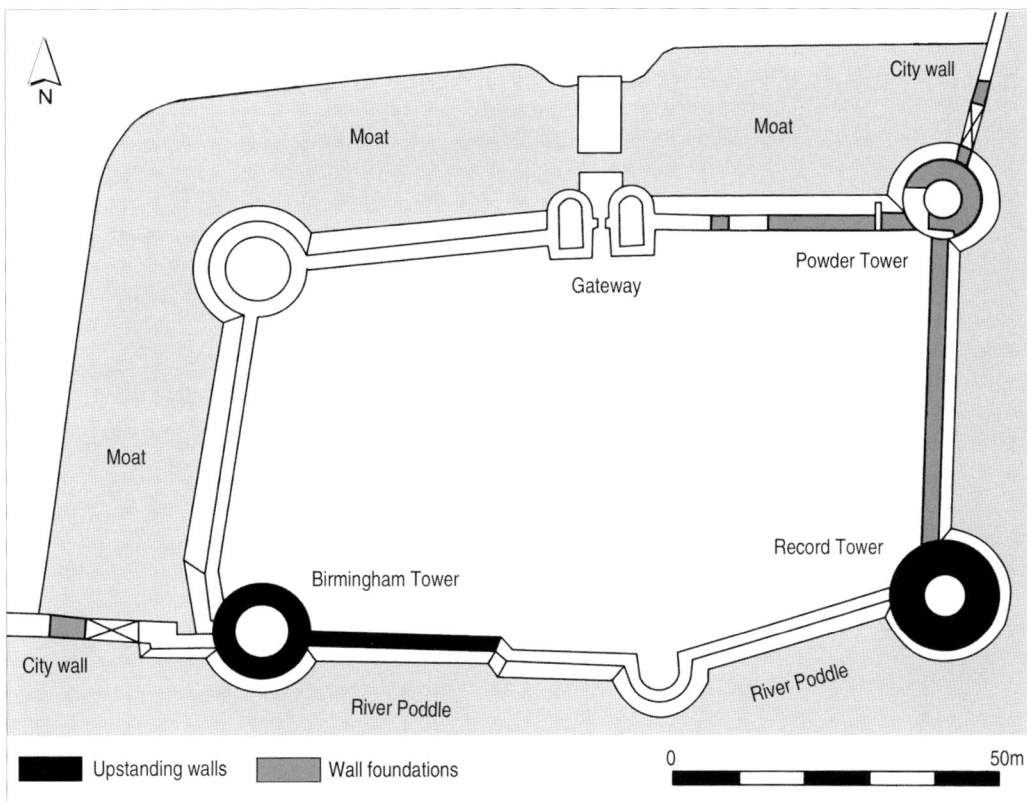

Figure 5.23 Plan of Dublin Castle, showing wall foundations revealed during recent archaeological excavations (after Sweetman, *Medieval castles of Ireland*, p. 50, fig. 36).

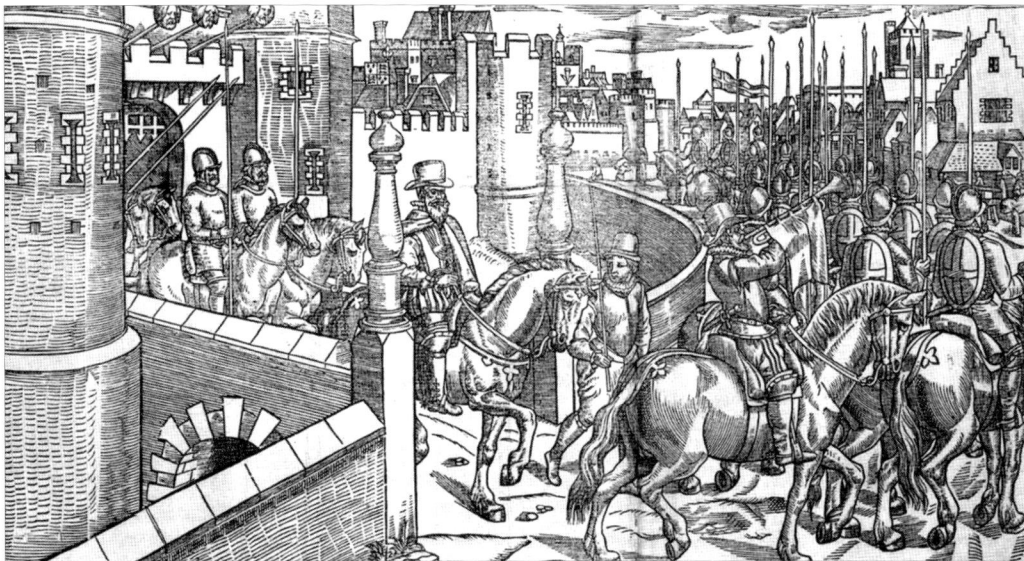

Figure 5.24 Sir Henry Sidney rides out of the gates of Dublin Castle with an armed force (taken from John Derricke, *The image of Irelande, with a discoverie of woodkerne*, ed. John Small (Belfast, 1985)).

almost all traces of the early castle.[129] What survives of the thirteenth-century complex once formed part of a keepless castle with a roughly rectangular circuit of walls and four corner towers (Figure 5.23).[130] It was one of the earliest of its type in Ireland or Britain, and it may well have influenced the design and construction of later castles. Extensive excavations at Dublin Castle have contributed significantly to our understanding of its form and development.[131]

The masonry castle at Maynooth may also have been commenced in the first years of the thirteenth century if not earlier, and the castle complex was soon to incorporate a chapel

129 But see Lynch and Manning, 'Dublin Castle: the archaeological project', 67; Lynch and Manning, 'Excavations at Dublin Castle, 1985–7', p. 183.   130 Tadhg O'Keeffe, 'Dublin Castle's donjon in context' in Bradley, Fletcher and Simms (eds), *Dublin in the medieval world* (2009), pp 277–94.   131 Lynch and Manning, 'Dublin Castle: the archaeological project'; Manning, 'Dublin Castle: the building of a royal castle in Ireland'; Lynch and Manning, 'Excavations at Dublin Castle, 1985–7'; Manning, 'The Record Tower, Dublin Castle'.

Figure 5.25 Aerial view of Maynooth, Co. Kildare, showing St Patrick's College in the foreground, with the medieval church and castle visible in the top-left quarter (CUCAP AVS032 image courtesy of Cambridge University Collection of Aerial Photographs).

and a series of other buildings and features.[132] The manor of Maynooth had been granted to Maurice Fitz Gerald by Strongbow and it was the FitzGeralds who built the first castle there.[133] The present remains include a large square keep, a gate-house, parts of the curtain walls and fosse and a tower at the south-east corner (Figure 5.25). Excavations at the site in the 1990s revealed evidence for at least seven phases of activity, including a medieval well, an arrowhead, a spur, Ham Green pottery and bones from fallow deer and immature seal.[134] Publication of the full results of the excavations is awaited.

Swords Castle was built *c.*1200 as the manorial residence of the archbishop of Dublin (Figures 5.25, 5.26).[135] It is close to the River Ward on low-lying ground. Little of the original castle survives above ground, and it is hard to know what form it took. The present remains include a late thirteenth-century hall (along the east wall), and a chapel (to the east of the gateway) of probable fourteenth-century date (Figure 5.26). The range of surviving buildings, including a great chamber and a series of barrel-vaulted rooms, suggests the former existence of elaborate domestic quarters.[136] Excavations in 1971 uncovered a remarkable tiled floor, in an area that must have formed part of the archbishop's private chambers.[137]

The castle's defences included a circuit of thin curtain walls pierced by a simple gateway (complete with Dundry stone window surrounds) to the south. The mural tower to the north, opposite the main gate, is probably fourteenth or fifteenth century in date.[138] The meagre defences, among other things, relative to the status of the site and that of its medieval owners, beg the question as to whether this really was a castle at all.[139] Roger Stalley concluded that the curtain walls are more likely to have served to keep livestock in the courtyard, rather than to keep an organised army out.[140] Swords was at the core of the

132 *RBK*, pp 98–100.   **133** Horner, *IHTA: Maynooth*, p. 1.   **134** Alan Hayden, 'Maynooth Castle, Maynooth' in *Excavations 1999*, pp 132–3; Alan Hayden, 'Maynooth Castle', DEHLG file 96E0391.   **135** McNeill (ed.), *Alen's register*, p. 104; Bradley, 'The medieval boroughs of Co. Dublin', p. 139.   **136** McNeill, *Castles in Ireland*, pp 108, 166. **137** Thomas Fanning, 'An Irish medieval tile pavement: recent excavations at Swords Castle, County Dublin', *JRSAI*, 105 (1975), 47–82.   **138** Sweetman, *Medieval castles of Ireland*, pp 127–9.   **139** Roger Stalley, 'The archbishop's residence at Swords: castle or country retreat' in Duffy (ed.), *Medieval Dublin VII* (2006), pp 152–76.   **140** Stalley,

archbishops' lands in north Co. Dublin, some of the most profitable farms in the country – the castle complex consequently included granaries, barns and stables.

The castles at Dublin, Maynooth and Swords were each the result of a large-scale multi-phased building project, both in terms of the main residential quarters and the ancillary buildings and defences. The remaining early masonry castle sites in the Dublin region were more modest in design.

Other early stone castles

It was possibly at the start of the thirteenth century, a generation into Anglo-Norman presence in Ireland, and a period of major stone building in the Dublin region, that the first masonry structure at Castleknock Castle was begun (Figures 5.18, 5.29). Unfortunately, only small fragments survive of the three- or four-storey polygonal keep shown by Francis Place on top of the motte in 1689.[141]

Situated on a ridge overlooking the River Slang, the late sixteenth-century castle at Dundrum incorporates part of a thirteenth-/fourteenth-century fortification (Figure 5.28).[142] This castle, which was surrounded by a moat, may have been built by the de Clahull family, who were granted the area in the 1170s, but the lands here went through a number of hands in the thirteenth and fourteenth centuries.[143] The present castle at Clontarf is a neo-Tudor building of mid-nineteenth-century date, but it occupies the site of the original Clontarf Castle, which was probably first built in the late twelfth century.[144] It was built by the Knights Hospitallers of St John of Jerusalem, but nothing is known of its form, or even whether it was of stone or of earth-and-timber construction.

There are some physical remains at Newcastle McKynegan and, although most of what is visible is post-medieval in date, the core of the castle/gate-house structure on the top of the ringwork is medieval (Figure 5.9).[145] The first masonry castle was built at this royal manor in the last quarter of the thirteenth century, probably in response to worsening relations between the English crown and the Irish in the Wicklow Mountains in the 1270s. The pipe rolls of the Irish exchequer record expenditure on the castle. For example, in 1280–1 a tower was built at a cost of £74 6s. 9d. and in subsequent years £30 was spent building a wall and carrying out works at the great hall and other houses there.[146] During the same decade, resources were being expended 12km away on the fortifications at Castlekevin, at a time when it too was in the king's hand.[147] Although the vestiges of some masonry structures can still be made out on the site (Figures 5.20, 5.21), the extent of the stone castle cannot be traced with any certainty.

The castle at Bray, which may originally have been sited where Herbert Road North is now, is first mentioned in the late twelfth century.[148] It is referred to again in 1284, and included a stone house and courtyard by no later than 1311.[149] These features, together with the church, mill, tenements and cottages mentioned in the same documents, were probably in existence from the early years of the thirteenth century.[150] All but the most meagre traces of the castle have now disappeared.

'The archbishop's residence at Swords', pp 171–5. **141** H.G. Leask, *Irish castles and castellated houses* (Dundalk, 1951; repr. 1995), pp 27, 43; Sweetman, *Medieval castles of Ireland*, p. 85. **142** Elizabeth O'Brien, 'Excavations at Dundrum Castle, Dundrum, Co. Dublin', *AI*, 3:4 (winter 1989), 136–7; Elizabeth O'Brien, 'Excavations at Dundrum Castle, Co. Dublin, E000419 (1987–91): final report, unpublished'; Peter Harbison (ed.), *Gabriel Beranger's drawings of the principal antique buildings of Ireland* (Dublin, 1998), pp 72–5, 90–1. **143** Ball, *A history of the county of Dublin*, 2, pp 66–7. **144** Harbison (ed.), *Beranger's drawings*, pp 160–1. **145** Grogan and Kilfeather, *Archaeological inventory of County Wicklow*, pp 181–2; Bradley and King, 'UAS 9: Wicklow', pp 63–4; Shanahan, 'The manor in east county Wicklow', pp 143–4. **146** *RDKPRI*, 36, p. 59; *RDKPRI*, 38, p. 47. **147** *CDI, 1252–84*, no. 1412, p. 267; *RDKPRI*, 36, p. 44. McNeill (*Castles in Ireland*, p. 140) describes Castlekevin as 'a strongly defended moated site'. **148** Scott, *The stones of Bray*, p. 215; Davies, *IHTA: Bray*, pp 1, 11. **149** *CDI, 1252–84*, no. 2340, p. 560; *RBO*, p. 24. **150** Bradley and King, 'UAS 9: Wicklow', pp 12–19; Davies, *IHTA: Bray*.

Figure 5.26 Swords Castle, Co. Dublin: general plan (above) and plan of south-eastern range (below) (after McNeill, *Castles in Ireland*, p. 108, fig. 63).

Figure 5.27 Swords Castle, Co. Dublin: the north tower (seen here) is probably fourteenth or early fifteenth century in date. It is sometimes referred to as the 'Constable's Tower'. The stepped battlements along the top of the curtain wall are typically late medieval in style.

The castle at the archiepiscopal manor of Ballymore is first referred to in the 1180s, when Prince John granted Archbishop John Cumin 'the half of the cantred of the abbey of Glendalough nearest to his castle of Ballymore'.[151] It was subsequently taken into the king's hand during a dispute with the archbishop, but was restored in 1203.[152] The fortifications were strengthened in 1274–5, but the castle was described as dilapidated by the time of the 1326 extent.[153] The extent records that there was still a hall and a chapel and several different chambers – including one for the archbishop when he chose to visit, and one for the constable. There was also a small chamber for clerks, a kitchen roofed with shingles, a stable and a thatched grange – the granary had been burnt down. The size of the castle precinct is indicated by the statement that it included three acres of meadow. A number of prisoners were incarcerated at the castle in the early fourteenth century.[154] While the castle continued to serve a variety of functions through the fifteenth, sixteenth and seventeenth centuries, little of it was left by the time it was drawn by Gabriel Beranger in 1773 (Figure 4.11).[155] Its exact location is now a matter of conjecture.

A stone castle was probably erected at Rathcoffey soon after 1312, when John de Wogan was granted lands here.[156] The surviving remains include a gatehouse and parts of the castle built into a nineteenth-century mansion (Figure 5.30). Excavations in 2003, just 400m from Rathcoffey Castle, uncovered a well-laid metalled surface, a small pit and part of a gully, as well as some slag associated with a 'relatively large quantity of medieval pottery sherds'.[157] It is not clear what the relationship was between this material and the castle.

The minor remains of the castle at Killegland, near Ashbourne, appear to have formed part of a tower house, but recent work has indicated that this may have superseded an earlier castle on the site.[158] The site is across the Broad Meadow River from a medieval millrace earthwork and a twelfth- to fourteenth-century farmstead excavated by Bill Frazer.

151 McNeill (ed.), *Alen's register*, p. 18.   152 *CDI, 1171–1251*, no. 180, pp 28–9.   153 *RDKPRI*, 36, p. 41; McNeill (ed.), *Alen's register*, p. 189.   154 *CJR, 1305–7*, p. 495.   155 Harbison (ed.), *Beranger's drawings*, pp 170–1.   156 Matthew Devitt, 'The barony of Okethy', *JCKAHS*, 8 (1917), 276–301 at 295–6.   157 Emmet Stafford, 'Rathcoffey, Co. Kildare' in *Excavations 2003*, p. 254.   158 W.O. Frazer, pers. comm.; W.O. Frazer, 'A medieval farmstead at Killegland,

Figure 5.28 Dundrum Castle, Co. Dublin. Overlooking the River Slang, this castle may have been built on the site of a pre-Anglo-Norman fort or dún. Although most of what is visible today dates to the sixteenth and later centuries, excavations directed by Elizabeth O'Brien have revealed parts of the thirteenth-century castle, as well as a section of its moat and a triple-slotted drawbridge (image courtesy of Elizabeth O'Brien).

Figure 5.29 Castleknock Castle, Co. Dublin, drawn c.1698 by Francis Place (1647–1728) (image courtesy of Castleknock College).

The earliest known reference to a castle at Leixlip dates to before 1212, and it is possible that this was a motte.[159] The present castle is still lived in, but it has gone through many phases of construction, alteration and restoration, and little of pre-1700-date survives. In 1303/4, work on Leixlip Castle necessitated the construction of a lime kiln, the breaking of stone and the cutting of timber – resources that would have been collected in the nearby countryside.[160] An extent for Leixlip dating to 1341 mentions some of the defensive features of the castle at that time:[161]

> There is a stone castle with a large tower and three smaller towers, which is worth nothing in time of war. The king for the custody of the same castle paid 10 marks each year for the fee of the constable. And for repairing and sustaining the castle a sum of 40s. p.a. is required.

The motte at Dunsany was superseded by a stone castle, some of which may be incorporated into the present building, much of which is eighteenth and nineteenth century in date (Figure 5.31). Just across the road from Dunsany is another Plunkett residence, Killeen

Ashbourne, Co. Meath' in Corlett and Potterton (eds), *Rural settlement in medieval Ireland* (2009), pp 109–24. **159** *RAST*, pp 142–3; Bradley, Halpin and King, 'UAS 7:3: Kildare', p. 309. **160** *RDKPRI*, 38, pp 86, 95. **161** TNA:PRO C47/10/20/1.

Castle. The present building at Killeen is mainly late eighteenth and early nineteenth century, but there is some evidence for the inclusion of earlier features. A major campaign of archaeological survey, testing, monitoring and excavation was carried out at Killeen, and while the focus of this was mostly away from the castle itself, a series of earth-cut ditches was excavated in proximity to the castle (Figure 5.32).[162] The excavator concluded that the second phase of these ditches – some of which appear to have been re-cuts of earlier features – 'may have either constituted the original castle ringwork or formed part of a motte and bailey'.[163]

Hall-houses

The term 'hall-house' is applied to a type of small castle or strong-house first built in Ireland in the early years of the thirteenth century.[164] They are generally two-storey buildings with narrow opes on the ground floor and larger windows and a main entrance on the first floor, where the hall was situated. Although hall-houses are generally isolated and without visible outer defences, Sweetman has shown that some functioned as manor houses, being associated with deserted settlements and churches. Hall-houses are most common in the west of Ireland, and they are rare in Leinster. Indeed, the only example in the Dublin region is Kindlestown Castle, near Delgany in Co. Wicklow, which was probably commenced

Figure 5.30 The gatehouse and castle at Rathcoffey, Co. Kildare, are set within large open fields that have been producing arable crops annually for the best part of a thousand years. Just out of view to the right is a ringfort, and the focus of settlement appears to have moved from there to the crest of the hill, where the Wogan family built a castle in the early fourteenth century.

162 Christine Baker, *The archaeology of Killeen Castle, Co. Meath* (Bray, 2009). **163** Ibid., p. 60. **164** David Sweetman, 'The hall-house in Ireland' in Kenyon and O'Conor (eds), *The medieval castle in Ireland and Wales* (2003), pp 121–32; Sweetman, *Medieval castles of Ireland*, pp 89–104; McNeill, *Castles in Ireland*, pp 149–55.

Figure 5.31 The first castle at Dunsany, Co. Meath, was a motte, which is now covered in trees and can be seen to the left of the ruined church in the foreground of this photograph. The present castle is lived in by the 20th Baron Dunsany and his family. The 1st Baron had the church built in the fifteenth century (CUCAP ATC40 image courtesy of Cambridge University Collection of Aerial Photographs).

*c.*1300 (Figures 5.33, 5.34). Kindlestown is generally regarded as a text-book example of a hall house.[165] It is a rectangular two-storey hall built of local limestone and felsitic rubble. The ground floor is barrel-vaulted and has projecting towers on both corners of the north side. A spiral stairs in the north-east tower lead to an intramural passage at first floor level. The entire site is surrounded by a rectangular four-metre-wide fosse (enclosing an area *c.*18m by 52m). Simpson has argued that the construction of Kindlestown was initiated as a result of the changing political circumstances in this frontier area, which included an increasing number of sporadic attacks, military campaigns and instability.[166]

Polygonal enclosure castles: the case of Ballyvolan, Co. Wicklow

The ringwork at Ballyvolan in Co. Wicklow contains within it the remains of a polygonal enclosure castle (Figure 5.35).[167] Overlooking a stream, it is situated about 100m from the ruins of the medieval church of Kilmartin, to which it is linked by an old road. Kilmartin was a small manor centre, probably held from the manor of Wicklow.[168] Liam Price, who believed that the fortification dates to the fourteenth century, speculated that it may have been built *c.*1350 by Sir Thomas de Rokeby, the justiciar.[169] In 1394, Kilmartin was one of the

---

165 Grogan and Kilfeather, *Archaeological inventory of County Wicklow*, p. 183; Sweetman, 'The hall-house in Ireland', pp 127–8. **166** Simpson, 'Dublin's southern frontier'. **167** Grogan and Kilfeather, *Archaeological inventory of County Wicklow*, p. 184; McNeill, *Castles in Ireland*, pp 154, 156. **168** Shanahan, 'The manor in east county Wicklow', pp 141, 145–6. **169** Liam Price, 'The Byrnes' country in County Wicklow in the sixteenth century: and the manor of Arklow',

Figure 5.32 Killeen Castle, Co. Meath, during archaeological excavations. Evidence for pre-masonry castle earthen fortifications was uncovered. The fifteenth-century church is also visible (image courtesy of Christine Baker, Margaret Gowen and Co. Ltd).

manors granted to Janico Dartas, the Navarrese esquire who Richard II established in Ireland.[170] Very little of the stonework survives at Ballyvolan, although in two places the walls reach *c*.4m in height, and three putlog holes are visible. Despite the meagre remains, the Ballyvolan enclosure appears to be the most extensive one known in Ireland. Only a handful of polygonal enclosures are recorded, and their dating to the thirteenth century is based on two examples from Ulster. McNeill has noted that these simple castles 'are not to be found at manorial centres but are associated with the frontiers of lordship and areas of military tension, rather like the mottes with baileys … The function of these small castles was to provide a base for troops stationed during times of tension. They were there to defend the area from raids by Irish while forces were prepared for counter-raids by the English'.[171] Such a characterisation would seem to suit Ballyvolan very well. O'Conor has presented evidence for the construction of castles elsewhere in the Leinster marches in response to increasing instability in the period following *c*.1270.[172] Ballyvolan may have functioned as a garrison in the late thirteenth century, but in the absence of further evidence, there is no way to be sure.

Later medieval masonry castles

Most castles that had been built before *c*.1320 continued in use through the fourteenth century and beyond, and many were renovated and/or extended during this time. After *c*.1320, very few new fortifications were constructed until well into the fifteenth century. New castles were being built in the Dublin region right up to the late sixteenth and seventeenth centuries, with examples such as Drumcondra, Dubber, Loughlinstown, Rathfarnham and Roebuck. Almost all of the surviving castles in the Dublin region exhibit evidence for multiple phases of construction and reconstruction. The late sixteenth-century castle at Dundrum, for instance, incorporates part of a thirteenth-/fourteenth-century

JRSAI, 66 (1936), 41–66 at 47. **170** Liam Price, *Placenames, VII: the baronies of Newcastle and Arklow* (Dublin, 1967), p. 412. **171** McNeill, *Castles in Ireland*, p. 155. **172** O'Conor, 'The later construction and use of motte and bailey castles in Ireland', passim.

Figure 5.33 Kindlestown Castle, Co. Wicklow, viewed from north. The outlets for the garderobe chutes can be seen in the projecting tower on the west side. This building is generally regarded as one of the finest hall-houses in Ireland.

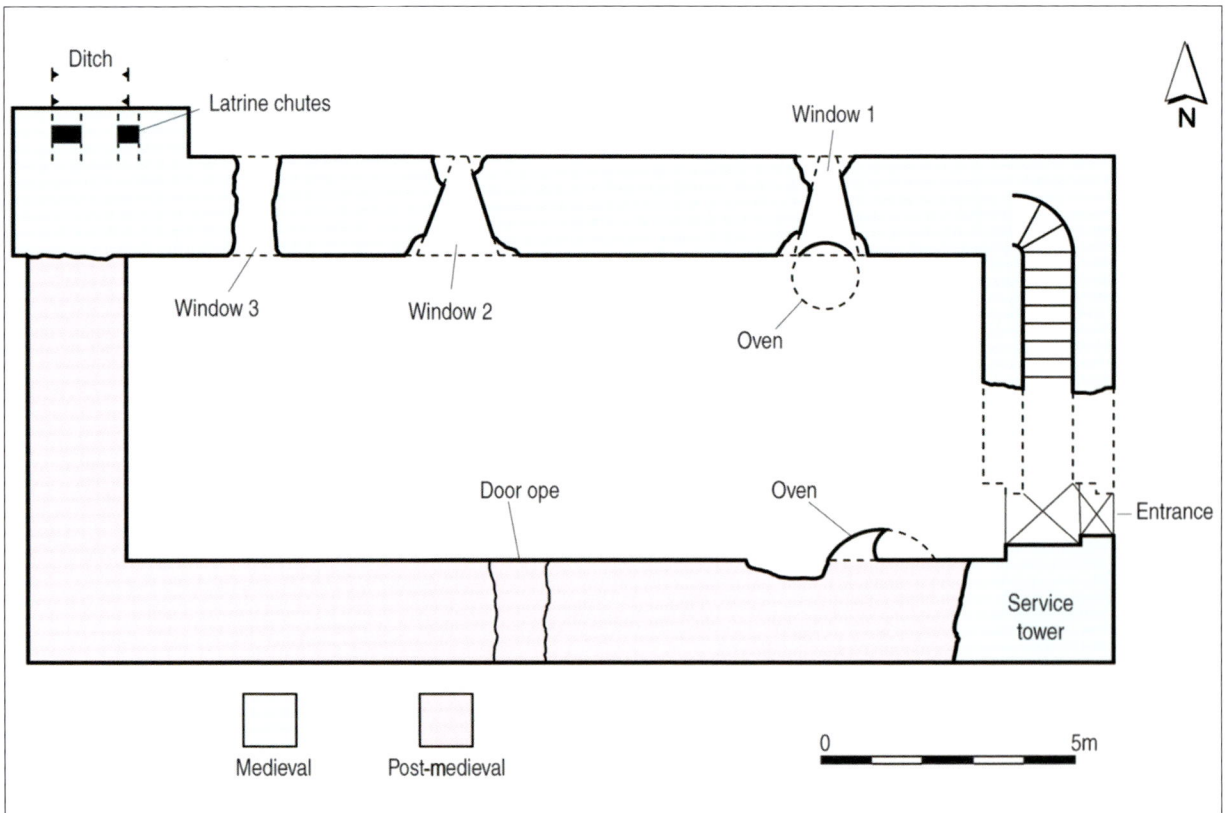

Figure 5.34 Kindlestown Castle, Co. Wicklow: plan of ground floor. The building is surrounded by a fosse that would originally have been water-filled (after Linzi Simpson, 'Dublin's southern frontier', p. 283, fig. 3).

fortification (see above, p. 137).[173] Drimnagh Castle also comprises features from a range of periods (Figures 5.37, 5.38).[174] In other cases, such as Newtown House (Blackrock), it is likely that post-medieval buildings have incorporated parts of earlier structures that are now difficult to discern.

In addition to the castles that are now shrouded beneath later façades, many of the fortified residences known to have existed across the Dublin region have all but vanished. In Meath, for example, no visible remains survive of the castles at Balsoon, Staffordstown and Vesingstown, while only minor traces can be seen at Balreask and Derrypatrick. Documentary and cartographic sources are all that remain to attest the former existence of masonry castles at Laragh East, Powerscourt Demesne, Rathdown Upper and Threecastles, all in Co. Wicklow. The distribution of stone fortresses in Kildare appears to have been denser than in the neighbouring counties of Meath and Wicklow, but the majority of these sites are known from paper sources only.[175] At Cloncurry, a masonry castle was built no later than the early fifteenth century, but its exact location is a matter of conjecture.[176] Five hundred metres to the north of the church at Laraghbryan, outside Maynooth, are some loose mortared stones and a series of low earthworks that may mark the site of a stone castle. In a field at Athgarrett known locally as 'Castle Field', finds of pewter plates, medieval tiles, a token and portions of two cauldrons hint at the former presence of a castle, although there is no visible trace of this today.[177] At Hartwell Upper, a series of large, seventeenth-century walls and some potentially earlier sections of masonry have been incorporated into farm buildings.[178]

Tentative references to buildings and fragmentary masonry remains, such as those mentioned above, are insufficient to recreate a picture of the form and type of the site. Some would have been fortified houses, particularly in coastal areas, but it is beyond any reasonable doubt that the overwhelming majority of castles built in the fifteenth and sixteenth century were tower houses.

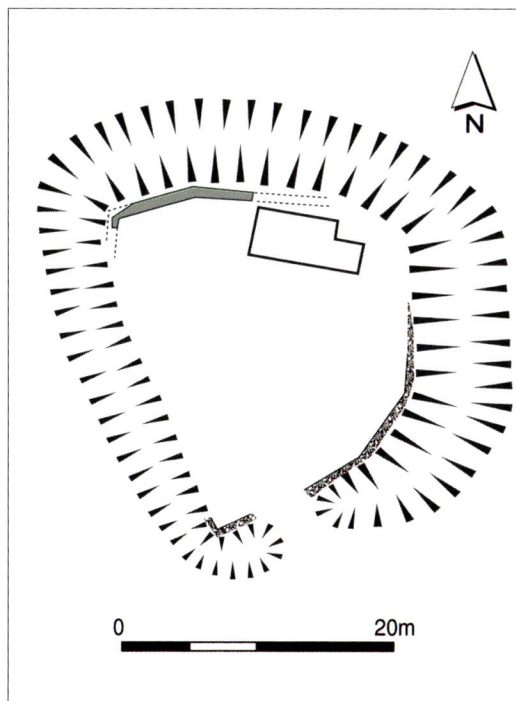

Figure 5.35 Plan of Ballyvolan Castle, Co. Wicklow. The polygonal masonry castle seems to be set within a pre-existing ringwork (after McNeill, *Castles in Ireland*, p. 156, fig. 100).

Tower houses

The tower house is a type of single-towered, fortified residence, or 'small castle', similar to the broadly contemporary 'peel towers' (or 'peles') along the Anglo-Scottish border.[179] Although only several hundred survive, it is estimated that as many as 3,500 were built across

173 O'Brien, 'Excavations at Dundrum Castle' (1989); O'Brien, 'Excavations at Dundrum Castle' (unpublished); Harbison (ed.), *Beranger's drawings*, pp 72–5, 90–1. 174 F.E. Ball, 'A descriptive sketch of Clondalkin, Tallaght and other places in west County Dublin', *JRSAI*, 29 (1899), 93–108 at 95–6; Ball, *A history of the county of Dublin*, 4, pp 125–32; E.R.McC. Dix, 'The lesser castles in the county Dublin', *Irish Builder*, 39 (1897), 49–50; Harbison (ed.), *Beranger's drawings*, pp 40–3; Rachel Corcoran, '"Ireland's forgotten castle": an archaeological study of Drimnagh Castle, Co. Dublin' (MA, UCD, 2005). 175 Blackhall (Bodenstown), Boleybeg (Gilltown), Castledillon Lower ('Rochford Castle'), Coghlanstown West, Confey, Gragadder, Lyons, Mullacash Middle, Mylerstown (Carnalway), Oldtown (Carnalway), Punchestown Great, Rathasker and Wolfestown. 176 Bradley, Halpin and King, 'UAS 7:2: Kildare', p. 172. 177 DEHLG file (KD025–005). 178 This was an Aylmer possession in the sixteenth century (Matthew Devitt, 'The barony of Okethy (continued)', *JCKAHS*, 8:6 (1917), 464–94 at 494). 179 See, for example, C.T. Cairns, 'The Irish tower house: a military view', *Fortress*, 11 (1991), 3–13; T.E. McNeill, 'The origins of tower houses', *AI*, 6:1 (spring 1992), 13–14; Terry Barry, 'The archaeology of the tower house in late medieval Ireland' in Hans Anderson and Jes Wienberg (eds), *The study of medieval archaeology* (Stockholm, 1993), pp 211–17; Terry Barry, 'Harold Leask's "single towers": Irish tower houses as part of larger settlement complexes', *Château Gaillard*, 22 (2006), 27–34; McNeill, *Castles in Ireland*; Tadhg O'Keeffe, *Barryscourt Castle and the Irish tower-house* (Cork, 1997); O'Conor, *Medieval rural settlement in Ireland*, pp 20–5; Sweetman, *Medieval castles of Ireland*, pp 137–74; David Sweetman, *The origin and development of the tower house* (Cork, 2000); O'Keeffe, *Medieval Ireland*, pp 146–56.

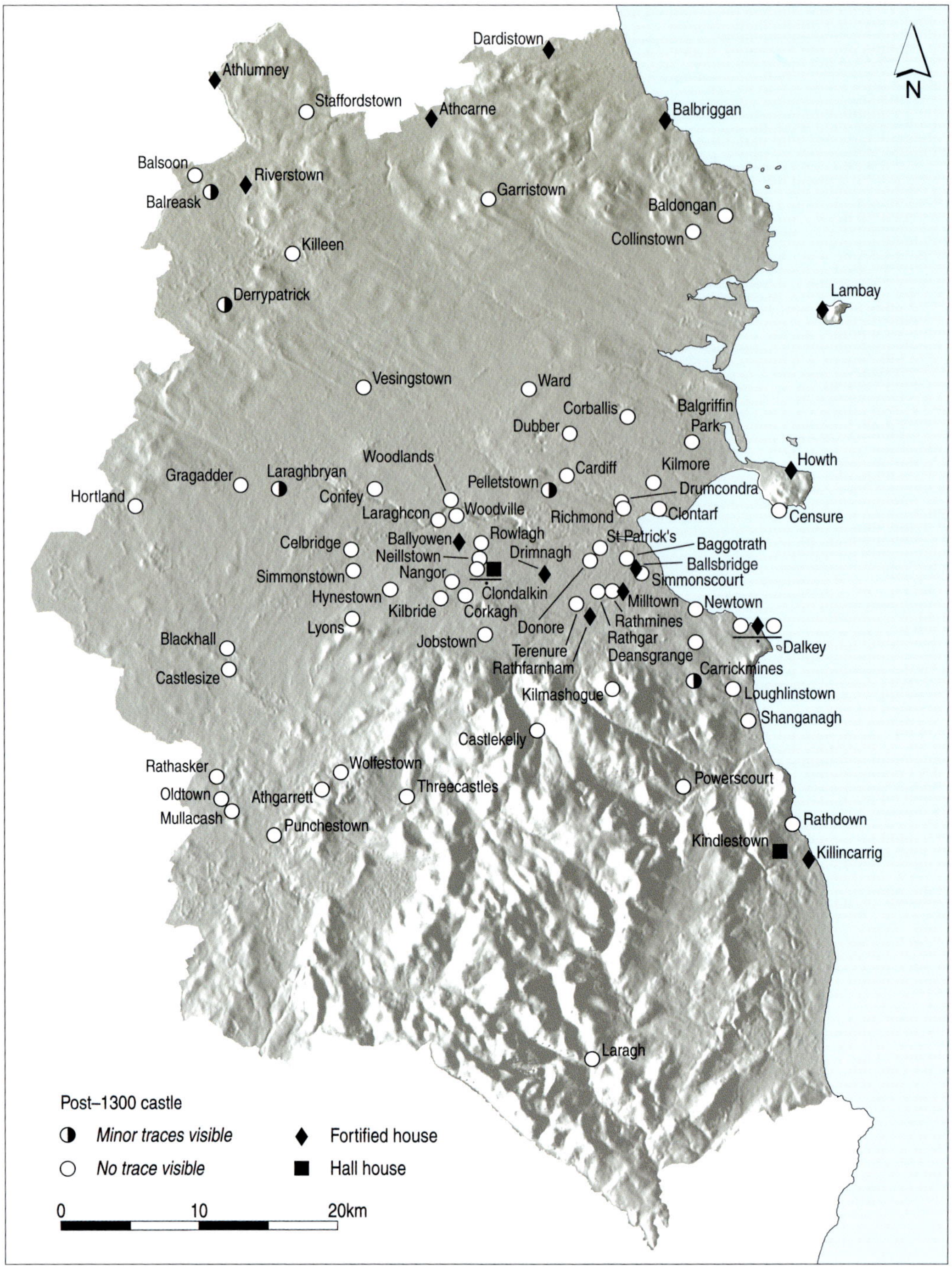

Figure 5.36 Distribution of masonry castles built in the Dublin region after *c.*1300, excluding those known to have been tower houses.

the country, making Ireland the most heavily castellated part of these islands by the seventeenth century.[180] Indeed, one estimate has put the number as high as 7,000.[181] Tower houses were typically the residences of wealthy Gaelic lords or Anglo-Norman/English gentry. They were to be found mainly in richer, more fertile areas; at least 410 are known from Co. Tipperary, 400 from Co. Limerick and 325 from Co. Cork.[182] Although an Anglo-Norman origin has been suggested for tower houses, they are also the first type of stone castle to be built extensively by the Gaelic Irish, and it is in areas that were predominantly Gaelic in the Middle Ages that the largest and most complex examples are found.[183] The

180 C.T. Cairns, *Irish tower houses: a Co. Tipperary case-study* (Athlone, 1987), pp 3, 21; O'Conor, *Medieval rural settlement in Ireland*, 17–25; O'Conor, 'Castle studies in Ireland: the way forward', 329–30. 181 Terry Barry, 'Rural settlement in Ireland in the Middle Ages: an overview', *Ruralia*, 1 (1996), 134–41 at 140; Terry Barry, 'The study of medieval Irish castles', 129. 182 Cairns, *Irish tower houses*, p. 155; McNeill, *Castles in Ireland*, pp 205–10; Barry, *The archaeology of medieval Ireland*, pp 186–90. 183 For an analysis of tower houses in terms of ethnicity, see Rory

Figure 5.37 Drimnagh Castle, Co. Dublin, is a multi-period building surrounded by a fosse and a stout curtain wall, creating an enclosed bawn that would have provided suitable protection for a range of out-buildings and workshops.

Figure 5.38 1772 drawing by Gabriel Beranger of Drimnagh Castle (image reproduced courtesy of the National Library of Ireland).

dating of tower houses is notoriously complicated, but most seem to fit into the bracket 1450 to 1620, although some – such as Derryhivenny, Co. Galway – are even later than this. Many were built before the middle of the fifteenth century, however, and there is some evidence that several were even constructed before the end of the fourteenth century.[184]

Sherlock, 'Cross-cultural occurrences of mutations in tower house architecture: evidence for cultural homogeneity in medieval Ireland?', *JIA*, 15 (2006), 73–91. See also Tadhg O'Keeffe, *The Gaelic peoples and their archaeological identities, AD1000–1650* (Quiggin pamphlets on the sources of mediaeval and Gaelic history, 7, Cambridge, 2004), esp. pp 12–16.
184 John Bradley and Ben Murtagh, 'Brady's Castle, Thomastown, Co. Kilkenny: a 14th-century fortified town house'

Figure 5.39 Distribution of tower houses in the Dublin region, based on DEHLG files, published sources and limited fieldwork.

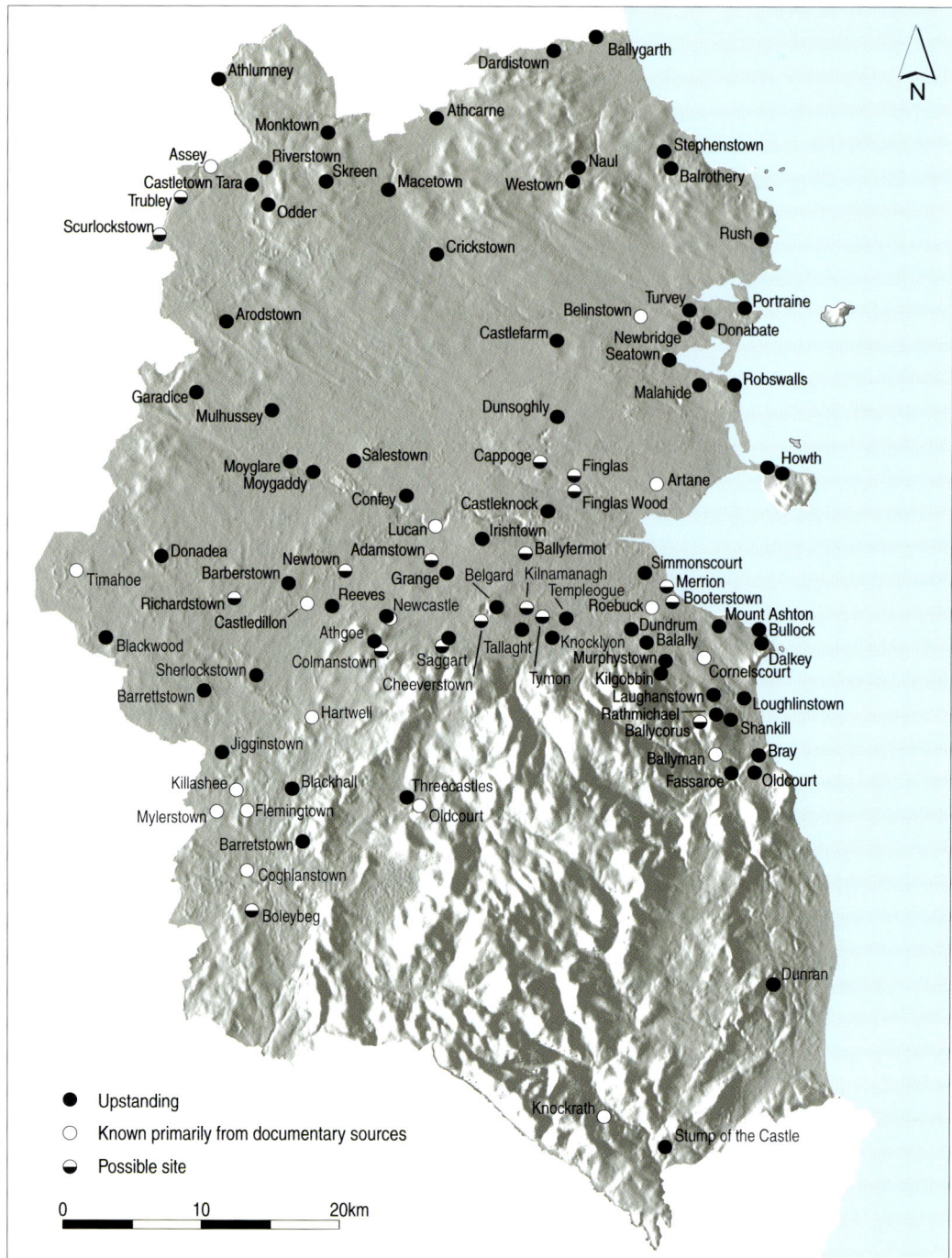

Ballygarth
Dardistown
Athlumney
Athcarne
Monktown
Stephenstown
Assey
Riverstown
Naul
Castletown Tara
Skreen
Westown
Balrothery
Trubley
Macetown
Odder
Scurlockstown
Rush
Crickstown
Turvey
Portraine
Belinstown
Arodstown
Castlefarm
Newbridge
Donabate
Seatown
Robswalls
Garadice
Malahide
Dunsoghly
Mulhussey
Salestown
Cappoge
Finglas
Howth
Moyglare
Artane
Moygaddy
Confey
Castleknock
Finglas Wood
Lucan
Irishtown
Donadea
Adamstown
Ballyfermot
Newtown
Simmonscourt
Barberstown
Grange
Belgard
Kilnamanagh
Merrion
Timahoe
Reeves
Templeogue
Booterstown
Richardstown
Newcastle
Roebuck
Mount Ashton
Castledillon
Dundrum
Bullock
Athgoe
Balally
Blackwood
Colmanstown
Tallaght
Knocklyon
Dalkey
Sherlockstown
Saggart
Murphystown
Cornelscourt
Cheeverstown
Tymon
Kilgobbin
Barrettstown
Laughanstown
Loughlinstown
Hartwell
Rathmichael
Shankill
Ballycorus
Jigginstown
Ballyman
Bray
Killashee
Blackhall
Threecastles
Fassaroe
Oldcourt
Mylerstown
Flemingtown
Oldcourt
Barretstown
Coghlanstown
Boleybeg
Dunran
Knockrath
Stump of the Castle

● Upstanding
○ Known primarily from documentary sources
◑ Possible site

0   10   20km

Sweetman has argued that tower houses developed from the earlier hall houses, specifically those like Kindlestown in Co. Wicklow (Figures 5.33, 5.34).[185] While the main rooms of hall houses, which tend to be of two storeys, are arranged on a horizontal plane, the rooms of tower houses are stacked vertically, rising three, four and five storeys tall. Most tower houses would probably have been surrounded, at least partially, by a bawn area or walled courtyard that sometimes had towers at the corners. Within the bawn area would have been the ancillary domestic and agricultural buildings. Most of the buildings within the bawn area would not have been of stone – some being of wattle-and-daub – and there is little above-ground evidence for their form and number. McNeill has questioned the

in Kenyon and O'Conor (eds), *The medieval castle in Ireland and Wales* (2003), pp 194–216; Brian Hodkinson, 'Thom Cor Castle: a 14th-century tower house in Limerick city', *JRSAI*, 135 (2005), 119–29.   **185** Sweetman, *The origin and development of the tower house*, p. 286; Sweetman, 'The hall-house in Ireland'.

widespread existence of bawn walls, however, and has drawn attention to their shortcomings in terms of serious defence, concluding that where they did exist, they were probably 'meant to prevent theft rather than [serving as] real defences'.[186]

It is possible that a spurt of building was stimulated by a statute of 1430, whereby a government subsidy of £10 was given to any liegeman within the counties of the Pale or in Down, Wicklow or Wexford, who constructed a small stone castle of certain specifications.[187] The tower was to measure sixteen by twenty feet and had to be forty feet in height. Later, tower houses in Meath were limited to a ground area of twelve by fifteen feet. The tower house at Donore, near Killyon in Co. Meath, fits these specifications almost exactly, but it is one of only a few that do.[188] Many commentators feel that the £10 subsidy was not a major factor in encouraging the construction of tower houses in the east of Ireland, and it certainly played no role whatsoever in the west.

From the outside, tower houses resemble smaller versions of the earlier masonry keeps, and although they are not as massive, usually have thinner walls, and are less fortress-like, they had a defensive role nonetheless. Many of the surviving examples display defensive characteristics such as double-stepped battlements, machicolations over doorways, slit-windows at lower levels, and 'murder-holes' at the entrance lobby. In a number of examples, the grooves can still be seen where a 'yett' (or iron grille) could be pulled across in front of the main door, which is almost always at ground level. From the late sixteenth century onwards, loops for guns become noticeable. In general, the upper floors have larger, ogee-headed windows with punch-dressed stone for the jambs. The number of corner turrets varies, but one – usually above the stairs – is sometimes higher than the others, and a second turret often contains the garderobe. The base of the roof gables was set within the parapet, a metre or so below the top of the surrounding walls. Materials for roofing varied: some were slated and some thatched, while roofs of stone slabs, oak timbers or shingles were also known.

As well as being fortresses, tower houses were administrative centres for agricultural estates, and storage depots for merchant families.[189] They were also self-contained houses. The principal rooms were usually located on the upper floors, which had larger windows and were therefore better lit. Windows at the higher levels were also more decorative. Where evidence for fireplaces remains, it is usually to be found on these upper floors. Many tower houses had no fireplaces when originally built, but had one or more inserted at a later date, usually at the expense of some of the windows. The interior of the rooms was usually whitewashed or plastered, and evidence for this remains at many sites around the country. In most cases, at least one floor was barrel-vaulted, frequently the ground floor, and in some instances other floors had vaulted ceilings too. Wicker mats were frequently used in the preparation of vaulting, and evidence for this practice was often left behind in the form of impressions in the mortar (such as at Salestown, Co. Meath).[190]

Dublin region tower houses

Over one hundred tower houses are known to have been built in the Dublin region (Figure 5.39).[191] Indeed, the figure may well be closer to 170, or even higher, as it is likely that the majority of the documented castles for which little or no physical trace survives were in

186 McNeill, *Castles in Ireland*, p. 217. See also O'Conor, *Medieval rural settlement in Ireland*, p. 23.   **187** *Stat. Ire., Hen. VI*, pp 33–5: 1429/30; Bradley and Murtagh, 'Brady's Castle', p. 212.   **188** Moore, *Archaeological inventory of County Meath*, p. 170.   **189** Muiris O'Sullivan and Liam Downey, 'Tower houses and associated farming systems', *AI*, 23:2:88 (summer 2009), 34–7.   **190** Moore, *Archaeological inventory of County Meath*, p. 175.   **191** This includes 95 listed in the SMR under the category 'Tower House' and a further 16 [probably 15 if Dundrum is duplicated] that are inexplicably included within the 'Castle' category.

fact tower houses. In addition to the ninety-five tower houses listed for the region in the SMR, ninety-four 'castles' are recorded. When the pre-1320 structures are excluded from this category, and the errant tower houses and fortified houses are removed to their appropriate listings, sixty-six entries are left. Of these, there are no visible remains of sixty-one, while five others each survives as minor vestiges only (that is, too little is left to form an impression of the form the building took originally). In cases where there are no visible remains, the evidence for the former existence of the castle is either documentary or cartographic (or both). While it is likely that many of these were tower houses, in the absence of excavation there is no way of being certain. Based on extensive archival research and surveying in Co. Roscommon, Kieran O'Conor has concluded that 'many castles have been levelled in Roscommon since the late sixteenth century',[192] and that there are hints from fieldwork that the great majority of these castles were in fact tower houses. The same pattern is likely to apply to the Dublin region and, overall, emerging evidence suggests that the high estimate for the number of tower houses built in Ireland could be right.

Although there is considerable variation in plan and size, most of the surviving examples in the Dublin region are quite simple in plan, and many have one or more projecting angle towers and evidence for a vaulted ceiling to the ground floor. O'Keeffe has studied the

---

192 O'Conor, 'Castle studies in Ireland: the way forward', 329–31.

distribution of masonry castles in the Dublin region, and identified a particularly high density in the countryside around the bend of the Liffey in south-west Co. Dublin and north-east Co. Kildare.[193] Most of these structures are fifteenth-century tower houses. Many differ slightly from the norm in that they have a projecting turret – a feature that is rare in other parts of the country (with the exception of east Co. Down).[194] Tower houses in Louth, Meath and the Pale in general tend to have certain features that are generally absent from other parts of the country, and lack other characteristics that are present elsewhere.[195]

Tower houses were often built close to, or even on top of, existing mottes and baileys, and they can sometimes be taken as indicators of settlement continuity. At the appropriately named Stump of the Castle, in Co. Wicklow, traces survive of the tower

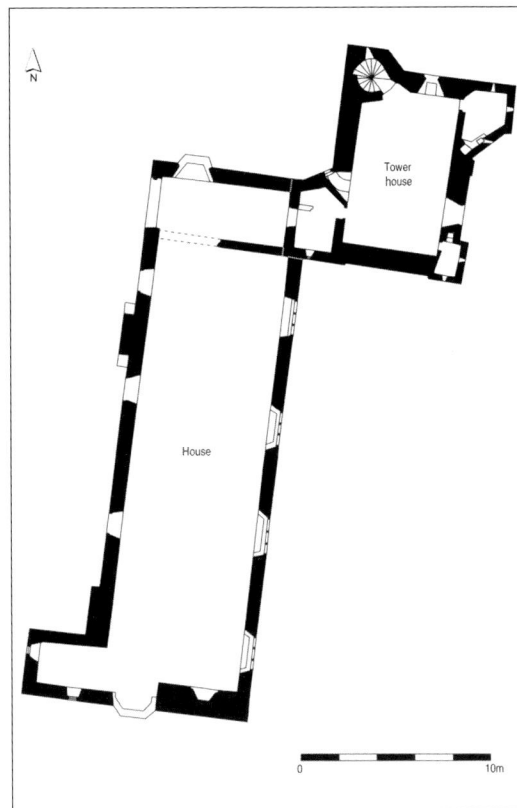

Figure 5.41 Plan of Athlumney Castle. Overlooking the Boyne and Blackwater Rivers, this two-part castle is less than 200m from a motte. Together, these represent three phases of lordly residence spanning over 400 years (after Sweetman, *Castles of Ireland*, p. 183, fig. 154).

house that was built within an earlier moated site.[196] At sites such as Athcarne (Figure 5.42), Athlumney (Figures 5.40, 5.41), Dardistown and Riverstown in Meath, continuity and expansion of tower houses in the late sixteenth and early seventeenth century are indicated by the addition of larger stone houses.[197]

Twenty tower houses are listed in the SMR for the Meath portion of the region, but upstanding examples (of at least one storey) survive at only fourteen of these sites.[198] Others are known from antiquarian accounts, drawings and even photographs. The tower house at Assey was illustrated by Francis Grose in 1791, but was demolished in the twentieth century.[199] Similarly, a description and illustration (by William Wakeman) of the tower house at Scurlockstown were published by William Wilde in 1849 (Figure 5.43), but a series of grass-covered mounds of stone are all that remain at the site now.[200] Wilde also mentioned a tower at Trubley, and part of this survived into the 1970s, when the last remaining walls blew down in a storm.[201] Skreen Castle is an eighteenth-century house that almost certainly incorporates a three-storey tower house.[202] The tower houses at Ballygarth, Dardistown and Odder are still inhabited.

In Kildare, all that remains above ground of the tower house at Confey is a small rectangular turret of un-coursed limestone blocks with wooden floors.[203] A series of

193 O'Keeffe, 'Medieval frontiers and fortifications', pp 68–70. **194** See also McNeill, *Castles in Ireland*, p. 213. **195** See, for example, McNeill, *Castles in Ireland*, pp 211–21, 222–3. **196** Grogan and Kilfeather, *Archaeological inventory of County Wicklow*, p. 191. **197** Moore, *Archaeological inventory of County Meath*, pp 166, 170, 175, 178, 179. **198** These are: Arodstown, Athcarne (Figure 5.42), Athlumney (Figures 5.40, 5.41), Ballygarth (Figure 5.44), Castletown Tara, Dardistown, Garadice, Monktown, Moygaddy, Moyglare (the SMR erroneously lists *two* tower houses for Moyglare at precisely the same location (292760E; 239870N), but with different monument numbers (ME049-023 and ME049A001)), Mulhussey, Odder, Riverstown and Salestown (Moore, *Archaeological inventory of County Meath*, pp 166–77). A 'tower house' at Crickstown is listed in the SMR (ME039-006), but it appears as a 'stone house' of possible seventeenth-century date in the *Archaeological inventory of County Meath* (p. 178). **199** Francis Grose, *The antiquities of Ireland* (2 vols, Dublin, 1791–5), 2, p. 17; Moore, *Archaeological inventory of County Meath*, p. 166. **200** Moore, *Archaeological inventory of County Meath*, p. 175; Wilde, *The beauties of the Boyne*, p. 104. **201** Moore, *Archaeological inventory of County Meath*, p. 175; Wilde, *The beauties of the Boyne*, p. 106. **202** Moore, *Archaeological inventory of County Meath*, p. 175. Mark Bence-Jones, *A guide to country houses, vol. 1: Ireland* (London, 1978), p. 260. The SMR erroneously lists *two* tower houses for Skreen at precisely the same location (295324E; 260176N), but with different monument numbers (ME032-035 and ME032-047002). **203** Tadhg O'Keeffe, 'The church and castle of

Figure 5.42 Athcarne
Castle, Co. Meath:
tower house and
attached house,
sketched before
further alterations
were made (image
reproduced courtesy
of the National
Library of Ireland).

earthworks are visible nearby. At least one half of it was still standing in the middle of the nineteenth century, when it was drawn by George du Noyer.[204] The castle clearly had a stone vault over the first floor, with four storeys above that, including the attic. It may have had four corner towers, like the tower house at Dunsoghly, and it certainly appears to have been similar to many other examples in the Pale.

The tower house at Donadea Demesne has undergone many phases of alteration and rebuilding and the present structure is a mixture of sixteenth- to nineteenth-century elements (Figure 5.45).[205] Barberstown Castle, which now functions as a hotel, incorporates a tower house of three floors over a basement. There are two projecting turrets, while the car park and yard probably mark the extent of the original bawn area. Some scattered pieces of masonry are all that survive of Richardstown Castle, a probable tower house that still stood to over sixty feet in height in the mid-nineteenth century.[206] Close to the site of a church, Sherlockstown House incorporates a tower house once held by the Dongan family.[207] The location and extent of the bawn that once adjoined the four-storey tower at Reeves can be identified on the basis of the layout of the surviving gateway and adjacent farm buildings and a series of crop-marks visible from the air.[208] Reeves Castle, which is similar to Athgoe and Kilteel, has a projecting stair turret, typical of towers in the Pale area. Newtown Castle, shown in a 1778 drawing by Austin Cooper and on Taylor's 1783 map of Kildare, was situated beside 'Temple Mills', but has subsequently been destroyed.[209]

In 1472, permission was sought for the erection of a £10 castle and bawn at 'Balablaght'.[210] This is probably the tower house illustrated at Boleybeg by Keenan and

Confey, Co. Kildare', *JCKAHS*, 16:5 (1985–6), 408–17.   **204** Conleth Manning, 'An illustration of Confey Castle, Co. Kildare', *JRSAI*, 131 (2001), 143–5.   **205** Seósamh Ó Muirthuile, 'Meascra de thaighdighthe maidir le dinnsheanchas Choill Chluana Gabhann agus na dúthaighe ina timcheall (Clongoweswood)', *JCKAHS*, 12:7 (1944–5), 375–95 at 382; R.A. Aylmer, 'Donadea Forest Park', *Oughterany*, 2:1 (1999), 41–55.   **206** DEHLG file KD014-012; Michael Herity (ed.), *Ordnance Survey letters: letters containing information relative to the antiquities of the county of Kildare collected during the progress of the Ordnance Survey in 1837, 1838 and 1839* (Dublin, 2002), p. 28.   **207** Walter FitzGerald, 'The Dongan family in the county of Kildare at the commencement of the seventeenth century', *JCKAHS*, 4:1 (1903), 67–70 at 68. **208** DEHLG file KD015-002. CUCAP BOC38–40.   **209** DEHLG file KD011-019; Walter FitzGerald, 'Historical notes on the O'Mores and their territory of Leix, to the end of the sixteenth century, with appendices', *JCKAHS*, 6:1 (1909), 1–88 at 20–1.   **210** Annaba Kilfeather, pers. comm.

Noble (1752), and Taylor (1783) and shown as ruinous on the 1837 Ordnance Survey map. There is some evidence that tower houses once stood at Castledillon, Castlesize, Flemingtown North, Hartwell Upper, Killashee, Mylerstown and Timahoe West.[211] A tower house at Barretstown (Figure 5.46), to the south of Naas, was modified and incorporated into a dwelling house in the nineteenth century. Sections of the west and south walls of a tower house survive at Barrettstown, to the north of Naas.

The tower house at Oughterard is a rectangular, four-floored limestone example, built on a ridge with good views of the Wicklow Mountains.[212] Part of the third floor was converted to accommodate a dovecot, but it is not clear when this took place. The manor of Oughterard passed through many hands in the fifteenth and sixteenth centuries and it is difficult to know who was responsible for the construction of the tower house there.

Within Co. Dublin, either complete tower houses or substantial remains are present at at least fourteen locations.[213] Entire tower houses or parts thereof, have been incorporated

Figure 5.43 Scurlockstown, Co. Meath. This drawing was made in c.1848 by William Wakeman. It depicts a tower house (now destroyed) with a round corner tower, comparable with extant examples at Causestown and Donore, Co. Meath, and typical of the tower house architecture of the Pale (image taken from William Wilde, *The beauties of the Boyne and its tributary, the Blackwater* (1849), p. 106).

Figure 5.44 Ballygarth Castle, Co. Meath, is a three-storey tower house attached to a later house with early nineteenth-century alterations (image courtesy of Jason Moore).

211 Ibid. **212** Bradley, Halpin and King, 'UAS 7:4: Kildare', pp 402–4. **213** Athgoe, Balrothery (the SMR erroneously lists *two* tower houses for Balrothery at precisely the same location (319920E; 261150N), but with different monument numbers (DU005-010 and DU005-057006)), Ballyman, Bullock (Figures 5.49, 13.2), Castlefarm, Castleknock, Dalkey, Donabate, Newcastle Lyons (Glebe), Newbridge Demesne, Portraine, Rathmichael, Robswalls

Figure 5.45 Donadea
Castle and demesne,
Co. Kildare, from the air.
Set among some of the
densest woodland in
the county, the multi-
phased crenellated
tower house can be
seen on the right,
overlooking the remains
of the medieval church
(middle of top half of
photograph) (©
Department of the
Environment, Heritage
and Local Government).

into later buildings at eight or more other places,[214] while five further examples survive as minor vestigial remains only.[215] There is evidence for the former existence of a tower house at at least twenty more locations where nothing now survives above ground.[216] Tragically, some of these have been demolished within the last fifty years or so (for example, Adamstown (1960s; Figures 5.47, 5.48), Cheeverstown (1980s), Saggart (1970s), Templeogue (1950s), Turvey (1980s), Tymon (1960s; Figures 5.50, 5.51)).

Compared to the neighbouring counties of Dublin, Kildare, Carlow and Wexford, Co. Wicklow is significantly underrepresented in terms of tower houses.[217] Wicklow is an anomaly in the distribution of many monument types in eastern Ireland, and much of the reason for this is the relatively inhospitable terrain of the Wicklow Mountains. The scarcity of tower houses in Wicklow may also reflect the disinterest shown by the Gaelic Irish of this

and Rush Demesne. The sixteenth-century tower house known as Grange Castle was sketched by Beranger in 1773 but is now in a poor state of repair (Harbison (ed.), *Beranger's drawings*, pp 168–9). **214** Finglas Wood (Ball, *A history of the county of Dublin*, 6, pp 89–91), Howth, Kilnamanagh, Laughanstown (Leo Swan, 'Lehaunstown Park, Co. Dublin: a forgotten tower house' in Manning (ed.), *Dublin and beyond the Pale* (1998), pp 163–8), Saggart, Seatown East, Shankill and Westown House (Knight of Glin, David Griffin and Nicholas Robinson, *Vanishing country houses of Ireland* (Dublin, 1988). **215** Cappoge (Harbison (ed.), *Beranger's drawings*, pp 68–9), Irishtown (Harbison (ed.), *Beranger's drawings*, pp 30–1), Murphystown, Naul and Stephenstown. **216** Adamstown (Dix, 'The lesser castles', 12; Ball, *A history of the county of Dublin*, 4, pp 58–60; Harbison, *Beranger's views of Ireland*, pp 20–1), Artane, Ballycorus, Ballyfermot Upper (Harbison (ed.), *Beranger's drawings*, pp 54–5), Belinstown (*Civil Survey*, 7, p. 104), Booterstown, Cheeverstown, Colmanstown (Paddy Healy, 'Report on monuments and sites of archaeological interest in County Dublin' (An Foras Forbartha, Conservation and Amenity Advisory Section, 1974), pp 23–4), Cornelscourt (D'Alton, *History of county Dublin*, p. 420; Austin Cooper in 1781 (Liam Price (ed.), *An eighteenth-century antiquary: the sketches, notes and diaries of Austin Cooper (1759–1830)* (Dublin, 1942)), Cornerpark (O'Keeffe, 'Medieval architecture and the village of Newcastle Lyons', p. 55, no. 6), Finglas (near St Canice's Church), Lucan, Meakstown (Melanie McQuade, 'Archaeological excavations on the site of Meakstown Castle, Finglas, Co. Dublin' in Duffy (ed.), *Medieval Dublin IX* (2009), pp 91–130), Merrion (associated with the Fitzwilliam family; Figure 5.53; Harbison (ed.), *Beranger's drawings*, pp 38–9), Mount Ashton (associated with the grange of St Mary's Abbey), Newcastle South (O'Keeffe, 'Medieval architecture and the village of Newcastle Lyons', 55, fig. 4.1:3), Saggart (*Civil Survey*, 7, p. 290), Templeogue, Turvey and Tymon North (Harbison (ed.), *Beranger's drawings*, pp 44–5; David Newman Johnson, 'Tymon: a lost Pale castle restored' in Mac Niocaill and Wallace (eds), *Keimelia* (1988), pp 557–72). The archiepiscopal palace at Tallaght included part of an earlier tower house, but nothing of this survives above ground (Harbison (ed.), *Beranger's drawings*, pp 28–9). **217** Sweetman, *The origin and development of the tower house*, p. 276.

Figure 5.46
Barrettstown,
Co. Kildare, from the air.
The tower house has
been incorporated into
a more extensive
complex of domestic
buildings and out-
houses that now form
part of a heavily
wooded demesne
(© Department of the
Environment, Heritage
and Local Government).

county in building castles of this type. Nonetheless, there are some important tower houses in Wicklow. The castle at Bray is shown as a tower house in the seventeenth century, while the three-storey example on a slope overlooking the River Liffey at Threecastles is probably the last remaining of the three that gave the townland its name (Figure 5.54).[218] Situated on naturally raised ground overlooking a stream at Oldcourt (Rathdown barony), there is a rectangular tower of un-coursed rubble with dressed granite and limestone quoins (Figure 5.55).[219] Sweetman has pointed out, however, that this tower was once attached to a late medieval hall and should not properly be described as a tower house.[220] The castle at Oldcourt (Talbotstown Lower barony), described in the Ordnance Survey letters for Co. Wicklow, but since destroyed, may have been a tower house.[221] Situated within a graveyard, the tower at Burgage (Figures 5.56, 5.57) was part of the medieval borough of Burgage More.[222] Although this structure is recorded as a tower house, it is in fact all that survives of a medieval church, being the remains of a west-end residential tower.[223] To facilitate the construction of the Poulaphouca Reservoir, the burials associated with the church were

218 Grogan and Kilfeather, *Archaeological inventory of County Wicklow*, p. 184; DEHLG file no. WI005-031. 219 Grogan and Kilfeather, *Archaeological inventory of County Wicklow*, pp 190–1. 220 Sweetman, *The origin and development of the tower house*, p. 267. 221 Grogan and Kilfeather, *Archaeological inventory of County Wicklow*, p. 189; Michael O'Flanagan (comp.), *Letters containing information relative to the antiquities of the county of Wicklow collected during the progress of the Ordnance Survey in 1838* (Bray, 1928), pp 28–9. 222 Grogan and Kilfeather, *Archaeological inventory of County Wicklow*, p. 187; Bradley and King, 'UAS 9: Wicklow', pp 21–2. 223 For example, Walter FitzGerald, 'Burgage churchyard', *JIMA*, 9 (1913–16), 395–7 at 395–6; Christiaan Corlett, *Beneath the Poulaphouca Reservoir: the 1939 Poulaphouca Survey of the lands flooded by the Liffey Reservoir Scheme* (Dublin, 2008), pp 285–300.

Figure 5.47 Adamstown Castle, Co. Dublin, was probably built by Thomas Adam (d. 1556) in the first half of the sixteenth century. It was still inhabited when this watercolour was drawn by Gabriel Beranger in 1775, but it was demolished in the 1960s. The thatched sheds beside the castle may have been part of the original complex of buildings within the bawn (image courtesy of the Royal Irish Academy, © RIA).

Figure 5.48 This is one of the last photographs taken of Adamstown Castle, Co. Dublin, before it was torn down. The scar on the wall probably marks the former position of the roof of one of the farm buildings shown in Beranger's eighteenth-century watercolour (Figure 5.47). (© Department of the Environment, Heritage and Local Government).

exhumed in 1939 and moved to a new site, along with several medieval grave-slabs and two high crosses. Much of the building that was left behind (the 'tower house') collapsed in the early 1990s (Figure 5.57), and this may be due in part to the proximity of the reservoir.

There is uncertainty about the dwelling places and fortifications of the Gaelic lords who came to control much of the Wicklow area in the later medieval period (see above, pp 102–3). Of course they opportunistically took over strongholds, such as Castlekevin, in the

Figure 5.49 1772 drawing by Gabriel Beranger of Bullock Castle, Co. Dublin (image reproduced courtesy of the National Library of Ireland).

lands that they conquered but there must have been residences that were constructed by the Irish themselves. There is some evidence that they were not all ephemeral, non-permanent structures. Froissart's Chronicle reports the capture of Henry Crystede by one Brin Costerec in the late fourteenth century.[224] Emmett O'Byrne identifies Costerec as 'probably an O'Byrne warlord'.[225] In Crystede's own words, he was taken 'to a very remote spot covered with thick bushes'. There, he found the residence of his captor, 'a fortified house and town surrounded by woods and stockades and stagnant waters'.

O'Byrne described the lands of the O'Byrnes of Glenmalure in the sixteenth century as 'a discontinuous territory, anchored by the chief residence of its lords at Ballinacor, lying at the mouth of Glenmalure, ranging from Glendalough southwards to Shillelagh and westwards into Carlow'.[226] A description of the taking of Ballinacor in the late sixteenth century implies that it was fortified – it was laid to siege but the O'Byrnes escaped out the back.[227] A lament poem written following the burning of Ballinacor in 1581 refers to this proud residence as a well-appointed mansion equipped with walls and ramparts as well as an ornamental lawn.[228]

Fortified houses

In the sixteenth and seventeenth centuries, a series of large, many-windowed, and gabled houses were built, which retained some defensive characteristics.[229] These are sometimes referred to as 'fortified houses', and O'Conor has estimated that as many as 200 or more may once have existed across the Irish countryside.[230] There was usually an oblong central

---

224 J.A. Buchon (ed.), *Collection des chroniques nationales françaises, vol. xiii: Chronique de Froissart* (Paris, 1825), p. 241. **225** O'Byrne, *War, politics and the Irish of Leinster*, p. 2. **226** Ibid., p. 170. **227** Ibid., p. 225. **228** Maginn, *'Civilizing' Gaelic Leinster*, pp 189–90; Harry Long, 'Three settlements of Gaelic Wicklow, 1169–1600: Rathgall, Ballinacor and Glendalough' in Hannigan and Nolan (eds), *Wicklow: history and society* (1994), pp 237–65. **229** See, for example, Sweetman, *Medieval castles of Ireland*, pp 175–98; O'Keeffe, *Medieval Ireland*, pp 55–7; Leask, *Irish castles*, pp 125–41; Hanneke Ronnes, *Architecture and elite culture in the United Provinces, England and Ireland, 1500–1700* (Amsterdam, 2006). **230** O'Conor, *Medieval rural settlement in Ireland*, p. 25.

Figure 5.50 This is one of few known photographs of Tymon Castle, Co. Dublin, of which no trace survives above ground. The castle was apparently already ruinous in 1547, but part of it was still inhabited in the 1770s and the remains visible in this photograph stood on a gravel hillock near Tallaght until they were finally pulled down in August 1960 (© Department of the Environment, Heritage and Local Government).

Figure 5.51 This drawing of Tymon Castle, Co. Dublin, was made by Gabriel Beranger in 1763. The tower house, which was attached to the prebend of St Patrick's Cathedral, was probably built in the fifteenth century, and it formed part of the southern defences of the Pale. In the seventeenth century, it was lived in by Nicolas Relly with a household including ploughmen, cowherds and gardeners (image reproduced courtesy of the National Library of Ireland).

building of three or more storeys, with a square tower at each angle. There was a symmetrical design that included gables at each end and some along the front and back. These were Renaissance-influenced manor houses incorporating a range of defensive features usually seen in tower-house architecture.

One of the first fortified houses in Ireland, Rathfarnham Castle was built by the Loftus family in the late sixteenth century, although it was substantially remodelled in the

Figure 5.52 Drawing by Gabriel Beranger of Simmonscourt Castle (1765). Only some small remains of this building survive close to the Victorian house now known as Simmonscourt Castle. The 'real' castle was probably built in the sixteenth century by either Christ Church Cathedral or the FitzWilliam family. It guarded the important Dodder crossing on the supply route from Dalkey to Dublin (image reproduced courtesy of the National Library of Ireland).

Figure 5.53 1772 drawing by Gabriel Beranger of Merrion Castle (image reproduced courtesy of the National Library of Ireland).

eighteenth century.[231] Drimnagh Castle was associated with the Barnewalls from the thirteenth century, but the present castle is a fortified house built considerably later (Figures 5.37, 5.38).[232] Unusually, the building is surrounded by a water-filled moat, fed by the Bluebell Stream, and it may have been built as a moated site. A fortified house in Dalkey,

---

231 Ball, *A history of the county of Dublin*, 2, pp 117–30; Harbison (ed.), *Beranger's drawings*, pp 184–5.   **232** Ball, 'Descriptive sketch of Clondalkin', 95–6; Ball, *A history of the county of Dublin*, 4, pp 125–32; Dix, 'The lesser castles',

Figure 5.54 (opposite) Threecastles Castle, Co. Wicklow, was probably one of the buildings that gave the townland its name. The other two castles are no longer extant (© Department of the Environment, Heritage and Local Government).

Figure 5.55 Oldcourt, Co. Wicklow. This was probably the service tower for a late medieval hall, now destroyed. Roof-scars are visible where the hall joined the tower.

known as Wolverston Castle, was demolished in the 1840s. A possible fortified house on Lambay parallels a type of plan, otherwise confined to Cos. Cork and Tipperary, in which there is a square tower at each angle.[233] In Co. Meath, a fortified house was attached to the tower house at Athlumney (in the late sixteenth century; Figures 5.40, 5.41).[234] Killincarrig Castle, Co. Wicklow, was built some time in the early seventeenth century for the Walsh family.[235] It had two storeys with an attic, a stair turret in the west wall, and an attached kitchen block to the north-east. Tall chimney stacks survive, but no cut stone remains.

The cultural geography of castles in the Dublin region in the later medieval period

Evidence as to who was responsible for the construction of individual castles in the Dublin region is patchy, and it is often difficult to trace the origin of local, or even widely known

49–50; Harbison (ed.), *Beranger's drawings*, pp 40–3. **233** Sweetman, *Medieval castles of Ireland*, p. 177. **234** Ibid., pp 183–4; Moore, *Archaeological inventory of County Meath*, p. 178. **235** Grogan and Kilfeather, *Archaeological inventory*

Figure 5.56 Burgage, Co. Wicklow, before the creation of the Poulaphouca Reservoir (© Department of the Environment, Heritage and Local Government).

or accepted associations. Nonetheless, it is possible in some cases to identify who is likely to have been behind the new building projects. In other instances, it is possible to determine who owned the castles at a slightly later date, even if he or she was not responsible for the original construction.

Situated on a natural rise at the foot of the Dublin Mountains, Balally Castle was built by William Walsh some time after 1407 when a grant from the crown conditioned that a castle be built on these lands.[236] Eight kilometres to the south-east, a tower house may have been built by a member of the Lawless family at Loughlinstown in 1408, but only parts of this castle survive. Parts of a tower house have been incorporated into a later building at Belgard, which was associated with the Talbot family in the fifteenth to seventeenth centuries. The Talbot family are also associated with Malahide Castle (Figure 5.59). The four-storey Dunsoghly Castle was built *c*.1450 by Thomas Plunkett, chief justice of the king's bench (Figure 5.58). This is a particularly fine example of a tower house and still has its original roof (Figures 11.5, 11.6). It is surrounded by a bawn and has an adjacent chapel.

At Fassaroe, in north Co. Wicklow, two walls, part of the barrel vaulting and some foundations survive of a granite tower built in 1535 by William Brabazon, treasurer of Ireland.[237] Hiram Morgan described Brabazon as a 'prototype New Englishman – a hard man with sticky fingers'.[238] He attacked the O'Mores and the O'Connors in 1546, and profited greatly through fraud after the Dissolution of the monasteries.

Ballyowen Castle, between Lucan and Clondalkin, may have been built by a certain Robert Taylor, who is known to have held the castle in 1558.[239] Cardiff (or Cardiff's) Castle was almost certainly built in the late sixteenth century by the Kerdiff family, close to the River Tolka in Finglas.[240] Beranger sketched the castle in 1773, but it has since been destroyed. Monkstown Castle was probably built by the Cistercian monks of St Mary's

of County Wicklow, p. 192.   **236** Ball, *A history of the county of Dublin*, 2, pp 73–4.   **237** Grogan and Kilfeather, *Archaeological inventory of County Wicklow*, p. 189; DEHLG file no. W1007-027.   **238** Hiram Morgan, 'Brabazon, Sir William' in Connolly (ed.), *The Oxford companion to Irish history* (1998), p. 56.   **239** Harbison (ed.), *Beranger's drawings*, pp 56–7.   **240** Ibid., pp 116–17.

Figure 5.57 Burgage, Co. Wicklow, today. A large part of the tower has collapsed since the first photograph (Figure 5.56) was taken (© Department of the Environment, Heritage and Local Government).

Abbey, Dublin.[241] It was given by Henry VIII to Sir John Travers in the 1540s. A second 'fortified dwelling' at Monkstown was drawn by Beranger in 1771, but there is no trace of this structure above ground today.[242] St Mary's was also the patron of Bullock Castle to the north of Dalkey (Figures 5.49, 13.2). There is some evidence that a tower house once stood at Knockrath Big, with commanding views over the Avonmore Valley, and a series of earthworks may well mark the site of this possible (sixteenth-/seventeenth-century?) O'Byrne residence.[243] Aodh Dubh O'Byrne was lord of Knockrath and constable of Arklow in the late sixteenth century.[244]

Tradition asserts there were once seven castles in Dalkey. Two of these fortified town houses survive: Goat's Castle, which now serves as the town hall, and which was probably built in the late fifteenth or early sixteenth century; and Archbold's Castle, just across the road. In the 1580s, and probably much earlier, Archbold's Castle appears to have been owned by Christ Church Cathedral.[245] The property boundary associated with Archbold's Castle survived until recent times, when it was redeveloped for a residential complex. Three other castles in Dalkey were owned by the archbishop of Dublin in the late sixteenth century.[246] It is not clear which ones these were, but one of them may have been the castle later known as Wolverston's. Another was perhaps Goat's Castle. A castle formerly located at the corner of

241 Ibid., pp 60–3.   242 Ibid., pp 98–9.   243 Grogan and Kilfeather, *Archaeological inventory of County Wicklow*, p. 189; Price, 'The Byrnes' country', 240–1.   244 O'Byrne, *War, politics and the Irish of Leinster*, pp 198, 210.   245 *CCCD*, p. 278. 246 M.C. Griffith, *Calendar of inquisitions formerly in the office of the chief remembrancer of the exchequer, prepared from*

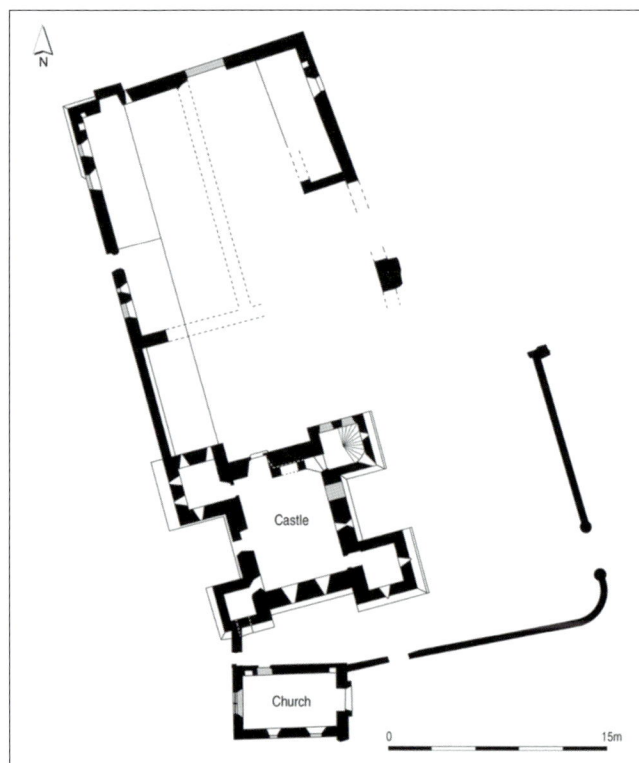

Figure 5.58 Dunsoghly Castle, Co. Dublin, was built in the middle of the fifteenth century by the Plunkett family. They also built a private chapel beside the castle (after Sweetman, *Castles of Ireland*, p. 138, fig. 112).

St Patrick's Road and Castle Street was owned by Richard Walsh in 1641,[247] and was later known as 'Castle House' after it was converted into a dwelling house by Robert Barry *c.*1765. Excavations on Castle Street and Dalkey Avenue in 2003 identified some of the foundations of another fortified house, and associated medieval artefacts included a bone spindle whorl, an iron knife, fragments of rotary querns, fragments of green glazed floor tiles and Leinster Cooking Ware.[248]

Dalkey's fortunes improved considerably in the fifteenth century when its port became one of the busiest on Ireland's eastern seaboard.[249] A similar pattern is observed at Ardglass, Co. Down, whose concentration of urban tower houses reflects the importance of maritime trade to the region. Families who were involved in trade through the busy harbour made large sums of money, and it is very likely that at least some of Dalkey's castles were erected by wealthy merchants. Combining residential and storage facilities, fortified houses were highly suitable for merchant families. Even if they were not built by them, some of the Dalkey castles were certainly leased by Dublin merchants in the sixteenth century. Christ Church rented its Dalkey castle to John Dungan, whose father appears to have been a fishmonger on Fishamble Street.[250] Two other castles were held by Henry Walsh of Killincarrig, Co. Wicklow, and later by his son Theobald.[251] Theobald may also have been responsible for the construction of the castle at Killincarrig itself, but his family had been active in Dalkey for generations. By the fifteenth century, the Walshes of Carrickmines and the Walshes of Killincarrig essentially controlled Dalkey. They were perceived by some as an unruly clan who had adopted Irish ways (indeed one of them, William Walsh, was also known as McHowell).[252] The Barnewalls, another local family of some standing, held a castle of the archbishop of Dublin in Dalkey in 1595.[253] This property seems to have passed to the Wolverstons in the following century and to have taken their name.

The present castle at Bremore, in the north of Co. Dublin, is mostly sixteenth century in date, but it may have replaced or incorporated (parts of) an earlier structure. Bremore is associated with the Russell family from the latter years of the thirteenth century, and they may have constructed or at least owned a castle there.[254] Bremore passed to the Barnewalls in the fourteenth century, possibly when Wolfran Barnewall married a daughter of Robert de Clahull.[255] It was the primary seat of the Bremore branch of the Barnewalls through the sixteenth century (the main branch being based at Drimnagh). Recent excavations confirmed that the land close to Bremore Castle was in agricultural use from at least the thirteenth or fourteenth century to the twentieth century.

the MSS of the Irish Record Commission (Dublin, 1991), pp 292, 299.   **247** M.R.L. Kelly, *Dalkey, Co. Dublin* (Ilfracombe, 1952), p. 15.   **248** John Kavanagh, '62 Castle Street, Dalkey' in *Excavations 2003*, pp 115–16.   **249** C.V. Smith, *Dalkey: society and economy in a small medieval Irish town* (Dublin, 1996), pp 45–53.   **250** Smith, *Dalkey: society and economy*, p. 32; Margaret Murphy, 'Historical report on Goat's Castle, Dalkey, Co. Dublin', unpublished report prepared for Dalkey Castle and Heritage Centre, Jan. 2008.   **251** Griffith, *Cal. inquisitions*, p. 292.   **252** Smith, *Dalkey: society and economy*, p. 33; Berry (ed.), *Statute rolls*, pp 461–2.   **253** Griffith, *Cal. inquisitions*, p. 299. **254** Finola O'Carroll, 'Bremore, Co. Dublin: the field by the castle' in Baker (ed.), *Axes, warriors and windmills* (2009), pp 75–87; Finola O'Carroll, 'A medieval and post-medieval farm landscape at Bremore, Co. Dublin' in Corlett and Potterton (eds), *Rural settlement in medieval Ireland* (2009), pp 157–70; *CGR*, p. 16.   **255** Ball, *A history of the county*

Figure 5.59 Malahide Castle, Co. Dublin, was built by the Talbot family. The present building incorporates several phases of construction (photograph by Martin Kuhn: www.flickr.com/photos/mkuhn/).

Like Dalkey, Newcastle Lyons has a tradition of seven castles and, as at Dalkey, only two of these survive.[256] These two fortified town houses – one on the road that leads to Athgoe, the other close to the church (Glebe townland) – belong to a standard architectural model that is adhered to by many tower houses in the Pale.[257] They have a simple rectangular plan, with projecting stair turrets and little architectural elaboration. The possible sites of four or five other castles can be tentatively identified at Newcastle, but it is impossible to be sure if these were among the village's seven reputed castles. In any case, the former presence of these buildings demonstrates the wealth and importance of Newcastle in the later medieval period. While it is not known who exactly built the castles, it must have been people with significant resources – probably wealthy townspeople and merchants. O'Keeffe has highlighted the possibility that 'the desertion and waste of other settlements and markets nearby enhanced Newcastle's commercial importance in Dublin's hinterland and facilitated mercantile settlement'.[258]

In Kildare, Celbridge Castle, which was first mentioned in 1403, was probably built by the earls of Kildare, but there is no sign of it now.[259] The small limestone tower house at Jigginstown, near Naas, was held by Roland FitzEustace in the 1480s and may have been built by a member of this family.[260] The castle that once stood at Coghlanstown and which

of Dublin, 4, p. 127.   256 The 'Book of Reference' to Down Survey maps 1655–6 records seven old castles in Newcastle townland: Civil Survey, 7, p. 291.   257 O'Keeffe, 'Medieval architecture and the village of Newcastle Lyons', p. 55.   258 Ibid., pp 53–6.   259 Bradley, Halpin and King, 'UAS 7:2: Kildare', p. 141; RPCH, p. 168, no. 23.   260 E.F. Tickell,

was mapped by Keenan and Noble (1752), and Taylor (1783), may also have been a tower house erected by the FitzEustace family in the fifteenth century or earlier.[261] At Blackhall, the roughly coursed limestone remains of a tower house can be seen incorporated into farm buildings, while faint traces of a possible bawn are also visible. The building is said to have been acquired by William Eustace in 1535.[262] The Eustaces were also probably responsible for building the now destroyed tower house at Confey, Co. Kildare.[263]

According to the Ordnance Survey letters, a stone castle once stood at Hortland, Co. Kildare, beside the motte and graveyard, but nothing remains of it now (Figure 5.60).[264] Hortland appears to have been held by the Flattisburys in the fourteenth century (and probably earlier),[265] and they may have been responsible for the masonry castle, if not the motte before it. Ten kilometres south of Hortland, the tower house at Blackwood was built by Pyers FitzGerald of Ballyshannon and Elinor his wife in 1584.[266]

Castles and landscapes of the elite

There has been an increasing interest in recent times in the role of medieval castles as part of elite, high-status landscapes, particularly in England.[267] There can be little doubt that castles served, above and beyond their practical residential and military functions, as symbols of status, wealth and power. The survival, scale and dominant position of castles – especially those of stone – makes them relatively easy to see, but it is much more of a challenge to visualise the carefully designed lordly landscapes that may once have surrounded them. Among the components of such landscapes were rabbit warrens, dovecots, deer parks, fishponds, artificial lakes, woodlands, gardens, orchards and viewing platforms.

While little scholarly attention has so far been paid to potential elite medieval landscapes in Ireland, a survey of the historical sources has led Kieran O'Conor to conclude that there are 'hints that designed landscapes occurred around castles in Ireland during the [high medieval] period, much like the situation in England'.[268] Some castles in Ireland were certainly the residences of very wealthy and powerful lords, many of whom also owned castles in England. There is evidence, in one form or another, for most of the individual components mentioned above, at various locations in Ireland – a dovecot in Tipperary, a late fishpond in Clare, a deer park in Carlow, and so on – but evidence for the combined package of ingredients that made up a 'landscape of lordship' remains elusive.[269]

To take one example, there is documentary evidence for parks in the Dublin region at Bray, Colonia, Finglas, Glencree, Kilmasantan, Lucan and Maynooth.[270] Place-name evidence indicates the former presence of parks at at least twenty-five locations across the region (Figure 11.1), and some of these are specifically related to deer. The site of Harristown Castle, Co. Kildare, for instance, is adjacent to an area called the 'Deer Park'.[271] The scientific analysis of excavated faunal remains from medieval contexts indicates that deer are more

'The Eustace family and their lands in County Kildare, Part III', *JCKAHS*, 13:8 (1960), 364–413 at 371. **261** Tickell, 'The Eustace family', 368. **262** DEHLG file KD024–011; Tickell, 'The Eustace family', 370. **263** Manning, 'An illustration of Confey Castle'. **264** Herity (ed.), *Ordnance Survey letters: Kildare*, p. 32; Des O'Leary, 'Hortland', *Oughterany*, 2:1 (1999), 56–69. **265** Otway-Ruthven, 'Knight's fees', 167. **266** DEHLG file KD013–016; Tickell says, however, that it was 'rebuilt' in 1584 ('The Eustace family', 371, fn 13). **267** David Austin, 'The castle and the landscape', *Landscape History*, 6 (1984), 70–81; O.H. Creighton, *Castles and landscapes: power, community and fortification in medieval England* (London and Oakville, CT, 2002); Robert Liddiard, *Landscapes of lordship: Norman castles and the countryside in medieval Norfolk, 1066–1200* (BAR 309, 2000); Robert Liddiard, *Castles in context: power, symbolism and landscape, 1066–1500* (Macclesfield, Cheshire, 2005); Robert Liddiard, 'Medieval designed landscapes: problems and possibilities' in Gardiner and Rippon (eds), *Medieval landscapes* (2007), pp 201–14. **268** O'Conor, 'Gaelic lordly settlement', p. 213. See also Tadhg O'Keeffe, 'Were there designed landscapes in medieval Ireland?', *Landscapes*, 5:2 (2004), 52–68. **269** Margaret Murphy and Kieran O'Conor, 'Castles and deer parks in Anglo-Norman Ireland', *Eolas*, 1 (2006), 53–70. **270** Ibid., 66–70. **271** Bradley, Halpin and King, 'UAS 7:2: Kildare', pp 189–95.

Figure 5.60 The motte at Hortland, Co. Kildare, is just 50m from the site of a church. There is now no trace above ground of either the church or the stone castle that is recorded at this site.

common at high-status sites, especially castles.[272] It is likely that at least some of these deer came from parks managed by the castle authorities. Excavations at the FitzGerald castle at Maynooth, Co. Kildare, uncovered the remains of fallow deer that may have come from the park mentioned there in 1328.[273]

Looking for and at the individual components of lordly landscapes is one thing; it is entirely another to investigate the existence and form of such landscapes in a holistic way. Future work in Ireland might follow some of the approaches outlined recently by Robert Liddiard.[274] Indeed, in remarking on the potential for the study of designed landscapes to give broader insights into social history, Liddiard notes that 'perhaps the most relevant example is that of Ireland'.[275]

Chapter summary

The Dublin hinterland was one of the most encastellated regions in medieval Ireland, containing some of the largest earthwork fortifications and the widest range of types of stone castles in the country. Castles were built from the late twelfth century right up to the seventeenth century. The motivation for castle-building was a combination of needs (defence, accommodation, facilities) and desires (comfort, ostentation, aesthetics). The weighting of these criteria varied greatly, however, both chronologically and spatially.

With regard to earthwork castles, it is clear that mottes were preferred to ringworks and over sixty were built across the region. They included some of the largest mottes in Europe, which is hardly surprising, as their builders were some of the wealthiest landowners in Ireland. Smaller mottes were associated with the tenants-in-chiefs of these lords and in the Dublin region it appears that castles of this type continued to be constructed through the

272 See, for example, Fiona Beglane, 'Meat and craft in medieval and post-medieval Trim' in Potterton and Seaver (eds), *Uncovering medieval Trim* (2009), pp 346–70.   273 Hayden, 'Maynooth Castle, Maynooth'; Hayden, 'Maynooth Castle', DEHLG file 96E0391; Murphy and O'Conor, 'Castles and deer parks in Anglo-Norman Ireland', 70.   274 Liddiard, 'Medieval designed landscapes: problems and possibilities'.   275 Ibid., p. 204.

thirteenth and into the fourteenth century. The earliest mottes were frequently sited at locations that were already centres of settlement, religious worship and commerce and that went on to become important boroughs, while later, often smaller, mottes were built to protect and provide prestigious residences for lesser manorial farmsteads. While mottes were built by individual lords, their distribution pattern on a regional level shows them combining to form a protective cordon around Dublin and points to the existence of a centralised policy of fortification, at least in the early decades of Anglo-Norman control. There were very few mottes within 10km of the city, and the royal anxiety about Castleknock indicates that castles in lay control close to the city were seen as a distinct threat.

The density of settlement and the differing levels of lordship may also partly account for the wide variety of types of stone castle built in the region. The earliest stone castles were built by the crown, the archbishop and wealthy lordly families. They included the innovatively designed Dublin Castle and the lightly fortified Swords Castle. More traditional castles with central keeps and strong curtain walls were also built, but were later superseded by structures in which the main components of the castle were incorporated into the surrounding walls, and especially the main entrance area. There are a couple of examples of hall-houses and polygonal enclosure castles, but many more may have been incorporated into the tower houses that were built in great numbers in the fourteenth and especially the fifteenth century. These new castles were multi-functional and served as rural fortifications, administrative centres for farm estates, and warehouses for wealthy merchants. Over a hundred were built in the Dublin region, many of them with the financial encouragement of the Dublin-based administration. The incentive was to protect the core area of Dublin as well as the peripheral settlements which were so necessary to the economic and political well-being of the entire region. In time, the distribution of these tower houses came to define the area known as the English Pale (see below).

The Dublin region was in the vanguard of castle-building trends in Ireland from the late twelfth to the late sixteenth century, when one of Ireland's first fortified houses was built at Rathfarnham. New ideas diffused out from the city to the hinterland just as the new rich moved from urban streets to country estates. The region was not characterised by a bland uniformity, however, and castle form and function varied just as much as the ownership patterns discussed in the previous chapter.

CHAPTER 6

Manor centres, tenants and rural settlement

Once the region had been secured by the castles of the early conquerors, the process of colonisation and rural settlement got underway. The conversion of castle territories into profitable agricultural units was extremely rapid in the Dublin region. This can be partly explained by the high level of agrarian exploitation that was already present in much of the area. Furthermore, Dublin would have acted as a staging post for the peasant migrants who started to flood into Ireland from Wales and south-west England. These people dispersed outwards from the city, looking for lands to hold and lords to protect them. Within a remarkably short space of time, the Dublin region was full of manors, the Anglo-Normans' favourite tool of settlement and colonisation.

Manor centres

The manorial centres that developed within the region were of different types. Firstly, there were the principal centres that developed from the original key strong-points of colonisation. Stone and sometimes earthwork castles are frequently found at these locations, and their lords were the king, the archbishop of Dublin and top-ranking lay magnates. Secondly, smaller or secondary manorial centres grew out of the process of subinfeudation. They are generally characterised by earthwork castles and their lords were the principal tenants-in-chief of the major magnates. Finally, ecclesiastical manors or out-farms, usually known as granges, developed on the dispersed holdings of religious houses.[1]

The main components of manorial centres were the residence of the lord with associated agricultural buildings and adjacent features, such as mills, bake-houses, barns, granaries, livestock houses, dovecots and warrens, which are sometimes labelled 'seigneurial monopolies', as they represented attempts by lords to control production (Table 6.1).[2] The manorial centre, of whatever type, was generally situated close to the parish church, and Simms and Fagan have found that in Co. Dublin forty-five of sixty identified medieval manors were located at parish centres.[3] A degree of nucleation has also been recognised, ranging from a collection of cottars' cottages to the fully-fledged borough with its burgesses.

There is a great deal of both documentary and archaeological material relating to the appearance and layout of manorial complexes in England and Wales;[4] much less is known

---

1 For a discussion of granges, see below, pp 257–63.   2 See O'Conor, *Medieval rural settlement in Ireland*, pp 26–35; Mark Hennessy, 'Manorial agriculture and settlement in early fourteenth-century Co. Tipperary' in Clarke, Prunty and Hennessy (eds), *Surveying Ireland's past* (2004), pp 99–118.   3 Simms and Fagan, 'Villages in Co. Dublin', p. 93.   4 See, for example, Higham and Barker, *Timber castles*; J.G. Hurst and L.A.S. Butler, 'Rural building in England and Wales' in Hallam (ed.), *The agrarian history of England and Wales, vol. 2* (1988), pp 854–965. See also Colin Platt, *The monastic grange in medieval England* (London, 1969); James Bond, *Monastic landscapes* (Stroud, Gloucestershire, 2004);

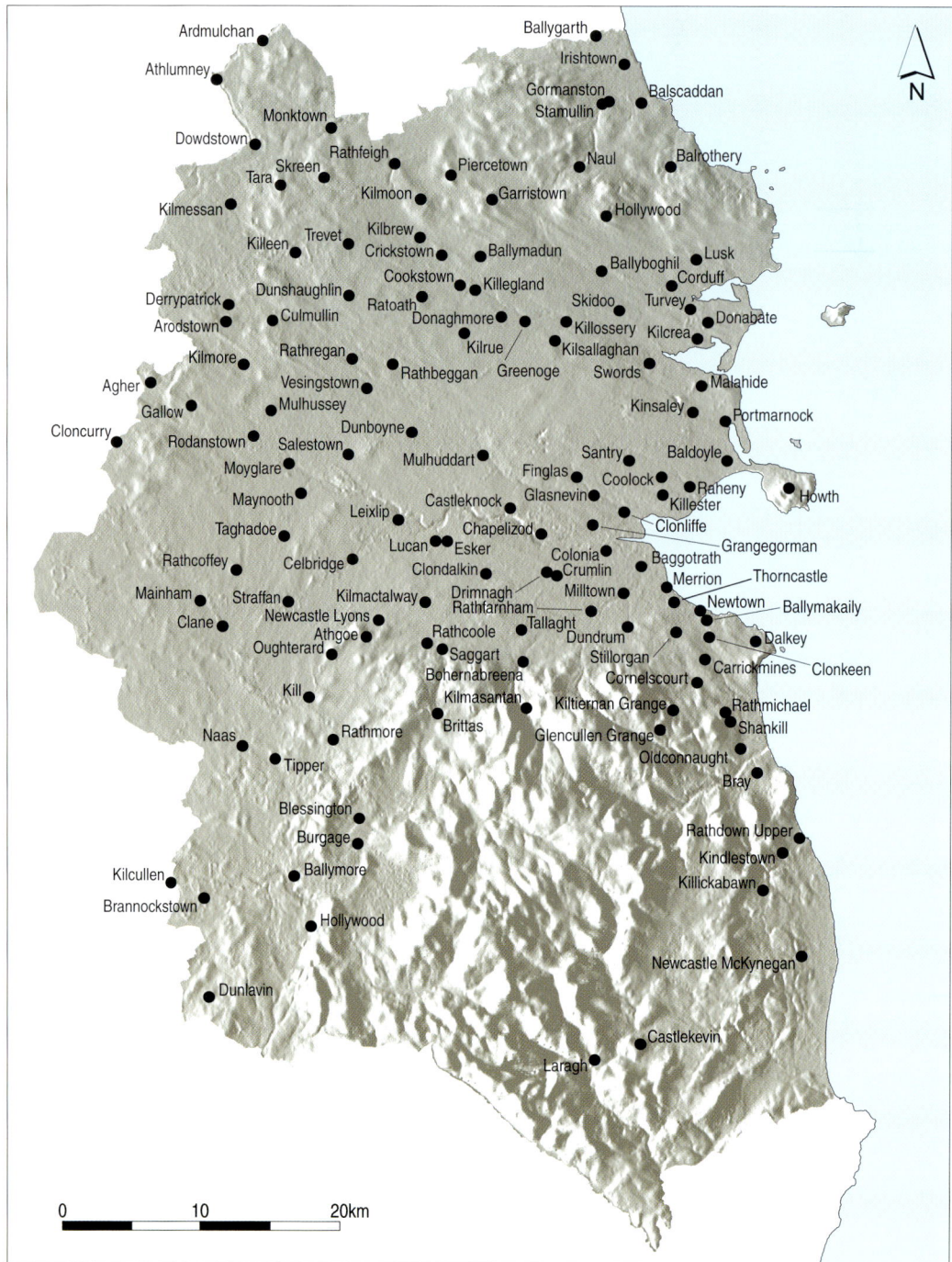

Figure 6.1 Distribution of principal medieval manor centres in the Dublin region.

about such centres in Ireland. From an archaeological perspective, Sweetman stated that the association between earthwork castles and ecclesiastical remains was not as pronounced in Ireland as it is in England and Wales, and he signalled the importance of historical records in simply identifying earthwork castles within a manor.[5] Even with regard to the larger masonry fortifications, there has been virtually no work on the nature and layout of the buildings close to or within the castle complexes, while O'Conor has shown that 'the archaeological evidence for most castles functioning as the centres of demesne farms on manors or as the agricultural cores of later freehold estates is minimal'.[6] In the small number of masonry castles that have been excavated, the courtyard areas, where it is likely that the wooden and clay-walled farm buildings were located, have been largely ignored. There has

Michael Aston, *Monasteries in the landscape* (Stroud, Gloucestershire, 2000). **5** Sweetman, *Medieval castles of Ireland*, p. 13. **6** O'Conor, *Medieval rural settlement in Ireland*, p. 28.

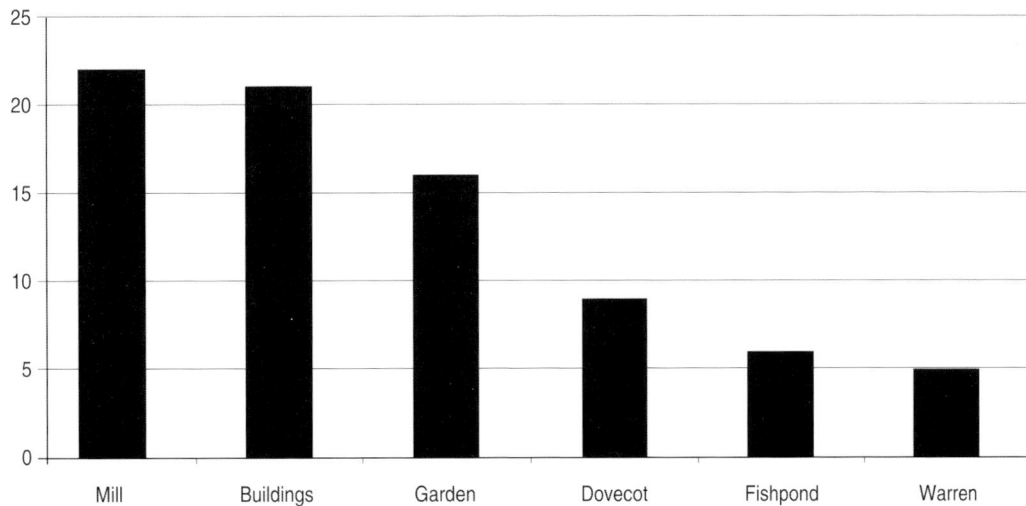

Figure 6.2 Dublin region extents, 1250–1358. This chart plots the number of surviving extents which record the existence of manorial buildings and associated structures.

been even less exploration of mottes, and virtually no excavation of baileys.[7] It is only in the last decade or so that this pattern is changing, and excavation has occurred on off-mound habitation beside free-standing mottes.[8] Some excavation of ringwork castles has taken place, although much of this remains to be published.[9] In addition, the publication of the large-scale excavation at Carrickmines, Co. Dublin, a medieval manor and castle site on the frontier of the Pale, will be an important contribution to the study of manor centres.[10]

In the case of religious houses, most research and excavation has concentrated on the visible architectural remains of churches and claustral buildings. There have been few explorations of the granges or out-farms of Cistercian and Augustinian houses (see below), although such research has been identified as a priority for future work on medieval rural settlement in Ireland.[11]

A partial picture of some of the manorial centres in the Dublin region can be reconstructed from the evidence of extents, a significant number of which include mention of manorial buildings and associated structures and monopolies.[12] An analysis of the information on resources contained in the sample of extents collected for the region shows that mills are most frequently included, with buildings and gardens also appearing in nearly half of the extents (Figures 6.2, 6.3). The occurrence of dovecots, fishponds and warrens also indicates that many of the manors in the Dublin region possessed these additional resources,

7 Barry, *The archaeology of medieval Ireland*, pp 37–40. Excavation in proximity to mottes has taken place at a number of locations. 8 For examples, see Duffy, 'Moat Commons, Clane'; Donal Fallon, 'Ladycastle Lower' in *Excavations 2003*, pp 247, 247–8, 248; Donal Fallon, 'Summary report on excavation (licence 02E1781) at Ladycastle Lower, Co. Kildare' (unpublished report, 2005); Donal Fallon, 'Summary report on excavation (licence 02E1782) at Ladycastle Lower, Co. Kildare' (unpublished report, 2005); Donal Fallon, 'Summary report on excavation (licence 03E0043) at Ladycastle Lower, Co. Kildare' (unpublished report, 2005); Robert O'Hara, 'Drumcondrath' in *Excavations 2003*, p. 369; Kieran Campbell, 'Castleknock' in *Excavations 2004*, p. 102; T.C. Breen, 'Site 3, Laracor' in *Excavations 2004*, pp 324–5; Cotter, 'Dunboyne Castle, Castlefarm'; Fiona Rooney, 'Newtown' in *Excavations 2001*, p. 136; Martin Fitzpatrick, 'Newtown' in *Excavations 2002*, p. 179; Goorik Dehaene, 'Medieval rural settlement beside Duncormick motte, Co. Wexford' in Corlett and Potterton (eds), *Rural settlement in medieval Ireland* (2009), pp 59–66. 9 Sweetman, *Medieval castles of Ireland*, pp 4–6; Sweetman, 'Archaeological excavations at Ferns Castle'; O'Conor, 'The origins of Carlow Castle'. 10 An initial programme of investigation was conducted by Niall Brady, 'Archaeological investigations, Carrickmines Great, South-Eastern Motorway, Co. Dublin. 004E0045', Valerie J. Keeley Ltd, Nov. 2000. The main excavations were conducted by Mark Clinton for Valerie J. Keeley Ltd, between 2000 and 2002 and are reported on by him in 'Carrickmines Castle, Carrickmines' in *Excavations 2000*, p. 72; 'Carrickmines Great' in *Excavations 2001*, pp 85–7; 'Carrickmines Castle, Carrickmines' in *Excavations 2002*, p. 131. Further work to complete elements of the main road project were conducted by Gary Conboy; see also Emmett O'Byrne, 'The Walshes and the massacre at Carrickmines', *AI*, 17:3 (autumn 2003), 8–11. 11 O'Conor, *Medieval rural settlement in Ireland*, p. 142. A doctoral thesis that is looking at the development of Augustinian estates in Ossory, and in particular at granges and rectories, has recently been begun at the National University of Ireland, Galway: Arnaud de Volder, pers. comm. 12 For documentary references to individual extents, see the list in Appendix 1, below.

whose primary function was to provide luxury items for lordly tables, but which also served to display the power and privilege of the manorial lord.[13]

The absence from certain extents of information relating to buildings and structures does not necessarily mean that such structures were not present. On occasion, it might just indicate that the jurors did not consider them worth mentioning as their contribution to manorial revenues was negligible. There are examples where the values of certain structures was said to be nothing because of their condition, and on occasion this description was applied to the whole manorial complex. The 1326 extent for Shankill, for instance, which had been one of most important of the archiepiscopal manors and a principal residence for the archbishop, commences: 'there are no buildings at Shankill; once there were but they are now burned and thrown down by Irish felons'.[14]

Many of the extents enumerate a series of farm buildings that lay beside, or close to, the seigneurial residence. Granges, barns and granaries are mentioned relatively often. At Cloncurry there was a small house for keeping threshed grain as there was 'neither barn nor granary' (see below). The two small cruck-built granges on this manor presumably served some other function. At Ballymore there was a thatched grange and a granary, while at Colonia there were a grange and a granary roofed with boards. In other instances only a grange or a granary is mentioned, as at Swords, where there was a cruck-built thatched grange and a granary roofed with boards. Only a grange is mentioned at Maynooth, while Castlewarden's sole agricultural building was a granary.

Ox-houses were described on the manors of Ballymadun, Cloncurry, Dunshaughlin, Maynooth and Swords. At Maynooth, the building was called 'the great ox-house', which suggests the possible presence of a smaller version as well. The ox-house at Swords appears to have been used to accommodate horses also, although there was a stable within the complex too. Perhaps the working horses, known as affers, were accommodated with the oxen, while the stable was restricted to riding horses. Stables are also mentioned at Ballymore, Clondalkin – 'a stone stable' – Colonia, Dunshaughlin and Santry, while excavation at Scurlockstown, Co. Meath, identified a stone building that is most probably a stable.[15] Specialised shelters for other animals (apart from dovecots, warrens and hen-houses) rarely appear in the documents. The documentary evidence does not suggest that the sty-rearing of pigs was a widespread practice. More surprising is the lack of documentary evidence for sheepfolds or cots. They are mentioned in some late medieval leases, and in 1560, for example, a lease of the manor of Grangegorman refers to the 'farm, barn, kiln, sheepfold and cow-house'.[16] Other buildings mentioned in the extents include a dairy (Swords), a workshop (*carpentaria*; Swords), bake-houses (Swords and Maynooth) and kilns (Ballymadun and Dunshaughlin; both thatched).

The extents rarely assign a monetary value to these agricultural buildings, usually stating that they are worth nothing beyond the cost of repair. This indicates that in the case of a manor being leased out, the lessee would pay no rent for the buildings but would be expected to fund their maintenance and repair. A document of 1302–3 relating to the manor of Santry does assign values to certain manorial buildings as compensation was being sought for their destruction.[17] The hall, which was built of timber, was valued at £20 and another chamber was given the same value. Two stables, a granary and a bake-house were each said to be worth ten marks (£6 6s. 8d.), and a third chamber was valued at twenty marks (£13 3s. 4d.). These are high values, possibly artificially high as a result of the circumstances of the case.

13 Murphy and O'Conor, 'Castles and deer parks in Anglo-Norman Ireland', 54–8.　　**14** McNeill (ed.), *Alen's register*, p. 194.　**15** Alan Hayden, 'Scurlockstown' in *Excavations 2003*, pp 390–1, described below, pp 174–5.　**16** *CCD*, no. 1268–9.　**17** *CDI, 1302–7*, no. 255, pp 86–7.

Table 6.1 Manorial components for selected manors in the Dublin region.

MANOR	RESIDENCE/DOMESTIC BUILDINGS	FARM BUILDINGS	SEIGNEURIAL MONOPOLIES	NUCLEATION
Ballymore	Castle complex – hall, 3 chambers, chapel, kitchen (shingled)	Grange (thatched), granary, dovecot	2 watermills Market Oven	Borough (160 burgages – 22 cottages)
Castlewarden/ Oughterard	Houses Garden	Granary	Mill	Borough (58 burgesses)
Cloncurry	Courtyard, close with hall (thatched), *mota* with chamber (roofed with boards) Garden	Old haggard close with 2 small granges each of 8 forks, kiln, small house for keeping threshed grain, ox-house Dovecot	Mill (leased)	Borough (burgesses hold 2 carucates for 112s. per annum)
Clondalkin	Chamber, chapel (shingled) 2 small houses (thatched) Garden Orchard	Stone stable Dovecot	Mill	Borough (33 burgages) 444 acres
Colonia	Stone hall (shingled), chamber with chapel adjoining, kitchen built of timber, garden	Grange, stable and granary roofed with boards	2 mills Fishery	
Leixlip	Stone castle with large tower and 3 smaller towers Garden		Mill Fishery	Borough (54 burgesses each holding a 3-acre burgage for which they render 54s. and 5 geese), 39 'frontes held for 6d. and one one 'placea' for 1lb of pepper/12d.
Lucan	Messuage Garden	2 dovecots	Fishpond Warren	120 acres in 'burgager'
Swords	Hall, stone chamber roofed with shingles Kitchen with larder whose walls are stone and roof of shingle and bake-house. Chapel with stone walls and shingle roof, chamber for friars with cloister. Near the gate a chamber for the constable and 4 chambers for knights and squires roofed with shingles	Dairy and workshop Grange of forks (thatched) Timber granary roofed with 'bords', cow house Dovecot	3 watermills Warren	122 burgages by the law of Breteuil along with 16 free cottages, 16 'burgag fornic' which render 22s. 8d. Burgagers of Lusk hold 36 burgages for 37s.
Maynooth	Stone castle Kitchen partly stone-built Hall (thatched) and chamber (shingled) Bake-house Garden	Grange 'Great' ox-house Stable	Mill	
Shankill	Buildings Garden		Mill Warren	Burgagers at Shankill holding 17 burgages for 17s. 1½d. Burgagers at Dalkey holding 39 burgages for 76s. 3d. 18½ burgages at Kilmacberne – 18s. 6d.

Figure 6.3 Agher, Co. Meath. The present church is in the south-west quadrant of the oval area delimited by hedgerows. Between the church and the Rye Water, which runs south-west/north-east, are the remains of at least six houses, a hollow way, an enclosure and a possible windmill (© Ordnance Survey Ireland).

Although not one motte in the Dublin region has been excavated, field-walking, aerial photography and some small-scale archaeological investigation have identified a range of features associated with earth-and-timber castles. Combined with what can be extracted from the documentary sources, there is evidence for the residential, agricultural and industrial functions of manorial centres across the region. The motte and bailey at Agher, Co. Meath, for instance, are adjacent to a deserted settlement comprising at least six house platforms, a 3m-wide hollow way leading to a banked enclosure, and the remains of a possible windmill mound (Figure 6.3).[18] The whole complex, which also includes a series of field boundaries and is next to a church, is set on well-drained, productive soils along the banks of the Rye Water. At Scurlockstown, the motte overlooking the River Boyne is also next to a medieval church and graveyard. A series of medieval gullies were identified on the productive land close to the site during archaeological excavations in 2001, and these may well be related to agriculture associated with the nearby motte.[19] Further investigation on the site revealed a sequence of settlement features that, based on pottery finds, suggest a date in the twelfth–thirteenth centuries, on which was built a stone stable (referred to as a barn by the excavator).[20] The stable measured 7m wide by 13m long, and had a wide centrally placed doorway on one long wall, while three stalls occupied one half of the building. The

18 Moore, *Archaeological inventory of County Meath*, pp 120, 127, 156, 164. **19** Alan Hayden, 'Scurlockstown' in *Excavations 2001*, p. 334. **20** Hayden, 'Scurlockstown' in *Excavations 2003*.

structure is broadly dated to the twelfth–fifteenth centuries, and a series of pit and gully features lay around the building while the burned remains of a smaller stone-footed timber building lay to the south. The motte built at Derrypatrick (Co. Meath) in the early 1170s was close to the Derrypatrick River and adjacent to a church. The motte was replaced by a stone fortification that is now situated within a *c.*6-acre field system, with two associated sunken roadways and a possible windmill mound.[21] Similar features are known close to ringworks, such as at Rathregan (Co. Meath), where the possible ringwork lies within a kilometre of the remains of a deserted medieval settlement including rectangular enclosures, house sites and a sunken roadway.[22]

In Co. Kildare, the physical evidence for features close to the motte at Cloncurry is greatly supplemented by the documentary sources. By 1297, Cloncurry had become the caput of the large Butler manor, and the 1304 extent refers to a number of elements within the complex:[23]

> *Jurati dicunt per sacramentum suum quod est apud Cloncorry una curia debiliter clausa in qua est quedam aula stramine cooperta cuius una pars est ruinosa et una parva domus debilis et una mota in qua una camera bordis cooperta sita est quas non extendunt eo quod nemo est qui illas voluit locare. Set gardinum quod est ibidem valet per ann. viiis. Est etiam ibidem quoddam hagardum debiliter clausum in quo sunt ii grangie parve quelibet de viii furcis. Et unum torellum male coopertum et una parva domus ad bladum trituratum imponendum quia non ibidem horreum vel granarium. Et est ibidem iuxta portam una boveria. Et valet hagardum cum domibus predictis ad locandum per ann. iis. Et est ibidem unum columbare quod extenditur per annum ad iiis.*

The jurors say under oath that there is at Cloncurry a courtyard [with] an old close in which there is a hall roofed with straw of which one part is ruinous and there is one small house which is old and a motte in which there is a chamber roofed with boards which is not extended because no-one wishes to lease it. But the garden which is there is worth 8*s.* per annum. There is also an old haggard close in which there are two small granges each of eight forks. And a kiln badly roofed and a small house for keeping threshed grain as there is neither barn nor granary. There is also there, beside the gate, an ox-house. And the haggard with the aforesaid buildings is worth for leasing 2*s.* There is a dovecot worth 3*s.* per annum.

The description suggests the presence of a thatched hall with a small house and a motte with a small building, all within a courtyard area. The garden appears to have been within or adjacent to this area. There was also a separate haggard or farmyard accessed through a gate in which were found the two granges, the grain store, the ox-house and the kiln. The location of the dovecot is not specified but it may have been in the garden. The manorial complex at Cloncurry therefore comprised two enclosed spaces, one of which accommodated the residential buildings, and the other the farm buildings.

Little trace of the manorial centre survives at Cloncurry, apart from the ruins of the parish church and the motte, which are located in close proximity to each other and occupy the north-west quadrant of a crossroads (Figure 6.5).[24] A curving boundary wall around part of the church site encloses the graveyard, while a patchwork of settlement has developed

21 Moore, *Archaeological inventory of County Meath*, pp 122, 170.   **22** Ibid., p. 164; Rice, *Norman Kilcloon*, p. xi. **23** *RBO*, p. 27; Holton, 'Medieval Cloncurry', 80.   **24** Bradley, Halpin and King, 'UAS 7:2: Kildare', pp 167–79; O'Conor, *Medieval rural settlement in Ireland*, p. 30, fig. 9. We are grateful to Niall Brady for discussion relating to the

Figure 6.4 A conjectural
reconstruction of the
medieval manor of
Cloncurry, Co. Kildare,
based on the extent of
1304. While much of
this is fanciful, it
provides an interesting
visual interpretation of
the written record.
(1) hall; (2) moat with
watch-house; (3) cow-
byre; (4) dovecot
(source O'Loan, 'The
manor of Cloncurry').

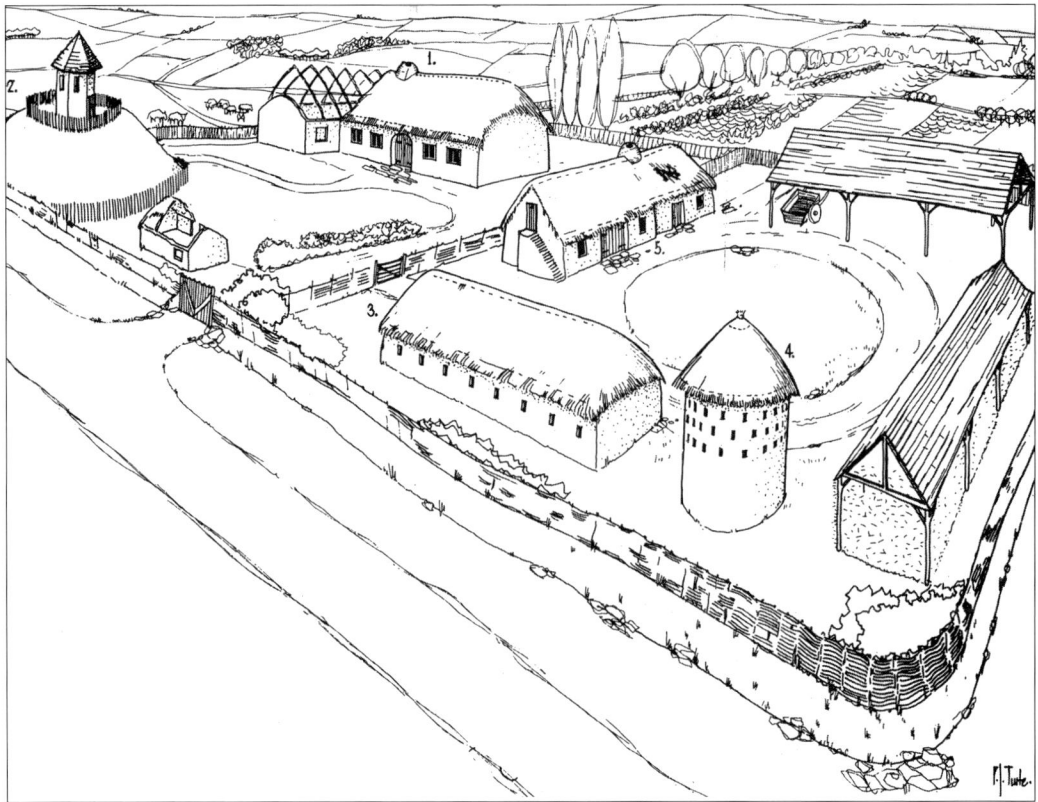

along the roadway to the south of the graveyard. There is no formal indication of burgage property boundaries arising from the settlement sites. In a field to the south of the crossroads, however, are the remains of a hollow way and the base of a cross. Bradley, Halpin and King pointed out the likelihood that these are the remains of the medieval main street and the market cross.[25] At certain times of the year, the growth pattern of nettles and other weeds in the fields at Cloncurry indicates the possible location of house-plots and perhaps even some of the buildings mentioned in the 1304 extent.

Excavations in association with the construction of a house at Cloncurry in 1995 unearthed little of archaeological significance, but investigations nearby in 2001 revealed a possible medieval field ditch and a sherd of 'late medieval pottery'.[26] A further thirty sherds of medieval pottery were recovered later in the same year, some of which were associated with the foundations of a stone building of unknown function.[27] Other features of medieval date included a hearth, a pit, possible boundaries and some burnt structures.

A further insight into the make-up of a medieval manor centre in the Dublin region can be gleaned from the combined archaeological and historical evidence for the caput of the FitzGerald manor of Rathmore (Figure 5.14).[28] The location of the deserted borough is indicated by some low banks in the surrounding fields, while excavations in the vicinity of the motte in 1998 uncovered a number of medieval refuse pits, some Leinster Cooking Ware and sherds of local pottery of probable thirteenth-/fourteenth-century date.[29] While little can be inferred from the physical remains, the documentary sources provide some details about the form and function of the manorial centre. Ownership of the manor was in dispute in the late thirteenth century and an incident there was the subject of a case heard by the justiciar's court in 1305.[30] Agnes de Valence complained that she had been attacked at

archaeology at Cloncurry. **25** Bradley, Halpin and King, 'UAS 7:2: Kildare', pp 169, 176. **26** Deirdre Murphy, 'Cloncurry' in *Excavations 1995*, p. 45; Finola O'Carroll, 'Ballyvoneen' in *Excavations 2001*, pp 175–6. **27** Hilary Opie, 'Cloncurry' in *Excavations 2001*, pp 181–2. **28** Bradley, Halpin and King, 'UAS 7:4: Kildare', pp 422–35, esp. p. 433. **29** Emmet Byrnes, 'Rathmore West' in *Excavations 1998*, p. 113. **30** *CJR, 1305–7*, pp 75–8, 240–1.

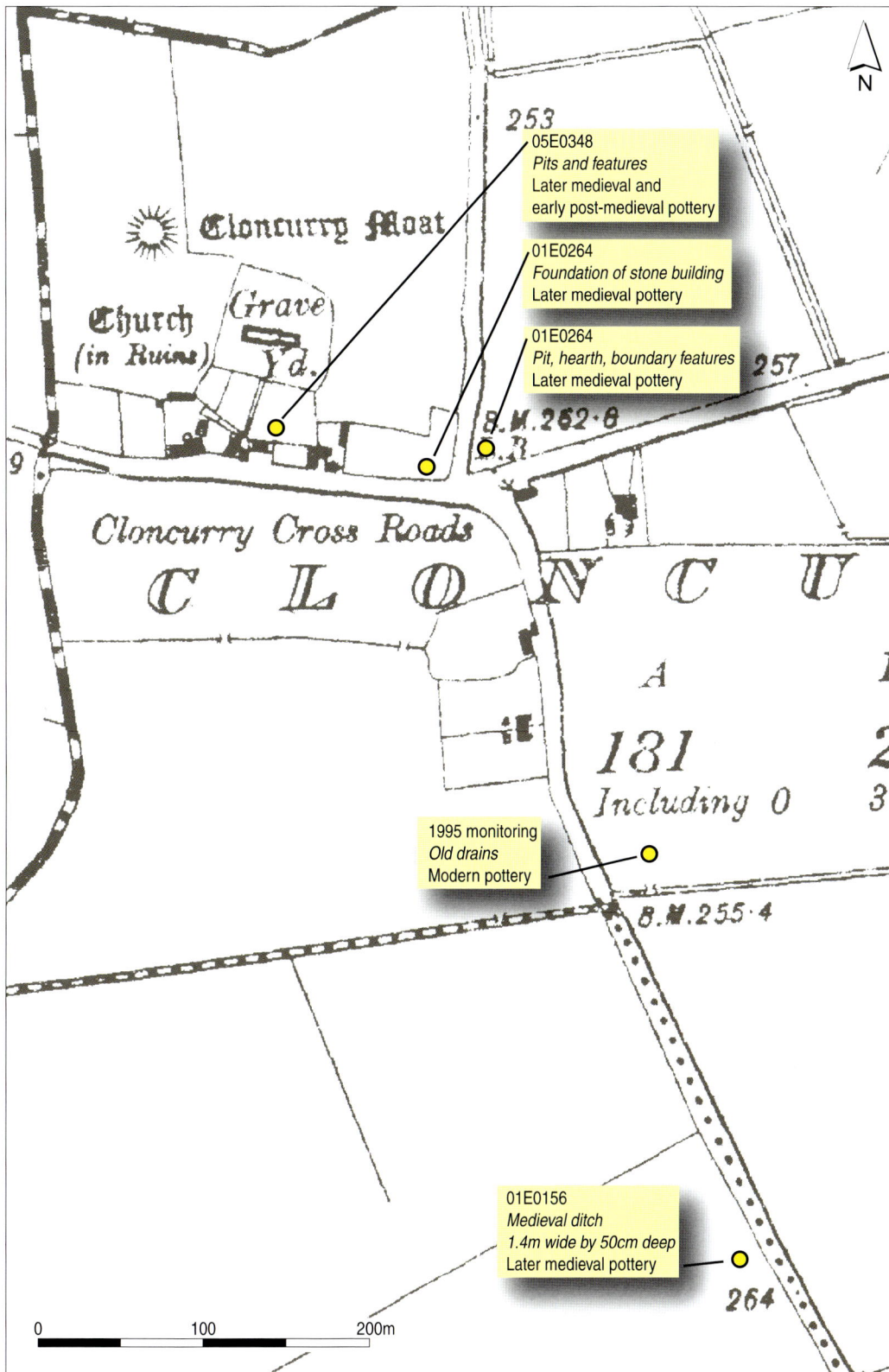

Figure 6.5 Archaeology at Cloncurry, Co. Kildare (map and accompanying text by Niall Brady).

Rathmore by John fitz Thomas FitzGerald. He had taken livestock and corn, as well as destroying farm equipment and agricultural and domestic buildings. The buildings are not named, but the quantities of grain and animals that were seized suggest the presence there of a range of farm buildings. The mill at Rathmore is mentioned in a document of 1331, while a dovecot appears in a rental for the manor dating to 1449.[31]

Excavations carried out adjacent to Ladycastle motte at Straffan in 2002–3 revealed a substantial ditch (5m wide; 2.2m deep; 50m long), as well as a dozen fragments of abraded medieval pottery.[32] Further work recovered several fragments of medieval crested ridge tiles, perforated roofing slate and mortar, while a medieval limekiln was exposed c.140m to the south-east of the site and this was 'presumably related to construction associated with occupation in the vicinity of the motte castle'.[33] The heavily disturbed remains of a stone structure with minimum dimensions of 3m by 12m were uncovered, and this was seen by the excavator as 'a building of some substance directly associated with occupation of the adjacent motte castle'.[34]

O'Conor surmised that the manorial court reported to take place at the motte at Kill in the sixteenth century would have been held in a timber building within the original motte and bailey complex.[35] Excavations adjacent to this motte in 1997 recovered some evidence for field drains and several sherds of medieval pottery.[36] A small conical mound to the south of the motte may have served some function within the manorial centre, perhaps as a windmill mound. Similar features are present close to the mottes at Agher (Figure 6.3) and Derrypatrick in Co. Meath. Early editions of the Ordnance Survey maps show a ruinous windmill c.750m to the north-west of the motte at Hortland, Co. Kildare. It is possible that this mill had medieval origins, but the motte is less than 200m from the Blackwater River, and may have had a water-powered mill.[37] The motte at Hortland, which lies 50m from a church site and graveyard, was superseded by a stone castle but nothing of this now remains.[38] The motte at Dunsoghly, Co. Dublin, which is 150m to the south of a tower house and church, is marked as 'Connaberry Moat' on early Ordnance Survey maps. It is possible that this name derives from 'Coney Burrow', suggesting the presence of rabbit warrens in the area. Archaeological monitoring close to Connaberry motte did not reveal any evidence for this, but a series of cultivation furrows and several sherds of north Leinster Cooking Ware and some wheel-thrown Dublin wares were found.[39] The excavator suggested that this was ridge-and-furrow cultivation associated with either the motte or the adjacent Dunsoghly Castle. Just 800m to the south-west of Dunsoghly, the motte and bailey at Newtown were destroyed in 1952, but they used to lie on a gentle rise in a field of tillage.[40] Traces of the earthworks are visible from the air, but when a series of archaeological test-pits were excavated in the vicinity in 2001, no features or artefacts were noted.[41] Less than 1300m to the north-west of Dunsoghly lies the motte at Kilshane. The proximity of these sites to one another, all close to the main road leading into Dublin from the north-west, is indicative of the density of settlement in this area at the end of the twelfth century.

Among the more detailed descriptions of manorial centres in the Dublin region are those associated with the early stone castles at Maynooth and Swords. In 1328, when dower

31 *RBK*, no. 131; Dryburgh and Smith, *Handbook*, p. 273.   **32** Fallon, 'Summary report on excavation (licence 02E1781)'; Fallon, 'Ladycastle Lower' in *Excavations 2003*, pp 247, 247–8, 248.   **33** Fallon, 'Summary report on excavation (licence 03E0043)'; Fallon, 'Summary report on excavation (licence 02E1782)'.   **34** Fallon, 'Ladycastle Lower' in *Excavations 2003*, pp 247, 247–8.   **35** *EIMP*, p. 39; O'Conor, *Medieval rural settlement in Ireland*, p. 33. **36** Rónán Swan, 'Killhill' in *Excavations 1997*, p. 93.   **37** For a more detailed discussion of mills and milling in the Dublin region, see pp 416–30.   **38** Herity (ed.), *Ordnance Survey letters: Kildare*, p. 30.   **39** Claire Walsh, 'Newtown link road, St Margaret's' in *Excavations 1999*, p. 92.   **40** DEHLG files (DU014-013).   **41** Rooney, 'Newtown'; Fitzpatrick, 'Newtown'.

was being assigned to Joanna de Burgh, countess of Kildare, a description was drawn up of the manorial complex at Maynooth:[42]

> *Quo die fuerunt infra claustrum manerii de Mainoth unum castrum lapideum, una aula cum quoquina ex lapidibus pro parte constructa, item una aula stramine cooperta cum camera cindula cooperta, una pistrina, una camera in gardino de novo constructa, item unum grangium, unum boverium, unum stabulum, unus torellus.*

> [The jurors say] that there was that day within the close of the manor of Maynooth a stone castle, a hall and kitchen partly stone built, a hall roofed with straw with a chamber roofed with shingles, a bake-house, a chamber newly built in the garden, a grange, an ox-house, a stable and a kiln.

The 1326 extent for Swords provides the fullest known description of the buildings at the core of a manor in the region:[43]

> [The jurors say] that there are a hall, a chamber for the archbishop annexed to it, of which the walls are stone and crenellated like a castle and roofed with shingles; and there are a kitchen there with a larder whose walls are stone and roof of shingle, a chapel with stone walls and shingle roof; there was a chamber for friars with a cloister now thrown down; near the gate there is a chamber for the constable and four chambers for knights and squires, roofed with shingles; under these, a stable and bake-house; there was a house for a dairy and workshop now thrown down. In the haggard a grange of poles (*furcae*) thatched, a timber granary roofed with 'bords', an ox-house for housing nags and kine; these easements they extend at no value for nothing is to be got from them either by letting or otherwise, since they need great repair, as they are badly roofed.

A recent analysis of Swords Castle concluded that the above description demonstrates that the complex of buildings was functioning as the headquarters of a manorial estate, while the fact that the chamber-block was described as 'crenellated like a castle' suggests that the writer did not regard Swords as a castle.[44] The author concluded that while Swords served many functions, one of its most important roles was as the headquarters of a substantial agricultural enterprise.

Manorial tenants and their holdings

The residence of the manorial lord and the associated buildings of the demesne farm or grange was only one of the settlement components that went to make up the medieval manor but the nature of documentary evidence results in it being the one most often described. Most manorial land was populated and farmed by tenants who belonged to a variety of social groupings defined by their status, size of holding and obligation to perform customary services for their lord. Extents and rentals indicate that some, or all, of the following groups were present on the manors of the region in the medieval period – free tenants, farmers (tenants who leased land for a term of years), gavellors or tenants 'at will', cottars, betaghs and burgesses.

---

42 Extent made on assignment of dower to Joanna de Burgh, 1328 (*RBK*, pp 98–100).   43 McNeill (ed.), *Alen's register*, p. 175.   44 Stalley, 'The archbishop's residence at Swords: castle or country retreat', pp 166–7.

The different categories of tenant and the different forms of tenurial relationships must be appreciated in order to understand manorial composition, structure and economy in the Dublin region. Research on the location of tenants' holdings within the geographical boundaries of the manors and the form of their habitations is seen as one of the core issues for investigation within the field of medieval rural settlement studies.[45] This research is hampered by the complex and often ambiguous nature of the documentary evidence, much of which dates to more than a hundred years after the original settlement of manors, and also by the lack of archaeological evidence for peasant settlement forms.

There is very little evidence relating to manorial tenants before the middle of the thirteenth century, although it is clear that much of Cos. Dublin and Meath was substantially manorialised by c.1210. A dozen settlements in Meath are described as 'manors' in the pipe roll of 1212 and the evidence in this document for extensive arable cultivation suggests a substantial labour force on these manors, and presumably in Co. Dublin also.[46] The surviving admission rolls to the Dublin guild merchant for the period 1190–1265 demonstrate the large numbers of people from England, Scotland, Wales and further afield who were coming to live and/or trade in Dublin, and it has always been assumed that there was a similar influx of immigrant workers into the Irish countryside.[47]

There are several indications, however, that there was a lack of labour on manors in the decades following the conquest. This is strongly suggested by the provision of the 1175 Treaty of Windsor, which called on fugitives to be compelled to return to the lands of the Anglo-Normans.[48] According to Gerald of Wales, Hugh de Lacy went to great trouble to conciliate those who had been conquered and forcibly ejected from their lands. 'He restored the countryside to its rightful cultivators and brought back cattle to pastures which had formerly been deserted'.[49] As has been noted, the new lords had no interest in slaughtering or driving out the existing rural population, just the Gaelic aristocracy.[50]

A partial explanation for the apparent speed with which military conquest turned to colonisation and economic exploitation in Meath and parts of Dublin may be the presence of this largely unchanged workforce. In this context, those archaeological sites which show continuity of occupation from the pre-Anglo-Norman to the post-Anglo-Norman period are particularly interesting. A site recently excavated at Castlefarm, just outside Dunboyne, Co. Meath, showed occupation from the fifth to the sixteenth centuries (Figure 6.6).[51] The re-cutting of one of the early medieval enclosures in the twelfth/thirteenth century led the excavator to suggest possible continuity of activity from the early to the later medieval periods. One proposal for the site is that on the eve of the conquest it was occupied by an Irish family group who pragmatically adapted themselves to the incoming regime in the person of the new lord of Dunboyne.[52] While the early medieval artefactual evidence pointed to a site of some status, the relatively sparse later medieval faunal remains and a significant

45 O'Conor, *Medieval rural settlement in Ireland*, pp 70–1; Tadhg O'Keeffe, 'Afterword' in Lyttleton and O'Keeffe (eds), *The manor in medieval and early modern Ireland* (2005), pp 188–97.   **46** Davies and Quinn, 'Irish pipe roll of 14 John'. See also Margaret Murphy 'Rural settlement in Meath, 1170–1660: the documentary evidence' in Mary Deevy and Donald Murphy (eds), *Places along the way: first findings on the M3* (Bray, 2009), pp 153–68 at p. 159.   **47** John Bradley, 'Planned Anglo-Norman towns in Ireland' in H.B. Clarke and Anngret Simms (eds), *The comparative history of urban origins in non-Roman Europe: Ireland, Wales, Denmark, Germany, Poland and Russia from the ninth to the thirteenth century* (2 vols, BAR International Series, 255, 1985), 2, pp 411–67 at pp 421–2; A.J. Otway-Ruthven, 'The character of Norman settlement in Ireland', *Historical Studies*, 5 (1965), 75–84 at 83.   **48** Otway-Ruthven, *Medieval Ireland*, p. 56. See also the mandate to the Irish justiciar c.1200 to assist the abbot of St Mary's Abbey in recovering the Irish tenants who had fled from their lands: *CSMA*, 1, p. 90.   **49** Gerald of Wales: *Expugnatio Hibernica*, p. 191.   **50** Frame, *Colonial Ireland*, p. 82.   **51** Aidan O'Connell, 'The many lives of Castlefarm', *Seanda*, 1 (2006), 19–21; Aidan O'Connell and Allister Clarke, 'Report on the archaeological excavation of Castlefarm 1, Co. Meath' (unpublished report, 2008).   **52** Margaret Murphy, 'Digging with documents: late medieval historical research on the M3 in County Meath' in Jerry O'Sullivan and Michael Stanley (eds), *Roads, rediscovery and research: proceedings of a public seminar on*

Figure 6.6 Aerial view of enclosure complex at Castlefarm, Co. Meath, looking east. The town of Dunboyne can be seen in the background (image courtesy of Aidan O'Connell, Allister Clarke and ACS Ltd; photograph by Studio Lab).

decline in the quality and quantity of later medieval artefactual assemblage suggested that the status and economy of the site deteriorated in this period. The fact that the native Irish were incorporated into the colonisation does not mean that they were necessarily integrated with the colonists or that they were economically on a par with them. For most Irish, the conquest resulted in a definite loss of status and the excavated evidence at sites like Castlefarm may underline this decline.

Some of the earliest information on the composition of manorial populations in the Dublin region comes from a series of inquisitions carried out on the archbishop of Dublin's manors in the period 1257–63.[53] These were enquiries into the exercise of jurisdiction by the archbishops from the time of John Cumin (1181–1212) onwards. They covered the manors of St Sepulchre, Swords, Ballymore, Clondalkin, Rathcoole, Shankill with Rathmichael and Dalkey, and Castlekevin. On each manor, a jury comprising between twelve and thirty-seven tenants was assembled to provide information on the practices and customs of that particular place. The majority of cases cited date to the period between 1228 and c.1260, but some refer to the episcopacy of Henry of London (1212–28) and some go back even earlier.

An analysis of the names in these inquisitions allows some conclusions to be drawn as to the racial origin of the settlers on the archiepiscopal manors. While in certain cases the documents themselves specify whether a person was English, Welsh, Irish or Hiberno-Norse (Ostman), in the majority of cases the identification has to be made on the basis of the person's surname. This, of course, is problematic as there are several examples of Irishmen using English names in order to use English law and have other benefits.[54] It is a reasonable assumption, however, that in most cases those who had English surnames were in fact of English descent.[55]

archaeological discoveries on national road schemes, August 2007 (Bray, 2008), pp 117–26.   **53** McNeill (ed.), *Alen's register*, pp 101–14.   **54** See, for example, *CJR, 1295–1303*, pp 119, 158, 342, 454.   **55** As concluded by Otway-Ruthven, 'Character of Norman settlement', 78.

On the manor of St Sepulchre, all seventeen jurors assembled appeared to have been of English or Welsh descent, and only three Irish or possibly Ostman names appear among the twenty-six people involved in the incidents described by them. Thirty-seven jurors were named in the Swords inquisitions, of whom thirty had English or Welsh names, six Irish and one Ostman. Forty people were mentioned by name in the course of the enquiries, of whom five were Irish and one was Ostman. Most of the Irishmen who appeared as jurors had English forenames, such as Roger and William, while the Irishmen who appeared as participants in the judicial proceedings tended to have Irish forenames and surnames. There was a high proportion of tenants on this manor with the surname 'Walens', denoting their Welsh origin. One of the earliest cases mentioned in the inquisitions occurred on the manor of Swords during the episcopacy of John Cumin and involved the murder of a Welshman by one Macdoc Maccursey.[56]

Eighty-one individuals were named in the inquisition that took place on the manor of Ballymore, Co. Kildare. Only a handful of these had Irish names and a similar ethnic breakdown applied with regard to Clondalkin and Rathcoole. The jurors at Clondalkin reported an interesting case that had occurred in the 1230s involving a dispute between Gyllakyne Okernekes, an Irishman described as 'Walter de Ridelesford's man', and Gillemolron McMankane, described as the archbishop's man. The two Irishmen fought a duel at Tallaght.[57]

The highest proportion of Irish tenants was found, not surprisingly, on the archbishop's manor of Castlekevin in the Wicklow Mountains. Nine Irishmen were numbered among the twenty-seven jurors, and a number of the cases involved men and women with Irish names. A notable feature of this extent is the high proportion of people whose ethnic origin is stated. The incorporation of Irish families, including the O'Tooles, into the manorial system is clear from the mention of Elias O'Toole holding the position of 'sergeant of the country'.[58]

The inquisition for the manor of Shankill with Dalkey and Rathmichael is comparatively short. The twelve named jurors all appear to have been of English or Welsh descent, although Roger Synnuche may have been Irish.[59] About half of the people named as participating in activities which led to judicial processes have both Irish forenames and surnames. One individual, Hodo McFoyde, was identified as an Ostman.

These inquisitions covering manors in both north and south Co. Dublin and Cos. Wicklow and Kildare show that people of English and Welsh origin predominated on the manors of the Dublin region by the middle of the thirteenth century. Nevertheless, on every manor there is evidence of tenants of Irish and Ostman descent, and on some manors, particularly those in south-east Dublin and north-east Wicklow, the percentage of Irish was fairly significant.

Evidence relating to the status of manorial tenants, the size of their holdings and the nature of their customary obligations dates from a slightly later period and is found predominantly in the manorial extents covering the period 1290–1330. The principal distinction normally made was between the free and the unfree tenants. Nonetheless, this division should not be given too much weight at the expense of ignoring equally important considerations of an economic nature. 'We must think of the manorial population as a body of people whose material circumstances were of the most varied nature'.[60]

56 McNeill (ed.), *Alen's register*, p. 104.   57 Ibid., p. 109.   58 Ibid., p. 111; O'Byrne, *War, politics and the Irish of Leinster*, pp 25–7.   59 McNeill (ed.), *Alen's register*, p. 112.   60 H.S. Bennett, *Life on the English manor: a study of peasant conditions, 1150–1400* (Gloucester, 1987), p. 63.

The free tenant

The actual social standing of the free tenant would have been determined by the size of his holding and the manner in which it was held. Apart from burgage tenure there were two basic forms of free tenure: military and non-military. The military tenant either provided a knight or paid scutage, a tax in lieu of military service, when required to do so. He was also subject to the usual feudal obligations, to do so such as payments for inheritance of the holding. He sometimes owed suit to the manor court and very occasionally owed a rent for his tenement.

It is clear that there was no standard form of military tenure. Some tenants merely paid scutage when military service was proclaimed, while others might also have owed suit of court and, in some cases, an annual rent. For example, the early fourteenth-century extent for the manor of Castlewarden, Co. Kildare, gives the following information in relation to the twenty-seven free tenants, the first two of whom are military tenants:[61]

> There are 27 free tenants, of whom Gerald Tyrell is one who holds 3 carucates and renders per annum 7s. with suit, ward and marriage and 20s. royal service when it runs.
>
> John le Blunt holds 5 carucates of land doing suit without render and he owes 20s. of royal service when it runs.
>
> Henry Penris hold ½ a carucate and renders 15s. with suit.
>
> John Quynton holds ½ a carucate without render, doing suit.
>
> The prior of the Hospital of St John of Jerusalem in Ireland holds ½ a carucate rendering per annum 12d. without suit.
>
> Henry Penris holds 12 acres and renders 10s.
>
> Henry le Reve, William le Reve, Stephen Colyn, William le Hunte, William Ballard, Stephen Baldone, Richard le Melmongere, William Juvene, Walter Moton, Reginald Albus, Simon Ballard, Walter le Reve, William Ive, John le Fogelere, William Malet, Richard le Wyte, John fitz William and Roger fitz Walter hold forty-eight acres of land and render 23s. 3d. per annum with suit.
>
> Thomas Rathmegan holds one messuage and 3 acres and renders 1lb of pepper and suit.
>
> Bardewyn Wodeman renders per annum 1d. without suit.
>
> Thomas Clericus hold one messuage and renders 1d. with suit.
>
> Sum of the rents of the free tenants – 62s. 5d.

Even within the same manor, different conditions could apply, both in regard to the amount of scutage paid for ostensibly the same unit of landholding (the knight's fee) and in relation to whether or not suit of court was required. There were three military tenants listed on the manor of Cloncurry in the 1304 extent.[62] Thomas, son of Alfred, who held a knight's fee in Donadea was liable to pay 40s. in scutage when royal service was proclaimed, together with an annual rent of 6d. Robert Flattisbury also held a knight's fee, paying 40s. when scutage ran and either making an annual render of a pair of gloves or paying 6d. Both men owed suit of court. By contrast, Hugo Possewyk held a fee attached to the manor of Cloncurry, which lay in one of the less stable areas of the Kildare/Offaly/Meath march, for which he paid an annual rent of 13s. 4d., and only 20s. in scutage when royal service was proclaimed. Here, the deciding factor appears to have been the location of the lands.

It was more usual for military tenants not to pay an annual rent. On the manor of Leixlip, for instance, four military tenants held some two-and-a-half knights' fees between them in 1341.[63] They each paid scutage of 20s. when required, and no other rent for holdings

61 TNA:PRO SC12/20/48.   62 *RBO*, pp 29–31.   63 TNA:PRO C47/10/20.

in excess of 200 acres. There is no mention of suit of court with reference to these tenements. It appears, therefore, that most military tenements were of financial advantage to the lord only during periods when he gained control of wardships and marriage of heirs and heiresses. Most of the time, their value was military rather than economic.

The position of non-military free tenants on manors in the region displayed, if anything, even greater variety than that of the military tenant. Rents in particular varied greatly from manor to manor, and even within the same manor. The relationship between the rents and what might be termed the 'market value' of the land is particularly difficult to gauge. The non-military tenements on the manor of Cloncurry brought in over £36 per annum, but the rents per acre varied from less than a farthing to 15*d.* In general, the smaller the holding, the higher the per acre rent, which suggests that some of the smallest holdings were granted out at a time when population pressure and demand for land was growing.[64]

It is clear that some of the larger free tenants held substantial blocks of land – up to and sometimes over four carucates (*c.*500 acres). Frequently, they gave their names to the lands they occupied and these have survived as townland names. There are several examples of this occurring at Swords, Co. Dublin – Fieldstown (de la Felde), Saucerstown (de Saucere), Marshallstown (le Marschalle) and Belinstown (Belyns).[65]

The betagh

The term *betagius* was used to denote a manorial tenant, or layman, who was personally unfree and virtually invariably of Irish origin.[66] There exists a substantial body of literature on the betagh and his status and in particular on the word and its derivation. There is a considerable, if not universal, acceptance that the origin of the term betagh – *betagius* – is the Irish word 'bíatach', used in old Irish law texts to describe, in the words of Mac Niocaill, the 'typical Irish commoner'.[67] One of the earliest documents in which the Latin word *betagius/betaci* occurs is the 1212 pipe roll of King John, which records that betaghs in Meath had to do carting for the lord and that there were poor betaghs who had to be provided with corn by way of assistance.[68] Another early use of the term *betagius* occurred in 1219 in relation to the king's lands at Othee, Okelly and Obrun in the Dublin/Wicklow Mountains, where settlements of betaghs owed both a monetary rent and a customary render in kind.[69] Thereafter, the term betagh passed into general usage and is encountered in a variety of different sources.

The betagh, therefore, can be seen as the Irish equivalent of the English villein (although, there were important differences between the economic positions of the Irish betaghs and the English villeins). The term *nativus*, used in English law to denote the villein or serf, tied to the land, is also found in Ireland, where it is used as an alternative term for betagh – that is, it is used to describe unfree Irish tenants.[70] The descriptive term *hibernicus* is also frequently used in connection with this class of unfree Irish tenants. It is also used as an ethnic label for people of Irish origin not burdened by the servile status of a villein. Where a manorial extent or rental lists the services owed by the *hibernici*, it is fairly clear that betaghs are being described. The situation is not always clear-cut, however, and it is worth remembering that while all betaghs were *hibernici* not all *hibernici* were betaghs.[71]

64 Lyons, 'Manorial economy', p. 322.   **65** Mills, 'Tenants and agriculture', 59.   **66** It is possible that, as Otway-Ruthven pointed out, some men of English origin may have 'fallen' into the betagh class, although there is no direct evidence for this. One possible example dates to 1541, when Nicholas Brymyngham, a tenant on the manor of Kilmainham, was described as a '*nativus*' (*EIMP*, p. 86).   **67** Gearóid Mac Niocaill, 'The origins of the betagh', *IJ*, new ser., 1 (1966), 292–8 at 297–8; see also Curtis, 'Rental of the manor of Lisronagh, 1333, and notes on 'betagh tenure in medieval Ireland', *PRIA*, 43C3 (1926), 41–76; G.J. Hand, 'The status of the native Irish in the lordship of Ireland, 1272–1331', *IJ*, new ser., 1 (1966), 93–115.   **68** Davies and Quinn, 'Irish pipe roll of 14 John', 21, 33.   **69** *RDKPRI*, 35, p. 29.   **70** As, for example, on the manor of Lucan, where there were seven *nativi* in 1359 (TNA:PRO C47/10/22/15).   **71** It is also worth noting that when James Mills was preparing his calendars of the rolls of the justiciar's court, he made a decision to leave *hibernicus* untranslated when he judged that it referred to betaghs or *nativi*, but to translate it as 'Irish' when he believed it to be

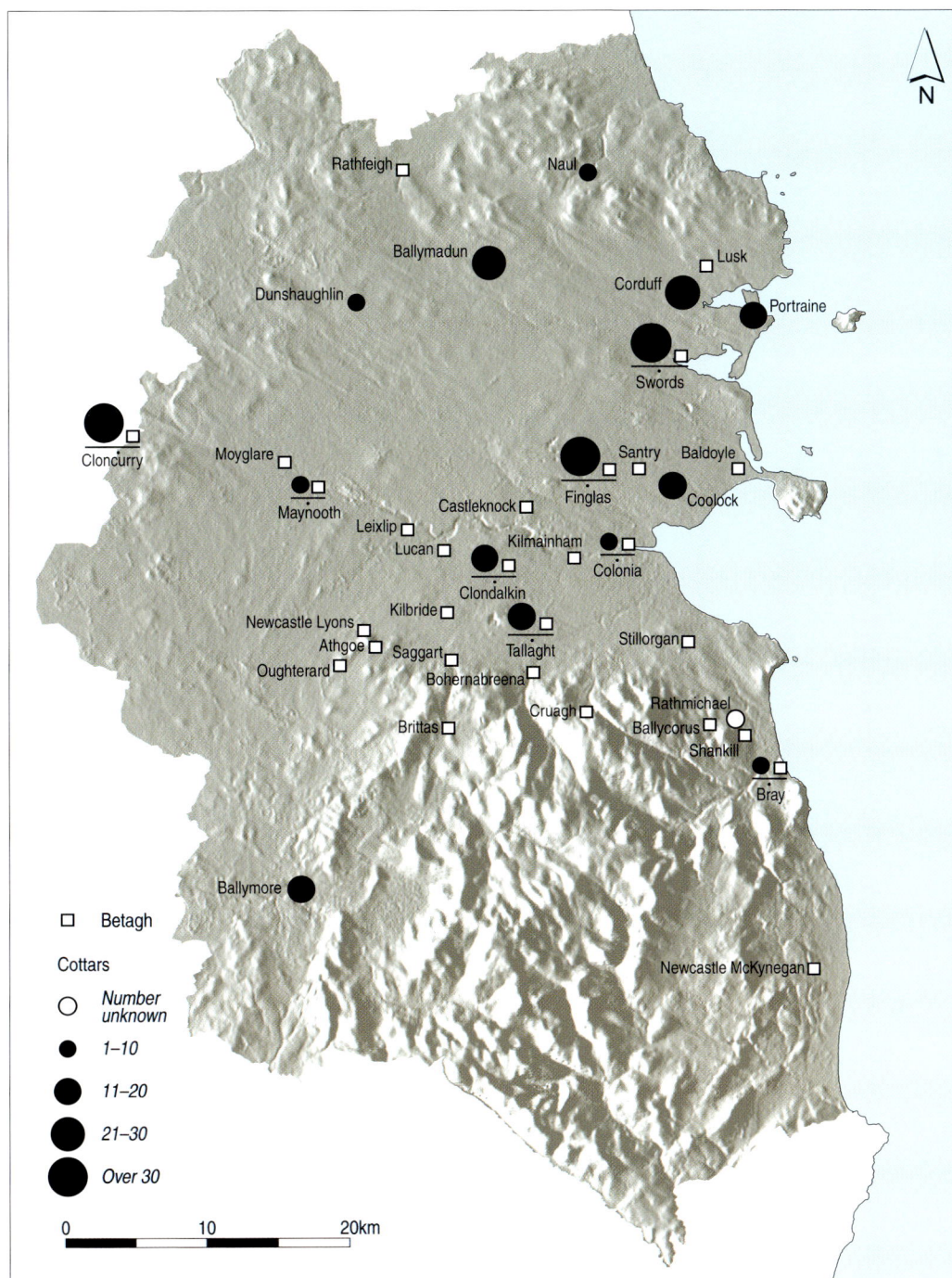

Figure 6.7 Distribution of betaghs and cottars mentioned in documentary sources *c.*1200–1360. Numbers of betaghs are rarely given in manorial extents, while cottars are frequently named and counted.

The '*bíatach*', was not servile or even semi-servile, and it is difficult to explain why the term was appropriated by the Anglo-Normans to describe a class of tenant equivalent to the English villein. In the Irish law texts, a semi-servile tenant bound to the land and transferable with the land was known as a *senchleithe*.[72] Certain charter evidence can be interpreted as demonstrating that something akin to betagh status had begun to emerge in eleventh-century Ireland together with an embryonic form of feudalism in Leinster. There is a grant, for example, from Diarmait Mac Murchada to the monastery of All Hallows, Dublin, of lands in Baldoyle, which specifies that the land was granted *with* its men, 'namely Máel Isu Macfeilecan with his sons and nephews'.[73]

an ethnic rather than a status description.   **72** Kelly, *Early Irish farming*, p. 429.   **73** Butler (ed.), *Registrum prioritas omnium sanctorum*, pp 50–1. But see K.W. Nicholls, 'Anglo-French Ireland and after', *Peritia*, 1 (1982), 370–403 at 378, where he proposes that Máel Isu was 'simply the taxpaying landowner of Baldoyle, no more unfree than any other

Some of the tenants described as betaghs on the Anglo-Norman manors of the Dublin region undoubtedly had been of servile status before 1170. It appears likely, however, that very many had not been servile, but were all grouped together into this unfree class by their new masters. This might explain the noticeable dichotomy that appears in the sources between betagh small-holders, often described as 'poor', and other betaghs who held comparatively large tenements and were people of consequence in their localities.

Irish tenants are mentioned in thirteen of the forty or so manorial extents that survive for the Dublin area between about 1250 and 1350. This is a slightly misleading statistic and needs to be qualified with the information that over half of the extents do not give any information on tenants or their holdings beyond a composite cash income from rents and services. Virtually all the extents that do enumerate tenants mention Irish tenants who can be recognised by their names and/or their description as betaghs, *hibernici* or natives. It would appear that, as shown by the inquisitions on the archiepiscopal manors, very few manors in the region had no Irish tenants. Figure 6.7, which plots references to betaghs in a range of documentary sources, indicates that they were least commonly found in the north-west of the region and most often found in the south and especially the south-east of the region.

In England, one of the underlying purposes of villeinage was to provide access to free labour in the form of customary services. Where the production of a saleable grain surplus was the aim, the need for these services increased. All of the surviving documentary sources relating to the performance of customary services by unfree tenants on the manors of the Dublin region, however, indicate that these services were extremely light and bore little resemblance to those in force in much of England.[74] Moreover, by the end of the thirteenth century, these services were already being commuted into cash payments.

In the 1322 extent for the Mortimer manor of Rathfeigh in Co. Meath, where some thirty-six betagh holdings are enumerated, the services consisted of between one and three days weeding per annum. At harvest time, the betaghs similarly owed between one and three days work and there is also mention of some unspecified carrying services.[75] The betaghs paid an average rent of 1s. per acre for their land and there does not appear to have been any discernable relationship between lands held and services owed.

The services required from the betaghs on the lands of the archbishop of Dublin in the early fourteenth century were even lighter. At Finglas, they were required to cut and gather the lord's hay (a service valued at 5s. per annum, suggesting that it had been commuted) and to watch the lords 'nags and kine' (a service valued at 6s. 8d.). The betaghs at Finglas held land in Kildonan and Kilshane.[76] Betaghs on the huge manor of Swords were also required to watch animals, but here this task was valued at 20s.[77] The money rents paid by the betaghs ranged from 6d. to 18d. per acre, depending on the quality of the land. The value of the customary services can be seen to decline as the fourteenth century progressed; the works and services of the seven *nativi* who held forty acres of land on the manor of Lucan in 1358, for instance, were worth only 3s. 6d. per annum.[78] Some of the extents list no customary services due from betaghs. The sixty-three betaghs listed on the manor of Cloncurry did not owe any customary services, but rather paid a high rent of 20d. an acre for their 341½ acres of land.[79] None of the betagh tenants at Maynooth in 1328 or at Leixlip in 1341 owed any services.

Lands farmed by betaghs frequently appear in consolidated holdings in specific parts of the manors. In the extents, betaghs are very often referred to in the plural and in a manner

Irishman outside a narrow group of the newly dominant nobility'. **74** Lyons, 'Manorial economy', p. 271. **75** TNA:PRO C47/10/18/13. **76** McNeill (ed.), *Alen's register*, pp 173–5. **77** Ibid., p. 176. **78** TNA:PRO C47/10/22/15. **79** *RBO*, pp 27–34.

that may imply grouping – for instance, 'land of the betaghs' and 'services of the betaghs' are terms that recur frequently. Judging by their surnames, where they are recorded, they lived in family groups and often their land appears to have been held and cultivated in common. This community was sometimes known as a betaghry. Certain place-names and townland names, like Baile Betagh, Bettystown and Betaghsland, indicate the location of some of these consolidated holdings. Another place-name element associated with betagh settlements is the suffix -park – for example at Trim, where the betagh community lived beside the park and was supervised by a sergeant who was also the park-keeper.[80] In the Dublin region, there is an association between betaghs and the place-name element Boly or Booley – a dairy place. In the archiepiscopal manor of Colonia/St Sepulchre in the early fourteenth century, for instance, there were betagh settlements at Boly maior and Boly minor, while at Swords betaghs are recorded as holding land at Boly.[81]

The records tend to refer to the betaghs and their holdings communally, leading to the proposition that on many Anglo-Norman manors in Ireland, these servile Irish tenants occupied a quite separate area to other manorial tenants, perhaps a definite townland.[82] It has been argued, for example, that betagh settlements were pre-existing bond settlements that the Anglo-Normans incorporated into their manorial structures.[83] Graham has identified at least a hundred medieval settlements in Meath which he has classified as 'house clusters' and which he considers may in fact have been betagh settlements.[84] Virtually all of these settlements were located within 4km of a manorial village.

It would be erroneous to believe that the Irish tenants were always to be found in dispersed settlements. It is evident from the documents that Irish tenants also occur in the classes of free tenants, farmers and cottars, although burgess names do appear to be almost exclusively of English origin. A study of the manorial village of Killeen (barony of Skreen) based on a fifteenth-century manuscript, partly compiled in the area, concluded that the local population had remained largely Irish in its descent.[85] Of eighty-eight individuals named in the document, at least forty-seven had surnames of Irish origin. Given the situation of Killeen, securely within the Pale, it was not deemed plausible that the Irish names represented a re-Gaelicisation of an English settlement. Rather, it was concluded that the individuals were descended from the Irish population which had been assimilated into the manorial village when it was first founded.

Judging by the rents they paid, the holdings of individual betaghs were frequently more extensive than those of some other classes of tenants, especially cottars. This acts as a reminder that betaghs should not necessarily be placed at the bottom of the tenurial pyramid. One source that gives an insight into the material conditions of betaghs are the inventories of goods found on the Irish memoranda rolls.[86] When a betagh resident on one of the king's manors died in suspicious circumstances, it was usual for a listing of his possessions to be made. Clement Ocathyll, one of the king's betaghs, was killed at Cruagh in 1303 and the sheriff of Dublin reported that he had the following possessions:

> Four cows with their calves, 16s.; an ox, 3s.; three affers (work horses) 6s. 8d.; thirty
> sheep, 40d. each, one pig, 4d., three small stacks of oats containing an estimated five
> crannocks; a small stack of wheat, beans and barley containing an estimated one

80 Potterton, *Medieval Trim*, pp 125–8.   81 McNeill (ed.), *Alen's register*, pp 170, 176.   82 Otway-Ruthven, 'Character of Norman settlement', 76.   83 Desmond McCourt, 'The dynamic quality of Irish rural settlement' in R.H. Buchanan, Emyr Jones and Desmond McCourt (eds), *Man and his habitat: essays presented to Emyr Estyn Evans* (London, 1971), pp 126–64 at p. 143.   84 Graham, 'Anglo-Norman settlement in County Meath', pp 228–9, 244. 85 Michael Benskin, 'An English township in fifteenth-century Ireland', *Collegium Medievale*, 4:1 (1991), 57–84 at 73–4. 86 Connolly, 'The Irish Memoranda Rolls', 68–73.

bushel of wheat, two bushels of beans and two bushels of barley, a stack of turf worth
6s. 8d., a brass pot, 6s. 8d. and a chest worth 6d.[87]

This was clearly an individual who had a modest small-holding and was engaged in a
mixture of arable and pastoral farming, which would have been beyond the capabilities of
the average cottar with their toft and croft.

In one important respect, however, Irish tenants were at a disadvantage, and that is
before the law. The Irish were not allowed to bring cases to court unless they were under the
advowery of an English protector, or in the case of the betaghs, in conjunction with the
king. Being accused of being Irish was legal defamation, while the murder of an Irishman
was not considered a felony. The lord of a slain Irishman, however, could, and often did, sue
the slayer for compensation. The price of a betagh appears to have been fixed at five marks
and 40d. (the equivalent of 70s.; about the price of a good horse).

It is possible of course to find cases where the courts appear to act fairly with regard to
Irish subjects. In 1309, for instance, the Dublin exchequer had to decide between two
claimants to twenty-seven acres of land held 'in betagio' of the king. One claimant was Irish
and the other was English and claimed in right of his wife (who was apparently the sister of
the Irish claimant). The court preferred the Irishman, who was 'verus betagius' and bound
to the soil.[88] In 1305, a woman called Grathagh, described as being 'of the race of O
Thotheles, married to Andrew le Deveneys, a tenant of the manor of Saggart', was accused
along with her husband of receiving one Kelt, a man of 'David McKilecoul O Tothil', a
common thief, and having part of his thefts.[89] The jurors, twelve men with clearly English
names, dismissed the case against them, saying that Grathagh is accustomed at the request
of faithful men of peace to go into the mountains where she stays with women of the parts
of peace, to see and search for cattle carried off by her race so that men of peace may more
easily recover their goods and cattle carried away.

The other guise in which the Irish appear in the manorial and administrative records of
the period is as marauders, evildoers and reducers of manorial profits. Many of the extents
that date from the last decades of the thirteenth century and the early decades of the
fourteenth century bear witness to the revival of Gaelic warfare that posed a serious threat
near the periphery of the study area, and sometimes struck at its heart. Frequently it was the
lands held by Irish tenants that were the first to come under threat. As early as the 1280s, the
betaghs of the king in the vale of Dublin were being paid compensation by the Irish
exchequer on account of the depredations of Art Mac Murchada, and soon afterwards
betaghs began leaving their lands because of war.[90] In the 1290s, William le Deveneys, who
had been granted land in the mountainous areas, prayed that the king would enable him to
recover the betagii who were wont to stay there but who, owing to the violent war prevailing,
had fled and were dwelling with others.[91] Whether he was successful or not is not known.

One of the measures taken by the English administration in Ireland to protect manorial
lands from Gaelic depredations was to compel manorial tenants to come to regular 'views',
where local officials ensured that they had weapons and armour.[92] Orders that betaghs as
well as English tenants should make view of arms still survive, and they demonstrate that
the Irish population of manors was also obliged to serve in the defence of the lordship. The
complaints, such as that cited above, however, suggest that more often than not betaghs fled

87 NAI RC8/2: Memoranda roll, p. 314.   **88** *CJR, 1295–1303*, pp 356–7.   **89** *CJR, 1305–7*, p. 480.   **90** *CDI, 1252–84*,
no. 1935, p. 440.   **91** *CDI, 1285–92*, no. 622, p. 309.   **92** Robin Frame, 'The Dublin government and Gaelic Ireland,
1272–1361' (PhD, TCD, 1971), pp 40–1, 470–1.

before Irish attacks and in some cases transferred their services to the local Irish when it was expedient to do so.[93]

There is also evidence of betaghs and other Irish tenants taking flight because of dissatisfaction with their lord. In 1306, Geoffrey McWyther, a *hibernicus* of Geoffrey de Brandewode in Co. Dublin, objected to the services being asked of his family, and together with his wife, household and cattle he removed himself to the lands of Geoffrey Sauvage, an enemy of his former lord.[94] In 1322, one Maurice Dongon, a betagh, volunteered the information that he had fled from Leixlip, where he had been first Ralph Pippard's betagh and subsequently the king's betagh.[95] He went first to the grange of Athgoe, a part of the royal manor of Newcastle Lyons, and finally settled on Arnald le Poer's lands on the manorial borough of Oughterard.

A writ of *de nativo habendo* was available in Ireland from the early years of the thirteenth century, and this could be used to get the authorities to find and return unfree tenants who had taken flight from their manors. It was very rarely used, however, perhaps because of the ease with which the Irish, by making for the nearest area of marchland or land of war, could put themselves beyond the reach of the law. This same factor – ease of escape – might also explain the lack of evidence for widespread unrest among the servile and smallholder tenants on Irish manors such as was found in England.

The position of the betagh on manors in the Dublin region and in particular the light nature of the labour services expected from him is an excellent example of how English manorialism was adapted to suit Irish conditions. Similarly, there is evidence that many of the Irish living on the manors pragmatically adapted themselves to new systems of agriculture and settlement. Conflict was always on the horizon, but interaction and cooperation were also present.

The cottar

The class of tenant known as the cottar occupied the lowest rung of the ladder in the hierarchy of manorial settlement.[96] This was due to the small size of their holdings, which were usually considerably less than an acre and consisted of the small plots or crofts which lay around their little dwellings. Although free, the economic position of the cottar placed him or her in a position of great dependence on the manorial lords and larger tenants. Numbers of cottars, the rent they paid for their cottages and their conditions of tenure varied greatly from manor to manor (Figure 6.7). For example, at Ballymadun in 1344 there were twenty-two cottars who rendered 2*s.* 6*d.* annually in rent 'and not more, apart from works which are worth 2*s.* 6*d.*'[97] Nearby at Dunshaughlin, in the same year, a smaller group of seven cottars rendered the larger rent of 3*s.* 8*d.* per annum, but appeared to have no customary services.[98] In general, manors in north Co. Dublin tended to have the largest populations of cottars. In 1311, there was a large group of cottars at the Ormond manor of Corduff in the parish of Lusk. Twenty-seven are recorded, paying 13*s.* 9½*d.* for their cottages per annum. Their works were said to be worth 8*s.* 5½*d.* per annum.[99] At Finglas, twenty-eight cottars held their cottages for 22*s.* and their work in autumn was valued at 12*d.*[100] At Lusk, there were forty-six cottages, which brought in 30*s.* a year plus 2*s.* in customary services.[101] At Swords, forty-four cottages and gardens 'built and unbuilt' were valued at 26*s.* 8*d.* a year, while at Portraine, part of the same manor, an unspecified number of cottars

93 Mills, 'Tenants and agriculture', 56; Otway-Ruthven, 'Organisation of Irish agriculture', pp 9–10.   94 *CJR, 1305–7*, pp 326–7.   95 Lyons, 'Manorial economy', p. 287.   96 Otway-Ruthven, 'Organisation of Anglo-Irish agriculture', 12. 97 TNA:PRO C135/75/3.   98 TNA:PRO C135/75/3.   99 *RBO*, pp 25–7.   100 McNeill (ed.), *Alen's register*, pp 173–5. 101 Ibid., p. 176.

Table 6.2 List of rents from cottars at Cloncurry, Co. Kildare, in 1304.

From David le ffouler for a cottage half a stang and 3 virgates 2*d*.
From Cristin McLothyr for a cottage 1 stang 12 virgates 3*d*.
From Crayn McTressy for a cottage half a stang 10 virgates 4*d*.
From Elyn McGalman for a cottage 1 stang 10 virgates 4*d*.
From Henry Ogillegan for 1 cottage 8 virgates 2*d*.
From Gillecrist O Hogan for a cottage half a stang 12 virgates 2*d*.
From Molrony McLude for a cottage half a stang 15 virgates 2*d*.
From Raynagh widow for a cottage half a stang 2*d*.
From Conelath McTressy for a cottage and 1 stang 2*d*.
From Evercath McTressy for a cottage and 1 stang 2*d*.
From Gilumtharog for a cottage and 10 virgates 2*d*.
From Eug'O Bygyn for a cottage and half a stang 10 virgates 4*d*.
From Mulrony O Kellan for a cottage half a stang 10 virgates 2*d*.
From Mardauth McTressy for a cottage half a stang and 5 virgates 2*d*.
From McTrahy McKun for a cottage and 16 virgates 2*d*.
From Comdino McLothyr for a cottage ½ a stang and 16 virgates 6*d*.
From Hugh O Haclan for a cottage 14 virgates 2*d*.
From Stephen O Donked for a cottage half a stang 6 virgates 2*d*.
From Gillecrist McKun for a cottage half a stang and 1 virgate 2*d*.
From Gilko de Balymaclothyr for 1 cottage and 16 virgates 2*d*.
From Adam ODoude for 1 cottage half a stang and 16 virgates 2*d*.
From Gillemyall medico for a cottage half a stang and 10 virgates 2*d*.
From Mannes McBroey for a cottage half a stang 8 virgates 2*d*.
From Emin OKarwill widow for a cottage 5 virgates 2*d*.
From Gillepedir Offynnog for a cottage 1 stang 30 virgates 6*d*.
From Nicholas Braynok for a cottage half a stang 2 virgates 2*d*.
From Mannes McBroyg for a cottage half a stang 6 virgates 2*d*.
From Katherine widow for a cottage half a stang 7 virgates 4*d*.
From Gillemyal Foil for a cottage 12 virgates 2*d*.
From Bryce McCoissyn for a cottage 7 virgates 2*d*.
From Ralph Ker for a cottage 2 virgates 2*d*.
From Gillekeyvyn McLorkan for a cottage 3 virgates 2*d*.
From Richard McLorkan for a cottage 1 stang 4*d*.
From Gillemory McKun for a cottage half a stang 4*d*.
From Kellath O Donked for a cottage 6 virgates 3*d*.
From Philip McKarwyll for a cottage and 10 virgates 2*d*.
From John le Waleys for a cottage half a stang 4 virgates 2*d*.
From Dovenold O Tagan for a cottage 3 virgates 2*d*.
From Kynnath McKeni for a cottage 12 virgates 2*d*.
From Grathini ODogry for a cottage 10 virgates 2*d*.
From Grathini OCorcran for a cottage 14 virgates 2*d*. Sum 8*s*. 4*d*.

rendered thirty-six hens, priced 1*d*. each, at Christmas for their cottages.[102] In addition, these last-mentioned paid 6*s*. 8*d*. a year 'to have their handmills and be relieved of suit of the mill'.

In north-east Kildare, cottars were recorded on the manors of Maynooth, Ballymore and Cloncurry. Nine cottars were listed at Maynooth in 1328, paying rents that totalled 11*s*. 4*d*.

102 Ibid.

and ranged between *6d.* and *3s. 4d.*[103] Five were given occupational designations – two shoemakers, a tailor, a merchant and an arblaster (crossbow-man). There were one widow and two possible Irish names. No labour services or commuted payments were listed. On the archiepiscopal manor of Ballymore, Co. Kildare, in 1326 there were sixteen cottars who paid no rent, but each was bound to reap a day with the lord in autumn for food supplied by him.[104] This work had presumably been commuted and was worth *16d.* It was also reported in the same extent that four cottages at Ballymore lay vacant and that all the cottages at Ballybough were waste and of no value. Cottages lying waste were also recorded at the archiepiscopal holdings at St Sepulchre, Clondalkin and Dalkey in 1326.[105]

The extent for the manor of Cloncurry, drawn up in 1304, names a total of forty-two cottars whose holdings ranged in size from one stang thirty virgates to three virgates (Table 6.2).[106] They paid rents of between *2d.* and *6d.* and appear to have owed no labour services. As can be seen, the group is dominated by people with Irish names, although some English and Welsh names, such as David le ffouler, John le Waleys and Nicholas Braynok, appeared. Up to seven of the names appear to be of women, including three described as widows.

Cottars are included among the tenants listed in the 1326 rentals for the Holy Trinity manors of Clonkeen, Grangegorman and Glasnevin.[107] At the last two named manors there appears to have been a mix of cottars who owed labour services and those who did not. Those who did not owe labour services did not appear to pay higher rents or to have held larger holdings. The labour services consisted of two days reaping, two days hoeing and some work at hay-making as well as the gift of a hen at Christmas. All of the cottars at Clonkeen owed either customary renders or labour services along with their rents. The labour services could be commuted to a money payment of *4d.* Most of the cottars were located in the hamlet called the 'vill of the grange'.

Farmers and gavellors

The designations of farmer and gavellor relate to the form of tenurial contract between lord and tenant rather than to the social condition of the tenant.[108] Both types of tenure were relatively common in the medieval Dublin region from the late thirteenth century on. The farmer held his tenement on contract for a fixed rent over a fixed number of years. This form of tenure could embrace any size of tenement from a mill to an entire manor. While the farmers were clearly personally free, their holdings tended to be smaller than those of the free tenants. Otway-Ruthven characterised them as the smaller free tenants who did not have enough land of their own and found it necessary to lease more.[109] Farmers could be English or Irish, although the majority appear to have been of English origin.

At Maynooth in 1328–9, twenty farmers constituted the largest single group of tenants on the manor.[110] At Ballymadun there were thirty-two parcels of land let out to farm, which comprised in total 482 acres of arable, meadow and pasture said to be worth £16 16d. annually. On this manor, the farmers were clearly expected to perform some customary services, and their 'works' were valued at *24s. 5d.*[111]

In terms of status, the gavellor came below the farmer as he held his land *ad voluntatem*, that is 'at the will' of the lord, and he could be ejected at the lord's pleasure. Most of the tenements held in this way were relatively small. At Swords in 1326, twenty-eight gavellors held 'one carucate, four score and three acres in diverse places about the town of Swords', at

103 *RBK*, pp 98–100. **104** McNeill (ed.), *Alen's register*, pp 189–94. **105** Ibid., pp 170–2, 185–9, 195. **106** *RBO*, pp 27–34. **107** Mills (ed.), *Account roll*, pp 189–98. **108** Lyons, 'Manorial economy', p. 295. **109** Otway-Ruthven, 'Organisation of Anglo-Irish agriculture'. **110** *RBK*, pp 54–7. **111** TNA:PRO C135/75/3.

10*d.* an acre.[112] This would have given each one slightly over seven acres. At Bray, two tenants were described as *gablarii* – John Park held thirteen acres and paid 8*d.* an acre per annum, while Robert, son of John, had a more substantial holding of twenty-three acres, for which he paid 12*d.* an acre.[113] One farmer on the manor paid the equivalent of 10*d.* per acre for his holding of twenty acres. The only difference was that a farmer owed suit of court while a gavellor appears not to have.

The eleven gavellors on the manor of Cloncurry held very small amounts of land for a couple of pence, the largest holding being a cottage and half an acre.[114] It is difficult to see what distinguished them from the cottars on the same manor, and their names display the same ethnic and gender mix as that of the latter group. Archbishop Alen commented in his register that the gavellor was a 'farmer at will or by deed, not cottier or betagh, they are, as it were, copyholders'.[115]

It is clear from the above discussion that the manors of the region were densely populated in the thirteenth century, and that high levels of rural population persisted in secure areas throughout the medieval period. A major question that arises is where did these people live? The following discussion focuses on two types of rural settlement – rural boroughs and moated sites.

Rural boroughs

A medieval borough was a nucleated settlement that enjoyed special privileges, enumerated and detailed in a borough charter, usually issued by the crown. More than 170 boroughs were established in Ireland, but many of these did not endure for very long and only about fifty or so developed into successful commercial centres. Although some boroughs existed in Ireland prior to 1169, the vast majority were founded by the Anglo-Normans. Excluding those that became towns during the Middle Ages, over thirty medieval boroughs were located within the Dublin region, and more than three-quarters of these were situated inside a 20km-wide corridor running from the south-west to the north-east of the region (Figure 6.8). The corridor is along the line of the River Liffey Valley as it makes its way down the Wicklow Mountains, and it suggests the importance that was attached to having access to the river and its floodplain as a primary communications routeway. The pattern reflects the relatively high number of boroughs in Kildare (twenty-five for the entire county), compared with Wicklow, which had few (eleven), and the south-east of Meath, which also had a (perhaps surprisingly) low number.[116] In some cases, attempts made to establish settlements on lower ground in Wicklow also failed, and Burgage, Hollywood, Killickabawn (Kilmacberne) and (possibly) Mulsoescourt were all abandoned.

While some boroughs (such as Donore and Lucan) were probably entirely new creations, the majority evolved out of existing, pre-Anglo-Norman ecclesiastical centres, such as at Burgage, Clane, Cloncurry, Clondalkin, Dunshaughlin, Kill, Lusk (Figure 6.9), Oughterard, Saggart, Swords, Tallaght and possibly Newcastle Lyons and Rathcoole. Most of these places retained their religious and other functions while simultaneously taking on new administrative and commercial roles.

Boroughs functioned as important market centres absorbing much of the agricultural surpluses of their own hinterlands while they also served, for an even wider hinterland, as stepping stones to the larger markets and ports such as Dalkey, Drogheda, Dublin, Naas and Swords. It was not simply one-way traffic, however, and the relationship between even the

---

112 McNeill (ed.), *Alen's register*, p. 176.   **113** *RBO*, pp 16–17.   **114** *RBO*, pp 27–34.   **115** McNeill (ed.), *Alen's register*, p. 179.   **116** Geoffrey Martin, 'Plantation boroughs in medieval Ireland, with a handlist of boroughs to *c.*1500' in

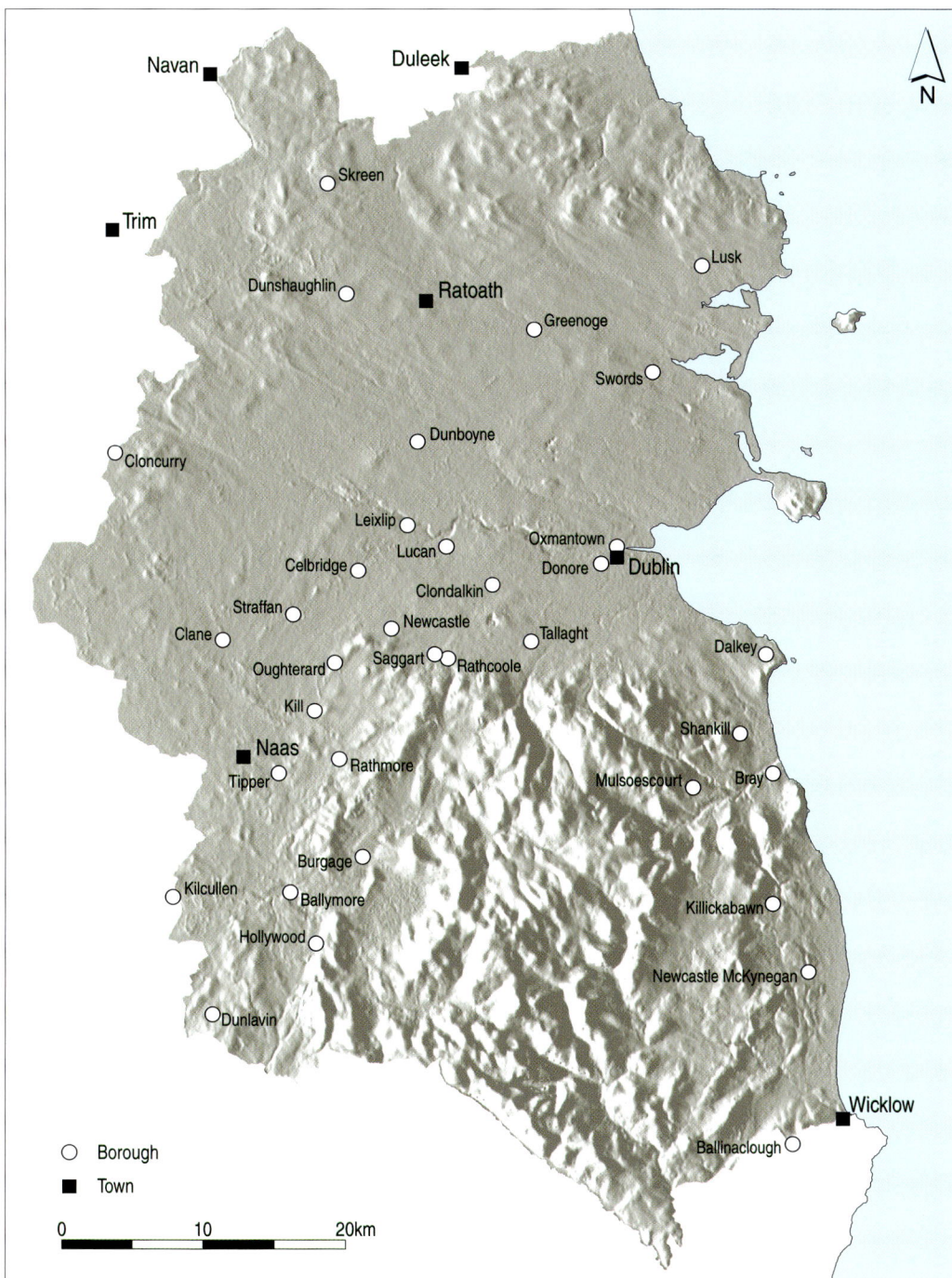

Figure 6.8 Distribution of towns and boroughs in the Dublin region.

smaller urban centres and their surrounding rural hinterland was symbiotic. Among the privileges granted to the burgesses of Rathcoole, for instance, was the right to pasture their animals and to cut turf on the mountain of 'Slestoll' (Slievethoul), and this was typical of burgesses' rights across the region.[117] The importance to the boroughs of their surrounding hinterland is perhaps best demonstrated by the rapid decline of Rathcoole, Saggart and Shankill once the neighbouring lands were lost to the Gaelic Irish in the fifteenth century.[118]

There were a dozen or more boroughs in Co. Dublin, and at least eight of these were founded by the church.[119] This situation is not typical of the rest of the country and it can be seen as a reflection of the dominant landholding position of the various ecclesiastical institutions in the Dublin region. The abbey of St Thomas was responsible for the creation

Harkness and O'Dowd (eds), *The town in Ireland* (1981), pp 23–53 at pp 33–51.   **117** McNeill (ed.), *Alen's register*, p. 84.
118 Bradley, 'The medieval boroughs of Co. Dublin', p. 142.   **119** Ibid.

Figure 6.9 Depiction of
church and houses at
Lusk, Co. Dublin, by
Joseph Moland, 1716
(© Representative
Church Body).

of the borough of Donore, which was effectively a suburb of the city of Dublin, while in the southern half of the county, the archbishops of Dublin established boroughs at Clondalkin, Dalkey, Rathcoole, Shankill and Tallaght. North of the Liffey, they also founded boroughs at Lusk (Figure 6.9) and Swords.

A transcript of a charter of confirmation issued by Archbishop Luke of Dublin to the burgesses of Rathcoole is preserved in Alen's register.[120] Although the confirmation refers to the laws and customs of Bristol, the actual terms point clearly to the law of Breteuil.[121] Each burgage tenement contained four acres and was held at an annual rent of 12*d*. Rathcoole also had a mill and those who produced grain on the nearby farms had to come there to have it ground. Swords was one of the largest and most influential boroughs in the Dublin region, and the castle there was one of the archbishops' principal seats. There was an annual eight-day fair and probably also a weekly market from 1193.[122] A confirmation issued by Archbishop Cumin to the burgesses of Swords, either in the closing years of the twelfth century or the early years of the thirteenth, stated that the burgesses there were liable to certain labour services such as reaping, carting the archbishop's hay and corn and repairing the millpond.[123]

Tallaght was one of the most important ecclesiastical manors in the region (Figure 6.10), and the borough there was home to one of the archbishop of Dublin's palaces.[124] The significance of Dalkey was as a deep-water port, particularly in the fourteenth century and after.[125] Saggart was a royal borough, one kilometre to the west of the archbishops' borough at Rathcoole. Both settlements were roughly halfway along the main thoroughfare from Dublin to Naas. The manor of Newcastle Lyons was also retained by the crown, but evidence for its status as a borough does not appear until the late fifteenth century (Figure 6.14). The borough of Lucan, established possibly by Alard Fitz William or Warisius de Pech, may have been founded on a green-field site close to a ford over the River Liffey.[126] Whatever the origins of this settlement, it quickly developed into an important regional focus, with a castle, a church and a mill.

120 McNeill (ed.), *Alen's register*, p. 84.　**121** For discussion of the laws of Breteuil, see Adolphus Ballard, 'The law of Breteuil', *EHR*, 30 (1915), 646–58; Mary Bateson, 'The laws of Breteuil', *EHR*, 15 (1900), 73–90, 302–18, 496–523, 754–7; 16 (1901), 92–110, 332–45.　**122** McNeill (ed.), *Alen's register*, p. 23; Bradley, 'The medieval boroughs of Co. Dublin', pp 138–9.　**123** McNeill (ed.), *Alen's register*, p. 32.　**124** This building was taken down in 1729 (W.D. Handcock, *A history of Tallaght* (2nd ed., Dublin, 1899), p. 17; Harbison (ed.), *Beranger's drawings*, pp 28–9).　**125** Smith, *Dalkey: society and economy*.　**126** Bradley, 'The medieval boroughs of Co. Dublin', pp 135, 142.

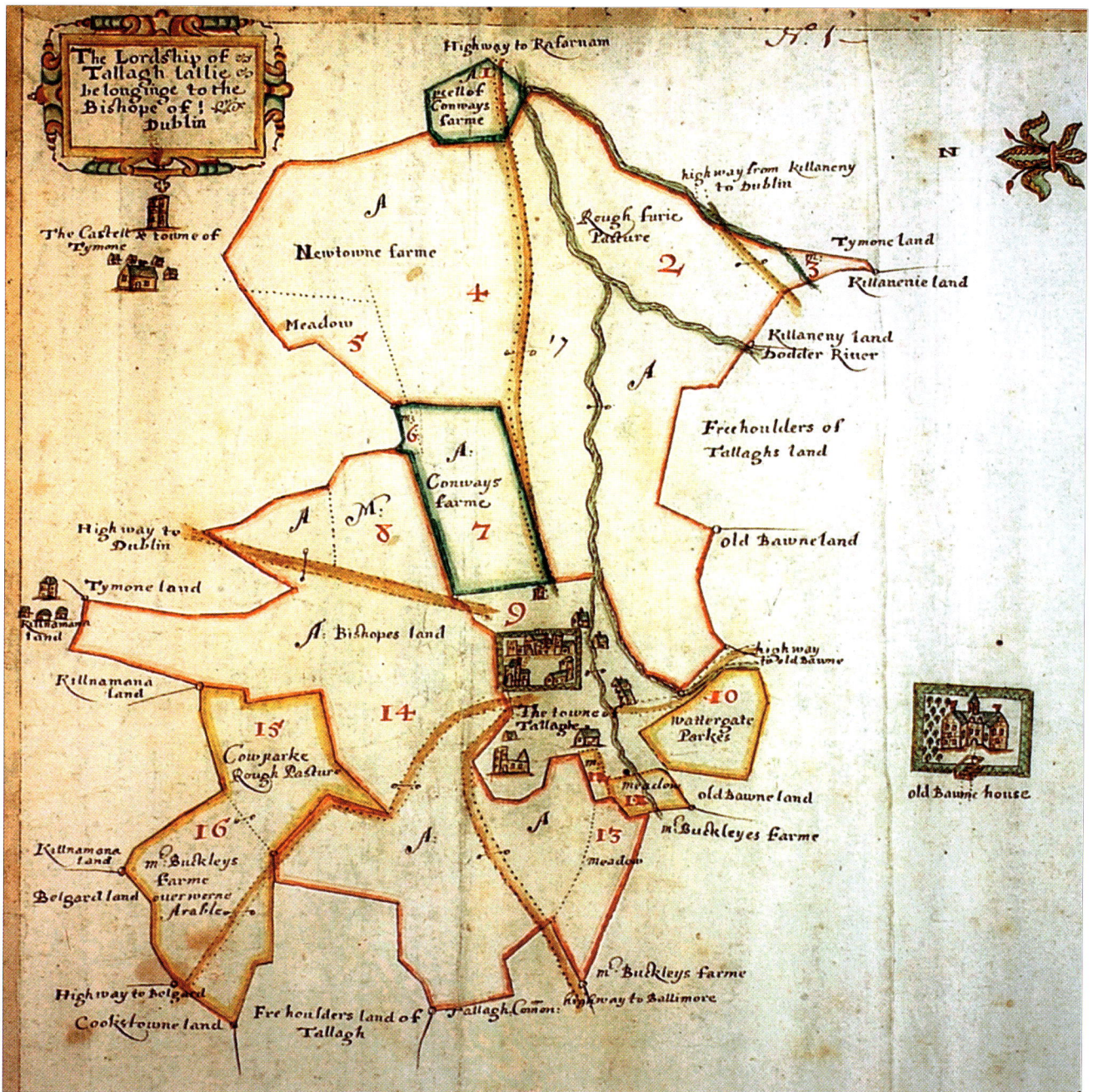

Figure 6.10 Map of Tallaght, Co. Dublin, by Robert Newcomen, 1654 (© Representative Church Body).

In Co. Kildare, the manor of Ballymore (Eustace) belonged to the archbishops of Dublin and the borough was established on the River Liffey on the main route from Dublin to the medieval towns of Athy, Carlow and Kilkenny.[127] The borough grew rapidly and soon had an annual fair, a weekly market, a church, a castle, two water-mills and a kiln. Ballymore is a rare example of a borough founded by the church in north-east Co. Kildare where, reflecting the landholding situation, most tended to be founded by lay-lords. In these cases, it was not unusual for the secular lords to hand over control of the borough church to one of the religious houses in Dublin.

The borough of Kill may have been founded by a de Hereford or a de Rochford, but there was significant involvement on behalf of the abbey of St Thomas from an early stage.[128] The church of Kill had been granted to St Thomas' by 1202, and not long after that, there is a record of them holding a grange, a croft, a garden and a haggard there too.[129] The

127 Bradley, Halpin and King, 'UAS 7:1: Kildare', pp 83–96.   128 Bradley, Halpin and King, 'UAS 7:3: Kildare', pp 292–303.   129 *RAST*, pp 298–9.

Figure 6.11 Map of
Newcastle Lyons,
Co. Dublin. The form,
layout and names of the
fields are relics of
medieval agricultural
organisation. In 1765,
the pattern of
ownership of the
fields – with three
tenants owning the
fields shaded here –
was also a medieval
inheritance (after
Geraldine Stout and
Matthew Stout, 'Early
landscapes: from
prehistory to plantation'
in Aalen, Whelan and
Stout (eds), Atlas of the
Irish rural landscape
(1997), pp 31–63,
fig. 68, p. 60).

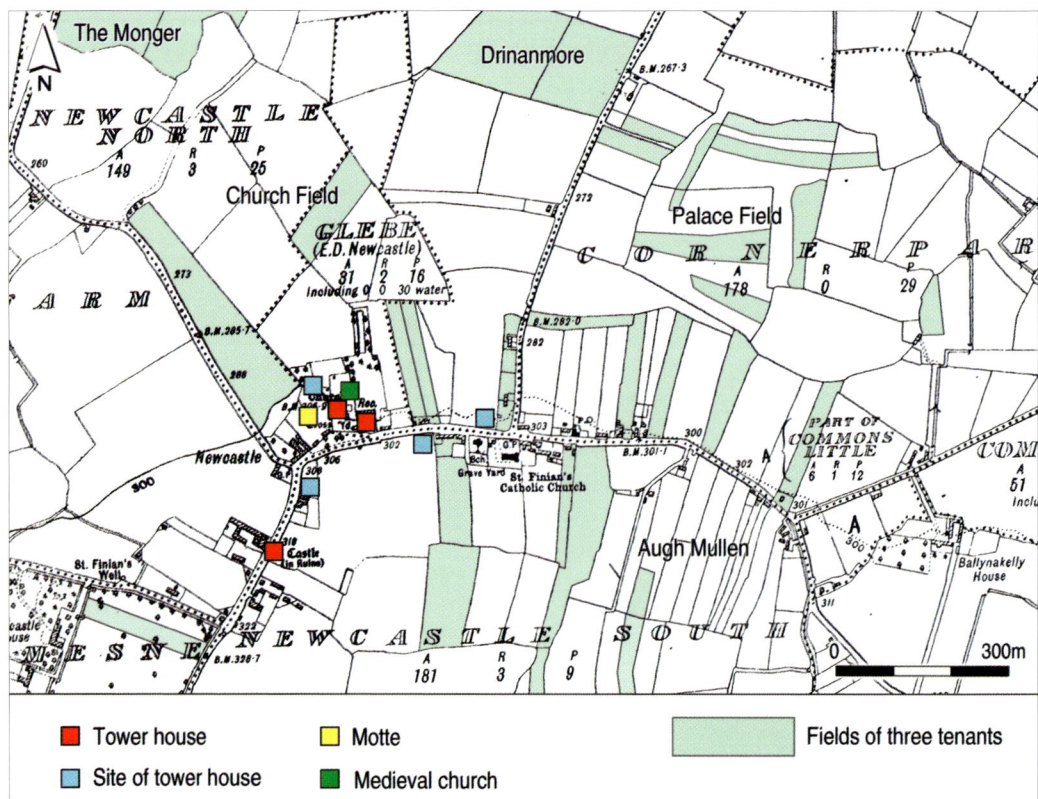

Figure 6.11 Map of Newcastle Lyons, Co. Dublin.

Legend: Tower house · Site of tower house · Motte · Medieval church · Fields of three tenants

borough of Leixlip was founded by Adam de Hereford, who granted the church and some other property to the abbey of St Thomas, and another burgage to St Mary's Abbey (Dublin) early in the thirteenth century.[130] Due to its riverine location and its arable hinterland, milling formed a very important part of Leixlip's economy.

The early ecclesiastical site at Clane was developed as a borough, possibly by the de Stauntons, and its religious functions were continued by the foundation of a Franciscan friary there c.1258 (possibly by Gerald fitz Maurice FitzGerald).[131] There was also a castle, a parish church, a mill and (from 1392) a stone bridge. The de Herefords or the Pippards founded a borough at Oughterard sometime before 1276, and from 1318 a weekly market and annual fair were held there.[132] As with so many of the ecclesiastical sites in the area, the church at Oughterard was granted to St Thomas' Abbey by Adam de Hereford before 1189.[133] The site is now abandoned, but phosphate analysis has indicated the former location of the borough to the south-east of the upstanding church.[134] This examination also identified evidence for agricultural activity close to the borough in the form of a series of linear banks and possible drainage channels.

Gerald fitz Maurice FitzGerald was granted a weekly market at Rathmore in the second half of the 1180s and a borough was established there no later than 1203.[135] An indication of the amount of land required to sustain a borough can be ascertained from the Rathmore burgesses' charter of c.1220.[136] Eighty-five of the burgages were to contain seven acres, while the other eleven were to have half an acre each. This means that the burgesses of Rathmore held about 600 medieval acres (or 1,500 statute acres).

The borough of Cloncurry may have been established by Adam de Hereford, but the first references to it do not appear until 1304.[137] Celbridge was also in the lands of the de

130 Bradley, Halpin and King, 'UAS 7:3: Kildare', pp 304–23.   131 MRHI, p. 245.   132 Bradley, Halpin and King, 'UAS 7:4: Kildare', pp 400–12.   133 RAST, p. 75.   134 Carl Heistermann, 'Appendix. Phosphate analysis at Oughterard, Co. Kildare' in Hall, Hennessy and O'Keeffe, 'Medieval agriculture and settlement in Oughterard and Castlewarden' (1985), 16–25 at 23–4; O'Keeffe, Medieval Ireland, pp 63–4.   135 Bradley, Halpin and King, 'UAS 7:4: Kildare', pp 422–35.   136 Mac Niocaill, Na buirgéisí, 2, pp 294–5.   137 Bradley, Halpin and King, 'UAS 7:2: Kildare',

Herefords, but the borough there may have been founded later by the earls of Kildare.[138] Three kilometres to the north of Old Kilcullen, the present village of Kilcullen developed beside a bridge built over the River Liffey in 1319.[139] It has been shown, however, that references to Kilcullen in medieval records actually refer to the borough of Old Kilcullen, which is just outside the Dublin study area.

The archbishops of Dublin also founded a series of boroughs in Co. Wicklow, but Burgage, Dunlavin, Hollywood and Killickabawn (Kilmacberne) all appear to have been unsuccessful ventures.[140] An important borough was established by the crown in conjunction with the royal manor of Newcastle McKynegan, but even this appears to have passed into the hands of the Gaelic Irish at the beginning of the fifteenth century.[141] In 1450, Sir Edmund Mulso was granted permission to establish a borough called Mulsoescourt, in the lordship of Fercullen (the Powerscourt area of the Dublin/Wicklow border).[142] It is not known if this borough was ever founded, but no further references to it are known and there is no visible physical evidence for its existence.

Boroughs founded by secular lords in Co. Wicklow seem to have been more successful. The borough of Wicklow is likely to have been founded by Maurice Fitz Gerald,[143] and in 1213 Walter de Ridelesford was granted a weekly market at Bray, and it was probably he who founded the borough there.[144] He granted property in the borough to St Mary's Abbey, Dublin, and further property was later given to St Thomas' Abbey.[145] The burgage he granted to St Mary's Abbey was situated opposite his castle and was described as being eighty paces in width and twenty perches in length. The burgage granted to St Thomas' lay beside that of St Mary's but was fifty paces in width and thirty perches in length.

Although no borough charter survives for Dunboyne, it is generally defined as being one of Meath's second stratum borough settlements.[146] This is by virtue of its being the centre of one of the major land grants of the subinfeudation and its possession of early market and fair charters.[147] It was probably founded in the early decades of the thirteenth century by Nicholas le Petit, son of William le Petit, the original grantee. The appearance of individuals with the locative surname 'Dunboyne' in the Dublin guild merchant roll of 1190–1265 is further proof of its nucleated nature.[148] Despite the various vicissitudes of the fourteenth century which resulted in the desertion of several Anglo-Norman boroughs, Dunboyne continued to exist if not flourish. In 1366, it was chosen as the venue for a meeting between the archbishop of Armagh and the chancellor of Ireland to discuss a controversy that had arisen between the archbishops of Dublin and Armagh.[149] In 1423, the provost and community of Dunboyne were asked to assist the town of Trim, which was coming under threat from the depredations of the O'Conors and O'Reillys.[150] At around the same time, various towns in Meath were assessed for a subsidy to raise money to help in the fight against the king's enemies. Dunboyne was assessed at 13s. 4d., while Ratoath, Skreen, Navan and Slane were assessed at 10s.[151] The borough received a boost in 1475 when Edmond (Esmond) Butler, eighth baron of Dunboyne, undertook to 'erect and complete a castle anew at Dunboyne at his great charge and costs'.[152]

pp 167–79. **138** Ibid., pp 137–47. **139** Ibid., pp 384–99. **140** Bradley and King, 'UAS 9: Wicklow', pp 20–7, 38–43, 48–52, 53–6. **141** Bradley and King, 'UAS 9: Wicklow', pp 61–7. **142** Stat. Ire. Hen. VI, pp 214–19; Liam Price, 'Powerscourt and the territory of Fercullen', JRSAI, 83 (1953), 117–32; Bradley and King, 'UAS 9: Wicklow', pp 57–60. **143** Bradley and King, 'UAS 9: Wicklow', pp 68–77. **144** Ibid., pp 12–19; Davies, IHTA: Bray. **145** CSMA, I, p. 29; RHJB, p. 170. **146** As, for example, in Graham's functional settlement hierarchy: see Graham, 'Anglo-Norman settlement in County Meath', 226. **147** CDI, 1171–1251, no. 1389, p. 210, no. 1673, p. 250. **148** DGMR, pp 44, 69, 83, 105. The admissions include 'Johannes medicus de Dunboyn'. **149** Brendan Smith (ed.), The register of Milo Sweteman, archbishop of Armagh, 1361–1380 (Dublin, 1996), p. 28. **150** RPCH, p. 225. **151** RPCH, p. 230. **152** Stat. Ire., 12–22 Edw. IV, p. 287.

Figure 6.12 (*left*) Cross-incised stone slab at Ballymore Eustace Church, Co. Kildare (image courtesy of Chris Corlett).

Figure 6.13 (*right*) Cross-incised stone slab at Donard Church, Co. Wicklow (image courtesy of Chris Corlett).

The barony of Ratoath contained two medieval boroughs, Dunshaughlin and Greenoge, as well as the town of Ratoath.[153] The earliest reference to Greenoge's existence as a borough occurs in 1228 when a burgage plot was granted to St Thomas' Abbey, Dublin.[154] Little further is known about this borough. An extent of 1344 for the manor of Dunshaughlin mentions an unspecified number of free tenants and burgesses paying rents amounting to £4 18s. 2d.[155] The 'works' of the burgesses are mentioned, implying some customary services, subsequently commuted to financial renders.

The borough at Skreen was established at an early date and is first referred to during the early thirteenth century, when one Geoffrey of Galetrum granted St Mary's Abbey, Dublin, a burgage in Skreen along with three acres of land.[156] The burgage was held by an individual called Macrath, whose name suggests that he was Irish. The rent paid by Macrath and his heirs was specified as 6d. to the abbey and 12d. to the lord. There are few references to the later history of the borough although, like Navan, Ratoath and Slane, it was assessed at 10s. in the early fourteenth-century subsidy.[157]

The existence of these rural boroughs suggests that there was a considerable degree of nucleated settlement across the Dublin region throughout the medieval period. Of course, not all nucleated settlements had borough status. The forty-two cottars named in the extent for Cloncurry, Co. Kildare, are likely to have held their cottages and small plots of land in the vicinity of the church and motte at Cloncurry, forming a distinct manorial village that also had a recorded market.[158] There were other centres that clearly supported significant population clusters without the benefit of borough status. Killeen, Co. Meath, provides a good example of a manorial village that supported a population of over eighty families in the fifteenth century.[159] There were very few recorded boroughs in north Co. Dublin, but it is likely that there were manorial villages at places such as Ballymadun, Corduff, Finglas and Malahide.[160]

153 Bradley, 'UAS 2: Meath'; John Bradley, 'The medieval towns of County Meath', *RnM*, 8:2 (1988–9), 30–49. **154** *RAST*, p. 59. **155** TNA:PRO/C135/75/3; Dryburgh and Smith (eds), *Handbook*, pp 58–9. **156** *CSMA*, I, p. 236. **157** *RPCH*, p. 230. **158** *CJR, 1295–1303*, p. 198. **159** Benskin, 'An English township in fifteenth-century Ireland'. **160** For example, 'your town of Corduff in the parish of Lusk' (*COD*, 4, p. 317).

Figure 6.14 Trevet, Co. Meath. Excavations in advance of road construction revealed the remains of a rectangular house of thirteenth-/fourteenth-century date, as well as a cobbled laneway and yard (image courtesy of Stuart Rathbone and ACS Ltd).

Many of these rural boroughs and manorial villages went on to become successful towns and villages. A significant number did not survive, however, and these deserted borough and village sites provide the best opportunity for archaeological investigation.

Excavations by Alan Hayden in the 1990s revealed evidence for medieval peasant houses within the medieval borough of Ballymore, Co. Kildare.[161] The presence of a number of late medieval cross-incised slabs at Ballymore is further evidence of settlement relating to the archiepiscopal manor and borough here (Figure 6.12). Similar slabs have been identified at Burgage, Donard (Figure 6.13) and Hollywood (all Co. Wicklow) and Templeogue and Saggart (Co. Dublin). Corlett has described them as an important addition to the evidence available for the analysis of medieval settlement in this region.[162]

At Macetown, Co. Meath, a deserted settlement covers almost eight acres and includes a series of rectangular house platforms.[163] The plots are arranged in a grid pattern and front onto sunken trackways, while the edges of the settlement are defined on two sides by a millrace. A tower house once stood at Macetown but is now a pile of rubble and is likely to mark the site of an earlier castle situated to the west of a ruinous church.

Three kilometres due north of Dunshaughlin, Co. Meath, the townland of Trevet is believed to have contained a manorial village in the Middle Ages.[164] Trevet was granted by Walter de Lacy to his younger brother Hugh in the 1190s. According to a charter that survives in the Gormanston Register, Walter granted 'all the land of Ratoath with all appurtenances as well and fully as I have held said land and, for increase, Trevet with all its appurtenances' (*totam terram de Rathtowtht cum omnibus pertinenciis suis sicut melius et plenius eandem terram unquam tenui et de incremento Treuthd cum omnibus pertinenciis suis*).[165] It is clear that Trevet was outside the area described as 'the land of Ratoath', as Trevet was

161 O'Conor, *Medieval rural settlement in Ireland*, p. 55.   **162** Christiaan Corlett, 'The Hollywood slabs: some late medieval grave-slabs from west Wicklow and neighbouring counties', *JRSAI*, 133 (2003), 86–110 at 105.   **163** Moore, *Archaeological inventory of County Meath*, pp 139, 164, 172.   **164** Graham, 'Anglo-Norman settlement in County Meath', fig. 3.   **165** *CGR*, pp 142–3, 190.

given in order to augment the holding. This may explain why part of the civil parish of Trevet is in the barony of Ratoath, while most is within the barony of Skreen.[166] In any case, Hugh de Lacy enfeoffed Walter de Scotot (or Escotot) with Trevet, and de Scotot then granted the church of Trevet to the abbey of St Thomas, Dublin.[167]

The present church at Trevet has an undivided nave and chancel with opposing doors near the west end (overall dimensions *c.*6m by 26m).[168] It contains several sixteenth- and seventeenth-century memorials to the Cusack family. In the early fourteenth-century ecclesiastical taxation, the church of the Holy Trinity, *alias* Trevet, was valued at ten marks (£6 13*s.* 4*d.*), while the vicarage of Trevet was valued at five marks (£3 6*s.* 8*d.*).[169] There was an important monastery at Trevet from at least the eighth century (abbot Albran died there *c.*769),[170] and perhaps from as early as the sixth century, as Colmcille is said to have visited there in 560.[171] The church was wealthy or important enough to warrant attacks by the Vikings in 848 and 917, and by Irish raiders in 1145 and 1152.[172] It is possible that the later medieval church was built on this early church site. Indeed, the field boundaries surrounding the present church, on both sides of the road, may follow the line of an earlier enclosure. A second possible location for the early church is in the neighbouring townland of Trevet Grange, which seems to have been the part of Trevet held by the abbey of St Thomas.[173] Early ecclesiastical connections here might explain the later grant of this land (and church?) to St Thomas'. Traces of a large oval enclosure around the present farmyard at Trevet Grange can be seen from the air as cropmarks. The surrounding fields are also replete with cropmarks and low earthworks.

In 1654, the Civil Survey recorded that Trevet had a church, a farmhouse and some cabins.[174] Ninety years later, Isaac Butler described the decayed village of Trevet, which then contained six poor cottages, a good farmhouse and a ruined church: 'Trevet was anciently a considerable town and colony of English … at present it is an obscure village'.[175] In 1862, Anthony Cogan recorded the desertion of the manorial village of Trevet: 'almost the whole population has been swept from the land. The country has been converted into pasture, a herd's house is all that remains of the poor town; sheep and oxen abound here in great numbers, but the bone and sinew of the country has passed away'.[176]

Although little is immediately visible at Trevet now, there are indications of the former presence of a range of medieval features. A raised rectangular area (*c.*30m north-south by *c.*33m east-west) is surrounded by a slight fosse with an entrance on the west side.[177] This may have been a moated site. An adjacent sunken roadway (*c.*15m in width) connects with a series of low earthwork field boundaries covering *c.*10 acres.[178] The roadway continues in the direction of the ruinous medieval church mentioned above.

Towards the western boundary of the townland, close to the laneway leading to the church, archaeological excavations in advance of the construction of the M3 motorway uncovered the very fragmentary remains of a rectangular building with estimated external dimensions of *c.*6m by 20m (Figure 6.14).[179] It seems that this was a house with stone foundations and lower wall courses, surmounted by a clay/cob superstructure. The excavator suggested that there would have been a cruck-frame to support the roof. There was an associated cobbled laneway and yard, as well as several pits and a ditch that partly

166 *Civil Survey*, 5, pp 74–5, 93.   **167** *RAST*, pp 10, 12, 15, 20, 261–2; *CDI, 1285–92*, no. 839, p. 381.   **168** Moore, *Archaeological inventory of County Meath*, p. 147.   **169** *CDI, 1302–7*, no. 713, p. 254.   **170** *AFM, s.a.* 769.   **171** A.O. Anderson and M.O. Anderson, *Adomnán's Life of St Columba* (London, 1961).   **172** *AFM, s.a.* 848, 917, 1145, 1152.   **173** *EIMP*, pp 32–3; *RAST*, pp 8, 26.   **174** *Civil Survey*, 5, pp 74–5, 93.   **175** Isaac Butler, 'A journey to Lough Derg', *JRSAI*, 22 (1892), 13–24, 126–36 at 17.   **176** Anthony Cogan, *The diocese of Meath, ancient and modern* (3 vols, Dublin, 1862–70), I, p. 155.   **177** Moore, *Archaeological inventory of County Meath*, p. 119.   **178** Ibid., p. 124.   **179** Stuart Rathbone, 'Trevet 1: draft interim excavation report', unpublished report, 2007.

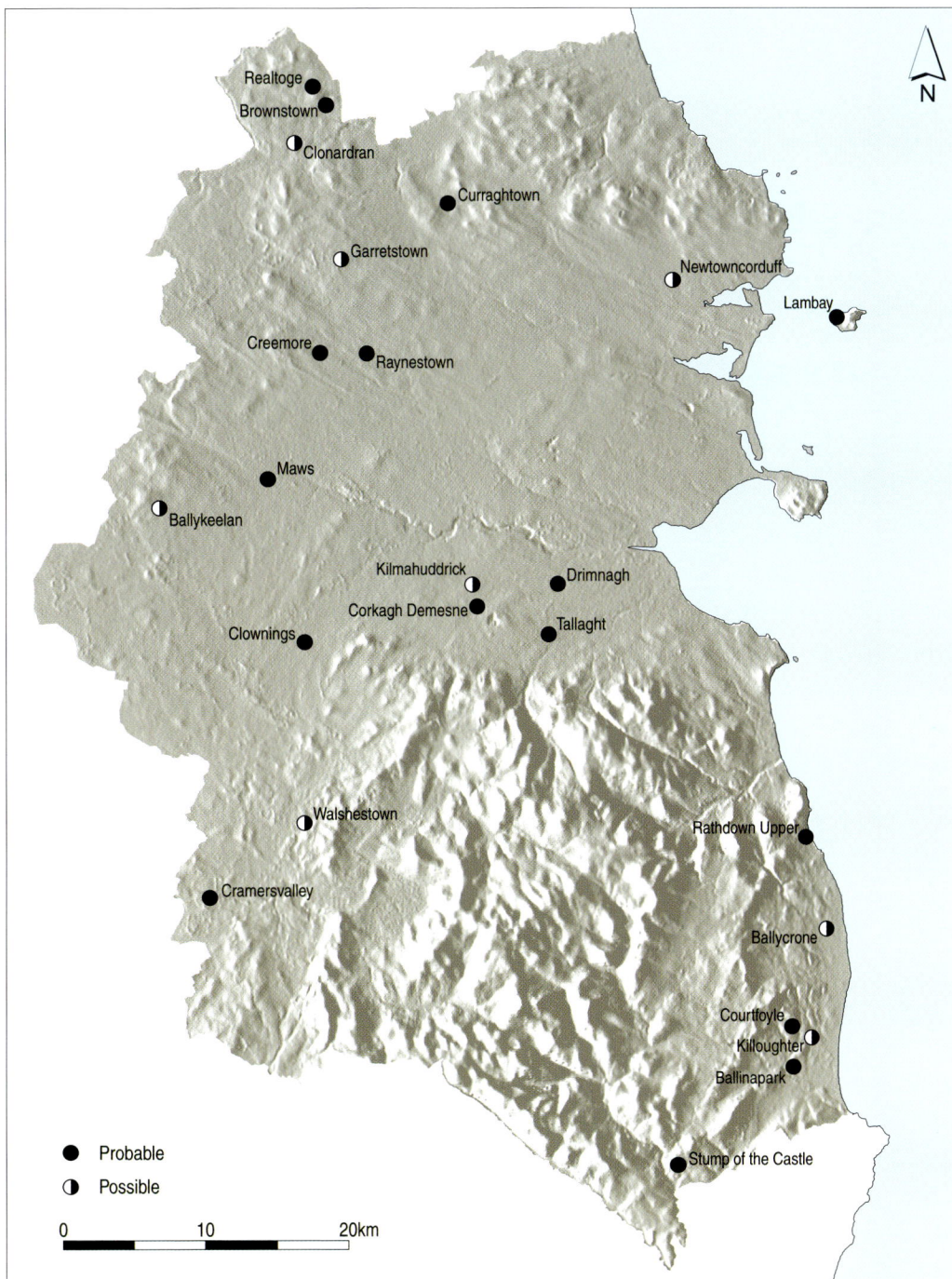

Figure 6.15 Distribution of moated sites in the Dublin region.

surrounded the house. The artefacts, which included over 3,000 sherds of medieval pottery, indicate a thirteenth-/fourteenth-century date for the complex. While the director of the excavations is reluctant to see this house as part of a manor centre, it would appear to be contemporary with other activity in this and the neighbouring townland.

Seven kilometres to the west of Trevet, at Tullykane, excavations by Christine Baker uncovered the remains of what appears to have been an Anglo-Norman tenant settlement.[180] Two possible houses were identified, as well as a series of ditches, gullies, pits, hearths and burnt spreads. Pottery from the site has been dated to between AD1250 and 1300, possibly extending to about 1350. After that time the site appears to have been abandoned.

---

180 Christine Baker, 'Tullykane, Co. Meath: a medieval rural settlement' in Corlett and Potterton (eds), *Rural settlement in medieval Ireland* (2009), pp 1–18.

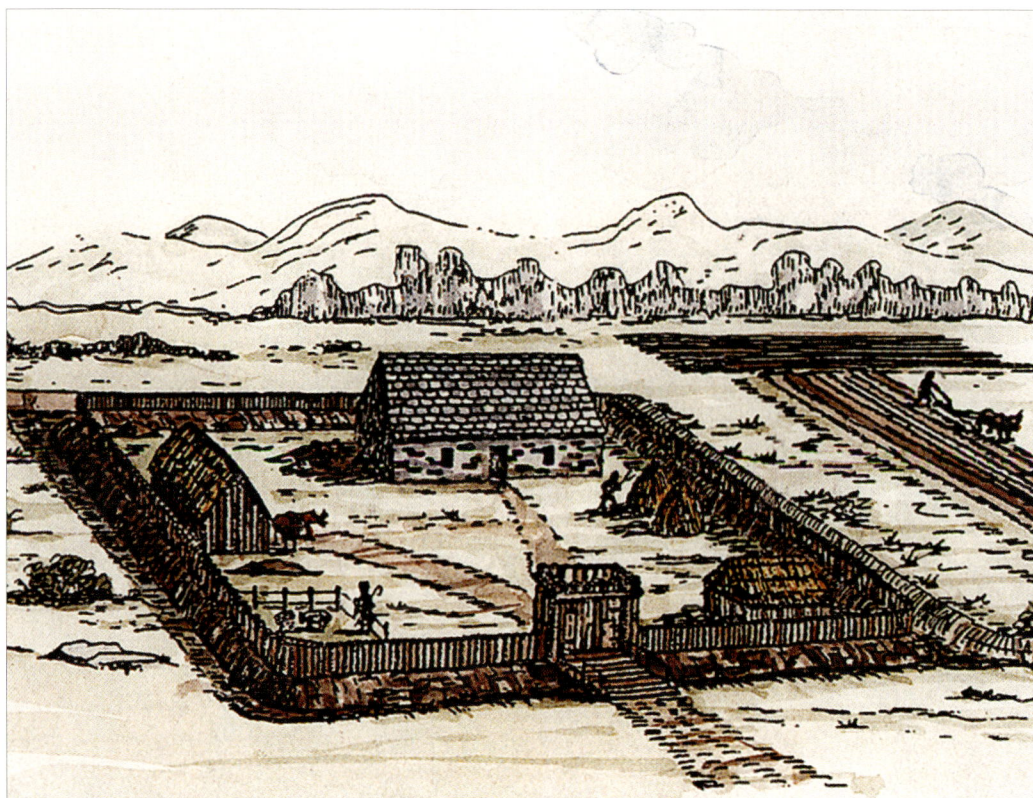

It is evident from the documentary sources that many manorial tenants lived in dispersed settlements away from the manor centres. In general, this dispersed settlement has left very little trace on the landscape but one monument type, the moated site, has been frequently associated with manorial free tenants.

Moated sites

A moated site can be defined as an area enclosed by a rectangular or sub-rectangular, often water-filled, ditch (Figure 6.16).[181] They are most frequently (but not exclusively) found in the south and east of the country, and on lands controlled by the Anglo-Normans. Their primary function was as defended farmsteads and, unlike in the case of many castles, there appears to be little association between moated sites and parish churches. This is significant in terms of both the role and chronology of the moated sites. They are not usually seen as part of the first phase of manorial development, and are more often associated with a later wave of settlement, whereby lands in more peripheral areas were granted to new settlers (especially in the second half of the thirteenth century). This latter point might well explain the relative rarity of moated sites in the Dublin region (Figure 6.15) – little land remained unaccounted for and uncultivated after the first wave of grants.

In his 1998 treatment of moated sites in Ireland, O'Conor noted that 'there has been little attempt to fit this settlement form into the different models of manorial settlement proposed by various historical geographers over the last fifteen years'.[182] It has been suggested, however, that many moated sites in Ireland served as the defended manor houses and farms

181 For discussion of moated sites, see Barry, *Medieval moated sites of south-eastern Ireland*; T.B. Barry, 'Moated sites in Ireland' in F.A. Aberg (ed.), *Medieval moated sites* (London, 1978), pp 56–9; T.B. Barry, 'The moated sites of Co. Waterford', *Decies*, 10 (1979), 32–6; T.B. Barry, 'The shifting frontier: medieval moated sites in Counties Cork and Limerick' in F.A. Aberg and A.E. Brown (eds), *Medieval moated sites in north-west Europe* (Oxford, 1981), pp 71–85; R.E. Glasscock, 'Moated sites and deserted boroughs and villages: two neglected aspects of Anglo-Norman settlement in Ireland' in Nicholas Stephens and R.E. Glasscock (eds), *Irish geographical studies in honour of E. Estyn Evans* (Belfast, 1970), pp 162–77; O'Conor, *Medieval rural settlement in Ireland*, pp 58–69; O'Keeffe, *Medieval Ireland*, pp 73–80. 182 O'Conor, *Medieval rural settlement in Ireland*, p. 58.

of minor Anglo-Norman gentry in the thirteenth and fourteenth centuries.[183] It is also possible that some moated sites mark the remains of monastic granges or hunting lodges, and some were certainly lived in by the Gaelic Irish.[184] The view that moated sites were farmsteads of free tenants who settled on assarts or newly cleared land-holdings, as opposed to the manor houses of minor Anglo-Norman gentry, has also been discussed.[185] It seems highly plausible that at least some moated sites in Ireland were

Figure 6.17 Old Bawn House, Co. Dublin, from a watercolour of 'the lordship of Tallagh latlie belonginge to the Bishope of Dublin' by Robert Newcomen (1654). This detail shows a three-storey house with high gables and tall chimneys, surrounded by a moat crossed by a bridge (© Representative Church Body).

constructed by free tenants of English origin (primarily), away from manorial centres, on marginal lands and/or in areas bordering with the Gaelic Irish. O'Conor concluded that 'at present [1998] the moated site series in Ireland can contribute little to the ongoing debate concerning the exact appearance of dispersed English peasant settlement within Anglo-Norman manors in eastern Ireland'.[186]

The handful of moated sites around Dublin includes Drimnagh,[187] Kilmahuddrick, Lambay (Figure 6.18), Newtowncorduff and a possible one at Castlewarden. McNeill suggests that the large earthwork at Castlekevin, Co. Wicklow, is best described as 'a strongly defended moated site', but the site looks more like a large rectangular motte.[188] A stone castle was built inside the area enclosed by a moated site at Stump of the Castle, also in Co. Wicklow.[189] Situated in low-lying grounds on Corkagh Demesne, Corkagh House (which is now destroyed) was once surrounded by a moat.[190] A map of the lordship of Tallaght drawn by Robert Newcomen in 1654 depicts Old Bawn House, built by William Bulkley, as a large edifice enclosed by what appears to be a rectangular moat traversed by a bridge (Figure 6.17).[191] The seventeenth-century house may have been constructed within an existing moated site.

The D-shaped, raised-platform enclosure at Castlewarden, Co. Kildare, could be described as a moated site, but at one end there is an oval mound that could be a small motte. The site is surrounded by an extensive system of earthworks including drainage channels, banks and enclosures.[192] One-hundred-and-fifty metres from the site is a rectangular building platform. It has been suggested that this possible moated site was associated with a phase of 'exploitation, although apparently not for cultivation, of marshland between Oughterard and Castlewarden'.[193] The site may also have been the manor house of the estate.

The *Archaeological inventory of County Wicklow* lists as a possible moated site the roughly square enclosure overlooking the sea at Rathdown Upper (Figure 6.19).[194] The earthwork

183 Barry, *Medieval moated sites of southeast Ireland*, pp 101–2; Barry, 'Rural settlement in Ireland in the Middle Ages', 137.   184 Brian Graham, *Anglo-Norman settlement in Ireland* (Athlone, 1985), p. 22; O'Conor, *Medieval rural settlement in Ireland*, pp 61, 87–9; Thomas Finan and Kieran O'Conor, 'The moated site at Cloonfree, Co. Roscommon', *Journal of the Galway Archaeological and Historical Society*, 54 (2002), 72–87.   185 McNeill, *Castles in Ireland*, pp 148–9; O'Conor, *Medieval rural settlement in Ireland*, pp 61–2.   186 O'Conor, *Medieval rural settlement in Ireland*, p. 69. 187 Ball, 'Descriptive sketch of Clondalkin', 95–6; Ball, *A history of the county of Dublin*, 4, pp 125–32; Dix, 'The lesser castles', 49–50; Harbison (ed.), *Beranger's drawings*, pp 40–3; Corcoran, '"Ireland's forgotten castle"'.   188 McNeill, *Castles in Ireland*, p. 140; O'Conor, 'The later construction and use of motte and bailey castles in Ireland', 24. 189 Grogan and Kilfeather, *Archaeological inventory of County Wicklow*, p. 191.   190 Liam Ua Broin, 'Clondalkin, Co. Dublin, and its neighbourhood: notes on place-names, topography and traditions, &c', *JRSAI*, 74 (1944), 191–218 at 203.   191 Raymond Refaussé and Mary Clark, *A catalogue of the maps of the estates of the archbishops of Dublin, 1654–1850* (Dublin, 2000), pp 43, 89 (n. 3), pl. 23.   192 Hall, Hennessy and O'Keeffe, 'Medieval agriculture and settlement in Oughterard and Castlewarden', 20–2.   193 Ibid., 22.   194 Grogan and Kilfeather, *Archaeological inventory of County Wicklow*, p. 170.

Figure 6.18 Aerial photograph showing moated site on Lambay, Co. Dublin (CUCAP AOZ44 image courtesy of Cambridge University Collection of Aerial Photographs).

measures *c*.43m by 43m and is represented by a distinct cropmark that indicates a fosse that retains a roughly 7m-wide causeway approximately half way along the north side. The continuation of the fosse right around the site is hinted at, but the southern half of the enclosure, which included the site of stone castle (perhaps sixteenth century in date), was developed as a sewerage treatment plant that has since been removed. An 'associated field system or medieval village' is evident as further cropmark features to the north of the squared enclosure, and a small church and graveyard lies to the south-west.[195] The site may have been a residence of the Mac Gilla Mo Cholmóc family.[196]

Situated in a slight natural hollow in gently undulating terrain, is the moated site at Ballinapark, Co. Wicklow.[197] It is roughly 30m square and is surrounded by a 4.5m-wide earthen bank that averages 1m in height. Outside this is a flat-bottomed fosse measuring 6.5m in width and 1.7–2.5m in depth. The moat is fed by a leat from a stream on the north side. The bank has been levelled at the north-east corner. There are no traces of an entrance or any features on the interior. Similar to Ballinapark in situation and shape, but almost three times the area (51m²), is the moated site at Stump of the Castle.[198] It was described in

195 DEHLG file, CUCAP BDP25; Grogan and Kilfeather, *Archaeological inventory of County Wicklow*, pp 185, 111, 134. 196 For discussion of moated sites and ethnicity, see Kieran O'Conor, 'The ethnicity of Irish moated sites', *Ruralia*, 3 (2000), 92–102; Tadhg O'Keeffe, 'Ethnicity and moated settlement in medieval Ireland: a review of current thinking', *Medieval Settlement Research Group Annual Report*, 15 (2000), 21–5. 197 Grogan and Kilfeather, *Archaeological inventory of County Wicklow*, p. 168; Simpson, 'Anglo-Norman settlement in Uí Briuin Cualann', p. 216. 198 Grogan

Figure 6.19 Aerial photograph of the moated site at Rathdown Upper, Co. Wicklow. Faint traces of the banks and ditch can be seen as cropmarks in the middle of the upper half of this photograph (CUCAP BDP26 image courtesy of Cambridge University Collection of Aerial Photographs).

1838 as having a deep wide fosse, but little of this is now visible.[199] The square moated site at Courtfoyle is also situated on a gentle south-facing slope, and is also 51m².[200] The earthen bank that surrounds it rises from 50cm on the interior to 2m on the exterior. It is faced with a dry-stone wall, outside which is a 4–6m-wide fosse. A possible entrance feature on the east side consists of a causeway across the fosse, which is fed by a stream. Sections of the moated site at Killoughter have been incorporated into farm buildings.[201] Further earthworks, consisting of field boundaries, platforms and linear features, are adjacent to the site and may be vestiges of a farm associated with it. The moated sites at Killoughter, Courtfoyle and Ballinapark are all within 3km of each other (Figure 6.15).

The oval enclosure at Ballykeelan, near Cloncurry, Co. Kildare, contains a sub-rectangular platform measuring c.12m by 15m (Figures 6.20, 6.21). The platform is surrounded by a slight bank inside a fosse. The fosse is 7m wide and 2m deep on average. The rectangular feature may be a small moated site.[202] Other moated sites in the Kildare portion of the study area include the roughly square (43m) 'Puddlehall Moat' at Clownings, and the large rectangular platform at Sallymount Demesne (also known as Cramersvalley). This latter example, which is c.50m², overlooks the River Liffey 2.5km east of Kilcullen. The moated site at Dunfierth is slightly raised and measures 36m by 31m. Like the sites at Clownings and Sallymount Demesne, it has a broad fosse (8–10m wide). The external bank at Dunfierth is partly stone-built, and a stone revetment is visible on the south corner of the platform. A well is shown at the west corner in the first edition Ordnance Survey map. A second moated site, 150m to the west, measures 30m by 31m and its shallow fosse is fed by a leat at the north-east corner.[203] Burgesses are recorded at 'Dunfert' in 1273, and Glasscock

and Kilfeather, *Archaeological inventory of County Wicklow*, p. 170. **199** O'Flanagan (comp.), *Ordnance Survey letters, Wicklow, 1838*, pp 121–2. **200** Grogan and Kilfeather, *Archaeological inventory of County Wicklow*, p. 169. **201** Ibid.; Simpson, 'Anglo-Norman settlement in Uí Briuin Cualann', p. 216. **202** Noel Murphy and Karina Holton, 'An aerial perspective on Oughterany', *Oughterany*, 2:1 (1999), 97–106. **203** DEHLG files.

Figure 6.20 Aerial photograph of earthworks at Ballykeelan, Co. Kildare (image courtesy of Noel Murphy and Karina Holton).

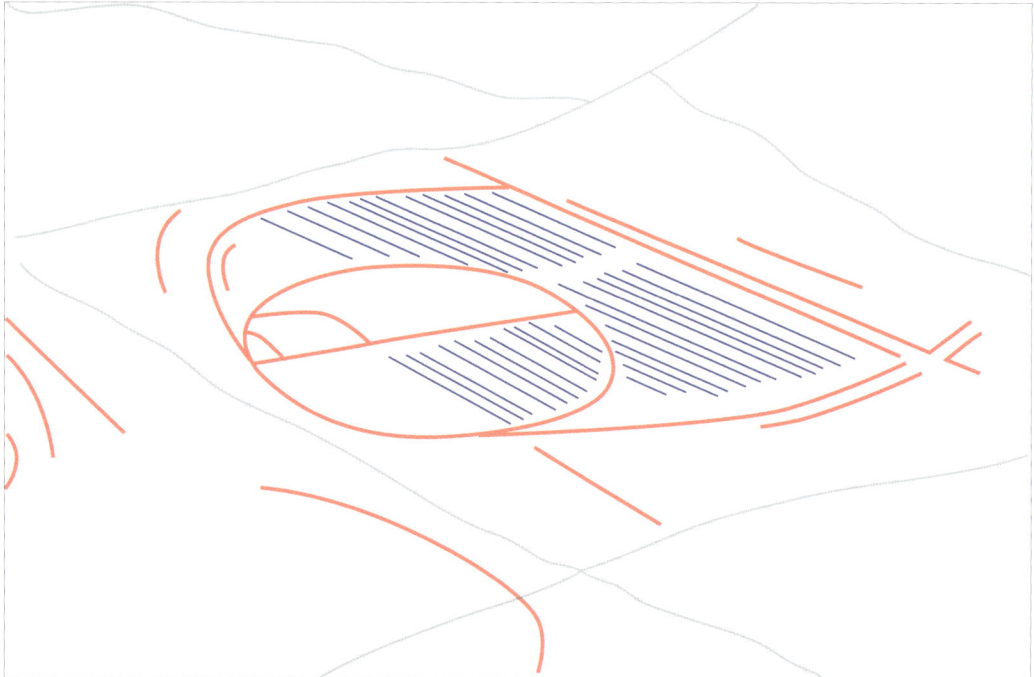

Figure 6.21 Sketch of earthworks at Ballykeelan, Co. Kildare, based on aerial photograph (after Murphy and Holton, 'An aerial perspective on Oughterany').

lists it as a deserted Anglo-Norman rural borough.[204] It is possible that one or both of the moated sites at Dunfierth, close to the parish church, were farmsteads associated with the rural borough.

The rectangular moated site at Maws, Co. Kildare, is situated on the south bank of the Rye Water, 2km to the east of Kilcock. It is 32m by 22m and its shorter north side is formed by the river only. On the other three sides, there is a shallow fosse (10–40cm deep by 3–6m wide).[205] There is a possible moated site at Walshestown at the south end of a linear field system. It is a rectangular embanked enclosure, rising at each corner.

204 R.E. Glasscock, 'The study of deserted medieval settlements in Ireland (to 1968)' in Maurice Beresford and J.G. Hurst (eds), *Deserted medieval villages: studies* (Gloucester, 1989), pp 279–91 at p. 294; J.C. Russell, *British medieval population* (Albuquerque, 1948), p. 353; Otway-Ruthven, 'Character of Norman settlement', 79; Martin, 'Plantation boroughs in medieval Ireland', p. 40.   **205** DEHLG files.

Set in the middle of a field surrounded by wet ditches, the moated site at Realtoge, Co. Meath, is defined by banks and an external fosse that is fed by a leat.[206] Less than 2km to the south-east, there is a pair of conjoined moated sites beside a tributary of the River Nanny at Brownstown.[207] The western site is *c*.62m by 67m, while the eastern one is *c*.62m by 70m. The 12m-wide fosse between them is shared by the two enclosures. Three kilometres to the south-west of Brownstown, the triple moated site at Clonardran is next to another tributary of the River Nanny.[208] It is really one large (*c*.90m east-west by 80m north-south) site, sub-divided by fosses into three rectangular enclosures. The remains of a stone gateway or bridge are present in the fosse at the west side. Other moated sites in Meath are at Curraghtown, Creemore, Raynestown and possibly Trevet (see above, p. 201).[209] Elsewhere in the county, recent excavations at Garretstown unearthed the remains of a smithing hearth, a possible charcoal-manufacturing kiln, and a group of ditches that may have formed part of a moated site and associated field system.[210] Geophysical investigation identified further elements of the moated site and field system, but full publication of this work is awaited. Initial indications that a 'new' moated site had been discovered close to Killeen Castle have recently been played down by Christine Baker.[211] The site seems to be more of a ditched enclosure than a moated site.

Chapter summary

There is strong documentary evidence for castles, both earthwork and stone, functioning as manorial centres, but to date the archaeological evidence is minimal. There has been some investigation recently of the areas adjacent to earthwork castles, but not a single motte within the Dublin region has been excavated. Documentary evidence indicates that most manor centres comprised a residence with garden, associated agricultural buildings and seigneurial resources such as mills, dovecots and warrens. The size and style of the residence varied greatly from the multi-chambered stone castles to simple thatched halls. The agricultural buildings were generally arranged in a courtyard area, often called a haggard, and most commonly comprised grain storage facilities and animal shelters. Additional structures such as kilns, bake-houses and brew-houses were found at some manor centres. Private chapels are sometimes documented on ecclesiastical manors and granges. There is some limited archaeological evidence for agricultural buildings – including stables and mills – close to mottes and ringworks.

The residence of the manorial lord and the associated buildings of the demesne farm or grange was only one of the settlement components that went to make up the medieval manor. Most of the manorial land was populated and farmed by tenants. Sources indicate that a wide range of tenants was found on the manors of the region, with a concomitant variety apparent in size of holding, nature of tenure and presumably type of residence. A large number of manorial tenants from England and Wales settled in the region, but there is also evidence for continued occupation by Irish and Ostman smallholders, some (but not all) of whom were incorporated into the unfree tenant class of betaghs.

While it is clear that the countryside of the Dublin region was densely populated, particularly in the thirteenth century, evidence for the location and nature of tenant residences is meagre and problematic. Some of the larger manorial free tenants may have constructed fortified manor centres of their own around an earthwork castle, later replaced

206 Moore, *Archaeological inventory of County Meath*, p. 163.   **207** Ibid., p. 162.   **208** Ibid.   **209** Ibid., pp 162–3. **210** Jonathan Dempsey, 'Garretstown' in *Excavations 2004*, pp 312–13; Stuart Rathbone, 'Seeing the light at Garretstown, Co. Meath', *Seanda*, 2 (2007), 55–6.   **211** Baker, *The archaeology of Killeen Castle*, p. 52.

by a tower house. They may also have lived in defended farmsteads or moated sites. The Dublin region contains some examples of this settlement type, although they do not appear to be associated, as they are elsewhere in Ireland, with a later settlement phase that took in peripheral lands.

There are some indications that existing rural habitations continued in use by the Irish tenants who were incorporated into the manorial structure, and it is possible that some of these habitations may have been adapted by new peasant settlers. It is feasible that many manors contained two areas of nucleated settlement: one occupied by the betaghs, who lived in large family groups; and one occupied by the burgesses (if the manor had borough status), alongside the small-scale tenants such as the cottars. Remnants of betagh settlements may be recognisable in the house-clusters that Graham classified for Co. Meath. A significant number of the regions' towns and villages have grown out of manorial villages and boroughs. Those settlements that were deserted offer the best opportunity for archaeological investigation of the nature of rural housing, property divisions and rural crafts.

CHAPTER 7

The church

The emphasis of the last two chapters has been on the fortification and occupation of the countryside and the form and function of castles and manors. The dwellers of the countryside looked to their lord and their manor for security, land and commercial opportunities. There was, however, another institution that had a vital role in their lives – the church. This chapter looks at the parish churches which formed such an important element of the rural landscape, as well as the religious houses and their granges.

Parochial development

There is an increasing argument in favour of the development of a parochial structure in Ireland before the coming of the Anglo-Normans.[1] While the degree to which this was a country-wide development is disputed, most commentators would agree that parishes were present in the Norse towns by the twelfth century.[2] It is also argued that a parish structure was present in the hinterland of Dublin, and, writing in 1961, Otway-Ruthven asserted that 'the organisation of the territorial parish … was no doubt substantially complete in Co. Dublin before the coming of the Normans'.[3] This process may have begun in the eleventh century, when the growing number of churches, both inside and outside Dublin, would have encouraged the bishops towards some basic level of parochial organisation.[4] The monastic sites that were scattered over the rural parts of the diocese must have played a role in the formation of a parochial system. There is some evidence that in the late eleventh century the reforming bishop of Dublin, Patrick (d. 1084), was attempting to assert jurisdiction over the monastic church of Clondalkin, possibly to create a parochial church there.[5] This policy was probably followed by his successors during the twelfth century, when many of the holdings associated with the monastic foundations were integrated within the rapidly expanding episcopal estate. Howard Clarke has drawn attention to the fact that some of the largest parishes in the Anglo-Norman archdiocese were centred on the ancient monastic sites of Clondalkin, Lusk, Santry, Swords and Tallaght, and proposed that in the initial stages of parochial development these could have functioned rather like minster churches in late Anglo-Saxon England, which served large and diffuse rural communities.[6] In the Dublin half-barony of Rathdown alone, Elizabeth O'Brien identified some seventeen pre-Anglo-Norman church sites and showed that many of these continued to function

1 Sinéad Ní Ghabhláin, 'Late twelfth-century church construction: evidence of parish formation?' in FitzPatrick and Gillespie (eds), *The parish in medieval and early modern Ireland* (2006), pp 147–67; Flanagan, 'Henry II and the kingdom of Uí Fáeláin', p. 235. 2 Adrian Empey, 'The layperson in the parish: the medieval inheritance, 1169–1536' in Raymond Gillespie and W.G. Neely (eds), *The laity and the Church of Ireland, 1000–2000* (Dublin, 2000), pp 7–48 at pp 11–12. 3 Otway-Ruthven, 'Medieval church lands', pp 55–6. 4 MacShamhráin identified 131 church sites of probable pre-twelfth-century date within Co. Dublin and a further 20 possible sites: MacShamhráin, 'The *Monasticon Hibernicum* project', p. 126. 5 This is the interpretation of Charles Doherty ('Cluain Dolcáin: a brief note', p. 187). 6 Clarke, 'Conversion, church and cathedral', p. 49.

through the Middle Ages.[7] Most of those that survive exhibit signs of pre-Anglo-Norman origin, with substantial rebuilding and renovation in the thirteenth century in particular.

Analysis of the names of the 233 parishes in the Dublin region adds weight to the theory of their pre-Anglo-Norman origin. W.J. Smyth calculated that only about 14 per cent of parish names in Co. Dublin are Anglo-Norman in origin or are translations of older Irish names.[8] Most parishes take their name from one of their component townlands, and this is often (although not exclusively) an Irish name rather than one in English. Some thirty-seven of these (or 16 per cent of all) include the prefix *kil-*, suggesting that the townland from which they derive their name was one in which an early church was located (perhaps the largest or most important church in the newly formed parish, and perhaps also the precursor to the parish church). *Kil-* parishes are scattered throughout the Dublin region (with the exception of mountainous areas), and examples include Kilbarrack (*Cill Berech*, Co. Dublin), Kilbride (*Cill Bride*, Co. Wicklow), Kilcock (*Cill Coca*, Co. Kildare) and Kilmore (*Cill Mór*, Co. Meath).

Other parish names that preserve the memory of an early ecclesiastical association include Chapelizod (*Seipeal Izod*, 'the chapel of Iseult'), Donnybrook (*Domhnac Broc*, 'the

---

7 O'Brien, 'Churches of south-east County Dublin'; see also Tomás Ó Carragáin, 'Habitual masonry styles and the local organisation of church building in early medieval Ireland', *PRIA*, 105C3 (2005), 99–149, esp. 111–12, 141.
8 Smyth, 'Exploring the social and cultural topographies', p. 150.

Figure 7.2 Skreen, Co. Meath, looking north-west. The church, which occupies the highest ground in the area, has a tall residential/belfry tower. The simplicity of this tower suggests that it might be early in the sequence of west-end towers, typical of churches in the greater Dublin region (CUCAP AYM98 image courtesy of Cambridge University Collection of Aerial Photographs).

church of Broc'), Donabate (*Domhnac Báite*, 'the church of Báite'), Saggart (*Teach Sagart*, 'Sacra's house'), Taney (*Tigh Naithí*, 'Naithí's house') and Templekeeran (*Teampull Ciaran*, 'Ciaran's church'). Viking influence closer to the urban centre is reflected in parish names of Scandinavian origin such as Dalkey, Howth and Leixlip (see pp 62–4, above). Smyth has pointed out that about 15 per cent of the parish names in Co. Dublin are hybrid in character, being a mixture of Irish, Scandinavian and Anglo-Norman origin (for example, Baldoyle, Balgriffin, Balrothery, Castleknock, Holmpatrick and possibly Rathmichael).[9]

The geography of parochial organisation

The manorial centre, of whatever type, was generally situated close to the parish church, and Simms and Fagan have found that forty-five of sixty identified manors for medieval Dublin were located at parish centres.[10] Writing in 1968, Otway-Ruthven categorically stated that 'nothing is clearer than the identification of manor and parish'.[11] Two years earlier, she had demonstrated in her pioneering study of parochial development in the rural deanery of Skreen, Co. Meath, how the land-grants of the primary subinfeudation were formed into distinct parishes over time.[12] This concordance between the territorial structures of parish and secular power has been recognised and confirmed by the subsequent work of settlement historians.[13] Similarly, the conjunction of early castle and parish church has become the visible landscape mark of this enduring association (see above, pp 112–22).

While there is growing evidence for parish organisation in the pre-Anglo-Norman period, as noted above, particularly in the area immediately around Dublin, this evidence is lacking for most of the rest of the country. O'Neill argued with regard to Meath, that there is evidence for the existence of a pastoral organisation centred on churches and possibly

9 Smyth, 'Exploring the social and cultural topographies', p. 150. **10** Simms and Fagan, 'Villages in Co. Dublin', p. 93. **11** Otway-Ruthven, *A history of medieval Ireland*, p. 119. **12** A.J. Otway-Ruthven, 'Parochial development in the rural deanery of Skreen', *JRSAI*, 94 (1965), 111–22. **13** For example, Mark Hennessy, 'Parochial organisation in medieval Tipperary' in William Nolan and Thomas McGrath (eds), *Tipperary: history and society* (1985), pp 60–70; Duffy, 'The shape of the parish', pp 43–4.

Figure 7.3 The 233
parishes in the Dublin
region. Many of the
parish boundaries
follow natural
topographical features
such as rivers and
streams. Some are
clearly coterminous
with ancient territorial
boundaries, but others
have undergone
considerable changes
over time.

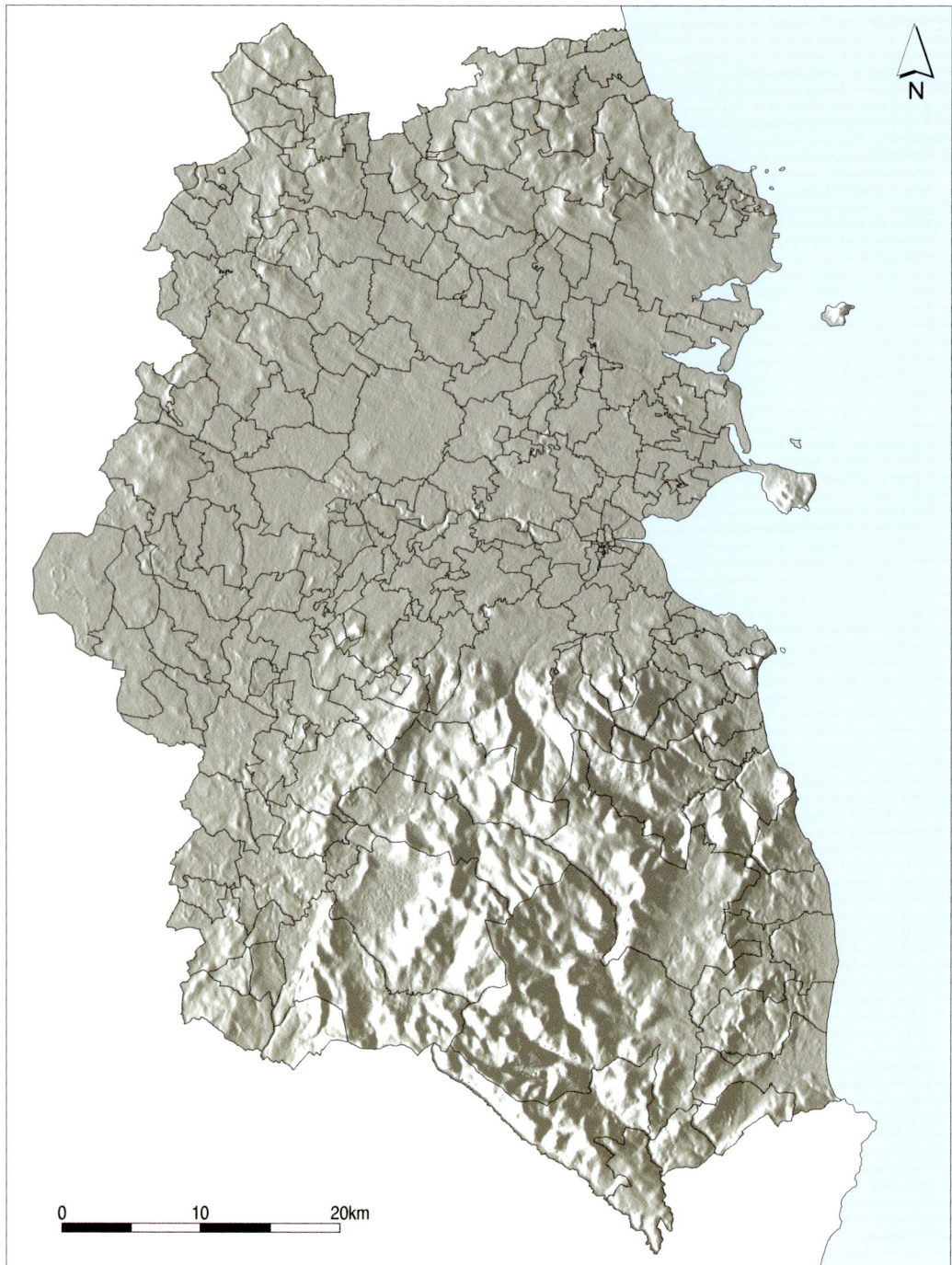

0   10   20km

involving the payment of tithes before the arrival of the Anglo-Normans.[14] He believes that
this organisation and these churches were taken over by the new manorial lords and
contributed to the rapid progress of the Anglo-Norman manorial settlement. Flanagan
similarly proposed that in parts of Kildare, rural deaneries and parishes may have been
present at the time of the conquest or they may have emerged shortly afterwards, under the
administration of Irish ecclesiastics.[15] In the absence of more compelling evidence, however,
it appears that many parishes in the study area came into being during the early years of
Anglo-Norman manor formation and territorial delineation, in a process similar to that
described for Skreen. In particular, as a recent commentator has concluded, the lack of
evidence for disputes over tithes in the years after conquest appears to suggest that these dues

14 O'Neill, 'The medieval parish churches in county Meath', 12–16.   15 Flanagan, 'The kingdom of Uí Fáeláin', p. 235.

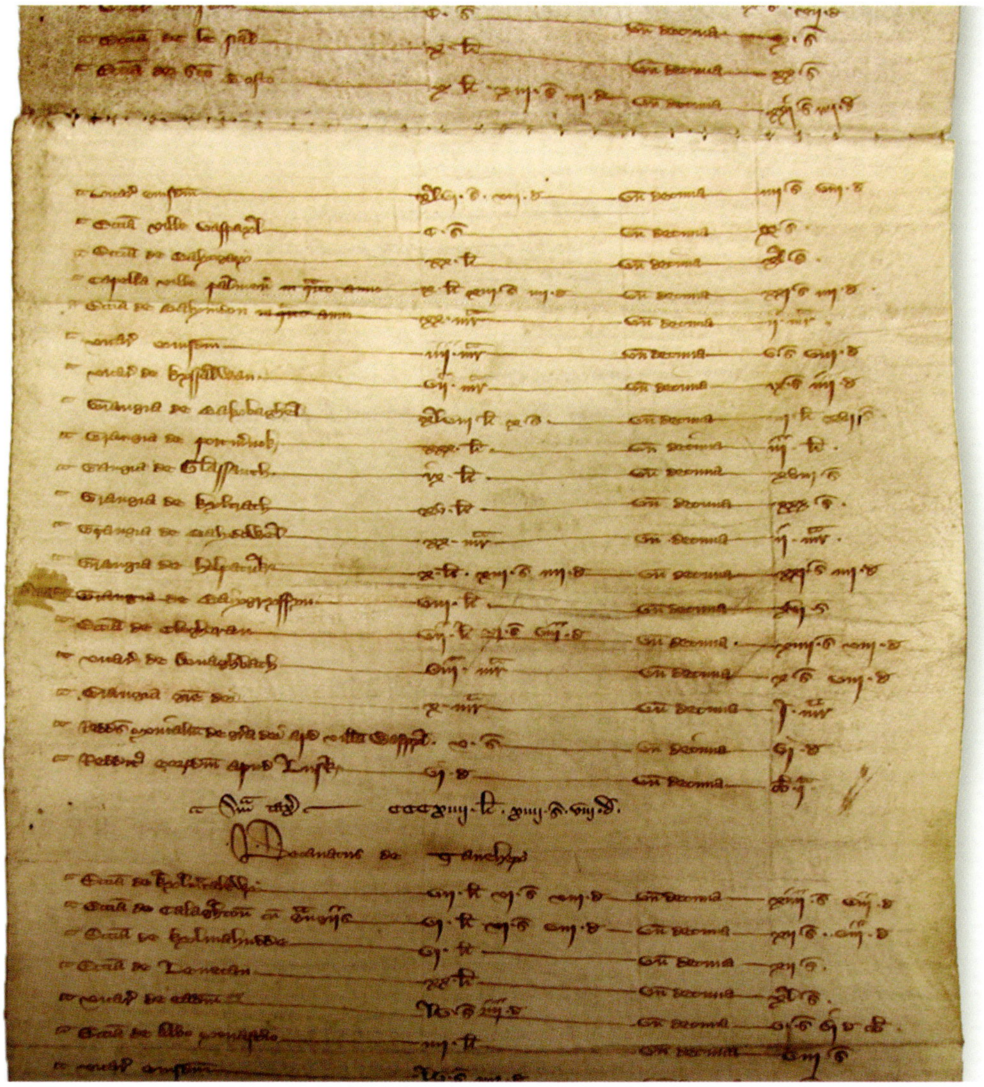

Figure 7.4 Part of the ecclesiastical taxation for the diocese of Dublin, showing the returns for the deaneries of Swords and Taney, 1306–7. The taxation lists churches, chapels and granges within each rural deanery, assigning to each a value based on the tithes or other payments made by parishioners and the income from lands and property (image reproduced courtesy of the National Archives of the UK, ref: TNA: PRO E101/233/21).

had not already been allocated, and to provide support for the statement of Gerald of Wales that the Irish did not pay tithes or first fruits.[16] There are countless instances in which Anglo-Norman lords disposed of the tithes of their own demesnes as well as the other tenements of their holdings to monastic houses of their own foundation or religious houses of their homelands. In Meath, for example, in the period between 1170 and 1300, at least thirty-six churches were placed, without dispute, in the control of the abbeys of St Thomas and St Mary, Dublin, and the monastery of Llanthony in Wales.[17]

Frequently, the first incumbents of these parish churches were relatives of the manorial lords. Thomas de Feypo, brother of Adam de Feypo, lord of Skreen, for instance, was named as the priest administering to the chapel of St Nicholas, whose tithes were granted to St Mary's Abbey, Dublin.[18] He went on to become a Cistercian monk in St Mary's. In Dunboyne, William le Petit, shortly after constructing his castle, granted the church and the tithes of the parishioners to Llanthony Prima.[19] His brother, Ralph le Petit, who held the bishopric of Meath from 1227 to 1230, appears to have been the first incumbent there.

---

16 Empey, 'The layperson in the parish', p. 12; Gerald of Wales, *The history and topography of Ireland*, trans. and intr. J.J. O'Meara (London, 1982), p. 106.   17 John Brady, 'Anglo-Norman organization of the diocese of Meath', *IER*, 67 (1946), 232–7 at 235. There is some evidence that later bishops of Meath came to regret this wholesale allocation of parish church tithes and attempted to redress the balance in favour of the diocesan clergy. See *RAST*, pp 243–52. 18 *CSMA*, 1, pp 91–3, 96, 156–7; 2, pp 21–2.   19 Brooks (ed.), *The Irish cartularies*, pp 74–5, 216–17.

The parish church was the focus of pastoral care for the laity of the manor and it also played an important part in supporting the religious houses or cathedrals that usually held the tithes and appointed the vicar. Once the area from which tithes were due to a parish church was defined, its territorial identity became fixed and inviolate, and the parishes that developed in the medieval period still exist today as civil parishes. There are 233 such parishes in the Dublin region. They average 1,375 hectares and cover a total area of 321,664.5 hectares (Figure 7.3). The smallest parish is formed by the Liberties of Christ Church and covers less than one hectare; the largest is Derrylossery in the Wicklow Mountains, and is 18,604 hectares. This pattern presents a microcosm of the national situation, where the smaller parishes tend to occur in the manorial regions colonised by the Anglo-Normans, while the larger ones are found in the upland regions that later became Gaelic enclaves.[20] There is an obvious topographical influence on parish size, both nationally and regionally, with the larger parishes found in the more marginal, thinly populated areas.

The first general review of Irish parishes is contained in the lists of valuations of Irish dioceses, which were produced in the early fourteenth century.[21] This valuation was undertaken to assess ecclesiastical income from glebe lands, tithes, donations and landed property for the purpose of calculating liability towards the tax granted on 18 March 1291 by Pope Nicholas IV to Edward I for his planned crusade to the Holy Land.[22] The tax was a tenth, to be collected from all ecclesiastical income in England, Wales, Scotland and Ireland. The returns for England, Wales and Scotland date to 1291–2, but those for the Irish dioceses are believed to date from 1303–7 and 1319–20.[23] Roll 2 of the manuscript, which contains the returns for the dioceses of Dublin, Meath and Kildare, dates to 1306–7 (Figure 7.4).

The total valuations of the parishes, vicarages and landed possessions of the archbishop and religious houses of the diocese of Dublin amounted to £2,280 14s. 4½d., making it by far the most valuable Irish diocese among those whose assessments have survived. An analysis of the diocesan assessments across Ireland and Britain that has mapped the valuations at the level of the square mile has revealed that land in the Dublin diocese was valued at between £2 and £3 per square mile.[24] While this valuation was high in an Irish context, it did not come close to matching the valuations for the richest English dioceses, which were well over £6 per square mile. Within Dublin, valuations ranged considerably, and it may be possible to use these variations as an indicator of settlement density and landed wealth across the region.[25] Mapping the valuations has proved problematic, however, due to changing parochial boundaries, difficulty in the identification of place-names and the omissions of property belonging to some of the religious orders.

Churches

The vestiges of almost 300 medieval churches and chapels lie dotted across the landscape of the Dublin region (Figure 7.5).[26] Many survive as mere foundations in open fields, others are more structurally sound but roofless, while some have been subsumed into the fabric of

20 Duffy, 'The shape of the parish', p. 41.   21 TNA:PRO E101/233/21. Printed (with many errors) in *CDI, 1302–7*, pp 202–323.   22 See W.E. Lunt, 'Papal taxation in England in the reign of Edward I', *EHR*, 30 (1915), 398–417 at 412–13; W.E. Lunt, *Financial relations of the papacy with England to 1327* (Cambridge, MA, 1939), pp 346–65.   23 G.J. Hand, 'Dating of the early fourteenth-century ecclesiastical valuation of Ireland', *Irish Theological Quarterly*, 24 (1957), 271–4.   24 B.M.S. Campbell, 'The medieval economy' in *The Penguin atlas of British and Irish history* (London, 2001), pp 100–3; B.M.S. Campbell, 'Benchmarking medieval economic development: England, Wales, Scotland and Ireland, *c*.1290', *EHR*, 61 (2008), 896–945.   25 This has been attempted for other parts of the country. See Barry, *Medieval moated sites of south-eastern Ireland*, pp 128–38; Sinéad Ní Ghabhláin, 'Church and community in medieval Ireland: the diocese of Kilfenora', *JRSAI*, 125 (1995), 61–84.   26 See, for example, Ní Mharcaigh, 'The medieval parish churches of south-west Dublin'; O'Neill, 'The medieval parish churches of County Kildare'; O'Brien, 'Churches of south-east County Dublin'; Michael O'Neill, 'St Patrick's Cathedral, Dublin, and its prebendal churches: Gothic architectural

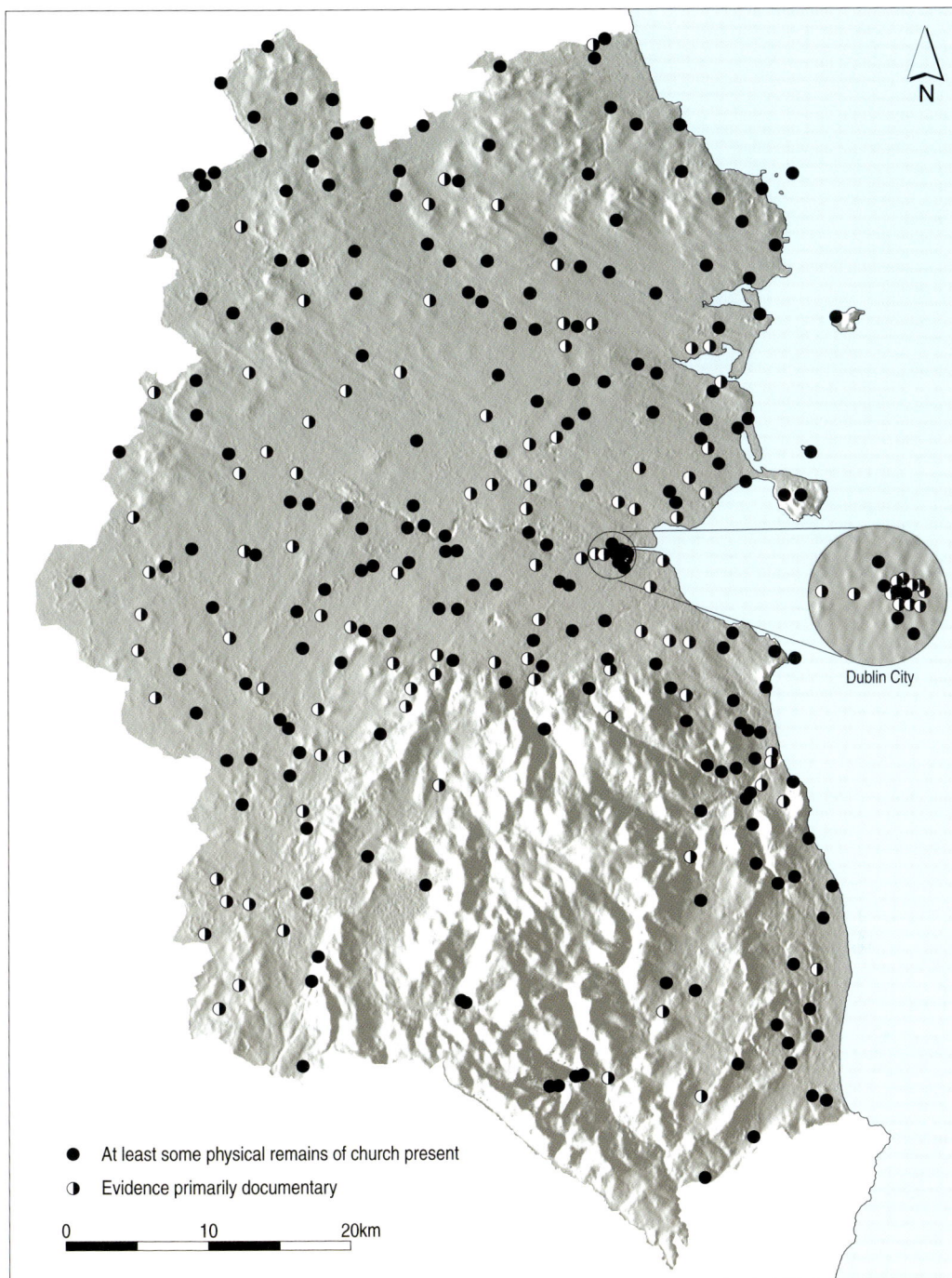

Figure 7.5 There are almost 300 churches of medieval date in the Dublin region, including parish churches, subsidiary churches and chapels of ease. Most have some visible remains – some are still functioning, some are largely intact but roofless, others have only minor structural remains. In some cases, all physical trace of the church has disappeared, but the site is known from documentary or cartographic sources or because of a place-name.

● At least some physical remains of church present

◑ Evidence primarily documentary

0   10   20km

Dublin City

later buildings. Almost all of them display evidence for multiple phases of construction, and a handful continue in use, serving the same purpose for which they were originally built. In all, something approaching 40 per cent of the known medieval churches have evidence of pre-Anglo-Norman origin.

Eighteen medieval parish churches have been identified in south-west Co. Dublin, from either historical sources or surviving architectural remains.[27] Seven of these have evidence for a pre-Anglo-Norman date, in the form of early documentary references, indications of a circular

relationships' in Duffy (ed.), *Medieval Dublin V* (2004), pp 243–76; O'Neill, 'The medieval parish churches in County Meath'; Mary McMahon, *Medieval church sites of north Dublin: a heritage trail* (Dublin, 1991); MacShamhráin, 'The *Monasticon Hibernicum* project'; FitzPatrick and Gillespie (eds), *The parish in medieval and early modern Ireland*. **27** Ní Mharcaigh, 'The medieval parish churches of south-west Dublin', 257. The churches are: Aderrig; Ballyfermot; Clondalkin; Cruagh; Crumlin; Drimnagh; Esker; Kilbride; Kilmactalway; Kilmahuddrick; Lucan; Newcastle; Palmerston; Rathcoole; Saggart; St Catherine's; St James'; Tallaght.

Figure 7.6 The early medieval granite cross in the graveyard at Newcastle Lyons, Co. Dublin, significantly predates the present church, much of which was built in the fifteenth century.

or oval enclosure around the church, or the presence of diagnostically pre-Anglo-Norman features including round towers, cross-slabs, fonts or architectural features (such as the gable-finial at Saggart or the chancel-arch and doorway at Palmerston).[28] On architectural grounds, Tadhg O'Keeffe has dated the churches at Palmerston and Killiney to the period before *c*.1120.[29] Both of these sites are included in a recent study by Nessa Walsh, in which ten pre-Romanesque churches are listed for the Dublin region – five south of the Liffey in Co. Dublin and five at Glendalough, Co. Wicklow.[30] The other three Dublin churches are at Kill of the Grange and Kiltiernan (Figure 7.8) and on Dalkey Island (Figure 7.1). It is interesting, and probably significant (especially in light of the distribution of Rathdown Slabs – see pp 64–5), that four of the five pre-Romanesque churches in Dublin are to be found within less than 10km of each other, and all within the barony of Rathdown.

Glendalough, 'the glen of two lakes', was home to a monastery founded by St Kevin (d. 618) in the sixth century (Figure 7.11).[31] It was to become one of the most famous religious centres in early medieval Ireland. Although few of the above-ground remains date to before the eleventh century, at least five of the churches were probably built within a generation or so either side of the year 1100.[32] The largest and oldest of these is the 'cathedral', a simple nave-and-chancel structure with a sacristy.[33] The earliest part is the nave, which has been entirely rebuilt using stones from an earlier, smaller church, probably on the same site. It may be tenth century in date, but the chancel is a twelfth-century addition. In a field to the west of the cathedral is the Church of St Mary, large parts of which may have been built *c*.1100. The most distinctive building in the valley is the nave-and-chancel church known as 'St Kevin's Kitchen'. This is in fact a two-storeyed oratory, given its name by the chimney-like round bell-turret projecting from the roof at the west end. It is of the same period and type as those of St Columba at Kells, St Flannan at Killaloe and St Mochta at Louth. It consists of a barrel-vaulted lower chamber with a loft above. A sacristy and chancel were later additions to the east end. The sacristy still stands, but the chancel, still standing in 1779, collapsed at a later date (Figures 7.9, 7.10).[34]

28 Ní Mharcaigh, 'The medieval parish churches of south-west Dublin', 262. The churches are: Aderrig; Clondalkin; Cruagh; Newcastle; Saggart; Palmerston; Tallaght.   **29** Tadhg O'Keeffe, *Romanesque Ireland: architecture and ideology in the twelfth century* (Dublin, 2003), pp 83–7.   **30** Nessa Walsh, 'Pre-Romanesque churches in County Dublin and its hinterland: the Golden Ratio' in Duffy (ed.), *Medieval Dublin VIII* (2008), pp 21–35.   **31** G.L. Barrow, *Glendalough and St Kevin* (Dundalk, 1992); Robert Cochrane, *Historical and descriptive notes, with ground plans, elevations, sections and details of the ecclesiastical remains at Glendalough, Co. Wicklow* (Dublin, 1912); H.G. Leask, *Glendalough, Co. Wicklow, National Monuments vested in the Commissioners of Public Works: official historical and descriptive guide* (Dublin, 1974). **32** Ó Carragáin, 'Habitual masonry styles'; Tomás Ó Carragáin, 'Rebuilding the 'city of angels': Muirchertach Ua Briain and Glendalough, *c*.1096–1111' in Sheehan and Ó Corráin (eds), *The Viking Age: Ireland and the West* (2010), pp 258–70. **33** Peter Galloway, *The cathedrals of Ireland* (Belfast, 1992), p. 117; Con Manning, 'A puzzle in stone: the cathedral at Glendalough', *AI*, 16:2 (summer 2002), 18–21; Tomás Ó Carragáin, 'Skeuomorphs and spolia: the presence of the past in Irish pre-Romanesque architecture' in Rachel Moss (ed.), *Making and meaning: studies in Insular art* (Dublin, 2007), pp 95–109 at pp 96, 100, 108, 109.   **34** Peter Harbison, 'Glendalough drawings of 1779 in the Royal Irish Academy Library' in Condit and Corlett (eds), *Above and beyond* (2005), pp 445–60.

Figure 7.7 The builders of the late medieval tower at the church in Lusk, Co. Dublin, constructed a circular turret at three corners of the new tower. It was built in such a way that the existing round tower (back left) fits into the fourth corner.

Figure 7.8 Kiltiernan Church, Co. Dublin, is associated with St Tigernán and is one of the oldest surviving churches in the Dublin region. The remains, viewed here from the north-west, consist of the lower courses of a single-cell church with a blocked-up square-headed doorway in the west end.

Churches with contemporary naves and chancels are very rare in Ireland before the second half of the twelfth century, but Glendalough has two examples – Reefert and Trinity.[35] Both of these churches probably date to the late eleventh or early twelfth century, and are among the earliest of their type anywhere in Ireland. The name Reefert possibly derives from *Ríogh-feart*, meaning royal cemetery, and the church stands on a site regarded as the burial place of the local chieftains, the O'Tooles.

Standing 6m above the south shore of the Upper Lake at Glendalough are the slight remains, mainly a reconstruction on old foundations, of a small rectangular church – *Temple na Skellig*. This church may also date to *c*.1100, as could the round tower (Figure 7.12), the 'Priests' House', St Kieran's Church, and the round-arched entrance gateway to the main monastic complex. The gateway, which is the only one of its type in Ireland, formerly had a second storey. Although it is not east-west in orientation, the structural evidence of an upper chamber, combined crucially with the presence of antae, suggest that this was a gateway-chapel.[36]

Little is known of the early history of Kilcroney Church, Co. Wicklow, but the present building contains some probable eleventh-century components (Figure 7.13).[37] There are antae on the east gable end, and these were probably matched on the west end, although an extension to the church has removed all trace of them. There is a small round-headed window in the south wall, as well as a doorway with a flat lintel. The church is generally well-built with blocks of granite, shale and sandstown, but the walls are now supported by buttresses.

Recent archaeological excavations in the townland of Glebe, Co. Wicklow, have uncovered the foundations of a medieval building believed to be Drumkay Church, and an associated cemetery and triple-ditched enclosure (Figures 7.14, 7.46).[38] The church was

35 O'Keeffe, *Romanesque Ireland*, pp 83–8; Máire Donovan, 'Reefert: a biography' (MA, UCD, 2009). **36** O'Keeffe, *Romanesque Ireland*, pp 83–8. **37** Grogan and Kilfeather, *Archaeological inventory of County Wicklow*, pp 126–7. **38** Edmond O'Donovan, 'Preliminary report: archaeological excavations on the Wicklow Port Access Town Relief Road' (unpublished report, Margaret Gowen and Co. Ltd, 2007).

Figure 7.9 St Kevin's Church, Glendalough, Co. Wicklow, in 2009, from the south-east. The roof-scars that mark the former position of the chancel can be seen clearly in the east gable. The arch that once allowed movement between the nave and chancel now functions as a door. The round tower, with its conical cap, can be seen in the background on the right.

Figure 7.10 St Kevin's Church, from the south-east and showing the now-vanished chancel, in a drawing attributed to Gabriel Beranger, 1779 (although stylistically it is unlike many of his known drawings). Note also the round tower, without its conical cap, which was restored in 1876 (image courtesy of the Royal Irish Academy, © RIA).

recorded in the *County inventory*, but its exact location was unknown.[39] A Romanesque doorway and a font had previously been removed from the site to the Church of Ireland church in Wicklow town.[40] The *c.*200 burials revealed during the excavation range in date from *c.*AD600 up to the seventeenth century, indicating the longevity of the site's use. The

39 Grogan and Kilfeather, *Archaeological inventory of County Wicklow*, p. 123.   **40** H.G. Leask, *Irish churches and monastic buildings, 1: the first phases and the Romanesque* (Dundalk, 1955), pp 160–1; Grogan and Kilfeather,

remains of the church provided evidence for several phases of construction, using some granite boulders but primarily limestone and shale. The earth-cut ditches enclosed an oval area measuring roughly 33m north-south by 47m east-west.

The early church at Clondalkin is well-attested historically, and its pre-Anglo-Norman origins are also evidenced by the presence of a round tower, two cross-slabs, an early granite font and traces of an enclosure.[41] Elsewhere, the evidence is less clear-cut. The earliest known record of the church at Aderrig dates to 1235, for instance, but the upstanding remains, which are not clearly datable, lie within a raised circular burial ground.[42] Traces of similar enclosures can be seen at other locations in the Dublin region such as at Balscadden, Colmanstown, Grange, Kilbride, Kilmartin, Loughtown, Oldtown and Newcastle.[43] Recent archaeological excavations in the vicinity of the church at Kilgobbin (whose name indicates an early origin) revealed traces of an enclosing ditch around the church site, as well as evidence for occupation and small-scale industrial activity in the period c.AD650–c.950.[44]

Similar architectural, documentary and archaeological evidence has been used to identify seventeen pre-Anglo-Norman church sites in the south Co. Dublin half barony of Rathdown.[45] Indeed, the south Dublin/north Wicklow area has the highest density of mortared pre-Anglo-Norman churches in Ireland. O'Brien noted the continued use of these sites as parish churches throughout the Middle Ages as a primary reason for their survival into the seventeenth century and, in some cases, beyond.[46] The earliest known reference to the church at Rathmichael dates to 1179, but pre-Anglo-Norman origins are suggested by the presence of the base of a round tower and several 'Rathdown Slabs' (see above, pp 64–5).[47] There is a tradition that St Finian founded a church at Newcastle, Co. Dublin, in the sixth century, and while most of the present building is of fifteenth-century date, a granite cross in the graveyard is early medieval (Figure 7.6).[48]

In the north of Co. Dublin, Lusk was an important church site founded in the fifth century by St Mac-Cuilinn, and a fair or óenach was held there from as early as AD800. The former boundaries of the early church site can be traced in the modern street pattern, but the round tower is the only upstanding survival of the pre-Anglo-Norman church (Figures 7.7, 7.16). Lusk was granted to the see of Dublin in the twelfth century. Recent archaeological excavations close to the church at Lusk revealed a curved section of an enclosing ditch (Figure 7.17), a burial ground and a souterrain.[49] A charcoal sample from an early fill in the ditch has been dated to the fifth to sixth century, confirming the early date of this enclosing feature. This ditch appears to be the outermost of three that were dug around the church at Lusk and it is one of the earliest church enclosures known in Ireland.

St Mary's collegiate parish church at Howth was built on the site of an eleventh-century church founded by Sitric, king of Dublin, in 1042.[50] The round tower and a cross-slab at

Figure 7.11 (opposite) Glendalough, Co. Wicklow, is home to one of the greatest concentrations of medieval ecclesiastical buildings anywhere in Ireland. The remains of at least ten churches survive, and others are known to have existed (© Department of the Environment, Heritage and Local Government).

Archaeological inventory of County Wicklow, p. 123.   **41** The remains of an early nave-and-chancel church in Clondalkin were identified and excavated in 1962–4 (Etienne Rynne, 'Excavation of a church site at Clondalkin, Co. Dublin', *JRSAI*, 97:1 (1967), 29–37).   **42** McNeill (ed.), *Alen's register*, p. 78. CUCAP images BDU 46–7 show the ploughed-out enclosure clearly.   **43** MacShamhráin, 'The *Monasticon Hibernicum* project', pp 123–5; Ailbhe MacShamhráin, 'An ecclesiastical enclosure in the townland of Grange, parish of Holmpatrick' in Ailbhe MacShamhráin (ed.), *The Island of St Patrick: church and ruling dynasties in Fingal and Meath, 400–1148* (Dublin, 2004), pp 52–60; Christine Baker, 'A lost ecclesiastical site in Fingal: Oldtown, Swords, Co. Dublin', *AI*, 18:3 (autumn 2004), 14–17.   **44** Teresa Bolger, 'Excavations at Kilgobbin Church, Co. Dublin', *JIA*, 18 (2008), 85–112.   **45** O'Brien, 'Churches of south-east County Dublin', pp 504, 522.   **46** See also Tomás Ó Carragáin, 'Church buildings and pastoral care in early medieval Ireland' in FitzPatrick and Gillespie (eds), *The parish in medieval and early modern Ireland* (2006), pp 91–123 at pp 101–4.   **47** MacShamhráin, 'The *Monasticon Hibernicum* project', pp 122–3.   **48** O'Keeffe, 'Medieval architecture and the village of Newcastle Lyons', pp 52–3; H.G. Leask, *Irish churches and monastic buildings, 3: medieval gothic: the last phases* (Dundalk, 1971), pp 18–19; Ní Mharcaigh, 'The medieval parish churches of south-west Dublin', 272–4.   **49** Aidan O'Connell, 'Excavations at Church Road and the early monastic foundation at Lusk, Co. Dublin' in Baker (ed.), *Axes, warriors and windmills* (2009), pp 51–63.   **50** Leask, *Irish churches and monastic buildings, 3*, p. 34; McMahon, *Medieval church sites of north Dublin*, p. 23.

Figure 7.12 The round tower at Glendalough, Co. Wicklow, was probably built in the late eleventh or early twelfth century. Its conical stone cap was reconstructed from stones found inside and around the base in 1876. Fine views could be had from the tower up and down the valley, but the steep hills on either side obstructed vision to the north and south.

Figure 7.13 This simple rectangular church at Kilcroney, Co. Wicklow, is built of sandstone, granite and shale blocks of various sizes. The antae projecting from the east end and the flat-lintelled doorway in the south wall indicate an eleventh-century date for its construction (© Department of the Environment, Heritage and Local Government).

Swords attest the pre-Anglo-Norman origins of the church there (Figure 7.15). A church was founded at Finglas by St Canice in the sixth century, and while a granite high cross is a visible survival of the pre-Anglo-Norman church, it is also likely that some parts of the church itself were built before the twelfth century.[51] Near Malahide, St Doolagh's Church is also a pre-Anglo-Norman foundation, refurbished under Anglo-Norman patronage in the thirteenth century and extended in the fifteenth century.[52] The east end of the church is probably twelfth century, and a small granite cross near the lane leading to the church was probably part of the early complex.[53] Recent archaeological investigations have identified the lines of two enclosing ditches in the fields around the church.[54] The massive stones used in the base of the south wall of St Fintan's Church in Sutton suggest that at least some parts of this church were built in the twelfth century if not earlier.[55]

O'Neill has argued cogently that parochial development was well advanced in Kildare before the coming of the Anglo-Normans, and there is clear evidence (either documentary, architectural or both) for the existence of a pre-Anglo-Norman church on many sites in the county.[56] The earliest known record of the church at Confey, in the extreme north-east of

51 McMahon, *Medieval church sites of north Dublin*, p. 30.   52 Brian de Breffny and George Mott, *The churches and abbeys of Ireland* (London, 1976), p. 78; Peter Harbison, 'Some old illustrations of St Doulagh's Church, Balgriffin, Co. Dublin' in Duffy (ed.), *Medieval Dublin IX* (2009), pp 152–65.   53 McMahon, *Medieval church sites of north Dublin*, pp 30–1.   54 D.L. Swan, '"St Doulagh's", Balgriffin' in *Excavations 1989*, pp 18–19; D.L. Swan, '"St Doulagh's", Balgriffin' in *Excavations 1990*, p. 24.   55 McMahon, *Medieval church sites of north Dublin*, p. 31.   56 Those in the Dublin region are: Ballymore Eustace; Clane; Cloncurry; Confey; Donaghmore; Killashee; Kilteel; Laraghbryan;

Co. Kildare, dates to 1179, but the building has early twelfth-century architectural elements (Figure 7.19).[57] What survives consists of three main phases: 1) a single-cell church with 2) an added chancel and 3) a fifteenth-century nave extension and renovation.[58] Con Manning has dated the first, single-cell phase to 'about the eleventh century', and similar early elements can be seen at Laraghbryan, near Maynooth (Figure 7.18).[59] The second phase at Confey – the addition of a chancel prior to the extension/alteration of the nave – has parallels at Donaghcumper and Donaghmore, and it is possible that these also existed as single-cell churches before 1170.[60]

Manning has posited that the Romanesque fragments incorporated into the church at Kilteel came from an earlier church at the site, probably built for Diarmait Mac Murchada (Figure 7.20), and some even earlier fragments are also visible.[61] The earliest known reference to the church at Ballymore (Eustace) dates to 1192,[62] but the presence of a pre-Anglo-Norman church is indicated by the two surviving granite high crosses (Figure 7.23).[63] A seventeenth-century watercolour sketch of the church survives among the maps of the estates of the archbishops of Dublin (Figure 7.21).

The circular graveyard at the parish church in Clane is indicative of an early ecclesiastical foundation, while traces are also visible of a circular enclosure around the church at Celbridge. Traces of an oval enclosure around the stone-roofed church at Ardrass – incorporating a curve in the road – suggest that the later medieval church was built on the footprint of an early medieval foundation (Figure 7.22).[64] The church, which was restored

Oughterard; Taghadoe and Timahoe (see O'Neill, 'The medieval parish churches of County Kildare', pp 156, 161 (fig. 6.2)).   **57** O'Neill, 'The medieval parish churches of County Kildare', p. 157.   **58** Ibid., p. 163; O'Keeffe, 'The church and castle of Confey'.   **59** Manning, 'A puzzle in stone'; O'Neill, 'The medieval parish churches of County Kildare', pp 163–7.   **60** Ibid., p. 168.   **61** H.G. Leask, 'Carved stones discovered at Kilteel, Co. Kildare', *JRSAI*, 65:1 (1935), 1–8; Leask, *Irish churches and monastic buildings, 1*, p. 165; Conleth Manning, 'Excavations at Kilteel Church, Co. Kildare', *JCKAHS*, 16:3 (1981–2), 173–229; Conleth Manning, 'Kilteel revisited', *JCKAHS*, 18:3 (1996–7), 296–300.   **62** McNeill (ed.), *Alen's register*, p. 20.   **63** Peter Harbison, *The high crosses of Ireland: an iconographical and photographic survey* (3 vols, Bonn, 1992), 1, pp 23–4.   **64** Walter FitzGerald, 'Description of the stone-roofed building called St Patrick's Chapel at Ardrass, County Kildare', *JRSAI*, 1 (1890–1), 456–8; Walter FitzGerald, 'The stone-roofed church at Ardrass', *JCKAHS*, 7:2 (1911), 410–14.

Figure 7.16 The early
ecclesiastical enclosure
at Lusk, Co. Dublin,
influenced the later
development of the
village, and the line of
the enclosure can be
traced clearly in the
modern street plan and
property boundaries
(photograph taken by
Leo Swan).

Figure 7.17 Lusk, Co.
Dublin: early medieval
ecclesiastical enclosure
ditch, looking south. This
ditch was recently
investigated by
archaeologists and a
sample from it was
radiocarbon dated to
the fifth or sixth century
AD, making it one of the
earliest known church
boundaries in Ireland
(image courtesy of
Aidan O'Connell and
ACS Ltd).

in 1888, is dedicated to St Patrick. There is clear evidence for the use of wicker centring in the construction of the roof. While no graveyard is visible, human remains were disturbed when the iron railings around the church were being erected in the late nineteenth century. The round tower at Oughterard may have been a component of an early monastic site, and the present church may incorporate some of the lower courses of an earlier building (Figure 7.35). The tufa stone in the rounded chancel arch at Oughterard, and also at Kerdiffstown and Tipper, may derive from earlier churches. The ruinous medieval church

Figure 7.18
Laraghbryan Church,
Co. Kildare, from the
south-east. Parts of this
building may date to the
eleventh century, but it
was significantly
remodelled in the
thirteenth, when it
became one of the
largest churches in
Kildare. Various phases
of construction and
modification can be
identified in the window
and door surrounds.

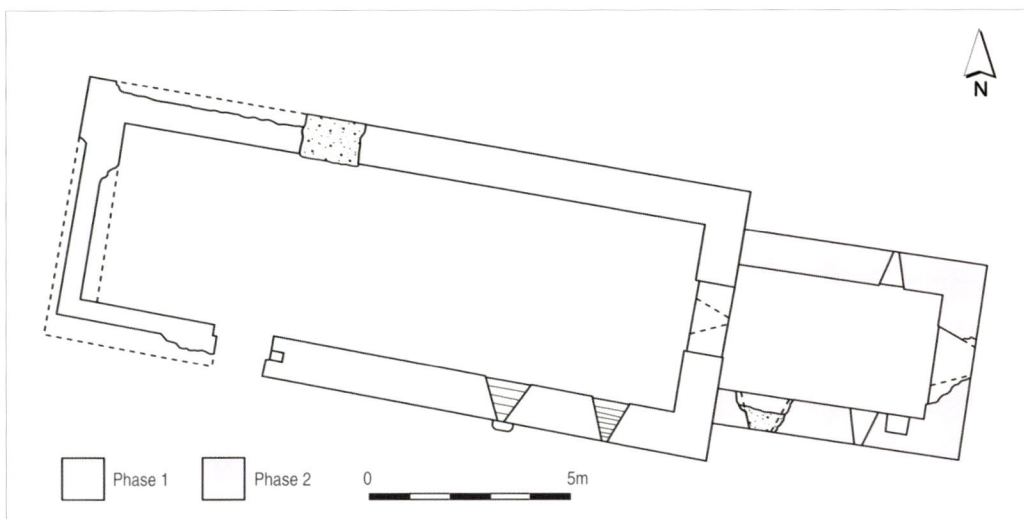

Figure 7.19 Confey
Church, Co. Kildare.
The earlier main phase
represented in the
extant remains is a
single-chamber
rectangular church. In a
later phase, a chancel
was added to the east
end of this structure.
A third phase, indicated
here by hachured lines,
included the extension
of the nave in the
fifteenth century (after
O'Keeffe, 'The church
and castle of Confey').

at Cloncurry is likely to have been built on the site of a pre-Anglo-Norman foundation
traditionally associated with St Ninian (Figures 5.10, 7.36).[65] Cloncurry was raided by the
Anglo-Normans in 1171 and the church was later granted by Adam de Hereford to St
Thomas' Abbey in Dublin. St Mary's Church at Leixlip, which, like so many other churches
in Kildare and in Meath, was granted to St Thomas' Abbey, may also have been built on the
site of a pre-Anglo-Norman church (Figure 7.34). Tradition maintains that the present Church
of Ireland building in Kill is on the site of an early foundation associated with St Brigit.[66] The
place-name 'Kill' (from *Cell*, 'church') certainly suggests that there was an early church here.[67]
St David's Church in Naas was also built on the site of a pre-Anglo-Norman church.[68]

St Mary's Church, Kilcoole ('Church of Comhgall'), Co. Wicklow, was probably built
in the twelfth century (Figure 7.24). It is a nave-and-chancel church and both parts had a

65 Bradley, Halpin and King, 'UAS 7:2: Kildare', pp 167–79; O'Conor, *Medieval rural settlement in Ireland*, p. 30, fig. 9.
66 Herity (ed.), *Ordnance Survey letters: Kildare*, p. 23.   **67** Joyce, *Irish names of places*, 3, p. 406.   **68** Bradley, Halpin
and King, 'UAS 7:4: Kildare', p. 359.

Figure 7.20 The church at Kilteel, Co. Kildare. Romanesque architectural fragments have been incorporated (in the wrong order) into the reconstructed building. This is the only chancel arch in Ireland with Romanesque figure sculpture (© Department of the Environment, Heritage and Local Government).

vaulted ceiling. The later extension at the west end may have been a clerical residence. Recent excavations at Killeen, Co. Meath, have revealed the remains of a pre-Anglo-Norman church and enclosure close to the fifteenth-century Plunkett church (Figure 5.32).[69]

Leixlip is one of the few churches in the region with demonstrably early thirteenth-century features (a blocked Dundry stone window in the chancel), and most of the evidence suggests that very little structural work was carried out on churches in Kildare in the period 1170–1230.[70] Co. Meath is similarly lacking in demonstrably late twelfth- or early thirteenth-century churches. While O'Keeffe states that there is 'considerable evidence that [the Anglo-Normans] were erecting new churches in the first decades after 1169', and FitzPatrick lists a range of thirteenth-century Anglo-Norman churches, O'Neill concludes that they engaged in very little new church building before the middle of the thirteenth century.[71]

69 Baker, *The archaeology of Killeen Castle.* 70 O'Neill, 'The medieval parish churches of County Kildare', p. 169. Dundry is a creamy/brown limestone imported from near Bristol. 71 O'Keeffe, *Medieval Ireland*, p. 156 (and see also Tadhg O'Keeffe, 'The built environment of local community worship between the late eleventh and early thirteenth centuries' in FitzPatrick and Gillespie (eds), *The parish in medieval and early modern Ireland* (2006), pp 124–46 at pp 133–6; Ní Ghabhláin, 'Late twelfth-century church construction', p. 148); Elizabeth FitzPatrick, 'The material world of the parish' in FitzPatrick and Gillespie (eds), *The parish in medieval and early modern Ireland* (2006), pp 62–75 at pp 68–9; O'Neill, 'St Patrick's Cathedral, Dublin, and its prebendal churches', p. 249.

Figure 7.23 The taller of the two granite crosses at Ballymore Eustace Church, Co. Kildare. The inscription '1689' on the south arm appears to be the year in which the cross was re-erected. It was probably also at this time that other inscriptions, including 'IHS' were added.

What little evidence there is for church building in the Dublin region in this period usually consists of additions or alterations to earlier buildings (such as at Cruicetown, Ardsallagh and Ballygarth, Co. Meath), rather than the erection of entirely new churches. One possible explanation for the apparent absence of stone churches of this period is that many of the early Anglo-Norman churches were replaced in subsequent centuries. In contrast to the early lacuna, Meath has many fine examples of later fourteenth- and fifteenth-century church buildings, and it is likely that large parts of the earlier structures were subsumed into these. Ballygarth is an example of a church with architectural components of several periods. It has mid-thirteenth-century features including a trefoil-headed west window and moulded capitals with filleted shafts in the north porch. It also has late fifteenth- or early sixteenth-century modifications, including a fine triple bell-cote and, in sandstone, a triple-light stepped round-headed window under a square hood-mould.[72] In many cases, such major renovations would have totally obliterated any diagnostic thirteenth-century features.

There are records of churches at Baldongan (Figure 7.28) and Balrothery (Figures 7.25, 7.26, 7.27) in the twelfth and thirteenth centuries, and both belonged to the prior of Kilbixy, near Tristernagh, Co. Westmeath.[73] The lands at Balrothery were held by Geoffrey de Costentin in the twelfth century and he granted the (revenues from) the church and a mill to Kilbixy. The hilltop church at Baldongan was granted to Kilbixy in the thirteenth century, but subsequently became part of the properties of Gracedieu. Close to Baldongan Castle (demolished in 1974), it probably served as a manorial church, and was held at various times by the Barnewalls, the de Berminghams and the St Lawrences of Howth.

Many of the Anglo-Norman castles in the Dublin region contained private chapels, and O'Keeffe has suggested that these may have provided pastoral ministry to manorial tenants.[74] If this were the case, it would help to explain the apparent absence of newly-built Anglo-

72 O'Neill, 'The medieval parish churches in County Meath', 9, 17, 30, 33 (fig. 47).   **73** Gilbert (ed.), *Crede Mihi, s.a.* 1275; McMahon, *Medieval church sites of north Dublin*, p. 16.   **74** O'Keeffe, 'The built environment of local community worship', p. 135.

Figure 7.24 St Mary's Church, Kilcoole, Co. Wicklow. This small nave-and-chancel church may have been built early in the twelfth century. Both parts were originally vaulted, and were roofed in stone. A granite cross-slab and font are present in the nave. A later extension, to the west end of the nave, may have been a priest's house.

Norman parish churches of late twelfth- and early thirteenth-century date. It is also possible that many of the early churches were built of timber, leaving no trace above the ground.[75]

There are indications that there was an increase in building work after 1230, and O'Neill has proposed that this represents 'the bedding down of the Anglo-Norman colony at the end of its period of expansion in this part of Ireland'.[76] The large but sympathetic extension at Laraghbryan, for instance, may have been added after that church became a prebend of St Patrick's Cathedral in 1248, and this made it one of the largest churches in thirteenth-century Kildare.[77] The style of the north door-jambs revealed during excavations at Artane Church, Co. Dublin, indicates a thirteenth- or fourteenth-century date for the construction of this church.[78] St David's Church in Naas underwent substantial renovations in the mid- to late thirteenth century.[79] Here, as elsewhere, however, it is difficult to disentangle the many phases of building and rebuilding, modification and renovation. O'Keeffe quite rightly noted that 'much more work needs to be done on the matter of Anglo-Norman parish churches, and there is probably scope for a refinement of their chronology so that we can distinguish between churches built at different times in the thirteenth century'.[80]

Some building activity took place in the fourteenth century and Leask suggested that the east window at Ardcath, Co. Meath, dated to this period (Figure 7.30).[81] In the same county, Stamullin, Ardmulchan and Skreen churches might also have significant fourteenth-century components.[82] There is a small, single-cell church at Grange, near Kilbarrack, Co. Dublin.[83] A fourteenth-century date for at least part of this church is suggested by the west

75 Empey, 'The layperson in the parish', p. 16.   76 O'Neill, 'The medieval parish churches of County Kildare', p. 173. 77 Ibid., pp 169–70, 173.   78 Mary McMahon, 'Artane Church, Kilmore Road, Dublin' in Manning (ed.), *Dublin and beyond the Pale* (1998), pp 155–62; Barry, *The archaeology of medieval Ireland*, p. 142.   79 O'Neill, 'The medieval parish churches of County Kildare', p. 162. See also Brendán Ó Ríordáin, 'St David's Church, Naas: a new dimension', *JCKAHS*, 17 (1987–91), 151–60.   80 O'Keeffe, *Medieval Ireland*, p. 156. Subsequent years have seen the publication of several studies, but major lacunae persist. See also O'Keeffe, 'The built environment of local community worship', p. 124. 81 H.G. Leask, *Irish churches and monastic buildings, 2: Gothic architecture to AD1400* (Dundalk, 1966), p. 145; Moore, *Archaeological inventory of County Meath*, p. 127.   82 O'Neill, 'The medieval parish churches in County Meath', 17. 83 Brian MacGiolla Phadraig, 'Grange Abbey, Baldoyle', *DHR*, 20:3/4 (1965), 129–32.

Figure 7.25 Balrothery
Church, Co. Dublin, by
Francis Grose,
1790×1800. The tower
is still standing today, but
the nave and chancel as
seen here have been
replaced by a modern
church (see Figure 7.27)
(image courtesy of the
National Library of
Ireland).

Figure 7.25 Balrothery Church, Co. Dublin, by Francis Grose, 1790×1800. The tower is still standing today, but the nave and chancel as seen here have been replaced by a modern church (see Figure 7.27) (image courtesy of the National Library of Ireland).

Figure 7.26 Balrothery Church, Co. Dublin, by James Saunders, 1801 (image courtesy of the National Library of Ireland).

twin-light sandstone window, which is a cusped and ogee-headed example with internal splay and evidence for plank-shuttering.[84] Records show that new windows were inserted into Glasnevin Church in 1345.[85] Although it has later modifications, the square tower at Swords Church may also have been built in the fourteenth century (Figures 7.15, 18.1). The church itself does not survive, but a scar on the south wall of the tower marks its original roof line.

The church on Ireland's Eye is associated with St Nessan, and the island itself is sometimes called *Inis mac Nessáin*.[86] The present remains are of a church of twelfth-century

84 McMahon, *Medieval church sites of north Dublin*, pp 20–1.   85 Mills (ed.), *Account roll*, pp 97–8.   86 MacShamhráin,

date (Figure 7.32). In 1235, a new church was built in Howth to replace the one on Ireland's Eye.[87] This move may have been part of an archiepiscopal policy to relocate island churches to the mainland (see below, p. 253). The present church at Howth appears to be mainly mid- to late fourteenth-century in date, however, with a range of later modifications. There is a long nave (35m), divided into two aisles. Twin-aisled naves and chancels are surprisingly common in Co. Dublin, with further examples at St Audoen's, Balrothery (Figures 7.25, 7.26), Clondalkin, Finglas and Lusk (Figures 6.9, 7.7, 7.16, 11.7). Yellow sandstone was used in the fourteenth-century west window in the north aisle at Howth, while limestone, granite and sandstone were used in the fine east window of the south aisle. This is a triple-light ogee-headed window with cusps and trefoil lights on top.[88] The limestone might represent fifteenth-century repairs to the original fourteenth-century window. Two fourteenth-century

Figure 7.27 Aerial photograph of the church at Balrothery, Co. Dublin, from the north-west. The west-end residential tower is a typical feature of medieval parish churches in the Dublin region, and this one is most similar to the example at Lusk. The corner turret – which contains a spiral stairs – is reminiscent of the tower-house architecture of the region (see, for example, Figure 5.42) (© Department of the Environment, Heritage and Local Government).

'The *Monasticon Hibernicum* project', p. 121; W.F. Wakeman, 'Ante-Norman churches in the county of Dublin', *JRSAI*, 22 (1892), 101–6 at 104.   **87** *MRHI*, p. 360; Leask, *Irish churches and monastic buildings, 3*, p. 34.   **88** McMahon, *Medieval church sites of north Dublin*, p. 24.

Figure 7.28 Baldongan Church from the air. There was a castle next to this church until it was demolished in 1974. The richness of the soils in this part of Co. Dublin is illustrated by the continued use of this land for growing fruit and vegetables to supply the city of Dublin (© Department of the Environment, Heritage and Local Government).

trefoil-headed sandstone piscinas are present in the south wall of the church. In the fifteenth century, the east end of the south aisle of the church served as a private chantry for the St Lawrence family of Howth Castle. Here stands the double effigial tomb of Christopher St Lawrence (d. 1462), and his wife Anne Plunkett of Ratoath, Co. Meath (Figure 7.31).[89] The tomb of Maud Plunkett (d. 1482), wife of Richard Talbot, is in Malahide Church (Figure 7.33).[90] Fragments of another fifteenth-century tomb of a female were found in the graveyard of Garristown Church and are now stored in the church at Lusk.[91] This tomb was similar to that of Maud Plunkett.

The late fourteenth and fifteenth centuries marked a period of considerable church expansion across the Dublin region. In Kildare, for example, new windows were inserted at Donaghcumper and Oughterard, rood lofts were added at Leixlip, Laraghbryan and Coghlanstown, and residential quarters were constructed at Celbridge (Figure 7.29), Leixlip (Figure 7.34), Maynooth, Straffan and Whitechurch. Most of the major extensions consisted of defensive residential towers, but renovations at some churches were dominated by the insertion of bell-cotes. Double- or even triple-bell-cotes were commonly added to the west gable of churches in the Pale in the fifteenth and sixteenth centuries.[92] O'Neill has interpreted this development as being 'symptomatic of the then tranquillity of the Pale'.[93] It is likely that the addition of belfries and bell-cotes at this time was also a reflection of the importance of bell-ringing as a part of the Mass. Bell-cotes were erected at Cloncurry,

89 John Hunt, *Irish medieval figure sculpture, 1200–1600: a study of Irish tombs with notes on costumes and armour* (2 vols, Dublin, 1974), 1, pp 144–5. 90 Ibid., pp 146–7. 91 McMahon, *Medieval church sites of north Dublin*, pp 10, 33. 92 O'Neill, 'St Patrick's Cathedral, Dublin, and its prebendal churches', pp 269–70. 93 O'Neill, 'The medieval parish churches of County Kildare', p. 179.

Figure 7.29 Celbridge Church, Co. Kildare, by Austin Cooper (1781). This view shows the residential tower before it was substantially remodelled as a mortuary chapel for the Connolly family (image reproduced courtesy of the National Library of Ireland).

Figure 7.30 This drawing of Ardcath Church, Co. Meath, by George du Noyer (1866) shows the now-collapsed triple bell-cote. Only the top of the east window can be seen (image courtesy of the Royal Society of Antiquaries of Ireland).

Coghlanstown, Killybegs, Killashee and Straffan, and it is interesting that the renovators at Oughterard (Figure 7.35) and Taghadoe (Figures 7.37, 7.38) chose to erect new bell-cotes rather than to re-use the adjacent round towers. The church at Ardcath, Co. Meath, had a fine triple bell-cote, and this was drawn by du Noyer in the nineteenth century (7.30). The bell-cotes on the towers at Tallaght, Baldongan and Balrothery indicate that the function of the tower (in these instances at least) was primarily as a residence more than as a bell-tower. Elsewhere in Dublin, there are bell-cotes at Howth, Malahide and St Fintan's in Sutton. The

Figure 7.31 Drawing of the double effigial tomb of Christopher St Lawrence (d. 1462), thirteenth baron of Howth, and his wife, Anne Plunkett of Ratoath, Co. Meath, in St Mary's Church, Howth, Co. Dublin (© Department of the Environment, Heritage and Local Government).

bells from the sixteenth-century triple bell-cote at Howth Church are now in front of the main entrance to Howth Castle.

The surge in ecclesiastical building and re-building across the Dublin region in the fifteenth century is epitomised by three major Plunkett projects in Co. Meath at Dunsany (Figure 5.31), Killeen (Figure 5.32) and Rathmore.[94] These churches exhibit signs of influence from the English Perpendicular style of Gothic architecture, albeit with several decades of delay.[95] Rae suggested that the twin-turreted west gables of Killeen and Dunsany may have been modelled on the west front of St Patrick's Cathedral, Dublin (c.1370–1400).[96] Further similarities between these buildings have been identified by Michael O'Neill, and he believes that the design of the Plunkett churches reflects the spread of architectural styles, and possibly even individual craftsmen, from the city out into its hinterland, the Pale.[97] The windows at Killeen (notably the triple-light west window) are so similar to those at St Patrick's that O'Neill argues 'it is practically certain that one or more of the masons who worked on Minot's Tower and the west front of St Patrick's held a later commission on Killeen'.[98] He suggests that Christopher Plunkett, sometime vice-deputy in Dublin, may

Figure 7.32 The remains of the simple rectangular church on Ireland's Eye probably date to the twelfth century. This church, which was held by the archbishop of Dublin, was replaced by a new building on the mainland, at Howth, in the 1230s (image courtesy of Hauke Steinberg).

94 Leask, *Irish churches and monastic buildings, 3*, pp 12–17; T.J. Westropp, 'The churches of Dunsany and Skreen, Co. Meath', *JRSAI*, 24 (1894), 222–31; O'Keeffe, *Medieval Ireland*, pp 150–1, 157–8. **95** O'Keeffe, *Medieval Ireland*, pp 150–1. **96** E.C. Rae, 'The medieval fabric of the cathedral church of St Patrick in Dublin', *JRSAI*, 109 (1979), 29–73 at 32. **97** O'Neill, 'The medieval parish churches in County Meath', 18–26; see also Michael O'Neill, 'The architectural history of the medieval cathedral' in John Crawford and Raymond Gillespie (eds), *St Patrick's Cathedral, Dublin: a history* (Dublin, 2009), pp 96–119. **98** O'Neill, 'St Patrick's Cathedral, Dublin, and its prebendal churches', pp 257–62, esp. p. 262.

Figure **7.33** The interior of the church beside Malahide Castle, Co. Dublin, looking west. The west wall has a triple-light ogee-headed window with a triple-arched bell-cote above. The tomb in the foreground is that of Maud Plunkett (d. 1482), and may be contemporary with the building of much of this nave.

Figure **7.33** The interior of the church beside Malahide Castle, Co. Dublin, looking west. The west wall has a triple-light ogee-headed window with a triple-arched bell-cote above. The tomb in the foreground is that of Maud Plunkett (d. 1482), and may be contemporary with the building of much of this nave.

have been responsible for introducing the latest architectural styles from the capital into the general Pale area. Another example of possible Dublin influence in Meath is the east window of Macetown Church. This is now badly damaged, but it can be seen in a late eighteenth-century drawing by Francis Grose (Figure 7.39). O'Neill has compared its form with a window recorded in the choir aisle of St Patrick's Cathedral and the triple-light sandstone window in the east wall of Malahide Church in the grounds of Malahide Castle.[99]

O'Neill has investigated the degree to which the architecture of churches that were prebends of St Patrick's Cathedral was influenced by their relationship with the cathedral.[100] Although the main fabric of St Patrick's dates to *c.*1225–70, it appears to have had little

99 O'Neill, 'The medieval parish churches in County Meath', 31, 36 (fig. 52). For further discussion of Malahide Church, see Leask, *Irish churches and monastic buildings, 3*, pp 32–4. **100** O'Neill, 'St Patrick's Cathedral, Dublin, and its prebendal churches'. Among the prebendal churches of St Patrick's were Aderrig, Artane, Baldongan, Balrothery, Clondalkin, Crumlin, Esker, Finglas, Kilmactalway, Lusk, Malahide, Maynooth, Mulhuddart, Newcastle Lyons, St Audoen's, St Brigit's (The Ward), St Margaret's, Rathcoole, Swords, Tallaght and Tipper.

Figure **7.34** (*left*) The residential tower at Leixlip Church, Co. Kildare.

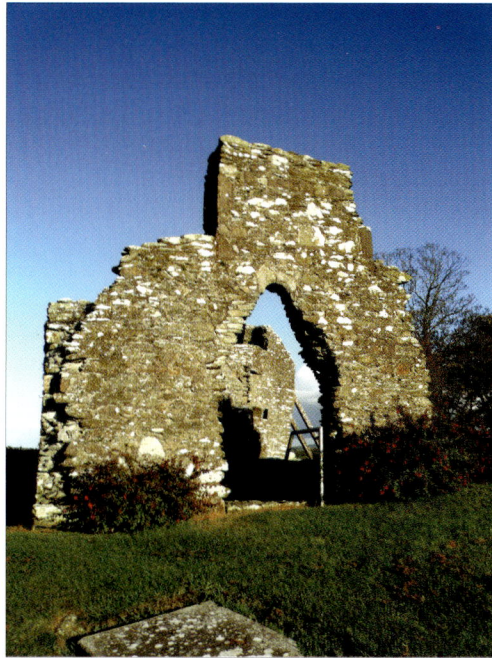

Figure **7.35** (*right*) The church at Oughterard, Co. Kildare, was fitted with a bell-cote (now largely missing), despite the fact that there was a round tower just 10m from it.

Figure **7.36** The church at Cloncurry, Co. Kildare, viewed from the top of the motte. The bell-cote is probably a fifteenth-century addition to a gable that has a slight base batter.

influence on other churches until the fifteenth century.[101] St Patrick's was responsible for the upkeep of the chancels of churches within the parishes put in its hands. One of its prebends was Lusk, and in 1502 the precentor of St Patrick's, Thomas Rochfort, donated to the church at Lusk a large alabaster table for the high altar, together with images of the Saviour, St Mac-Cuilinn (patron saint of Lusk) and St Patrick.[102] O'Neill has also suggested that St Patrick's may have provided the inspiration for some of the windows in Lusk (depicted in a drawing of 1833).[103] Medieval line-impressed floor-tiles recovered during maintenance work in Lusk

101 O'Neill, 'St Patrick's Cathedral, Dublin, and its prebendal churches', pp 145, 256ff.   **102** William Monck-Mason, *The history and antiquities of the collegiate and cathedral church of St Patrick's, Dublin* (Dublin, 1820), p. 142; O'Neill, 'St Patrick's Cathedral, Dublin, and its prebendal churches', p. 244.   **103** O'Neill, 'St Patrick's Cathedral, Dublin, and

Figure 7.37 Taghadoe Church and round tower, Co. Kildare, drawn by Austin Cooper in October 1794. The church seen here was demolished in 1831, to be replaced by the present church, now also ruinous (image reproduced courtesy of the National Library of Ireland).

Figure 7.38 Taghadoe Church and round tower, Co. Kildare, 2009. This church was erected with a grant from the Board of First Fruits in 1831.

Church in the 1970s are similar in style to those found at other Dublin churches, including St Audoen's, which was another of St Patrick's prebendal churches.[104] There are further hints of St Patrick's influence on the churches of Howth and Newcastle Lyons.[105]

The fifteenth-century west tower at Lusk is all that remains of the medieval church, which had two aisles and a seven-arched arcade (Figures 6.9, 7.7, 7.16, 11.7). It has been

its prebendal churches', pp 264–5. **104** McMahon, *Medieval church sites of north Dublin*, p. 10; Mary McMahon, *St Audoen's Church, Cornmarket, Dublin: archaeology and architecture* (Dublin, 2006). **105** O'Neill, 'St Patrick's

Figure 7.39 Macetown Church, Co. Meath, by Francis Grose (1790×1800). This is one of the few representations of the church with its window tracery relatively intact. The east window is comparable to windows at St Patrick's Cathedral and the church in Malahide Demesne. The ivy-clad remains of Macetown Church stand to the east of a deserted medieval settlement and next to the ruins of a tower house (see above, p. 199) (image courtesy of the National Library of Ireland).

Figure 7.40 Effigial tombs of (left) James Bermingham (d. 1637) and (right) Sir Christopher Barnewall (d. 1575) and Marion Sharl (d. 1578) at Lusk Church, Co. Dublin (© Department of the Environment, Heritage and Local Government).

suggested that this four-storey tower may have been built by the same masons who were responsible for the belfry tower at Balrothery Church.[106] The tower at Balrothery (Figures 7.25, 7.26, 7.27) is the earliest upstanding remnant on the site and is one of a series of comparable belfries at the west end of churches in north Co. Dublin that are characteristic of the Pale.[107] At Baldongan, much survives of the nave and chancel, but the best-surviving part is the three-storey west-end belfry (Figure 7.24). The ground floor is vaulted and there

Cathedral, Dublin, and its prebendal churches', pp 266–7.   **106** Leask, *Irish churches and monastic buildings, 3*, p. 23; McMahon, *Medieval church sites of north Dublin*, p. 9.   **107** McMahon, *Medieval church sites of north Dublin*, p. 16.

Figure 7.41 The present St James' Church, Coghlanstown, Co. Kildare, was built on the site of an earlier building. A cross-base in the churchyard was probably associated with the earlier church (image courtesy of Margaret and Ronald Eustice, Eustace Families Association).

is a bell-cote (originally double) on the top of the tower. The chancel may be fifteenth-century, but the nave and tower could be later.

After the Reformation, prominent families continued to patronise their local parish churches and to build their own family chapels. Foremost among these families were the Barnewalls, Bellews, Cruises, Nugents, de Verduns, St Laurences, Flemings and Plunketts. Aside from the Plunketts of Dunsany, Killeen and Rathmore (Figure 4.9), another branch of the family was based at Dunsoghly Castle in north Co. Dublin. John Plunkett built a chapel beside the parish church at St Margaret's and, in 1573, he built a small, private chapel close to the castle at Dunsoghly (Figure 5.58). This chapel has been much altered over the years and its chancel is now missing. A fine effigial tomb in Lusk Church commemorates Christopher Barnewall of Turvey and his wife Marion Sharl, who died in 1575 and 1578 respectively (Figure 7.40).[108]

The church at Coghlanstown, Co. Kildare, has the appearance of 'a late medieval Anglo-Norman manorial church' (Figure 7.41), but an earlier cross-base in the churchyard reveals its early origin.[109] In the fifteenth-century renovations at Coghlanstown, O'Neill has identified some architectural similarities with the church at Rathmore, Co. Meath, and postulates a connection with the Plunketts.[110] Late window inserts often include cusped ogee-headed windows under square hood-mouldings, and examples of this can be seen in Co.

108 Hunt, *Irish medieval figure sculpture*, 1, pp 145–6.   109 O'Neill, 'The medieval parish churches of County Kildare', p. 157.   110 Ibid., p. 180.

Figure 7.42 The church at Mainham, Co. Kildare, was built on a site overlooking the Gollymochy River. The present building, which has undergone extensive reconstruction, consists of a long nave and an unusual square tower with four protruding corner turrets.

Figure 7.43 (*above*) This cusped ogee-headed window under a square hood-moulding is in one of the tower walls of the church at Mainham, Co. Kildare.

Kildare at Cloncurry, Mainham (Figures 7.42, 7.43), Laraghbryan and Lyons. There are also twin-light windows at Coghlanstown (Figure 7.41), Donaghcumper and Killybegs. O'Neill has noted how poorly these architectural features compare with examples in Dublin and Meath, and he sees this as a reflection of variable fortunes within and beyond the Pale.[111]

St Mary's Church, Howth, was a collegiate parish church, and the ruins of the priest's residence or 'college' are in the south-east corner of the graveyard. This is a rare example of a free-standing priest's house in Ireland.[112] From the fifteenth century, and perhaps slightly earlier in some instances, priests would have been accommodated in the newly-built west-end residential towers. Co. Meath has a particularly high density of these extensions, as has north Co. Dublin. Elsewhere, evidence for galleries at churches such as Drimnagh, Esker (Figure 7.44), Kilmahuddrick and Lucan in south Co. Dublin has been interpreted by Helen Bermingham as indicative of priest's residences within the church buildings.[113]

From the available evidence, it seems that the majority of late medieval churches in Ireland were roofed with straw thatch or timber shingles.[114] While some churches had floor tiles, at least in the chancel, this was not ubiquitous in the towns and was very rare in the countryside.[115] Clay floors were the norm. Windows would generally – but not always – have been glazed.[116] It is hard to know exactly what the interiors of the churches would have looked like,[117] but the will of Christopher Plunkett (d. 1461) of Dunsany, Co. Meath, provides an idea of the range of furnishings that would have been present in a wealthy

III Ibid., p. 182.   112 Helen Bermingham, 'Priests' residences in later medieval Ireland' in FitzPatrick and Gillespie (eds), *The parish in medieval and early modern Ireland* (2006), pp 168–85 at p. 176.   113 Ibid., p. 173.   114 Siobhán Scully, 'Medieval parish churches and parochial organisation in Muintir Eolais' (MA, UCG, 1999), pp 109, 110–11; Elizabeth FitzPatrick and Caimin O'Brien, *The medieval churches of County Offaly* (Dublin, 1998), p. 132. 115 FitzPatrick and O'Brien, *Medieval churches of Offaly*, p. 131; Scully, 'Medieval parish churches', p. 111; V.M. Buckley and P.D. Sweetman, *Archaeological survey of County Louth* (Dublin, 1991), p. 257, no. 981; H.A. King, 'A tile from Greenoge, Co. Meath', *RnM*, 7:3 (1984), 63–6; H.A. King, 'A tiled floor at Greenoge, Co. Meath', *RnM*, 8:4 (1992–3), 92–3. See below, pp 457–9.   116 Scully, 'Medieval parish churches', pp 129–33.   117 See, for example, Rachel Moss, 'Permanent expressions of piety: the secular and the sacred in later medieval stone sculpture' in Rachel Moss, Colmán Ó Clabaigh and Salvador Ryan (eds), *Art and devotion in late medieval Ireland* (Dublin, 2006), pp 72–97 at pp 72–3, 96.

Figure 7.44 Esker
Church, Co. Dublin:
there may have been a
priest's residence over
the west end of the
church.

church in the fifteenth century.[118] Among the items that he bequeathed to the church at Dunsany were two silver censers, a cross and a chalice, four 'antiphoners', three graduals, three mass books, a legend, two 'salters and hymners', a salter's epistolary, a versiculary, a martyrology, a cope of gold, a chasuble of cloth of gold, and a chasuble of red satin.

Many of the churches in the Dublin region would have had paintings on their interior plastered walls.[119] At Christ Church Cathedral, there was a timber-panelled wall behind the rood, 'wher the story of the passion was painted'.[120] In 1559, on foot of the Reformation, orders were issued to 'newe paynt the walls of Christ Church and St Patrick's and in sted of pictures and popish fancies to place passages or text of scripture on the walls'.[121] Some of the column capitals in St Patrick's bare traces of paint but,[122] in general, very little of the medieval paintwork survives. In the 1880s, 'a fresco in vivid colours' of apparently fifteenth-century date or earlier was revealed when some arches were being unblocked inside St Audoen's Church in Dublin.[123] One of the scenes possibly depicted St Anne teaching the Virgin, but very little trace of these paintings survives. Several authors commented on the presence of wall-paintings in the baptistery beside St Doolagh's Church, near Malahide. In 1772, Gabriel Beranger noted that they were badly defaced, and that the small statues of the twelve apostles that were once present had been removed.[124] Over a hundred years later, however, it was noted that the frescoes included depictions of SS Patrick, Columba, Brigit and Doolagh.[125] Traces of paint can be seen on the walls of the baptistery, but individual scenes can no longer be identified.

Altar furnishings included silver and bronze crosses, bells and candlesticks, such as those found at Sheephouse, Co. Meath, in the nineteenth century (Figure 7.45).[126] The metal

118 *Cal. Carew MSS, Howth*, pp 357–9; Westropp, 'The churches of Dunsany and Skreen', 222.   **119** Karena Morton, pers. comm.   **120** Raymond Gillespie (ed.), *The proctor's accounts of Peter Lewis, 1564–1565* (Dublin, 1996), p. 39.   **121** N.B. White, 'The annals of Dudley Loftus', *Analecta Hibernia*, 10–11 (1941), 223–4.   **122** Rae, 'The medieval fabric', p. 47.   **123** T.N. Deane, '55th report of the Commissioners of Public Works (C5 142), Appendix E (1886–7)', p. 63; Robert Cochrane, '81st annual report of the Commissioners of Public Works, Appendix E:II (1912–13)', p. 44; T.J. Westropp, 'Clare Island Survey: history and archaeology', *PRIA*, 31 (1911–15 [1911]), section 1, pt 2, 1–78 at 31; H.M. Roe, 'Illustrations of the Holy Trinity in Ireland, 13th to 17th centuries', *JRSAI*, 109 (1979), 144–5; M.V. Ronan, *S. Anne her cult and her shrines* (London, 1927), pp 110–11.   **124** Harbison, *Beranger's antique buildings*, p. 136. See also Francis Grose, *The antiquities of Ireland*, 2 (2nd ed., Kilkenny, 1982), p. 78.   **125** J.S. Slone, 'Antiquities of Fingal, no. 1: St Doulagh's', *Irish Builder*, 1 Oct. 1879.   **126** Raghnall Ó Floinn, 'Later medieval Ireland, AD1150–1550' in P.F. Wallace

Figure 7.45 Processional cross, bell and candlestick from Sheephouse, Co. Meath, *c.*1500. This hoard of altar furnishings was found in a quarry in the late nineteenth century (image courtesy of the National Museum of Ireland).

Figure 7.46 Metal candle-holder found during recent excavations at Drumkay Church, Co. Wicklow (max. length 15cm). This would have been set into the wall of the church (courtesy of Edmond O'Donovan and Margaret Gowen and Co. Ltd).

candle-holder recovered during excavations at Drumkay Church, Co. Wicklow, was probably fitted to the wall of the church to light the interior (Figure 7.46). A medieval hand-bell recently discovered close to the site of the church of Michael le Pole, Dublin, may have been rung from the round tower that formerly stood at this location (Figure 7.47). The very fine sculpted stone shaft from Ratoath Church, Co. Meath, is a reflection of the wealth of some of the churches in the Dublin region in the later Middle Ages (Figure 7.48).[127]

Religious houses in the Dublin region

Cistercian houses

The monastery at Mellifont, Co. Louth, founded by St Malachy in 1142, was the first Cistercian house in Ireland.[128] Its first daughter house, at Bective, Co. Meath, was founded in 1147. On the north-west bank of the River Boyne, Bective Abbey lies just 100m outside the study area. Mellifont's second daughter house was established at Baltinglass, Co. Wicklow, in 1148, but this too lies beyond the (southern) boundary of the study area. Indeed, the only Cistercian monastery within the entire area being studied is St Mary's Abbey, Dublin, and this was in fact founded as a Savigniac house in 1139, becoming Cistercian only in 1147 when the two orders merged (Figure 7.49).[129] As it was founded three years before Mellifont, there appears to have been some controversy regarding seniority between the two.[130]

St Mary's was situated on the north bank of the Liffey, and much of it survived until the late seventeenth century.[131] Now, however, nothing remains apart from the four-bay, rib-vaulted chapter house and an adjoining passage to the south (Figure 7.50).[132] Fragments of a Perpendicular-style cloister arcade discovered on Cook Street on the opposite side of the river in 1975 may once have formed part of the monastic complex.[133] In addition to its church buildings, the 1539 extent for St Mary's lists mills, stables, a granary and a brew-house, among other agricultural and semi-industrial buildings.[134] The monastery managed at least

and Raghnall Ó Floinn (eds), *Treasures of the National Museum of Ireland: Irish antiquities* (Dublin, 2002), pp 257–300 at pp 272, 299; Colum Hourihane, '"Holye Crossys": a catalogue of processional, altar, pendant and crucifix figures for late medieval Ireland', *PRIA*, 100C1 (2000), 1–85 at 10–11, 30, 44–5.   **127** H.M. Roe, 'The presidential address, 26 January 1966: Some aspects of medieval culture in Ireland', *JRSAI*, 96 (1966), 105–9; Potterton, *Medieval Trim*, pp 400–1, 402 (fig. 11.11).   **128** Roger Stalley, *The Cistercian monasteries of Ireland* (London and New Haven, 1987), passim; Roger Stalley, *Architecture and sculpture in Ireland, 1150–1350* (Dublin, 1971), pp 92–7.   **129** Gwynn, 'The origins of St Mary's Abbey'.   **130** Stalley, *The Cistercian monasteries of Ireland*, p. 244.   **131** Bill Doran and Linda Doran, 'St Mary's Cistercian abbey, Dublin: a ghost in the alleyways' in Bradley, Fletcher and Simms (eds), *Dublin in the medieval world* (2009), pp 188–201.   **132** P.J. Donnelly (comp.), *Remains of St Mary's Abbey, Dublin: their exploration and researches, AD1886* (Dublin, 1887).   **133** Stalley, *The Cistercian monasteries of Ireland*, p. 244.   **134** *EIMP*, pp 1–2; *CSMA*, 2,

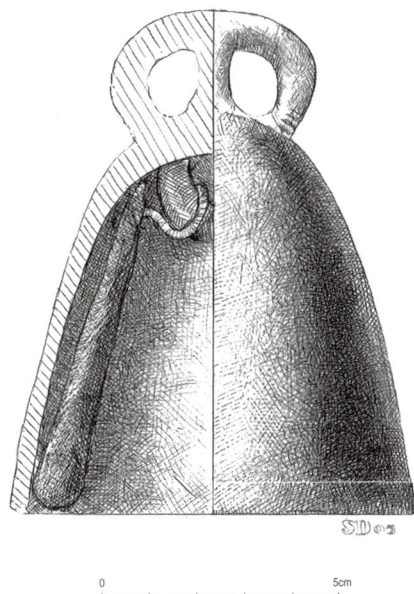

Figure 7.47 (*left*) Drawing by Simon Dick of a medieval hand-bell found during excavations at the site of the church of Michael le Pole. The pit from which this copper-alloy bell was recovered contained pottery dating to the twelfth to fourteenth centuries. The bell may have been rung from the top floor of the round tower that is known to have stood on the site in the Middle Ages. The remains of a rope attached to the bell were identified during conservation (courtesy of Margaret Gowen and Co. Ltd).

Figure 7.48 This sculpted hexagonal shaft once stood in Ratoath Church, Co. Meath, but it was moved to St Patrick's Cathedral, Trim. It is one of the finest pieces of stone carving from medieval Ireland.

half a dozen granges, and even before the arrival of the Anglo-Normans in Ireland, it had accumulated blocks of land all across the region (see pp 68–9). Further grants were made to them in Dublin, Meath and Wicklow after 1170, by both Anglo-Norman and Gaelic Irish families. St Mary's may have been responsible for the building of castles at Monkstown and at Bullock (Figures 5.49, 13.2), where they operated a port and a fishery.[135] St Mary's was to become the richest Cistercian house in Ireland, and maintained this position right up to the Dissolution in 1539, when it was valued at almost £540.[136]

Augustinian houses

As with the Cistercians, the first Augustinian communities in Ireland seem to have emerged in the mid-twelfth century. Unlike their Cistercian counterparts, however, the first Augustinian houses were pre-existing communities that adopted the Augustinian rule. Further houses were founded after 1170, many of which were patronised by Anglo-Norman lords. The Augustinians were a mendicant order, and as such their foundations were usually located outside towns, but close enough to allow them to carry out their pastoral roles among the people. Among the Augustinian houses, some followed the Arrouaisian rule, and others followed the rule of St Victor.

The abbey of Arrouaise in Artois, France, had adopted special observances based partly upon those of the Cistercians and approved by St Bernard.[137] According to the Cartulary of Arrouaise, Malachy, who worked as papal legate in Ireland from 1140 until his death in 1148, introduced this rule in many places in Ireland.[138] The three Arrouaisian houses in the Dublin region were St Saviour's Priory, Glendalough, Co. Wicklow, the priory of All Hallows and

pp xli–xliii; Purcell, 'Land-use in medieval Oxmantown', pp 203–4.   **135** *CSMA*, 1, pp 307–11.   **136** Stalley, *The Cistercian monasteries of Ireland*, p. 244; *MRHI*, pp 130–1; *EIMP*, pp 1–25.   **137** Neville Hadcock, 'The origin of the Augustinian order in Meath', *RnM*, 3:2 (1964), 124–31 at 124–5; Sarah Preston, 'The canons regular of St Augustine: the twelfth-century reform in action' in Stuart Kinsella (ed.), *Augustinians at Christ Church: the canons regular of the Cathedral priory of the Holy Trinity* (Dublin, 2000), pp 23–40.   **138** P.J. Dunning, 'The Arroasian order in medieval Ireland', *IHS*, 4 (1945–6), 297–315 at 299–300, referring to J.-P. Migne (ed.), *Patrologiae latinae cursus completus* (221 vols, Paris, 1844–64), 217, cols 67–8; the original MS (no. 1077), 'Cartulaire de l'abbaye d'Arrouaise … rédigé sous l'administration de l'abbé Gaultier de Cambrai (1180–93) avec additions: actes de 1097 à 1287', is in the Bibliothèque Municipale at Amiens, France. See also Ludo Milis, *L'ordre des chanoines réguliers d'Arrouaise: son histoire et son organisation, de la fondation de l'abbaye-mère (vers 1090) a la fin des chapitres annuels (1471)* (2 vols, Bruges, 1969), 2, pp 338–77; M.T. Flanagan, 'St Mary's Abbey, Louth, and the introduction of the Arrouaisian observance into Ireland',

Figure 7.49 (above) Reconstruction drawing of St Mary's Abbey, c.1450, from the south-east, with Oxmantown in the background (image from *Dublin: one thousand years* by Stephen Conlin, published by the O'Brien Press Ltd, Dublin. © Stephen Conlin).

Figure 7.50 The chapter-house of St Mary's, built c.1200. This is the only surviving part of St Mary's Abbey. Excavations in 1886 unearthed tiles and the footings of walls and piers, but no detailed report was made of the findings (© Department of the Environment, Heritage and Local Government).

the priory of Holy Trinity, Dublin. The priory at Glendalough, on the south bank of the Glendasan River, just 1km east of the earlier monastic complex, was founded in the 1150s by Laurence O'Toole (Lorcán Ua Tuathail) under the patronage of Diarmait Mac Murchada. Among the later benefactors of the priory were the Mac Gilla Mo Cholmóc family[139] and Strongbow, who appropriated St Saviour's as part of his royal grant of Leinster in 1171. The twelfth-century nave-and-chancel church of St Saviour's is heavily restored, but the nineteenth-century restoration seems quite faithful to its original appearance.[140] The Romanesque chancel arch has three orders carved with various small motifs set within

Clogher Record: Journal of the Clogher Historical Society, 10 (1978–81), 223–34. **139** McNeill (ed.), *Alen's register*, p. 21. **140** O'Keeffe, *Romanesque Ireland*, pp 234, 239–43; Barrow, *Glendalough and St Kevin*, pp 45–8; Cochrane, *Historical*

Figure 7.51 Distribution of religious houses in the Dublin region.

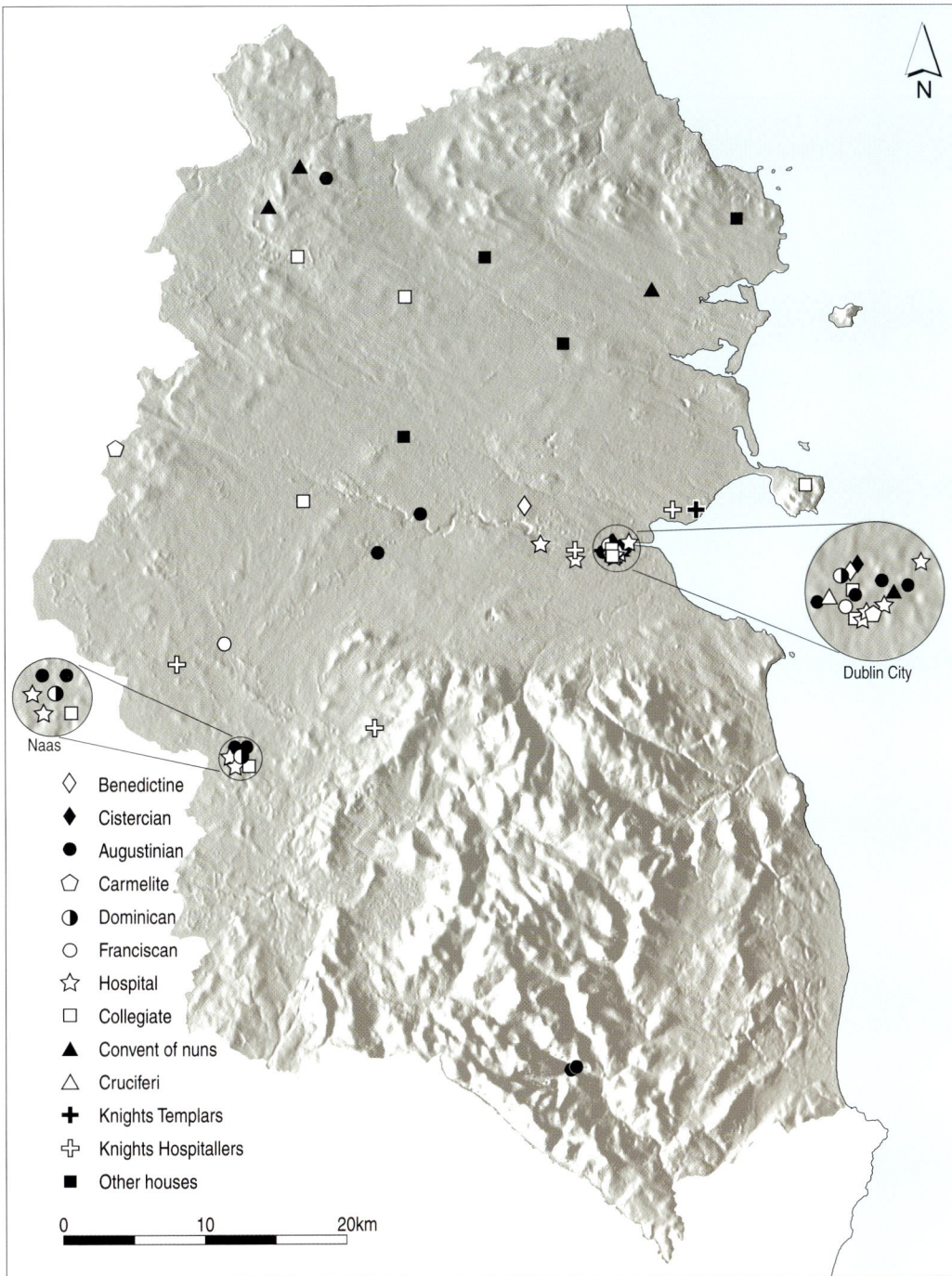

lozenges, while the east window also has some fine carving. Apart from the church, nothing of the monastic complex survives above ground.

The Arrouaisian priory of All Hallows was founded in Dublin's eastern suburb by Diarmait Mac Murchada *c.*1166.[141] The original grant was witnessed by the bishop of Glendalough, and by the former abbot of the Arrouaisian house at Glendalough, Laurence O'Toole, who had become archbishop of Dublin in 1162. The association with Glendalough was a strong one, and after the union of the dioceses of Dublin and Glendalough in 1216, the priory of St Saviour's in the Wicklow Mountains was granted to All Hallows.[142] The Dublin priory also held lands in Meath, Kildare, Louth, Tipperary and elsewhere in Ireland.[143] The site of the priory of All Hallows is now occupied by Trinity College

---

and descriptive notes, Leask, *Glendalough*, pp 36–41.   **141** *MRHI*, pp 171–2; Roland Budd, The platforme of an universitie: *All Hallows Priory to Trinity College, Dublin* (Dublin, 2001).   **142** McNeill (ed.), *Alen's register*, p. 38.   **143** *MRHI*, p. 172.

Figure 7.52 'Plott of a colledg or hospice' (*c.*1592). This is the oldest surviving illustration of Trinity College Dublin. The monastic range of All Hallows previously occupied this site and it is possible that some of the buildings depicted here incorporate earlier structures (from the library at Hatfield House (CPM 1/6), reproduced by permission of the Marquess of Salisbury).

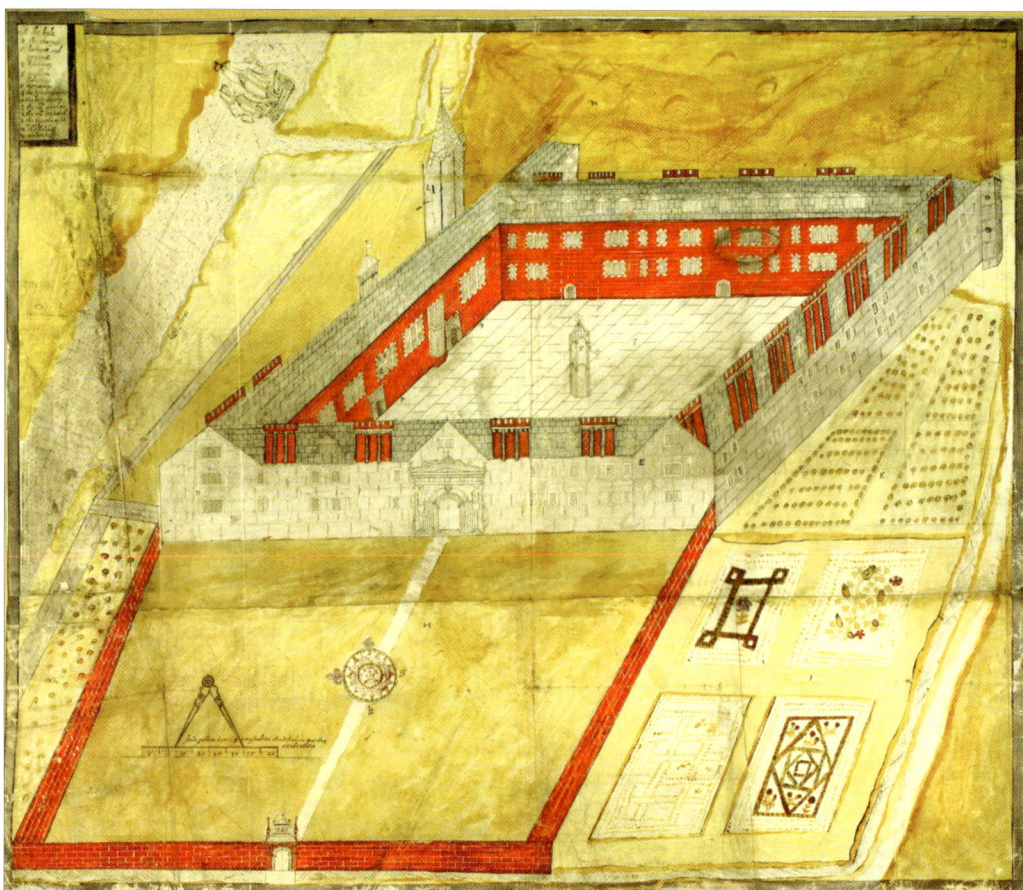

(Figure 7.52), and it seems that nothing of it survives above ground. In addition to the range of monastic buildings, documentary sources confirm the presence of twelve acres of meadow and nine acres of pasture as well as seven orchards.[144] Through close analysis of the historical and cartographical sources, Linzi Simpson has been able to create a good picture of how the whole complex might have appeared. Subsequent archaeological investigations revealed burials that appear to have been within the priory cemetery, as well as the foundations of medieval walls.[145]

After his appointment as archbishop of Dublin in 1162, Laurence O'Toole had the secular canons of Christ Church Cathedral become regular canons under the rule of St Augustine.[146] After his death in Normandy in 1180, some of O'Toole's bones were placed among the large collection of relics at Holy Trinity – among which was the famous wooden *Bachall Iosa* (or 'Staff of Jesus'), which was publicly burnt in 1538 by Archbishop George Browne, a nominee of Henry VIII.[147] At the time of the taxation of 1302–6, the priory of Holy Trinity, with all of its churches and granges, was valued at over £182, making it the wealthiest of all Irish monasteries recorded at that time. Most of the early canons seem to have been of Irish birth, but in the thirteenth and fourteenth centuries an increasing number of Englishmen became part of the community. In 1380, it was enacted that no mere Irishman should be professed in the priory. A new cathedral was begun at the priory of Holy Trinity *c.*1175, with support from Strongbow, and building continued under Archbishop Cumin in

144 Linzi Simpson, 'The priory of All Hallows and Trinity College, Dublin: recent archaeological discoveries' in Duffy (ed.), *Medieval Dublin III* (2002), pp 195–236. **145** Simpson, 'The priory of All Hallows', pp 229–35. **146** *MRHI*, pp 170–1. **147** M.V. Ronan, 'St Patrick's Staff and Christ Church' in Clarke (ed.), *Medieval Dublin: the living city* (1990), pp 123–31; Raghnall Ó Floinn, 'The foundation relics of Christ Church Cathedral and the origin of the diocese of Dublin' in Duffy (ed.), *Medieval Dublin VII* (2006), pp 89–102; Raghnall Ó Floinn, 'The late medieval relics of Holy Trinity Church, Dublin' in Bradley, Fletcher and Simms (eds), *Dublin in the medieval world* (2009), pp 369–89.

Figure 7.53 St Wolstan's Priory, Co. Kildare: four of the five structures depicted in these Austin Cooper sketches survive. They were drawn in 1781 and 1782 (image reproduced courtesy of the National Library of Ireland).

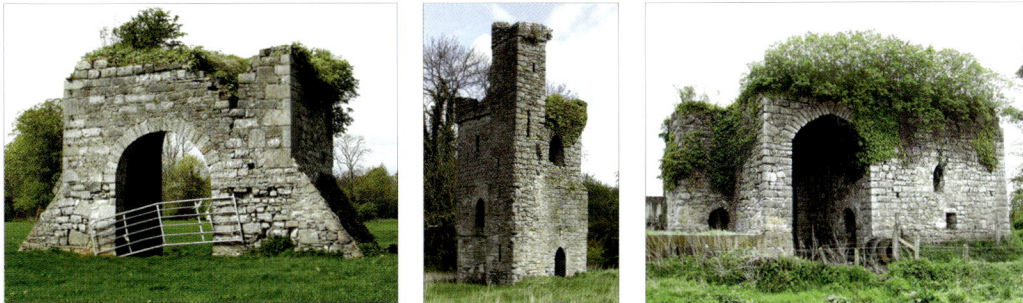

Figure 7.54 (*left*) St Wolstan's Priory, Co. Kildare: one of three surviving gateways, viewed from the south. It is likely that this one was significantly remodelled after the Dissolution.
Figure 7.55 (*centre*) This four-storey tower at St Wolstan's Priory has also undergone major renovations.
Figure 7.56 (*right*) This gateway is the largest and apparently least altered of the three upstanding examples at St Wolstan's Priory, Co. Kildare. A fourth gate was still standing in 1939, but it is no longer present.

the 1180s and 1190s. The present transept dates to this period, but the nave is a generation or so later (*c.*1220).[148] This later phase exhibits strong influences from the architecture of western England, and indeed much of the stone was imported from there. Various other phases of building took place; some in response to disasters such as fires or collapses (such as in 1283, 1316, 1461 and 1562).[149] Among the benefactors of Holy Trinity were wealthy families from the surrounding counties, and in 1512 the earl of Kildare had a chapel built and dedicated to Mary in the choir.[150] A major campaign of restoration took place at the cathedral in 1872–8.[151]

The three congregations of Victorine canons in the Dublin region were St Catherine's, Lucan, Co. Dublin, St Thomas the Martyr's, Dublin, and St Wolstan's, Co. Kildare. The priory of St Thomas the Martyr was founded in 1177 by William Fitz Audelin on behalf of Henry II.[152] It followed the Victorine rule from *c.*1192 and had close ties with the Augustinian

---

148 Roger Stalley, 'The construction of the medieval cathedral, *c.*1030–1250' in Milne (ed.), *Christ Church Cathedral* (2000), pp 53–74; Rachel Moss, 'Tales from the crypt: the medieval stonework of Christ Church Cathedral, Dublin' in Duffy (ed.), *Medieval Dublin III* (2002), pp 95–114. **149** Roger Stalley, 'The architecture of the cathedral and priory buildings, 1250–1530' in Milne (ed.), *Christ Church Cathedral* (2000), pp 95–128; Máire Geaney, 'Christ Church Cathedral, Dublin: a survey of the nave and chancel transept roofs' in Duffy (ed.), *Medieval Dublin VII* (2006), pp 233–49; Stuart Kinsella, 'Mapping Christ Church Cathedral, Dublin, *c.*1028–1608' in Bradley, Fletcher and Simms (eds), *Dublin in the medieval world* (2009), pp 143–67. See also Thomas Drew, 'The ancient chapter-house of the priory of Holy Trinity, Dublin' in Clarke (ed.), *Medieval Dublin: the making of a metropolis* (1990), pp 173–82. **150** Lyons, *Church and society*, p. 85. **151** Roger Stalley, 'George Edmund Street and the restoration of the cathedral, 1868–78' in Milne (ed.), *Christ Church Cathedral* (2000), pp 353–73. **152** *MRHI*, pp 172–3; A.C. Elliot, 'The abbey of St Thomas the Martyr, near Dublin' (Dublin, 1892), reprinted in Clarke (ed.), *Medieval Dublin: the living city* (1990), pp 62–77; Aubrey Gwynn, 'The early history of St Thomas Abbey, Dublin', *JRSAI*, 84 (1954), 1–35; see also Laureen Buckley,

house in Bristol.[153] It was granted lands, churches and other properties at various locations across the Dublin region, especially at Donore, where it held mills, meadows and other appurtenances.[154] St Thomas' was one of the most extensive monastic complexes in medieval Ireland, but nothing survives of it above ground.[155] Excavations revealed a variety of floor tiles and possible fragments of the church and cloister walls, including several blocks of Dundry stone. Evidence for a medieval garden was also uncovered. The extent of October 1540 confirmed that St Thomas' held over 2,300 acres of land and properties including three castles and five mills, altogether worth more than £450.[156] Excavations directed by Franc Myles in 2003–4 revealed the remains of a millpond at the site, and this may have been associated with at least one of those recorded in 1540 and used for many years before that.[157]

A priory dedicated to St Catherine was founded by Warisius de Pech in *c.*1219.[158] Among its benefactors were the lord of Lucan and Adam de Hereford. St Catherine's was closely linked with the priory of St Thomas the Martyr, to which it was finally annexed in 1327.[159] De Hereford had co-founded a priory of Victorine canons at St Wolstan's, on the south bank of the Liffey near Celbridge, Co. Kildare, with its first prior, Richard, in *c.*1205.[160] St Wolstan's was suppressed in September 1536, when its possessions included gardens, orchards, cottages, four watermills (Figure 7.57) and over a thousand acres of land.[161] The structural remains at the site consist of one tower and three gateways, most of which have

'Health status in medieval Dublin: analysis of the skeletal remains from the abbey of St Thomas the Martyr' in Duffy (ed.), *Medieval Dublin IV* (2003), pp 98–126. **153** Claire Walsh, 'Archaeological excavations at the abbey of St Thomas the Martyr, Dublin' in Duffy (ed.), *Medieval Dublin I* (2000), pp 185–202. **154** For example, see *CPI*, p. 2; *EIMP*, pp 32–3; *RAST*, pp 8, 26, 45–6, 50, 59, 75, 298–9; *RHJB*, p. 170; Otway-Ruthven, 'Medieval church lands', pp 70–1; Clarke, '*Urbs et suburbium*', p. 51; Duddy, 'The western suburb of medieval Dublin'; Bradley, Halpin and King, 'UAS 7:3: Kildare', p. 298. **155** Walsh, 'Archaeological excavations at the abbey of St Thomas'; Cathal Duddy, 'The role of St Thomas's Abbey in the early development of Dublin's western suburb' in Duffy (ed.), *Medieval Dublin IV* (2003), pp 79–97. **156** *MRHI*, pp 172–3. **157** Franc Myles, 'Archaeological excavations at the millpond of St Thomas's Abbey, Dublin' in Duffy (ed.), *Medieval Dublin IX* (2009), pp 183–212. **158** *MRHI*, p. 192. **159** *MRHI*, pp 172, 192. **160** *MRHI*, p. 193; Nolan, 'Kildare from the documents of conquest'. **161** *MRHI*, p. 193.

been substantially remodelled (Figures 7.53, 7.54, 7.55, 7.56). One of the gates has a round-arched passageway with a chamber on the west, a projecting stair turret to the east, and a second, residential chamber at first-floor level. A fourth gate is visible on the 1939 Ordnance Survey map, but only minor earthworks survive there now.

Other houses of Augustinian canons in the Dublin region were founded at Naas and St Patrick's Island. The priory of St John the Baptist at Naas was founded by a baron of Naas in the twelfth century.[162] It had an associated hospital. When the extent was drawn up in 1540, it was found that the priory church was being used as a barn, and that the other buildings, including a tower, were also being used by the farmer.[163] Among its possessions were a castle, several cottages and gardens, and a mill (which was initially concealed from the commissioners).[164]

A priory of Augustinian canons appears to have been founded on St Patrick's Island, off the coast of Dublin, by Sitric Mac Murchada, but this was moved by Henry of London, archbishop of Dublin, to Holmpatrick on the mainland in 1220.[165] In 1540, the possessions of the priory included a thousand acres of land and a watermill.[166] It is possible that there were other priories of Augustinian canons at Ballymadun, Co. Dublin, and at Dunboyne and Ratoath in Co. Meath.[167]

There were houses of Augustinian friars at Dublin, Naas and Skreen. The Dublin friary, which was dedicated to the Holy Trinity, may have been founded by a member of the Talbot family in the late 1270s or early 1280s.[168] A certain Thomas de Carlow was prior there in 1328, and two professors of sacred writings are recorded later in the fourteenth century – one of whom was licensed to lecture at the University of Oxford. At the time of the Dissolution, the prior was seized of various buildings as well as about a hundred acres of land and a mill.[169]

The Augustinian friary was founded in Naas in the second half of the fourteenth century, but its subsequent history is vague.[170] The founder may have been a Cullen from Dublin and the Eustaces may have been among its patrons. It was referred to as the 'Monastery of the Moat', and this may have been due to its proximity to the motte at Naas, or to the town defences. A large ruinous church stood close to the town boundary until 1835, but nothing survives of it now. Holy Trinity Priory at Skreen, Co. Meath, was established on lands leased from Francis de Feypo in 1341.[171] Little is known of the history of this Augustinian house, but when it was valued in 1539 it included a church, a chapter house, a dormitory, two chambers, a hall, a kitchen and other buildings as well as a park and at least one garden.[172]

Benedictine houses

It has recently been suggested that 'the origins of the diocese of Dublin owe much to the involvement of Irish Benedictine monks based … in Germany'.[173] The Benedictines had only a small number of foundations in Ireland, and the only one with any substantial remains is at Fore in Co. Westmeath.[174] This was founded by Hugh de Lacy c.1180. The only Benedictine house in the Dublin region was the priory of St Brigit, Castleknock, which was

162 *MRHI*, p. 189.   163 *EIMP*, p. 155.   164 *MRHI*, p. 189.   165 *MRHI*, pp 178, 193; D'Alton, *History of the county of Dublin*, p. 445.   166 *EIMP*, pp 49–53.   167 *MRHI*, pp 174, 191, 198.   168 *MRHI*, pp 298–9; Seán Duffy and Linzi Simpson, 'The hermits of St Augustine in medieval Dublin: their history and archaeology' in Bradley, Fletcher and Simms (eds), *Dublin in the medieval world* (2009), pp 202–48.   169 *EIMP*, pp 79–80.   170 *MRHI*, p. 301. 171 *MRHI*, pp 301–2.   172 *EIMP*, pp 306–7; *MRHI*, p. 302.   173 Colmán Ó Clabaigh, 'The Benedictines in medieval and early modern Ireland' in Martin Browne and Colmán Ó Clabaigh (eds), *The Irish Benedictines: a history* (Dublin, 2005), pp 79–121 at p. 84.   174 Rory Masterson, 'The alien priory of Fore, Co. Westmeath in the Middle Ages', *Archiv. Hib.*, 53 (1999), 73–9; Rory Masterson, 'The Church and the Anglo-Norman colonisation of Ireland: a case study of the priory of Fore', *RnM*, 11 (2000), 58–70; Rory Masterson, 'The early Anglo-Norman colonisation of Fore, Co. Westmeath', *RnM*, 13 (2002), 44–60; Ó Clabaigh, 'The Benedictines in medieval and early modern Ireland', pp 100–4.

Figure 7.58 Naas 'Abbey', Co. Kildare, drawn by Austin Cooper in July 1781. The two-storey wall to the left of the tower may have been part of the domestic range of buildings associated with the friary. The whole complex was demolished in 1835 and this may be the only drawing of it (image reproduced courtesy of the National Library of Ireland).

founded *c*.1185 by Hugh Tyrell, as a dependency of the Benedictine priory of Little Malvern, Worcestershire.[175] Its holdings included lands in Dublin and Meath. In 1336, Brother Nicholas de Upton, of the community of Little Malvern, was excused from having to travel to the priory at Castleknock, living as he did in fear of crossing the sea and visiting a barbarous land.[176] In 1486, the priory of Castleknock, together with its churches and lands in Meath, were purchased by the abbot of St Mary's, Dublin.[177]

Dominican houses

Another mendicant order, the Dominicans, or Friars Preachers, first reached Ireland in 1224 from England, establishing houses in Drogheda and Dublin.[178] By the end of the thirteenth century, twenty-four communities had been formed in Ireland.[179] St Saviour's 'Black Friary' was established in Oxmantown on land belonging to the Cistercian house of St Mary's.[180] The site is now occupied (in part) by the Four Courts. In 1285, the Dominicans were granted thirty oaks for the fabric of their church.[181] In the following decades, various fires, repairs and other events associated with the friary are recorded.[182] The King's Inns were established on the site *c*.1582. Apart from St Saviour's, the only Dominican friary in the Dublin region was at Naas, Co. Kildare (Figure 7.58).[183] This was founded by the Eustaces in the mid-fourteenth century and was dedicated to St Eustace.

Franciscan houses

It appears that the first Franciscan houses in Ireland were founded in the 1220s, and by 1282 there were twenty-seven friaries.[184] Repairs were already being carried out at the friary in

175 Ó Clabaigh, 'The Benedictines in medieval and early modern Ireland', pp 99–100.   **176** Ibid., p. 100.   **177** *MRHI*, p. 105; *CSMA*, 2, pp 16–18.   **178** TCD MS 579/2, fo. 343; Aquilla Smith (ed.), Annales de Monte Fernandi *(Annals of Multifernan)* (Dublin, 1842; repr. Dublin, 1843), *s.a.* 1224, p. 12.   **179** Thomas Flynn, *The Irish Dominicans, 1536–1641* (Dublin, 1993), p. 2; Finbar Ryan and Ambrose Coleman, *St Dominic and the Dominicans in Ireland, 1216–1916* (Dublin, n.d.), p. 18; Hugh Fenning (ed.), *Medieval Irish Dominican studies: Benedict O'Sullivan OP* (Dublin, 2009).   **180** *MRHI*, pp 224–5; Benedict O'Sullivan, 'The Dominicans of medieval Dublin' in Clarke (ed.), *Medieval Dublin: the living city* (1990), pp 83–99; see also Bernadette Williams, 'The Dominican annals of Dublin' in Duffy (ed.), *Medieval Dublin II* (2001), pp 142–68.   **181** *CDI, 1285–92*, no. 92, p. 38.   **182** *MRHI*, p. 225.   **183** *MRHI*, p. 228.   **184** *MRHI*, p. 260; Luke Wadding,

Dublin by January 1233, so it must have been founded before then.[185] The friary at Clane (Figure 7.59), Co. Kildare, was founded *c*.1258, probably by Gerald FitzMaurice, lord of Offaly, who was buried there in 1287 (a mutilated effigy still present in the friary may represent FitzMaurice).[186] After the Dissolution, materials from the Clane friary were used to repair Maynooth Castle.

Carmelite houses

The first Carmelites probably came to Ireland in the 1260s, and St Mary's Priory, Dublin was founded in 1274, possibly by Robert Bagod, Chief Justice.[187] It was located in the 'southern suburbs' of the city. At the Dissolution, its possessions included seven gardens and two meadows, but most of its buildings were destroyed soon after that. Edward III granted a licence to John Roche to found a house of Carmelites at Cloncurry, Co. Kildare, in 1347. In 1539, the priory complex consisted of a church with belfry, a chapter house, a dormitory, a hall, two chambers, a kitchen, an orchard, three cottages and twelve acres of land.[188] Remarkably, by the following year, there were apparently no buildings left on the site.[189]

Houses of the Fratres Cruciferi and Fratres de Poenitentia

The priory and hospital of St John the Baptist, outside the New Gate, Dublin, was founded by Ailred the Palmer and confirmed by Pope Clement III in November 1188.[190] This was a house of the *Fratres Cruciferi* or 'crutched friars', who got their name from the wooden staff that they each carried with them, which was topped by a cross. It was for both brethren and sisters, and looked after the poor and infirm. The church was demolished at the Dissolution.

Annales Minorum seu trium ordinum A.S. Francisco institutorum (7 vols, Lyon, 1625–54; new ed., 32 vols, Quarrachi, 1931–64), 15, p. 417; Patrick Conlon, *Franciscan Ireland* (Mullingar, 1988); Colmán Ó Clabaigh, *The Franciscans in Ireland, 1400–1534* (Dublin, 2002). **185** *CDI, 1171–1251*, no. 2004, p. 298; *MRHI*, pp 248–9. **186** *AFM, s.a.* 1287; *MRHI*, p. 245. **187** *MRHI*, p. 289. **188** *MRHI*, p. 288. **189** *EIMP*, p. 172. **190** *MRHI*, p. 212; Mark Hennessy, 'The priory and hospital of Newgate: the evolution and decline of a medieval monastic estate' in W.J. Smyth and Kevin Whelan (eds), *Common ground: essays on the historical geography of Ireland* (Cork, 1988), pp 41–54; Charles McNeill, 'Hospital of St John without the New Gate, Dublin', *JRSAI*, 55 (1925), 58–64; repr. in Clarke (ed.), *Medieval Dublin: the living city* (1990), pp 77–82; Grace O'Keeffe, 'The hospital of St John the Baptist in medieval Dublin' in Duffy (ed.),

At this time, its possessions included three watermills, gardens and a house with beds for fifty patients, as well as over 1,700 acres of land in Cos. Dublin, Meath, Kildare, Carlow, Cork and Tipperary.[191]

The only foundation in Ireland of the *Fratres de Poenitentia*, or *Saccati* ('friars of the sack'), was established in Dublin in 1268.[192] The order had been founded before the middle of the thirteenth century, but they were abolished in 1274 and nearly all were extinct by 1315. Where this friary was located is a matter of conjecture, but in 1766 Walter Harris suggested that it was in 'the west part of Dublin [near] the pool of the house of St Thomas the Martyr'.[193]

Convents of nuns

Most medieval convents in Ireland followed the Arrouaisian rule, and all of those in the Dublin region did.[194] Most were also dedicated to Mary, and most were situated in rural locations. The main exception to this latter characteristic was the abbey of St Mary de Hogges, Dublin, founded by Diarmait Mac Murchada *c*.1146 on the south side of Hoggen Green.[195] It was a convent of Arrouaisian nuns, initially under the jurisdiction of Clonard, Co. Meath, but later becoming independent (*c*.1200?). At the Dissolution, materials from St Mary de Hogges were used to repair Dublin Castle. The priory of St Mary at Gracedieu, Co. Dublin, was transferred from Lusk by Archbishop Cumin in the 1190s.[196] The church at Lusk was later appropriated to the priory of All Hallows, Dublin, but in 1540 the properties of Gracedieu still included over a hundred acres and several cottages in Lusk. In the early thirteenth century, the church of Ballymadun was also granted to Gracedieu by Archbishop Henry of London (1213–28). At the Dissolution, the properties of Gracedieu included over 800 acres as well as a watermill, a horse mill and a dovecot.[197] The remains of a medieval mill were excavated by archaeologists at the site in 1999 (see below, p. 421).[198] The church at Odder, near Tara, Co. Meath, was dedicated to St Brigit, which suggests an early origin.[199] It became Arrouaisian, however, possibly in the 1140s. In the early 1380s, it replaced Clonard as the main Augustinian convent in Ireland. The priory of Holy Trinity at Lismullin, Co. Meath, was founded *c*.1240 by Avicia de la Corner, who was also its first prioress.[200] Just 2km to the south-east of Lismullin, St Mary's Church at Skreen was confirmed to the Arrouaisian nuns of Clonard in 1195, but it had probably gone out of existence before the foundation of Lismullin.[201] The name Calliaghstown (from the Irish *caille*, 'veil'; *cailleach*, 'nun'), is often associated with nunneries. The church of Calliaghstown, near Duleek, Co. Meath, was confirmed to the nuns of Clonard in 1195, but it appears to have been shared between canons and canonesses from the 1140s.[202] It was probably abandoned before 1500.

Knights Hospitallers and Knights Templars

The Knights Hospitallers, who were both knights and monks, cared for pilgrims to Jerusalem, and increasingly for the sick.[203] Their preceptories were more akin to fortified manor houses or castles than to conventional monasteries. Each group of preceptories was governed by a priory. The Hospitallers in Ireland were richly endowed with lands by Anglo-Norman lords. Some Irish names appear in the order by the early fourteenth century. The priory of Kilmainham was founded by Strongbow *c*.1174 on the site of St Maignenn's

Medieval Dublin IX (2009), pp 166–82. **191** *EIMP*, pp 55–68. **192** *MRHI*, p. 306. **193** *MRHI*, p. 306. **194** Margaret MacCurtain, 'Late medieval nunneries of the Irish Pale' in Clarke, Prunty and Hennessy (eds), *Surveying Ireland's past* (2004), pp 129–43. **195** *MRHI*, pp 150, 316–17; Clarke, 'Conversion, church and cathedral', p. 49. **196** *MRHI*, pp 317, 322–3. **197** *EIMP*, p. 73; see also *Civil Survey*, 7, p. 56. **198** Malachy Conway, 'Gracedieu' in *Excavations 1999*, pp 83–4; Malachy Conway, 'Gracedieu', DEHLG file 99E0217. **199** *MRHI*, p. 323. **200** *MRHI*, p. 322; J.P. Kelly, 'Lismullin priory, 1240–1539', *RnM*, 2:3 (1961), 53–6. **201** *MRHI*, p. 324. **202** *MRHI*, p. 314. **203** C.H. Lawrence, *Medieval monasticism: forms of religious life in Western Europe in the Middle Ages* (London and New

Church.[204] It was also an almshouse and a hospital for the sick, as well as being the headquarters of an agricultural estate. The roof of the great barn was burnt by Thomas FitzGerald *c*.1535 and all of the grain was destroyed.[205] When it was dissolved, the buildings were considered to be among the best in the kingdom. The site was surrounded by stone walls with four towers and a fortified gatehouse and other buildings. The priory held over 10,000 acres of land across the country, as well as a variety of manors, castles, cottages and mills.

The preceptory of Killybegs was confirmed to the Knights Hospitallers in 1212.[206] In 1540, Killybegs was found to own 180 acres of arable and 100 acres of commonage. A stipendary priest served the church there. Maurice FitzGerald, second baron of Offaly, founded a preceptory of the Knights Hospitallers at Kilteel, Co. Kildare, in *c*.1250.[207] It was dedicated to St John the Baptist. The preceptory may have been founded on the site of a pre-Anglo-Norman church.

The Knights Templars arrived in Ireland before 1180.[208] The vill of Clontarf was granted to them by Henry II, and this became their chief house.[209] They had a castle and various other properties at Ballyman, Co. Dublin.[210] The Templars were suppressed in 1312, and all of their possessions were allocated to the Hospitallers (although the transfer of property was complicated and prolonged). The house at Clontarf was allocated in 1333 to the prior of Kilmainham, Roger Outlaw, whenever his term of office should end.[211]

Monastic granges

Several large farms or granges in the Dublin region were administered by monastic owners. Some may have had features that underlined their ecclesiastical associations, such as chapels and dormitory accommodation, but it is likely that the requirements of agriculture played the major part in their planning and organisation.[212] In addition to the granges, the monasteries and abbeys themselves frequently had complexes of farm buildings in their outer courts. Many of the religious houses situated in suburban areas of Dublin displayed characteristics of manorial centres (Figure 7.51). St Mary's Abbey, which occupied a large precinct on the eastern side of Oxmantown, had, in addition to the usual conventual buildings, mills, stables, a haggard, a barn, a granary, a tan house and a brew house.[213]

The preceptory of the Knights Hospitallers at Kilmainham comprised an inner and an outer enclosure. The inner enclosure was surrounded by a strong wall with corner towers and was described as a 'castle'.[214] The chapel, dormitories, residence of the prior and guests, great hall and prison were all located in this inner enclosure. The outer enclosure, which surrounded the 'castle' on all sides, formed what was known as the 'manor close'. It too was surrounded by a strong wall, on the eastern side of which was located the great entrance gate of the hospital. This survived into the seventeenth century and was shown on William Petty's map of the district. In 1540, the jurors reported that there were two stables, a granary roofed with tiles, a malt-house and a barn with stone walls within this enclosure.[215] The

York, 1989), pp 206–15; *MRHI*, pp 332–3; H.J.A. Sire, *The Knights of Malta* (New Haven, 1994), pp 180–2. **204** *Reg. Kilmainham*; *MRHI*, pp 334–5; C.L. Falkiner, 'The hospital of St John of Jerusalem in Ireland', *PRIA*, 26C (1906–7), 275–317; Linzi Simpson, 'Dublin's famous "Bully's Acre": the site of the monastery of Kilmainham?' in Duffy (ed.), *Medieval Dublin IX* (2009), pp 38–83; Laurence O'Dea, 'The hospitals of Kilmainham', *DHR*, 20:3/4 (1965), 82–99. **205** *EIMP*, p. 81. **206** *MRHI*, p. 337. **207** *MRHI*, p. 338; Earl of Mayo, 'Kilteel Castle', *JCKAHS*, 1:1 (1891), 34–7; Walter Fitzgerald, 'The preceptory, or commandery, of Kilteel, County Kildare', *JCKAHS*, 8:4 (July 1916), 267–75; Conleth Manning, 'Excavations at Kilteel Church, Co. Kildare', *JCKAHS*, 16:3 (1981–2), 173–229; H.G. Leask, 'Carved stones discovered at Kilteel, Co. Kildare', *JRSAI*, 65:1 (1935), 1–8; Leask, *Irish churches and monastic buildings, 1*, p. 165. **208** Herbert Wood, 'The Templars in Ireland', *PRIA*, 26 (1906–7), 327–77; M.J. Carroll, *The Knights Templar and Ireland* (Bantry, Co. Cork, 2006). **209** *MRHI*, p. 329. **210** *MRHI*, p. 329. **211** *MRHI*, p. 335. **212** As shown in Britain by Platt, *The monastic grange*, and Bond, *Monastic landscapes*, pp 124–70. **213** *EIMP*, pp 1–2; *CSMA*, 2, pp xli–xliii; Purcell, 'Land-use in medieval Oxmantown', pp 203–4. **214** *Reg. Kilmainham*, pp 24–7, 141. **215** *EIMP*, p. 81.

Figure **7.60** Extract
from the Down Survey
map for the parish of
Kilmainham, Co. Dublin
(1654–6). Watermills
are depicted on both
the River Camac and
the River Liffey, and
several bridges are
shown.

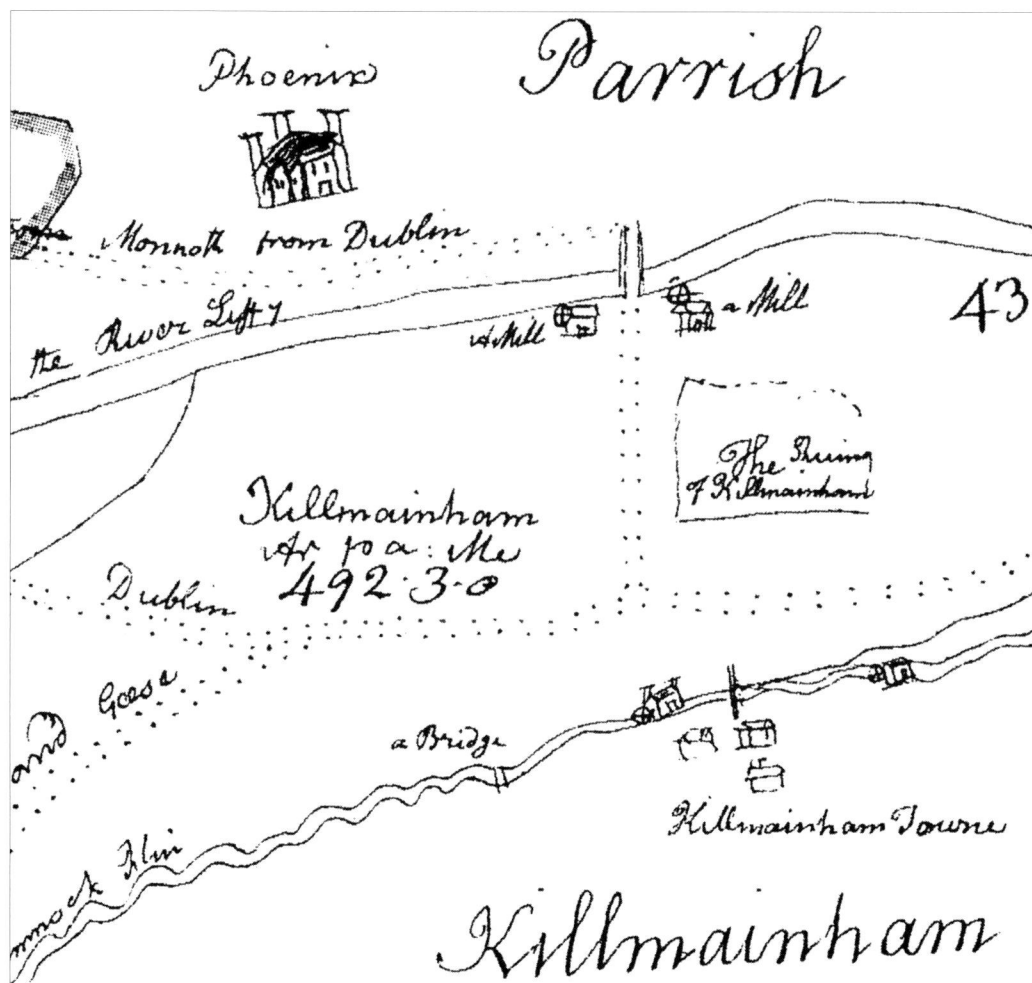

Figure **7.60** Extract from the Down Survey map for the parish of Kilmainham, Co. Dublin (1654–6). Watermills are depicted on both the River Camac and the River Liffey, and several bridges are shown.

register of Kilmainham, which was compiled in the early fourteenth century, contains references to a dairy, a brew-house, a carpenter's shop, stables, a forge and a livestock-house.[216]

Less is known about the religious houses in the countryside of the Dublin region. The Augustinian priory of Holmpatrick near Skerries, Co. Dublin, was described at its Dissolution in 1540 as comprising a precinct of three acres, which, in addition to the church, gardens and orchards, contained 'certain buildings necessary for the farmer'.[217] The nuns of Gracedieu convent, near Lusk, inhabited a precinct in excess of three acres, which contained several buildings, a watermill, a horse mill and a dovecot.[218] In the nineteenth century, an ornamental moat that surrounded the nunnery garden was still visible, along with a paved path-way leading to Swords.[219] In 1988, excavations were carried out in the vicinity of the standing remains of the thirteenth-century nunnery site.[220] No ecclesiastical structures of medieval date were revealed, but several cobbled surfaces were uncovered, along with substantial sections of walls. Medieval pottery and ridge-tiles were found in this area. A 6m-wide lane was also revealed running north-south through the western limit of the excavated area.

The most comprehensive descriptions to have survived of ecclesiastical granges in the region are for the three home farms or granges of Holy Trinity (Christ Church). These were located at Grangegorman, Glasnevin and Clonkeen (Deansgrange), and their buildings are mentioned in the priory account rolls, which have survived for 1337–46.[221] The buildings that comprised the Augustinian grange at Grangegorman lay inside an enclosure that was

216 *Reg. Kilmainham*, pp 8, 12, 17, 23–5.   **217** *EIMP*, p. 49.   **218** *EIMP*, p. 73.   **219** Dianne Hall, *Women and the church in medieval Ireland, c.1140–1540* (Dublin, 2003), p. 121.   **220** Margaret Gowen, 'Gracedieu' in *Excavations 1988*, pp 16–17.   **221** Mills (ed.), *Account roll*, passim.

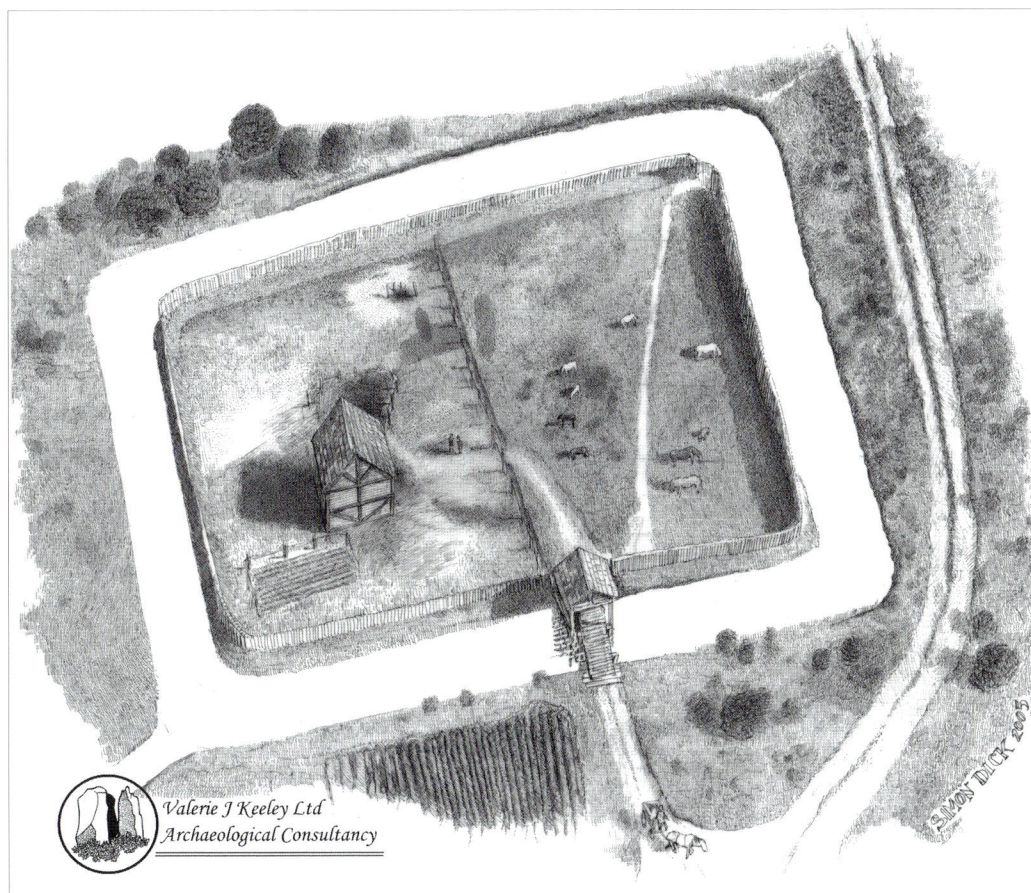

Figure 7.61
Reconstruction drawing, by Simon Dick, of the moated site at Coolamurry, Co. Wexford, based on excavated evidence. The monastic grange buildings at Grangegorman, Co. Dublin, may have been enclosed by a similar moat with wooden gateway (image courtesy of Grace Fegan, Valerie J. Keeley Ltd and the National Roads Authority).

probably constructed of earth and wood. A sixteenth-century lease mentioned the ditch and fortification of Grangegorman.[222] Entrance was via the 'great gate' and there was at least one other gate, perhaps a small pedestrian entrance.[223] A gatekeeper was mentioned, and the presence of a gatehouse can be interpolated from the entry recording the purchase of a key for the gatekeeper's door.[224] The description sounds like one of a moated site, and the reference to a gated entrance recalls the features excavated by Grace Fegan and her team at Coolamurry, Co. Wexford (Figure 7.61).[225]

The farm buildings at Grangegorman appear to have been constructed of a mixture of wattle-and-daub and wooden planks with straw thatched roofs. At least ten different buildings are mentioned in the accounts and it is possible to partially reconstruct the layout of the grange from the various references.[226] The *granarius* – granary or, in this context, a barn – was a large building with a roof supported by nine couples of oak wood. This matches the description of a cruck-roofed structure, and if the complex of buildings were situated, as seems likely, within a moated site, then the overall picture is reminiscent of Cloonfree, Co. Roscommon.[227] The barn at Grangegorman was probably the largest agricultural building in the complex, large enough to store the manorial grain and the tithe grain received by the priory from its rectories north of the Liffey. It had an earthen floor and a thatched roof. Next to it was a house and next to that was the hall with a further chamber beside it. It is clear that the ox-house and grange (*grangia*) were situated side-by-side, because a wall between them was mentioned. There was a stable fitted with mangers and stalls, a workshop, a kiln-house and another private chamber. The entry recording the cost of

222 *CCCD*, nos. 1268–9. **223** Mills (ed.), *Account roll*, pp 23, 37. **224** Ibid., p. 40. **225** Grace Fegan, 'Discovery and excavation of a medieval moated site at Coolamurry, Co. Wexford' in Corlett and Potterton (eds), *Rural settlement in medieval Ireland* (2009), pp 91–108. **226** Mills (ed.), *Account roll*, pp 28, 36–40. **227** Finan and O'Conor, 'The moated site at Cloonfree'; O'Conor, 'Housing in later medieval Gaelic Ireland'.

Figure 7.62 Beranger's painting of 'Monckstown Abby' – formerly the Carrickbrennan grange of St Mary's Abbey. The courtyard arrangement of farm buildings that was typical of lay and ecclesiastical manor centres can clearly be seen (image reproduced courtesy of the National Library of Ireland).

making windows and doors for two inner chambers beside the hall may indicate the presence of a further building or alternatively that the hall formed part of a larger structure. There was a well beside the kiln-house and also a cistern, which may have been used for storing water. The internal space was occupied by a cattle yard and a haggard. When the manor of Grangegorman was leased in 1560, the buildings included a barn, a kiln, a sheepfold and a cow-house.[228]

The priory's principal grange in south Co. Dublin was situated at Clonkeen (Deansgrange).[229] It appears to have been organised in much the same way as Grangegorman, with a series of wooden buildings inside an enclosure with a large entrance gate. The accounts mention the kiln-house, grange, cow-house and ox-house.[230] The kiln-house, which was built in 1344–5, was four perches in length and had a roof supported by two couples or tie-beams. It took the thatcher, assisted by two men, ten days to thatch the kiln-house. The cow-house was rebuilt in the same year, with timber purchased partly in Glencree, Co. Wicklow. The carpenter spent eight days working on the walls, which were also four perches in length. There is no mention of a barn, but sheaves of corn were brought into the haggard, where they were bound and heaped into stacks that were then thatched for protection from the elements.[231] It is clear from the accounts that domestic buildings such as a kitchen and hall were present, although not specifically mentioned. On one occasion, bread was baked for sixty-four people who were working in the fields.[232] The prior and seneschal of Holy Trinity were entertained along with their retinues when they visited Clonkeen, and the archbishop of Dublin also dined at the manor.

There are no references to the agricultural buildings at Glasnevin, but the accounts refer to the hall, the prior's chamber and the church, the chancel of which was furnished with

228 *CCCD*, nos. 1268–9; Katharine Simms, 'Native sources for Gaelic settlement: the house poems' in Duffy, Edwards and FitzPatrick (eds), *Gaelic Ireland* (2001), pp 246–67.   **229** For a discussion of the location of the grange, see Liam Clare, 'The kill and the grange of medieval Clonkeen' in Karina Holton, Liam Clare and Brian Ó Dálaigh (eds), *Irish villages: studies in local history* (Dublin, 2004), pp 17–45 at p. 20.   **230** Mills (ed.), *Account roll*, pp 60–1.   **231** Ibid., pp 67–8.   **232** Ibid., p. 77.

two new windows in 1345.[233] The abbey of St Thomas, Dublin, did not have any monastic farms in Co. Dublin outside the extensive holdings surrounding the abbey precincts (see above, p. 252). They did, however, have granges in Meath and Kildare. In 1540, the grange of Donaghmore, near Greenoge in Co. Meath, was described as consisting of 'a hall and certain rooms with a garden and a parcel of ground called a haggard'.[234] The monastic extents also contain an interesting description of the grange held by the abbey in Kill, Co. Kildare. They note that 'there is a small mountain surrounded by a dry ditch on which the capital messuage of the manor was situated and where the Court Baron is still held' (Figure 5.13).[235] A grant of c.1206–23 mentions the grange of the canons at Kill, which at that time included a garden and haggard, and appears to have been demarcated by a fosse.[236] This may be a reference to the motte and bailey, but there is no way to be sure.

The Cistercian abbey of St Mary's had at least six granges in Co. Dublin. These were Clonliffe, Portmarnock and Ballyboghill in north Co. Dublin, and Ballichelmer (barony of Newcastle), Balgeeth or the Grange in the Marsh (south of Rathfarnham) and Carrickbrennan (Monkstown/Bullock) to the south. Its holdings in Meath at Monktown and Brownstown in the barony of Skreen, and Bracetown in the barony of Dunboyne were probably also farmed from granges. There is little information on the layout of these granges before the sixteenth-century extents. A document of 1318 mentions the haggard of St Mary's grange of Clonliffe and the grange of Portmarnock, both of which contained large quantities of grain and livestock.[237] In 1312, the grange of Carrickbrennan was attacked by the Irish and livestock and other valuables were stolen.[238]

The authors of the Dissolution extents were most interested in recording the presence of large stone buildings with defensive features, which could be profitably leased out, and consequently they rarely enumerated farm buildings. Furthermore, by the sixteenth century, much monastic land had been leased out to farmers, and the agricultural buildings of the granges had become redundant. The only building mentioned at Clonliffe was a residence of the abbot, but at Dubber, in the parish of Santry, a messuage with a fortalice, dovecot, garden and 'haygarde' (haggard) were recorded in 1540.[239] At Carrickbrennan, there was a 'capital messuage with three towers surrounded by stone walls' occupied by the bailiff.[240]

Some information on the layout of Cistercian granges can be gleaned from the instructions sent by Stephen of Lexington following his visitation of the Cistercian monasteries of Jerpoint and Graiguenamanagh in Co. Kilkenny in 1228.[241] It is clear that, following Cistercian practice, the granges were run by lay brothers of the order who were accommodated in dormitory-type buildings and operated under the supervision of a 'master of the lay brothers'. The instructions mentioned barns and livestock sheds that were to be arranged around the sides of the grange's boundary. Some buildings dedicated to craft workers also appear to have been present, as there is a reference to a 'cobbler's stall'.

There have been no excavations of granges within the Dublin region, but at Knowth in Co. Meath, excavations on the top of the main passage tomb mound have exposed the remains of farm buildings of the Cistercian grange (Figure 7.63).[242] They formed a rectangular courtyard (36m long and 25m wide) enclosed by a masonry wall with lean-to buildings and an entrance in the south-east. One of the buildings had plastered walls, well-finished with shaped sandstone blocks. A number of the structural stones in this building

233 Ibid., pp 97–8.   234 *EIMP*, pp 32–3.   235 *EIMP*, p. 39.   236 *RAST*, pp 298–9.   237 *CSMA*, I, p. 263. According to Ó Conbhuí, the agricultural buildings of Clonliffe grange were probably located close to the Tolka, to the east of what is now Clonliffe College: Ó Conbhuí, 'The lands of St Mary's Abbey', 30.   238 *CSMA*, I, p. 275. 239 *EIMP*, pp 2, 8.   240 *EIMP*, p. 10.   241 B.W. O'Dwyer (trans.), *Stephen of Lexington: letters from Ireland, 1228–1229* (Kalamazoo, MI, 1982), pp 157–71.   242 F.J. Byrne, William Jenkins, Gillian Kenny and Catherine Swift, with George Eogan, *Historical Knowth and its hinterland* (Dublin, 2008), pp 136–40; Geraldine Stout, *Newgrange and the*

Figure 7.63 Aerial view of Knowth, Co. Meath, showing outline of buildings of the Cistercian grange as reconstructed by the Office of Public Works (© Department of the Environment, Heritage and Local Government).

were dressed and its windows were glazed. The recovery of a font provided conclusive proof of this building's religious function, and the excavator proposed that it was an oratory, serving the lay brothers in the grange. A series of low-lying enclosures north of the passage tomb cemetery at Knowth may be additional remnants of this medieval farm and fields. Overall, the evidence suggests that the grange dates to the late twelfth century and continued in use until the late thirteenth or early fourteenth century. Four kilometres to the west of Knowth, at Stalleen, Co. Meath, recent archaeological excavations have revealed the remains of a fourteenth-century stone gateway that seems to have been part of another monastic grange belonging to Mellifont.[243]

There has also been research on two granges that formed part of the Llanthony estates in Ireland. The cells of Duleek and Colp, both situated in the barony of Lower Duleek, just outside the study area, were described in extents dated to 1381 and 1408 respectively.[244] The description of the buildings at Duleek is probably the best surviving depiction of a monastic grange in Ireland. The buildings were organised around a rectangular courtyard. On the east side were the church, a hall, two further rooms, a small stable, a kitchen and a dairy; on the south were a bakery, a brew-house and a small granary; on the north was a sheep-pen and a

Bend of the Boyne (Cork, 2002), pp 87–8; George Eogan, *Excavations at Knowth, 1* (Dublin, 1984), p. 7. **243** Jessica Smyth (comp. and ed.) et al., *Brú na Bóinne World Heritage Site: research framework* (Kilkenny, 2009), pp 49, 50. **244** Brooks (ed.), *The Irish cartularies*, pp 178–82, 289–95.

long stable. There was a stone gate called the high gate on the north and to the west there was another gate leading into the haggard. Beside the west gate there was another small granary under which was a pig-sty. There was no building to store unthreshed grain, and corn and hay were stacked in the haggard, as they were at Clonkeen. The surviving remains at Duleek were surveyed and described by Bradley, but regrettably they do not reflect the arrangement of buildings as laid out in 1381.[245] The conclusion was that the grange was re-built in the fifteenth century or later and that the fourteenth-century buildings will only be revealed by archaeological excavation.

Chapter summary

The parish church was the focus of pastoral care for the majority of the people who lived in the Dublin hinterland and this study has identified almost 300 medieval churches and chapels across the region. The evolution of the parish church as the centre of a tithe-rendering community was closely linked with the formation of Anglo-Norman manors. It would appear, however, that existing church sites and buildings were frequently re-used, albeit with substantial rebuilding and renovation. There was an increase in church construction in the second half of the thirteenth century, and the fourteenth and fifteenth centuries witnessed significant church expansion across the Dublin region. Meath in particular has many fine examples of church buildings of this period. Later structural developments at church-sites saw the building of defensive residential towers and the insertion of bell-cotes. Dublin's influence on its hinterland is evident in several aspects of church architecture; for example, St Patrick's Cathedral influenced the building styles of its prebendal churches. In the fifteenth and sixteenth centuries, hinterland families, many of them with strong links to the capital, were responsible for the erection of distinctive effigial sculptures and the provision of rich furnishings in the parish churches of the region.

In contrast to the ubiquitous parish churches, there was a scarcity of religious houses and hospitals in a rural region that in earlier times had been home to several large monastic establishments. In the later medieval period, most religious houses were situated in and around Dublin and to a lesser extent in Naas, probably the only other true town in the region. There were a few exceptions to this, including nunneries patronised by the lesser gentry families as convenient outlets for unmarried daughters, and collegiate establishments associated with some of the larger parish churches. There were also some small houses or cells attached to or taken over by the Dublin houses.

The Dublin religious houses were, of course, closely linked to the rural hinterland by virtue of their ownership of large estates and also their position as rectors of many of the parish churches. The tithes paid by rural parishioners were more than likely destined to increase the food stocks of the religious houses of Dublin, with surpluses sold by monastic agents. The monastic granges which were scattered around the countryside acted as convenient collection points for these tithes, as well as functioning as centres of agrarian exploitation in their own right. In the early fourteenth-century assessment for ecclesiastical taxation, Dublin was revealed as by far the most valuable Irish diocese, while the Dublin religious houses also emerged as the richest in the country. This ecclesiastical wealth was derived, in great part, from the agrarian and natural resources of the region, which ensured substantial congregations for the parish churches and considerable tithes for their rectors.

245 Simms and Bradley, 'The geography of Irish manors'.

CHAPTER 8

The English Pale

Background

While the English Pale in Ireland emerged from the political circumstances of the fifteenth century, its origins can be traced at least three hundred years before that. Even though the Anglo-Normans ultimately established counties and liberties all across the island, the most intensively settled part was to remain the region around Dublin. As seen above (pp 111–22), Anglo-Norman territories were secured with a network of fortifications and, by the beginning of the thirteenth century, the borderlands of north Meath and Louth were among the most encastellated parts of Europe. As the manorial agricultural economy thrived and expanded through the thirteenth century, grain- and wool-surpluses were shipped overseas through the growing port-towns of Dublin and Drogheda. Dublin was the capital and the seat of royal administration in Ireland, while inland market towns flourished at Ardee, Athboy, Kells, Trim and Naas. These centres of trade were sufficiently far from Dublin to have their own commercial viability and their own hinterland, and not too close either to Dublin or to each other to be redundant. Indeed, already in the thirteenth century, it could be argued that these towns and their fortifications were the genesis of a line inside which Anglo-Norman manorial and commercial organisation thrived, and beyond which, Dublin's authority was, at best, diluted.

If the thirteenth century was a boom-time for the colony, then the fourteenth century was generally a period of decline. Bad weather, poor harvests, plagues, famine and war had already taken their toll before the Black Death arrived in the late 1340s. The towns – such as those mentioned – that had been at the core of the Anglo-Norman success in Ireland were hit hardest.

Following the pattern of most colonies, there had been increasing contact between the colonisers and the colonised. Indeed, statutes were considered necessary to forbid members of the colony from dressing in the Irish style, speaking the Irish language, taking Irish names, using Irish law or – worse still – marrying into Irish families.[1] Despite, or perhaps more accurately *because of*, laws like these, the English colony came under ever-increasing pressure from the resurgent Gaelic Irish. By the end of the fourteenth century, it was necessary for King Richard II to make two visits to Ireland to try and stop the rot.[2] Royal intervention was ultimately unsuccessful, however, and the English continued to suffer military defeats, encroachments and losses of territory – especially to the O'Neills, O'Briens, Mac Murchadas

---

[1] James Hardiman (ed.), 'The statute of Kilkenny, which was enacted there in the time of Lionel Duke of Clarence, in the xlth year of the reign of Edward III', *Tracts relating to Ireland* (Dublin, 1843), vol. 2; *Stat. Ire., John-Hen. V*, pp 430–69; G.J. Hand, 'The forgotten statutes of Kilkenny: a brief survey', *IJ*, 1:2 (winter 1966), 299–312; Watt, 'The Anglo-Irish colony under strain', esp. pp 386–90. [2] Edmund Curtis, *Richard II in Ireland, 1394–5, and submissions of the Irish chiefs* (Oxford, 1927); Otway-Ruthven, *A history of medieval Ireland*, pp 309–38; Watt, 'The Anglo-Irish colony under

and O'Byrnes. A particular flashpoint continued to be the Dublin-Wicklow Mountains. Even when the Anglo-Norman colony was at its strongest, this area had remained a Gaelic-Irish stronghold, with the O'Byrnes and the O'Tooles making regular raids and sorties into Anglo-Norman settlements – such as Saggart, Tallaght and Rathcoole – in the foothills of the Mountains and closer to Dublin.[3]

Gaelic resurgence was a catalyst to colonial retreat, and by 1400 the colony was greatly weakened and depleted. The crown committed only limited resources to Ireland in the early fifteenth century, and by 1428 Archbishop Swayne of Armagh claimed that the territory under the effective control of the Dublin administration amounted to little more than one English shire.[4] In 1435, the king was informed that his writ was confined to an area thirty miles long by twenty miles wide, in Cos. Dublin, Meath, Louth and Kildare.[5] The colony had fragmented and its core had contracted back to the area around Dublin – the area subsequently known as the 'English Pale'.

The physical expression of the Pale

The line of the Pale

The 'English Pale' was a contemporary term applied to the region around Dublin in which language, law, culture and government remained closely aligned with England in the fifteenth and sixteenth centuries. On the ground, the area witnessed the construction of many strategic fortifications and, towards the end of the fifteenth century, it was considered necessary to enclose the Pale with a palisaded earthen rampart and ditches. Indeed the very word 'Pale', like palisade, comes from the Latin *palus*, meaning a 'stake'.[6] The use of the term is both illustrative of the defensive mindset of the retreating colony and indicative of the nature of the physical defences that were envisaged.

The term itself was probably inspired by the 'Pale of Calais' – the territory around that city (and the last part of France) that was retained by the English in the fifteenth century.[7] According to David Grummitt, the term 'Pale of Calais' was first coined in 1436, but it was not until about 1494 that more definite references occur.[8] At this time, the deputy lieutenant at Calais was Sir Edward Poynings. Poynings left Calais later that year when he was appointed as governor of Ireland, and there can be no coincidence that the first use of the term 'Pale' in an Irish context dates to Poynings' Drogheda parliament of 1494–5.[9] The thirty-fourth act of that parliament stated that

> as the marches of four shires lie open and not fensible in fastness of ditches and castles, by which Irishmen do great hurt in preying the same: it is enacted that every inhabitant, earth-tiller, and occupier in said marches, i.e. in the county of Dublin, from the water of Anliffy to the mountains of Kildare, from the water of Anliffy to Trim, and so forth to Meath and Uriel … do build and make a double ditch of six feet high above ground, at one side, or part which mireth next unto Irishmen, betwixt this and next Lammas [1 August], the said ditches to be kept up and repaired as long as they shall occupy said land, under pain of forty shillings.

strain', pp 391–3.   **3** O'Byrne, *War, politics and the Irish of Leinster*, passim; S.G. Ellis, *Ireland in the age of the Tudors, 1447–1603: English expansion and the end of Gaelic rule* (New York, 1998), pp 70–1.   **4** D.A. Chart (ed.), *The register of John Swayne, archbishop of Armagh and primate of Ireland, 1418–1439* (Belfast, 1935), p. 108; Art Cosgrove, 'The emergence of the Pale, 1399–1447' in Cosgrove (ed.), *A new history of Ireland: II* (1993), pp 533–56, esp. pp 533, 541, 546. **5** Cosgrove, *Late medieval Ireland, 1370–1541*, pp 44–5, referring to Betham, *Dignities*, p. 361.   **6** *OED*.   **7** S.G. Ellis, 'Pale' in Connolly (ed.), *The Oxford companion to Irish history* (1998), pp 424–5, referring to S.G. Ellis, 'The emergence of the English Pale in Ireland', *IHS* (forthcoming); Mary Ann Lyons, 'Pale, or English Pale' in Duffy (ed.), *Medieval Ireland: an encyclopedia* (2005), pp 852–3.   **8** David Grummitt, *The Calais garrison: war and military service in England, 1436–1558* (Woodbridge, Suffolk, 2008).   **9** Hardiman (ed.), 'The statute of Kilkenny', ii, p. 4, fn. The purported

Figure 8.1 The Pale in the later fifteenth century, based primarily on the places mentioned in the acts of 1488 and 1495.

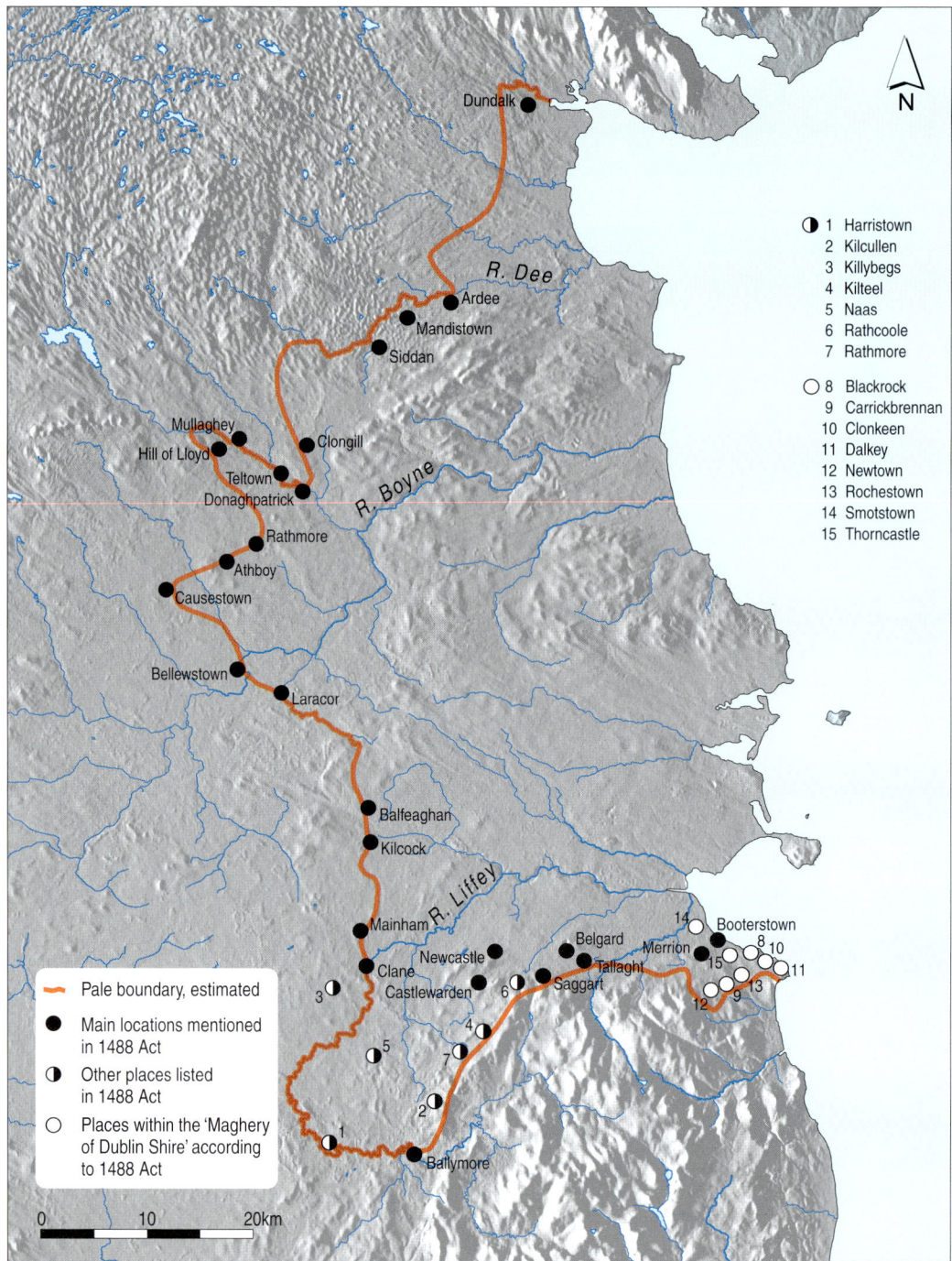

While this may have been the first explicit reference to the construction of a physical cordon around the Dublin region, an act of parliament of 1488 had given clearer definition to the boundary of the Pale – on paper at least (Figure 8.1):[10]

> Booterstown, Merrion, Tallaght, Belgard, Saggart and the lordship of Newcastle, and so to Castlewarden, and so by the mountain to Ballymore, and there joins the Liffey, and so as the Liffey runs to Clane in the maghery,[11] and also Mainham, and so to the

reference to the English Pale in 1446–7 has been shown to be a subsequent Tudor interpolation [Aodh Ruadh Mac Mathghamhna promised to 'carrie nothing owte of the inglshe pale contrarie to the statutes' (*Cal. Carew MSS*, 1, p. 290; E.P. Shirley, *Some account of the territory or dominion of Farney* (London, 1845), p. 24)]. **10** McNeill (ed.), *Alen's register*, pp 250–1 (place-names, where identifiable, have been modernised here). **11** Moody, Martin and Byrne (eds), *A new history of Ireland: IX*, pp 44 (map 46), 109.

waters of Rye by Kilcock, also Balfeaghan, and so to the parish of Laracor, and so to Bellewstown by the Boyne, and so as the Blackwater runs from Athboy, and so to *Blakcavsey* [Causestown?] by Rathmore to the Hill of Lloyd, and then to Mullaghey and the parish of Teltown and Donaghpatrick, Clongill and so to Siddan, and so down to Mandistown? by the west of Ardee, and so to the water of Dundalk, and so as that water goes to the sea.

A second paragraph in the 1488 act included seven more locations in the bend of the Liffey: Rathcoole, Kilteel, Rathmore [Kildare], Kilcullen, Harristown, Naas and Killybegs, and specified that to the south of Dublin city, Dalkey, Carrickbrennan, Newtown, Rochestown, Clonkeen, Smotstown, Booterstown, Thorncastle and Blackrock were within the maghery of 'Dublin Shire'. Dalkey had become one of the most important ports on the eastern seaboard in the fifteenth century and it was imperative to keep it on the 'right' side of the line. Smotstown, or Simmonscourt, was on the supply route from Dalkey to Dublin, and a castle was built there to guard the important crossing over the River Dodder (Figure 5.52). Similarly, in the 1460s, Stephen FitzWilliam built houses, a castle and other necessary defences at Thorncastle, 'near the highway between the ports of Dublin and Dalkey'.[12]

The Act of 1488 was entitled the 'Act of Marches and Maghery'. The term 'maghery' had been mentioned as early as 1428 and referred to the inner 'land of peace', as opposed to the marchlands surrounding it. The word 'maghery' is a transliteration of the Irish word *machaire*, meaning 'a plain', and there is a certain irony in the adoption of this term into English, given the promulgation of various statutes forbidding the use of the Irish language in the previous decades. In recent times, the term 'maghery' has been used by Kenneth Nicholls to define a larger area beyond the Pale in which common law and the authority of the Dublin government functioned.[13]

Tower houses and the Pale boundary

The proposed construction of an enclosing defensive earthen ditch around the Pale was neither the first nor the only strategy by which the government sought to physically defend the 'English Pale'. Successive parliaments had offered subsidies to those who would build castles at strategic locations within the region. A statute of 1429, for instance, offered a government subsidy of £10 to any liegeman dwelling in Co. Louth who constructed a stone castle of certain specifications.[14] The following year, the offer was extended to Cos. Meath, Kildare and Wicklow.[15] These tower houses have been compared to the 'peel towers' (or 'peles') along the Anglo-Scottish border.[16] Indeed, it is interesting to note that, like pale and palisade, the term 'pele' itself also derives from the Latin *palus*.[17] One of the advantages of these tall single towers was that they had commanding views of the surrounding countryside and could provide warning of approaching enemies. In 1454, parliament promoted further statutes to erect fortresses in the marches of the 'four obedient shires' and to repair the key border castles at Ballymore and Tallaght.[18] The fact that nothing survives now of Ballymore Castle is perhaps an indication of just how besieged the southern reaches of the Pale were. Some recent commentators have tended to downplay the role of the ten-pound grant in the story of castle-building in fifteenth-century Ireland, but there are many examples of the grant in action – ten-pound subsidies aided the construction or reconstruction of castles

12 *Stat. Ire., 1–12 Edw. IV*, pp 225, 565.   13 Moody, Martin and Byrne (eds), *A new history of Ireland: IX*, pp 44 (map 46), 109.   14 *Stat. Ire., Hen. VI*, p. 17.   15 *Stat. Ire., Hen. VI*, 33–5: 1429/30; Bradley and Murtagh, 'Brady's Castle', p. 212.   16 See, for example, Sweetman, *The origin and development of the tower house*; McNeill, *Castles in Ireland*, pp 201–23; Sweetman, *Medieval castles of Ireland*, pp 137–74.   17 *OED*.   18 *Stat. Ire., Hen. VI*, p. 299.

Figure 8.2 Distribution
of castles on the
borders of the Pale in
the sixteenth century.
Most of these were
tower houses.

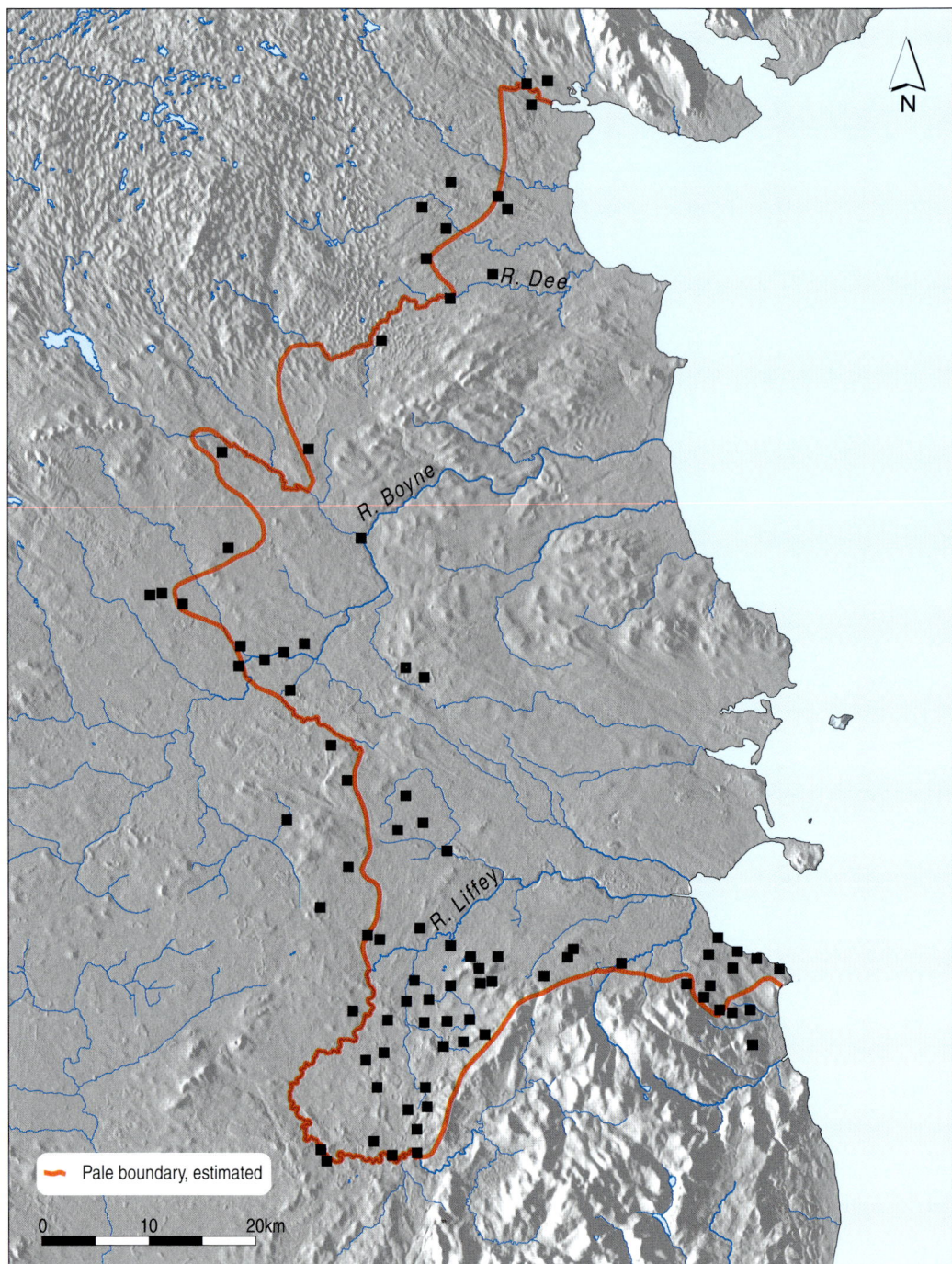

along the Pale boundary at sites including Boleybeg near Ballymore (1472), Kilcullen (1457), Kilcullenbridge (1467), Windgates (1474), Clondalkin (1477), and Jamestown (1478).[19] In 1474, a grant was given to Edward Wellesley to build a castle at Laracor, which was 'on the frontier of the march of the county of Meath'.[20] The castle would be 'a great succour and relief to all Meath'. Similarly, in 1480 Richard Bellew built a tower 'on the frontier of the march of the county of Louth', at Castletown Dundalk, and proposed to erect another as 'a signal refuge for the inhabitants of the said county'.[21] In 1473, Robert Missete complained that his lands at Bellewstown, where he had recently built a castle and other fortresses, were 'day by day assaulted by the O'Connors and the Berminghams'. His fortifications were

19 Balablaght: Annaba Kilfeather, pers. comm; Kilcullen: *Stat. Ire., Hen. VI*, p. 457; Kilcullenbridge: *Stat. Ire., 1–12 Edw. IV*, pp 609–11; Windgates: *Stat. Ire., 12–22 Edw. IV*, p. 49; Jamestown: *Stat. Ire., 12–22 Edw. IV*, pp 517–19. **20** *Stat. Ire., 12–22 Edw. IV*, p. 123.   **21** *Stat. Ire., 12–22 Edw. IV*, p. 715.

regarded as the 'key and safeguard of all this part', and he was granted a tax exemption in recognition of this.[22] Several of these locations are later specifically mentioned as being on the line of the Pale boundary.

By the end of the fifteenth century, the Pale boundary was already dotted with castles, and more were to appear in the following decades. Over 300 were built within the Pale, with a particular density along the boundary, especially at the southern extremity of the region, around the bend in the Liffey.[23] The southern reaches of the Pale had now overtaken the northern boundaries as the most densely castled part of Europe. Although there is considerable variation in plan and size, most of the surviving tower houses within the Pale are quite simple. There is an architectural uniformity to Pale tower houses: many have evidence for a vaulted ceiling to the ground floor and over three-quarters of them have one or more projecting angle towers.[24]

In addition to tower houses, other forms of fortifications and defended homesteads may have been built along the line of the Pale. At Pitchfordstown, for example, less than 1km to the south-west of Kilcock, Co. Kildare, there is a large rectangular turreted enclosure that appears to be of late medieval date.[25] The enclosure is surrounded by a bank and ditch, which is fed with water by a natural spring. A range of faint earthworks on the interior of the enclosure indicate the former presence of structures or buildings, but their function and make-up remain unclear.

Towns and the Pale boundary

The Pale boundary was also dotted with market towns, many of which had multiple urban tower houses – Naas had at least eight, Dalkey and Newcastle had seven each, Athboy and Dundalk had at least four each, Ardee had at least three, Trim had two, not to mention its enormous Anglo-Norman castle.[26] Like their rural cousins, the urban tower houses of the Pale have a range of common architectural traits that unites them as a group.

The fifteenth century witnessed increased attention on the defences of Pale towns. New murage grants to support the construction and maintenance of town defences were issued to Nobber in 1436, Athboy in 1446, Kells in 1468 and Kilcullen in 1478.[27] Naas received murage grants in 1415, 1452 and again in 1468, when it was described as a 'key of the county of Kildare in resistance of their Irish enemies'.[28] Saggart was to be enclosed by defences in 1472, and in 1477 the portreeve and burgesses of Siddan appealed for permission to collect tolls towards the construction of an enclosing wall.[29] A review carried out in 1462 of the defences of Athboy, Kells, Naas, Navan and Trim concluded that funding for murage should continue to be made available to these centres, to avoid 'the utter annihilation of the said towns'.[30] All of these towns were on the borders of the Pale.

Further provision was made for the defence of these frontier towns, both individually and collectively. In 1455, for instance, an order was made that fines paid by those who refused to come to defend the marches of Co. Louth were to be used to purchase bows, arrows and other defensive armour for the town of Ardee.[31] In 1466, it was enacted that each English-

22 *Stat. Ire., 12–22 Edw. IV*, p. 627.   **23** O'Keeffe, 'Medieval frontiers and fortifications', pp 68–70.   **24** See, for example, McNeill, *Castles in Ireland*, pp 211–21, 222–3.   **25** Séamus Cullen and Tadhg O'Keeffe, 'A turreted enclosure at Pitchfordstown, Co. Kildare', *JRSAI*, 124 (1994), 215–17.   **26** Ben Murtagh, 'The castles of Naas', *JCKAHS*, 16:4 (1983–4), 355–61; Ben Murtagh, 'St David's Castle: a fortified town house, Naas, Co. Kildare', *JCKAHS*, 16:5 (1985–6), 468–78; Ben Murtagh, 'The fortified town houses of the English Pale in the later Middle Ages' (MA, UCD, 1982).   **27** *Stat. Ire., 12–22 Edw. IV*, p. 615; Avril Thomas, *The walled towns of Ireland* (2 vols, Dublin, 1992), I, p. 155.   **28** *Stat. Ire., 1–12 Edw. IV*, p 607–9.   **29** Matthew Seaver, 'Practice, spaces and places: an archaeology of boroughs as manorial centres in the barony of Slane' in Lyttleton and O'Keeffe (eds), *The manor in medieval and early modern Ireland* (2005), pp 70–104 at 100–1; *Stat. Ire., 12–22 Edw. IV*, p. 366.   **30** *Municipal corporations (Ireland), appendix to the first report of the commissioners (part I: southern, midland, western and south-eastern circuits, and part of the north-eastern circuit)*, HC 1835, vol. 28, p. 119; *Stat. Ire., 1–12 Edw. IV*, pp 24–6.   **31** *Stat. Ire., Hen. VI*, p. 317.

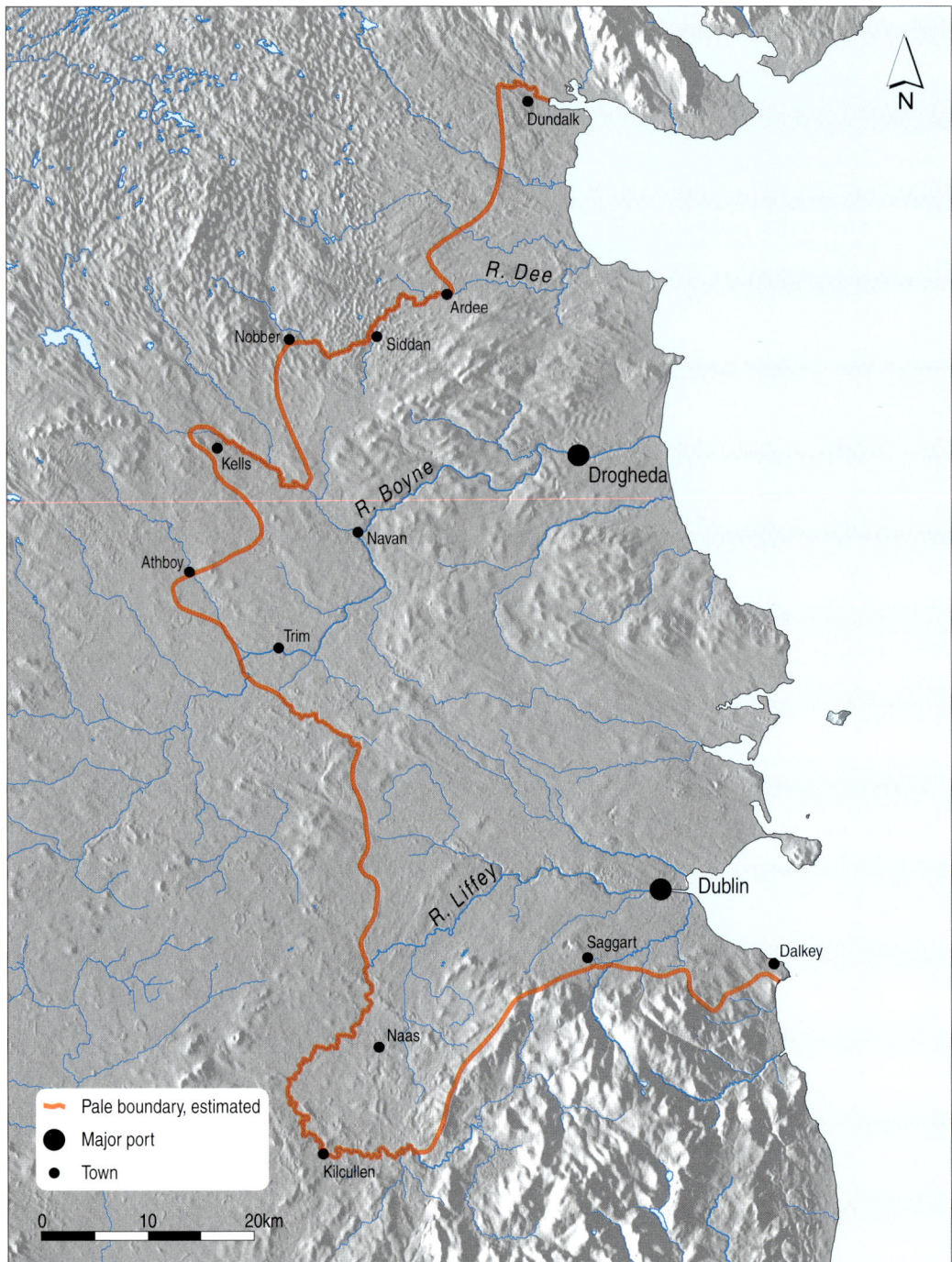

speaking male between the ages of sixteen and sixty, whether Irish or English, was to have a bow equivalent to his height and a quiver of a dozen arrows.[32] Every 'English' town in Ireland was to be equipped with a pair of archery butts for these men to practice regularly.

Provisions for the defence of urban areas were extended to the surrounding countryside in 1472 when parliament agreed to retain a force of 80 archers for three months for the defence of the Pale during war season.[33] The following year the force grew to 160 archers and 63 spearmen, and when it was formalised as the Brotherhood of Arms of St George, it comprised 120 archers and 40 horsemen. It expanded to 300–500 archers, with a further 100 men from 1475. This 'border-patrol unit' operated each war season until it was disbanded by Poynings in 1495.

32 *Stat. Ire., 1–12 Edw. IV*, p. 293.   **33** Ellis, *Ireland in the age of the Tudors*, pp 72–4.

Churches and the Pale boundary

The fifteenth century also witnessed a wave of church expansion across the Dublin region. New buildings were erected and old ones were renovated, being fitted with new windows, rood lofts and, especially, west-end belfry towers. These should more accurately be described as defended residential towers, as in most cases their role as belfries was secondary at best. Such towers are most evident along or close to the Pale boundary at places such as Celbridge, Clane, Maynooth, Straffan, Seatown (Dundalk), Newcastle, Whitechurch, Athboy, Trim, Tallaght and elsewhere. Like secular tower houses in many ways, these tall church towers, most of which were fitted with wall-walks, crenellated parapets and arrow-slit windows, could have functioned as look-out posts and their bells may even have served as warning signals. Like tower houses, they continued to be built through the sixteenth century. Soon, the bounds of the Pale were dotted with new or renovated churches, many of which had defended residential towers at one end.

The Pale ditch

Although Poynings' 1495 act specified that the marches of the four shires lay 'open and not fensible in fastness of ditches', there is some evidence that at least some sections of defensive ditches and banks had been erected in the previous decades. In 1454, for example, statutes were passed requiring the four 'obedient shires' to employ labourers and workmen to dig trenches upon the borders and the marches.[34] In 1457, certain fines that had been received were allocated to pay for 'the works and the defences to be made in Meath'.[35] And in 1481, an act ordained that labourers were to help 'throw up entrenchments around Cookstown', near Ardee, 'for the succour of the adjoining English country'.[36] It is, of course, impossible to be sure whether any of these statutes and proposals were fully implemented. A statute of 1477, however, is more enlightening.[37] It refers to a defensive dyke from Tallaght to Saggart that had been built by royal authority to protect Co. Dublin. Having been broken down in several places by the king's enemies and rebels, the dyke had recently been repaired. It was ordained that 'no passage, way or road shall henceforth be made on, in, by or over the said dyke', and that pigs, goats, cows and any other cattle, which by rooting, pasturing or any other means break the said dyke, should be forfeited.

Cattle-raiding was an important aspect of Gaelic Irish society and it is likely that a major factor in the decision to erect banks and ditches was the need to thwart cattle-rustlers. Even at its largest, the Pale ditch could not have kept out a marauding gang of Irish rebels, intent on wreaking havoc, but it would have prevented the movement of cattle, and probably horses, and certainly wheeled transport.

When government officials were drawing up the 1488 list of places on the borders of the Pale, they may have considered the locations of some existing sections of banks and ditches. They checked to see who held what lands and one can also imagine them referring to their archives of grants, levies and ordinances to ascertain the locations of newly-built or re-fortified castles. Also at a local level, the existence of long stretches of double-ditched boundaries – built expressly to retain cattle – negated the need to construct new earthen defences. At locations including Baltracey (Figure 8.5) and Clonshanbo near Clane, pre-Pale double ditches survive along territorial divisions such as townland boundaries, and these were almost certainly on the lines of property boundaries between neighbouring proprietors. Substantial pre-existing banks and ditches like these, in the right places, are likely to have been used opportunistically to fill some of the gaps between newly-built sections of Pale boundary.

---

34 *Stat. Ire., Hen. VI*, p. 299. **35** *Stat. Ire., Hen. VI*, p. 455. **36** *Stat. Ire., 12–22 Edw. IV*, p. xlvii. **37** *Stat. Ire., 12–22 Edw. IV*, pp 443–5.

Figure 8.4 Distribution
of churches on the
borders of the Pale in
the sixteenth century.

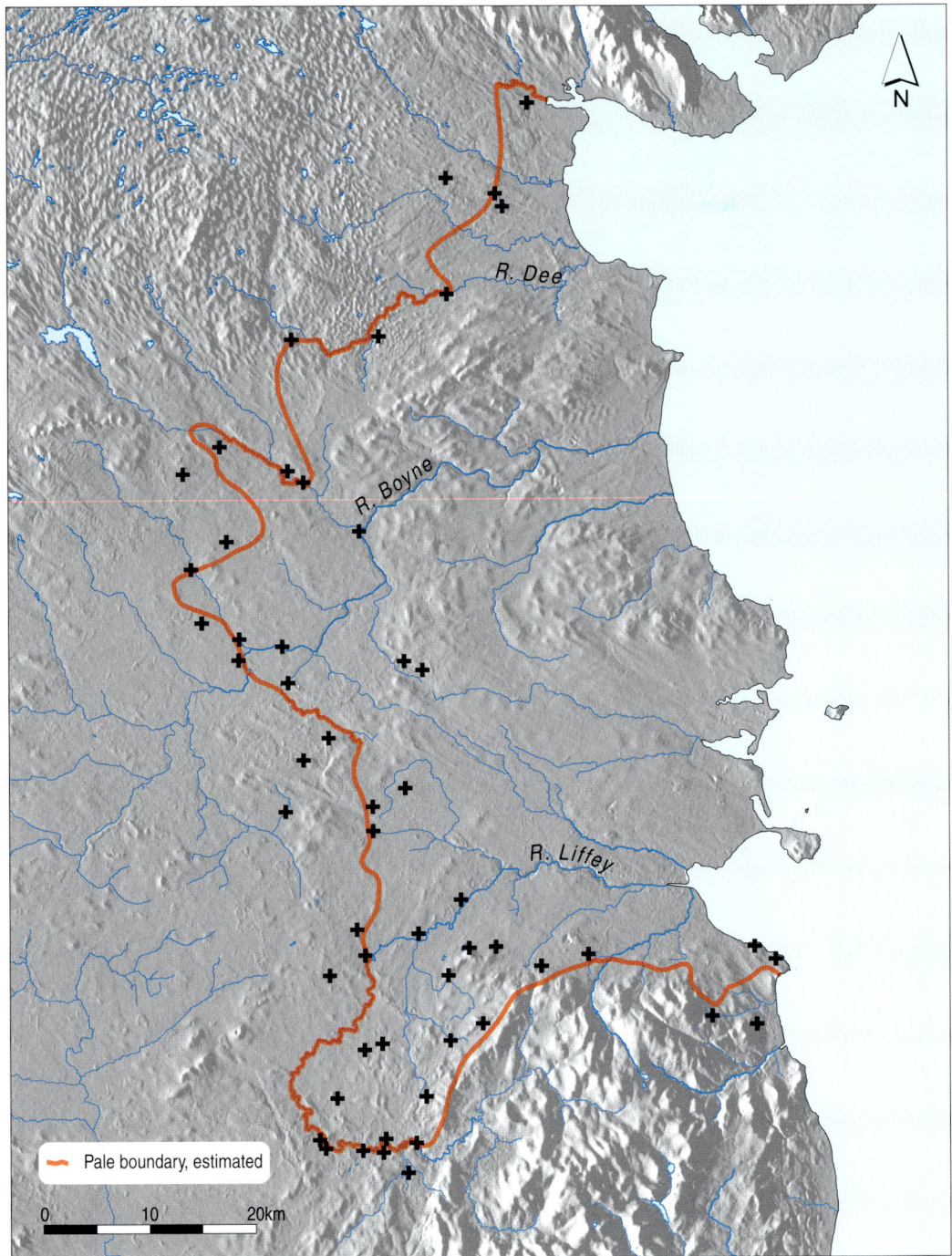

Where possible, natural topographical features such as hills and glacial kames were also used, and the documents of 1488 and 1495 make it clear that rivers such as the Dodder, the Liffey, the Blackwater, the Boyne and the Dee played a role in delimiting the Pale. From the perspective of the twenty-first-century researcher, it is important to bear in mind the landscape changes that have or may have taken place since the fifteenth century. For instance, place-name and cartographic evidence for the area around Clane indicates the former presence of lakes and moors that have since dried up. Seamus Cullen has demonstrated that gaps between long stretches of the Pale ditch in this area were once occupied by lakes – such as Loughbollard – and moors – such as Moortown (Figure 8.6).[38] He has concluded that where natural boundaries existed, no Pale ditch was needed and none

38 Seamus Cullen, 'The Pale in the Donadea area', *Oughterany*, 1:1 (1993), 9–22.

was built. Cullen has also shown that the line of the Pale in the vicinity of Clane is reinforced with castles, such as at Clongowes and Painstown. Clongowes Castle in particular occupied a strategic location, on a wide neck of dry land between the lake at Loughbollard and the bogs of Moortown. South of Loughbollard, the River Liffey connects Clane with Ballymore (Eustace). Again, natural topography, this time in the form of a river, negated the need for a Pale ditch.

Despite the 1495 parliamentary stipulation that 'a double ditch of six feet high' was to be constructed under pain of a forty-shilling fine, there are no further references to this project and no records of any expenses or claims relating to it. Poynings was replaced as governor of Ireland in 1495 and it is likely that his orders were never carried out fully. The digging of the banks and ditches was the responsibility of individual land-holders in the marches and some of them appear to have been more willing or indeed eager to comply than others. Consequently, some significant sections of the boundary were completed but the envisaged enceinte never materialised.

Probable sections of the Pale defences survive at at least twenty-five locations in Dublin, Kildare, Meath and Louth (Figure 8.7). In general, where sections of the boundary survive relatively well, they tend to be in the form of an earthen bank flanked by a ditch on either side. The absence of an over-arching plan for the project is also evident on the ground in the orientation and morphology of the surviving earthworks. While some builders appear to have adhered reasonably closely to the specifications laid down by the parliamentary act, others were less strict, with the result that profiles recorded across the banks and ditches vary considerably from location to location. In some places, such as at Ballyloughan, Clonduff, Clonfert and Graiguepottle, Co. Kildare, the earthworks do not run in a straight line but make several sharp turns, as if to enclose certain fields or properties and not others (Figure 8.8). This would have been a most inefficient way of constructing a delimiting ditch and bank, and the unusual alignment almost certainly reflects patterns of late fifteenth-century land-ownership.

Figure 8.6 The line of
the pale in the vicinity
of Clane, Co. Kildare,
showing the location of
nearby castles and
natural features (bogs
and lakes) in the vicinity
(image courtesy of
Seamus Cullen).

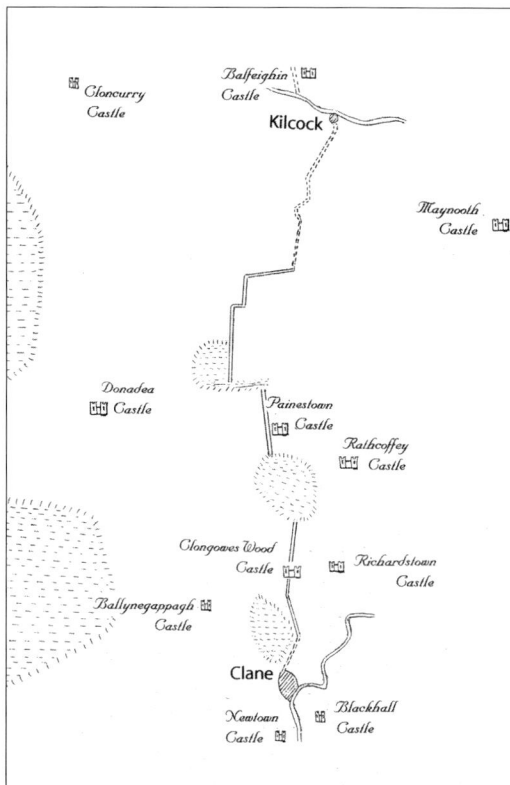

The bank is usually about 1–2m high and 2–4m wide, while the ditches are usually in the range of 1.5–2m wide and 50cm to 1m deep, although these dimensions do vary considerably (Table 8.1). Stretches of the bank that were wide enough also functioned as pathways in the past and indeed some sections now have a modern road running along them. P.W. Joyce described the Pale boundary in the Merrion-Donnybrook area of Co. Dublin as an 'old double-ditch and pathway', and remarked that the Corporation used to take that route when riding the franchises.[39] At Neillstown, Co. Meath, a modern laneway runs along the top of a possible stretch of the Pale boundary.[40] North of Rathcoffey, Co. Kildare, a stretch of c.3.5km of the earthwork survives in the townlands of Ballyloughan, Clonduff and Graiguepottle. Although it is quite overgrown, it is still possible to walk along the top of the bank here, and it is easy to see how it could have doubled as a roadway in the past. Indeed, at Clonfert South the modern road does run along the top of the bank for almost one kilometre, with a steep ditch on each side of the road, except in some places where this has been in-filled to give access to houses (Figure 8.8). Ironically, the development of a road on top of the Pale boundary, in some instances, may well be the only reason that the earthworks have survived at all, in these locations.

Several surveys and archaeological excavations have taken place along the known or presumed line of the Pale boundary (over twenty-five licences have been issued by the DEHLG and the NMI for such work). Some of these investigations have shed a great deal of light on the construction and form of the earthworks, but in some cases not even a trace of it was found. In 1988, for instance, an investigation on what was thought to be the line of the Pale boundary in Dalkey revealed no evidence for it either below or above ground.[41] At Woodside, near Stepaside, Co. Dublin, archaeological monitoring of topsoil-stripping in an area adjacent to the supposed line of the Pale boundary revealed nothing related to that feature in 2002.[42] In 2003, however, archaeologists returned to Woodside to carry out further test excavations.[43] On this occasion, an overgrown earthen bank was identified beside the Ballyogan Stream. It was 45cm in height and c.2.4m in width. Elsewhere on the site, another stretch of overgrown bank was surveyed. This measured c.1.5m in height and c.3.2m in width. Part of the bank was faced with granite stones. No dateable evidence was uncovered and the original function of the banks could not be determined.

A section of the Pale boundary survives at Balally, Co. Dublin.[44] In 1895, Ball and Hamilton recorded that the Pale boundary 'crossed the Parish of Taney to the south of that part of the lands of Balally now called Moreen'.[45] Healy surveyed the visible remains in the

39 O'Keeffe, 'Medieval frontiers and fortifications', p. 70.   40 Ibid., p. 71.   41 Margaret Gowen, 'Dalkey' in *Excavations 1988*, p. 14.   42 Susan McCabe, 'Woodside' in *Excavations 2002*, pp 191–3.   43 Angela Wallace, 'Woodside' in *Excavations 2003*, pp 186–7.   44 Paddy Healy, 'A report on the importance of an earthwork believed to be part of the Pale ditch at Balally, Co. Dublin' (An Foras Forbartha Teoranta, Dublin, 1978), p. 1; Rob Goodbody, *On the borders of the Pale: a history of the Kilgobbin, Stepaside and Sandyford area* (Bray, 1993), p. 29; Rob Goodbody, 'Pale ditch in south County Dublin', *AI*, 7:3 (autumn 1993), 24–5; O'Keeffe, 'Medieval frontiers and fortifications', p. 71.   45 F.E. Ball

Figure 8.7 The locations of sections of the Pale boundary that are still visible in the twenty-first century.

1970s and noted that they consisted of a linear earthwork 220m in length.[46] The flat-topped bank was 3–4m wide on top, 6m wide at the base and 1–1.2m in height. Its flanking ditches were 2m wide on average, and had a depth of 30cm. Part of the earthwork can be seen in a housing estate at Kilcross, although the ditches here have been in-filled. In 1996, during archaeological testing in advance of the construction of a motorway, the remains of a ditch were uncovered near the Central Bank of Ireland building at Balally.[47] A 63m length of the ditch was exposed, and it was in line with the section of the Pale boundary that survives to the south at Kilcross. Full excavation of this feature took place in 2000, and it was found to be the foundation trench of an eighteenth-century mortared granite wall.[48] Clinton suggested that the stretch that runs through Kilcross 'represents an unfinished section of the

and E. Hamilton, *The parish of Taney: a history of Dundrum near Dublin, and its neighbourhood* (Dublin, 1895), p. 8. **46** Healy, 'A report on the importance of an earthwork', pp 1–2. **47** C.D. Gracie, 'Central Bank of Ireland, Balally' in *Excavations 1996*, p. 16. **48** Mark Clinton, 'Balally' in *Excavations 2000*, pp 65–8.

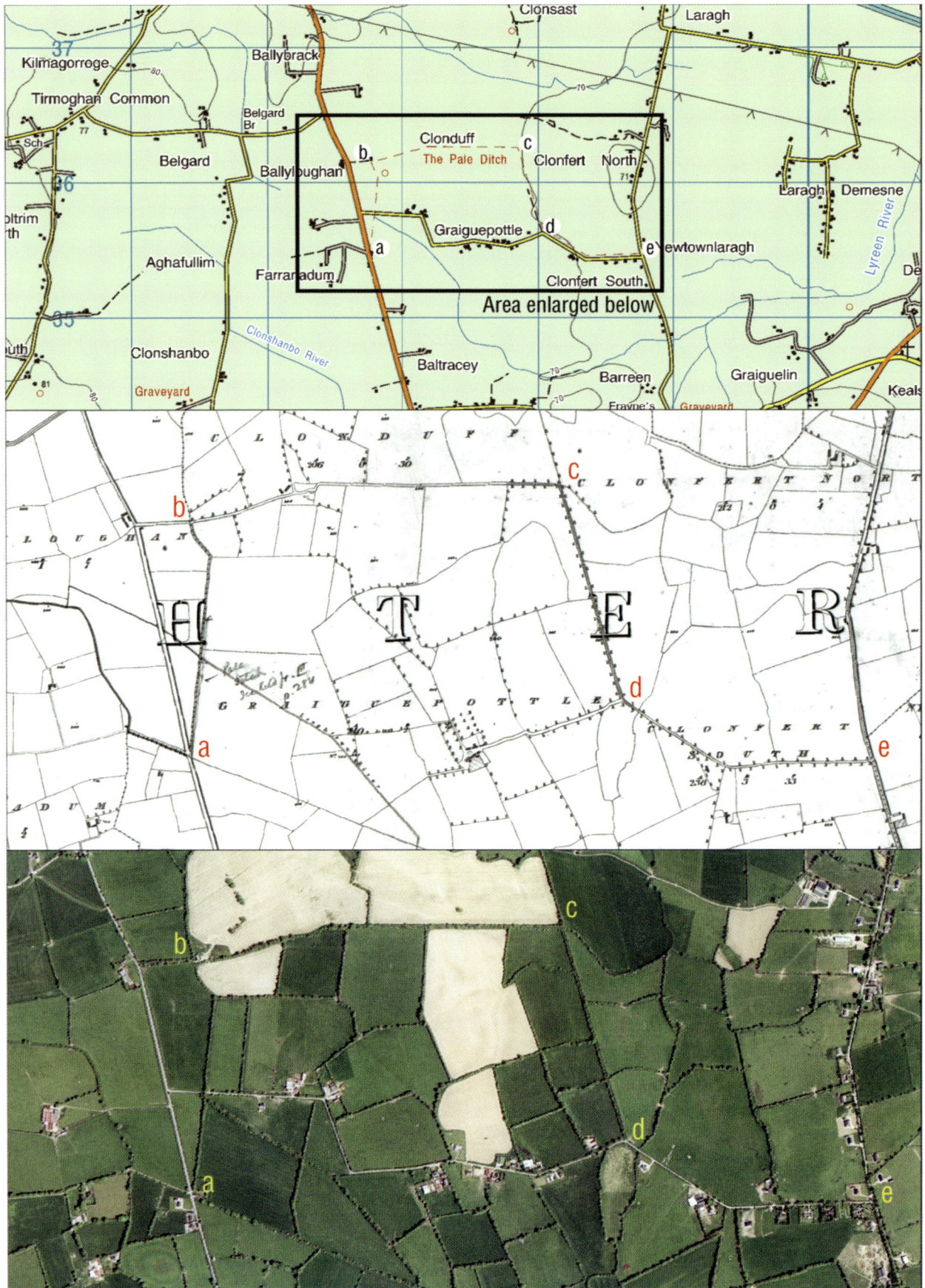

Figure 8.8 The Pale boundary at Ballyloughan, Clonduff, Graiguepottle and Clonfert, Co. Kildare. The top image is an extract from the OS Discovery Series Sheet 49, with 'The Pale Ditch' marked; the middle image is an extract showing the core of this area from the OS 25-inch map, c.1900; the bottom image is an aerial photograph of the same area in 2005. Section a–b consists of a partly levelled bank and ditch; section b–c is in better condition but is overgrown with vegetation; section c–d consists of a large bank with a deep fosse on either side (Figures 8.9, 8.10). It once functioned as a laneway; the modern road runs along the top of section d–e. Archaeological excavations in the vicinity of section d–e revealed little (see below, p. 280)(© Ordnance Survey Ireland).

Figures 8.9–8.10
Photographs of the Pale boundary at Graiguepottle, Co. Kildare.

Pale ditch', and that its builders took advantage of a natural moraine or causeway across marshy ground. He concluded that this section can still only be considered a 'possible' part of the Pale boundary.

At Jamestown, Co. Dublin, a well-preserved 55m section of the Pale boundary is visible as an overgrown earthen bank flanked by a ditch on each side (SMR 26:1). It is situated between a sloping meadow to the north and a flat marshy area bounded by the Ballyogan Stream to the south. The man-made bank and ditches use the natural topography to augment their defensive capabilities. According to O'Carroll, this stretch of the Pale boundary was constructed by the Walsh family 'to connect their castles at Kilgobbin and Carrickmines, which were some 3km apart'.[49] This part of the Pale was close to the Wicklow Mountains, and a defensive barrier here was probably a priority.

A number of archaeological investigations have taken place in the vicinity of the Pale boundary at Ballyogan and Jamestown. In 1997, testing took place in advance of construction near Ballyogan tip-head, but nothing relating to the Pale was found.[50] In 1998, the laying of sewerage pipes on the Ballyogan Road at Jamestown was monitored by archaeologists.[51] The profile of the base of one of the Pale boundary ditches was revealed in one trench. It was 1.6m wide and up to 1.2m deep. The bank was present but unclear due to disturbance. Further work was carried out at the same location in 2001 in advance of development at the Ballyogan Recycling Park.[52] Three trackways breach the Pale boundary here and two of these were to be developed into roadways. Excavation revealed the eroded bank and the recently back-filled ditches of the Pale boundary. Both ditches were cut through 'compact, moderately stony, yellowish-orange natural clay which had some iron flecking'. The northern (inner) ditch was 1.8–2.2m wide at the top, with a steep, V-shaped profile. It reached a depth of 1.1m below modern ground level. The southern (outer) ditch was 2.2–2.4m wide, and 1.2m deep. Nothing of pre-modern date was recovered from the ditches. Where it could be identified, the bank was 4m wide between the ditches. Beyond the cuttings, the bank survived better and had steeply-sloping sides and a rounded top. A survey of its profile was carried out at this location. On the north side, the bank was 1.05m above the surrounding ground, and 1.95m above the base of the ditch. On the south side, it reached 1.75m above ground level and 2.9m above the bottom of the flanking ditch. Assessment in 2002 in a field abutting the Pale boundary (SMR 26:115) at Ballyogan identified a possible extension of the boundary, but a geodetic survey and small-scale excavation proved inconclusive.[53]

49 Ellen O'Carroll, 'Ballyogan Recycling Park, Jamestown' in *Excavations 2001*, pp 123–4. **50** Martin Reid, 'Ballyogan and Stepaside' in *Excavations 1997*, p. 24. **51** Niall Brady, 'Carrickmines and Jamestown' in *Excavations 1998*, pp 39–40; Laurence Dunne, 'Ballyogan Road, Jamestown' in *Excavations 1998*, p. 61; Martin Reid, 'Ballyogan, Jamestown' in *Excavations 1998*, p. 61. **52** John O'Connor, 'Ballyogan Road, Jamestown' in *Excavations 2002*, p. 162; O'Carroll, 'Ballyogan Recycling Park, Jamestown'. **53** John Ó Néill, 'Ballyogan Road, Jamestown' in *Excavations 2002*, p. 162.

Table 8.1 Dimensions of Pale boundary ditch and bank at selected locations.

Location	BANK DIMENSIONS (CM)		DITCH DIMENSIONS (CM)	
	Height	Width	Depth	Width
Ballyogan 1	45	240	–	–
Ballyogan 2	150	320	–	–
Balally	100–120	300–400	30	200
Jamestown 1	–	–	120	160
Jamestown 2	105	400	110	180–220
Jamestown 3	173	400	120	220–240
Kilgobbin	200	–	–	–
Cupidstown	127	200	23	223
Bishopsland	–	–	50	220
Clongowes 1	75	300–400	100–150	–
Clongowes 2	75	300–400	100–150	–
Clongowes 3	–	200	120	200
Clongowes 4	–	200	100	250
Ballynamona	200	600	150	800
Kilteel	60	650	60	350

A test excavation was carried out in advance of pipe-laying on the Ballyogan Road at Kilgobbin in 2000.[54] At one location the pipeline cut through a 2m high bank and adjacent watercourse. This feature is generally regarded as being a section of the Pale boundary, but no archaeological material was recovered and the feature was found to be of natural origin. It is still possible that it formed part of the Pale boundary, of course, but the evidence from this assessment was inconclusive.

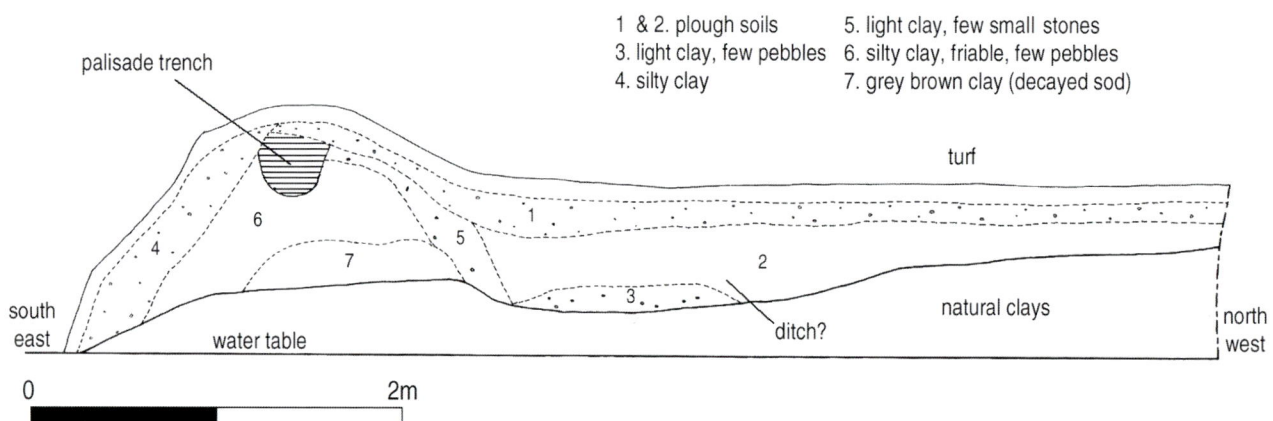

1 & 2. plough soils
3. light clay, few pebbles
4. silty clay
5. light clay, few small stones
6. silty clay, friable, few pebbles
7. grey brown clay (decayed sod)

Figure 8.11 Section through excavated portion of Pale boundary at Cupidstown, Co. Kildare, showing location of apparent palisade trench (after O'Donnell, 'Cupidstown').

A survey and small-scale excavation of a tree-lined earthwork at Kiltalown House, Tallaght, were carried out in March 1998 in advance of development.[55] The earthwork, which curves gradually, is c.330m long. A shallow, flat-bottomed gully was revealed at the crest of the bank. It was 80cm wide at the top and 50cm wide at the base and had been cut directly

54 Teresa Bolger, 'Kilgobbin' in *Excavations 2000*, pp 103–4; Bolger, 'Excavations at Kilgobbin Church, Co. Dublin'.
55 Tadhg O'Keeffe, 'Kiltalown House, Tallaght' in *Excavations 1999*, pp 94–5.

Figure 8.12 A probable section of the Pale ditch at Kilteel, Co. Kildare. The fact that the bank is on the inside of the ditch, rather than the other way around, suggests that the primary role of these earthworks was to keep animals in and not to keep people out (image courtesy of Terry Barry).

into the natural soil to an average depth of 20cm. A single post-hole at the base of the gully measured *c.*20 by 25cm and was at least 25cm deep. Two stones found in the post-hole may have been used as packing to secure a post. The bank was apparently formed by scarping away natural soil on either side, rather than by piling up soil at the centre. Tadhg O'Keeffe, who excavated the site, concluded that 'the Kiltalown earthwork belongs to the late medieval tradition of protective enclosure that reaches its apogee in the attempted enclosure of the English Pale in 1494–5, and the identification of it as part of the Pale is a reasonable one, but it may equally have enclosed an area of medieval parkland'.

Excavation on the Pale boundary at Cupidstown, to the north-east of Kilteel village, Co. Kildare, in 1981, was the first recorded archaeological investigation of the boundary.[56] A cutting through the boundary revealed that the bank was 1.27m high and 2m wide. It was flanked by a ditch that was 2.26m wide and 23cm deep. The ditch on the other flank had been re-cut in modern times and this removed any trace of the earlier fosse. The excavation demonstrated that the bank had been constructed by putting down a layer of sods, 1.25m wide and 20cm deep. This was then covered by layers of soil and hard-packed silty clay. The lowest two layers were still *in situ* and reached 83cm in height. As at other locations along its course, the builders of the Pale boundary at Cupidstown took advantage of the local terrain to boost the overall height of the bank. The bank was topped by a trench 34cm deep and 38cm wide at the top, narrowing to 24cm wide at its rounded base. It is likely that this trench once held a timber palisade (Figure 8.11).

The excavation at Cupidstown was carried out in advance of the laying of the Cork to Dublin gas pipeline, and it is likely that this pipe cut through the Pale boundary at several other locations – Coghlanstown, near Tipperkevin, between Rathcoole and Kilteel, and at Saggart.[57] At two locations, archaeologists monitoring the pipe-laying noted the presence of a bank and ditch in section.

56 M.G. O'Donnell, 'Cupidstown, Co. Kildare: the Pale earthwork' in Cleary, Hurley and Twohig (eds), *Archaeological excavations on the Cork-Dublin gas pipeline* (1987), pp 106–10.   **57** O'Donnell, 'Cupidstown', p. 110.

Close to the church at Kilteel, Co. Kildare, a low denuded bank with wide, shallow outer ditches and low outer banks might also be part of the boundary (Figures 8.12, 8.13, 8.14). The bank is so badly eroded that it is difficult to distinguish from other field boundaries. In some places, the bank survives to a height of 1.5m, but the flanking ditches have been filled in almost everywhere. In 2002, an archaeological assessment was carried out by Ines Hagen at Kilteel Upper.[58] The site was close to the recorded line of the Pale boundary but nothing associated with that feature or its construction was found during testing.

To the west of Ballymore Eustace, a substantial stretch of the Pale boundary runs towards Coghlanstown in the direction of Harristown. At Bishopsland, close to Ballymore Eustace, Paul Stevens carried out an archaeological assessment at the site of a proposed water treatment plant.[59] A section of the Pale boundary is thought to survive in a field ditch at this location. This section is 380m long and consists of a ditch flanked by a low bank on either side. The ditch is 2.2m wide and 50cm deep. At one location, the ditch is truncated by a road, and further to the south it has been completely removed. The archaeological trial-trenches revealed nothing but modern disturbance.

At Castlebrown or Clongowes, Co. Kildare, near Clongowes Wood College, the Pale boundary survives as a flat-topped bank flanked by ditches, with a footpath along the top. Two sections are extant – one to the north of the college and one to the south. The northern portion (SMR 14:8 (01)/10:21) runs for over 500m. The bank ranges from 3m to 4m in width and is c.75cm above the level of the surrounding fields. The ditches are 1–1.5m deep. The second section (SMR 14:8 (02)) at Clongowes is similar in profile, and is also c.500m long, running south towards Clane. It is likely that these two sections joined, but that the middle portion was levelled by the college. In 1993, new sewerage pipes were installed at Clongowes and one section cut through the line of the Pale. The breach was made at an existing gateway and bridge, and this was monitored by archaeologists.[60] Nothing of the original Pale boundary survived at this location, but the opportunity was taken to cut a section through the surviving earthworks 4m to the north. Here, the overall width of the bank and ditches was 8.5m, with the flat top of the bank measuring 2m in width. The ditch to the west of the bank appears to have been re-cut as a drain. It is 2m wide at the top and has a V-shaped profile. Its base is 1.2m below the level of the field and 2.2m below the top of the bank. The other (east) ditch is c.2.5m wide and has a rounded base. It is 1.5m below the top of the bank and less than 1m below the level of the field, although the ground in this area is disturbed. Nothing dateable was recovered.

Five kilometres to the north of Clongowes is a 3.5km stretch of Pale earthworks that includes some of the best-surviving sections anywhere (Figures 8.8–8.10). In this context, it is useful to note what little trace remains once the earthworks are levelled, for it was adjacent to these upstanding remains, at Clonfert South, that Alan Hayden excavated a total of fifteen trenches along the 'supposed line of the Pale boundary' (SMR 10:00101) on four separate dates between November 2000 and October 2001.[61] Nothing of archaeological significance was found in any of these trenches. Seven more trenches were cut in April 2003 and, while 'a number of shallow gulleys/ditches filled with silt containing medieval (thirteenth–fourteenth-century) pottery were uncovered', nothing associated with the Pale boundary was found.[62] Two kilometres to the west, at Ballyloughan, Coughlan carried out

58 Ines Hagen, 'Kilteel Upper' in *Excavations 2002*, p. 257.   59 Paul Stevens, 'Bishopsland, Co. Kildare' in *Excavations 2001*, p. 176.   60 Caroline Donaghy, 'Castlebrown/Clongowes' in *Excavations 1993*, pp 46–7.   61 Alan Hayden, 'Clonfert South' in *Excavations 2000*, p. 162; Alan Hayden, 'Clonfert South' in *Excavations 2001*, p. 182; Alan Hayden, 'Clonfert South' in *Excavations 2001*, p. 182; Alan Hayden, 'Clonfert South' in *Excavations 2001*, p. 182.   62 Alan Hayden, 'Clonfert South 5, Clonfert South' in *Excavations 2003*, p. 238; Alan Hayden, 'Clonfert South 6, Clonfert

Figure 8.13 Kilteel, Co. Kildare. Remnants of the Pale boundary can be seen in the bottom right and left (from Manning, 'Excavation at Kilteel', p. 219).

Figure 8.14 Kilteel, Co. Kildare: from this interpretative tracing by Con Manning it can be seen that, as noted elsewhere, the earthworks (from 'C' to 'D' to 'E' to 'F') do not run in a straight line, instead making several sharp turns. At one point, to the west of 'E', there is a 'bastion-like projection' that may somehow have formed part of the defences. For a stretch, east of 'F', the ditch is fed by a diverted stream (after Manning, 'Excavation at Kilteel', p. 219).

an assessment of the route of a proposed water pipeline.[63] The route passed within 30m of the recorded Pale boundary and a trial-trench here uncovered part of an arched, mortared-stone culvert. 'Although this may represent an extension of the Pale boundary, it is felt that this is unlikely because of the lack of further archaeological evidence from Trench 2'.

South' in *Excavations 2003*, p. 238.   **63** Tim Coughlan, 'Ballyloughan' in *Excavations 2002*, pp 230–1.

If it was ever completed, the Pale boundary must have crossed from Kildare into Meath somewhere in the vicinity of Kilcock, but nothing is visible in this area. This is one of the most intensively farmed parts of Ireland and it is possible that the Pale earthworks have been removed entirely. Further north in Meath, however, at Neillstown (between Trim and Athboy), a modern laneway runs along what may be the former Pale boundary. This is identified as such by the Ordnance Survey, but Tadhg O'Keeffe has some reservations.[64] There is a more convincing stretch of the Pale boundary at Ballynamona, between Athboy and Kells.[65] This is an 'earthen bank running N–S for *c.*200m'. It is up to 2m high and 6m wide, while the ditch running parallel to the east side of the bank is up to 1.5m deep and 8m wide. It is marked as 'The Pale' on the first edition of the Ordnance Survey maps. At Woodtown, Co. Meath, monitoring by an archaeologist of ground-works for a one-off house adjacent to the possible Pale boundary revealed 'nothing of archaeological interest'.[66] From Kells, the assumed line of the boundary, following the act of 1488, crossed into Co. Louth and passed via Siddan, Ardee and Darver before meeting the coast at Dundalk.

Chapter summary

The concept of constructing a massive linear boundary across dozens of miles of countryside was certainly not new in the fifteenth century. Offa's Dyke, Hadrian's Wall, the Danevirke and the Great Wall of China are also variations of the same principle. In Ireland, the Black Pig's Dyke may have been built to counteract Iron-Age cattle-raiders. It is likely that this was also the primary function of the Pale ditch.

To date, most research on the English Pale in Ireland has focused on the history, culture and politics of the area, and – with some notable exceptions – little work has been carried out on the physical and material expression of the region. It is understandable that people prefer to study the Pale as a concept and a state of mind, rather than as a physical entity. And while there is little doubt that the proposed defensive cordon around the Pale was never finished, perhaps more was achieved than has previously been appreciated. It is also worth noting that one of the factors that attracted settlers in the first place and one of the reasons that this area was so economically successful for so long was the fertility of the soil, which lent itself ideally to intensive agriculture of many types. Through hundreds of years of rigorous farming, many of the earthworks must have been lost to the plough and the bulldozer.

It is clear that the earthworks were only one part of the defences, and the dozens of fifteenth- and sixteenth-century tower houses and church towers along the line of the Pale are a reminder of the various methods used in its defence. Pre-existing double ditches and various natural topographical features were also used opportunistically to supplement or even act as substitutes for new banks and ditches (Figure 8.5). The result of all of this was a close coincidence of geographical, cultural, administrative, political and military boundaries, all clustered thickly together.

The Pale boundary was part of an attempt to consolidate control within the region and to stem the flow of cattle and goods out into Gaelic hands. Ultimately, it would seem that the defences of the Pale were a failure. But for a time at least, and for some residents, they may just have had the desired effect. In the 1520s, for instance, there were complaints that lords were abandoning fortified dwellings for stately houses as in England: they kept 'little ordinary houses as [if] they were in a land of peace'.[67] Generally, however, Gaelic incursions

64 O'Keeffe, 'Medieval frontiers and fortifications', p. 71.   **65** Moore, *Archaeological inventory of County Meath*, p. 115.
66 P.D. Sweetman, 'Woodtown' in *Excavations 2003*, p. 395.   **67** S.G. Ellis, *Tudor Ireland: crown, community and the*

and sieges continued unabated throughout the early sixteenth century. The Dissolution of the monasteries in the 1530s provided the English with further opportunity for fortification within and along the boundary of the Pale. Royal commissioners were particularly quick to seize the properties of larger houses such as Mellifont, St Wolstan's, Great Connell, Bective and Baltinglass.[68] Strong towers were soon built at the former Cistercian houses at Bective and Mellifont and at the former house of the Crutched Friars at Newtown Trim.[69]

Considering the intensity of Anglo-Norman settlement and fortification in the Dublin region in the buoyant twelfth and thirteenth centuries, it stands to reason that this would become the heartland of the contracting English colony when things got tough. Whether the emergence of the Pale was an expression of resignation that this was all that was left of a once-great colony, or a confident assertion of the region's 'Englishness' and the recognition of a generation of recovery, and hope for the future, a lot more remains to be understood about its extent, its defences, its architecture, and the ways in which its boundaries fluctuated over time.

conflict of cultures, 1470–1603 (London and New York, 1985), p. 57; *Letters and papers, foreign and domestic, Henry VIII* (21 vols, London, 1862–1932), 4.2, p. 1076.   **68** *MRHI*, pp 123, 139 [Mellifont], 155, 193 [St Wolstan's], 154, 177 [Great Connell], 122, 128 [Bective], 122, 127 [Baltinglass].   **69** Sweetman, *Medieval castles of Ireland*, p. 147.

PART III

EXPLOITATION OF RESOURCES

CHAPTER 9

Agriculture

Land-use

The predominant agricultural land-uses in the Dublin region throughout the medieval period were arable, meadow and pasture. While gardens, woods, parks and bogs also had agricultural functions, their primary roles were in other spheres and they are dealt with separately in following chapters.

Arable land (*terra arabilis*) was land that was 'under the plough' and on which grains, legumes and industrial crops were cultivated. It was frequently measured in carucates, a unit of land equivalent to that which could be ploughed by a team of eight oxen in a year – usually 120 medieval acres or in the region of 250–300 statute acres.[1] Grassland was usually defined as being either meadow (*pratum*) or pasture (*pastura*), the difference being that meadow could be mown to yield a hay crop whereas pasture normally could not.

Virtually all landholding units, from small peasant holdings to large demesnes, were comprised of some combination of these three land-uses. Investigating the balance between these resources can reveal much about the practice of agriculture and the presence and location of specialisms. Most land-use information relates to the demesne – that part of the manor under the direct management of the lord. Manorial extents frequently contain information relating to the amount of demesne land under different land-uses. A database containing information drawn from thirty-eight extents for the study area has been assembled (see above, pp 46–9). Twenty-one of these extents include fairly robust land-use data, and this information is presented below (Tables 9.1, 9.2 and Figure 9.1).

Table 9.2 summarises the land-use information across the entire sample. In the Dublin region *c*.1300, the average demesne was 427 acres, where the arable acreage amounted to 74 per cent of the total demesne land-use. Such averaged figures do subsume considerable differences in both size of demesne and relative areas under different land-uses. While the majority of the demesnes had between 200 and 400 acres, three (Ballymore, Gormanston and Swords) are recorded as having over 800.[2] A spatial pattern in the relative distributions of different sizes of demesnes is not immediately apparent, but there is a discernable pattern in the relative importance of different land-uses (see Figure 9.1). Overall, arable accounted

---

1 See, for example, the grant of lands in Crumlin in 1291: 'there are 128 acres of land whereof 120 acres are reputed as one carucate', *CDI, 1285–92*, no. 855, p. 387. James Mills calculated that in the Dublin area the medieval acre was equivalent to about two-and-one-eighth statute acres: Mills, 'Tenants and agriculture', 58. Otway-Ruthven uses a multiplier of 2.5 to convert medieval acres to statute acres: Otway-Ruthven, *A history of medieval Ireland*, p. 117.
2 Many demesnes in the Dublin region were significantly larger than those in the London region at a similar period, even when a larger acre size is taken into consideration. See B.M.S. Campbell, J.A. Galloway and Margaret Murphy, 'Rural land-use in the metropolitan hinterland, 1270–1339: the evidence of *Inquisitiones post mortem*', *AHS*, 40:1 (1992), 1–22. Extents indicate that the average demesne in the London region comprised some 180–90 acres, although this figure should be revised upwards to take account of the under-recording of fallow arable.

Figure 9.1 Land-use in
the Dublin region,
c.1300. This map plots
data from manorial
extents relating to the
size of manorial
demesne and the
proportion of demesne
acreage under the four
major land-uses.

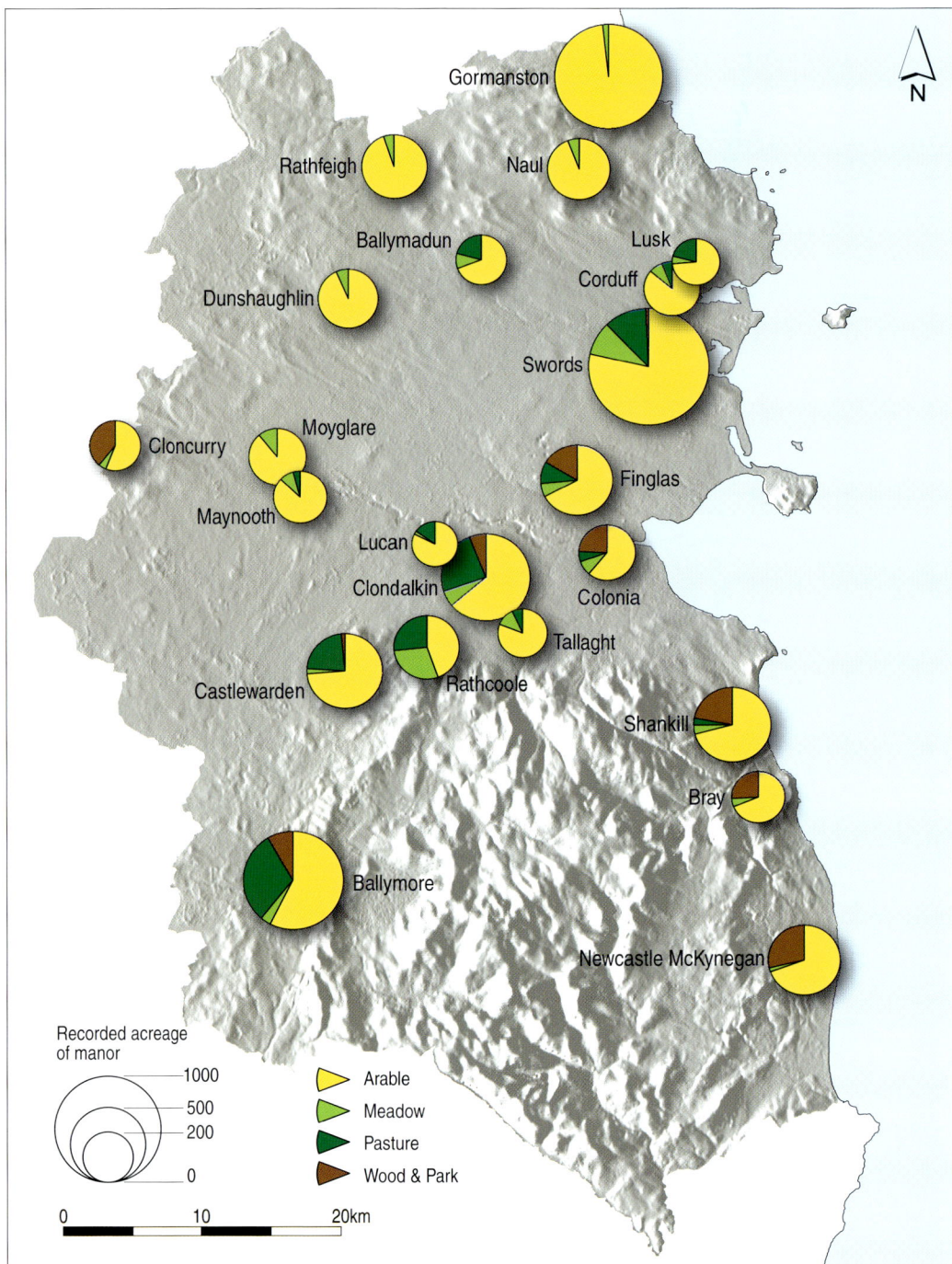

Figure 9.1 Land-use in the Dublin region, c.1300. This map plots data from manorial extents relating to the size of manorial demesne and the proportion of demesne acreage under the four major land-uses.

for 74 per cent of the land surveyed in the extents. In the north of the region, arable was by far the most important land-use, with four manors (Dunshaughlin, Gormanston, Naul, and Rathfeigh) recording over 90 per cent of their demesnes under the plough. Pasture was the next most important land-use, and 13 per cent of land fell into this category. The south-west of the region, however, showed much higher relative percentages of pasture on manors such as Clondalkin, Rathcoole, Castlewarden and Ballymore. It should also be noted that on six demesnes (Bray, Cloncurry, Dunshaughlin, Gormanston, Naul and Newcastle McKynegan), the extents make no reference to pasture. Some of these cases may indicate the existence of arable intensive regimes where livestock were stall-fed or pastured on fallow arable. Other cases may be the result of the under-recording of unenclosed or common pastoral resources. Therefore, the predominance of arable on these manors may be somewhat exaggerated.

All demesnes recorded some land as mowable meadow, and across the region 6 per cent of land fell into this category. It can be argued that proximity to Dublin exercised some influence on the importance of this land-use, with virtually all the manors with proportions of meadow over the average situated close to the city. Perhaps the clearest spatial pattern can be seen with reference to wood. Manors to the north of the Liffey, with the sole exception of Finglas, recorded no woodland and, apart from Cloncurry in the far west of the region, all the well-wooded demesnes were situated along the south-east coastal fringe.

These spatial patterns in the distribution of different land-uses accord well with the varying environmental attributes of the region, which bolsters confidence in the reliability of the source. North of Dublin, the low-lying land with light and fertile grey-brown podzolic soil was most suitable for arable agriculture and, while arable was also important in the south of the region, the soils and topography there favoured a more mixed farming economy. It might also be argued that the patterns in distribution of meadow and woodland, while undoubtedly influenced by environmental factors, were somewhat influenced by the requirements of the city of Dublin for hay, fuel and building materials. This possibility is explored below (pp 324–6).

Table 9.1 Acreage under different land-uses on demesnes in the Dublin region, c.1300.

MANOR	ARABLE[3]	MEADOW	PASTURE	WOOD & PARK	TOTAL	% ARABLE
Ballymadun	140	20	42	–	202	69
Ballymore [incl. Ballybough]	483	29	257	70	839	58
Bray	160	12	–	60	232	69
Castlewarden	366.5	11	111	8	496.5	74
Cloncurry	125.5	11.5	–	87	224	56
Clondalkin	425.5	40	160	40	665.5	64
Colonia	166	23	16	66	271	61
Corduff	218	20	15	–	253	86
Dunshaughlin	280	20	–	–	300	93
Finglas	292	27.5	44	71	434.5	67
Gormanston	920	17	–	–	937	98
Lucan	142	4	26	–	172	82
Lusk	137	10.5	39	–	186.5	73
Maynooth	209	21	10	–	240	87
Naul	304	19	–	–	323	94
Newcastle McKynegan	292.5	8.5	–	120	421	69
Rathcoole	160	104	96	–	360	44
Rathfeigh	330	18	–	–	348	95
Shankill	348	19.5	15	108	490.5	71
Swords [incl. Werne]	934	111.5	136.5	8	1190	78
Tallaght	160	24	14	–	198	81

3 This includes fallow arable put to pastoral uses.

Table 9.2 Land-use information on twenty-one manorial demesnes in the Dublin region, 1292–1358 (note that figures can only be used from those extents which record these four land-uses).

AVERAGE TOTAL ACREAGE	ARABLE	MEADOW	PASTURE	WOOD/PARK
427	314 (74%)	27 (6%)	55 (13%)	30 (7%)

It is interesting to compare the information on land-use *c.*1300 with what is known for the 1650s. The Civil Survey recorded land-use in some detail at a townland level, and the data survives for roughly two-thirds of the study area.[4] As in the early fourteenth century, the predominant land-use was arable, accounting for over 90 per cent of all farmland in some places, and averaging over 74 per cent across the region. Comparing the percentages under different land-uses from the two sources appears to show very little change over this 350-year period – in particular, the arable component constituted 74 per cent of land at both times (see Figure 9.2). Nonetheless, it would be dangerous to argue for continuity in land-use patterns without the same level of detail for any time in the intervening period. It is likely that there were shifts – by 1400 for instance, with a drop in population after a disastrous fifty years, there is a good deal of anecdotal evidence for a retreat from arable agriculture. The 1650 figures may reflect a pattern of taking pasture land back into arable cultivation in response to demands from a resurgent population.

Figure 9.2 Land-use in the Dublin region, *c.*1300 (*left*; source: manorial extents) and *c.*1650 (*right*; source: Civil Survey).

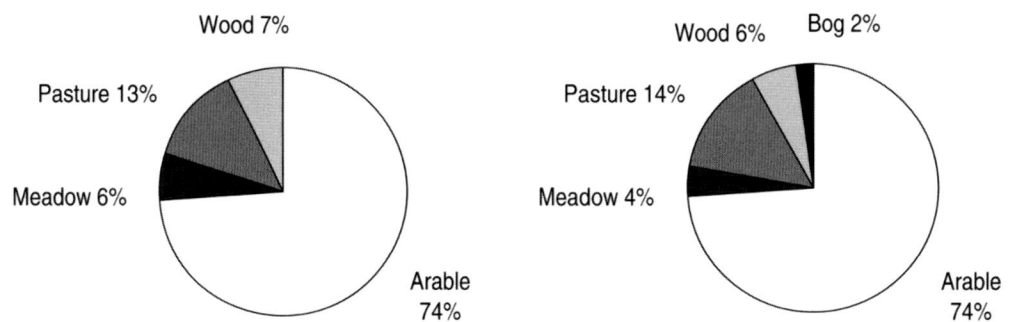

Relative value of different land-uses

As well as quantifying the different land-uses, extents frequently assigned a value-per-acre to each category. This value represented the estimated annual rental value of each resource rather than its capital or asset value.[5] The value placed on land varied from demesne to demesne and also within demesnes. It is not unusual to encounter three or more differing values per acre of arable land on the same manor. On the archiepiscopal manor of Clondalkin in 1326, arable land was valued variously at 4*d.*, 3½*d.*, 3*d.* and 2*d.* per acre.[6] In addition, 134½ acres of fallow arable were given a nominal composite value of 30*d.* The average value for arable land on this manor was therefore 2*d.* per acre.

A variety of factors could influence the value placed on a particular piece of land at a particular time. Low valuations were sometimes explained by reference to the quality of the land and its potential for cultivation. For example, low-valued arable on the manors of Clondalkin and Colonia/St Sepulchre was described as 'poor and worn out' or 'exhausted

4 *Civil Survey*, vols 5, 7, 8. Unfortunately, the details of the survey for Co. Wicklow do not survive. For a fuller discussion of this, see Margaret Murphy and Michael Potterton, 'Mapping a medieval landscape? The Civil Survey and land-use in County Dublin' in Bradley, Fletcher and Simms (eds), *Dublin in the medieval world* (2009), pp 316–44. 5 Bailey, *The English manor*, pp 24–5.   6 McNeill (ed.), *Alen's register*, pp 185–9.

and poor'.[7] It is interesting to note that while arable land at Colonia was assigned an averaged value of 2*d.* per acre in 1326, arable on the same manor was valued at 17*d.* an acre in 1288.[8] Environmental factors such as flooding and excessive dryness are also cited.[9] At Colonia, six acres of meadow were given a low value because they lay near the highway and were trampled by carters.[10] On three of the archbishop of Dublin's manors, meadow land was said to be worth nothing or very little because it had been wasted in digging sods. At Ballymore Eustace, Co. Kildare, nine acres had been affected, at Clondalkin four acres and at Rathcoole eight-and-a-half acres.[11] This practice appears to have been aimed at replenishing the fertility of the arable land by digging in fresh sods from meadow land.

The political situation, and, in particular, the activities of the Irish were frequently cited as a reason for low or zero valuations on manors towards the south of the study area. Although these references are more habitually encountered after 1300, some are as early as 1277. In that year, jurors testifying about the value of land on the holding of Walshestown (part of the manor of Ballymore Eustace) stated that 'there are 99 acres of arable and each acre is extended with the easements of the manse and garden at 9*d.* if there was peace but now the land is laid waste by war'.[12]

The 1326 extents for the archiepiscopal manors of Ballymore Eustace, Colonia, Shankill and Tallaght all refer to 'the war' and land lying waste because of the Irish or because it lay 'near the Irish'. At Ballymore, arable land was said to be worth ½*d.* an acre in time of peace, nothing in time of war.[13] At Shankill, the jurors reported that 'there are 76 acres of the demesne which used to be under the lord's ploughs, sown this year by divers tenants, 3*d.* an acre in peace, nothing in war; nine score and five acres of the same demesne which used to be under the lord's ploughs, waste and untilled for want of tenants, because it is near Irish malefactors'.[14] For purposes of comparison, average 'value-per-acres' have been calculated for each land-use on a number of manors across the region (Table 9.3).

The sample of land values for the Dublin region is too small to be very meaningful statistically, and the large number of variables that can affect the values placed on land such as acre size, vulnerability to attack and environmental considerations prevent spatial analysis from being carried out. The 1326 extents of the archiepiscopal manors presented the lowest value for arable land in relation to meadow and this suggests a pattern similar to that found on many English manors.[15] On several other manors in the Dublin region, however, the values for arable and those for meadow were similar (Ballymadun, Bray, Castlewarden, Cloncurry, Dunshaughlin, Gormanston, Newcastle McKynegan, Rathfeigh, Walshestown) and in one instance (Naul) the value of arable far outstripped that of meadow. These manors are located throughout the study region, which suggests that environmental attributes were not a causative factor. In most cases it appears that a high arable value was responsible for the parity, rather than a low meadow value. Therefore, it could be argued that the arable land in these locations was of a superior productivity.

Crop cultivation

Fields and drainage

The expanding cultivation of cereals in the Dublin region resulted in a significant restructuring of the use and occupation of land.[16] There is, for example, evidence for the

---

7 Ibid., pp 170, 186.   **8** Ibid., p. 152.   **9** Both at Swords in 1326. Pasture near the sea was subject to flooding, while meadow gave a poor crop because it was poor and dry. McNeill (ed.), *Alen's register*, p. 176.   **10** McNeill (ed.), *Alen's register*, p. 170.   **11** Ibid., pp 184, 186, 189.   **12** TNA:PRO C133/16.   **13** McNeill (ed.), *Alen's register*, p. 189.   **14** Ibid., p. 194.   **15** Campbell, *Seigniorial agriculture*, p. 90. Across England, on average, meadow had a unit value 4.7 times that of arable. There were, however, considerable spatial variations.   **16** Britnell, *Britain and Ireland*, p. 195.

Table 9.3 Value per acre of arable, meadow and pasture on demesnes in the Dublin Region, c.1300 (in pence).

MANOR/HOLDING	ARABLE	MEADOW	PASTURE
Ardinode	12	8	–
Ballymadun	13	13	13
Ballymore [incl. Ballybough]	0.5	2	0.5
Bray	12	12	–
Castlewarden	12	12	4
Cloncurry	20	20	–
Clondalkin	2	10.5	0.5
Colonia	2	3	1
Corduff	12	24	12
Dunshaughlin	6	6	–
Finglas	3	3	2
Gormanston	3	3	2
Kilmactalway	4	6	2
Leixlip	9	–	–
Lucan	4	10	3
Lusk	6	18	–
Naul	11	2	–
Newcastle McKynegan	8	8	–
Rathcoole	8	4	1
Rathfeigh	11	12	–
Shankill	1	1	–
Swords [incl. Werne]	3	21	6
Tallaght	2	12	3
Walshestown	9	9	–
Mean Value Per Acre	**7.2**	**9.5**	**4.1**

clearance of woodland to create more arable in the early thirteenth century, and some blocks of land were clearly the result of individual enterprise in forest-clearance and reclamation. In about 1220, the archbishop of Dublin granted to William Gascoing sixteen acres that Robert Blund the smith held and which he cleared from the wood lying between the archbishop's land and the land of Reginald de Bernevale.[17] In 1229, Henry III granted Luke, archbishop of Dublin, an extensive charter of disafforestation of his lands stretching from Wicklow in the south-east over to Naas in the west and up as far as Shankill.[18] The archbishop was to be allowed to enclose the woods and make parks but also 'to take, give, sell and assart these woods at will'.

The sources refer to a rotation system on many demesnes, and this has been used to suggest that a three-field system in Ireland was an innovation associated with the Anglo-Normans.[19] The occasional reference to autumn-sown cereals in earlier sources might be an indication of at least a two-crop rotation in use before the late twelfth century.[20] The evidence of the extents suggests that the arable land was organised into large blocks or

17 *RHJB*, no. 338.   18 McNeill (ed.), *Alen's register*, p. 62.   19 Down, 'Colonial society and economy', p. 467, referring to J.Z. Titow, *English rural society, 1200–1350* (London, 1969), pp 20–3.   20 Kelly, *Early Irish farming*, pp 230–1.

'sesona', which may be translated as 'sowing areas'. On some manors these sesona would appear to equate with open fields, while on others they incorporated several fields and perhaps multiple boundaries. At Cloncurry, Co. Kildare, in 1304, three sesona are mentioned – one sown with wheat, one sown with oats and the third lying fallow.[21] The same division was recorded at Clondalkin in 1326, where some of the sesona appear to have spanned townland boundaries and incorporated land of varying quality.[22] An extent of the same year for Swords mentions three sesona, each measuring 220 acres and one stated to lie 'in diverse fields'.[23] Other archiepiscopal manors at Colonia and Finglas employed the same system of land management. On the Kildare manor of Maynooth in 1328, 80 acres lay in the *seisona frumenti* (the wheat sowing area), 66 acres in the *seisona avene* (the oat sowing area), and 73 acres in the *seisona warect* (the fallow sowing area).[24] At Naul, the term sesona was not used and here the arable was divided between two large fields – the carrot field (*le carret feld*), containing 140 acres, and the mill field, containing 120 acres.[25]

There is also evidence relating to the organisation of manorial lands held by tenants. Some of these holdings appear to have been self-contained parcels or blocks. The extent of 1344 for Ballymadun in north Co. Dublin, for example, mentions thirty-two parcels of land let out to farm 'that is 482 acres of arable, meadow and pasture'.[26] Other records show quite clearly the existence of scattered holdings consisting of many small strips in a number of different fields.[27] Even very small holdings were divided up into different strips. In 1318, John Elysauder granted Thomas de Mateshale two acres of arable land in Rathcoole.[28] The land was said to lie 'in the field which is called le Brodefold' and was made up of four half-acre strips:

> half an acre lie in width between the land of Adam del Rath to the east and that of John Chaumpneys to the west; half an acre between the land of Roger le Deveneys to the east and that of Alicia Gyllot to the west; half an acre between the land of Roger Aleyn to the east and that of Roger Aylmer to the west and half an acre between the land of John le Long on both sides to the east and west.

Another deed from the same year grants land in Rathcoole in a field called Lyteslade and mentions another field called Halfesoulonde.[29] These deeds appear to indicate the existence of three large open fields with a number of small strip-holdings in each. In some cases these land divisions show impressive continuity over several centuries. The late fifteenth-century rent roll of Richard Stanihurst, a merchant of Dublin, lists twenty-six acres of arable and an acre of meadow, which he held in Rathcoole.[30] The arable was held in twenty small parcels and the meadow in four. Some of the parcels were contained in the fields called 'Brodeffeld' and 'Lytillslade' mentioned in 1318.

A fifteenth-century deed relating to land in the manor of Crumlin illustrates the complex landholding pattern that evolved when tenants acquired strips of land scattered throughout many fields.[31] In 1468, Isabella FitzRichard granted a total of twenty-five acres to Thomas Archbold:

21 RBO, p. 27. 22 McNeill (ed.), *Alen's register*, p. 185. One sesona was partially situated at Clondalkin and at Ballymacnegin. 23 McNeill (ed.), *Alen's register*, p. 175. 24 *RBK*, pp 98–100. 25 TNA:PRO C133/63/15. 26 TNA:PRO C135/75/3. 27 Otway-Ruthven, 'Organisation of Anglo-Irish agriculture', 2. 28 J.G. Smyly, 'Old Latin deeds in the library of Trinity College I', *Hermathena*, 66 (1945), 25–39 at 37. 29 Ibid. 30 Smyly, 'Old Latin deeds V', *Hermathena*, 71 (1948), 36–51 at 38–9. 31 Smyly, 'Old Latin deeds IV', *Hermathena*, 70 (1947), 1–21 at 19.

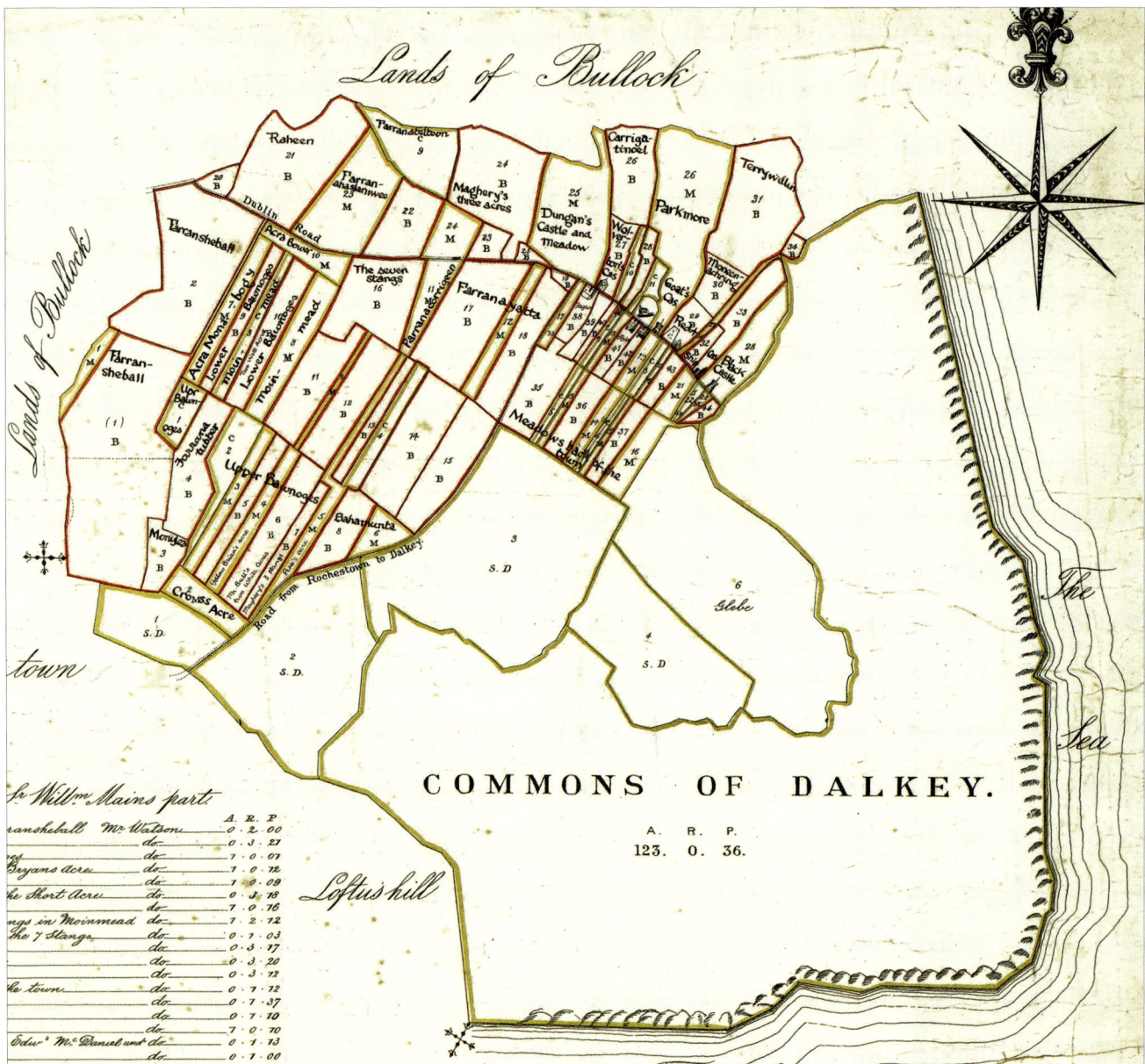

Figure 9.3 Detail from Thomas Reading's 1765 map of Dalkey. Reproduced from an 1892 lithograph of the original map held by the Royal Society of Antiquaries of Ireland. The whereabouts of the original map are unknown.

viz: an acre and a half near Biggeslie, called Hollowcrofte; an acre and a stang of meadow and another stang near the said croft; 2 acres of land in le Stonywayfeld, an acre and a half in le Yoghillfeld; an acre in a park at Minganesborres called le Langhers; half an acre in le Kingesfeld; 5 acres in le Camyshefeld; an acre and a half in le Coilaghfeld; two acres and a half in le Firrewode; 7 acres in le Cuokefeld; half an acre in a park near Lawles is place; an acre in Cuokefeld atte the Popell.

Cartographic evidence indicates that the system of strip-holdings survived in some areas into the eighteenth and nineteenth centuries. Thomas Reading's 1765 map of the lands of Dalkey and its accompanying schedule clearly shows separate parcels of tenant-held land dispersed in long narrow strips (Figure 9.3).[32] Many of the strips are less than an acre in size, while some of the larger holdings display consolidation of adjacent strips. Similar patterns are visible on an eighteenth-century map of Clondalkin (Figure 9.4).

The existence of such field arrangements is difficult to trace archaeologically. Whether dealing with expanses of land that preserve relict field boundaries that have dissolved into the present-day landscape, or considering the possibility that ancient and/or medieval field

32 Chris Corlett, *Medieval Dalkey in the 1760s* (Archaeology Ireland Heritage Guide 33, 2006).

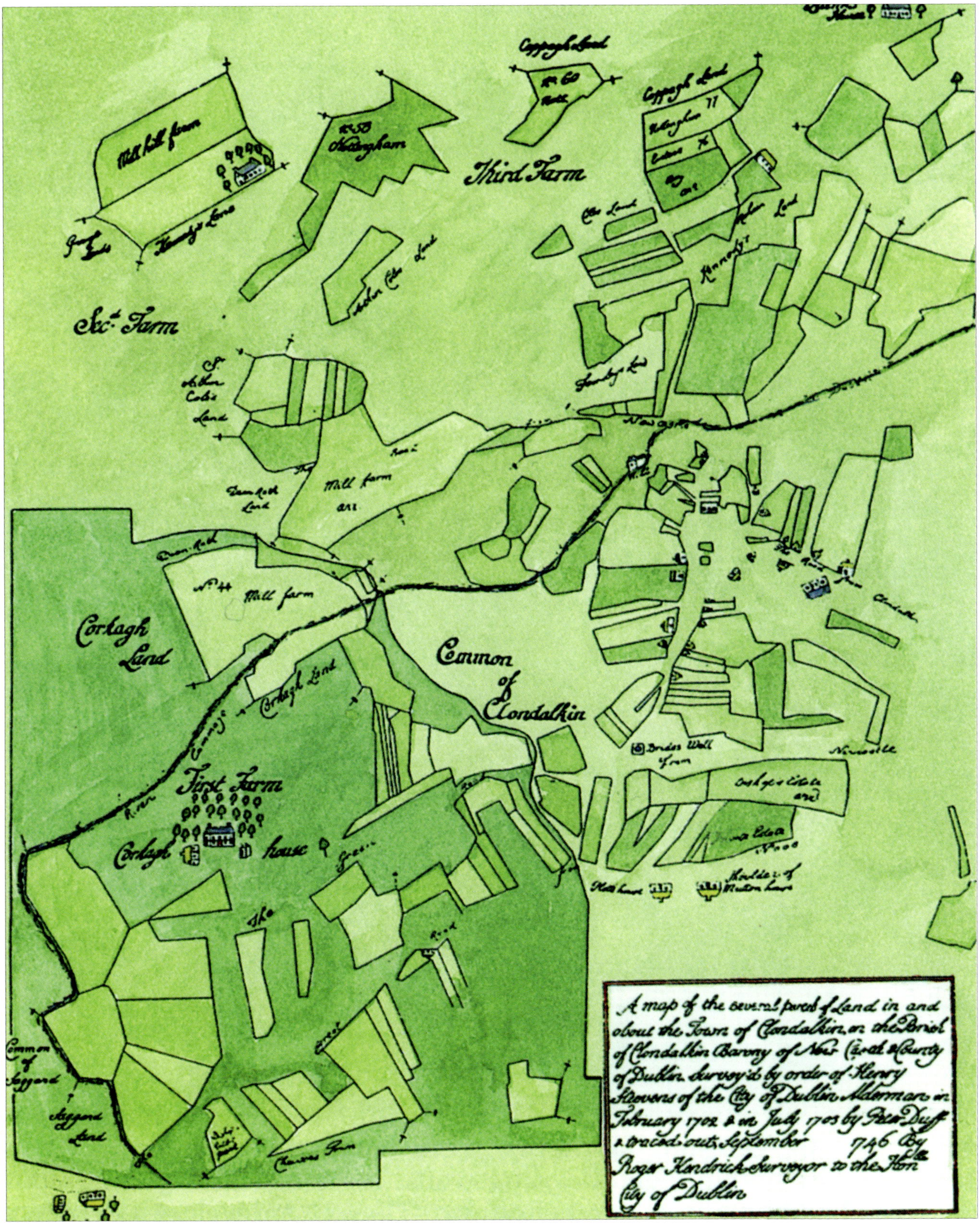

Figure 9.4 Map of Clondalkin in 1746. This map was based on a survey carried out in 1702–3, and shows landholdings in and around the 'town' of Clondalkin. The landscape was clearly still heavily influenced by the tradition of open fields, with scattered strip-holdings (image from F.H.A. Aalen and Kevin Whelan, 'Fields' in Aalen et al. (eds), *Atlas of the Irish rural landscape*, pp 134–44 at p. 137, fig. 9, after 'A map of the several parcels of land in and about the town of Clondalkin surveyed in February 1702 and July 1703 by Peter Duff and traced out September 1746 by Roger Kendrick'. Roger Caldwell Collection EC2553, Box 3782, Land Commission Papers, NAI).

divisions may be preserved in modern boundaries, little research has been carried out on the question of land division anywhere in medieval Ireland.[33] Modern changes in agricultural practices have, in turn, led farmers to favour larger fields and this has been achieved through the large-scale removal of field boundaries such as hedges, hedgerows, ditches and banks across the study area. Beneath the surface, however, some traces of these levelled features survive, and excavations at a number of sites have uncovered their remains.[34] At Kilgobbin, for instance, Hagen revealed a series of features relating to drainage, land enclosure and other agricultural activity.[35] One boundary ditch, cut into the natural subsoil, was 1.2–1.3m deep, c.4.5m wide at the top, and c.1.5m wide at the base. Generally, it had a U-shaped profile with a flat base, but one edge was stepped and this was seen by the excavator to indicate the use of a spade in its construction.[36] When the ditch was being dug, the material removed from it was used to construct a parallel bank, remains of which also survived. The basal and middle fills of the ditch contained some gravel, medieval pottery and animal bone. A second, smaller ditch may have functioned as an internal field boundary. It was 40–70cm deep, 1.4m wide at the top and 50cm wide at the base. Among its contents were charred cereal remains, charcoal, ash, animal bone and two sherds of pottery. Two nearby pits contained a similar range of medieval debris.

At Brookfield House, on the north bank of the Camac River in Clondalkin, Donal Fallon excavated two phases of medieval agricultural activity.[37] The earlier phase featured the remains of a bank and double ditch (22m long, 2.4m wide, 40cm deep) with associated cultivation furrows. A second, larger ditch (23m long, 2–4m wide, 1m deep) was also uncovered, and it too was associated with a series of furrows. Two-hundred-and-twenty-six sherds of medieval pottery were recovered, consisting primarily of a range of locally produced thirteenth- to fourteenth-century wares. Fallon suggested that the earlier phase represented strip cultivation within a large, open-field unit, the vestiges of which are indicated on an early eighteenth-century estate map (Figure 9.4).[38] He saw the later phase in the context of later medieval enclosure and a general pattern of decline in communal agriculture.

Excavations by David O'Connor at Kilmessan, Co. Meath, uncovered a series of cultivation furrows, ditches and boundaries. O'Connor interpreted some of the furrows as part of a 'lazy-bed' field-system.[39] A medieval iron sickle was also found on this site. At Dunshaughlin, less than 10km to the south-east of Kilmessan, an extensive network of medieval gullies, trenches and furrows were found, and the excavator inferred from the extent of the evidence that 'the entire area was under cultivation, probably as part of the Anglo-Norman manor'.[40] The gullies and trenches may well have been dug in an effort to drain the land, which was low-lying and probably prone to flooding. Evidence for medieval field drainage has also been excavated at Dalkey, and at Hammond Lane in Dublin, where the gullies and channels were of thirteenth- and fourteenth-century date.[41] At Ballymount Great, Co. Dublin, the excavation of a series of shallow thirteenth- and fourteenth-century trenches and gullies uncovered large quantities of locally produced pottery.[42] To the excavator, it seemed likely that the pottery 'was introduced to the gullies to assist drainage'.

33 An overview of research carried out is presented in Niall Brady, Rory McNeary and Brian Shanahan, 'A new study of land enclosure and settlement in north Roscommon', *Journal of the Roscommon Historical and Archaeological Society*, 10 (2006), 99–104.   **34** DEHLG file 00E0283 (Laughanstown); DEHLG file 00E0758 (Glebe); DEHLG file 01E0094 (Naas: Dublin Road); DEHLG file 02E0074 (Carmanhall: site 55m); DEHLG file 02E0078 (Ballough); DEHLG file 00E0754 (Nangor); O'Donnell, 'Cupidstown, Co. Kildare'.   **35** DEHLG file 02E1173 (Kilgobbin).   **36** DEHLG file 02E1173 (Kilgobbin), p. 20.   **37** Donal Fallon, 'Brookfield House, Ninth Lock Road, Clondalkin' in *Excavations 2002*, pp 136–7. **38** Fallon, 'Brookfield House', pp 136–7.   **39** David O'Connor, 'Kilmessan, Co. Meath: stratigraphic report and post-excavatoin assessment (04E1352)', unpublished report, 2005.   **40** DEHLG file 94E0178 (Dunshaughlin, Co. Meath), p. 46; Linzi Simpson, 'Church of St Secundinus, Dunshaughlin' in *Excavations 1995*, pp 70–1.   **41** DEHLG file 97E0393 (Dalkey: 59 Castle Street); DEHLG file 02E0096 (Hammond Lane).   **42** Franc Myles, 'Ballymount Great' in *Excavations 2001*, p. 81; Franc Myles, 'Ballymount Great' in *Excavations 2002*, pp 124–5.

Figure 9.5 A fifteenth-century Irish medical manuscript with marginal drawings depicting agricultural tasks (see Figure 9.14, below, for detail) (image reproduced courtesy of the Council of King's Inns, Dublin: MS 17, fo. 5v).

Preparing the land (by Niall Brady)

Cultivation ridges are a relatively common occurrence in the Irish landscape but the identification of medieval cultivation is more challenging. In the absence of excavation, where it would be hoped to recover medieval potsherds from 'night soil' and other manuring additives, the dating of expanses of ridges in the landscape remains difficult. That is not to say that relict areas of cultivation remain undated in Ireland. Furrows are commonly found during excavation. Where the intervening ridges have disappeared or dissolved into the general sod level, the furrows invariably represent a surface level of activity below the grass that has cut into the underlying natural soil levels, and survive as obvious linear intrusions into the B-horizon. Within the area that would have been enclosed by the boundaries at Kilgobbin, and perpendicular to the larger ditch, a series of cultivation furrows were uncovered, some of which produced medieval pottery. The furrows ranged in depth from 2cm to 5cm, and were 30cm to 60cm wide. An extensive series of similar furrows was excavated at St Margaret's, close to the stream that flows north-eastwards from Clonaberry motte.[43] These varied from 2cm to 6cm in depth and were 10cm to 55cm wide. Sherds of Leinster Cooking Ware and wheel-thrown Dublin wares were found in the topsoil covering the furrows. The furrows were regularly spaced, being *c.*3m apart, and the excavator compared them to similar furrows examined at Bishopsland, Ballymore Eustace, Co. Kildare, and at Agnes Road, Crumlin, which were spaced at *c.*3m and 2m intervals respectively.[44] Excavation at Cupidstown in Co. Kildare revealed a series of ridges and furrows enclosed by two field boundaries.[45] The field had been cultivated at least three times using this method, and a small field-drain had been re-cut twice (having silted up).[46]

The most convincing evidence for the employment of an open-field approach to land management in the larger Dublin area has been identified around the manor centres of Oughterard and Castlewarden, Co. Kildare, where plough headlands, or furlong boundaries have been recorded (Figures 9.6, 9.7).[47]

The headlands are a product of ploughing, and are formed over time when a plough is turned around at the end of its run; the soil that has clung to the plough gradually falls away and comes to form a broad low bank that extends at right angles to the main direction of ploughing. The headlands themselves would in turn be ploughed as they represent part of the cultivable area. In Kildare, the headlands were reported as measuring up to 20m wide and 50cm high, and they ran for up to 1km in length. The distance between the banks was *c.*200m. The headlands run along the natural contours, around the principal area of settlement at Oughterard, between the early church site to the north and a tower house to the south. Headlands were also noted to the east of the principal settlement area, where they are formed around a moated site.

Where headlands occur in England, they are classically associated with ridge-and-furrow cultivation, with the main ploughing forming a series of reverse S-shaped ridges and associated furrows through the plough area.[48] The form has come to epitomise medieval agriculture and the search continues for the ideal medieval field in Ireland. Early ridges may survive at two locations in the Curragh, Co. Kildare, where it is understood that the lands

43 DEHLG file 99E0028 (St Margaret's). 44 DEHLG file 99E0305 (Crumlin: 1–7 St Agnes Road); DEHLG file (Bishopsland, Ballymore Eustace). 45 O'Donnell, 'Cupidstown, Co. Kildare'. 46 For other examples of furrows identified as medieval in date by the associated small finds, see: DEHLG file 96E0188 (Tallaght: St Maelruan's); DEHLG file 96E0391 (Maynooth Castle); DEHLG file 02E1454 (Ratoath); DEHLG file 94E0178 (Dunshaughlin, Co. Meath); DEHLG file 97E0393 (Dalkey: 59 Castle Street); DEHLG file 02E0096 (Hammond Lane) DEHLG files 98E0526, 99E0517, 99E0518, 99E0519, 99E0523 (Cherrywood); DEHLG file 97E0152ext (Kill: Killihill). 47 Hall, Hennessy and O'Keeffe, 'Medieval agriculture and settlement in Oughterard and Castlewarden'. 48 D.N. Hall, *Medieval fields* (Princes Risborough, Buckinghamshire, 1982).

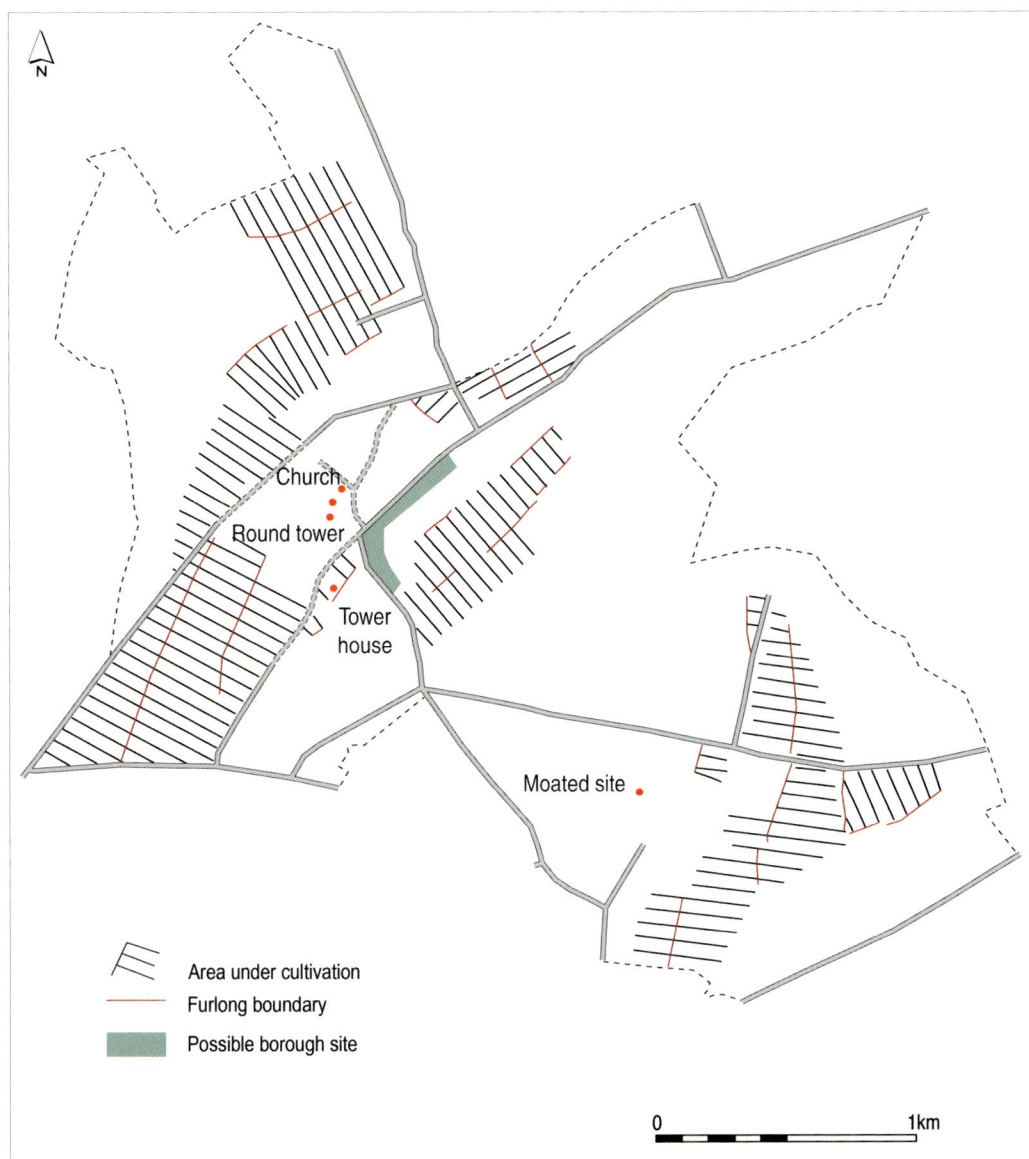

Figure 9.6 Plan of plough headlands in Castlewarden and Oughterard, Co. Kildare (after Hall, Hennessy and O'Keeffe, 'Medieval agriculture and settlement').

Church

Round tower

Tower house

Moated site

Area under cultivation
Furlong boundary
Possible borough site

0   1km

have not been cultivated since the sixteenth and the seventeenth century respectively.[49] The same is the case at Ballysax, Co. Kildare, and at Moyaliff, Co. Tipperary.[50] It should be noted, however, that ridge-and-furrow is essentially an adaptation to the heavy wet clays that dominate the central and west midlands of England, where it was necessary to raise the seedbed and ensure adequate drainage on either side. The absence or low representation of ridge-and-furrow in Ireland should not be considered problematic.

The creation of a suitably tilled surface was achieved principally by ploughing the land. It is likely that the plough was not the only tool used, and that the earth would also have been turned by hand-spading, although the extent to which spades were employed in the medieval period is not clear.[51] The spade was certainly used to assist in ploughing in the early modern period, and the 'potato-ridge' of the nineteenth century was largely prepared using spades.

There is little doubt that a range of plough-types were used to cultivate the land. The early fourteenth-century account roll of Holy Trinity Priory, Dublin, notes that a carpenter was hired to make two summer ploughs and five winter ploughs.[52] Heavy ground-breaking

---

49 Muiris O'Sullivan and Liam Downey, 'Ridges and furrows', *Archaeology Ireland*, 21:2 (summer 2007), 34–7 at 36.
50 Ibid., 36–7.   **51** See, for instance, the wooden shovel and iron spade shoe from Back Lane, Dublin, in the National Museum of Ireland medieval display: 92E0051172 and 96E3008402 (KS.GA.17).   **52** Mills (ed.), *Account roll*, p. 30.

Figure 9.7 View of plough headlands at Oughterard, Co. Kildare, as they survive crossing a field today. The second fence-post is on top of one headland, and another headland is visible as a darker ridge further down the field, at the seventh fence-post (image courtesy of Tadhg O'Keeffe).

Figure 9.7 View of plough headlands at Oughterard, Co. Kildare, as they survive crossing a field today. The second fence-post is on top of one headland, and another headland is visible as a darker ridge further down the field, at the seventh fence-post (image courtesy of Tadhg O'Keeffe).

devices would have been used for bringing previously un-worked land (such as woodland or old pasture) into cultivation, while lighter ploughs (perhaps scratch ploughs, or ards) would have helped to turn light soils, as well as to cover over seed that was sown on heavier soils. The archaeological evidence for ploughs indicates an element of continuity between the tenth century and the early sixteenth century.[53] It also shows certain developments. The plough irons that survive consist of small, symmetrically shaped shares, and short, knife-shaped coulters. The share would have been positioned horizontally on the base of the plough to undercut the sod. The coulter would have been set slightly in front of and above the share to slice through the side of the sod and define the furrow's width. It appears that the best comparison for the Irish plough irons is found on a plough that survived in use on Orkney into the nineteenth century (Figure 9.8). The Orkney plough may therefore be similar to the one that was used in Ireland for much of the medieval period. Unfortunately, no plough irons have been recovered from later medieval contexts in the Dublin region, and what is known about this plough-type comes from finds across the country.

The Dublin area has produced a large number of plough pebbles, however, and these represent the most direct evidence for ploughing across the region in the thirteenth century.[54] Plough pebbles are small field stones, generally of quartz or flint, and measuring 3–4cm in length (Figure 9.9). They were inserted into the base of timber ploughs to protect the frame from wear. The pebbles would have protruded beyond the surface of the wooden frame and stood out from it. Over time, the outer face of the pebble was worn back, creating a sharply defined and lightly scratched surface. The pebbles would eventually fall out of the plough onto the field. Plough pebbles are known outside Ireland in similarly dated horizons, but they also occur in earlier and later contexts. Pebbles have been found *in situ* on medieval ploughs from Denmark, where they were used on heavy, wheeled ploughs.[55]

53 Niall Brady, 'Reconstructing a medieval Irish plough', *Primeras Jornadas Sobre Technologia Agraria Tradicional* (1993), 31–44. **54** Niall Brady, 'The plough pebbles of Ireland', *Tools and Tillage*, 6 (1988), 47–60; Niall Brady, 'Just how far can you go with a pebble? Taking another look at ploughing in medieval Ireland' in Joseph Fenwick (ed.), *Lost and found II* (Bray, 2009), pp 61–9. **55** Grith Lerhce, *Ploughing implements and tillage practices in Denmark from the Viking*

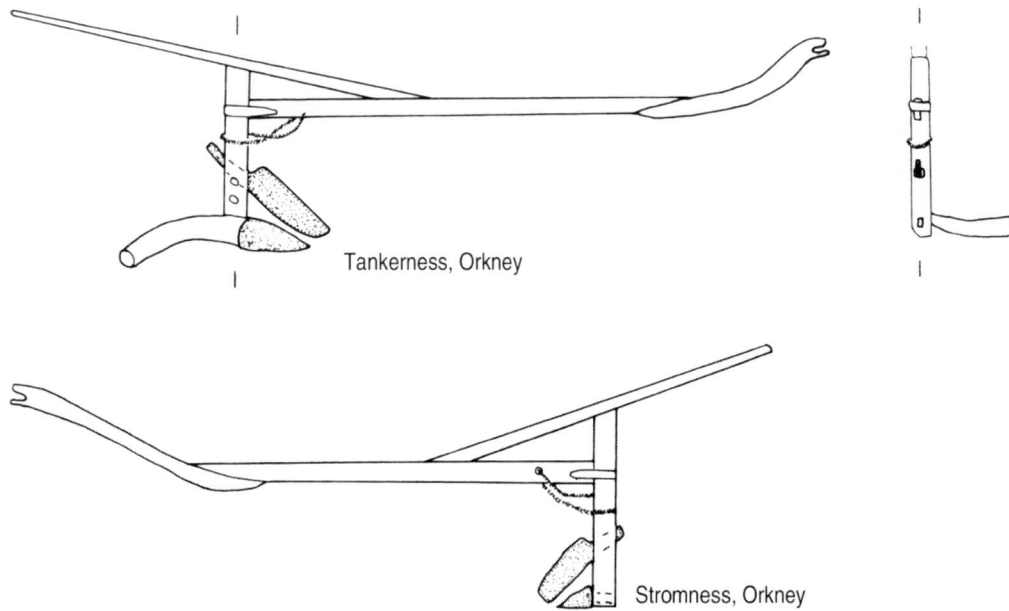

Figure 9.8 Line-drawings of Orkney ploughs (image courtesy of Niall Brady).

Tankerness, Orkney

Stromness, Orkney

In Ireland, the pebbles are consistently thirteenth century in date and seem therefore to have a particularly narrow period of use. The national distribution highlights north Dublin and Cos. Meath and Louth as the area of principal concentration, and their presence recalls the pipe roll for 1211–12, which refers to the employment of eight-ox plough-teams on certain of the de Lacy manors in Meath.[56] The distribution of pebbles can be combined with that of medieval cultivation furrows across the Dublin region, to see one indication of the extent of arable cultivation during the later

Figure 9.9 Plough pebble from Brownstown, Co. Dublin. This is one of a collection of pebbles picked up during field-walking on lands formerly belonging to the manor of Swords. The sharply defined abraded surface at the top of the picture is the facet that is worn back by the earth as the plough is pulled through the soil.

medieval period (Figure 9.10). The distributions show a focus of ploughing on the low-lying and relatively flat landscape of the Liffey Valley's lower reaches and the agriculturally rich lands to the north. There is, however, an absence of pebbles and medieval cultivation furrows in the upper reaches of the Liffey Valley and from the coastal belt south of Bray, where data from the extents indicates that there was significant arable husbandry (compare Figure 9.1). This is surely an artificial discordance between the sources that archaeologists should be able to resolve with more careful attention to the dating of furrows and surveillance for plough pebbles in these areas.

The distribution and dating context of the plough pebble in Ireland suggests that it was associated with an innovation in ploughing technology, and it occurred during a period of intensive economic activity. The pipe roll for 1211–12 preserves the only documentary reference to ploughing activity during the thirteenth century, but there are more frequent references in the fourteenth century. The account roll of Holy Trinity Priory, Dublin, for instance, notes in 1343:

period to about 1800, experimentally substantiated (Poul Kristensen, Herning, 1994).   **56** Davies and Quinn, 'Irish pipe roll of 14 John', 40.

Figure 9.10 Distribution of plough pebbles and medieval cultivation furrows in the Dublin region. Plough pebbles represent the single-most numerous artefactual witness to medieval ploughing in Ireland, while cultivation furrows also reveal the practice of arable activities. It is noticeable, however, that the picture is at a slight variance to the pattern of land-use indicated from the extent data, presented on Figure 9.1.

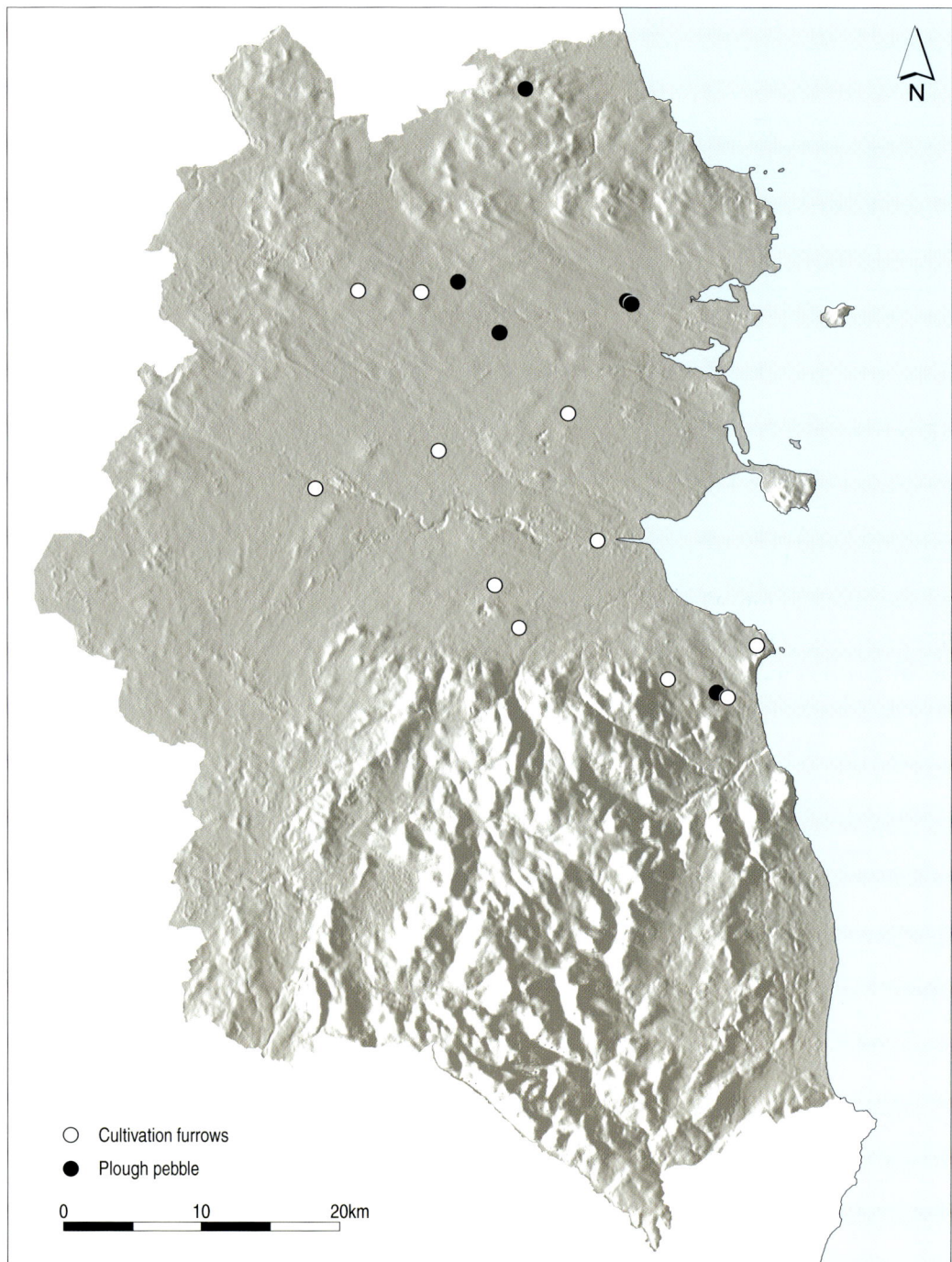

○　Cultivation furrows

●　Plough pebble

0　　　　10　　　　20km

Also in hire of a carpenter, making 2 summer ploughs and 5 winter ploughs, for 7 days at full wages [...] Also another time for 6 plough beams, 4 axle-trees, and timber for chippes (soles) of ploughs bought, 15½d.[57]

The distinction between summer ploughs and winter ploughs may reflect the different plough-types or different sowing regimes. The mention of axle-trees in the context of ploughing seems to refer to the use of wheeled ploughs. If this is the case, it represents the earliest reference to their presence in Ireland. The axle-tree is a beam or bar connecting two wheels that constitute the wheel carriage which supported the plough beam.

The extent for the manor of Cloncurry in 1304 provides information on the investment required to construct and maintain ploughs.[58] Four new ploughs were sufficient for each

---

57 Mills (ed.), *Account roll*, p. 30.　**58** *RBO*, pp 27–8.

carucate of land per annum, which suggests that ploughs had a short working-life and were expected to be renewed each year. A plough cost 3*d.*, or 2*d.* if made from one's own timber, but the expense associated with the iron components was considerably more. At Cloncurry, six stone weight of iron was deemed sufficient to provide the annual iron requirements for each plough with two garbs (a measurement of weight) of steel, while the cost of making the iron parts of the plough amounted to 4*s.* per year.[59] The estate of Adam Jordan, an escapee from Dublin Castle, included a pair of plough irons worth 10*d.*[60] When one considers that an agricultural labourer was paid 1*d.* a day, for a job that would have run from dawn to dusk, the value attached to the irons can be appreciated.

In addition to ploughing, the seed bed was prepared by harrowing, which broke down the sod further and helped prepare a friable till. Documents refer to harrowing in the context of labour inputs, but there is no indication of what the harrows looked like, and no pieces have been recognised archaeologically. Based on comparison with England, where pictures of harrows survive in medieval sources, it is likely that the harrows were made from an openwork timber frame that secured pointed tips to cut into the earth. The harrow would be pulled perhaps by a two-horse team.

Once tilled, the lands were then sown and the growing cycle began. Once again, we must refer to English sources to appreciate that sowing was presumably achieved using a broad-cast method, where a sower would carry the seed in a basket or other receptacle and perhaps simply a sack cloth secured around his neck, grab handfuls of the seed and cast the seed widely onto the tilled soil as he walked forward.[61]

The balance between crops

Most of the arable fields in the Dublin region were sown with grains (wheat, oats, barley, rye and mixtures of the same), legumes (peas and beans) and occasionally mixed crops of grains and legumes. There is no direct documentary evidence for the field cultivation of vegetables in the region during the Middle Ages, although there is a reference to a field called 'the carrotfield' in Naul, north Co. Dublin, in 1292.[62] At Kilsaran, Co. Louth, just outside the study area, fields were sown with leeks in the early fourteenth century.[63] The documentary evidence for the cultivation of industrial crops such as flax, hemp and madder is similarly scarce, although the archaeological material fills out the picture slightly.

Table 9.4 Cropped acreages on Dublin demesnes, *c.*1300–30.

MANOR	YEAR	WHEAT	OATS	BARLEY	PEAS & BEANS	PEAS & WHEAT
Cloncurry	1304	44.5	48.25			
Clondalkin	1326	116.5	104.25			
Clontarf	1308	170.5	154.5	8	8	
Colonia	1326	50	48			
Finglas	1326	96	98			
Maynooth	1328	72	74			
Swords	1326	200	5			201
Tallaght	1326	60.5	48	3		

59 A garb was a weight for thirty pieces of steel; R.E. Zupko, *A dictionary of weights and measures for the British Isles: the Middle Ages to the twentieth century* (Philadelphia, 1985), p. 168. **60** *CJR, 1308–14*, p. 153. **61** For example, Bodl. MS Rawl. D939, Section 2, a late fourteenth-century calendar, labour of the month for October, reproduced in J.W.Y. Higgs (intr.), *English rural life in the Middle Ages* (Oxford, 1965, repr. 1977). **62** TNA:PRO C133/63. **63** Gearóid

Table 9.5 Crops attached from individuals in the Dublin region, 1305–10.

NAME	PLACE	CROPS ATTACHED	YEAR	REF. (*CJR*)
Warin Oweyn	Co. Dublin	24 crannocks wheat 60 crannocks oats 6 crannocks beans & peas	1305	ii, p. 144
Nigel le Brun	Roebuck, Co. Dublin	50 crannocks wheat 40 acres wheat	1305	ii, p. 164
Thomas de Penkeston	Ballybrittan, Co. Kildare	22 crannocks wheat 18 crannocks oats 3 crannocks beans 3 crannocks peas 2½ crannocks barley	1306	ii, p. 307
Milo McBridyn	Co. Dublin	4 acres wheat & rye	1305	ii, p. 479
Geoffrey Omolan	Cruagh, Co. Dublin	3 crannocks rye 1½ acres wheat	1305	ii, p. 479
Patrick *medicus*	Co. Dublin	Barley, oats & peas	1305	ii, p. 479
Walter FitzWilliam	Co. Dublin	16 crannocks wheat 40 acres wheat & barley	1308	iii, p. 17
William le Blund	Balrothery, Co. Dublin	20 acres wheat 20 acres oats	1308	iii, p. 76
Eustace de Glenmethan	Clonmethan?, Co. Dublin	5 acres wheat & hastivell[64] 9 acres beans & peas	1308	iii, p. 86
Simon de Colbroc	Co. Dublin	5 acres wheat 1 acre barley 3 acres oats 2 acres beans & peas	1308	iii, p. 116
Richard de Grange	Co. Kildare	1 acre hastivell 1 acre wheat 4 acres oats	1310	iii, pp 147–8

The vast majority of relevant documentary references relate to the cultivation of grains and legumes. The evidence for demesne cultivation is mostly supplied by manorial extents, where details on crops are included to supplement the arable information. Judicial records frequently include valuations of sown acres and harvested crops in cases of trespass, debt or when goods are distrained. This data does not lend itself to any degree of systematic analysis as it is subject to many qualifications. It can, however, be used to highlight general distribution patterns in the cultivation of particular crops. Further evidence is supplied from municipal regulations concerned with the supply of crops into Dublin and from the records of purveyance and export which give relative quantities of various grains and legumes leaving the region. The fifteenth-century inventories for Dublin area testators also frequently list cropped acres as well as stores of grain 'in the haggard'.[65]

Mac Niocaill, 'Documents on the suppression of the Templars in Ireland', *Anal. Hib.*, 24 (1961), 183–226 at 196. **64** Hastivell appears to have been an early ripening variety of barley: see below, pp 306, 310–11.   **65** These can be found in Berry (ed.), *Register of wills and inventories*.

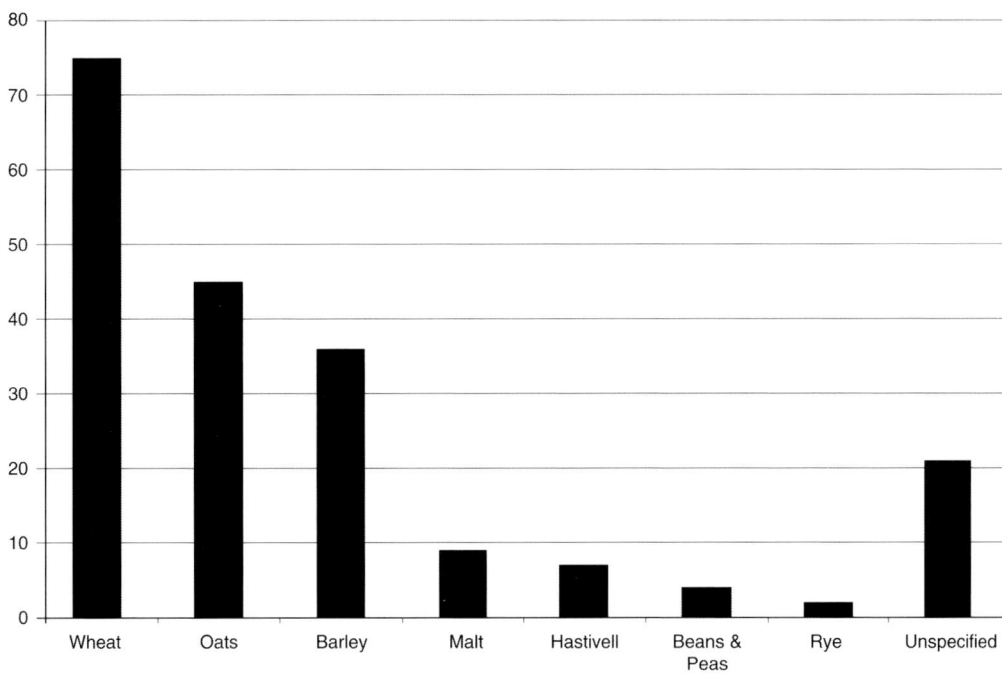

Figure 9.11 Crop data from fifty-six Dublin will inventories, 1467–83 (all of these inventories listed crops in haggards or barns, threshed or in stacks). The chart plots the percentage of wills that mention each crop.

The cultivation of wheat and oats dominated on the manorial demesnes of the region. Indeed demesnes are frequently found growing no other crops. Table 9.4 summarises information from extents and other sources *c*.1300–30. It can be seen that there was a general tendency on these manors to divide the sown arable fairly equally between wheat and oats. The information for Swords is problematic, as in this case the sown arable is taken up with wheat and a crop of 'wheat and peas', with only five acres devoted to oat cultivation. The extent for Swords also includes information relating to the sub-manors of Lusk and Werne, but no details are given on the crops grown on their arable land, which amounted to over 400 acres.[66] Perhaps some or all of this arable was devoted to oat cultivation in 1326. A valuation of the archiepiscopal manors made in 1323 records 120 acres sown with wheat and 140 acres sown with oats at Swords.[67]

This balance between wheat and oats and their preponderance over all other crops on demesnes in the late thirteenth and early fourteenth centuries is borne out by other evidence for the Dublin area and indeed for other parts of Leinster.[68] The sown acreage on the Holy Trinity manor of Clonkeen is not known but the quantities of crops harvested and received as tithes in 1344 are given in the haggard account of that year.[69] The indications are that wheat was slightly more widespread than oats, and that barley was the third crop grown. The same relationship between these three cereals can be observed in the quantities of grain recorded as received from payments of tithe.

Evidence relating to the crops of the non-demesne sector can be gleaned from an examination of the property distrained from small farmers who had defaulted on a debt or committed a felony (Table 9.5). This indicates that a wider range of crops was grown by the smaller farmers. Although wheat and oats were present in the majority of examples, the cultivation of barley, rye and legumes appears much more frequently than in those records relating to demesne agriculture.

For the fifteenth century, it is possible to examine the balance between the different crops listed in the inventories of testators from the Dublin county area (Figure 9.11). These

---

66 McNeill (ed.), *Alen's register*, p. 176.   **67** NAI RC8/13: Memoranda roll, pp 238–40.   **68** Down, 'Colonial society and economy', pp 470–1.   **69** Mills (ed.), *Account roll*, pp 77–83.

indicate that wheat retained or perhaps even exceeded its former position as the premier grain in the region. Three-quarters of the inventories that listed crops included wheat. Oats, however, had declined somewhat in prominence and the brewing grains, barley and hastivell, now equalled it in importance. Hastivell appears to have been an early ripening variety of barley, probably sown in the winter.[70] The evidence for different time periods is drawn from a variety of source-types and this must be taken into consideration when trying to track real shifts in emphasis over time. Some general patterns in crop cultivation do emerge from the documentary sources however. Firstly, the dual cultivation of wheat and oats dominated the demesne sector, particularly in the late thirteenth and early fourteenth centuries. Smaller farmers grew a wider variety of crops throughout the period, and barley and other brewing grains gradually increased their share of arable acreages in the later medieval period.

Crop types: wheat, rye, barley, oats and legumes

Wheat Wheat, more than any other grain, was grown for human consumption. Throughout the medieval period it was recognised as a standard food crop in eastern Ireland and was the preferred bread grain of the people in this area. It commanded the highest price and its high status ensured its widespread cultivation throughout the region. In the documents it is most usually called *frumentum*, although on occasion the generic term for corn (*bladum*) can be shown by its price profile to refer to wheat. There is no documentary reference to the different botanical varieties of wheat grown, and nor is there archaeological evidence for selective breeding of specific varieties of crop during the medieval period. Archaeo-botanical analysis, however, has provided some indications of the broad species type cultivated.

The most important wheats in the medieval period were bread wheat (*Triticum aestivum*) and rivet wheat (*Triticum turgidum*). The medieval pits, gullies and furrows that were excavated at Bremore (Balbriggan) contained large quantities of the former.[71] Rivet wheat is increasingly being identified at medieval sites in England but it has not yet been identified in Ireland. It is a tall and productive grain when it grows well but it is sensitive to bad weather and poor soil.[72] Spelt wheat (*Triticum spelta*), on the other hand, has a reputation for surviving a worse climate than any other wheat but it very rarely appears in medieval deposits in England. Spelt was found during excavations in Tallaght, however, where part of the boundary ditch of the medieval borough and a parallel property boundary were exposed.[73]

Excavations at Killeen Castle, Co. Meath, revealed features of early medieval and later medieval date.[74] Palaeo-environmental samples from the early medieval contexts were dominated by oats and barley with very little wheat.[75] The later medieval levels, associated with the Anglo-Norman castle and settlement, were dominated by wheat, with much less oats and very little barley. This is a pattern that is replicated across the Dublin region – there is a shift away from barley to wheat in Anglo-Norman settled areas. Anglo-Norman levels at Killeen also produced peas and beans, in percentages sufficient to suggest that crop-rotation was being practised here too.

70 R.E. Latham, *Revised medieval Latin word-list from British and Irish sources* (Oxford, 1965), p. 222.　**71** Penny Johnston, 'Analysis of plant remains, Bremore, Balbriggan, Co. Dublin (01E0370)', unpublished report, 4 Dec. 2002. **72** James Greig, 'Plant resources' in Astill and Grant (eds), *The countryside of medieval England* (1988), pp 108–27 at p. 110. **73** DEHLG file E000555 (Tallaght: Old Bawn Road); John Tierney, 'A report on the archaeo-botanical remains recovered from sites at Old Bawn Road and rere of Main Street, Tallaght, Co. Dublin' (unpublished report submitted to DEHLG, n.d.), p. 9.　**74** Baker, *The archaeology of Killeen Castle*.　**75** Mary Dillon and Penny Johnston, 'Plant remains' in Baker, *The archaeology of Killeen Castle* (2009), pp 101–11.

Figure 9.12a–d Wheat, oats and barley were the three main arable crops grown in the Dublin region throughout the Middle Ages. Rye was also grown, but to a lesser extent: (a) wheat at Brownstown, Swords, Co. Dublin (image courtesy of Fionnuala Parnell); (b) oats at Rathdown Upper, Co. Wicklow (image courtesy of Michael Connaughton); (c) barley at Naas, Co. Kildare (image courtesy of Shawn McFarlane); (d) rye at Ashbourne, Co. Meath.

Table 9.6 Disposal of wheat on two Holy Trinity manors: Clonkeen (1344–5) and Grangegorman (1343–4).

	RECEIPT OF WHEAT (PECKS)	USED IN SEED	SENT TO HOLY TRINITY	ON-MANOR FOOD LIVERIES	MALTED	SOLD
Clonkeen	1,483.75	190.50 (13%)	763 (51%)	364.75 (25%)	91 (6%)	54 (4%)
Grangegorman	761.5	241 (32%)	238 (31%)	278.5 (37%)	0	0

Wheat was rarely, if ever, used as animal fodder, but there is some evidence from the Dublin region that it was malted for brewing into ale. The survival of haggard accounts for the Holy Trinity manors of Clonkeen (1344–5) and Grangegorman (1343–4) allow the disposal pattern for wheat on these two manors to be reconstructed (Table 9.6). As the 'home manors' of a conventual institution, these manors should not be taken as typical of the demesnes in the area. One of their primary functions was to supply foodstuffs to central households. Sales, which were significant on many manors and holdings, were therefore of marginal importance.

At both Clonkeen and Grangegorman, wheat was used to bake bread for the harvest workers and it also formed the bulk of the food liveries given to manorial servants. Legumes made up the remainder of these liveries (see below). This would suggest that peasants in the Dublin region may have been more accustomed to wheaten bread than their counterparts in Britain.

Rye Rye (*secale cerale*) was primarily grown as a bread grain, and was rarely malted or used as animal feed. It produced a dark and heavy bread that was regarded mainly as food for poorer consumers.[76] Rye straw was extremely long and consequently was sought after as a roofing material. Rye can grow on much poorer soils than wheat and does well on sandy soils. On English demesnes, it was grown principally for consumption by the manorial workforce and close to London it was marketed to poor urban consumers.[77]

There is no mention of rye cultivation on manorial demesnes in the Dublin region, although there is evidence that it was grown by lords in some other parts of the country.[78] What evidence there is, relates to its cultivation by small-holders and in the early fourteenth century by Irish farmers. According to Fergus Kelly, rye was of considerable importance in the early Irish economy and it appears second to wheat in the eighth-century law-text *Bretha déin chécht*, which lists seven cereal-grains in order of their relative prestige.[79] In 1305, rye was mentioned among the chattels of various Irish felons who lived in the south of Co. Dublin, probably in the area around Cruagh (see Table 9.5).[80] Milo Mcbridyn had four acres sown with wheat and rye, probably a reference to the cultivation of the mixed crop maslin, while Geoffrey Omolan had three crannocks of rye in his possession.

In the fifteenth century, rye and maslin were cultivated in sufficient quantities in Ireland for them to form part of an export trade. In 1471, a petition of the Commons of the Irish parliament claimed that great dearth and famine had befallen the king's people of Ireland 'through the shipping of wheat, malt, rye, maslin and other grains to England, Scotland and Wales'.[81] References to its cultivation in the Dublin area remain scarce in the fifteenth

76 Greig, 'Plant resources', p. 112.   **77** Campbell, Galloway, Keene and Murphy, *A medieval capital*, pp 39, 121–2. **78** It was grown in Co. Wexford on the earl of Norfolk's manor of Old Ross and on the Templar manor of Kilcloggan: PRO SC6/1238/43; Mac Niocaill, 'Suppression of the Templars', 201.   **79** Kelly, *Early Irish farming*, pp 219–22. **80** *CJR, 1305–7*, pp 479, 485.   **81** *CARD*, 1, pp 172–3.

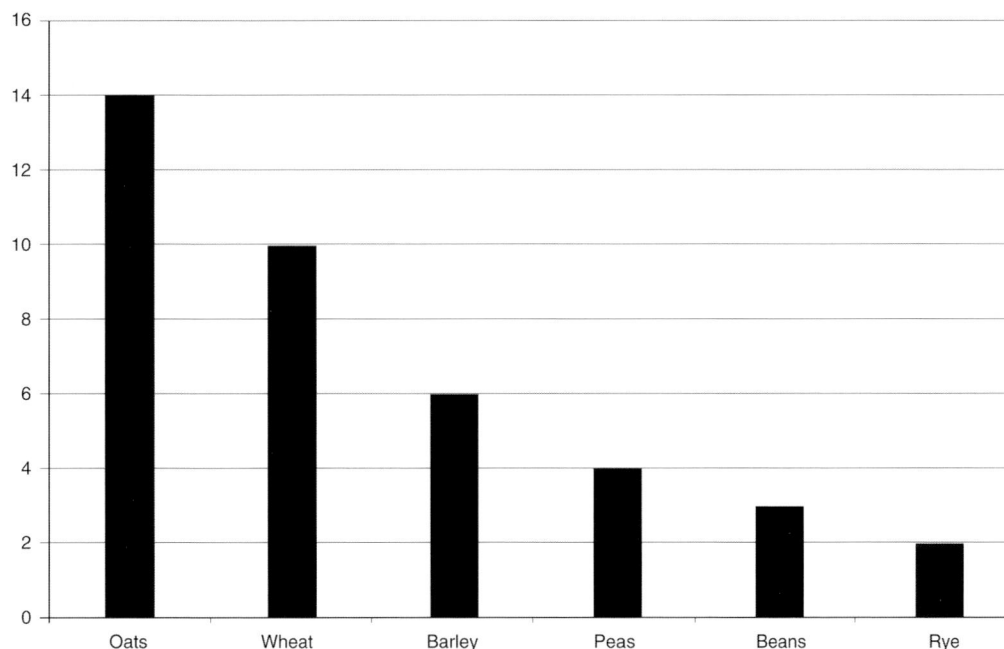

Figure 9.13 Percentage of archaeological excavations in the Dublin region on which selected plant remains occur in medieval contexts (based on an analysis of fifty reports).

century. Only one of the Dublin testators appears to have been growing rye in the region at the end of the century. John Kempe of Hollywood, Co. Dublin, who made his will in 1471, left two acres of rye to the fraternity of Hollywood, another field of rye to the vicar of Hollywood, half an acre of rye to the chapel of Grallagh and two acres of rye to a certain John Bowill.[82] He also left a total of twelve 'measures' of rye to a variety of individuals. His bequests include a small quantity of oats, but there is no mention of wheat. It appears likely that a good proportion of his twelve acres was sown with rye.

When preservation is adequate, rye can be identified from its tapering grains and also from its chaff and elongated pollen grains. On medieval sites in England, it is frequently found and is sometimes the most abundant or second most abundant cereal represented.[83] It has also been found widely on early medieval sites in Ireland, although it forms only a small percentage of the total cereal sample.[84] The archaeo-botanical record for the Dublin area, however, adds weight to the conclusion based on the documentary sources that rye was a minority crop in Dublin and its region (Figure 9.13). Some grains of rye were found at Nangor, Co. Dublin, and rye was also present in twelfth-century levels in Fishamble Street and thirteenth-century contexts at Skreen, Co. Meath.[85]

Barley Barley (*Hordeum vulgare*), which was most often grown as a spring-sown crop, could be used in a variety of different ways. It was used for human food in the form of coarse bread, it was brewed into ale and it was also fed to animals, particularly those being fattened for the table.[86] In some parts of Britain, notably lowland Scotland, north-west England and parts of Wales and Cornwall, barley bread was a staple food.[87] In areas where wheat grew well, however, the principal use of barley was for malting. Barley is particularly tolerant of climatic changes and grows well on light to medium soils.

82 Berry (ed.), *Register of wills and inventories*, pp 13–15.   **83** Greig, 'Plant resources', p. 112.   **84** M.A. Monk, 'The archaeobotanical evidence for field crop plants in early historic Ireland' in J.M. Renfrew (ed.), *New light on early farming: recent developments in palaeo-ethnobotany* (Edinburgh, 1991), pp 315–28 at p. 318.   **85** Penny Johnston, 'Environmental analysis of samples from Nangor townland (Grange Castle International Business Park), Clondalkin, Dublin 22 (00E754)', unpublished report, 5 Aug. 2001; G.F. Mitchell, *Archaeology and environment in early Dublin* (Dublin, 1987), p. 30; Grainne Kelly, 'Analysis of the plant remains: Skreen 05E0321', unpublished report, 2006.   **86** Charles Parain, 'The evolution of agricultural technique' in M.M. Postan (ed.), *The Cambridge economic history of Europe, vol. 1: the agrarian life of the Middle Ages* (Cambridge, 1966), pp 125–79 at p. 161.   **87** Greig, 'Plant resources',

Both two-row and four-row varieties appear to have been widely cultivated in early medieval Ireland. Barley bread is mentioned in the historic sources although frequently linked with austerity or abstinence.[88] In the Dublin region, barley dominated the cereal remains at Rosepark, Balrothery (where radiocarbon dates suggest that the site was occupied in the seventh century).[89] At Flemington, Co. Dublin, barley and oats were found together in early medieval samples in a context that suggests they may have been deliberately sown together.[90] This mixture of crops appears to have been widespread; it is termed 'dredge' in England and 'siprys' in Wales.[91] These are grain crops that are deliberately sown together to reduce the risk of total crop failure and is a recognised risk-buffering strategy in traditional farming societies.[92] The yield from mixed crops of barley and oats was used primarily for brewing. At Fishamble Street in Dublin (c.AD917–80), two deposits contained mixtures of barley and oat grains. These were found in a ratio of about five-to-one (barley to oats) in both samples. The similar ratios in both samples suggested that this was a preferred mixture.[93] In the mixture at Flemington, however, the proportions were almost half and half.

The palaeo-environmental samples from late thirteenth-/early fourteenth-century contexts at Tullykane, Co. Meath, contained barley, wheat and oats, and one possible bean.[94] According to John Tierney, who carried out the post-excavation analysis, the plant remains seem to represent fully-processed crops that had been threshed, winnowed and sieved. The fact that wheat, barley and oats were present together in most samples, indicates that they may have been grown as mixed crops.

It comes as something of a surprise to find barley so poorly represented on archaeological sites and in the records for crop cultivation on demesnes in the Dublin region before the mid-fourteenth century. On those manors represented in Table 9.4, only Clontarf and Tallaght devoted small acreages to barley. On both these manors barley represented between 2 and 3 per cent of grain acreages. Dredge is not mentioned on any of these manors. This represents a marked difference between crop cultivation on demesnes in the Dublin region and those in England at a similar period. In the early fourteenth century, demesnes close to London for example, devoted, on average, 20 per cent of their grain acreages to these crops. This rose to 32 per cent in the later fourteenth century due to increased demand for brewing grains from both urban and rural consumers.[95] This pattern was not confined to the Dublin region, and there is little evidence for the cultivation of barley on demesnes outside the area either. The earl of Norfolk's demesnes situated in Cos. Kildare, Carlow and Wexford, devoted very little land to barley.[96]

It may be that barley cultivation was more widespread on the small holdings of the Dublin region. The evidence from the judicial distraints suggests that this might have been the case (Table 9.5). In 1306, a felon in Co. Kildare had an acre sown with 'winter barley' and a further two acres sown with oats and barley (which may be a rare reference to dredge).[97] In 1308, the goods of Simon de Colbroc of Co. Dublin included one acre of barley, while Eustace de Glenmethan (Clonmethan, Co. Dublin) had five acres sown with wheat and hastivell in the same year.[98] An acre of hastivell was also sown by Richard le Graunger,

pp 110–11.   **88** Kelly, *Early Irish farming*, pp 330, 344.   **89** Penny Johnston, 'Analysis of plant remains, Rosepark, Balrothery, Co. Dublin, Licence no. 99E0155' (unpublished report, Feb. 2002).   **90** Penny Johnston, 'Analysis of plant remains, Flemington Site 4, Co. Dublin, Licence no. 02E0296' (unpublished report, June 2003).   **91** Kelly, *Early Irish farming*, p. 227.   **92** Glynis Jones and Paul Halstead, 'Maslins, mixtures and monocrops: on the interpretation of archaeological crop samples of heterogenous composition', *Journal of Archaeological Science*, 22 (1995), 103–14. **93** Geraghty, *Viking Dublin*, p. 49.   **94** John Tierney, 'An assessment of the plant remains from Tullykane, Kilmessan, Co. Meath', unpublished report, 2001.   **95** J.A. Galloway, 'Driven by drink? Ale consumption and the agrarian economy of the London region, c.1300–1400' in Carlin and Rosenthal (eds), *Food and eating in medieval Europe* (1998), pp 87–100 at p. 97.   **96** Down, 'Colonial society and economy', p. 471.   **97** *CJR, 1305–7*, p. 494. It is not clear what Mills translated as 'winter barley'.   **98** *CJR, 1308–14*, pp 86, 116.

who was accused of a murder committed in Clane in 1310.[99] Adam Jordan, who escaped from Dublin Castle in 1310, had some barley among his chattels, while John Arthur, a *hibernicus* who lived on the manor of Leixlip, had two crannocks and six pecks of barley in his possession when he died in 1324.[100]

The documentary evidence for barley cultivation increases from the mid-fourteenth century. Two types of barley were cultivated at Clonkeen in the 1340s: one was hastivell and the other was *ordeum*, which is taken to be the two-rowed, spring-sown variety.[101] In 1344, hastivell was the first crop to be harvested at Clonkeen, suggesting that it was sown early.[102] Four crannocks of each variety were harvested from the demesne lands and an additional two crannocks of hastivell and ten crannocks of barley were received as tithes. Apart from some barley set aside as seed, all this grain was malted on the manor. The hastivell malt was expended on the manor while the barley malt (along with wheat and oat malt) was sent into Dublin to be used in the monastery.

A range of other sources include references to barley and mixtures of barley from the late fourteenth to the sixteenth century. The inventory of John Hamound, a Dublin tanner and shoemaker, who had land in the Luttrelstown area, lists eight acres sown with barley in 1388.[103] In 1450, a list of customs leviable on agriculturalists bringing grain into Dublin included barley, oat malt, dredge malt and wheat malt.[104] The evidence from the fifteenth-century Dublin inventories shows that barley cultivation and consumption was fairly widespread across the region at this date. Thirty-six per cent of the inventories that list crops included barley, 7 per cent listed hastivell and 9 per cent noted malt (which may have been oat). In 1513, Thomas Plunkett was growing barley at Dunsoghly as it was included among the crops he gave to Holy Trinity at that time.[105] While the use of barley for malting does appear to have increased throughout the medieval period, it did not completely displace oats. In the sixteenth century, the vicars choral of Christ Church continued to receive food liveries which included oat malt as well as barley malt.[106]

As mentioned above, barley was very commonly found in early medieval deposits in the Dublin region. In the later period, however, it becomes less visible in the archaeo-botanical record. Barley was found at rural sites in Bremore, Kindlestown, Skreen, Naas and (in larger quantities) at Nangor. At Kindlestown, a very small amount was found, while at Bremore barley represented just one per cent of the cereal sample. At Nangor, however, 10 per cent of the sample was made up of barley. Barley appears to have been absent from the samples at Dundrum Castle and Tallaght – this last mentioned being the location of one of the few demesnes known from documentary sources to have grown barley.

Oats Oats were widely used and grown in virtually all parts of Ireland throughout the medieval period and they are frequently cited as the dominant cereal type.[107] This may be related to climate, as oats are seen as being more tolerant of difficult growing conditions than any other crop. 'They were the staple grain in much of the north and west of England where low temperatures and high rainfall hindered other grains from germinating and ripening'.[108] The common oat (*Avena sativa*) and the bristle oat (*Avena strigosa*) were both widely cultivated as a spring crop in Britain, either on their own or together with barley as dredge.[109] The grains of oats are not determinable to species unless chaff fragments are also

99 *CJR, 1308–14*, pp 147–8.   **100** *CJR, 1308–14*, p. 153; NAI RC8: Memoranda roll, pp 94–7. For further discussion of *hibernici*, see pp 184–5, this volume.   **101** Mills (ed.), *Account roll*, pp 79–80, 213.   **102** Ibid., p. 64 – six men were hired to reap the *hastivell* before the main harvest commenced on 5 Aug.   **103** *CARD*, I, pp 127–9.   **104** *CARD*, I, p. 275.   **105** *CCCD*, no. 400.   **106** *CCCD*, no. 1265.   **107** M.A. Monk, 'Evidence from macroscopic plant remains for crop husbandry in prehistoric and early historic Ireland: a review', *JIA*, 3 (1985/6), 31–6 at 34.   **108** Campbell, *Seigniorial agriculture*, p. 225.   **109** Greig, 'Plant resources', p. 111.

Table 9.7 Plant remains from selected medieval excavations in Dublin and its region.

		DUBLIN CITY										DUBLIN REGION								
Category	Plant	Dublin excavations (Mitchell)	Patrick Street: 14th century	Patrick Street: 13th century	Patrick Street: 12th century	Thomas Street (96E0280)	Bride Street (93E0153) [EM*]	Ship Street Great (01E0772)	High Street, 9–12 (E000548)	Cook Street, 16–17 (92E0083)	John Dillon Street (98E0158)	Carmanhall (55m) (02E0074)	Tallaght: Old Bawn Road	Naas: Burke's Pharmacy	Parkwest: Galanstown	Nangor (00E0754)	Bremore (01E0370)	Dundrum Castle (E000419)	Kindlestown (01E0084)	Skreen (05E0321)
Fruits	Apple	•	•		•		•		•						•					
Fruits	Cherry	•																		
Fruits	Fig	•	•							•									•	
Fruits	Grape	•	•																	
Fruits	Prunus											•								
Fruits	Plum	•							•		•									
Berries	Sloe	•			•				•		•				•				•	
Berries	Haw				•															
Berries	Elder	•			•		•						•	•						•
Berries	Bilberry		•		•						•									
Berries	Strawberry	•								•										
Berries	Raspberry		•		•															
Berries	Rowan	•																		
Berries	Frochan	•																		
Berries	Blackberry	•	•	•	•	•	•		•	•	•								•	•
Cereals	Barley	•					4	•	•			•		•		10%	1%		•	1%
Cereals	Oat	•	•	•	•		43	•	•				•	•		28%	10%		•	26%
Cereals	Spelt												•							
Cereals	Wheat	•	•	•			6	•						•		37%	48%		•	35%
Cereals	Rye (secale)	•														•				3%
Cereals	Straw					•			•	•	•									
Vegetables	Bean																		•	1%
Vegetables	Peas												•		•				•	11%
Vegetables	Legumes																			
Vegetables	Lentils												•							
Vegetables	Brassica	•							•											
Vegetables	Horsebean											•								
Vegetables	Mallow	•																		
Vegetables	Vetch	•					•													
Vegetables	Radish	•																		•
Weeds	Black bindweed																		•	
Weeds	Knotgrass						•												•	•
Weeds	Dock			•																
Weeds	Fat hen	•					•						•						•	•
Weeds	Clover	•																		
Weeds	Corn cockle	•	•		•	•			•	•	•									
Weeds	Corn marigold	•	•		•					•										
Edible plants	Watercress		•																	
Edible plants	Wild carrot	•		•																
Edible plants	Wild celery	•	•																	
Edible plants	Wild radish																		•	
Nuts	Hazelnut	•	•	•	•		•	•	•		•	•							•	•
Nuts	Walnut	•																		
Seeds	Black mustard	•			•															
Seeds	Mustard	•																		
Seeds	Rape	•																		
Herbs	Parsley		•																	
Herbs	Hemlock	•																		
Herbs	Fennel	•																		
Indust. crop	Flax	•	•		•				•	•	•			•						
Indust. crop	Hemp		•		•															
Indust. crop	Hops															•				
Miscellaneous	Corn salad																		•	
Miscellaneous	Hedge	•																		
Miscellaneous	Lucern	•																		
Miscellaneous	Meld	•																		
Miscellaneous	Sedge		•	•			•													•

found; however the cultivated or common oat (*Avena sativa*) has been recognised at several sites in the Dublin region.

Oats were put to a number of different uses, depending on the availability of other grains and to some extent on personal taste. They were a cheap and plentiful source of human food, either baked into flat cakes or added as an ingredient to stews and pottages. They were also malted and brewed into somewhat inferior ale. They were important as a fodder crop for horses, which were used extensively for farm work, transport, hunting and warfare (see below, pp 327–32). Oat cultivation is thus frequently seen as characteristic of areas where there was both a large market for fodder, such as urban hinterlands, and a concentration of poorer consumers.

Both documentary and archaeo-botanical information for the Dublin region indicate the importance of oats from an early date. As can been seen above (Table 9.4), it was the largest crop (in terms of sown acres) on three demesnes in the region – Cloncurry, Finglas and Maynooth – and it came a close second to wheat on several others. Oats were present in virtually all cereal deposits from both rural and urban sites in the region (Table 9.7). It was the most common cereal at Kindlestown Castle, but at Dundrum Castle it was second in importance to wheat by a long way. Such conflicting evidence makes it difficult to formulate any 'status'-type explanations for the relative importance of cereals, particularly given the uncertainty as to whether the deposits represented human or animal food.

It is possible to track the disposal of oats on the two Holy Trinity manors of Clonkeen and Grangegorman (Table 9.8). Clonkeen received a considerable quantity of oats from the demesne harvest and from tithes (roughly half from each source). Of this, 19 per cent was set aside as seed for the following year's crop. The cart horses on the manor, along with the horses of visitors and the prior's palfreys, consumed some 10 per cent of the stock of oats. A very small proportion went towards human food, in the form of pottage, but the greatest use was for converting into malt for brewing. Some of this malt was used on the manor to provide ale for the harvest workers, but most was delivered to the cellarer of Holy Trinity to be brewed for the uses of the community.

Grangegorman harvested a very small quantity of oats in 1343–4 and also received small quantities through tithe and purchase. There is no account of seed set aside for the next year, although a small quantity of the receipt remains unaccounted for. Fifteen pecks were expended as fodder for the prior's riding horses but, as was the case at Clonkeen, most of the oats was malted. It would be dangerous to extrapolate too much from this evidence, but it does underline the importance of oats as a brewing grain in the region and its very minor role as a food grain. Its secondary use as a fodder grain for horses is also apparent.

The evidence above, combined with the lack of evidence for barley cultivation, would suggest that up to the early fourteenth century at least, most of the ale drunk in the Dublin region was brewed from oat malt, with a smaller quantity of wheat malt used to supply a superior drink to the upper end of the market. Moreover, there is no evidence that barley or barley malt was sent out of Ireland during the great purveyances of the late thirteenth and early fourteenth centuries, while wheat and oat malt was sent in some quantities. In 1296, for example, one hundred quarters of oat malt and twenty-two quarters of wheat malt were purchased in Dublin for shipment to Wales.[110]

---

110 *CDI, 1293–1301*, no. 345, p. 159.

Table 9.8 Disposal of oats on two Holy Trinity manors: Clonkeen (1344–5) and Grangegorman (1343–4).

	RECEIPT OF OATS (PECKS)	USED IN SEED	FODDER FOR HORSES	ON-MANOR FOOD LIVERIES	MALTED	SOLD
Clonkeen	1,869	357 (19%)	186 (10%)	21 (1%)	1305 (70%)	0
Grangegorman	91	0	15 (16%)	0	74 (81%)	0

Studies of brewing grains in England suggest that barley gradually overtook oats as the preferred brewing grain at some time during the thirteenth century, although the 'conservative' practice of using oats did continue, especially in some religious houses.[111] It is possible that the same trend, with an element of time-lag, also occurred in the Dublin region.

Legumes The cultivation of legumes – peas, beans and vetches – as field crops was widespread in medieval England on demesnes and small holdings.[112] They were cultivated alone, as a mixed crop (that is, peas and beans) and as grain-legume mixtures. They were used as human food and animal fodder in a variety of ways. The importance of legumes as an element in the diet of poorer consumers emerges in the analysis of maintenance agreements where peas and beans together represented 9 per cent of the total crops mentioned.[113] White and green peas were dried and either ground down for use as a bread ingredient or added whole to soups and pottages where they formed a useful source of protein. Green peas were also eaten fresh as peascods. There were also different varieties of beans – some used for human consumption in the same way as peas, and others, such as the coarse bean or 'horse bean', used for animal fodder. Horse bread, which was usually made from ground beans, was a popular fodder. Vetches were grown principally as a fodder, but became human food in times of famine.[114]

Legumes also played an important role in replenishing the fertility of the soil as they acted as nitrogen fixers. This quality was recognised by medieval farmers and in some regions of England legume cultivation formed part of intensive cropping systems.[115] Legumes were sown on arable land to provide a nitrogen boost between successive grain crops, and they were also sown on land before it was left fallow. Further benefits were obtained by feeding animals on standing crops of legumes and then ploughing in the remaining stalks together with the animal dung.

There is little evidence to suggest that the cultivation of legumes in medieval Ireland formed part of intensive cropping regimes. In the Dublin region, it appears that they were primarily grown for consumption by humans and animals. They were grown on some (but by no means all) of the demesnes for which evidence survives. Eight acres sown with peas and beans were recorded on the Templar manor of Clontarf in the early fourteenth century and apparently over 200 acres were sown with a mixture of wheat and peas on the

111 Campbell, Galloway, Keene and Murphy, *A medieval capital*, p. 25. On the merits/demerits of ale brewed from oats, see H.S.A. Fox, 'Devon and Cornwall' in Miller (ed.), *The agrarian history of England and Wales, vol. 3*, pp 303–7. **112** Campbell, *Seigniorial agriculture*, pp 228–30. **113** Christopher Dyer, 'English diet in the later Middle Ages' in T.H. Aston, P.R. Coss, C.C. Dyer and Joan Thirsk (eds), *Social relations and ideas: essays in honour of R.H. Hilton* (Cambridge, 1983), pp 191–216 at p. 201. **114** C.A. Wilson, *Food and drink in Britain* (London, 1973), p. 183; John Gerarde, *The herbal or generall historie of plantes: very much enlarged and amended by Thomas Johnson* (London, 1633), p. 1226. **115** B.M.S. Campbell, 'Agricultural progress in medieval England: some evidence from eastern Norfolk', *EHR*, 36 (1983), 26–46 at 31–3; F.J. Green, 'The archaeological and documentary evidence for plants from the medieval period in England' in Willem van Zeist and W.A. Casparie (eds), *Plants and ancient man: studies in palaeoethnobotany*

archiepiscopal manor of Swords in 1326.[116] Cultivation of legumes does appear to have been important on the archiepiscopal lands in the thirteenth century, as they were in a position to supply 124 crannocks of beans and peas to the king's armies in Wales in 1290.[117] A quantity of beans was stolen from one of the archbishop's haggards in the manor of Colonia/St Sepulchre in the mid-thirteenth century.[118] Lay lords also grew legumes: Fromond le Brun was reported to have sixty acres sown with wheat, peas and oats at Donnybrook in 1313.[119]

Beans and peas were grown on the Holy Trinity manor of Clonkeen, where they formed an important element in the food liveries for the manorial *famuli*. In 1334–5, a total of five crannocks, seven pecks of '*fabe et pise*' was harvested on the demesne, but a further thirteen crannocks, one peck were received as tithes, indicating that legumes were widely grown in the locality.[120] Over 50 per cent of the beans and peas were given as food liveries to the Clonkeen servants and a further half a crannock was given to Brother John Comyn, seneschal of Holy Trinity, 'to bake bread for his horse'. The remainder was sent to the bailiffs of the Holy Trinity manors of Glasnevin and Grangegorman, in all probability to form part of the food liveries on those manors (Grangegorman did not grow any legumes that year). No legumes were sown in Clonkeen the following year, suggesting that these three manors may have been part of a reciprocal system whereby one manor cultivated legumes and supplied the other two.

The importance of legumes in the food liveries of Clonkeen is notable, as they formed almost 30 per cent of the *mixtura*, as it was called, which was shared out between the bailiff, sergeant, janitor, carter, four ploughmen, cowherd, shepherd and the woman who made the malt.[121] If Clonkeen was in any way typical of settlements in the region, it would suggest that legumes formed an important part of the diet of poorer consumers in the Dublin countryside. No legumes were sent from the manor to Holy Trinity, apart from the beans for horse bread, which would suggest that it did not form part of the normal diet of the monks.[122]

The quantities of legumes received as tithes into Clonkeen also suggest their widespread cultivation outside the manorial demesnes.[123] Further evidence is provided by the records of the justiciar's court, which include numerous references to thefts and distraints of small quantities of peas and beans as well as their cultivation on small-holdings. In the early fourteenth century, several men were accused of stealing three pecks of peas worth 5*s.* from the church of St Stephen near Dublin.[124] These may have been tithes, and their high price – in excess of 13*s.* a crannock – suggests that this was a year of severe scarcity, if not famine. In a debt case in Dublin in 1313, the debtor was obliged to forfeit a crop of beans worth 4*s.*[125]

Large quantities of legumes, particularly beans, were shipped out of Ireland in the late thirteenth and early fourteenth centuries to feed the king's armies in Wales and Scotland. It is not stated whether they were for human or animal consumption but it may be supposed that a lot of the beans were intended for feeding the horses in the form of horse bread.

Archaeo-botanical evidence for legumes is relatively rare; their straw was not usually used as a fuel and therefore charred remains are infrequent.[126] Peas and beans were identified among the remains from a hearth at Kindlestown Castle.[127] A possible pea was found among the samples (otherwise dominated by wheat) from Merrywell, Co. Meath.[128] Some legumes,

(Rotterdam, 1984), pp 99–114 at p. 107.   **116** Mac Niocaill, 'Suppression of the Templars', 214; McNeill (ed.), *Alen's register*, p. 176.   **117** *CDI, 1285–92*, no. 736, pp 344–5.   **118** McNeill (ed.), *Alen's register*, p. 103.   **119** NAI KB 1/1: Justiciar roll 6–7 Ed. II, m.92.   **120** Mills (ed.), *Account roll*, pp 80–1.   **121** Ibid., pp 83–5.   **122** It was an important element in the monastic diet in some English houses: see James Bond, 'Production and consumption of food and drink in the medieval monastery' in G.D. Keevill, Mick Aston and T.A. Hall (eds), *Monastic archaeology* (Oxford, 2001), pp 54–87 at p. 65.   **123** Sheaves of beans and peas are also recorded among the tithes of the rectory of Slane in 1288 (*CDI, 1285–92*, p. 293).   **124** NAI KB 2/7: Justiciar roll 8–9 Ed. II, m.14.   **125** NAI KB 1/1: Justiciar roll 6–7 Ed. II, m.76. **126** Greig, 'Plant resources', p. 113.   **127** Penny Johnston, 'Analysis of plant remains' in Simpson, 'Dublin's southern frontier' (2003), pp 361–5.   **128** Archaeological Services Durham University (ASDU), 'Merrywell 1, M3 Motorway

including peas, were found at Nangor and horse bean was found at Old Bawn in Tallaght.[129] Samples from the medieval pits, gullies and furrows that were excavated at Bremore (Balbriggan) contained large amounts of bread wheat mixed with smaller components of legumes (a composition similar to the documented food liveries at Clonkeen mentioned above).[130] At Nangor, legumes were found more often in samples from furrows and gullies than in pit fills. Carbonised pulses (probably peas and beans) were found at Baltrasna, Co. Meath, in a ditch fill which contained waste material from processing. This suggests that they were being ground for consumption by humans or animals.[131] Among the palaeo-environmental remains recovered from a thirteenth-century cereal-drying kiln at Skreen, Co. Meath, were beans and peas, with the latter being 'particularly abundant', and accounting for 11 per cent of the sample.[132] More peas were found in a nearby pit.

There does not appear to be documentary evidence for the cultivation of vetches or lentils (*Lens culinaris*) in medieval Ireland. However, both have appeared in plant remains assemblages from the Dublin region. Excavations of a medieval site in Naas produced remains of lentils along with peas, while one charred vetch seed turned up at Dundrum Castle.[133] Vetches were also identified in Dublin city excavations, including at Bride Street, although in these cases it is impossible to tell whether they were weeds or remains from cultivated crops.

Industrial crops

Archaeological evidence indicates that industrial crops such as flax, hemp and madder were grown in the Dublin region during the medieval period (see Table 9.7). Flax could be grown for its seeds (to be eaten whole or refined for oil) as well as for fibre. It was also used as a medicine and as animal food. When grown for use as a fibre, it would be sown in spring, pulled up when ripe, retted (soaked) in a pool of water, then processed (to separate the linen fibres), spun and finally woven.[134] Linseed, the seed of the flax plant, can be eaten in bread and stews. Seeds and capsules of cultivated flax have been found at several sites in Dublin, and were particularly numerous in early twelfth-century contexts on Fishamble Street.[135] Some of these seeds may have been ground to produce linseed oil, as the recovery of fragments of the seed capsules and occasional seeds may be the waste from this process. Seeds and fragments from flax were found in cess deposits at John Dillon Street, which suggests that they were being eaten.[136] Nonetheless, Geraghty suggests that this was not an important part of the diet in medieval Dublin.[137]

In thirteenth-century levels at Fishamble Street, both ripe seeds and immature capsules were found which may have come from plants that had been retted. There were also occasional fibres which may have been from linen. Weeds of wet ground were sometimes found, and these may have been carried in from the ponds where the flax was retted.[138] A flax-retting pit was found at Wood Quay and a pit at High Street contained cultivated flax

Project, Co. Meath, Ireland: environmental analysis, Report 1752' (unpublished report on behalf of Archaeological Consultancy Services Ltd, 2008). **129** Johnston, 'Environmental analysis of samples from Nangor'; DEHLG file E000555 (Tallaght: Old Bawn Road). **130** Johnston, 'Analysis of plant remains, Bremore'. **131** Donal Fallon, 'Continuity: the archaeological and documentary evidence for medieval to modern rural settlement and landholding in the townland of Baltrasna, Ratoath, Co. Meath' in Corlett and Potterton (eds), *Rural settlement in medieval Ireland* (2009), pp 79–90; Susan Lyons, 'N2 Finglas-Ashbourne road scheme – Site 17/18: flot assessment' (unpublished Headland Archaeology report, 2006). **132** Kelly, 'Analysis of the plant remains: Skreen 05E0321'. **133** DEHLG file 02E0955 (Burkes Pharmacy, Main Street Naas) – environmental report by Penny Johnston; DEHLG file E000419 (Dundrum Castle): appendix 4, Meriel McClatchie, 'The archaeobotanical material'. **134** James Greig, 'Plant resources', p. 122. **135** Mitchell, *Archaeology and environment*, p. 10. **136** Penny Johnston, 'Plant remains, John Dillon Street (98E0158)'. **137** Geraghty, *Viking Dublin*. **138** Mitchell, *Archaeology and environment*, p. 22.

bolls (capsules) identified as waste from processing of flax to linen.[139] There is less evidence of flax from rural sites, although it was represented in the samples taken from the medieval (post-1170) site at Old Bawn Road, Tallaght.[140] Flax seeds are very hard to move naturally, and so their discovery in an area is a very good indicator of the former cultivation of flax there.

The paucity of documentary references to flax cultivation may indicate that in the region it was largely grown by small-holders in plots and gardens and not on the better-documented holdings of the lords and tenants-in-chief. In the early sixteenth century, the lease of the manor of Clonkeen included a 'flax yard'.[141] Although this is not referred to in earlier documentary sources, it may have been linked to processing of the tenants' flax. In medieval England, although flax and hemp were extensively grown on peasant holdings, they rarely appear on demesnes apart from occasionally as a garden crop.[142] Furthermore, while it is clear from the extensive export trade in linen that flax was widely grown in the north and west of Ireland, documentary references to flax-growing are 'curiously rare' here also.[143]

Yields and seeding rates

Information on yields and seeding rates is scarce and problematic. The only completely reliable source for this information is a grange account with marginal yield figures inserted by the manorial auditor or a consecutive series of demesne accounts which allow the quantities harvested to be matched with the quantities sown the previous year.[144] The one surviving clear statement of crop yields from the Dublin region is contained in the 1304 extent for the manor of Cloncurry, Co. Kildare. On this manor, wheat was sown at a rate of five bushels to an acre and oats at twelve bushels. An acre of wheat was said to yield two-and-a-half crannocks on average and an acre of oats, two crannocks. This would indicate a four-fold return for wheat and a return of 2.7 for oats.

There is considerable doubt though, as to the size of the acre used at Cloncurry, primarily because of the unusually high value placed on an acre of arable (20*d*. – see above) but also because of the seeding rates cited above. For example, in the London region *c.*1300, the average seeding rate per acre for wheat was 2.8 bushels, while oats were sown at a rate of 4.8 bushels per acre.[145] High or very high seeding rates were classified as over 3.5 bushels for wheat and 6 bushels for oats and were associated with the most intensive cropping systems found on the best soils of central and eastern Kent. The return for seed recorded at Cloncurry, however, is on a par with that encountered in the London region, where wheat yielded on average between 3.8 and 4.1 bushels for each bushel sown and oats 2.7–2.8 bushels.

With regard to the Holy Trinity manor of Clonkeen, it is possible to apply a method of yield calculation known as the 'internal method'.[146] This involves comparing the quantity of grain harvested in one year with that sown in the next and is based on the assumption that on average the amounts and acreages sown remained much the same from one year to the next. On this basis, in 1344–5, the yield of wheat at Clonkeen was 4.2; barley was 2.3 and oats 2.6. These figures compare closely with those pertaining in medieval England. It is not possible to estimate the seeding rates at Clonkeen, as the acreage sown is not known, but it is possible to calculate the percentage of harvested grain set aside for seed in 1344–5. Wheat seed represented 26 per cent of harvested grain, while 36 per cent of the recorded harvest of

139 Brenda Collins, 'Plant remains, High Street, 9–12'.   **140** John Tierney, 'Archaeo-botanical remains from Old Bawn Road'.   **141** *CCCD*, no. 1189.   **142** Campbell, *Seigniorial agriculture*, p. 213.   **143** K.W. Nicholls, 'Gaelic society and economy' in Cosgrove (ed.), *A new history of Ireland: II* (1993), pp 412–13.   **144** On methods of calculating medieval yields, see R.V. Lennard, 'Statistics of corn yields in medieval England: some critical questions', *Economic History*, 3:11 (1936), 173–92; J.Z. Titow, *Winchester yields: a study in medieval agricultural productivity* (Cambridge, 1972), pp 2–9; D.L. Farmer, 'Grain yields on the Winchester manors in the later Middle Ages', *EHR*, 2nd ser., 30 (1977), 555–66.   **145** Campbell, Galloway, Keene and Murphy, *A medieval capital*, pp 40, 136–8, fig. 21.   **146** This method was

oats was set aside for seed. These percentages are strikingly similar to those calculated for a sample of 200 demesnes in the London region *c.*1300. There, wheat seed represented 27 per cent of harvested grain and oat seed 37 per cent.[147] Thus, there appear to be regularities in medieval arable husbandry which transcend regional and national boundaries.

Weeding and fertilising

One of the reasons cited for the low productivity of medieval arable is the weediness of the soil. One study of manorial practices in England, however, concluded that although weediness may have contributed to poor yields of grain, efforts were actively made to combat the problem.[148] There certainly was an awareness that time expended on weeding would be repaid in increased yields and better crops, and medieval agricultural treatises advocated weeding at particular times during the year. Walter of Henley suggested that weeding should be done in the period following the feast of St John the Baptist (24 June), as this was the best time for eradicating thistles and other noxious weeds.[149]

Two principal methods of removing weeds were employed – one involved hoeing the soil, while the other involved ploughing the demesne fallow in the summer (a practice known as the *rebinatio*). An account rendered by the custodian of the vacant lands of the archbishopric of Dublin in 1310 gives values for land at Swords and Clondalkin described as fallow and 'rebinand'.[150] This indicates that the practice was used on the archiepiscopal manors. It is possible that the reference in the extent for Cloncurry to the triple ploughing of the land to be sown with wheat is an indication that the fallow on this manor was ploughed as a means of weed reduction.[151] In addition, the same extent contains the information that weeding an acre costs 1*d.*, which suggests that it represented a full day's work for one individual. Presumably some weeding was done by hand, but the removal of deep-rooted species and plants such as nettles and thistles would have necessitated the use of implements like hoes or sickles attached to long rods such as that shown in the Luttrell Psalter and also perhaps in a fifteenth-century Irish manuscript (Figure 9.14).

Weeding was labour intensive and potentially very expensive. Some manors were able to call on the services of customary tenants for this task and rentals and extents frequently mention weeding as a customary service. Tenants on the manor of Glasnevin were required to weed the lord's corn for two days with one man.[152] When manors employed wage labour for weeding, the amounts expended were generally small, suggesting that only a proportion of the arable was weeded. For example, at Grangegorman in 1339 a sum of 2*s.* 1½*d.* was expended on weeding the corn, in comparison to the £8 5*s.* 3¼*d.* which was spent on the harvest.[153]

Archaeological evidence for the presence of weeds and species types can be found in environmental samples. Geraghty noted that some Fishamble Street pits contained finely ground fragments of corn cockle, probably as a result of having been milled, consumed with cereal food, and passed through the digestive system.[154] Similar results were obtained from pit samples at Waterford and in Dublin at Temple Bar West and Patrick Street.[155] The frequency with which corn cockle seeds turn up in cess-pits suggests that they were a normal

pioneered by Campbell, see *Seigniorial agriculture*, p. 317.   **147** Campbell, Galloway, Keene and Murphy, *A medieval capital*, p. 146.   **148** David Postles, 'Cleaning the medieval arable', *AHS*, 37:2 (1989), 130–43.   **149** Dorothea Oschinsky, *Walter of Henley and other treatises on estate management and accounting* (Oxford, 1971), pp 322–3.   **150** NAI RC8/5: Memoranda roll, pp 284–91.   **151** *RBO*, pp 27–8.   **152** Mills (ed.), *Account roll*, p. 189.   **153** Ibid., p. 23.   **154** Geraghty, *Viking Dublin*.   **155** John Tierney and Martha Hannon, 'Plant remains' in Hurley et al., *Late Viking-Age and medieval Waterford* (1997), pp 854–93 at pp 888–9, 890–1; Penny Johnston, 'Macroscopic plant remains from excavations at Temple Bar West' (unpublished report – DEHLG file 96E0245); Brenda Collins, 'Plant remains' in Walsh, *Archaeological excavations at Patrick, Nicholas and Winetavern Streets* (1997), pp 228–36 at p. 229.

constituent of the prepared crop. Although corn cockle has now almost vanished from Ireland, Dickson and Dickson noted that 'for a long time no effort was made to remove [its] seeds form the corn crop, and indeed the floury nature of the seeds was regarded as adding to the crop'[156] – this was despite the fact that corn cockle is poisonous, due to its content of *sapogenin githogenin*.[157] Corn marigold appears to have been a late arrival, and probably came in from the Mediterranean, taking advantage of new farming methods in Ireland. At Fishamble Street in Dublin, there were three instances of corn marigold in eleventh-century samples, but thirteen in thirteenth-century deposits.[158]

Soil fertility and crop yields were also improved by the application of fertilisers. Various techniques of fertilising were known to medieval farmers. The most common method comprised the spreading of animal and human dung on the fields prior to ploughing. Evidence for this practice occurs in both the documentary and archaeological record for the Dublin region.

The discovery of pottery sherds and fragments of animal bones in so many of the furrows and fields investigated indicates that domestic refuse was being spread on the land as fertiliser. At Ship Street Great, the abraded nature of the many small sherds recovered suggested that the soil here was turned constantly, probably during cultivation in the twelfth and thirteenth centuries.[159] At Beaverstown (Donabate, Co. Dublin), sherds of abraded medieval pottery were recovered from the ploughsoil and the excavator surmised that these may have been introduced indirectly with domestic waste being applied as fertiliser.[160] At Muckerstown, Co. Meath, manuring of a possible medieval kitchen garden was suggested by the recovery from bedding trenches of pottery sherds, charcoal, animal bones and organic material.[161] It is possible that domestic waste from the associated settlement was used to fertilise the soil. Excavations at Merrywell, Co. Meath, revealed substantial quantities of twelfth-, thirteenth- and fourteenth-century pottery sherds and burnt animal bone in association with ridge-and-furrow cultivation, indicating that household waste was spread here as manure.[162]

At Ballough, 2.5km north-west of Lusk, a linear field ditch with steep, concave sides was found to contain sherds of medieval pottery, animal bones, berry seeds and carbonised grain.[163] Near St Luke's Church in the Coombe, the presence in the cultivation soil of broken pieces of pottery, tiles, bones and shells was seen by the excavator as evidence that rubbish

156 C.A. Dickson and J.H. Dickson, 'The plant remains' in Mitchell, *Archaeology and environment* (1987), pp 22–32 at p. 24.   **157** Dickson and Dickson, 'The plant remains', p. 24; J.M. Kingsbury, *Poisonous plants in the United States and Canada* (Englewood Cliffs, NJ, 1964).   **158** Mitchell, *Archaeology and environment*, p. 25.   **159** DEHLG file 01E0772 (Ship Street Great).   **160** Kevin Lohan, 'Beaverstown, Donabate' in *Excavations 2004*, pp 108–9.   **161** Donal Fallon, 'Muckerstown/Wotton' in *Excavations 2004*, pp 328–9; Donal Fallon, 'Muckerstown/Wotton: final excavation report' (unpublished report, 2008).   **162** Aidan O'Connell and Vicky Ginn, 'Report on the archaeological excavation of Merrywell 1, Co. Meath' (unpublished report, 2009), p. 8.   **163** R.M. Chapple, 'Site 17, Ballough' in *Excavations 2002*,

from the town was being spread on the fields.[164] One other source of fertiliser for Dublin's hinterland was the manure produced by humans and animals, especially horses, within the city. There is a reference to carters and carmen drawing dung out of Dublin in 1460.[165] This was probably applied to the nearby fields.

The discovery of a series of plough pebbles in Brownstown, Co. Dublin, suggests that ploughing took place on lands belonging to, and at some remove from, the archiepiscopal manor at Swords.[166] The pebbles were picked up during field-walking, and there was an absence of contemporary pottery sherds and other indicators that household and farmyard manure had spread in the area.[167] The fields at Brownstown are some 4km north of Swords, and the lack of habitation-derived additives may be an indication that manure was only used as fertiliser in areas close to the holdings that produced it. It is possible that further away alternative fertilising agents were used, such as sand or marl. It is also possible that livestock were allowed in to graze the stubble and fertilise it directly.[168] Another method, mentioned above, was the practice documented on some of the archiepiscopal manors of taking sods out of the meadow or pasture land and digging them into the arable to introduce fresh nutrients to the soil.[169]

Harvesting and storage (by Niall Brady)

In common with practice across the temperate zone of the medieval west, harvesting in Ireland was conducted manually using the sickle. The harvest typically began in August and was one of the busiest periods in the agricultural year, as it is today, since it was vitally important to get the crop cut and stored before the wet weather of autumn. The detailed account of the 1344 harvest on the Christ Church manor of Clonkeen reveals that the harvest continued for eighteen days with breaks for Sundays and feast-days, drawing to a close on 4 September.[170] Eighty-eight reapers set to work on the first day and thereafter varying numbers were employed, with a total of 562 man-days required from start to finish of the harvest. Labours of the Month scenes in English and continental manuscripts show the harvest during its various stages, and the scenes from the richly illustrated Luttrell Psalter are typical (Figure 9.16).[171] The grain was reaped by teams of men and women using sickles. The stalks were then gathered together and left to dry for a few days before they were bound into sheaves, and the sheaves assembled into stooks or heaps in the field, where they would spend several further days drying. Gleaning is not specifically mentioned in Irish sources, but it must have occurred in a manner that was similar to its practice in England, where the gleaners followed behind the harvesters to pick up the ears of grain that had fallen from the sheaves or were otherwise left behind. It was lighter work than reaping and was generally done by the children and the feeble. Once this work was completed, the sheaves were brought in from the fields and stored for the longer term.

Sickle blades are sometimes found on Irish later medieval sites and they appear to change little in design from the early medieval period (Figure 9.15).[172] Other aspects of the harvest are difficult to see archaeologically, but written sources provide some insight. There is recurrent reference to open-air stacks, such as at Cloncurry, where the stacks were carried

pp 123–4.   **164** DEHLG files 93E0066 and 01E0614 (Coombe Relief Road/St Luke's Church).   **165** *CARD*, 1, p. 306. **166** Our thanks to Fionnuala Parnell for bringing these stones to our attention.   **167** Personal observation during field inspection, 2007.   **168** On the leasing of fallow arable for pasture by the manor of Swords, see p. 326 below. **169** McNeill (ed.), *Alen's register*, pp 184, 186, 189.   **170** Mills (ed.), *Account roll*, pp 64–7.   **171** For example, Janet Backhouse, *The Luttrell Psalter* (London and New York, 1989); Janken Myrdal, *Medeltidens Åkerbruk. Agrarteknik i Sverige ca 1000 till 1520* (Stockholm, 1986), pp 120–35.   **172** A medieval sickle was excavated at Grange Castle (00E0754:824) (Figure 9.15), while an early medieval one was excavated recently at Laracor, Co. Meath, in proximity to a short-handled plough coulter (Thaddeus Breen, pers. comm.). An iron sickle was recovered in 2004 from medieval

into the haggard and covered, and at Clonkeen the corn and hay were stacked in the haggard. Open air stacks, or ricks, had advantages over storage in buildings such as barns. According to Sigaut, 'the European weevil, *sitophilus granarius*, the main insect pest of former times, cannot survive winters outside granaries or barns – whereas in well-built ricks, being set on a new plot, the grain was not damaged by weevils and less by rodents than a layman might expect'.[173] The stacks would have been raised from the ground on mushroom-shaped pedestals, where short, stone pillars or timber posts were capped with disc-shaped stones to deter rats and other vermin. The archaeological imprint of stacks in Ireland is difficult to see. No *in situ* remains have been identified, and the excavation signature may amount to one or more occasional post-holes, which would have accommodated a central pole to support the rick. The disc-shaped stones, in contrast, are a common find across much of Ireland, typically lying abandoned in modern farmyards or being re-used as garden ornaments. They do not come from dated contexts, however, and may have supported hay ricks in the early modern period and more recent times.

Grain would have been stored in barns (*grangia* and *horreum*) and granaries (*granaria*). This was certainly the case across southern England, where unthreshed grain was stored in heaps and stacks in large ventilated timber and stone barns. Barns could accommodate large quantities of grain, and they provided the advantage of sheltered drying and added security for the harvested crop. The sheaves could also be threshed piecemeal, which was not the case in an open-air stack. Once opened, the rick's contents had to be threshed immediately because it was not easily resealed against the elements. The presence of barns in the Dublin region is described above in Chapter 5, and other references from around Ireland complement the picture. An extent for the manor of Knocktopher, Co. Kilkenny, in 1312, for example, indicates the presence of a timber grange and a byre in the lower courtyard of the castle, while a large wooden barn existed within the haggard on the manor of Callan, Co. Kilkenny, in 1307, along with a building for housing oxen and stone-built stables.[174] A barn may also have existed at the manor of Odagh, Co. Kilkenny, in 1324, while a *grangia* of 'ten forks' is listed on the Bigod manor of Forth in 1307.[175] The reference to forks (*furcae*) reflects the use of cruck-frames in the construction of these buildings.[176] It also gives some indication of the building's relative size, where the forks would have divided the building into a series of bays. It is another matter to observe any standard for bay size, however, and the absolute size of such a documented building remains unknown. Medieval barns survive in large numbers across southern England, often achieving considerable size, and these may have appealed to lordly senses of prestige display and authority.[177] The barns built in Ireland were more modest structures, no doubt reflecting the smaller arable base.

Once sufficiently dry, the stacks would be opened up and the grain threshed to remove the kernels from the stalks. Threshers at Cloncurry were paid 2½*d.* to thresh a crannock of wheat and 2*d.* for one of oats.[178] A fifteenth-century Irish medical manuscript shows a threshing scene using flails (Figure 9.5). This practice was typical across temperate Europe. The stalks were re-used for thatching, bedding and fodder, while the threshed grain was re-stored for consumption, or sale. The Cloncurry extent mentions 'a small house for

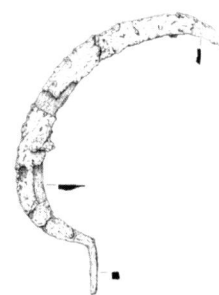

Figure 9.15 Iron sickle found in association with medieval pottery during excavations at Grange Castle, Co. Dublin. Maximum length, from tip to tip: 50cm (image courtesy of Ian Doyle and Margaret Gowen and Co. Ltd).

contexts at a site in Kilmessan, Co. Meath (O'Connor, 'Kilmessan, Co. Meath'). **173** François Sigaut, 'A method for identifying grain storage techniques and its application for European agricultural history', *Tools and Tillage*, 6 (1988), 3–32 at 16. **174** *RBO*, pp 127–31; *CIPM*, 4, no. 435, and cited in O'Conor, *Medieval rural settlement in Ireland*, pp 29, 31. **175** *CIPM*, 4, no. 518; *CDI, 1302–7*, no. 617, p. 174, *CIPM*, 4, no. 434, *CJR, 1305–7*, p. 346, and cited in O'Conor, *Medieval rural settlement in Ireland*, p. 33. **176** N.W. Alcock (ed.), *Cruck construction: an introduction and catalogue* (CBA Research Report, 42, 1981), p. 28. **177** Niall Brady, 'The gothic barn of England: icon of prestige and authority' in Elizabeth Smith and Michael Wolfe (eds), *Technology and resource use in medieval Europe: cathedrals, mills and mines* (Aldershot and Brookfield, 1997), pp 76–105. **178** *RBO*, pp 27–8.

Figure 9.16 Illuminations from the Luttrell Psalter showing harvest scenes: reaping (*top*); stacking (*middle*); and carting (*bottom*). The Psalter is one of most lavishly illustrated manuscripts in an English collection that displays scenes from everyday life. It dates to c.1320–40 and was written and illuminated for Geoffrey Luttrell of Irnham, Lincolnshire (BL Add. MS 42130 fos. 172v, 173, 173v © The British Library Board, all rights reserved).

keeping threshed grain as there is neither barn nor granary'. Medieval granaries and barns have yet to be identified clearly in Ireland. The majority of these buildings would have been of earth and timber, leaving little indication of their former presence on the ground today. As work-buildings used for storage, it would not be expected for organic debris to accumulate in barns as layers or fills over floor surfaces. The traces of these buildings may be ephemeral, and perhaps only identifiable when large areas are uncovered manually, ensuring the slow exposure through the topsoil levels.

Arable: labour inputs

Arable agriculture, of the type that was practiced on the demesnes of the Dublin region, was extremely labour intensive. Tasks that required large inputs of labour were fertilising, ploughing, harrowing, sowing, weeding, reaping, stacking, carrying, threshing and winnowing. Mark Hennessy has proposed that in Co. Tipperary in the early fourteenth century an average of fourteen man-days of work were required for every demesne arable acre.[179] A similar figure might be estimated for the Dublin region.

The 1304 extent for the manor of Cloncurry, Co. Kildare, estimated the labour requirements of an acre of demesne arable in terms of its financial cost:

> they say that weeding each acre costs 1*d*. and reaping, tieing and stooking in the field of each acre of wheat costs 10*d*. and reaping each acre of oats 8*d*. And the carriage of the stacks into the haggard and covering them costs 3*d*. per acre. Cost of threshing a crannock of wheat is 2½*d*. and each crannock of oats 2*d*. Five crannocks of wheat and oats can be winnowed for a penny.

Weeding, harvesting and preparing the grain from an acre of wheat at Cloncurry cost 21¼*d*. The costs of ploughing and harrowing added a further 11*d*. to each acre. If any manuring was carried out, this resulted in an additional cost. In comparison, the work of mowing and making hay from an acre of meadow was reckoned at 9*d*. The extent reveals, however, that the expected yield from an acre sown with wheat was two-and-a-half crannocks. In the early fourteenth century, this quantity of grain could be sold for at least 10*s*., which would produce a significant profit even after deduction of labour costs, tithes and seed set aside for next year's sowing.

All the labour calculations included in the Cloncurry extent were expressed in monetary terms and it would appear that no customary services were required of the tenants. Although over one hundred betaghs and cottars were tenants of the manor in 1304, the extent mentions no labour services connected with their tenancies. Many other manors in the Dublin area did require their tenants to perform some services, but these appear to have been only a small proportion of what was needed. According to rentals of 1326, tenants on the Christ Church manors of Glasnevin and Grangegorman were expected to provide four days of ploughing, two each at winter and Lent as well as two days weeding, two days reaping and two days carrying at harvest time.[180] These services continued to feature in leases well into the fifteenth century. When a new lease was drawn up for land in the parish of Glasnevin in 1475, the lessee was required 'to perform customary service in meadow, ploughing, reaping and weeding days as other tenants of Glassnewyn'.[181] At the other Christ Church manor of Clonkeen, tenants were required to perform a varying amount of

179 Mark Hennessy, 'Manorial agriculture and settlement in early fourteenth-century Co. Tipperary' in Clarke, Prunty and Hennessy (eds), *Surveying Ireland's past* (2004), pp 99–117 at p. 106. **180** Mills (ed.), *Account roll*, pp 189–93. **181** *CCCD*, no. 1005.

customary service or provide a monetary substitute. The detailed account that survives of the 1344 harvest on this manor reveals that although customary services were called upon, they contributed only a small proportion of the total labour required.[182] On three days, the hired workers were joined by customary tenants of the manor who numbered sixty on one day. The overall contribution of these labour services was small, however, comprising just 91 (or 16 per cent) of the 562 man-days.

Grassland

The provision of adequate pasture and meadow was vital because of the important role played by livestock in the cultivation and manuring of arable land. Oxen were largely grass-fed and required substantial amounts of winter fodder in the form of hay.[183] Horses were also stall-fed on hay, and on-farm demands were matched or perhaps exceeded by the significant requirements generated by urban horse populations. Meadow, which could be mown each year to produce a hay crop, was the most valuable type of grassland. It required fertile soil in areas with a high water table – river valleys were ideal – and dry, sunny conditions during the mowing season, usually June to early July. Mowing was probably carried out using scythes, as indicated on manuscripts across the medieval west, but no scythe blades have yet been identified from archaeological contexts in Ireland, and scythes are not referred to in the written sources.

The setting aside of meadows for mowing, the making of hay and winter feeding of stock are usually seen as innovations of Anglo-Norman agriculture in Ireland. There is a quantity of convincing evidence, certainly for the early medieval period, to suggest that the Irish did not cut meadow grass to make hay for winter feeding of stock but rather left certain lands unused during the summer in order to preserve the grass for winter feeding. Gerald of Wales stated categorically that 'the meadows are not cut for fodder, nor do they [the Irish] ever build stalls for their beasts'.[184] In general, it appears that the Irish trusted that there would be sufficient grass growth to support their animals over the winter. This was a high-risk strategy, however, and during years of heavy snowfalls there could be large-scale livestock losses.[185]

Meadow was recorded on virtually all the demesnes in the Dublin region for which extents survive. It occupied on average 6 per cent of demesne land equating to a mean area of twenty-seven acres (Tables 9.1; 9.2). There was, however, a great deal of variation in both the quantity and the value of meadow land across the region and there is some evidence for specialisation in hay production in areas with environmental advantages.

Meadow land could be found in different areas of a manor, but because of the labour required in bringing hay into the haggard for storage it was normally located fairly near to the manor centre. At Ballymore in 1326, the jurors recorded that three acres of meadow were situated *within* the castle.[186] In addition, there were seventeen acres of meadow in a location called Incheboye and a further nine acres in Paynesput. At Maynooth in 1328, twenty-one acres of meadow were situated close to the castle, divided between le Loghmede next to the park and an area beside the River Rye.[187] Hayfields were frequently given names incorporating the element *mede*, as can be seen in the extract from the Rathcoole extent (below). The archiepiscopal manor of Colonia/St Sepulchre had hayfields called Bishopsmede, Brodemede, Strifmede and Crokemede.[188] At Swords, meadow land was organised into the great meadow

182 Mills (ed.), *Account roll*, pp 64–7. 183 J.L. Langdon, 'The economies of horses and oxen in medieval England', *AHS*, 30 (1982), 31–40 at 32–5. 184 Gerald of Wales, *The history and topography of Ireland*, p. 53. 185 Nicholls, 'Gaelic society and economy', p. 415. 186 McNeill (ed.), *Alen's register*, p. 189. 187 *RBK*, p. 98. 188 McNeill (ed.), *Alen's register*, pp 170, 172.

where there were seventy-one acres and the lesser meadow which had just six acres.[189] A further fifteen-and-a-half acres were found 'in divers places'. There was also a great meadow associated with the manor of Glasnevin. In 1542, a lessee had to agree to 'keep the great meadow of Glasnevin in meadow and mow, save and rick the hay'.[190]

The most valuable meadow in the study area (24d. per acre) was in north Co. Dublin on the manorial demesnes of Swords and Corduff.[191] The extent for Cloncurry recorded that eleven-and-a-half acres of meadow there could be let each year for 20d. an acre.[192] Furthermore, the cost of mowing an acre of meadow was given as 5d. and spreading and gathering the hay cost a further 4d. an acre. Occasionally, a low value for meadow was explained by environmental factors such as the meadow at Werne, a sub-demesne of Swords which was valued at 8d. an acre and 'no more because poor and dry'.[193] Some of the meadow land at Colonia/St Sepulchre, which lay outside Newgate, was worth less than it should have been because it was damaged by carts and carters *en route* into the city, while the war with the Irish was cited as the explanation for the low-valued meadow at Shankill and Tallaght in 1326.[194]

The surviving evidence for one Dublin manor suggests a marked specialism in hay production. This was the archiepiscopal manor of Rathcoole, situated in the south-west of Co. Dublin, where meadow constituted some 44 per cent of demesne land-use by area. The 1326 extent for this manor provides considerable detail about the distribution of 104 acres of meadow land throughout the demesne, and this is always a sign that the resource is accorded more than average importance. Rathcoole was drained by two rivers that flowed northwards out of the parish and it may have been environmentally suited to the production of hay in large fields or water meadows. As can be seen from the following extract, the meadow was divided into several sizeable fields, many of them over ten acres in area.[195]

> … in Flottergres 10½ acres meadow for mowing at 12d., 10s. 6d.; at Grencolmede 13½ acres meadow at 3d. 3s. 4½d.; in Litilmede 10½ acres meadow 10s. 6d. at 12d. an acre; in Flagges, called le Middel flagges 10½ acres meadow 6s. 3d. at 6d. an acre, in le North flagges and le Seneschallesmede 11½ acres at 3d. 2s. 10½d.; in le Fyve acres 5a meadow, whereof the archbishop gave 4 acres to John son of Adam for life, and nothing to be got therefrom; the remaining acre, 6d. a year; in le Midweye 6a of meadow which Robert Graff holds 12d. an acre, 6s.; in Hagarde 1 acre meadow 12d.; 2 acres called le Hende acres, 6d. an acre, 12d.; Lesemourmede 8½ acres 1d. an acre 8½d. and no more because wasted in time past by digging sods.

The extent contains a range of values which, when averaged out, give a mean value for meadow of 4d. per acre – only half the average value given for arable land in the same extent (Table 9.3). This is a result of the very low value (1d./acre) given for Lesemourmede, where sods had been dug out, presumably to use in increasing the fertility of the demesne arable. This practice was also recorded on the archiepiscopal demesne lands at Clondalkin and Ballymore. A significant portion of the meadow at Rathcoole was valued at 10d. and 12d. an acre, and this is a reflection of its profitability.

It is unlikely that animals would have been grazed on meadow land which was specifically reserved for the production of hay. Most manors set aside land to provide permanent grazing for livestock. Across the demesnes of the region, land described as 'pasture' came second in importance to arable in terms of area, with an average of fifty-five

189 Ibid., p. 175.   **190** *CCCD*, no. 1186.   **191** McNeill (ed.), *Alen's register*, p. 175; *RBK*, p. 25.   **192** *RBK*, p. 28.   **193** McNeill (ed.), *Alen's register*, p. 176.   **194** Ibid., pp 170, 181, 195.   **195** Ibid., pp 183–4.

acres or 13 per cent of land devoted to this land-use (Table 9.2; Figure 9.1). It is clear from the documentary sources that different grades of pasture land were recognised and put to different purposes. On the manor of Naul in north Co. Dublin, a number of different pastoral resources were utilised by the manorial lords.[196] Seventeen acres of mountain pasture were extended at *6d.* an acre. In addition, there was a pasture called la Roche said to be useful for sheep, which was valued at *6s. 8d.* and a moor useful for oxen, valued at *8s.*

Pastoral resources were particularly plentiful on manors situated in the south-west of the study area (Figure 9.1). On the archiepiscopal manor of Ballymore, for example, the jurors recorded that there were 124 acres of pasture 'lying around the demesne lands in different places'.[197] In addition, there was another pasture called Inchboy, which contained ten acres, and a further forty acres in 'Barrets mountayn'. The burgesses of Ballymore held a pasture at 'Brodley', which contained two carucates (240 acres). As there were 160 burgesses, this suggests that each had one-and-a-half acres of pasture.

The extents for a number of manors in the Dublin region record no pasture among the demesne resources. This does not necessarily mean that the manorial lord had no access to pastoral resources. At Bray, for example, no demesne pasture was listed, but it was stated that the lord of the manor could avail of a certain external (*forinsecus* – outside the manor) pasture, which was sufficient to sustain one hundred ewes.[198] At Cloncurry, the extent records no pasture but does state that part of the value of the eighty-seven acres of demesne woodland lies in its use as providing grass and pasturage.[199] Indeed, according to the extent, 'eighteen oxen and thirty cows can be well sustained in the said woods'.

The extent for Rathfeigh, Co. Meath, states clearly that no pasture was available to the demesne apart from fallow arable.[200] This may have been a common occurrence in the arable dominated parts of north Co. Dublin and south-east Meath. At Swords, where there was permanent pasture land, the manor still leased 120 acres of fallow arable for pasture but only got *1d.* an acre because of the lack of animals.[201] Elsewhere, scattered throughout the manor, there were 115 acres of pasture valued at *6d.* an acre. Of this, it was stated that eighty-six acres were grazed by the lord's horses and cattle. Fifteen acres at Lusk were also valued at *6d.*, but a further twenty-four acres were worth only *1d.* an acre because they were subject to flooding from the sea.[202]

The extent for Clondalkin mentioned two pastures, one at Keppach (twenty acres) and another at Ceskin (forty acres). They were valued at a very low level and proximity to the Irish and lack of beasts were cited as reasons for this.[203] These factors were similarly cited at Shankill and Tallaght. It appears that on many manors, pasture land lay in peripheral areas, at some distance from the security afforded by the caput, and as it was unsafe to leave animals on these lands, their value declined.

When pasture was in a secure position and close to Dublin, its value rose accordingly. The prior of the hospital of St John's Newgate held a pasture in Terenure from the archbishop of Dublin. It comprised twenty-six acres and the prior made an annual payment of *20s. 8d.* (over *9½d.* an acre) for it.[204] The pasture at Corduff was also valuable – fifteen acres 'for oxen and cows' was valued at *12d.* an acre, the same value as the arable.[205]

Livestock

Animal husbandry in the medieval period served three principal purposes: it produced work animals for agriculture and transport; it provided meat and other foodstuffs (such as dairy

196 TNA:PRO C133/63. **197** McNeill (ed.), *Alen's register*, p. 189. **198** *RBO*, p. 24. **199** Ibid., p. 28. **200** TNA:PRO C47/10/18/13. **201** McNeill (ed.), *Alen's register*, p. 175. **202** Ibid., p. 176. **203** Ibid., p. 186. **204** Ibid., p. 171. **205** *RBO*, p. 26.

products, eggs and fat); and it furnished raw materials (such as wool, skins, horns and feathers).[206] Wild animals were hunted as a source of meat, fur, antlers and entertainment. Domestic animals on demesne lands were often housed in specialised buildings such as stables and byres, as well as piggeries and sheepcotes (discussed in Chapter 5).[207]

Horses and oxen

The primary functions of horses and oxen were to provide a source of power through their ability to haul ploughs and heavy loads, and to transport people and goods.[208] Oxen had a secondary function as providers of meat (and by-products such as hides and horns) when they had reached the end of their working lives. Horses were occasionally eaten, but in general their roles beyond agriculture were primarily in the realms of transport, warfare and display.

By the start of the thirteenth century, the eight-ox plough-team was in use on some of the de Lacy manors in the liberty of Meath, including some in the Dublin region. The 1211–12 pipe roll, for instance, records the purchase of twenty-four oxen to stock three plough-teams in Coolock (*xxiiij boves ad staurandum iij carrucas de Culoch*).[209] In all, 906 oxen were recorded on these manors, with up to eight plough-teams occurring in some places. By contrast, only eighteen affers or draught-horses are mentioned. These affers may have been a heavy breed of horse introduced by the Anglo-Normans. They were strong enough to be used for ploughing and were about 50 per cent faster than oxen. Although there is no archaeological evidence to support the presence of large horses in Ireland at this time, it is reasonable to conclude that horses played some role in ploughing at this early stage. Unless a document specifically calls them 'plough horses', however, their function is unclear.

---

206 Sandor Bokonyi, 'The development of stockbreeding and herding in medieval Europe' in Del Sweeney (ed.), *Agriculture in the Middle Ages: technology, practice and representation* (Philadelphia, 1995), pp 41–61 at p. 55. **207** O'Conor, *Medieval rural settlement in Ireland*, pp 29–33. **208** It has been estimated that 70% of the power available to English society at the time of Domesday Book was supplied by animals, the remaining 30% or so being provided by mill- and manpower together (J.L. Langdon, *Horses, oxen and technological innovation: the use of draught animals in English farming from 1066 to 1500* (Cambridge, 1986), p. 20). **209** Davies and Quinn, 'Irish pipe roll of 14 John', 40.

Horses were certainly used as traction animals on manors in Ireland, for carting and carrying and increasingly for harrowing. A range of archaeological evidence indicates the exploitation of horses for farm-work in the Dublin region. The exostosis or bony growth on several of the bones from excavations at Nangor suggest that the horses here had been ridden or used for traction purposes before eventually being eaten.[210] Two horse mandibles from fourteenth- to sixteenth-century samples on Patrick Street displayed evidence for wear possibly caused by a bit.[211] All of the horses represented on this site were adults and the one for which a height could be estimated would have stood at about thirteen hands – roughly the size of a modern Connemara Pony (although this animal may have come from post-medieval levels). A horse from Arran Quay was of a similar size.[212] The equine remains found at Dundrum Castle came from horses larger than those normally found on sites in Ireland, and these large animals may have been particularly prized for agricultural work.[213] Simon Turrell noted that while the average size of a horse in medieval Ireland was roughly similar to that of a modern Connemara Pony, horse sizes increased gradually through the Middle Ages.[214]

In the absence of demesne accounts, it is difficult to draw a livestock profile of any large holding in the Dublin area. Nonetheless, references from various sources indicate that oxen were the preferred beast of traction on the royal and archiepiscopal manors in the region. Central exchequer accounts frequently record the purchase of oxen for the royal manors. In 1275–6, the king's treasurer accounted for £2 6s. 8d. spent on the purchase of seven oxen for ploughing on the royal manor of Chapelizod.[215] This gives a unit price of 6s. 8d. or half a mark, a figure similar to that paid in Dublin in 1282 for the forty oxen and cows bought to send to the earl marshal (Roger Bigod) in Wales.[216] There are similar purchases for the archiepiscopal manors of Swords and Colonia during periods when they were being administered by royal officials.[217]

In England, during the thirteenth century, mixed plough-teams comprising oxen and affers started to become more common, particularly in the south and east of the country, and it is likely that this was also the case in parts of Ireland. In 1306, Agnes de Valence had twenty-four oxen and twelve affers on the manor of Rathmore, Co. Kildare, and forty-eight oxen and twenty-four affers at Maynooth.[218] One of the early fourteenth-century inquisitions for the Templar manor of Clontarf, Co. Dublin, records the presence of thirty oxen for five ploughs as well as ten affers.[219] This might indicate that there were five plough-teams each comprising six oxen and two affers. There were also ten ox carcases in the larder. A second, apparently later, inquisition lists forty-two oxen and eight affers and makes no mention of any ox carcases. In addition to the plough animals, the Templars had nine cart-horses, two pack-horses and several riding horses.

The account roll of the priory of Holy Trinity records purchases of both oxen and horses for the granges at Grangegorman and Clonkeen. In 1334, nine oxen and six horses were purchased for the plough at Grangegorman, indicating the presence on this manor of at least two plough- teams.[220] The prices paid for the oxen ranged from 5 to 8s. a head, while the horses were more expensive at between 6s. 8d. and 10s. There is one record of the sale of two oxen described as old and debilitated.[221] The oxen netted 5s. a head, which might indicate

210 Melanie McQuade, 'Analysis of the faunal remains from excavations in Nangor townland', unpublished report submitted to the DEHLG.   211 Finbar McCormick and Eileen Murphy, 'Mammal bones' in Walsh, *Archaeological excavations at Patrick, Nicholas and Winetavern Streets* (1997), pp 199–218 at p. 205.   212 McCormick, 'The mammal bone' in Hayden, 'Arran Quay' (2004), pp 221–31 at p. 229.   213 Emily Murray, 'Reports on the faunal and molluscan material from excavations at Dundrum Castle, Co. Dublin (appendix 5), Dundrum Castle (E000419)' (unpublished report), p. 5.   214 Turrell, 'Archaeozoology of medieval Dublin', pp 50–1.   215 *IEP*, p. 14.   216 *CDI, 1252–84*, no. 2009, p. 460: 40 oxen and cows bought for £12 11s. 9d., giving a unit price of 6s. 4d.   217 *CDI, 1302–7*, pp 8, 10.   218 *CJR, 1305–7*, pp 240–1.   219 Mac Niocaill, 'Suppression of the Templars'.   220 Mills (ed.), *Account roll*, pp 22–3, 35–6, 62.   221 Ibid., p. 56.

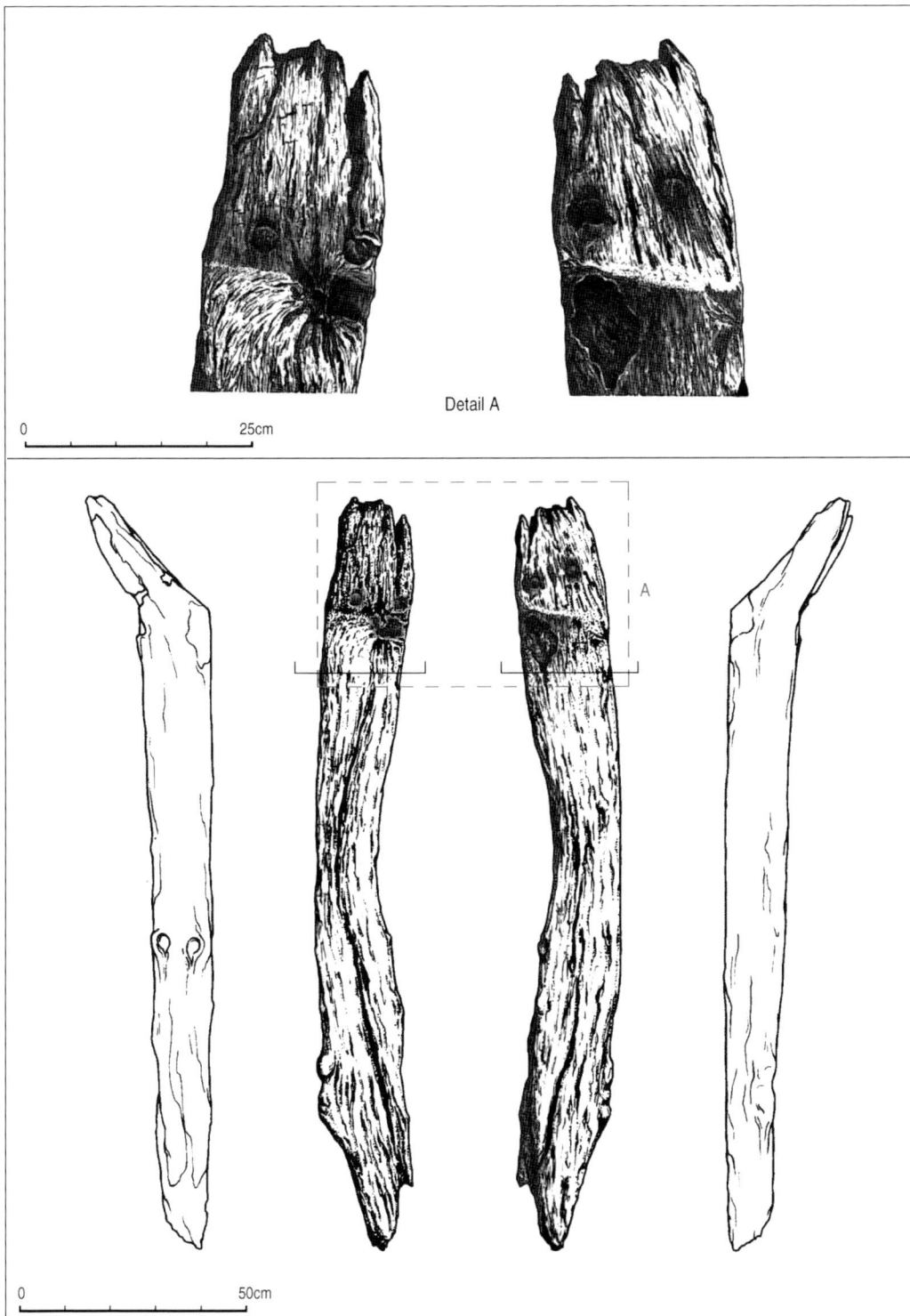

Detail A

0   25cm

A

0   50cm

Figure 9.18 Wooden
yoke from Merrywell,
Co. Meath. This yoke
was recovered from the
fill of a well in 2005
(image courtesy of
Aidan O'Connell, Vicky
Ginn and ACS Ltd).

that they had been deliberately fattened up prior to sale as was recommended in some of the medieval treatises on animal husbandry. Zoo-archaeological evidence from English sites indicates that many of the cattle eaten in towns, castles and villages may have served several years as plough beasts before being fattened up for the table.[222]

There is similar evidence from Dublin – abnormalities noted on some of the skulls from fourteenth- to sixteenth-century levels at Patrick Street were interpreted as possible evidence for 'the use of yokes for draught purposes'.[223] Further pathological abnormalities identified

222 Annie Grant, 'Animal resources' in Astill and Grant (eds), *The countryside of medieval England* (1988), pp 149–87 at p. 156. For example, cattle bones at Winchester showed a high incidence of injuries to the hip joint, likely to have been induced by traction. **223** McCormick and Murphy, 'Mammal bones', p. 201.

included bruising to the jaw of one animal, possibly caused by a strike or knock, and evidence for some degenerative joint disease. A large wooden yoke with dowels still *in situ* was recovered from the secondary fill of the well at Merrywell, Co. Meath (Figure 9.18).[224] This fill also contained sherds of late twelfth- to thirteenth-century pottery. The yoke, which was made of oak, measured 1.67m in length and between 13cm and 18cm in thickness. It may have been dumped into the well once it had become broken and useless.

At Nangor, some of the bovine bones displayed evidence for arthropathy, and possible joint and muscular strain, and this may be the result of a life of draught and toil.[225] Bones from male cattle over three years old are rare, and when they do occur it is likely that they are the remains of working animals. Some of the fourteenth-century bones from Arran Quay exhibited signs of wear and strain, potentially resulting from traction, and these may derive from old oxen that were slaughtered once they had reached the end of their working life.[226] Draught animals generally start their working lives at about two years of age, and after three to five years they are fattened for food. Working oxen could be kept for up to ten years before being slaughtered.[227] In general, however, it is very difficult to definitively identify animals that have been used for traction from their skeletal remains and, if anything, the bovine fossils from the Dublin region demonstrate their primary function as meat producers.

Extents sometimes contain references to livestock, particularly in relation to pasture for stock. What emerges is the adaptability of oxen to different types of grazing – one of their chief advantages over horses. At Corduff there were fifteen acres of pasture for oxen and cows, while at Cloncurry there was a wood in which eighteen oxen and thirty cows could be sustained.[228] At Naul there was a moor 'useful for oxen'.[229] The accounts for the earl of Norfolk's manors (all outside the Dublin region) indicate some of the advantages of oxen over horses in terms of their feeding. On these demesnes, the affers consumed oats during the winter at the rate of half a bushel a night, while in many accounts the oxen do not appear to have consumed any oats at all.[230] Another consideration was that oxen did not normally require shoeing, which was a considerable expense with regard to horses.[231] In 1343, the steward of Holy Trinity accounted for 5s. 4½d. for shoeing the affers and cart-horses ahead of harvest time.[232] Both oxen and horses required further expenditure for medical treatment when injured or ill. On the manors of Clonkeen and Grangegorman, butter and sulphur were bought to rub into the injured necks of the oxen and affers, and a *medicus* was paid 15d. for attending to them.[233]

It is difficult to assess the degree to which oxen were used outside demesnes, as the sources for peasant agriculture and small-holdings are so sparse. John Langdon's work has shown a definite correlation in England between size of holding and the choice of draught animal. Horses were especially favoured on small-holdings, where the quantity of land did not justify having a full plough-team.[234] Tenants who were required to do harrowing and carrying services were also more likely to keep horses. There is some evidence from the earl of Norfolk's ministers' accounts that horses were more numerous than oxen among the peasantry in the late thirteenth century.[235]

224 O'Connell and Ginn, 'Report on the archaeological excavation of Merrywell', p. 3; Ellen O'Carroll, 'An analysis of the wood remains from Merrywell 1, A017–029, Co. Meath' (unpublished report on behalf of Archaeological Consultancy Services Ltd, 2006).   **225** McQuade, 'Faunal remains from Nangor'.   **226** McCormick, 'The mammal bone (from Arran Quay)', p. 226.   **227** P.L. Armitage, 'Post-medieval cattle horns from the Greyfriars site, Chichester, West Sussex, England', *Circaea*, 7:2 (1990), 81–90 at 87.   **228** *RBO*, pp 25–7, 27–34.   **229** *CDI, 1285–92*, no. 1066, pp 467–8.   **230** Down, 'Colonial society and economy', p. 475.   **231** Oxen were sometimes shod, but much less frequently than horses: see Langdon, *Horses, oxen*, p. 17.   **232** Mills (ed.), *Account roll*, p. 30.   **233** Ibid., p. 29.
234 Langdon, *Horses, oxen*, pp 194–5.   **235** Down, 'Colonial society and economy', p. 475.

The collection of fifteenth-century will inventories which has survived for the Dublin region provides some insight into the livestock profiles on a range of holdings (Table 9.9). Only two of the testators listed oxen among their livestock, although the majority were involved in arable agriculture. John Palmer of Kilsallaghan had two oxen and four horses, while Peter Highley, a well-off citizen of Dublin, had three oxen in addition to eight horses.[236] Highley held forty acres near Killeigh from the baron of Skreen, including nine acres sown with wheat and barley. His possessions also included three ploughs 'with iron etc.' The average value of an ox, according to these examples, was 7s. 5d.

Table 9.9 Livestock data from fifty-nine Dublin will inventories, 1467–83.[237]

	HORSES	CATTLE	SHEEP	PIGS
No. and % of inventories	47 (80%)	53 (90%)	43 (73%)	48 (81%)
Total no. of animals	288	469	1,134	434
Average no. per inventory	6	9	26	9

Forty-seven (or 80 per cent) of the testators had horses variously described as *caballus, affrus* and occasionally *equus*. It seems likely that the term 'equus' was used to denote a riding horse. Testators rarely owned more than two *equi* and their average value was 15s. 6d. It is not clear whether there was any difference between animals described as *caballus* and those described as *affrus*.[238] Both types are similarly valued at about 5s. a head and they never appear together in inventories. This would suggest that the variation in nomenclature is a reflection of the scribe rather than of any real difference. Affers appear in just twelve inventories, while *caballi* are found in thirty-one. Only one inventory gives information about the precise function of the animals and that relates to the possessions of Michael Tregury, archbishop of Dublin (d. 1471). He had fourteen horses for the plough (*item xiiij^or caballos pro aratro*) and six horses for carts or wains (*item vi caballos pro bigis sive criborum*).[239]

The average number of horses kept by the testators was six and these were probably used for ploughing, harrowing and general carting jobs. The majority of the testators can be classified as small to middling farmers, but as the inventories include only sown acres and exclude fallow arable and pastoral resources, the overall size of holdings cannot be calculated. It is interesting to note that oxen were absent even on larger holdings, such as that of the archbishop of Dublin. This suggests that there was a general move towards the use of horses for ploughing by the late fifteenth century. This move is further reflected in the archaeo-logical evidence, where the decline in the numbers of male cattle represented on medieval sites (proportionate to females) is mirrored by an increase in the numbers of horse bones found.[240] This appears to be related to the increasing importance of horses in traction duties, and the concomitant decrease in the use of oxen for agricultural work.

Draught oxen, plough-horses and cart-horses had average working lives of between five and seven years. There was a recurrent need for the replacement of working animals. Working horses could be male or female, and so there was the possibility of breeding replacement animals from the working mares. Large estates were more likely to have

236 Berry (ed.), *Register of wills and inventories*, pp 128–33.   **237** Note: statistics have been calculated from all inventories that include livestock. Those which do not are excluded from the calculation. Foals, calves, lambs and piglets are counted as 0.5. In a small number of inventories where numbers are omitted and values given, numbers of animals have been calculated using unit prices from equivalent inventories.   **238** Langdon found *caballus* 'on a few occasions, primarily in twelfth- and early thirteenth-century documents' and translates it as 'work-horse' (*Horses, oxen*, p. 295). Berry, who edited the inventories in 1898, translated *caballus* as 'cart-horse' and *affrus* as 'farm horse'.   **239** Berry (ed.), *Register of wills and inventories*, p. 25.   **240** Andrea Cremin, 'Animal bones from Christ Church Place, Dublin: 10th to 12th century' (MA, QUB, 1996), p. 49.

dedicated stud-farms for horse breeding. The earl of Kildare in the early fourteenth century had three studs at Kildare, each in the charge of an Irish stud-keeper.[241] There were three stallions at each stud and a total of 184 mares and 64 colts and fillies. In 1310, two Dublin men were accused of stealing 'the stud of Robert Darditz in the liberty of Trim and driving it into the county of Dublin'.[242] This presumably refers to the theft of several mares and foals and perhaps some stallions.

It is clear from the example of the Holy Trinity manors cited above that some lords did not attempt to be self-sufficient in terms of their work animals. This may have been because they had recourse to the market to supply their needs. In the case of Holy Trinity, it appears that replacement animals were frequently sourced from tenants of the manor. There are references in Gaelic sources to large numbers of horses being kept by the Irish chiefs.[243] It is possible that they were supplying some of the Anglo-Norman lords. In the fifteenth century, mares and foals – usually just one or two – are recorded in the will inventories, indicating that small-scale horse-breeding was fairly widespread.

The absence of butchery marks on most horse bones from medieval sites in the Dublin region supports the documentary evidence that horses were not generally exploited for their meat.[244] This is not universally true, however, and some equine bones from sites at Nangor, Dundrum Castle, Fishamble Street, Back Lane and Wood Quay displayed evidence of butchery.[245] Finbar McCormick has argued that horse meat, while not preferred, was not uncommon in medieval Ireland.[246]

Cows

As oxen were invariably male, the presence of cows (*vacca*) on a manor or holding indicates that breeding and/or dairying was being carried out. The documentary sources do not allow any systematic numerical study of any livestock type before the late fifteenth century. They do indicate, however, that cattle (other than oxen) were present in some numbers throughout the Dublin region. The archaeological evidence suggests that cattle were generally of the *Bos longifrons*, or Celtic short-horn variety.[247] Anglo-Norman agriculture is thought to have placed less emphasis on the socio-economic role of the milk cow than did Gaelic agriculture.[248] Nevertheless, the demand for replacement oxen to service the large plough-teams, coupled with the growing demands for meat and dairy products from urban communities and hides from leather-workers, ensured that cattle numbers remained at a high level throughout the region.

Some manors had significant cow herds. In 1303, it was claimed that Agnes de Valence had forty-two cows on her manor of Rathmore, Co. Kildare.[249] In 1308, the vaccary, or cowshed at the Templar manor of Clontarf had ten cows and one bull, and this was probably less than was needed to breed replacements for their five plough-teams.[250] The absence of any juvenile cattle from the records is puzzling, although they may have been sold off before the inquisition was drawn up. A second inquisition, which is more informative in some

241 *RBK*, p. 104; the earl of Norfolk also had a stud-farm attached to his manor of Forth, Co. Carlow, from which 20 mares were stolen by the O'Nolans in 1311: *CJR, 1308–14*, p. 172.   **242** *CJR, 1308–14*, p. 163.   **243** J.A. Watt, 'Gaelic polity and cultural identity' in Cosgrove (ed.), *A new history of Ireland: II* (1993), pp 314–51 at p. 330.   **244** V.G. Butler, 'Report on the animal bones from C46, C48, C50, C53, C54, C56, C58 and C60' in McMahon, 'Bridge Street Lower' (1991), 41–71 at 67–8; Murray, 'Reports on the faunal and molluscan material from excavations at Dundrum Castle'; McQuade, 'Faunal remains from Nangor'; Andrea Cremin, 'Animal bone', appendix III, Thomas St. (96E0280) DEHLG, p. 59; McCormick, 'The mammal bone (from Arran Quay)', pp 228–9.   **245** Murray, 'Reports on the faunal and molluscan material from excavations at Dundrum Castle'; McQuade, 'Faunal remains from Nangor'; Mitchell, *Archaeology and environment*, p. 10; Vincent Butler, 'Animal bone studies in archaeology', *AI*, 3:3 (autumn 1989), 104–7 at 106–7; Turrell, 'Archaeozoology of medieval Dublin', p. 54.   **246** Finbar McCormick, 'The effect of the Anglo-Norman settlement on Ireland's wild and domesticated fauna' in P.J. Crabtree and Kathleen Ryan (eds), *Animal-use and cultural change* (MASCA Research Papers in Science and Archaeology, supplement to vol. 8 (1991), pp 41–52 at p. 44; McCormick, 'The animal bones (Waterford)', p. 832.   **247** Butler, 'Animal bone studies in archaeology', 106; Cremin, 'Animal bone, Thomas St.', p. 59; Turrell, 'Archaeozoology of medieval Dublin', pp 36–7.   **248** McCormick, 'The effect of Anglo-Norman settlement', p. 46.   **249** *CJR, 1308–14*, p. 240.   **250** Mac Niocaill, 'Suppression of the

respects, records the presence of four stone of cheeses in the larder.[251] This might suggest that dairying rather than stock-breeding was the primary function of the herd. Holy Trinity does not appear to have had cattle on its manors of Clonkeen and Grangegorman in the 1340s. Replacement oxen were acquired through purchase: on one occasion, three were bought from the bailiff of Grangegorman.[252] Cheese and butter were also purchased, while there is mention of a cowman at Clonkeen and a reference to the sale of a single cowhide, which may indicate that cows had been there formerly.[253]

It is also clear that tenants frequently had significant numbers of cattle. In 1311, fifty cows and bulls were taken from the tenants on the manor of Mainham in Co. Kildare and driven to Saggart in Co. Dublin.[254] In the same year, the tenants of Cloncurry, also in Co. Kildare, were robbed of fourteen cows.[255] John Arthur, an Irish tenant of the king on the manor of Leixlip, had in his possession when he died in 1324, one bull, eleven cows and ten calves.[256] In 1305, sixteen cows were stolen from the abbot of St Mary's manor at Portmarnock.[257]

In terms of meat consumed, cattle certainly dominated the human diet in the Dublin region throughout the Middle Ages. This was despite the increasing importance of sheep (and in some areas pig) and their numerical dominance on many sites.[258] Within the city alone and on the basis of the bone assemblage from twelfth-century Fishamble Street, it has been calculated that 'small mature cattle, probably brought in, provided 90 per cent of the meat consumed'.[259] Cattle accounted for about 84 per cent of the meat consumed by the residents of a site on Thomas Street in the thirteenth century.[260] Bovine remains also dominated the faunal assemblage from thirteenth-century contexts at Skreen, Co. Meath.[261] Analysis of the animal bone assemblage from medieval contexts at Nangor, Co. Dublin, suggests that cattle and sheep were present in roughly equal numbers.[262] Multiplying the minimum number of individuals (MNI) by the established average meat weight for each species (cattle 408kg, sheep 56.7kg, pig 90.7kg), Melanie McQuade estimated relative meat contributions of 82.4 per cent for cattle, 11.5 per cent for sheep and 6.1 per cent for pig. Evidence from eight separate contexts on Patrick Street, High Street and Arran Quay indicates that cattle consistently provided over 70 per cent of the meat consumed from the twelfth to the eighteenth century.[263] Indeed, when all available figures for the Dublin region are averaged, the impression is that, of the three main domesticates, cattle provided as much as 79 per cent of the meat, pig 18 per cent and sheep only 3 per cent (Figure 9.19).[264]

Cattle dominated the faunal assemblage from later medieval contexts at Killeen Castle, Co. Meath, but less so than in the early medieval levels.[265] There was an increased representation of sheep/goat and pigs, with horse, dog and cat also present. The remains of red deer, rabbit, fowl and geese were also found. The age-profile of the cattle is more in line with a dairy-economy than a beef one, but the meat was undoubtedly consumed.

Cow dung found in samples taken from Dublin's twelfth-century waterfront indicates the presence of cattle. Frank Mitchell commented that 'the cattle in the town will have been held in very close confinement, and their owners may have been glad to have given them some exercise on the beach'.[266] It is unlikely that cattle were kept in the town for any length of time, however, and the range of bones present on many urban sites indicates that the

Templars', 188.   **251** Ibid., 215.   **252** Mills (ed.), *Account roll*, p. 22.   **253** Ibid., pp 57, 62, 85.   **254** *CJR, 1308–14*, p. 219.   **255** Ibid., p. 226.   **256** NAI RC/8: Memoranda roll, pp 94–7.   **257** *CJR, 1305–7*, p. 483.   **258** Turrell, 'Archaeozoology of medieval Dublin', pp 32–9.   **259** Mitchell, *Archaeology and environment*, p. 10.   **260** Cremin, 'Animal bone, Thomas St.', p. 62.   **261** Patricia Lynch, 'The animal bone from Skreen, Co. Meath: licence 05E0321', unpublished report, 2006.   **262** McQuade, 'Faunal remains from Nangor'.   **263** McCormick and Murphy, 'Mammal bones', p. 201; Finbar McCormick, 'The mammal bones from the excavations at rear 9–12 High Street, Dublin (unpublished report deposited with the DEHLG)', p. 4; McCormick, 'The mammal bone (from Arran Quay)', p. 224.   **264** Information from sites of twelfth- to sixteenth-century dates was used.   **265** Geber, 'The faunal remains [from Killeen Castle]'.   **266** Mitchell, *Archaeology and environment*, p. 15.

Figure 9.19 Relative percentage of faunal remains of three main domesticates on medieval sites in the Dublin region, and relative percentage of meat provided by each. Figures derived from an analysis of thirty published and unpublished reports.

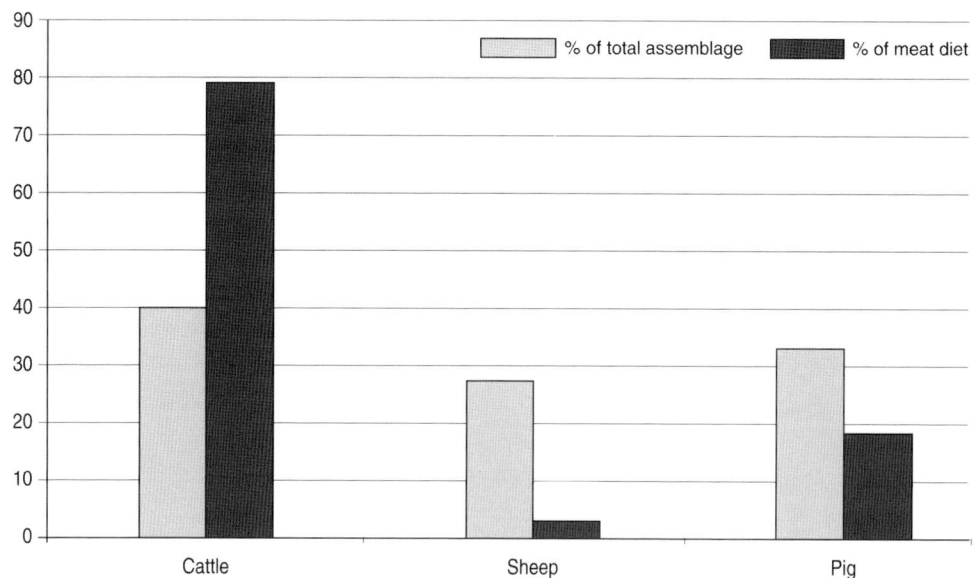

animals were brought into the town on the hoof and were then slaughtered and butchered, probably immediately.[267] Evidence from thirteenth-century samples from Thomas Street suggests that cattle were suspended by their hind legs while being butchered, that they were chopped into three parts (the two sides and the vertebral column), and that the skull was chopped open to enable the removal of the brain.[268] The bones from meat-yielding parts of the animal tend to have far greater numbers of cut and chop marks. The horns of cattle are regularly found among the skeletal remains and these often exhibit signs of having been cut from the skull.[269] Cattle horns were worked into drinking vessels, handles and other objects. The high numbers of cattle horn cores from fourteenth-century Arran Quay 'clearly represent an industrial deposit'. As they appear to derive from young animals (otherwise absent from the assemblage), they were seen by the analyst to be a by-product, traded on to urban merchants or craftsmen, of the slaughter of young males in rural areas.[270] Further, as the horns of young animals are not usually solid enough for horn-working, McCormick concluded that these may have ended up at Arran Quay attached to calfskins destined for use as parchment.

The optimum meat-producing age for cattle is usually considered to be approximately twenty-seven months. This fits the pattern from the majority of sites in the Dublin region, where most cattle whose age could be determined were in the eighteen-to-thirty-month bracket, suggesting that they were farmed and killed primarily for their meat.[271] Most cattle from urban sites tend to be over two years old and McCormick has inferred from this that 'outside producers found it more profitable to send semi-mature or fully grown beasts to the Dublin market'.[272] Some 85 per cent of the cattle analysed from thirteenth-century contexts at Wood Quay were mature at the time of death.[273]

The vast majority of cattle that found their way onto the meat market in Dublin were female. At Patrick Street, cows accounted for 85 per cent of the identifiable bovine remains from twelfth- to fourteenth-century contexts, 94 per cent in the fourteenth- to sixteenth-century levels, and 100 per cent in the sixteenth- to eighteenth-century phases.[274] Similarly

267 Ibid.; Nora Bermingham, 'John Dillon Street, Dublin 8 (98E0158)'; Cremin, 'Animal bone, Thomas St.', p. 62. 268 Cremin, 'Animal bone, Thomas St.' 269 Tallaght: St Maelruan's (96E0188); Cremin, 'Animal bone, Thomas St.'; Vincent Butler, Bridge St. Upr (92E0078); Butler, 'Report on the animal bones (from Bridge St. Lower)', 68. 270 McCormick, 'The mammal bone (from Arran Quay)', p. 226. 271 McQuade, 'Faunal remains from Nangor'; Cremin, 'Animal bone, Thomas St.' 272 McCormick and Murphy, 'Mammal bones', p. 200; McCormick, 'The mammal bone (from Arran Quay)', p. 224. 273 Butler, 'Animal bone studies in archaeology', 106. 274 McCormick

high figures (91.1 per cent) were noted from fifteenth- to sixteenth-century levels at Arran Quay.[275] There is some evidence that in primitive cattle, females fattened at a faster rate than males.[276] This would have made them more economically viable, while another clear advantage of females over males is that they can replace themselves before being sent for slaughter. McCormick sees the rising percentage of female animals noted from across medieval sites in Dublin as evidence for a 'decline in the use of ox for ploughing within the hinterland of Dublin'.[277]

Sheep

Sheep were 'one of the most complex components of medieval agriculture'.[278] Although technically 'non-working' animals, they played a role in arable agriculture. The practice of sheep-folding – moving animals onto arable land to be penned in folds at night – is documented in medieval Ireland. The dung walked into the fields increased fertility and yields. Sheep dung is richer than cattle dung in nitrogen, potassium and phosphorus and therefore makes better manure.[279] Arable land needs regular manuring in order to maintain optimum yields, and an expansion of arable agriculture can sometimes be concomitant with an increase in sheep numbers.[280] Such a pattern is identifiable in the Dublin region.

As a food animal, sheep were kept for their milk and for their meat, but it was as a source of wool that they tended to give their best returns.[281] Sheep yield a very small amount of meat per animal in comparison with cattle and pigs, and mutton was essentially a by-product of the wool industry, rather than vice versa. A study of medieval sheep-types based on documentary, skeletal and illustrative evidence concluded that the predominant sheep type in the Middle Ages was a small medium-wool type 'perhaps comparable with the surviving short-tailed and vari-coloured Orkney/Shetland breeds'.[282] The Irish evidence fits well with this, and analysis of the bones from thirteenth-century contexts at Thomas Street in Dublin suggests that the sheep were small in stature with long slender legs.[283] As much as 17 per cent of the Patrick Street sheep were polled (hornless), and no multi-horned sheep were present.[284] Evidence also indicates that the sheep were becoming larger through the generations, and this may reflect the importation of new breeds, producing more or better quality wool.[285]

There have been various studies of wool-yields of medieval sheep in England, Scotland and Wales.[286] These show that there was considerable variation depending on breed, environment and management techniques. On average, however, the mean fleece weights produced by these studies agree closely and a figure of about 1.4lbs (*c.*640g) of wool per fleece would appear to be representative. In order to yield a good quality fleece, sheep must be fed very well.[287] Irish wool was regarded as inferior to English and Scottish wool and it is possible that Irish fleeces were also lighter than many English equivalents (see below, Chapter 17).

It is difficult to assess the importance of sheep to the rural economy of the medieval Dublin region, given the nature of the surviving sources. The biggest landowner in the region, the archbishop of Dublin, was able to sell fifty-one sacks of wool to merchants in 1216.[288] Depending on how one calculates the number of fleeces in a sack, this represented

and Murphy, 'Mammal bones'. **275** McCormick, 'The mammal bone (from Arran Quay)', p. 225. **276** Ibid. **277** Ibid. **278** Campbell, *Seigniorial agriculture*, p. 157. **279** K.D. White, *Roman farming* (London, 1970), pp 127–8. **280** McCormick, 'The effect of Anglo-Norman settlement', p. 46. **281** Campbell, *Seigniorial agriculture*, p. 155. **282** M.L. Ryder, 'British medieval sheep and their wool types' in D.W. Crossley (ed.), *Medieval industry* (CBA Research Report, 40, 1981), pp 16–27 at p. 27. **283** Cremin, 'Animal bone, Thomas St.' **284** McCormick and Murphy, 'Mammal bones', p. 204. **285** Ibid.; McCormick, 'The mammal bone (from Arran Quay)', p. 228. **286** M.J. Stephenson, 'Wool yields in the medieval economy', *EcHR*, 41 (1988), 368–91; Robert Trow-Smith, *A history of British livestock husbandry to 1700* (London, 1957), pp 166–9; Miller (ed.), *The agrarian history of England and Wales, vol. 3*; Campbell, *Seigniorial agriculture*, pp 155–6. **287** Cremin, 'Animal bones from Christ Church Place', p. 78. **288** *CDI,*

the clip of between 12,750 and 21,420 sheep.[289] Assuming that the wool was all produced by the archbishop's own sheep, the figures indicate large flocks on the archiepiscopal manors, although of course the wool might have accumulated over a number of years.

Some lay manors in the region had impressive numbers of sheep, although none could match the manor of Old Ross in Co. Wexford, which specialised in sheep and had 2,423 in 1289.[290] In 1303, Agnes de Valence had 400 wethers, 420 ewes and 400 lambs on her manor of Rathmore, Co. Kildare.[291] Ballysax, also in Co. Kildare, had 365 sheep in 1280/1.[292] Not all sheep were kept on the large demesnes, however. On aggregate, more were probably found on the holdings of lesser farmers and peasants. Judicial records that give details of the chattels of individuals distrained for debts or felonies abound with instances of people owning small flocks of sheep of thirty or less. In 1310, Adam Jordan, who escaped from Dublin Castle, had ten sheep and six lambs, while in 1305 two Irish felons had six sheep each and a third had a stone-and-a-half of wool.[293] A family of *hibernici* in Ballykene, Co. Dublin, had thirty sheep in 1306, while an unspecified group of 'men of Cloncurry' suffered the theft of 140 of their sheep in 1311.[294] Information is rarely given regarding the sex and age of the sheep, which makes it difficult to determine whether they were being kept primarily for their wool. Identification of a sheep as a 'wether' (an adult castrated male) indicates a primary use as a wool-producer. The fleece of a wether was about a third heavier than that of a ewe, and consequently they dominated the specialist wool-producing flocks.[295]

Forty-three (or 73 per cent) of the Dublin testators who left inventories in the period 1467–83 kept a total of 1,134 sheep between them (Table 9.9).[296] In aggregate terms, sheep were the largest animal category listed, even though 27 per cent of testators did not keep any. The average number of sheep was twenty-six and very few testators kept fewer than ten. Sheep had the lowest unit price of the four livestock types encountered, with 4*d.* a head being the most commonly cited value.[297] The term used in the inventories is '*ovis*', which can be translated as 'sheep' but is more likely to mean specifically a ewe. The term 'wether' is completely absent, and the presence in many lists of lambs indicates a predominance of breeding females. Jonet Cristore of Glasnevin had forty sheep with lambs and Margaret Browneusyn of Killadoon had fifteen sheep with fifteen lambs.[298] Most of the people with sheep and lambs also had cows and calves, perhaps indicating an interest in dairying rather than wool production. Not one of the testators mentioned wool among their possessions, although John Wyde, an English merchant, had eleven packs (pakkys) of sheepskins and lambskins worth ten marks when he died in Dublin in 1471.[299]

While a significant number of testators had meat stocks in their larder, mutton is never mentioned. In England before the fifteenth century, sheep were rarely kept for their meat.[300] As a food animal, they were kept much more for their milk. There are no references to the production of ewe's milk and cheese in the Dublin region, although it undoubtedly occurred. The sheep were milked and cheeses were made on the earl of Norfolk's manors at

1171–1251, no. 712, p. 109.   **289** The wide range reflects the uncertainty about the size of the sack and the weight of the fleece. O'Neill states that, for customs purposes, the sack was a standard weight of 364lbs of shorn wool representing the clip of 250 sheep (*Merchants and mariners*, p. 59); this is represented above by the lower figure. There are several documentary references to a sack of wool containing 42 stone or 588lbs, however, which (using an average fleece weight of 1.4lbs) gives the larger figure above. The Irish fleece may have been lighter than the English average, which would give a larger figure again. Mary Lyons states that 'it is apparent from figures in the Fothered (Forth) demesne accounts that a stone of wool contained between nine and eleven fleeces of mature sheep' ('Manorial administration', p. 62). This would give an average fleece weight of between 1.27 and 1.55lbs.   **290** TNA:PRO SC6/1238/55.   **291** *CJR, 1305–7*, p. 240.   **292** TNA:PRO SC6/1237/1.   **293** *CJR, 1308–14*, p. 153; *CJR, 1305–7*, p. 479.   **294** *CJR, 1305–7*, pp 326–7; *CJR, 1308–14*, p. 226.   **295** Trow-Smith, *British livestock husbandry*, p. 149; Stephenson, 'Wool yields', 373.   **296** Berry (ed.), *Register of wills and inventories*.   **297** Occasionally, higher values occur – even 12*d.* a head in one case.   **298** Berry (ed.), *Register of wills and inventories*, pp 3–5.   **299** Ibid., p. 16.   **300** Campbell, *Seigniorial agriculture*, p. 154; Grant, 'Animal resources', pp 154–5.

Table 9.10 Livestock data from selected faunal assemblages in Dublin city and region.

	Arran Quay (14thc.): MNI%	Arran Quay (15–16thc.): MNI%	Bridge St. Upr (92E0078): 12–13thc. (no. of frags)	Dundrum Castle (13/14thc.)	Fishamble Street (10–11thc.): MNI%	Fishamble Street (11–12thc.): MNI%	George's Hill (93E0106): no. of bones	High Street (12–E13thc.): MNI	High Street (12–E13thc.): MNI%	John Dillon Street (98E0158)	Kindlestown (01E0084): L13–14thc.	Naas (02E0955): MNI	Nangor (meat contribution): %	Patrick St. A (L13–L14thc.): MNI%	Patrick St. B (L13–L14thc.): MNI%	Ship Street (E12thc.): MNI%	Ship Street Great (01E0772)	Skreen (05E0321): MNI	Thomas Street	Thomas Street: carcass weight %	Wood Quay (13thc.): meat %	Wood Quay (13thc.): MNI%
Cattle	35.5	34	561	5	34.4	58.8	25	19	43.2	12	1	82.4	33.3	33.3	47.8	1	30	8	84	83	40	
Sheep/Goat	35.5	42.4	62	6	10.4	11.3	16	8	13.6	5	5	2	11.5	52.8	23.5	13	1	6	20	2.4	4	36
Pig	29	23	229	4	55.3	30	6	19	43.2	1	2	6.1	13.9	43.1	39.1	1	17	1	13.6	13	24	
Horse	1	2	1	1	1	2																
Dog	2	2	2	1	4																	
Cat	1	2	2	1														1				
Hare	7	1																				
Deer	2	2	1	1	1																	
Rat	2	1																				
Bird	49	1	12	1	5																	
Rabbit	1																					

Ballysax and Old Ross in the 1280s, and it was stated that the milk produced by ten ewes was equal in value to that produced by one cow.[301]

The increasing economic importance of sheep in medieval Ireland is clearly attested in the archaeological record for the Dublin region. Analyses of pre-Anglo-Norman samples suggest that sheep/goat (the two are notoriously difficult to tell apart on the basis of their skeletal remains alone) were relatively unimportant, with 10–13 per cent of assemblages being made up of caprovine remains.[302] Twelfth-century samples from Bridge Street Upper also contained a very low proportion of sheep remains. Thirteenth- and fourteenth-century deposits from Patrick Street and Wood Quay indicated that by this time the importance of sheep/goat had increased considerably, with recorded values of 36 and 53 per cent respectively.[303] Thirteenth-century samples from Thomas Street yielded similarly high figures.[304] Outside the town, sheep also dominated the samples from thirteenth-/fourteenth-century remains at Kindlestown Castle, Naas, Dundrum Castle and Nangor townland.[305] As ovine numbers increased, so the porcine population decreased, and by the sixteenth century, sheep had overtaken pig in many places, particularly in Dublin.[306] By this time, sheep even overtook cattle numerically.[307]

From the thirteenth century onwards, bones from non meat-yielding animals become less frequent in urban assemblages and lambs are increasingly rare.[308] This was not the case on rural sites, however, and at Dundrum Castle some lambs were present side-by-side with the mature animals.[309] A similar pattern was identified at Nangor, where most of the sheep

301 Lyons, 'Manorial administration', p. 62. This is close enough to the figure of twelve ewes to one cow cited by Trow-Smith, *British livestock husbandry*, pp 121–2. **302** McCormick and Murphy, 'Mammal bones', pp 199–200. **303** V.G. Butler, 'Cattle in thirteenth-century Dublin: an osteological examination of its remains' (MA, UCD (NUI), 1984); McCormick and Murphy, 'Mammal bones', pp 199–200. **304** Cremin, 'Animal bone, Thomas St.' **305** Melanie McQuade, 'Analysis of faunal remains' in Simpson, 'Dublin's southern frontier' (2003), pp 357–61; Burkes Pharmacy, Main Street Naas (02E0955), Animal bone report by Melanie McQuaid, pp 14–16; Murray, 'Reports on the faunal and molluscan material from excavations at Dundrum Castle', p. 2; McQuade, 'Faunal remains from Nangor'. **306** Turrell, 'Archaeozoology of medieval Dublin', pp 39–44. **307** Ibid., p. 32. **308** McCormick and Murphy, 'Mammal bones', p. 202. **309** Murray, 'Reports on the faunal and molluscan material from excavations at Dundrum Castle', p. 2.

Figure 9.20 Shanganagh
Castle, Co. Dublin,
drawn by Gabriel
Beranger, 1760. The
flesh of goats was a
popular meat at this
time, and many were
reared in south
Co. Dublin (image
reproduced courtesy of
the National Library of
Ireland).

were two years of age or more, but one or two were immature or neonatal.[310] The evidence indicates that sheep were being farmed in the area, while the high number of non-meat-bearing bones present indicates that slaughter and/or primary butchering was also being carried out nearby.

Bones often display evidence for butchery, in the form of cut and chop marks, while long bones in particular were regularly broken open in order to extract marrow. Where cranial remains are found on urban sites, it is possible that the heads were exploited for food – a sheep skull from Bridge Street Lower had been cleaved apart down the centre, and it was suggested that this was in order to extract the brain. In general, the pattern appears to be that the age at which animals were slaughtered increased over time.[311] Older animals, past their wool-producing best, were probably then sent on to the urban meat market.

The increasing numbers of sheep must have been reflected in the agricultural landscape around the city, as sheep (unlike pig) could not be reared easily within the town and were supplied by outside producers. Evidence for sheep management, the employment of shepherds and the construction and use of purpose-built sheep-shelters or sheepcotes is difficult to find for the Dublin region. Sheepcotes are very frequently mentioned in English documents of the medieval period and their remains constitute a common archaeological site.[312] They are associated with efficient and progressive husbandry 'which sought to make the best use of resources and which involved considerable effort to keep animals warm, healthy and well fed'.[313] The surviving evidence for the Dublin region unfortunately does not provide information on the nature of sheep husbandry in the medieval period.

Goats

A recent study of goats in medieval England has concluded that goat husbandry was an appropriate way to exploit the resources of areas ill-suited to conventional mixed corn and

310 McQuade, 'Faunal remains from Nangor'.   **311** McCormick and Murphy, 'Mammal bones', pp 202–3; McCormick, 'The mammal bone (from Arran Quay)', p. 228.   **312** Christopher Dyer, 'Sheepcotes: evidence for medieval sheepfarming', *Med. Arch.*, 39 (1995), 136–62.   **313** Dyer, 'Sheepcotes', 160.

Figure 9.21 Feral goat in the Wicklow Mountains. It is possible that the wild goats in Wicklow are the descendants of the commercially reared goats of the eighteenth century (© Department of the Environment, Heritage and Local Government).

sheep farming or dairying.[314] They were occasionally kept by lords to provide kid for the table but more often kept by peasants in small numbers for their milk and meat. While most goats were undoubtedly to be found in the countryside, they were also an ideal source of milk in towns, where they were easier to keep than any other milk-producing domesticate.[315] Goats also have the advantage that they lactate continuously as long as they are milked.

One of the most satisfactory ways of telling the difference between goats and sheep from their skeletal remains is by means of the horns. The fact that goat horns are more often recovered than those of sheep on medieval sites in Ireland has been seen as evidence that goat horns (which are straighter and harder) were preferred by horn-workers, but it has also been pointed out that the prevalence of goat horns might be related to the fact that they tend to survive better than those of sheep.[316] When goat horns do occur on urban sites, they are usually from females, underlining the role of the goat as a dairy animal. When the animal had reached the end of its life, its skin and horns could be removed, prepared and sold. Goat horns were well-represented in thirteenth-century levels at Thomas Street, and all were from females, one of which was *c*.25–6 months old.[317] At Arran Quay, all nine goats from fourteenth- to sixteenth-century samples were female.[318] At Bridge Street Lower, a single horn core from a female goat had apparently been hacked from her skull and was seen by the analyst as possible waste from a horn-worker.[319] Goat horn cores found at John Dillon Street had also been cut from the skull.[320]

Documentary references to the keeping of goats in the Dublin region are not numerous but they do occur. In 1280, the tenants of Saggart petitioned the king, informing him that

---

314 C.C. Dyer, 'Alternative agriculture: goats in medieval England' in R.W. Hoyle (ed.), *People, landscape and alternative agriculture: essays for Joan Thirsk* (Exeter, 2004), pp 20–38 at p. 37. **315** McCormick and Murphy, 'Mammal bones', p. 202. **316** Ibid.; McCormick, 'The mammal bone (from Arran Quay)', p. 227; McCormick, 'The effect of Anglo-Norman settlement', pp 46–7; McCormick, 'Bones from High Street', p. 10. **317** Cremin, 'Animal bone, Thomas St.' **318** McCormick, 'The mammal bone (from Arran Quay)', p. 227. **319** Butler, 'Report on the animal bones (from Bridge St. Lower)', figs 6 and 7, C46. **320** Bermingham, 'John Dillon Street'.

during a recent raid by the Irish they had lost a considerable number of livestock, including a number of goats.[321] In 1314, William and Henry McGochi of Ballycorus in south-east Co. Dublin were robbed of livestock including forty goats.[322] There are no references to goats in the fifteenth-century will inventories, but in 1444 two tenants on the manor of Lucan were fined 'for their goats'.[323] This presumably refers to an incident involving damage caused by these animals. The documentary evidence therefore suggests that goats were kept by tenants rather than lords and were often found in the uplands of south Dublin, where they were probably grazed alongside sheep on hilly pasture (Figure 9.21). In the eighteenth century goat flesh was a popular meat on Dublin tables and kids were reared in the mountainous parts of south Dublin to supply this demand.[324]

Pigs

Pigs are specialised meat-producing animals – 'game and poultry apart, they were the single most productive source of meat available to medieval farmers'.[325] They are more prolific and they mature at a faster rate than any other domestic animal. The domestic sow can average up to eleven piglets per litter and will farrow at least twice a year, and one pig is capable of providing bacon for a family of four to six for most of the year.[326] Unlike cattle and sheep, they can be kept in urban spaces with relatively little difficulty, as they do not require grazing and can be fed on scraps of food and other waste (if, as has been suggested above, goats were kept for dairying purposes, then it is also possible that the by-products of the manufacture of butter and cheese could be fed to the pigs).[327] While they were certainly kept in towns, pigs were more common in rural areas, where they were herded into woods to feed on roots, fungi, beech mast, acorns and other wild food.[328] In general, all males and most females were slaughtered once they reached full size. Pigs clearly had advantages over other farm animals, but they could also be difficult to control. They are competitors with humans as they eat a similar range of food and, unlike most other animals, they provide very few useful by-products either when dead or when alive. Their sole contribution to the medieval economy was meat, and little of this was wasted – indeed archaeological evidence from the Dublin region demonstrates that pigs' trotters and brains were consumed.[329]

In Anglo-Norman Ireland, pigs were particularly associated with provisioning castle garrisons and military expeditions. In the early years of the colony, pigs were sent to Ireland in great numbers, but by 1217 the movement had reversed, with 1,000 pigs being sent to England.[330] In 1282, pigs were driven from the manor of Ballysax, Co. Kildare, to Dublin and fifty-five were shipped to Wales to supply Roger Bigod, who was on campaign there.[331]

There is no direct evidence for the Dublin area of the intensive pig-husbandry found on some English manors, where sty-based animals were fed on legumes and the by-products of brewing and dairying.[332] Some Leinster manors did support large numbers of pigs, however, and in 1308, for instance, there were one hundred pigs at Clontarf.[333] In general, rural and

321 Sayles, *Documents on the affairs of Ireland*, no. 41, p. 32.   **322** NAI KB2/7: Justiciar roll 8–9 Ed. II, m.2.   **323** Dryburgh and Smith (eds), *Handbook*, p. 238.   **324** John Rutty, *An essay towards a natural history of the county of Dublin* (Dublin, 1772), quoted by John Feehan, *Farming in Ireland: history, heritage and environment* (Dublin, 2003), p. 187.   **325** Campbell, *Seigniorial agriculture*, p. 165.   **326** Alexander Fenton, 'Pork in the rural diet of Scotland' in Theo Gantner and Hans Trumpy (eds), *Festschrift fur Robert Wildhaber* (Basel, 1973), pp 98–110 at p. 98.   **327** J.W. King, 'Pigs', *Biologist*, 20:5 (1983), 267–73; McCormick, 'The animal bones (Waterford)', p. 830; Butler, 'Animal bone studies in archaeology', 106.   **328** Turrell, 'Archaeozoology of medieval Dublin', pp 44–8.   **329** Emily Murray, 'Animal bone report [Maynooth Castle]' (unpublished report – DEHLG file 96E0391); Emmet Byrnes, 'Archaeological test excavation at Rathmore West, Co. Kildare (excavation no. 98E0145; file no. 1248/2345)', unpublished report, April 1998, p. 6; Emmet Byrnes, 'Archaeological monitoring at Rathmore West, Co. Kildare (excavation no. 98E0145; file no. 1248/2345)', unpublished report, Aug. 1998.   **330** *CDI, 1171–1251*, pp 1–3, no. 756, p. 114; McCormick 'The effect of Anglo-Norman settlement', p. 48.   **331** *CDI, 1252–82*, no. 2009, pp 459–61.   **332** See, for example, Kathleen Biddick, 'Pig husbandry on the Peterborough Abbey estate from the twelfth to the fourteenth century AD' in Juliet Clutton-Brock and Caroline Grigson (eds), *Animals and archaeology* (Oxford, 1985), pp 161–77.   **333** Mac Niocaill, 'Suppression

urban pigs appear to have been free-ranging foragers, with woodlands in particular being associated with the feeding of swine. In 1544, when Christ Church leased the manor of Cabra, one of the terms of the lease was that the lessee was allowed to keep forty pigs in Salcock's Wood, which the abbey retained possession of.[334]

After cattle, pigs were the animal most likely to feature in the inventories of fifteenth-century Dubliners. They were kept by forty-eight testators and the average number kept was nine (Table 9.9). Many of the inventories distinguish between adult pigs, sows and piglets, although boars are only mentioned twice. The average price for a pig was about 1s., although values twice that and more are sometimes encountered. Piglets were valued at between 4d. and 8d. The adult pig's value was therefore at least three times that of the sheep. Testators who were not otherwise implicated in agricultural pursuits were more likely to have pigs than any other animal. John Kyng and Jacoba Payn, whose possessions suggest that they were brewers or inn-keepers and who lived in the parish of St Nicholas Without, owned eighteen pigs, and these were their only livestock (perhaps they were fattening them on the brewing by-products?).[335] Bacon, gammon and pork were by far the most likely meats to be found in the larders of the testators. A gammon of bacon could be worth as much as 3s. 4d.

Analysis of the bone assemblage from Maynooth Castle revealed the importance of pigs in the diet of the site's occupants.[336] The increased importance of pig was coincident with a decrease in cattle numbers. This change in species exploitation was particularly noticeable from the pre-Anglo-Norman period to the post-1170 period, and may be related to wider agricultural changes in which more arable land meant less grazing land and consequently relatively fewer cattle.[337] Cattle accounted for some 27.3 per cent of the animals represented in the pre-Anglo-Norman samples at Maynooth, but only 10 per cent in the later phases. While most of the cattle represented were female, almost all of the pigs were male. Sheep were rare. There is evidence that pigs were reared on-site, and this tallies with the information from Dundrum Castle, where bones of both adult pigs (mostly over two years old) and several neonatal individuals were identified, leading Emily Murray to suggest that 'pigs may have been bred in pens in the grounds of the castle'.[338] This age pattern was repeated on Arran Quay and at Patrick Street and again this can be seen as evidence for pig rearing on site.[339] Of course the presence of bones of young pigs cannot in itself be taken as concrete evidence for pig rearing, and McCormick has suggested that suckling pigs were seen (and consumed) by some as a delicacy.[340] The pig-sties and farrowing pens excavated by Wallace at the rear of Viking-Age houses on Fishamble Street are more conclusive evidence, however, and it is likely that structures such as these also existed at later sites, both urban and rural.[341]

The evidence from thirteenth-century contexts on Thomas Street suggests that pigs made up 21.5 per cent of the animals consumed on that particular site, a figure that probably equates with about 13.6 per cent of the meat eaten.[342] Analysis of this and other Dublin sites indicates that pigs decreased in relative importance over the years, particularly when compared to sheep. Comparing the figures, one can see that pigs made up 43.2 per cent of the animal remains in twelfth- to thirteenth-century High Street, 24 per cent in thirteenth-century Wood Quay, 16.7 per cent in twelfth- to fourteenth-century Nicholas Street and 9.7 per cent in the same place in the sixteenth to eighteenth centuries.[343]

of the Templars', 188. **334** *CCCD*, no. 1195. **335** Berry (ed.), *Register of wills and inventories*, pp 156–8. **336** Murray, 'Maynooth Castle (96E0391)'. **337** Finbar McCormick, 'Farming and food in medieval Lecale' in Lindsay Proudfoot (ed.), *Down: history and society* (1997), pp 33–46 at pp 39–41. **338** Murray, 'Reports on the faunal and molluscan material from excavations at Dundrum Castle', p. 3. **339** McCormick and Murphy, 'Mammal bones', p. 204. **340** McCormick, 'The animal bones (Waterford)', p. 831. **341** P.F. Wallace, 'The archaeological identity of the Hiberno-Norse town', *JRSAI*, 122 (1992), 35–66 at 57, 62; P.F. Wallace, *The Viking-Age buildings of Dublin* (2 vols, Dublin, 1992), I, pp 124, 126. **342** Cremin, 'Animal bone, Thomas St.'. **343** Ibid., p. 61.

It has been suggested that the high incidence of pig remains in an assemblage can sometimes be attributed to the proximity of extensive forest that could supply mast (acorns) for pig fodder.[344] McCormick highlighted the important role played by acorns in the diet of pigs and wondered if this might be linked to references to mast being sold as a cash crop in Armagh in the eleventh century.[345] While mast may have been fed to pigs in the Dublin region in the Middle Ages, there is no direct evidence for this and it is possible that the diet of most pigs, particularly in urban contexts, consisted mainly of miscellaneous scraps.

The archaeological record provides evidence for an overall decrease in pig numbers over the course of the Middle Ages. It has been suggested that an increasing human population may have put pressure on the numbers of pigs kept in towns, while a factor in their decrease in rural areas may have been a reduction in woodland area.[346]

Rabbits

It would appear that rabbits were introduced into Ireland very shortly after the arrival of the Anglo-Normans, who prized their meat and fur.[347] One of the earliest documentary references to rabbits can be found in a grant of c.1185 from Prince John to his chamberlain, Alard Fitz William.[348] Fitz William was given lands in the hinterlands of Waterford, Wexford and Dublin (probably Lucan) along with the 'hunting of stag, doe, pig, hare, wolf and rabbit'. The wording of this grant may be rather stereotypical and not reflect the actual situation in these areas. An unambiguous reference to a warren in the Dublin area can however be found c.1200, when the first Anglo-Norman archbishop of Dublin, John Cumin, granted the canons of Holy Trinity, Dublin, one hundred rabbits yearly from his warren at Portraine.[349] The warren must have been large and well developed by this date, given the expected yield of rabbits. In 1326, it was valued at 20s. 'in grass and other issues'.[350] The archbishop had a much larger warren or warrens on Lambay, valued at 100s. in 1326.[351] According to Archbishop Alen, John Cumin had given the tithes of rabbits from Lambay to the nunnery of Gracedieu at its foundation in 1195.[352] It is possible, therefore, that Cumin, who before his elevation to Dublin had served Henry II in an ambassadorial capacity, had developed a taste for rabbit on his visits to the Continent and was responsible for their introduction into Ireland.[353]

Some of the earliest references to rabbits in English documentary sources also relate to warrens on natural islands.[354] The references are for the late twelfth and early thirteenth centuries and relate to the Scilly Isles, Lundy Island and the Isle of Wight. It has been proposed, therefore, that rabbits first became established in the twelfth century on small islands off the English coast and only in the mid- to late thirteenth century started to appear on some mainland estates. Our limited Irish evidence would suggest the same progression. Rabbits favoured the sandy soils found in coastal and riverine locations and on islands where they were relatively free from large predators (Figure 9.21). O'Conor has also suggested that in Ireland rabbits may have been encouraged to use deserted ringforts with their dry interiors and earthen banks, although this theory awaits further investigation.[355]

344 McCormick, 'Farming and food in medieval Lecale', p. 39.   345 AFM, s.a. 1031, 1097 (the latter entry notes that there was a 'great abundance of nuts throughout Ireland in general this year, so that the swine of Ireland were fatted'). 346 Turrell, 'Archaeozoology of medieval Dublin', p. 45.   347 McCormick, 'The effect of Anglo-Norman settlement', p. 49; Murphy and O'Conor, 'Castles and deer parks in Anglo-Norman Ireland', 57.   348 COD, 1, p. 4.   349 McNeill (ed.), Alen's register, p. 30.   350 Ibid., p. 178.   351 Ibid.   352 Ibid., p. 19.   353 Margaret Murphy, 'Archbishops and Anglicisation: Dublin, 1181–1271' in Kelly and Keogh (eds), History of the Catholic diocese of Dublin (2000), pp 72–91 at p. 75.   354 E.M. Veale, 'The rabbit in England', AHS, 5 (1957), 85–90 at 86.   355 Kieran O'Conor, 'Medieval rural settlement in Munster' in John Ludlow and Noel Jameson (eds), The Barryscourt Lectures I–X (Cork, 2004), pp 227–56 at pp 237–8.

Figure 9.22 This nineteenth-century depiction of Waterford by George du Noyer is based on a drawing in the Great Charter Roll of Waterford, c.1370. It shows rabbit warrens on the north bank of the River Suir. The sandy soil found on estuaries and river banks was an ideal habitat for rabbits, and their meat formed part of the urban diet in Waterford as in Dublin (image courtesy of the Royal Society of Antiquaries of Ireland).

Figure 9.23 Extract
from the Down Survey
map of the barony of
Coolock, showing a
large 'conyburry' or
rabbit warren at
Portmarnock.

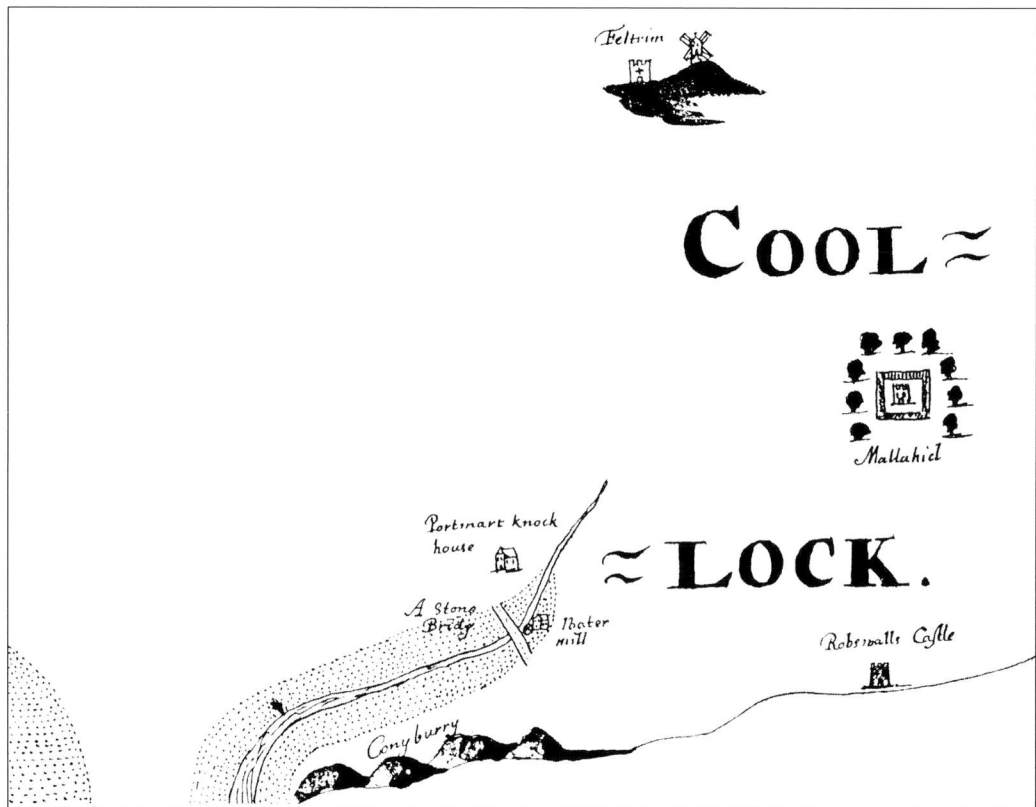

By the late thirteenth century, rabbit warrens had become part of the Irish manorial landscape and in the Dublin region are mentioned in extents for Chapelizod, Gormanston, Lucan, Shankill and Swords. These warrens provided food for the lord's table but were probably also exploited commercially, particularly on manors where the lord was non-resident. The values assigned to them in the extents reflected their size and productive capacity. The archbishop of Dublin's warrens at Lambay and Portraine were certainly the best in the Dublin region. The warren at Gormanston was worth 6s. 8d., while those at Chapelizod and Lucan were valued at 3s. 4d.[356] In 1326, the warren at Shankill was said to be worth nothing because it was all wasted and nothing could be got from it.[357] It may have been the Irish who destroyed the Shankill warren, although predators and poachers could also pose a serious threat to rabbit farming. An extent dated to 1299 for the manor of Shanid, Co. Limerick, recorded nothing from the manorial warrens because the rabbits had been destroyed by foxes.[358]

The value of rabbits lay in both their meat and their fur. Early fourteenth-century municipal legislation for Dublin fixed the price of two good rabbits at 1½d.[359] In 1286, rabbits in Co. Carlow were selling for ½d. each, while rabbit skins sold at just under 1d.[360] Rabbit featured on the menu of the prior of Christ Church in the 1340s and an individual was paid for going to Holmpatrick to fetch rabbits.[361] Rabbit fur became increasingly popular in England in the thirteenth century and presumably in Ireland also.[362] Rabbit warrens were usually culled in the autumn when the rabbit's fur was at its thickest, and the usual method of trapping was with ferrets and nets.[363] At Ballysax, Co. Kildare, in the 1280s, the ferret-keeper or handler was given a proportion of the rabbits culled from the warren as his payment.[364]

356 TNA:PRO C134/21/6; C143/50/16; C47/10/22/15.   **357** McNeill (ed.), *Alen's register*, p. 196.   **358** *CDI, 1293–1301*, no. 551, p. 259.   **359** *HMDI*, pp 232–5.   **360** TNA:PRO SC6/1237/51.   **361** Mills (ed.), *Account roll*, pp 111, 117. **362** E.M. Veale, *The English fur trade in the later Middle Ages* (Oxford, 1966), ch. 1.   **363** Mark Bailey, 'The rabbit and the medieval East-Anglian economy', *AHS*, 36 (1988), 1–20 at 7.   **364** TNA:PRO SC6/1237/4.

Rabbits were not able to survive in a feral state until the eighteenth century and consequently for many centuries they lived in protected confines. Specially constructed warrens provided safe habitats for them and facilitated their management and annual culling. The seventeenth-century Civil Survey recorded warrens at many locations in the Dublin region, including Portraine and a large example at 'Howth Island'.[365] The surveyors also noted that along the banks of the Liffey, there was an 'aboundance of Connyburroughs which are profitable to the proprietors' (Figure 9.23).[366]

In Britain, rabbit farming is associated with the distinctive cigar-shaped earthworks, known as pillow mounds, which are found all over the countryside and some of which are believed to date to the medieval period.[367] No pillow mound has yet been recognised in the Irish countryside and in fact there is virtually no archaeological evidence for rabbit farming in Ireland in the medieval period.[368] The rabbit bones recovered from thirteenth-century contexts some 250m from the motte at Skreen, Co. Meath, are among the earliest found in Ireland.[369] Rabbit remains were also found in medieval levels at Killeen Castle, Co. Meath.[370]

Poultry

Poultry and other domesticated fowl including ducks, geese, swans, pigeons, pheasants and peacocks were popular among the Anglo-Normans and were kept on most manors to provide eggs, meat and feathers. Thirteenth-century manorial accounts frequently include numbers of poultry at the end of the stock account and documents for the earl of Norfolk's manors of Ballysax, Co. Kildare, Forth, Co. Carlow and Old Ross, Co. Wexford, list hens, geese, swans and peacocks.[371] In the absence of such documents for the Dublin region, it must be assumed that domestic fowl were similarly a common sight in manorial farmyards.

Poultry, especially hens, were also found on small-holdings and even the poorest peasant would have been able to keep a few birds. The evidence of rentals would suggest indeed that poultry functioned as a sort of substitute currency for rural dwellers. Rents and dues were often paid in hens. The 1326 rental for the Christ Church properties of Grangegorman and Glasnevin reveals that each tenant was required to pay a hen or 1*d.* to the priory at Christmas.[372]

Hens would no doubt have been accommodated at night in coops or small sheds to protect them from predators. One judicial record from Co. Dublin mentions such a structure. In 1311, Laurence Manfras was accused of entering the hen house of Andrew Tyrell by night and stealing six capons and hens worth 12*d.*[373] The jurors found that the accused was drinking in Andrew's house and when leaving found one capon and one hen sitting in a tree in Andrew's garden and took them. As he had already spent a long time imprisoned in Dublin Castle for the offence, he was pardoned by the court.

Finbar McCormick has suggested that domesticated fowl played a relatively minor role in the agriculture and diet of the Gaelic Irish.[374] It was, however, an important component of the Anglo-Norman diet, as shown by the prior of Christ Church's consumption of goose, capons and pigeons.[375] Like pigs, poultry was also considered as suitable provisioning for troops, and geese and chickens were mentioned in connection with castle garrisons in 1211–12.[376]

Although early Irish literature contains many references to the dove, Fergus Kelly found no mention of their rearing for food in monasteries or elsewhere in early medieval Ireland

365 *Civil Survey*, 7, pp 54, 149. 366 Ibid., p. 288. 367 Michael Aston, *Interpreting the landscape: landscape archaeology and local history* (London, 1985), p. 115. 368 O'Conor, 'Medieval rural settlement in Munster', p. 237. 369 Lynch, 'The animal bone from Skreen'. 370 Jonny Geber, 'The faunal remains' in Baker, *The archaeology of Killeen Castle* (2009), pp 131–56. 371 TNA:PRO SC6/1237/1–6; 1237/40; 1238/44. 372 Mills (ed.), *Account roll*, pp 190–3. 373 *CJR, 1308–14*, pp 217–18. 374 McCormick, 'The effect of Anglo-Norman settlement', p. 49. 375 Mills (ed.), *Account roll*, passim. 376 Davies and Quinn, 'Irish pipe roll of 14 John', p. 15.

(seventh and eighth centuries).[377] It therefore appears that it was the Anglo-Normans who introduced the dovecot and the farming of doves into Ireland. By the early fourteenth century, dovecots were a common feature of the landscape of manors and granges and were usually situated close to the central farm buildings for protection and ease of access.[378] These structures produced meat for the table and also valuable fertiliser for gardens and plots and were, initially at least, counted along with warrens and fishponds among the preserves of lordship. In the later medieval period, there is some evidence that they became more widely dispersed and were found on smaller holdings and farms.

In the Dublin region, dovecots were recorded on the manors of Ballymore Eustace, Cloncurry, Clondalkin, Corduff, Lucan, Maynooth, Moyglare, Rathcoole, Rathfeigh, Swords and Turvey. In many cases they were said to be worth nothing or very little, frequently because they had been allowed to fall into disrepair. There were some exceptions, however, and the two dovecots on the manor of Turvey in 1311 were said to be worth 10s. per annum.[379] In 1288, the archbishop of Dublin leased half a carucate of land in his manor of Colonia to David de Callen, citizen of Dublin, allowing him to erect a dovecot on the land provided that he surrender it at the end of the lease.[380] This might be an indication that dovecots were starting to be more widely dispersed among different ranks of landholders. There are some indications that they were found on small holdings and farms in the fifteenth century. When Christ Church leased a vacant place within a croft in Glasnevin in 1473, they required the lessee to erect a dovecot.[381]

The vast majority of dovecots in Anglo-Norman Ireland were most likely constructed of wood or clay walls and were covered by a roof of thatch or wooden shingles. The 1344 extent for Moyglare, Co. Meath, mentions that the dovecot there was roofed with straw.[382] The medieval dovecots that have survived were stone-built, such as those at Kilcooly, Co. Tipperary, Danesfort, Co. Kilkenny, and Fore, Co. Westmeath. Occasionally, existing structures were adapted to accommodate dovecots; for example, part of the third floor of the tower house at Oughterard was modified for use as a dovecot. To date, very few dovecots have been recognised through archaeological investigation.

Birds were also kept for hunting and as pets. In 1319, Richard de Exeter, a chief justice of the king's bench, complained that the prior of All Hallows, Dublin, had lost a crane that he, Richard, had given to him to keep safely until he should call for it.[383] As a result, he claimed 60s. compensation, an indication of the value placed on such pet birds. The prior confessed that the bird had escaped out of his custody and was pardoned from paying the damages. In his works on Ireland, Gerald of Wales remarked on the abundance of cranes in the country and also on the reluctance of the Irish to eat the flesh of this bird,[384] although they did so when requested to by Henry II.

Chapter summary

The majority of land in the Dublin region was dedicated to agricultural uses, as arable, pasture or meadow. The balance between these land-uses can be investigated by using the evidence provided by medieval extents. It was found that across the Dublin region, arable was the most important agricultural land-use on manorial demesnes. Analysis of the spatial pattern in the relative importance of land-uses revealed that arable assumed most importance in the north of the region, while pasture was most significant in the south, especially the

377 Kelly, *Early Irish farming*, p. 107.   378 Murphy and O'Conor, 'Castles and deerparks in Anglo-Norman Ireland', 56.   379 *RBO*, p. 27.   380 McNeill (ed.), *Alen's register*, p. 152.   381 *CCCD*, no. 1002.   382 TNA:PRO C135/75/13. 383 Butler (ed.), *Registrum prioritas omnium sanctorum*, p. xxi.   384 Gerald of Wales, *The history and topography of Ireland*, pp 40-1; Gerald of Wales: *Expugnatio Hibernica*, p. 97. See also Kelly, *Early Irish farming*, pp 125–9.

south-west. These spatial patterns have an obvious relationship with environmental attributes, but can also be seen to be partly influenced by the requirements of Dublin. Manorial demesnes in the south-east of the region were markedly more wooded than those elsewhere, and wood was almost entirely absent from northern parts.

Extents also give information on the relative value of different land-uses, and this data revealed that arable was frequently valued as highly as meadow land. This contrasts with equivalent data from England, which valued meadow at about three times the rate of arable. It is difficult to discern spatial patterns in the values placed on land because of the variety of factors that could affect value. The valuations, however, expose a sophisticated under-standing of the varying productivity of land and the environmental factors that could impact upon land value.

There is a significant amount of documentary and cartographic evidence for the organisation of arable land into large blocks or 'sesona', which may be translated as open-field sowing areas. Tenants frequently held strips of land scattered across several fields – a system that survived in some areas into the eighteenth and nineteenth centuries. Most of the arable fields in the Dublin region were sown with grains (wheat, oats, barley, rye and mixtures of the same), legumes (peas and beans) and occasionally mixed crops of grains and legumes.

The cultivation of wheat and oats dominated on the manorial demesnes of the region. Indeed, demesnes are frequently found growing no other crops. There are indications, however, that a wider range of crops, including barley, rye and legumes, was grown by the smaller farmers. Wheat was the principal bread grain and it also formed the bulk of the food liveries given to manorial servants. Both the documentary and the archaeo-botanical record for the Dublin area point to rye being a minority crop in Dublin and its region. Barley is poorly represented on archaeological sites and in the records for crop cultivation on demesnes in the Dublin region before the mid-fourteenth century. Thereafter, it appears to have gradually increased its share of arable acreages. Oats were very widely grown and were put to a number of different uses. A particular feature of the Dublin region appears to be the widespread use of oats for brewing throughout the period. While the use of barley for malting does appear to have increased throughout the medieval period, it did not completely displace oats.

Information on yields and seeding rates is scarce and problematic. What evidence there is appears to point to patterns that are similar to those found on English manors for the same period. Various methods were used to increase yields, such as weeding and fertilising. References to the practice of spreading animal and human dung on the fields prior to ploughing occur in both the documentary and the archaeological record for the Dublin region. There is little evidence to suggest that the cultivation of legumes in medieval Ireland formed part of intensive cropping regimes. In the Dublin region, it appears that they were primarily grown for consumption by humans and animals at home and abroad.

Meadow was recorded on virtually all of the demesnes in the Dublin region for which extents survive. It was usually located close to the manor centre and some manors recorded 'great meadows' containing up to seventy acres. There is clear evidence for specialisation in hay production in areas with environmental advantages, such as the manor of Rathcoole, where meadow constituted some 44 per cent of demesne land-use by area. Pastoral resources overall were particularly plentiful on manors situated in the south-west of the study area, in contrast to parts of the north, where only the fallow arable was available to graze livestock.

Oxen and horses – the working animals – had the first call on pastoral resources where they were in short supply. By the start of the thirteenth century, the eight-ox plough-team was in common use across the region, although there is some evidence for mixed teams of oxen and horses. It is difficult to assess the degree to which oxen were used outside demesnes, as the sources for peasant agriculture and small-holdings are so sparse. There was a general move towards the use of horses for ploughing by the late fifteenth century, a move which is reflected in the documentary sources as well as the archaeological evidence. A decline in the numbers of male cattle represented on medieval sites (proportionate to females) is mirrored by an increase in the numbers of horse bones found.

The need for replacement oxen as well as demand for meat and dairy products ensured that manors with sufficient pastoral resources maintained large cow herds. Tenants also kept significant numbers of cattle. In terms of meat consumed, cattle certainly dominated the human diet in the Dublin region throughout the Middle Ages. Sheep and pigs were important livestock components on large and small holdings; sheep primarily for their wool and pigs for their meat. Goats were also present, but the evidence suggests that they were kept by tenants rather than lords, and particularly in the uplands of south Dublin.

By the late thirteenth century, rabbit warrens had become part of the Irish manorial landscape. They were used to provide food for the lord's table and were also exploited commercially. Dovecots were common features at manorial centres in the thirteenth and fourteenth centuries. By the fifteenth century, they could be found on smaller farms and holdings.

A great deal of the documentary evidence for the practice of agriculture in the Dublin region comes from sources of the thirteenth and early fourteenth centuries, and relates to the large lay and ecclesiastical manorial demesnes. The documentary material for agriculture on small and peasant holdings is sparse, although the archaeological evidence can provide valuable clues. The nature of the sources also means that it is difficult to chart change over time in any statistically meaningful way. In terms of overall land-use patterns, the evidence of the Civil Survey suggests that the balance between arable and pastoral resources in the region remained remarkably stable between the early fourteenth and the mid-seventeenth century, with arable accounting for three-quarters of agricultural land. The growing of crops clearly persisted as the most popular and profitable form of agrarian exploitation in many parts of Dublin's hinterland, although the importance of pastoral farming, particularly to the south of the city, should not be underestimated. There were, of course, other ways to exploit the resources of the region for subsistence and for commercial gain and these will be explored over the next four chapters.

CHAPTER 10

Horticulture

Introduction

Horticulture was a widespread activity in the medieval period and gardens were a commonplace feature of daily life for all classes of people.[1] The percentage of productive land dedicated to horticultural uses and the income generated by this activity were nonetheless very small. The real importance of gardens and gardening was in the sphere of the domestic economy, especially with regard to the largely self-sufficient rural peasant or low-income urban dweller. It is in this sphere, however, that the evidence is for the most part meagre. As Chris Dyer put it, 'gardens were embedded in the interstices of the domestic economy and were bound up in a cycle of auto-consumption which is often hidden from our view'.[2] The vast majority of gardens were in the form of small plots or enclosures located to the rear of smallholders' crofts or cottages. Here, a range of vegetables, fruit and herbs was grown and found its way directly into the owner's stew-pot or onto his or her plate. Apart from labour, little was expended and any surplus was more likely to be bartered than sold.

When gardens do appear in the sources it is usually because they were large enough to generate a profit or confer prestige and therefore could be assigned a monetary value. Manorial extents frequently include a separately valued garden and/or orchard and occasionally give additional information regarding its form and function.[3] In addition, gardens and orchards appear in land transactions when their enclosures are used to delimit boundaries. This is the form in which most references to urban gardens appear. A third source of information is the records of religious houses, as gardens were particularly associated with these establishments. Some idea of the numbers and locations of monastic gardens and orchards can be obtained from the extents of monastic possessions taken in 1540.[4] A century later, the Civil Survey recorded over 110 orchards and 300 gardens for the Dublin region.[5]

There are a number of different archaeological indicators of the presence of gardens and past horticultural activity. The term 'garden soil' is commonly used in the archaeological literature to describe a soil rich in organic matter.[6] This soil type is most frequently encountered on medieval sites across Dublin,[7] but it has also been identified outside the

---

1 For general works on medieval gardens and horticulture, see J.H. Harvey, *Mediaeval gardens* (London, 1981); J.H. Harvey, 'Vegetables in the Middle Ages', *Garden History*, 12 (1984), 89–99; Teresa McLean, *Medieval English gardens* (London, 1981). For gardens in Ireland, see Keith Lamb and Patrick Bowe, *A history of gardening in Ireland* (Dublin, 1995); Terence Reeves-Smyth, *Irish gardens and gardening before Cromwell* (Cork, 1999).   2 Christopher Dyer, *Everyday life in medieval England* (London, 1994), p. 113.   3 See below, pp 350–2.   4 *EIMP.*   5 R.C. Simington (ed.), *The Civil Survey, AD1654–56* (10 vols, 1931–61), passim.   6 Brenda Collins, 'Garden soil', *IAPA News: Bulletin of the Irish Association of Professional Archaeologists*, 23 (1996), 6–7.   7 For example, see Andrew Halpin, 'Bride St./Golden Lane, Dublin' in *Excavations 1992*, pp 17–18; Alan Hayden, 'Jury's Hotel site, Christchurch Place, Dublin' in *Excavations 1992*, p. 20; Alan Hayden, 'Mercer's Hospital, Digges Lane, Dublin' in *Excavations 1992*, pp 21–2; Eoin Halpin, 'Church and hospital of St Stephen, Mercer's Hospital, Digges Lane, Dublin' in *Excavations 1992*, p. 22; Andy Halpin, 'Francis St./Hanover Lane, Dublin' in *Excavations 1992*, p. 24; Alan Hayden, 'Coombe Relief Rd, Dublin' in *Excavations 1993*,

medieval town, at locations such as Donnybrook, Finglas and Tallaght.[8] While it is unlikely that all deposits referred to as 'garden soils' were actually used for gardening (and in fact many probably had no role in gardening whatever), some of them are certainly the result of horticultural activity. These soils regularly contain abraded fragments of bone, shell and ceramic, indicating the manuring and regular cultivation of the soil. Palaeo-environmental analysis of these soils can also reveal the presence of pests known to favour various vegetables, and insects that may have been brought into the garden plots along with soil enhancers such as seaweed.

Investigation of palaeo-environmental assemblages of medieval date from both urban and rural sites can further indicate the range of domesticated fruits and plants grown in nearby gardens and orchards or imported from overseas. Furthermore, gardens were virtually always enclosed and these enclosures occasionally leave an imprint in the archaeological record.

Manorial and monastic gardens

There is a general perception that enclosed gardens and orchards were introduced into Ireland by the Anglo-Normans along with various other aspects of manorialisation. Sources for pre-Anglo-Norman agriculture in Ireland, however, clearly demonstrate that this was not the case.[9] Plant cultivation was particularly associated with the church: monastic gardeners are frequently mentioned and herbs and vegetables appear to have played an important role in monastic diets. The sources also make it clear that secular farmers often had an enclosed garden near the farmhouse. Small irregularly shaped fields around ringforts may well attest to the presence of such gardens.[10]

Linguistic evidence does suggest, however, that the Anglo-Normans had a profound impact on horticulture in Ireland. Loan-words in Irish can indicate the adoption of Anglo-Norman farming practices and the arrival of new species. The Irish word for pear (*péire*) is a borrowing from Norman French or Middle English, as is the Irish word for the cultivated cherry (*sirín*). Other loan words include those for rake and garlic.[11] Some of the earliest references to horticulture practiced by the Anglo-Normans in Ireland come from the Irish pipe roll for 1211–12, where receipts from manors in the king's hand are listed. There are

pp 19–20; Neil O'Flanagan, 'Fyffes Yard, Beresford Lane, Dublin' in *Excavations 1994*, p. 21; Deirdre Murphy, '56–7 Dame St./28 Eustace St./1A Temple Lane, Dublin' in *Excavations 1995*, p. 18; Margaret Gowen, '29–34 Thomas St. (rear), Dublin' in *Excavations 1995*, p. 22; Margaret Gowen, 'National College of Art and Design, Thomas St./Oliver Bond St./John's Lane/John's St., Dublin' in *Excavations 1995*, p. 23; Margaret Gowen, 'Statoil, Thomas St., Dublin' in *Excavations 1995*, p. 23; Georgina Scally, '1 Essex Gate/10 Exchange St. Upper' in *Excavations 1996*, pp 23–4; Margaret Gowen, 'Bridge St., Swords' in *Excavations 1996*, p. 3; Linzi Simpson, 'Essex Street West/Lower Exchange Street, Dublin' in *Excavations 1997*, pp 41–2; Claire Walsh, '123–133 Francis Street, 1–4 Swift's Alley, Dublin' in *Excavations 1997*, pp 44–5; Claire Walsh, '17–35 Carman's Hall (odd nos. only)/1–7 Ash Street/33–34 Garden Lane, Dublin' in *Excavations 1998*, pp 46–7; Claire Walsh, 'Carman's Hall, Dublin' in *Excavations 1999*, pp 60–1; Franc Myles, 'Iveagh Market, Francis Street, Dublin' in *Excavations 1999*, pp 67–8; John Ó Néill, 'Bow Street/Church Street, Dublin' in *Excavations 2000*, pp 81–2; Linzi Simpson, 'St James's Hospital, James's Street, Dublin' in *Excavations 2000*, pp 88–9; John Ó Néill, 'Longford Street Little' in *Excavations 2000*, pp 89–90; Linzi Simpson, '46–50, 52–57 South Great George's Street/58–67 Stephen Street Lower, Dublin' in *Excavations 2000*, pp 96–7; Linzi Simpson, 'Ship Street Great, Dublin' in *Excavations 2001*, pp 112–13; Edmond O'Donovan, '119–21 Thomas Street, Dublin', DEHLG file 95E0280; Cia McConway, 'Digges Lane, Dublin', DEHLG file 96E0006; Claire Walsh, '97 Francis Street, Dublin', DEHLG file 99E0692; Claire Walsh, 'Mark's Alley, Dublin', DEHLG file 01E1142; Linzi Simpson, '161–168 Church Street, 3–15 Hammond Lane, Dublin', DEHLG file 02E0096. **8** Cia McConway, 'St Mary's, Brookvale Rd, Donnybrook' in *Excavations 1995*, p. 13; Tim Coughlan, 'Jamestown Road, Finglas East' in *Excavations 1996*, p. 34; Claire Walsh, 'St Maelruan's, Tallaght', DEHLG file 96E0188. **9** Kelly, *Early Irish farming*, pp 250–71. **10** An overview is presented by Edwards, *The archaeology of early medieval Ireland*, pp 52–6, while recent work particularly on infrastructural projects associated with large-scale geophysical surveys and excavation, has highlighted new sites, such as on the M3 motorway scheme at Boyerstown 3 and Dowdstown, Co. Meath. See also Aidan O'Sullivan and Lorcan Harney, 'Early Medieval Archaeology Project: investigating the character of early medieval archaeological excavations, 1970–2002' (unpublished report for the Heritage Council, 2008 rev. ed.), pp 180–3. **11** Kelly, *Early Irish farming*, pp 262–3, 468.

some significant sales of apples from manors in Co. Meath, and at Rathfeigh a gardener was paid an annual stipend of 4s.[12]

Manorial documents frequently refer to the existence and value of gardens and orchards as part of the demesne complex. These values show considerable variation within the Dublin region. There were some relatively valuable gardens; the garden at Cloncurry was worth 8s. per annum in 1304, and another garden attached to a lordly residence – at Rathfeigh, Co. Meath – was valued at 6s. 8d. in 1322.[13] The archiepiscopal garden at Swords was valued at 6s., while one of the three gardens attached to the manor of Colonia/St Sepulchre, also belonging to the archbishop of Dublin, was said to be worth half a mark (that is, 6s. 8d.).[14] On the other hand, a significant number of manorial gardens were said to be worth 2s. or less per annum. These were the gardens at Castlewarden, Clondalkin, Corduff, Finglas, Leixlip, Lucan, Shankill and Tallaght.[15]

The terms 'garden' and 'orchard' are often used interchangeably, and it is clear that most manorial gardens included fruit trees. There were some very extensive orchards in the Dublin region, and these must have been involved in the commercial production of fruit. Such an orchard was found on the de Feypo manor of Santry, Co. Dublin, and in 1303 this orchard was reported to have 200 apple trees and 100 pear trees, implying an area of at least three acres.[16] The de Feypos originated in Herefordshire, a part of England noted for fruit growing, and it is possible that they had particular expertise in fruit production.[17]

Reasons given for low valuations of gardens often include the non-fruiting of trees due to their age, or indeed the lack of fruit trees. In the extent for Castlewarden (c.1315), the jurors said that the garden was worth nothing as it did not bear fruit because the trees were old. In contrast, the herbage (grass crop) of the garden was worth 2s. per annum.[18] At Clondalkin (in 1326) a curtilage and old orchard were said to be of no value, because they were unenclosed and without apple trees; herbage of the garden was worth 12d.[19] At Corduff and Finglas, it is again the lease of pasture or herbage that is valued.[20] Finglas was one of three archiepiscopal manors whose gardens and orchards were recorded as being damaged during the upheavals of 1315–17.[21]

Monastic gardens were extended and developed in the Anglo-Norman period, although less is known about horticulture in Irish monasteries than in their better documented English counterparts.[22] The mid-fourteenth-century register of the priory of Kilmainham contains brief mentions of a number of different gardens and orchards scattered within the inner and outer precincts of the Kilmainham preceptory.[23] Some of these gardens provided produce for the central kitchen, while others were attached to the residences of various priory officials and permanent guests who lived within the Kilmainham enclosure. At the time of the Dissolution, the priory had within its precincts, three small gardens with an orchard surrounded by a stone wall with four towers.[24] It had interests in a further fifteen gardens in the vill of Kilmainham, including 'certain gardens called the king's yards on both sides of the [River] Cammok on the west called Sangwenslands'. These were leased to a Dublin baker for 8s.[25]

12 Davies and Quinn, 'Irish pipe roll of 14 John', 30, 46 (21s. 4d. recorded from sales of apples).   13 RBO, pp 27–34; TNA:PRO C47/10/18/13.   14 McNeill (ed.), Alen's register, p. 172. This was the garden by St Kevin's Church. 15 TNA:PRO SC12/20/48; McNeill (ed.), Alen's register, pp 185–9; RBO, pp 25–7; McNeill (ed.), Alen's register, p. 174; TNA:PRO C47/10/20/1; TNA:PRO C47/10/22/15; McNeill (ed.), Alen's register, pp 196, 182.   16 CDI, 1302–7, no. 255, pp 86–7.   17 A view expressed by Elizabeth Hickey: Skryne and the early Normans, p. 136.   18 TNA:PRO SC12/20/48. 19 McNeill (ed.), Alen's register, p. 187.   20 RBO, pp 25–7.   21 HMDI, pp 366–71.   22 For a general overview, see Bond, Monastic landscapes, ch. 9.   23 Reeves-Smyth, Irish gardens, pp 114–15; There was also apparently a nursery for seedlings and grafts (J.C. Walker, 'Essay on the rise and progress of gardening in Ireland', Transactions of the Royal Irish Academy, 4 (1799), 3–19; D'Alton, History of the county of Dublin, p. 313).   24 EIMP, p. 81.   25 EIMP, p. 83.

At least one hundred gardens are mentioned in the extents made at the time of the Dissolution of the Dublin religious houses in 1540.[26] There was a particular concentration in the western suburb, where St Thomas' Abbey had two gardens and eight orchards in its precincts and also had interests in a further thirteen gardens.[27] In 1477, Richard Stanihurst had a madder yard and garden 'by Saint Thomas Cowrte'.[28]

The northern suburb of Oxmantown also had a decided horticultural aspect. St Mary's Abbey owned a garden and an orchard called Comyn Orchard within its precincts in eastern Oxmantown, while Holy Trinity had an orchard, known as the Great Orchard, north of Oxmantown Green.[29] The nuns of St Mary de Hogges had a garden leased for 10s., while the nuns of Gracedieu had a garden and a large orchard.[30] The priory of Holmpatrick had 'gardens and orchards'.[31] Christ Church, Dublin, had a large 'Convent Garden' which was leased to a Dublin merchant in 1536.[32]

It is clear from various sources that manorial and monastic gardens were often enclosed in some way. According to Terence Reeves-Smith, 'physical boundaries were considered an integral part of a garden's layout; walls, banks, hedges and fences were all employed, and these served to keep livestock and people out and to provide shelter for the plants within'.[33] Wattle fences and thorn fences are known to have been used to enclose some manorial gardens, while stone walls were preferred in monastic precincts.[34] In 1404, when the earl of Ormond leased the manor of Turvey, he included 'all the commodities and profits of his orchard there'.[35] The lessees were obliged to ditch and clear the orchard 'and make a palisaded fence at their own cost'. Similarly, in 1545, when Holy Trinity leased an orchard outside St Nicholas' Gate, the lessee had to agree to ditch and fence it on two sides.[36] It was bounded on the west and north by the River Poddle.

There is some evidence for structures within gardens. In the assignment of dower granted to Lady Joanna de Burgh, countess of Kildare, in 1328, the countess was assigned a third part of the garden at Maynooth Castle, 'extending in length from the gate of the garden to the ditch lying towards the land of Robert Baker, chaplain, and from the water towards the dovecot to the herbarium'.[37] Lady Joanna was also assigned a newly built chamber in the garden, which may have been an ornamental feature.

Small urban and rural gardens

Occasionally, extents and rentals contain information regarding the gardens and orchards of manorial tenants. A tenant of the archiepiscopal manor of Swords had a garden (with fishpond) attached to his residence at Skidoo in 1276, while another archiepiscopal tenant at Walshestown, part of the manor of Ballymore Eustace, Co. Kildare, had a garden of half an acre.[38] The 1351 rental of the manor of Coolock recorded that one Adam Cromelyn held a messuage with an orchard at 6s. 8d. a year, while another tenant held a garden for 16d.[39] In 1477, mention was made of 'six houses with gardens' in Rathcoole.[40] In 1506, Holy Trinity leased a messuage with a garden in Grangegorman, 'adjoining the arable land, to be held for the purpose of planting and cutting down trees, plants and other necessaries'.[41]

Although they were not called gardens, the small parcels of land, frequently less than a quarter of an acre, held by the forty-one cottars on the manor of Cloncurry in 1304 must have been gardens or crofts attached to their cottages and used to keep small animals such

26 *EIMP*, passim.   27 *EIMP*, pp 26–8.   28 Smyly, 'Old Latin deeds V', 37–8.   29 Purcell, 'Land-use in medieval Oxmantown', pp 204, 226.   30 *EIMP*, pp 69, 73.   31 *EIMP*, p. 49.   32 *CCCD*, no. 1162.   33 Reeves-Smyth, *Irish gardens and gardening*, pp 103–4.   34 Garden boundaries at Old Ross were sheltered by thorn hedging, palisades and ditching: see TNA:PRO SC6/1238/44.   35 *COD*, 2, p. 272.   36 *CCCD*, no. 1198.   37 *RBK*, pp 98–100.   38 TNA:PRO C133/16.   39 TNA:PRO SC12/18/18 (PD).   40 Smyly, 'Old Latin deeds V', 37–8.   41 *CCCD*, no. 1114.

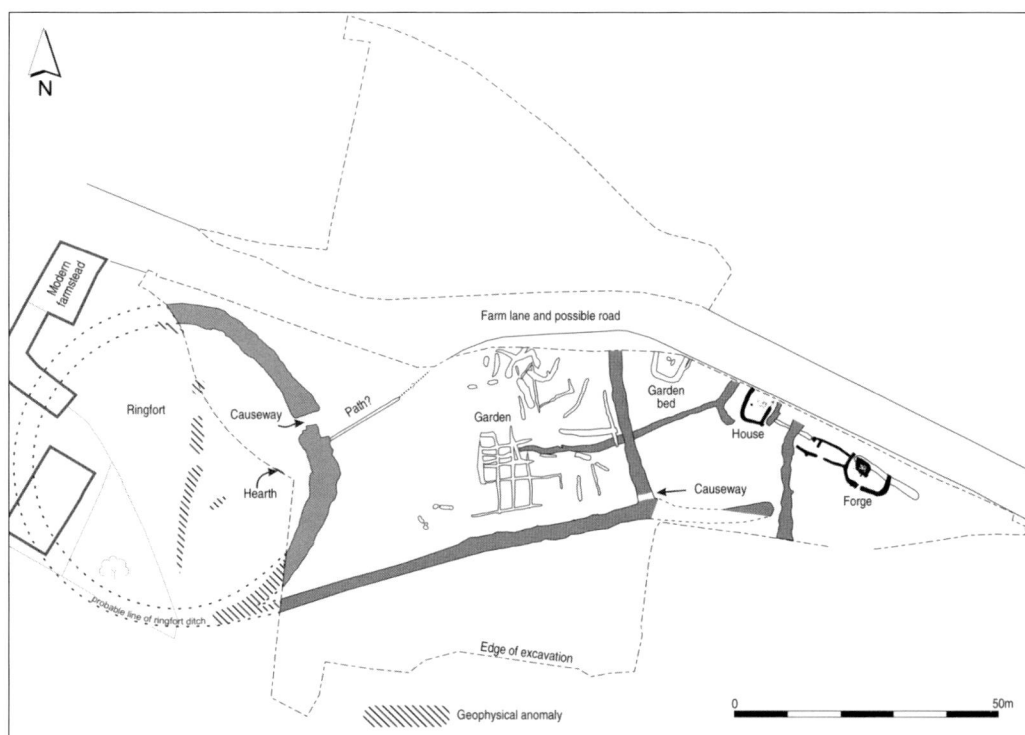

Figure 10.1 Plan of excavated features at Cookstown, Co. Meath, showing line of possible medieval road, and garden (image courtesy of Richard Clutterbuck and CRDS Ltd).

as pigs and poultry as well as for the cultivation of vegetables.[42] These multiple gardens were certainly delimited in some way. At Oughterard, Co. Kildare, features possibly representing 'the end boundaries of enclosures (crofts) associated with houses' were identified by field survey.[43] Laboratory analyses of samples from this area identified high levels of phosphate, and these were seen by the analyst as possible evidence for 'intensive manuring of possible crofts'.[44] Medieval garden boundaries have also been recognised at Newcastle Lyons, Co. Dublin.[45]

At Cookstown, Co. Meath, a garden was found in association with a house and forge believed to have been the holding of a relatively humble manorial tenant in the thirteenth/ fourteenth century (Figure 10.1).[46] Protective ditches were found surrounding the garden and within it, hand-dug furrows created a regular pattern of garden beds. The primary function of this garden appears to have been to supply the settlement's household with fruit, vegetables and herbs, and remains of pea, legume and radish were identified among the environmental samples.

It is clear that, in addition to the gardens associated with religious houses, there were numerous other gardens within or just outside the walls of Dublin, and primary documentary references to over 120 gardens are listed by Howard Clarke for medieval Dublin.[47] The hinterland area played an important part in the maintenance and manuring of these gardens, however. Carters and carmen regularly brought loads of dung into the city for spreading on the citizens' gardens. This practice became so widespread in the fifteenth century that the city authorities legislated that all dung brought in had to be left in designated areas and spread the same day by the city gardeners.[48]

Excavations at St Stephen's Hospital, Dublin, revealed the presence of a layer of garden soil, up to 80cm thick, containing pottery sherds and organic material. The excavator

42 *RBO*, pp 27–34.   **43** Hall, Hennessy and O'Keeffe, 'Medieval agriculture and settlement in Oughterard and Castlewarden', 20.   **44** Heistermann, 'Phosphate analysis at Oughterard', 24.   **45** Edwards, Hamond and Simms, 'The medieval settlement of Newcastle Lyons'; Simms, 'Rural settlement in medieval Ireland' pp 141, 143.   **46** Richard Clutterbuck, 'Cookstown, Co. Meath: a medieval rural settlement' in Corlett and Potterton (eds), *Rural settlement in medieval Ireland* (2009), pp 27–48.   **47** Clarke, *IHTA: Dublin Part I, to 1610*, pp 24–5.   **48** *CARD*, I, p. 326.

identified evidence for continued manuring and likened the deposits to plaggen soil, explaining that

> although, strictly speaking, the term plaggen refers to the addition of heather sods, forest litter, grasses and dung in a rural context, the term can loosely be ascribed to the urban practice of importing organic matter and manure into inner city plots as an aid to soil fertility. It is likely, therefore, that these soils were imported onto the site for use in the cultivation of crops.[49]

The value of seaweed as a fertiliser was appreciated by medieval cultivators, and it is likely that it was brought into the city to spread on gardens. This may explain the presence of seaweed, seashells and the remains of insects associated with seaside or coastline environments in the garden soil deposits from Essex Street in Dublin. Palaeo-environmental analysis of these samples of medieval garden soils also demonstrated the presence of pests known to favour various beans including broad beans, as well as insects usually only found in the roots of turnips.[50] Excavations at a site on the east side of Bride Street in Dublin revealed deposits of 'garden-type' soil that were loamy, loose in texture, with a silty clay content.[51] They contained fragments of animal bone, fish bone and mussel shell, as well as small deposits of both charred and unburnt human waste.[52] Sherds of pottery were present, in addition to charcoal, charred grains (wheat, oats and possibly barley), charred hazelnut shell fragments and charred seeds of vetch (*Vicia* sp.) and fat hen (*Chenopodium album*). Large quantities of organic waste were included in the deposits and regular digging and cultivation resulted in the mixing of materials. The loamy quality of the soil resulted from the inclusion of rotting foliage and plant remains. The soils appear to have been used for 'agricultural or horticultural activities' and, according to the excavator, this may be the garden referred to in documentary sources as 'Earl Hascalf's Garden'.[53]

The so-called 'garden soils' are rarely recorded on sites outside Dublin and its neighbouring boroughs. One of the few locations where they have been found is Naas. Excavations on Main Street revealed evidence for a vegetable garden of medieval date.[54] A single sherd of sixteenth-century Isabella polychrome ware was retrieved, while among the environmental samples were the remains of a range of common weeds, lentils and peas. Further archaeological evidence for horticultural activity in Naas was found on the site of the new courthouse, where deposits containing sherds of thirteenth-/fourteenth-century pottery were interpreted as 'a cultivated "garden" soil'.[55]

At Muckerstown, Co. Meath, a complex of features was excavated close to a deserted settlement.[56] The remains of a medieval yard enclosure as well as field boundaries, nearfields and gardens were investigated, while bedding trenches of a kitchen garden may have been represented by small gullies containing thirteenth-century pottery, charcoal, bones and other organic waste probably applied as fertiliser.

49 Eoin Halpin, 'Excavations at St Stephen's Hospital, Dublin, 1992', DEHLG file 92E0117, p. 4.   **50** Simpson, 'Essex Street West' in *Excavations 1997*, pp 41–2; Linzi Simpson, 'Essex Street West/Lower Exchange Street, Dublin', DEHLG file 96E0245.   **51** Mary McMahon, 'Early medieval settlement and burial outside the enclosed town: evidence from archaeological excavations at Bride Street, Dublin', *PRIA*, 102C4 (2002), 67–135 at 69, 70.   **52** McMahon, 'Excavations at Bride Street', 83, 86; Brenda Collins, 'Macroscopic plant remains' in McMahon, 'Excavations at Bride Street', 108–10 at 109–10.   **53** McMahon, 'Excavations at Bride Street', 86.   **54** Edmond O'Donovan, 'Burke's Pharmacy, 3 Main Street, Naas', DEHLG file 02E0955.   **55** Margaret Gowen, 'New Courthouse, Naas, County Kildare', DEHLG file 95E0251.   **56** Fallon, 'Muckerstown/Wotton' in *Excavations 2004*, pp 328–9; Fallon, 'Muckerstown/Wotton: final excavation report'.

Production and consumption

Documentary sources often reveal little of what was grown in gardens beyond generic 'fruit' and 'vegetables'. There is very little evidence for the cultivation of flowers or decorative plants in medieval Irish gardens, although the remains of the sweet smelling guelder rose identified in samples from an excavation at Parkwest in Tallaght were interpreted by the analyst as possible evidence for the former existence of a garden there.[57] With regard to fruit, apples and pears are the most frequently mentioned. Undoubtedly, apples predominated in Irish orchards, and most likely included varieties of costards, pearmains and bitter-sweets, the latter being used for cider-making.[58] Cider may never have been as popular in Ireland as it was in England at this time, but cider presses are occasionally mentioned in Irish medieval documents. There was one, for instance, on the Templar manor at Kilsaran in Co. Louth.[59] The most widely appreciated pears of the period included wardens, sorells, caleols and gold knopes, all of which were usually cooked and put into preserves, puddings and pies. In 1545, when a garden in Crumlin was leased out, the lessee covenanted to plant it with apples, pears and wardens (a type of culinary pear).[60] Dessert pears may have been comparatively rare, though there is one apparent reference to a bon chrétien in the prior's garden of St John's Priory, Kilkenny.[61]

Documentary sources for the consumption of fruit and vegetables are similarly sparse. The most detailed record to have come down to us from medieval Dublin in relation to standards of living is a seneschal's account from Holy Trinity for the years 1337–46. Vegetables appear infrequently in the account apart from a small purchase of onions.[62] The only fruits to feature were imported items. Two pounds of figs were purchased for the prior's table and there was a special purchase of dessert pears ahead of a visit by the archbishop.[63]

It is very likely that the priory's garden supplied the monks with a range of fruit, herbs and vegetables, but as no cash transaction occurred, this escaped the notice of the accountants. Barbara Harvey has cautioned against assumptions that vegetables played little or no part in the urban monastic diets, based solely on the evidence of central accounts.[64] It is interesting to note that in 1536 when the priory leased its garden to Richard Hankoke, a Dublin merchant, the lessee was required to supply herbs to the convent kitchen, 5s. or two pecks of onions at the feast of the nativity of the Blessed Virgin Mary, leeks in Lent and herbs for the 'coppys' to the convent hall and the prior's chamber.[65]

The chance survival of two fragments of diet accounts relating to the household of Roger Mortimer and his wife Joan at Ardmulchan, Co. Meath (about 50km north-west of Dublin), dated to the first decade of the fourteenth century, allows some insight into the consumption patterns of a lordly household in Ireland. The accounts cover the period of Lent and purchases of fish predominate. Most items were purchased at local markets such as Trim and Skreen, but certain items were bought in Dublin, including oysters and other shellfish and, interestingly, 1,000 onions were bought from a 'man of Dublin'.[66]

Archaeo-botanical evidence reveals more about the variety of horticultural products found in Dublin and its hinterland.[67] Finds include a range of pips, seeds, stones and other fossil remains of domesticated fruits and plants likely to have been grown in gardens and orchards. Among the garden produce represented are beans, fennel, mustard, parsley, peas,

57 Avril Purcell, 'Parkwest, Gallanstown', DEHLG file 00E0267.   **58** Reeves-Smyth, *Irish gardens and gardening*, p. 117.
59 Dermot MacIvor, 'The Knights Templar in County Louth', *Senchas Ardmhacha*, 4 (1960–2), 72–91 at 82.
60 *CCCD*, no. 1198.   **61** Lamb and Bowe, *History of gardening*, p. 12, fn 31.   **62** Mills (ed.), *Account roll*, p. 14.
63 Ibid., pp 5, 112.   **64** B.F. Harvey, *Living and dying in England, 1100–1540: the monastic experience* (Oxford, 1993),
p. 60.   **65** *CCCD*, no. 1162.   **66** C.M. Woolgar, *Household accounts from medieval England* (2 vols, Oxford, 1992), 1,
pp 173–7.   **67** See Murphy and Potterton, 'Investigating living standards', pp 243–8.

radish, raspberries and strawberries.[68] Tree fruit remains include apples, cherries and plums and many of these are likely to have been grown in orchards.[69]

An important archaeological find from Dublin's High Street reveals that cultivated and wild fruits were being processed in the town in the early thirteenth century.[70] A square wooden chute was uncovered, packed with the remnants of cherries, plums, sloes and strawberries, with smaller quantities of blackberry, fig and frochan also present. Mitchell suggested that the chute may have led to a fruit-press where the fruit was crushed for juice extraction. The structure was dated, on the grounds of dendrochronology and associated artefacts, to the first quarter of the thirteenth century.

The remains of figs have been found on a number of medieval sites in the Dublin region.[71] As mentioned above, figs were purchased by Holy Trinity in the fourteenth century. These were probably imported, although the climatic conditions that prevailed in Ireland prior to the fourteenth century would have suited figs and indeed grape vines, for which there is some evidence in the form of both vineyards and winepresses.[72] Grape seeds have been recovered on several sites; but, like the hemp seeds and serradella remains from Patrick Street and the walnuts from a thirteenth-century drain at Winetavern Street, they seem likely to derive from imports.[73]

Chapter summary

The evidence points to the existence of many gardens and much horticultural activity in the Dublin region. There are few indications, however, that this activity was carried out on a commercial scale. The low value placed on all but imported fruit and vegetables makes it difficult to view it as a profitable endeavour. The function of the majority of gardens, whether rural or urban, was to supply the household. For the wealthy lords and denizens of religious houses, garden produce provided welcome seasonal additions to the daily fare: for poorer folk, horticultural activity played an important role in delivering vital nutrients and calories to their diets.

68 Brenda Collins, 'Plant remains' in Walsh, *Archaeological excavations at Patrick, Nicholas and Winetavern Streets* (1997), pp 228–36; O'Sullivan, 'Woodmanship and the supply of underwood', p. 59; Mitchell, *Archaeology and environment*, passim; Margaret Gowen, '9–12 High Street, Dublin', DEHLG file E000548; Kelly, 'Analysis of the plant remains: Skreen 05E0321'.   **69** Collins, 'Plant remains', pp 228–36; O'Sullivan, 'Woodmanship and the supply of underwood', p. 59; Mitchell, *Archaeology and environment*, passim; Gowen, '9–12 High Street'; Elizabeth O'Brien, 'Old Bawn Road, Tallaght', DEHLG file E000555; Claire Walsh, 'John Dillon Street, Dublin', DEHLG file 98E0158.   **70** Mitchell, *Archaeology and environment*, p. 27; Brendán Ó Ríordáin, 'Excavations at High Street and Winetavern Street, Dublin', *Med. Arch.*, 15 (1971), 73–85.   **71** Mitchell, *Archaeology and environment*, pp 21, 25, 27; Collins, 'Plant remains', pp 228–36; Ó Ríordáin, 'Excavations at High Street and Winetavern Street', 77; Elizabeth O'Brien, 'Final report on excavations at Dundrum Castle, Co. Dublin (E419), 1987–1991', DEHLG file E000419.   **72** There was a vineyard at Old Ross in Co. Wexford in the thirteenth century and there is a possible reference to a winepress in one of the Cistercian houses in Co. Kilkenny – probably Jerpoint. See Reeves-Smyth, *Irish gardens and gardening*, p. 139, fn 93.   **73** Collins, 'Plant remains', pp 228–36; Mitchell, *Archaeology and environment*, p. 25.

CHAPTER 11

Woods and woodlands

Introduction

It was for long believed that down to the seventeenth century Ireland was a much wooded country, and place-names that contain elements relating to woodland and forests are numerous (Figure 11.1). Research in a range of scientific and academic fields has shown, however, that this widespread assumption was probably unfounded.[1] Most of Ireland's natural forests were cleared long before 1600, and indeed it now appears that much of this clearance took place in prehistoric times. It is difficult to estimate just how much of early medieval Ireland was covered in woodland, but the documentary evidence suggests that there were only scattered woods and copses, often privately owned, whose resources were limited and needed to be protected carefully by law.[2] This picture fits well with the results of palynological analyses, which also indicate a generally open landscape dotted with woods and forests.[3] Oak was an especially valuable resource in medieval times, and while there is evidence for a reasonably healthy supply in the Dublin region up to the thirteenth century, from then on there was increasing reliance on forests further afield.

In addition to the predictable or planned availability of certain woodland resources at regular intervals, some far greater cyclical patterns have been distinguished as a result of the scientific analysis of a large amount of ancient Irish timber.[4] It has been demonstrated that there were clear periods of oak abundance in the sixth and seventh centuries, the twelfth century, and the fifteenth and sixteenth centuries. These periods were separated by times when relatively few timbers appear in the archaeological or architectural record, in the ninth, fourteenth and late seventeenth centuries.

Place-name evidence for woods: in Irish

Place-names containing elements relating to trees or woods are widespread in Ireland, and the Dublin region is no exception (Figure 11.1). What is perhaps most noticeable is the absence of woodland elements in the immediate environs of the city and the coastal belt to the north. The higher regions of the Dublin/Wicklow Mountains are also largely devoid of woodland, which may be expected from such exposed elevations, where the ability for trees

---

1 For example, see Eileen McCracken, *The Irish woods since Tudor times: distribution and exploitation* (Newton Abbot, 1971); Oliver Rackham, 'Looking for ancient woodland in Ireland' in Pilcher and Mac an tSaoir (eds), *Wood, trees and forests in Ireland* (1995), pp 1–12 at p. 1; V.A. Hall, 'Woodland depletion in Ireland over the last millennium' in Pilcher and Mac an tSaoir (eds), *Wood, trees and forests in Ireland* (1995), pp 23–33; Aidan O'Sullivan, 'Trees, woodland and woodmanship in early medieval Ireland', *BJS*, 46:4 (1994), 674–81; Kelly, *Early Irish farming*, pp 389–90; M.G.L. Baillie and D.M. Brown, 'Some deductions on ancient trees from dendrochronology' in Pilcher and Mac an tSaoir (eds), *Wood, trees and forests in Ireland* (1995), pp 35–50. See also A.C. Forbes, 'Some legendary and historical references to Irish woods and their significance', *PRIA*, 41B (1932), 15–36.　**2** Kelly, *Early Irish farming*, pp 389–90.　**3** O'Sullivan, 'Trees, woodland and woodmanship', 674; Michael Ryan, 'Furrows and browse: some archaeological thoughts on agriculture and population' in Smyth (ed.), *Seanchas* (2000), pp 30–6.　**4** Baillie and Brown, 'Some deductions on ancient trees', pp 37–8.

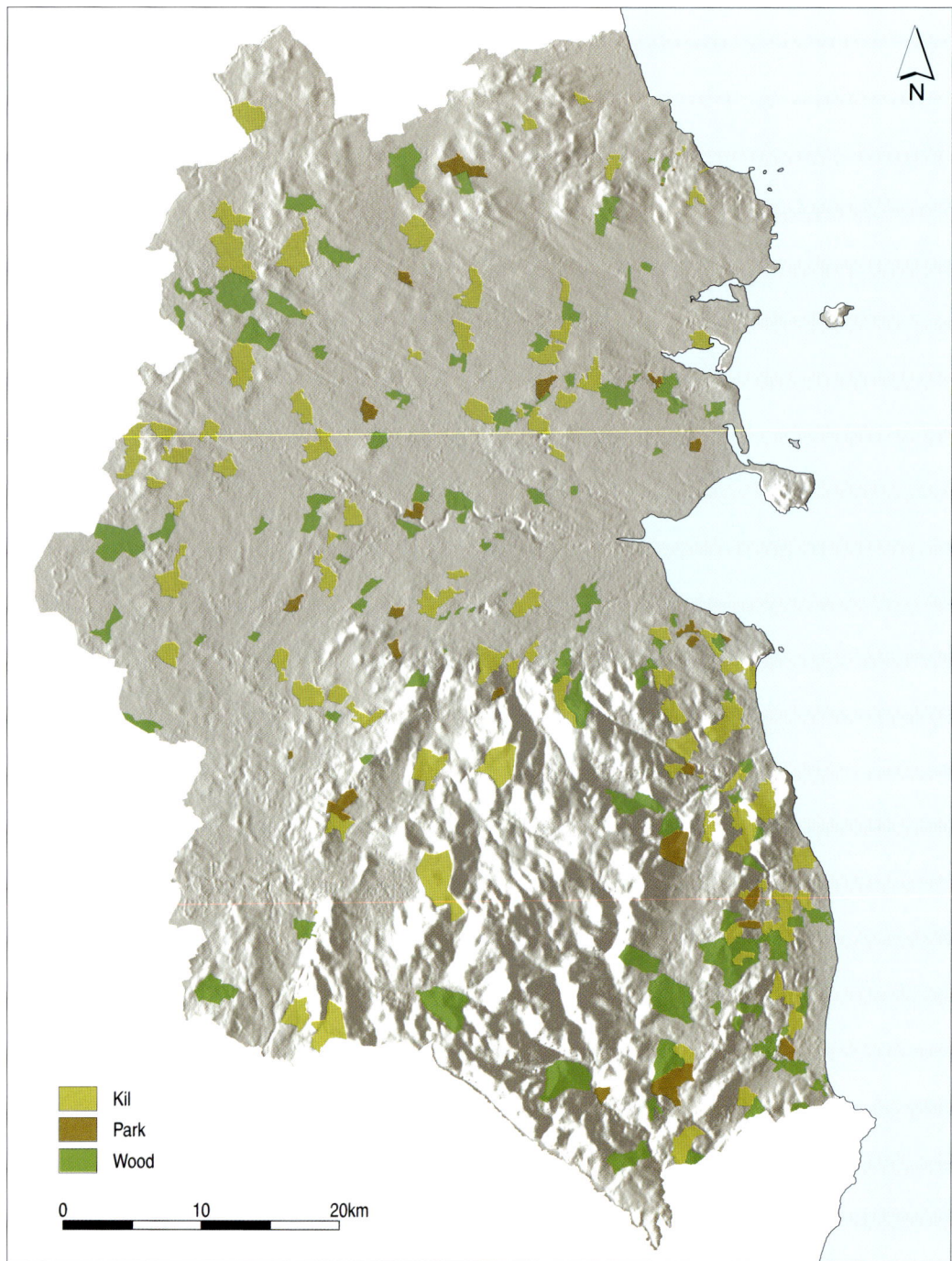

Kil
Park
Wood

0   10   20km

to take root and flourish is challenged. In contrast, woodland name elements are densely distributed along the narrow strip of low-lying land that forms the Wicklow coastline.

There are several words in Irish for a wood, the most common being *fid* and *caill*. Fidorfe (Ratoath parish) derives its name from *fid*. *Caill* is sometimes Anglicised kyle or coyle, and while most place-names prefixed *kil-* or *kill-* are generally thought to relate to early church sites, Joyce estimated that about 20 per cent of these are in fact derived from *caill*, although it is often hard to identify the true root of such names.[5] Barnacullia (Kilgobbin), near Dublin translates as 'the top of the wood' (Barr-na-Coille). While the word *ros* can mean either a point or a wood, it is likely to be the latter in the following toponyms in the Dublin region: Roscall (Ballyboghill); Ross (Skreen); Ross (Tara); Rossana (Rathnew); Ballyross (Powerscourt); and Cooldross (Newcastle Lower).

5 Joyce, *Irish names of places*, 1, p. 492.

Most 'wood' place-names relate to specific species of tree, however, with oak being the most prevalent. *Daire* is the common Irish word for an oak-wood, and this gives rise to townland names such as Ballinderry (Rathdrum), Derrybawn (Derrylossery), Derryclare (Galtrim), Derrycrib (Ballynafagh), Derrypatrick, Derrypatrick Grange (Derrypatrick) and Derryvarroge (Timahoe), as well as the parish names Derrylossery and Derrypatrick. Derreens (Carragh) and Derrinstown (Taghadoe) also take their names from oak woods (*derreen*; little oak-wood), while Beldaragh (Hollywood), Glendarragh (Newcastle Upper), Lackandarragh (Powerscourt), Tomdarragh (Derrylossery) all terminate with the genitive *dara/darach*. *Rál* also means oak and can be identified in place-names such as Railpark (Laraghbryan), Rowlagh (Esker), Rowlestown (Ardcath), Rowlestown West and Rowlestown East (both Killossery).

A range of other tree species are recorded in the toponyms of the Dublin region, and these include ash (*fuinnse* – Ballinahinch (Calary), Inch (Balrothery), Inchanappa (Killiskey), Tinnehinch (Powerscourt), and Hinchoge (Raheny)); birch (*beith* – Bahana (Powerscourt), Bahana (Kilcommon)); elder (*tromm* – Galtrim (Galtrim), Cooltrim North and Cooltrim South (Donadea), Feltrim (Kinsaley)); elm (*leamh* – Ballykillavane (Glenealy), Dunlavin (Dunlavin)); hazel (*coll* – Callowhill (Newcastle Upper), Barnacoyle (Killiskey), Tomcoyle (Killiskey)); rowan (*caerthainn* – Caureen (Rathmore), Templekeeran parish) and yew (*iubhair* – Terenure, Newrath (Rathnew)).[6]

Place-names relating to bushes and 'scrubbywood' are also plentiful in the Dublin region. The whitethorn bush or haw-tree (*skeagh*) gives its name to Augherskea (Knockmark), Clonskeagh (Donnybrook), Coolnaskeagh (Delgany), Killiskey (Killiskey), Skeagh (Newcastle) and Skephubble (Finglas), while the blackthorn (*draeigheann*) forms part of the names Cooldrinagh (Aderrig), Crockaunadreenagh (Rathcoole), Drinan (Kinsaley) and Killadreenan (Newcastle Lower). Sloe bushes (*airne*) are commemorated in the names Bollarney (Rathnew) and Killarney (Bray). The townland and parish Cruagh, at the base of the mountains south of Dublin, means 'branchy or bushy land',[7] while a brake or shrubbery is indicated by the names Moneenalion (Saggart), Monenstown (Galtrim), Moneyatta (Saggart), Moneycarroll (Newcastle Upper), Moneycooly (Laraghbryan) and Moneystown (Derrylossery).

In defining the extent of the townland of Stuckens in Co. Kildare, the Civil Survey noted that it 'meareth on the east from a high tree or bush on the lands of Downewer'.[8] This is almost certainly the same bush, 'called Skeaghnecroghery', mentioned as delimiting the neighbouring townland of Downings.[9]

Place-name evidence for woods: in English

Forty-four townlands in the Dublin region contain the word 'wood', and all but two of these appear to have been named after woods that were once present there (the exceptions being Woodcockstown and Woodenbooley, and even these names suggest the presence of woods locally).[10] Some of the names are not very informative (Woodfarm, Woodland, Woodlands,

6 *An Uragh*, a place abounding in Yew trees, becomes Newragh, which is corrupted into Newrath, see Joyce, *Irish names of places*, 1, p. 513. 7 Joyce, *Irish names of places*, 1, p. 501. 8 *Civil Survey*, 8, p. 157. 9 Ibid., p. 159. 10 Allenswood (Leixlip), Allenswood (Jarretstown), Beechwood (Portmarnock), Birchwood (Killiskey), Bishopswood (Finglas), Blackwood (Downings), Cherrywood (Killiney), Finglas Wood (Finglas), Garranswood or Kingswood (Tallaght), Glenwood (Derrylossery), Greenwood (Kinsaley), Hamwood (Dunboyne), Hoganswood and Hoganswood East (Clane), Hollywood (Mulhuddart), Hollywood (Hollywood, WW, x3), Hollywood Great (Hollywood), Hollywood Little (Hollywood), Hollywoodrath (Mulhuddart), Kingswood (Clondalkin), Naulswood (Dunboyne), Oakwood (Hollywood, WW), Priorswood (Coolock, x2), Ringwood (Newcastle), Roundwood (Derrylossery), Shortwood (Whitechurch), Woodfarm (Palmerstown), Woodland (Stillorgan), Woodland (Rathregan), Woodlands (Clonsilla), Woodlands (Kilcoole), Woodpark (Lusk), Woodpark (Kill), Woodpark (Dunboyne), Woodside (Kilgobbin), Woodstock (Newcastle Lower), Woodtown (Cruagh), Woodtown (Culmullin), Woodville (Esker), Woodcockstown

Woodpark, Woodside, Woodstock, Woodtown, Woodville), but others give indications as to the former owners of the woods (for example, Allenswood, Hoganswood, Garranswood), the nature or shape of the wood (Blackwood, Greenwood, Ringwood, Roundwood, Shortwood), or the main species of tree growing there (Beechwood, Birchwood, Cherrywood, Hollywood, Oakwood). The ownership of the townlands Bishopswood, Kingswood and Priorswood is also demonstrated in the names. The townlands of Forestfields, Forrest Great and Forrest Little are all in the parish of Swords, while Copse is in Rathdrum.

Most of these place-names came about in the Middle Ages and, while it is impossible to be certain, it is likely that they relate to considerable tracts of woodland. It is interesting to note, however, that by the time of the Civil Survey in the mid-seventeenth century, some of the 'wood' townlands were entirely treeless. Despite its name, for instance, Finglas Wood, in the barony of Nethercross, is recorded as having 'no wood but the seventy acres of shrubbywood aforesaid [seventy acres of shrub and furze]'.[11]

Pre-1170 use of timber in Dublin and its region

Fergus Kelly quotes compelling literary evidence for the practice of coppicing in Ireland prior to the arrival of the Anglo-Normans, and there are indications of woodland management in the Dublin region from as early as the sixth century.[12] At St Maelruan's in Tallaght, excavations of sixth- to eighth-century contexts yielded a collection of rods of hazel (20 per cent) and ash (80 per cent), which had been cut in spring.[13] Hazel was often sought out for post-and-wattle structures as it produces strong, flexible rods. Excavations of tenth-century levels in Dublin have revealed that post-and-wattle construction was employed in houses, fences, breakwaters, animal pens and pits, while wattle screens were also used for paths and flooring.[14] Larger posts and planks were found in palisades, pits and, less commonly, as structural elements in otherwise post-and-wattle houses.[15] Wood was put to similar uses in eleventh- and twelfth-century Dublin, but the archaeological record suggests an increasing use of heavier posts and jambs in house construction through the twelfth century.[16] The ephemeral nature of most timber structures, combined with the effects of flooding and fire, meant that the houses, fences and paths of Viking Dublin were in constant need of repair and renewal.[17]

According to Aidan O'Sullivan, increased demands on local woodland in the vicinity of Dublin, from the tenth century or earlier, must have led to organised and controlled woodland management strategies.[18] He suggests that the vast amounts of quality rods and

(Culmullin), Woodenbooley (Hollywood, WW).   **11** *Civil Survey*, 7, p. 134.   **12** Kelly, *Early Irish farming*, pp 389–90.   **13** Ellen O'Carroll, 'Wood identification report' in Claire Walsh, 'Archaeological excavation of a development site to the south-east of St Maelruan's, Tallaght, Co. Dublin (96E0188)' (report lodged with NMI, Aug. 1997), no page numbers given.   **14** Claire Walsh, 'Dublin's southern town defences, tenth to fourteenth centuries: the evidence from Ross Road' in Duffy (ed.), *Medieval Dublin II* (2001), pp 88–127; Alan Hayden, 'The excavation of pre-Norman defences and houses at Werburgh Street, Dublin: a summary' in Duffy (ed.), *Medieval Dublin III* (2002), pp 44–68; Lynch and Manning, 'Excavations at Dublin Castle, 1985–7'; Linzi Simpson, 'Excavations on the southern side of the medieval town at Ship Street Little, Dublin' in Duffy (ed.), *Medieval Dublin V* (2004), pp 9–51; Linzi Simpson, 'Forty years a-digging: a preliminary synthesis of archaeological excavations in medieval Dublin' in Duffy (ed.), *Medieval Dublin I* (2000), pp 11–68, passim.   **15** Margaret Gowen with Georgina Scally, *Archaeology in Temple Bar: a summary report on excavations at Exchange Street Upper/Parliament Street, Dublin* (Temple Bar Archaeological Reports, 4, Dublin, 1996), pp 15–16; Georgina Scally, 'The earthen banks and walled defences of Dublin's north-east corner' in Duffy (ed.), *Medieval Dublin III* (2002), pp 11–33 at pp 19, 20–5; Walsh, 'Dublin's southern town defences', pp 49–53; Lynch and Manning, 'Excavations at Dublin Castle, 1985–7', p. 178.   **16** See, for example, M.E. Byrne, '26–29 Castle Street/20 Lord Edward Street: a brief introduction' (unpublished report submitted to NMI, 1993); Gowen with Scally, *Summary report on excavations at Exchange Street Upper/Parliament Street*, p. 19; Ó Ríordáin, 'Excavations at High Street and Winetavern Street'; Bride Street (02E0163).   **17** See, for example, Gowen with Scally, *Summary report on excavations at Exchange Street Upper/Parliament Street*, p. 16; Walsh, 'Dublin's southern town defences', pp 98–102; Simpson, 'Excavations on the southern side of the medieval town at Ship Street Little', pp 27–8; H.A. Murray, *Viking and early medieval buildings in Dublin* (BAR British Series, 119, 1983), pp 204–5.   **18** O'Sullivan, 'The wooden waterfronts', p. 77.

underwood required in the Viking town 'indicate a close relationship with the nearby, native hinterland, possibly involving organised trading of woodland products'.[19] The felling and transport of timber from source to construction site probably involved specialised woodsmen, and such expertise was already being alluded to in seventh-century Ireland.[20] John Tierney has estimated that Viking Dublin must have had consistent access to approximately one hundred acres of managed hazel coppice to build and renew its housing stock, though the figure may well have been even higher.[21] Studies by Raymond Tabor have shown that a well-tended hazel coppice with 600 stools per acre can produce as much as 12,000 rods per acre every seven years.[22] Hilary Murray notes that it is ash, in fact, that dominates the post-and-wattle structures of Dublin prior to the arrival of the Anglo-Normans.[23]

In addition to its ubiquitous use in house construction, wood was needed as a fuel for heating, cooking and lighting and in a range of industrial activities.[24] The woodlands of the Dublin region were not only a source of timber and fuel; referring to the evidence from an eleventh-/twelfth-century latrine pit found in Winetavern Street, palaeo-botanists noted that the species of moss found there (which is 'very suitable for wiping') 'must have been specifically gathered from the partially-shaded tree-trunks, rocks and soils of deciduous woodlands'.[25] Sheets of this moss were found interspersed with human faecal matter. The remains of fruits and nuts typically found in woodlands and hedgerows have also been retrieved on many excavations in the Dublin region. Among the most frequently represented are apples, bilberries, blackberries, elderberries, haws, hazelnuts, raspberries, rowans and sloes, while the remains of a fruit processing structure of c.1200 were found on High Street (see above, p. 356).[26]

Post-1170 use of timber in Dublin and its region

Large urban centres required access to considerable supplies of wood for both building and fuel, and medieval Dublin was no exception.[27] The town's rapidly increasing population after the advent of the Anglo-Normans inflated the need for wood, with a greater number and range of consumers than ever before. In tandem with this, the growth of other urban foci in the Dublin region imposed further pressures on their respective hinterlands.

The documentary references to wood and woodlands increase greatly after 1170, as the exploitation of this resource started to be recorded in Anglo-Norman manorial documents. Woodland is recorded in just under a quarter of the extents collected for the Dublin region, but the information they contain varies considerably (Table 11.1; Figure 11.1). At Ballymore (1326), Bray (1311) and Shankill (1326), the woods are said to be worth nothing because of war with the Irish, reflecting the perilous location of the woodlands in the south of the Dublin region.[28] The woods at Kilmasantan attached to the archiepiscopal manor of Tallaght

19 O'Sullivan, 'Trees, woodland and woodmanship', 676, 678–9. **20** Ibid., 679, referring to Seán Connolly and J.-M. Picard, 'Cogitosus: life of St Brigit', *JRSAI*, 117 (1987), 5–27. **21** Tierney, 'Woods and woodlands in early medieval Munster', pp 53–8. **22** Raymond Tabor, *Traditional woodland crafts* (London, 1994); O'Sullivan, 'The wooden waterfronts', p. 80. **23** Murray, 'Viking and early medieval buildings', p. 22. **24** See, for example, Ruth Johnson, 'Decorated wood from Temple Bar West, Dublin' in Duffy (ed.), *Medieval Dublin III* (2002), pp 69–80; Ó Ríordáin, 'Excavations at High Street and Winetavern Street', 80, fig. 22; Alan Hayden [with Sarah Cross (species and conversion identification)], 'Wooden objects' in Walsh, *Archaeological excavations at Patrick, Nicholas and Winetavern Streets* (1997), pp 159–62 at p. 159; Ruth Johnson, 'Decorated wood from Temple Bar West, Dublin' in Duffy (ed.), *Medieval Dublin III* (2002), pp 69–80 at p. 79. **25** Dickson and Dickson, 'The plant remains', pp 24, 28–9. **26** Collins, 'Plant remains' in Walsh, *Archaeological excavations*, pp 228–36; O'Sullivan, 'Woodmanship and the supply of underwood', p. 59; Mitchell, *Archaeology and environment*, p. 27. **27** For a general discussion on the importance of urban wood and fuel supplies, see Paul Bairoch, *Cities and economic development from the dawn of history to the present* (London, 1988), pp 14–15; Ad van der Woude, Akira Hayami and Jan de Vries (eds), *Urbanization in history: a process of dynamic interactions* (Oxford, 1990), pp 8–12. **28** McNeill (ed.), *Alen's register*, p. 189; *RBO*, 24–5; McNeill (ed.), *Alen's register*, p. 195.

were similarly affected by the political situation in the 1320s, but the extent does mention their previous value of 37s. a year, equating to over 7d. per acre.[29] The 120 acres of woodland attached to the royal manor of Newcastle McKynegan were still productive at the time of the extent (1304), and herbage and sales of wood were valued at 6d. per acre.[30] The high value (8d. an acre) recorded for the fifteen acres of wood at Leixlip (the former Pippard manor, which by the date of the extent – 1341 – was in royal hands) reflects the value of the underwood; herbage is not mentioned.[31]

Table 11.1 Manorial extent data relating to woodland.

MANOR	AREA OF WOODLAND (ACRES)	PENCE PER ACRE
Ballymore	70	0
Bray	–	0
Castlewarden	8	3
Chapelizod	–	8
Cloncurry	87	5/6
Clondalkin	40	1.5
Colonia	66	3.5
Leixlip	15	8
Newcastle McKynegan	120	6
Shankill	104	0
Swords	8	1.5
Tallaght	60	7.4

The 1304 extent for Cloncurry is more informative about the type of woodland and the nature of the valuation. There are three woods which, although named, cannot now be identified. One twenty-six-acre wood contained only scrub so nothing could be sold, but the herbage of each acre was valued at 8d. per annum.[32] Another sixty-one-acre wood yielded £1 6s. 8d. per annum, including herbage and pasture, while a third wood had been granted to a free tenant who got the ground, bark and crop (*fundum, scorcium et cruppum*). The lord retained the right to take as much timber as he required for building his houses. Individual tree species, with the exception of oaks and thorns, are not mentioned in any of the extents.[33]

In addition to the extents, there are other documents that shed light on the distribution of managed woodland in the Dublin region. One is an account of 1302–3 of an official named as William de Moenes, who was in charge of outfitting ships then assembled at Dublin to make them suitable for transporting the horses of the earl of Ulster to Scotland to join in Edward I's campaigns (Figure 11.2).[34] It includes details of payments made to men cutting rods in the woods of *Balikey, Karybican* (Carrickbrennan?), *Clonkene, Glassagh, Coulock, Kinsale, Ballygryffen* and *Newcastle of McKynegan*. The location of Balikey is uncertain, but it seems likely that it can be identified with Balgeeth, a grange of St Mary's Abbey situated in the west of the barony of Rathdown. Balgeeth appears in a number of

29 McNeill (ed.), *Alen's register*, p. 181. **30** TNA:PRO C47/10/17/10. **31** TNA:PRO C47/10/20/1. **32** *RBO*, pp 27–34. **33** Mentioned at Shankill 'a park of oaks and thorns, 30 acres, no value either in herbage or sale of underwood because of war' and Swords 'a grove of 8 acres, partly oaks, partly thorns, 12d. a year for pasture and underwood'. **34** TNA:PRO E101/11/3. This account is discussed by James Lydon, 'Edward I, Ireland and war in Scotland, 1303–1304' in Lydon (ed.), *England and Ireland in the later Middle Ages* (1981), pp 43–61 at pp 48–9. It has been printed in translation (with some errors) by Patrick O'Connor, 'Hurdle making in Dublin, 1302–3', *DHR*, 13 (1952–4), 18–22.

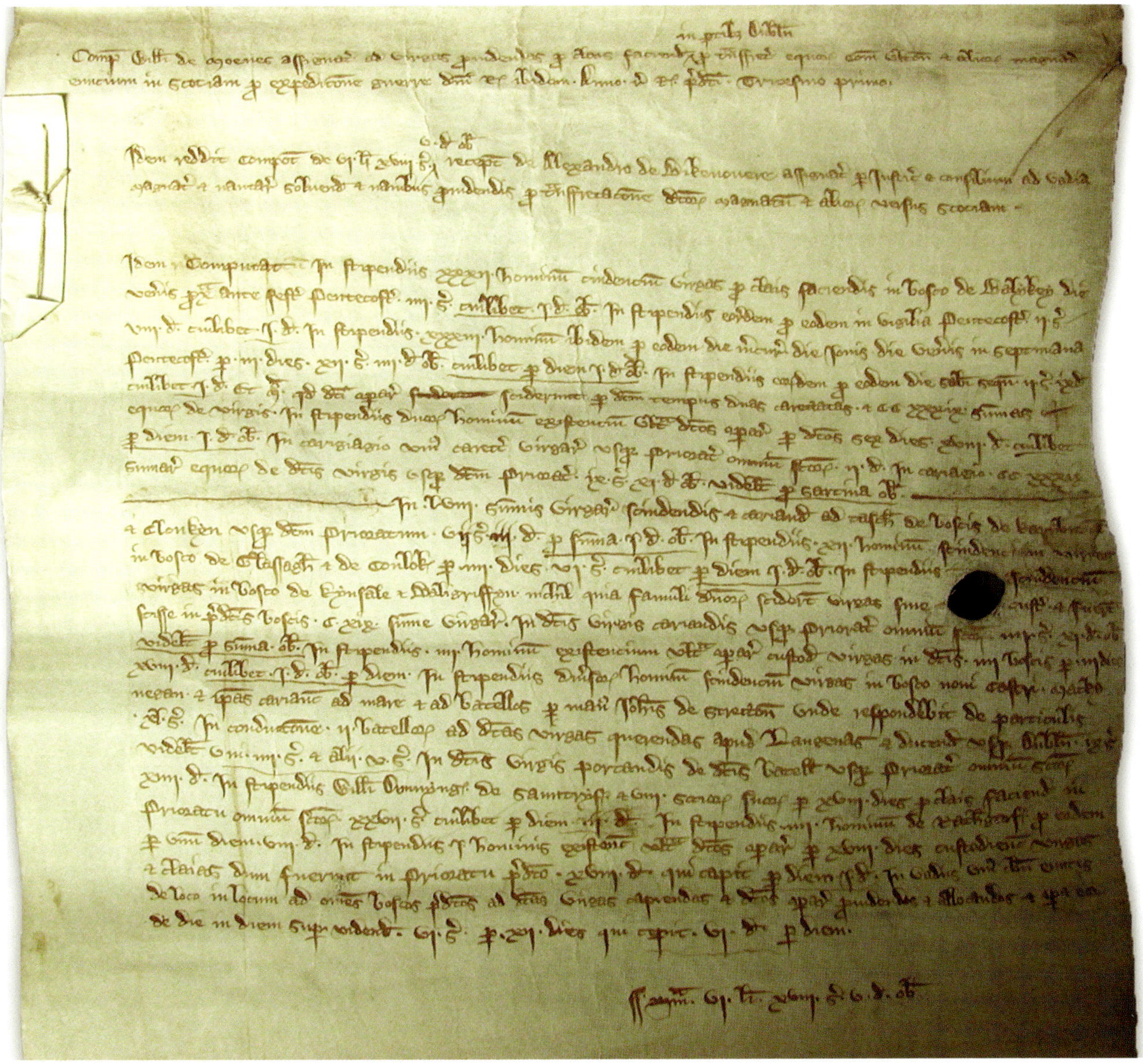

Figure 11.2 Account of William de Moenes, appointed to provide 'rods for hurdles in the parts of Dublin for the crossing of horses to Scotland, 1302–3' (image reproduced courtesy of the National Archives of the UK, ref: TNA:PRO E101/11/3).

documents in the cartularies of St Mary's under a variety of forms, including Balikech and Balioketh. It sometimes appears in association with another grange of St Mary's, Carrickbrennan (Monkstown), which is also a source of wood in de Moenes' account.[35] Of the other woodlands named, Clonkeen (Kill of the Grange) and Newcastle McKynegan are located to the south-east of the study area, while Glassagh, Coolock, Balgriffin and Kinsaley are in the north-east of Co. Dublin.

Religious houses, particularly those with large resident communities and those which provided hospitality, accommodation and facilities for the sick, had particular need for regular supplies of wood. Fuel was required for baking, brewing and cooking as well as for heating. Building and fencing works required timber, rods and poles of various sizes, and it is no surprise that religious houses were among the foremost proponents of woodland management. According to Rackham, writing of medieval England, 'Norwich Cathedral Priory and Beaulieu Abbey set standards of woodmanship which have never been surpassed'.[36]

---

35 For example, in 1312, William, Abbot of St Mary's was pardoned for having negotiated with Irish enemies of the king to obtain restitution of goods which had been carried away from the granges of the abbey at Carrickbrennan and Balioki: *CSMA*, i, p. 275.   **36** Oliver Rackham, *Ancient woodland: its history, vegetation and uses in England* (London, 1980), p. 137; see also Bond, *Monastic landscapes*, ch. 6.

With reference to Ireland, Rackham concluded that Irish monasteries did not invariably include woodland among their assets as they did in England.[37] Nevertheless, the necessity of ensuring timber and fuel supplies is evident in the land transactions involving religious houses in the Dublin region. Grants of land to religious houses frequently included designated woodland or rights to wood in adjoining areas, the usual wording being 'sufficient for their buildings and their fires'.[38] When religious houses were leasing out their lands, they frequently excluded the woodland or placed restrictions on its use.

When the abbot of St Thomas' in Dublin granted land in Killiskey to William Lawless, it was on condition that nothing be taken or sold from the wood there except for building purposes.[39] Such conditions are found in other leases and testify to the value placed on woodland and the awareness that damage to this resource caused long-term loss of profit. In the thirteenth century, Archbishop Luke of Dublin confirmed to the O'Tooles their holding in the manor of Castlekevin, Co. Wicklow, but reserved to himself the wood called *Fythgonerogy*.[40] Meiler O'Toole was allowed to take 'all needful deadwood and underwood for him and his men abiding in the same wood and its lands and have pasture of the wood for their own beasts'. None of the wood was to be reduced to cultivation without the archbishop's consent. Similarly, in 1431, when four chaplains granted custody of a wood in Crumlin called *Giffardesgrowe* to John Arthur, the lessee was allowed wood 'to make bread' and 'wattles and scollops' to repair buildings but was not to admit any beasts to the wood that would cause damage.[41]

In the almost total absence of central accounts for Irish religious houses, there is little detailed evidence for the management of woodland. The survival of accounts for the priory of Holy Trinity for the 1340s allows a certain insight.[42] The priory had woodland attached to their manor at Clonkeen – one of the woods used to supply rods for the outfitting of ships in 1302–3 (see above, pp 362–3). This wood was used in the 1340s to supply fuel for the abbey's baking and brew-houses. In the autumn of 1344, the bailiff of Clonkeen paid two men cutting underwood in the wood of Clonkeen for fourteen days 'for brewing and baking for the abbey'.[43] Not all firewood was supplied from the abbey's woods, however, and an undated entry in the *Liber niger* records the purchase of 101 loads of firewood – fifty-eight loads at 3½d. each and forty-three loads at 2½d.[44] The abbey also purchased wood and wood products needed for various maintenance and building works on their manors. Nine couples of oak (presumably tie-beams for a timber-framed building) and one hundred planks of Wicklow boards were bought for a new barn as well as six beams of oak for the well.[45] Timber was also bought for making ploughs, and 'he [the bailiff] renders account in timber bought for making new ploughs, to have in stock, of a certain Irishman, 3s.'[46]

From at least 1178, Christ Church also owned an extensive area of woodland called Salcock's Wood, located between Grangegorman and Cabra.[47] This conveniently situated wood must have been carefully managed throughout the medieval period and it was still productive in the sixteenth century. When the manor of Cabra was leased in 1544, the lessee was allowed to take away six cartloads of wood for fuel from Salcock's Wood.[48] Twenty years later, during the reconstruction of the nave of Christ Church, local timber was supplied from Salcock's Wood as well as from Castleknock.[49] Wattles for constructing the scaffolding were supplied from Kilmainham, where the 'wood-keeper' was paid for his good will.[50] In

37 Rackham, 'Looking for ancient woodland', p. 6.   38 *RAST*, pp 24–5, 32, 78, 85, 142.   39 *RAST*, pp 180–1.
40 McNeill (ed.), *Alen's register*, pp 81–2.   41 *CCCD*, no. 911.   42 Mills (ed.), *Account roll*.   43 Ibid., p. 64.   44 H.J. Lawlor (ed.), 'A calendar of the *Liber niger* and *Liber albus* of Christ Church, Dublin', *PRIA*, 27C (1907–9), 1–93, no. 3.
45 Mills (ed.), *Account roll*, pp 36, 40.   46 Ibid., p. 57.   47 McNeill (ed.), *Alen's register*, p. 256.   48 *CCCD*, no. 240.
49 Gillespie, *The proctor's accounts*, pp 65, 103–4. See Roger Stalley, 'The 1562 collapse of the nave and its aftermath' in Milne (ed.), *Christ Church Cathedral* (2000), pp 218–36.   50 Gillespie, *The proctor's accounts*, pp 27, 36.

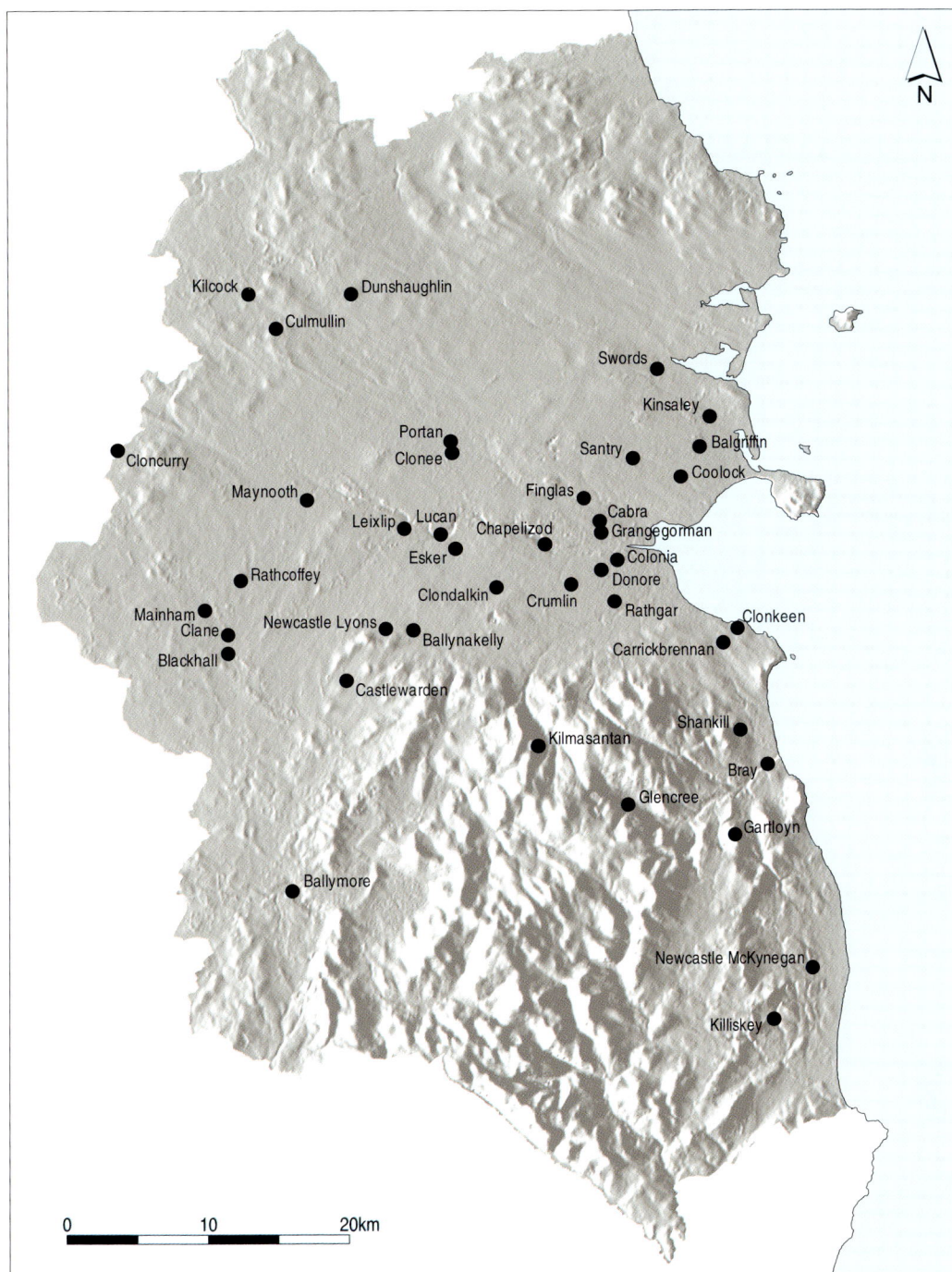

Figure 11.3 Map
showing location of
woodlands mentioned
in medieval
documentary sources.

1578, the bishop of Meath was granted a plot of wood containing three acres, parcel of the main wood called Salcock's Wood, Co. Dublin, and the scrubby park, part of John Kelly's farm.[51]

In addition to the numerous grants of land that included provisions of wood for fuel and building, the abbey of St Thomas had a large area of woodland in the carucate of Donore, close to their precincts. In the thirteenth century, this wood was sufficiently large to contain seven acres of arable land within it and in the sixteenth century, ten acres of underwood were recorded there.[52]

The house of the Hospitallers at Kilmainham maintained considerable woodland in proximity to the city. The 1540 extent of the preceptory's possessions mentions a wood called the 'Grete' wood, containing forty-one acres on the north side of the Liffey and a wood called 'Inscore' (Inchicore), containing sixteen acres of underwood, on the south side.[53] All

51 *CCCD*, 1578, no. 1352.   **52** *RAST*, p. 3; *EIMP*.   **53** *EIMP*.

of this woodland was said to be reserved for the hospice. The Hospitallers also had two acres of underwood around their manor of Clontarf and a wood called 'Priorswood' at Coolock, containing twenty-four acres. Other religious houses that carefully husbanded their woodland resources included the nunnery of Gracedieu, situated near Lusk. In 1540, the convent had three acres close to the precincts on which ash trees and oaks were reserved solely for the repair of their buildings.

Buildings

Post-and-wattle houses continued to be built in Dublin in the late twelfth century.[54] When Henry II camped outside Dublin in 1171, he is said to have ordered the construction of 'a palace [made] out of twigs after the fashion of the country'.[55] This suggests that such post-and-wattle buildings were viewed as peculiarly Irish, but the method of construction appears to have been adopted by the Anglo-Normans, who continued the tradition into the thirteenth century.[56] Part of the reason for this was almost certainly the established and regular supply of the appropriate raw materials for this building method. While some Gaelic Irish lords continued to use post-and-wattle buildings right up to the seventeenth century, the Anglo-Normans and their descendants appear not to have done so.[57]

The remains of a rectangular house of early thirteenth-century date were excavated by Claire Walsh at Back Lane.[58] The house had internal roof supports, and walls of post-and-wattle construction. The upright posts included willow, alder, hazel, ash and holly, and it appears that these posts were being taken from suitably sized poles of random species in a mixed woodland.[59] In contrast, the rods were almost exclusively of hazel. Analysis by Aidan O'Sullivan and Mary Deevy of wood from other structures at Back Lane revealed that much of the wood was probably coppiced at four- to eight-year intervals.[60] Almost all of the post-and-wattle structures examined from sites across Dublin were dominated by hazel rods, but alder, ash, birch, elm, holly, oak and willow also occurred occasionally.[61] In the wattle fences on Patrick Street, for instance, 84 per cent of the rods were of hazel, but ash (*c.*5 per cent) and willow (*c.*11 per cent) were also used.[62]

Despite the continued construction of post-and-wattle buildings, sill-beamed houses with plank walls began to be built as well.[63] At Back Lane, for instance, twelfth-century post-and-wattle houses were replaced in the thirteenth century with sill-beamed structures (incorporating some timbers previously used for other purposes).[64] The same sequence was found in High Street and Winetavern Street, as well as at Ship Street Little, where the base-plates, planks and roof supports of the later structure were all of oak.[65] The floors of wattles and wood chips may have derived from the preparation on site of some of the larger structural timbers.

In some places, the change of building style seems to have been abrupt rather than gradual.[66] It is likely to have been the result of the arrival new people with different building

54 Simpson, 'Forty years a-digging', pp 57–9; Simpson, 'Excavations on the southern side of the medieval town at Ship Street Little', pp 25, 27–8.   55 Simpson, 'Forty years a-digging', p. 57, referring to William Stubbs (ed.), *The chronicle of the reigns of Henry II and Richard I, AD1169–1192, known commonly under the name of Benedict of Peterborough* (2 vols, London, 1867), i, pp 28–9.   56 Tim Coughlan, 'The Anglo-Norman houses of Dublin: evidence from Back Lane' in Duffy (ed.), *Medieval Dublin I* (2000), pp 203–34; Margaret Gowen, 'Archaeology and Christchurch Place, 1993', unpublished report, 1993; Margaret Gowen, 'Hotel and car park development at Christchurch Place: archaeology' (preliminary post-excavation report submitted to the Office of Public Works, 1992).   57 K.D. O'Conor, 'Housing in later medieval Gaelic Ireland', *Ruralia*, 4 (2002), 201–10.   58 Claire Walsh, 'Back Lane, Dublin', DEHLG file 92E0005.   59 O'Sullivan, 'Trees, woodland and woodmanship', 677–8.   60 O'Sullivan, 'The wooden waterfronts', p. 78.   61 Gowen, '9–12 High Street'; Gowen, 'Archaeology and Christchurch Place'; Simpson, 'Excavations on the southern side of the medieval town at Ship Street Little', p. 25; Bride Street (02E0163); Walsh, 'Structural timbers', pp 196–8; Mary McMahon, 'Archaeological excavations at Bridge Street Lower, Dublin', *PRIA*, 91C3 (1991), 41–71 at 47–52.   62 Walsh, 'Structural timbers', pp 196–8.   63 Simpson, 'Forty years a-digging', pp 59–62; Celie O'Rahilly, 'Bridge Street, Dublin', DEHLG file (1980).   64 Coughlan, 'The Anglo-Norman houses of Dublin', pp 203–34.   65 Ó Ríordáin, 'Excavations at High Street and Winetavern Street'; Simpson, 'Excavations on the southern side of the medieval town at Ship Street Little', p. 36.   66 Coughlan, 'The Anglo-Norman houses of Dublin', p. 220.

traditions and the change was probably catalysed by improving techniques and technology at the same time. The change in building methods had knock-on effects – oak replaced ash as the most frequently used building material, and more advanced carpentry techniques began to emerge.[67] These changes are evidenced not only in the houses, but also in a range of other structures. Water pipes of oak were found during excavations at Francis Street, and similar pipes on Bridge Street were interpreted by the excavator as part of Dublin's water supply network, initiated in 1244.[68] A dendrochronologically dated thirteenth-century sluice gate uncovered at Inns Quay was fashioned from well-seasoned oak (and all faces had adze marks).[69] The excavator suggested that the gate and associated stone drains and features may have been part of a mill.[70] Large oak timbers were also used in the construction and repair of the thirteenth- and fourteenth-century mill at Patrick Street.[71]

Wood was also used for purposes such as the lining of graves, pits, troughs, drains and water channels.[72] It was used in the construction of coffins, beams, pathways, fences and jetties.[73] The high-quality oak timbers used to line a pit in Thomas Street in the first decade of the thirteenth century had a very regular ring-pattern, suggesting that the timber was harvested from slow-grown trees.[74] Wood debris at the base of the pit was dominated by oak (79 per cent of all identifiable chips), with some ash (18 per cent) and cherry (3 per cent) also present. In contrast, oak planks used in a second pit had rings that indicated poor growing conditions.[75] Some timber from a crab apple tree was also found in this pit.

Fuel

In the medieval period, Dublin was the focus of the most substantial aggregate demand for fuel in Ireland. Firstly, there were the needs of baking, brewing, food preparation and domestic heating. In common with other large towns and cities of northern Europe, the long and relatively cold winters would have necessitated a substantial energy expenditure on home heating. Furthermore, most methods of food and drink preparation required considerable fuel inputs. Pottages and stews, which rendered edible various grains, legumes, dried fish and cheap cuts of meat, required long periods of simmering. Brewing and baking were similarly fuel hungry, and the various hospitals, inns and hostelries clustered together in the capital were significant consumers of fuel.[76] Dublin and its suburbs would have generated a

67 Barry, *The archaeology of medieval Ireland*, p. 111; Walsh, 'Structural timbers', p. 189; Murray, *Viking and early medieval buildings*, p. 3; Wallace, *Viking-Age buildings of Dublin*, 1, p. 41; Coughlan, 'The Anglo-Norman houses of Dublin', p. 232; O'Sullivan, 'Medieval boat and ship timbers', p. 121.   **68** Claire Walsh, '123–33 Francis Street, Dublin', DEHLG files 96E0349 and 97E0129; McMahon, 'Archaeological excavations at Bridge Street Lower', 54–6 (pls III–IV), 66.   **69** Mary McMahon, 'Archaeological excavations at the site of the Four Courts extension, Inns Quay, Dublin', *PRIA*, 88C9 (1988), 271–319 at 271, 276, 280–5.   **70** McMahon, 'Excavations at the site of the Four Courts extension', 311. **71** Linzi Simpson, 'Historical background to the Patrick Street excavation' in Walsh, *Archaeological excavations at Patrick, Nicholas and Winetavern Streets* (1997), pp 17–33 at p. 28; David Brown, 'Dendrochronological report on the timbers' in Walsh, *Archaeological excavations at Patrick, Nicholas and Winetavern Streets* (1997), pp 185–8.   **72** Coughlan, 'The Anglo-Norman houses of Dublin', pp 220–5; Simpson, 'Excavations on the southern side of the medieval town at Ship Street Little', p. 38; Conway, *Director's first findings from excavations in Cabinteely*, p. 21; O'Donovan, '119–21 Thomas Street, Dublin', DEHLG file 95E0280 [plank-lined pit, early thirteenth century]; Walsh, *Archaeological excavations at Patrick, Nicholas and Winetavern Streets*, p. 79; Simpson, 'Forty years a-digging', pp 42–3; Hayden, 'West Side story', pp 106, 108–9; Ellen O'Carroll, 'Appendix 3: Wood analysis of samples from Dundrum Castle' in O'Brien, 'Final report on excavations at Dundrum Castle', DEHLG file E000419; Ó Ríordáin, 'Excavations at High Street and Winetavern Street'; Simpson, 'Excavations on the southern side of the medieval town at Ship Street Little', passim; Edmond O'Donovan, 'The growth and decline of a medieval suburb? Evidence from excavations at Thomas Street, Dublin' in Duffy (ed.), *Medieval Dublin IV* (2003), pp 127–71 at pp 134–9.   **73** P.F. Wallace, 'Carpentry in Ireland, AD900–1300: the Wood Quay evidence' in Seán McGrail (ed.), *Woodworking techniques before AD1500: papers presented to a symposium at Greenwich in September, 1980, together with edited discussion* (BAR International Series, 129, 1982), pp 263–99; Margaret Gowen, 'Excavations at the site of the church and tower of St Michael le Pole, Dublin' in Duffy (ed.), *Medieval Dublin II* (2001), pp 13–52 at pp 36, 41; O'Sullivan, 'The wooden waterfronts', p. 63; Coughlan, 'The Anglo-Norman houses of Dublin', pp 212–13; Simpson, 'Excavations on the southern side of the medieval town at Ship Street Little', pp 30–1; Lynch and Manning, 'Excavations at Dublin Castle', p. 194; Rosanne Meenan, '27–30 Merchant's Quay, Dublin' in *Excavations 1989*, p. 25; Rosanne Meenan, '20–23 Merchant's Quay, Dublin' in *Excavations 1990*, p. 31.   **74** O'Donovan, 'The growth and decline of a medieval suburb?', p. 136.   **75** Ibid., pp 138–9.   **76** A late thirteenth-century source from Kent, England, states that one large,

large industrial demand for fuel as well – the manufacture of pottery and tiles, metal working, glass-making and the production of lime all required fuel for kilns and braziers.

The primary fuel was wood, and evidence from a site at Carmanhall suggests that species such as alder, hazel, ash and *prunus* species (such as blackthorn) were used for firewood, while oak was mainly reserved for structural purposes.[77] Ellen O'Carroll concluded that most of the wood may have originated from mixed woodlands, while the alder suggests a slightly wetter environment and the *prunus* is indicative of hedges. Among the findings from the analysis of insect remains from Back Lane were indicators of dead or decaying oak or pine, and Fiona Reilly suggested that these species may have been brought into the town with consignments of firewood.[78] In the late twelfth century, the burgesses of Trim in Co. Meath were permitted to take old wood from the floor of the forest of Trim for use as firewood, under the supervision of Hugh de Lacy's foresters.[79] Such a permit was relatively common in the late twelfth and early thirteenth centuries.[80] The list of goods on which taxes applied in Trim in 1290 included ½*d.* on each cartload of logs for sale, ¼*d.* on each horse-load of logs and ½*d.* on each ship laden with logs.[81] Some at least of Dublin's wood fuel came into the city by boat, and it is recorded that the construction of a weir at Lucan in 1306 hindered the passage of boats carrying firewood into the town.[82]

Dublin undoubtedly needed the output of a considerable area of managed woodland to satisfy its fuel requirements if woodfuel was largely used by the populace (see below, pp 480–1). The Dublin region extents, however, indicate that the demesne acreage given over to woodland was comparatively low, and this was especially so in the area immediately adjacent to and south of the city, where one might expect a focus on fuel exploitation to support the urban demand (Figure 9.1, Tables 9.1 and 11.1). Only 16 per cent of the demesne at Finglas, for instance, was used for woodland/park (71 of 434.5 acres); and 6 per cent at Clondalkin (40 of 665.5 acres), while 24 per cent was used at Colonia (66 of 271 acres). Some of these patterns may be explained by the availability of other fuels. Turf was certainly available and used as a fuel in Dublin. There is also evidence that fuels such as furze were widely used in Dublin, at least in the early modern period and very likely earlier.

London's great demand for fuel of various types resulted in the development of a specialised trade involving large numbers of wood-mongers who occupied designated areas within the city with wharves and landing places.[83] There is little evidence for such specialised trade in the Dublin region. What can be seen, however, is a definite involvement of Irish people in the selling of timber and, to a lesser extent, fuel.

Waterfront revetments

A significant market for the oak resources of the Dublin region, particularly in the thirteenth century, was the erection and maintenance of timber structures used in the reclamation and consolidation of the Liffey foreshore (Figure 11.4). The early to mid-thirteenth century witnessed the construction of complex revetments, primarily of oak, at (among other locations) Church Street, Cornmarket, Patrick Street, Strand Street Great, Usher's Quay, Wood Quay and Winetavern Street, all of which have been examined archaeologically.[84] The

---

horse-drawn wagon-load of wood was needed to produce 8 bushels of malt. This would have produced about 70 gallons of medium ale (K.P. Witney, 'The woodland economy of Kent, 1066–1348', *AHS*, 38 (1990), 20–39 at 31). J.A. Galloway, 'Driven by drink? Ale consumption and the economy of the London region, *c.*1300–1400' in Carlin and Rosenthal (eds), *Food and eating in medieval Europe* (1998), pp 87–100 at p. 91.   **77** Fiona Reilly, 'Carmanhall (site 55m)', DEHLG file 02E0074 (wood analysis by Ellen O'Carroll).   **78** Reilly, 'The contribution of insect remains', pp 56–8. **79** *CPI*, p. 10; Mac Niocaill, *Na buirgéisí*, 1, pp 74–5; 2, pp 327, 481; Russell Library, Maynooth, MS O'Renehan, 3RB1, p. 17; Nat. Archives, MS 2–504/9, no. 190, pp 159–60.   **80** Adolphus Ballard (ed.), *British borough charters, 1042–1216* (Cambridge, 1913), pp 52–7.   **81** *CDI, 1285–92*, no. 560, p. 278   **82** *HMDI*, p. 536.   **83** Galloway, Keene and Murphy, 'Fuelling the city'; Margaret Murphy, 'The fuel supply of medieval London, 1300–1400', *Franco-British Studies*, 20 (1995), 85–96.   **84** Simpson, '161–168 Church Street, 3–15 Hammond Lane, Dublin', DEHLG file 02E0096; Hayden,

very name Wood Quay, documented from the Middle Ages, is indicative of the prevalence of timber as a building material in medieval Dublin.[85] Evidence suggests that there were professional 'quay builders' in operation in Dublin at this time.[86] These specialists may have worked further afield as well, and timber revetments have also been excavated in Drogheda, at both Shop Street and Dyer Street.[87]

At Patrick Street, all but two of the structural timbers (in the foreshore revetment) were of oak derived from slow-grown trees, while dowels were made from hazel, ash, birch and oak, with the latter predominating.[88] Intensive analysis of the Winetavern Street wood assemblage has revealed significant information about its source and management.[89] The earliest revetment, of late twelfth-century date, was predominantly of strong willow and ash, with smaller amounts of holly, alder, birch and hazel also present. The larger structural timbers of the later revetments were almost exclusively of oak, with occasional pieces of ash and alder also appearing. Some of the oak was characteristic of timbers extracted from trees in either regenerated secondary, wild woodland or, more probably, mature managed oak-woods.[90] A similar picture is given by the large timbers excavated elsewhere on Winetavern Street.[91] Much of the timber used in the smaller structural elements – the vertical posts and subsidiary base-plates – was sourced from either fast-grown oak saplings or coppiced mature

'West Side story', pp 95–6, 99–100; Walsh, *Archaeological excavations at Patrick, Nicholas and Winetavern Streets*; D.L. Swan, 'Archaeological excavations at Usher's Quay, 1991' in Duffy (ed.), *Medieval Dublin I* (2000), pp 126–58 at pp 146–56; Claire Walsh, 'Archaeological excavation of the Anglo-Norman waterfront at Strand Street Great, Dublin' in Duffy (ed.), *Medieval Dublin VI* (2005), pp 160–87; Helen Kehoe, '24–28 St Mary's Abbey' in *Excavations 2003*, p. 141; Helen Keogh, 'St Mary's Abbey/Strand Street Little, Dublin' in *Excavations 2004*, pp 136–7; D.L. Swan, 'Wood Quay found at Usher's Quay!', *AI*, 5:2 (1991), 6; Wallace, 'Carpentry in Ireland', pp 263–99; O'Sullivan, 'The wooden waterfronts', pp 62–92; Aidan O'Sullivan, 'Medieval boat and ship timbers' in Halpin, *The port of medieval Dublin* (2000), pp 118–36. **85** Linzi Simpson, 'Historical background' in Halpin, *The port of medieval Dublin* (2000), pp 23–7 at p. 25. **86** P.F. Wallace, 'Dublin's waterfront at Wood Quay, 900–1317' in G. Milne and R. Hobley (eds), *Waterfront archaeology in Britain and northern Europe* (CBA Research Report, 41, 1981), pp 108–18. **87** Sweetman, 'Archaeological excavations at Shop St., Drogheda', *PRIA*, 84C (1984), 171–224; Malachy Conway, 'Caffrey's Monumental Works, Dyer Street, Drogheda', DEHLG file 99E0242. **88** Claire Walsh, 'Structural timbers' in Walsh, *Archaeological excavations at Patrick, Nicholas and Winetavern Streets* (1997), pp 189–98. **89** O'Sullivan, 'The wooden waterfronts', pp 62–92. **90** Ibid., pp 79–80. **91** Walsh, *Archaeological excavations at Patrick, Nicholas and Winetavern Streets*, pp 99–103.

THE DUBLIN REGION IN THE MIDDLE AGES

oak-wood.[92] Trees of this type are, according to O'Sullivan, best found in periodically felled woodland. In addition to the oak from managed or secondary woodland, some timbers were hewn from long-lived trunks, such as those typically found in hedgerows or open ground.

Some of the largest oak timbers were up to 11m in length.[93] They were probably transported to the site by boat and may have come from woods close to the sea – perhaps the Wicklow lowlands. The use in Dublin at this time of timber from coastal broad-leaved woodland was also indicated by the presence of certain insect remains in samples from Back Lane (in the form of *Mesites tardii*, et al.).[94]

While the larger timbers at Winetavern Street were mostly oak, a much wider range of species was exploited for post-and-wattle and other lighter structures. Hazel accounted for over half of these, while ash was the second most common species. These were closely clustered in age, unlike the other species used, and it was suggested by O'Sullivan that some of the wood was sourced in high quality, managed woodland, while the rest came from poorer scrub woodland.[95] The posts in a nearby wattle fence were predominantly of willow roundwood, while the wattles were of hazel with some willow. The hazel rods were aged between four and ten and the age distribution indicated a range of managed coppice cycles on a rotation of four, seven and ten years. Similarly, an area of hazel brushwood was made up of rods between six and thirteen years of age, with a peak at eight years suggesting planned coppice rotation. In some structures, the hazel age/size relationships demonstrated an even increase in diameter with age, indicating a common source for the wood.[96]

Many of the ash roundwoods were also clustered in the four-, seven- and ten-year slots, and the overall pattern suggests that wood may have been extracted at defined intervals of 4, 7–8 and 10–11 years. Summarising the evidence, O'Sullivan suggested that large oak trunks and hazel and ash rods were being specifically obtained for the waterfront construction at Winetavern Street, with a range of other species used incidentally.[97]

> The fast-grown hazel and ash would probably have grown best on dry, lime-rich soils, although occasional hazel and willow trunks that were longer lived but with narrower growth rate indicate that stressed or scrubby trunks were also exploited. The alder and willow would have thrived best on waterlogged mineral soils, perhaps adjacent to the River Liffey wetlands. More acidic, upland soils may be indicated by the oak, holly and birch. It is also possible, however, that the predominant woodland used was of hazel/ash with additional stands of holly, willow, elm and dogwood growing on its fringes.[98]

The wood used in the Strand Street Great waterfront structures may have come from mixed woodlands nearby, and the variety of species present indicated 'a mixed, fairly open forest consisting of oak and ash'.[99]

Oak was still exploited for the construction of riverside revetments in the fourteenth century, and this was demonstrated in 1990 by excavations at Arran Quay.[100] Oak was used in the manufacture of the base-plates and in most of the uprights and planks, but a possible shortage of oak timbers was suggested by the presence of ash uprights (*c*.20 per cent) and planks. In some places, it appears that large posts were not available at all, and here smaller

92 O'Sullivan, 'The wooden waterfronts', pp 78, 80.   **93** Ibid., p. 79.   **94** Reilly, 'The contribution of insect remains', pp 56–8.   **95** O'Sullivan, 'The wooden waterfronts', pp 69, 77, 80.   **96** Ibid., pp 72–3, 77.   **97** Ibid., pp 76, 77 (fig. 37), 78.   **98** Ibid., p. 77; Rackham, *Ancient woodland*.   **99** Ellen O'Carroll, 'Wood identification from Strand Street Great, Dublin' in Walsh, 'Archaeological excavation of the Anglo-Norman waterfront' (2005), pp 185–7.   **100** Alan Hayden, 'Excavation of the medieval river frontage at Arran Quay, Dublin' in Duffy (ed.), *Medieval Dublin V* (2004), pp 149–242.

Rafter
foot

Dunsoghley: Roof.

Top of truss

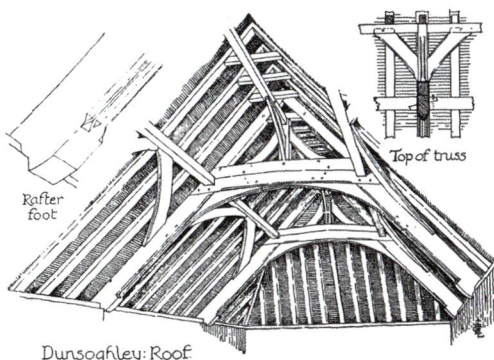

Figure 11.5 (*left*) Dunsoghly Castle, Co. Dublin, roof timbers. This is one of the very few, if not the only, timber roof-frames to survive on any tower house in Ireland (© Department of the Environment, Heritage and Local Government).

Figure 11.6 (*right*) Drawing by Harold Leask of the roof timbers at Dunsoghly Castle. 'It is a straightforward arch-braced collar roof with short crown-posts carrying a medial purlin and braced downwards to the collar and upwards to the purlin. It has curved windbraces and the ends are treated as a gambrel roof' (Craig, *The architecture of Ireland*, p. 107; image from Leask, *Irish castles and castellated houses*, p. 120).

Figure 11.7 Lusk Church, Co. Dublin. This belfry tower was built in the fifteenth century and while there has been no analysis of the timbers, some of them may be early. They would certainly be worth sampling for dating (© Department of the Environment, Heritage and Local Government).

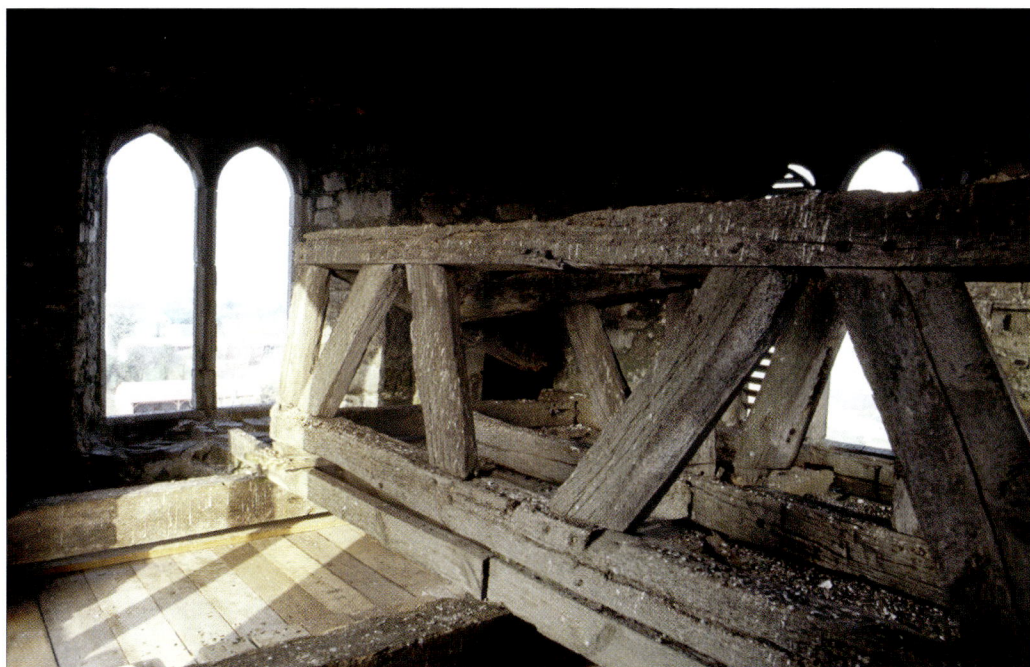

posts were hammered in side-by-side to form 'composite posts'.[101] The short lifespan of revetments (and consequent need for a large supply of timber) was also illustrated at Arran Quay, where three successive examples were built in the first sixty years or so of the fourteenth century. Most of the timbers in the second revetment were of oak, but one flimsy ash base-plate was also present. Most of the wooden structures at Arran Quay were superseded in the fifteenth century, when a stone quay wall was built.[102]

Despite the increasing use of stone, the use of wood was still prevalent on Dublin's quaysides at the end of the sixteenth cemtury. The 'great explosion' of 11 March 1597 serves as a reminder of this fact.[103] The extent of the damage caused by the gunpowder explosion was exacerbated by the prevalence of timber structures on the quays – apart from the boats and houses, the crane and crane-tower were wooden, and there were wooden barrels, carts and fish-crates. Most of the timber would have been sourced in the hinterland.

Stone structures using wood

A large amount of archaeological evidence has been found for the destruction of medieval wooden structures by fire, and a number of major burnings are recorded historically.[104] It is possibly as a consequence of the inescapable risk of fire that, from as early as the middle of the thirteenth century, houses of stone began to become more commonplace in Dublin.[105]

101 Hayden, 'Arran Quay', p. 169.   **102** Ibid., pp 176–83.   **103** Colm Lennon, 'The great explosion in Dublin, 1597', *DHR*, 42:1 (Dec. 1988), 7–20.   **104** See, for example, J.F. Lydon, 'The medieval city' in Art Cosgrove, *Dublin through the ages* (Dublin, 1988), pp 25–45 at p. 34.   **105** Coughlan, 'The Anglo-Norman houses of Dublin', p. 232.

While this must have had a knock-on effect on the relative importance of wood, large quantities of timber were still required in the construction of stone buildings. In fact, wood was now required for an even wider range of purposes than before. Lime-kilns had to be fuelled, heavy scaffolding had to be erected and temporary timber supports were needed for the erection of arches, vaults, lintels and roofs. The impressions created by wattle, wicker and plank centring survive in upstanding stone monuments across the Dublin region, while putlog holes attest the former presence of timber scaffolding and, in some cases, hoarding. Indeed, parts of the original twelfth- and thirteenth-century oak timbers were found to survive in the putlog holes at Trim Castle.[106] Rows of socket holes for timber floor and roof supports are a common feature of ruinous masonry buildings of medieval date and at Dunsoghly Castle in north Co. Dublin the medieval roof-timbers survive intact (Figures 11.5, 11.6).[107] The timbers in some other buildings, such as church towers, may also turn out to be medieval (Figure 11.7).

At Kindlestown Castle, Co. Wicklow, where no medieval timbers survive, there is a range of evidence for the extensive use of wood in a variety of forms.[108] The architectural remains feature putlog holes and sockets that once accommodated heavy timber supports, and clear evidence for the use of plank centring can be seen on the barrel vault. Excavations revealed a series of large post-holes, impressions of laths in the clay, and indications of the previous existence of plank partitions in the form of staining left by burnt and rotting wood. Chips of slate told of the former presence of timber roof supports and laths.

Dendrochronological analysis of timbers in the roof of St Patrick's Cathedral in Dublin has indicated that some of them derive from trees felled in the thirteenth century, and that these were sourced 'within the Dublin region'.[109] Other timbers came from trees felled in the 1360s. These later trees may have been more than 350 years old when cut, but significantly, they appear *not* to have come from the Dublin region, but from further north (perhaps Antrim). The implication is that good-quality oaks could be found in the Dublin region in the thirteenth century (as confirmed by the timbers at St Patrick's and Salisbury Cathedrals (see below, p. 375)), but that by the mid-fourteenth century, alternative sources of long oak timbers had to be used. The widespread evidence for re-use of large timbers at other sites across the city also attests the increasing difficulty that existed in sourcing new supplies. It is possible that less timber was available in the Dublin region, or that there was still a supply, but that getting access to it had become more difficult in the fourteenth century, perhaps for political reasons.

Turners, carvers, coopers and shipwrights

Aside from the structural projects, wood was required to supply specialist craftsmen such as turners, carvers, coopers and shipwrights. Fragments of five lathe-turned bowls were recovered from thirteenth-century levels at Winetavern Street. All were of ash, a suitable medium for carving vessels, and the 'preferred species for turned ware in Dublin'.[110] A turned bowl of willow was found during excavations on Patrick Street, while one of ash was uncovered at a site on Thomas Street.[111] Excavations on High Street yielded a series of bowls, a lathe-turned handle and a large amount of woodturning waste, and this was interpreted by the excavator as evidence for the presence of a lathe-turning workshop in the vicinity.[112]

106 Tom Condit, 'Rings of truth at Trim Castle', *AI*, 10:3 (autumn 1996), 30–3; P.D. Sweetman, 'The development of Trim Castle in the light of recent research', *Château Gaillard*, 18 (Caen, 1998), 224–30.   107 Leask, *Irish castles*, fig. 83 and pp 118–21; M.G.L. Baillie, *Tree ring dating and archaeology* (London, 1982), p. 147; Maurice Craig, *The architecture of Ireland, from the earliest times to 1880* (London and Dublin, 1982), p. 107.   108 Simpson, 'Dublin's southern frontier', pp 311, 334–5.   109 Charles Lyons, 'Dublin's oldest roof? The choir of St Patrick's Cathedral' in Duffy (ed.), *Medieval Dublin VI* (2005), pp 177–213 at pp 206–8.   110 Aidan O'Sullivan and Mary Deevy, 'Wooden artefacts' in Halpin, *The port of medieval Dublin* (2000), pp 162–7 at p. 164.   111 Hayden, 'Wooden objects'; O'Donovan, 'The growth and decline of a medieval suburb?', p. 161.   112 Ó Ríordáin, 'Excavations at High Street and Winetavern Street', 76–7.

Ash was probably readily obtainable in the vicinity of Dublin, and the Winetavern Street bowls appear to have been fashioned from wood that came from 'very fast-grown timber, ash trees which were of no great age but measured up to 25cm in diameter. It is possible that the bowls were made from stout poles and small trunks growing in hedgerows or areas of mature coppiced woodland'.[113] Parts of at least two wooden bowls of probable twelfth- to thirteenth-century date were recovered during excavations at Dunboyne Castle, Co. Meath.[114] At Merrywell, in the same county, seven pieces of a turned ash bowl were found in a well, in association with thirteenth-century pottery (Figure 11.8).[115]

Other wooden artefacts recovered from thirteenth- and fourteenth-century contexts in Dublin include needles, pins, toggles, pegs, dowels, combs, gaming pieces, lids and handles.[116] The species most frequently used for these were birch, willow, hazel, alder and oak, with yew and pine being used less frequently. There is a range of indirect evidence for the preparation and use of timber in medieval Dublin, and this includes the discovery of woodworking tools such as saws, axes, chisels, wedges, mallets, punches, boring bits and gimlets.[117] Analyses of insect remains have demonstrated the presence of very large numbers of wood-dependent taxa.[118] Samples from medieval contexts at Back Lane and Christ Church Place comprised a range of indicators of broad-leaved woodland (such as *Mesites tardii*, *Saperda Scalaris*, *Gracilia minuta*).[119] Bark, particularly from oak trees, contains tannic acid, which is an important component of the tanning process, and evidence for its use has been found on a number of sites in Dublin.[120]

The craft of the cooper was an important one and barrels were widely used for storage and transport. The remains of timber barrels have been found on many medieval sites in Dublin.[121] The discovery on High Street of a large number of staves, some of which were

113 O'Sullivan and Deevy, 'Wooden artefacts', p. 164.   **114** Cotter, 'Dunboyne Castle, Castlefarm'.   **115** O'Carroll, 'An analysis of the wood remains from Merrywell', p. 6.   **116** Hayden, 'Wooden objects'; O'Sullivan and Deevy, 'Wooden artefacts', pp 162–7; Lynch and Manning, 'Excavations at Dublin Castle', p. 178; Hayden, 'Arran Quay', pp 209–11; Gowen, '9–12 High Street'; O'Donovan, 'The growth and decline of a medieval suburb?', pp 139, 161. **117** Barry, *The archaeology of medieval Ireland*, p. 113; Andrew Halpin, *The port of medieval Dublin: archaeological excavations at the Civic Offices, Winetavern Street, Dublin, 1993* (Dublin, 2000), p. 167, no. 122.2; Lynch and Manning, 'Excavations at Dublin Castle', pp 178, 181, fig. 6; Hayden, 'Arran Quay', p. 185; O'Sullivan, 'Medieval boat and ship timbers', p. 121.   **118** Reilly, 'The contribution of insect remains', pp 56–8.   **119** Ibid.; G.R. Coope, 'Report on the coleoptera from an eleventh-century house at Christ Church Place, Dublin' in Hans Bekker-Nielsen, Peter Foote and Olaf Olsen (eds), *Proceedings of the eighth Viking Congress, 1977* (Odense, 1981), pp 51–6.   **120** Mitchell, *Archaeology and environment*, p. 22.   **121** McMahon, 'Archaeological excavations at Bridge Street Lower', pp 54, 62–3 (fig. 10.181); Gowen, '9–12 High Street'; O'Donovan, 'The growth and decline of a medieval suburb?', pp 161–3; Hayden, 'Wooden

unfinished, led Brendán Ó Ríordáin to suggest that coopers were settled in this part of the town.[122] The staves, lids and bases recovered from most excavations are generally made of oak, and three oak bungs were also found on Patrick Street.[123] Hoops and dowels (if present) are most commonly of hazel, but examples made from birch, ash and yew are also known.[124] The remains of several barrels were found re-used in a thirteenth-century barrel-lined pit on Thomas Street and these were the subject of specialist analysis.[125] All of the staves, which had evidence for adze-tooling on the internal faces, were fashioned from regularly growing oak, showing stable growing conditions. The wood was hard and of good quality. The staves were held in place by eighteen thin hazel hoops, bound together with strips of willow. There were some hazel dowels. The hazel rods were four to seven years old and the willow was one to two.

Analysis of the archaeological and dendrochronological evidence has led a number of commentators to conclude that medieval Dublin had its own shipbuilding industry, 'perhaps with a boatyard situated along the Liffey Valley'.[126] Seán McGrail has argued convincingly that the great majority of nautical timbers uncovered in the Wood Quay excavations were parts of boats and ships built in the Dublin region.[127] Indeed, some of the ships' timbers were unfinished, and this is viewed as further evidence for a boat- and shipbuilding 'yard' in medieval Dublin.[128] This suggestion is supported by the documentary evidence, which includes an order from Henry III in July 1222 to the men of Dublin (and of Waterford, Drogheda and Limerick) that they build galleys for the defence of Ireland.[129] There is a reference dated October 1233 to a great galley that the men of Dublin had recently constructed, and in 1241 the king ordered Dubliners to construct another such ship.[130]

Recent studies have also demonstrated that the late eleventh-century warship Skuldelev 2, found at Roskilde in Denmark, was built of oaks grown in the Dublin region (although it is not clear where the ship was actually built).[131] Excavations on Winetavern Street yielded parts of a number of boats, one of which was possibly used 'for fishing or for use as a ferry across the river'.[132] According to O'Sullivan, 'a range of woodland sources is possible for [these] timbers, including hedgerows or large woodland trees for the planks, pasture-grown or open woodland oaks for the stems, knees and bulkhead'.

It was not only large structural timbers that were required for constructing and finishing ships, and this is illustrated by the account of William de Moenes (1302–3)(Figure 11.2).[133] The account details the felling of rods and the construction of hurdles for use in ships. The hurdles (*claie*) were made of pliable rods woven together and were used for making stalls to accommodate the horses on board and prevent them from injuring themselves or the sides of the ships. A sum of £6 18s. 5½d. was spent on cutting the rods (*virge*), transporting them to All Hallows in Dublin and making the hurdles.[134] William Dunning of Santry was in charge of the hurdle-makers assembled at All Hallows, while another group was employed making hurdles at Rathgar.

objects'; P.F. Wallace, 'The survival of wood in tenth- to thirteenth-century Dublin' in *Waterlogged wood study and conservation: proceedings of the second ICOM Waterlogged Wood Group Conference* (Grenoble, 1985), pp 81–7 at p. 85; Simpson, 'Excavations on the southern side of the medieval town at Ship Street Little', pp 31, 39, 40; O'Donovan, '119–21 Thomas Street, Dublin', DEHLG file 95E0280, pp 23–4, 54–6, 85. **122** Ó Ríordáin, 'Excavations at High Street and Winetavern Street', 77. **123** Hayden, 'Wooden objects', p. 162. **124** Gowen, '9–12 High Street'; Simpson, 'Excavations on the southern side of the medieval town at Ship Street Little', pp 31, 39, 40. **125** O'Donovan, '119–21 Thomas Street, Dublin', DEHLG file 95E0280, pp 23–4; 54–6, 85; O'Donovan, 'The growth and decline of a medieval suburb?', p. 140. **126** O'Sullivan, 'Medieval boat and ship timbers', p. 121. **127** Seán McGrail, *Medieval boat and ship timbers from Dublin* (Dublin, 1993). **128** McGrail, *Medieval boat and ship timbers from Dublin*, p. 87. **129** *CDI, 1171–1251*, no. 1049, p. 161. **130** *CDI, 1171–1251*, nos. 2066–7, p. 307, no. 2532, p. 377. **131** Niels Bonde and Ole Crumlin-Pedersen, 'The dating of wreck 2 from Skuldelev, Denmark', *NewsWARP*, 7 (Exeter, 1990), 3–6. **132** O'Sullivan, 'Medieval boat and ship timbers', p. 121. **133** TNA:PRO E101/11/3. This account is discussed by Lydon, 'Edward I, Ireland and war in Scotland', pp 48–9. It has been printed in translation (with some errors) by O'Connor, 'Hurdle making in Dublin'. **134** A much larger sum of £17 13s. 8d. was spent on hurdles and boards for repairs at Dublin, but no particulars survive of how this was spent: Lydon 'Edward I, Ireland and Scotland', p. 58, n. 30.

Re-used ship timbers are a feature of many of the timber structures revealed in medieval Dublin. The Wood Quay carpenters re-used the dismembered hulk of a ship in the thirteenth-century timber revetments, and on Fishamble Street a ship's keel was recycled.[135] Some of the re-used planks appear to have come from ships built in Ireland late in the twelfth century.[136] Further nautical timbers were recycled on sites at Castle Street and at Winetavern Street.[137] Most were of oak, but an oar re-used in a revetment at Winetavern Street was made of 'straight-grained, fast-grown ash'.

As a large number of timbers in a decommissioned ship are usually salvageable, it stands to reason that many will be re-used in other projects, but the frequency with which such recycled material is found in medieval Dublin may suggest that purpose-cut, primary timber was in limited supply. In addition to those from boats and ships, there is widespread evidence for the secondary use of timbers originally used in paths, fences, barrels, houses, wainscots and revetments.[138] On the other hand, there is evidence for the existence of an ample supply of timber, or at least one sufficient enough to supply overseas markets, and it is possible that the widespread re-use of timber was simply an economical and efficient use of resources.

The exportation of timber

It is thought that the export of Irish oak to England for use in cathedrals and municipal buildings did not take place on a large scale.[139] There is evidence, however, for the exportation of at least some timber from the Dublin region in the Middle Ages. Recent analysis of the oak timbers used in the construction of the roof of Salisbury Cathedral revealed that roughly half of the wood was imported from Dublin in the first half of the thirteenth century.[140] The research, carried out by the Oxford dendrochronology laboratory, has shown that many of the trees were felled in the Dublin region in the spring of 1222. It appears that the wood was 'natural' oak from 'virgin Irish forests' and that it differed significantly from the 'cultivated' English oak, which was also exploited for roof timbers at Salisbury.[141] The English trees came from managed woodland and were encouraged to grow quickly. This resulted in widely spaced tree rings. In contrast, the 'wild' Irish trees grew much more slowly and had narrowly spaced rings. Timber sourced in Ireland was used throughout the building campaigns from the 1220s to the 1250s, not only in roofing, but also in some of the doors. Many of the trees were 300 years old when felled. It seems that the builders of Salisbury, who were in search of 'wood of the highest quality', were tapping into a rich source of timber in the area around Dublin, access to which had been made easier thanks to the strong links between Dublin and Bristol. The timber was bought from a certain William of Dublin, who assisted in its transport across the Irish Sea.[142]

135 Wallace, 'Carpentry in Ireland, AD900–1300', p. 277.   **136** Wallace, 'The survival of wood', p. 85.   **137** Byrne, '26–29 Castle Street/20 Lord Edward Street'; Halpin, *The port of medieval Dublin*, p. 35; O'Sullivan, 'The wooden waterfronts', pp 64–5, 67; O'Sullivan, 'Medieval boat and ship timbers', pp 118–36, esp. p. 121.   **138** Wallace, 'Carpentry in Ireland, AD900–1300', p. 277; Wallace, 'The survival of wood', p. 85; Gowen with Scally, *Summary report on excavations at Exchange Street Upper/Parliament Street*, p. 16; Scally, 'The earthen banks and walled defences', pp 20–5; Hayden, 'The excavation of pre-Norman defences and houses at Werburgh Street', pp 47, 62; McMahon, 'Excavations at the site of the Four Courts extension'; Coughlan, 'The Anglo-Norman houses of Dublin', p. 222; O'Donovan, '119–21 Thomas Street, Dublin', DEHLG file 95E0280, pp 23–4; 54–6, 85; O'Donovan, 'The growth and decline of a medieval suburb?', pp 138, 140; Simpson, 'Excavations on the southern side of the medieval town at Ship Street Little'; Hayden, 'West Side story', pp 108–9; Swan, 'Archaeological excavations at Usher's Quay', p. 152; Hayden, 'Arran Quay', pp 160, 162, 166–7, 172, 174; O'Sullivan, 'The wooden waterfronts', p. 73; Walsh, 'Structural timbers', pp 195–6.   **139** O'Sullivan, 'The wooden waterfronts', pp 84–5.   **140** *Daily Telegraph* (5 March 2003), p. 10. See also D.W.H. Miles, 'The tree-ring dating of the roof carpentry of the eastern chapels, north nave triforium, and north porch, Salisbury Cathedral, Wiltshire', *Centre for Archaeology Report*, 94, English Heritage (2002).   **141** Tim Tatton-Brown and Dan Miles, 'Salisbury Cathedral', *Current Archaeology*, 188 (2003), 364–9.   **142** O'Neill, *Merchants and mariners*, p. 100.

During the thirteenth century, sawn timber was sent to England for use in construction and shipbuilding, and timber boards and prefabricated wooden brattices were shipped from Dublin to Wales for use in Edward I's campaign there.[143] Timber to make brattices was also sent to Gascony.[144] Much of Ireland's timber trade with England passed through the port of Bristol, and records of this appear in the ships' cargo inventories in the Bristol customs accounts.[145] Timber boards were among the exports to England and a list of customs to be collected at Ipswich in c.1300 included a tax of 4d. on every hundred 'borde of Irlond'.[146] Timber exports were not confined to England and Wales, and in the fifteenth century, carpenters at Rouen Cathedral in Normandy carved the choir stalls from Irish oak.[147]

Forests

'Forests', in the general sense of regions subject to the jurisdiction of forest law, are documented in many sources for the Dublin region, particularly in the thirteenth century. Most were the property of the crown but other persons often held land within the bounds of the forest. The primary function of these lands was to provide opportunities for hunting. There were at least three royal forests in the south-east of the study area in the region known as Uí Briúin Cualann.[148]

One vast area of royal forest encompassed the entire valley of Glencree, the probable boundaries of which have been described by le Fanu.[149] The royal forest at Glencree would probably have been too extensive to enclose,[150] but part of it at least seems to have been bounded by a deep fosse and bank, traces of which can still be seen near Curtlestown Church. In 1913, it was described as a bank standing 3m wide with the fosse 4m wide and 1.6m deep.[151] Today, the bank and fosse are still visible, although they have eroded considerably; a large stone wall runs along the top of the bank.[152] Perhaps this was part of the enclosure of a deer park on the edge of the forest?[153] In 1244, sixty does and twenty bucks were sent from the royal forest at Chester to Dalkey to stock the forest of Glencree and the earthwork may have been constructed at this time to prevent the deer from escaping and to protect them from poaching (Figure 11.9).[154] The king was able to bestow gifts of deer from Glencree on some of his faithful subjects by 1296 when he granted Eustace le Poer twelve fallow deer from Glencree.[155] Poaching was a problem, however, and some of the offenders were of rather high status. In 1291, the abbot of St Mary's Abbey, Dublin, which held lands in nearby Kiltiernan and Glencullen, was accused of hunting in the king's forest with nets, greyhounds and other apparatus.[156]

In addition to providing hunting, the forest was a valuable source of timber. There are records of gifts of between seven and twenty oaks from Glencree to various individuals and institutions in Dublin during the thirteenth century, including St Patrick's Cathedral, St Mary's Abbey, St Thomas' Abbey and the Dominican friary.[157] Sales of copse wood from

143 Down, 'Colonial society and economy', p. 488; J.F. Lydon, 'The years of crisis, 1254–1315' in Cosgrove (ed.), *A new history of Ireland: II* (1993), pp 179–204 at p. 182; *CDI, 1171–1251*, nos. 2735–6, p. 408.   **144** *CDI, 1252–84*, no. 346 [*recte* 446], p. 71.   **145** O'Neill, *Merchants and mariners*, p. 101.   **146** Ibid.   **147** Ibid., p. 100.   **148** Mary Kelly Quinn, 'The evolution of forestry in County Wicklow from prehistory to the present' in Hannigan and Nolan (eds), *Wicklow: history and society* (1994), pp 823–54.   **149** T.T. Le Fanu, 'The royal forest of Glencree', *JRSAI*, 12 (1883), 268–80 at 269. See above, p. 89.   **150** Large areas of forest and park *could* be enclosed, but it was a massive undertaking. Clarendon Park in Wiltshire, England, for instance, was enclosed by a massive earthwork bank and ditch that ran for 16.5km. It was complete by the fourteenth century, and even now the bank survives up to 3.5m high in places (see Tom Beaumont James and Christopher Gerrard, *Clarendon: landscape of kings* (Macclesfield, Cheshire, 2007), esp. pp 13, 45–69).   **151** J.T. Westropp, 'Earthwork near Curtlestown, Co. Wicklow', *JRSAI*, 43 (1913), 185–6.   **152** Simpson, 'Anglo-Norman settlement in Uí Briuin Cualann', p. 207.   **153** Margaret Murphy and Kieran O'Conor, 'Castles and deer parks in Anglo-Norman Ireland', *Eolas: Journal of the American Society of Irish Medieval Studies*, 1 (2006), 53–70 at 61–2.   **154** *CDI, 1171–1251*, no. 2671, p. 398   **155** *CDI, 1293–1301*, no. 352, p. 167.   **156** *CSMA*, 1, p. 4.   **157** *CDI, 1252–84*, no. 2195, p. 509; *CDI, 1285–92*, no. 92, p. 38.

Figure 11.9 Wild deer in the Wicklow Mountains, near Glencree. The indigenous red deer of these mountains became extinct in the nineteenth century, and most of the deer there now are red/sika hybrids. Red deer were not well-suited to hunting, and the Anglo-Normans brought in smaller fallow deer to stock their deer parks (image courtesy of John Kenny).

Glencree were accounted for along with the issues of the royal manor of Obrun.[158] A more systematic removal of timber commenced in the last decades of the thirteenth century when the forest was held by Queen Eleanor, wife of Edward I. In 1290, William de Moenes, 'keeper of the queen's timber works in Glencree', was granted £100 from the Irish treasury to pay the wages of carpenters and other workmen employed in producing timber in Glencree for the queen's use in Wales (see above, pp 362–3).[159] This coincided with Eleanor's programme of building at Haverford Castle.[160]

There were many disputes concerning the royal forest, especially with the archbishop of Dublin, who also held forests in Wicklow.[161] In 1229, however, he managed to get a disafforestation charter for his vast forest at Coillacht.[162] A third royal forest is recorded at Garfloun in the manor of Obrun, somewhere between Powerscourt and Kilmacanogue.[163]

The Irish in the forests

The Wicklow woods were a source of much profit to the English crown in the thirteenth century, but in later periods their role in sheltering hostile Irishmen was a cause of dismay.

---

158 Michaelmas 1285 – 33s. from the copse wood of Glencree accounted for, along with the rent of Obrun (*CDI, 1285–92*, p. 52 and another 58s. [1286 – term of St John the Baptist] (*CDI, 1285–92*, no. 251, p. 112). **159** *CDI, 1285–92*, no. 641, p. 323. **160** Ibid., no. 796, p. 363. Wood was also exported from the woods of Newcastle McKynegan for the works at Haverford. **161** *CDI, 1171–1251*, no. 1317, p. 199; McNeill (ed.), *Alen's register*, p. 62. **162** This covered most of the barony of Lower Talbotstown – McNeill (ed.), *Alen's register*, pp 25–6. **163** *CDI, 1171–1251*, no. 2409, pp 359–60.

Figure 11.10 Meeting of Gloucester and Mac Murchada in Co. Wicklow in 1399, from an early fifteenth-century manuscript by Jean Creton, who was with Richard II in Ireland in 1399. The drawing shows the heavily armoured English knights assembled at the edge of the forest, with the Irish appearing from a narrow pass or ravine (BL Harleian MS 1319 © The British Library Board; reproduced from J.T. Gilbert, *Facsimiles of national manuscripts of Ireland*, 3 (1879), pl. xxxiii).

The survival and later resurgence of Gaelic society under the noses of the English adminis-tration was due in large part – perhaps even solely, as Smyth asserts – to the protection afforded by the high mountain areas of Wicklow and the forest cover on the perimeter of these regions.[164] It was the Leinster forest that led to the failure of Richard II's expeditions in spite of his employment of 2,500 people to cut a way through the forest for the royal army on its disastrous trek from the Barrow Valley to the Wicklow coast via the Glen of Imaal and Glenmalure.[165] The king apparently claimed that if Art Mac Murchada was not captured by the autumn of 1399 he would burn all the woods, great and small (Figure 11.10).[166]

Legal protection of woods and forests

A measure of the importance of woodland is the frequent documentary references to steps taken to prevent its despoliation by unauthorised tree-felling or other illegal usages. Wood was often a cause of dispute both between lord and tenant and between lords themselves. On the royal manors in the Dublin region, one of the duties of the official known as the seneschal of demesnes was to oversee the use of the royal woodland and punish any infringements by tenants or manorial officials.[167] Grants of wood were made but restrictions were placed on the felling and cutting processes. When wood was required for the repair of the mill at Newcastle Lyons in 1321, the seneschal had to supervise the cutting to minimise waste.[168] Enquiries carried out in 1374 into waste on royal manors found that theft of wood or trees was particularly common on the manor of Esker.[169] Sometimes those accused of

164 Smyth, *Celtic Leinster*, p. 109. **165** Ibid. **166** J.J. Webb, 'Translation of a French metrical history of the deposition of King Richard the Second', *Archaeologia*, 20 (1824), 45, 308–9 (quoted by Smyth, *Celtic Leinster*, p. 111). For a discussion of medieval Gaelic military tactics, see O'Conor, *Medieval rural settlement in Ireland*, pp 98–100; O'Conor, 'Gaelic lordly settlement', p. 218. **167** Lyons, 'Manorial administration', pp 48–9. **168** NAI RC8/12: Memoranda roll, pp 515–16. **169** Lyons, 'Manorial administration', p. 49.

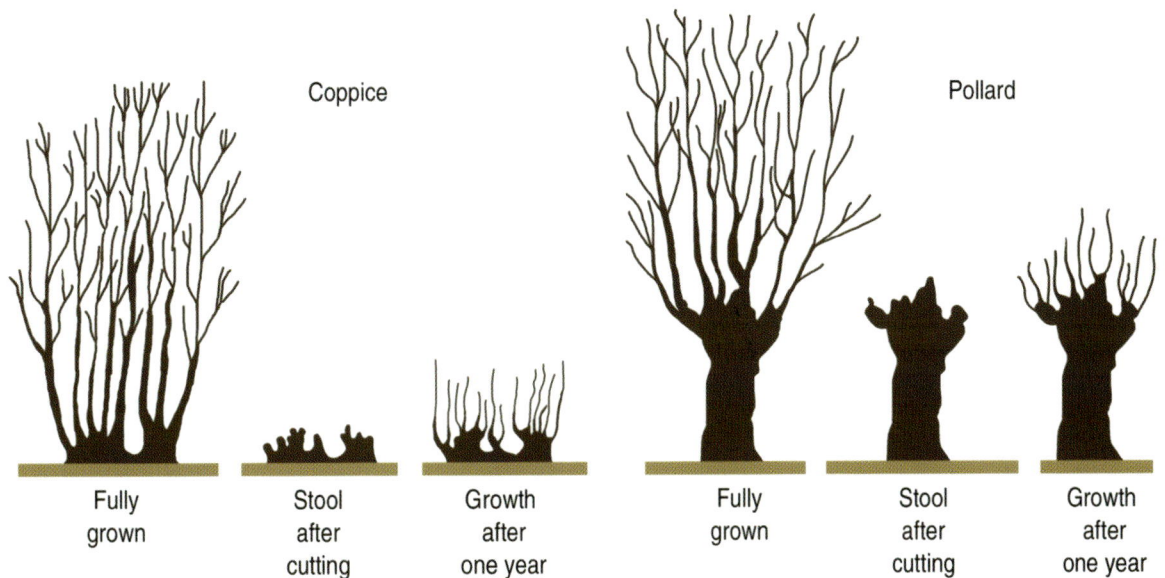

Coppice   Pollard

Fully grown   Stool after cutting   Growth after one year   Fully grown   Stool after cutting   Growth after one year

Figure 11.11 The main methods of woodland management are coppicing and pollarding. In the former, the young stems are cut back regularly so that a lot of shoots, rather than one larger trunk, will grow. When they have reached an appropriate height, they are harvested as rods and the cycle begins again. Pollarding is coppicing done higher up on the tree, in order to protect new shoots from grazing animals. It is often carried out in woodlands in which there are deer or other large herbivores. If for some reason the new branches are not harvested, coppiced or pollarded trees will continue to grow normally, and their characteristic form can make them readily identifiable many years later (see Figure 11.12).

infringements were the officials whose positions placed them in ideal circumstances for illegal practices. In 1292, William de Prene, the king's carpenter, was imprisoned for levelling and carrying away oak trees in the king's wood at Newcastle McKynegan.[170]

There were frequent disputes over rights of estover – the privilege allowed to certain tenants to take from the lord's wood what was required for repairing dwellings (known as housebote), for repairing gates and fences (known as heybote) and for general fuel. In a case of 1305, William le Deveneys claimed estover for enclosing, burning and building in forty acres of wood in Keppoc, Clane (in the manor of Blackhall). This was disputed by another party who claimed that William had no such right but rather that he and his men, 'as if by stealth, entered the wood, and cut and carried away certain trees'.[171] In 1496–7, jurors on the Christ Church manor of Grangegorman found that one tenant, 'the wife of Donald Swynard', had cut down two ash trees, while another tenant had broken the ditch of the wood of Litelcobragh and put eight cows into it without licence.[172]

The most extreme case of woodland destruction in the Dublin region was alleged to have occurred on the manor of Santry. In 1302, Simon de Feypo brought a case against Theobald de Verdun who, as his overlord, had been administering the manor of Santry during the minority of the heir – sometime in the period 1274–96.[173] Simon claimed that de Verdun had committed serious damage to the manorial buildings and resources. In particular, he had destroyed 200 apple trees valued at £20, 100 pear trees valued at £10, 30,000 great ash trees valued at £200 and 1,000 great alders valued at £60. De Verdun denied the charge, saying that he had only cut down twelve alders and twelve ash trees during his wardship. Whatever the truth of the claim, it cannot be doubted that there was a substantial and valuable area of woodland attached to the manor of Santry. According to Elizabeth Hickey,

the great ash forest and the alder trees are likely to have been part of the native forest running north to Swords and east to Clontarf and flourishing on this rich limestone land; the ash valuable for every sort of farm implement, the alder valued for its property of absorbing water without decaying and much used for underpinning bridges and for trackways across boggy lands. Alder and ash grow naturally together.

170 CDI, 1285–92, no. 1151, p. 519. 171 CJR, 1305–7, p. 94. 172 CCCD, no. 1105. 173 CJR, 1295–1303, no. 386.

This great forest of north Co. Dublin is mentioned as late as 1689 when, on the approach of Schomberg towards Dublin, the woods of Santry and Clontarf were cut and the ways palisaded between Swords and Dublin.[174]

A generation earlier, the Forest of Swords is referred to in the Civil Survey, where mention is made of the 'highway leading from Swords to the fforest'.[175] This woodland does not appear on the Down Survey barony maps, however. In the Civil Survey, twenty-nine acres of wood are recorded in the parish of Santry and thirty-seven acres and ninety acres in the neighbouring parishes of St Margaret's and Coolock respectively. A small area of woodland survives at Santry to the present day, and it contains a number of 'uncommon species that tend to be associated with old woodlands, most notably hairy St John's-wort (*Hypericum hirsutum*)'.[176]

Where other possibly ancient woods survive in the Dublin region, evidence of woodland management can be identified. Post-medieval coppicing is known to have been practiced in the Glen of the Downs, Co. Wicklow, and at Kilteel, Co. Kildare, for instance, and ancient oak-woods with giant stools or stumps are still present in both locations (Figure 11.12).[177]

Chapter summary

Timber was one of the most important natural resources in the Middle Ages. Dublin, like all major urban centres, required a constant supply of wood, and most of this was sourced in its immediate hinterland. Wood was used in the construction of all sorts of buildings, from domestic to agricultural to religious to administrative. It was needed for the manufacture of waterfront revetments, boats and ships, bridges, pipes, barrels and a wide range of smaller items. It also served as the main fuel for domestic heating, baking, brewing, cooking and lighting and in a range of industrial activities such as metal working, lime production and the manufacture of pottery, tiles and glass. Some timber from the Dublin region was exported to England, Wales and France.

Before the coming of the Anglo-Normans, post-and-wattle houses were the norm in Dublin. While this building technique continued to be used in some quarters in the thirteenth century and later, it was mostly superseded by masonry construction. Large quantities of timber were still required for roofs and floors, for scaffolding and supports and to fuel lime-kilns. With the change in building methods, oak replaced ash as the most commonly used building material. There is evidence for a good supply of oak in the Dublin region up to the thirteenth century, but from then on there was increasing reliance on forests further away. Thirteenth-century timbers in the roof of St Patrick's Cathedral derive from trees sourced within the region, but the fourteenth-century timbers seem to have come from further north, possibly Antrim.

There is increasing evidence that much of Ireland's natural forest-cover had been cleared long before 1600, and probably much earlier than that. It is likely that the Dublin region in the Middle Ages consisted of largely open landscape dotted with stands of trees and some larger forests. Analysis of the place-name evidence for woodland, in both Irish and English, highlights the absence of 'wood' elements in the immediate environs of the city and the coast to the north of the city, while they are most frequent between the mountains and the sea to the south of the city. Some place-names give indications as to the former owners of the woods, the nature or shape of the wood, or the main species of tree growing there.

174 Hickey, *Skryne and the early Normans*, p. 136.   **175** *Civil Survey*, 7, pp 89, 90, 93, 96, 101, 186.   **176** Daniel Kelly, Margaret Norton and Declan Doogue, 'Woodlands and hedges' in Declan Doogue, David Nash, John Parnell, Sylvia Reynolds and Peter Wyse Jackson (eds), *Flora of County Dublin* (Dublin, 1998), pp 85–93 at p. 86.   **177** Rackham, 'Looking for ancient woodland in Ireland', p. 9.

Figure 11.12 This tree in woodland at Kilteel, Co. Kildare, is one of a number at this location that were clearly coppiced at an early age.

Documentary references to wood and woodlands are more frequent after 1170, as their exploitation began to be recorded in Anglo-Norman manorial documents. The sources provide evidence for the location of the woodland and the value of the timber. There are frequent references to efforts to protect the woods from despoliation by unauthorised tree-felling or other illegal usages. 'Forests' – in the sense of regions that were governed by forest law – are well-documented in the Dublin region. Most were held by the crown, and their primary function was to provide opportunities for hunting. One extensive royal forest covered the entire valley of Glencree and included a purpose-built deer park. In addition to providing hunting, however, the forest was a valuable source of timber.

Although some evidence for woodland management can be found at several locations in the Dublin region, and archaeological research indicates that coppicing was practiced, there is little detailed documentary evidence for the management of woodland. Some woodlands in the south of the Dublin region had particularly low values due to their proximity to Gaelic Irish strongholds. These woods had been a source of much profit for the English crown in the thirteenth century, but their increasing role in sheltering the enemy was a cause of concern for the government.

Woods were probably the most valuable natural resource available in the Dublin hinterland. There were other natural resources, however, which could be exploited for fuel, fodder and building materials. The next chapter looks at these resources.

CHAPTER 12

Natural resources

Bogs

Productive peat bogs were found in several locations in the Dublin region and it is clear from the documentary sources that they were perceived as an important source of fuel throughout the medieval period, particularly for domestic heating. Access to this alternative fuel supply was especially important in those parts of the region where wood was scarce or entirely absent. In this way, relatively infertile land assumed an important function in energy production. Turf was not simply a second-choice fuel to which people turned only when local forests were cut down and wood became hard to get. Recent research has stressed the advantages of peat over wood as a pre-industrial fuel:

> A year's supply was cut with less labour. It needed only one tool that did not need sharpening or replacing. Wood was difficult to process and hard to transport, and not clearly of calorific advantage, ton for ton. It took even longer to dry. Peat was safer, spark-free and flexible to use in the home.[1]

Turbaries were exploited by both manorial lords and their tenants. The sums of money associated with them in manorial documents reflect both the value of the fuel for demesne use and the value of grants of rights to tenants. It is rarely possible to discover who exactly was using the fuel. At Clondalkin in the early fourteenth century, the rents paid by the burgesses included an element for common turbary rights.[2] On Ballymore, another archiepiscopal manor, tenants in the thirteenth century held rights of turbary as part of their leases, sometimes for a specified period of twenty years. A small turbary was reserved for demesne use.[3]

Turbaries were also valued on the manors of Finglas, Leixlip, Maynooth and Ratoath.[4] The values were generally small, usually between one and two shillings. The 'per acre' values could, however, be on a par with good value arable or meadow land. The 1½ acres valued on the manor of Ratoath in 1333 were worth 12*d.* or 8*d.* per acre.[5] At Finglas in 1326, there were twelve acres of moor with turbary, valued at 3*s.* 4*d.* 'and no more, because all wasted in time past'. This equates with a per acre value of over 3*d.*, which presumably had been considerably higher before the peat had been dug out.[6] In the thirteenth century, the priory

---

1 T.C. Smout, 'Energy rich, energy poor: Scotland, Ireland and Iceland, 1600–1800' in David Dickson and Cormac Ó Grada (eds), *Refiguring Ireland: essays in honour of L.M. Cullen* (Dublin, 2003), pp 19–36 at p. 21. See also A.T. Lucas, 'Notes on the history of turf as a fuel in Ireland to 1700', *Ulster Folk-life*, 15–16 (1969–70), 172–4. 2 McNeill (ed.), *Alen's register*, p. 186. An early fifteenth-century document mentions both the common moor of Clondalkin and a field called 'Turfmorefield' (McNeill (ed.), *Alen's register*, pp 235–6). 3 McNeill (ed.), *Alen's register*, pp 121, 189. 4 Ibid., p. 173; TNA:PRO C47/10/20/1; *RBK*, pp 98–101; TNA:PRO C135/36. 5 TNA:PRO C135/36. This is a very high valuation. By comparison, a medieval reference to a bog for digging peat in Pembrokeshire gives a per acre value of 4*d.* T.M. Owen, 'Historical aspects of peat-cutting in Wales' in Jenkins (ed.), *Studies in folk life* (1969), pp 124–55 at p. 128. 6 McNeill (ed.), *Alen's register*, p. 173.

of All Hallows, Dublin, was granted a turbary at Finglas, where turf might be dug out for the supply of all the houses of the priory.[7] Finglas bog was clearly still in use in 1315–16 when the escheator, who was administering the archiepiscopal temporalities during a vacancy in the see, reported a loss for the turbary at Finglas. This loss was caused not by the turf being exhausted but by the 'raininess of the season and the great floods' which prevented it being cut.[8]

Grants and assignments of land frequently included specific mention of rights over turbary. In *c.*1247, the prior and canons of Holy Trinity were granted land 'near the red moor' with turbary in *Clonemachgillegrie.*[9] This may be the same red moor mentioned in a document of a similar date that granted to Richard son of Stephen of Killcollin 'common turbary for firing' of the red moor between the vills of Dergory (possibly Delgany) and Cnochoille.[10] As part of her assignment of dower in 1328, Joanna de Burgh, countess of Kildare, got an acre of turbary in *le More dil Rathen.* As she was granted one-third of each resource, this implies that there were three acres of turbary in total.[11]

Turbary rights, like woodland rights such as estover (the right to take firewood) were seen as an integral part of the package of resources that made up a manor or grange. This is evident in a grant of 1268 from St Mary's Abbey to the prior of Holy Trinity of right of turbary in Balykeeth 'sufficient for the grange of Kilmashogue'.[12] Almost seventy years later, in 1335, when Holy Trinity leased the manors of Kilmashogue and Ballyardor to a Dublin merchant, they retained their turbary rights.[13] The lessee was obliged to supply from every house 'a day's work to make turf at digging time and a day from those having pack horses there, to carry the turf of the manor'.

Cutting and carrying turf were labour-intensive activities. It has been estimated that during the early modern period an expert turf-cutter could dig out eight tons of raw peat in a day, equivalent to three tons of air-dried peat.[14] This may have been enough fuel to supply the annual needs of a small household. In practice, few would have worked at that pace, and

7 Butler (ed.), *Registrum prioritas omnium sanctorum,* p. 55.   8 *HMDI,* pp 366–71.   9 *CCCD,* no. 59.   10 McNeill (ed.), *Alen's register,* pp 80–1.   11 *RBK,* pp 98–101.   12 *CCCD,* no. 95.   13 *CCCD,* no. 593.   14 Smout, 'Energy rich, energy poor', p. 28.

considerable time and energy was also expended in transporting the peat from the bogs to the place of consumption. It is not surprising, therefore, to find that tenurial obligations often included the digging and transport of peat. The monastic extents of 1540–1 detail how each of the four tenants of St Mary's Abbey in Haroldsgrange ('the Grange in the Marsh') were required to make and bring four cart-loads of turf from the turbary to the grange; the value of this work was 1s. per tenant or 4s. in total.[15] Tenants of the nunnery of Gracedieu in the vills of Lusk, Dunganstown and Irishtown were also required to supply turf to the religious community on an annual basis.[16]

Consumers without access to their own turbaries were obliged to obtain their supplies through the market. While there is no evidence of an extensive trade in peat, it is clear that turf was brought into Dublin for sale. Carts of turf were included among the items on which customs were to be paid in the early seventeenth century.[17] Sometimes turf was sold by manors. In 1344, the bailiff of Clonkeen accounted for 3s. 1d. for turf sold that year.[18] It is also possible that turf was marketed by individuals and that the Irish may have played a major role in this particular trade. On a number of occasions, chattels of Irishmen included quantities of turf. This may have been for personal use; however the quantities appear to be quite large. In 1303, the chattels of Clement Ocathyll, the king's betagh, killed at Cruagh, included a stack of turf valued at 6s. 8d., and in 1306 a felon associated with Clonloragh, Co. Kildare, had twelve cart loads of turf in his possession.[19]

Turf is only once listed in the inventories of late fifteenth-century testators in the Dublin region. Agnes Bourke of Balscadden had turf worth 3s. among her possessions when she made her will in 1472.[20] Nor are prices of turf often found in the records, but in general it appears to have been a fairly cheap commodity – certainly cheaper than wood. In 1542, the account of the economy rents of Christ Church included 4d. for two loads of turf.[21] If this represents the market price for cart-loads of turf in the sixteenth century, then the 6s. 8d. of turf in the hands of the Irishman mentioned above must have represented a very substantial supply in the fourteenth century.

The evidence leads to the conclusion that bogs were intensively exploited across the study area and turf was commonly used as a fuel in urban and rural households of all types – rich and poor, lay and ecclesiastical. This intensive usage had an impact and it appears that some raised bogs were cut away as early as the fourteenth century.[22] Finglas Bog was wasted by 1326, while Garristown Bog, along the River Delvin in the north of the county (the 'Redmore in Gariestown'), was under cultivation in 1337, and was common pasture by 1348.[23] Some of the later history of the depletion of Garristown Bog is recorded cartographically (Figures 12.2, 12.3). The earliest mapped extent is shown on the Down Survey map of 1654, but drainage of the area and presumably continued cutting away of the bog had further reduced its extent by the time of the Ordnance Survey first edition mapping in the 1830s, while more recent mapping shows the rather small extent of the bog in the twentieth century. There is also a suggestion that 'the bog at Newlands near Tallaght may have disappeared in medieval times'.[24] The removal of many raised bogs close to Dublin appears therefore to have been partly due to demand for turf for domestic heating and partly to the increased pressure in the thirteenth and early fourteenth centuries to create as much productive arable land as possible.

15 *EIMP*, p. 10. For the identification of the Grange in the Marsh, see Ó Conbhuí, 'The lands of St Mary's Abbey', 54–5. 16 *EIMP*, p. 74. 17 *CARD*, I, p. 262. 18 Mills (ed.), *Account roll*, p. 55. 19 NAI RC8/2: Memoranda roll, p. 314; *CJR, 1305–7*, p. 494. See also *CJR, 1305–7*, p. 485, where the chattels of another felon in Co. Dublin included a stack of turf. 20 Berry (ed.), *Register of wills and inventories*, p. 45. 21 *CCCD*, no. 434. 22 John Feehan and Grace O'Donovan, *The bogs of Ireland: an introduction to the natural, cultural and industrial heritage of Irish peatlands* (Dublin, 1996), pp 7, 37. 23 McNeill (ed.), *Alen's register*, p. 173; *CGR*, p. 46. 24 Feehan and O'Donovan, *The bogs of Ireland*, p. 37.

Figure 12.2 Extract
from the Down Survey
map of the barony of
Balrothery, showing
'Garristowne moore'.

Place-name evidence

The exploitation of bogs through the years has been so complete in some cases that it is difficult to pinpoint where they once were. Combined with documentary and cartographic sources such as those mentioned above, place-names can provide useful clues in this regard. There are several Irish words used to denote a marsh or bog and, as Joyce noted in 1869, 'in thousands of cases the marshes have been drained, and the land placed under cultivation, the names alone remaining to attest the existence of swamps in days long past'.[25] In the Dublin region, many places have names containing elements relating to bogland or marshy ground. *Móin* is the word most commonly associated with bog[26] and it forms part of over twenty place-names, including Ballynamona (Galtrim parish) 'the townland of the bog'; Ballymoneen (Killiskey) 'the townland of the little bog'; Newtownmoneenluggagh (Scullogestown) 'the little bog of the holes' (that is, bog-holes); and Moneycooly (Laraghbryan) 'the bog of the hazel'. *Carcach* is a word often used to denote marshy or swampy ground, and it gives rise to the place-names Corkagh and Corkagh Demesne (both Clondalkin), Corkeragh (Ballynafagh; Figure 13.1), Cork Great and Cork Little (Oldconnaught). Other words associated with marsh or marshy ground include *eanach*, *riasc* and *seiscenn*, and these words are at the root of the names Annaghaskin (Rathmichael), meaning the marsh of the eels (*easgan*, an eel), Reask (Kilbrew), Balreask (Balsoon), Balseskin (Finglas) and Mountseskin (Tallaght).[27] There are two townlands called Redbog in the Dublin region, one in Co. Meath (Dunshaughlin) and one in Co. Kildare (Rathmore).

Furze

Furze belongs to the family *leguminosae*, which also includes plants such as peas, beans, clover etc. Nowadays it is regarded as a weed, but formerly it played an important role in

25 Joyce, *Irish names of places*, 1, p. 461. **26** Ibid., pp 467–8. **27** Ibid., pp 461–8.

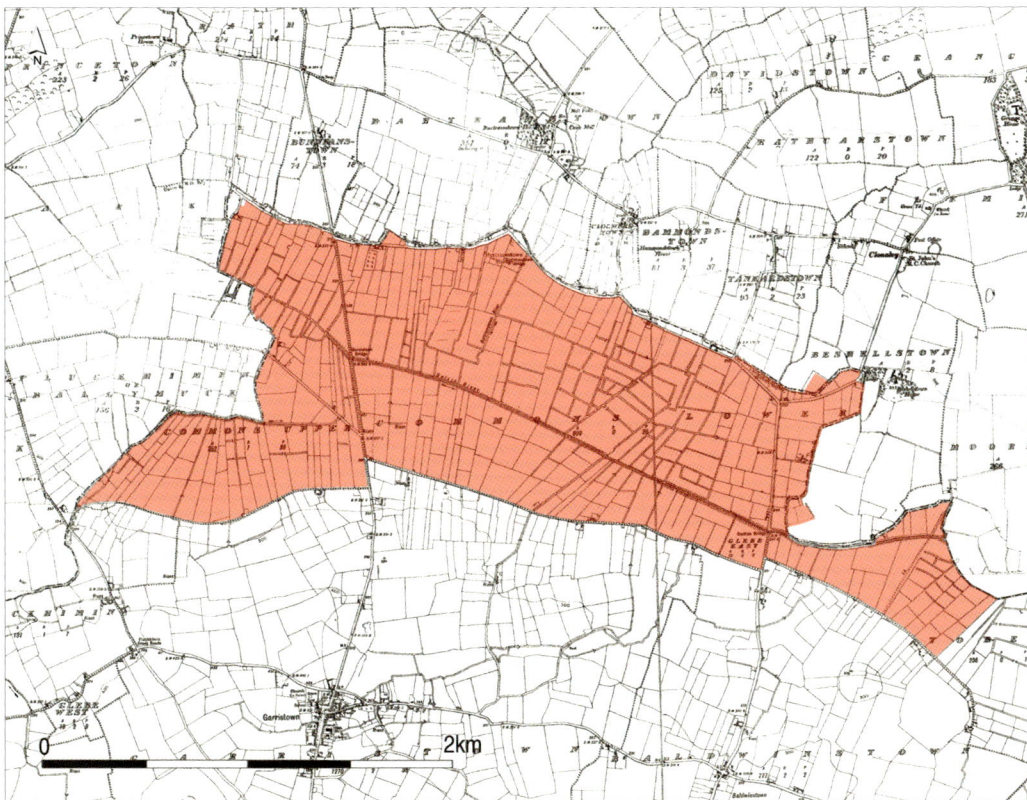

Figure 12.3 Extract from the second edition of the Ordnance Survey map of Meath, with Garristown Bog (digitised from the first edition map) super-imposed, revealing the progress of the bog's depletion in recent times.

the rural economy of much of Ireland, being used for, among other things, fuel, fodder and fencing. According to A.T. Lucas, 'there can hardly be any other plant in the Irish flora which has been pressed into service for so many and for such a variety of purposes'.[28] There are two species of furze found in Ireland: one, the taller and more robust, is the common furze (*Ulex europaeus*); the other is the dwarf furze (*Ulex galii*). Both species are found in the Dublin region, but the dwarf furze is rarely found north of a line drawn from Malahide westwards.[29]

There are few references to furze and its uses in pre-Anglo-Norman sources, although what little there is does seem to indicate that it was a plant of some economic importance. A thirteenth-century memoranda regarding the lands of St Thomas' Abbey, Dublin, mentions two fields opposite the '*januam silve*' or yellow wood, which might be translated as furze wood.[30] From the fifteenth century onwards, specific references to furze ('furs, firres') begin to appear in the documents in a manner that indicates that it was recognised as an asset. For example, in 1475–6, Jenet Rocheford, gentlewoman, was seised of a park in Co. Meath, near the hill of Bray [Hill of Bree?], which contained three acres of furze and two acres of arable.[31]

The extents of Irish monastic possessions (1540–1) contain several references to 'fir trees', some of them occurring in the Dublin region. For example, the priory of Holmpatrick had twelve acres of pasture and fir-trees as part of its demesne at Holmpatrick, as well as one acre of fir trees in the vill of Killinure, parish of Duleek.[32] Lucas argues convincingly that these are references to furze, as it is extremely unlikely that plantations of fir-trees were established at this date.[33] Moreover, it is believed that pine (*Pinus sylvestris*) became extinct in Ireland long before the medieval period or, at best, only survived in very isolated locations.[34] With

28 A.T. Lucas, *Furze: a survey of its uses in Ireland* (Dublin, 1960), p. 1. **29** Ibid., p. 5. **30** *RAST*, p. 3. **31** *Stat. Ire., 12–22 Edw. IV*, p. 397 – cited by Lucas (*Furze*, p. 17). **32** *EIMP*, pp 49, 51. **33** Lucas, *Furze*, p. 17. **34** Recently, however, pine pollen has been found in late medieval horizons: see V.A. Hall and Lynda Bunting, 'Tephra-dated pollen studies of medieval landscapes in the north of Ireland' in Duffy, Edwards and FitzPatrick (eds), *Gaelic Ireland* (2001), pp 207–22 at pp 218–19 – so the possibility should not be totally ruled out.

Figure 12.4 Extract
from the Down Survey
map of the barony of
Clane, Co. Kildare,
showing 'a great red
bog … called the bog
of Munroe'.

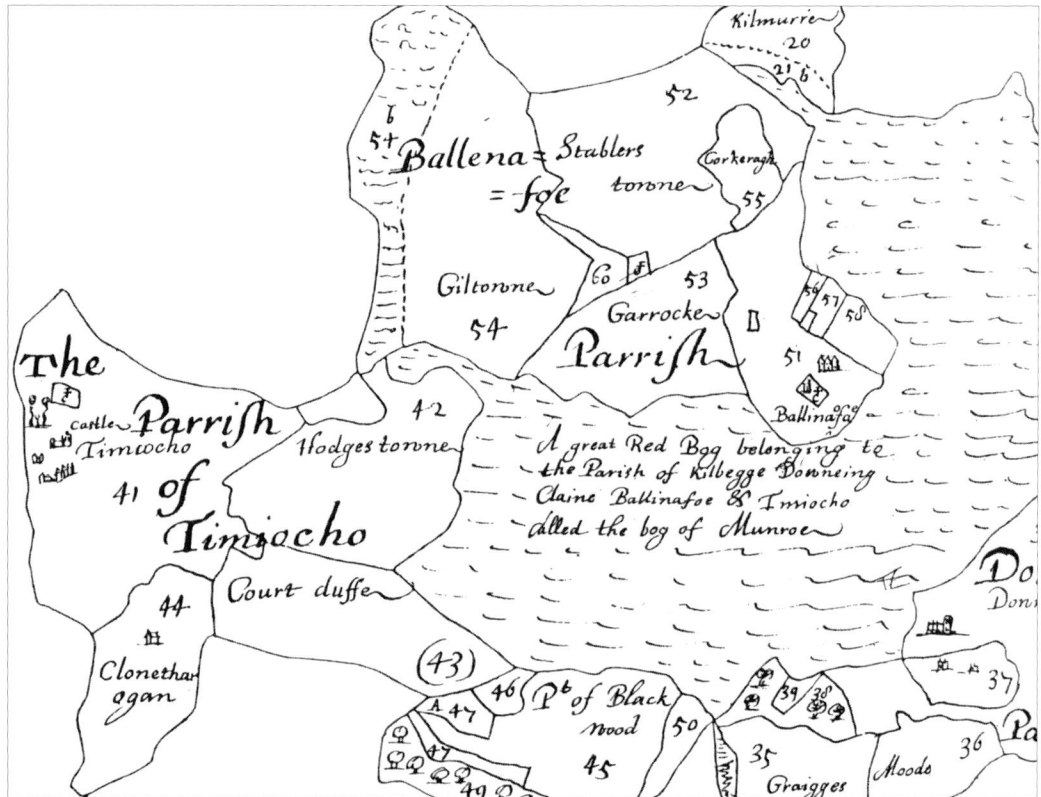

Figure 12.4 Extract from the Down Survey map of the barony of Clane, Co. Kildare, showing 'a great red bog … called the bog of Munroe'.

regard to the 'fir trees' at Holmpatrick, it is interesting to note that the grant of the demesne there to the earl of Thomond in 1605 refers to sixteen acres of furze and mountain as part of the demesne lands.[35]

From an agricultural point of view, furze can be a particularly useful asset in winter, because in addition to providing fodder for animals, it also gives good shelter from the wind. As a fuel, it was particularly suited to baking and brewing – that is, where the fire was intended to last a certain length of time, and where the continual feeding with the combustible branches, instead of being a drawback, gave a measure of control over the heating. Furze heats up very quickly once dried, and it was also preferred because it left little ash. In 1568, the Dublin bakers are specifically mentioned in a regulation regarding the purchase of 'fyrris, fagots and other fuell'.[36]

Furze was also used as a domestic fuel. Along with coal, furze was the common firing of Pembrokeshire and a legal document of 1542 referring to illegal cutting of ten acres of furze near the town of Pembroke describes furze as 'the chief and principal fuel of that country'.[37] Regulations regarding the use and storage of furze in Dublin occur frequently. When it was brought into the city for sale to the citizens it was apparently heaped up in great ricks or stacks that constituted a considerable fire risk. The regularity with which the city authorities attempted to curtail this practice indicates the widespread use of furze as a fuel.[38] The complaints continued into the seventeenth century, when one states that 'the great firr and faggott reekes built close to the city walls doe overtop the said walles in height'.[39] Furze was commonly measured in sheaves, and the earliest mention of its value can be found at this date, when it was ordained that a sheaf of furze was to sell for a penny.[40] In 1586, at the court of the archbishop of Dublin, held at St Sepulchre's, John Caddel of Morton was found guilty of taking '20 shewes of ffurres from William Dicson that he had upon the commons'.[41]

35 M.C. Griffith (ed.), *Irish patent rolls of James I* (Dublin, 1966), p. 3.   36 *CARD*, 2, p. 51.   37 Owen, 'Historical aspects of peat-cutting in Wales', p. 138.   38 *CARD*, 2, pp 83, 134, 166, 253, 274, 446, 466.   39 *CARD*, 3, pp 77–8.   40 *CARD*, 3, p. 88.   41 Herbert Wood (ed.), *Court book of the liberty of Saint Sepulchre, 1586–1590* (Dublin, 1930), p. 3.

Building stone and quarries

There was a small number of stone buildings in pre-Anglo-Norman Dublin. On the eve of the Anglo-Norman arrival, there was a royal hall, a cathedral, seven parish churches inside the town's stone walls and about the same number of extramural churches as well as two suburban monasteries.[42] Other stone churches were dotted across the Dublin region.[43] During the late twelfth and thirteenth centuries, there was an explosion in stone building in Dublin city and suburbs, as the new castle, walls, gates, towers, religious houses, parish churches and residential buildings were constructed. Christ Church Cathedral, whose original construction is generally dated to between 1028 and 1036, saw substantial new works in the period 1190–1210.[44] The archiepiscopal residence was built at Swords Castle *c.*1200, and new building works were carried out at Dublin Castle in 1204. There are references to substantial stone residences in Dublin from as early as 1220.[45] In about 1231, the priory of Holy Trinity was granted land on which Sir Gilbert de Lyvet had built his great stone hall, with its loft, cellar and portico and detached stone-built kitchen.[46] It is widely accepted that the fourteenth century witnessed a major downturn in the number and range of building projects in Ireland. It has been shown, however, that this trend was not uniform across the country. At Trim, Co. Meath, for instance, several prominent stone buildings were erected or renovated during this time.[47] Certainly by the turn of the fifteenth century and beyond, there is clear evidence for renewed construction in stone, especially in the form of tower houses, friaries and parish churches.

Most building stone was quarried locally. This is clear from the granite churches and tower houses distributed across south Co. Dublin and north Wicklow, for instance. Here, the underlying geology is a rich vein of granite running south-west across the mountains from Dun Laoghaire-Dalkey (Figure 1.5). Limestone is the main rock-type in the central and northern parts of the region, and the buildings here reflect this. Transporting stone was expensive, but costs were reduced when water shipment was possible. Research has shown that medieval quarry sites in Norway and Yorkshire were invariably located close to water for precisely this reason.[48] There is a reference to ships and boats loaded with stones plying up and down the Liffey in 1220.[49] In 1322–3, 400 free stones (*libere petre*) were sent by ship from Drogheda to Dublin for repairs to the castle.[50]

There is evidence for a number of quarries in and around the city of Dublin in the Middle Ages. A document of 1236 refers to the 'old quarry of the Ostmen', located beside Oxmantown Green.[51] It continued in use until sometime before 1291, when it was described as disused.[52] There was a quarryman living in the suburb of Oxmantown at this time, and also a functioning lime-pit.[53] Quarrying was still taking place in the area in the seventeenth century, as John Foster, alderman, was given permission to 'dig stones in Oxmantown Green sufficient to burn 200 hogsheads of lime'.[54] There was a stone quarry near Capel Street in 1285 and one near Stephen Street in 1357.[55] In 1337, a grant of land included vacant land called 'the quarel [quarry] pits', adjoining the Liffey and the lands of St Patrick's.[56] A small

42 Clarke, *IHTA: Dublin Part I, to 1610*, p. 5.   **43** The dating of these buildings has been assessed by Tomás Ó Carragáin ('Habitual masonry styles').   **44** Stalley, 'The construction of the medieval cathedral', pp 53–61.   **45** *RHJB*, pp 55–6; see section on Anglo-Norman stone buildings in Linzi Simpson, 'Forty years a-digging', pp 62–5 and also the listing of residences in Clarke, *IHTA: Dublin Part I, to 1610*, pp 29–31.   **46** *CCCD*, no. 47.   **47** Potterton, *Medieval Trim*, p. 356.   **48** Irene Baug, 'Prehistoric quarrying on the west coast of Norway – the production of quernstones, millstones and crosses in Hyllestad, Sogn of Fjordane', *Ruralia*, 6 (2007), 219–25; Stephen Moorhouse, 'The quarrying of building stone and stone artefacts in medieval Yorkshire: a multi-disciplinary approach', *Ruralia*, 6 (2007), 295–319.   **49** *CDI, 1171–1251*, no. 74, p. 149.   **50** RIA 12D13, p. 85 – cited by O'Neill, in *Merchants and mariners*, p. 143.   **51** *CARD*, 1, p. 81.   **52** *CSMA*, 1, p. 500.   **53** Purcell, 'Land-use in medieval Oxmantown', p. 224.   **54** Ibid.   **55** Lawlor (ed.), '*Liber niger* and *Liber albus*', 40; Smyly, 'Old Latin Deeds II', 28.   **56** *CARD*, 1, pp 131–2.

number of quarries have been uncovered during routine excavation. At Church Road in Swords, Finola O'Carroll revealed two phases of medieval outcrop quarrying.[57] During excavations at Essex St West, Dublin, the remains of an extensive quarry pit, dating to the thirteenth century, were found.[58] A high ridge of bedrock had been quarried into a series of large steps with several 'rough-out' blocks recovered from the lowest levels. In addition, extensive deposits of waste limestone chippings had been dumped in the centre of the trench. At Chancery Lane in Dublin, the remains of a stone quarry of late medieval date were excavated.[59] Finds from the quarry pit included a complete timber block wheel and axle and a range of leather and cloth artefacts.

Stone was sourced from various locations in 1564–5 for rebuilding the nave of Christ Church Cathedral, Dublin.[60] Most came from quarries in the immediate locality of the city – Clontarf, Finglas and Milltown. None of these quarries was organised on a professional basis, and in each case masons from Christ Church were sent to cut the stone themselves. Several sites were exploited along the Dodder Valley, some of them in the middle of the river itself. Once the limestone was extracted from the river bed, it had to be cut into manageable pieces and loaded onto carts for the journey to Christ Church. The carts cost 3s. 6d. per day, and this was a considerable part of the overall expense. This particular element of the cost could be avoided when Clontarf stone was used, as it could be loaded straight into boats and brought up the Liffey to Wood Quay, just below the cathedral. The boats were loaded at low tide and floated off at high water. Quarrying at Clontarf was difficult, however, as the beds were located on the shoreline and were flooded at high tide. An 'old quarry' marked on various maps is located just east of the confluence of the River Tolka with the sea, and may have served as such a site.[61] The stone was so tough that it broke the points of picks and crowbars, forcing the workers to return to the quarries in the Dodder Valley. In both quarries, the stone in question was dark-coloured carboniferous limestone, often described as Dublin 'calp', a notoriously hard stone to cut. Some quarrying also took place at Finglas, but the bulk of the stone used at Christ Church came from the River Dodder.

The Civil Survey records over fifteen quarries in the Dublin region, all but one of which were situated in Co. Dublin (the other was at Confey in Co. Kildare).[62] Most are referred to as 'open' quarries, presumably to distinguish them from mines or tunnels from which stone might be extracted. All are specified as 'stone' quarries, but at Holmpatrick there was a quarry for both stone and slate, and at Howth there was a dedicated slate quarry.[63] While there is no mention of a quarry at Rickenhore and Saucerstown in Swords, the commissioners noted that there was 'stone sufficient for building'. This may indicate that the bedrock was sufficiently close to the surface in this area to allow easy access, and it ties in well with the archaeological evidence from elsewhere in Swords for the extraction of stone from outcrops in the Middle Ages.[64]

Slate

Fragments of medieval roofing slates have been found on a number of sites in Dublin and its region.[65] It is likely that most if not all of these were sourced locally. Large numbers of

57 Finola O'Carroll, 'Church Road, Swords', DEHLG file 98E0082. 58 Simpson, 'Essex Street West' in *Excavations 1997*, pp 41–2; Simpson, 'Essex Street West', DEHLG file 96E0245. 59 Claire Walsh, 'Chancery Lane, Dublin' in *Excavations 2003*, p. 125. 60 Gillespie, *The proctor's accounts*, passim; see Stalley, 'The 1562 collapse', pp 229–30. 61 Jason Bolton, pers. comm. 62 *Civil Survey*, 7, pp 26 (2), 27, 30, 36, 49, 54, 102, 125, 138, 141, 169, 223, 231 (2), 242; *Civil Survey*, 8, p. 13. 63 *Civil Survey*, 7, pp 54, 169. 64 *Civil Survey*, 7, p. 102; O'Carroll, 'Church Road, Swords', DEHLG file 98E0082. 65 Joanna Wren, 'Roof tiles' in Walsh, *Archaeological excavations at Patrick, Nicholas and Winetavern Streets* (1997), p. 140; Hayden, 'Arran Quay', pp 206–7; Abi Cryerhall, 'Excavations at Hammond Lane, Dublin: from hurdle-ford to iron-foundry' in Duffy (ed.), *Medieval Dublin VII* (2006), pp 9–50 at p. 30; Simpson,

both red and grey slates were found during excavations at Arran Quay in Dublin, for instance. According to the excavator, the red ones 'derive from eastern Leinster'.[66]

Clay

In 1344, the bailiff of Clonkeen accounted for 4s. received for clay sold by the hands of Dowenild O'Helyn, for making earthenware pots.[67] James Mills, who edited the Holy Trinity account roll in 1890, remarked that coarse pottery and tiles were still being made at Kill of the Grange in his day, at a location known previously as 'Pollaughs'. Explaining that Pollagh in Irish means 'a place of holes', he concluded that this would have been a very apt description of ground used for excavating potter's clay.[68] Recent analysis of pottery sherds from Thomas Street indicates that the clay for the pots was sourced close to the city (see below, p. 451).[69] In 1460, the city authorities legislated that carters and carmen were to charge no more than 1½d. for drawing a cart of clay or 1½d. for three cars of clay into the city. This suggests that clay was regularly brought into the city for building and other purposes and that it was sourced relatively nearby.[70]

A late fifteenth-century building account that details repairs carried out to the parish church of St John in the city of Dublin contains some information on the cost and use of clay in the city.[71] Six carts of clay were purchased at a cost of 2d. per cart and there were two further purchases of clay, one specifically 'to make a chimney'. Three shillings and one penny were spent on lime, which was used to whitewash the chimney and which was measured in 'carnoks' and 'peckyse'.

Chapter summary

As the population increased and industry grew, the exploitation of the hinterland's natural resources became more important. Peat bogs provided fuel, for instance, especially for domestic heating in areas in which wood was scarce or inaccessible. Certain tracts of bog were designated as common turbaries, and manorial tenants were given specific rights in relation to these. In return, tenurial obligations often included cutting and transporting peat. Turf from the hinterland made its way into the city for sale, and it seems that Gaelic Irish merchants played a role in this trade. The intensive exploitation of the region's peatlands led to the complete disappearance of some bogs by as early as the fourteenth century. Apart from turf-extraction for fuel, the need for more and more land for agricultural purposes also seems to have precipitated the demise of some bogs. Several place-names in the Dublin region derive from the presence of bogs – Ballynamona, Corkagh, Reask and Redbog, for example – and in some cases the names are just about the only trace left of the bog.

In most places, furze is considered to be a weed. Formerly, however, it was used for a variety of purposes, including as a fuel and for fencing. It also provides good wind-shelter for animals, while simultaneously acting as a fodder. It has several beneficial features as a fuel, notably that it leaves little ash and that it heats very quickly once dried. Like turf, furze was supplied to the medieval city of Dublin from the surrounding countryside, being stored in large stacks that constituted a considerable fire hazard.

As timber was replaced by stone in many construction projects, there was an increased demand for building stone, and for limestone to be heated and made into lime for mortar (lime was also used as a fertiliser and in the tanning process). Most building stone was

'Dublin's southern frontier', pp 355–6. **66** Hayden, 'Arran Quay', pp 206–7. **67** Mills (ed.), *Account roll*, p. 55. **68** Ibid., p. 174. **69** DEHLG file 96E0280 (Thomas Street; Clare McCutcheon). **70** *CARD*, 1, p. 306. **71** James Lydon, 'A fifteenth-century building account from Dublin', *IESH*, 9 (1982), 73–5.

quarried locally, as transport was difficult and expensive. There were several quarries close to the city, near Oxmantown Green, Capel Street and Stephen Street, and at Clontarf, Finglas and Milltown, for example. The remains of others have been found through archaeological excavation, including at Essex Street West, at Chancery Lane and on Church Road in Swords. The banks and bed along the course of the River Dodder were quarried. When stone had to be transported over longer distances, it was mostly by river or along the coast. The roofs of some buildings in Dublin were slated, and it is likely that these were also sourced locally. Clay was used in pottery making and in building. One possible source for this clay was at Kill of the Grange. Carters and carmen were employed to take clay into the city, and the prices they could charge were strictly regulated.

Having examined the various natural resources that were available for exploitation by both town and country dwellers, the next chapter moves on to look at the rich resources of the rivers and coast.

CHAPTER 13

Water resources

Fish, fishermen and fishing

Dublin's coastal position and the presence of so many rivers and streams in the Dublin region meant that the diet of many people living in this area included a wide variety of fish and molluscs. Bones from bream, cod, eel, gurnard, haddock, hake, ling, plaice, ray and other fish as well as the shells of cockles, mussels, oysters, periwinkles, scallops and crabs have been recovered from a wide range of twelfth- to sixteenth-century deposits.[1] A herring bone was found embedded in human coprolite in a medieval cess-pit on High Street, while further examples were recovered from deposits on Thomas Street.[2] The remains of a possible herring fishery were excavated on the south of Dublin's Hammond Lane.[3] Oyster shells have been recovered on many medieval excavations in urban areas, but outside the city they are more frequently found on high-status sites, such as Dunboyne Castle, Dundrum Castle and Maynooth Castle (where cockle shells were also recovered).[4]

Excavations by Alan Hayden at Arran Quay revealed evidence for fish processing.[5] Small wooden pins were likened by the excavator to those used in the production of stockfish (salted and dried cod and related species).[6] The great number of large cod and ling heads recovered suggests that these species were being prepared for consumption.[7] While ling and cod were the main species represented, the remains of bass, conger eel, flounder, hake, plaice and sea-bream were present in smaller quantities.[8] The majority of the cod and ling bones were from heads, probably resulting from the preparation of stockfish. There was also evidence that cod and ling, which is usually slimmer, were prepared in different ways. Some of the ling bones showed definite butchery marks. Calculations indicated that most of the cod and ling were over 1m in length and were probably in the range of 8 to 10kg. Two of the conger eel were probably *c*.1.15m and 2.7kg, while the third was significantly larger, at nearly

1 Collins, 'Plant remains', passim; Mitchell, *Archaeology and environment*, pp 23, 37–9; V.G. Butler, 'Report on the animal bones from layers 01 and 03' in McMahon, 'Excavations at the site of the Four Courts extension' (1988), 313–17, esp. 314; Butler, 'Report on the animal bones (from Bridge St. Lower)'; Sheila Hamilton-Dyer, 'Bird, fish and marine invertebrates from Site G' in Walsh, *Archaeological excavations at Patrick, Nicholas and Winetavern Streets* (1997), pp 220–1; McCormick and Murphy, 'Mammal bones', p. 199; Abi Cryerhall, '3–15 Hammond Lane/161–168 Church Street, Dublin' in *Excavations 2003*, pp 133–6; Cryerhall, 'Excavations at Hammond Lane', pp 40–3; Melanie McQuade, '46–47 Castle Street, Dalkey' in *Excavations 2003*, pp 114–15; Dermot Nelis, '27–31 Church St., Dublin' in *Excavations 2003*, pp 125–6; Sinclair Turrell, '32 Cook Street, Dublin' in *Excavations 2004*, pp 116–17; Rosanne Meenan, '16–17 Cooke Street, Dublin', DEHLG file 92E0083: Brenda Collins, 'The plant remains'; Linzi Simpson, 'Ship Street Great, Dublin', DEHLG file 01E0772; Gowen, '9–12 High Street'.   2 Gowen, '9–12 High Street'; O'Donovan, '119–21 Thomas Street, Dublin', DEHLG file 95E0280, p. 66.   3 Simpson, '161–168 Church Street, 3–15 Hammond Lane, Dublin', DEHLG file 02E0096.   4 Cotter, 'Dunboyne Castle, Castlefarm'; Murray, 'Reports on the faunal and molluscan material from excavations at Dundrum Castle'; Alan Hayden, 'Maynooth Castle', DEHLG file 96E0391.   5 Hayden, 'Arran Quay', p. 189.   6 Ibid.; J. Lindh, 'Aspects of sea-level changes, fishing, and fish processing in Tønsberg in the Middle Ages' in G.L. Good, R.H. Jones and M.W. Ponsford (eds), *Waterfront archaeology: proceedings of the third international conference, Bristol, 1988* (CBA Research Report, 74, 1991), pp 67–75 at pp 74–5.   7 Hayden, 'Arran Quay', p. 189; Sheila Hamilton-Dyer, 'The fish bone' in Hayden, 'Arran Quay' (2004), pp 235–8.   8 Hamilton-Dyer, 'The fish bone', pp 235–8.

2m and *c.*15kg. The plaice and flounder were comparable in size to modern flatfish, at about 30–35cm.

The cod may have been caught locally, but ling are not normally found in waters shallower than 60m and their presence in the Arran Quay assemblage indicates that fishermen were travelling quite some distance to catch them. Sheila Hamilton-Dyer pointed out that the hake and sea-bream that were represented in the assemblage might have been incidental catches with the cod and ling. She also suggested that the other species (especially the flatfish) were simply the remains of fish living at the quayside. A potential explanation for the almost total absence of otoliths is that they were being extracted for use as medicines (Hamilton-Dyer suggested that this practice was carried out in England and France in the Middle Ages).[9]

In addition to the expected range of seafood, a number of rarer species have also turned up on excavations in the Dublin region. While it is not clear that they were exploited for food, the remains of a seal were recovered in Maynooth, a walrus in Temple Bar, a dolphin on Arran Quay, and a porpoise on High Street.[10] A porpoise was also sent to England from Ireland in 1241.[11] Perhaps surprisingly, fish bones were not found in large numbers during the excavations on Fishamble Street, but there were occasional seal and whale bones in twelfth-century contexts.[12] The bones of a pilot whale were found in fourteenth-century deposits on Patrick Street and another in twelfth- to thirteenth-century levels on Bridge Street Upper.[13] The whale-bone fragment from Bridge Street Upper was a lumbar vertebra that had been hacked with a cleaver-type implement. The discovery of pilot whales on medieval sites in Dublin, particularly the Patrick Street example, may tie in with a documentary reference to the beaching of a shoal of pilot whales at the mouth of the River Dodder in 1331. There was a famine in Ireland at this time:

> … and the city of Dublin suffered miserably. The lord justice, Sir Anthony Lucy, with his servants and many of the citizens of Dublin, killed above 200 of [the whales], and gave leave to the poor to carry them away at their pleasure.[14]

In addition to the fish remains themselves, there is a range of archaeological evidence for fishing in the medieval Dublin region. Among the artefacts catalogued by Thaddeus Breen are fish hooks from Fishamble Street, Werburgh Street, Cook Street and Nicholas Street, a line-sinker from Howth and two prongs from possible eel-spears from the Christ Church/Fishamble Street area.[15] A hazel netting-needle was recovered from probable late sixteenth-century levels on Patrick Street.[16] Substantial squared timbers of possible thirteenth-century date may originally have formed part of fish traps.[17] Parts of at least one small boat, 'possibly for fishing or for use as a ferry across the river', were found during excavations at Winetavern Street/Wood Quay.[18] Other boats represented in the same timber assemblage may also have been used for fishing.

9 Otoliths are tiny sensory organs that can be used to identify fish species, and in some cases to determine the age of the fish. During the medieval period, they were used in folk-medicine as a cure for various complaints and also as an aphrodisiac (see Hamilton-Dyer, 'The fish bone').   **10** Alan Hayden, 'Maynooth Castle', DEHLG file 96E0391: Animal bone report (Emily Murray); Simpson, 'Essex Street West' in *Excavations 1997*, pp 41–2; Simpson, 'Essex Street West', DEHLG file 96E0245; McCormick, 'The mammal bone (from Arran Quay)', p. 229; Gowen, '9–12 High Street'. **11** *CDI, 1171–1251*, no. 2529, p. 376.   **12** Mitchell, *Archaeology and environment*, p. 10.   **13** McCormick and Murphy, 'Mammal bones', pp 205–6; Alan Hayden, 'Bridge Street Upper, Dublin', DEHLG file 92E0078: Animal bone report (Vincent Butler).   **14** McCormick and Murphy, 'Mammal bones', pp 205–6; W.R. Wilde, *Tables of deaths, census of Ireland for the year 1851*, part 5, vol. 1 (Dublin, 1856), p. 84; see also William Camden, *Britannia: a chronological description of Great Britain and Ireland together with the adjacent islands* (6th ed., 1607; repr. Hildesheim and New York, 1970).   **15** Thaddeus Breen, 'Finds from Dublin city and county listed in the registers of the Irish antiquities division, National Museum of Ireland' (unpublished catalogue).   **16** Hayden [with Cross], 'Wooden objects', p. 159. **17** Martin Reid, 'Meeting House Square, 10–14 Sycamore Street/31–32 Essex Street, Dublin', DEHLG file 93E0194. **18** O'Sullivan, 'Medieval boat and ship timbers', p. 121.

Documentary records contain few references to the actual mechanism of fishing. This is probably due to the fact that most fishing was carried out by less well-off individuals, and the lords had little direct involvement in it. The occupational designation 'fisherman' does appear frequently in the records. In the thirteenth century, the Dublin guild merchant roll included twenty-seven fishermen among its members.[19] Most of them may have been involved in riverine fishing, but Hugh of Howth was probably a sea fisherman. The fifteenth-century Dublin franchise roll, which contains fewer occupational designations, records eleven fishermen.[20] In the miracle plays performed in Dublin to celebrate the feast of Corpus Christi, an occupational group referred to as the 'salmon takers' was required along with the mariners, vintners and ship-carpenters to enact the scene of 'Noe (Noah) with his shipp'.[21]

Some fifteenth-century will inventories reveal the types of fishing equipment belonging to the better-off individuals who lived in the north Dublin coastal settlements of Malahide and Lusk. Boats and nets were prized and highly valued possessions: one couple owned a boat worth £4 and fourteen sea-nets worth a further £2; another man owned a fourth share of a skiff valued at 26s. 8d., which suggests the skiff was worth £5 6s. 8d.[22] A century later, Thomas Morgan of Dalkey was accused by a Wicklow man of detaining his boat, valued at £14 (the sources are unfortunately silent regarding the size of these vessels).[23] The inventories also include stocks of fish and salt and other preserving materials. In socio-economic terms, these testament-makers represent the upper end of the group of people involved in coastal exploitation. They, and others like them, would be classed as 'hunters' – people who set out with moveable nets in pursuit of quarry.[24] Lower on the scale were the 'trappers', who set up snaring devices (fixed nets) on the shore and waited for the fish to come into them. Lower still were the 'gatherers', who possessed no special equipment but their hands and perhaps a wooden bucket and who were involved in the sometimes treacherous business of collecting shellfish at low tide.

Riverine fisheries

The value of the fisheries of the River Liffey in the medieval period can be gauged from the number of disputes that arose over their exploitation.[25] Dublin religious houses such as Holy Trinity Priory, the abbey of St Thomas, the abbey of St Mary, and the hospitals of Kilmainham and St John the Baptist all claimed fisheries on the Liffey or rights to maintain fishing boats on the river or receive tithes of fish caught there. King Henry II appears to have laid claim to the fisheries on the Liffey during his visit to Dublin, as his son John is soon afterwards found granting to St Thomas' Abbey 'the tithe of salmon due to my kitchen in Dublin Castle', as well as the right to have a boat on the river.[26] As king, John firstly gave the citizens half of his rights over the Liffey and then gave them his half of the river as well.[27] John, however, excluded from the grant all boat fishings that he had already granted as alms or that he had confirmed as belonging to individuals or institutions by customary right. This included St Thomas' Abbey, St Mary's Abbey, Holy Trinity Priory and the archbishop of Dublin. In addition, the crown acknowledged the right of John son of Diarmait son of Domnall Mac Gilla Mo Cholmóc to have a boat on the river as his ancestors before him had.[28] He subsequently granted this right to have a fishing boat on the Liffey to the monastery of All Hallows.[29]

19 *DGMR*, pp 16, 47, 48, 53, 55, 66, 69–72, 74–77, 79, 81, 87, 88, 90, 91, 93, 94, 115.   **20** *DCFR*, pp 4, 5, 6, 8, 11, 12, 20, 21, 33, 43, 61.   **21** *CARD*, I, p. 239.   **22** Berry (ed.), *Register of wills and inventories*, pp 52, 109.   **23** Wood (ed.), *Court book of the liberty of St Sepulchre*, p. 20.   **24** This follows the classification of Pawley, cited by Harold Fox in *The evolution of the fishing village: landscape and society along the south Devon coast, 1086–1550* (Oxford, 2001).   **25** See A.E.J. Went, 'Fisheries of the River Liffey', *JRSAI*, 83 (1953), 163–73, repr. in Clarke (ed.), *Medieval Dublin: the living city* (1990), pp 182–91.   **26** Duffy, 'Town and crown', p. 97; *CARD*, I, p. 166.   **27** *CDI, 1171–1251*, no. 138, p. 23.   **28** *CDI, 1171–1251*, no. 903, p. 135.   **29** Butler (ed.), *Registrum priorates omnium sanctorum*, p. 23.

With all these conflicting rights to fish the river, it is not surprising that disputes frequently arose. As early as 1220, the citizens complained that the prior and brethren of the hospital at Kilmainham had made a pool upstream of the city that was preventing boats from travelling up and down and was also preventing the fish from reaching their fisheries downstream.[30] Later on, the Hospitallers removed the fixed net that the citizens had attached to the bridge, complaining that it was injurious to their fisheries. A jury found that it was the citizens' right to have such a net, which was valued at £10.[31] Complaints about traps, nets and pools continued throughout the medieval period.[32] These complaints rarely contain much detail about fish species, but salmon and eels are sometimes mentioned.

There remains little archaeological evidence for the weirs and fish-traps mentioned in documentary sources. The Ballast Office's construction of the Great North Wall, or Bull Wall, between 1819 and 1824, created a formal straight-line navigation channel through what had been a maze of meandering estuarine sandbars.[33] The subsequent development of the estuary has largely buried or destroyed the evidence for earlier fish-traps, while the construction of the formal quays along the Liffey and through the city has had a similar effect upriver to Kilmainham.[34] Perhaps surprisingly, there is no clear indication of fish-traps being used on the Broad Meadow or Ward Rivers, which empty into the expansive Malahide Estuary.

Fishponds

Fishponds were artificially constructed structures whose function was to produce freshwater fish for the table. Their construction was expensive and regular outlays had to be made on stocking and cleaning. Therefore, they were generally the preserve of a wealthy minority. The earliest fishponds in England were associated with the king's castles and houses, but by the thirteenth century they were a common feature of lay and monastic estates.[35] Dyer has written that the ponds, which were located behind park pales or joined to moats, 'were associated with the physical barriers that helped to separate the aristocracy from the rest of society'.[36]

The physical remains of some fishponds of post-medieval date are known from Ireland, but to date no medieval fishponds have been recognised.[37] Documentary references are similarly sparse. A fishpond which was constructed at Limerick Castle in 1211–12 cost £33 6s. 8d., and this gives some indication of the expense involved.[38] Some of the larger religious houses and seigneurial residences in the Dublin region did have fishponds (Figure 6.2), but the records tell us nothing of their construction or stocking. It is likely that some of the religious houses would also have had fishponds, but no definite reference has been located.

Coastal resources

The documentary sources reveal that in the medieval period the coastal area to the north and south of the city of Dublin was extensively exploited for its fishing. As with the rest of Co. Dublin, a great deal of the coastal area was in ecclesiastical ownership. The archbishop of Dublin, the Cistercian abbey of St Mary's, the Hospitallers of Kilmainham and the

30 *CDI, 1171–1251*, no. 974, p. 149.   **31** *HMDI*, pp 216–19.   **32** *HMDI*, p. 149; *CJR, 1305–7*, p. 258.   **33** Gerald Daly, 'George Semple's charts of Dublin Bay, 1762', *PRIA*, 93C (1993), 81–105 at 100, 105.   **34** The potential for insight was revealed recently with the discovery of Mesolithic period traps during development works on Spencer Dock, North Wall Quay; see Melanie McQuade, 'Gone fishin'', *AI*, 22:1 (2008), 8–11.   **35** J.M. Steane, 'The royal fishponds of medieval England' in Mick Aston (ed.), *Medieval fish, fisheries and fishponds in England* (BAR British Series, 182, 1988), pp 39–68.   **36** Christopher Dyer, 'The consumption of fresh-water fish in medieval England' in Aston (ed.), *Medieval fish* (1988), pp 27–38 at p. 27.   **37** Murphy and O'Conor, 'Castles and deerparks in Anglo-Norman Ireland', 54–6.   **38** Davies and Quinn, 'Irish pipe roll of 14 John', 70.

Figure 13.1 Extract
from the Down Survey
map of the barony of
Rathdown, Co. Dublin,
showing a windmill at
Clontarf and a ship
sailing into the mouth of
the Liffey.

Augustinian abbey of Holmpatrick were among the major ecclesiastical landlords. A great deal of documentary material survives relating to these owners and their efforts to enforce seigneurial rights over fishing dues, customs and tithes.

There is little evidence that the major lords, whether ecclesiastical or secular, exploited coastal resources themselves with their own boats and nets. One possible exception is the seigneurial construction of artificial fish pools on the sandy coastal strip belonging to the manor of Thorncastle in the Booterstown area, probably between Merrion and Blackrock. In 1299, the king granted a carucate-and-a-half of land (180 acres), rent and a fishery at Thorncastle with a total value of 108s. 4d. per annum to William le Deveneys.[39] In 1306, le Deveneys asked the king to grant him in addition wreck of the sea, the escheats that might be found on the sand and the pools near the sea coast.[40] These may have been artificially constructed fishponds.

Most lords exploited the foreshore parts of their manors by exacting payments, often called customs, or portions of the catch from fishing boats that used the havens and harbours on their lands. Another form of seigneurial exploitation took the form of exercising rights to buy fish at preferential rates. In many cases, the best fish of a catch was to be handed over by the fishermen, and this became known as 'the lord's fish'. These privileges were carefully guarded and enumerated and continued to be enforced up to the seventeenth century and probably later. The religious houses, whose communities consumed even more fish per caput than the populace at large, were particularly zealous in guarding their rights.

39 TNA:PRO C143/27.   **40** *CDI, 1302–7*, no. 47, pp 160–1.

Figure 13.2 Bullock Harbour, and the tower house built by St Mary's Abbey to protect their fishery interests. The medieval landing area may well have been under the current road that skirts the bottom of the castle (image courtesy of Niall Brady).

In a legal case of 1345–6, it was asserted that the abbot of St Mary's Abbey was unjustly exacting a toll of fish from the fishermen who used their port of Bullock.[41] This port (*portus*) formed one of the appurtenances of the manor of Carrickbrennan (Monkstown). The jury in the case found in favour of the abbey, but limited the levy to one fish from every boat that sought refuge in that port.

On occasions, when lands of a manor were sub-leased, the lord specifically excluded his custom of fish. For example, when in 1519 Richard FitzWilliam leased the manor of Merrion to Owen Albanagh, a physician, he specifically reserved to himself the annual custom of herrings and other fish.[42] The records also contain examples of rents being paid in fish, or leases containing a condition stipulating a certain supply of fish to the lord.[43]

The settlements along the coast also played an important role in coastal trade, a role that the city of Dublin increasingly sought to control. By the fourteenth century, the city authorities were claiming to exercise jurisdiction over the neighbouring coast, and during the riding of the city franchises it became customary for the water-bailiff to ride into the sea and to cast a spear as far as he could to symbolise this jurisdiction.[44] In 1375, Edward III granted to Dublin the customs of all ports between Skerries and Arklow. In 1561, the city sheriff was ordered to ride along the coast from Nanny (the point at which the River Nanny enters the sea, north of Balbriggan) to Arklow to seek out and punish offences at every creek and road along the coast.

The coastal settlements, therefore, and the people who lived and worked in them, were subject to a variety of controls, the majority of which were articulated through the city of Dublin. They were perhaps more fully integrated into the hinterland of the medieval Irish capital and more aware of their connection with Dublin than some geographically closer inland areas.

41 *CSMA*, I, pp 307–11.   **42** One source mentions that the Fitzwilliams received a toll of 500 choice herrings from their fisheries between Blackrock and Ringsend.   **43** See, for example, lease of lands in Dalkey, *CCCD*, no. 1341.
44 For a discussion of these claims, see Smith, *Dalkey: society and economy*, pp 50–2.

Supplying the market

Although the remains of sea-fish have been found on inland excavations (for example, at Trim Castle), and they frequently appear as taxable items on murage charters,[45] the primary market for the fish and shellfish from the Dublin coastline was the city of Dublin itself. In various royal and municipal statements seeking to regularise the supply of fish to the citizens of Dublin, the phrase 'all harbours from Holmpatrick in the north to Dalkey in the south' is used. This appears to represent the limits of the coastal area from which supplies were normally obtained.

Municipal regulations indicate that fish were brought into the city by packhorse, but also that fishmongers and their wives would go out to the 'seaside' to purchase fish and bring it into the city themselves.[46] Transporting large quantities of fish was expensive. In the sixteenth century, the proctors of Holy Trinity paid 2*s.* to transport a barrel of herrings from Dalkey to Dublin – almost 10 per cent of the cost of the fish itself.[47] Within the city, the marketing of fish was restricted to the fish shambles and to certain times of the day, with penalties imposed for infringements.[48] Demand for fish was always high, as all citizens needed to eat fish on fast days, days of abstinence and throughout the period of Lent. When households or officials were undertaking a journey, special arrangements were set in place to ensure a supply of fresh fish. In 1383, merchants from Malahide and Howth were contracted to supply fish to the justiciar's household as it travelled around Ireland.[49]

The biggest demand for fish came with the infrequent royal expeditions to Ireland. It appears that in these circumstances the resources of the Irish fisheries were put under strain. Prior to Richard II's expedition to Ireland in 1394, his household officials ordered the arrest in England of 'as many fishermen with the vessels, boats, nets, instruments and other engines as will suffice for catching fish at sea for the use of the household during the present expedition to Ireland'.[50]

Not all of the fish sold in Dublin therefore were destined for consumption by the city dwellers. There are records of foreign merchants buying fish in Dublin in the thirteenth century, while in the fourteenth century the mayor and citizens of Dublin were given licence to export fish to England.[51] Households as far away as Ardmulchan near Skreen, Co. Meath, obtained some of their fish supplies in Dublin.[52] In the period 1308–11, the household of Roger Mortimer was supplied with shellfish from Dublin. On one occasion, 3,000 oysters were purchased in Dublin for this household. This account covers the Lenten period and provides an excellent illustration of the range of fish and shellfish consumed by a noble household. The fish consumed included eels, herrings, cod and salmon, while shellfish including scallops, oysters, whelks, rasers, mussels and '*scarbardis*' were also purchased.

The fourteenth-century accounts for the priory of Holy Trinity record numerous purchases of fish, and occasionally reveal the provenance of the supplies.[53] Edward the fisherman was owed 19*d.* by the abbey's kitchener, and John Kendal, a tenant of the lands of the priory in Dalkey, sold them 200 herrings in 1344.[54] Apart from oysters, the monks appear to have consumed less shellfish than the noble Mortimer household, but the range of fresh fish purchased was impressive, comprising eels, herrings, white fish, salmon, tublings, plaice, trout, turbot and gurnard.

45 Murage charters gave permission for tax (on goods traded at urban markets) to be collected in order to raise funds for the construction and maintenance of the town's defences.   **46** *HMDI*, p. 130; *CARD*, 1, p. 274.   **47** Gillespie, *The proctor's accounts*, p. 64.   **48** *CARD*, 1, p. 124.   **49** James Graves (ed.), *A roll of the proceedings of the king's council in Ireland, 1392–93* (London, 1877), p. 163.   **50** J.F. Lydon, *Ireland in the later Middle Ages* (Dublin, 1973), p. 113. **51** *HMDI*, p. 130; *CARD*, 1, p. 124.   **52** Woolgar (ed.), *Household accounts*, 1, pp 173–7.   **53** Mills (ed.), *Account roll*. **54** Ibid., pp 21, 74, 195.

The range of fish consumed by less well-off consumers was undoubtedly less extensive and plentiful. There are some annalistic references to Dubliners enjoying fish, but they highlight unusual occurrences rather than day-to-day consumption patterns. As mentioned above, the beaching of a large number of pilot whales in 1331 appears in at least two chronicle sources. In addition, the Book of Howth records that in 1338 when the Liffey was frozen over in Dublin, the people played football on the ice and made a fire on it with timber and turf on which they roasted eels.[55]

The analysis of environmental samples taken from early thirteenth-century contexts in Dublin has thrown light on the range of fish available to urban consumers either through the marketplace or through exploitation of coastal resources by the urban community itself.[56]

Further exploitation of the shoreline: sand, seaweed, salt and wreck

Apart from fish and shellfish, there were other foreshore resources that were certainly exploited. It seems highly likely that those who lived near the coast were frequently employed in collecting, transporting and spreading sand on their own and others' agricultural land. English demesne accounts include extensive evidence for the use of sand to improve soil fertility in the medieval period and sand was certainly used in Ireland on the Bigod manors of Fennagh, Forth and Old Ross in the 1280s.[57] Manors in the Dublin area, particularly those close to the coast, no doubt also used sand in their tillage regimes, but the lack of manorial accounts for the area deprives us of our chief source for this practice. It appears that the hospital of St John the Baptist without the New Gate, Dublin, had access to a sand-pit in 1312, and that sand was used on its lands in north Co. Dublin.[58]

In his study of the exploitation of the foreshore of Devon, H.S.A. Fox found extensive evidence that the inhabitants of fishing villages and hamlets were employed in collecting and transporting sand, often for use on manors far inland. He noted 'a network of hundreds of tracks linking small coastal coves and estuarine beaches and mudflats to settlements inland', and concluded that the passage of heavy sand carts had left its trace.[59]

Other commodities that might be gathered on the shore include seaweed (for food and fertiliser) and 'wreck'– various goods that might be cast up, particularly following a shipwreck. Technically, 'wreck' belonged to the crown, but there are instances of people helping themselves to items found on the foreshore and also to parts of wrecked vessels. In 1308, a group of people were charged before the justiciar with robbing the goods of a merchant bound for England when his ship was wrecked near Dalkey.[60] Sometimes, a landowner might petition the crown for right to 'wreck' and other 'escheats' of the sea, as William le Deveneys did with regard to his manor of Thorncastle in 1306.[61]

Foreshores also offered opportunities for salt-making, through the evaporation of sea water in specially constructed pans. The records indicate the large-scale import of salt into Ireland in the medieval period and this leads to the conclusion that very little salt was manufactured in the country.[62] There are some references to salt manufacture, but none for the immediate Dublin area.[63]

55 *Cal. Carew MSS*, 5, p. 161.　**56** See Reilly, 'The contribution of insect remains', pp 54–5, 59.　**57** Down, 'Colonial society and economy', pp 471–2. See A.T. Lucas, 'Sea sand and shells as manure' in Jenkins (ed.), *Studies in folk life* (1969), pp 184–203.　**58** *RHJB*, p. 144.　**59** Fox, *Evolution of the fishing village*, p. 68. A deed relating to land in the vicinity of Ardmore, Co. Waterford, states that the owner 'is to have lawful way to the sea for sand for his land, without challenge' (*COD*, 1, p. 93).　**60** Smith, *Dalkey: society and economy*, p. 50.　**61** See above, p. 397.　**62** O'Neill, *Merchants and mariners*, pp 84–90.　**63** *CDI, 1252–84*, no. 582, p. 95, no. 1918, p. 433.

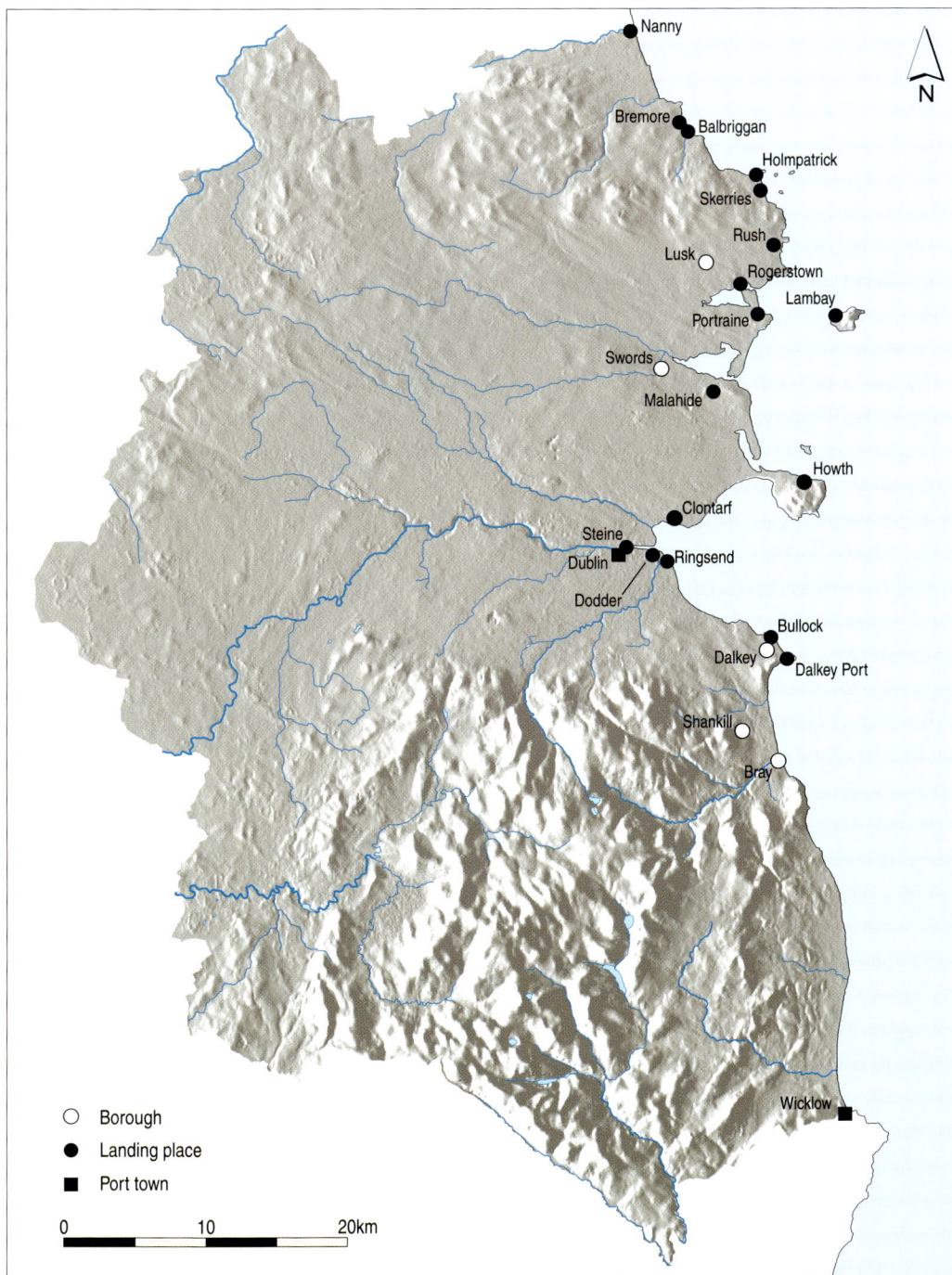

Figure 13.3 The known medieval landing places in the Dublin region, attested in the sources (map by Niall Brady). The map also shows the medieval boroughs adjacent to the coast. With the exception of the Dublin city excavations along the medieval quays, the archaeological study of the landing places within the Dublin region has not been undertaken (see Niall Brady, 'Dublin's maritime setting and the archaeology of its medieval harbours' in Bradley, Fletcher and Simms (eds), Dublin in the medieval world (2009), pp 295–315).

Classification of coastal settlements

Fox divided the settlements along the Devon coast into port towns, fishing villages and cellar settlements that comprised just a few dwellings. His criteria for defining a port town include: adequate anchorage for ships; facilities for loading and unloading cargoes and repair and outfitting of ships and also evidence for residence by ship-owners, merchants, masters and mariners. By these criteria, only Dublin itself could be classified as a port town. It possessed quays, warehouses and a crane. The names of six mariners and three steersmen appear in the thirteenth-century guild merchant roll of Dublin, while the fifteenth-century Dublin franchise roll records nine mariners.[64] Steersmen would have been employed both on board ships and on land, to guide vessels into safe moorings.

64 *DGMR*, pp 48, 55, 65, 66, 83, 89, 98, 117, 118; *DCFR*, pp 1, 2, 3, 12, 22, 27, 30, 33, 48.

The description '*portus*' (port) is used, however, in connection with several other settlements along the Dublin coastline. In the early fourteenth century, Bullock is described as a port of St Mary's Abbey.[65] A regulation of Henry IV (1399–1413) concerns exports from the ports of Clontarf, Dalkey, Steine, Dodder and 'le Kay de Dyvelyne'. In 1455, the collection of the tolls in the ports of Rush, Rogerstown and Portraine is mentioned, and there are several references to customs and tolls on merchandise arriving at Skerries (Holmpatrick). Facilities such as quays and cranes were not essential for the unloading of ships. In 1437–8, Dublin merchants complained that some merchants were unloading and selling in Howth, Baldoyle, Malahide, Portraine, Rogerstown, Rush and Skerries.[66] 'Haven' and 'harbour' are words frequently encountered in references to these coastal settlements, and were applied to places such as Skerries, Rogerstown, Portraine and Howth (Figure 13.3). Writing in Holinshed's 'Irish Chronicle' (first published in 1577), Richard Stanihurst listed eighty-seven haven towns in Ireland, including Balbriggan, Bremore, Baldoyle, Holmpatrick, Skerries, Howth, Malahide, Rogerstown and Rush.[67] In 1559, a licence was issued to John Parker, master of the rolls, for eight months to export wool from various Irish havens including Skerries, Malahide, Howth, Bullock and Dalkey.[68]

References to buildings and structures

There are some references in the documents to the building of harbours, jetties and quays. There was a proposal at the end of the fifteenth century to build a fortified harbour of wood and stone at Skerries, and there is a reference to wares and merchandise 'on the quay of Skerries' some years later.[69] The absence of formal quays and jetties is more typical, however, and it suggests that much of the sea traffic was landed on the foreshore from boats. Fortified dwellings were sometimes constructed by lords wishing to guard their coastal rights. St Mary's Abbey is attributed with building Bullock Castle to oversee its lucrative fishery there (Figures 5.49, 13.2). The castle also provided shelter and hospitality for those visiting from overseas. Dublin merchants were apparently responsible for the late medieval fortified town houses in Dalkey, which provided secure storage as well as underlining their presence and control of this settlement.[70] In 1463, Stephen FitzWilliam of Thorncastle (Booterstown) petitioned parliament for remission of his rent to the crown to enable him to build a castle. He was granted the relief on the grounds that if the castle were not built and the said place were allowed to lie waste, it would be a great injury to merchants, mariners and other subjects of the king.[71] In 1582, the corporation of Dublin erected a fort at Ringsend to secure the dues that they charged ships using that port.[72]

There is little information regarding the houses and living conditions of fishermen, apart from what can be gleaned from the fifteenth-century will inventories. A sixteenth-century source refers to 'cottages in the vills of Holmpatrick and Skerries' and indicates that some had land attached. In the early sixteenth century, St Mary's Abbey was leasing a messuage in Howth along with two acres of land to a fisherman.[73] This indicates that fishing need not have been the sole occupation of those described as fishermen and that they may also have carried out a certain amount of farming.

There is an interesting reference from the seventeenth century regarding the building of a town or village for the habitation of fishermen on Lambay. In 1551, Archbishop Browne of

65 *CSMA*, 1, pp 307–11.   66 *CARD*, 1, p. 30.   67 Maighréad Ní Mhurchadha, *Fingal, 1603–60: contending neighbours in north Dublin* (Dublin, 2005), p. 25; Raphael Holinshed: *Holinshead's Irish chronicles*, ed. Liam Miller and Eileen Power (Atlantic Highlands, NJ, 1979).   68 *RPCH*, p. 96.   69 D'Alton, *History of the county of Dublin*, p. 450.   70 Kelly, *Dalkey, Co. Dublin*, p. 18.   71 Smith, *Dalkey: society and economy*, p. 50.   72 *CARD*, 2, p. 168.   73 *EIMP*, p. 15.

Figure 13.4 Lambay, Co. Dublin, was a focus of fishing activity throughout the medieval period (image courtesy of Tony Kavanagh).

Dublin got a licence to grant to John Challoner and his heirs the entire island of Lambay, with the whole coast of the said island at a rent of £6 13s. 4d., provided that he or his heirs should within six years build on said island a town or village for the habitation of fishermen, with a place of refuge 'circumvallated with a mound, to which they might resort in case of any sudden irruption'.[74] The place of refuge might have been within the confines of the presumably earlier moated site that overlooks the harbour area today (Figure 6.18). The conditions also included that the grantee should make within the said term a harbour for the fishermen's boats, on whatever part of the shore of said island he should think fit. It appears that Challoner had brought over to the island a colony of the king's subjects to inhabit and render it safe from pirates and smugglers. A seventeenth-century description of Lambay mentions a 'fine little castle of freestone and close by it a village, wherein dwell divers families, of fishers and husbandmen, who plough part of this island'.[75]

Many of the people involved in fishing and other forms of foreshore exploitation may have lived at a little distance from the coast but would have maintained collections of storage huts on the beach that were utilised as bases for fishing operations. These structures may have served as temporary dwellings during periods when night-time fishing was required. The mobile and uncertain life of the herring fisherman is illustrated by some legislation of the Irish parliament in 1470.[76] The statute describes how herring fishing is movable by

74 D'Alton, *History of the county of Dublin*, p. 436. 75 Ní Mhurchadha, *Fingal, 1603–60*, pp 24–5. 76 *Stat. Ire., 1–12 Edward IV*, p. 665.

storms and winds from one place to another and how fishers must follow and take the fish before they are gone. The statute decreed therefore that fishermen were to be allowed into ports 'to draw and cast nets for herrings at all hours of the day and night'.

Hemp was often grown close to fishing communities, as it was used for fishing nets, ropes and sails for the fishing boats. One north Co. Dublin testator who owned sea nets and nautical equipment was owed a quantity of hemp by two debtors. The only evidence for hemp cultivation close to the coast, however, comes from the 1540 extents of monastic possessions, in which the nuns of the convent of Gracedieu were said to have a hemp garden in Portraine.[77]

Chapter summary

Both the archaeological and the documentary sources indicate the importance of fish as a dietary component in Dublin and its region, although most of the evidence relates to the city rather than the countryside. A wide range of marine fish and shellfish was available, and there were structured and organised methods of market supply. The fish-markets of Dublin drew in purchasers from inland parts of the hinterland and may have been an incentive for rural producers to bring their products into the city markets. There were fewer types of

77 D'Alton, *History of the county of Dublin*, p. 321.

freshwater fish available, with salmon and eels predominating. These supplies were also constrained by the competing claims of religious houses and the Dublin citizens. The mechanisms used for trapping fish frequently caused conflict. There is surprisingly little evidence for the construction and use of freshwater fishponds by the monasteries. This may be an indication that the Liffey fisheries, combined with the ready supply of fresh fish from the estuary and coast, were deemed sufficient.

The evidence allows a general picture of foreshore exploitation along the Dublin coastline to be reconstructed, but evidence of specific methods, structures and equipment is rare. It is clear that coastal fishing was extensive and organised and that some of the people involved in fishing and the fish trade were comparatively affluent. Despite some complaints of the high price of fresh fish, there does not appear to have been a problem in supplying the needs of domestic urban centres and maintaining a lucrative export trade. Outside the city, it appears that most settlements lacked what might be termed 'port facilities', such as quays, warehouses and cranes. This did not stop them being called 'ports', however, and it did not mean that large ships were unable to discharge goods or load cargoes. It appears that during the fifteenth and sixteenth centuries, a preoccupation with safety developed, as coastal piracy and attacks by the Irish started to increase in frequency. The construction of the fortified harbour at Skerries, the establishment of a colony on Lambay and the building of a new wave of castles can all be seen as responses to these threats.

The hinterland of Dublin was the most densely settled and populated region in medieval Ireland, and the available resources were exploited in order to feed, fuel and provide raw materials for the inhabitants of the city and countryside, as well as to provide surpluses for trade with more distant areas. There were some direct links between producers and consumers, but frequently the products of the land had to be processed and marketed before they arrived at their final form and destination. The next part of the book investigates the topics of processing and distribution in the region.

PART IV

PROCESSING AND DISTRIBUTION

CHAPTER 14

The processing of cereal products

(by Niall Brady, Margaret Murphy and Michael Potterton)

Introduction

Apart from the grain used as animal fodder and set aside for the following year's seed, the cereals harvested in the countryside around Dublin went through a number of processes before being converted into human foodstuffs. On occasion, raw grain and other products were sent outside the region and exported overseas for processing elsewhere, but most of the ingredients for the bread and meal that was eaten and the ale that was drunk by urban and rural dwellers of the Dublin region were processed very close to the site of consumption. There was an abundance of structures involved in these processes and people employed to run them.

Corn-drying and malting

The drying of grain is an essential part of its processing for consumption. In Ireland, as in Britain, the relatively short growing season invariably left the crops with a high moisture content. Some drying occurred naturally as the harvested grain stood in sheaves in the field, and further drying was achieved when the harvest was brought into the haggard for storage, either in open-air stacks or in a barn. Kilns were also used to dry the grain more completely before it was stored, although it is not clear how much of the harvest was put into a kiln at this stage. Kilns were also used post-storage, when the grain was further dried prior to milling.[1] Mick Monk argues that the presence of corn-drying kilns is indicative of large-scale production, since small quantities of grain can be dried by passing the sheaf through burning straw or by being placed in a pot over a domestic hearth. Within the Dublin region, the presence of corn-drying kilns is well attested and they were commonly used in the early medieval period. Their distribution highlights the importance of the Dublin-Meath-Louth area for large-scale cereal cultivation throughout the Middle Ages (Figure 14.2).[2] Sites with multiple-kilns were already in existence during the early medieval period, as at Raystown, Co. Meath, where five kilns were uncovered along with bowl-furnaces, millraces and six watermills, indicating the presence of a substantial agricultural processing unit that developed between the sixth and the twelfth century AD.[3]

Most kilns were set into a pit in the ground, and had a kiln chamber with an attached flue, often forming a keyhole shape. The subterranean features could be lined with stone

---

[1] M.A. Monk, 'Post-Roman drying kilns and the problem of function: a preliminary statement' in Donnchadh Ó Corráin (ed.), *Irish antiquity: essays and studies presented to Professor M.J. O'Kelly* (Dublin, 1981, repr. 1994), pp 216–30 at pp 217–18. [2] M.A. Monk and Ellen Kelleher, 'An assessment of the archaeological evidence for Irish corn-drying kilns in the light of the results of archaeological experiments and archaeobotanical studies', *JIA*, 14 (2005), 77–114 at 82; Niall Brady, 'Agricultural tools and agrarian development in early medieval Ireland', *Ruralia*, 6 (2007), 245–50 at 248. [3] Matthew Seaver, 'Run of the mill? Excavation of an early medieval site at Raystown, Co. Meath', *AI*, 19:4 (winter

Figure 14.1 Image of a
reconstructed medieval
corn-drying kiln by
David Simon, from Piers
Dixon, *Puir labourers and
busy husbandmen*, a
publication in the
Making of Scotland
Series (general editor
Gordon Barclay)
(reproduced by
permission of Birlinn
Ltd: www.birlinn.co.uk).

and the chamber was covered, probably with flat timbers.[4] The grain, possibly still in its sheaves, was spread out across wattles or brushwood. A fire would be lit at the mouth of the flue, from which the heat would be drawn into the chamber, where it would permeate up through the grain, ripening, drying and hardening it. Drying grain in this manner also served to kill pests such as the weevil.[5] Straw was readily available and the roof of the kiln would usually be thatched, perhaps fitted with a door or other mechanism to vary the draught and ensure that the moisture-laden air escaped and did not linger to re-saturate the grain.[6] This form of roofing allowed the smoke to escape easily, while keeping the rain off and retaining ample heat to dry the grain, but of course it usually leaves little trace in the archaeological record. The manner of drying cereals did not change much from the earliest times to the nineteenth century.[7] The above-ground elements of kilns rarely survive, but at Clonfad, Co. Westmeath, a fill layer comprising burnt daub with intact wattle twigs was interpreted as the collapsed cupola or dome.[8] It is more usual for only the flues and drying chambers to survive. Keyhole-shaped cereal-drying kilns appear to have been standard in Ireland from the thirteenth century onwards, with origins that lay somewhat earlier.[9]

The documentary evidence for cereal-drying in the Dublin region consists primarily of incidental references to kilns and their appurtenances. The 1304 extent for the manor of Cloncurry, Co. Kildare, for instance, notes the existence in the farmyard there of a badly roofed corn-drying kiln as well as two barns, a cow-byre, a dovecot and a house for threshed grain.[10] The kiln beside the well at Clonkeen, Co. Dublin, is mentioned in a document of 1343, while a later reference specifies that this was the well *for* the kiln.[11] One of the key

2005), 9–12; Matthew Seaver, 'Silent mills', *British Archaeology* (March–April 2006), 40–5. **4** Piers Dixon, *Puir labourers and busy husbandmen: the countryside of lowland Scotland in the Middle Ages* (Edinburgh, n.d.), p. 54. **5** Gavin Bowie, 'Corn-drying kilns, meal milling and flour in Ireland', *Folklife: a Journal of Ethnological Studies*, 17 (1979), 5–13 at 5. **6** Monk and Kelleher, 'An assessment', 101. **7** Alan Gailey, 'Irish corn-drying kilns', *Ulster Folklife*, 15–16 (1970), 52–71. **8** Paul Stevens, 'N6 Kinnegad to Kilbeggan dual carriageway: archaeological resolution preliminary report, A001/036 E2723 Site Clonfad 3, Clonfad townland, Co. Westmeath' (unpublished report by Valerie J. Keeley Ltd, 2007), p. 8. **9** M.F. Hurley, 'Kilferagh, Co. Kilkenny: corn-drying kiln and settlement site' in Cleary, Hurley and Twohig (eds), *Archaeological excavations on the Cork-Dublin gas pipeline* (1987), pp 88–100 at p. 96; Monk and Kelleher, 'An assessment', 105–6. **10** *RBO*, pp 27–31; O'Loan, 'The manor of Cloncurry', 14–15. **11** Mills (ed.), *Account roll*, pp 39, 40.

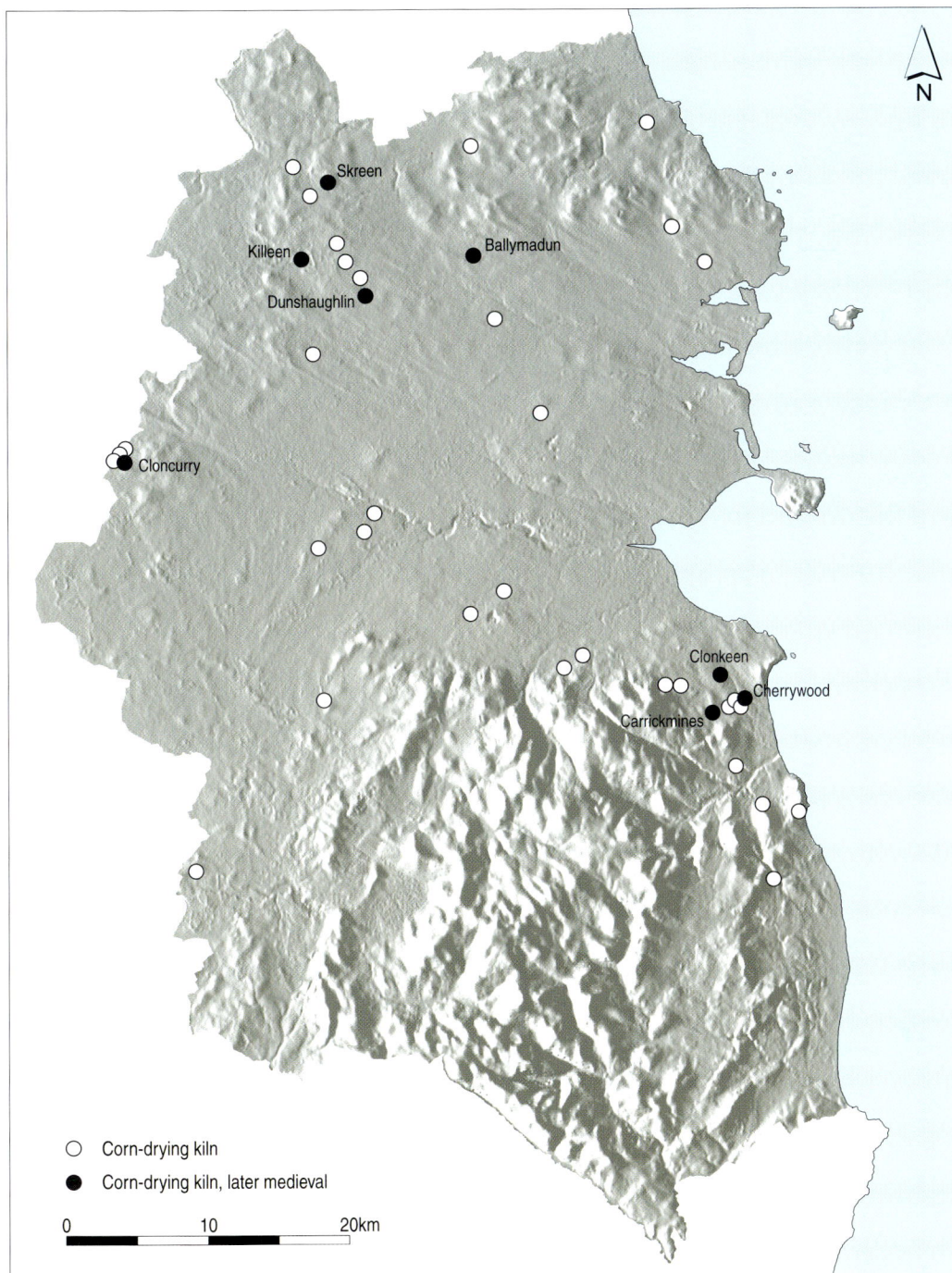

Figure 14.2 Distribution of corn-drying sites in the Dublin region, from archaeological and documentary sources. Note the absence of clear dating evidence for most of the kiln sites. The strikingly linear pattern of discoveries reflects the national road scheme excavation projects of recent years.

points about drying grain properly is that the heating process has to be stopped at just the right moment.[12] It is possible that the proximity of an accessible source of water at Clonkeen facilitated this. Lime and tar were purchased to repair the vessels (*vasorum*) in the Clonkeen kiln house, and boards were bought to repair the door.[13] It is not clear what these vessels were, but they may have been used for transporting water and/or for storing grain. The Clonkeen kiln appears to have been a large enterprise and in 1344/5 further money was spent on making new walls, seven perches long.[14] A carpenter was hired for three days to prepare and erect the roof supports and hurdles, while another man was employed to gather wattles. A thatcher and two assistants were hired to roof the kiln, which took ten days to complete. The 1344 extent for the manor of Ballymadun, Co. Dublin, specifies that the kiln there was

12 Bowie, 'Corn drying kilns', 7.   **13** Mills (ed.), *Account roll*, p. 40.   **14** Ibid., p. 60.

'roofed with straw', and the one at Dunshaughlin, Co. Meath, was also thatched.[15] A record survives of a theft from the kiln of the abbot of the priory of St Thomas the Martyr at Newbury, Co. Meath, in 1310, and fear of a similar occurrence at Grangegorman was probably the reason that the lock was repaired on the kiln there in the 1340s.[16]

Medieval cereal-drying kilns are distributed across Ireland, and excavation since the 1980s has revealed a concentration on the more fertile soils of the east as well as north Munster and the Shannon Estuary.[17] Kiln sites have been excavated at a range of rural and urban locations, including Kilferagh, Co. Kilkenny, Ballynaraha, Co. Tipperary, Lough Gur, Co. Limerick, and Ballybofey, Co. Donegal.[18] The evidence from Kilferagh demonstrated that kilns during the thirteenth/early fourteenth centuries could be well made, lined with stones and associated with a stable stone platform, while the presence of a small wattle-and-daub structure next to the kiln was interpreted as a small barn.[19] The excavation plan suggests that the building was approximately 4m wide internally. Analysis of the plant remains indicated the presence of peas and bean fragments as well as grain, suggesting that a wide spectrum of the harvest could have been kiln-dried.[20] Kilns are also found in urban contexts, and the Waterford City excavations uncovered a series of mostly keyhole-shaped kilns and a possible oven in the back yards of medieval properties on Peter Street and Back Lane, dating to the late twelfth/early thirteenth centuries.[21] In the Dublin region, excavated corn-drying kilns are distributed in linear patterns south of the city and also to the north-west (Figure 14.2). The distribution reflects recent discoveries along the M50 and M3 motorway schemes respectively. Indeed, the majority of kiln sites in the region have been discovered as a result of major road-building projects.

Most of the excavated sites have been greatly disturbed by post-medieval activity, and the dating of many kilns remains unspecified. The sequence of five kilns excavated at Jordanstown, Co. Dublin, typifies the challenges facing researchers, as here the assemblage of features is undated despite environmentally rich deposits.[22] Each of the five kilns was a variation on the classic figure-of-eight plan, and all five were located several metres apart in a 25m-long area. The kilns were cut into the underlying clay, and the bowls and flue areas were lined with reddened, oxidised clay and were filled with single uniform fills of charcoal-rich deposits.

Other evidence for cereal drying is more securely later medieval in date but often the kiln structure itself is absent. At Balrothery, the remains of a complex of features next to a silted up watercourse included pits containing charcoal and carbonised grain associated with stone-lined drains. This suggested the presence of a corn-drying kiln, but it seems that the kiln itself was destroyed by truncation in the early modern period.[23] A probable grain-drying kiln of sixteenth-century date was found at Killegland, Co. Meath, where the kiln appears

15 TNA:PRO C135/75/3. 16 CJR, 1308–14, p. 162; Mills (ed.), Account roll, p. 120. 17 Writing in the 1980s, Maurice Hurley observed that the majority of keyhole-shaped kilns were distributed in the west and north-west, but this pattern has changed radically in the intervening years; see Hurley, 'Kilferagh, Co. Kilkenny'; Margaret Gowen, Three Irish gas pipelines: new archaeological evidence in Munster (Dublin, 1988), pp 158–62 at p. 96; Monk and Kelleher, 'An assessment'; Brady, 'Agricultural tools and agrarian development', 248. 18 Hurley, 'Kilferagh'; R.M. Cleary, 'Excavations at Lough Gur, Co. Limerick: part III', JCHAS, 88 (1983), 51–80 at 67–8; Eoghan Kieran (Ballybofey, pers. comm.). See also Niall Brady, 'Abbeyland/Blackcastle Demesne, Co. Meath' in Excavations 1998, p. 160; Ciara MacManus, 'Gorteen, Co. Limerick' in Excavations 1999, p. 166; Finola O'Carroll, 'Haggardstown, Co. Louth' in Excavations 1999, pp 183–6; Michael Tierney, 'Excavating feudalism? A medieval moated site at Carrowreagh, Co. Wexford' in Corlett and Potterton (eds), Rural settlement in medieval Ireland (2009); Muiris O'Sullivan and Liam Downey, 'Corn-drying kilns', AI, 19:3 (autumn 2005), 32–5. 19 Hurley, 'Kilferagh', pp 90–1. 20 M.A. Monk, 'Appendix II: charred seed and plant remains' in Hurley, 'Kilferagh' (1987), pp 98–9. 21 M.F. Hurley and C.M. Sheehan, 'Ovens and kilns' in Hurley et al., Late Viking-Age and medieval Waterford (1997), pp 276–7. 22 Redmond Tobin, 'Jordanstown (BGE 6/12/1)' in Excavations 2002, pp 163–5; see also his entry in Eoin Grogan, Lorna O'Donnell and Penny Johnston (eds), The Bronze-Age landscapes of the pipeline to the west (Dublin, 2007), pp 221–5. 23 Teresa Bolger, 'Old Coach Road, Balrothery' in Excavations 2001, pp 82–5.

to represent re-use of an earlier building.[24] Indications of grain-processing in the medieval period were also found at Darcystown, Co. Dublin, where a kiln of unspecified type was uncovered.[25] At the Coombe in Dublin, a truncated pit that had been used for corn-drying or baking was excavated within an area where tanning also took place.[26] The pit contained charred cereal remains, and over 2,000 sherds of medieval pottery were found in the vicinity.

At Cherrywood, Co. Dublin, the remains of a keyhole-shaped kiln were uncovered, measuring 4.26m long.[27] A 3.1m-long U-shaped gully lay against a small pit that was 1.2m in diameter. Both features were simply cut into the underlying clay, while charred oats located to the west of the kiln were determined to be associated with discard from its use, and returned a radiocarbon determination of AD1020–1190. An adjacent area of paving may indicate the location of the flue, while a post-hole could originally have held a support for the roof of the kiln chamber. A number of re-used stones including part of a granite millstone and two possible pivot-stones were also found, and it is likely that some of these came from a nearby mill. Some sherds of local cooking ware and glazed wares of mid-twelfth- to fourteenth-century date were recovered among the stones. Deposits of charred cereal grains were dominated by wheat (73 per cent of those identified), but also contained oats (21 per cent) and barley (6 per cent). The prevalence of wheat was also noted in samples from a fourteenth-/fifteenth-century kiln at Ardee (Co. Louth).[28]

The excavation of a medieval farmstead and field system at Baltrasna, Co. Meath, revealed concentrations of carbonised wheat, with successively lesser quantities of oats, barley and rye, found in association with charred oat chaff and part of a rotary quern.[29] No formal cereal-processing structures were uncovered in these thirteenth- to fourteenth-century contexts, but the remains of at least two grain-drying kilns of sixteenth- to seventeenth-century date were exposed elsewhere on the site. Here, grains of both wheat and barley were recovered from the primary fills of one of the kiln bowls, while further evidence for cereal processing, in a nearby shallow hearth, included carbonised wheat, oat and rye grains as well as oat chaff.

The remains of a thirteenth-century farmstead were uncovered by archaeologists at a site just 250m from the motte at Skreen, Co. Meath.[30] There was evidence for two houses, a latrine, a grain-drying kiln and a series of associated pits. The keyhole-shaped kiln contained carbonised oat and bread-wheat, as well as barley, beans, peas and rye. The presence of large quantities of peas in the kiln suggests that crop-rotation was being practised. The ratio of cultivated grain to wild-seeds suggests that the crop was clean, and that it was intended for human consumption. The minimal levels of chaff identified support this theory.

Overall, the archaeological evidence has been somewhat frustrating insofar as many of the excavated kiln sites are not closely dated.[31] The fact that the process of corn-drying took place away from habitation *per se*, no doubt to avoid the risks of fire, might explain the absence of pottery and other occupation debris that is more usually available for dating later

24 W.O. Frazer, 'Killegland, Ashbourne' in *Excavations 2004*, pp 283–5; Frazer, 'A medieval farmstead at Killegland'. **25** Frank Ryan, 'Darcystown' in *Excavations 2004*, pp 106–7. **26** Melanie McQuade, '105–109 The Coombe, Dublin' in *Excavations 2004*, pp 117–18. **27** Ó Néill, 'Excavation of pre-Norman structures', pp 71–2; DEHLG file 99E0519 (Cherrywood; John Ó Néill). **28** DEHLG file 02E0831 (Ardee); Penny Johnston, pers. comm. **29** Donal Fallon, 'Continuity: the archaeological and documentary evidence'; Susan Lyons, 'N2 Finglas-Ashbourne road scheme – Site 17/18: flot assessment' (unpublished Headland Archaeology report, 2006). **30** Ciara McCarthy, 'Final excavation report: Skreen, Co. Meath (licence 05E0321)', unpublished report, 2006; Kelly, 'Analysis of the plant remains: Skreen 05E0321'. **31** An exception to this are the recent discoveries lying just outside the study area at Phoenixtown, Co. Meath, where excavations directed by Ed Lyne for ACS Ltd on the M3 motorway scheme have revealed a rich assemblage of features, including a roadway, a probable horse mill and three corn-drying kilns that are dated by associated pottery to the thirteenth/fourteenth centuries (Ed Lyne, pers. comm.). The excavation area lies away from the main habitation site. Documentary evidence also indicates that this land was intensively cultivated at this time, and suggests that it lay within the manor of Martry, which was held by the de Say family up to the early fourteenth century;

medieval deposits. This is not always the case, however, as witnessed at Kilferagh, Co. Kilkenny. Rich environmental deposits, such as the charred oats adjacent to the Cherrywood kiln, can provide sufficient material for dating, although it seems that many kiln fills are not yet processed in this manner. The bulk of the evidence suggests that corn-drying kilns were quite common in the early medieval period. It also suggests that individual cereal-drying kilns were used intensively but that they had a relatively short life-span, being back-filled and replaced periodically. That they were an efficient means of preparing grain for the milling process is indicated by their presence in the archaeological record over many centuries. The relatively small number of clearly attested later medieval sites may be increased with future excavations. An avoidance of manorial centres as sites for excavation may have led to their under-representation in the archaeological record. The discovery of a keyhole-shaped kiln at Carrickmines Castle demonstrates the presence of kilns at manor centres, and supports the indications from documentary sources described above.[32] With the centralisation of seigneurial resources, it is likely that corn-drying was also located closer to the centre of the manor than was the case previously, and perhaps the kilns at Phoenixtown, lying adjacent to the mill, are a case in point. Alternatively, or possibly in addition, the pattern may reflect a change in the methods for drying grain in the later Middle Ages, but the details of such remain elusive at present. The storage of grain in barns was primarily to dry the grain, which could then be threshed on the barn floor. The addition of kilns suggests that air-drying within barns was not always entirely successful and perhaps the usage of both barn and kiln is an indicator of the damp weather in Ireland at this time. Alternatively, it might reflect inadequate ventilation within Irish barns.

The use of corn-drying kilns continued into the sixteenth century and later. A pair of kilns dated to this period was excavated in Baltrasna, Co. Meath.[33] The seventeenth-century Civil Survey lists seven 'kill houses' for the Dublin region, and it is likely that these were in fact corn-drying kilns (Figure 14.3).[34] Two were recorded at Garristown, one each at Balscadden, Barberstown (Swords), Rallekaystown (Lusk) and Kilshane, and a thatched example at Old Court.

Kilns were also used for malting. In this process, grain that has been artificially encouraged to germinate is dried quickly to halt germination at the optimum time. Barley and other grains malted in this way were then used for brewing or, less commonly, distilling. A well-constructed kiln at Friary Street, Kilkenny, yielded a sample in which oats represented 60 per cent of the cereal grain present. The fact that many of the grains were sprouting led to the conclusion that the oats were being dried for malting to produce ale.[35] Sufficient quantities of malt were produced in the Dublin region to service an export market. In 1296, one hundred quarters of oat malt and twenty-two quarters of wheat malt were shipped from Dublin to Wales, while a parliamentary petition of 1471 indicates that malt was being exported at that time from Ireland to England, Scotland and Wales.[36] On the manor of Clonkeen in 1344/5, roughly 6 per cent of the wheat was malted, and 70 per cent of the oats.[37] At about the same time, as much as 81 per cent of the oats accounted for on the manor of Grangegorman were processed into malt.[38] In the mid-fifteenth century, customs were levied in Dublin on all barley malt, oat malt, dredge malt and wheat malt being brought into the city for sale, while in the sixteenth century, the vicars' choral of Christ Church received food liveries including beer (barley) malt and oat malt.[39]

see Murphy, 'Digging with documents'. **32** Clinton, 'Carrickmines Great'. **33** Fallon, 'Continuity: the archaeological and documentary evidence'. **34** *Civil Survey*, 7, pp 17, 18, 70, 116, 121, 140. **35** Paul Stevens, 'Four excavations in Kilkenny city (1999–2001), Part 2: the late medieval/post-medieval findings', *Old Kilkenny Review*, 59 (2007), 18–37 at 35. **36** *CDI, 1293–1301*, no. 345, p. 159; *CARD*, 1, pp 172–3. **37** See above, p. 308 and Table 9.6. **38** See above, p. 308 and Table 9.6. **39** *CARD*, 1, p. 275; *CCCD*, no. 1265.

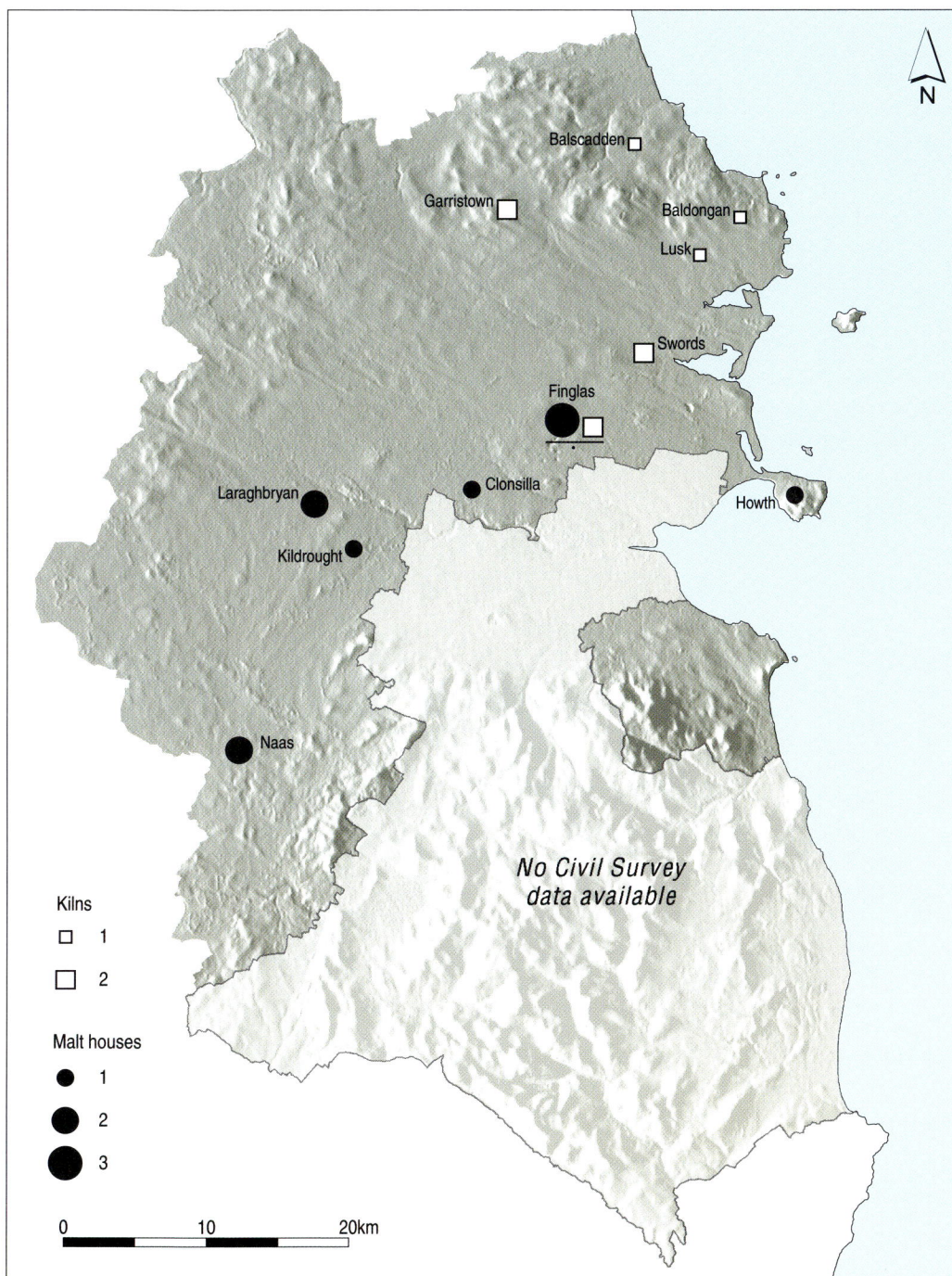

Figure 14.3 Location of kilns and malt houses in the Dublin region (as recorded in the Civil Survey).

Some religious houses, such as Christ Church, had their grain malted on-manor and then sent into the central household for brewing. Other houses, such as that of the Hospitallers at Kilmainham, amalgamated malting and brewing on one site. The prioral seat had two malt kilns, an old one and a new one, at Kilmainham in *c*.1330.[40] These kilns must have been substantial structures given the scale of the brewing activity at Kilmainham.[41] Malting and brewing were very frequently carried out by women, and the manors of Grangegorman and Clonkeen both employed female maltsters in the 1340s.[42]

The Civil Survey lists ten malt houses for the Dublin region (Figure 14.3), and it is likely that many of these were on the sites of earlier examples. In Co. Dublin, those at Finglas, Portmarnock and Clonsilla were slated, nothing is known of the one at Old Court (Finglas),

40 *Reg. Kilmainham*, p. 25.   **41** Murphy and Potterton, 'Investigating living standards'.   **42** Mills (ed.), *Account roll*, pp 35, 54, 62, 82, 84.

while the one at Little Cabragh was tiled.[43] In Kildare, the commissioners noted that Nicholas Walsh owned a stone house in Kildrought (Celbridge), worth £20, which was 'intended for a malt house'; two small malt houses had been built at Maynooth 'since the rebellion [of 1641]'; and at Naas one malt house was owned by the church and another by the Augustinians.[44]

Milling

Following kiln-drying, the next step in the processing of grain was milling. This process firstly separated the husks from the grains and then reduced the kernels to flour in the case of wheat and rye, and meal in the case of oats. If corn-drying kilns testify to large-scale production, the presence of mills to grind the grain into flour and meal reveals further the scale of arable production in medieval Ireland. Watermills were commonly used in the early medieval period, especially in the east and south of the country, but it is the scale of production after 1170 that sets later medieval milling apart. Various aspects of the form and function of medieval mills and the technology of milling have been covered in recent publications relating to Ireland and Britain.[45] The focus here is the distribution of mills in the Dublin region, their relationship with the arable economy, and the value of milling resources to lords.

Hand-mills

Rotary quern-stones are a common find on medieval sites in Ireland. This is despite the fact that manorial lords endeavoured to limit the use of hand-querns by their tenants so that they were obliged to grind their grain at the manorial mill. Tenants had to obtain special permission to have hand-mills and, in England, their continued use became a cause of considerable tension. A dispute between the tenants and abbey of St Albans, for example, resulted in the smashing of dozens of hand-mills by the abbey authorities.[46] There are few documentary references to the use of hand-mills in the Dublin region, although the activity must have been comparatively widespread. It is known that 'hand-grindstones' were shipped to Ireland in the later Middle Ages, and in the early fourteenth century, cottar tenants at Portraine on the archiepiscopal manor of Swords collectively paid 6s. 8d. per year 'to have their hand-mills and be relieved of suit of the mill'.[47] When mills were damaged or went out of use, tenants resorted to grinding grain in the home and it is likely that those who lived some distance from mills regularly did so.

Watermills

Most milling took place in purpose-built water-powered mills. Research has demonstrated that in the early medieval period Ireland showed a 'remarkable precocity' with regard to the development of water-powered grain mills.[48] At Raystown, Co. Meath, for example, the remains of at least four early medieval horizontal watermills and associated millraces have recently been found.[49] It is thought that the mills were not contemporary with each other and that a new one was built when the existing mill went out of use. On the eve of the

43 *Civil Survey*, 7, pp 133, 140, 142, 174, 231.   **44** *Civil Survey*, 8, pp 7, 21, 226, 227.   **45** Richard Holt, *The mills of medieval England* (Oxford, 1988); Colin Rynne, 'The development of milling technology in Ireland, *c*.600–1875' in Andy Bielenberg (ed.), *Irish flour milling: a history, 600–2000* (Dublin, 2003), pp 13–38; J.L. Langdon, *Mills in the medieval economy: England, 1300–1540* (Oxford, 2004); Adam Lucas, *Wind, water, work: ancient and medieval milling technology* (Leiden, 2005); Niall Brady, 'Mills in medieval Ireland: looking beyond design' in Steve Walton (ed.), *Wind and water in the Middle Ages: fluid technologies from antiquity to the Renaissance* (Tempe, AZ, 2006), pp 39–68.   **46** P.A. Rahtz, 'Medieval milling' in Crossley (ed.), *Medieval industries* (1981), pp 1–15 at pp 2–3; Holt, *Mills of medieval England*, pp 40–1. Holt does not regard this quarrel as typical.   **47** O'Neill, *Merchants and mariners*, p. 92; McNeill (ed.), *Alen's register*, pp 175–80.   **48** Rynne, 'Development of milling technology', p. 20.   **49** Seaver, 'Run of the mill?'; Seaver, 'Silent mills'.

Anglo-Norman invasion, the Dublin region already contained a large number of water-mills. A mill considered to date to the tenth and eleventh century has been uncovered at Chapelizod.[50] The mill was well preserved and the associated stone construction extended to a length of nearly 30m. It was situated downriver from the well-documented mills of the Anglo-Norman period.

Figure 14.4 Granite runner stone and bed stone from Kilbaylet Upper, Co. Wicklow (image courtesy of Chris Corlett).

Following the arrival of the Anglo-Normans, there was a significant increase in milling activity in the region. The growth and development of Dublin as an urban centre resulted in the establishment of a great number of watermills in its immediate environs. Some of the earliest references to mills must reflect newly constructed edifices, although more than likely on the site of earlier buildings. The mill of Glasnevin was confirmed as part of the possessions of Christ Church in 1179.[51] In 1191, Archbishop John Cumin granted to the canons of the newly instituted cathedral of St Patrick's in Dublin the tithes of all his manorial mills excepting those of his mills at Swords.[52]

Horizontal watermills, where the water powering the mill falls onto a wheel of wooden paddles aligned horizontally below the mill-house, continued to be used into the later medieval period, as did vertical undershot watermills, where the water drove a mill wheel that was aligned vertically and usually to one side of the mill. The mill-house, or wheel-house, was a relatively small building, often measuring less than 4–5m long by the same in width, but it was sufficiently spacious to accommodate the millstones and the associated apparatus of a wooden hopper to feed the grain onto the millstones, the shaft and devices to propel the stones, and certain space to place the ground grain (Figure 14.6). A mill-house excavated at Patrick Street in Dublin is considered to be the remains of Forde's Mill, which occupied the west side of the street and which appears in the documentary sources c.1230.[53] The excavation revealed that the mill was of a vertical undershot type and that it functioned between the thirteenth and seventeenth centuries.[54] It was extensively rebuilt in the later fourteenth century, when it was accompanied by substantial stone revetments to the inlet and outlet channels that were part of a process of canalisation of the underlying river.

The 'footprint' of a watermill was far larger than the wheel-house itself, and it could extend over some considerable distance to include a sequence of millrace channels that would carry water to the mill from a river or stream, as well as one or more millponds that acted as localised reservoirs to manage the flow of water to the mill. Tail-races would also help to channel the water away from the mill, and all these water channels could have simple timber sluice gates to help manage and control the passage of the water. Excavations within Dublin city have encountered water management channels in some number. Work conducted in the Coombe area, to the south of the castle, revealed an artificial channel along the northern boundary of the site that would have carried water from the Coombe Stream in the late twelfth century.[55] An investigation south of Kilmainham revealed where the

50 Claire Walsh, 'The Island/Martin's Row, Chapelizod' in *Excavations 2002*, p. 135.   **51** McNeill (ed.), *Alen's register*, p. 3.   **52** Ibid., p. 19.   **53** Clarke, *IHTA: Dublin Part I, to 1610*, p. 26; *RHJB*, p. 101.   **54** Colin Rynne, 'The Patrick Street watermills' in Walsh (ed.), *Archaeological excavations at Patrick, Nicholas and Winetavern Streets* (1997), pp 81–9.   **55** McQuade,

Figure 14.5 Distribution
of mills in the Dublin
region, from various
sources. The excavated
evidence includes sites
investigated up to 2004.

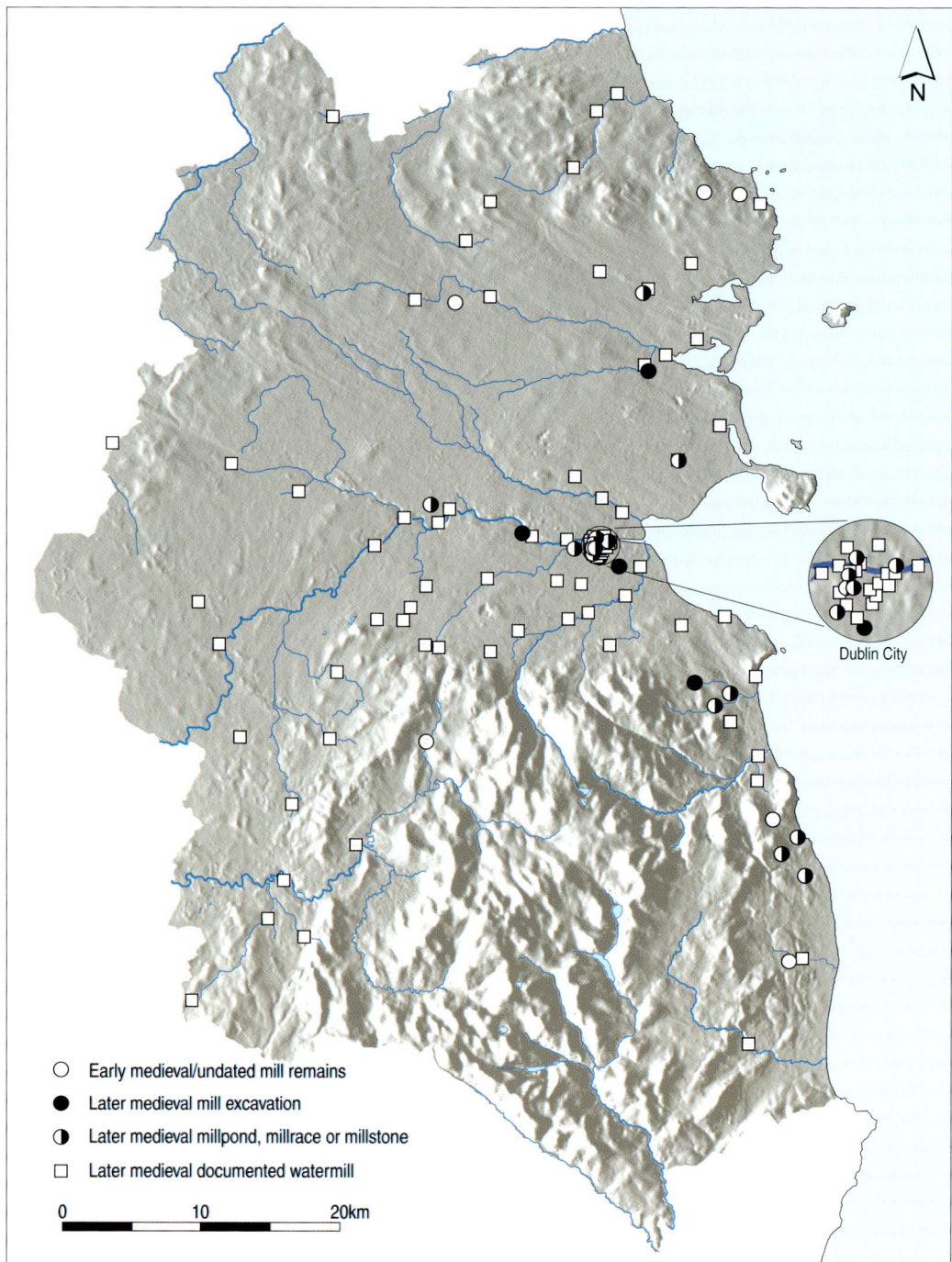

Figure 14.5 Distribution of mills in the Dublin region, from various sources. The excavated evidence includes sites investigated up to 2004.

○ Early medieval/undated mill remains

● Later medieval mill excavation

◐ Later medieval millpond, millrace or millstone

☐ Later medieval documented watermill

0   10   20km

Camac River, a tributary of the Liffey, was confined by stone walls defining the rear of twelfth- or thirteenth-century property plots. The channel was subsequently developed into a series of five tanneries in the late seventeenth century.[56] At Reuben Street, an unlined watercourse was identified as a branch of the diverted River Poddle, which measured less than 50cm in depth. Subsequent excavation revealed the watercourse to be thirteenth century in date, and that it was formalised in 1605 with the addition of a stone lining.[57]

Excavations at the abbey of St Thomas the Martyr in the western suburb of Dublin uncovered a watercourse possibly associated with the documented Watte Mill.[58] A large oak

'105–109, The Coombe'.   56 Alan Hayden, 'Old Kilmainham, Dublin' in *Excavations 2004*, p. 129.   57 Alan Hayden, 'Reuben Street, Dublin' in *Excavations 2002*, p. 153; Emer Dennehy, 'Reuben Street/Dolphin's Barn Street, Dolphin's Barn, Dublin' in *Excavations 2004*, pp 135–6.   58 Walsh, 'Archaeological excavations at the abbey of St Thomas', p. 192; *EIMP*, p. 26; *CARD*, 1, p. 155.

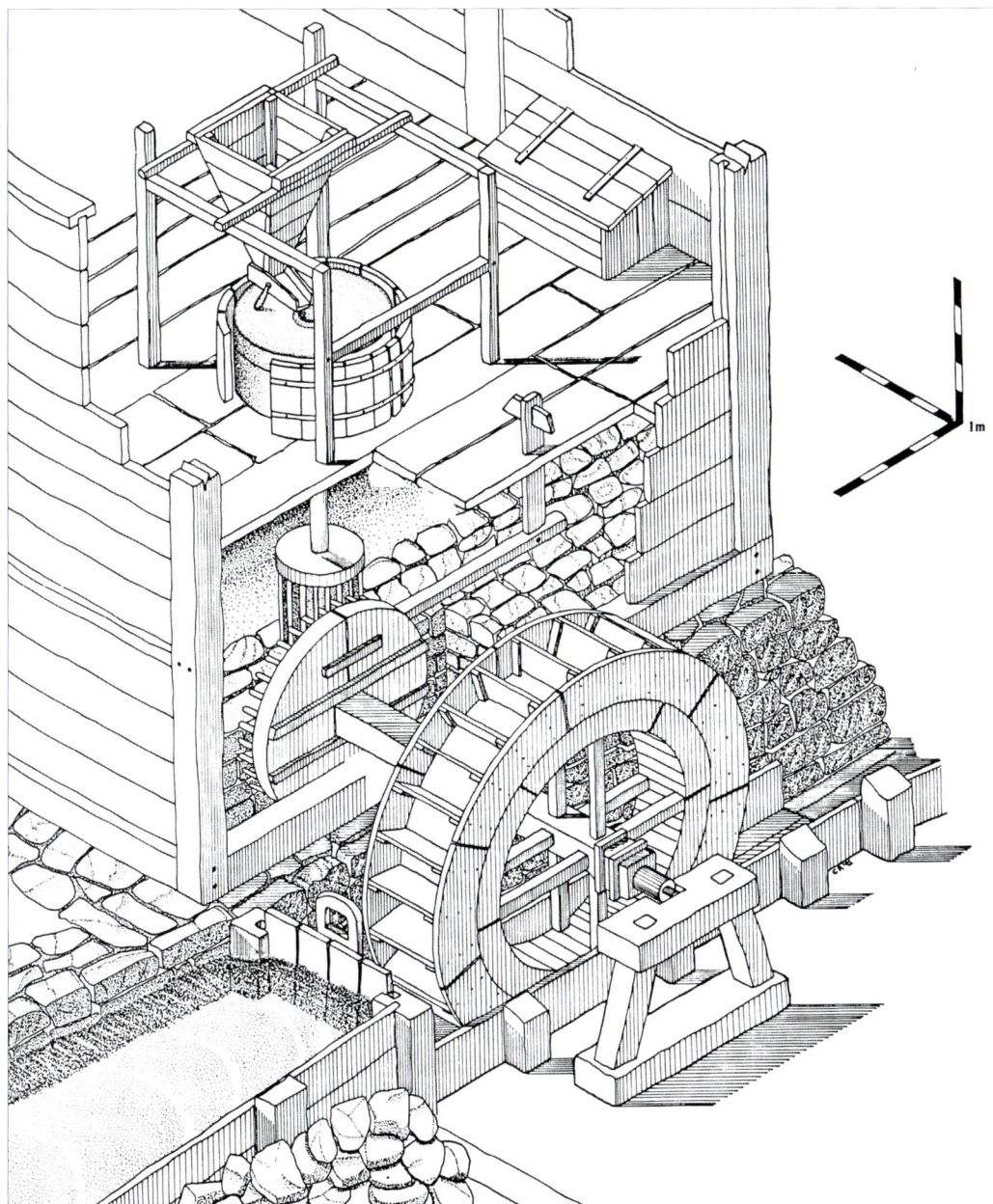

Figure 14.6
Reconstruction of
watermill excavated at
Patrick Street, Dublin
(image courtesy of
Colin Rynne).

beam was also discovered at a site close to the abbey of St Thomas' Double Mills in 2004.[59] The timber, which had been re-used in the nineteenth-century Poddle culvert, was dated by dendrochronology to the late twelfth or early thirteenth century. Claire Walsh noted that it 'is likely that some of the timber structure of the mill remains beneath the floor level of the culvert'. A thirteenth-century sluice gate uncovered during excavations at the site of the Four Courts extension at Inns Quay on the north side of the Liffey may be the remains of a millrace associated with documented mills in the area.[60] Excavations at Little Ship Street on a site perhaps related to the well-documented Pole Mills revealed two water channels bordered by strong post-and-wattle fences and structures that may have been the remains of outhouses or stores.[61] At Arran Quay, a 12m long timber revetment was exposed that 'formed the southern wall of a strong water-course … and probably represents the race of a mill

59 Claire Walsh, 'Eircom Depot, Mill Street, Dublin' in *Excavations 2004*, p. 126.   60 McMahon, 'Excavations at the site of the Four Courts extension'; Purcell, 'Land-use in medieval Oxmantown', p. 212.   61 DEHLG file 93E0132 (Little Ship Street; Linzi Simpson); Linzi Simpson, 'Excavations on the southern side of the medieval town at Ship Street Little, Dublin' in Duffy (ed.), *Medieval Dublin V* (2004), pp 9–51; *RDKPRI*, 20, p. 107; *RDKPRI*, 23, pp 104, 116, 141; *RDKPRI*, 24, pp 107, 137, 149.

Figure 14.7 The River Liffey near Celbridge, Co. Kildare. The power of the Liffey and its tributaries was harnessed to drive mill-wheels throughout the Middle Ages. Conflict frequently arose between millers and those who used the river for navigation, and weirs and other 'obstructions' often had to be removed.

situated close to the western side of the bridge which spanned the Liffey at the north-west corner of the city. Associated pottery suggests a thirteenth-century date. Documentary sources record a "mill near the bridge", but this was clearly on the southern side of the Liffey. It may represent an undocumented mill associated with St Saviour's priory'.[62] Still another watercourse possibly associated with a medieval mill was exposed on Francis Street.[63] Excavations at Ardee Street uncovered a millpond built shortly after 1603. It was a saucer-shaped shallow depression measuring *c.*50m by 53m, and it is thought to have been fed by the Commons Water to provide water for nearby mills that belonged to the abbey of St Thomas.[64]

While the evidence for watermills outside the city is much less concentrated, the abundance of watermills along the river systems clearly demonstrates the importance of water power and grain milling throughout much of the Dublin region (Figure 14.5). The Liffey was exploited for its potential to drive mill wheels, although until the river entered its lower levels from Leixlip, downstream of its confluence with the Rye Water, most of the known mills were sited on its tributary streams rather than on the main river channel. The crossing of the Liffey at Leixlip for a water mains pipe provided an opportunity to observe a previously unnoticed section of lime-mortared river-wall associated with some medieval pottery. It is thought that the wall may have been associated with St Catherine's Priory, which is known to have operated a mill and weir on the river.[65]

South of the city, the Dargle, the Loughlinstown River, the Dodder and the Poddle were all dotted with watermills, while to the north of the city, the lower reaches of the Tolka, the Ward, the Broad Meadow and the Delvin were equally exploited to power mills. At Killegland, near Ashbourne, Co. Meath, archaeological investigations were carried out on

62 Linzi Simpson, 'Arran Quay, Dublin' in *Excavations 1993*, p. 14.   **63** Ciara MacManus, 'Francis Street, Dublin' in *Excavations 2003*, pp 130–1.   **64** Franc Myles, 'Ardee Street, Dublin' in *Excavations 2003*, pp 119–21; Franc Myles, '24–26 Ardee Street, Dublin' in *Excavations 2004*, pp 111–12.   **65** David McCullough, 'Archaeological monitoring of excavations in the River Liffey at Leixlip, Co. Dublin: Leixlip/Ballycoolen Water Supply, 07E0265' (unpublished report by the Archaeological Diving Company Ltd, 2008).

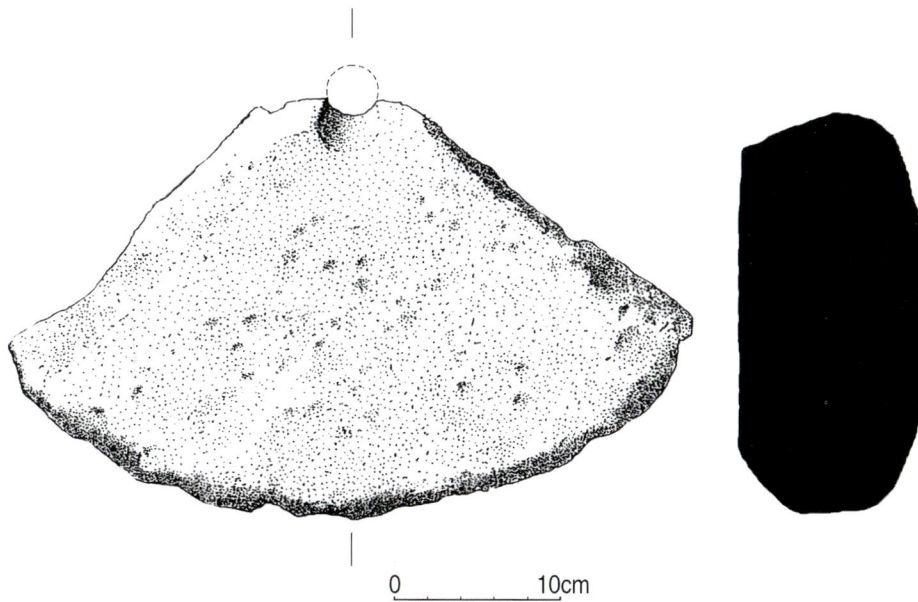

Figure 14.8 Fragment of a millstone found during excavations at Kindlestown Castle, Co. Wicklow (after Simpson, 'Dublin's southern frontier under siege: Kindlestown Castle', p. 355).

an earth-built millrace channel to the north of the Broad Meadow River, close to the site of Killegland tower house (which was possibly erected for Walter Wafre after 1400).[66] A low platform (20m by 45m) next to the millrace may be the remains of a mill, while two shallow ditches could indicate the location of the tail-race. The pottery recovered suggests a medieval date for the features. Nearby, two ponds (c.8–10m in diameter) appear to have been once linked to the river by a shallow channel that is now silted up. These may have functioned as fishponds; the first edition Ordnance Survey maps indicate the presence of unusual earthworks at the site of the ponds. The abbey of St Thomas' in Dublin was granted the mill and fishery at Killegland c.1300 along with the messuage held by Hugh the miller and common pasture for six cows.[67]

A re-used millstone fragment was found in association with some sherds of medieval pottery on a site at Charlesland, Co. Wicklow.[68] Similarly, a fragment of a millstone was recovered during excavations at Kindlestown Castle in the same county, and this may be all that remains of the documented mill on that site.[69] The undercroft of a wheelhouse with some timber workings were excavated at Carrickmines, Co. Dublin, with the timbers returning a dendro-date of 1123+/–9. In one part of this very large site, a series of gullies and water channels formed part of the millraces that fed water to the mill.[70] Remains of what appear to be the documented medieval mill of the Augustinian nunnery at Gracedieu were found during gas pipeline excavations in 1999.[71] A millrace was investigated and was found to have to have been faced with a strong mortar-bonded wall. A substantial wall to the north of the millrace may have served 'some related structural purpose'. The structures were believed to be medieval and 'related to the occupation of the nunnery'. At the time of the Dissolution, the nunnery had a watermill and a horse mill with a combined value of £2;[72] a century later, the Civil Survey recorded 'an old mill in use' at Gracedieu with a value of £8.[73]

The frequency with which mills are mentioned in medieval documents is a measure of their importance as a source of lordly income. There are references to at least eighty

66 Edmond O'Donovan, 'Ashbourne town centre' in *Excavations 2002*, pp 399–400; DEHLG file 02E0708 (Ashbourne; Edmond O'Donovan); Frazer, 'A medieval farmstead at Killegland'. 67 *RAST*, pp 45–6, 50. 68 Sinéad Phelan, 'Charlesland' in *Excavations 2004*, p. 480. 69 Simpson, 'Dublin's southern frontier', p. 355. 70 Clinton, 'Carrickmines Great', p. 87; David Brown (pers. comm.), and personal observation, Niall Brady 2002. 71 Conway, 'Gracedieu'; DEHLG file 99E0217 (Gracedieu; Malachy Conway). 72 *EIMP*, p. 73. 73 *Civil Survey*, 7, p. 56.

individual mills in Dublin city and region in the period 1179–1540 – although they were clearly not all functioning at the same time. The references include valuations of mills in manorial extents, details of leasing out of mills, accounts of accidents occurring in and around mills, disputes concerning milling rights, and costs of repair and maintenance of mill buildings and equipment.

A great deal of milling in the region was controlled by religious houses. Rural houses such as the Augustinian priory at Holmpatrick and the nunnery at Gracedieu had mills near their precincts.[74] Urban houses, such as the Cistercian abbey of St Mary's, had mills situated in, or close to, their precincts and mills located on their rural granges. These mills played a vital role in processing the monastic community's own grain and also produced income through the payment of tolls or *multure* (grain levied as toll from tenants using the mill) by the tenants who were required to bring their grain to the mill for grinding. At the time of the Dissolution, St Mary's had a watermill and a horse mill within the precincts in Dublin, and watermills in its granges at Balgeeth, Ballyboghill, Clonliffe, Kilcrea and Portmarnock (all Co. Dublin), and at Monktown Grange, Co. Meath.[75] There is also an earlier reference to a mill at their grange in Carrickbrennan (Monkstown, Co. Dublin).[76] Despite early prohibitions on the Cistercians using mills as a source of revenue, many of these mills were leased to laymen.

A significant number of mills in the region were under royal control. Mills were located near Dublin Castle from at least 1243, when they are mentioned as being 'new'.[77] These must have processed a great deal of grain for Dublin consumers. In addition to these, there were mills on the royal demesne manors of Chapelizod, Esker, Saggart and Newcastle Lyons. The two mills at Newcastle McKynegan were valued at 100s. in 1305.[78] Mills at Saggart and Newcastle Lyons were leased to individuals from the late thirteenth century onwards.[79] Thomas the miller at Newcastle Lyons was leasing the mill for 40s. in 1296.[80] Fourteenth-century leases of this mill included sixty acres of land at Kilmactalway, worth 1s. per acre.[81] Sometimes, entrepreneurial individuals would lease several royal mills – like Henry Ash, who is recorded in 1295 as paying rents for the royal mills at Dublin Castle (£4 13s. 4d.) and the mills at Saggart and Newcastle Lyons (£2 10s.).[82] There does not appear to have been a mill at Crumlin, but there was a mill at Esker that was recorded as prostrated in 1325.[83] The two mills at Chapelizod were valued at five marks (£3 6s. 8d.) in 1304.[84]

There were two mills on the manor of Leixlip, which was acquired by the king in 1302 and both were of considerable value. In 1341, one was assessed as being worth ten marks (£6 13s. 4d.) per annum beyond five marks in repairs and routine maintenance. The other was valued at five marks (£3 6s. 8d.) per annum, while an associated fishery was worth £1 10s. Both mills were held by Robert Lengynour in the 1320s for £6 13s. 4d.[85] Castlewarden, also acquired by the king in the early fourteenth century, had two mills, but these were much less valuable, being farmed for one mark and two marks respectively in c.1315.[86]

Another significant mill-owner in the region was the archbishop of Dublin. The extents of 1326 mention a total of fifteen mills on eight archiepiscopal manors of Ballymore, Clondalkin, Colonia, Finglas, Rathcoole, Shankill, Swords and Tallaght.[87] The large manors of Swords and Ballymore had the greatest concentration of mills. Ballymore had five, two of which were located at the borough and one each at Ballybough, Dunlavin and

74 *EIMP*, pp 41, 73.   75 *EIMP*, pp 2, 10–14, 17. There were two watermills at Portmarnock and Kylragh.   76 *CJR, 1305–7*, p. 478.   77 Butler (ed.), *Registrum prioritas omnium sanctorum*, p. 27.   78 *CDI, 1302–7*, no. 335, p. 115.   79 *CDI, 1293–1301*, no. 264, pp 112–17, no. 300, pp 136–41.   80 *CDI, 1293–1301*, no. 300, pp 136–41.   81 NAI RC8/24: Memoranda roll, pp 337–9; Lyons, 'Manorial administration', p. 28.   82 *CDI, 1293–1301*, pp 112, 116.   83 NAI RC8/14: Memoranda roll, pp 228–9.   84 TNA:PRO C143/50/16.   85 *RDKPRI*, 43, p. 31.   86 TNA:PRO SC12/20/48.   87 McNeill (ed.), *Alen's register*, pp 170–96.

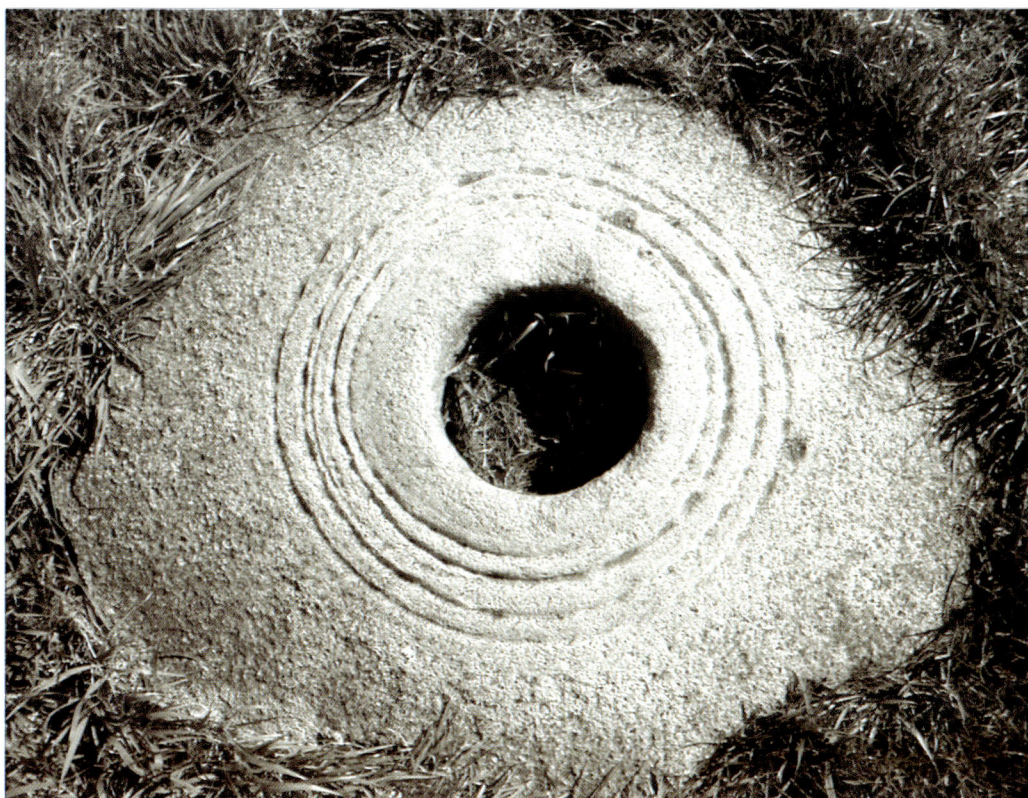

Figure 14.9 Millstone unearthed at Trim, Co. Meath.

'Donnahymelaghe'. Swords had three mills and possibly another two at Seatown, which may not have been among the three extended in 1326. The watermills at Ballymore were more valuable than those at Swords, which possibly reflects the fact that the tenants at Swords had access to other mills in the area.[88] In 1296, when the manor was under royal administration, the keeper accounted for profit from the 'troll mill' and the tidal mill.[89] The 'troll' mill may have been a horse mill, as an early meaning of the verb to troll was to move in a circular fashion. The presence of a horse mill might suggest that the capacity of the watermills was not sufficient. The archbishop had two valuable mills on the manor of Colonia, of which one – the 'Wodemill' – was held by the prior of Holy Trinity.[90]

There were documented mills on many of the lay manors in the region, such as at Baggotrath, Cloncurry, Gormanston, Killiney, Maynooth, Naul, Rathmore, Ratoath and Templeogue. The sources for these mills are generally less informative than for the better-documented royal or episcopal mills. Due to the constant partitioning of lay estates and resources, references are often to fractions of mills. Thus, Joanna de Burgh was granted a third part of two parts of two mills in Maynooth in 1328.[91]

Information on the value placed on mills comes from a variety of sources. Manorial extents, which survive from the period 1250–1350, frequently include a value for the mill if there was one. It would appear that what was being valued in the extent was the yearly profit accruing to the owner from the mill. This would represent the value of sales from multure, if the mill was under the lord's direct management, or the 'farm' or rent of the mill if it was being leased out. It is not possible to determine the rate of mill toll levied in Ireland. Apparently, the toll charged at the king's mills at Dublin Castle in 1319 was one sixteenth of the grain to be milled, but there is no way of ascertaining if this was typical of the region as a whole.[92]

88 Suggested by Lyons ('Manorial administration', p. 114).   89 *RDKPRI*, 38, p. 46.   90 McNeill (ed.), *Alen's register*, p. 171.   91 *RBK*, p. 98.   92 Lyons, 'Manorial administration', p. 79, quoting Richard Bennett and John Elton, *A history of corn milling* (4 vols, London/Liverpool, 1898–1904), 4, pp 16–20.

In the period 1250–1350, the average annual value of a watermill was somewhere between £1 and £2. There were some mills with values significantly greater than this, for example, the mills at Dublin Castle (£5) and at St Sepulchre's (£3 10s.).[93] In 1292, following the destruction of the royal mill at Chapelizod by an inundation of the River Liffey, the exchequer allowed the keeper £6 for loss of issues of the mill.[94] The mills at Leixlip, mentioned above, had an impressive combined value matched by the two mills at Ballymore (£10 in 1326). Other valuable mills included those in Co. Wicklow, at Newcastle McKynegan and Dunlavin, said to be worth £5 and £4 respectively.[95] Much higher values are recorded for mills in other parts of Ireland however. In 1306, four mills in Gowran, Co. Kilkenny, produced £42 per annum in rent, and in 1305 two mills in Ardmayle in Co. Tipperary were worth twenty-four marks (£16) per annum.[96]

The extent values display a great deal of variation and were obviously conditional on the state of repair of the mill, its capacity and efficiency, and the number of people bringing their grain to be milled there. Lack of tenants using the mill was cited as a reason for the comparatively low valuation at Kilmactalway, Co. Dublin (£2 13s. 4d.) in 1351.[97] Sometimes the appurtenances of the mill formed an element of the calculated value and this might include accommodation for the miller and a small amount of land. On occasion, the annual yield of eels from the millpond is also part of the calculation. The ownership of the mill did not necessarily affect the value. The two archiepiscopal mills at Ballymore were valued at £10 in 1326, while one mill at Tallaght was valued at £1 6s. 8d. in the same year.[98]

The extents of monastic possessions taken in 1540 provide valuations for eighteen mills in the region that were in ecclesiastical ownership at the end of the medieval period. Not one of the mills valued could match the £5 valuations cited above. The average value, however, had risen to between £3 and £4 per annum. Two mills were valued at £4, one of which (that belonging to the hospital at Kilmainham) was a double mill with two pairs of millstones under one roof (Figure 7.60).[99]

Another source of valuations are leases or rents for when the mill was 'farmed' out, and these too display a great deal of variation. Frequently, the value of the mill is said to be 'less' the cost of repairs and maintenance and sometimes it is said to be 'over and above' the cost of upkeep. When a mill was leased out, the lessee was usually in charge of maintenance. On occasion, the terms of the lease included a remission of the first year's rent in order to allow the lessee to make necessary repairs and sometimes even rebuild the mill. In 1373, when Archbishop Minot of Dublin granted Thomas FitzEustace the mill of Ballymore Eustace, the lease required FitzEustace to keep the mill 'styff and staunch' at his own expense.[100] In 1540, the extent of the possessions of St Mary's Abbey, Dublin, reported an arrangement at the abbey's mill in Kilrea (north of Malahide), whereby the lord provided timber and stone for repairs and the lessee paid the wages of the workmen.[101]

Most valuations therefore represent the productive capacity of the mill rather than the inherent value of the structure and its equipment. An exception to this is the valuation for the mill at Leyiston, Co. Kildare, in 1302. In legal proceedings following the accidental death of the miller, a value of £1 7s. 8d. was assigned to the mill, including mill wheels, iron and timber.[102] The profits of the mill were separately valued at £1 6s. 8d. In 1282, a mill was constructed on the earl of Norfolk's manor of Fennagh in Co. Carlow at a cost of £4 9s., and this provides some indication of the expense of building a modest watermill from scratch.[103]

93 *CDI, 1285–92*, no. 215, p. 100; McNeill (ed.), *Alen's register*, p. 171.   **94** *RDKPRI*, 37, p. 52.   **95** TNA:PRO C47/10/17/10; McNeill (ed.), *Alen's register*, p. 190.   **96** *RBO*, pp 40, 62.   **97** TNA:PRO C47/10/22/7.   **98** McNeill (ed.), *Alen's register*, pp 182, 190.   **99** *EIMP*, p. 82.   **100** McNeill (ed.), *Alen's register*, p. 222.   **101** *EIMP*, p. 14. **102** CJR, 1295–1303, pp 444–5.   **103** TNA:PRO SC6/1239/2.

Figure 14.10 Sixteenth-
century depiction of
'the King's Myll' at
Ogmore in Wales
(image reproduced
courtesy of the
National Archives of
the UK, ref: TNA:PRO
MCP 1/49).

Constructing a new mill at Chapelizod in 1292 following the destruction of the old mill apparently cost £18 5s. 7¾d.[104] The sum included materials, wages of craftsmen and millstones, but the mill itself must have been a substantial building. Mills obviously varied greatly in size but were often very modest structures; the sixteenth-century depiction of the King's Myll at Ogmore in Wales (Figure 14.10) may give an impression of the appearance of some of the mills in the Dublin region.

The value assigned to the mill at Leyiston appears to be relatively low, given the known costs of repairs that were carried out on some mills. The three royal mills in Ardee, Co. Louth, were repaired at a cost of £12 10s. in 1304.[105] In 1314, Nicholas Balscote, keeper of the king's mills in Dublin, spent £2 13s. 2d. on timber boards, nails, posts and other 'necessaries' bought for reconstructing the wheels of the mills, £2 6d. on wages of carpenters, £1 5s. 6½d. on iron and steel bought for shafts and other apparatus and £1 8s. 9d. on a Welsh millstone, including its carriage.[106] Good quality millstones that were sourced in England, France and Wales were often the biggest single item of expenditure, particularly as they were bulky and therefore expensive to transport. Richard de Wodehouse of Chapelizod, who died in 1322, had among his possessions two millstones valued at 20s. and a mill-spindle with a brazen mill-rind worth 6s. 8d.[107] When the royal mills at Leixlip were repaired c.1330, two French millstones were purchased for £7 6s. 8d., which presumably included their transport from the French quarries to Dublin.[108] A separate payment of 6s. 8d. was made for their transport from Dublin to Leixlip.

It is clear that there was a great deal of continuity in the use of mill sites but that the scale and value of milling in the region varied considerably in the course of the period 1200–1600. The decades spanning 1300 probably marked a peak in terms of the value and productivity of milling, especially in areas close to the city and to the ports. The enormous contribution made by Ireland and the Dublin region in particular to the supply of the king's armies in Scotland during the years 1296–1324 would have provided a significant boost not just to the agrarian economy but to mills and millers.[109] In 1298, 8,000 quarters of wheat were ordered to be sent to Scotland. Six thousand of these were 'to be of bolted [sifted] flour, free from bran, packed in barrels'.[110] The milling of this quantity of grain must have occupied mills in Dublin and the region for a considerable period. When the flour was received from the millers it had to be bolted to extract the bran, and special sieves were purchased for this

104 RDKPRI, 37, p. 52.   105 J.F. Lydon, 'The mills at Ardee in 1304', CLAHJ, 4 for 1980 (1981), 259–63.   106 HMDI, pp 471–2.   107 NAI RC8/13: Memoranda roll, pp 227–33.   108 O'Neill, Merchants and mariners, p. 92.   109 James Lydon, 'The Dublin purveyors and the wars in Scotland, 1296–1324' in Mac Niocaill and Wallace (eds), Keimelia (1988), pp 435–48.   110 CPR, 1292–1301, p. 388.

Figure 14.11
Depiction of houses
and windmill at
Ballough, Lusk,
Co. Dublin, by Joseph
Moland, 1716
(© Representative
Church Body).

purpose. The bolting took place in a temporary stall or granary set up on the quay at Dublin. There is evidence that in this period Dublin gained a reputation for having facilities for milling considerable quantities of grain. In 1300, a shipload of wheat was sent from Kirkudbright in Scotland to Dublin, where it was ground into flour and then shipped back to Ayr for the army.[111]

Many of the records of large expenditures on mill repairs and equipment date from the first quarter of the fourteenth century when it was obviously considered a good economic investment. The series of setbacks to the economy and population that was encountered in the course of the fourteenth century also had their impact on mills and milling. The scarcity of documentary evidence for milling in the period 1350–1500 is partly due to the poor survival of source material from this period but must also reflect a period of recession and retrenchment in the industry – a trend that is similarly noticeable in the archaeological record. There is some evidence that mills were leased out on terms much more favourable to the lessee, with long terms and low rents. In 1371, Archbishop Minot leased the site of the mill formerly called 'Shyreclap', in St Patrick's Street, to John Pasvaund.[112] The mill was described as 'altogether thrown down' and had to be rebuilt at the lessee's expense. However, the site, with associated pond, bridge and floodgates, was granted for a term of sixty years at the low rent of 20s. per annum and the lessee paid nothing for the first two years. In 1373, the same archbishop included the mill in Ballymore Eustace as part of the grant of the constableship of the castle there. The grantee had only to agree to keep it in good repair.

Windmills

Windmills provided an alternative to watermills, which could be frozen, flooded or might dry up. Windmills were also more self-contained, and did not require associated millponds and millraces to power them. The mechanism to drive the wheels was powered by a set of framed sails that were attached to an axle on the elevated side of the mill house. The whole structure could be rotated manually on its central base-frame to catch the best wind. The freedom that this conveyed to choose location unshackled the association of mills with riverine and tributary locations. Yet, despite this locational opportunity, windmills were not numerous in later medieval Ireland. There are only a few specific documentary references to

111 Lydon, 'The Dublin purveyors', p. 445.   **112** McNeill (ed.), *Alen's register*, p. 220.

Figure 14.12
Foundation trenches of
medieval post-mill,
Mount Gamble, Swords,
Co. Dublin, viewed from
the west (the lesser
crossing trench on the
south side is a later
feature, not associated
with the mill) (image
courtesy of Edmond
O'Donovan and
Margaret Gowen and
Co. Ltd).

windmills in Ireland before the seventeenth century, although it is possible that some of the many undifferentiated references to a *molindinum* may in fact refer to windmills. There was a windmill worth 40*s.* a year at the manorial borough of Old Coillacht (Coolaghmore, barony of Kells, Co. Kilkenny) in the late thirteenth century, while the 1307 extent for the Templar manor of Kilcloggan on the Hook Peninsula in Co. Wexford included an expenditure of 2*s. 6d.* for iron for the repair of the broken sail of the windmill.[113] Closer to Dublin, an extent of the lands of William de Vescy at Kildare in 1297 mentions 'a windmill worth 26*s. 8d.* a year'.[114] The priory of Holy Trinity had a windmill on Oxmantown Green to the north-west of the city that was functioning at some time before 1330.[115]

Archaeologically, the most prominent indicator of the former presence of a windmill is the mound on which the timber super-structure would have been positioned.[116] While such mounds are identifiable in many parts of England, very few have been recorded in Ireland. A small number of possible examples have been identified in the Dublin region, but all remain undated. One of these is at Agher, Co. Meath, where the mound in question appears to form part of a deserted settlement.[117] The complex consists of a motte and bailey, at least six house platforms, a sunken roadway leading to a rectangular enclosure, and a series of field divisions covering *c.*15 acres (*c.*6 hectares)(Figure 6.3). Other possible windmill mounds in Co. Meath have been identified at Bartramstown, Derrypatrick, Diamor and Hurdlestown. The Bartramstown example is located within a complex of apparently medieval features including a field system (of seven acres) and a church.[118] The group of medieval features at Derrypatrick consists of a rectangular field system (of six acres), the site of a castle and two sunken roadways, in addition to the possible windmill mound.[119] A small conical mound close to the motte at Kill, Co. Kildare, may once have supported a windmill, while early

113 Dryburgh and Smith (eds), *Handbook*, p. 252; Mac Niocaill, 'Suppression of the Templars', 201.   114 *CDI, 1293–1301*, no. 481, p. 225.   115 *CCCD*, no. 578.   116 M.W. Beresford and J.K.S. St Joseph, *Medieval England: an aerial survey* (2nd ed., Cambridge, 1979), pp 64–5.   117 Moore, *Archaeological inventory of County Meath*, p. 164; see also pp 120, 127, 156; Matthew Devitt, 'Summerhill and its neighbourhood, part i', *JCKAHS*, 6:3 (1910), 214–21 at 221.   118 Moore, *Archaeological inventory of County Meath*, p. 121; see also p. 129.   119 Ibid., p. 122; see also pp 117, 133, 170.

editions of the Ordnance Survey maps show a ruinous windmill *c.*750m to the north-west of the motte at Hortland, also in Co. Kildare. It is possible that this mill had medieval origins, but the motte is less than 200m from the Blackwater River, and may have had a water-powered mill instead, or as well. The mound depicted by Beranger in 1768 close to Castleknock Castle is also likely to have supported a windmill.[120]

At Mount Gamble in Swords, the foundation trenches of a timber windmill were excavated in 2003, just off the top of a low hill (Figure 14.12).[121] According to the excavator, 'the morphology of the surviving archaeological feature is very similar to timber windmill sites excavated in medieval and early post-medieval Britain'. Straight-sided foundation trenches, measuring 8.25m and 9.4m long, 0.75m and 1m wide, and 1.31m and 1.38m deep would have accommodated the cross-trees timbers that supported the base frame on which the windmill would have rotated. Soil samples collected on the site contained cereal remains. The possible site of the windmill in Raheny was excavated in 1999, but no traces of it were found.[122]

These two medieval windmills are in the northern part of the region, close to the coast: one in the city area at Oxmantown; the other to the north at Swords (Figure 14.5). The locations are in keeping with the pattern of early windmill development elsewhere in medieval Europe, where the first sites appeared along shorelines in the late twelfth century.[123] The absence of windmills in similar locations south of Dublin, and inland, suggests that the existing network of watermills predominated throughout the period. The use of windmills in the Dublin region is reminiscent of the pattern in France and England, where their usage complemented established patterns of production.[124] The distribution in the Dublin region again highlights north Dublin/south Meath as the area of most intensive arable productivity.

The records from the seventeenth and eighteenth centuries show a similar distribution, focused to the north of the city, with some additional sites inland.[125] The Civil Survey for Dublin records four windmills – three in the barony of Coolock (Clontarf (Figure 14.13), Raheny and Swords – the latter being worth £5 per year) and one in the barony of Lusk (also worth £5).[126] This last-mentioned example may be the one at Ballough depicted in Joseph Moland's 1716 map (Figure 14.11).[127] Two of these appear to be shown on the Down Survey barony map, which also depicts one at Newcastle and two in Co. Meath (at Kilmoon and Kilbride). Jean Rocque's 1762 map of Co. Dublin shows eleven windmills, all of which are located in the northern third of the county.[128] The 1703 estate map of Holmpatrick depicts a windmill that may be the one 'on Channon Hill' referred to in a lease of 1565.[129] An eighteenth-century windmill on Windmill Hill at Newcastle could well be on the site of a windmill referred to in 1418.[130] This in turn may be the one shown on the Down Survey map.

120 Harbison (ed.), *Beranger's drawings*, pp 86–7.   **121** Edmond O'Donovan, 'Mount Gamble, Townparks, Swords' in *Excavations 2003*, pp 181–2; Edmond O'Donovan, 'Archaeological excavations, Mount Gamble, Townparks, Swords, Co. Dublin, 02E0608' (unpublished report by Margaret Gowen and Co. Ltd, 2005), pp 32–3.   **122** DEHLG file 99E0702 (St Francis Hospice, Raheny; Tim Coughlan).   **123** Georges Comet, 'Technology and agricultural expansion in the Middle Ages: the example of France north of the Loire' in Grenville Astill and J.L. Langdon (eds), *Medieval farming and technology: the impact of agricultural change in north-west Europe* (Leiden, New York and Köln, 1997), pp 11–39 at p. 31.   **124** For a comparative distribution of watermill and windmill sites in England, based on documentary sources of early fourteenth-century date, see Langdon, *Mills in the medieval economy*, p. 10.   **125** See a national distribution of windmills in Colin Rynne, *Industrial Ireland, 1750–1930: an archaeology* (Cork, 2006), p. 28.   **126** *Civil Survey*, 7, pp 95, 120, 172, 176, 184.   **127** Refaussé and Clark, *Maps of the estates of the archbishops of Dublin*, pp 58–9.   **128** These windmills are at Balcumin, Ballough, Borandstown, Feltrim, Garristown, Jamestown, Nutstown, Skerries, Swords, nr. Balruddery, nr. Bow Hill.   **129** DEHLG RMP file 02701; K.W. Nicholls and T.G Ó Canann (eds), *The Irish fiants of the Tudor sovereigns: during the reigns of Henry VIII, Edward VI, Philip and Mary, and Elizabeth I* (4 vols, Dublin, 1994), 2 (1558–86), p. 90, no. 831 (619).   **130** DEHLG RMP file 038—021; Healy, 'Monuments and sites of archaeological interest', p. 25; D'Alton, *History of the county of Dublin*, p. 677 (1418).

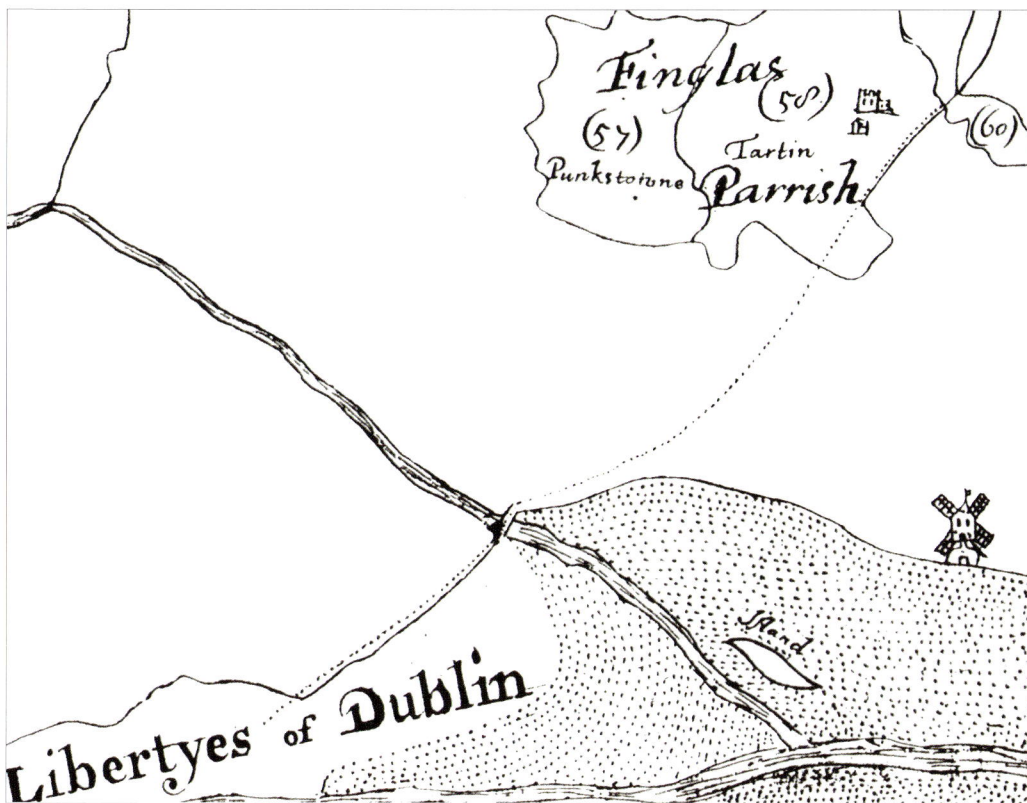

Figure 14.13 Extract from the Down Survey map of the barony of Coolock, Co. Dublin, showing a windmill at Clontarf.

Horse mills

Horse mills are generally regarded as marking an intermediate stage in milling technology between the manual quern stone and the mechanised watermill or windmill. The grinding power was supplied by a horse walking on a circular track around a set of grinding stones. Rynne suggested that they were introduced into Ireland from Britain in the early medieval period.[131] The earliest known reference to a horse mill in England dates to 1183, but Holt believes that they were in use long before this date.[132] In their simplest form, they were little more than large hand-mills, but some were nevertheless substantial structures. The horse mill that was constructed at Ivinghoe in Buckinghamshire in 1408–9 used a considerable quantity of timber and had wattle-and-daub walls and a thatched roof.[133]

While many horse mills must have operated in a domestic sphere, most of the documented examples from the Dublin region occur in conjunction with known seigneurial watermills, and therefore appear to have acted as an additional or back-up source of power. It is also possible that horse mills may have been used exclusively for one type of milling. John Langdon found that in England, horse mills were closely associated with malt grinding, while Holt pointed out that grinding both bread grains and malt through the same set of millstones resulted in the tainting of meal and flour by the distinctively flavoured and sticky malt.[134]

The earliest recorded horse mill in the Dublin region appears to be that in Dublin Castle, which in c.1224 had harnesses but no horses.[135] It must have resumed operations, however, for in 1314 the keeper of the king's mills in Dublin spent 60s. 7½d. on a horse servicing the mills and for shoeing him.[136] There was a horse mill on the archiepiscopal manor of Swords in 1279 and one at Lusk in 1326.[137] In the 1540 extents of monastic possessions, both the abbey of St Mary's in Dublin and the nunnery at Gracedieu are recorded as having a watermill and a horse mill in their precincts, while the hospital of St

131 Colin Rynne, *Technological change in Anglo-Norman Munster* (Cork, 1998), repr. in Ludlow and Jameson (eds), *Medieval Ireland* (2004), pp 65–95 at p. 72. 132 Holt, *Mills of medieval England*, p. 17. 133 Langdon, *Mills in the medieval economy*, p. 255. 134 Ibid., pp 151–2; Holt, *Mills of medieval England*, p. 148. 135 CDI, 1171–1251, no. 1227, p. 187. 136 HMDI, pp 471–2. 137 TCD MS 804, p. 199; McNeill (ed.), *Alen's register*, p. 177.

John the Baptist had a piece of meadow called 'the myll horse park', containing three stangs, situated near Darndale by Coolock.[138] The Civil Survey notes the presence of two horse mills in Co. Dublin in the 1650s – one 'now out of use', at Carnhill (Lusk) and a second, valued at £6 per annum, at Stapolin (Howth).[139]

Archaeological evidence for horse mills in Ireland is scant. At Hammond Lane in Dublin, a central circular base 3.9m in diameter surrounded by a 2m-wide track that measured nearly 15m in diameter was interpreted by the excavator as a horse mill used for grinding grain at the edge of the suburb.[140] The central depression would have housed the mechanism of the mill, while the track would have been worn by the animals that moved in a circle to turn a wheel on the central pivot.[141] A watercourse and trough were found in close proximity to the mill, but if and how these features functioned together was unclear. The site is close to the thirteenth-century sluice-gate channel uncovered at the site of St Saviour's priory in the 1980s.[142] A similarly dated watercourse with wooden revetments, running parallel and to the south of Hammond Lane, may also have been part of a mill.[143] Abi Cryerhall suggested that all of this activity may have been part of the same milling complex.[144] Excavations at Phoenixtown to the north of Navan, Co. Meath, exposed a similar sunken central feature surrounded by a shallow trough that indicates the former presence of a horse mill.[145] The features were part of a larger complex of medieval features indicative of a general work area. Phoenixtown was part of the manor of Martry, which was held by the de Say family up to the early fourteenth century and subsequently by the Darcys.[146]

Brewing and baking

Brewing

The process of steeping, boiling and fermenting grain with other ingredients provided an important supply of ale and other alcoholic beverages. Most religious houses had their own breweries and there are references to brew-houses at the priory of Holy Trinity (1327), the hospital at Kilmainham (c.1330) and Christ Church Cathedral (1591).[147] A number of brewers are mentioned in the Dublin guild merchant roll for the period 1190–1265.[148] In c.1306, the city regulations stipulated that no brewer was to brew with straw, and this presumably refers to its use as a fuel rather than as an ingredient in the process.[149] It was probably quite easy for brewers to source straw when they were procuring grain, but it tended to be a fire hazard.

It was common, in many parts of Ireland, for brewing tolls (tollbolls), which usually consisted of a stipulated measure of ale from each brewing, to be granted as a form of revenue to churches. Such tolls are well attested as a form of income enjoyed by ecclesiastics, churches and, occasionally, secular lords in the pre-Anglo-Norman period and in some cases these customary renders were adopted and formalised in the post-invasion period.[150] The nunnery of Gracedieu, Co. Dublin, for example, had the right to a flagon of ale from every brewing at Lusk.[151] This render may have originally been associated with the important early monastery at Lusk. St Thomas' Abbey, Dublin, was granted a valuable toll of ale from every brewing offered for sale in Dublin. This frequently brought the abbey into conflict with the innkeepers and city authorities.[152]

138 *EIMP*, pp 2, 58, 73.   139 *Civil Survey*, 7, pp 61, 170.   140 Cryerhall, 'Excavations at Hammond Lane', pp 32–5. 141 For a discussion on animal power and milling, see Rynne, *Industrial Ireland*, pp 16–23.   142 McMahon, 'Excavations at the site of the Four Courts extension', 271–319.   143 Simpson, 'Arran Quay'.   144 Cryerhall, 'Excavations at Hammond Lane', p. 35.   145 The excavation was carried out as part of the M3 enabling works for the NRA and Meath County Council by Ed Lyne, on behalf of Irish Archaeological Consultancy Ltd.   146 Lyne, 'Phoenixtown: lives through time'.   147 *CSMA*, 2, p. 380; *Reg. Kilmainham*, pp 12, 25, 27, 72; Raymond Gillespie (ed.), *The first chapter act book of Christ Church Cathedral, Dublin, 1574–1634* (Dublin, 1997), pp 54, 69. It is possible that the 1327 and 1591 references are to the same brew-house.   148 *DGMR*, pp 75, 84.   149 *HMDI*, pp 232–5. 150 Flanagan, *Irish royal charters*, pp 93–5.   151 McNeill (ed.), *Alen's register*, p. 180.   152 H.F. Berry, 'Proceedings in

Most noble households would have brewed for their own use, and small-scale brewing was no doubt very common. Inventories or lists of household goods sometimes mention equipment used for brewing. In 1335, the goods and chattels of Robert Bagod, proprietor of the manor of Baggotrath near Dublin, included a large vat with four trundles and other vessels for brewing.[153] Among his grain stores were seven crannocks of undried malted oats. Brewing pans were also mentioned in the inventories of fifteenth-century testators in the Dublin region.[154] The involvement of women in brewing both in the home and professionally was a feature of most medieval towns and Dublin was no exception.[155] Municipal legislation survives forbidding Dublin women from brewing inferior ale and selling it in taverns.[156]

There are indications that brewing declined in Dublin through the Middle Ages. For instance, an arbiter in the 1524 dispute regarding the rights of St Thomas' Abbey to tollboll found that brewers in the time of King John were wont to brew thirty or forty bushels at a time, while now, in 1524, brewers brewed only two, four or eight bushels, and that this ale was consumed, for the most part, at home rather than in taverns.[157] A bushel was equivalent to a gallon and, from 1524 on, the abbot of St Thomas' was to collect tollboll from brewers producing sixteen bushels or more. The mayor was to pay the abbot 10s. per year on behalf of all 'petty' brewers producing less than this. Part of the reason for the decline in brewing may have been the provision of better access to drinking water.

Brewing may have declined, but it was still practised across the region in the seventeenth century. There was a brewery at Thomas Court in 1603, while outside the city, brew-houses operated in most nucleated settlements.[158] In 1654, the Civil Survey recorded one at Little Cabragh (Finglas), one at Lusk (Corduff), which was slated, and one at Swords (Saucerstown), which was built of stone and lime and had a thatched roof.[159]

Baking

Much of the grain brought into the city was used to make bread, a staple in the diet of virtually all citizens. From c.1195 or earlier, the 'city bake-house' was located on Schoolhouse Lane, and it is referred to on a number of occasions from then until the sixteenth century.[160] There were also bake-houses at Dublin Castle, as well as those run by the priory of Holy Trinity and St Patrick's Cathedral.[161] In the sixteenth century, there were further bake-houses at Church Street (in the former St Mary's Chapel) and at Exchange Street Upper.[162] Excavations at Francis Street in 1997 unearthed the remains of a small hearth that may have functioned as part of a bake-oven.[163] In the Coombe, a pit containing charred cereal remains was excavated in 2004 and the excavator felt that it may also have been used for baking in the medieval period.[164]

There were many commercial bakers in the city who supplied hucksters selling in the markets. Not all of the bread consumed in the city was baked *intra-muros*, however, and from 1462 if not earlier, anybody who hindered those delivering fresh bread from outside the city was to be fined 100s.[165] Similar ordinances stipulated that the city bakers were to

the matter of the custom called tollboll, 1308 and 1385: St Thomas Abbey v. some early Dublin brewers etc.', *PRIA*, 28C (1910), 116–73. **153** NAI RC8/18: Memoranda roll, pp 559–64. Printed in translation in Connolly, 'The Irish memoranda rolls', 72. **154** Berry (ed.), *Register of wills and inventories*, pp 34–5, 58–60. **155** See Judith Bennett, *Ale beer and brewsters in England: womens' work in a changing world, 1300–1600* (Oxford, 1996). **156** *CARD*, 1, p. 219. **157** *CARD*, 1, pp 178ff. **158** *CSPI, 1601–3*, p. 574. **159** *Civil Survey*, 7, pp 65, 102, 133. **160** *CCCD*, no. 475; H.F. Berry, 'History of the religious gild of S. Anne, in S. Audoen's Church, Dublin, 1430–1740, taken from its records in the Haliday Collection, RIA', *PRIA*, 25C (1904–5), 21–106 at 65, 80; *CARD*, 2, pp 14, 35. **161** Dublin Castle: *RDKPRI*, 35, p. 29; *RDKPRI*, 36, p. 75; A.T. Robinson, 'The history of Dublin Castle to 1684' (PhD, UCD, 1994), p. 73; Christchurch Place (Holy Trinity): Mills (ed.), *Account roll*, p. 98; St Patrick's Cathedral: James Mills, 'Notices of the manor of St Sepulchre, Dublin, in the fourteenth century', *JRSAI*, 19 (1889), 31–41, 119–26 at 33, 119. **162** Report on the manuscripts of Lord De L'Isle and Dudley preserved at Penshurst Place, 1 (London, 1925), p. 398; *CARD*, 2, p. 90. **163** DEHLG files 96E0349 and 97E0129 (Francis Street; Claire Walsh). **164** McQuade, '105–109, The Coombe'. **165** *CARD*, 1, p. 313.

purchase corn at the city market and nowhere else, on pain of a 20s. fine.[166] Bread and ale were considered the two staples of life and therefore their sale was subject to a much greater degree of regulation than virtually any other commodity. Those dealing in their sale and manufacture had to comply with standard weights and measures on pain of fine or punishment.[167] In 1224, reference was made to bakers of the archbishop's land who were convicted of selling false – presumably underweight – bread in the city market.[168]

As so little rye appears to have been grown in Dublin's hinterland, it can be assumed that most bread baked in the city and region was made from wheaten flour. It is clear, however, that different grades of bread were available, based on the degree of processing of the wheat flour and the proportion of bran that was extracted. The finest of all breads, made from virtually white flour and used by the royal and great households was known as *pain-demain*.[169] This was being produced by some Dublin bakers in the middle of the fourteenth century, when it was purchased by the prior of Holy Trinity.[170] The corrodians who were fed at the hospital in Kilmainham received bread of four different types depending on their wealth and status.[171] The best quality white bread, 'such as is served to the prior', was reserved for the grandest recipients; next in quality came the white loaves, 'such as were served to the brethren'; and then 'brown loaves', which appear to have been eaten by the servants, and 'trencher loaves', given with hot dishes to act as plates.

Chapter summary

Most of the grain grown in the Dublin region was dried in keyhole-shape kilns before being ground in one of the water-powered mills on the region's major rivers and their tributaries. There were some wind-powered and horse-powered mills in the region, but these were in the minority. Mills were built and controlled by manorial lords and in the Dublin hinterland these included royal, ecclesiastical and lay owners. Mills were expensive to build and maintain but the potential profits rendered the expenditure worthwhile. The scale of milling in the region probably reached a peak *c*.1285–1315, and exports to feed the king's armies in Scotland would certainly have provided a boost to those involved in the process. The Dublin region at this date was so noted for its milling capacity that grain was sent here from Scotland to be processed. It seems that there was a prolonged downturn from the middle of the fourteenth century onwards, however, and this is observable in both the documentary and the archaeological record.

The primary use of grain in the city and countryside was in bread-making. Most bread appears to have been baked using wheat flour, but it is clear that there was a range of different grades of bread available. Small quantities of wheat were malted and brewed into ale, but oats were most commonly processed in this manner. It was not until the fifteenth century that barley malt and ale started to appear with any frequency. Ale was widely consumed, particularly in the religious houses and hospitals. Some religious houses had their grain malted at their manor centres, and then brought into the central household for brewing; other houses combined malting and brewing at one location. Both tasks were frequently carried out by women. The scale of brewing declined sharply over the fourteenth and fifteenth centuries, partly due to falling population levels but also perhaps because of the improved supply of clean drinking water.

---

166 *CARD*, i, pp 219ff.   **167** *HMDI*, p. 162.   **168** *HMDI*, p. 82.   **169** See C.M. Woolgar, *The great household in late medieval England* (New Haven and London, 1999), p. 124.   **170** Mills (ed.), *Account roll*, p. 96.   **171** McNeill, 'Hospitallers'; Murphy and Potterton, 'Investigating living standards', p. 242.

CHAPTER 15

The processing of animal products

Dairying

The Dublin region was well endowed with pasture land and the documentary and archaeological sources indicate that there were large numbers of cows, sheep and goats present throughout the medieval period.[1] There is, however, very little evidence of any type; for the processing of milk into butter and cheese, for purpose-built dairies, employment of specialised dairymen or maids or equipment used in these processes. What evidence there is for dairying in the region comes from the consumption end of the process.

In medieval England, dairy products were important in monastic diets and in the diets of children and poorer consumers. Chris Dyer's research on the changing diet of harvest workers shows a decline in the importance of dairy products as living standards and meat consumption rose.[2] In her study of the diet of the monks of Westminster Abbey, Barbara Harvey found that dairy produce was an important part of the monastic diet.[3] Except during Lent, all monks probably had cheese at dinner and many had more again at supper. Milk was also drunk at the rate of about half a pint a day per capita and butter was used in cooking.

With a couple of exceptions, the accounts for Holy Trinity in Dublin do not itemise purchases of dairy products. A small amount of butter and cheese was purchased for the prior when he was visiting Drogheda in c.1339, while in c.1343 the seneschal accounted for five cheeses bought and sent in various directions by command of the prior.[4] These cheeses cost just over 6d. each, which suggests that they were fairly substantial. It seems likely that the priory received dairy products from its granges or in the form of tithes and rents in kind. In 1483, the priory leased various issues of the church of St David near Arklow for a money rent and 'eight gallons of good butter in the first year and ten gallons of good butter thereafter'.[5]

In 1308, the inquisition into the Templar manor of Clontarf listed four stone of cheese, valued at 5d. per stone.[6] It is not clear whether this was cows' or ewes' cheese, as both of these animals were found on the manor. In England, the milking of sheep and production of sheep's cheese was widespread.[7] There are no references to the production of ewes' milk and cheese in the Dublin region, but it almost certainly occurred. Sheep were milked and cheeses made on the earl of Norfolk's manors at Ballysax, Forth and Old Ross in the 1280s and it was stated that the milk produced by ten ewes was equal in value to that produced by one cow.[8] In 1282, the supplies sent from Dublin to the household of the earl marshal then

---

1 See above, pp 332–9.   2 Christopher Dyer, *Standards of living in the later Middle Ages: social change in England*, *c.1200–1520* (Cambridge, 1989), pp 157–60.   3 Harvey, *Living and dying in England*, pp 61–2.   4 Mills (ed.), *Account roll*, pp 2, 41.   5 *CCCD*, no. 1045.   6 Mac Niocaill, 'Suppression of the Templars', 215.   7 Campbell, *Seigniorial agriculture*, p. 154; Grant, 'Animal resources', pp 154–5.   8 TNA:PRO SC6/1237/49 and 55; this is close to the figure of 12 ewes to 1 cow cited by Trow-Smith (*British livestock husbandry*, pp 121–2).

Figure 15.1 This sketch by
Thomas Dineley (c.1680)
shows a woman milking a cow
with its feet tethered together
(image courtesy of the
National Library of Ireland).

on campaign in Wales included forty-two stone of cheese.[9] Thirty stone was provided by the
earl's manors at Ballysax (Co. Kildare) and Old Ross (Co. Wexford) and twelve stone was
purchased in Dublin.

There is evidence to suggest that the southern part of the Dublin region was associated
with dairying (for example, the reference to butter from Arklow mentioned above), and
indeed on the manor of Ballymore, 31 per cent of the land in 1300 was devoted to pasture
and a further 8 per cent to woodland park (Table 9.1). Furthermore, in the early seventeenth-
century account of the riding of the franchises of Dublin, there is mention of the Butter
Cross, where it was said 'in ould tyme the provision of butter that came from the marches
and Tooles' country to Dublin was sold'.[10] According to another seventeenth-century
reference, butter was brought into the city in pails or buckets.[11]

Wool and cloth

Most of the evidence relating to wool in the region is concerned with its trade and export and
is covered below. As has been seen above (Chapter 9), sheep were fairly ubiquitous throughout
the region, both in large seigneurial flocks and on smallholdings. While Dublin does not
appear to have been a major exporter of wool, there is enough evidence to suggest that it was
an important commodity in the economic life of the region. Most of the evidence relating
to the processing of cloth within the region is fairly indirect and unspecific as to location.

9 *CDI, 1252–84*, no. 2009, p. 459.   10 *CARD*, 1, p. 193. Although the location of Butter Cross is not known, Butter
Lane is now Bishop Street (Clarke, *IHTA: Dublin Part I, to 1610*, p. 13).   11 *CARD*, 1, p. 262.

Figure 15.2 Iron shears found during excavations at High Street, Dublin (image courtesy of the National Museum of Ireland).

One of the few references to the shearing of sheep within the region comes from the manor of Clonkeen, where, in 1344–5, the bailiff sold 14¾ stones of sheep's wool and three stones of lambs' wool.[12] The sheep's wool was the product of two shearings, one in May and one in November, while the lambs were shorn in late June. It is not clear whether the same sheep were shorn twice – which appears unlikely – or a different group of sheep were shorn each six months. Shearing, undertaken with hand shears, was a labour-intensive task. Several shears from the Dublin region are held by the National Museum of Ireland (Figure 15.2).[13] Others have been recovered on archaeological excavations in the area.[14]

The markets for Irish wool were predominantly the great cloth manufacturing centres of Flanders, where it was used for making less expensive cloth.[15] The production of fine quality cloth required superior yarn from sheep with silky fleeces. There is considerable evidence to suggest that Irish fleeces in the medieval period were not considered suitable for this type of processing. A Flemish drapery regulation from Bruges in the year 1282 stated that cloth made from English wool was to be marked with three crosses, from Scottish wool with two crosses and from Irish wool with one cross (local Flemish wool merited only half a cross).[16]

Further evidence confirms the inferiority of Irish wool. There is reference to a complaint in 1276 by Irish merchants that the king's collectors of the custom on wool were charging them 10s. for each sack, whereas sacks of English wool were only charged at 6s. 8d.[17] This discrepancy was because the Irish sack was bigger but as the Irish merchants pointed out, the English sack *though of less weight is of equal value*. The complaint was accepted and the custom on Irish sacks was thereafter to be 6s. 8d. In 1356, a shipment of about fifty sacks of Irish wool remained unsold at the English ports of Plymouth and Dartmouth, as 'merchants refused to buy it because of its poor quality'.[18] As the factors that produce better quality wool also produce heavier fleeces, it is plausible that Irish fleeces were also lighter than many English ones. Fleeces from Wales and the West Midlands were somewhat lighter (about 1.1 to 1.2lbs) and they may have come from a smaller and rather more primitive type of sheep.[19] Sheep in medieval Ireland may have been more similar to this type than to those found in the Midlands and south of England.

The production of cloth necessitated spinning and weaving, and this was done manually. Weaving was a common occupation among the members of Dublin guild merchant in the period 1190–1265,[20] and there were several 'challoners' (makers of hangings, rugs and coverlets that were woven on a chalon loom).[21] A 'burel-maker' (the maker of a

12 Mills (ed.), *Account roll*, p. 56.   **13** NMI R2368 (RIA reg., 1 (1859–83)); NMI 1887:115 (RIA reg., 2 (1886–1928)); NMI 1917:90 (RIA reg., 2 (1886–1928)); NMI Wk39 (Wakeman reg., 1, p. 130); NMI E191:413 (Ray Collection). **14** Alan Hayden and Claire Walsh, 'Small finds' in Walsh (ed.), *Archaeological excavations at Patrick, Nicholas and Winetavern Streets* (1997), pp 132–44 at pp 138–9; DEHLG file E000132 (Wood Quay; Patrick Wallace); DEHLG file E000162 (Nevinstown, Co. Meath; Mary Cahill); Mary Cahill, 'Nevinstown' in *Excavations 1977–9*, p. 76.   **15** O'Neill, *Merchants and mariners*, p. 59.   **16** J.H.A. Munro, *Wool, cloth and gold; the struggle for bullion in Anglo-Burgundian trade, 1340–1478* (Toronto, 1972), pp 2–3, quoted by O'Neill (*Merchants and mariners*, p. 59).   **17** *CDI, 1252–84*, no. 1305, p. 243.   **18** *CPR, 1354–8*, p. 405.   **19** Trow-Smith, *British livestock husbandry*, p. 167.   **20** *DGMR*, pp 20, 27, 34, 36, 37, 43, 48, 57, 71, 72, 74, 75, 79, 81, 82, 90, 92, 94, 96, 109, 115.   **21** *DGMR*, pp 49, 53, 65, 66, 75, 96.

Figure 15.3 Weaver's sword of yew, from High Street, Dublin (after Ó Ríordáin, 'Excavations at High Street', p. 80, fig. 22).

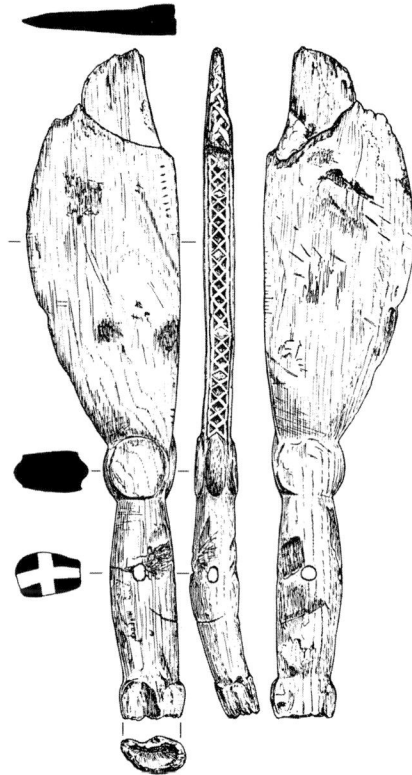

cheap cloth of poor quality wool) appears in 1229, as well as a spindle-maker, who presumably supplied the town's spinners.[22] Spindle whorls, which were used for spinning thread, have been found on a number of medieval excavations in the Dublin region, including Cornmarket, Nicholas Street and Winetavern Street (all Dublin city), Dalkey and Castleknock, Co. Dublin, and Tullykane, Co. Meath.[23] The Tullykane example may be of late twelfth-century date, and its relatively light weight suggests that it might have 'been used to spin flax fibre or wool fibres of a shorter length'.[24] A possible loom dog was also recovered from early thirteenth-century levels at Winetavern Street.[25] Among the weaving equipment that has come to light are a bone weaving-comb from Glassamucky Brakes, a weaver's sword of yew from near Christ Church Cathedral, and a 'weaver's smoothing bone' from St Audoen's.[26]

The maximum charges for the various processes in cloth production were fixed by the municipality of Dublin in the early fourteenth century. Carding wool was priced at 1*d.* per stone, weaving 300 ells of cloth of one colour at 16*d.*, and weaving fine red cloth at ¾*d.* per ell. Fulling thirty ells cost 3*s.*, while fullers were paid 2*d.* a day.[27]

There is evidence that by the thirteenth century the manufacture of woollen cloth was expanding within Ireland.[28] The mechanisation of fulling with the introduction of the water-powered fulling mill was a key element in this process. Fulling was a process whereby newly woven woollen cloth was treated in order to give it greater density and a softer finish.[29] Until the appearance of the fulling mill in the later medieval period, fulling took place in large tubs or vats where cloth was trampled in an alkaline liquor containing fuller's earth, vegetable ash or stale human urine. The fulling mill replaced the action of stamping feet by the beating action of swinging wooden hammers. Fulling mills were introduced into England in the latter part of the twelfth century and two such mills appear in a survey of land belonging to the Knights Templars in 1185.[30] Research in Britain has found a concentration of early fulling mills in south Wales, an area with which many of the people who settled in Ireland in the late twelfth and thirteenth century had strong links.[31] Fulling is referred to in the pipe roll of 1211–12, but it is not clear whether the activity is being carried

22 *DGMR*, pp 60, 86. **23** DEHLG file 92E0109 (Cornmarket/Bridge Street Upper); Halpin, *The port of medieval Dublin*, p. 162; Hayden and Walsh, 'Small finds [Patrick, Nicholas and Winetavern Streets]', pp 142–3; Alan Hayden, 'Stone objects' in Walsh, *Archaeological excavations at Patrick, Nicholas and Winetavern Streets* (1997), pp 156–8; Kavanagh, '62 Castle St., Dalkey'; Campbell, 'Castleknock'; Baker, 'Tullykane', pp 5, 15–16 (appendix by Maria Fitzgerald). **24** Baker, 'Tullykane', p. 15. **25** O'Sullivan and Deevy, 'Wooden artefacts', pp 164–5 (fig. 82), 166. **26** NMI annual reg. 1944:535; Bradley and King, 'UAS 8:4: County Dublin', p. 338 (Glassamucky Brakes); RIA reg., 2 (1886–1928): 1887:143, Wk393 B5:25 indexed (Christ Church); SA 28:1900 (St Audoen's). **27** O'Neill, *Merchants and mariners*, p. 66, citing Mac Niocaill, *Na buirgéisí*, 2, p. 380. An ell is a unit of length equating to about 1.14m, used mainly for measuring cloth. **28** Rynne, *Technological change*, p. 85. **29** A.T. Lucas, 'Cloth finishing in Ireland', *Folk Life: Journal of the Society for Folk Life Studies*, 11 (1968), 18–68; Rynne, *Technological change*, pp 85–6. **30** E.M. Carus-Wilson, 'An industrial revolution of the thirteenth century' in E.M. Carus Wilson (ed.), *Essays in economic history* (London, 1954), pp 41–60 at pp 45–6. **31** Langdon, *Mills in the medieval economy*, p. 3, quoting R.A. Pelham, *Fulling mills: a study in the application of water power to the woollen industry* (London, 1958), esp. pl. iv.

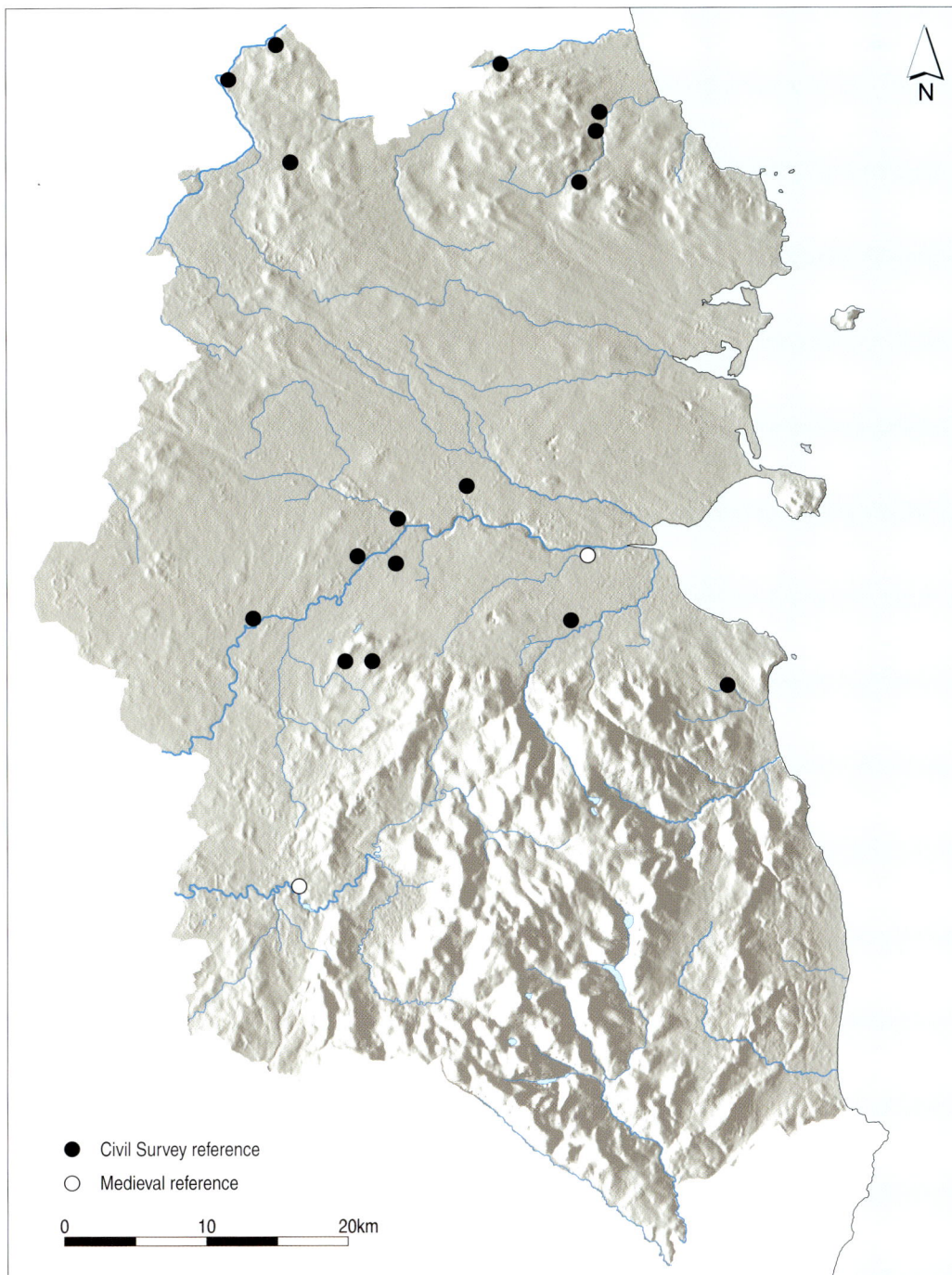

Figure 15.4 Fulling mills in the Dublin region. No Civil Survey data is available for the southern part of the region.

out in a mill.[32] Indirect evidence for fulling mills comes from the existence of specialised fullers in the documentary sources. Several individuals with the occupation of fuller appear in the Dublin guild merchant roll (1190–1265), and their toponymics identify them as coming from Kilmainham and Dundalk in Ireland, and Lincoln and Stamford in England.[33] Fulled cloth has been recovered on excavations of thirteenth-century levels in Dublin, and if this was manufactured in the city it probably indicates the presence of horizontal looms, which had come into general use by this time.[34]

There is a mention of a fulling mill in 1276–7 in an extent of the lands which Henry de Barbedor held from the archbishop of Dublin in the manor of Ballymore Eustace.[35] Henry

32 Davies and Quinn, 'Irish pipe roll of 14 John', 52–3. **33** *DGMR*, pp 2, 21, 23, 32, 47, 53, 65, 71, 76, 77, 81, 91, 119. **34** Elizabeth Wincott Heckett, 'Textiles, cordage, basketry and raw fibre' in Hurley et al., *Late Viking-Age and medieval Waterford* (1997), pp 743–60 at p. 749. **35** TNA:PRO C133/16.

held lands at Ardinode and had a fulling mill there – two parts of which brought in a rent of 6s. A more valuable mill is recorded in 1279–80, when the Irish exchequer accounted for receipt of 40s. rent for a fulling mill in Louth paid by 'Thomas the fuller'.[36] It is likely that at sites where several mills are recorded, one of these was a fulling mill. James Lydon believed that one of the three mills at Ardee was used for fulling, while the other mills dealt with corn and malt.[37] There is a reference to a fulling mill owned by the hospital of Kilmainham in 1540.[38] It was on the River Camac and was leased by Richard Rawson of Bristol, who paid 40s. per annum for it. Despite the fact that many of the watercourses in the Dublin region would have been conducive to the operation of fulling mills in the Middle Ages, none has yet been identified archaeologically.

By the mid-seventeenth century, fulling mills, or 'tuck mills' as they are also known, are more evident (Figure 15.4). The Civil Survey records sixteen tuck/fulling mills in the Dublin region. In Meath, there were examples in the parishes of Templekeeran (fulling mill), Stamullin (two tuck mills, one of which was associated with a corn mill), Duleek, Athlumney (with a water mill) and Ardmulchan, while in Dublin there were tuck mills at the Naul ('one corne mill & one tuck mill in use worth fifteen pounds, [the] buildings are valued by ye jury at 200 pounds'), Chapelizod, Clonsilla ('one corne mill and a tuck mill both in use worth anno 1640 twenty pounds p ann') and Rathmichael (one tuck mill and one corn mill).[39] A tuck mill at Templeogue and one on the lands of St Wolstan's in Co. Kildare are also recorded.[40] They also note that on the branch of the Dodder between Rathfarnham and Ringsend there 'stood many corn and tuck mills which have been ruinated by the late warr but some of them have been lately repaired'. The former presence of tuck mills is demonstrated in the place-names Tuckmill Upper, Tuckmill Lower and Tuckmill Hill in Co. Wicklow, and in Tuckmilltown in Co. Kildare.

The increased numbers by the 1650s demonstrates a pattern of development in the Dublin region from the late 1200s, and it is evident that the Liffey Valley became a focus for fulling activities. The pattern of medieval land-use described in Figure 9.1 indicates that pastoral activities were of greater importance on manors along the Liffey Valley. Grain milling exploited the same water channels, but the discrete distribution of fulling mills may suggest the emergence of areas of specialisation where the comparative advantages of the local terrain helped to secure the direction of economic energy into the early modern period. Even for the later period, the archaeological imprint is small; in describing developments since the eighteenth century, Colin Rynne suggests that the fulling machinery would be housed in the same building as a grain mill, and might even share the same water-wheel.[41]

Tanning and leatherworking

The conversion of animal skins and hides into leather was, for a number of reasons, primarily a suburban industry, but the three main commodities that this process required – animal skins, water and (oak) bark – all originated in the surrounding countryside.[42] Tanning involved various processes, most of which required water and all of which were malodorous – hence the location of tanneries away from centres of population. Firstly, the hides were washed and then they were left to sit long enough for the hair follicles to rot and loosen. This process could be catalysed by the addition of urine, ash or lime. Once the hair had been loosened and scraped away, and both sides of the hide were smooth, the lime

36 CDI, 1252–84, no. 1740, p. 359.   37 Lydon, 'The mills at Ardee', p. 260.   38 EIMP, p. 82.   39 Civil Survey, 5, pp 11, 12, 18, 60, 62, 64; Civil Survey, 7, pp 32, 223, 231, 276.   40 Civil Survey, 7, p. 289; Civil Survey, 8, p. 19.   41 Rynne, Industrial Ireland, p. 221.   42 John Cherry, 'Leather' in Blair and Ramsay (eds), English medieval industries (1991), pp 295–318 at p. 301.

Figure 15.5 Possible tanning pit excavated on Patrick Street, Dublin (image courtesy of Claire Walsh).

would be removed and the hide softened by being immersed in a vat of bird dung, dog excrement, urine or stale beer. The hide would be washed once more before being placed and regularly agitated in a pit of weak tanning liquor and finally being left for up to a year or more in a pit containing vegetable remains such as oak bark or wood chips, and water.

The frequency with which the occupational designation of 'tanner' is encountered in the documentary sources from the late twelfth century onwards is a measure of the importance of the process in the region. Many tanners are listed in the Dublin guild merchant roll for *c*.1190–1265 and in the Dublin franchise roll for 1468–1512.[43] In most cases in the guild merchant roll, the tanner's name includes reference to where he originated, and a wide geographical spread is evident. Places in the Dublin region referred to are Carbury, Clane, Clonard, Naas and Ratoath, while places further afield include Adare, Ardee, Castledermot, Dundalk, Ferns, Kilkenny, Louth, Mullingar and Slane. It is likely that some of these men carried out their trade as tanners in their home towns and became members of the Dublin guild merchant in order to trade there. Many tanners from overseas appear to have settled in Dublin in the first half of the thirteenth century. Tanners from England came from Birmingham, Bristol, Cornwall, Gloucester, Keynsham, Kidderminster, Leighton, Lincoln, London, Nottingham, Pontefract, Shrewsbury, Warwick and Worcestershire, while *Willelmus de Fontenay Tannator* was almost certainly originally from Fontenay-le-Comte in France, and *Johannes de Cally Tannator* may have been from Calais in Normandy. The presence of two whit-tawyers in the guild merchant indicates that this process, whereby hides were tanned with alum to produce a white leather, was also undertaken in the Dublin area.[44] Many of these tanners would have operated in suburban areas around Dublin, like their fourteenth-century equivalent William Brown, a tanner who was based 'in the suburbs of Dublin in the street of St George' in 1330.[45] In 1305, Adam le Tanner of Naas was involved

43 *DGMR*, pp 10–12, 16, 21, 23, 26, 29, 30, 36–8, 40, 42, 45, 46, 48, 50, 51, 54, 56, 58, 61, 62, 65–7, 69–70, 76, 77, 79, 80, 82, 86, 87, 90, 91, 93–4, 96, 98, 101, 103, 108, 109, 114–19; *DCFR*, pp 5, 6, 16, 20, 22, 26, 32, 34, 36, 38, 40, 43, 45, 46, 48, 51, 56, 57, 61. **44** *DGMR*, pp 52, 77. **45** Smyly, 'Old Latin deeds II', 15.

in a court case relating to unlawful activities at the market there.[46] The tanners of Dublin were significant enough by 1289 to be granted their own charter.[47]

The archaeological evidence for medieval tanning in and around Dublin is relatively meagre. The sites where tanning was indicated include Back Lane and Digges Lane (formerly Goat Lane), near St Luke's Church on the Coombe Relief Road, New Row South, Thomas Street and Fumbally Lane.[48] A series of tanneries of late seventeenth-century date and later were excavated at Old Kilmainham.[49] Excavations on Patrick Street revealed an oak-stave-lined tanning pit that seems to have been part of a larger, thirteenth-century tanning complex on the banks of the Poddle (Figure 15.5).[50] The pit contained barrel staves, cattle horn cores and a substance that may have been lime, while five small wooden barrels recovered near the pit contained horn cores, wood chips and bark which were 'very likely residue from the tanning process'. Because skins and hides most frequently became available as a by-product of meat consumption, they were supplied to tanners by butchers, who left horns and hooves attached. The tanner would remove these, and so the discovery of a preponderance of horns or hooves on an archaeological site can be a good indication of the former presence of a tannery.[51] The small size of the barrels at Patrick Street (90–110cm in diameter) suggests that they were used in the preparation of skins rather than hides (the skins of larger animals such as cattle and horse are generally referred to as hides, while those of smaller animals such as sheep, goats, calves and dogs are referred to as skins).[52] There is some documentary evidence for the presence on Patrick Street of tanneries in the fifteenth and early seventeenth centuries.[53] It appears that this area of suburban Dublin, close to the River Poddle, was a focus for the tanning industry over a period of several centuries.

Excavations at the Coombe in 2004 revealed several pits containing organic waste, two of which had wooden barrels at their base.[54] These pits seem to have been used for tanning, while nearby, two circular pits and a stone-lined pit contained basal fills of lime. A strong smell of urea from one of these suggested that it may have been used for soaking hides. A later pit at this location contained some cattle horn cores, hinting that tanning may have continued here, albeit on a smaller scale. A hearth, two post-holes, a rubbish pit and several soaking pits were excavated nearby, and leather fragments and the soles from three shoes were found.

On New Street South, near the banks of the Poddle in Dublin, a tannery was discovered that had been in use from the medieval period up to the seventeenth century.[55] The street immediately behind the site is called Blackpitts, and this name almost certainly derives from the pits or vats of dark tanning liquor in which the hides would have been steeped. The site consisted primarily of almost 200 unlined circular and rectangular pits, half of which were medieval, and the other half were of seventeenth-century date (although there was no physical difference between the earlier and later pits). Many of them contained dark, organic fills with bark chips, twigs, nutshells and other vegetation, smelling strongly of ammonia. The pits were connected to the Poddle by a series of drains and channels. A large ditch

46 *CJR, 1305–7*, p. 149.   47 O'Rourke, 'Leather finds [from Patrick, Nicholas and Winetavern Streets]', p. 163; J.J. Webb, *The guilds of Dublin* (Dublin, 1929), p. 4.   48 Turrell, 'Archaeozoology of medieval Dublin', pp 43–4; DEHLG files 01E0614/93E0066 (Coombe Relief Road/St Luke's Church); 96E0342 (New Row South; Georgina Scally); 95E0110 and 95E0110ext (Frawley's: Thomas Street (rere); Margaret Gowen); 00E0253 (Fumbally Lane; Georgina Scally). 49 Alan Hayden, 'Old Kilmainham, Dublin' in *Excavations 2004*, p. 129.   50 Walsh, *Archaeological excavations at Patrick, Nicholas and Winetavern Streets*, pp 39–41; DEHLG file 93E0173 (St Patrick's Street; Eoin Halpin).   51 Dale Serjeantson, 'Animal remains and the tanning trade' in Serjeantson and Waldron (eds), *Diet and crafts in towns* (1989), pp 129–46 at pp 136–7, 139.   52 Serjeantson, 'Animal remains and the tanning trade', p. 129.   53 Mason, *The cathedral church of St Patrick*, p. 141; James Morrin (ed.), *Calendar of the patent and close rolls of chancery in Ireland, from the 18th to the 45th of Queen Elizabeth* (Dublin, 1862), p. 622.   54 McQuade, '105–109 The Coombe'.   55 Antoine Giacometti, '48 New Street South, Dublin' in *Excavations 2004*, pp 127–8.

found here may once have served to divert water from the river to the tannery, but it had filled up by the seventeenth century. According to the excavator, a series of later pits on the site may have functioned as 'layaway pits for the cleaning of the hides before and/or after the tanning process'.

The rectangular pit which was uncovered during excavations at Ship Street Little was over 1.8m in length and would certainly have been large enough to process hides.[56] The pit was found in association with three wooden barrels and foul-smelling deposits containing lime and wood chips, all of which indicate tanning. There is documentary evidence for tanning in the area in the fifteenth century. In July 1485, John Warynge, parson of Mulhuddart, was granted 'a messuage and tan-house with a bawn and haggard place without the Pole gate in St Bride's parish'.[57] Further evidence for tanning in various periods has been revealed in the vicinity of this site.[58]

Documentary evidence indicates that Oxmantown, which formed the northern suburb of Dublin, was also a centre of tanning in the medieval period. In c.1195, a grant of land in this northern suburb was made to a certain Richard, the tanner.[59] Purcell has deduced that the property granted to Richard was probably next to the river, which would have been suitable for a tanner, and that one of his new neighbours was also a tanner. The site must also have been relatively close to the dung pits and limekiln near Oxmantown Green, and this would also have facilitated anyone involved in the tanning industry.[60] Purcell has also shown that 'a large number of tenants with cattle- or farming-related occupations' held land in this area, as well as leatherworkers and saddlers.[61]

There are fewer indications of tanning in rural areas, although evidence from England suggests that tanners operated in some villages and forest areas.[62] It is possible that tanning, like ironworking, was carried out as a part-time activity by rural dwellers. William Neill of Clondalkin, who made his will in 1471, had eighteen acres of land sown with wheat, oats and barley as well as an assortment of stock. His principal asset, however, was a tan-house worth twenty marks.[63] He was owed money by a variety of individuals from Co. Dublin – Kilmainham, Clondalkin, Ballyfermot, Lucan, Saggart, Newcastle and Rathcoole. Some of these individuals bear the surname 'Corviser', perhaps indicating they were shoemakers or general leatherworkers who obtained tanned leather from Neill.

During the 1970s excavations at High Street and Winetavern Street, 'an abundance of worked leather ascribable ... to the late twelfth and early thirteenth centuries' was found.[64] Cattle hides and, to a lesser extent, goat skins had been used to make knife-sheaths and, particularly, footwear. Excavations at Merchants Quay Ward/New Row South uncovered leather off-cuts and a small quantity of leather soles of post-fourteenth-century date.[65] The proximity of the site to the Poddle and Coombe Rivers, together with the discovery of medieval tanning pits in the vicinity, suggests that this may have been an industrial area associated with leatherworking. Assemblages of medieval leather objects, mostly dominated by shoes, but also including belts, sheaths and straps, have been recovered on a range of sites in Dublin and its region.[66] The thirteenth-century leather assemblage from Winetavern

56 Simpson, 'Excavations on the southern side', pp 18, 30–4, 39–42, 43.   **57** *CCCD*, no. 348, p. 99.   **58** DEHLG file 97E0161 (Ship Street Little/Ship Street Great: Osmond House; Margaret Gowen); DEHLG file 92E0207 (Little Ship Street; Georgina Scally).   **59** Purcell, 'Land-use in medieval Oxmantown', pp 201–2, referring to *CCCD*, no. 475, p. 125.   **60** Purcell, 'Land-use in medieval Oxmantown', pp 217, 224.   **61** Ibid., pp 223–4.   **62** Cherry, 'Leather', p. 301. **63** Berry (ed.), *Register of wills and inventories*, pp 94–8.   **64** Ó Ríordáin, 'Excavations at High Street and Winetavern Street', 75.   **65** DEHLG file 96E0342 (New Row South).   **66** Dáire O'Rourke, 'Leather' in Hayden, 'Arran Quay' (2004), pp 211–17; Dáire O'Rourke, 'The leather finds' in Halpin, *The port of medieval Dublin* (2000), pp 143–58; O'Rourke, 'Leather finds [from Patrick, Nicholas and Winetavern Streets]'; Catherine Johnson, 'The small finds' in Edmond O'Donovan, 'The growth and decline of a medieval suburb? Evidence from excavations at Thomas Street, Dublin' in Duffy (ed.), *Medieval Dublin IV* (2003), pp 154–63 at p. 158; Helen Kehoe, '24–28 St Mary's Abbey' in

Street was dominated by items made from bovine hides, but sheepskins (7 per cent), goatskins (1 per cent) and deerskins (8 per cent) were also used.[67] The bovine to caprovine ratio from these excavations is very similar to that from Patrick, Nicholas and Winetavern Streets,[68] and this may reflect the dominance of cattle-rearing the city's hinterland.

Further evidence for the preparation of hides and skins is present in the roll of the Dublin guild merchant, which included among its members leather carvers, a leather dresser, scabbard makers and saddlers.[69] Simon 'le curier' was almost certainly involved in 'finishing' the leather.[70] The first reference to a company of shoemakers in Dublin appears in 1427, when the guild of shoemakers was granted a royal charter.[71] There had, of course, been an important shoemaking industry in Dublin for many generations before that, however, and John Hamound, who died in 1388, ran what was evidently a large business.[72] On his death, he had a number of skins and hides in stock, as well as 116 pairs of shoes. He was owed money by twenty-two individuals for boots and shoes and he must also have been a supplier to larger dealers, as one person owed him for thirty pairs of shoes, and another for 168 pairs. There is evidence for a trade in hides beyond the markets of Dublin and, for instance, when Christopher Plunkett of Dunsany, Co. Meath, died in 1462, he owed two marks to one Awly O'Doffermoth for an undisclosed number of hides.[73] The wills of two overseas merchants (one of whom was from Coventry and died in Dublin in the second half of the fifteenth

Excavations 2003, p. 141; Helen Keogh, 'St Mary's Abbey/Strand Street Little, Dublin' in *Excavations 2004*, pp 136–7; Cotter, 'Dunboyne Castle, Castlefarm'; Cryerhall, 'Excavations at Hammond Lane', pp 40–3; Claire Walsh, 'Chancery Lane, Dublin' in *Excavations 2003*, p. 125; Turrell, '32 Cook Street'; McQuade, '105–109 The Coombe'; DEHLG file 96E0280 (Thomas Street); DEHLG file 96E0300 (Back Lane/Lamb Alley); DEHLG file 92E0109 (Cornmarket/Bridge Street Upper); Dáire O'Rourke, 'The leather finds from the Dublin Castle excavations' (forthcoming); Dáire O'Rourke, 'The leather finds from High St., Dublin' (forthcoming). **67** O'Rourke, 'The leather finds [port of medieval Dublin]', p. 152. **68** O'Rourke, 'Leather finds [from Patrick, Nicholas and Winetavern Streets]', p. 164. **69** *DGMR*, pp 1, 5, 7–9, 11, 15, 17, 18, 27, 30, 40, 52, 54, 57, 73, 95, 96, 99, 102, 107, 111, 113, 117. **70** O'Rourke, 'Leather finds [from Patrick, Nicholas and Winetavern Streets]', p. 163. **71** Ibid., p. 165; Webb, *The guilds of Dublin*, p. 63. **72** O'Neill, *Merchants and mariners*, p. 82. **73** *Cal. Carew MSS, Howth*, p. 358.

century), mention quantities of lambskins, goatskins and sheepskins, suggesting that the men were involved in the export of these commodities from Dublin.[74]

Chapter summary

Milk, butter and cheese formed important dietary components in the medieval period, but evidence for the processing and sale of dairy products in the Dublin region is very sparse. Religious houses appear to have received butter and perhaps cheese in the form of tithes or rents in kind. The pastoral lands in the south of the region were the main source of dairy products and, in the later medieval period, trade in butter was associated with the Irish and their lands.

Wool and hides were important commodities in the economic life of the region. Irish wool was considered to be of low quality, but it was still much in demand in the cloth-manufacturing centres of Flanders. Hides were also exported to the markets of continental Europe. Cloth was produced in the Dublin region and the regulation of prices for various cloth production processes indicates that it was a fairly widespread occupation. There are references to fulling and fulling mills, although no such mill has yet been identified archaeologically. Tanners operated in the suburbs of Dublin, particularly in Oxmantown, where they lived alongside butchers, leatherworkers and saddlers. There are fewer indications of tanning in rural areas, but some country dwellers profitably combined tanning with farming.

In contrast to the processing of grain, which was usually under seigneurial control and frequently a fairly large-scale operation, the processing of livestock products was smaller scale, local and sometimes combined with other occupations. As such, it had more in common with the products whose processing is examined in the next chapter.

---

74 Berry (ed.), *Register of wills and inventories*, pp 8–11, 15–18.

CHAPTER 16

The importation and processing of natural resources

Metal

Iron

Iron was an indispensable commodity for the inhabitants of the medieval Dublin region. It was needed for the building and maintenance of castles, houses and ships and it was the raw material from which smiths and other craftsmen made a great variety of tools, implements, bolts, nails, horseshoes, arms and armour. The purchases listed in the account roll of the Augustinian priory of Holy Trinity give a good indication of the variety of uses to which iron was put on a medieval farm. Iron for the repair and manufacture of ploughs and cartwheels constituted a major expenditure.[1] Implements such as iron-tipped spades, an axe, and an iron fork 'for lifting sheaves' were also purchased, while a hammer 'for breaking stones' was repaired.[2] Nails of different sizes were bought for various building and repair jobs, including for making the prior's coffin.[3] Other items included a bucket and chain for the well, locks and keys, window hooks, horseshoes, stirrups and spurs.[4]

Iron was one of the staple Irish imports, frequently coming into the country along with cargoes of salt in great ships from Brittany and Spain.[5] A fourteenth-century statute regarding the export of raw iron from England shows that it also came in from English ports.[6] Some of the iron purchased by the priory of Holy Trinity came from Spain, and most of it is described as being bought in pieces or 'bends'.[7] In the fifteenth century, Dublin authorities attempted to control the sale of iron by legislating in 1454 and 1458 that iron brought by foreigners to the city was to be first offered for sale to one of the 'four buyers of the city'.[8] In 1455/6, mention is made of customs payable on ships containing iron.[9] Colin Rynne assumed that imported iron 'was extensively traded within the hinterland of Munster's ports'.[10] The same is likely to have been true of the hinterland of Dublin.

Despite the fact that much iron was imported, there was also a strong tradition of mining, smelting and forging iron throughout medieval Ireland, with bog ore and rock-based ores being exploited. Haematite and siderite ores are known in the Dublin region, in the area of Rush and Lusk north of the Liffey, and more especially in the Wicklow Mountains.[11] The evidence for medieval mining is hardly visible today, however, due to the continued activities of ironworkers in the seventeenth century and later, and the extraction of peat from the bogs.[12] In contrast, the work of the blacksmith seems ubiquitous. In the

---

1 Mills (ed.), *Account roll*, pp 22, 24, 29, 30–1, 58, 99.   2 Ibid., pp 41, 63.   3 Ibid., pp 31–2, 38, 59, 99, 113.   4 Ibid., pp 33–4, 40, 97, 98, 120.   5 Wendy Childs and Timothy O'Neill, 'Overseas trade' in Cosgrove (ed.), *A new history of Ireland: II* (1993), pp 492–524 at pp 508–9; O'Neill, *Merchants and mariners*, pp 90–1.   6 *CPR, 1354–8*, p. 267.   7 Mills (ed.), *Account roll*, p. 99.   8 *CARD*, 1, pp 283, 299–300.   9 Ibid., p. 290.   10 Rynne, *Technological change*, p. 89.   11 Brian Scott, *Early Irish ironworking* (Belfast, 1990), p. 153.   12 Ibid., p. 155.

Figure 16.1 Medieval and post-medieval iron knives recovered during excavations at Cookstown, Co. Meath (photograph by John Sunderland for CRDS Ltd on behalf of Meath County Council).

early medieval period, the blacksmith enjoyed high status, and had an honour-price that was equal to that of the physician, the coppersmith and the silversmith.[13] Iron slag and related metalworking debris are regularly recovered on medieval sites. The preferred method of smelting throughout much of the period was to use the simple bowl furnace.[14] A small circular pit was dug into the ground, and air was introduced from a bellows through a nozzle or tuyère to assist the burning or roasting of the ore. In this way, the metallic iron was reduced from the ore and separated from the unwanted material. The pit could be re-used for smithing, or the smithing could be conducted separately.

One of the clearest indicators of iron smelting is slag, a waste-material produced when the metal is separated from its ore during this industrial process. Much of the slag recovered on medieval excavations in Ireland has a high metal content, indicating that the temperature in the bloomery did not reach 1,000 degrees Celsius. With time, techniques and technology improved and higher temperatures were attained, with the result that slag from later sites tends to contain less residual metal (and sometimes none at all). Two bowl furnaces were identified at Kilcoole, Co. Wicklow, where round-bottomed pits were filled with charcoal-rich dark grey clay loam.[15] The bowl and flue of each furnace contained fragments of iron slag and charcoal derived from brushwood and twigs. A burnt sheep's tooth and a rim sherd of glazed medieval ware were also recovered. Excavations at Kindlestown Castle, Co. Wicklow, uncovered a large stone with two hollowed basins and this was interpreted by Linzi Simpson as a mortar that may have been used in ore-smelting.[16] Evidence for medieval metal preparation was discovered at Killickaweeny, Co. Kildare, where a square pit or furnace was connected to a shaft that may have acted as an air-intake or stoke-hole.[17] Heavy burning was indicated in the pit and shaft, but the absence of slag or melted ore suggests that this was not a smelting furnace. The excavator proposed that the site, which yielded medieval pottery, might have functioned as an ore-roasting and preparation facility. To the west of these features, a flat stone surface may have been used to crush and clean the ore,

13 Fergus Kelly, *A guide to early Irish law* (Dublin, 1988), p. 62. 14 Rynne, *Technological change*, p. 89. 15 Emmet Byrnes, 'Archaeological monitoring and rescue excavation at Lott Lane, Co. Wicklow (excavation no. 98E0244)', unpublished report, Aug. 1998. 16 Simpson, 'Dublin's southern frontier', p. 355. 17 Tim Coughlan, 'Site 23, Killickaweeny' in *Excavations 2002*, pp 251–2; Fintan Walsh and John Harrison, 'Early medieval enclosure at Killickaweeny, Co. Kildare', *AI*, 17:1 (spring 2003), 33–6.

Figure 16.2 The post-excavation traces of a medieval forge and associated features at Cookstown, Co. Meath (image courtesy of Richard Clutterbuck and CRDS Ltd).

before it was transported elsewhere for smelting. Bowl furnaces were excavated at Kilgobbin, Co. Dublin, in 2004.[18] Iron objects, iron slag and a furnace bottom were also recovered during excavations at Tallaght.[19]

Similar evidence for smelting has come to light in urban locations. At Vicar Street in Dublin, for instance, an ironworking furnace and two pits were found in association with a shallow pit lined with small stakes and wattle.[20] These were interpreted by the excavator as indicative of iron-smelting. Over 200 sherds of late twelfth-/thirteenth-century local pottery provided dating evidence for the features, while fragments of iron slag, animal bone and oyster shells were also recovered. A small iron furnace was excavated on Cornmarket Street by Alan Hayden in 1992, at a site where metalworking activity was concentrated in the thirteenth century.[21] The remains of a post-and-wattle workshop for metalworking were uncovered, and artefacts of lead, iron and copper alloy were also found. At Werburgh Street, close to the medieval town wall, the discovery of iron slag and a tuyère attested smelting in the Middle Ages.[22] Similar activity on Francis Street was suggested by the recovery of an iron furnace bottom and slag, together with some locally produced pottery.[23]

18 Emer Dennehy, 'Block 7, Belarmine, Kilgobbin' in *Excavations 2004*, p. 142.   19 Walsh, 'St Maelruan's, Tallaght'.   20 Judith Carroll, 'Vicar Street/58–59 Thomas Street, Dublin' in *Excavations 1997*, p. 55; DEHLG file 97E0380 (Vicar Street/Thomas Street; Judith Carroll).   21 Hayden, 'West Side story', pp 106, 108; Alan Hayden, 'Cornmarket/Bridge Street Upper, Dublin', DEHLG file 92E0109.   22 Linzi Simpson, 'Hoey's Court, Werburgh Street, Dublin', DEHLG file 99E0228.   23 Claire Walsh, '95–7, Francis Street, Dublin', DEHLG file 99E0692.

John Hurst points out that secondary ironworking and smithing was a village industry, and that each village would have had at least one specialist smith who was also a part-time farmer.[24] Metalworking was carried out in forges which were often situated in rural locations. A forge is documented at Kilmainham, and a fine example has recently been excavated at Cookstown, Co. Meath (Figure 16.2).[25] Cookstown lies close to the Broad Meadow River, 1km to the west of Ashbourne. The forge, which appears to have been in operation in the thirteenth century, is next to a ringfort that may have been reoccupied at this time. The forge would have been built of timber, but the remains of its earthen floor were littered with fragments of charcoal, metal slag and sherds of pottery. A quenching trough was also present, as well as evidence for a workbench and an adjacent workshop. Metal artefacts from the area included a horseshoe, a piece of a rowel spur, a buckle, a pin and a range of copper-alloy fragments.

At Ballyman, excavations revealed important evidence relating to small-scale ironworking in this part of south Co. Dublin in the thirteenth to fourteenth centuries.[26] Anvil stones and a stone mortar or hammer-stone were found, as well as nails, spikes, small knives, an iron stick-pin and a Jews' harp. The excavator, Elizabeth O'Brien, noted that 'the source of the ore used (limonite, an iron-bearing stone) was located nearby at St Kevin's Well, and the evidence from the site suggests that this stone was crushed, heated, smelted and smithed in the one spot'. Samples associated with the metalworking area yielded radiocarbon dates of 1285–1410 (one sigma) and 1280–1440 (two sigma). It is possible that the iron was being smelted and worked as part of building works carried out at Ballyman Church by the Knights Templars.

Excavations close to the site of a medieval parish church at Laracor, Co. Meath, revealed a shallow square pit containing a large quantity of charcoal and slag and at least two phases of stake-holes.[27] Beside this was a hearth with a small flat stone structure at its core. The complex was interpreted by the excavator as a possible medieval metalworking site. Also in Co. Meath, the remains of a smithing hearth and a possible charcoal-manufacturing kiln were excavated at Garretstown in 2004.[28] At Castlefarm, which was within the Anglo-Norman manor of Dunboyne, charcoal and metallurgical waste were recovered, and may result from small-scale metalworking activity at the site.[29]

Further indications of minor metalworking activity were unearthed on Church Street in Finglas.[30] The excavator suggested that the medieval features exposed here, which included a small well, might be associated with the archbishop's manor of Finglas. On Merrion Road in Dublin, metal artefacts associated with ironworking, carpentry and horse shoeing were recovered.[31] Pottery and radiocarbon dates indicate occupation of the site from the late thirteenth to the early fifteenth century. It was interpreted by the site director as a 'working/processing area located at the periphery of the manor of Merrion'.

There is as yet no evidence for industrial-scale metalworking in the Dublin region during the later medieval period. The application of waterpower to industrial processes is seen across medieval Europe, where watermills were adapted to serve fulling, tanning, timber-cutting, tool-sharpening, and metallurgical processes. The process was less common in Britain, and even rarer in Ireland.[32] While it is possible that the various water courses

24 J.G. Hurst, 'Rural building in England and Wales – England' in Hallam (ed.), *Agrarian history of England and Wales, vol. 2* (1988), pp 884–930 at p. 927 ('ironworking'). **25** *Reg. Kilmainham*, pp 25, 118; Clutterbuck, 'Excavations at Cookstown, Co. Meath'; Richard Clutterbuck, pers. comm. **26** Elizabeth O'Brien, 'Ballyman', DEHLG file E000182. **27** Breen, 'Site 3, Laracor'. **28** Dempsey, 'Garretstown'; Rathbone, 'Seeing the light at Garretstown'. **29** Robert O'Hara, 'Testing Area 1, Castlefarm' in *Excavations 2004*, p. 296. **30** Kavanagh, '4–8 Church Street, Finglas'. **31** Christine Baker, 'Merrion Road, Dublin' in *Excavations 2004*, p. 125; Christine Baker, 'Excavations within the manor of Merrion Castle, Co. Dublin' in Duffy (ed.), *Medieval Dublin VIII* (2008), pp 228–86. **32** Lucas, 'The role of

identified in the Dublin city excavations fed mills other than grain mills, only one medieval water-powered forge has been discovered in Ireland. It was found at the North Gate Bridge in Cork city, and Rynne has suggested that this thirteenth-century site would have been suitably located to process cargoes of bar iron that would have arrived into the city along the River Lee.[33] Rynne has also discussed the introduction of the blast furnace, where water was used to power a mill wheel that in turn operated a sequence of bellows.[34] If the later medieval usage of watermills in grain processing represented a heightened degree of production compared with early medieval milling, so the blast furnace represented an industrialisation of iron-smelting in Ireland, but this did not occur until the very end of the sixteenth century and was mostly focused in the Munster region.

Lead

Lead is a commodity that turns up from time to time in both the archaeological and the documentary sources for the Dublin region. It was used for a range of purposes in the Middle Ages, but most frequently for windows, roofs, water pipes, coffins, weights and glaze for pottery and tiles. It is found more frequently on wealthier urban sites than in the country, but its ultimate source was generally rural. One of the advantages of lead over other materials such as stone, wood, clay, leather and even other metals, is that it could be melted down again and again, remodelled and re-used. This partly explains its relative rarity on excavations, compared to, say, iron. Nonetheless, there is a growing body of evidence for the use of lead in both Dublin and its hinterland. Medieval window lead has been recovered during excavations at Bridge Street Upper and Nicholas Street in Dublin, as well as at Muckerstown, Co. Meath.[35] Other lead items found on excavations include weights (Christ Church Place), seal matrices (High Street), an ingot (Coolock), a hook (Exchange Street), and pieces of waste (Bride Street; Francis Street).[36]

   One of the main uses to which lead was put in medieval Dublin was in the provision of pipes to bring water to the townspeople, a major project that was undertaken in the thirteenth century. Indeed, the importance of lead pipes in transporting water is reflected in the occupation name 'plumber', which is derived from the Latin word for lead. *Robertus Plumbator* and *Robertus Longus Plumbator*, both listed in the Dublin guild merchant roll in the early thirteenth century, would almost certainly have spent a large part of their day working with lead.[37] Lead-alloy was used in about 7 per cent of all ring-brooches examined by Deevy, and many of these are from Dublin and the surrounding area.[38] Potters in Dublin also required lead, which they used to make glaze. In June 1367, Edward III ordered the custodians of Trim Castle to 'rebuild the tower beyond the west gate of the castle … including walls, wooden planks, iron, lead and all other necessary roofing'.[39] Those working on the roof would probably have been able to purchase the necessary iron and lead at the market in Trim, and these materials are included in the town's tariff lists for 1290 and 1308.[40] Murage tax was charged by the cart-load for these metals, suggesting that they were available in considerable quantities, although their ultimate source is not known.

monasteries in the development of medieval milling', p. 105.   **33** Maurice Hurley, *Excavations at the North Gate, Cork, 1994* (Cork, 1997), pp 44–9; Rynne, *Technological change*, p. 89.   **34** Rynne, *Industrial Ireland*, pp 114–25; Colin Rynne, 'The origins and technical development of the blast furnace in Ireland, *c*.1596–*c*.1740' in Conleth Manning (ed.), *From ringforts to fortified houses: studies on castles and other monuments in honour of David Sweetman* (Dublin, 2007), pp 387–97. **35** Cornmarket/Bridge St. Upr (92E0109); Hayden and Walsh, 'Small finds [Patrick, Nicholas and Winetavern Streets]', p. 140; Fallon, 'Muckerstown/Wotton' in *Excavations 2004*, pp 328–9; Fallon, 'Muckerstown/Wotton: final excavation report'.   **36** Ó Ríordáin, 'Excavations at High Street and Winetavern Street', 73; D.L. Swan, '"Church of St John the Evangelist", Coolock' in *Excavations 1990*, p. 25; DEHLG file 98E0198 (Exchange St: 8–10; Georgina Scally); McMahon, 'Excavations at Bride Street', 83, 104; DEHLG file 95E0058ext. (78–89 Francis Street: Alan Hayden).   **37** *DGMR*, pp 36, 58.   **38** M.B. Deevy, *Medieval ring brooches in Ireland: a study of jewellery, dress and society* (Bray, 1998), p. 40.   **39** NAI RC8/29: Memoranda roll, pp 500–1, no. 508.   **40** *CDI, 1285–92*, no. 560, pp 277–8; *CPR, 1307–13*, p. 70.

A more precise idea of the price of lead can be ascertained from a number of incidental references dating to the early fourteenth century. In 1305, for instance, four stone weight of lead in Drogheda was valued at 16d.[41] This figure is comparable to the price being paid for lead at the mine in England in 1330, where a pound weight of lead cost about 1/3d.[42] While it was a relatively inexpensive commodity, it was beyond the means of some, and in 1311 a man was charged with breaking a pipe and stealing lead from a weir at Dundalk.[43]

Due to its low melting point (327 degrees Celsius), the smelting of lead was simpler and more energy-efficient than the smelting of iron. Little is known about the mining and smelting of lead in medieval Ireland however. It is quite possible that both activities were quite rare and that where they did take place they left little trace in the archaeological record and even less in the documents. Some metal mining was carried out in Munster, as is indicated by the record of payments being made to borers and miners there in 1296, but it is not clear what metals were being extracted.[44] Edward I had established a silver mine in Co. Tipperary in 1276, and the following year he ordered the opening of 'other mines of silver, copper, lead, iron, or other metals lately found in Ireland'.[45] Despite the order, however, it is unlikely that any lead mine was opened at this time.[46]

It is perhaps significant that lead was imported to Ireland from Wales in 1286–7, when ten stones of lead were brought in for use in the roofing of a castle at Great Island, Co. Waterford.[47] Importing such a heavy commodity suggests that it was not readily available locally (although it was not unusual for lead to be transported over long distances in medieval England).[48] The timing of this import from Wales is also interesting, as the massive programme of castle-building initiated by Edward I in the principality in the 1280s had stimulated the development of an indigenous industry there.[49] In the Middle Ages, the northern English mines produced the largest output of lead in Europe, and although little of this was exported, it seems logical that some of it would have made its way into Ireland through ports on the Irish Sea.[50] Lead was certainly *worked* in Ireland – *Willelmus le Ledbetere*, listed in the roll of the Dublin guild merchant in 1238–9,[51] was surely a lead-beater – but evidence for its extraction and smelting is minimal. Indeed, there can be little doubt that 'the bulk of Ireland's metal requirement was imported'.[52] As yet, no direct evidence has come to light for the extraction or smelting of lead in the Dublin region.

Silver

In medieval Ireland, silver was used in the minting of coins, in jewellery manufacture and in the production of a range of other items such as bowls, cups and other vessels. Goods such as these sometimes turn up on archaeological excavations in the Dublin region, and also appear in contemporary documents. Silver could be obtained in three main ways: by melting down existing silver objects; through importation; or through local extraction. The extraction of silver was closely related to the smelting of lead, as most lead ores in Ireland are silver-bearing (argentiferous) – and silver could be separated from the lead after smelting. Some silver mining took place near Knockaunderrig, Co. Tipperary, in the 1270s,[53] and it is

41 *CJR, 1305–7*, p. 82.   **42** R.F. Homer, 'Tin, lead and pewter' in Blair and Ramsay (eds), *English medieval industries* (1991), pp 57–80 at p. 63.   **43** *CJR, 1308–14*, p. 169.   **44** *CDI, 1293–1301*, no. 346, pp 163–4.   **45** D.F. Gleeson, 'The silver mines of Ormond', *JRSAI*, 67 (1937), 101–16; M.D. O'Sullivan, *Italian merchant bankers in Ireland in the thirteenth century: a study in the social and economic history of medieval Ireland* (Dublin, 1962); Des Cowman, 'The metal mines of Tipperary', *Tipperary Historical Journal*, 5 (1992), 105–15.   **46** Down, 'Colonial society and economy', p. 489. **47** O'Neill, *Merchants and mariners*, p. 93.   **48** Homer, 'Tin, lead and pewter', p. 64.   **49** I.S.W.B. Blanchard, 'Lead mining and smelting in medieval England and Wales' in Crossley (ed.), *Medieval industries* (1981), pp 72–84 at pp 82–3. **50** Blanchard, 'Lead mining', p. 72.   **51** *DGMR*, p. 74.   **52** Down, 'Colonial society and economy', p. 490; Wendy Childs and Timothy O'Neill, 'Overseas trade' in Cosgrove (ed.), *A new history of Ireland: II* (1993), pp 492–524 at pp 508–9.   **53** Gleeson, 'The silver mines of Ormond'; O'Sullivan, *Italian merchant bankers*; Cowman, 'The metal mines of Tipperary'; Barry, *The archaeology of medieval Ireland*, p. 108.

likely that other ore sources were exploited in other parts of Munster and elsewhere. *The Libelle of Englysche Polyce*, an English poem written in the 1430s, claims that silver 'ore' was available in Ireland but that the Gaelic Irish did not exploit it: 'For of sylvere and golde there is the oore | Amonge the wylde Yrishe, | though they be pore, | For thye ar rude and can thereone no skylle; | So that, if we had there pese and gode wylle | To myne and fyne and metall for to pure, | In wylde Yrishe might we fynde the cure'.[54] It seems that some Irishmen found it easier to collect silver by carefully clipping tiny fragments off the edges of coins. They would melt this down and use it to mint new coins. The best known example of this is 'O'Reilly's money', a type of counterfeit silver coinage produced by Gaelic Irish forgers in Bréifne. It was outlawed by an act of the Trim parliament of 1447, and denounced again at the Naas parliament of 1456.[55]

Silver was a relatively rare commodity in medieval Ireland and there are indications that merchants from Dublin looked well beyond the Dublin region to source it. In 1457, a Dublin merchant by the name of William Willeston was granted licence to work certain mines (possibly at Clonmines) in Co. Wexford for twenty years.[56] From 1460 or earlier, a royal mint operated at Trim Castle, and this would have required a regular supply of silver.[57] For a time in the 1470s, the Trim mint was supervised by Patrick Keyn, a goldsmith from Dublin. It has been suggested that gold-smithing (which included silver-smithing) was one craft that bridged the ethnic divide in medieval Ireland.[58] It is likely that the Dermot Lynchy who was admitted to the franchise of Dublin in 1473, was a Gaelic Irishman from outside the town, and the same may be true of Patrick Keyn, who had been trained in London.[59]

Other metals

Although copper mines in Cos. Cork and Kerry are among the oldest in north-western Europe,[60] there is little evidence for the extraction of copper anywhere in Ireland in the Middle Ages (see above). Nonetheless, artefacts made from alloys of copper are frequently found on medieval excavations in urban settings in Ireland, and on occasion in the countryside. Most of these are relatively high quality objects, with bronze being the preferred alloy. While it is likely that some copper was mined in medieval Ireland, much of it was probably imported, either as a raw material or in the form of finished products. Evidence for the working of copper is remarkably rare in Ireland, considering the number of finished items that have come to light over the years. *Henricus le Kopersmit*, listed in the Dublin guild merchant roll for 1263–4, is likely to have been a coppersmith working in the city.[61]

In addition to lead and silver, tin was the third non-ferrous metal to be mined in medieval Ireland, although this too was on a very small scale. When alloyed with copper, tin forms bronze, and when alloyed with smaller amounts of copper (usually less than 15 per cent) or more often lead, it forms pewter. Medieval pewter tokens have been recovered on a number of excavations in Dublin and its region, including Winetavern Street and Rathfarnham.[62] A pewter pilgrim's badge, of a type known to have been made in Rome, was found in thirteenth-century levels on High Street.[63] It is likely that most pewter objects in

54 Down, 'Colonial society and economy', pp 489–90. 55 Michael Dolley and W.A. Seaby, 'Le money del Oraylly (O'Reilly's money)', *BNJ*, 36 (1967), 114–17; Michael Dolley, *Medieval Anglo-Irish coins* (London, 1972), pp 18–19; Edward Colgan, *For want of good money: the story of Ireland's coinage* (Bray, 2003), pp 35–6; Richard Butler, *Some notices of the castle and of the ecclesiastical buildings of Trim* (3rd ed., Trim, 1854), pp 76–8. 56 Barry, *The archaeology of medieval Ireland*, p. 108, referring to RIA Halliday Collection, 2, pp 178–9. 57 Potterton, *Medieval Trim*, pp 227–9. 58 O'Neill, *Merchants and mariners*, pp 95–6. 59 *DCFR*, p. 7; O'Neill, *Merchants and mariners*, pp 95–6. 60 William O'Brien, *Mount Gabriel: Bronze-Age mining in Ireland* (Galway, 1994). 61 *DGMR*, p. 109. 62 R.H.M. Dolley and W.A. Seaby, 'A find of thirteenth-century pewter tokens from the National Museum excavations at Winetavern Street, Dublin', *Spinks Numismatic Circular* (1971), 446–8; DEHLG file 97E0140 (Orchard Inn, Rathfarnham, Butterfield Avenue). 63 Ó Ríordáin, 'Excavations at High Street and Winetavern Street', 73.

medieval Ireland were imported, especially from England. The south-west of England was one of the greatest tin-producing regions of north-western Europe in the Middle Ages.[64]

Pottery

Pottery is a unique artefact type; it was manufactured and used extensively across Europe throughout the Middle Ages; it survives remarkably well; and is consequently available in statistically significant quantities. From the end of the Bronze Age until the coming of the Anglo-Normans in the second half of the twelfth century, however, most of Ireland was essentially aceramic. That is to say, almost no indigenous ware was produced, and what little pottery was present was imported (from Anglo-Saxon and Saxo-Norman England as well as from Normandy and northern France). Some hand-made ceramics were produced locally however. These are known as crannog ware, everted rim ware and souterrain ware and are most commonly found in the north-east of Ireland. With the arrival of the Anglo-Normans, this changed dramatically – in the south and east of the country at least. The English and French preference for pottery vessels spread, and new trade routes were soon opened up. Initially, most of the pottery was imported but local production centres were quickly established to meet the rising demand.

By about 1175, local potteries appear to have been up and running in the Dublin region, and by the early thirteenth century the majority of pottery in Dublin and surrounding areas was of local manufacture. While the medieval pottery industry did not usually generate much in the way of documentary records – potters did not form into guilds, their produce was usually tax free, and their kilns were generally situated away from town centres – Dublin had one of the best-documented colonies of potters in Britain and Ireland. A street of potters (*vicus pottorum*) is documented there by 1190, and was situated in the suburbs outside the town's west gate – presumably because at that location the kilns would not pose a fire threat to the many timber buildings and structures within the town.[65] The guild merchant roll, which covers the period from 1190 to 1265, lists several dozen potters and crockers associated with Dublin at that time (including one *Willelmus le Crockere de Nas* [Naas]).[66] There are also several documentary references to pots being bought and sold in the town. In 1335, one penny was paid for three little earthenware pots to contain mustard at the priory of Holy Trinity, while the same priory purchased several earthenware pots at the market the following summer.[67] There are also references to the sale of clay for the purpose of making pots, and James Mills surmised that this clay may have been extracted from the ground close to Kill of the Grange (see above, p. 391).[68] The analysis by Clare McCutcheon of some locally made vessels recovered on Thomas Street in Dublin indicated a source for the clay somewhere close to Dublin.[69]

Excavations across the Dublin region (as well as chance finds of pottery sherds) have demonstrated that from early in the thirteenth century locally made pottery significantly outnumbered imported wares. This was the case on high-status sites as much as on low-status sites and in urban areas as well as rural ones. Local wares dominated the pottery assemblages recovered on most sites in Dublin city as well as at sites in Leixlip, Naas and Tallaght.[70] Local wares were as prevalent at the castles of Dundrum, Kindlestown and

---

64 R.F. Homer, 'Tin, lead and pewter' in Blair and Ramsay (eds), *English medieval industries* (1991), pp 57–80 at 58–62. **65** D.J. Keene, 'Suburban growth' in Holt and Rosser (eds), *The English medieval town* (1990), pp 97–119 at p. 116; *RHJB*, p. 22. **66** *DGMR*, pp 6, 14, 21, 23, 25, 33–5, 38, 43, 47, 48, 57, 58, 68, 69, 74–6, 87, 91, 93 (Willelmus le Crockere de Nas), 95, 102, 109. **67** Mills (ed.), *Account roll*, p. 10. **68** Ibid., pp 55, 174. **69** DEHLG file 96E0280 (Thomas Street; Clare McCutcheon). **70** DEHLG files 95E0041 (Earl Street South); 97E0129 (Francis St/Swift's Alley); E000217 (Ship Street); 02E0096 (Hammond Lane); E000548 (High Street); 01E0206 (Leixlip); 00E0754

Maynooth as they were at Carmanhall and Nangor.[71] In rural medieval England, potting was often pursued as a part-time occupation in conjunction with small-scale agriculture,[72] and it is quite likely that a similar situation existed in the Dublin region.

Leinster Cooking Ware

The indigenous pottery type known as Leinster Cooking Ware (LCW) is the single most widespread medieval pottery type in Leinster,[73] having been found in varying quantities on both urban and rural sites from the south of Co. Wexford to the north of Co. Louth (Figure 16.4a). Sherds of LCW had been found on approximately twenty-five sites in the Dublin region by the time Raghnall Ó Floinn published his seminal paper on the subject in 1988.[74] The increased number of excavations in this area has seen the figure rise by over 200 per cent to at least seventy-five sites by 2004 (Figure 16.3a).[75] Only about 15 per cent of these sites were in Dublin city, however, and even on these urban sites LCW made up a relatively small proportion of the overall local assemblage. At Wood Quay, for instance, LCW accounted for only 3.6 per cent of all locally made wares.[76] Such low figures are a reflection of the strength of the locally made Dublin cooking wares (which were roughly contemporary with LCW) on the one hand and, on the other, the fact that LCW was made, used and traded predominantly *outside* the city. That it is present at all in Dublin is consequently a particularly good indicator of trade between the city and its hinterland.

Microscopic petrological analysis of thin sections of sherds of locally produced pottery from the Wood Quay excavations in Dublin revealed that the clay used in the manufacture of LCW (as well as Dublin-type coarseware and Dublin-type cooking ware; see below) came from a source in a volcanic region.[77] This source may have been the North Wicklow/Leinster granites, or clays transported from here by river. Furthermore, the temper used was crushed granite, 'presumably Leinster granite'. This scientific evidence serves to corroborate the pre-existing widely held view that the characteristic mica and quartz inclusions in most sherds of LCW betray a granite origin for the clay, with the Leinster Granite Massif being the most likely source.

There is some documentary evidence that clay for pottery-making was extracted in the south of Co. Dublin, close to the mountains. In 1344, clay for making earthenware pots was sold by Dowenild O'Helyn, presumably a Gaelic Irishman, on the manor of Clonkeen.[78] In medieval England, 'tileries and potteries were frequently sited on clay sub-soils which support managed woodland and tend to be in rural areas'.[79] In addition to a good supply of clay, pottery-making needs water and plenty of wood, and so the Dublin/Wicklow Mountains area was particularly conducive to this rural industrial activity. Peat could also be used as a fuel to fire the kilns, and this too would have been in good supply in this area.

The general distribution of LCW implies that there may have been a central location or locations for the production of these vessels, with an excellent distribution system covering places right across the province and beyond.[80] As yet, however, no definite kiln or production site has been found for LCW and the documentary evidence is equally scant. It is likely that

(Nangor); 02E0955 (Naas); 91E0016 (Nicholas Street); Walsh, 'St Maelruan's, Tallaght'.   **71** DEHLG files E000419 (Dundrum Castle); Clare McCutcheon, 'The pottery from Dundrum Castle, Co. Dublin (licence number E419)', unpublished report; 01E0844 (Kindlestown); 96E0391 (Maynooth Castle); 98E0254/99R0002 (Carman Hall).   **72** John Cherry, 'Pottery and tile' in Blair and Ramsay (eds), *English medieval industries* (1991), pp 189–209 at pp 204, 207.   **73** Raghnall Ó Floinn, 'Handmade pottery in S.E. Ireland: Leinster Cooking Ware' in Mac Niocaill and Wallace (eds), *Keimelia* (1988), pp 325–64 at p. 340.   **74** Ibid., p. 334.   **75** Based on an analysis of excavation reports to 2004. The figure is likely to be considerably greater than this, but detailed breakdowns of the pottery assemblages were not available for many sites.   **76** By sherd count. Clare McCutcheon, *Medieval pottery from Wood Quay, Dublin: the 1974–6 waterfront excavations* (Dublin, 2006), pp 60, 85.   **77** R.M. Cleary, 'Appendix D: petrological analysis of thin section' in McCutcheon, *Medieval pottery from Wood Quay* (2006), p. 155.   **78** Mills (ed.), *Account roll*, p. 55.   **79** Cherry, 'Pottery and tile', p. 189.   **80** DEHLG files E000419 (Dundrum Castle); McCutcheon, 'The pottery from Dundrum Castle', p. 2.

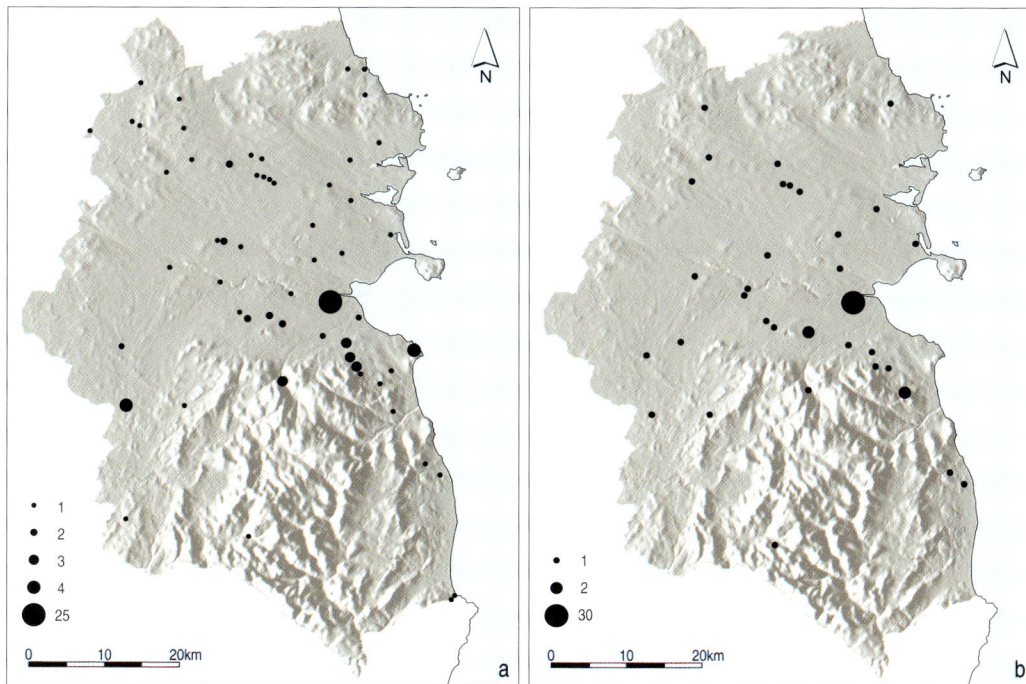

Figure 16.3
(a) Distribution of Leinster Cooking Ware in the Dublin region; (b) Distribution of Dublin-type wares in the Dublin region (sources: published reports; unpublished archives; DEHLG files; *Excavations bulletins*; www.excavations.ie).

many of the kiln sites were located outside towns and have not yet been discovered due to the urban nature of so many excavations. Temporary or 'simple bonfire' kilns were also used commonly, but these have left very little physical trace.[81] There was probably a network of kilns across the Dublin region, with each one serving a small local market. It has been calculated that the products of the Downpatrick kiln had a distribution range of about 15km, and similar distances have been recorded for medieval kiln products in England.[82]

The remains of a pottery kiln that may have made LCW were excavated within a ditched enclosure on the side of Ballynabarny Hill, Co. Wicklow, in 2001.[83] Although the natural underlying soil was a sandy till with no stones, large numbers of small stones were found scattered among the broken pottery sherds. The stones were all of a similar size (*c.*1cm by 2cm) and shape (almond) and had clearly been gathered and brought onto the site. There was a small furnace with evidence for extensive burning, and a series of small stake-holes around and under it. The stake-holes were in two groups forming an 'S'-shaped line. The feature was described by the excavator as 'a rural clamp-style kiln'. He suggested that the small stones had been brought in for use as 'spacers', to put between wet pots during the firing process, to stop them sticking together. Some larger rocks had also been brought onto the site to cover the kiln. The excavator suggested that they may have been used for shelving or drying pottery. Two thousand seven hundred sherds of crude, handmade medieval pottery were recovered from within a series of ash and charcoal spreads. The pottery, which had inclusions of quartzite and mica, included rim and body sherds, with thumb-impressed notches on the rims. It was comparable to LCW and was probably made in the period between the twelfth and the early fourteenth century. At the base of some of the trenches, sherds of Saintonge pottery were found among the local pottery, while some red earthen wares (including a jug handle) were also recovered. The earthen ware was probably wheel-thrown.

81 Ó Floinn, 'Handmade pottery in S.E. Ireland: Leinster Cooking Ware', pp 327, 340–1. **82** Maureen McCorry, *The medieval pottery kiln at Downpatrick, Co. Down: an investigation of its working life, its products and their distribution* (BAR British Series, 326, 2001), fig. 2; K.G. Barton, *Pottery in England from 3500BC–AD1730* (Newton Abbot, 1975), p. 46. **83** Information from a paper by Angus Stephenson given at NRA seminar; www.adsireland.ie/pdf/n11.pdf (most recently accessed 7 Dec. 2007).

Excavations at the Old Mart on Magdalene Street in Drogheda revealed a series of medieval pottery kilns and several of these appear to have been in operation simultaneously.[84] The kilns were 'double-flued with a stoking hole at either end, and an oval-shaped firing chamber with a raised central platform'. They contained sherds of thirteenth-/fourteenth-century pottery 'as well as fragments of kiln furniture and medieval roof tiles'. The kilns may have been served by drainage gullies and a series of associated pits may have been used for clay preparation or settling. The Magdalene Street kilns were near to the site of a medieval tile kiln excavated in the early 1980s.[85] The double-flued kiln was similar in many ways to one excavated in 1978 at Carrickfergus, Co. Antrim.[86]

Within 400m of the motte and castle at Castleknock, Co. Dublin, a possible medieval pottery kiln was excavated in association with the remains of a small shelter or work area with a hearth and refuse pits.[87] It was a small kiln of dry-stone construction. Most of the 3,000 sherds of pottery that were recovered could be dated to the late thirteenth or early fourteenth century. The assemblage included pottery wasters, ladles or pipkins with hooked handles, cooking vessels and jugs. Copper and iron objects were also recovered, including a possible iron scissors, as well as a spindle whorl and a fragment of rotary quern. Kieran Campbell concluded that there was evidence, albeit inconclusive, for the production of pottery during the medieval period, juxtaposed with small-scale domestic or semi-industrial activity. A potter would have required more than just a kiln – there would also have been a need for a workshop and a covered area to dry and store the pots after firing.[88] In this regard, it is significant that the Castleknock kiln was found in association with a shelter and pits.

Dublin-type wares

If LCW is the most commonly found medieval pottery type in the countryside around Dublin, then Dublin-type wares are the most frequently recovered within the city itself. Dublin-type wares are so called because Dublin is the place that they most often occur, and while no kiln has been found to confirm that they were manufactured in Dublin, there can be little doubt that they were.[89] There are four sub-categories of Dublin-type wares: Dublin-type coarseware (late twelfth to early thirteenth century; Figure 16.4b); Dublin-type ware (thirteenth century); Dublin-type fineware (late thirteenth to fourteenth century) and Dublin-type cooking ware (late twelfth to thirteenth century). Unsurprisingly, Dublin-type wares tend to dominate the assemblages of local pottery recovered on excavations in Dublin city.[90] For instance, at Wood Quay, they made up over 96 per cent of all Irish wares present.[91] Dublin-type ware in particular (as opposed to Dublin-type coarseware, cooking ware or fineware), is, according to Clare McCutcheon, the most commonly found thirteenth-century ware in the wider Dublin area.[92]

As much as the discovery of LCW on city-centre sites can be seen as reflecting trade between Dublin and its hinterland, so too the presence of Dublin-type wares on rural sites can be viewed as a sign of commercial interaction between town and country (Figure 16.3b). Of particular interest in the Maynooth Castle pottery assemblage, for instance, was the 'further evidence of the distribution of Dublin glazed wares outside the medieval city'.[93] Dublin-type wares have been found on a range of sites and site-types across the Dublin

84 Eoin Halpin, 'Old Mart, Magdalene Street, Drogheda' in *Excavations 2004*, pp 259–60; Eoin Halpin, pers. comm. **85** Kieran Campbell, 'A medieval tile kiln site at Magdalene Street, Drogheda', *CLAHJ*, 21 (1985), 48–54. **86** M.L. Simpson, P.S. Bryan, T.T. Delaney and Anthony Dickson, 'An early thirteenth-century double-flued pottery kiln at Carrickfergus, County Antrim', *Medieval Ceramic*, 3 (1979), 41–51. **87** Campbell, 'Castleknock'. **88** Cherry, 'Pottery and tile', p. 202. **89** McCutcheon, *Medieval pottery from Wood Quay*, pp 58–9. **90** Here, the term 'Dublin-type wares' includes Dublin-type coarseware, Dublin-type ware, Dublin-type fineware and Dublin-type cooking ware. **91** By sherd count. McCutcheon, *Medieval pottery from Wood Quay*, p. 59. **92** McCutcheon, *Medieval pottery from Wood Quay*, p. 73. **93** Alan Hayden, 'Maynooth Castle' (unpublished report), p. 26.

Figure 16.4 (a) Leinster Cooking Ware; (b) Dublin-type coarseware jug; (c) Ham Green B jug; (d) Saintonge chequerboard jug from Winetavern Street, Dublin (images courtesy of Hugh Kavanagh (a), Clare McCutcheon and the National Museum of Ireland (a–d)).

region, including at Kilgobbin, Portmarnock (both Co. Dublin), Clane, Straffan (both Co. Kildare), Harlockstown, Muckerstown (both Co. Meath), Charlesland and Templeteenaun (Figure 16.5) (both Co. Wicklow).[94]

Laboratory analysis has shown that the clay for Dublin-type coarseware and Dublin-type cooking ware, like that for LCW, was probably sourced in the north Wicklow/Leinster Mountains. Examination of Dublin-type ware and Dublin-type fineware, however, which are generally slightly later than the coarseware and cooking ware, has shown that the clay had come from an area where volcanically derived clays do not exist – that is, possibly west or north of Dublin.[95] Rose Cleary makes the interesting point that the Anglo-Normans might first have used 'the clay source already being used in the later twelfth century in the production of Leinster Cooking Ware. Subsequently, a different clay source, without the need for added temper, may have been sourced away from the North Wicklow/Leinster granite region'. An ordinance of 1460 refers to the fees to be charged by carters and carmen drawing loads of clay into Dublin city.[96] It is likely that this clay was destined for the city's potters and tile-makers.

Imported pottery

Pottery can be a particularly useful indicator of commercial contacts, having been traded for its own qualities or as an adjunct to trade in other commodities (contained within the pots and vases), such as wine. At coastal and riverine ports it is a particularly good guide to trade.[97] Imported pottery is frequently found on medieval sites in Dublin city, and here it can be seen as direct evidence for overseas trade (Figures 16.4c, 16.4d, 16.6a, 16.6b). Predictably, sites on or near the east coast tend to turn up a higher proportion of English wares, while places closer to the south coast yield a greater amount of material from France. Imported wares come mainly from England and France, but pottery from the Low Countries, northern Germany and the Rhineland and from the Mediterranean is also found.[98] Pottery was just one component of Ireland's overseas trade, and in the late twelfth century Gerald of Wales noted that 'Poitou out of its own superabundance sends plenty of wine [to Ireland], and Ireland is pleased to send in return the hides of animals and the skins of flocks and wild beasts'.[99]

While it is impossible to say for sure through which port a piece of pottery entered the country, it is likely that the majority of imported wares discovered in most of the Dublin region arrived through Dublin itself, particularly in the years before Dalkey gained greater importance. To the north of the region, goods also came in through Drogheda, and the Boyne was navigable as far as Trim, Co. Meath, where a range of imported wares have been found.[100] Much of the English pottery found in the Dublin region, especially from the late twelfth and thirteenth centuries, comes from the Bristol area, and the close contacts between Dublin and Bristol, the two most important ports on the Irish Sea in the Middle Ages, are well-documented.[101]

---

94 Emer Dennehy, 'Block 7, Belarmine, Kilgobbin' in *Excavations 2004*, p. 142; Sinéad Phelan, 'Portmarnock' in *Excavations 2004*, p. 151; M.E. Byrne, 'Prosperous Road/Millicent Road, Clane' in *Excavations 2003*, p. 238; Donal Fallon, 'Ladycastle Lower, Straffan' in *Excavations 2003*, p. 248; Stuart Halliday, 'Testing Area 18, Harlockstown' in *Excavations 2003*, pp 372–3; Fallon, 'Muckerstown/Wotton' in *Excavations 2004*, pp 328–9; Fallon, 'Muckerstown/Wotton: final excavation report'; Bernice Molloy, 'Charlesland' in *Excavations 2004*, pp 480–1; Aidan O'Sullivan and Graeme Warren, 'Templeteenaun, Ballinagee' in *Excavations 2004*, pp 474–5. Other sites in the Dublin region, outside Dublin itself, where Dublin-type wares have been recovered include: Balally, Ballymount Great, Carrickmines, Clonee, Cookstown, Dundrum, Finglas, Grange Castle, Kindlestown, Leixlip, Naas, Nangor, Rathfarnham, St Margaret's and Swords. **95** McCutcheon, *Medieval pottery from Wood Quay*, p. 73; Cleary, 'Appendix D', p. 155. **96** *CARD*, 1, p. 306. **97** Schofield and Vince, *Medieval towns*, p. 166. **98** O'Keeffe, *Medieval Ireland*, pp 118–24. **99** Gerald of Wales, *The history and topography of Ireland*, p. 35. **100** Potterton, *Medieval Trim*, pp 149–51, 160–1; Clare McCutcheon and Rosanne Meenan, 'Pottery in medieval Trim' in Michael Potterton and Matthew Seaver (eds), *Uncovering medieval Trim: archaeological excavations in and around Trim, Co. Meath* (Dublin, 2009), pp 333–45. **101** See, for example, Bradley, 'A tale of three cities'. See also pp 73–5, 375–6, above.

Archaeologically, foreign-made pottery becomes increasingly uncommon with distance from sea-ports. This marked falling off in frequency can be seen as a reflection of the relative non-integration of inland locations with direct overseas trade, as well as giving an indication of the degree to which an area traded with and formed part of the hinterland of its nearest sea-port. Even on the wealthiest of sites across the Dublin region – such as the large castles at Dundrum and Maynooth – local wares outnumbered imported pottery by as much as one hundred to one.[102] Only a handful of sites in the Dublin region have yielded imported medieval pottery – Cookstown, Dundrum, Maynooth and Nangor.[103] It is becoming apparent that the presence of imported pottery on a site is not so much an indicator of wealth or status, as was previously thought.[104] Imported pottery has recently been recovered at Cookstown and Nangor, for instance, and these sites were never of the status of the castles at Maynooth or Trim. The presence of imported pottery may be seen less as a diagnostic of status and more as an indicator of proximity to a trading port and interaction with that port. Commenting on the ceramic assemblage from Nangor, McCutcheon noted that 'the paucity of imported wares is an interesting indication of the distribution of such material outside the port cities, and a similar trend was also noted from the large assemblages at Dundrum Castle, Maynooth Castle and Kells Priory'.[105] It is true that very little imported pottery was recovered at Nangor, but the fact that *any* was present at all is significant nonetheless.

Figure 16.5 Selected sherds of medieval pottery from Templeteenaun, Co. Wicklow (image courtesy of Aidan O'Sullivan).

An example of the fall-off in imported pottery away from urban centres has been demonstrated in a study of the hinterland of medieval Southampton.[106] On sites within the port of Southampton itself, imported wares are recovered in large quantities, and are found on sites of all kinds. At Winchester, however, which is fourteen miles inland, imported pottery is much less frequent and is mostly found on high-status sites. At Newbury, a small market town some forty-one miles from Southampton, imported wares are hardly ever found.

Floor tiles

As far as we know, earthenware tiles were first used to pave floors in Ireland in the thirteenth century.[107] The earliest examples were probably imported from the south-west of England and Wales through Bristol, but Thomas Fanning surmised 'that within a relatively short time of their introduction, a local tile industry, using local clays, would have grown up particularly in the Dublin, Meath and Kilkenny areas'.[108] Marcus le Teler and Willelmus le Tieler were both members of the Dublin guild merchant in the thirteenth century.[109] The vast majority of the tiles found in Ireland have come from religious houses, and many of these are from the Dublin region. Terry Barry's 1987 map of the distribution of medieval pavement tiles in Ireland shows three main concentrations – one in the south-east of the country stretching from Waterford north to Kilkenny, one around Drogheda, Co. Louth, and a third in the Dublin region.[110] The following year saw the publication of the Eames and Fanning monograph on *Irish medieval tiles*, and this updated and refined the distribution greatly.[111] Since the publication of these maps, further investigation has served to consolidate these concentrations.[112]

102 Maynooth Castle (96E0391); DEHLG files E000419 (Dundrum Castle); McCutcheon, 'The pottery from Dundrum Castle'. **103** Clare McCutcheon, 'The medieval pottery from the N2 Finglas-Ashbourne bypass at Site 25, Cookstown, Co. Meath (03E1252)'; DEHLG files E000419 (Dundrum Castle); McCutcheon, 'The pottery from Dundrum Castle'; Maynooth Castle (96E0391); 00E0754 (Nangor), Clare McCutcheon pottery report. **104** John Hurst, 'Medieval pottery imported into Ireland' in Mac Niocaill and Wallace (eds), *Keimelia* (1988), pp 229–53 at pp 234–5. **105** 00E0754 (Nangor), Clare McCutcheon pottery report. **106** Alejandra Gutiérrez, *Mediterranean pottery in Wessex households (13th to 17th centuries)* (BAR International Series, 306, 2000). **107** E.S. Eames and Thomas Fanning, *Irish medieval tiles: decorated medieval paving tiles in Ireland with an inventory of sites and designs and a visual index* (Dublin, 1988), pp v, 6. **108** Fanning, 'An Irish medieval tile pavement', 81. **109** *DGMR*, pp 21, 72. **110** Barry, *The archaeology of medieval Ireland*, p. 102, fig. 24. **111** Eames and Fanning, *Irish medieval tiles*, pp 15, 18, 30, 38, 39, 47, 52. **112** See, for example, Hayden, 'Arran Quay', pp 194–7; Alan Hayden, 'Medieval floor tiles' in Walsh, *Archaeological excavations at Patrick, Nicholas and Winetavern Streets* (1997), pp 145–8; Halpin, *The port of*

Figure 16.6
(a) Distribution of Ham
Green pottery and
(b) Distribution of
Saintonge wares
recovered from
excavations in the
Dublin region (sources:
published reports;
unpublished archives;
DEHLG files; NMI files;
Excavations bulletins;
www.excavations.ie).

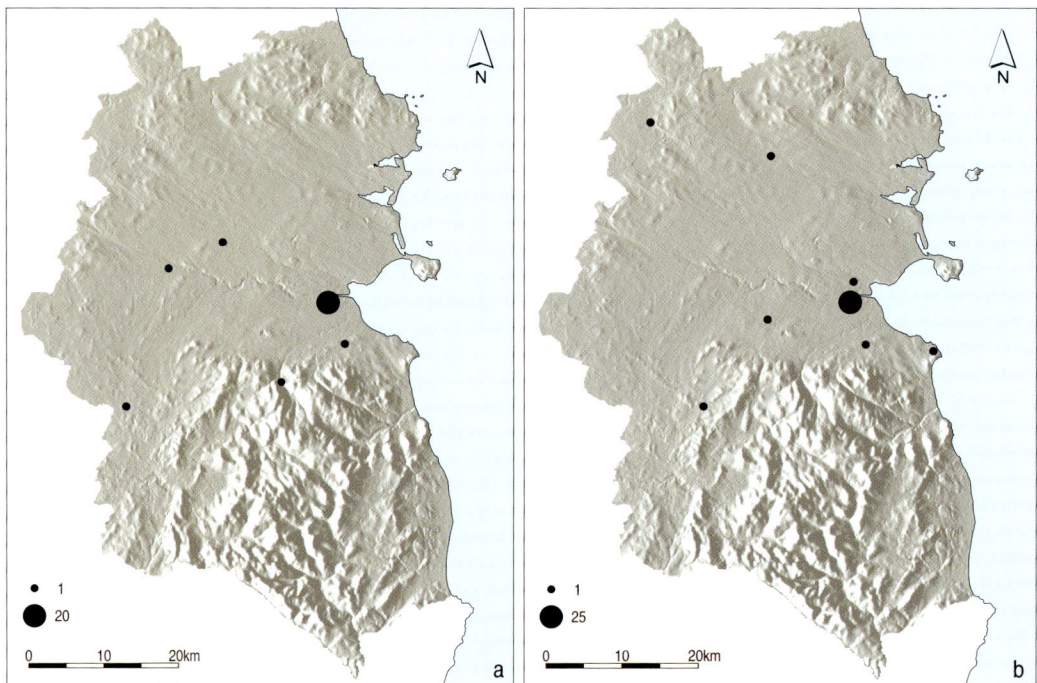

It is probable that each of these areas was served by a number of tileries, and excavations have located one kiln close to the Dominican friary in Drogheda, and another at the Augustinian priory at Kells, Co. Kilkenny.[113] There were probably others at Kilkenny (near St Canice's Cathedral) and at Waterford, and perhaps even at some of the rural religious houses as well (such as at Graiguenamanagh, Co. Kilkenny). For Dublin, it is likely that 'a locally based industry using popular designs with kilns situated somewhere in or close to medieval Dublin would have supplied the tilers' needs'.[114] This assertion is backed up by the archaeological evidence. All of the floor tiles from Patrick Street, for instance, appeared to be of local manufacture, with fabric closely resembling that of locally produced pottery.[115] Floor tiles and roof tiles found during excavations at John Dillon Street were also 'locally made'.[116] Similarly, the tile fragments from Winetavern Street 'appear to be manufactured from local fabrics, with calcite and mica inclusions evident'.[117] Abundant mica flecks were also present in the tiles found on Arran Quay, and the presence of a number of wasters

medieval Dublin, p. 141; Thomas Fanning, 'Some observations on the medieval pavement tiles from the site of St Nicholas's Church, Dublin' in Manning (ed.), *Dublin and beyond the Pale* (1998), pp 71–3; Thomas Fanning and E.S. Eames, 'A line-impressed mosaic tile from Lusk Church, Co. Dublin, 1324' in Mac Niocaill and Wallace (eds), *Keimelia* (1988), pp 365–74; Gowen, 'St Michael le Pole', pp 46–7; Lynch and Manning, 'Excavations at Dublin Castle, 1985–7', p. 203; Johnson, 'The small finds' (2003), pp 159–60; Alan Hayden, 'Excavation of a medieval house in the grounds of Howth House, County Dublin' in Duffy (ed.), *Medieval Dublin VII* (2006), pp 103–12; Brendán Ó Ríordáin, 'St David's, Naas: a new dimension', *JCKAHS*, 17 (1989–91), 151–60; Joanna Wren, *Floor tiles: a guide to the medieval and 19th-century floor tiles of Christ Church Cathedral, Dublin* (Dublin, n.d.); DEHLG file 01E0229 (Tram Street/Phoenix Street, Dublin); DEHLG file 01E0614 (=93E0066) (Coombe Relief Road/St Luke's Church, Dublin); DEHLG file 01E0772 (Ship Street Great, Dublin); DEHLG file 01E1142 (Marks Alley, Dublin); DEHLG file 91E0016 (Nicholas Street, Dublin); DEHLG file 92E0109 (Cornmarket/Bridge Street Upper, Dublin); DEHLG file 92E0143 (Patrick Street/Dillon Street, Dublin); DEHLG file 95E0041 (30–2 Earl Street South, Dublin); DEHLG file 96E0245 (Essex Street, Dublin); DEHLG file 96E0300 (Back Lane/Lamb Alley, Dublin); DEHLG file 96E0357 (2–5 Meath Market, Dublin); DEHLG file 97E0129 (Francis Street/Swifts Alley, Dublin); DEHLG file 97E0220 (Earl Street, Dublin); DEHLG file 98E0158 (John Dillon Street, Dublin 8); DEHLG file 98E0254/99R0002 (Carman Hall, Dublin); DEHLG file 99E0386 (Abbeylands, Clane, Co. Kildare); Walsh, '95–7, Francis Street, Dublin', DEHLG file 99E0692; DEHLG file E000544 (St David's Church, Naas, Co. Kildare); DEHLG file E000557 (9–14 Arran Quay, Dublin); DEHLG file E000630 (31–3 Stephen Street Lower, Dublin).   **113** Kieran Campbell, 'The floor tiles' in Miriam Clyne, *Kells Priory, Co. Kilkenny: archaeological excavations by T. Fanning and M. Clyne* (Dublin, 2007), pp 234–59; Kieran Campbell, 'A medieval tile kiln site at Magdalene Street, Drogheda', *CLAHJ* (1985), 48–54.   **114** Fanning, 'Some observations on the medieval pavement tiles from the site of St Nicholas's Church', p. 73.   **115** Hayden, 'Medieval floor tiles' in Walsh, *Archaeological excavations at Patrick, Nicholas and Winetavern Streets* (1997), p. 148.   **116** DEHLG file 98E0158 (John Dillon Street, Dublin 8).   **117** Halpin, *The port of medieval Dublin*, p. 141.

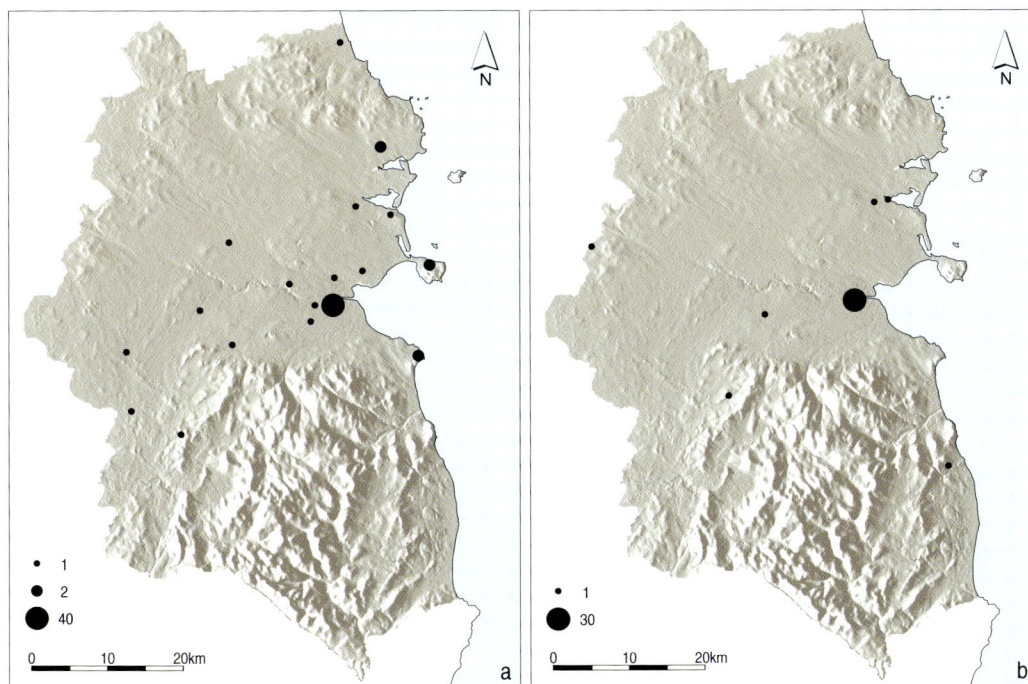

Figure 16.7 (a) Distribution of floor tiles in the Dublin region; (b) Distribution of roof tiles in the Dublin region (sources: published reports; unpublished archives; DEHLG files; NMI files; *Excavations bulletins*; www.excavations.ie).

(unusable tiles) among this assemblage suggests that tiles may have been produced locally, perhaps at St Mary's Abbey.[118] Excavations at Hanbury Lane unearthed the remains of a kiln used to produce a range of line-impressed and relief-decorated tile types over several centuries.[119] There must have been other kilns, perhaps even one at each of the cathedrals and major religious houses, but these have not yet come to light. It is beyond any reasonable doubt that Dublin tile-makers and Dublin potters sourced their clay in the same area, probably somewhere in the foothills of the mountains. Having imported their raw materials from the hinterland, it is likely that the city's tile-makers then supplied local consumers and also exported the products of their kilns to building projects across the region – at places like Celbridge, Howth, Kilmainham, Kilteel, Lusk, Malahide, Naas and Swords (Figures 16.7a, 16.8). Indeed, it has been suggested that tiles produced in Dublin might even have been exported to Wales.[120]

Neutron activation analysis of floor tiles from Cheshire, Kells and Swords, carried out in the 1980s, could not pinpoint the source of the clay, but it demonstrated that the Irish tiles were manufactured in Ireland, and that the Kells and Swords tiles did not share a common clay source.[121] The tests provided scientific proof to an existing assumption.

Roof furniture

The earliest roof tiles used in Ireland may have been imported to Dublin from the north of England *c.*AD1000.[122] These were rare and would have been used on prestigious buildings only. By the thirteenth century, if not earlier, tiles, louvers and finials were being manufactured in Dublin and had become a more common sight both here and in other towns in Leinster.[123] Excavations have unearthed assemblages of medieval roof furniture at a range of locations across the city and in the surrounding region (Figure 16.7b).[124]

118 Hayden, 'Arran Quay', pp 196–7.   **119** Walsh, 'Archaeological excavations at the abbey of St Thomas', pp 198–200; Wren, 'Appendix H', pp 179, 188; Joanna Wren, 'The roof tiles' in Claire Walsh, *Excavations at Hanbury Lane, Dublin* (forthcoming).   **120** Fanning, 'Some observations on the medieval pavement tiles from the site of St Nicholas's Church', p. 71.   **121** M.J. Hughes and John Cherry, 'Neutron activation analysis of medieval decorated floor tiles from Ireland and Cheshire' in Eames and Fanning, *Irish medieval tiles* (1988), pp 136–9.   **122** Joanna Wren, 'Appendix H: medieval and post-medieval roof tiles' in McCutcheon, *Medieval pottery from Wood Quay* (2006), pp 177–95 at pp 178–9. **123** Joanna Wren, 'Crested ridge tiles from medieval towns in Leinster, 1200–1500AD' (MA, UCD, 1987).   **124** See, for example, Fanning, 'An Irish medieval tile pavement', 75; Manning, 'Excavation at Kilteel Church'; Wren, 'Roof

Figure 16.8 Some of
the floor tiles revealed
during excavations at
Swords Castle, Co.
Dublin (© Department
of the Environment,
Heritage and Local
Government).

Three roof tiles of thirteenth- to fifteenth-century date from the excavations at Patrick, Nicholas and Winetavern Streets in Dublin were submitted for petrological analysis.[125] The results indicated that the raw materials used in their manufacture most likely came from 'an area adjacent to both the Caledonian granite and the Carboniferous limestone'. The only area in the Dublin region that fits these criteria is a narrow band running from the coast at Dun Laoghaire to Stepaside (see Figure 1.5). This area was within easy reach of Dublin and would have been an accessible source of raw materials for the city's tile-makers.

tiles (Patrick, Nicholas and Winetavern Street)'; Joanna Wren, 'Roofing tiles and slates' in Halpin, *The port of medieval Dublin* (2000), pp 139–41; Gowen, 'St Michael le Pole', pp 46–7; Joanna Wren, 'Roof tiles' in McMahon, 'Excavations at Bride Street' (2002), 97–8; Lynch and Manning, 'Excavations at Dublin Castle', p. 203; Johnson, 'The small finds' (2003), pp 158–9; Joanna Wren, 'Clay building material' in Simpson, 'Dublin's southern frontier' (2003), pp 353–4; Joanna Wren, 'The roof tiles' in Hayden, 'Arran Quay' (2004), pp 198–9; Wren, 'Appendix H'; DEHLG file 00E0263 (Grangecastle Business Park, Dublin); DEHLG file 01E0229 (Tram Street/Phoenix Street, Dublin); DEHLG file 01E1142 (Marks Alley, Dublin); DEHLG file 02E0163 (Bride Street, Dublin); DEHLG file 92E0078 (Bridge Street Upper, Dublin); DEHLG file 92E0143 (Patrick Street/Dillon Street, Dublin); DEHLG file 93E0074 (Arran Quay, Dublin); DEHLG file 93E0143 (Parliament Street, Dublin); DEHLG file 95E0041 (30–2 Earl Street South, Dublin); DEHLG file 96E0245 (Essex Street, Dublin); DEHLG file 97E0129 (Francis Street/Swifts Alley, Dublin); DEHLG file 97E0220 (Earl Street, Dublin); DEHLG file 98E0254/99R0002 (Carman Hall, Dublin); Walsh, '95–7, Francis Street, Dublin', DEHLG file 99E0692; DEHLG file E000547 (Usher's Quay, Dublin); DEHLG file E000557 (9–14 Arran Quay, Dublin); DEHLG file E000630 (31–3 Stephen Street Lower, Dublin). Also Joanna Wren, 'The roof tiles' in Alan Hayden, *Excavations at the Cornmarket, Dublin* (forthcoming); Wren, 'The roof tiles (Hanbury Lane)'; Joanna Wren, 'The roof tiles' in Ann Lynch and Conleth Manning, *Excavations at Dublin Castle* (forthcoming); Joanna Wren, 'The roof tiles' in Linzi Simpson, *Excavations Temple Bar West (Essex Street), Dublin* (forthcoming); Joanna Wren, 'The roof tiles' in Mary McMahon, *Excavations at the Four Courts, Dublin* (forthcoming); Joanna Wren, 'The roof tiles' in Martin Reid, *Excavations at Meeting House Square, Dublin* (forthcoming).   **125** Maureen McCorry, 'Petrological report on the roof tiles' in Walsh, *Archaeological excavations at Patrick, Nicholas and Winetavern Streets* (1997), pp 153–4.

One of the types analysed (DT1) has been dated to the first half of the thirteenth century and, due to the large number of waster sherds in this fabric found at Cornmarket in Dublin, it seems likely that there was a tile kiln in operation in this area at this time.[126] Indeed, the name 'Cornmarket' is now applied to this type of tile (DT1). The clay source used for DT1 appears to have been exploited for both DT2 (early thirteenth to late fourteenth century) and DT3 (late fourteenth and fifteenth century) as well, and such continuity suggests both accessibility and security.

A second Dublin kiln, at Hanbury Lane, produced peg tiles as well as floor tiles in the fourteenth to sixteenth centuries.[127] Pantile wasters were found during excavations at Dublin Castle, and it is possible that another kiln was in operation here too.[128] As with the pottery and the pavement tiles, it is likely that locally manufactured roof tiles in Dublin were produced using clay from the south hinterland. Products from these kilns have been found on sites across the city, and it is likely that regional finds – such as those from Kilteel, Kindlestown and Swords – also derive from the Dublin kilns.

Limekilns

Limekilns were furnaces used to produce lime by heating limestone at high temperatures.[129] The resultant lime was used mainly to make mortar for use in building, but also for agricultural purposes. According to Muiris O'Sullivan and Liam Downey, 'the burning of limestone for the specific purpose of applying the lime produced to soil was commonly practised [in Ireland] between the twelfth and seventeenth centuries'.[130] Limekilns required large amounts of fuel, and roughly equal quantities of limestone. In the Middle Ages, wood was the primary fuel, but peat could also be used, and furze burned with a particularly high temperature. Wet limestone and wet fuel helped to produce a better quality lime. To make mortar, the lime would have been mixed with sand. The process of converting stone to lime can take up to four days.

Limestone underlies much of the Dublin region, and there is evidence from both urban and rural contexts for the tapping of this resource. Although limekilns were often situated at a distance from habitation, due to the noxious gases produced during the firing process, this was not always the case. Excavations within the confines of a thirteenth-century Augustinian friary at Cecilia Street, in the Temple Bar area of Dublin, revealed the remains of a limekiln thought to relate to the construction of the friary.[131] Elsewhere in Temple Bar, part of what appeared to be a blackstone-built kiln for the production of mortar was uncovered.[132] It is likely that the kiln was used to provide mortar for the building of the medieval walls and towers in the vicinity. Excavation at the north end of Nicholas Street in Dublin revealed a limekiln that may have been used during the construction of the town wall in this area.[133] The kiln contained deposits of pure, soft white lime 'interspersed with patches of brown peaty organic material and lumps of burnt orange clay overlay the floor'. Burnt timbers were also present, as well as pottery sherds of approximately thirteenth-century date. The kiln may once have had a clay and wicker superstructure, but little of this survived. The excavator determined that the kiln was of the periodic or 'flare' type, in which

126 Wren, 'Appendix H', p. 181; Wren, 'The roof tiles (Cornmarket, Dublin)'.   127 Walsh, 'Archaeological excavations at the abbey of St Thomas', pp 198–200; Wren, 'Appendix H', pp 179, 188; Wren, 'The roof tiles (Hanbury Lane)'. 128 Wren, 'Roof tiles (Patrick, Nicholas and Winetavern Street)', p. 152.   129 Muiris O'Sullivan and Liam Downey, 'Lime kilns', *AI*, 19:2 (summer 2005), 18–22.   130 O'Sullivan and Downey, 'Lime kilns', 21.   131 Linzi Simpson, '5–6 Cecilia Street West' in B.S. Nenk, Cathy Haith and John Bradley, 'Medieval Britain and Ireland in 1996', *Med. Arch.*, 41 (1997), 241–328 at 304–5; Linzi Simpson, '5–6 Cecilia Street West, Dublin' in *Excavations 1996*, p. 21.   132 Helen Keogh, '14 Exchange Street Lower, Temple Bar, Dublin' in *Excavations 2004*, pp 120–1.   133 Walsh, *Archaeological excavations at Patrick, Nicholas and Winetavern Streets*, pp 60–2.

the stone is not placed in contact with the fuel, but is exposed to the heat and flames given off by the burning fuel.

In the suburbs, there was a limekiln near Oxmantown Green in the Middle Ages.[134] Further to the north, two limekilns were excavated in the vicinity of Corr Castle, Howth.[135] This was an ideal location for limekilns, and indeed the area was quarried for limestone through much of the nineteenth and twentieth centuries. At Ladycastle Lower, Straffan, Co. Kildare, a limekiln was excavated by Donal Fallon within 150m of the motte.[136] It consisted of a central firing bowl with two flues lined with clay-bonded stone packing. The upper part of the bowl and flues had been truncated by later disturbance, but the flues appear to have been covered over by capstones originally. Fills contained charcoal, burnt clay and fractured limestone, while a fragment of thirteenth-/fourteenth-century Dublin-type pottery was recovered from the clay bonding of the kiln. The excavator concluded that the kiln was 'presumably related to construction associated with occupation in the vicinity of the motte castle'. There was a lime pit at Maynooth in 1328, and this may be the same one that was recorded by royal surveyors in 1518–19.[137] The Dublin guild merchant roll records the names of two lime-burners in the thirteenth century – *Hugo le Limbernere* (1225–6) and *Walter le Grant Limbernarius* (1241–2).[138]

The remains of a medieval limekiln were uncovered during archaeological excavations at Ballymount Great in Co. Dublin.[139] It was 1.2m wide and *c*.70cm deep, with a flat base of limestone slabs and vertical walls of irregularly shaped stones. Deposits inside the kiln included a basal layer of white lime mortar, a layer of mixed brown soil with orange clay flecks, and a 20cm-deep layer of boulder infill. Sherds of LCW and Dublin-type wares from inside the kiln indicated a date in the thirteenth or fourteenth century for its construction and use. The medieval limekiln excavated at Killeen Castle, Co. Meath, was probably fifteenth century in date.[140]

Chapter summary

Iron was the most commonly used metal in the medieval Dublin region. Much of it was imported from England, Brittany and Spain, but there is good evidence for local mining, smelting and forging as well. Bog ore was used in addition to rock-based ores. Slag is the most frequent indicator of smelting, and analysis of this indicates that the quality of iron produced improved through the Middle Ages. Iron furnaces have been excavated at a number of locations around the region, including Kilcoole, Co. Wicklow, and Kilgobbin, Co. Dublin, as well as at Cornmarket Street and Vicar Street in the city. Ironworking was carried out in forges such as that documented at Kilmainham or the one excavated at Cookstown, Co. Meath. As yet, there is no evidence for industrial-scale metalworking in the medieval Dublin region.

Lead was used for a variety of purposes, especially on higher status sites. Although most lead seems to have been imported, there were specialised lead-workers in Dublin. Silver was used in the manufacture of jewellery, altar-plate and coins, but there is little evidence for its extraction in the Dublin region. Copper was worked – by craftsmen like *Henricus le Kopersmit*, whose name appears in the Dublin guild merchant roll for 1263–4 – but there is no evidence for its extraction locally. The same is true of tin, which was alloyed with copper

---

134 Purcell, 'Land-use in medieval Oxmantown', pp 217, 224.   **135** DEHLG file 98E0349 (Rónán Swan; Howth: Corr Castle).   **136** Fallon, 'Ladycastle Lower' in *Excavations 2003*, p. 248.   **137** *RBK*, pp 97, 99; *Crown surveys, 1540–1*, p. 280.   **138** *DGMR*, pp 54, 117.   **139** Malachy Conway, 'Ballymount Great' in *Excavations 1997*, pp 22–3; DEHLG file 97E0316 (Ballymount Great: Malachy Conway).   **140** Baker, *The archaeology of Killeen Castle*, pp 79–83.

to make bronze, and with lead to make pewter (although most pewter appears to have been imported from England).

In the early years of Anglo-Norman control, almost all pottery in Dublin was imported, but local production centres were soon established, and within a generation or so most pottery in the city and surrounding region was made locally. Leinster Cooking Ware is the most commonly found medieval type across the province, and by 2004, it had been recorded on over seventy-five sites in the Dublin region. It was manufactured, used and traded outside the city, by and large, and is rarely found in urban areas. When it *is* found in the city, it is a good indicator of urban-rural trade, or at least contact. While no definite LCW kiln has yet been found, a possible candidate was excavated at Ballynabarny Hill in Co. Wicklow in 2001.

Within the city, a greater range of pottery types were to be found. The four most commonly occurring wares produced in Dublin have been categorised under the general term 'Dublin-type wares'. These are all late twelfth to fourteenth century in date and tend to dominate assemblages on city excavations. When these wares are found outside the city, they can be taken as further evidence of trade between Dublin and its hinterland. So far, Dublin-type wares have been found on over thirty sites in the region, but they become rarer with distance from the city. Clay for the manufacture of at least some Dublin-type wares originated in the countryside surrounding the city, so the return of finished vessels to the hinterland completed a trade-cycle and epitomised the symbiotic interdependence between town and country.

Medieval pottery from England and France, and lesser quantities from the Low Countries, Germany and the Mediterranean, are found on excavations in Dublin city. The majority of English pottery from twelfth- and thirteenth-century levels in Dublin is from the Bristol region, reflecting the strong links between the two ports during that period. Imported medieval pottery is rarely found in Dublin's hinterland (occurring on about a dozen sites, including Cookstown, Dundrum, Maynooth and Nangor), but when it *is* found, it can be seen as a good indicator of Dublin's role as a port that connected its hinterland with a network of overseas trade. It might be expected that the frequency of imported pottery would be proportional to the status of the site, but the evidence shows that the relationship is less clear-cut; while wealth was certainly a factor in access to foreign goods, proximity to a major sea-port was at least as influential. A wealthy site inland is no more likely to have had access to imported pottery than a poorer one close to a port.

As with pottery vessels, the first earthenware floor tiles to be used in Anglo-Norman Ireland were imported via Bristol from England and Wales. A local industry soon developed in Dublin, however, and tiles were manufactured in large quantities. Most were destined for the floors of religious houses, both in the city and in the surrounding counties. A tile kiln has been excavated at Hanbury Lane, and it is likely that there were many more across the city and in the suburbs. Tiles found as far apart as Celbridge, Kilteel, Lusk, Naas and Swords may all have been made in Dublin, while some may even have been exported overseas. Analysis of medieval roof tiles from Dublin city suggests that the clay for their manufacture was sourced in south Co. Dublin.

Lime was a key component of the construction industry, as well as being used as a fertiliser and for a range of other purposes. Kilns were used to heat limestone to a powder at very high temperatures. They were established at building sites as the need arose, but usually away from residential areas due to the noxious gases produced during the burning process. Medieval limekilns have been excavated at Nicholas Street and Cecilia Street in

Dublin city, near Corr Castle (Howth), at Ballymount Great, and at Ladycastle Lower, Straffan, Co. Kildare. The names of two lime-burners are listed in the Dublin guild merchant roll for the thirteenth century. The stone and the fuel used to burn it were both sourced as locally as possible. In some cases, sand was added to the lime-mix to make mortar, and this would have been collected on the seashore.

Having considered the processing of agricultural and natural products, the next chapter explores the movement of these products around the region, starting with a discussion of the towns, markets and transport routes which facilitated exchange. The focus shifts from producer to consumer and the chapter ends with an examination of the demands of Dublin and how they were met.

CHAPTER 17

Distribution and provisioning

Urban development

Following the definition of an Anglo-Norman town proposed by John Bradley in 1985, three of the nucleated settlements in the Dublin region can be classified as true towns.[1] These were Dublin itself, Naas and Ratoath, while the towns of Duleek, Navan, Trim and Wicklow were just on the perimeter of the study area (Figure 6.8).

Almost exactly 30km from the centre of medieval Dublin, Naas is surrounded by low-lying, well-drained and fertile lands at the eastern edge of the Liffey Valley. Little is known of its earliest history, but through the eighth, ninth and tenth centuries, Naas served for several generations as the royal seat of the kingdom of Leinster, and was also the site of an early monastery.[2] It was almost certainly the presence of this ecclesiastical foundation that attracted Anglo-Norman settlers to this location in the twelfth century. The fortunes of the town were improved in *c*.1186 when it was granted a weekly market by Prince John.[3] It quickly became the principal town in Kildare and was to remain important throughout the Middle Ages – indeed such was its pre-eminence that at least nine parliaments and thirteen councils were held there between 1355 and 1484.[4] Naas was enclosed by a stone wall and from the mid-fifteenth century the 'gentlemen and commons of Kildare' were required to pay towards its upkeep.[5] Mary Ann Lyons has shown clearly how Naas was regarded as 'an indispensable outpost for the Dublin administration' in the early sixteenth century.[6] At this time the town had many craftsmen, and most of these were Gaelic Irish. Most of the property and surrounding lands were held by the religious houses, the FitzGeralds and a handful of gentry families.

Among the factors that promoted the success of Naas during the Middle Ages was its rich agricultural hinterland. In a similar way, though on a smaller scale, Ratoath, in Co. Meath, developed as an urban centre surrounded by fertile and productive lands (Figure 17.1). Ratoath was not as successful as Naas, however, and by 1468 thirty-seven burgages lay waste there.[7] There are several references to burgesses and burgages at Ratoath, the earliest occurring in a charter of *c*.1200 from Hugh de Lacy to St Thomas' Abbey, Dublin.[8] In 1333, the burgage rents at Ratoath amounted to £6 16*s.* 4*d.*, which might suggest a burgess population of 136 (if the usual rent of 1*s.* per burgage plot pertained).[9]

In August 1227, Hugh de Lacy was granted the right to have an annual fair at Ratoath on the vigil and feast of St Mary Magdalen, and thirteen days following – that is 21 July to 4 August.[10] As most fairs lasted for eight days, the duration of the Ratoath fair may reflect

---

1 Bradley, 'Planned Anglo-Norman towns in Ireland', 2, pp 420, 447–55.   2 T.J. de Burgh, 'Ancient Naas (Parts I and II)', *JCKAHS*, 1:3 (1893), 184–201 at 184–6; T.J. Westropp, 'On Irish mottes and early Norman castles', *JRSAI*, 34 (1904), 313–45 at 326; Bradley, Halpin and King, 'UAS 7:4: Kildare', p. 343.   3 *CGR*, p. 145; *CPI*, p. 5.   4 Moody, Martin and Byrne (eds), *A new history of Ireland: IX*, pp 596–602.   5 Lyons, *Church and society*, pp 24–5.   6 Ibid., passim.   7 *Stat. Ire., 12–22 Edw. IV*, p. 169.   8 *RAST*, p. 8.   9 TNA:PRO C135/36.   10 *CDI, 1171–1251*, no. 1544, pp 232–3.

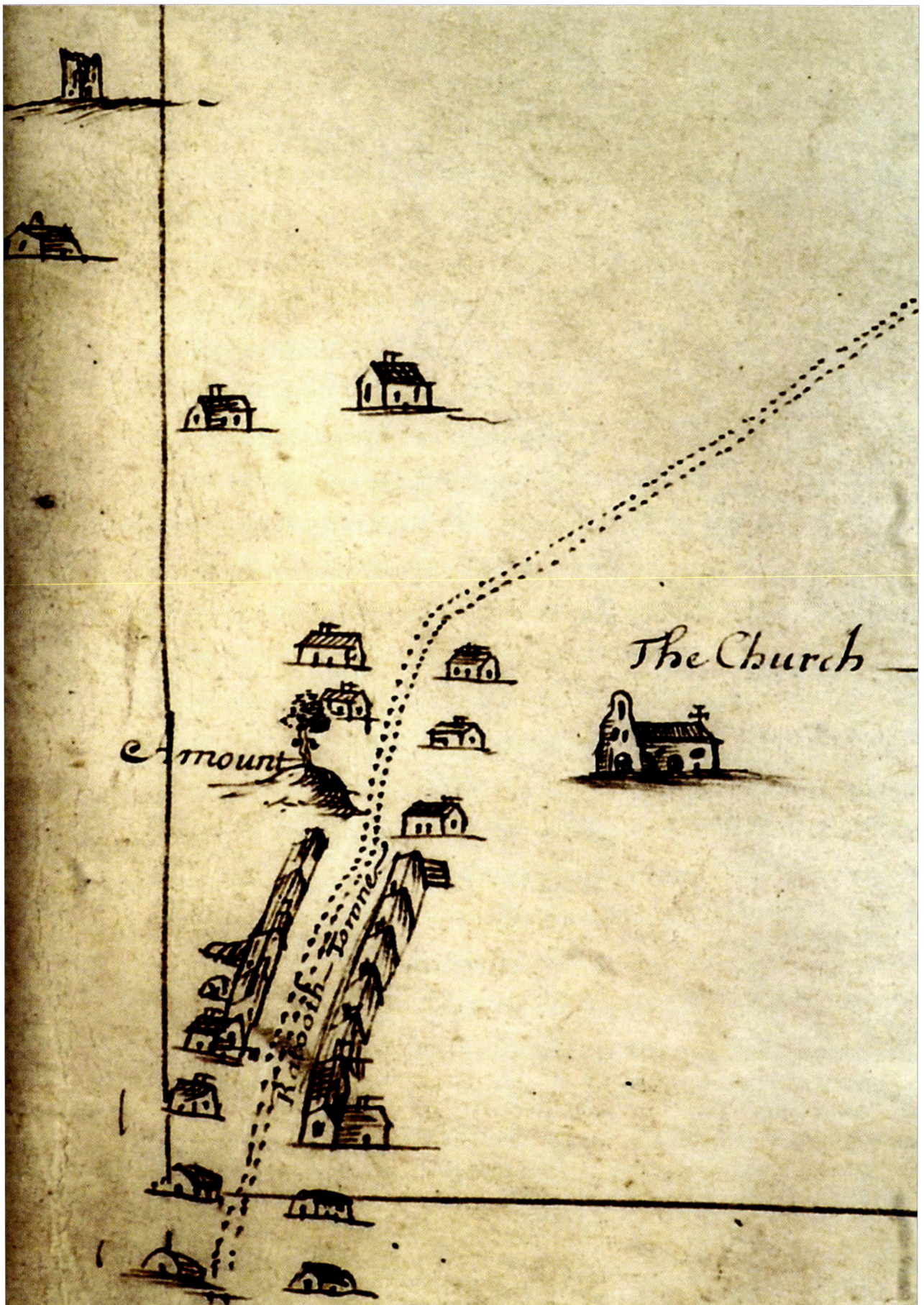

Figure 17.1 'Ratooth Towne', Co. Meath, in 1659. The fourth house from the bottom on the left appears to have a flag flying outside it – possibly a sign that it was an inn (BL Harley 4784, fo. 9 © the British Library Board, all rights reserved).

the expectation of a substantial amount of trade at this location.[11] There is no record of a weekly market at Ratoath, Greenoge or Dunshaughlin, but these boroughs are very likely to have functioned as market centres, serving the day-to-day exchange needs of the local populations. Individuals from Ratoath, Dunshaughlin and Greenoge are found as members of the Dublin guild merchant in the early thirteenth century, including chapmen (travelling provincial merchants), mercers and tanners.[12] This implies that the settlements acted as foci for trade and processing activities.

Trade and commercial activity

Evidence for the supply of agricultural produce to pre-Anglo-Norman Dublin as well as the export of grain overseas in the eleventh century indicates that farming in the Dublin region had been producing a surplus for some time. Following the arrival of the Anglo-Normans and the institution of the manorial system, rural trade underwent something of a revolution. Manorial lords, stimulated by rising prices, were eager to acquire money to improve their housing and standards of living as well as to spend on luxuries for themselves. Manorial tenants needed cash to pay their rents and other dues as well as to buy essential commodities like salt for preserving food and tools for cultivating the land.

The number of purchasers of agricultural produce started to rise steadily in the thirteenth century. Firstly, there was the rapidly expanding population of Dublin, whose requirements were substantial (see below, pp 481–6). There was also an expanding customer base in the countryside. Not all of the people who flooded into rural Ireland in the late twelfth and thirteenth centuries came to farm. Many came to practice trades in rural boroughs and villages and these people resorted to the marketplace for their daily necessities. Export markets also expanded, and in the later thirteenth and early fourteenth centuries, Ireland started to play an important role in the victualling of royal armies campaigning in Wales, Scotland and France.

There were a variety of ways in which buyers and sellers in the Dublin region could come together in order to make a transaction. At a very basic level of exchange, manorial demesnes could sell produce to tenants or tenants could supply demesnes with replacement livestock for example. One can see this at work on the Holy Trinity manor of Clonkeen in the 1340s, when the demesne purchased oxen and work horses from manorial tenants.[13] Other sales could take place very close to the point of production, for example when travelling wholesalers like wool merchants visited manors and farms to purchase in bulk or even in advance. At a further remove, produce could be taken to one of the many local weekly markets or annual fairs. At a regional level, trade could be conducted directly with the large urban market. Different commodities were suited to different marketing strategies, and this often bore a close relation to aspects of their transportability, as will be seen in the following discussions.

The institutionalisation of rural trade

Markets

While many of the people who lived in the countryside pursued a largely self-sufficient lifestyle, there was, in the twelfth and thirteenth centuries, a growing reliance on trade.[14] Rural trade became institutionalised with the foundation of markets. The estate policies of

11 Karina Holton, 'From charters to carters: aspects of fairs and markets in medieval Leinster' in D.A. Cronin, Jim Gilligan and Karina Holton (eds), *Irish fairs and markets: studies in local history* (Dublin, 2001), pp 18–44 at p. 20. 12 *DGMR*, pp 30, 66, 70, 81, 113.   13 Mills (ed.), *Account roll*, pp 22–3.   14 Britnell, *Britain and Ireland*, p. 158.

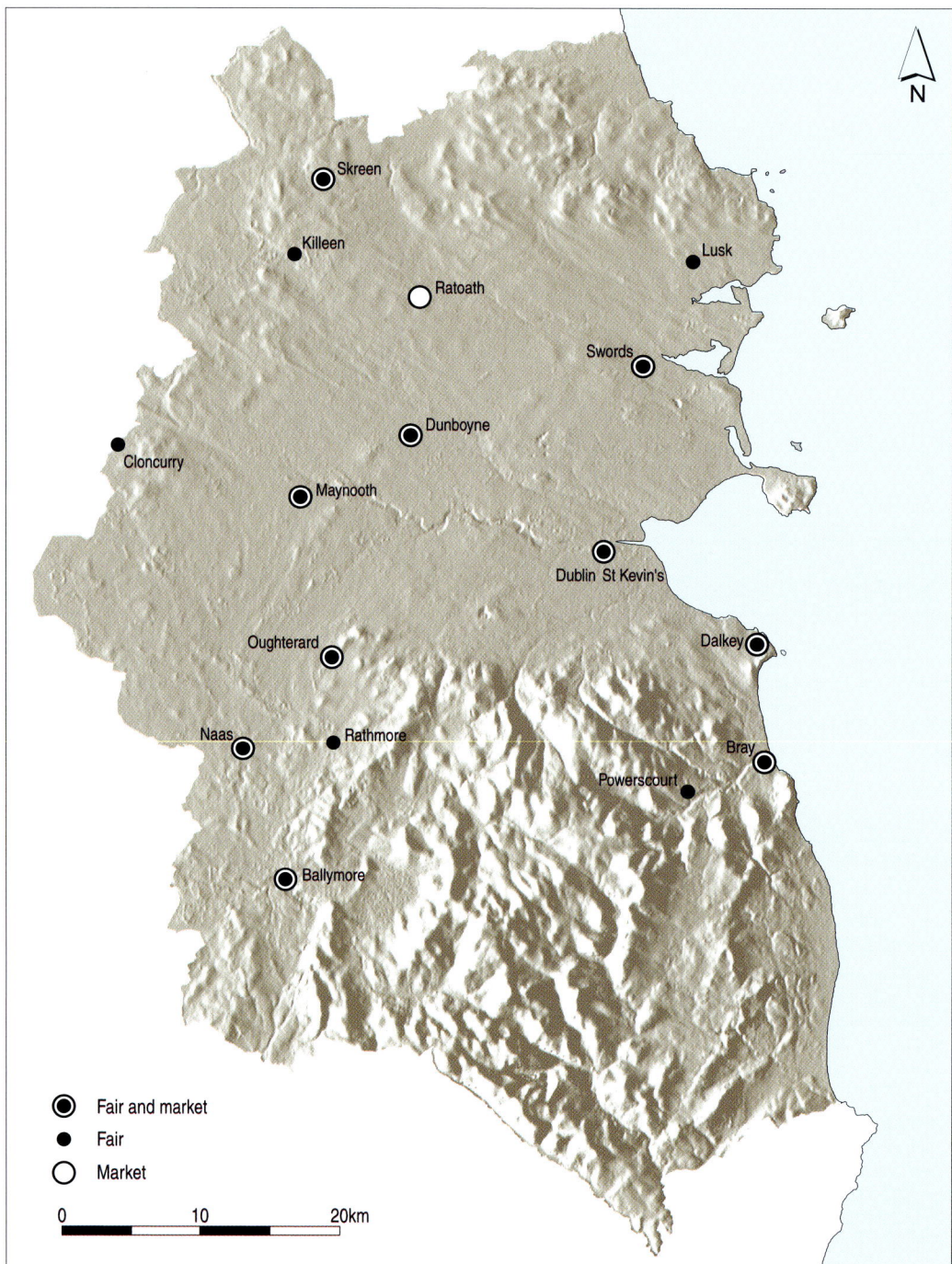

landlords were a powerful agent in bringing about this change. Following the arrival of the Anglo-Normans, the right to grant markets and fairs was considered to be a royal franchise and the thirteenth century saw a large number of grants of both institutions.[15] By granting the right to hold a market or fair, monarchs transferred to the grantees the right to hold and control these events and collect from them revenues including the profits of justice.[16] Lords wanted markets partly to provide an outlet for the surplus produce of their demesnes, but more importantly, perhaps, markets represented to them a regular source of income. The lord collected tolls on goods sold, rents for stalls and profits of the market court if there was one. In the same way that borough privileges attracted people to settle in a particular place, so too the provision of a market and/or fair would have proved an incentive. For the

15 Holton, 'From charters to carters'.   16 Samantha Letters, *Gazetteer of markets and fairs in England and Wales to 1516* (List and Index Society, Special Series, 32, 2003), p. 14.

inhabitants of boroughs and villages, a regular market was essential to attract outsiders with their produce and to provide them with outlets for their goods.

Analysis of the granting of English and Welsh markets and fairs, for which the evidence is much more plentiful and systematic, has identified certain peak periods in the cycle of grants – for example the 1220s and the 1250s. Although certain economic factors may have been at work, it appears that some of the peaks reflect the course of political events.[17] It has been noted that grants to certain individuals coincide with periods when they were in royal favour or when the king was in particular need of their support. This no doubt happened in Ireland also. It is no coincidence, for example, that Geoffrey de Turville, bishop of Ossory, was granted a string of markets and fairs in the 1240s, at a time when he had undergone 'immense labour' and 'no small odium' in attending to the king's business.[18]

There is no satisfactory way of ascertaining how many towns or villages within the Dublin region had functioning markets and/or fairs in the period under consideration. Some of the markets that were granted were never actually held and, conversely, other places without surviving record of official warranty are known to have been centres of trading. Market grants survive for Ballymore, Bray, Dunboyne, Maynooth, Naas, Powerscourt, Swords, Tipperkevin and the vill of St Kevins (Figure 17.2). There are documented markets at several other places, however, including Cloncurry, Dunbro and Lusk. Apart from the market at St Kevin's,[19] just outside the city, what is noticeable from the map is the cordon around Dublin in which no markets or fairs are documented. In 1275, the citizens of Dublin complained to the king about a market that was held in a street outside Dublin on the lands of the archbishop.[20] This market, they claimed, was close to the gate of the city and was selling grain, quires, wool and all manner of merchandise to the prejudice of the king and to the damage of the town. The result of the petition is not known, but it shows the resentment that a rival market close to the city could cause. Swords, 12km to the north, was the next nearest place to the city to have a market while, until the fifteenth century, Dunboyne (c.16km) and Bray (c.18km) were the next closest. In the fifteenth century, Dalkey (c.13km) was granted a market and fair to replace the market at Stagonnil (Powerscourt), which was 'wasted and destroyed by the king's Irish enemies and English rebels'.[21] Earlier attempts to set up a market at Dalkey may have been stymied by the Dublin merchants who had strong connections with the settlement (see above, pp 163–4).

Fairs

The largest and most important fair in the region was the Dublin fair, which must have attracted people from all over the hinterland area. The right to hold a fair was originally granted to the city of Dublin in 1204 by King John. It was to start on 3 May each year and last eight days in total.[22] The grant was renewed in 1215, when the duration of the fair was extended to fifteen days with the proviso that the archbishop of Dublin should have all the profits of the first two days.[23] In 1252, the date of the fair was changed from May to July and its duration was again fixed at fifteen days.[24] English town regulations often forbade shops and traders from operating during the time of the fair. The markets and shops of Winchester closed during the St Giles' fair and the king ordered London's shops to shut during the fair at Westminster.[25] It is likely that this also happened in Dublin. The Dublin fair, which took place on the Fair Green just outside the great western defensive ditch of the city, was visited by many international as well as local merchants.

---

17 Letters, *Gazetteer of markets and fairs*, p. 36.   18 *CDI, 1171–1251*, no. 2780, p. 415, no. 2827, p. 422.   19 *CDI, 1171– 1251*, no. 1351, p. 203.   20 Sayles, *Documents on the affairs of Ireland*, no. 16, p. 11.   21 McNeill (ed.), *Alen's register*, pp 247–8.   22 *CDI, 1171–1251*, no. 226, p. 35; *HMDI*, p. 62.   23 *CDI, 1171–1251*, no. 573, p. 89.   24 *CDI, 1252–84*, no. 1694, p. 349.   25 Farmer, 'Marketing the produce of the countryside', p. 343.

One of the principal functions of the fair was to redistribute imported and manufactured goods. Rural traders would have used it to stock up on goods to be taken to smaller fairs or village markets. The Dublin fair also played a part in marketing agricultural produce. A list of customs or 'stallage' fees payable at the fair of Dublin survives in the 'Dublin chain book' and indicates the goods that might change hands at the fair.[26] Locally produced goods include livestock (cattle, horses, pigs and sheep) and their products (wool, hides, skins, grease and bacon), but not grain. Taking place as it did in July, the fair was too early in the year to trade in grain from the current harvest. Nevertheless, there is some evidence for grain being purchased at the fair. A purveyance account of 1298 lists corn and malt 'bought at the fair and elsewhere in Dublin'.[27] The fair may also have been used as a place where wool was assembled for export.

Regional and local fairs also played an important part in agrarian marketing. During the thirteenth century, the right to hold a fair was granted to seven settlements within the region (Ballymore, Dunboyne, Maynooth, Naas, Ratoath, Skreen and Swords) and there may have been many more whose grants have not survived. Fairs in locations slightly further afield, such as Castledermot, Drogheda, Duleek, Nobber and Trim, also attracted rural dwellers from within Dublin's hinterland. Fairs that occurred during the autumn and early winter were particularly associated with livestock and their products, as animals that had been fattened up during the summer were sold off before the leaner grazing days of winter. These fairs would also have taken place at the right time for the marketing of newly threshed grain. The September fair at Maynooth and the October fairs at Naas and Skreen may have been particularly important. Very few of the fairs for which grants have survived took place during the months of December to April, an exception being the fair at Trim, which was held for eight days during February. Cereals formed an important element of the merchandise traded at Trim in the thirteenth century.[28]

There is some evidence that fairs were used as occasions to mint money. In the 1280s, the Irish exchequer accounted for 'monies minted at divers fairs'.[29] Growing monetisation served to improve the efficiency and scope of exchange. Increasingly, workers were paid daily rates in cash, and customary services were commuted into money payments. It is not clear, however, to what extent most ordinary people (as distinct from merchants and traders) had daily dealings in cash.[30]

Coins, tokens and jettons

One of the most useful forms of non-documentary evidence for trade is coinage. Many coin hoards of thirteenth- to seventeenth-century date have been found in the Dublin area. A large number of the coins were minted in England and others from Scotland, Germany and France have also come to light, reflecting the international trade network of which this region was part. Most of these coins came into the country through Dublin or other ports on the east coast, and made their way inland through trade and exchange. Many more of the coins were produced at local mints such as those at Dublin, Drogheda and Trim.

Some of the hoards were recovered in Dublin city, but others were found away from major urban centres at places such as Three Rock Mountain, Loughlinstown, St Margaret's (all Co. Dublin), Ballynapark and Killiskey (both Co. Wicklow).[31] The provenance of other

26 *CARD*, 1, pp 232–3. The 'Dublin chain book' was an early fourteenth-century collection or cartulary of Dublin records which acquired its name because it was kept on public display in the Tholsel in Dublin chained to a lectern. 27 *CDI, 1293–1301*, no. 572, p. 272. 28 Potterton, *Medieval Trim*, pp 143–53, 157, 162–3. 29 *CDI, 1252–84*, no. 2336, p. 555. 30 See Murphy and Potterton, 'Investigating living standards', pp 228–39. 31 RIA MS 24H9, fo. 19v; Michael Dolley and W.D. Hackman, 'The coinages for Ireland of Henry VIII', *BNJ*, 38 (1969 [1970]), 84–108 at 86, 95–6, 107;

hoards of medieval coins is given simply as 'Dublin district' or Dublin area'.[32] One of these hoards, deposited c.1240, contained coins from Canterbury and Münster, as well as some from the Dublin mint. Other English coins of the late thirteenth century found their way to Ballyshannon (Co. Kildare) and Duleek (Co. Meath).[33] A hoard found at Portmarnock contained fifteenth-century silver groats from Bristol, London, York and Calais.[34]

Besides the hoards, a number of single coin finds have been made in the Dublin region. A silver *denier tournois a I'o rond* was discovered at Swords Castle in 1971.[35] It was struck at Tours for Philip IV of France (1285–1314), and Michael Dolley noted the significance of the discovery of such a coin in the 'immediate hinterland of Dublin'.

Merchants' tokens and jettons (used in accounting) of medieval date have also been found in the Dublin region.[36] The National Museum of Ireland has a collection of medieval coins, tokens and jettons from Dublin.[37] A number of coins have been recovered on archaeological excavations across the region.[38] Several merchants' tokens and a number of Nuremberg jettons, minted by Hans Kravwinckel between 1562 and 1586, were found during an excavation at the Smithfield Market in Dublin and attest commercial activity at this location even before the formal establishment of the market here in the seventeenth century.[39]

Dublin was the first mint established by the Anglo-Normans in Ireland and was operational from c.1185. Coins minted here have been found across Ireland from Antrim (Carrickfergus) to Cork (Bantry) and from Mayo (Kilmaine) to Meath (Oldcastle).[40] Dublin-minted coins have also been found in many parts of Scotland, including Aberdeen,

Figure 17.3 Medieval coins minted in Dublin: (a) groat, Edward IV, 'Heavy cross and pellets', 1465–7; (b) penny, Edward IV, 'Heavy cross and pellets', 1465–7; (c) penny, Henry III, Davi of Dublin (Class 1A), 1251–4; (d) penny, Henry III, Ricard of Dublin (Class 1Jd, 1251–4 (after Colgan, *For want of good money*, pp 20, 46).

I.D. Brown and Michael Dolley, *A bibliography of coin hoards of Great Britain and Ireland, 1500–1967* (London, 1971), pp 70, 71, 74; J.D.A. Thompson, *Inventory of British coin hoards, AD600–1500* (Royal Numismatic Society, special publications, 1, 1956), pp 8, 52; Dolley, *Medieval Anglo-Irish coins*, pp 60, 62, 64, 69, 83; R.H.M. Dolley, 'Was there an Anglo-Irish coinage in the name of Edward VI?', *NC*, 77 (1969), 274–5; Michael Dolley and W.A. Seaby, *Sylloge of coins of the British Isles: Anglo-Irish coins: John-Edward III, Ulster Museum, Belfast* (London, 1968), pp xlviii, xlix, l. **32** Thompson, Inventory of coin hoards, p. 52; Dolley, Medieval Anglo-Irish coins, p. 60; Dolley and Seaby, Sylloge of coins: John-Edward III, p. xlix; Dolley and Hackman, *The coinages for Ireland*, pp 86, 95–6, 107. **33** Thompson, Inventory of coin hoards, p. 8; Dolley, *Medieval Anglo-Irish coins*, p. 60; Dolley and Seaby, *Sylloge of coins: John-Edward III*, p. l. **34** Michael Dolley and S.N. Lane, 'A find of fifteenth-century English groats from Co. Dublin', *JRSAI*, 102 (1972), 143–50; Dolley, *Medieval Anglo-Irish coins*, p. 83. **35** Fanning, 'An Irish medieval tile pavement', 71 (fig. 31a), 75–6. **36** G.D. Liversage, 'Excavations at Dalkey Island, Co. Dublin, 1956–1959', *PRIA*, 66C (1968), 55–234 at 181–2; Michael Kenny, 'Coins' in Walsh, *Archaeological excavations at Patrick, Nicholas and Winetavern Streets* (1997), p. 132; Dolley and Seaby, 'A find of thirteenth-century pewter tokens', 446–8; Michael Kenny, 'Token' in Hayden, 'Arran Quay', p. 199; DEHLG file 96E0276 ext. (College Street/Fleet Street/Westmoreland Street; Sylvia Desmond and Judith Carroll). **37** NMI 60/AMB533; 64/AMB5561o; 1872:17; 1873:14–23; 1873:34; 1902:20–2; 1914:43; 1969:40–57; 1976:88; 1981:8; 1995:27–6; 11.2.1865; 68/AMB611; R1085–1133; R1812; R1858; 1874:23–24; 1899:25; 1899:26; 1914:50; 1917:11; 1932:5616; 1955:15. There are many coins from the Dublin region in the British Museum, London, and in other repositories. **38** See, for example, McMahon, 'Excavations at Bride Street', 104; Kenny, 'Coins', p. 132; Karl Brady and Connie Kelleher, 'Swords, plague and pestilence', *AI*, 14:3 (autumn 2000), 8–11 at 11; Gowen, 'St Michael le Pole', pp 44–5; Lynch and Manning, 'Excavations at Dublin Castle', pp 169–204; Simpson, 'Dublin's southern frontier', p. 356; DEHLG file 97E0343 (Augustine Street/John Street West; Una Cosgrave); DEHLG file 95E058ext. (Francis Street; Alan Hayden); DEHLG file 98E0013ext. (Bride Street; Una Cosgrave); DEHLG file 98E0398 (Phoenix Street/Stable Lane, Smithfield; Una Cosgrave); DEHLG file 99E0690 (Turvey Avenue, Donabate; Claire Walsh); DEHLG file E000508 (St Doologue's, Balgriffin; D.L. Swan); DEHLG files E000296–8 (Dublin Castle; Ann Lynch). **39** Franc Myles, 'Smithfield, Dublin' in *Excavations 2003*, pp 154–5. **40** Thompson, *Inventory of coin hoards*, pp 10, 23, 79; Michael Dolley, Noel Nesbitt and David Rebbeck, 'Three unpublished nineteenth-century Irish finds of coins', *UJA*, 30 (1967), 89–94 at 91–4. Dublin-minted coins have also been found at Ardquin (Co. Down), Ballymahon (Co. Longford), Belfast, Carrick-on-Suir (Co. Waterford), Drumercool (Co. Roscommon), Kilmallock (Co. Limerick), Newry (Co. Down), Portrush (Co. Derry), Scarva (Co. Monaghan) and Sligo (Thompson, *Inventory of coin hoards*, pp 4, 14–15, 23, 78, 109, 117, 125; Dolley, *Medieval Anglo-Irish coins*, p. 83; Herbert Grueber, *Handbook of the coins of Great*

Ayr, Dumfries and Dunblane, and these were almost exclusively pennies of Edward I.[41] In England, Dublin coins have turned up at Chester, Colchester, Coventry, London, Oxford and York, but also at a number of less important market centres and rural sites.[42] Three Edward I pennies minted in Dublin were found at Swansea in Wales, in 1840,[43] while Dublin-minted coins have also been unearthed in Normandy and elsewhere in France at Montpellier and Le Poiré-sur-Velluire (La Vendée).[44] Over 1,600 authentic Dublin coins and a number of forgeries came to light in Brussels in 1908 and three separate hoards found in Denmark included a range of Dublin-made coins.[45] Of a slightly later date, a silver penny of Elizabeth I, minted in Ireland, was found during the excavations at Castle Rushen on the Isle of Man.[46] The recovery of Dublin coins in such a variety of places is further evidence of the extensive trade network of which it was part.

Transport

From early times, Dublin was a 'nexus of communications' by land and sea.[47] It occupied a commanding position in the system of overland communications. The Dublin region was crossed by a number of significant highways (*slighte*), four of which converged on the site of Dublin and the lowest regular crossing point of the River Liffey.[48] From at least the ninth century, the Liffey ford was regarded as one of the three most notable in Ireland.[49]

Viking Dublin would have utilised and probably maintained these existing routeways as well as extending the network, initially for raiding and thereafter for trading. Clarke maintains that a great deal of Viking raiding was done on horseback.[50] With the growth of Dublin as a market town, overland transport routes assumed greater importance as resources flowed both into and out of the urban area.[51] Some of this trade would have been undertaken on foot, but commodities such as grain would probably have been transported by cart. The wood which was required in large amounts for building as well as for fuel would also have required wheeled transportation. Cattle would probably have been driven into the town on the numerous *bóthair* or drove-ways.

With the arrival the Anglo-Normans, there came a massive increase in the use of the communications system. James Lydon speaks of the 'commercial revolution' brought about by the Anglo-Normans, manifested partly in the foundation of towns and markets, but

Britain and Ireland (London, 1899), p. 215, no. 7).   **41** Thompson, *Inventory of coin hoards*, pp 1, 4, 6, 15, 16, 22, 23–4, 37, 48–9, 53, 62, 79, 86, 102, 104–5, 106, 114–15, 137. Other Dublin-minted coins have been found in Scotland at Arkleton, Blackhills, Borscar, Canonbie, Carsphairn, Craigie, Dornock, Giffnock, Kinghorn, Lochmaben, Mellendean, Monifieth, Montraive, Netherfield, Penicuick and Tom Fuaraich.   **42** Thompson, *Inventory of coin hoards*, pp 32, 33–5, 37, 88–9, 91–2, 113, 150; David Clarke, 'The 1969 Colchester Hoard', *BNJ*, 44 (1974), 41–61 at 43–8. Dublin coins have also been found in England at Beaumont, Boyton, Derby, Eccles, Hesleyside, Hickleton, Hornchurch, Hounslow, Newbury, Newminster, Newport (Isle of Wight), Skipton, Steppingley, Stow Hill, Sudbourne, Thrapston, Tutbury, Wyke (Thompson, *Inventory of coin hoards*, pp 13, 17–18, 44–5, 57–8, 68, 69, 70–1, 107, 108–9, 124–5, 129–30, 136, 138, 148–9).   **43** Thompson, *Inventory of coin hoards*, p. 131.   **44** Michael Dolley, 'The continental hoard-evidence for the chronology of the Anglo-Irish pence of John', *NC*, 74 (1966), 30–2; J. Béranger, 'Une trouvaille de monnaies anglo-normandes', *Bulletin de Numismatique*, 12 (1905), 67–72; Émile Bonnet, 'Note sur un trésor de monnaies anglaises découvert a Montpellier', *Revue Numismatique*, 4th ser., 37 (1934), 169–73; H. Gillard, 'Le trésor du Poiré de Velluire', *Bulletin de Numismatique*, 4 (1897), 21–3.   **45** Michael Dolley and W.A. Seaby, 'The anomalous long-cross coins in the Anglo-Irish portion of the Brussels hoard' in R.A.G. Carson (ed.), *Mints, dies and currency: essays in honour of Albert Baldwin* (London, 1971), pp 291–317; Michael Dolley, 'The King John portion of the Anglo-Irish element in the 1908 Brussels hoard', *JRSAI*, 100C (1970), 67–70; Clarke, 'The 1969 Colchester Hoard', 43; Dolley and Seaby, *Sylloge of coins: John-Edward III*. See also L.A. Lawrence [on Brussels Hoard], *BNJ*, 9 (1912), 170; B.H.I.H. Stewart [on Brussels Hoard], *BNJ*, 29 (1960), 91; Michael Dolley and W.A. Seaby, 'The thirteenth-century Anglo-Irish coins in the Kirial find from Denmark', *JRSAI*, 102 (1973), 86–92; Dolley, 'The continental hoard-evidence'; Georg Galster, 'A find of English coins at Ribe, Denmark', *Numismatic Chronicle*, 11 (1911), 378–98.   **46** M.M. Archibald, 'Coins' in P.J. Davey, D.J. Freke and D.A. Higgins, *Excavations in Castletown, Isle of Man, 1989–1992* (Liverpool, 1996), p. 35.   **47** Clarke, *IHTA: Dublin Part I, to 1610*, p. 2.   **48** These were the Slige Chualann, Slige Dála, Slige Mhór and Slige Midlúachra. Another unnamed road from Tara is likely to have headed in a south-easterly direction towards the main fording-point on the lower Liffey: see O'Lochlainn, 'Roadways in ancient Ireland', pp 465–74.   **49** Clarke, *IHTA: Dublin Part I, to 1610*, p. 2.   **50** Ibid., pp 2–3.   **51** Valante, 'Dublin's economic relations', p. 71.

also in the improvement of communications, the building of roads and bridges, the establishment of ferries and the clearing of waterways.[52] It is apparent from the documentary evidence that distance proved no obstacle to transport in thirteenth- and early fourteenth-century Ireland. Millstones were brought to manors, timber transferred to building sites, and loads of grain sent to provision castles.

There are many incidental references to the communications network that linked Dublin to its hinterland. In the thirteenth century, for instance, there are mentions of the Donnybrook Road (c.1250), the highway from Dublin to Thorncastle and the Dodder Bridge (c.1238), the road from Dublin to Ballymore (c.1250), and the king's highway from Finglas (c.1202).[53] The way from Dublin to Cabra and the way from Dublin to Ashtown are mentioned in 1470.[54]

Most rivers would have been crossed at fording points, but increasingly the later medieval period saw the construction of bridges, and they are frequently mentioned in documentary sources. Even before it was built in stone, the bridge over the Liffey linking Dublin with Oxmantown was described as 'great'.[55] In August 1214, the citizens of Dublin were granted permission to demolish the existing bridge over the Liffey and to erect a new one in its place.[56] This bridge collapsed in 1385 and two masons were appointed to repair it while the fares charged on ferries operating across the river were diverted to offset the cost.[57] In 1455, tolls were charged on carts going over Dublin Bridge.[58] These ranged from 4d. for a cart carrying a millstone to ½d. for a cart of hay or wood.

The bridge over the Liffey at Kilmainham, 1.75km west of the city, was another important link in the transportation system.[59] In 1541, it was described as 'a stone bridge … built in ancient times with six arches, now very ruinous and dilapidated, to the great loss of the manor (of Kilmainham) and the surrounding countryside'.[60] There were several smaller bridges in and around Dublin, over the Rivers Poddle, Camac and Steine.[61] A bridge over the Dodder at Donnybrook is mentioned in a grant of 1238 and Glasnevin Bridge is documented in 1558.[62]

King John's Bridge is one of the few remaining bridges in the Dublin region whose origins are considered to be medieval. The site crosses the River Griffeen, south of Lucan. The bridge is thought to date from 1199–1216, with disuse occurring sometime between 1773 and 1837. Originally a three-span masonry bridge, only one arch (central span) and two piers remain today.[63] An indication of the third arch exists in the form of a 50cm-long segment that protrudes from one corner. The existing structure measures 5.9m long and stands 2.8m from the riverbed at its highest point. Each pier measures 3.7m in length and 1.2m in width, and both have triangular cutwaters protruding on the upstream side. Cutwaters are absent on the downstream side. Footings remain and extend 40cm from the inner side of each pier. The pier-construction is of good quality mortar and coursed stone masonry, while the arch is formed using roughly worked limestone blocks. The bridge appears to have undergone re-pointing and has had various modern additions to its structure, which probably relate to nineteenth-century work.

Keeping bridges in repair was a costly business and in general was seen as the responsibility of those communities who made use of them. From a security point of view,

52 Lydon, *Ireland in the later Middle Ages*, p. 14.　53 *CARD*, 1, pp 87, 490; *CCCD*, no. 490; Lawlor, '*Liber Niger* and *Liber Albus*', no. 114; M.P. Sheehy, 'The *Registrum Novum*: a manuscript of Holy Trinity Cathedral', *Reportorium Novum: Dublin Diocesan Historical Record*, 3 (1963–4), 249–81 at 264.　54 *CARD*, 2, p. 988.　55 *RAST*, p. 284.
56 *CDI, 1171–1251*, no. 511, p. 81.　57 *RPCH*, p. 128; *CARD*, 1, pp 26–7.　58 *CARD*, 1, p. 284.　59 *CARD*, 1, p. 162.
60 *EIMP*, p. 82.　61 For a listing, see Clarke, *IHTA: Dublin Part I, to 1610*, pp 26–7.　62 *CCCD*, nos. 490, 1256.
63 Rex Bangerter, 'Archaeological assessment, River Griffeen flood alleviation scheme, Lucan Co. Dublin, 02D025, 02R041' (unpublished report for the Archaeological Diving Company Ltd, 2002); see also Peter O'Keeffe and Tom

however, it was necessary for the administration to maintain bridges in strategic areas. In 1358–9, the Irish exchequer spent £60 building a new bridge over the river-bank of Wicklow, in place of an old bridge which was ruinous.[64] This was quite an elaborate structure, however, described as having a crenellated watch-tower and drawbridge in the middle.

The documentary sources stress the importance of keeping transport routes open and removing obstacles. The enactments of the 1297 parliament included one relating to the maintenance of roads and bridges.[65] The king's highway was to be kept sufficiently wide and open and clear of briars and trees, while bridges and causeways were to be repaired. The motivation in this instance was to enable felons and thieves to be quickly pursued but the benefit to trade and commerce may also have been a factor. The main obstacle to river transport was the construction of weirs and fishtraps and there are several instances when Dubliners complained about such structures and the hindrance they posed to trade.[66]

The modern roadmap of the east of Ireland shows a series of major routeways radiating out from Dublin like the spokes of a bicycle wheel. This pattern very much reflects the medieval network of roadways connecting Dublin with its hinterland and beyond. The remains of many of these roads lie buried beneath their modern successors, but from time to time other elements of the medieval communications network come to light. At Killegland, near Ashbourne in Co. Meath, archaeologists uncovered a metalled surface and associated pillar bases, 'possibly representing controlled access to this crossing point on the Broad Meadow River, directly opposite the stepping stones indicated on the first-edition map.[67] This was probably a medieval ford, and the presence of small islands at this point in the river, like those at Oldbridge, Co. Meath, 'supports its use as a crossing point on the river'. 'Material traces of an ancient roadway exist in the landscape; for example, the water-filled boundary which cuts through the site to the west may represent part of a field system which respected the line of an earlier road'. At Phoenixtown, Co. Meath, excavators uncovered the remnants of a metalled road defined by drainage gullies on either side.[68] Intensive agricultural activity, including milling, took place on either side of the road, which seems to have served the local manor.

The trade in grain

Although it had a high value relative to its bulk, grain was still an expensive commodity to transport, and shipping by water had significant cost advantages on reliable river and coastal routes. Merchants and others active in the supply of the grains required by Dublin's bakers and brewers and for export might be expected to have used water transport wherever possible. It is evident, however, that overland carriage by cart and packhorse accounted for a significant element of the city's supply. In part, this doubtless derived from the comparative shortness of the Liffey (particularly of its fully navigable stretch), the periodic obstructions to navigation, and the distance of many grain-producing districts from the coast or a major waterway. It may also have been quicker to bring supplies by road in some cases, avoiding delays in loading and unloading boats and possible transhipment to circumvent obstructions. Thus, in 1282, wheat and oats from Ballysax in Co. Kildare, required as part of the supplies for Wales in that year, were carried to Dublin overland, two horses being hired for the purpose for a period of six weeks.[69] A total of ninety-three quarters

Simington, *Irish stone bridges: history and heritage* (Dublin, 1991), pp 27–9.   **64** *IEP*, p. 491.   **65** Philomena Connolly, 'The enactments of the 1297 Parliament' in James Lydon (ed.), *Law and disorder in thirteenth-century Ireland: the Dublin parliament of 1297* (Dublin, 1997), pp 139–62 at p. 159.   **66** *HMDI*, p. 149; *CJR, 1305–7*, p. 258.   **67** Finola O'Carroll, 'Killegland, Ashbourne' in *Excavations 2003*, p. 359.   **68** Ed Lyne, 'Phoenixtown: lives through time', *AI*, 22:2 (2008), 17–21.   **69** *CDI, 1252–84*, no. 2009, p. 459.

and six bushels of grain were carried which, if loaded into carts of three quarters carrying capacity drawn by two horses, would have necessitated thirty-one return journeys.[70] Despite the lack of evidence for grain being brought into the city by water, the location of many manor centres close to navigable rivers and to the coast suggests that it should not be discounted as a possibility.

Most goods that were sold at the market at Trim, Co. Meath, were transported by horse or horse-and-cart, but the murage lists of 1290 and 1308 also stipulate the taxes payable on each 'ship-load' of wood coming into the town.[71] This indicates that some goods were brought to the market by boat along the Boyne. Indeed Walter de Lacy's 1194 charter to the burgesses of Drogheda granted them the right to free passage on the Boyne from the sea to the bridge at Trim, and states that weirs and all other obstacles were to be removed.[72]

Dublin murages of the thirteenth and early fourteenth centuries – beginning with that of 1233, the earliest to mention grain – imposed toll upon sales of wheat and oats by the crannock or the weigh, leaving open the means by which such grains might be carried to the city.[73] Similarly, the unauthorised toll on grain levied by the Dublin citizens during the turbulent years of the Bruce wars amounted to 4d. per crannock.[74] In the mid-fifteenth century, custom was leviable upon all men and women bringing 'peke bags' of wheat, bere (barley), peas, beans, and malted oats, wheat and dredge to market in Dublin.[75] This clearly suggests an active overland trade in small parcels of grain. As mentioned above (pp 431–2), some of Dublin's bread was baked outside the city and transported in for sale.[76]

Dubliners were supposed to wait for grain to arrive in the city market-places before making their purchases, and not go out into the countryside or to other markets, thereby 'forestalling' the Dublin market. The repeated admonitions in this regard clearly suggest that Dubliners were indeed actively seeking out supplies. The city bakers were prohibited from purchasing grain outside the city gates or anywhere except the city market in an undated ordinance of the fourteenth or fifteenth century.[77] In 1452, city haggard-men (owners of granaries) were forbidden from going into the country to buy corn.[78] Sometimes the Dubliners' actions may have been carried out with the intention of preventing royal purveyors from acquiring supplies in the city, as was alleged in 1309–10.[79] Similarly, it was alleged in 1333 that the actions of royal officials in requisitioning conveyances, horses and carts entering the city was deterring people bringing in victuals and other merchandise and impoverishing the citizens.[80]

It is likely that a city of Dublin's size drew upon the grain trade of smaller centres, which acted as bulking centres and were visited by Dublin merchants seeking large consignments of grain. A commission to purveyors in 1315 specified Lusk and Swords as markets at which wheat should be acquired and brought to Dublin, while in c.1284 corn had been bought at Swords and Dunbro (in the parish of St Margaret's, close to Dunsoghly).[81]

A detailed account survives of the monies spent by Nicholas Goldyng and Hugh de Castleknock, royal purveyors of victuals at Dublin, during the years 1314–15 (Figure 17.4).[82] The commodities which they purchased and transported were wheat, oats and wine. Most

70 The average cartload of wheat in the London region c.1300 – Campbell, Galloway, Keene and Murphy, *A medieval capital*, p. 31. 71 *CDI, 1285–92*, no. 560, pp 277–8; *CPR, 1307–13*, p. 70. 72 Mac Niocaill, *Na buirgéisí*, 2, pp 172–3; Edmund Curtis and R.B. McDowell (eds), *Irish historical documents, 1172–1922* (London, 1943), pp 27–8. 73 *CDI, 1171–1251*, no. 2068, p. 308. Grain and various other commodities were measured in Ireland in crannocks and pecks. A crannock of wheat contained 8 pecks and various sources in the thirteenth century equate it with the English quarter which contained 8 bushels. See *CDI, 1293–1301*, no. 345, p. 159. A bushel of wheat had a weight equivalent of about 53lbs c.1300. See Campbell, Galloway, Keene and Murphy, *A medieval capital*, p. 41. 74 *CARD*, 1, p. 12. 75 Ibid., p. 275. Interestingly, unmalted oats were to be exempt from the toll, which may suggest that this grain was in short supply. 76 *CARD*, 1, p. 313. 77 Ibid., pp 219ff. 78 Ibid., p. 275. 79 *HMDI*, pp 504–5. 80 *CARD*, 1, p. 160. 81 *HMDI*, pp 336–7; *CDI, 1252–84*, no. 2336, p. 555. 82 TNA:PRO E101/14/40.

Figure 17.4 Account of purchases made by the king's purveyors in Dublin, 1314–15 (image reproduced courtesy of the National Archives of the UK, ref: TNA: PRO E101/14/40).

were destined for Skinburness in Cumberland to provision the king's army then campaigning in Scotland. Some supplies were diverted, however, for the war in Leinster and for the provisioning of castles in Ireland such as Carrickfergus. By this date, the grain production capacity of the Dublin hinterland had been exploited for many years by the king's purveyors, who were accustomed to using the marketing structure of the region. The 1314–15 account therefore sheds important light on grain availability and marketing within the region.

During the period May-October 1314, the purveyors itemised forty-seven separate purchases of wheat from a variety of named individuals. Most of the purchases were of ten crannocks or less and they totalled over 451 crannocks. The prices varied, and on occasion quantities purchased on the same day from different individuals showed variation. This suggests either that the quality of the grain differed from seller to seller, or that certain individuals drove a harder bargain or were treated preferentially for some reason. A significant number of sales appear to be from groups of two, three or four individuals or from one individual '*et sociis suis*' (and his companions), indicating that a number of sellers from a particular location or manor banded together to strike a deal. One of the largest single purchases was of forty-five crannocks of wheat from the procurator of the rector of Clonmethan. This parish, situated in arable rich north Co. Dublin, formed one of the prebends of St Patrick's Cathedral and the rector was probably selling some of his parishioners' tithes. The purveyors made one large purchase of oats in this period – seventy-seven crannocks from the attorney of Alexander de Bicknor, archbishop of Dublin.

In 1315, the purveyors were again active – this time making fifty-three separate purchases of wheat (over 667 crannocks) and fifty purchases of oats (over 493 crannocks). Several purchases of both grains were made from individuals from Maynooth, while Carbury and Kilcock are also mentioned. The archbishop's attorney appears again – this time selling wheat. There is a separate section detailing purchases of oats at Swords, a market frequently mentioned by the purveyors. Just fewer than 114 crannocks of oats were purchased in this market in a number of separate transactions.

The purveyors' account reveals a marketing structure in which potential purchasers could obtain grain in a number of different ways. Large purchases were made as the result of deals struck with the representatives of important landowners, such as the archbishop of Dublin, or managers of grains stocks obtained as tithes. Medium purchases of between five and ten crannocks were made from dozens of individuals, some of whom may have been operating in cooperative groups. Furthermore, market towns in the region were visited at times when it was likely to meet with rural producers selling surplus grain. The account suggests that the rural markets at Swords and Maynooth played a particularly important role in the grain trade in the early fourteenth century.

The system operating in the Dublin area can be compared with that in the Drogheda region, for which a number of similar purveyors' accounts survive.[83] A purveyance carried out there between May and November 1314 shows that the purchase of both wheat and oats was dominated by small parcels, suggesting that many of those whose grain was drawn upon were peasant farmers or small-scale traders. Of forty purchases of wheat made by the Drogheda purveyors, thirty-three were of less than five crannocks. Three larger purchases, however, including one from the prior of Duleek, accounted for 46 per cent of the total, which, at just over 155 crannocks, was considerably smaller than the amount purchased in and around Dublin in the same year.

Little is known of the merchants who handled medieval Dublin's grain supplies, or of the balance between citizens and outsiders in the grain trade. Much of the trade may have been in the hands of general merchants, who traded in grain among a range of other commodities. In the haggard-men who appear in fifteenth-century records, however, Dublin may have possessed a group of organised corn-dealers, who both purchased and stored grain for re-sale. While the city authorities attempted to prevent haggard owners from seeking out country corn, and sought to compel them to sell to their neighbours at below the market rate, it seems probable that this group was playing a significant role in the city's grain supply.[84] Specialised dealing in grain was uncommon in medieval English towns apart from London, which had a numerous and organised guild of *bladarii* or corn-mongers *c.*1300, and the Dublin haggard-men may have been responding to particular difficulties and opportunities in the fifteenth-century lordship.[85] At the same time that the Dublin authorities were seeking to control the activities of those storing and trading grain, the Irish parliament was concerned with preventing the export of grain from Ireland. A petition to the parliament of 1471 complained of the 'gret derthe and famyn' which had befallen the king's subjects in Ireland because of 'the grete ladyng of graynes of whete, malt, ry, meslon and other graynes out of this lande into diverse parties of England, Scotland and Walys'.[86]

Whatever the precise organisation of the trade, there is some evidence to suggest that, at least in the thirteenth and fourteenth centuries, the grain market in the Dublin region operated in a reasonably efficient manner. Supplies were readily available in the city, and much of the grain purveyed was purchased in the city's market-places, rather than having to be sought in the countryside.

Grain prices

The price of grain was of vital interest to all levels of medieval society as cereals formed such an important element in the diet of all classes. It has been estimated that the wealthiest households spent about a third of their food budgets on cereals, while the proportion rose accordingly in the case of the less well off.[87]

83 TNA:PRO E101/14/35; we are grateful to Jim Galloway for sharing the results of his on-going research into the Drogheda purveyance accounts. **84** *CARD*, i, pp 275, 341. **85** For a study of the London corn-mongers, see Campbell, Galloway, Keene and Murphy, *A medieval capital*, pp 81–6. **86** *CARD*, i, p. 172. **87** Dyer, 'English diet

Historical investigations of market structure and integration commonly draw upon price evidence, and while medieval Irish price data are scant, they do permit some observations to be made. Dublin wheat prices from the late thirteenth century moved broadly in tandem with those in England, suggesting that the market was responsive to external stimuli.[88] The Dublin prices were generally below average English prices, a factor which clearly underlay the repeated sourcing in Ireland of wheat, oats and other supplies required by English armies, as well as the buoyant commercial export trade of the thirteenth and early fourteenth centuries. That the gap was not always substantial, however, is testified by Henry III's discovery that 'corn, wine and other supplies are dearer in Ireland than the king believed'.[89] That prices varied within the Dublin hinterland in a logical manner is suggested by the comparison of the price of wheat in the city in 1283 and that obtained by the manorial officers of Ballysax in Co. Kildare in the same year. The Ballysax price was almost exactly equal to the Dublin price minus the recorded price of transport between the two places of 3d. per crannock.[90] This is consistent with the Dublin market being the major influence upon the price of grain within its hinterland, and with the proposition that, at least in this part of Ireland and at this period, the grain market operated efficiently.

The graph (Figure 17.5) shows prices, in shillings, for a crannock (quarter) of wheat. It appears to indicate that wheat prices in Dublin moved in a similar way to those in England, with low prices in the late 1280s and significantly higher prices in the mid-1290s. Overall, the Dublin price was 13 per cent lower than the average English price, although in two of the nine years for which direct comparison can be made, the Dublin price was slightly above the English price level. In the period 1280–1300, therefore, Dubliners were paying, on average, 5s. 4d. for a crannock of wheat, or about 10d. less than the 6s. 1¾d. that consumers in England were paying in the same period.

It is more difficult to construct a price series based on market prices for any part of Ireland after about 1300. For the Dublin area, it is possible to put together a collection of price material from various sources, including judicial valuations, purveyance payments and chronicle evidence, for the period 1300–50.[91] This collection, while not in any way statistically robust, can furnish some rough idea of prevailing levels. The period saw considerable variation in prices. On average, however, wheat prices ranged between 4s. 6d. and 5s. 6d. a crannock, and again can be seen to mirror the movements of English prices. After 1350, price material becomes even thinner, but having established a broad correlation with English price series it can be postulated that Dublin wheat prices continued to move in the same general direction as English ones. This would mean therefore that they declined in the later fourteenth century and remained low throughout the fifteenth century.

The trade in livestock and meat

The trade in livestock was potentially the most complex of the provisioning systems operating within and beyond the Dublin hinterland. The fact that livestock could be driven to market on the hoof meant that the live animal supply hinterland of a major town or city could be considerably more extended than those for grain and fuel, with distant cattle-rearing districts linked to urban consumers via intermediate fattening districts and regular droving routes.[92] In England, fairs constituted one of the major venues for the sale and purchase of livestock in the medieval and early modern periods, frequented by peasants and

in the later Middle Ages', p. 193.　**88** Murphy and Potterton, 'Investigating living standards', pp 236–9.　**89** *CDI, 1171–1251*, no. 2835, p. 423.　**90** *CDI, 1252–84*, no. 2009, pp 459–60.　**91** A large collection of price material was assembled by M.C. Lyons ('Manorial administration').　**92** J.A. Galloway, 'Metropolitan market networks: London's economic hinterland in the later Middle Ages', *London and Middlesex Archaeological Society Transactions*, 50 (1999), 91–7 at 94–5.

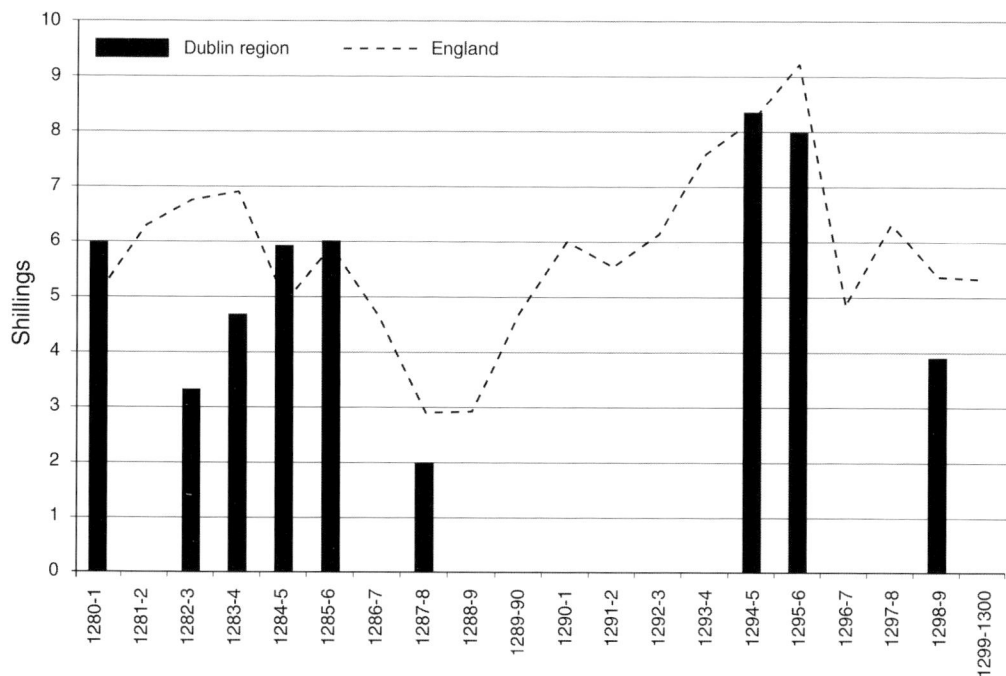

Figure 17.5 Wheat prices in Dublin and England, 1280–1300. Sources: prices for the Dublin region, 1280–1, 1283–4, 1284–5, 1285–6, 1287–8 from TNA: PRO SC6/1237/1, 3–6 (ministers' accounts for the manor of Ballysax); 1282–3 from CDI, 1252–84, pp 459–61, no. 2009; 1294–5, 1295–6, 1298–9 from CDI, 1285–92, p. 99, no. 215, pp 159ff, p. 272, no. 559. All English prices from Farmer, 'Some grain price movements in thirteenth-century England', EcHR, 2nd ser., 102 (1957), 207–20. We are particularly grateful to Jim Galloway for advice on presenting this price material.

manorial officers seeking to sell or replace their farm stock, and by the urban butchers and professional cattle-dealers who coordinated longer-distance networks of supply. Weekly markets also saw much trade in live animals, however, and private dealing in town and countryside was common.[93]

The role played in the live-animal trade of fairs and small-town markets in and adjacent to the Dublin hinterland can be seen from various references. In 1305, Thomas de Cantelou was abused in the market-place of Naas while engaged in selling the lambs of his lord, Philip le Flemeng.[94] Kildare markets may have acquired their specialism in horse-trading by c.1300. On one occasion in 1298, men of the sheriff of Kildare were able to find as many as eighty affers (work-horses) in the market at Cloncurry, which they took for carriage, while a horse was stolen from the market-place at Maynooth in 1311.[95] Dublin's fair and markets were major sources of both live and dead animals for the purveyors of the late thirteenth century.[96] Supplies may normally have been abundant, although a 'dearth of flesh meat' was noted in 1364 as a reason to limit prices charged by city butchers.[97] 'Foreign merchants' brought skinned carcases of oxen and cows for sale at the butchers' stalls at the Dublin fair; undated late medieval provisions required payment of custom of one penny per carcase from dealers, but exempted those who sold 'through need'.[98] In 1470, it was ordained that country butchers bringing meat to the city should be [toll] free.[99] These references imply that a considerable amount of slaughtering of animals must have been carried out in the rural districts and small towns of the Dublin hinterland. Indeed, from 1366, if not earlier, butchers were prohibited from slaughtering beasts within the walls of Dublin.[100]

Early sixteenth-century references show that parts of Co. Meath were involved in the supply of cattle to Dublin butchers. In 1530, two Athboy merchants were found to have forestalled the Athboy market by buying cows at 'Windmillhill', half a mile outside the town, which they then sold at a profit to the Dubliners William White, a butcher, and Donald Dyrney. Five years later, six Athboy merchants were found to have done the same

93 Farmer, 'Marketing the produce of the countryside', pp 377–94.   94 CJR, 1305–7, pp 149, 218.   95 CJR, 1294–1302, p. 198; CJR, 1308–14, p. 218.   96 CDI, 1252–84, no. 2009, p. 459.   97 CARD, I, p. 235.   98 Ibid., p. 232.   99 Ibid., p. 341.   100 Ibid., p. 236.

thing, intercepting cattle at Windmillhill and selling on to Dyrney and to William Corkran, a butcher from Dublin.[101]

Arising from the Dublin meat and livestock trade was a trade in fresh hides, which might be exported or supplied to tanners within the city or elsewhere. Tanners formed a noticeable element in the new freemen admitted in the thirteenth century, and again in the surviving late fifteenth- and early sixteenth-century admissions (see above, pp 439–40), and regulations were put in place to ensure that city butchers did not sell fresh hides to 'foreigners'.[102]

The trade in wool

A recent study has estimated that by 1300 there were possibly one million sheep in Ireland producing wool for export.[103] The customs levied on wool exports for New Ross, Waterford and Wexford indicate that in the region of three million fleeces may have left these three ports in the period 1275–9.[104] The markets for Irish wool were predominantly the great cloth manufacturing centres of Flanders, where it was used for making less expensive cloth.[105] The bulk of the wool exports left from Waterford and New Ross and most of the surviving evidence suggests that the main wool-producing area of medieval Ireland was the south-eastern region.[106] When three wool staples were set up in Ireland in 1326, however, Dublin and Drogheda were included along with Cork, while Waterford was added later (staples were places through which the exports of wool, woolfells and hides were compulsorily directed). Dublin does not appear to have been a major exporter of wool, but there is enough evidence to suggest that this was an important commodity in the economic life of the region.

Dubliners were involved in the wool trade, and carts loaded with wool sacks were a common sight heading into the city. In 1221, the citizens of Dublin were allowed to levy a murage payment of 3*d*. on each sack of wool being brought into Dublin for sale.[107] In c.1240, permission was given for the construction of a gate for carts laden with hides and wool to have access to the Liffey, presumably to load for export.[108] In 1255, Prince Edward was in Bazas (in Gascony) and, presumably short of money, instructed his Irish treasurer in Dublin to deliver fifty sacks of wool to a citizen of Bordeaux.[109] This again implies an abundance of sheep in the region. Towns on the fringes of the Dublin region acted as bulking centres for wool and merchants could purchase wool there to bring to Dublin for export. In 1305, a merchant, Richard Snow, complained that nine sacks of wool belonging to him had been confiscated and that he was out of pocket to the tune of 100*s*.[110] He had purchased the wool in the town of Naas and intended to carry it to Dublin.

The trade in fuel

The fuel trade was characterised by bulky and comparatively low-value produce, and transport considerations were thus of great significance. Water transport was several times cheaper than overland haulage when safe and navigable routes were available, but the presence of natural and man-made obstructions necessitating transhipment could significantly narrow the cost differential. In England, London's great demand for fuel of various types resulted in the development of a specialised trade along the River Thames, with overland carriage of firewood normally restricted to areas within some 14–20km of the city in the

101 Griffith, *Cal. inquisitions*, pp 30, 42. **102** *DCFR, passim; CARD*, I, p. 219. **103** Campbell, 'The medieval economy', p. 103. **104** James Lydon, 'The expansion and consolidation of the colony 1215–54' in Cosgrove (ed.), *A new history of Ireland: II* (1993), p. 167. This figure is an estimate – the sums given represent a mixture of fleeces and hides which unfortunately cannot be differentiated. **105** O'Neill, *Merchants and mariners*, p. 59. **106** Ibid., p. 61. **107** *CDI, 1171–1251*, no. 1002, p. 154. **108** *CARD*, I, p. 84. **109** *CDI, 1252–84*, no. 429, p. 69. **110** *CJR, 1305–7*, p. 107.

fourteenth century. The London trade was characterised by a large group of specialised wood-mongers, who dealt both in firewood and in timber for building, and who occupied particular areas of the city, owned river-boats and had commercial interests in smaller towns and landing places along the valley of the River Thames.[111] There is little evidence for the existence of such specialised fuel traders in the Dublin region, presumably because of the smaller aggregate demand, but it is clear that both water and overland transport were drawn upon to bring fuel to the city. The Dublin murage of 1312 imposed tolls upon carts and boats carrying firewood and upon packhorses carrying both firewood and charcoal, an easily damaged fuel which was less suited to transportation in bumpy wheeled vehicles.[112]

Land and water carriage were to some extent complementary, as heavy firewood and building timber would have had to be carted or dragged to places where it could be loaded onto boats or directly floated. While quantification is impossible, the River Liffey and coastal trade from Wicklow seem likely to have been the most important arteries by which fuel came to the city. Complaints about obstruction of the Liffey by weirs and fish-traps at Chapelizod, Kilmainham, Lucan, Palmerstown and elsewhere make specific reference to a regular trade in firewood, both carried in boats and floated as bundles (*busca colligata*).[113] As early as 1220, the prior of Kilmainham was said to have obstructed the Dubliners' trade in victuals, stone and firewood through the construction of a weir.[114] Much of the wood brought from Wicklow was in the form of building timber and boards, but this coastal trade certainly also included firewood. A late sixteenth-century lease of the rectory of Killaharlot or Killaharlan in the lordship of Arklow included the provision that the lessee should deliver fourteen tons of firewood yearly at Wood Quay in Dublin.[115] Mid-fifteenth-century regulations required that wood from Wicklow should be exposed on the quay for twenty days before retail sale, and attempted to prevent the storage of wood in houses, probably for safety reasons as well as to prevent private trading away from the quayside market.[116]

Documentary sources hardly ever specify from what species of trees firewood was taken. English evidence suggests that ash was the premier coppiced wood-fuel, although many other species were also drawn upon. Evidence from a site at Carmanhall suggests that species such as alder, hazel, ash and *prunus* species (such as blackthorn) were used for fuel, while oak was reserved for structural purposes only.[117] Ellen O'Carroll concluded that most of the wood may have originated from mixed woodlands, while the alder suggests a slightly wetter environment, and the *prunus* is indicative of hedges. Among the findings from the analysis of insect remains from Back Lane were indicators of dead or decaying oak or pine, and Eileen Reilly suggested that these species may have been brought into the town with consignments of firewood.[118] In the late twelfth century, the burgesses of Trim, Co. Meath, were permitted to take old wood from the floor of the forest of Trim for use as firewood, under the supervision of Walter de Lacy's foresters.[119] Such a permit was relatively common in the late twelfth and early thirteenth centuries.[120]

Provisioning Dublin

The single most important market for the rural surpluses of the region throughout the period under consideration was of course the city of Dublin. Although the size of the

111 Murphy, 'The fuel supply of medieval London', pp 90–4. **112** *HMDI*, pp 308–12. **113** *CJR, 1305–7*, p. 258. **114** *HMDI*, p. 149. **115** *CCCD*, no. 1391. **116** *CARD*, 1, pp 284–5. A marginal illustration in the manuscript here apparently shows 'a drawing of a horse with a bundle of wood', which suggests that the clerk at least was thinking of firewood in recording these regulations. **117** DEHLG file 02E0074 (Carmanhall: site 55m; analysis by Ellen O'Carroll). **118** Reilly, 'The contribution of insect remains', pp 56–8. **119** *CPI*, p. 10; Mac Niocaill, *Na buirgéisí*, 1, pp 74–5; 2, pp 327, 481. **120** Ballard (ed.), *Charters 1042–1216*, pp 52–7.

medieval city is the subject of considerable debate (see Chapter 1), the scale of Dublin's demands would have surpassed by far the demands of any other urban centre in Ireland. Within the region there were few other fully fledged towns and there were none within the county of Dublin itself.

A method which has been used recently in several provisioning studies has been to estimate the aggregate demand for specific commodities generated by urban settlements and then to estimate the rural area needed to meet these demands.[121] This is most often done for grain because of the essential place it occupied in the medieval diet. Whether consumed as bread, brewed into ale, or taken as a component of pottages and soups, cereals were responsible for at least 70 per cent of calorific intake in the diets of the thirteenth and early fourteenth centuries.[122] There has already been an attempt to estimate elements of the resource consumption of Dublin *c*.1100. Siobhán Geraghty calculated that at this period Dublin may have required the cereal production of some 10,000 acres for its bread.[123] She estimated the town's population at 4,500 and used a rather high allocation of 2.2 quarters of grain per head per annum. However, she did not include an allowance for ale.

In calculating London's grain consumption *c*.1300, the Feeding the City project used an allowance of 1.65 quarters of grain per head of population.[124] The estimate was more nuanced in that it took into account the extraction rates for converting bread grains to flour and brewing grains to ale, and the total allowance also included an element for the fodder requirements of the horses needed to transport the grain into the city. The allowance of grain was believed to be equivalent to 1¼lbs of coarse bread and a pint of weak ale per person per day.

Population figures for Dublin *c*.1300 range from 10,000 to 26,000. One might roughly estimate that the average consumption of grain was two quarters per head per annum, giving a minimum requirement of 20,000 quarters and a maximum of 52,000. It is generally believed that an acre of medieval arable land would produce a quarter of grain each year. Therefore, if the population of Dublin *c*.1300 was a modest 10,000, 20,000 acres of grain would be needed to supply its bread and ale needs. In reality, only about half of the total yield from each acre would have been available for disposal, and a proportion of this would not have made it as far as the city. In addition, a third of the arable land would have been fallow each year. We might therefore surmise that the footprint of medieval Dublin in terms of the area needed to supply its grain needs *c*.1300 was in the region of 60,000 acres of arable. If the population *c*.1300 reached 20,000, then the arable area needed to supply it with grain would have been 120,000 acres. There were some 400,000 acres of land within a 30km radius of Dublin. Even if only 50 per cent of this land area was under arable cultivation then Dublin's grain needs could be comfortably met from within it. In addition, however, the needs of the people dwelling in the countryside had to be met, and there was also a considerable export market.

In estimating the area of Dublin's hinterland most likely to have met its market needs it is useful to examine research on English cities and towns.[125] The 'Feeding the City' project attempted to define London's grain-supply area *c*.1300 by a variety of independent measures, each of which tended to support the other. They included the range of activity of London

121 For a discussion of this method, see Murphy, 'Feeding medieval cities'.   **122** Separate studies of soldiers in Scotland, harvest workers in the English midlands and households of the English lay-nobility revealed diets where between 65% and 80% of calorific intake was provided by grains in the form of bread, ale, oatmeal flour, pasties and pastries: Michael Prestwich, 'Victualling estimates for English garrisons in Scotland during the early fourteenth century', *EHR*, 52 (1967), 536–43; Christopher Dyer, 'Changes in diet in the late Middle Ages: the case of harvest workers', *AHS*, 36 (1988), 21–37; J.M. Thurgood, 'The diet and domestic households of the English lay nobility, 1265–1531' (MPhil., University of London, 1982).   **123** Geraghty, *Viking Dublin*, pp 57–71.   **124** Campbell, Galloway, Keene and Murphy, *A medieval capital*, pp 31–6.   **125** See the papers in Galloway (ed.), *Trade, urban hinterlands and market*

corn-mongers, the pattern of transport costs to the city, the integration of London and local prices, and the evidence for the production and disposal of different grains in the hinterland. The cost of transport emerged as the prime but not the sole determinant of the shape of the supply region. In normal years, London's grain supply area appears to have extended to include market towns up to about twenty miles from the city when only land transport was available, and up to about sixty miles (as the crow flies) when water transport could be used.[126] York, England's northern capital, with around 15,000 inhabitants c.1300, also had a noticeable effect on its agrarian hinterland. A similar case might be made for Bristol, third in rank with at least 12–13,000 inhabitants in the later fourteenth century.[127] Recent research on the hinterland of medieval Cambridge, a town with a population of between 4,000 and 5,000 for much of the Middle Ages, demonstrated that 'for many economic purposes, the town was served by its local region of about 10 to 15 miles in radius'.[128] Although this area appears to be quite restricted, it is clear that between 1450 and 1560 at least, the local hinterland was just one of 'three inter-connecting regions linked to the town'– the others being 'a regional hinterland stretching to just over 50 miles away, and more distant ties with other urban centres'.[129] Lower-value consumables generally came from closer to the town, with more expensive goods being transported over greater distances.[130] In time, the colleges at Cambridge appear to have had to look further afield for charcoal and firewood – supplies closer to the town may have been exhausted as forestry was felled to make way for food crops.[131] The author of the Cambridge study concluded by suggesting that the hinterland of most English towns in the Middle Ages was more restricted than might otherwise be assumed.[132]

The population of later fourteenth-century Winchester was in the region of 8,000 and the town appears to have been supplied with grain from within a radius of about twelve miles.[133] It lacked a navigable river and was situated in a region of relatively unintensive farming. In contrast, however, Exeter in the same period, even smaller than Winchester (3–4,000), seems to have drawn its supplies from up to twenty miles away, from a hinterland more intractable and less productive than Winchester.[134] Colchester, which was probably smaller than Exeter, appears in this period regularly to have drawn its grain from places up to eight miles distant by road.[135]

The research on English towns confirms that the correlation between an urban centre's size and the extent and shape of its normal supply region was complex and affected by factors such as topography, the range of transport options available, and the proximity of other local and regional centres. While the population of medieval Dublin is uncertain, indications are that in the late thirteenth century it was larger than urban centres such as Cambridge, Winchester and Exeter and may have been of a similar size to Bristol and even York.

The parts of the region from which Dublin received its essential supplies were probably defined at an early stage when the Ostman town developed an infrastructure of transport and exchange linking urban and rural settlements. This infrastructure was further expanded following the foundation of religious houses in the town and their endowment with country estates. Substantial transfers of provisions from rural granges to central monastic cellars not only served to feed the resident religious, but also would have provided surpluses for sale in the urban market. In the pre-Norman period the provisioning hinterland of Dublin may

integration, c.1300–1600. **126** Campbell, Galloway, Keene and Murphy, *A medieval capital*, pp 172–3. **127** Galloway, 'Town and country in England, 1300–1570', p. 119. **128** J.S. Lee, *Cambridge and its economic region, 1450–1560* (Hatfield, Herefordshire, 2005), pp 6–7. **129** Ibid., p. 203. **130** Ibid., p. 172. **131** Ibid., p. 159. **132** Ibid., p. 204. **133** Keene, *Survey of medieval Winchester*, pp 251–5, fig. 27. **134** Maryanne Kowaleski, 'The grain trade in fourteenth-century Exeter' in E.B. DeWindt (ed.), *The salt of common life: individuality and choice in the medieval town, countryside and church: essays presented to J. Ambrose Raftis* (Kalamazoo, MI, 1995), pp 1–52. **135** Britnell, *Growth and decline in Colchester*, p. 44.

have included most of Co. Dublin, with the zone within 10km of the town experiencing the most profound impact.[136] This zone would have been elongated north and south along the coast which supplied the fish and shellfish consumed in the town.[137]

When the Anglo-Normans arrived there was therefore a provisioning infrastructure in place which could serve as a framework for the system needed to support a much larger town and colonial capital in the thirteenth century. The rapid organisation of manorial centres and granges, endowing of new religious houses, incorporation of boroughs and foundation of markets and fairs in the hinterland all served to bring a wider area into the normal provisioning zone of Dublin. Population growth within Dublin created a large market for agrarian produce, in particular for cereals needed for the staple foodstuffs of bread and ale. A growing labour force in the manorialised countryside promoted the intensification of cereal production and the expansion of land under the plough. Documentary evidence suggests that c.1300 an average of 70 per cent of the land in the Dublin region was devoted to cereal cultivation (Figure 9.1 and Table 9.2). In north Co. Dublin, south-east Meath and parts of north-east Kildare the proportion of land under the plough was even higher. These areas can be characterised as forming Dublin's grain provisioning zone although lands in the very north of Co. Dublin and in parts of Meath were probably equally affected by the demands of Drogheda, the next largest settlement on the east coast. In the seventeenth century, Richard Stanihurst described this area as 'the barn of Ireland'.[138] The evidence of the Dublin purveyance discussed above ties in to a large extent with the land-use pattern with Swords and Maynooth emerging as the two most important rural markets for the purchase of wheat and oats. These areas also emerge with some of the highest values per acre for arable land, reflecting the profits expected from cereal production (Table 9.3).

Despite the apparent dominance of arable farming across much of the county, there is abundant evidence that dairying and livestock-rearing were also a significant feature of the region. Meat formed an important part of the diet in medieval Dublin and it is likely that in common with most other European towns, the proportion of meat eaten increased during the fourteenth and fifteenth centuries.[139] If the diet of the prior of Holy Trinity Priory in the fourteenth century can be taken as being in any way typical of the diet of a wealthy consumer, then meat featured very heavily on the tables of well-to-do Dubliners.[140] Faunal evidence suggests that cattle provided as much as 79 per cent of the meat eaten in Dublin, pig 18 per cent and sheep only 3 per cent (Figure 9.19). As so much of the land to the north was dominated by arable agriculture, it appears likely that Dublin looked to the south for its meat and dairy produce, although draught cattle undoubtedly found their way onto the capital's tables when they reached the end of their useful lives. Land-use data and incidental references support the view that Dublin was largely provisioned with meat and dairy produce from the south, where pastoral farming had always been important. In the later medieval period when supplies from this area were affected by the political situation, it is probable that Dublin butchers had to look further afield for their supplies. As a commodity which could be transported on the hoof, livestock was not subject to the same transport cost constraints. Perhaps the reference to Dublin butchers sourcing supplies 65km from the city in Athboy, Co. Meath, in the early sixteenth century reflects a widening and reorientation of Dublin's livestock provisioning zone.

Much closer to the city, supplies of vegetables, fruit and poultry from the many orchards and gardens belonging to citizens and religious houses played some part in the provisioning

136 See Valante, 'Dublin's economic relations', pp 71–6.   **137** Geraghty, *Viking Dublin*, p. 67.   **138** Colm Lennon, *Richard Stanihurst the Dubliner* (Dublin, 1981), p. 143.   **139** Murphy and Potterton, 'Investigating living standards', pp 239–45.   **140** Mills (ed.), *Account roll*, passim.

of Dublin. The rivers and the coast played a more important part, however, and faunal remains demonstrate that fish and shellfish made a crucial contribution to the diet.[141] The documentary sources reveal that, in the medieval period, the coastal area to the north and south of Dublin was extensively exploited for its fishing and much of this catch found its way into the city. The fact that religious houses zealously guarded their customary rights to renders of fish from their coastal properties testifies to the importance of this dietary element. As stated above (p. 398), the coastal fishing settlements may have been more closely integrated into Dublin's provisioning hinterland than some geographically closer inland areas.

The challenge of meeting urban society's need for fuel was just as great as the challenge of feeding it, and it too placed considerable demands on hinterlands and distributive systems.[142] In the medieval period, Dublin would have been the focus of the most substantial demand for fuel in Ireland. Firstly there were the needs of baking, brewing and food preparation. Furthermore, the long, cold winters would have necessitated a substantial energy expenditure on home heating. Medieval methods of food and drink preparation required considerable fuel inputs, with pottages and stews requiring long periods of simmering, while brewing and baking were similarly energy hungry.[143] The various hospitals, inns and hostelries clustered together in the capital were significant consumers of fuel. Dublin and its suburbs would also have generated a large industrial demand for fuel – the manufacture of pottery and tiles, metalworking, glass-making and the manufacture of lime all required fuel for kilns and braziers.

There are no contemporary records of total quantities of fuel consumed in medieval Dublin, but recent work on the fuel requirements of medieval London can provide some basis for comparison.[144] This research has put forward an estimated per caput annual fuel requirement of 1.76 tons of wood for each Londoner in the medieval period. The figure covers both the domestic needs of the general population and the fuel consumed by industry. Using an estimated output figure of two tons of wood per intensively managed woodland acre, it was proposed that London's total fuel needs in 1300 required the entire underwood output of some 70,000 acres.[145] Using the same figures with reference to medieval Dublin's proposed requirement, it can be estimated that c.1300, with a possible population of 15,000 persons, the output of some 13,200 acres of intensively managed woodland would have been needed. This figure is almost certainly a gross overestimate. Leaving aside the uncertainty as to the size of medieval Dublin, it should be noted that industrial activity in London was undoubtedly far greater. Furthermore, while turf was not used to any extent in London, it was certainly available and used as a fuel in Dublin. An undated, but probably seventeenth-century reference to customs payable on horse-loads of fuel in the city itemises 'faggotts, wood, furs, fern, turfe and straw', and it is probable that all of these items had also formed elements of the medieval city's fuel supply.[146]

Geographical models such as that of Johann Von Thünen propose that as wood is so bulky and expensive to transport, there should be a zone of woodland located very close to an urban centre.[147] Research on medieval London revealed that areas close to the city or within easy reach of navigable water retained significant areas of woodland throughout the

141 Murphy and Potterton, 'Investigating living standards', pp 246–8. 142 Murphy, 'The fuel supply of medieval London'. 143 Witney, 'The woodland economy of Kent', 31; see above, pp 367–8. 144 Galloway, Keene and Murphy, 'Fuelling the city'. 145 Ibid., p. 456. 146 CARD, 1, p. 262. 147 Peter Hall (ed.) and C.M. Wartenberg (trans.), Von Thünen's Isolated State: an English edition of Der Isolierte Staat by Johann Heinrich von Thünen (London, 1966).

period. There is some evidence that this was also the case in the Dublin region. Most of the land within 4–5km of the city was in the hands of ecclesiastical owners who appear to have carefully managed pockets of woodlands to supply their own needs into the sixteenth century (see above, pp 364–6). At a further remove, a combination of land-use information and documentary evidence suggests that timber and wood fuel supplies came from coastal Wicklow and parts of the Liffey Valley, where water transport could be utilised. By the seventeenth century, there was a chronic shortage of wood in much of Co. Dublin and alternative fuels such as turf and furze were being increasingly exploited.

Chapter summary

In conclusion, it would appear that the provisioning relationship between Dublin and its rural hinterland was moulded by a number of factors. Patterns of landownership had an impact, particularly the preponderance of ecclesiastical lands close to the city, as religious houses were to some extent immune to market forces and pursued their own provisioning strategies. For most of the inhabitants of Dublin, the regular supply of affordable commodities was of great importance, and efforts were made to source the staple necessities in the most economic way possible. Dublin's role as colonial capital and gathering point for military provisioning aided the development of an integrated transport and marketing structure in the hinterland, but the activities of royal officials were sometimes resented by the populace when they interfered with normal supply patterns. In the fourteenth and fifteenth centuries when the 'land of war' approached ever closer to the city, different strategies had to be employed to source some products, and the provisioning hinterland shifted accordingly.

Apart from crisis years when weather, crop failure or severe political instability threatened supplies, Dublin appears to have been comfortably provisioned from its hinterland. The limits of this hinterland differed depending on the product. The documentary evidence suggests that most grain came into the city overland in horse-drawn carts and was brought in by rural producers. The practical limits of such direct provisioning has been estimated at *c.*30–40km or the maximum distance a farmer could conveniently carry grain and return the same day, or, at most, spending one night away. It therefore appears likely that Dublin's grain requirement was largely met from within a 30km zone. It is not clear whether Dublin's demand for food had a structured impact upon its region such as has been revealed in the study of medieval London. It seems that the city's grain needs were substantially met by the region to the north, while the requirement for meat, dairy produce and wood was largely satisfied by the southern hinterland. The demands of the city may have had a role in shaping this spatial specialisation, but environmental factors exerted an equal if not greater influence.

PART V

CONCLUSIONS

CHAPTER 18

Conclusions

The principal aim of this book has been to produce a detailed regional study of settlement in Ireland in the medieval period using a combination of archaeological and documentary source material. The region under investigation is large, comprising over twenty baronies and 200 parishes. At the core of the region lay Dublin, the biggest urban centre in Ireland and an important administrative, commercial and judicial hub of the English colony in Ireland. Dublin, with a population of at least 10,000 in the thirteenth and early fourteenth century, was firmly placed at the apex of the medieval Irish urban hierarchy and exerted an unparalleled level of influence over its surrounding area.[1] Virtually all parts of the study region lay within 35km of the centre of medieval Dublin and were potentially within the city's provisioning zone.

Notwithstanding the important defining role of Dublin, the focus of the book has been on rural settlement and the ownership and occupation of land which was primarily exploited agriculturally. Outside of the city and suburbs of Dublin, the character of the region was essentially rural, with only Naas and possibly Ratoath, both on the fringes of the region, achieving anything close to urban status during the medieval period. There was a scatter of chartered boroughs across the region, but even the most successful of these, at locations such as Swords, cannot be seen as urban. Burgesses at Swords, for example, were required to perform labour services such as reaping the lord's corn and carting his hay.[2]

The field of medieval Irish settlement studies has seen the publication of several regional studies where the research area has been defined by a combination of geographical, political and administrative factors.[3] The present book, however, represents the first intensive study of a hinterland area in medieval Ireland. As a result, in addition to providing a comprehensive description of patterns of settlement, landholding, agriculture, industry and economy, this book addresses and explores other issues. The size of Dublin, its long history as an urban centre, and the fact that it was home to the largest religious establishments, the wealthiest bishop and the most influential and affluent households in Ireland, resulted in a complex and far-reaching relationship with its hinterland. This inevitably had an impact on patterns of rural settlement and the practice of agriculture. In describing these patterns and practices, this book assesses the particular role which Dublin played in their formation.

In the course of the book, certain themes have emerged which are presented here as a framework for the conclusions. They are: the importance of the environment; continuity

1 See above, pp 30–1. Very few reliable population estimates exist for other Irish towns. Russell estimated that the ports of New Ross, Waterford and Galway may have had populations of around 3,000 in the late thirteenth century, but some of his propositions are questionable (Russell, 'Late thirteenth-century Ireland as a region', 506). The largest inland town was Kilkenny, and Bradley has proposed a figure of between 1,800 and 3,500 for the combined boroughs of Hightown and Irishtown in the thirteenth and early fourteenth centuries (John Bradley, *IHTA: Kilkenny* (Dublin, 2000), pp 2, 4). 2 See above, p. 194. 3 Examples of book-length regional studies which focus on settlement patterns and employ both documentary and archaeological sources include Tom McNeill, *Anglo-Norman Ulster: the history and*

and change; lordship and land; the practice of agriculture; and the interdependence of town and country.

The importance of the environment

The growth of Dublin into Ireland's largest town can be attributed to many factors, but it would certainly not have been possible without the presence of a fertile and productive hinterland. Most of the countryside around Dublin was ideally endowed for agriculture. The low-lying lands to the north were perfect for arable cultivation, while mixed farming predominated in the south, with the well-drained upland areas being particularly suitable for livestock rearing. The north Wicklow hills provided wood for building and for fuel, while the long coastline with its numerous harbours ensured plentiful supplies of fish as well as opportunities for trade and travel. These factors determined patterns of settlement from earliest times and continued to exert a strong influence in the period under consideration and beyond. In 1577, when Richard Stanihurst described the pleasant situation of Dublin with easy access to hills, champion ground, fresh water and the coast, he was largely concerned with portraying the city as attractive to the visitor.[4] The features he accurately described, however, had played a vital role in shaping the city and provisioning its inhabitants over the course of many centuries.

The physical environment – in particular topography, soils and the varying suitability of land for different types of agriculture – was probably the most important factor in determining patterns of settlement across the hinterland. In considering the degree to which settlement forms and features were associated with geological and topographical patterns, a central theme which emerges is the contrast between the areas north of Dublin and those which lay to the west and south. Differences between the settlement forms found in the north and south of the region are apparent from at least the early medieval period, and these differences can in large part be attributed to variations in the exploitation of agricultural land.

North of Dublin, the low-lying land with light and fertile grey-brown podzolic soil was most suitable for arable agriculture, and ringforts appear much less frequently here than in the more pastoral areas of the south. It is impossible to know whether this absence is due to the area never having many of these dispersed defended farmsteads in the first place, or to the possibility that their use here declined much earlier than elsewhere. It could be that the environmental predisposition to arable agriculture encouraged a more nucleated pattern of settlement. This is perhaps what is being reflected in the unenclosed dwelling and processing clusters currently being discovered in north-east Leinster.[5] This area supported a number of large monasteries in the early medieval period, but also increasingly came under the influence of Scandinavian Dublin. From the tenth century onwards, the growing population of Dublin created demand for grain and north Co. Dublin's designation as the 'bread-basket' of the capital can probably be traced back to this period. The environmental attributes of the area were obvious to the Anglo-Normans when they arrived, and the introduction of new farming methods and the growing market for cereal crops sustained, and even augmented, the dominance of arable cultivation. Some of the largest manors in Leinster were located here and substantial manorial villages developed at locations like Lusk and Swords.

archaeology of an Irish barony, 1177–1400 (Edinburgh, 1980); George Cunningham, *The Anglo-Norman advance into the south-west midlands of Ireland, 1185–1221* (Roscrea, 1987); Billy Colfer, *Arrogant trespass: Anglo-Norman Wexford, 1169–1400* (Wexford, 2002). **4** Lennon, *The lords of Dublin in the age of Reformation*, p. 19. **5** Geraldine Stout and Matthew Stout, *Excavation of an early medieval secular cemetery at Knowth Site M, County Meath* (Bray, 2008); Matthew Seaver, 'Against the grain: early medieval settlement and burial on the Blackhill – excavations at Raystown, Co. Meath' in Corlett and Potterton (eds), *Death and burial in early medieval Ireland* (2010), pp 261–79; Seaver, 'Run of the mill?'; Matthew Seaver, 'Through the mill: excavations of a complex early medieval site at Raystown, County Meath' in Jerry O'Sullivan

Fertile lands were also found to the west and south of Dublin in the Liffey and Dodder Valleys, towards the plain of Kildare and down the coastal strip into Wicklow. Here, the topography and soils favoured more mixed farming and in the early medieval period there was a dense distribution of ringforts and monastic centres. Archaeological and place-name evidence indicates that this area saw significant Scandinavian and Hiberno-Norse settlement. Following the arrival of the Anglo-Normans, large parts of south-west Dublin were incorporated into the royal demesne, while the south-east became a dense patchwork of ecclesiastical and lay manors.

Further south again, the challenging environment of the Wicklow uplands offered protection for those who could manage to live there. This environment enabled the survival of members of the dispossessed Gaelic elites along with their families and retainers, with obvious consequences for the security of the English colony. These Gaelic rulers had formerly controlled the lowlands of the Liffey where they no doubt pursued a mix of arable and pastoral farming, but they adapted to the uplands and forests of Wicklow. Over the course of time, this landscape became particularly associated with Gaelic kingship and the continuance of the Gaelic way of life. Its destruction in the seventeenth century was a deliberate policy of the Dublin administration 'to sever the bond between the people and the landscape'.[6] Meanwhile, in the interstices between the ordered and largely English lowlands and the Gaelic uplands, a frontier or marcher society struggled obstinately to endure.

The correlation between the density of Anglo-Norman settlement forms and the availability of fertile, productive land is obvious from any distribution map. Had the pace of colonial settlement continued unchecked into the last third of the thirteenth century and beyond, a different pattern may have emerged. Nicholls advised against uncritical acceptance of the received wisdom that the Anglo-Normans never ventured above 500-foot contour.[7] By the mid-thirteenth century, the Anglo-Normans had clearly established themselves in the heart of the Wicklow Mountains, around Glendalough and Castlekevin and in the Glen of Imaal. It was a good deal more common, however, to find manorial tenants of English and Welsh origin on the low-lying arable lands which characterised much of the Dublin hinterland. At the same time, Irish betagh communities occupied the higher lands less suitable for growing cereals, particularly wheat.

The importance of other environmental features in shaping settlement in the region must be noted. The early monastic and secular settlements, at *Dubhlinn* and *Áth Cliath* respectively, owed their origin to topographic conjunctions. The safe moorings provided by Dublin Bay, the Liffey and its tributaries first attracted the Viking raiders into the region, while the low ridge of boulder clay overlooking the black pool provided the ideal location for their encampment. The siting of Dublin at the lowest crossing point of a major east-flowing river echoed the positioning of its much larger neighbouring capital and, like London, Dublin looked to the east for many of its trading connections. The presence of small harbours and ports on the coast to the south and especially to the north of Dublin Bay increased the region's seaborne connectivity with the rest of Ireland, Britain and the Continent.

The River Liffey and other smaller rivers and streams played an important role in moulding the settlement landscape of the region. Rivers frequently functioned as delimiters of landholding units throughout the period, and a variety of settlement forms – including mottes, manorial centres and boroughs – were situated close to waterways. More than three-quarters of the boroughs in the Dublin region were situated in a corridor which runs along

and Michael Stanley (eds), *Settlement, industry and ritual: archaeology and the National Roads Authority monograph series no. 3* (Bray, 2006), pp 73–87.   **6** Smyth, *Celtic Leinster*, p. 116.   **7** Nicholls, 'Anglo-French Ireland and after', 372–3.

the line of the River Liffey Valley. This highlights the importance that was attached to having access to the river and its floodplain as a primary communications routeway, as well as the significant role of rivers in generating power and providing food. Moreover, the soil in the river valleys was fertile and suitable for a range of agricultural uses including the management of water meadows.

Over the course of the medieval period, the natural environment of the region was frequently changed by human agency. Changes were particularly marked during the thirteenth century when increasing population in both city and hinterland led to the clearance of woodland and exhaustion of peat bogs. Thereafter, economic forces combined with the political situation to halt and perhaps partially redress landscape change.

Continuity and change

Variations in environmental factors clearly played a major role in influencing types of settlement and systems of agriculture across the region. Another variable to be inserted into the mix is the degree of continuity between early and late medieval settlement structures.

The period covered by this study, c.1100 to c.1600, was one that witnessed profound changes but was also characterised by enduring continuities. With the benefit of historical hindsight, the capture of Dublin and the expulsion of the Hiberno-Scandinavian elite in 1170–1 appear as crucial events which ushered in a period of significant change in the region. It is becoming increasingly apparent, however, that events which are retrospectively labelled as 'watersheds' may have had very little impact at the time on the majority of the population. The people in control changed and, over time, waves of new settlers arrived in the region, but the continued observance of existing territorial boundaries, many of them defined by natural features, and the re-use of settlement foci ensured that there were elements of permanence in the landscape which inevitably lessened the impact of change.

This study has also concluded that, rather than introducing a number of completely new practices, the Anglo-Normans were frequently just quickening the pace of change that was already underway. The Dublin region, more than any other part of Ireland, had already undergone significant transformation in the centuries before the arrival of the Anglo-Normans. Culturally, the population was already a mixture of native Irish, Scandinavian, Welsh and possibly some English. All of these groups exerted influence on land-use, agriculture and settlement forms in the countryside. There is growing evidence for Scandinavian rural settlement in dispersed farmsteads across the Dublin region. This evidence suggests that we should be looking for the possible influence of Scandinavians on agriculture and developments previously seen as Anglo-Norman innovations – such as the introduction of open fields and commercial agriculture. Even a small amount of Scandinavian rural settlement could have acted as a catalyst for change, as has been suggested by a recent study of East Anglian enclosures.[8] It has also been suggested that the influence of the Vikings, particularly their value systems based on silver bullion and slaves, encouraged a move away from livestock towards more intensive arable farming as a way of accumulating wealth.[9]

In order to estimate the degree to which the post-invasion landscape was shaped by pre-existing settlement patterns and administrative boundaries, it is necessary to construct a model of what it was like before. Tadhg O'Keeffe proposed a model for eastern Ireland whereby a dispersed settlement pattern of ringforts gives way c.1000 to a pattern of

8 Edward Martin, '"Wheare most inclosures be": the making of the East Anglian landscape' in Gardiner and Rippon (eds), *Medieval landscapes* (2007), pp 122–38.   9 McCormick and Murray, *Knowth and the zooarchaeology of Early Christian Ireland*, pp 112–15.

clustering around church sites and settlement mounds.[10] These clusters then become the manorial centres of the Anglo-Normans who founded markets and boroughs, but who also introduce dispersed settlement in the form of secondary mottes and moated sites. This model must also take into account the possibility that manorial centres had begun to emerge before the arrival of the Anglo-Normans, a possibility that O'Keeffe himself does not dismiss. The case for pre-Anglo-Norman manors might be advanced in particular for those parts of the Dublin region which saw the emergence of a parochial structure in the twelfth century. Moreover, locations such as Clondalkin, Dalkey, Swords and Tallaght were clearly important central places and possibly even boroughs before 1170.[11]

Continuities are particularly manifest with regard to the church (Figure 18.1). The lands of the large monasteries which surrounded Dublin were in the course of the twelfth century transformed into the archiepiscopal estates. Monastic enclosures were fossilised into the street plans of medieval boroughs at locations like Lusk and Swords in north Co. Dublin (Figures 7.16, 18.1). Customary renders of monastic retainers lived on in the formalised tenurial obligations of manorial tenants. The vast majority of civil parish centres reach back into the early medieval period and many parish churches retained their early medieval fabric.

Figure 18.1 Aerial view of Swords Church, Co. Dublin. Together, the pre-Anglo-Norman round tower, the fifteenth-century belfry and the nineteenth-century church illustrate the continuity that was characteristic of ecclesiastical sites throughout the Dublin region (© Department of the Environment, Heritage and Local Government).

---

10 Tadhg O'Keeffe, 'Rural settlement and cultural identity in Gaelic Ireland, 1000–1500', *Ruralia*, 1 (1996), 142–53 at 147–8. 11 Bradley, 'The medieval boroughs of Co. Dublin', p. 142.

Almost 40 per cent of the known medieval churches in the region have evidence of pre-Anglo-Norman origin. Burial places, and indeed burial practices, show significant continuity from the early to late medieval period.

Continuity with regard to ownership of land by the church persisted throughout the medieval period up to the time of the Dissolution. Lay landholding patterns showed less permanence as families died out, marriage alliances were forged and holdings were forfeited as magnates fell out of favour with the crown. While the people in control of lands may have changed, the location of dwellings and strongholds frequently remained the same. General patterns in monument distribution show little substantial variation over the whole medieval period and there is a clear continuity in the location of sites which can be classed as 'significant' from either a secular or an ecclesiastical perspective. Tower houses were often built close to, or even on top of, existing mottes and baileys which themselves had been sited on early medieval strongholds and mounds. Maynooth and Trim Castles, and probably others like them, were constructed right on top of older ringwork castles, while later fortified houses were often built close to and sometimes even incorporated earlier tower houses. Continuity over long periods is also evident in the use of mill sites, quarries and clay sources for pottery and tiles, while excavations have demonstrated that industrial sites such as tanneries were used and re-used for the same purposes for periods spanning several centuries.

Patterns of land-use across the region also display a significant level of stability as is evidenced by comparing data from the late thirteenth-/early fourteenth-century extents with the seventeenth-century Civil Survey.[12] While caution must be employed in taking these figures at face value, there is nevertheless sufficient evidence to question whether the Dublin region and in particular north Co. Dublin might have constituted an exception to the general pattern of agriculture in eastern and southern Ireland, which saw a marked decrease in land under the plough from 1300 onwards.[13] In areas where land-use remained unchanged through the medieval centuries, it is also possible to find evidence of small individual holdings and field-names persisting.[14]

All this evidence does not take away from the fact that the arrival of the Anglo-Normans in the Dublin region and the evolution and consolidation of their settlement landscape was of crucial significance. They did not set to work on a blank canvas but they did rework their inheritance in some significant ways. The argument that the townland structure placed a significant constraint on manorial settlement is one which maximises the importance of continuity over change. It is evident that the Anglo-Normans did use existing territorial divisions and frequently retained Irish place-names, but there is also evidence for knights' fees and vills bearing no relationship to pre-existing units and large swathes of north Co. Dublin and south-east Meath display heavy concentrations of place-names ending in 'town'. There was undoubtedly a great variety both between and within manors. Demesne lands may have been subject to significant reorganisation, while the lands that remained in the hands of native tenants may have retained their traditional organisation and layout.

Lordship and land

Following the arrival of the Anglo-Normans in the Dublin region, the process of colonisation and subsequent settlement owed much to the individual efforts of Strongbow and Hugh de Lacy. These great magnates, along with the archbishops of Dublin and those representatives of the crown with responsibility for the king's demesnes, combined to mould

12 See above, pp 287–8.   **13** As has already been suggested by Jäger, 'Land-use in Ireland', p. 65, and Lennon, *Sixteenth-century Ireland*, p. 33.   **14** See above, p. 293, with reference to Rathcoole.

a settlement landscape based around the dual needs of military support and commercially based agriculture. This initial community of purpose between lay magnates, archbishop and crown resulted in a more homogenous settlement pattern than was found in much of the rest of colonised Ireland, which was characterised by often competing, semi-autonomous lordships and liberties.

The Dublin region was more densely settled by the Anglo-Normans than any other part of Ireland. Lack of evidence for the early phases of settlement prevents the reconstruction of the precise process by which manorial tenants were recruited and introduced into the region. It is clear, however, that the efforts of individual lords played a major role in the process. It was in many ways a plantation, an impression underlined by the use in a contemporary source of the verb *herberger* – 'to plant' – with reference to de Lacy's subinfeudation of Meath.[15]

Before introducing settlers into their new lands, lords had to ensure that these lands were properly fortified. The actions of some of the major magnates, such as de Lacy, who was involved in the construction of castles on lands outside those that he retained for himself, suggest that they had an overall plan for the arrangement of fortifications across their lordships. Variations in the size and complexity of these early castles can be linked to differentials in importance of lordships, with the largest mottes and baileys associated with the most important centres and lords. Some of the most important Anglo-Norman magnates were involved in the settlement of the Dublin region and it is no accident that some of the largest mottes in the country, indeed in Europe, are found in a ring some 15km from the centre of the city. These fortifications were not built solely to shield the lands of the individual magnates; collectively they were intended as a defensive cordon to protect the wider territory and the city of Dublin itself.

Lords played the principal role in founding markets and chartered boroughs and in the Dublin region there was a clear distinction between the types of lord who founded markets and boroughs and those who did not. The archbishops of Dublin emerged as the most prolific founders of boroughs, being responsible for seven in Co. Dublin, six in Co. Wicklow and one in Co. Kildare. This, in part, reflects the dominant landholding position of the see of Dublin. Religious houses, however, whose combined holdings matched those of the archbishop, founded remarkably few boroughs and markets. Only the abbey of St Thomas, Dublin, formed an exception to this rule, fostering the suburban borough of Donore and possibly Greenoge in Co. Meath. It may be that religious houses such as Holy Trinity (Christ Church) and St Mary's Abbey operated a conservative system of direct provisioning from many of their granges and were less motivated by the need to enhance opportunities for trade and profit. The archbishop, the king and the lay lords who founded the rest of the boroughs in the region were more conscious of the advantages both for themselves and for their tenants of offering borough privileges and fostering trade.

In addition to their castles and boroughs, lords left other marks on the landscape. Resources such as deer parks, fishponds, dovecots and warrens, often found close to castles, were potent symbols of seigneurial power (see pp 166–7). In providing delicacies for the lord's table, they emphasised privilege and also afforded opportunities for lordly largesse. From the fourteenth century onwards, however, it can be observed that these monopolies diffused down the social ladder and became associated with smaller holdings and less powerful landowners.

---

15 '*E Huge de Laci, qui tant iert fer, pur sa terre herberger, vers Mithe s'en est turné, od meint vassal alosé*': Mullally (ed.), *The deeds of the Normans*, p. 128.

Over time, the fortunes of different lords had a direct bearing on the success or failure of the settlements associated with them. Large castles may have been a potent symbol of lordly power, but without a resident lord and household the associated settlement could decline and even disappear. Absence of lordship at a local level had consequences for the wider community and during the later medieval period the Dublin region suffered from what can only be described as a crisis of lordship. The community of purpose which had promoted a certain degree of homogeneity in the thirteenth century became fragmented as central authority broke down, absenteeism was rife and individual lords pursued their own strategies to deal with worsening economic and political conditions. Indeed, it is hard to see a strategy in lordship for much of the fourteenth and fifteenth centuries, as landholders lurched from crisis to crisis. The construction of the Pale ditch in the late fifteenth century underlines the divisions between central and local authority and within the local community itself. The creation of a defensive cordon around the Dublin region was put forward by the Dublin administration and promulgated by parliamentary decree, but the building work was left to individual lords and landholders. The resulting earthwork followed a circuitous route, lacked a standard design and did not join up where it should have.

The practice of agriculture

This book has endeavoured to provide a systematic survey of medieval agriculture across the Dublin region. By combining data from a range of sources, it has attempted to refine generalities and provide some yardsticks by which different elements of agricultural practice in the region can be measured and compared with other parts of Ireland and Britain.

As mentioned above in the discussion of continuity, the view that the Anglo-Normans revolutionised Irish agriculture should be tempered somewhat with regard to the Dublin region. While knowledge of farming practices before the twelfth century remains sparse, there are indications that the size and demands of Dublin had already resulted in an intensification of farming methods in the hinterland and that this may have promoted the collective management of open fields, nucleation and commercialisation. The arrival of the Anglo-Normans, with their fully formed conceptions of manorial structure, their knowledge of intensive farming techniques and their understanding of the workings of a monetised economy, acted as a catalyst on these incipient practices. The speed at which parts of Dublin and Meath were colonised, manorialised and set to producing marketable surpluses, suggests that the conditions already prevailing here were more conducive to these developments than elsewhere in the lordship.

The collection of manorial extents assembled during the course of the research, while small in comparison to many regions of England, can still furnish some general statistics relating to manorial demesnes in the Dublin region in the late thirteenth and early fourteenth centuries. On average, the demesnes were large – some very large – and by far the greater proportion of the land was devoted to arable agriculture. There were of course spatial variations in both size and land-use, many of which reflect variations in the physical environment of the region and some of which reflect the different strategies of different types of landholders.

The biggest demesnes and the ones with the largest proportions of arable land tended to occur in the north of the region. Woodland was almost completely absent and frequently pasture also was absent or unrecorded. Manorial demesnes to the west and south of the city also had high proportions of arable land but recorded more meadow, pasture and woodland. On some manors in the Liffey Valley, meadow land assumed equal if not greater importance than arable land in terms of its value, indicating the intensive production of hay. Proportions of woodland were markedly high on manors situated on the south-east littoral. All of these findings appear to correspond with what is known of the environmental attributes of different parts of the region. Extents for some demesnes within 5km to 10km of Dublin, however, show significant acreages of woodland, and other sources indicate a deliberate policy of preserving and nurturing pockets of woodland in proximity to the city. These lands were often in the hands of religious houses whose constant requirements for fuel and building material could be met in this way without incurring prohibitive transport costs.

The evidence for demesne farming in large open fields is fairly undisputed, as is the evidence for tenant farming in unenclosed strips. There remains some ambiguity about whether the tenant strips were incorporated into the demesne's open fields and to what degree the land was farmed communally. The balance between nucleated and dispersed settlement forms in the region has obvious implications for assessing the extent of communal farming. Some manors had a definite village settlement at their core, often, though not invariably, with borough status. There were significant populations of manorial tenants at, for example, Ballymore Eustace, Clonkeen, Cloncurry, Lusk and Swords, and at these places it is likely that fields were farmed in common. At other locations, the manorial centre may have comprised just a castle, mill and church with only a handful of cottars' cottages. If most of a manor's population was dispersed, the opportunities for cooperative farming were clearly reduced. It might be argued that over time the deteriorating political situation acted as a spur to more nucleated settlement forms and the adoption of communal farming practices. The shift from arable to pastoral farming in frontier acres, however, may have had an opposing effect.

A three-course system operated on the open arable fields of many of the region's demesnes in the late thirteenth and early fourteenth centuries, usually divided equally between winter sown wheat, spring sown oats and fallow. There is little evidence for the demesne cultivation of crops, other than wheat and oats in this period, although the complete lack of manorial accounts for the region is a major obstacle to the reconstruction of farming practices. It would appear that smallholders grew a wider variety of crops on their arable lands and also that the cultivation of barley increased on both large and small holdings after about 1340. The concentration on wheat and oats in the late thirteenth century reflects the fact that these were the most readily marketed grains and also the ones most in demand by the royal purveyors who frequently operated out of Dublin in this period. The apparent avoidance of barley cultivation is intriguing and inevitably resulted in a predominance of oat-based brewing in city and countryside. As barley was cultivated in later periods, it must be assumed that the preference for malting oats was in part culturally determined. Therefore, the crops that were grown appear to have been those best suited to supplying the urban and overseas markets.

Variability in the value of arable land suggests variability in the productivity of land, but there is no hard evidence that this was a result of intensive practices employed in some areas. There is an absence of references to techniques such as the elimination of fallow or the extensive cultivation of legumes. Yields and seeding rates appear to have been universally low and, while various methods of manuring and replenishing soil fertility were utilised, their effect was to stabilise, rather than increase, productivity. In areas where wood, hay or dairy production assumed importance, it is perhaps possible to identify strategies of intensive production which may have been influenced by the demands of Dublin. There is also evidence across the whole period for investment by landowners in farm buildings, kilns and mills.

Interdependence of town and country

Dublin was connected to its hinterland by economic, political, religious and cultural ties. In some ways, it can be seen as a consuming capital, drawing in supplies of food, fuel, raw materials and replacement population from a countryside that came increasingly under its control. In many respects, however, the relationship was more symbiotic. Dublin's location on the Irish Sea, and its proximity and ease of access to other ports made it of great importance to its hinterland. While the city undoubtedly laid claim to the surpluses of the hinterland to feed its citizens, it also provided rural producers with opportunities to trade with England and the Continent. Dublin merchants were also responsible for distributing manufactured and imported goods into the countryside. Furthermore, it can be argued that the capital acted as an agent of economic growth, influencing agricultural practices, land-use and commercialisation in its surrounding area. The city also provided rural dwellers with legal, administrative and religious services, with opportunities for education and leisure and with models and stimuli in fields as diverse as personal ornament, funerary monuments and architectural styles. The symbiotic nature of the relationship between capital and countryside can be seen in the fortunes of the Dublin merchant class in the later medieval period. The wealth of many of the capital's mercantile families was based on the marketing of rural produce. Frequently, however, they spent their wealth on acquiring rural landholdings where they built tower houses and patronised local parish churches. In this way, a significant proportion of the wealth coming into the city through exports from the hinterland eventually found its way back to the region. The merchants did not sever their ties with the city, indeed some managed to remain civic office-holders, but their rural activities often resulted in their being accepted into the gentry society of the countryside, thereby allowing them to enjoy the best of both worlds.

Many of the links between the city and the nucleated and dispersed settlements of its hinterland can be traced archaeologically. The discovery of French or English pottery, coins or other items in the countryside around Dublin is a good indicator of trade and contact with the city. Items such as pots, roof tiles and coins that were produced in Dublin and ended up on rural sites across the hinterland are further proof of contact. Rurally produced goods and animals that are found in urban contexts form another strand of evidence. The trenches that archaeologists dig, even in the heart of medieval Dublin, are often filled with material derived from the hinterland and with indicators as to what the countryside was like in the Middle Ages.

The links between city and countryside were facilitated by a complex trade and transport infrastructure that had developed in the Dublin region from at least the eleventh century. This system was adopted and developed by the Anglo-Normans, who built and maintained roads and bridges and utilised navigable water in order to maximise trade and security. The transport system, coupled with the productive agricultural regime of the hinterland, allowed medieval Dublin to be comfortably supplied with necessary foodstuffs in all but a few crisis years. Additionally, substantial quantities of agricultural products, particularly grain, were exported through the capital. Dublin's provisioning hinterland for grain was c.30–40km. Livestock might be sourced from further afield. Water transport enabled wood to be brought in from more distant regions. However, the question of whether medieval Dublin was large enough to structure its hinterland spatially is still unresolved. Environmental factors and topography appear more important than urban demand in determining the location of particular specialisms.

The marketing pull of medieval Dublin, particularly in the decades around 1300, when the city reached its peak medieval population, was considerable. Drogheda, 56km to the north, was the capital's nearest competitor and some manors in north Co. Dublin and south-east Meath were probably drawn into its provisioning hinterland. The role of markets such as that at Swords, a borough of the archbishop of Dublin and a focus of activity by Dublin merchants, may have drawn in grain and other products from further north and channelled them towards the city. Geographical proximity was of course not always the most reliable indicator of a location's integration into the city's supply zone. Patterns of land-ownership also played an important part. Dublin's religious houses owned over a quarter of the land in Co. Dublin and some of them employed strategies of direct provisioning well into the fourteenth century. Even when they moved towards a system of leasing their lands, they frequently required some rents to be paid in kind. Thus, for example, the priory of Holy Trinity was receiving annual rents of ten gallons of butter from lands near Arklow, Co. Wicklow, at the end of the fifteenth century. Availability of water transport was also a key factor in promoting links between capital and hinterland, and many coastal settlements were more closely integrated into Dublin's region than geographically closer areas. As an extension of this, it might be argued that much of Wales and the south-west of England also formed part of Dublin's medieval hinterland. These regions supplied the Irish capital with Dundry stone, Ham Green pottery (Figures 16.4c, 16.6a), mill stones, iron, and other raw materials, as well as immigrant workers and other people with new skills, techniques and ideas. They also provided markets for Dublin's exports of grain, hides, cattle and wool – so much so that by 1640, Chester was dependent on Dublin trade for its survival.[16]

The region under study was initially defined by an artificial geometric boundary or buffer representing the probable limits of direct provisioning in pre-industrial societies. The research has in part validated the proposition that the area within 30km of Dublin felt the effect of the city most profoundly and responded to it most directly. It has also highlighted the importance of factors other than geographical proximity. Politically, Dublin's medieval hinterland area can be traced from the Dyflinarskiri of the ninth century to the Pale of the sixteenth century. Economically, the city's region might be seen as ending only when it was intersected by the provisioning zones of other towns.

The Dublin region was unique in medieval Ireland as the only block of territory which had to support an urban settlement of over 10,000 people. The impacts that this had on rural settlement are discussed in this study, although the extent to which distinctive settlement features and patterns were present cannot be accurately quantified until a sufficient number of other regional studies have been undertaken. It is hoped that the present work, and in particular its promotion of an interdisciplinary approach, will encourage such studies to be carried out.

This book is based on a rich archaeological and documentary record, the potential of which is far from exhausted. Future archaeologists and historians will have the opportunity to interrogate these sources further, posing many more questions, and opening up new and exciting areas of research.

---

16 Gillespie, 'Dublin 1600–1700: a city and its hinterlands', p. 94.

Appendix

Extents for manors/places in the Dublin region, 1253–1358

(for explanation of abbreviations, see list below, pp 501–4)

MANOR/PLACE	TYPE	DATE	HELD BY	SOURCE
Ardinode	IPM	1276	Elias de Waleys (of the archbishop of Dublin)	TNA:PRO C133/16
Athgoe	IQD	1320	William Douce (of the king)	TNA:PRO C143/136/14
Ballymadun	IPM	1344	Walter de la Hide	TNA:PRO C135/75
Ballymore	IM	1326	Archbishop of Dublin	McNeill (ed.), *Alen's register*, p. 189
Balrothery	IPM	1253	Geoffrey de Costentin	TNA:PRO C132/14
Balscadden	IM	1255	Holy Trinity (of the king)	*CDI, 1252–84*, no. 482, p. 79
Bohernabreena	IM	1311	Butler	*RBO*, 23–4
Brannockstown	IPM	1276	Elias de Waleys (of the archbishop of Dublin)	TNA:PRO C133/16
Bray	IM	1311	Butler	*RBO*, 24–5
Castlewarden	IM	c.1315	Le Poer (of the king)	TNA:PRO SC12/20/48
Chapelizod	IQD	1304	Royal/lay	TNA:PRO C143/50
Cloncurry	IM	1304	Butler	*RBO*, 27–34
Clondalkin	IM	1326	Archbishop of Dublin	McNeill (ed.), *Alen's register*, p. 186
Colonia	IM	1326	Archbishop of Dublin	McNeill (ed.), *Alen's register*, p. 170
Corduff	IM	1311	Butler	*RBO*, 25–7
Dunshaughlin	IPM	1344	Walter de la Hide	TNA:PRO C135/75
Finglas	IM	1326	Archbishop of Dublin	McNeill (ed.), *Alen's register*, p. 173
Garristown	IPM	1318	Drogo de Merlawe	TNA:PRO C134/59/8
Gormanston (with Balscaddan)	IPM	1310	Aylmer [de St Aumand]	TNA:PRO C134/21
Kilmactalway	IM	1351/2	William de Barton	TNA:PRO C47/10/22/7
Leixlip	IM	1341	The king (formerly Pippard)	TNA:PROC47/10/20/1
Lucan	IM	1358	Thomas de Rokeby	TNA:PRO C47/10/22/15
Lusk (land in)	IQD	1311	Simon FitzRichard (of the archbishop of Dublin)	TNA:PRO C143/82
Maynooth	IM/AD	1328	Joanna de Burgh, countess of Kildare	*RBK*, 98–101
Moyglare	IPM	1344	Walter de la Hide	TNA:PRO C135/75
Naul	IPM	1292	Robert de Cruise	TNA:PRO C133/63
Newcastle Lyons (land in)	IM	1285	Henry le Marshal (of the king)	*CDI, 1252–84*, no. 2344, pp 561–2
Newcastle McKynegan	IM	1304	John FitzThomas (of the king)	TNA:PRO C47/10/17/10
Rathcoole	IM	1326	Archbishop of Dublin	McNeill (ed.), *Alen's register*, p. 184
Rathfeigh	IM	1322	Mortimer	TNA:PRO C47/10/18/13
Ratoath	IPM	1333	De Burgh	TNA:PRO C135/36
Shankill with Dalkey & Rathmichael	IM	1326	Archbishop of Dublin	McNeill (ed.), *Alen's register*, p. 195
Saggart	IQD	1312	William Douz (of the king)	TNA:PRO C143/91
Skidoo with Roganstown	IPM	1276	Robert de Shardelowe	TNA:PRO C133/16
Swords (with Lusk & Clonmethan)	IM	1326	Archbishop of Dublin	McNeill (ed.), *Alen's register*, p. 176
Tallaght	IM	1326	Archbishop of Dublin	McNeill (ed.), *Alen's register*, p. 181
Thorncastle	IQD	1297	William le Deveneys (of the king)	TNA:PRO C143/27
Turvey	IM	1311	Butler	*RBO*, 27
Vale of Dublin	IPM	1260	Walter de Ridelesford	TNA:PRO C132/46

Abbreviations

AConn	*Annála Connacht: the annals of Connacht (AD1224–1544)*, ed. A.M. Freeman (Dublin, 1944)
AFM	*Annála ríoghachta Éireann: annals of the kingdom of Ireland by the Four Masters from the earliest period to the year 1616*, ed. and trans. John O'Donovan (7 vols, Dublin, 1851; repr. New York, 1966)
AHS	*Agricultural History Review*
AI	*Archaeology Ireland* (Bray, 1987–)
app.	appendix; appendices
Arch. Hib.	*Archivium Hibernicum* (Maynooth, 1912–)
ATig.	'The annals of Tigernach', ed. Whitley Stokes, in *Revue Celtique*, 16–18 (1895–7) (repr. 2 vols, Felinfach, Wales, 1993)
AU	*Annála Uladh, annals of Ulster: otherwise annála senait, annals of senat: a chronicle of Irish affairs, 431–1131, 1155–1541*, ed. W.M. Hennessy and Bartholomew MacCarthy (4 vols, Dublin, 1887–1901)
AU2	*The annals of Ulster (to AD1131), pt i: text and translation*, ed. Seán Mac Airt and Gearóid Mac Niocaill (Dublin, 1983)
BAR	British Archaeological Reports
BJS	*Botanical Journal of Scotland*
BL	British Library
BM	British Museum
BNJ	*British Numismatic Journal*
Bodl.	Bodleian Library, Oxford
Cal. Carew MSS, 1515–74 [etc.]	*Calendar of the Carew manuscripts preserved in the archiepiscopal library at Lambeth, 1515–74* [etc.] (6 vols, London, 1867–73)
CARD	*Calendar of ancient records of Dublin*, ed. J.T. Gilbert (19 vols, Dublin, 1889–1944)
CBA	The Council for British Archaeology
CChR, 1226–57 [etc.]	*Calendar of the charter rolls, 1226–57* [etc.] (6 vols, London, 1903–27; repr. Nendeln, 1972)
CDI, 1171–1251 [etc.]	*Calendar of documents relating to Ireland, 1171–1251* [etc.] (5 vols, London, 1875–86)
CGR	*Calendar of the Gormanston register*, ed. James Mills and M.J. McEnery (Dublin, 1916)
Civil Survey, I [etc.]	*The Civil Survey, AD1654–56*, ed. R.C. Simington (10 vols, Dublin, 1931–61)
CJR, 1295–1303 [etc.]	*Calendar of the justiciary rolls, or proceedings in the court of the justiciar of Ireland … 1295–1303* [etc.], ed. James Mills (2 vols, Dublin, 1905, 1914)
CLAHJ	*County Louth Archaeological and Historical Journal* (Dundalk, 1904–)
comp.	compiler; compilation; compiled by
cont.	continued
CPI	*Chartae, privilegia et immunitates, being transcripts of charters and privileges to cities, towns, abbeys, and other bodies corporate, … 1171–1395* (Dublin, 1889)
CPR Ire., 18–45, Eliz.	*Calendar of the patent and close rolls of chancery in Ireland, from the 18th to the 45th of Queen Elizabeth*, ed. James Morrin (Dublin, 1862)
CPR Ire., Hen. VIII–Eliz.	*Calendar of patent and close rolls of chancery in Ireland, Henry VIII to 18th Elizabeth*, ed. James Morrin (Dublin, 1861)

CPR, 1232–47 [etc.]	*Calendar of the patent rolls, 1232–47* [etc.] (London, 1906–)
Crown surveys, 1540–1	*Crown surveys of lands, 1540–41, with the Kildare rental begun in 1518*, ed. Gearóid Mac Niocaill (Dublin, 1992)
CS	*Chronicum Scotorum: a chronicle of Irish affairs … to 1135, and supplement … 1141–1150*, ed. W.M. Hennessy (London, 1866)
CSMA	*Chartularies of St Mary's abbey, Dublin, … and annals of Ireland, 1162–1370*, ed. J.T. Gilbert (2 vols, London, 1884)
CSPI, 1509–73 [etc.]	*Calendar of the state papers relating to Ireland, 1509–73* [etc.] (24 vols, London, 1860–1911)
DEHLG	Department of the Environment, Heritage and Local Government
DHR	*Dublin Historical Record* (Dublin, 1938–)
DHSG	Dublin Historic Settlement Group
DNB	*Dictionary of national biography*, ed. Sir Leslie Stephen and Sir Sidney Lee (66 vols, London, 1885–1901; repr. with corrections, 22 vols, London, 1908–9)
EcHR	*Economic History Review* (Oxford, 1927–)
ed.	editor(s); edition; edited by
EHR	*English Historical Review* (London, 1886–)
EIMP	*Extents of Irish monastic possessions, 1540–1541, from manuscripts in the Public Record Office, London*, ed. N.B. White (Dublin, 1943)
Excavations 1971 [etc.]	*Excavations 1971* [etc.]: *summary accounts of archaeological excavations in Ireland*, ed. T.G. Delaney (1971–6), Claire Cotter (1985–6), Isabel Bennett (1987–) [1977–84 incorporated in *Irish Journal of Archaeology/The Journal of Irish Archaeology*] (Bray (since 1986))
fo./fos.	folio/folios
GEC, Peerage	*GEC[okayne], The complete peerage of England, Scotland, Ireland, Great Britain and the United Kingdom …* (8 vols, Exeter, 1887–98; ed. Vicary Gibbs et al., 13 vols, London, 1910–40)
Griffith, *Cal. inquisitions*	M.C. Griffith, *Calendar of inquisitions formerly in the office of the chief remembrancer of the exchequer, prepared from the MSS of the Irish Record Commission* (Dublin, 1991)
HMDI	*Historic and municipal documents of Ireland, 1172–1320*, ed. J.T. Gilbert (London, 1870)
IEP	*Irish exchequer payments, 1270–1446*, ed. Philomena Connolly (Dublin, 1998)
IESH	*Irish Economic and Social History, Journal of the Economic and Social History Society of Ireland* (Derry, 1974–)
IG	*Irish Geography*
IHS	*Irish Historical Studies: the Joint Journal of the Irish Historical Society and the Ulster Society for Irish Historical Studies* (Dublin, 1938–)
IHTA	Irish Historic Towns Atlas
IJ	*The Irish Jurist*, new ser. (Dublin, 1966–)
IM	Inquisition miscellaneous
IM/AD	Inquisition miscellaneous/Assignment of dower
intr.	introduction; introduced by
IPM	Inquisition *post mortem* (extent)
IQD	Inquisition *ad quod damnum* (extent)
Ir. fiants, Hen. VIII–Eliz. I	*The Irish fiants of the Tudor sovereigns: during the reigns of Henry VIII, Edward VI, Philip and Mary, and Elizabeth I*, ed. K.W. Nicholls and T.G. Ó Canann, (4 vols, Dublin, 1994)
JCKAHS	*Journal of the County Kildare Archaeological and Historical Society* (Dublin, 1891–)
JGAHS	*Journal of the Galway Archaeological and Historical Society* (Galway, 1900–)
JIA	*Journal of Irish Archaeology* (Dublin, 1983–)

JIMA	*Journal of the Irish Memorials Association*, formerly the Association for the Preservation of the Memorials of the Dead in Ireland, and now incorporating the Dublin Parish Register Society (Dublin, 1921–)
JRSAI	*Journal of the Royal Society of Antiquaries of Ireland* (Dublin, 1892–)
MARG	Medieval Archaeology Research Group
McNeill (ed.), Alen's register	*Calendar of Archbishop Alen's register, c.1172–1534*, ed. Charles McNeill (Dublin, 1950)
Med. Arch.	*Medieval Archaeology: Journal of the Society for Medieval Archaeology* (Leeds, 1957–)
Mills (ed.), Account roll	*Account roll of the priory of the Holy Trinity, Dublin, 1337–1346*, ed. James Mills (Dublin, 1891)
MRHI	Aubrey Gwynn and R.N. Hadcock, *Medieval religious houses: Ireland* (Dublin, 1970)
MS[S]	Manuscript[s]
MSRG	Medieval Settlement Research Group
NAI	National Archives of Ireland, Dublin
NC	*Numismatic Circular*
n.d.	no date
NHI	A new history of Ireland, under the auspices of the RIA, ed. T.W. Moody, T.D. Williams, J.C. Beckett, F.X. Martin, F.J. Byrne, W.E. Vaughan, Art Cosgrove, J.R. Hill (Dublin and Oxford, 1968–)
NLI	National Library of Ireland
NMI	National Museum of Ireland
n.p.	no place
NUI	National University of Ireland
ODNB	*Oxford dictionary of national biography* (Oxford, 2004)
Ormond deeds, 1172–1350 [etc.]	*Calendar of Ormond deeds, 1172–1350* [etc.], ed. Edmund Curtis (6 vols, Dublin, 1932–43)
Orpen, *Ireland under the Normans*	G.H. Orpen, *Ireland under the Normans, 1169–1333* (4 vols, Oxford, 1911–20; repr. Oxford, 1968, Dublin, 2005, in 1 vol.)
OSI	Ordnance Survey Ireland
Oughterany	*Oughterany: Journal of the Donadea Local History Group* (Naas, 1993–)
'Pipe roll Ire. 1211–12'	'The Irish pipe roll of 14 John, 1211–1212', ed. Oliver Davies and D.B. Quinn, in *UJA*, 3rd ser., 4, supp. (July 1941)
PRIA	*Proceedings of the Royal Irish Academy* (Dublin, 1836–)
PRO	Public Record Office (now TNA: The National Archives of England, Wales and the United Kingdom)
pt	part
QUB	Queen's University, Belfast
RAST	*Register of the abbey of St Thomas the Martyr, Dublin*, ed. J.T. Gilbert (London, 1889)
RBK	*The Red Book of the earls of Kildare*, ed. Gearóid Mac Niocaill (Dublin, 1964)
RBO	*The Red Book of Ormond*, ed. N.B. White (Dublin, 1932)
RCB	Representative Church Body, Dublin
RCh	*Rotuli chartarum in Turri Londinensi asservati, 1199–1216* (London, 1837)
RDKPRI, 1 [etc.]	*First [etc.] report of the deputy keeper of the public records in Ireland* (Dublin, 1869–)
reg.	register
Reg. Kilmainham	*Registrum de Kilmainham: register of chapter acts of the hospital of St John of Jerusalem in Ireland, 1326–1339*, ed. Charles McNeill (Dublin, 1932)
repr.	reprint; reprinted

rev.	revision; revised
RHJB	*Register of the hospital of St John the Baptist without the New Gate of Dublin*, ed. Eric St John Brooks (Dublin, 1936)
RIA	Royal Irish Academy
RnM	*Ríocht na Midhe: Records of the Meath Archaeological and Historical Society* (Drogheda, 1955–)
RPCH	*Rotulorum patentium et clausorum cancellariae Hiberniae calendarium*, ed. Edward Tresham (Dublin, 1828)
RSAI	Royal Society of Antiquaries of Ireland
ser.	series
Stat. Ire., 1–12 Edw. IV	*Statute rolls of the parliament of Ireland, 1st to the 12th years of the reign of King Edward IV*, ed. H.F. Berry (Dublin, 1914)
Stat. Ire., 12–22 Edw. IV	*Statute rolls of the parliament of Ireland, 12th and 13th to the 21st and 22nd years of the reign of King Edward IV*, ed. J.F. Morrissey (Dublin, 1939)
Stat. Ire., Hen. VI	*Statute rolls of the parliament of Ireland, reign of Henry VI*, ed. H.F. Berry (Dublin, 1910)
Stat. Ire., John–Hen. V	*Statutes and ordinances, and acts of the parliament of Ireland, King John to Henry V*, ed. H.F. Berry (Dublin, 1907)
Stat. Ire., Ric. III– Hen. VIII	*Statutes rolls of the Irish parliament, Richard III–Henry VIII*, ed. Philomena Connolly (Dublin, 2002)
'Stat. Ire., Hen. VII & VIII'	'The bills and statutes of the Irish parliaments of Henry VII and Henry VIII', ed. D.B. Quinn, in *Analecta Hibernica*, 10 (Dublin, 1941)
TCD	Trinity College Dublin
TNA:PRO	The National Archives of England, Wales and the United Kingdom (formerly the Public Record Office and the Historical Manuscripts Commission)
trans.	translation; translated by
TRHS	*Transactions of the Royal Historical Society* (London, 1872–)
TRIA	*Transactions of the Royal Irish Academy* (Dublin, 1787–1907)
UAS	The Urban Archaeology Survey (directed by John Bradley, 1982–95)
UC	University College
UCC	University College Cork
UCD	University College Dublin
UJA	*Ulster Journal of Archaeology* (Belfast, 3 ser.: 1853–62, 9 vols; 1895–1911, 17 vols; 1938–)

Bibliography

Manuscript sources

Library of the King's Inns, Dublin
MS 17: Irish medical manuscript of the fifteenth century.

NAI: National Archives of Ireland
EX 1/1–2: Memoranda rolls, 1309–10, 1319–20.
KB 1/1: Justiciary roll, 1312–13.
KB 1/2: Justiciary roll, 1317–18.
KB 2/1–12: Calendar of justiciary rolls, 1313–18.
RC 8/1–43: Record Commission's calendar of memoranda rolls.

TNA: The National Archives of the United Kingdom
PRO C47: Chancery miscellanea.
PRO C132: Chancery: inquisitions *post mortem* Henry III.
PRO C133: Chancery: inquisitions *post mortem* Edward I.
PRO C134: Chancery: inquisitions *post mortem* Edward II.
PRO C135: Chancery: inquisitions *post mortem* Edward III.
PRO C143: Chancery: inquisitions *ad quod damnum* Henry III to Richard III.
PRO E101: Exchequer: king's remembrancer: accounts various.
PRO SC2: Special Collections: court rolls.
PRO SC6: Special Collections: ministers' and receivers' accounts.
PRO SC8: Special Collections: ancient petitions.
PRO SC12: Special Collections: rentals and surveys.

NLI: National Library of Ireland
Down Survey (1654–6) parish and barony maps.
GO MSS 760–1: Betham Irish pipe roll extracts, Henry III–Edward III.
MSS 1–19: *Collectanea de rebus Hibernica*, compiled by Walter Harris.

RIA: Royal Irish Academy
MS 12D9: Transcript of the pipe roll for 1261–2.
MS 12D10: Extracts from pipe rolls, thirteenth and fourteenth centuries.
MS 12D12: Calendar of memoranda rolls, 1272–1327.
MS 24H9. Catalogue of Irish coins in the cabinet of the Reverend Henry Richard Dawson, 1834.

TCD: Trinity College Dublin
MS 579/1–2: *Collectanea de rebus monasticis Hiberniae ex registris domuum religiosarum.*
MS 804: *Miscellanea de rebus Hibernicis.*

Printed sources

Aalen, F.H.A., and Kevin Whelan (eds), *Dublin city and county: from prehistory to present: studies in honour of J.H. Andrews.* Dublin, 1992.

Aalen, F.H.A., Kevin Whelan and Matthew Stout (eds), *Atlas of the Irish rural landscape*. Cork, 1997.

Aberg, F.A. (ed.), *Medieval moated sites*. CBA Research Report, 17. London, 1978.

Aberg, F.A., and A.E. Brown (eds), *Medieval moated sites in north-west Europe*. BAR International Series, 121. Oxford, 1981.

Abraham, Kennedy, 'Upward mobility in later medieval Meath', *History Ireland*, 5:4 (1997), 15–20.

Addyman, P.V., 'York in its archaeological setting' in Addyman and Black (eds), *Archaeological papers from York* (1984), pp 7–21.

Addyman, P.V., and V.E. Black (eds), *Archaeological papers from York presented to M.W. Barley*. York, 1984.

Albarella, Umberto, 'Meat production and consumption in town and country' in Giles and Dyer (eds), *Town and country in the Middle Ages* (2005), pp 131–48.

Alcock, N.W. (ed.), *Cruck construction: an introduction and catalogue*. CBA Research Report, 42. London, 1981.

Allen, D.F., 'An Irish find of forged Scottish coins', *BNJ*, 26 (1949/51), 90–1.

Allen, J.R., and Joseph Anderson, *The Early Christian monuments of Scotland*. Edinburgh, 1903.

Almqvist, Bo, and David Greene (eds), *Proceedings of the seventh Viking Congress, Dublin, 15–21 August 1973*. Dundalk, 1976.

Anderson, A.O., and M.O. Anderson, *Adomnán's Life of St Columba*. London, 1961.

Andersson, Hans, and Jes Wienberg (eds), *The study of medieval archaeology*. Stockholm, 1993.

Andersson, Thorsten, and K.I. Sandred (eds), *The Vikings*. Stockholm, 1978.

Andrews, D.D. (ed.), *Cressing Temple: a Templar and Hospitaller manor in Essex*. Chelmsford, 1993.

Andrews, J.H., 'Medium and message in early 6-inch Ordnance maps: the case of Dublin city', *IG*, 6:5 (1973), 579–93.

Andrews, J.H., 'The oldest map of Dublin', *PRIA*, 83C (1983), 205–37.

Anon, 'Wooden house in Drogheda', *Dublin Penny Journal*, 1:12 (15 Sept. 1832), 89.

Anon, *Calendar of ancient deeds and muniments preserved in the Pembroke Estate Office*. Dublin, 1891.

Anon, *L'approvisionnement des villes de l'Europe occidentale au moyen age et aux temps modernes: Cinquièmes journées internationales d'histoire*, 1985; Auch, Centre culturel de l'abbaye de Flaran.

Anon, *Archaeology 2020: repositioning Irish archaeology in the knowledge society*. Dublin, 2006.

Archaeological Services Durham University (ASDU), 'Merrywell 1, M3 Motorway Project, Co. Meath, Ireland: environmental analysis, report 1752'. Unpublished report on behalf of Archaeological Consultancy Services Ltd, 2008.

Archibald, M.M., 'Coins' in Davey, Freke and Higgins, *Excavations in Castletown* (1996), p. 35.

Aris, Mary, 'Aerial photography and historic landscape on the Great Orme Llandudno' in Edwards (ed.), *Landscape and settlement in medieval Wales* (1997), pp 71–8.

Armitage, P.L., 'Post-medieval cattle horns from the Greyfriars site, Chichester, West Sussex, England', *Circaea*, 7:2 (1990), 81–90.

Armstrong, E.C.R. (ed.), 'Catalogue of the silver and ecclesiastical antiquities in the collection of the Royal Irish Academy by the late Sir William Wilde, M.D., M.R.I.A', *PRIA*, 32C (1915), 287–312.

Astill, G.G., and Annie Grant (eds), *The countryside of medieval England*. Oxford, 1988.

Aston, Michael, *Interpreting the landscape: landscape archaeology and local history*. London, 1985.

Aston, Michael, *Monasteries in the landscape*. Stroud, Gloucestershire, 2000.

Aston, T.H., P.R. Coss, Christopher Dyer and Joan Thirsk (eds), *Social relations and ideas: essays in honour of R.H. Hilton*. Cambridge, 1983.

Ault, W.O., 'Open-field husbandry and the village community: a study of agrarian by-laws in medieval England', *Transactions of the American Philosophical Society*, 55:7 (1965), 5–102.

Austin, David, 'The castle and the landscape', *Landscape History*, 6 (1984), 70–81.

Aylmer, Fenton, 'Sir Gerald Aylmer, knight and baronet', *JCKAHS*, 11 (1930–3), 267–385.

Aylmer, H.H., 'The Aylmer family', *JCKAHS*, 1 (1891–5), 295–307.

Aylmer, R.A., 'Donadea Forest Park', *Oughterany*, 2:1 (1999), 41–55.

Backhouse, Janet, *The Luttrell Psalter*. London and New York, 1989.

Bailey, Mark, 'The rabbit and the medieval East-Anglian economy', *AHS*, 36 (1988), 1–20.

Bailey, Mark, *The English manor, c.1200–c.1500*. Manchester, 2002.

Baillie, M.G.L., 'A horizontal mill of the eighth century AD at Drumard, Co. Derry', *UJA*, 38 (1975), 25–32.

Baillie, M.G.L., 'Dating of ships' timbers from Wood Quay, Dublin' in John Fletcher (ed.), *Dendrochronology in Europe*. BAR International Series, 51 (1977), pp 259–62.

Baillie, M.G.L., *Tree ring dating and archaeology*. London, 1982.

Baillie, M.G.L., and D.M. Brown, 'Some deductions on ancient trees from dendrochronology' in Pilcher and Mac an tSaoir (eds), *Wood, trees and forests in Ireland* (1995), pp 35–50.

Bairoch, Paul, *Cities and economic development from the dawn of history to the present*. London, 1988.

Baker, Christine, 'A lost ecclesiastical site in Fingal: Oldtown, Swords, Co. Dublin', *AI*, 18:3 (autumn 2004), 14–17.

Baker, Christine, 'Dry Goods Market, Iveagh Markets, Francis Street, Dublin' in *Excavations 2003*, p. 131.

Baker, Christine, 'Merrion Road, Dublin' in *Excavations 2004*, p. 125.

Baker, Christine, 'Excavations within the manor of Merrion Castle, Dublin' in Duffy (ed.), *Medieval Dublin VIII* (2008), pp 228–86.

Baker, Christine (ed.), *Axes, warriors and windmills: recent archaeological discoveries in north Fingal*. Dublin, 2009.

Baker, Christine, *The archaeology of Killeen Castle, Co. Meath*. Bray, 2009.

Baker, Christine, 'Tullykane, Co. Meath: a medieval rural settlement' in Corlett and Potterton (eds), *Rural settlement in medieval Ireland* (2009), pp 1–18.

Ball, F.E., 'A descriptive sketch of Clondalkin, Tallaght and other places in west County Dublin', *JRSAI*, 29 (1899), 93–108.

Ball, F.E., 'Monkstown Castle and its history', *JRSAI*, 30 (1900), 109–17.

Ball, F.E., *A history of the county of Dublin*. 6 vols, Dublin, 1902–20.

Ball, F.E., *An historical sketch of the Pembroke township*. Dublin, 1907.

Ball, F.E., and E. Hamilton, *The parish of Taney: a history of Dundrum near Dublin, and its neighbourhood*. Dublin, 1895.

Ballard, Adolphus (ed.), *British borough charters, 1042–1216*. Cambridge, 1913.

Ballard, Adolphus, 'The law of Breteuil', *EHR*, 30 (1915), 646–58.

Barnard, F.P., *The casting-counter and the casting-board*. Oxford, 1916.

Barrow, G.L., *The round towers of Ireland*. Dublin, 1979.

Barrow, G.L., *Glendalough and St Kevin*. Dundalk, 1992.

Barry, T.B., *The medieval moated sites of south-eastern Ireland: Counties Carlow, Kilkenny, Tipperary and Wexford*. BAR, 35. Oxford, 1977.

Barry, T.B., 'Moated sites in Ireland' in Aberg (ed.), *Medieval moated sites* (1978), pp 56–9.

Barry, T.B., 'The moated sites of Co. Waterford', *Decies*, 10 (1979), 32–6.

Barry, T.B., 'The shifting frontier: medieval moated sites in Counties Cork and Limerick' in Aberg and Brown (eds), *Medieval moated sites in north-west Europe* (1981), pp 71–85.

Barry, T.B., 'Anglo-Norman ringwork castles: some evidence' in Reeves-Smyth and Hamond (eds), *Landscape archaeology in Ireland* (1983), pp 295–314.

Barry, T.B., *The archaeology of medieval Ireland*. London, 1987.

Barry, T.B., 'The archaeology of the tower house in late medieval Ireland' in Andersson and Wienberg (eds), *The study of medieval archaeology* (1993), pp 211–18.

Barry, T.B., 'The last frontier: defence and settlement in late medieval Ireland' in T.B. Barry, Robin Frame and Katharine Simms (eds), *Colony and frontier in medieval Ireland: essays presented to J.F. Lydon* (London, 1995), pp 217–28.

Barry, T.B., 'Rural settlement in Ireland in the Middle Ages: an overview', *Ruralia*, 1 (1996), 134–41.

Barry, T.B., 'Harold Leask's "single towers": Irish tower houses as part of larger settlement complexes', *Château Gaillard*, 22 (2006), 27–34.

Barry, T.B., 'The study of medieval Irish castles: a bibliographical survey', *PRIA*, 108C (2008), 115–36.

Barry, John (intr.), *Sir John Davies, The discovery of the true causes why Ireland was never entirely subdued, 1612*. Shannon, 1969.

Barton, K.J., 'The medieval pottery of Dublin' in Mac Niocaill and Wallace (eds), *Keimelia* (1988), pp 271–324.

Barton, K.J., *Pottery in England from 3500BC–AD1730*. Newton Abbot, 1975.

Bateson, Mary, 'The laws of Breteuil', *EHR*, 15 (1900), 73–90, 302–18, 496–523, 754–7; 16 (1901), 92–110, 332–45.

Baug, Irene, 'Prehistoric quarrying on the west coast of Norway: the production of quernstones, millstones and crosses in Hyllestad, Sogn of Fjordane', *Ruralia*, 6 (2007), 219–25.

Beaumont James, Tom, and Christopher Gerrard, *Clarendon: landscape of kings*. Macclesfield, Cheshire, 2007.

Beglane, Fiona, 'Meat and craft in medieval and post-medieval Trim' in Potterton and Seaver (eds), *Uncovering medieval Trim* (2009), pp 346–70.

Bekker-Nielsen, Hans, Peter Foote and Olaf Olsen (eds), *Proceedings of the eighth Viking Congress, 1977*. Odense, 1981.

Bélier, A.-C., 'A sherd of Terra Sigillata from Wood Quay, Dublin', *UJA*, 94–5 (1981–2), 192–4.

Bell, Jonathan, and Mervyn Watson, *A history of Irish farming, 1750–1950*. Dublin, 2008.

Bence-Jones, Mark, *A guide to country houses, vol. 1: Ireland*. London, 1978.

Bennett, H.S., *Life on the English manor: a study of peasant conditions, 1150–1400*. Gloucester, 1987.

Bennett, Judith, *Ale, beer and brewsters in England: womens' work in a changing world, 1300–1600*. Oxford, 1996.

Bennett, Richard, and John Elton, *A history of corn milling*. 4 vols, London/Liverpool, 1898–1904.

Benskin, Michael, 'An English township in fifteenth-century Ireland', *Collegium Medievale*, 4:1 (1991), 57–84.

Béranger, J., 'Une trouvaille de monnaies anglo-normandes', *Bulletin de Numismatique*, 12 (1905), 67–72.

Beresford, M.W., and J.K.S. St Joseph, *Medieval England: an aerial survey*. 2nd ed., Cambridge, 1979.

Beresford, M.W., and J.G. Hurst (eds), *Deserted medieval villages: studies*. Gloucester, 1989.

Bermingham, Helen, 'Priests' residences in later medieval Ireland' in FitzPatrick and Gillespie (eds), *The parish in medieval and early modern Ireland* (2006), pp 168–85.

Bermingham, Nora, 'Animal bone report [John Dillon Street]'. Unpublished report. DEHLG file 98E0158 [n.d.].

Berry, H.F. (ed.), *Register of wills and inventories of the diocese of Dublin, 1457–1483*. Being the extra volume of the *RSAI* for 1896–1897. Dublin, 1898.

Berry, H.F., 'History of the religious gild of S. Anne, in S. Audoen's Church, Dublin, 1430–1740, taken from its records in the Haliday Collection, RIA', *PRIA*, 25C (1904–5), 21–106.

Berry, H.F., 'Proceedings in the matter of the custom called tollboll, 1308 and 1385: St Thomas' Abbey v. some early Dublin brewers etc.', *PRIA*, 28C (1910), 116–73.

Bhreathnach, Edel, 'The documentary evidence for pre-Norman Skreen, County Meath', *RnM*, 9:2 (1996), 37–45.

Bhreathnach, Edel, 'Authority and supremacy in Tara and its hinterland, c.950–1200', *Discovery Programme Reports: 5* (Dublin, 1999), 1–23.

Bhreathnach, Edel, 'Medieval Irish history at the end of the twentieth century: unfinished work', *IHS*, 32:126 (2000), 260–71.

Bhreathnach, Edel, Joseph MacMahon and John McCafferty (eds), *The Irish Franciscans, 1534–1990*. Dublin, 2009.

Biddick, Kathleen, 'Pig husbandry on the Peterborough Abbey estate from the twelfth to the fourteenth century AD' in Juliet Clutton-Brock and Caroline Grigson (eds), *Animals and archaeology* (Oxford, 1985), pp 161–77.

Bintliff, John, Phil Howard and Anthony Snodgrass, *Testing the hinterland: the work of the Boeotia Survey (1989–1991) in the southern approaches to the city of Thespiai*. Cambridge, 2007.

Blackburn, M.A.S. (ed.), *Anglo-Saxon monetary history: essays in memory of Michael Dolley*. Leicester, 1986.

Blackmore, Lyn, 'Aspects of trade and exchange evidenced by recent work on Saxon and medieval pottery from London', *London and Middlesex Archaeological Society Transactions*, 50 (1999), 38–54; repr. in *Medieval London: recent archaeological work and research: papers given at the CBA Mid-Anglia Group Conference held at the Museum of London, 14th February 1998*. London, 2000.

Blair, John, and Nigel Ramsay (eds), *English medieval industries: craftsmen, techniques, products*. London, 1991.

Blake Butler, Theobald, 'The barony of Dunboyne', *Irish Genealogist*, 2 (1943–55), 66–81, 107–21, 130–6, 162–4.

Blanchard, I.S.W.B., 'Lead mining and smelting in medieval England and Wales' in Crossley (ed.), *Medieval industries* (1981), pp 72–84.

Blunt, C.E., 'Coin hoards in the National Museum of Ireland, Dublin', *BNJ*, 27 (1952–4), 213–15.

Bochaca, Michel, 'L'aire d'influence et l'espace de relations économiques de Bordeaux vers 1475' in Noël Coulet and Olivier Guyotjeannin (eds), *La ville au moyen age* (Paris, 1998), pp 279–92.

Bokonyi, Sandor, 'The development of stockbreeding and herding in medieval Europe' in Del Sweeney (ed.), *Agriculture in the Middle Ages: technology, practice and representation* (Philadelphia, 1995), pp 41–61.

Bolger, Teresa, 'Kilgobbin' in *Excavations 2000*, pp 103–4.

Bolger, Teresa, 'Old Coach Road, Balrothery' in *Excavations 2001*, pp 82–5.

Bolger, Teresa, 'Kilgobbin, Stepaside' in *Excavations 2004*, pp 156–8.

Bolger, Teresa, 'An analysis of the environmental history of medieval County Dublin based on Archbishop Alen's register, *c.*1172–1534' in Duffy (ed.), *Medieval Dublin VIII* (2008), pp 287–317.

Bolger, Teresa, 'Excavations at Kilgobbin Church, Co. Dublin', *JIA*, 18 (2008), 85–112.

Bolton, J.L., *The medieval English economy, 1150–1500*. London, 1980.

Bond, James, 'Production and consumption of food and drink in the medieval monastery' in G.D. Keevill, Michael Aston and T.A. Hall (eds), *Monastic archaeology* (Oxford, 2001), pp 54–87.

Bond, James, *Monastic landscapes*. Stroud, Gloucestershire, 2004.

Bonde, Niels, and Ole Crumlin-Pedersen, 'The dating of wreck 2 from Skuldelev, Denmark', *NewsWARP*, 7 (1990), 3–6.

Bonnet, Émile, 'Note sur un trésor de monnaies anglaises découvert a Montpellier', *Revue Numismatique*, 4th ser., 37 (1934), 169–73.

Bourdillon, Jennifer, 'Countryside and town: the animal resources of Saxon Southampton' in Della Hooke (ed.), *Anglo-Saxon settlements* (Oxford and New York, 1988), pp 177–95.

Bourdillon, Jennifer, 'The animal provisioning of Saxon Southampton' in D.J. Rackham (ed.), *Environment and economy in Anglo-Saxon England*. CBA Research Report, 89 (York, 1994), pp 120–5.

Bowie, Gavin, 'Corn-drying kilns, meal milling and flour in Ireland', *Folklife: a Journal of Ethnological Studies*, 17 (1979), 5–13.

Bradley, John (ed.), *Viking Dublin exposed: the Wood Quay saga*. Dublin, 1984.

Bradley, John, 'Planned Anglo-Norman towns in Ireland' in Clarke and Simms (eds), *The comparative history of urban origins in non-Roman Europe* (1985), 2, pp 411–67.

Bradley, John (ed.), *Settlement and society in medieval Ireland: studies presented to F.X. Martin, O.S.A.* Kilkenny, 1988.

Bradley, John, 'The interpretation of Scandinavian settlement in Ireland' in Bradley (ed.), *Settlement and society in medieval Ireland* (1988), pp 49–78.

Bradley, John, 'The medieval towns of County Meath', *RnM*, 8:2 (1988–9), 30–49.

Bradley, John, 'Scandinavian rural settlement in Ireland', *AI*, 9:3 (autumn 1995), 10–12.

Bradley, John, 'The medieval boroughs of Co. Dublin' in Manning (ed.), *Dublin and beyond the Pale* (1998), pp 129–44.

Bradley, John, *Kilkenny: IHTA, no. 10*. Dublin, 2000.

Bradley, John, 'A tale of three cities: Bristol, Chester, Dublin and "the coming of the Normans"' in Clarke and Phillips (eds), *Ireland, England and the Continent in the Middle Ages and beyond* (2006), pp 51–66.

Bradley, John, 'Some reflections on the problem of Scandinavian settlement in the hinterland of Dublin during the ninth century' in Bradley, Fletcher and Simms (eds), *Dublin in the medieval world* (2009), pp 39–62.

Bradley, John, Alan Fletcher and Anngret Simms (eds), *Dublin in the medieval world: studies in honour of Howard B. Clarke*. Dublin, 2009.

Bradley, John, and Ben Murtagh, 'Brady's Castle, Thomastown, Co. Kilkenny: a 14th-century fortified town house' in Kenyon and O'Conor (eds), *The medieval castle in Ireland and Wales* (2003), pp 194–216.

Bradley, John, and H.A. King, 'UAS, 2: Co. Meath'. Unpublished report [Dublin, 1984].

Bradley, John, and H.A. King, 'UAS, 8:4: Co. Dublin'. Unpublished report [Dublin, 1988].

Bradley, John, and H.A. King, 'UAS, 9: Co. Wicklow'. Unpublished report [Dublin, n.d.].

Bradley, John, Andrew Halpin and H.A. King, 'UAS, 7: Co. Kildare'. 4 vols, unpublished report [Dublin, n.d.].

Bradshaw, Brendan, *The Dissolution of the religious orders in Ireland under Henry VIII*. Cambridge, 1974.

Brady, John, 'Anglo-Norman organisation of the diocese of Meath', *IER*, 67 (1946), 232–7.

Brady, John, 'Anglo-Norman Meath', *RnM*, 2:3 (1961), 38–45.

Brady, Karl, and Connie Kelleher, 'Swords, plague and pestilence', *AI*, 14:3 (autumn 2000), 8–11.

Brady, Karl, 'Bull Island North, Bull Strand North' in *Excavations 2002*, pp 128–9.

Brady, Karl, *Shipwreck inventory of Ireland: Louth, Meath, Dublin and Wicklow*. Dublin, 2008.

Brady, Karl, and Connie Kelleher, 'Preliminary report of rescue excavation at Windmill Lands, River Ward, Swords, County Dublin'. Unpublished report. DEHLG file 99E0554 [n.d.].

Brady, Niall, 'The plough pebbles of Ireland', *Tools and Tillage*, 6 (1988), 47–60.

Brady, Niall, 'Reconstructing a medieval Irish plough', *Primeras Jornadas Sobre Technologia Agraria Tradicional* (1993), 31–44.

Brady, Niall, 'The sacred barn: barn-building in southern England, 1100–1550: a study of grain storage technology and its cultural context'. PhD, Cornell University, 1996.

Brady, Niall, 'The gothic barn of England: icon of prestige and authority' in Elizabeth Smith and Michael Wolfe (eds), *Technology and resource-use in medieval Europe: cathedrals, mills and mines* (Aldershot and Brookfield, 1997), pp 76–105.

Brady, Niall, 'Abbeyland/Blackcastle Demesne, Co. Meath' in *Excavations 1998*, p. 160.

Brady, Niall, 'Archaeological investigations, Carrickmines Great, South-Eastern Motorway, Co. Dublin. 004E0045'. Unpublished report for Valerie J. Keeley Ltd, Nov. 2000.

Brady, Niall, 'Carrickmines and Jamestown' in *Excavations 1998*, pp 39–40.

Brady, Niall, 'Jamestown' in *Excavations 1999*, p. 84.

Brady, Niall, *Exploring Irish medieval landscapes: the Discovery Programme's Medieval Rural Settlement Project, 2002–2008*. Dublin, 2003.

Brady, Niall, 'Mills in medieval Ireland: looking beyond design' in Walton (ed.), *Wind and water in the Middle Ages* (2006), pp 39–68.

Brady, Niall, 'Agricultural tools and agrarian development in early medieval Ireland', *Ruralia*, 6 (2007), 245–50.

Brady, Niall, 'Dublin's maritime setting and the archaeology of its medieval harbours' in Bradley, Fletcher and Simms (eds), *Dublin in the medieval world* (2009), pp 295–315.

Brady, Niall, 'Just how far can you go with a pebble? Taking another look at ploughing in medieval Ireland' in Joseph Fenwick (ed.), *Lost and found II* (Bray, 2009), pp 61–9.

Brady, Niall, Stephen Balfe and John Nicholls, 'Archaeological Assessment, D'Arcy's Field, Greystones, Co. Wicklow: Greystones Harbour Development, 06R0157'. Unpublished report for the Archaeological Diving Company Ltd, 2006.

Brady, Niall, Rory McNeary and Brian Shanahan, 'A new study of land enclosure and settlement in north Roscommon', *Journal of the Roscommon Historical and Archaeological Society*, 10 (2006), 99–104.

Breen, Colin, *The Gaelic lordship of the O'Sullivan Beare: a landscape cultural history*. Dublin, 2005.

Breen, T.C., 'A pre-Norman grave-slab at Rathfarnham, County Dublin', *JRSAI*, 111 (1981), 120–3.

Breen, T.C., 'Site 3, Laracor' in *Excavations 2004*, pp 324–5.

Breen, T.C., 'Finds from Dublin city and county listed in the registers of the Irish Antiquities Division, National Museum of Ireland'. Unpublished catalogue, Dublin, 1995.

Briggs, C.S., and Michael Dolley, 'An unpublished hoard from north County Dublin with pennies of Eadgar', *Seaby's Coin and Medal Bulletin*, 654 (1973), 47–50.

Brisbane, Mark (ed.), *The archaeology of Novgorod, Russia: recent results from the town and its hinterland*. Society for Medieval Archaeology Monograph Series, 13. Lincoln, 1992.

Brisbane, Mark, and David Gaimster (eds), *Novgorod: the archaeology of a Russian medieval city and its hinterland*. British Museum Occasional Paper, 141. London, 2001.

Britnell, R.H., *Growth and decline in Colchester, 1300–1525*. Cambridge, 1986.

Britnell, R.H., *The commercialisation of English society, 1100–1500*. Cambridge, 1993.

Britnell, R.H., *Britain and Ireland, 1050–1530: economy and society*. Oxford, 2004.

Britnell, R.H., 'Rural and urban elites in England during the later Middle Ages'. www.dur.ac.uk/r.h.britnell/articles/Elites.htm (accessed 29 Nov. 2004).

Brooks, Eric St John, 'The grant of Castleknock to Hugh Tyrel', *JRSAI*, 63 (1933), 206–20.

Brooks, Eric St John (ed.), *Register of the hospital of St John the Baptist without the New Gate of Dublin*. Dublin, 1936.

Brooks, Eric St John, 'The Tyrels of Castleknock', *JRSAI*, 76 (1946), 151–4.

Brooks, Eric St John (ed.), *Knights' fees in Counties Wexford, Carlow and Kilkenny*. Dublin, 1950.

Brooks, Eric St John, 'The de Ridelesfords', *JRSAI*, 81 (1951), 115–38.

Brooks, Eric St John (ed.), *The Irish cartularies of Llanthony Prima and Secunda*. Dublin, 1953.

Broudy, Eric, *The book of looms: a history of the handloom from ancient times to the present*. Hanover and London, 1979.

Brown, A.E. (ed.), *Garden archaeology*. CBA Research Report, 78. York, 1991.

Brown, D.H., 'Pots from houses', *Medieval Ceram*, 21 (1997), 83–94.

Brown, David, 'Dendrochronological report on the timbers' in Walsh, *Archaeological excavations at Patrick, Nicholas and Winetavern Streets* (1997), pp 185–8.

Brown, David, 'Dendrochronological analysis of oak wood samples' in Halpin, *The port of medieval Dublin* (2000), pp 93–5.

Brown, H.P., and S.V. Hopkins, *A perspective of wages and prices*. London, 1981.

Brown, I.D., and Michael Dolley, *A bibliography of coin hoards of Great Britain and Ireland, 1500–1967*. London, 1971.

Brown, R.A., H.M. Colving and A.J. Taylor, *The history of the king's works*. 2 vols, London, 1963.

Browne, Martin, and Colmán Ó Clabaigh (eds), *The Irish Benedictines: a history*. Dublin, 2005.

Buchanan, R.H., R.A. Butlin and Desmond McCourt (eds), *Fields, farms and settlement in Europe*. Belfast, 1976.

Buchon, J.A. (ed.), *Collection des chroniques nationales françaises, vol. 13, Chronique de Froissart*. Paris, 1825.

Buckley, Laureen, 'Health status in medieval Dublin: analysis of the skeletal remains from the abbey of St Thomas the Martyr' in Duffy (ed.), *Medieval Dublin IV* (2003), pp 98–126.

Buckley, Laureen, 'Skeletal report, Tallaght, Co. Dublin'. Unpublished report. DEHLG file 96E0188 [n.d.].

Buckley, Laureen, and Alan Hayden, 'Excavations at St Stephen's leper hospital, Dublin: a summary account and analysis of burials' in Duffy (ed.), *Medieval Dublin III* (2002), pp 151–94.

Buckley, V.M., and P.D. Sweetman, *Archaeological survey of County Louth*. Dublin, 1991.

Budd, Roland, The platforme of an universitie: *All Hallows Priory to Trinity College Dublin*. Dublin, 2001.

Butler, Isaac, 'A journey to Lough Derg', *JRSAI*, 22 (1892), 13–24, 126–36.

Butler, Richard, *Some notices of the castle and of the ecclesiastical buildings of Trim*. 1st ed., Trim, 1835; 2nd ed., Trim, 1840; 3rd ed., Trim, 1854; repr. 1978; 4th ed., Dublin, 1861.

Butler, Richard, *Jacobi Grace, Kilkeniensis: Annales Hiberniae*. Dublin, 1842.

Butler, Richard (ed.), *Registrum prioritas omnium sanctorum juxta Dublin*. Dublin, 1845.

Butler, V.G., 'Cattle in thirteenth-century Dublin: an osteological examination of its remains'. MA, UCD, 1984.

Butler, V.G., 'Report on the animal bones from layers 01 and 03' in McMahon, 'Four Courts extension' (1988), 271–319 at 313–17.

Butler, V.G., 'Animal bone studies in archaeology', *AI*, 3:3 (autumn 1989), 104–7.

Butler, V.G., 'The animal bones from 1–3 High Street, Dublin (E476)'. Unpublished excavation report, Dúchas, 1990.

Butler, V.G., 'Report on the animal bones from C46, C48, C50, C53, C54, C56, C58 and C60' in McMahon, 'Bridge Street Lower' (1991), 41–71 at 67–8.

Butler, V.G., 'Report on the animal bones from 35 Parliament Street, Dublin'. Unpublished excavation report. Dúchas, 1992.

Butler, V.G., 'Animal bone report' in Hayden, 'Bridge Street Upper'. Unpublished report. DEHLG file 92E0078 [n.d.].

Butler, V.G., 'The animal bones [from George's Hill]'. Unpublished report. DEHLG file 93E0106 [n.d.].

Byrne, F.J., 'The trembling sod: Ireland in 1169' in Cosgrove (ed.), *A new history of Ireland: II* (1993), pp 1–42.

Byrne, F.J., William Jenkins, Gillian Kenny and Catherine Swift, with George Eogan, *Historical Knowth and its hinterland*. Dublin, 2008.

Byrne, M.E., '26–29 Castle Street/20 Lord Edward Street: a brief introduction'. Unpublished report submitted to NMI, 1993.

Byrne, M.E., 'Prosperous Road/Millicent Road, Clane' in *Excavations 2003*, p. 238.

Byrne, M.E., 'Abbeylands, Clane'. Unpublished report. DEHLG file 99E0386 [n.d.].

Byrnes, Emmet, 'Archaeological monitoring and rescue excavation at Lott Lane, Co. Wicklow (excavation no. 98E0244)'. Unpublished report, 1998.

Byrnes, Emmet, 'Rathmore West' in *Excavations 1998*, p. 113.

Cahill, Mary, 'Nevinstown' in *Excavations 1977–1979*, p. 76.

Cahill, Mary, 'Nevinstown, Co. Meath'. Unpublished report. DEHLG file E000162 [n.d.].

Cairns, C.T., *Irish tower houses: a Co. Tipperary case-study*. Athlone, 1987.

Cairns, C.T., 'The Irish tower house: a military view', *Fortress*, 11 (1991), 3–13.

Calendar of inquisitions post mortem and other analogous documents in the Public Record Office, Henry III–Richard II. 15 vols, London, 1901–70.

Camden, William, *Britannia: a chronological description of Great Britain and Ireland together with the adjacent islands*. 6th ed., 1607; repr. Hildesheim and New York, 1970.

Campbell, B.M.S., 'Agricultural progress in medieval England: some evidence from eastern Norfolk', *EcHR*, 36 (1983), 26–46.

Campbell, B.M.S., *English seigniorial agriculture, 1250–1450*. Cambridge, 2000.

Campbell, B.M.S., 'The medieval economy' in *The Penguin atlas of British and Irish history* (2001), pp 100–3.

Campbell, B.M.S., 'Benchmarking medieval economic development: England, Wales, Scotland and Ireland, c.1290', *EHR*, 61 (2008), 896–945.

Campbell, B.M.S., J.A. Galloway and Margaret Murphy, 'Rural land-use in the metropolitan hinterland, 1270–1339: the evidence of IPMs', *AHS*, 90 (1992), 1–22.

Campbell, B.M.S., J.A. Galloway, Derek Keene and Margaret Murphy, *A medieval capital and its grain supply: agrarian production and distribution in the London region, c.1300*. Historical Geography Research Series, 30 (1993).

Campbell, Kieran, 'A medieval tile kiln site at Magdalene Street, Drogheda', *CLAHJ*, 21 (1985), 48–54.

Campbell, Kieran, 'Naas (Black Castle)' in *Excavations, 1977–9*, pp 73–4.

Campbell, Kieran, 'Castleknock' in *Excavations 2004*, p. 102.

Campbell, Kieran, 'The floor tiles' in Clyne, *Kells Priory* (2007), pp 234–59.

Campbell, Kieran, 'Ship Street'. Unpublished report. DEHLG file E000217 [n.d.].

Carlin, Martha, and Joel Rosenthal (eds), *Food and eating in medieval Europe*. London, 1998.

Carlyon-Britton, Raymond, 'On the Irish coinage of Lambert Simnel as Edward VI', *Numismatic Chronicle*, 6th ser., 1 (1941), 133–5.

Carlyon-Britton, Raymond, 'On the proposed attribution of certain Irish coins to Edward V', *Numismatic Chronicle*, 6th ser., 1 (1941), 128–32.

Carlyon-Britton, Raymond, 'Two unpublished Irish coins [*1. Edward halfpenny of Dublin, 2. Richard III penny of Waterford*]', *BNJ*, 26 (1949–51), 350–1.

Carroll, Judith, 'Vicar Street/58–59 Thomas Street, Dublin' in *Excavations 1997*, p. 55.

Carroll, Judith, *Dublin city: sources for archaeologists*. Dublin, 2003.

Carroll, Judith, 'The Old Orchard Inn, Butterfield Avenue, Rathfarnham'. Unpublished report. DEHLG file 97E140 [n.d.].

Carroll, Judith, 'Vicar Street/Thomas Street'. Unpublished report. DEHLG file 97E0380 [n.d.].

Carroll, M.J., *The Knights Templar and Ireland*. Bantry, Co. Cork, 2006.

Carruthers, James, 'On hoards of coins found in Ireland', *UJA*, 1 (1853), 164–7.

Carson, R.A.G. (ed.), *Mints, dies and currency: essays in honour of Albert Baldwin*. London, 1971.

Carus-Wilson, E.M., 'An industrial revolution of the thirteenth century' in E.M. Carus Wilson (ed.), *Essays in economic history* (London, 1954), pp 41–60.

Case, H.J., G.W. Dimbleby, G.F. Mitchell, M.E.S. Morrison and V.B. Proudfoot, 'Land-use in Goodland, Co. Antrim, from Neolithic times until today', *JRSAI*, 99 (1969), 39–54.

Chambers, Richard, Andrew Fleming, Julian Munby and John Steane, 'Swalcliffe: a New College farm in the fifteenth century', *Oxoniensia*, 60 (1995), 333–78.

Chapple, R.M., 'Site 17, Ballough' in *Excavations 2002*, pp 123–4.

Chapple, R.M., 'Site 17, Ballough'. Unpublished report. DEHLG file 02E0078 [n.d.].

Charles-Edwards, T.M., *Early Christian Ireland*. Cambridge, 2000.

Chart, D.A. (ed.), *The register of John Swayne, archbishop of Armagh and primate of Ireland, 1418–1439*. Belfast, 1935.

Chartrand, Jeffrey, J.D. Richards and B.E. Vyner, 'Bridging the urban-rural gap: GIS and the York Environs Project' in Jens Andersen, Irwin Scollar and Torsten Madsen (eds), *CAA92: computer applications and quantitative methods in archaeology* (Aarhus, 1993), pp 159–66.

Cherry, John, 'Leather' in Blair and Ramsay (eds), *English medieval industries* (1991; pbk 2001), pp 295–318.

Cherry, John, 'Pottery and tile' in Blair and Ramsay (eds), *English medieval industries* (1991; pbk 2001), pp 189–209.

Childs, Wendy, and Timothy O'Neill, 'Overseas trade' in Cosgrove (ed.), *A new history of Ireland: II* (1993), pp 492–524.

Clare, Liam, 'The kill and the grange of medieval Clonkeen' in Holton, Clare and Ó Dálaigh (eds), *Irish villages* (2003), pp 17–45.

Clare, Linda, *On the edge of the Pale: the rise and decline of an Anglo-Irish community in County Meath, 1170–1530*. Dublin, 2006.

Clark, Mary, *The book of maps of the Dublin city surveyors, 1695–1827: an annotated list with biographical notes and an introduction*. Dublin, 1983.

Clark, Mary, 'Dublin surveyors and their maps', *DHR*, 39:4 (1986), 140–8.

Clark, Mary, 'People, places and parchment: the medieval archives of Dublin city' in Duffy (ed.), *Medieval Dublin III* (2002), pp 140–50.

Clark, Mary, and Raymond Refaussé (eds), *Directory of historic Dublin guilds*. Dublin, 1993.

Clark, Peter, and Bernard Lepetit (eds), *Capital cities and their hinterlands in early modern Europe*. Aldershot, Hampshire, 1996.

Clarke, David, 'The 1969 Colchester Hoard', *BNJ*, 44 (1974), 41–61.

Clarke, H.B., 'The mapping of medieval Dublin: a case-study in thematic cartography' in Clarke and
    Simms (eds), *The comparative history of urban origins in non-Roman Europe* (1985), 2, pp 617–43.

Clarke, H.B. (ed.), *Medieval Dublin: the living city*. Dublin, 1990.

Clarke, H.B. (ed.), *Medieval Dublin: the making of a metropolis*. Dublin, 1990.

Clarke, H.B., 'The bloodied eagle: the Vikings and the development of Dublin', *Irish Sword*, 18
    (1991), 91–119.

Clarke, H.B., 'The Vikings in Ireland: a historian's perspective', *AI*, 9:3 (autumn 1995), 7–9.

Clarke, H.B., 'London and Dublin' in Francesca Bocchi (ed.), *Medieval metropolises: proceedings of
    the congress of the Atlas working group International Commission for the History of Towns* (Bologna,
    1998), pp 103–25.

Clarke, H.B., '*Urbs et suburbium*: beyond the walls of medieval Dublin' in Manning (ed.), *Dublin
    and beyond the Pale* (1998), pp 45–58.

Clarke, H.B., 'Conversion, church and cathedral: the diocese of Dublin to 1152' in Kelly and Keogh
    (eds), *History of the Catholic diocese of Dublin* (2000), pp 1–50.

Clarke, H.B., *Dublin, part I, to 1610: IHTA, no. 11*. Dublin, 2002.

Clarke, H.B., *The four parts of the city: high life and low life in the suburbs of medieval Dublin*. Dublin,
    2003.

Clarke, H.B., 'Population' in Duffy, *Medieval Ireland* (2005), pp 383–4.

Clarke, H.B., and Anngret Simms (eds), *The comparative history of urban origins in non-Roman
    Europe: Ireland, Wales, Denmark, Germany, Poland and Russia from the ninth to the thirteenth
    century*. BAR International Series, 255. 2 vols, Oxford, 1985.

Clarke, H.B., and J.R.S. Phillips (eds), *Ireland, England and the Continent in the Middle Ages and
    beyond: essays in memory of a turbulent friar, F.X. Martin, O.S.A*. Dublin, 2006.

Clarke, H.B., Jacinta Prunty and Mark Hennessy (eds), *Surveying Ireland's past: multidisciplinary essays
    in honour of Anngret Simms*. Dublin, 2004.

Clarke, H.B., Maire Ní Mhaonaigh and Raghnall Ó Floinn (eds), *Ireland and Scandinavia in the early
    Viking Age*. Dublin, 1998.

Clarke, H.B., Sarah Dent and Ruth Johnson, *Dublinia: the story of medieval Dublin*. Dublin, 2002.

Clarke, Helen, and Erik Schia (eds), *Coins and archaeology*. MARG: proceedings of the first meeting
    at Isegran, Norway, 1988. BAR International Series, 556. Oxford, 1989.

Clarke, Michael, 'The Black Castle, Wicklow', *JRSAI*, 74 (1944), 1–22.

Cleary, R.M., 'Excavations at Lough Gur, Co. Limerick: part III', *JCHAS*, 88 (1983), 51–80.

Cleary, R.M., 'Appendix D: petrological analysis of thin section' in McCutcheon, *Medieval pottery
    from Wood Quay* (2006), p. 155.

Cleary, R.M., and M.F. Hurley (eds), *Cork City excavations, 1984–2000*. Cork, 2003.

Cleary, R.M., M.F. Hurley and E.A. Twohig (eds), *Archaeological excavations on the Cork–Dublin gas
    pipeline (1981–82)*. Cork, 1987.

Clinton, Mark, 'The souterrains of Co. Dublin' in Manning (ed.), *Dublin and beyond the Pale* (1998),
    pp 117–28.

Clinton, Mark, 'Settlement patterns in the kingdom of Leinster (7th to mid-12th centuries)' in Smyth
    (ed.), *Seanchas* (2000), pp 275–98.

Clinton, Mark, 'Balally' in *Excavations 2000*, pp 65–8.

Clinton, Mark, 'Carrickmines Castle, Carrickmines' in *Excavations 2000*, p. 72.

Clinton, Mark, 'Carrickmines Great' in *Excavations 2001*, pp 85–7.

Clinton, Mark, 'Carrickmines Castle, Carrickmines' in *Excavations 2002*, p. 131.

Clutterbuck, Richard, 'Cookstown, Co. Meath: a medieval rural settlement' in Corlett and Potterton
    (eds), *Rural settlement in medieval Ireland* (2009), pp 27–48.

Clyne, Miriam, *Kells Priory, Co. Kilkenny: archaeological excavations by T. Fanning and M. Clyne*.
    Dublin, 2007.

Cochrane, Robert, 'The ecclesiastical antiquities of Howth: the church of St Mary', *JRSAI*, 26 (1896),
    1–21.

Cochrane, Robert, *Historical and descriptive notes, with ground plans, elevations, sections and details of the ecclesiastical remains at Glendalough, Co. Wicklow*. Dublin, 1912.

Cochrane, Robert, '81st annual report of the Commissioners of Public Works, Appendix E:II (1912–13)'.

Coffey, George, 'A pair of brooches and chains of the Viking period, recently found in Ireland', *JRSAI*, 32 (1902), 71–3.

Coffey, George, and E.C.R. Armstrong, 'Scandinavian objects found at Islandbridge and Kilmainham', *PRIA*, 28C (1910), 107–22.

Coffey, George, *Guide to the collection of Irish antiquities* (*Royal Irish Academy Collection*): *Anglo-Irish coins*. Dublin, 1911.

Cogan, Anthony, *The diocese of Meath, ancient and modern*. 3 vols, Dublin, 1862–70; repr. Dublin, 1992.

Cole, G.A.J., and R.L. Praeger (eds), *Handbook to the city of Dublin and the surrounding district*. Dublin, 1908.

Colfer, Billy, *Arrogant trespass: Anglo-Norman Wexford, 1169–1400*. Enniscorthy, 2002.

Colgan, Edward, *For want of good money: the story of Ireland's coinage*. Bray, 2003.

Colles, J.A.P., 'Proposal to restore churches at Glendalough', *JRSAI*, 1 (1870), 194–201.

Collingwood, W.G., *Northumbrian crosses of the pre-Norman age*. London, 1927.

Collins, Brenda, 'Garden soil', *IAPA News: Bulletin of the Irish Association of Professional Archaeologists*, 23 (1996), 6–7.

Collins, Brenda, 'Plant remains' in Walsh, *Archaeological excavations at Patrick, Nicholas and Winetavern Streets* (1997), pp 228–36.

Collins, Brenda, 'Macroscopic plant remains' in McMahon, 'Bride Street' (2002), 108–10.

Collins, Brenda, 'Botanical remains from the Dublin Castle excavations'. Forthcoming.

Collins, Brenda, 'The plant remains [from High Street]'. Unpublished report. DEHLG file E000548 [n.d.].

Collins, Brenda, 'The plant remains [from Cooke St]'. Unpublished report. DEHLG file 92E0083 [n.d.].

Collins, Brenda, 'Plant remains [from Thomas Street]'. Unpublished report. DEHLG file 96E0280 [n.d.].

Comet, Georges, 'Technology and agricultural expansion in the Middle Ages: the example of France north of the Loire' in Grenville Astill and John Langdon (eds), *Medieval farming and technology: the impact of agricultural change in north-west Europe* (Leiden, New York and Köln, 1997), pp 11–39.

Condit, Tom, 'Rings of truth at Trim Castle, Co. Meath', *AI*, 10:3 (autumn 1996), pp 30–3.

Condit, Tom, and Christiaan Corlett (eds), *Above and beyond: essays in memory of Leo Swan*. Bray, 2005.

Conlin, Stephen, *Dublin: one thousand years*. Dublin, 1988.

Conlon, Patrick, *Franciscan Ireland*. Mullingar, 1988.

Connolly, Elizabeth, 'Kill Hill' in *Excavations 2003*, p. 245.

Connolly, Philomena, 'The Irish memoranda rolls: some unexplored aspects', *IESH*, 3 (1976), 66–74.

Connolly, Philomena, 'The enactments of the 1297 parliament' in James Lydon (ed.), *Law and disorder in thirteenth-century Ireland: the Dublin parliament of 1297* (Dublin, 1997), pp 139–62.

Connolly, Philomena (ed.), *Irish exchequer payments, 1270–1446*. Dublin, 1998.

Connolly, Philomena, *Medieval record sources*. Dublin, 2002.

Connolly, Philomena, and Geoffrey Martin (eds), *The Dublin guild merchant roll, c.1190–1265*. Dublin, 1992.

Connolly, S.J. (ed.), *The Oxford companion to Irish history*. Oxford, 1998.

Connolly, Seán, and J.-M. Picard, 'Cogitosus: life of St Brigit', *JRSAI*, 117 (1987), 5–27.

Conway, Malachy, 'Ballymount Great' in *Excavations 1997*, pp 22–3.

Conway, Malachy, *Director's first findings from excavations in Cabinteely*. Dublin, 1999.

Conway, Malachy, 'Gracedieu' in *Excavations 1999*, pp 83–4.

Conway, Malachy, 'Ballymount Great'. Unpublished report. DEHLG file 97E0316 [n.d.].

Conway, Malachy, 'Gracedieu'. Unpublished report. DEHLG file 99E0217 [n.d.].

Conway, Malachy, 'Caffrey's Monumental Works, Dyer Street, Drogheda'. Unpublished report. DEHLG file 99E0242 [n.d.].

Cooney, Gabriel, *Archaeology in Ireland: a vision for the future*. Royal Irish Academy Forum. Dublin, 2007.

Coope, G.R., 'Report on the coleoptera from an eleventh-century house at Christ Church Place, Dublin' in Bekker-Nielsen, Foote and Olsen (eds), *Proceedings of the eighth Viking Congress, 1977* (1981), pp 51–6.

Corcoran, Rachel, '"Ireland's forgotten castle": an archaeological study of Drimnagh Castle, Co. Dublin'. MA, UCD, 2005.

Corlett, Christiaan, *Antiquities of old Rathdown: the archaeology of south County Dublin and north County Wicklow*. Bray, 1999.

Corlett, Christiaan, 'Two recently discovered Rathdown Slabs from Taney graveyard, Dundrum, Co. Dublin', *JRSAI*, 132 (2002), 139–43.

Corlett, Christiaan, 'The Hollywood slabs: some late medieval grave-slabs from west Wicklow and neighbouring counties', *JRSAI*, 133 (2003), 86–110.

Corlett, Christiaan, 'The Rathdown Slabs: Vikings and Christianity', *AI*, 17:4 (winter 2003), 28–30.

Corlett, Christiaan, *Medieval Dalkey in the 1760s*. Archaeology Ireland Heritage Guide, 33 (2006).

Corlett, Christiaan, *Beneath the Poulaphouca Reservoir: the 1939 Poulaphouca Survey of the lands flooded by the Liffey Reservoir Scheme*. Dublin, 2008.

Corlett, Christiaan, and Mairéad Weaver (eds), *The Liam Price notebooks: the placenames, antiquities and topography of County Wicklow*. 2 vols, Bray, 2002.

Corlett, Christiaan, and Michael Potterton (eds), *Rural settlement in medieval Ireland in the light of recent archaeological excavations*. Bray, 2009.

Corlett, Christiaan, and Michael Potterton (eds), *Death and burial in early medieval Ireland in the light of recent archaeological excavations*. Bray, 2010.

Cornwall, I.W., *Bones for the archaeologist*. London, 1956.

Cosgrave, Una, 'Augustine Street/John Street West'. Unpublished report. DEHLG file 97E0343 [n.d.].

Cosgrave, Una, 'Bride Street'. Unpublished report. DEHLG file 98E0013ext. [n.d.].

Cosgrave, Una, 'Phoenix Street/Stable Lane, Smithfield'. Unpublished report. DEHLG file 98E0398 [n.d.].

Cosgrove, Art, *Late medieval Ireland, 1370–1541*. Dublin, 1981.

Cosgrove, Art (ed.), *A new history of Ireland II: medieval Ireland, 1169–1534*. Oxford, 1987; repr. 1993.

Cosgrove, Art, *Dublin through the ages*. Dublin, 1988.

Cosgrove, Art, 'The emergence of the Pale, 1399–1447' in Cosgrove (ed.), *A new history of Ireland: II* (1993), pp 533–56.

Cotter, Claire, 'Dunboyne Castle, Castlefarm, Dunboyne' in *Excavations 2004*, pp 308–9.

Coughlan, Tim, 'Jamestown Road, Finglas East' in *Excavations 1996*, p. 34.

Coughlan, Tim, 'The Anglo-Norman houses of Dublin: evidence from Back Lane' in Duffy (ed.), *Medieval Dublin I* (2000), pp 203–34.

Coughlan, Tim, 'Excavations at the medieval cemetery of St Peter's Church, Dublin' in Duffy (ed.), *Medieval Dublin IV* (2003), pp 11–39.

Coughlan, Tim, 'Ballyloughan' in *Excavations 2002*, pp 230–1.

Coughlan, Tim, 'Site 23, Killickaweeny' in *Excavations 2002*, pp 251–2.

Coughlan, Tim, 'Back Lane/Lamb Alley, Dublin'. Unpublished report. DEHLG file 96E0300 [n.d.].

Coughlan, Tim, 'St Francis Hospice, Raheny'. Unpublished report. DEHLG file 99E0702 [n.d.].

Courtney, Paul, 'Ceramics and the history of consumption: pitfalls and prospects', *Medieval Ceram*, 21 (1997), 95–108.

Cowman, Des, 'The metal mines of Tipperary', *Tipperary Historical Journal*, 5 (1992), 105–15.

Craig, Maurice, *The architecture of Ireland, from the earliest times to 1880*. London and Dublin, 1982.

Crawford, H.S, 'Ancient roof at Dunsoghley Castle, Co. Dublin', *JRSAI*, 52 (1922), 85–6.

Crawford, John, and Raymond Gillespie (eds), *St Patrick's Cathedral, Dublin: a history*. Dublin, 2009.

Creighton, O.H., *Castles and landscapes: power, community and fortification in medieval England*. London and Oakville, CT, 2002.

Cremin, Andrea, 'Animal bones from Christ Church Place, Dublin: 10th to 12th century'. MA, QUB, 1996.

Cremin, Andrea, 'Animal bone [from Thomas Street]'. Unpublished report. DEHLG file 96E0280 [n.d.].

Crossley, D.W. (ed.), *Medieval industries*. CBA Research Report, 40. York, 1981.

Crossley, D.W., 'Medieval iron smelting' in Crossley (ed.), *Medieval industries* (1981), pp 29–41.

Crowley, Caroline, James Walsh and David Meredith, *Irish farming at the Millennium: a census atlas*. Maynooth, 2008.

Cryerhall, Abi, '3–15 Hammond Lane/161–168 Church Street, Dublin' in *Excavations 2003*, pp 133–6.

Cryerhall, Abi, 'Excavations at Hammond Lane, Dublin: from hurdle-ford to iron-foundry' in Duffy (ed.), *Medieval Dublin VII* (2006), pp 9–50.

Cullen, Seamus, 'The Pale in the Donadea area', *Oughterany*, 1:1 (1993), 9–22.

Cullen, Seamus, and Tadhg O'Keeffe, 'A turreted enclosure at Pitchfordstown, County Kildare', *JRSAI*, 124 (1994), 215–17.

Cunliffe, Barry, Robert Bartlett, John Morrill, Asa Briggs and Joanna Bourke (eds), *The Penguin atlas of British and Irish history*. London, 2001.

Cunningham, George, *The Anglo-Norman advance into the south-west midlands of Ireland, 1185–1221*. Roscrea, 1987.

Curriculum Development Unit, *Viking settlement to medieval Dublin*. Dublin, 1978.

Curtis, Edmund, *Richard II in Ireland, 1394–5, and submissions of the Irish chiefs*. Oxford, 1927.

Curtis, Edmund (ed.), *Calendar of Ormond deeds*. 6 vols, Dublin, 1932–43.

Curtis, Edmund, 'Janico Dartas, Richard the Second's "Gascon Squire": his career in Ireland, 1394–1426', *JRSAI*, 63 (1933), 182–205.

Curtis, Edmund, 'Rental of the manor of Lisronagh, 1333, and notes on "betagh" tenure in medieval Ireland', *PRIA*, 43C3 (Feb. 1936), 41–76.

Curtis, Edmund, 'Norse Dublin', *DHR*, 4 (1942), 96–108; repr. in Clarke (ed.), *Medieval Dublin: the making of a metropolis* (1990), pp 98–109.

Curtis, Edmund, and R.B. McDowell (eds), *Irish historical documents, 1172–1922*. London, 1943.

D'Alton, John, *The history of county Dublin*. Dublin, 1838; repr. Cork, 1976.

Daly, Gerald, 'George Semple's charts of Dublin Bay, 1762', *PRIA*, 93C (1993), 81–105.

Davey, P.J., and Richard Hodges (eds), *Ceramics and trade: the production and distribution of late medieval pottery in north-west Europe*. Sheffield, 1983.

Davey, P.J., D.J. Freke and D.A. Higgins, *Excavations in Castletown, Isle of Man, 1989–1992*. Liverpool, 1996.

Davies, K.M., *Bray: IHTA, no. 9*. Dublin, 1998.

Davies, K.M., *That favourite resort: the story of Bray, Co. Wicklow*. Bray, 2007.

Davies, Oliver, and D.B. Quinn (eds), 'The Irish pipe roll of 14 John, 1211–12', *UJA*, 3rd ser., 4, supplement (1941).

Davies, R.R., 'Mortimer, Roger (VII), fourth earl of March and sixth earl of Ulster (1374–1398)' in *ODNB*.

Davies, R.R., *Lordship and society in the March of Wales, 1282–1400*. Oxford, 1978.

Davis, S.J.M., *The archaeology of animals*. New Haven, CT, 1987.

Davison, B.K., 'The origins of the castle in England', *Archaeological Journal*, 124 (1967), 202–11.

de Breffny, Brian, and George Mott, *The churches and abbeys of Ireland*. London, 1976.

de Burgh, T.J., 'Ancient Naas (Parts I and II)', *JCKAHS*, 1:3 (1893), 184–201.

de Courcy, John, 'Medieval banks of the Liffey Estuary' in Bradley (ed.), *Viking Dublin exposed* (1984), pp 164–6.

de Meulemeester, Johnny, and Kieran O'Conor, 'Fortifications' in Graham Campbell with Valor (eds), *The archaeology of medieval Europe* (2007), pp 316–41.

de Paor, Máire, and Liam de Paor, *Early Christian Ireland*. London, 1958.

de Varebeke, H.J., 'The Benedictines in medieval Ireland', *JRSAI*, 80 (1950), 92–6.

Deane, T.N., '55th report of the Commissioners of Public Works (C5 142), Appendix E (1886–7)'.

Deevy, M.B., *Medieval ring brooches in Ireland: a study of jewellery, dress and society*. Bray, 1998.

Dehaene, Goorik, 'Medieval rural settlement beside Duncormick motte, Co. Wexford' in Corlett and
    Potterton (eds), *Rural settlement in medieval Ireland* (2009), pp 59–66.

Dempsey, Jonathan, 'Garretstown' in *Excavations 2004*, pp 312–13.

Dennehy, Emer, 'Block 7, Belarmine, Kilgobbin' in *Excavations 2004*, p. 142.

Dennehy, Emer, 'Reuben Street/Dolphin's Barn Street, Dolphin's Barn, Dublin' in *Excavations 2004*,
    pp 135–6.

Derricke, John, *The image of Irelande, with a discoverie of woodkerne*, ed. John Small. Belfast, 1985.

Desmond, Sylvia, and Judith Carroll, 'College Street/Fleet Street/Westmoreland Street'. Unpublished
    report. DEHLG file 96E0276 ext. [n.d.].

Devitt, Matthew, 'Summerhill and its neighbourhood, part i', *JCKAHS*, 6:3 (1910), 214–21.

Devitt, Matthew, 'The barony of Okethy', *JCKAHS*, 8:6 (1917), 276–301, 464–94.

Devitt, Michael, 'Rathcoffey', *JCKAHS*, 3 (1899–1902), 79–98.

Devitt, Michael, 'The rampart of the Pale at Clongowes Wood', *JCKAHS*, 3 (1899–1902), 284–8.

DeWindt, E.B. (ed.), *The salt of common life: individuality and choice in the medieval town, countryside
    and church: essays presented to J. Ambrose Raftis*. Kalamazoo, MI, 1995.

Dickson, C.A., and J.H. Dickson, 'The plant remains' in Mitchell (ed.), *Archaeology and environment
    in early Dublin* (1987), pp 22–32.

Dillon, Mary, and Penny Johnston, 'Plant remains' in Baker, *The archaeology of Killeen Castle* (2009),
    pp 101–11.

Dix, F.R.McC., 'The lesser castles in the county Dublin', *Irish Builder*, 29 (1897), 199.

Dixon, Piers, *Puir labourers and busy husbandmen: the countryside of lowland Scotland in the Middle
    Ages*. Edinburgh [n.d.].

Doherty, Charles, 'Exchange and trade in early medieval Ireland', *JRSAI*, 110 (1980), 67–89.

Doherty, Charles, 'The Vikings in Ireland: a review' in Clarke, Ní Mhaonaigh and Ó Floinn (eds),
    Ireland and Scandinavia in the early Viking Age (1998), pp 288–330.

Doherty, Charles, 1985, 'The monastic town in early medieval Ireland' in Clarke and Simms (eds),
    The comparative history of urban origins in non-Roman Europe (1985), i, pp 45–75.

Doherty, Charles, 'Cluain Dolcáin: a brief note' in Smyth (ed.), *Seanchas* (2000), pp 182–8.

Dolley, Michael, 'The earliest German imitations of Anglo-Irish coins' in Peter Berghaus and Gertz
    Hatz (eds), *Dona Numismatica: Walter-Hävernick zum 23. Januar dargebracht* (Hamburg, 1965),
    pp 213–18.

Dolley, Michael, *Viking coins of the Danelaw and of Dublin*. London, 1965.

Dolley, Michael, 'Dr George Petrie's hoard of Anglo-Irish coins of King John', *NC*, 24 (1966), 127–9.

Dolley, Michael, 'Four neglected Irish finds of Anglo-Irish coins for John', *UJA*, 3rd ser., 29 (1966),
    130–7.

Dolley, Michael, *Sylloge of coins of the British Isles: the Hiberno-Norse coins in the British Museum*.
    London, 1966.

Dolley, Michael, 'The "Ireland" find (*c*.1842) of profile halfpence of John', *NC*, 74 (1966), 66–7.

Dolley, Michael, 'The continental hoard-evidence for the chronology of the Anglo-Irish pence of
    John', *NC*, 74 (1966), 30–2.

Dolley, Michael, 'Some unpublished early nineteenth-century Irish finds', *BNJ*, 36 (1967), 96–105.

Dolley, Michael, 'The Irish mints of Edward I in the light of the coin-hoards from Ireland and Great
    Britain', *PRIA*, 66C3 (1967–8), 235–97.

Dolley, Michael, 'Medieval coins and jettons' in Liversage, 'Excavations at Dalkey Island' (1968), 55–
    234 at 179–83.

Dolley, Michael, 'Anglo-Irish monetary policies, 1172–1637' in J.C. Beckett (ed.), *Historical Studies:
    VII* (London, 1969), pp 45–64.

Dolley, Michael, 'The sequence and chronology of the "portrait" Anglo-Irish groats of Henry VII', *NC*, 77 (1969), 370–4.

Dolley, Michael, 'Was there an Anglo-Irish coinage in the name of Edward VI?', *NC*, 77 (1969), 274–5.

Dolley, Michael, 'Medieval British and Irish coins as dating evidence for the archaeologist', *World Archaeology*, 1 (1969–70), 200–7.

Dolley, Michael, 'A critical unpublished penny Irish of Elizabeth', *NC*, 78 (1970), 190–1.

Dolley, Michael, 'A small find of "Dominick Grotes" from Co. Donegal', *NC*, 78 (1970), 330.

Dolley, Michael, 'An Anglo-Irish hybrid forgery from the 1280s', *NC*, 78 (1970), 286.

Dolley, Michael, 'Irish hoards with thirteenth- and fourteenth-century Scottish coins', *Seaby's Coin and Medal Bulletin*, 617 (Jan. 1970), 4–10.

Dolley, Michael, 'The King John portion of the Anglo-Irish element in the 1908 Brussels Hoard', *JRSAI*, 100 (1970), 67–70.

Dolley, Michael, 'Aspects of George Petrie III: George Petrie and a century of Irish numismatics', *PRIA*, 72C (1972), 165–93.

Dolley, Michael, *Medieval Anglo-Irish coins*. London, 1972.

Dolley, Michael, 'Découverte en France d'un groat anglo-irlandais du XVè siècle', *Club Français de médaille*, 51/52 (1976), 144–50.

Dolley, Michael, 'The Dublin pennies in the name of Sitric Silkbeard in the Hermitage Museum in Leningrad' in Clarke (ed.), *Medieval Dublin: the living city* (1990), pp 135–44.

Dolley, Michael, 'Coinage to 1534: the sign of the times' in Cosgrove (ed.), *A new history of Ireland: II* (1993), pp 816–26.

Dolley, Michael, and S.N. Lane, 'A find of fifteenth-century English groats from Co. Dublin', *JRSAI*, 102 (1972), 143–50.

Dolley, Michael, and W.A. Seaby, 'Le money del Oraylly (O'Reilly's money)', *BNJ*, 36 (1967), 114–17.

Dolley, Michael, and W.A. Seaby, *Sylloge of coins of the British Isles: Anglo-Irish coins: John–Edward III, Ulster Museum, Belfast*. London, 1968.

Dolley, Michael, and W.A. Seaby, 'A find of thirteenth-century pewter tokens from the National Museum excavations at Winetavern Street, Dublin', *Spinks Numismatic Circular* (1971), 446–8.

Dolley, Michael, and W.A. Seaby, 'The anomalous long-cross coins in the Anglo-Irish portion of the Brussels Hoard' in Carson (ed.), *Mints, dies and currency* (1971), pp 291–317.

Dolley, Michael, and W.A. Seaby, 'The thirteenth-century Anglo-Irish coins in the Kirial find from Denmark', *JRSAI*, 102 (1973), 86–92.

Dolley, Michael, and W.D. Hackman, 'The coinages for Ireland of Henry VIII', *BNJ*, 38 (1969 [1970]), 84–108.

Dolley, Michael, and William O'Sullivan, 'The chronology of the first Anglo-Irish coinage' in Etienne Rynne (ed.), *North Munster Studies* (Limerick, 1967), pp 437–78.

Dolley, Michael, Noel Nesbitt and David Rebbeck, 'Three unpublished nineteenth-century Irish finds of coins', *UJA*, 30 (1967), 89–94.

Donaghy, Caroline, 'Castlebrown/Clongowes' in *Excavations 1993*, pp 46–7.

Donnelly, P.J. (comp.), *Remains of St Mary's Abbey, Dublin: explorations and researches*. Dublin, 1886.

Donovan, Máire, 'Reefert: a biography'. MA, UCD, 2009.

Doogue, Declan, David Nash, John Parnell, Sylvia Reynolds and Peter Wyse Jackson (eds), *Flora of County Dublin*. Dublin, 1998.

Doran, Bill, and Linda Doran, 'St Mary's Cistercian abbey, Dublin: a ghost in the alleyways' in Bradley, Fletcher and Simms (eds), *Dublin in the medieval world* (2009), pp 188–201.

Dowle, Anthony, and Patrick Finn, *The guide book to the coins of Ireland, 995 to 1969*. London, 1969.

Down, Kevin, 'Colonial society and economy' in Cosgrove (ed.), *A new history of Ireland: II* (1993), pp 439–91.

Downham, Clare, 'Fine Gall' in Duffy, *Medieval Ireland: an encyclopedia* (2005), pp 170–1.

Doyle, Ian, 'Final report on archaeological excavations at Nangor townland (Grange Castle International Business Park), Clondalkin, Dublin 22'. Unpublished report lodged with National Museum of Ireland, July 2002.

Doyle, Ian, 'Grange/Kilmahuddrick/Nangor (Grange Castle International Business Park), Clondalkin'. Unpublished report. DEHLG file 00E0263 [n.d.].

Doyle, Ian, 'Nangor (Grange Castle International Business Park), Clondalkin'. Unpublished report. DEHLG file 00E0754 [n.d.].

Doyle, Ian, '7 The Mall, Leixlip'. Unpublished report. DEHLG file 01E0206 [n.d.].

Doyle, Niamh, 'Appendix 3: Medieval and post-medieval pottery from Carrowreagh' in Michael Tierney and Penny Johnston, 'Archaeological report: Carrowreagh N25 Narristown to Rathsillagh, Co. Wexford: medieval moated site and pottery kiln'. Unpublished report by Eachtra Archaeological Projects for Wexford County Council, 2006.

Doyle, Niamh, 'Medieval and post-medieval pottery: Trevet 1, Contract 2, M3, County Meath'. Unpublished report for ACS Ltd, 2007.

Drew, Thomas, 'The ancient chapter-house of the priory of the Holy Trinity, Dublin', *JRSAI*, 1 (1890), 36–43; repr. in Clarke (ed.), *Medieval Dublin: the making of a metropolis* (1990), pp 173–82.

Dryburgh, Paul, and Brendan Smith (eds), *Handbook and select calendar of sources for medieval Ireland in the National Archives of the United Kingdom*. Dublin, 2005.

Dúchas: the Heritage Service, *Monuments in the past: photographs, 1860–1936*. Dublin, 1991.

Duddy, Cathal, 'The western suburb of medieval Dublin: its first century', *IG*, 34:2 (2001), 157–75.

Duddy, Cathal, 'The role of St Thomas's Abbey in the early development of Dublin's western suburb' in Duffy (ed.), *Medieval Dublin IV* (2003), pp 79–97.

Duffy, Carmel, 'Headfort Place, Kells' in *Excavations 2003*, p. 375.

Duffy, Carmel, 'Moat Commons, Clane' in *Excavations 2003*, pp 237–8.

Duffy, Carmel, 'Newtown, Trim' in *Excavations 2004*, pp 352–3.

Duffy, Carmel, 'Tierney Street, Ardee'. Unpublished report. DEHLG file 02E0831 [n.d.].

Duffy, P.J., 'The shape of the parish' in FitzPatrick and Gillespie (eds), *The parish in medieval and early modern Ireland* (2006), pp 33–61.

Duffy, P.J., *Exploring the history and heritage of Irish landscapes*. Dublin, 2007.

Duffy, P.J., David Edwards and Elizabeth FitzPatrick (eds), *Gaelic Ireland, c.1250–c.1650: land, lordship and settlement*. Dublin, 2001.

Duffy, Seán, 'Irishmen and Islesmen in the kingdoms of Dublin and Man, 1052–1171', *Ériu*, 43 (1992), 93–133.

Duffy, Seán, 'Ostmen, Irish and Welsh in the eleventh century', *Peritia*, 9 (1995), 378–96.

Duffy, Seán, *Ireland in the Middle Ages*. Dublin, 1997.

Duffy, Seán, 'Ireland's Hastings: the Anglo-Norman conquest of Dublin', *Anglo-Norman Studies*, 20 (1998), 69–86.

Duffy, Seán (ed.), *Medieval Dublin I: proceedings of the Friends of Medieval Dublin Symposium, 1999*. Dublin, 2000.

Duffy, Seán (ed.), *Medieval Dublin II: proceedings of the Friends of Medieval Dublin Symposium, 2000*. Dublin, 2001.

Duffy, Seán (ed.), *Medieval Dublin III: proceedings of the Friends of Medieval Dublin Symposium, 2001*. Dublin, 2002.

Duffy, Seán (ed.), *Medieval Dublin IV: proceedings of the Friends of Medieval Dublin Symposium, 2002*. Dublin, 2003.

Duffy, Seán, 'Town and crown: the kings of England and their city of Dublin', *Thirteenth-Century England*, 10 (2003), 95–117.

Duffy, Seán (ed.), *Medieval Dublin V: proceedings of the Friends of Medieval Dublin Symposium, 2003*. Dublin, 2004.

Duffy, Seán (ed.), *Medieval Dublin VI: proceedings of the Friends of Medieval Dublin Symposium, 2004*. Dublin, 2005.

Duffy, Seán (ed.), *Medieval Ireland: an encyclopedia.* New York, 2005.

Duffy, Seán (ed.), *Medieval Dublin VII: proceedings of the Friends of Medieval Dublin Symposium, 2005.* Dublin, 2006.

Duffy, Seán (ed.), *Medieval Dublin VIII: proceedings of the Friends of Medieval Dublin Symposium, 2006.* Dublin, 2008.

Duffy, Seán (ed.), *Medieval Dublin IX: proceedings of the Friends of Medieval Dublin Symposium, 2007.* Dublin, 2009.

Duffy, Seán, and Linzi Simpson, 'The hermits of St Augustine in medieval Dublin: their history and archaeology' in Bradley, Fletcher and Simms (eds), *Dublin in the medieval world* (2009), pp 202–48.

Duignan, Michael, 'Irish agriculture in early historic times', *JRSAI*, 94 (1944), 124–45.

Dunlevy, Mary, 'A classification of early Irish combs', *PRIA*, 88C (1988), 341–422.

Dunne, Laurence, 'Ballyogan Road, Jamestown' in *Excavations 1998*, p. 61.

Dunne, Laurence, 'Sutton' in *Excavations 2001*, pp 140–1.

Dunne, Laurence, 'Bull Island North, Bull Strand North' in *Excavations 2002*, pp 127–8.

Dunning, G.C., 'The trade in medieval pottery around the North Sea' in J.G. Renaud (ed.), *Rotterdam Papers*, 1 (Rotterdam, 1968), pp 35–58.

Dunning, P.J., 'The Arroasian order in medieval Ireland', *IHS*, 4 (1945–6), 297–315.

Dyer, Christopher, 'English diet in the later Middle Ages' in Aston, Coss, Dyer and Thirsk (eds), *Social relations and ideas* (1983), pp 191–216.

Dyer, Christopher, 'Changes in diet in the late Middle Ages: the case of harvest workers', *AHS*, 36 (1988), 21–37.

Dyer, Christopher, *Standards of living in the later Middle Ages: social change in England, c.1200–1520.* Cambridge, 1989.

Dyer, Christopher, 'The hidden trade of the Middle Ages: evidence from the west midlands of England', *Journal of Historical Geography*, 18 (1992), 141–57.

Dyer, Christopher, *Everyday life in medieval England.* London, 1994.

Dyer, Christopher, 'Sheepcotes: evidence for medieval sheepfarming', *Med. Arch.*, 39 (1995), 136–62.

Dyer, Christopher, 'Alternative agriculture: goats in medieval England' in R.W. Hoyle (ed.), *People, landscape and alternative agriculture: essays for Joan Thirsk* (Exeter, 2004), pp 20–38.

Dykes, D.W., 'The Irish coinage of Henry III', *BNJ*, 32 (1963), 99–116.

Dykes, D.W., 'The Anglo-Irish coinage and ancient arms of Ireland', *JRSAI*, 96 (1966), 111–20.

Düwel, Klaus, Herbert Jankhun, Harald Siems and Dieter Timpe (eds), *Untersuchungen zu Handel und Verkehr der vor- und fruhgeschichtlichen Zeit in Mittel-und Nordeuropa iv.* Gottingen, 1987.

Eames, E.S., and Thomas Fanning, *Irish medieval tiles: decorated medieval paving tiles in Ireland with an inventory of sites and designs and a visual index.* Dublin, 1988.

Edwards, K.J., F.W. Hamond and Anngret Simms, 'The medieval settlement of Newcastle Lyons, County Dublin: an interdisciplinary approach', *PRIA*, 83C14 (1983), 351–76.

Edwards, Kathleen, *The English secular cathedrals in the Middle Ages.* Manchester, 1967.

Edwards, Nancy, *The archaeology of early medieval Ireland.* London, 2000.

Edwards, Nancy, 'The archaeology of early medieval Ireland, c.400–1169: settlement and economy' in Ó Cróinín (ed.), *A new history of Ireland: I* (2005), pp 235–300.

Elliot, A.C., 'The abbey of St Thomas the Martyr, near Dublin', *JRSAI*, 22 (1892), 25–41; repr. in Clarke (ed.), *Medieval Dublin: the living city* (1990), pp 62–77.

Ellis, S.G., 'The struggle for control of the Irish mint: 1460–1506', *PRIA*, 78C2 (1978), 17–36.

Ellis, S.G., 'The destruction of the liberties: some further evidence', *Bulletin of the Institute of Historical Research*, 54:130 (1981), 150–61.

Ellis, S.G., *Tudor Ireland: crown, community and the conflict of cultures, 1470–1603.* London and New York, 1985.

Ellis, S.G., *Ireland in the age of the Tudors, 1447–1603: English expansion and the end of Gaelic rule.* New York, 1998.

Ellis, S.G., 'Pale' in Connolly (ed.), *The Oxford companion to Irish history* (1998), pp 424–5.

Ellis, S.G., 'An English gentleman and his community: Sir William Darcy of Platten' in V.P. Carey and Ute Lotz-Heumann (eds), *Taking sides? Colonial and confessional* mentalités *in early modern Ireland: essays in honour of Karl S. Bottigheimer* (Dublin, 2003), pp 19–41.

Ellis, S.G., 'The emergence of the English Pale in Ireland', *IHS*, forthcoming.

Elmes, R.M., *Catalogue of Irish topographical prints and original drawings*. Dublin, 1975.

Empey, C.A., 'The manor of Carrick-on-Suir in the Middle Ages', *Journal of the Butler Society*, 2 (1982), 206–14.

Empey, C.A., 'Medieval Knocktopher: a study in manorial settlement', *Old Kilkenny Review*, 2:4 (1982), 329–42; 2:5 (1983), 441–52.

Empey, C.A., 'The layperson in the parish: the medieval inheritance, 1169–1536' in Raymond Gillespie and W.G. Neely (eds), *The laity and the church of Ireland, 1000–2000* (Dublin, 2000), pp 7–48.

Epstein, S.R. (ed.), *Town and country in Europe, 1300–1800*. Cambridge, 2001.

Etchingham, Colmán, 'Evidence of Scandinavian settlement in Wicklow' in Hannigan and Nolan (eds), *Wicklow: history and society* (1994), pp 113–38.

Falkiner, C.L., 'The hospital of St John of Jerusalem in Ireland', *PRIA*, 26C (1906–7), 275–317.

Fallon, Donal, 'Brookfield House, Ninth Lock Road, Clondalkin' in *Excavations 2002*, pp 136–7.

Fallon, Donal, 'Summary report on excavation (licence 02E1781) at Ladycastle Lower, Co. Kildare'. Unpublished report, 2005.

Fallon, Donal, 'Summary report on excavation (licence 02E1782) at Ladycastle Lower, Co. Kildare'. Unpublished report, 2005.

Fallon, Donal, 'Summary report on excavation (licence 03E0043) at Ladycastle Lower, Co. Kildare'. Unpublished report, 2005.

Fallon, Donal, 'Ladycastle Lower' in *Excavations 2003*, p. 247.

Fallon, Donal, 'Muckerstown/Wotton' in *Excavations 2004*, pp 328–9.

Fallon, Donal, 'Muckerstown/Wotton: final excavation report'. Unpublished report, 2008.

Fallon, Donal, 'Continuity: the archaeological and documentary evidence for medieval to modern rural settlement and landholding in the townland of Baltrasna, Ratoath, Co. Meath' in Corlett and Potterton (eds), *Rural settlement in medieval Ireland* (2009), pp 79–90.

Fanning, Thomas, 'An Irish medieval tile pavement: recent excavations at Swords Castle, County Dublin', *JRSAI*, 105 (1975), 47–82.

Fanning, Thomas, *Viking-Age ringed pins from Dublin*. Dublin, 1994.

Fanning, Thomas, 'Some observations on the medieval pavement tiles from the site of St Nicholas's Church, Dublin' in Manning (ed.), *Dublin and beyond the Pale* (1998), pp 71–3.

Fanning, Thomas, and E.S. Eames, 'A line-impressed mosaic tile from Lusk Church, Co. Dublin' in Mac Niocaill and Wallace (eds), *Keimelia* (1988), pp 365–74.

Farley, Eileen, 'Report on rock types from architectural stone fragments' in McMahon, 'Four Courts extension' (1988), 271–319.

Farmer, D.L., 'Some grain price movements in thirteenth-century England', *EcHR*, 2nd ser., 10:2 (1957), 207–20.

Farmer, D.L., 'Grain yields on the Winchester manors in the later Middle Ages', *EcHR*, 2nd ser., 30 (1977), 555–66.

Farmer, D.L., 'Marketing the produce of the countryside, 1200–1500' in Miller (ed.), *The agrarian history of England and Wales, vol. 3* (1991), pp 324–430.

Feehan, John, and Grace O'Donovan, *The bogs of Ireland: an introduction to the natural, cultural and industrial heritage of Irish peatlands*. Dublin, 1996.

Feehan, John, *Farming in Ireland: history, heritage and environment*. Dublin, 2003.

Fegan, Grace, 'Discovery and excavation of a medieval moated site at Coolamurry, Co. Wexford' in Corlett and Potterton (eds), *Rural settlement in medieval Ireland* (2009), pp 91–108.

Fenning, Hugh (ed.), *Medieval Irish Dominican studies: Benedict O'Sullivan OP*. Dublin, 2009.

Fenton, Alexander, 'Pork in the rural diet of Scotland' in Theo Gantner and Hans Trumpy (eds), *Festschrift fur Robert Wildhaber* (Basel, 1973), pp 98–110.

Ferguson, Paul, *The A–Z of Georgian Dublin: John Rocque's maps of the city in 1756 and the county in 1760*. Lympne Castle, Kent, 1998.

Ferguson, Paul, 'Irish map history: bibliography and guide to secondary works, 1850–1995, on the history of cartography in Ireland'. Unpublished report [n.d.].

Ffrench, J.F.M., 'Notes on the family of Sherlock: chiefly gathered from the state papers and other official documents', *JCKAHS*, 2 (1896–9), 39–47.

Finan, Thomas, and Kieran O'Conor, 'The moated site at Cloonfree, Co. Roscommon', *JGAHS*, 54 (2002), 72–87.

FitzGerald, Walter, 'Description of the stone-roofed building called St Patrick's Chapel at Ardrass, County Kildare', *JRSAI*, 1 (1890–1), 456–8.

FitzGerald, Walter, 'The Dongan family in the county of Kildare at the commencement of the seventeenth century', *JCKAHS*, 4:1 (1903), 67–70.

FitzGerald, Walter, 'Notes on the St Lawrences, lords of Howth, from the end of the twelfth to the middle of the sixteenth century, with a description of the family altar-tomb in St Mary's Church at Howth', *JRSAI*, 37 (1907), 349–59.

FitzGerald, Walter, 'Historical notes on the O'Mores and their territory of Leix, to the end of the sixteenth century, with appendices', *JCKAHS*, 6:1 (1909), 1–88.

FitzGerald, Walter, 'The stone-roofed church at Ardrass', *JCKAHS*, 7:2 (1911), 410–14.

FitzGerald, Walter, 'Burgage churchyard', *JIMA*, 9 (1913–16), 395–7.

FitzGerald, Walter, 'The preceptory, or commandery, of Kilteel, County Kildare', *JCKAHS*, 8:4 (1916), 267–75.

FitzPatrick, Elizabeth, 'The material world of the parish' in FitzPatrick and Gillespie (eds), *The parish in medieval and early modern Ireland* (2006), pp 62–75.

FitzPatrick, Elizabeth, and Caimin O'Brien, *The medieval churches of County Offaly*. Dublin, 1998.

FitzPatrick, Elizabeth, and Raymond Gillespie (eds), *The parish in medieval and early modern Ireland: community, territory and building*. Dublin, 2006.

FitzPatrick, Elizabeth, Madeleine O'Brien and Paul Walshe (eds), *Archaeological investigations in Galway city, 1987–1998*. Bray, 2004.

Fitzpatrick, Martin, 'Newtown' in *Excavations 2002*, p. 179.

Fitzpatrick, Martin, 'Ratoath'. Unpublished report. DEHLG file 02E1454 [n.d.].

Flanagan, M.T., 'St Mary's Abbey, Louth, and the introduction of the Arrouaisian observance into Ireland', *Clogher Record: Journal of the Clogher Historical Society*, 10 (1978–81), 223–34.

Flanagan, M.T., 'Henry II and the kingdom of Uí Fáeláin' in Bradley (ed.), *Settlement and society in medieval Ireland* (1988), pp 229–39.

Flanagan, M.T., *Irish society, Anglo-Norman settlers, Angevin kingship: interactions in Ireland in the late twelfth century*. Oxford, 1989.

Flanagan, M.T., 'Anglo-Norman change and continuity: the castle of Telach Cail in Delbna', *IHS*, 28:112 (1993), 385–9.

Flanagan, M.T., 'Lacy, Hugh de (d. 1186)', *ODNB*, 2004. www.oxforddnb.com/view/article/15852 (accessed 11 Dec. 2004).

Flanagan, M.T., 'High-kings with opposition, 1072–1166' in Ó Cróinín (ed.), *A new history of Ireland: I* (2005), pp 899–933.

Flanagan, M.T., *Irish royal charters: texts and contexts*. Oxford, 2005.

Flavin, Susan, and E.T. Jones, *Bristol's trade with Ireland and the Continent, 1503–1601*. Dublin, 2009.

Flynn, Thomas, *The Irish Dominicans, 1536–1641*. Dublin, 1993.

Forbes, A.C., 'Some legendary and historical references to Irish woods and their significance', *PRIA*, 41B (1932), 15–36.

Fox, H.S.A., 'Some ecological dimensions of medieval field systems' in Kathleen Biddick (ed.), *Archaeological approaches to medieval Europe* (Kalamazoo, MI, 1984), pp 119–58.

Fox, H.S.A., 'Devon and Cornwall' in Miller (ed.), *The agrarian history of England and Wales, vol. 3* (1991), pp 303–7.

Fox, H.S.A., *The evolution of the fishing village: landscape and society along the south Devon coast, 1086–1550*. Oxford, 2001.

Frame, Robin, 'The Dublin government and Gaelic Ireland, 1272–1361'. PhD, TCD, 1971.

Frame, Robin, 'Power and society in Ireland, 1272–1377', *Past and Present*, 76 (1977), 17–18.

Frame, Robin, *Colonial Ireland, 1169–1369*. Dublin, 1981.

Frame, Robin, *English lordship in Ireland, 1318–1361*. Oxford, 1982.

Frazer, W.O., 'Killegland, Ashbourne' in *Excavations 2003*, pp 356–9.

Frazer, W.O., 'Killegland, Ashbourne' in *Excavations 2004*, pp 283–5.

Frazer, W.O., 'A medieval farmstead at Killegland, Ashbourne, Co. Meath' in Corlett and Potterton (eds), *Rural settlement in medieval Ireland* (2009), pp 109–24.

Frazer, William, 'Description of a great sepulchral mound at Aylesbury Road, near Donnybrook, in the county of Dublin …', *PRIA*, 16 (1879), 29–55.

Frazer, William, 'On two finds of silver coins of Edward 1st and 2nd, obtained in Ireland, and also some foreign sterlings', *PRIA*, 2nd ser., 1 (1879), 70–2.

Frazer, William, 'The Aylesbury Road sepulchral mound …', *PRIA*, 16 (1882), 116–18.

Frazer, William, 'On Irish half-timbered houses', *JRSAI*, 21 (1891), 367–9.

Frazer, William, 'Early pavement tiles in Ireland', *JRSAI*, 23 (1893), 357–66.

Frazer, William, 'Early pavement tiles in Ireland: part II – tiles displaying shamrock and fleur-de-lis', *JRSAI*, 24 (1894), 136–8.

Frazer, William, 'Early pavement tiles in Ireland: part III', *JRSAI*, 25 (1895), 171–5.

French, E.J., 'Finds of coins, Co. Dublin', *JRSAI*, 54 (1924), 89.

Gaffney, Vincent, R.H. White and S.T.E. Buteux, 'Wroxeter, the Cornovii, and the urban process: final report on the work of the Wroxeter Hinterland Project and Wroxeter Hinterlands Survey, 1994–1999'. Forthcoming.

Gahan, Audrey, and Claire Walsh, 'Medieval pottery' in Walsh, *Archaeological excavations at Patrick, Nicholas and Winetavern Streets* (1997), pp 109–23.

Gailey, Alan, 'Irish corn-drying kilns' in Desmond McCourt and Alan Gailey (eds), *Studies in folklife presented to Emyr Estyn Evans* (Belfast, 1970), pp 52–71.

Galloway, J.A., 'London's grain supply: changes in production, distribution and consumption during the fourteenth century', *Franco-British Studies*, 20 (1995), 23–34.

Galloway, J.A., 'Driven by drink?: ale consumption and the agrarian economy of the London region, *c.*1300–1400' in Carlin and Rosenthal (eds), *Food and eating in medieval Europe* (1998), pp 87–100.

Galloway, J.A., 'Metropolitan market networks: London's economic hinterland in the later Middle Ages', *London and Middlesex Archaeological Society Transactions*, 50 (1999), 91–7.

Galloway J.A. (ed.), *Trade, urban hinterlands and market integration, c.1300–1600*. Centre for Metropolitan History Working Papers, 3. London, 2000.

Galloway, J.A., 'Town and country in England, 1300–1570' in Epstein (ed.), *Town and country in Europe* (2001), pp 106–31.

Galloway, J.A., 'Urban hinterlands in later medieval England' in Giles and Dyer (eds), *Town and country in the Middle Ages* (2005), pp 11–131.

Galloway, J.A., Derek Keene and Margaret Murphy, 'Fuelling the city: production and distribution of firewood and fuel in London's region, 1290–1400', *EcHR*, 49:3 (1996), 447–72.

Galloway, Peter, *The cathedrals of Ireland*. Belfast, 1992.

Galster, Georg, 'A find of English coins at Ribe, Denmark', *Numismatic Chronicle*, 11 (1911), 378–98.

Galster, Georg, Michael Dolley and J.S. Jensen, *Royal collection of coins and medals, National Museum, Copenhagen, pt v: Hiberno-Norse and Anglo-Irish coins*. London, 1975.

Gardiner, Mark, and Stephen Rippon (eds), *Medieval landscapes*. Macclesfield, Cheshire, 2007.

Geaney, Máire, 'Christ Church Cathedral, Dublin: a survey of the nave and chancel transept roofs' in Duffy (ed.), *Medieval Dublin VII* (2006), pp 233–49.

Geber, Jonny, 'The faunal remains' in Baker, *The archaeology of Killeen Castle* (2009), pp 131–56.

Geddes, Jane, 'Iron' in Blair and Ramsay (eds), *English medieval industries* (1991; 2001), pp 167–88.

Geraghty, Siobhán, *Viking Dublin: botanical evidence from Fishamble St.: medieval Dublin excavations, 1962–81*, ser. C, 2. Dublin, 1996.

Gerald of Wales: *Expugnatio Hibernica, the conquest of Ireland: by Giraldus Cambrensis*, ed. A.B. Scott and F.X. Martin. Dublin, 1978.

Gerald of Wales: *The history and topography of Ireland*, trans. and intr. J.J. O'Meara. London, 1982.

Gerarde, John, *The herbal or generall historie of plantes: very much enlarged and amended by Thomas Johnson*. London, 1633.

Giacometti, Antoine, '48 New Street South, Dublin' in *Excavations 2004*, pp 127–8.

Gibson, Annemarie, 'Medieval corn-drying kilns at Capo, Kincardineshire and Abercairny, Perthshire', *Proceedings of the Society of Antiquaries of Scotland*, 118 (1989), 219–29.

Gilbert, J.T., *A history of the city of Dublin*. 3 vols, Dublin, 1845–9.

Gilbert, J.T. (ed.), *Historic and municipal documents of Ireland, 1172–1320*. London, 1870.

Gilbert, J.T. (ed.), *Chartularies of St Mary's Abbey, Dublin*. 2 vols, London, 1884.

Gilbert, J.T. (ed.), *Register of the abbey of St Thomas, Dublin*. London, 1889.

Gilbert, J.T. (ed.), *Calendar of ancient records of Dublin*. 19 vols, Dublin, 1889–1944.

Gilbert, J.T. (ed.), *Crede Mihi: the most ancient register book of the archbishops of Dublin before the Reformation*. Dublin, 1897.

Giles, Kate, and Christopher Dyer (eds), *Town and country in the Middle Ages: contrasts, contacts and interconnections, 1100–1500*. Leeds, 2005.

Gillard, Henri, 'Le trésor du Poiré de Velluire', *Bulletin de Numismatique*, 4 (1897), 21–3.

Gillespie, Raymond, 'Dublin, 1600–1700: a city and its hinterlands' in Clark and Lepetit (eds), *Capital cities and their hinterlands* (1996), pp 84–104.

Gillespie, Raymond (ed.), *The proctor's accounts of Peter Lewis, 1564–1565*. Dublin, 1996.

Gillespie, Raymond (ed.), *The first chapter act book of Christ Church Cathedral, Dublin, 1574–1634*. Dublin, 1997.

Gillespie, Raymond, 'Small worlds: settlement and society in the royal manors of sixteenth-century Dublin' in Clarke, Prunty and Hennessy (eds), *Surveying Ireland's past* (2004), pp 197–217.

Gittos, Brian, and Moira Gittos, 'Irish Purbeck: recently identified Purbeck marble monuments in Ireland', *Church Monuments: Journal of the Church Monuments Society*, 13 (1998), 5–14.

Glasscock, R.E., 'Moated sites and deserted boroughs and villages: two neglected aspects of Anglo-Norman settlement in Ireland' in Stephens and Glasscock (eds), *Irish geographical studies* (1970), pp 162–77.

Glasscock, R.E., 'The study of deserted medieval settlements in Ireland (to 1968)' in Beresford and Hurst (eds), *Deserted medieval villages* (1989), pp 279–91.

Glasscock, R.E., and Thomas McNeill, 'Mottes in Ireland: a draft list', *Bulletin of the Group for the Study of Irish Historic Settlement*, 3 (1972), 27–51.

Gleeson, D.F., 'The silver mines of Ormond', *JRSAI*, 67 (1937), 101–16.

Glin, Knight of, David Griffin and Nicholas Robinson, *Vanishing country houses of Ireland*. Dublin, 1988.

Goodall, I.H., 'The medieval blacksmith and his products' in Crossley (ed.), *Medieval industries* (1981), pp 51–62.

Goodbody, Rob, *On the borders of the Pale: a history of the Kilgobbin, Stepaside and Sandyford area*. Bray, 1993.

Goodbody, Rob, 'Pale ditch in south County Dublin', *AI*, 7:3 (autumn 1993), 24–5.

Goodburn, Damian, 'Waterlogged wood and timber as archives of ancient landscapes' in John Coles and Damian Goodburn (eds), *Wet site excavation and survey* (Exeter, 1991), pp 51–3.

Goodburn, Damian, 'Trees underground: new insights into trees and woodmanship in south-east England, *c*.AD800–1300', *BJS*, 46 (1994), 658–62.

Goodman, P.J., *The Roman city and its periphery: from Rome to Gaul*. London and New York, 2007.

Gowen, Margaret, *Three Irish gas pipelines: new archaeological evidence in Munster*. Dublin, 1988.

Gowen, Margaret, 'Dalkey' in *Excavations 1988*, p. 14.

Gowen, Margaret, 'Gracedieu' in *Excavations 1988*, pp 16–17.

Gowen, Margaret (ed.), 'Hotel and car park development at Christchurch Place: archaeology. Preliminary post-excavation report submitted to the Office of Public Works'. Unpublished report, 1992.

Gowen, Margaret, 'Archaeology and Christchurch Place, 1993'. Unpublished report, 1993.

Gowen, Margaret, '29–34 Thomas St. (rear), Dublin' in *Excavations 1995*, p. 22.

Gowen, Margaret, 'National College of Art and Design, Thomas St./Oliver Bond St./John's Lane/John's St., Dublin' in *Excavations 1995*, p. 23.

Gowen, Margaret, 'Statoil, Thomas St., Dublin' in *Excavations 1995*, p. 23.

Gowen, Margaret, 'Bridge St., Swords' in *Excavations 1996*, p. 3.

Gowen, Margaret, 'Excavations at the site of the church and Lower of St Michael le Pole, Dublin' in Duffy (ed.), *Medieval Dublin II* (2001), pp 13–52.

Gowen, Margaret, 'Corke Abbey, Bray' in *Excavations 2002*, p. 533.

Gowen, Margaret, '9–12 High Street, Dublin'. Unpublished report. DEHLG file E000548 [n.d.].

Gowen, Margaret, 'High Street 9–12 (rear of)'. Unpublished report. DEHLG file E000548 [n.d.].

Gowen, Margaret, 'Frawley's: Thomas Street (rear)'. Unpublished reports. DEHLG files 95E0110 and 95E0110ext. [n.d.].

Gowen, Margaret, 'New Courthouse, Naas, County Kildare'. Unpublished report. DEHLG file 95E0251 [n.d.].

Gowen, Margaret, 'Ship Street Little/Ship Street Great: Osmond House'. Unpublished report. DEHLG file 97E0161 [n.d.].

Gowen, Margaret, with Georgina Scally, *Archaeology in Temple Bar: a summary report on excavations at Exchange Street Upper/Parliament Street, Dublin.* Temple Bar Archaeological Reports, 4. Dublin, 1996.

Gracie, C.D., 'Site 1: Balally' in V.J. Keeley (ed.), *Additional archaeological assessment of Routes A and S South-Eastern Motorway*, 1 (1996), pp 6–7.

Gracie, C.D., 'Central Bank of Ireland, Balally' in *Excavations 1996*, p. 16.

Graham, B.J., 'Anglo-Norman settlement in Co. Meath', *PRIA*, 75C11 (1975), 223–48.

Graham, B.J., 'The evolution of the settlement pattern of Anglo-Norman Eastmeath' in Buchanan, Butlin and McCourt (ed.), *Fields, farms and settlement in Europe* (1976), pp 38–47.

Graham, B.J., *Medieval Irish settlement: a review.* Geography Research Series, 3. Norwich, 1980.

Graham, B.J., 'The mottes of the Norman liberty of Meath' in Murtagh (ed.), *Irish midland studies* (1980), pp 39–56.

Graham, B.J., 'Anglo-Norman manorial settlement in Ireland: an assessment', *IG*, 18 (1985), 4–15.

Graham, B.J., *Anglo-Norman settlement in Ireland.* Athlone, 1985.

Graham Campbell, James, 'The Viking-Age silver hoards of Ireland' in Almqvist and Greene (eds), *Proceedings of the seventh Viking Congress* (1976), pp 39–74.

Graham Campbell, James, with Magdalena Valor (eds), *The archaeology of medieval Europe, vol. 1: eighth to twelfth centuries AD.* Aarhus, 2007.

Grant, Annie, 'Animal resources' in Astill and Grant (eds), *The countryside of medieval England* (1988), pp 149–261.

Grant, Annie, 'Food, status and religion in the Middle Ages: an archaeo-zoological perspective' in Liliane Bodson (ed.), *L'animal dans l'alimentation humaine: les critères de choix* (*Anthropozoologia*: second special number, London, 1988), pp 139–46.

Grant, Annie, 'The use of tooth wear as a guide to the age of domestic ungulates' in Bob Wilson, Caroline Grigson and Sebastian Payne (eds), *Ageing and sexing animal bones from archaeological sites.* BAR British Series, 109 (1982), pp 91–108.

Grantham, G.W., 'Espaces privilégiés: productivité agraire et zones d'approvisionnement des villes dans l'Europe préindustrielle', *Annales*, 52 (1997), 695–726.

Graves, James (ed.), *A roll of the proceedings of the king's council in Ireland, 1392–93.* London, 1877.

Green, F.J., 'The archaeological and documentary evidence for plants from the medieval period in England' in Willem van Zeist and W.A. Casparie (eds), *Plants and ancient man: studies in palaeoethnobotany* (Rotterdam, 1984), pp 99–114.

Greene, David, 'The influence of Scandinavian on Irish' in Almqvist and Greene (eds), *Proceedings of the seventh Viking Congress* (1976), pp 75–82.

Greene, David, 'The evidence of place-names in Ireland' in Andersson and Sandred (eds), *The Vikings* (1978), pp 119–23.

Greig, James, 'Garderobes, sewers, cess-pits and latrines', *Current Archaeology*, 85:2 (1982), 49–52.

Greig, James, 'Plant resources' in Astill and Grant (eds), *Countryside of medieval England* (1988), pp 108–27.

Griffith, M.C. (ed.), *Calendar of justiciary rolls, 1308–14*. Dublin, 1956.

Griffith, M.C. (ed.), *Irish patent rolls of James I*. Dublin, 1966.

Griffiths, R.A., 'Mortimer, Edmund (V), fifth earl of March and seventh earl of Ulster (1391–1425)' in *ODNB*.

Grogan, Eoin, and Annaba Kilfeather (comp.), *Archaeological inventory of County Wicklow*. Dublin, 1997.

Grogan, Eoin, and Tom Hillery, *A guide to the archaeology of County Wicklow*. Greystones, Co. Wicklow, 1993.

Grose, Daniel, *The antiquities of Ireland*. 2 vols, London, 1791.

Grueber, Herbert, *Handbook of the coins of Great Britain and Ireland in the British Museum*. London, 1899.

Grummitt, David, *The Calais garrison: war and military service in England, 1436–1558*. Woodbridge, Suffolk, 2008.

Guinness, Desmond, and William Ryan, *Irish houses and castles*. London, 1971.

Gutiérrez, Alejandra, *Mediterranean pottery in Wessex households (13th to 17th centuries)*. BAR British Series, 306. Oxford, 2000.

Gwynn, Aubrey, 'The origins of St Mary's Abbey', *JRSAI*, 19 (1949), 110–25.

Gwynn, Aubrey, 'The early history of St Thomas, Abbey, Dublin', *JRSAI*, 84 (1954), 1–35.

Gwynn, Aubrey, 'The origins of the see of Dublin' in Gwynn, *The Irish church in the eleventh and twelfth centuries* (1992), pp 50–67.

Gwynn, Aubrey, *The Irish church in the eleventh and twelfth centuries*, ed. Gerard O'Brien. Dublin, 1992.

Hadcock, Neville, 'The origin of the Augustinian order in Meath', *RnM*, 3:2 (1964), 124–31.

Hagen, Ines, 'Kilteel Upper' in *Excavations 2002*, p. 257.

Hagen, Ines, 'Kilgobbin'. Unpublished report. DEHLG file 02E1173 [n.d.].

Hale, William (ed.), *The Domesday of St Paul's of the year MCCXXII; or,* Registrum de visitatione maneriorum per Robertum Decanum. Camden Society, 69. London, 1858.

Hall, A.R., and H.K. Kenward (eds), *Urban-rural connexions: perspectives from environmental archaeology*. Oxbow Monograph, 47. Oxford, 1994.

Hall, D.N., Mark Hennessy and Tadhg O'Keeffe, 'Medieval agriculture and settlement in Oughterard and Castlewarden, Co. Kildare', *IG*, 18 (1985), 16–25.

Hall, D.N., *Medieval fields*. Princes Risborough, Buckinghamshire, 1982.

Hall, Dianne, *Women and the church in medieval Ireland, c.1140–1540*. Dublin, 2003.

Hall, Peter (ed.), and C.M. Wartenberg (trans.), *Von Thünen's* Isolated State: *an English edition of* Der Isolierte Staat *by Johann Heinrich Von Thünen*. London, 1966.

Hall, R.A., 'A check list of Viking-Age coin finds from Ireland', *UJA*, 3rd ser., 36–7 (1973–4), 71–86.

Hall, R.A., 'A Viking grave in the Phoenix Park, Co. Dublin', *JRSAI*, 104 (1974), 39–43.

Hall, R.A., 'A Viking-Age grave at Donnybrook, Co. Dublin', *Med. Arch.*, 22 (1978), 64–83.

Hall, V.A., 'Ancient agricultural activity at Slieve Gullion, Co. Armagh: the palynological and documentary evidence', *PRIA*, 90C5 (1990), 123–34.

Hall, V.A., 'Woodland depletion in Ireland over the last millennium' in Pilcher and Mac an tSaoir (eds), *Wood, trees and forests in Ireland* (1995), pp 23–33.

Hall, V.A., 'A comparative study of the documentary and pollen analytical records of the vegetational history of the Irish landscape, 200–1650AD', *Peritia*, 14 (2000), 342–71.

Hall, V.A., 'The documentary and pollen analytical records of the vegetational history of the Irish landscape, AD200–1650', *Peritia*, 14 (2000), 342–71.

Hall, V.A., and Lynda Bunting, 'Tephra-dated pollen studies of medieval landscapes in the north of Ireland' in Duffy, Edwards and FitzPatrick (eds), *Gaelic Ireland* (2001), pp 207–22.

Hallam, H.E. (ed.), *The agrarian history of England and Wales, vol. 2: 1042–1350*. Cambridge, 1988.

Halliday, Stuart, 'Testing Area 18, Harlockstown' in *Excavations* 2003, pp 372–3.

Halpin, Andrew, 'Bride Street/Golden Lane, Dublin' in *Excavations 1992*, pp 17–18.

Halpin, Andrew, 'Francis St./Hanover Lane, Dublin' in *Excavations 1992*, p. 24.

Halpin, Andrew, *The port of medieval Dublin: archaeological excavations at the Civic Offices, Winetavern Street, Dublin, 1993*. Dublin, 2000.

Halpin, Eoin, 'Church and hospital of St Stephen, Mercer's Hospital, Digges Lane, Dublin' in *Excavations 1992*, p. 22.

Halpin, Eoin, 'Clongowes' in *Excavations 2003*, p. 239.

Halpin, Eoin, 'Old Mart, Magdalene Street, Drogheda' in *Excavations 2004*, pp 259–60.

Halpin, Eoin, 'Excavations at St Stephen's Hospital, Dublin, 1992'. Unpublished report. DEHLG file 92E0117 [n.d.].

Halpin, Eoin, 'St Patrick's Street'. Unpublished report. DEHLG file 93E0173 [n.d.].

Hamilton-Dyer, Sheila, 'Bird, fish and marine invertebrates from Site G' in Walsh, *Archaeological excavations at Patrick, Nicholas and Winetavern Streets* (1997), pp 220–1.

Hamilton-Dyer, Sheila, 'The fish bone' in Hayden, 'Arran Quay' (2004), pp 235–8.

Hamilton-Dyer, Sheila, 'Bird, fish and marine invertebrates from Back Lane, Dublin'. Forthcoming.

Hamilton-Dyer, Sheila, 'Fish and bird remains [from Dundrum Castle]'. Unpublished report. DEHLG file E000419 [n.d.].

Hamilton-Dyer, Sheila, 'Fish and bird remains [from Trim Castle]'. Unpublished report [n.d.].

Hand, G.J., 'Medieval cathedral chapters', *Proceedings of the Irish Catholic Historical Committee* (1956), 11–14.

Hand, G.J., 'Dating of the early fourteenth-century ecclesiastical valuation of Ireland', *Irish Theological Quarterly*, 24 (1957), 271–4.

Hand, G.J., 'The forgotten statutes of Kilkenny: a brief survey', *IJ*, 1:2 (1966), 299–312.

Hand, G.J., 'The status of the native Irish in the lordship of Ireland, 1272–1331', *IJ*, 1:2 (1966), 93–115.

Handcock, W.D., *A history of Tallaght*. 2nd ed., Dublin, 1889.

Hannigan, Ken, and William Nolan (eds), *Wicklow: history and society – interdisciplinary essays on the history of an Irish county*. Dublin, 1994.

Harbison, Peter (ed.), *Beranger's views of Ireland*. Dublin, 1991.

Harbison, Peter, *The high crosses of Ireland: an iconographical and photographic survey*. 3 vols, Bonn, 1992.

Harbison, Peter (ed.), *Gabriel Beranger's drawings of the principal antique buildings of Ireland*. Dublin, 1998.

Harbison, Peter, *Cooper's Ireland: drawings and notes from an eighteenth-century gentleman*. Dublin, 2000.

Harbison, Peter, *Beranger's rambles in Ireland*. Bray, 2004.

Harbison, Peter, 'Glendalough drawings of 1779 in the Royal Irish Academy Library' in Condit and Corlett (eds), *Above and beyond* (2005), pp 445–60.

Harbison, Peter, 'Some old illustrations of St Doulagh's Church, Balgriffin, Co. Dublin' in Duffy (ed.), *Medieval Dublin IX* (2009), pp 152–65.

Hardiman, James (ed.), 'The statute of Kilkenny, which was enacted there in the time of Lionel, duke of Clarence, in the xlth year of the reign of Edward III', *Tracts relating to Ireland* (Dublin, 1843), ii.

Harkin, Mary, 'St Nathi's Church and graveyard, Dundrum, Co. Dublin' in Condit and Corlett (eds), *Above and beyond* (2005), pp 171–86.

Harkness, D.W., and Mary O'Dowd (eds), *The town in Ireland: papers read before the Irish conference of historians, Belfast, 30 May–2 June 1979*. Belfast, 1981.

Harris, E.J., 'Notes on Irish coins', *Seaby's Coin and Medal Bulletin* (Dec. 1964), 408.

Harris, E.J., 'Notes on the Irish hammered coinage', *Seaby's Coin and Medal Bulletin*, 569 (Dec. 1966), 366–9.

Hartnett, P.J., 'Malahide "Abbey", Co. Dublin', *JRSAI*, 84 (1954), 179.

Hartnett, P.J., and George Eogan, 'Feltrim Hill, Co. Dublin: a Neolithic and Early Christian site', *JRSAI*, 94 (1964), 1–37.

Harvey, B.F., 'Work and *Festa Ferianda* in medieval England', *Journal of Ecclesiastical History*, 23 (1972), 289–308.

Harvey, B.F., *Living and dying in England, 1100–1540: the monastic experience*. Oxford, 1993.

Harvey, J.H., *Mediaeval gardens*. London, 1981.

Harvey, J.H., 'Vegetables in the Middle Ages', *Garden History*, 12 (1984), 89–99.

Harvey, J.H., 'The first English garden book: Mayster Jon Gardener's treatise and its background', *Garden History*, 13 (1985), 83–101.

Hayden, Alan, 'Jury's Hotel site, Christchurch Place, Dublin' in *Excavations 1992*, p. 20.

Hayden, Alan, 'Mercer's Hospital, Digges Lane, Dublin' in *Excavations 1992*, pp 21–2.

Hayden, Alan, 'Coombe Relief Road, Dublin' in *Excavations 1993*, pp 19–20.

Hayden, Alan, 'Medieval floor tiles' in Walsh, *Archaeological excavations at Patrick, Nicholas and Winetavern Streets* (1997), pp 145–8.

Hayden, Alan, 'Stone objects' in Walsh, *Archaeological excavations at Patrick, Nicholas and Winetavern Streets* (1997), pp 156–8.

Hayden, Alan, 'Maynooth Castle, Maynooth' in *Excavations 1999*, pp 132–3.

Hayden, Alan, 'West Side story: archaeological excavations at Cornmarket and Bridge Street Upper, Dublin: a summary account' in Duffy (ed.), *Medieval Dublin I* (2000), pp 84–116.

Hayden, Alan, 'Clonfert South' in *Excavations 2000*, p. 162.

Hayden, Alan, 'The excavation of pre-Norman defences and houses at Werburgh Street, Dublin: a summary' in Duffy (ed.), *Medieval Dublin III* (2002), pp 44–68.

Hayden, Alan, 'Clonfert South' in *Excavations 2001*, p. 182 (no. 622).

Hayden, Alan, 'Clonfert South' in *Excavations 2001*, p. 182 (no. 623).

Hayden, Alan, 'Clonfert South' in *Excavations 2001*, p. 182 (no. 624).

Hayden, Alan, 'Scurlockstown' in *Excavations 2001*, p. 334.

Hayden, Alan, 'Excavation of the medieval river frontage at Arran Quay, Dublin' in Duffy (ed.), *Medieval Dublin V* (2004), pp 149–242.

Hayden, Alan, 'Reuben Street, Dublin', *Excavations 2002*, p. 153.

Hayden, Alan, 'Excavation of a medieval house in the grounds of Howth House, County Dublin' in Duffy (ed.), *Medieval Dublin VII* (2006), pp 103–12.

Hayden, Alan, 'Clonfert South 5, Clonfert South' in *Excavations 2003*, p. 238.

Hayden, Alan, 'Clonfert South 6, Clonfert South' in *Excavations 2003*, p. 238.

Hayden, Alan, 'Scurlockstown' in *Excavations 2003*, pp 390–1.

Hayden, Alan, 'Clonee' in *Excavations 2004*, pp 298–9.

Hayden, Alan, 'Old Kilmainham, Dublin' in *Excavations 2004*, p. 129.

Hayden, Alan, 'Trim Castle, Co. Meath: excavations, 1995–8'. Forthcoming.

Hayden, Alan, '9–14 Arran Quay, Dublin'. Unpublished report. DEHLG file E000557 [n.d.].

Hayden, Alan, '31–33 Lower Stephens Street, Dublin'. Unpublished report. DEHLG file E000630 [n.d.].

Hayden, Alan, 'Bridge Street Upper, Dublin'. Unpublished report. DEHLG file 92E0078 [n.d.].

Hayden, Alan, 'Cornmarket/Bridge Street Upper, Dublin'. Unpublished report. DEHLG file 92E0109 [n.d.].

Hayden, Alan, 'Coombe Bypass and Cork Street realignment, Dublin'. Unpublished report. DEHLG file 01E0614 (=93E0066) [n.d.].

Hayden, Alan, 'Francis Street'. Unpublished report. DEHLG file 95E0058 ext. [n.d.].

Hayden, Alan, 'Maynooth Castle'. Unpublished report. DEHLG file 96E0391 [n.d.].

Hayden, Alan, 'Mark's Alley, Dublin 8'. Unpublished report. DEHLG file 01E1142 [n.d.].

Hayden, Alan, and Claire Walsh, 'Small finds' in Walsh, *Archaeological excavations at Patrick, Nicholas and Winetavern Streets* (1997), pp 132–44.

Hayden, Alan [with Sarah Cross (species and conversion identification)], 'Wooden objects' in Walsh, *Archaeological excavations at Patrick, Nicholas and Winetavern Streets* (1997), pp 159–62.

Healy, Paddy, 'Report on monuments and sites of archaeological interest in County Dublin'. Unpublished report for An Foras Forbartha, Conservation and Amenity Advisory Section, Dublin, 1974.

Healy, Paddy, 'A survey of surviving portions of the Pale in County Kildare. An Foras Forbartha'. Unpublished report, Dublin, 1976.

Healy, Paddy, 'A report on the importance of an earthwork believed to be part of the Pale ditch at Balally, Co. Dublin'. An Foras Forbartha Teoranta, Dublin, 1978.

Heistermann, Christoff, 'Appendix. Phosphate analysis at Oughterard, Co. Kildare' in Hall, Hennessy and O'Keeffe, 'Medieval agriculture and settlement in Oughterard and Castlewarden, Co. Kildare' (1985), 16–25.

Helmig, Guido, Barbara Scholkmann and Matthias Untermann (eds), *Medieval Europe, centre, region, periphery: proceedings of the 3rd International Conference of Medieval and Later Archaeology, Basel, 2002*. 3 vols, Hertingen, 2002.

Hencken, H.O'N., 'Ballinderry Crannog I', *PRIA*, 43C5 (1936), 103–239.

Hencken, H.O'N., 'Lagore Crannog: an Irish royal residence of the 7th to 10th centuries AD', *PRIA*, 53C (1953), 1–247.

Henigfeld, Yves, 'Production et diffusion de la céramique dans le nord de l'Alsace de la fin du 10e au début du 17e siècle' in Helmig, Scholkmann and Untermann (eds), *Medieval Europe, centre, region, periphery* (2002), 1, pp 133–9.

Hennessy, Mark, 'Parochial organisation in medieval Tipperary' in William Nolan and Thomas McGrath (eds), *Tipperary: history and society – interdisciplinary essays on the history of an Irish county* (Dublin, 1985), pp 60–70.

Hennessy, Mark, 'The priory and hospital of Newgate: the evolution and decline of a monastic estate' in Smyth and Whelan (eds), *Common ground* (1988), pp 41–54.

Hennessy, Mark, 'Manorial organisation in early thirteenth-century Tipperary', *IG*, 24:2 (1996), 116–25.

Hennessy, Mark, 'Manorial agriculture and settlement in early fourteenth-century Co. Tipperary' in Clarke, Prunty and Hennessy (eds), *Surveying Ireland's past* (2004), pp 99–118.

Herity, Michael (ed.), *Ordnance Survey letters: letters containing information relative to the antiquities of the county of Kildare collected during the progress of the Ordnance Survey in 1837, 1838, and 1839*. Dublin, 2002.

Hickey, Elizabeth, *Skryne and the early Normans: papers concerning the medieval manors of the Feypo family in Ireland in the 12th and early 13th centuries*. Navan, 1994.

Higgs, J.W.Y., *English rural life in the Middle Ages*. Oxford, 1965; repr. 1977.

Higham, N.J., 'Changing spaces: towns and their hinterlands in the north-west, AD900–1500' in Gardiner and Rippon (eds), *Medieval landscapes* (2007), pp 57–70.

Higham, R.A., 'Timber castles in Great Britain' in Hartmut Hofricher (ed.), *Holz in der Burgearchitektur* (Braubach, 2004), pp 199–204.

Higham, R.A., and Philip Barker, *Timber castles*. London, 1992.

Hill, Michael, 'Insect assemblages as evidence for past woodlands around York' in Hall and Kenward (eds), *Urban-rural connexions* (1994), pp 45–54.

Hodkinson, Brian, 'Thom Cor Castle: a 14th-century tower house in Limerick city', *JRSAI*, 135 (2005), 119–29.

Hogan, Arlene, *The priory of Llanthony Prima and Secunda in Ireland, 1172–1541: lands, patronage and politics*. Dublin, 2008.

Holinshed, Raphael: *Holinshead's Irish chronicles*, ed. Liam Miller and Eileen Power. Atlantic Highlands, NJ, 1979.

Hollingsworth, T.H., *Historical demography*. London, 1969.

Holm, Ingunn, Sonja Innselset and Ingvild Øye (eds), *'Utmark': the outfield as industry and ideology in the Iron Age and the Middle Ages*. Bergen, 2005.

Holmes, Margaret, 'The palace of St Sepulchre', *DHR*, 42:4 (1989), 122–6.

Holt, Richard, *The mills of medieval England*. Oxford, 1988.

Holt, Richard, 'Gloucester in the century after the Black Death' in Holt and Rosser (eds), *The English medieval town* (1990), pp 141–59.

Holt, Richard, and Gervase Rosser (eds), *The English medieval town, 1200–1540*. London, 1990.

Holton, Karina, 'Medieval Cloncurry', *RnM*, 9:3 (1997), 73–88.

Holton, Karina, 'Cloncurry, County Kildare' in Paul Connell, D.A. Cronin and Brian Ó Dálaigh (eds), *Irish townlands: studies in local history* (Dublin, 1998), pp 43–68.

Holton, Karina, 'From charters to carters: aspects of fairs and markets in medieval Leinster' in D.A. Cronin, Jim Gilligan and Karina Holton (eds), *Irish fairs and markets: studies in local history* (Dublin, 2001), pp 18–44.

Holton, Karina, Liam Clare and Brian Ó Dálaigh (eds), *Irish villages: studies in local history*. Dublin, 2003.

Homer, R.F., 'Tin, lead and pewter' in Blair and Ramsay (eds), *English medieval industries* (1991; 2001), pp 57–80.

Hore, H.F., 'Woods and fastnesses and their denizens in ancient Leinster', *JRSAI*, 4 (1856–7), 229–40.

Hore, H.F., 'The Scandinavians in Leinster', *JRSAI*, 4 (1856–7), 430–44.

Horner, Arnold, *Maynooth: IHTA, no. 7*. Dublin, 1995.

Hourihane, Colum, '"Holye Crossys": a catalogue of processional, altar, pendant and crucifix figures for late medieval Ireland', *PRIA*, 100C1 (2000), 1–85.

Howlett, Liam, 'The Killester charter', *DHR*, 32 (1979), 69–71.

Hughes, M.J., and John Cherry, 'Neutron activation analysis of medieval decorated floor tiles from Ireland and Cheshire' in Eames and Fanning, *Irish medieval tiles* (1988), pp 136–9.

Hunt, John, *Irish medieval figure sculpture, 1200–1600: a study of Irish tombs with notes on costumes and armour*, 2 vols, Dublin, 1974.

Hurley, F.M., 'Patrick Street/Dillon Place, Dublin'. Unpublished report. DEHLG file 92E0143 [n.d.].

Hurley, M.F., 'Kilferagh, Co. Kilkenny: corn-drying kiln and settlement site' in Cleary, Hurley and Twohig (eds), *Archaeological excavations on the Cork–Dublin gas pipeline* (1987), pp 88–100.

Hurley, M.F., *Excavations at the North Gate, Cork, 1994*. Cork, 1997.

Hurley, M.F., and C.M. Sheehan, 'Ovens and kilns' in Hurley and Scully with McCutcheon (eds), *Late Viking-Age and medieval Waterford* (1997), pp 273–7.

Hurley, M.F., and O.M.B. Scully with S.W.J. McCutcheon (eds), *Late Viking-Age and medieval Waterford: excavations 1986–1992*. Waterford, 1997.

Hurst, J.G., 'Spanish pottery imported into medieval Britain', *Med. Arch.*, 21 (1977), 68–105.

Hurst, J.G., 'The dating of late twelfth- and early thirteenth-century pottery in Ireland', *UJA*, 98 (1985), 138–41.

Hurst, J.G., 'Medieval pottery imported into Ireland' in Mac Niocaill and Wallace (eds), *Keimelia* (1988), pp 229–53.

Hurst, J.G., 'Rural building in England and Wales – England' in Hallam (ed.), *Agrarian history of England and Wales, vol. 2* (1988), pp 884–930.

Hurst, J.G., and L.A.S. Butler, 'Rural building in England and Wales' in Hallam (ed.), *The agrarian history of England and Wales* (1988), pp 854–965.

Jacques, David, 'The techniques and uses of garden archaeology', *Journal of Garden History*, 17:1 (special issue, 1997), 1–99.

Jäger, Helmut, 'Land-use in medieval Ireland, a review of the documentary evidence', *IESH*, 10 (1983), 51–65.

Jenkins, Geraint (ed.), *Studies in folk life: essays in honour of Iorwerth C. Peate*. London, 1969.

Johnson, Catherine, 'The small finds' in O'Donovan, 'The growth and decline of a medieval suburb?' (2003), pp 154–63.

Johnson, Gina, *Review of urban archaeology research*. Kilkenny, 2000.

Johnson, Ruth, 'Decorated wood from Temple Bar West, Dublin' in Duffy (ed.), *Medieval Dublin III* (2002), pp 69–80.

Johnson, Ruth, *Viking-Age Dublin*. Dublin, 2004.

Johnston, Penny, 'Analysis of Plant Remains, Rosepark, Balrothery, Co. Dublin, Licence no. 99E0155'. Unpublished report, Feb. 2002.

Johnston, Penny, 'Analysis of Plant Remains, Flemington Site 4, Co. Dublin, Licence no. 02E0296'. Unpublished report, June 2003.

Johnston, Penny, 'Analysis of plant remains' in Simpson, 'Dublin's southern frontier under siege: Kindlestown Castle' (2003), pp 361–5.

Johnston, Penny, 'Macroscopic plant remains from excavations at Temple Bar West'. Unpublished report. DEHLG file 96E0245 [n.d.].

Johnston, Penny, 'Analysis of plant remains [from John Dillon Street]'. Unpublished report. DEHLG file 98E0158 [n.d.].

Johnston, Penny, 'Analysis of plant remains [from Parkwest: Galanstown]'. Unpublished report. DEHLG file 00E0267 [n.d.].

Johnston, Penny, 'Environmental analysis of samples from Nangor townland'. Unpublished report. DEHLG file 00E0754 [n.d.].

Johnston, Penny, 'Analysis of plant remains, Bremore, Balbriggan, Co. Dublin'. Unpublished report. DEHLG file 01E0370 [n.d.].

Johnston, Penny, 'Analysis of plant remains [from Ship Street Great]'. Unpublished report. DEHLG file 01E0772 [n.d.].

Johnston, Penny, 'Analysis of plant remains [from Main Street, Naas]'. Unpublished report. DEHLG file 02E0955 [n.d.].

Jones, Glynis, and Paul Halstead, 'Maslins, mixtures and monocrops: on the interpretation of archaeological crop samples of heterogenous composition', *Journal of Archaeological Science*, 22 (1995), 103–14.

Jope, E.M., H.M. Jope and E.A. Johnson, *An archaeological survey of County Down*. Belfast, 1966.

Joyce, P.W., *The origin and history of Irish names of places*. 3 vols, Dublin, 1873–1913.

Kavanagh, John, 'Excavation at Church Street, Finglas, Dublin'. Unpublished excavation report submitted to the DEHLG, 2005.

Kavanagh, John, '62 Castle Street, Dalkey' in *Excavations 2003*, pp 115–16.

Kavanagh, John, '4–8 Church Street, Finglas' in *Excavations 2004*, pp 139–40.

Keeley, V.J., '"Toole's Moat", Old Connaught' in *Excavations 1989*, p. 20.

Keene, D.J., *Survey of medieval Winchester, Winchester Studies, 2*. Oxford, 1985.

Keene, D.J., 'Medieval London and its regions', *London Journal*, 14 (1989), 99–111.

Keene, D.J., 'Suburban growth' in Holt and Rosser (eds), *The English medieval town* (1990), pp 97–119.

Kelly, Daniel, Margaret Norton and Declan Doogue, 'Woodlands and hedges' in Doogue, Nash, Parnell, Reynolds and Wyse Jackson (eds), *Flora of County Dublin* (1998), pp 85–93.

Kelly, Fergus, *A guide to early Irish law*. Dublin, 1988.

Kelly, Fergus, *Early Irish farming*. Dublin, 2000.

Kelly, Grainne, 'Analysis of the plant remains: Skreen 05E0321'. Unpublished report, 2006.

Kelly, J.P., 'Lismullin priory, 1240–1539', *RnM*, 2:3 (1961), 53–6.

Kelly, James, and Dáire Keogh (eds), *History of the Catholic diocese of Dublin*. Dublin, 2000.

Kelly, Liam, *Photographs and photography in Irish local history*. Dublin, 2008.

Kelly, M.R.L., *Dalkey, Co. Dublin*. Ilfracombe, Devon, 1952.

Kelly, Maria, *The great dying: the Black Death in Dublin*. Stroud, Gloucestershire, 2003.

Kelly Quinn, Mary, 'The evolution of forestry in County Wicklow from prehistory to present' in Hannigan and Nolan (eds), *Wicklow: history and society* (1994), pp 823–54.

Kenny, Michael, 'The geographical distribution of Irish Viking-Age coin hoards', *PRIA*, 87C8 (1987), 507–25.

Kenny, Michael, 'Coins' in Walsh, *Archaeological excavations at Patrick, Nicholas and Winetavern Streets* (1997), p. 132.

Kenny, Michael, 'Token' in Hayden, 'Arran Quay' (2004), p. 199.

Kenny, James, *A short history of Coolock parish*. Dublin, 1934.

Kenward, Harry, and Enid Allison, 'Rural origins of the urban insect fauna' in Hall and Kenward (eds), *Urban-rural connexions* (1994), pp 55–77.

Kenyon, J.R., and Kieran O'Conor (eds), *The medieval castle in Ireland and Wales: essays in honour of Jeremy Knight*. Dublin, 2003.

Keogh, Helen, '24–28 St Mary's Abbey' in *Excavations 2003*, p. 141.

Keogh, Helen, '14 Exchange Street Lower, Temple Bar, Dublin' in *Excavations 2004*, pp 120–1.

Keogh, Helen, 'St Mary's Abbey/Strand Street Little, Dublin' in *Excavations 2004*, pp 136–7.

Killanin, M.M., and M.V. Duignan, *The Shell guide to Ireland*. London, 1967.

King, D.J.C., and Leslie Alcock, 'Ringworks of England and Wales', *Chateau Gaillard*, 3 (1969), 90–127.

King, J.W., 'Pigs', *Biologist*, 30:5 (1983), 267–73.

King, H.A., 'A tile from Greenoge, Co. Meath', *RnM*, 7:3 (1984), 63–6.

King, H.A., 'A tiled floor at Greenoge, Co. Meath', *RnM*, 8:4 (1992–3), 92–3.

King, H.A., 'Usher's Quay, 6–9'. Unpublished report. DEHLG file E000547 [n.d.].

Kingsbury, J.M., *Poisonous plants in the United States and Canada*. Englewood Cliffs, NJ, 1964.

Kinsella, Stuart, 'Mapping Christ Church Cathedral, Dublin, *c*.1028–1608' in Bradley, Fletcher and Simms (eds), *Dublin in the medieval world* (2009), pp 143–67.

Kinsella, Jonathan, 'Research for the townland of Merrywell'. Unpublished report, 2006.

Kissane, Noel, *Historic Dublin maps*. Dublin, 1988.

Kolata, Alan, 'Tiwanaku and its hinterland', *Archaeology*, 40:1 (Jan./Feb. 1987), 36–41.

Kolata, Alan, *Tiwanaku and its hinterland: agroecology vol. 1: archaeology and palaeoecology of an Andean civilization*. Washington, DC, 1996.

Kolata, Alan, *Tiwanaku and its hinterland: urban and rural archaeology vol. 2: archaeology and paleoecology of an Andean civilization*. Washington, DC, 2003.

Kowaleski, Maryanne, *Local markets and regional trade in medieval Exeter*. Cambridge, 1995.

Kowaleski, Maryanne, 'The grain trade in fourteenth-century Exeter' in DeWindt (ed.), *The salt of common life* (1995), pp 1–52.

Lacey, Jim, *A candle in the window: a history of the barony of Castleknock*. Dublin, 1999.

Lamb, J.G.D., 'The apple in Ireland: its history and its varieties', *Economic Proceedings of the Royal Dublin Society*, 4 (1951), 1–61.

Lamb, Keith and Patrick Bowe, *A history of gardening in Ireland*. Dublin, 1995.

Lambrick, George, and Klara Spandl, *Urban archaeological practice in Ireland*. Kilkenny, 2000.

Landsberg, Sylvia, *The medieval garden*. London, 1997.

Lane, S.N., 'The medieval coinage of Ireland'. MLitt., TCD, 1965.

Lang, J.T., *Viking-Age decorated wood: a study of its ornament and style*. Dublin, 1988.

Langdon, J.L., 'The economies of horses and oxen in medieval England', *AHS*, 30 (1982), 31–40.

Langdon, J.L., *Horses, oxen and technological innovation: the use of draught animals in English farming from 1066 to 1500*. Cambridge, 1986.

Langdon, J.L., *Mills in the medieval economy: England, 1300–1540*. Oxford, 2004.

Latham, R.E., *Revised medieval Latin word-list from British and Irish sources*. Oxford, 1965.

Lawlor, H.J., 'A calendar of the *Liber Niger* and *Liber Albus* of Christ Church, Dublin', *PRIA*, 27C1 (1908), 1–93.

Lawlor, H.J. (ed.), 'Calendar of the *Liber Ruber* of the diocese of Ossory', *PRIA*, 27C19 and 20 (1908–9), 159–208.

Lawlor, H.J. (ed.), 'The chapel of Dublin Castle', *JRSAI*, 53 (1923), 34–73.

Lawrence, C.H., *Medieval monasticism: forms of religious life in Western Europe in the Middle Ages*. London and New York, 1989.

Lawrence, L.A. [on Brussels Hoard]. *BNJ*, 9 (1912), 170.

Lawrence, L.A., 'English and Irish coins of Henry VIII bearing initials of his queens', *BNJ*, 21 (1931/33), 89–92.

Le Fanu, T.P., 'The royal forest of Glencree', *JRSAI*, 23 (1893), 268–80.

Leask, H.G., 'Carved stones discovered at Kilteel, Co. Kildare', *JRSAI*, 65:1 (1935), 1–8.

Leask, H.G., *Irish castles and castellated houses*. Dundalk, 1951; repr. 1995.

Leask, H.G., *Irish churches and monastic buildings, I: the first phases and the Romanesque*. Dundalk, 1955.

Leask, H.G., *Irish churches and monastic buildings, II: Gothic architecture to AD1400*. Dundalk, 1966.

Leask, H.G., *Irish churches and monastic buildings, III: Medieval Gothic: the last phases*. Dundalk, 1971.

Leask, H.G., *Glendalough, Co. Wicklow, National Monuments vested in the Commissioners of Public Works: official historical and descriptive guide*. Dublin, 1974.

Lee, J.S., 'Feeding the colleges: Cambridge's food and fuel supplies, 1450–1560', *EcHR*, 56:2 (2003), 243–64.

Lee, J.S., *Cambridge and its economic region, 1450–1560*. Hatfield, Herefordshire, 2005.

Lennard, R.V., 'What is an extent?', *EHR*, 44 (1929), 256–62.

Lennard, R.V., 'Statistics of corn yields in medieval England: some critical questions', *EcHR*, 3:11 (1936), 173–92.

Lennon, Colm, *Richard Stanihurst the Dubliner*. Dublin, 1981.

Lennon, Colm, 'The great explosion in Dublin, 1597', *DHR*, 42:1 (Dec. 1988), 7–20.

Lennon, Colm, *The lords of Dublin in the age of reformation*. Dublin, 1989.

Lennon, Colm, *Sixteenth-century Ireland: the incomplete conquest*. Dublin, 1994.

Lennon, Colm, and James Murray (eds), *The Dublin city franchise roll, 1468–1512*. Dublin, 1998.

Lerhce, Grith, *Ploughing implements and tillage practices in Denmark from the Viking period to about 1800: experimentally substantiated*. Herning, 1994.

Letters, Samantha, *Gazetteer of markets and fairs in England and Wales to 1516*. List and Index Society, Special Series, 32. Kew, 2003.

Letters and papers, foreign and domestic, Henry VIII. 21 vols, London, 1862–1932.

Liddiard, Robert, *Landscapes of lordship: Norman castles and the countryside in medieval Norfolk, 1066–1200*. BAR British Series, 309. Oxford, 2000.

Liddiard, Robert, *Castles in context: power, symbolism and landscape, 1066–1500*. Macclesfield, Cheshire, 2005.

Liddiard, Robert, 'Medieval designed landscapes: problems and possibilities' in Gardiner and Rippon (eds), *Medieval landscapes* (2007), pp 201–14.

Limberger, Michael, *Sixteenth-century Antwerp and its rural surroundings: social and economic changes in the hinterland of a commercial metropolis (ca.1450–ca.1570)*. Studies in European Urban History, 14 (1100–1800). Turnhout, Belgium, 2008.

Lindh, Jan, 'Aspects of sea-level changes, fishing, and fish processing in Tønsberg in the Middle Ages' in G.L. Good, R.H. Jones and M.W. Ponsford (eds), *Waterfront archaeology: proceedings of the third international conference, Bristol, 1988*. CBA Research Report, 74 (London, 1991), pp 67–75.

Lindsay, John, *A view of the coinage of Ireland*. Cork, 1839.

Lindsay, John, *Notices of remarkable Greek, Roman and medieval coins in the cabinet of the author*. Cork, 1860.

Liversage, G.D., 'Excavations at Dalkey Island, Co. Dublin, 1956–1959', *PRIA*, 66C (1968), 55–234.

Lohan, Kevin, 'Beaverstown, Donabate' in *Excavations 2004*, pp 108–9.

Long, Harry, 'Three settlements of Gaelic Wicklow, 1169–1600: Rathgall, Ballinacor and Glendalough' in Hannigan and Nolan (eds), *Wicklow: history and society* (1994), pp 237–65.

Lucas, A.T., 'The horizontal mill in Ireland', *JRSAI*, 83 (1953), 1–37.

Lucas, A.T., *Furze: a survey of its uses in Ireland*. Dublin, 1960.

Lucas, A.T., 'Cloth finishing in Ireland', *Folk Life: Journal of the Society for Folk Life Studies*, 11 (1968), 18–68.

Lucas, A.T., 'Sea sand and shells as manure' in Jenkins (ed.), *Studies in folk life* (1969), pp 184–203.

Lucas, A.T., 'Irish ploughing practices', *Tools and Tillage*, 2 (1974), 149–60.

Lucas, A.T., *Cattle in ancient Ireland*. Kilkenny, 1989.

Lucas, Adam, *Wind, water, work: ancient and medieval milling technology*. Leiden, 2005.

Lucas, Adam, 'The role of the monasteries in the development of medieval milling' in Walton (ed.), *Wind and water in the Middle Ages* (2006), pp 89–127.

Ludlow, John and Noel Jameson (ser. eds), *Medieval Ireland: the Barryscourt Lectures I–X*. Kinsale, 2004.

Lunt, W.E., 'Papal taxation in England in the reign of Edward I', *EHR*, 30 (1915), 398–417.

Lunt, W.E., 'Financial relations of the papacy with England to 1327'. MA, University of Cambridge, 1939.

Lydon, J.F., 'Survey of the memoranda rolls of the Irish exchequer, 1295–1509', *Analecta Hibernica*, 23 (1966), 49–134.

Lydon, J.F., *The lordship of Ireland in the Middle Ages*. Dublin, 1972; repr. 2003.

Lydon, J.F., *Ireland in the later Middle Ages*. Dublin, 1973.

Lydon, J.F., 'Edward I, Ireland and war in Scotland, 1303–1304' in Lydon (ed.), *England and Ireland in the later Middle Ages* (1981), pp 43–59.

Lydon, J.F. (ed.), *England and Ireland in the later Middle Ages: essays in honour of Jocelyn Otway-Ruthven*. Dublin, 1981.

Lydon, J.F., 'The mills at Ardee in 1304', *CLAHJ*, 4 (for 1980) (1981), 259–63.

Lydon, J.F., 'A fifteenth-century building account from Dublin', *IESH*, 9 (1982), 73–5.

Lydon, J.F., 'The Dublin purveyors and the wars in Scotland, 1296–1324' in Mac Niocaill and Wallace (eds), *Keimelia* (1988), pp 435–48.

Lydon, J.F., 'The medieval city' in Cosgrove, *Dublin through the ages* (1988), pp 25–45.

Lydon, J.F., 'A land of war' in Cosgrove (ed.), *A new history of Ireland: II* (1993), pp 240–74.

Lydon, J.F., 'The expansion and consolidation of the colony, 1215–54' in Cosgrove (ed.), *A new history of Ireland: II* (1993), pp 156–78.

Lydon, J.F., 'The years of crisis, 1254–1315' in Cosgrove (ed.), *A new history of Ireland: II* (1993), pp 179–204.

Lydon, J.F., 'Medieval Wicklow: a land of war' in Hannigan and Nolan (eds), *Wicklow: history and society* (1994), pp 151–89.

Lydon, J.F., 'Introduction' in Mills (ed.), *Account roll* (1996), pp ix–xxii.

Lydon, J.F., 'Dublin in transition: from Ostman town to English borough' in Duffy (ed.), *Medieval Dublin II* (2001), pp 128–41.

Lydon, J.F., 'Dublin Castle in the Middle Ages' in Duffy (ed.), *Medieval Dublin III* (2002), pp 115–27.

Lynch, Ann, 'Dublin Castle'. Unpublished report. DEHLG files E000296–8 [n.d.].

Lynch, Ann, and Conleth Manning, 'Dublin Castle: the archaeological project', *AI*, 4:2 (summer 1990), 65–8.

Lynch, Ann, and Conleth Manning, 'Excavations at Dublin Castle, 1985–7' in Duffy (ed.), *Medieval Dublin II* (2001), pp 169–204.

Lynch, Patricia, 'The animal bone from Skreen, Co. Meath: licence 05E0321'. Unpublished report, 2006.

Lyne, Ed, 'Phoenixtown: lives through time', *AI*, 22:2 (spring 2008), 17–21.

Lynn, Chris, 'Deer Park Farms, Glenarm, Co. Antrim', *AI*, 1:1 (1987), 11–15.

Lyon, B.D. (ed.), *The high Middle Ages, 1000–1300*. New York and London, 1964.

Lyons, Charles, 'Dublin's oldest roof? The choir of St Patrick's Cathedral' in Duffy (ed.), *Medieval Dublin VI* (2005), pp 177–213.

Lyons, M.C., 'The manor of Ballysax, 1280–1288', *Retrospect*, 1 (1981), 40–50.

Lyons, M.C., 'Manorial administration and the manorial economy in Ireland, *c*.1200–*c*.1377'. PhD, TCD, 1984.

Lyons, M.C., 'Weather, famine pestilence and plague in Ireland, 900–1500' in E.M. Crawford (ed.), *Famine: the Irish experience, 900–1900: subsistence crises and famines in Ireland* (Edinburgh, 1989), pp 31–74.

Lyons, Mary Ann, 'Pale, or English Pale' in Duffy (ed.), *Medieval Ireland: an encyclopedia* (2005), pp 852–3.

Lyons, Mary Ann, *Church and society in County Kildare, c.1470–1547*. Dublin, 2000.

Lyons, Susan, 'N2 Finglas-Ashbourne road scheme – Site 17/18: flot assessment'. Unpublished Headland Archaeology report, 2006.

Lyttleton, James, and Tadhg O'Keeffe (eds), *The manor in medieval and early modern Ireland*. Dublin, 2005.

MacAlister, R.A.S., 'A catalogue of the Irish traders' tokens in the collection of the Royal Irish Academy', *PRIA*, 40C2 (Dec. 1931), 19–185.

MacCotter, Paul, *Medieval Ireland: territorial, political and economic divisions*. Dublin, 2008.

MacCurtain, Margaret, 'Late medieval nunneries of the Irish Pale' in Clarke, Prunty and Hennessy (eds), *Surveying Ireland's past* (2004), pp 129–43.

MacDougall, E.B. (ed.), *Mediaeval gardens*. Dumbarton Oaks, Washington, DC, 1986.

MacGiolla Phádraig, Brian, 'Grange Abbey, Baldoyle', *DHR*, 20:3/4 (1965), 129–32.

MacGiolla Phádraig, Brian, 'Fourteenth-century life in a Dublin monastery' in Clarke (ed.), *Medieval Dublin: the living city* (1990), pp 112–22.

MacGregor, Arthur, 'Bone, antler and horn industries in the urban context' in Serjeantson and Waldron (eds), *Diet and crafts in towns* (1989), pp 107–28.

MacIlwaine, J.B.S., 'Notes on some Irish coins found at Trim', *BNJ*, 1st ser., 10 (1913), 309–12.

MacIvor, Dermot, 'The Knights Templar in County Louth', *Seanchas Ard Mhacha*, 4 (1960–2), 72–91.

MacLeod, Caitriona, 'Some late mediaeval wood sculptures in Ireland', *JRSAI*, 77 (1947), 53–62.

MacManus, Ciara, 'A study of excavated animal bones from thirteenth- to eighteenth-century Dublin'. BSc, QUB, 1995.

MacManus, Ciara, 'Francis Street, Dublin' in *Excavations 2003*, pp 130–1.

Mac Niocaill, Gearóid, 'Documents relating to the suppression of the Templars in Ireland', *Analecta Hibernica*, 24 (1961), 183–226.

Mac Niocaill, Gearóid, 'An unpublished fragment of the register of the hospital of St John the Baptist, Dublin', *JRSAI*, 92 (1962), 67–9.

Mac Niocaill, Gearóid, *Na buirgéisí XII–XV aois*. 2 vols, Dublin, 1964.

Mac Niocaill, Gearóid (ed.), *The red book of the earls of Kildare*. Dublin, 1964.

Mac Niocaill, Gearóid, 'The origins of the betagh', *IJ*, new ser., 1 (1966), 292–8.

Mac Niocaill, Gearóid, 'Socio-economic problems of the late medieval town' in Harkness and O'Dowd (ed.), *The town in Ireland* (1981), pp 7–21.

Mac Niocaill, Gearóid, and P.F. Wallace (eds), *Keimelia: studies in medieval archaeology and history in memory of Tom Delaney*. Galway, 1988.

MacShamhráin, Ailbhe, '*Prosopographica Glindelachensis*: the monastic church of Glendalough and its community, sixth to thirteenth centuries', *JRSAI*, 119 (1989), 79–97.

MacShamhráin, Ailbhe, *Church and polity in pre-Norman Ireland: the case of Glendalough*. Maynooth, 1996.

MacShamhráin, Ailbhe, 'The emergence of the metropolitan see: Dublin, 1111–1216' in Kelly and Keogh (eds), *History of the Catholic diocese of Dublin* (2000), pp 51–71.

MacShamhráin, Ailbhe, 'An ecclesiastical enclosure in the townland of Grange, parish of Holmpatrick' in Ailbhe MacShamhráin (ed.), *The island of St Patrick: church and ruling dynasties in Fingal and Meath, 400–1148* (Dublin, 2004), pp 52–60.

MacShamhráin, Ailbhe, 'The *Monasticon Hibernicum* project: the diocese of Dublin' in Duffy (ed.), *Medieval Dublin VI* (2005), pp 114–43.

Maginn, Christopher, *'Civilizing' Gaelic Leinster: the extension of Tudor rule in the O'Byrne and O'Toole lordships*. Dublin, 2004.

Maguire, J.B., 'Seventeenth-century plans of Dublin Castle', *JRSAI*, 104 (1974), 5–14; repr. in Clarke (ed.), *Medieval Dublin: the making of a metropolis* (1990), pp 193–201.

Manchester, Keith, and Charlotte Roberts, *The archaeology of disease*. Stroud, Gloucestershire, 1997.

Manning, Conleth, 'Excavation at Kilteel Church, Co. Kildare', *JCKAHS*, 16:3 (1981–2), 173–229.

Manning, Conleth, 'Excavations at Glendalough', *JCKAHS*, 16:4, (1983–4), 342–7.

Manning, Conleth, 'Dublin Castle: the building of a royal castle in Ireland', *Chateau Gaillard*, 18 (1990), 119–22.

Manning, Conleth, 'Kilteel revisited', *JCKAHS*, 18:3 (1996–7), 296–300.

Manning, Conleth (ed.), *Dublin and beyond the Pale: studies in honour of Patrick Healy*. Bray, 1998.

Manning, Conleth, 'Some early masonry churches and the round tower at Clonmacnoise' in Heather King (ed.), *Clonmacnoise Studies, vol. 2: seminar papers, 1998* (Dublin, 2003), 63–95.

Manning, Conleth, 'An illustration of Confey Castle, Co. Kildare', *JRSAI*, 131 (2001), 143–5.

Manning, Conleth, 'A puzzle in stone: the cathedral at Glendalough', *AI*, 16:2 (summer 2002), 18–21.

Manning, Conleth, 'The Record Tower, Dublin Castle' in Kenyon and O'Conor (eds), *The medieval castle in Ireland and Wales* (2003), pp 72–95.

Manning, Conleth (ed.), *From ringforts to fortified houses: studies on castles and other monuments in honour of David Sweetman*. Dublin, 2007.

Martin, Edward, '"Wheare most inclosures be": the making of the East Anglian landscape' in Gardiner and Rippon (eds), *Medieval landscapes* (2007), pp 122–38.

Martin, F.X., 'Diarmait Mac Murchada and the coming of the Anglo-Normans' in Cosgrove (ed.), *A new history of Ireland: II* (1993), pp 43–66.

Martin, Geoffrey, 'Plantation boroughs in medieval Ireland, with a handlist of boroughs to *c.*1500' in Harkness and O'Dowd (eds), *The town in Ireland* (1981), pp 23–53.

Mason, W.M., *The history and antiquities of the collegiate and cathedral church of St Patrick, near Dublin …* Dublin, 1819.

Masschaele, Jim, *Peasants, merchants and markets: inland trade in medieval England, 1150–1350.* New York, 1997.

Massey, Eithne, *Prior Roger Outlaw of Kilmainham.* Dublin, 2000.

Masterson, Rory, 'The alien priory of Fore, Co. Westmeath, in the Middle Ages', *Archiv. Hib.*, 53 (1999), 73–9.

Masterson, Rory, 'The Church and the Anglo-Norman colonisation of Ireland: a case study of the priory of Fore', *RnM*, 11 (2000), 58–70.

Masterson, Rory, 'The early Anglo-Norman colonisation of Fore, Co. Westmeath', *RnM*, 13 (2002), 44–60.

Mayhew, Nicholas, 'Modelling medieval monetisation' in R.H. Britnell and B.M.S. Campbell (eds), *A commercialising economy: England, 1086 to c.1300* (Manchester, 1995), pp 55–77.

Mayo, earl of, 'Kilteel Castle', *JCKAHS*, 1:1 (1891), 34–7.

McAllister, K.W., 'A geographical and historical survey of medieval churches and ecclesiastical buildings in the county of Fingal'. BA dissertation, UCD, 2004.

McCabe, Susan, 'Woodside' in *Excavations 2002*, pp 191–3.

McCarthy, Ciara, 'Final excavation report: Skreen, Co. Meath (licence 05E0321)'. Unpublished report, 2006.

McClatchie, Meriel, 'The archaeobotanical material [from Dundrum Castle]'. Unpublished report. DEHLG file E000419 [n.d.].

McConway, Cia, 'St Mary's, Brookvale Rd., Donnybrook' in *Excavations 1995*, p. 13.

McConway, Cia, 'Digges Lane, Dublin'. Unpublished report. DEHLG file 96E0006 [n.d.].

McCormick, Finbar, 'The domesticated cat in Early Christian and medieval Ireland' in Mac Niocaill and Wallace (eds), *Keimelia* (1988), pp 218–28.

McCormick, Finbar, 'The effect of the Anglo-Norman settlement on Ireland's wild and domesticated fauna' in P.J. Crabtree and Kathleen Ryan (eds), *Animal use and cultural change.* MASCA Research Papers in Science and Archaeology supplement to vol. 8 (1991), pp 40–52.

McCormick, Finbar, 'Farming and food in medieval Lecale' in Lindsay Proudfoot (ed.), *Down: history and society* (Dublin, 1997), pp 33–46.

McCormick, Finbar, 'The animal bones' in Hurley and Scully with McCutcheon (eds), *Late Viking-Age and medieval Waterford* (1997), pp 819–53.

McCormick, Finbar, 'Early evidence for wild animals in Ireland' in Norbert Benecke (ed.), *The Holocene history of the European vertebrate fauna: modern aspects of research (workshop, 6th to 9th April 1998, Berlin)* (Rahden, 1999), pp 355–70.

McCormick, Finbar, 'The mammal bone' in Hayden, 'Arran Quay' (2004), pp 221–31.

McCormick, Finbar, 'The mammal bones from the excavations at rear 9–12 High Street, Dublin'. Unpublished report. DEHLG file E000548 [n.d.].

McCormick, Finbar, and Eileen Murphy, 'Mammal bones' in Walsh, *Archaeological excavations at Patrick, Nicholas and Winetavern Streets* (1997), pp 199–218.

McCormick, Finbar, and Emily Murray, *Knowth and the zooarchaeology of Early Christian Ireland*. Dublin, 2007.

McCormick, Finbar, and Emily Murray, 'The animal bones from Trim Castle'. Unpublished report.

McCorry, Maureen, 'Petrological report on the roof tiles' in Walsh, *Archaeological excavations at Patrick, Nicholas and Winetavern Streets* (1997), pp 153–4.

McCorry, Maureen, *The medieval pottery kiln at Downpatrick, Co. Down: an investigation of its working life, its products and their distribution*. BAR British Series, 326. Oxford, 2001.

McCourt, Desmond, 'The dynamic quality of Irish rural settlement' in R.H. Buchanan, Emrys Jones and Desmond McCourt (eds), *Man and his habitat: essays presented to Emyr Estyn Evans* (London, 1971), pp 126–64.

McCracken, Eileen, *The Irish woods since Tudor times: distribution and exploitation*. Newton Abbot, Devon, 1971.

McCullough, David, 'Archaeological monitoring of excavations in the River Liffey at Leixlip, Co. Dublin. Leixlip/Ballycoolen water supply, 07E0265'. Unpublished report for the Archaeological Diving Company Ltd, 2008.

McCutcheon, Clare, 'Medieval pottery in Dublin: new names and some dates' in Duffy (ed.), *Medieval Dublin I* (2000), pp 117–25.

McCutcheon, Clare, 'The pottery from excavations in Nangor townland, Clondalkin, Dublin 22' in Doyle (ed.), 'Final report on archaeological excavations at Nangor townland', pp 96–101.

McCutcheon, Clare, *Medieval pottery from Wood Quay, Dublin: the 1974–6 waterfront excavations*. Dublin, 2006.

McCutcheon, Clare, 'The medieval pottery from the N2 Finglas-Ashbourne bypass at Site 25, Cookstown, Co. Meath (03E1252)'. Unpublished report, 2007.

McCutcheon, Clare, 'Excavation 03E1328 – medieval pottery report: Muckerstown/Wotton'. Unpublished report for CRDS Ltd, 2008.

McCutcheon, Clare, 'The medieval pottery from Merrywell 1, Co. Meath (A017/029)'. Unpublished report on behalf of Archaeological Consultancy Services Ltd.

McCutcheon, Clare, 'The pottery from Dundrum Castle, Co. Dublin (licence number E419)'. Unpublished report.

McCutcheon, Clare, 'Thomas Street'. Unpublished report. DEHLG file 96E0280 [n.d.].

McCutcheon, Clare, and Catherine Johnson, 'Medieval/post-medieval pottery [from Thomas Street]'. Unpublished report. DEHLG file 96E0280 [n.d.].

McCutcheon, Clare, and Rosanne Meenan, 'Pottery in medieval Trim' in Potterton and Seaver (eds), *Uncovering medieval Trim* (2009), pp 333–45.

McCutcheon, S.W.J, 'The stone artefacts' in Hurley and Scully with McCutcheon (eds), *Late Viking-Age and medieval Waterford* (1997), pp 404–32.

McEnery, M.J., 'Address on the state of agriculture and the standard of living in Ireland in the years 1240–1350', *JRSAI*, 50 (1920), 1–18.

McEnery, M.J., and Raymond Refaussé (eds), *Christ Church deeds*. Dublin, 2001.

McErlean, Thomas, and Aidan O'Sullivan, 'Foreshore tidal fish traps' in McErlean, McConkey and Forsythe, *Strangford Lough* (2003), pp 144–85.

McErlean, Thomas, Rosemary McConkey and Wes Forsythe, *Strangford Lough: an archaeological survey of the maritime cultural landscape.* Belfast, 2003.

McGowan, Laurence, 'Cherrywood' in *Excavations 2004*, pp 103–4.

McGrail, Seán (ed.), *Woodworking techniques before AD1500: papers presented to a symposium at Greenwich in September 1980, together with edited discussion.* BAR International Series, 129. Oxford, 1982.

McGrail, Seán, *Medieval boat and ship timbers from Dublin.* Dublin, 1993.

McGrail, Seán, 'Ships' timbers from Wood Quay, Dublin, and other medieval sites in Ireland', *Bullán* 1 (1994), 49–61, repr. in Seán McGrail (ed.), *Studies in maritime archaeology.* BAR British Series, 256 (1997), pp 257–62.

McLean, Tom, *Medieval English gardens.* London, 1981; 2nd ed. 1994.

McLoughlin, E.P., *Report on the anatomical investigation of the skeletal remains unearthed at Castleknock in the excavation of an Early Christian cemetery in the summer of 1938.* Dublin, 1950.

McMahon, Mary, 'Archaeological excavations at the site of the Four Courts extension, Inns Quay, Dublin', *PRIA*, 88C9 (1988), 271–319.

McMahon, Mary, 'Archaeological excavations at Bridge Street Lower, Dublin', *PRIA*, 91C3 (1991), 3–71.

McMahon, Mary, *Medieval church sites of north Dublin: a heritage trail.* Dublin, 1991.

McMahon, Mary, 'Artane Church, Kilmore Road, Dublin' in Manning (ed.), *Dublin and beyond the Pale* (1998), pp 155–62.

McMahon, Mary, 'Early medieval settlement and burial outside the enclosed town: evidence from archaeological excavations at Bride Street, Dublin', *PRIA*, 102C4 (2002), 67–135.

McMahon, Mary, *St Audoen's Church, Cornmarket, Dublin: archaeology and architecture.* Dublin, 2006.

McManus, Ciara, 'Gorteen, Co. Limerick' in *Excavations 1999*, p. 166.

McNeill, Charles, 'The secular jurisdiction of the early archbishops of Dublin', *JRSAI*, 45 (1915), 81–108.

McNeill, Charles, 'The Hospitallers at Kilmainham and their guests', *JRSAI*, 54 (1924), 15–30.

McNeill, Charles (ed.), *Registrum de Kilmainham: register of chapter acts of the hospital of St John of Jerusalem in Ireland, 1326–1339.* Dublin, 1932.

McNeill, Charles, 'Notes on Dublin Castle', *JRSAI*, 70 (1940), 194–9.

McNeill, Charles (ed.), *Calendar of Archbishop Alen's register, c.1172–1534.* Dublin, 1950.

McNeill, Charles, 'Hospital of St John without the New Gate, Dublin', *JRSAI*, 55 (1925), 58–64; repr. in Clarke (ed.), *Medieval Dublin: the living city* (1990), pp 77–82.

McNeill, T.E., *Anglo-Norman Ulster: the history and archaeology of an Irish barony, 1177–1400.* Edinburgh, 1980.

McNeill, T.E., 'Early castles in Leinster', *JIA*, 5 (1989–90), 57–64.

McNeill, T.E., 'The origins of tower houses', *AI*, 6:1 (spring 1992), 13–14.

McNeill, T.E., *Castles in Ireland: feudal power in a Gaelic world.* London, 1997.

McNeill, T.E., 'The archaeology of Gaelic lordship east and west of the Foyle' in Duffy, Edwards and FitzPatrick (eds), *Gaelic Ireland* (2001), pp 346–56.

McNeill, T.E., 'Where should we place the boundary between the medieval and the post-medieval periods in Ireland?' in Audrey Horning, Ruairí Ó Baoill, Colm Donnelly and Paul Logue (eds), *The post-medieval archaeology of Ireland, 1550–1850* (Bray, 2007), pp 7–13.

McQuade, Melanie, 'A consideration of the significance of pathological animal bone from Irish archaeological sites'. MA, UCC, 1998.

McQuade, Melanie, 'Analysis of faunal remains' in Simpson, 'Dublin's southern frontier under siege: Kindlestown Castle' (2003), pp 357–61.

McQuade, Melanie, '46–47 Castle Street, Dalkey' in *Excavations 2003*, pp 114–15.

McQuade, Melanie, 'Schoolhouse Lane, Swords Road, Santry' in *Excavations 2003*, p. 180.

McQuade, Melanie, '105–109 The Coombe, Dublin' in *Excavations 2004*, pp 117–18.

McQuade, Melanie, 'Gone fishin'', *AI*, 22.1 (spring 2008), 8–11.

McQuade, Melanie, 'Archaeological excavations on the site of Meakstown Castle, Finglas, Co. Dublin' in Duffy (ed.), *Medieval Dublin IX* (2009), pp 91–130.

McQuade, Melanie, 'Faunal report [Ship Street Great]'. Unpublished report. DEHLG file 01E0772 [n.d.].

McQuade, Melanie, 'Faunal report [Naas]'. Unpublished report. DEHLG file 02E0955 [n.d.].

Meenan, Rosanne, '27–30 Merchant's Quay, Dublin' in *Excavations 1989*, p. 25.

Meenan, Rosanne, '20–23 Merchant's Quay, Dublin' in *Excavations 1990*, p. 31.

Meenan, Rosanne, 'A survey of late medieval and early post-medieval Iberian pottery from Ireland' in David Gaimster and Mark Redknap (eds), *Everyday and exotic pottery from Europe* (Exeter, 1992), pp 186–93.

Meenan, Rosanne, 'Archaeological excavations at 16–17 Cook Street, Dublin' in Duffy (ed.), *Medieval Dublin III* (2002), pp 128–39.

Meenan, Rosanne, 'Stephen Street Lower'. Unpublished report. DEHLG file 92E0086 [n.d.].

Mellor, Maureen, 'Making and using pottery in town and country' in Giles and Dyer (eds), *Town and country in the Middle Ages* (2005), pp 149–64.

Metcalf, D.M. (ed.), *Coinage in medieval Scotland (1100–1600): the second Oxford symposium on coinage and monetary history.* BAR British Series, 45. Oxford, 1977.

Migne, J.-P. (ed.), *Patrologiae latinae cursus completus.* 221 vols, Paris, 1844–64.

Miles, D.W.H., *The tree-ring dating of the roof carpentry of the eastern chapels, north nave triforium, and north porch, Salisbury Cathedral, Wiltshire.* Centre for Archaeology Report, 94. Eastney, Portsmouth, 2002.

Milis, Ludo, *L'ordre des chanoines réguliers d'Arrouaise: son histoire et son organisation, de la fondation de l'abbaye-mère (vers 1090) a la fin des chapitres annuels (1471).* 2 vols, Bruges, 1969.

Miller, Edward (ed.), *The agrarian history of England and Wales, vol. 3.* Cambridge, 1991.

Miller, Edward, and John Hatcher, *Medieval England: rural society and economic change, 1086–1348.* London and New York, 1978.

Mills, James, 'Notices of the manor of St Sepulchre, Dublin, in the fourteenth century', *JRSAI*, 19 (1889), 31–41, 119–26.

Mills, James, 'Tenants and agriculture near Dublin in the fifteenth century', *JRSAI*, 21 (1891), 54–63.

Mills, James, 'The Norman settlement in Leinster: the cantreds near Dublin', *JRSAI*, 24 (1894), 161–75.

Mills, James, 'Sixteenth-century notices of the chapels and crypts of the Church of the Holy Trinity, Dublin', *JRSAI*, 30 (1900), 195–203.

Mills, James, 'Peter Lewys: his work and workmen', *JRSAI*, 31 (1901), 99–108.

Mills, James (ed.), *Calendar of justiciary rolls, 1295–1303.* Dublin, 1905.

Mills, James (ed.), *Calendar of justiciary rolls, 1305–7.* Dublin, 1914.

Mills, James, and M.J. McEnery (eds), *Calendar of the Gormanston register.* Dublin, 1916.

Milne, Kenneth (ed.), *Christ Church Cathedral, Dublin: a history.* Dublin, 2000.

Mitchell, G.F., *Archaeology and environment in early Dublin.* Dublin, 1987.

Molloy, Bernice, 'Charlesland' in *Excavations 2004*, pp 480–1.

Molloy, Bernice, 'The excavation of a medieval enclosure at Charlesland, Co. Wicklow' in Corlett and Potterton (eds), *Rural settlement in medieval Ireland* (2009), pp 149–56.

Monck-Mason, William, *The history and antiquities of the collegiate and cathedral church of St Patrick's, Dublin.* Dublin, 1820.

Monk, M.A. 'Post-Roman drying kilns and the problem of function: a preliminary statement' in Donnchadh Ó Corráin (ed.), *Irish antiquity: essays and studies presented to Professor M.J. O'Kelly* (Cork, 1981), pp 216–30.

Monk, M.A., 'Evidence from macroscopic plant remains for crop husbandry in prehistoric and early historic Ireland: a review', *JIA*, 3 (1985/6), 31–6.

Monk, M.A., 'Appendix II: charred seed and plant remains' in Hurley, 'Kilferagh' (1987), pp 98–9.

Monk, M.A., 'The archaeobotanical evidence for field crop plants in early historic Ireland' in J.M. Renfrew (ed.), *New light on early farming: recent developments in palaeo-ethnobotany* (Edinburgh, 1991), pp 315–28.

Monk, M.A., and Ellen Kelleher, 'An assessment of the archaeological evidence for Irish corn-drying kilns in the light of the results of archaeological experiments and archaeobotanical studies', *JIA*, 14 (2005), 77–114.

Monk, M.A., and John Sheehan (eds), *Early medieval Munster: archaeology, history and society*. Cork, 1998.

Moody, T.W., F.X. Martin and F.J. Byrne (eds), *A new history of Ireland, III: early modern Ireland, 1534–1691*. Oxford, 3rd ed., 1989.

Moody, T.W., F.X. Martin and F.J. Byrne (eds), *A new history of Ireland, IX: maps, genealogies, lists: a companion to Irish history, ii*. Oxford, 1984.

Moore, Caitríona, 'Fleenstown Little' in *Excavations 2004*, p. 311.

Moore, M.J. (comp.), *Archaeological inventory of County Meath*. Dublin, 1987.

Moorhouse, Stephen, 'The medieval pottery industry and its markets' in Crossley (ed.), *Medieval industries* (1981), pp 96–125.

Moorhouse, Stephen, 'The quarrying of building stone and stone artefacts in medieval Yorkshire: a multi-disciplinary approach', *Ruralia*, 6 (2007), 295–319.

Morant, R.W., *The monastic gatehouse*. Lewes, 1995.

Morgan, Hiram, 'Brabazon, Sir William' in Connolly (ed.), *The Oxford companion to Irish history* (1998), p. 56.

Morley, Neville, *Metropolis and hinterland: the city of Rome and the Italian economy, c.200BC–AD200*. Cambridge, 1996.

Moss, Rachel, 'Tales from the crypt: the medieval stonework of Christ Church Cathedral, Dublin' in Duffy (ed.), *Medieval Dublin III* (2002), pp 95–114.

Moss, Rachel, 'Permanent expressions of piety: the secular and the sacred in later medieval stone sculpture' in Moss, Ó Clabaigh and Ryan (eds), *Art and devotion* (2006), pp 72–97.

Moss, Rachel, Colmán Ó Clabaigh and Salvador Ryan (eds), *Art and devotion in late medieval Ireland*. Dublin, 2006.

Mount, Charles, and V.J. Keeley, 'An early medieval strap-tag from Balally, County Dublin', *JRSAI*, 120 (1990), 120–5.

Moylan, T.K., 'Vagabonds and sturdy beggars: poverty, pigs and pestilence in medieval Dublin' in Clarke (ed.), *Medieval Dublin: the living city* (1990), pp 192–9.

Mullally, Evelyn (ed.), *The deeds of the Normans in Ireland,* La geste des engleis en Yrlande*: a new edition of the chronicle formerly known as* The song of Dermot and the earl. Dublin, 2002.

Municipal corporations (Ireland), appendix to the first report of the commissioners (part I: southern, midland, western and south-eastern circuits, and part of the north-eastern circuit), HC 1835, vol. 27, pp 199–644; vol. 28, pp 1–356.

Munro, J.H.A., *Wool, cloth and gold; the struggle for bullion in Anglo-Burgundian trade, 1340–1478*. Toronto, 1972.

Murphy, Deirdre, '56–7 Dame St./28 Eustace St./1A Temple Lane, Dublin' in *Excavations 1995*, p. 18.

Murphy, Deirdre, 'Cloncurry' in *Excavations 1995*, p. 45.

Murphy, Donald, '1–7 St Agnes Road, Crumlin'. Unpublished report. DEHLG file 99E0305 [n.d.].

Murphy, Margaret, 'The high cost of dying: an analysis of *pro anima* bequests in medieval Dublin' in W.J. Sheils and Diana Wood (eds), *The church and wealth: Studies in Church History*, 25 (Oxford, 1987), pp 111–22.

Murphy, Margaret, 'The fuel supply of medieval London, 1300–1400', *Franco-British Studies*, 20 (1995), 85–96.

Murphy, Margaret, 'Feeding medieval cities: some historical approaches' in Carlin and Rosenthal (eds), *Food and eating in medieval Europe* (1998), pp 117–32.

Murphy, Margaret, 'Archbishops and Anglicisation: Dublin, 1181–1271' in Kelly and Keogh (eds), *History of the Catholic diocese of Dublin* (2000), pp 72–91.

Murphy, Margaret, 'Digging with documents: late medieval historical research on the M3 in County Meath' in O'Sullivan and Stanley (eds), *Roads, rediscovery and research* (2008), pp 117–26.

Murphy, Margaret, 'Historical report on Goat's Castle, Dalkey, Co. Dublin'. Unpublished report prepared for Dalkey Castle and Heritage Centre, 2008.

Murphy, Margaret, 'Rural settlement in Meath, 1170–1660: the documentary evidence' in M.B. Deevy and Donald Murphy (eds), *Places along the way: first findings on the M3* (Bray, 2009), pp 153–68.

Murphy, Margaret, 'The "key of the county": Saggart and the manorial economy of the Dublin March, *c.*1200–1540' in Clare Downham, Jenifer Ní Gradaigh and Emmett O'Byrne (eds), *The march in the medieval west* (forthcoming).

Murphy, Margaret, and Kieran O'Conor, 'Castles and deerparks in Anglo-Norman Ireland', *Eolas: the Journal of the American Society of Irish Medieval Studies*, 1 (2006) [2008], 53–70.

Murphy, Margaret, and Michael Potterton, 'Investigating living standards in medieval Dublin and its region' in Duffy (ed.), *Medieval Dublin VI* (2005), pp 224–56.

Murphy, Margaret, and Michael Potterton, 'Mapping a medieval landscape? The Civil Survey and land-use in County Dublin' in Bradley, Fletcher and Simms (eds), *Dublin in the medieval world* (2009), pp 316–44.

Murphy, Noel, and Karina Holton, 'An aerial perspective on Oughterany', *Oughterany*, 2:1 (1999), 97–106.

Murray, Hilary, 'Documentary evidence for domestic buildings in Ireland, *c.*400–1200, in the light of archaeology', *Med. Arch.*, 23 (1979), 81–97.

Murray, Hilary, *Viking and early medieval buildings in Dublin*. BAR British Series, 119. Oxford, 1983.

Murray, Emily, 'Reports on the faunal and molluscan material from excavations at Dundrum Castle, Co. Dublin'. Unpublished report. DEHLG file E000419 [n.d.].

Murray, Emily, 'Animal bone report [Maynooth Castle]'. Unpublished report. DEHLG file 96E0391 [n.d.].

Murtagh, Harman (ed.), *Irish midland studies: essays in commemoration of N.W. English*. Athlone, 1980.

Murtagh, Ben, 'The fortified town houses of the English Pale in the later Middle Ages', MA, UCD, 1982.

Murtagh, Ben, 'The castles of Naas', *JCKAHS*, 16:4 (1983–4), 355–61.

Murtagh, Ben, 'St David's Castle: a fortified town house, Naas, Co. Kildare', *JCKAHS*, 16:5 (1985–6), 468–78.

Murtagh, Ben, 'The Kilkenny Castle archaeological project, 1990–1993: interim report', *Old Kilkenny Review*, 45 (1993), 101–17.

Myles, Franc, 'Iveagh Market, Francis Street, Dublin' in *Excavations 1999*, pp 67–8.

Myles, Franc, 'Ballymount Great' in *Excavations 2001*, p. 81.

Myles, Franc, 'Ballymount Great' in *Excavations 2002*, pp 124–5.

Myles, Franc, 'Ardee Street, Dublin' in *Excavations 2003*, pp 119–21.

Myles, Franc, 'Smithfield, Dublin' in *Excavations 2003*, pp 154–5.

Myles, Franc, '24–26 Ardee Street, Dublin' in *Excavations 2004*, pp 111–12.

Myles, Franc, 'Archaeological excavations at the millpond of St Thomas's Abbey, Dublin' in Duffy (ed.), *Medieval Dublin IX* (2009), pp 183–212.

Myles, Franc, 'Tram Street/Phoenix Street, Dublin'. Unpublished report. DEHLG file 01E0229 [n.d.].

Myrdal, Janken, *Medeltidens Åkerbruk. Agrarteknik i Sverige ca 1000 till 1520*. Stockholm, 1986.

Mytum, Harold, *The origins of Early Christian Ireland*. London and New York, 1992.

Nayling, Nigel, *The Magor Pill medieval wreck*. CBA Research Report, 115. York, 1998.

Nelis, Dermot, '27–31 Church St., Dublin' in *Excavations 2003*, pp 125–6.

Nelson, E.C., '"This garden to adorne with all varieties": the garden plants of Ireland in the centuries before 1700', *Moorea*, 9 (1990), 37–54.

Nelson, E.C., '"Reserved to the fellows": four centuries of gardens at Trinity College Dublin' in H.C. Holland (ed.), *Trinity College Dublin and the idea of a university* (Dublin, 1991), pp 185–222.

Nelson, E.C., and Wendy Walsh, *Trees of Ireland, native and naturalised*. Dublin, 1993.

Nenk, B.S., Cathy Haith and John Bradley, 'Medieval Britain and Ireland in 1996', *Med. Arch.*, 41 (1997), 241–328.

Newman Johnson, David, 'Tymon: a lost Pale castle restored' in Mac Niocaill and Wallace (eds), *Keimelia* (1988), pp 557–72.

Newton, D.P., 'Found coins as indicators of coins in circulation', *European Journal of Archaeology*, 9:2/3 (Aug./Dec. 2006 [2008]), 211–28.

Ní Ghabhláin, Sinéad, 'Church and community in medieval Ireland: the diocese of Kilfenora', *JRSAI*, 125 (1995), 61–84.

Ní Ghabhláin, Sinéad, 'Late twelfth-century church construction: evidence of parish formation?' in FitzPatrick and Gillespie (eds), *The parish in medieval and early modern Ireland* (2006), pp 147–67.

Ní Mharcaigh, Máirín, 'The medieval parish churches of south-west Dublin', *PRIA*, 97C5 (1997), 245–96.

Ní Mhurchadha, Maighréad, *Fingal, 1603–60: contending neighbours in north Dublin*. Dublin, 2005.

Nicholls, K.W., 'Anglo-French Ireland and after', *Peritia*, 1 (1982), 370–403.

Nicholls, K.W., 'The Land of the Leinstermen', *Peritia*, 3 (1984), 535–58.

Nicholls, K.W., 'Three topographical notes', *Peritia*, 5 (1986), 409–15.

Nicholls, K.W., 'Gaelic society and economy' in Cosgrove (ed.), *A new history of Ireland: II* (1993), pp 412–13.

Nicholls, K.W., *Gaelic and Gaelicized Ireland in the Middle Ages*. Dublin, 2003.

Nicholls, K.W., 'Woodland cover in pre-modern Ireland' in Duffy, Edwards and FitzPatrick (eds), *Gaelic Ireland* (2001), pp 181–206.

Nolan, Patrick, *A monetary history of Ireland*. 2 vols, London, 1926–8.

Nolan, William, 'Kildare from the documents of conquest: the monastic extents and the Civil Survey, 1654–1656' in Nolan and McGrath (eds), *Kildare: history and society* (Dublin, 2006), pp 233–71.

Nolan, William, and Thomas McGrath (eds), *Kildare: history and society – interdisciplinary essays on the history of an Irish county*. Dublin, 2006.

O'Brien, Elizabeth, 'Churches of south-east County Dublin, seventh to twelfth century' in Mac Niocaill and Wallace (eds), *Keimelia* (1988), pp 504–24.

O'Brien, Elizabeth, 'Excavations at Dundrum Castle, Dundrum, Co. Dublin', *AI*, 3:4 (winter 1989), 136–7.

O'Brien, Elizabeth, 'A tale of two cemeteries', *AI*, 9:3 (autumn 1995), 13–15.

O'Brien, Elizabeth, 'A reconsideration of the location and context of Viking burials at Kilmainham/ Islandbridge, Dublin' in Manning (ed.), *Dublin and beyond the Pale* (1998), pp 35–44.

O'Brien, Elizabeth, 'The location and context of Viking burials at Kilmainham and Islandbridge, Dublin' in Clarke, Ní Mhaonaigh and Ó Floinn (eds), *Ireland and Scandinavia in the early Viking Age* (1998), pp 203–21.

O'Brien, Elizabeth, 'Ballyman'. Unpublished report. DEHLG file E000182 [n.d.].

O'Brien, Elizabeth, 'Excavations at Dundrum Castle, Co. Dublin, E000419 (1987–1991)'. Unpublished report. DEHLG file E000419 [n.d.].

O'Brien, Elizabeth, 'Old Bawn Road, Tallaght'. Unpublished report. DEHLG file E000555 [n.d.].

O'Brien, William, *Mount Gabriel: Bronze-Age mining in Ireland*. Galway, 1994.

O'Byrne, Emmett, 'A much disputed land: Carrickmines and the Dublin Marches' in Duffy (ed.), *Medieval Dublin IV* (2003), pp 229–52.

O'Byrne, Emmett, 'The Walshes and the massacre at Carrickmines', *AI*, 17:3 (autumn 2003), 8–11.

O'Byrne, Emmett, *War, politics and the Irish of Leinster, 1156–1606*. Dublin, 2003.

O'Byrne, Emmett, 'Conflict and change: the Irish of Kildare, 1000–1269' in Nolan and McGrath (eds), *Kildare: history and society* (2006), pp 129–52.

O'Byrne, Emmett, 'One world: the communities of the southern Dublin marches', *History Ireland*, 13:3 (2005), 17–21.

Ó Carragáin, Tomás, 'Habitual masonry styles and the local organisation of church building in early medieval Ireland', *PRIA*, 105C3 (2005), 99–149.

Ó Carragáin, Tomás, 'Church buildings and pastoral care in early medieval Ireland' in FitzPatrick and Gillespie (eds), *The parish in medieval and early modern Ireland* (2006), pp 91–123.

Ó Carragáin, Tomás, 'Skeuomorphs and spolia: the presence of the past in Irish pre-Romanesque architecture' in Rachel Moss (ed.), *Making and meaning: studies in Insular art* (Dublin, 2007), 95–109.

Ó Carragáin, Tomás, 'Rebuilding the "city of angels": Muirchertach Ua Briain and Glendalough, *c.*1096–1111' in Sheehan and Ó Corráin (eds), *The Viking Age: Ireland and the West* (2010), pp 258–70.

O'Carroll, Ellen, 'Wood identification report' in Claire Walsh, 'Archaeological excavation of a development site to the south-east of St Maelruan's, Tallaght, Co. Dublin (96E0188)'. Unpublished report lodged with National Museum of Ireland, 1997.

O'Carroll, Ellen, 'Ballyogan Recycling Park, Jamestown' in *Excavations 2001*, pp 123–4.

O'Carroll, Ellen, 'Wood identification from Strand Street Great, Dublin' in Walsh, 'Archaeological excavation of the Anglo-Norman waterfront' (2005), pp 185–7.

O'Carroll, Ellen, 'An analysis of the wood remains from Merrywell 1, A017–029, Co. Meath'. Unpublished report on behalf of Archaeological Consultancy Services Ltd, 2006.

O'Carroll, Ellen, 'Appendix 3: Wood analysis of samples from Dundrum Castle' in Elizabeth O'Brien, 'Final report on excavations at Dundrum Castle, Co. Dublin (E419), 1987–1991'. Unpublished report lodged with National Museum of Ireland [n.d.].

O'Carroll, Finola, 'Haggardstown, Co. Louth' in *Excavations 1999*, pp 183–6.

O'Carroll, Finola, 'Ballyvoneen' in *Excavations 2001*, pp 175–6.

O'Carroll, Finola, 'Killegland, Ashbourne' in *Excavations 2003*, p. 359.

O'Carroll, Finola, 'Bremore, Co. Dublin: the field by the castle' in Baker (ed.), *Axes, warriors and windmills* (2009), pp 75–87.

O'Carroll, Finola, 'A medieval and post-medieval farm landscape at Bremore, Co. Dublin' in Corlett and Potterton (eds), *Rural settlement in medieval Ireland* (2009), pp 157–70.

O'Carroll, Finola, 'Church Road, Swords'. Unpublished report. DEHLG file 98E0082 [n.d.].

O'Carroll, Finola, 'Carnalway, Naas'. Unpublished report. DEHLG file 00E0303 [n.d.].

Ó Clabaigh, Colmán, *The Franciscans in Ireland, 1400–1534*. Dublin, 2002.

Ó Clabaigh, Colmán, 'The Benedictines in medieval and early modern Ireland' in Browne and Ó Clabaigh (eds), *The Irish Benedictines* (2005), pp 79–121.

Ó Conbhuí, Colmcille, 'The lands of St Mary's Abbey, Dublin', *PRIA*, 62C3 (1962), 21–84.

O'Connell, Aidan, 'The many lives of Castlefarm', *Seanda*, 1 (2006), 19–21.

O'Connell, Aidan, 'Excavations at Church Road and the early monastic foundation at Lusk, Co. Dublin' in Baker (ed.), *Axes, warriors and windmills* (2009), pp 51–63.

O'Connell, Aidan, and Allister Clarke, 'Report on the archaeological excavation of Castlefarm 1, Co. Meath'. Unpublished report, 2008.

O'Connell, Aidan, and Vicky Ginn, 'Report on the archaeological excavation of Merrywell 1, Co. Meath'. Unpublished report, 2009.

O'Connell, Michael, 'Early land-use in north-east Co. Mayo: the palaeoecological evidence', *PRIA*, 90C9 (1990), 259–79.

O'Connor, David, 'Kilmessan, Co. Meath: stratigraphic report and post-excavation assessment (04E1352)'. Unpublished report, 2005.

O'Connor, John, 'Ballyogan Road, Jamestown' in *Excavations 2002*, p. 162.

O'Connor, Patrick, 'Hurdle-making in Dublin, 1302–3', *DHR*, 13:1 (1952), 18–21.

O'Connor, T.P., 'What shall we have for dinner? Food remains from urban sites' in Serjeantson and Waldron (eds), *Diet and crafts in towns* (1989), pp 13–23.

O'Conor, K.D., 'The later construction and use of motte and bailey castles in Ireland: new evidence from Leinster', *JCKAHS*, 17 (1987–1991), 13–29.

O'Conor, K.D., 'Irish earthwork castles', *Fortress*, 12 (1992), 1–12.

O'Conor, K.D., 'The earthwork castles of medieval Leinster'. PhD, University of Wales, College of Cardiff, 1993.

O'Conor, K.D., 'The origins of Carlow Castle', *AI*, 11:3 (autumn 1997), 13–16.

O'Conor, K.D., *The archaeology of medieval rural settlement in Ireland*. Discovery Programme Monographs, 3. Dublin, 1998.

O'Conor, K.D., 'Anglo-Norman castles in Co. Laois' in P.G. Lane and William Nolan (eds), *Laois: history and society – interdisciplinary essays on the history of an Irish county* (Dublin, 1999), pp 183–212.

O'Conor, K.D., 'The ethnicity of Irish moated sites', *Ruralia*, 3 (2000), 92–102.

O'Conor, K.D., 'Housing in later medieval Gaelic Ireland', *Ruralia*, 4 (2002), 201–10.

O'Conor, K.D., 'Motte castles in Ireland: permanent fortresses, residences and manorial centres', *Château Gaillard: études de castellologie medievale*, 20 (2002), 173–82.

O'Conor, K.D., 'Medieval rural settlement in Munster' in Ludlow and Jameson (eds), *Medieval Ireland* (2004), pp 225–56.

O'Conor, K.D., 'Gaelic lordly settlement in the 13th and 14th century in Ireland' in Ingunn Holm, Sonja Innselset and Ingvild Øye (eds), *'Utmark': the outfield as industry and ideology in the Iron Age and the Middle Ages* (Bergen, 2005), pp 209–21.

O'Conor, K.D., 'Castle studies in Ireland: the way forward', *Château Gaillard: études de castellologie medievale*, 23 (2008), 329–39.

Ó Cróinín, Dáibhí, *Early medieval Ireland, 400–1200*. London and New York, 1995.

Ó Cróinín, Dáibhí (ed.), *A new history of Ireland, I: prehistoric and early Ireland*. Oxford, 2005.

O'Dea, Laurence, 'The hospitals of Kilmainham', *DHR*, 20:3/4 (1965), 82–99.

O'Donnell, M.G., 'Cupidstown, Co. Kildare: the Pale earthwork' in Cleary, Hurley and Twohig (eds), *Archaeological excavations on the Cork–Dublin gas pipeline* (1987), pp 106–10.

O'Donovan, Edmond, 'The growth and decline of a medieval suburb? Evidence from excavations at Thomas Street, Dublin' in Duffy (ed.), *Medieval Dublin IV* (2003), pp 127–71.

O'Donovan, Edmond, 'Ashbourne town centre' in *Excavations 2002*, pp 399–400.

O'Donovan, Edmond, 'Archaeological excavations, Mount Gamble, Townparks, Swords, Co. Dublin, 02E0608'. Unpublished report, Margaret Gowen and Co. Ltd, 2005.

O'Donovan, Edmond, 'Mount Gamble, Townparks, Swords' in *Excavations 2003*, pp 181–2.

O'Donovan, Edmond, 'Preliminary report: archaeological excavations on the Wicklow Port Access Town Relief Road'. Unpublished report, Margaret Gowen and Co. Ltd, 2007.

O'Donovan, Edmond, '119–21 Thomas Street, Dublin'. Unpublished report. DEHLG file 95E0280 [n.d.].

O'Donovan, Edmond, 'Ashbourne'. Unpublished report. DEHLG file 02E0708 [n.d.].

O'Donovan, Edmond, 'Burke's Pharmacy, 3 Main Street, Naas'. Unpublished report. DEHLG file 02E0955 [n.d.].

O'Driscoll, James, *Cnucha: a history of Castleknock and district*. [n.p.], 1977.

O'Dwyer, B.W. (trans.), *Stephen of Lexington: letters from Ireland, 1228–1229*. Kalamazoo, MI, 1982.

O'Flanagan, Neil, 'Fyffes Yard, Beresford Lane, Dublin' in *Excavations 1994*, p. 21.

O'Flanagan, Michael (comp.), 'Letters containing information relative to the antiquities of the county of Wicklow collected during the progress of the Ordnance Survey in 1838'. Typescript, Bray, 1928.

Ó Floinn, Raghnall, 'Handmade pottery in S.E. Ireland: Leinster Cooking Ware' in Mac Niocaill and Wallace (eds), *Keimelia* (1988), pp 325–64.

Ó Floinn, Raghnall, 'The archaeology of the early Viking Age in Ireland' in Clarke, Ní Mhaonaigh and Ó Floinn (eds), *Ireland and Scandinavia in the early Viking Age* (1998), pp 131–65.

Ó Floinn, Raghnall, 'Two Viking burials from Wicklow', *Wicklow Archaeology and History*, 1 (1998), 29–35.

Ó Floinn, Raghnall, 'Later medieval Ireland, AD1150–1550' in Wallace and Ó Floinn (eds), *Treasures of the National Museum of Ireland* (2002), pp 257–300.

Ó Floinn, Raghnall, 'The foundation relics of Christ Church Cathedral and the origin of the diocese of Dublin' in Duffy (ed.), *Medieval Dublin VII* (2006), pp 89–102.

Ó Floinn, Raghnall, 'The late medieval relics of Holy Trinity Church, Dublin' in Bradley, Fletcher and Simms (eds), *Dublin in the medieval world* (2009), pp 369–89.

Ó hÉailidhe, P[adraig], 'The Rathdown Slabs', *JRSAI*, 87 (1957), 75–88.

Ó hÉailidhe, P[adraig], 'Some unpublished antiquities of the Early Christian period in the Dublin area', *JRSAI*, 89 (1959), 205–7.

Ó hÉailidhe, P[adraig], 'Early Christian grave-slabs in the Dublin region', *JRSAI*, 103 (1973), 51–64.

Ó hÉailidhe, P[adraig], and Ellen Prendergast, 'Two unrecorded graveslabs in Co. Dublin', *JRSAI*, 107 (1977), 139–42.

O'Hara, Robert, 'Drumcondrath' in *Excavations 2003*, p. 369.

O'Hara, Robert, 'Testing Area 1, Castlefarm' in *Excavations 2004*, p. 296.

Ó hInnse, Séamus (ed.), *Miscellaneous Irish annals (AD1114–1437)*. Dublin, 1947.

O'Keeffe, Grace, 'The hospital of St John the Baptist in medieval Dublin' in Duffy (ed.), *Medieval Dublin IX* (2009), pp 166–82.

O'Keeffe, Peter, and Tom Simington, *Irish stone bridges: history and heritage*. Dublin, 1991.

O'Keeffe, Tadhg, 'The church and castle of Confey, Co. Kildare', *JCKAHS*, 16:5 (1985–6), 408–17.

O'Keeffe, Tadhg, 'Medieval architecture and the village of Newcastle Lyons' in O'Sullivan (ed.), *Newcastle Lyons* (1986), pp 45–61.

O'Keeffe, Tadhg, 'Medieval frontiers and fortification: the Pale and its evolution' in Aalen and Whelan (eds), *Dublin city and county* (1992), pp 57–78.

O'Keeffe, Tadhg, 'Tower-houses of the Pale in east County Kildare', *Oughterany*, 1:2 (1995), 4–11.

O'Keeffe, Tadhg, 'Rural settlement and cultural identity in Gaelic Ireland, 1000–1500', *Ruralia*, 1 (1996), 142–53.

O'Keeffe, Tadhg, 'Ethnicity and moated settlement in medieval Ireland: a review of current thinking', *MSRG Annual Report*, 15 (2000), 21–5.

O'Keeffe, Tadhg, *Medieval Ireland: an archaeology*. Stroud, Gloucestershire, 2000.

O'Keeffe, Tadhg, 'Kiltalown House, Tallaght' in *Excavations 1999*, pp 94–5.

O'Keeffe, Tadhg, 'Concepts of castle and the construction of identity in medieval and post-medieval Ireland', *IG*, 34:1 (2001), 69–88.

O'Keeffe, Tadhg, *Romanesque Ireland: architecture and ideology in the twelfth century*. Dublin, 2003.

O'Keeffe, Tadhg, *The Gaelic peoples and their archaeological identities, AD1000–1650*. Quiggin pamphlets on the sources of mediaeval and Gaelic history, 7. Cambridge, 2004.

O'Keeffe, Tadhg, 'Were there designed landscapes in medieval Ireland?', *Landscapes*, 5:2 (2004), 52–68.

O'Keeffe, Tadhg, 'Afterword' in Lyttleton and O'Keeffe, *The manor in medieval and early modern Ireland* (2005), 188–97.

O'Keeffe, Tadhg, 'The built environment of local community worship between the late eleventh and early thirteenth centuries' in FitzPatrick and Gillespie (eds), *The parish in medieval and early modern Ireland* (2006), pp 124–46.

O'Keeffe, Tadhg, 'Dublin Castle's donjon in context' in Bradley, Fletcher and Simms (eds), *Dublin in the medieval world* (2009), pp 277–94.

O'Leary, Des, 'Hortland', *Oughterany*, 2:1 (1999), 56–69.

O'Loan, J.J., 'The manor of Cloncurry, Co. Kildare, and the feudal system of land tenure in Ireland', *Department of Agriculture Journal*, 58 (1961), 14–36.

O'Loan, J.J., 'A history of early Irish farming', *Department of Agriculture Journal*, 60 (1963), 178–219.

O'Lochlainn, Colm, 'Roadways in ancient Ireland' in Ryan (ed.), *Feilsgribhinn Eoin Mhic Neill* (1940), pp 465–74.

Ó Muirthuile, Seósamh, 'Meascra de thaighdighthe maidir le dinnsheanchas Choill Chluana Gabhann agus na dúthaighe ina timcheall (Clongoweswood)', *JCKAHS*, 12:7 (1944–5), 375–95.

Ó Néill, John, 'A Norse settlement in rural County Dublin', *AI*, 13:4 (winter 1999), 8–10.

Ó Néill, John, 'Cherrywood Science and Technology Park, Cherrywood' in *Excavations 1999*, pp 54–6.

Ó Néill, John, 'Bow Street/Church Street, Dublin' in *Excavations 2000*, pp 81–2.

Ó Néill, John, 'Longford Street Little' in *Excavations 2000*, pp 89–90.

Ó Néill, John, 'Ballyogan Road, Jamestown' in *Excavations 2002*, p. 162.

Ó Néill, John, 'Excavation of pre-Norman structures on the site of an enclosed Early Christian cemetery at Cherrywood, County Dublin' in Duffy (ed.), *Medieval Dublin VII* (2006), pp 66–88.

Ó Néill, John, 'Science and Technology Park, Cherrywood'. Unpublished report. DEHLG file 98E0526 [n.d.].

Ó Néill, John, 'Cherrywood Science and Technology Park, Cherrywood'. Unpublished report. DEHLG file 99E0517 [n.d.].

Ó Néill, John, 'Cherrywood Science and Technology Park, Cherrywood'. Unpublished report. DEHLG file 99E0518 [n.d.].

Ó Néill, John, 'Cherrywood'. Unpublished report. DEHLG file 99E0519 [n.d.].

Ó Néill, John, 'Cherrywood Science and Technology Park, Cherrywood'. Unpublished report. DEHLG file 99E0523 [n.d.].

Ó Néill, John, and Jennie Coughlan, 'An enclosed early medieval cemetery at Cherrywood, Co. Dublin' in Corlett and Potterton (eds), *Death and burial in early medieval Ireland* (2010), pp 239–50.

O'Neill, Michael, 'The medieval parish churches in County Meath', *JRSAI*, 132 (2002), 1–56.

O'Neill, Michael, 'St Patrick's Cathedral, Dublin, and its prebendal churches: Gothic architectural relationships' in Duffy (ed.), *Medieval Dublin V* (2004), pp 243–76.

O'Neill, Michael, 'The medieval parish churches of County Kildare', *JCKAHS*, 19:3 (2004–5), 406–46.

O'Neill, Michael, 'The medieval parish churches of County Kildare' in Nolan and McGrath (eds), *Kildare: history and society* (2006), pp 153–93.

O'Neill, Michael, 'The architectural history of the medieval cathedral' in Crawford and Gillespie (eds), *St Patrick's Cathedral, Dublin* (2009), pp 96–119.

O'Neill, Timothy, *Merchants and mariners in medieval Ireland*. Dublin, 1987.

O'Rahilly, Celie, 'A classification of bronze stick-pins from the Dublin excavations, 1962–72' in Manning (ed.), *Dublin and beyond the Pale* (1998), pp 23–34.

O'Reilly, Eileen, 'Insect remains [from Thomas Street]'. Unpublished report. DEHLG file 96E0280 [n.d.].

Ó Ríordáin, Brendán, 'Excavations at High Street and Winetavern Street, Dublin', *Med. Arch.*, 15 (1971), 73–85.

Ó Ríordáin, Brendán, 'The High Street Excavations' in Almqvist and Greene (eds), *Proceedings of the seventh Viking Congress* (1973), pp 135–40; repr. in Clarke (ed.), *Medieval Dublin: the making of a metropolis* (1990), pp 165–72.

Ó Ríordáin, Brendán, *Dublin city: Christchurch Place*. Dublin, 1975.

Ó Ríordáin, Brendán, 'St David's Church, Naas: a new dimension', *JCKAHS*, 17 (1987–1991), 151–60.

Ó Ríordáin, Brendán, 'Naas, St David's Church'. Unpublished report. DEHLG file E000544 [n.d.].

Ó Ríordáin, S.P., 'Excavations at Cush, Co. Limerick', *PRIA*, 45C (1940), 83–181.

O'Rourke, Dáire, 'Leather finds' in Walsh, *Archaeological excavations at Patrick, Nicholas and Winetavern Streets* (1997), pp 163–78.

O'Rourke, Dáire, 'The leather finds' in Halpin, *The port of medieval Dublin* (2000), pp 143–58.

O'Rourke, Dáire, 'Leather' in Hayden, 'Arran Quay' (2004), pp 211–17.

O'Rourke, Dáire, 'The leather finds from High St., Dublin'. Forthcoming.

O'Rourke, Dáire, 'The leather finds from the Dublin Castle excavations'. Forthcoming.

O'Sullivan, Aidan, 'The craft of the carpenter in medieval Ireland: some hints from book illuminations', *IAPA Newsletter*, 19 (1994), 18–22.

O'Sullivan, Aidan, 'Trees, woodland and woodmanship in early medieval Ireland', *BJS*, 46:4 (1994), 674–81.

O'Sullivan, Aidan, 'Woodmanship and the supply of underwood and timber to Anglo-Norman Dublin' in Manning (ed.), *Dublin and beyond the Pale* (1998), pp 59–70.

O'Sullivan, Aidan, 'Medieval boat and ship timbers' in Halpin, *The port of medieval Dublin* (2000), pp 118–36.

O'Sullivan, Aidan, 'The wooden waterfronts: a study of their construction, carpentry and use of trees and woodlands' in Halpin, *The port of medieval Dublin* (2000), pp 62–92.

O'Sullivan, Aidan, and Graeme Warren, 'Templeteenaun, Ballinagee' in *Excavations 2004*, pp 474–5.

O'Sullivan, Aidan, and Lorcan Harney, 'Early Medieval Archaeology Project: investigating the character of early medieval archaeological excavations, 1970–2002'. Unpublished report for the Heritage Council, 2008 rev. ed.

O'Sullivan, Aidan, and Mary Deevy, 'Wooden artefacts' in Halpin, *The port of medieval Dublin* (2000), pp 162–7.

O'Sullivan, Aidan, and Mary Deevy, 'Trees, woodland and woodmanship in Anglo-Norman Dublin: the Back Lane evidence'. Forthcoming.

O'Sullivan, Benedict, 'The Dominicans of medieval Dublin' in Clarke (ed.), *Medieval Dublin: the living city* (1990), pp 83–99.

O'Sullivan, Jerry (ed.), *Archaeology and the National Roads Authority monograph series no. 1.* Bray, 2003.

O'Sullivan, Jerry, and Michael Stanley (eds), *Recent archaeological discoveries on National Road Schemes, 2004: archaeology and the National Roads Authority monograph series no. 2.* Bray, 2005.

O'Sullivan, Jerry, and Michael Stanley (eds), *Settlement, industry and ritual: archaeology and the National Roads Authority monograph series no. 3.* Bray, 2006.

O'Sullivan, Jerry, and Michael Stanley (eds), *New routes to the past: archaeology and the National Roads Authority monograph series no. 4.* Bray, 2007.

O'Sullivan, Jerry, and Michael Stanley (eds), *Roads, rediscovery and research: archaeology and the National Roads Authority monograph series no. 5.* Bray, 2008.

O'Sullivan, M.D., 'Some Italian merchant bankers in Ireland in the later thirteenth century', *JRSAI*, 79 (1949), 10–19.

O'Sullivan, M.D., *Italian merchant bankers in Ireland in the thirteenth century: a study in the social and economic history of medieval Ireland.* Dublin, 1962.

O'Sullivan, Muiris, and Liam Downey, 'Lime kilns', *AI*, 19:2 (summer 2005), 18–22.

O'Sullivan, Muiris, and Liam Downey, 'Corn-drying kilns', *AI*, 19:3 (autumn 2005), 32–5.

O'Sullivan, Muiris, and Liam Downey, 'Ridges and furrows', *AI*, 21:2 (summer 2007), 34–7.

O'Sullivan, Muiris, and Liam Downey, 'Fieldscapes: Anglo-Norman footprints', *AI*, 21:4 (winter 2007), 32–5.

O'Sullivan, Muiris, and Liam Downey, 'Tower houses and associated farming systems', *AI*, 23:2 (summer 2009), 34–7.

O'Sullivan, Peter (ed.), *Newcastle Lyons: a parish of the Pale.* Dublin, 1986.

O'Sullivan, William, 'The earliest Irish coinage', *JRSAI*, 79 (1949), 190–235.

O'Sullivan, William, *The earliest Anglo-Irish coinage.* Dublin [1964].

O'Sullivan, William, *The earliest Irish coinage.* Dublin, 1969.

O'Sullivan, T., 'The exploitation of birds in Viking Dublin: an avi-faunal analysis of a sample from Fishamble Street'. MA, NUIG, 1995.

Oftedal, Magne, 'Scandinavian place-names in Ireland' in Almqvist and Greene (eds), *Proceedings of the seventh Viking Congress* (1976), pp 125–33.

Opie, Hilary, 'Cloncurry' in *Excavations 2001*, pp 181–2.

Orpen, G.H. (ed.), *The song of Dermot and the earl.* Oxford, 1892.

Orpen, G.H., 'Mote and bretesche building in Ireland', *EHR*, 21 (1906), 417–44.

Orpen, G.H., 'Motes and Norman castles in Ireland', *EHR*, 22 (1907), 228–54, 440–67.

Orpen, G.H., 'Motes and Norman castles in Ireland', *JRSAI*, 37 (1907), 123–52.

Orpen, G.H., '*Castrum Keyvini*: Castlekevin', *JRSAI*, 38 (1908), 17–27.

Orpen, G.H., '*Novum Castrum McKynegan*, Newcastle, County Wicklow', *JRSAI*, 38 (1908), 126–40.

Orpen, G.H., *Ireland under the Normans, 1169–1333.* Oxford, 1911–20; repr. Oxford, 1968; Dublin, 2005.

Oschinsky, Dorothea, *Walter of Henley and other treatises on estate management and accounting.* Oxford, 1971.

Otway-Ruthven, A.J., 'The organisation of Anglo-Irish agriculture in the Middle Ages', *JRSAI*, 81 (1951), 1–13.

Otway-Ruthven, A.J., 'The medieval county of Kildare', *IHS*, 11:43 (1958–9), 181–99.

Otway-Ruthven, A.J., 'Knight service in Ireland', *JRSAI*, 89 (1959), 1–15.

Otway-Ruthven, A.J., 'Knight's fees in Kildare, Leix and Offaly', *JRSAI*, 91:2 (1961), 163–81.

Otway-Ruthven, A.J., 'The medieval church lands of County Dublin' in Watt, Morrall and Martin (eds), *Medieval studies presented to Aubrey Gwynn, S.J.* (1961), pp 54–73.

Otway-Ruthven, A.J., 'Parochial development in the rural deanery of Skreen', *JRSAI*, 94 (1965), 111–22.

Otway-Ruthven, A.J., 'The character of Norman settlement in Ireland', *Historical Studies*, 5 (1965), 75–84.

Otway-Ruthven, A.J., 'The chief governors of medieval Ireland', *JRSAI*, 95 (1965), 227–36.

Owen, T.M., 'Historical aspects of peat-cutting in Wales' in Jenkins (ed.), *Studies in folk life* (1969), pp 124–55.

Palliser, D.M. (ed.), *The Cambridge urban history of Britain: volume 1, 600–1540*. Cambridge, 2000.

Papazian, Cliona, 'The medieval pottery from the Dublin Castle excavations'. MA, UCC, 1989.

Papazian, Cliona, 'Medieval and later pottery from Site G' in Walsh, *Archaeological excavations at Patrick, Nicholas and Winetavern Streets* (1997), pp 124–8.

Papazian, Cliona, 'The medieval pottery' in Halpin, *The port of medieval Dublin* (2000), pp 103–17.

Papazian, Cliona, 'The medieval pottery from Back Lane, Dublin'. Forthcoming.

Papazian, Cliona, 'The medieval pottery from Christchurch Place, Dublin'. Forthcoming.

Papazian, Cliona, 'The medieval pottery from Cornmarket and Bridge Street Upper, Dublin'. Forthcoming.

Papazian, Cliona, 'The medieval pottery from High Street, Dublin'. Forthcoming.

Parain, Charles, 'The evolution of agricultural technique' in M.M. Postan (ed.), *The Cambridge economic history of Europe, vol. 1: the agrarian life of the Middle Ages* (Cambridge, 1966), pp 125–79.

Parsons, David, 'Stone' in Blair and Ramsay (ed.), *English medieval industries* (1991), pp 1–28.

Parsons, H.A., 'Remarks on a Trim groat marked B on the obverse', *Numismatic Chronicle*, 6th ser., 5 (1945), 142–7.

Pelham, R.A., *Fulling mills: a study in the application of water power to the woollen industry*. London, 1958.

Penn, S.A.C., 'Female wage-earners in late fourteenth-century England', *AHS*, 35 (1987), 1–14.

Perring, Dominic, *Town and country in England: frameworks for archaeological research*. CBA Research Report, 134. York, 2002.

Petrie, George [A notice on some Roman coins lately found near Rathfarnham]. *PRIA*, 6 (1858), 441–5.

Phelan, Sinéad, 'Baldonnell Lower' in *Excavations 2003*, p. 106.

Phelan, Sinéad, 'Charlesland' in *Excavations 2004*, p. 480.

Phelan, Sinéad, 'Portmarnock' in *Excavations 2004*, p. 151.

Pilcher, J.R., and S.S. Mac an tSaoir (eds), *Wood, trees and forests in Ireland*. Dublin, 1995.

Platt, Colin, *The monastic grange in medieval England*. London, 1969.

Pollock, A.J., and D.M. Waterman, 'A medieval pottery kiln at Downpatrick', *UJA*, 25 (1963), 79–104.

Postles, David, 'Cleaning the medieval arable', *AHS*, 37:2 (1989), 130–43.

Potterton, Michael, *Medieval Trim: history and archaeology*. Dublin, 2005.

Potterton, Michael, and Matthew Seaver (eds), *Uncovering Medieval Trim: archaeological excavations in and around Trim, Co. Meath*. Dublin, 2009.

Power, Catryn, 'Human remains' in Walsh, *Archaeological excavations at Patrick, Nicholas and Winetavern Streets* (1997), pp 222–7.

Preston, Sarah, 'The canons regular of St Augustine: the twelfth-century reform in action' in Stuart Kinsella (ed.), *Augustinians at Christ Church: the canons regular of the Cathedral priory of the Holy Trinity* (Dublin, 2000), pp 23–40.

Prestwich, Michael, 'Victualling estimates for English garrisons in Scotland during the early fourteenth century', *EHR*, 82 (1967), 536–43.

Price, Liam, 'The Byrnes' country in County Wicklow in the sixteenth century', *JRSAI*, 63 (1933), 224–42.

Price, Liam, 'The Byrnes' country in County Wicklow in the sixteenth century: and the manor of Arklow', *JRSAI*, 66 (1936), 41–66.

Price, Liam (ed.), *An eighteenth-century antiquary: the sketches, notes and diaries of Austin Cooper (1759–1830)*. Dublin, 1942.

Price, Liam, *The place-names of Co. Wicklow: barony of Ballinacor North*. Dublin, 1945.

Price, Liam, 'Powerscourt and the territory of Fercullen', *JRSAI*, 83 (1953), 117–32.

Price, Liam, 'The grant to Walter de Ridelesford of Brien and the land of the sons of Turchil', *JRSAI*, 84 (1954), 72–7.

Price, Liam, *The place-names of Co. Wicklow: barony of Rathdown*. Dublin, 1957.

Price, Liam, 'Rock-basins or "bullauns" at Glendalough and elsewhere', *JRSAI*, 89 (1959), 161–88.

Price, Liam, *Placenames, VII: the baronies of Newcastle and Arklow*, Dublin, 1967.

Prior, Stuart, *A few well-positioned castles: the Norman art of war*. Stroud, Gloucestershire, 2006.

Pryor, Francis, 'A descriptive catalogue of some ancient Irish metalwork in the collections of the Royal Ontario Museum, Toronto', *JRSAI*, 106 (1976), 73–91.

Purcell, Avril, 'Parkwest, Gallanstown'. Unpublished report. DEHLG file 00E0267 [n.d.].

Purcell, Emer, 'Land-use in medieval Oxmantown' in Duffy (ed.), *Medieval Dublin IV* (2003), pp 193–228.

Purcell, Emer, 'The city and the suburb: medieval Dublin and Oxmantown' in Duffy (ed.), *Medieval Dublin VI* (2005), pp 188–223.

Quinn, D.B., 'Aristocratic autonomy, 1460–94' in Cosgrove (ed.), *A new history of Ireland: II* (1993), pp 591–618.

Rackham, Oliver, *Ancient woodland: its history, vegetation and uses in England*. London, 1980.

Rackham, Oliver, 'The growing and transport of timber and underwood' in McGrail (ed.), *Woodworking techniques before AD1500* (1982), pp 199–218.

Rackham, Oliver, 'Looking for ancient woodland in Ireland' in Pilcher and Mac an tSaoir (eds), *Wood, trees and forests in Ireland* (1995), pp 1–12.

Rackham, Oliver, *The history of the countryside*. London, 1986.

Rackham, Oliver, *The illustrated history of the countryside*. London, 1994.

Rae, E.C., 'The medieval fabric of the cathedral church of St Patrick in Dublin', *JRSAI*, 109 (1979), 29–73.

Raftis, J.A., *Assart data and land values*. Toronto, 1974.

Rahtz, P.A., 'Medieval milling' in Crossley (ed.), *Medieval industry* (1981), pp 1–15.

Rathbone, Stuart, 'Seeing the light at Garretstown, Co. Meath', *Seanda*, 2 (2007), 55–6.

Rathbone, Stuart, 'Trevet 1: draft interim excavation report'. Unpublished report, 2007.

Reeves-Smyth, Terence, *Irish gardens and gardening before Cromwell*. Cork, 1999; repr. in Ludlow and Jameson (eds), *Medieval Ireland* (2004), pp 97–144.

Reeves-Smyth, Terence, and Fred Hamond (eds), *Landscape archaeology in Ireland*. Oxford, 1983.

Refaussé, Raymond, and Mary Clark, *A catalogue of the maps of the estates of the archbishops of Dublin, 1654–1850*. Dublin, 2000.

Reid, Martin, 'Ballyogan and Stepaside' in *Excavations 1997*, p. 24.

Reid, Martin, 'Ballyogan, Jamestown' in *Excavations 1998*, p. 61.

Reid, Martin, 'Meeting House Square, 10–14 Sycamore Street/31–32 Essex Street, Dublin'. Unpublished report. DEHLG file 93E0194 [n.d.].

Reilly, Eileen, 'The contribution of insect remains to an understanding of the environment of Viking-Age and medieval Dublin' in Duffy (ed.), *Medieval Dublin IV* (2003), pp 40–62.

Reilly, Fiona, 'Site 55, Carmanhall'. Unpublished report. DEHLG file 02E0074 [n.d.].

Report on the manuscripts of Lord De L'Isle and Dudley preserved at Penshurst Place. London, 1925.

Rice, Gerard, *Norman Kilcloon, 1171–1700*. Kilcloon, Co. Meath, 2001.

Richardson, H.G., and G.O. Sayles, *The administration of Ireland, 1172–1377*. Dublin, 1963.

Rigby, S.H., *Medieval Grimsby: growth and decline*. Hull, 1993.

Rippon, Stephen, 'Emerging regional variation in historic landscape character: the possible significance of the "long eighth century"' in Gardiner and Rippon (eds), *Medieval landscapes* (2007), pp 105–21.

Robinson, A.T., 'The history of Dublin Castle to 1684'. PhD, UCD, 1994.

Roe, H.M., 'The presidential address, 26 January 1966: some aspects of medieval culture in Ireland', *JRSAI*, 96 (1966), 105–9.

Roe, H.M., 'Illustrations of the Holy Trinity in Ireland, 13th to 17th centuries', *JRSAI*, 109 (1979), 144–5.

Ronan, M.V., *S. Anne, her cult and her shrines*. London, 1927.

Ronan, M.V., 'Union of the dioceses of Glendaloch and Dublin in 1216', *JRSAI*, 60 (1930), 56–72.

Ronan, M.V., 'Killadreenan and Newcastle', *JRSAI*, 63 (1933), 172–81.

Ronan, M.V., 'Mulhuddard and Cloghran-Hiddert', *JRSAI*, 70 (1940), 182–93.

Ronan, M.V., 'St Patrick's Staff and Christ Church', *DHR*, 5 (1943), 121–9; repr. in Clarke (ed.), *Medieval Dublin: the living city* (1990), pp 123–31.

Ronnes, Hanneke, *Architecture and elite culture in the United Provinces, England and Ireland, 1500–1700*. Amsterdam, 2006.

Rooney, Fiona, 'Newtown' in *Excavations 2001*, p. 136.

Russell, J.C., *British medieval population*. Albuquerque, NM, 1948.

Russell, J.C., 'Late thirteenth-century Ireland as a region', *Demography*, 3 (1966), 500–12.

Russell, J.C., *Medieval regions and their cities*. Newton Abbot, Devon, 1972.

Rutty, John, *An essay towards a natural history of the county of Dublin*. Dublin, 1772.

Ryan, Finbar, and Ambrose Coleman, *St Dominic and the Dominicans in Ireland, 1216–1916*. Dublin [n.d.].

Ryan, Frank, 'Darcytown' in *Excavations 2004*, pp 106–7.

Ryan, John (ed.), *Feilsgribhinn Eoin Mhic Neill*. Dublin, 1940.

Ryan, Michael, 'Furrows and browse: some archaeological thoughts on agriculture and population' in Smyth (ed.), *Seanchas* (2000), pp 30–6.

Ryder, M.L., 'British medieval sheep and their wool types' in Crossley (ed.), *Medieval industry* (1981), pp 16–27.

Rymer, Thomas (ed.), *Foedera, conventiones, litterae et cujuscunque generis acta publica inter reges Angliae et alios quosuis imperatores, reges, pontifices, principes, vel communitates (1101–1654)*. 20 vols, London, 1704–35.

Rynne, Colin, 'The introduction of the vertical watermill into Ireland: some recent archaeological evidence', *Med. Arch.*, 33 (1989), 21–31.

Rynne, Colin, 'The Patrick Street watermills' in Walsh, *Archaeological excavations at Patrick, Nicholas and Winetavern Streets* (1997), pp 81–9.

Rynne, Colin, 'Waterpower in medieval Ireland' in Paolo Squatriti (ed.), *Working with water in medieval Europe: technology and resource-use* (Leiden, Boston and Köln, 2000), pp 1–50.

Rynne, Colin, 'The development of milling technology in Ireland, *c*.600–1875' in Andy Bielenberg (ed.), *Irish flour milling: a history, 600–2000* (Dublin, 2003), pp 13–38.

Rynne, Colin, *Technological change in Anglo-Norman Munster*. Cork, 1998; repr. in Ludlow and Jameson (eds), *Medieval Ireland* (2004), pp 65–95.

Rynne, Colin, *Industrial Ireland, 1750–1930: an archaeology*. Cork, 2006.

Rynne, Colin, 'The origins and technical development of the blast furnace in Ireland, *c*.1596–*c*.1740' in Manning (ed.), *From ringforts to fortified houses* (2007), pp 387–97.

Rynne, Etienne, 'Excavation of a church site at Clondalkin, Co. Dublin', *JRSAI*, 97 (1967), 29–38.

Salter, Mike, *Castles and stronghouses of Ireland*. Worcester, 1993.

Salzman, L.F., *Building in England down to 1540*. Oxford, 1952.

Sayles, G.O., *Documents on the affairs of Ireland before the king's council*. Dublin, 1979.

Scally, Georgina, '1 Essex Gate/10 Exchange St. Upper' in *Excavations 1996*, pp 23–4.

Scally, Georgina, 'The earthen banks and walled defences of Dublin's north-east corner' in Duffy (ed.), *Medieval Dublin III* (2002), pp 11–33.

Scally, Georgina, '33–34 Parliament St./5–7 Exchange St. Upr, Dublin'. Unpublished report. DEHLG file 93E0143 [n.d.].

Scally, Georgina, '44–9 New Row South, Dublin'. Unpublished report. DEHLG file 96E0342 [n.d.].

Scally, Georgina, 'Exchange St.: 8–10'. Unpublished report. DEHLG file 98E0198 [n.d.].

Scally, Georgina, 'Fumbally Lane'. Unpublished report. DEHLG file 00E0253 [n.d.].

Scally, Georgina, 'Little Ship Street'. Unpublished report. DEHLG file 92E0207 [n.d.].

Scannell, M.J.P., 'Handlist of species of wood identified' in Lang, *Viking-Age decorated wood* (1988), p. 100.

Scantlebury, Charles, 'Tallaght, Co. Dublin: its monastery and its castle', *DHR*, 16:2 (1960), 65–71.

Schofield, John, and Alan Vince, *Medieval towns*. Leicester, 1994.

Scott, Brendan, *Religion and reformation in the Tudor diocese of Meath*. Dublin, 2006.

Scott, Brian, *Early Irish ironworking*. Belfast, 1990.

Scott, G.D. *The stones of Bray*. Dublin, 1913; repr. Bray, 1984.

Scott, Lindsay, 'Corn-drying kilns', *Antiquity*, 25 (1951), 196–208.

Scully, Siobhán, 'Medieval parish churches and parochial organisation in Muintir Eolais'. MA, UCG, 1999.

Seaby, B.A., *Catalogue of the coins of Great Britain and Ireland*. London, 1934.

Seaby, Peter, *Coins and tokens of Ireland*. London, 1970.

Seaby, Peter, and P.F. Purvey, *Standard catalogue of British coins, 2: coins of Scotland, Ireland and the Islands*. London, 1984.

Seaby, Wilfred, *Sylloge of coins of the British Isles, 32, Ulster Museum: Belfast, part ii: Hiberno-Norse coins*. London, 1984.

Seaver, Matthew, 'From mountain to sea: excavations in the townlands of Glebe and Laughanstown, County Dublin' in O'Sullivan and Stanley (eds), *Recent archaeological discoveries on National Road Schemes* (2005), pp 51–63.

Seaver, Matthew, 'Practice, spaces and places: an archaeology of boroughs as manorial centres in the barony of Slane' in Lyttleton and O'Keeffe (eds), *The manor in medieval and early modern Ireland* (2005), pp 70–104.

Seaver, Matthew, 'Run of the mill? Excavation of an early medieval site at Raystown, Co. Meath', *AI*, 19:4 (winter 2005), 9–12.

Seaver, Matthew, 'Silent mills', *British Archaeology* (Mar.–Apr. 2006), 40–5.

Seaver, Matthew, 'Through the mill: excavations of a complex early medieval site at Raystown, County Meath' in O'Sullivan and Stanley (eds), *Settlement, industry and ritual* (2006), pp 73–87.

Seaver, Matthew, 'Against the grain: early medieval settlement and burial on the Blackhill – excavations at Raystown, Co. Meath' in Corlett and Potterton (eds), *Death and burial in early medieval Ireland* (2010), pp 261–79.

Seaver, Matthew, 'Laughanstown'. Unpublished report. DEHLG file 00E0283 [n.d.].

Seaver, Matthew, 'Glebe'. Unpublished report. DEHLG file 00E0758 [n.d.].

Serjeantson, Dale, 'Animal remains and the tanning trade' in Serjeantson and Waldron (eds), *Diet and crafts in towns* (1989), pp 129–46.

Serjeantson, Dale, and Tony Waldron (eds), *Diet and crafts in towns: the evidence of animal remains from the Roman to the post-medieval period*. BAR British Series, 199. Oxford, 1989.

Shanahan, Brian, 'The manor in east County Wicklow' in Lyttleton and O'Keeffe (eds), *The manor in medieval and early modern Ireland* (2005), pp 132–59.

Sheehan, John, 'Early Viking-Age silver hoards from Ireland' in Clarke, Ní Mhaonaigh and Ó Floinn (eds), *Ireland and Scandinavia in the early Viking Age* (1998), pp 166–202.

Sheehan, John, and Donnchadh Ó Corráin (eds), *The Viking Age: Ireland and the west: papers from the Proceedings of the fifteenth Viking Congress, Cork, 18–27 August 2005*. Dublin, 2010.

Sheehy, M.P., 'The *Registrum Novum*: a manuscript of Holy Trinity Cathedral', *Reportorium Novum: Dublin Diocesan Historical Record*, 3 (1963–4), 249–81.

Sheppard, A.O., *Ceramics for the archaeologist*. Washington, 1976.

Sherlock, Rory, 'Cross-cultural occurrences of mutations in tower house architecture: evidence for cultural homogenieity in late medieval Ireland?', *JIA*, 15 (2006), 73–91.

Shetelig, Haakon (ed.), *Viking antiquities in Great Britain and Ireland, part III: Norse antiquities in Ireland*. Oslo, 1940.

Shirley, E.P., *Some account of the territory or dominion of Farney*. London, 1845.

Sigaut, François, 'A method for identifying grain storage techniques and its application for European agricultural history', *Tools and Tillage*, 6 (1988), 3–32.

Sikora, Maeve, 'The Finglas burial: archaeology and ethnicity in Viking-Age Dublin' in Sheehan and Ó Corráin (eds), *The Viking Age: Ireland and the West* (2010), pp 402–17.

Simington, R.C., *Civil Survey, 1654–6, county of Dublin*. Dublin, 1945.

Simms, Anngret, 'Rural settlement in medieval Ireland: the example of the royal manors of Newcastle Lyons and Esker in south County Dublin' in B.K. Roberts and R.E. Glasscock (eds), *Villages, fields and frontiers: studies in European rural settlement in the medieval and early modern periods (papers presented at the meeting of the Permanent European Conference for the Study of the Rural Landscape, held at Durham and Cambridge, England, 10–17 September 1981)*. BAR International Series, 185 (1983), pp 133–52.

Simms, Anngret, and John Bradley, 'The geography of Irish manors: the example of the Llanthony cells of Duleek and Colp in Co. Meath' in Bradley (ed.), *Settlement and society in medieval Ireland* (1988), pp 291–326.

Simms, Anngret, and Patricia Fagan, 'Villages in Co. Dublin: their origins and inheritance' in Aalen and Whelan (eds), *Dublin city and county* (1992), pp 79–119.

Simms, Katharine, 'Native sources for Gaelic settlement: the house poems' in Duffy, Edwards and FitzPatrick (eds), *Gaelic Ireland* (2001), pp 246–67.

Simms, Katharine, *Medieval Gaelic sources*. Dublin, 2009.

Simon, James, *An essay towards an historical account of Irish coins, and of the currency of foregin* [sic] *monies in Ireland*. 1st ed. Dublin, 1749; 2nd ed. Dublin, 1810.

Simpson, Linzi, 'Anglo-Norman settlement in Uí Briúin Cualann' in Hannigan and Nolan (eds), *Wicklow: history and society* (1994), pp 191–236.

Simpson, Linzi, 'Arran Quay, Dublin' in *Excavations 1993*, p. 14.

Simpson, Linzi, *Archaeology in Temple Bar: excavations at Isolde's Tower, Dublin*. Temple Bar Archaeological Reports 1. Dublin, 1994.

Simpson, Linzi, *Archaeology in Temple Bar: excavations at Essex Street West, Dublin*. Temple Bar Archaeological Reports 2. Dublin, 1995.

Simpson, Linzi, 'Church of St Secundinus, Dunshaughlin' in *Excavations 1995*, pp 70–1.

Simpson, Linzi, '5–6 Cecilia Street West' in B.S. Nenk, Cathy Haith and John Bradley, 'Medieval Britain and Ireland in 1996', *Med. Arch.*, 41 (1997), 241–328 at 304–5.

Simpson, Linzi, '5–6 Cecilia Street West, Dublin' in *Excavations 1996*, p. 21.

Simpson, Linzi, *Archaeology in Temple Bar: director's findings: Temple Bar West*. Temple Bar Archaeological Reports 5. Dublin, 1997.

Simpson, Linzi, 'Historical background to the Patrick Street excavation' in Walsh, *Archaeological excavations at Patrick, Nicholas and Winetavern Streets* (1997), pp 17–33.

Simpson, Linzi, 'Essex Street West/Lower Exchange Street, Dublin' in *Excavations 1997*, pp 41–2.

Simpson, Linzi, 'Forty years a-digging: a preliminary synthesis of archaeological excavations in medieval Dublin' in Duffy (ed.), *Medieval Dublin I* (2000), pp 11–68.

Simpson, Linzi, 'Historical background' in Halpin, *The port of medieval Dublin* (2000), pp 23–7.

Simpson, Linzi, '46–50, 52–57 South Great George's Street/58–67 Stephen Street Lower, Dublin' in *Excavations 2000*, pp 96–7.

Simpson, Linzi, 'St James's Hospital, James's Street, Dublin' in *Excavations 2000*, pp 88–9.

Simpson, Linzi, 'The priory of All Hallows and Trinity College, Dublin: recent archaeological discoveries' in Duffy (ed.), *Medieval Dublin III* (2002), pp 195–236.

Simpson, Linzi, 'Dublin's southern frontier under siege: Kindlestown Castle, Delgany, County Wicklow' in Duffy (ed.), *Medieval Dublin IV* (2003), pp 279–368.

Simpson, Linzi, 'Ship Street Great, Dublin' in *Excavations 2001*, pp 112–13.

Simpson, Linzi, 'Excavations on the southern side of the medieval town at Ship Street Little, Dublin' in Duffy (ed.), *Medieval Dublin V* (2004), pp 9–51.

Simpson, Linzi, 'Dublin's famous "Bully's Acre": the site of the monastery of Kilmainham?' in Duffy (ed.), *Medieval Dublin IX* (2009), pp 38–83.

Simpson, Linzi, 'The first phase of Viking activity in Ireland: archaeological evidence from Dublin' in Sheehan and Ó Corráin (eds), *The Viking Age: Ireland and the West* (2010), pp 418–29.

Simpson, Linzi, 'Arran Quay/Lincoln Lane/Church St.'. Unpublished report. DEHLG file 93E0074 [n.d.].

Simpson, Linzi, 'Little Ship Street'. Unpublished report. DEHLG file 93E0132 [n.d.].

Simpson, Linzi, 'Church of St Secundinus, Dunshaughlin'. Unpublished report. DEHLG file 94E178 [n.d.].

Simpson, Linzi, 'Essex Street West/Lower Exchange Street, Dublin'. Unpublished report. DEHLG file 96E0245 [n.d.].

Simpson, Linzi, 'Hoey's Court, Werburgh Street, Dublin'. Unpublished report. DEHLG file 99E0228 [n.d.].

Simpson, Linzi, 'Kindlestown Castle, Delgany'. Unpublished report. DEHLG file 01E0844 [n.d.].

Simpson, Linzi, '161–168 Church Street, 3–15 Hammond Lane, Dublin'. Unpublished report. DEHLG file 02E0096 [n.d.].

Simpson, Linzi, 'Molyneaux Hse, Bride St., Dublin'. Unpublished report. DEHLG file 02E0163 [n.d.].

Simpson, M.L., P.S. Bryan, T.T. Delaney and Anthony Dickson, 'An early thirteenth-century double-flued pottery kiln at Carrickfergus, County Antrim', *Medieval Ceram*, 3 (1979), 41–51.

Sire, H.J.A., *The Knights of Malta*. New Haven, CT, 1994.

Sloane, Rachel, 'Analysis of mammalian bone remains from Merrywell 1, Co. Meath'. Unpublished report on behalf of Archaeological Consultancy Services Ltd, 2007.

Slone, J.S., 'Antiquities of Fingal, no. 1: St Doulagh's', *Irish Builder*, 1 Oct. 1879.

Smith, Aquilla, 'On the Irish coins of Edward IV', *TRIA*, 19 (1838–43), 3–49.

Smith, Aquilla, 'On the Irish coins of Henry the Seventh', *TRIA*, 19 (1838–43), 50–83.

Smith, Aquilla (ed.), Annales de Monte Fernandi *(Annals of Multifernan)*. Dublin, 1842; repr. Dublin, 1843.

Smith, Aquilla, 'Catalogue of leaden and pewter tokens issued in Ireland', *JRSAI*, 5 (1858–9), 215–21.

Smith, Aquilla, 'On inedited silver farthings coined in Ireland', *Numismatic Chronicle*, new ser., 3 (1863), 149–61.

Smith, Aquilla, 'Irish silver coins of Henry VIII', *Numismatic Chronicle*, new ser., 19 (1879), 157–84.

Smith, Aquilla, 'Irish silver coins of Richard III', *Numismatic Chronicle*, 3rd ser., 1 (1881), 310–33.

Smith, Brendan (ed.), *The register of Milo Sweteman, archbishop of Armagh, 1361–1380*. Dublin, 1996.

Smith, Brendan (ed.), *Ireland and the English world in the late Middle Ages: essays in honour of Robin Frame*. London, 2009.

Smith, C.V., *Dalkey: society and economy in a small medieval Irish town*. Dublin, 1996.

Smout, T.C., 'Energy rich, energy poor: Scotland, Ireland and Iceland, 1600–1800' in David Dickson and Cormac Ó Grada (eds), *Refiguring Ireland: essays in honour of L.M. Cullen* (Dublin, 2003), pp 19–36.

Smyly, J.G., 'Old (Latin) deeds in the library of Trinity College', *Hermathena*, 66 (1945), 25–39; 67 (1946), 1–30; 69 (1947), 31–48; 70 (1947), 1–21; 71 (1948), 36–51; 72 (1948), 115–20; 74 (1949), 60–7.

Smyth, A.P., *Celtic Leinster: towards an historical geography of early Irish civilisation, AD500–1600*. Dublin, 1982.

Smyth, A.P. (ed.), *Seanchas: studies in early and medieval Irish archaeology, history and literature in honour of Francis J. Byrne*. Dublin, 2000.

Smyth, Jessica (comp. and ed.), with contributions from Conor Brady, Jill Chadwick, Tom Condit, Gabriel Cooney, Ian Doyle, Loreto Guinan, Michael Potterton, Geraldine Stout and Clare Tuffy, *Brú na Bóinne World Heritage Site: research framework*. Kilkenny, 2009.

Smyth, W.J., 'Exploring the social and cultural topographies of sixteenth- and seventeenth-century County Dublin' in Aalen and Whelan (eds), *Dublin city and county* (1992), pp 121–79.

Smyth, W.J., and Kevin Whelan (eds), *Common ground: essays on the historical geography of Ireland*. Cork, 1988.

St John Joyce, Weston, *The neighbourhood of Dublin*. Dublin, 1912; repr. 1988.

Stafford, Emmet, 'Rathcoffey, Co. Kildare' in *Excavations 2003*, p. 254.

Stalley, Roger, *Architecture and sculpture in Ireland, 1150–1350*. Dublin, 1971.

Stalley, Roger, 'Irish Gothic and English fashion' in James Lydon (ed.), *The English in medieval Ireland* (Dublin, 1984), pp 65–86.

Stalley, Roger, *The Cistercian monasteries of Ireland*. London and New Haven, CT, 1987.

Stalley, Roger (ed.), *Daniel Grose (c.1776–1838): the antiquities of Ireland: a supplement to Francis Grose*. Dublin, 1991.

Stalley, Roger, *Irish high crosses*. Dublin, 1996.

Stalley, Roger, 'George Edmund Street and the restoration of the cathedral, 1868–78' in Milne (ed.), *Christ Church Cathedral* (2000), pp 353–73.

Stalley, Roger, 'The 1562 collapse of the nave and its aftermath' in Milne (ed.), *Christ Church Cathedral* (2000), pp 218–36.

Stalley, Roger, 'The architecture of the cathedral and priory buildings, 1250–1530' in Milne (ed.), *Christ Church Cathedral* (2000), pp 95–128.

Stalley, Roger, 'The construction of the medieval cathedral, *c*.1030–1250' in Milne (ed.), *Christ Church Cathedral* (2000), pp 53–74.

Stalley, Roger, 'The archbishop's residence at Swords: castle or country retreat' in Duffy (ed.), *Medieval Dublin VII* (2006), pp 152–76.

Stanley, Michael, Ed Danaher and James Eogan (eds), *Dining and dwelling: proceedings of a public seminar on archaeological discoveries on national road schemes, August 2008: archaeology and the National Roads Authority monograph series no. 6*. Bray, 2009.

State papers, Henry VIII. 11 vols, London, 1830–52.

Stenning, Dave, 'The Cressing barns and the early development of barns in south-east England' in Andrews (ed.), *Cressing Temple* (1993), pp 51–75.

Stephens, Nicholas, and R.E. Glasscock (eds), *Irish geographical studies in honour of E. Estyn Evans*. Belfast, 1970.

Stephenson, M.J., 'Wool yields in the medieval economy', *EcHR*, 41 (1988), 368–91.

Stevens, Paul, 'Bishopsland, Co. Kildare' in *Excavations 2001*, p. 176.

Stevens, Paul, 'Four excavations in Kilkenny city (1999–2001), part 2: the late medieval/post-medieval findings', *Old Kilkenny Review*, 59 (2007), 18–37.

Stevens, Paul, 'N6 Kinnegad to Kilbeggan dual carriageway: archaeological resolution preliminary report, A001/036 E2723, Site: Clonfad 3, Clonfad Townland, Co. Westmeath'. Unpublished report for Valerie J. Keeley Ltd, 2007.

Stevens, Paul, 'Testing Area 11, Blundellstown/Philpotstown' in *Excavations 2004*, pp 292–3.

Stewart, B.H.I.H., [on Brussels Hoard], *BNJ*, 29 (1960), 91.

Stokstad, Marilyn, and Jerry Stannard, *Gardens of the Middle Ages: an exhibition catalogue*. Lawrence, KS, 1983.

Stout, Geraldine, *Newgrange and the Bend of the Boyne*. Cork, 2002.

Stout, Geraldine, and Matthew Stout, *Excavation of an early medieval secular cemetery at Knowth Site M, County Meath*. Bray, 2008.

Stout, Matthew, 'Early medieval boundaries' in Condit and Corlett (eds), *Above and beyond* (2005), pp 139–48.

Stubbs, William (ed.), Gesta regis Henrici Secundi*: the chronicle of the reigns of Henry II and Richard I, AD1169–1192, known commonly under the name of Benedict of Peterborough*. 2 vols, London, 1867.

Stuijts, Ingelise, 'Analysis of charcoal samples from excavations in Nangor townland, Dublin 22' in Doyle (ed.), 'Final report on archaeological excavations at Nangor townland', pp 113–18. Unpublished report.

Swan, D.L., 'Monastic proto-towns in early medieval Ireland: the evidence of aerial photography, plan analysis and survey' in Clarke and Simms (eds), *The comparative history of urban origins in non-Roman Europe* (1985), 1, pp 77–103.

Swan, D.L., '"St Doulagh's", Balgriffin' in *Excavations 1989*, pp 18–19.

Swan, D.L., '"Church of St John the Evangelist", Coolock' in *Excavations 1990*, p. 25.

Swan, D.L., '"St Doulagh's", Balgriffin' in *Excavations 1990*, p. 24.

Swan, D.L., 'Archaeological excavations at Usher's Quay, 1991' in Duffy (ed.), *Medieval Dublin I* (2000), pp 126–58.

Swan, D.L., 'St Doologue's, Balgriffin'. Unpublished report. DEHLG file E000508 [n.d.].

Swan, D.L., and Damien McGarry, 'Wood Quay found at Usher's Quay!', *AI*, 5:2 (summer 1991), 6.

Swan, Leo, 'Enclosed ecclesiastical settlement sites and their relevance to settlement patterns of the first millennium AD' in Reeves-Smyth and Hamond (eds), *Landscape archaeology in Ireland* (1983), pp 269–94.

Swan, Leo, 'Lehaunstown Park, Co. Dublin: a forgotten tower house' in Manning (ed.), *Dublin and beyond the Pale* (1998), pp 163–8.

Swan, Rónán, 'Killhill' in *Excavations 1997*, p. 93.

Swan, Rónán, '3C–4 South Earl Street, Dublin'. Unpublished report. DEHLG file 97E0220 [n.d.].

Swan, Rónán, '59 Castle Street, Dalkey'. Unpublished report. DEHLG file 97E0393 [n.d.].

Swan, Rónán, 'Howth: Corr Castle'. Unpublished report. DEHLG file 98E0349 [n.d.].

Swan, Rónán, 'Killhill'. Unpublished report. DEHLG file 97E0152 [n.d.].

Sweetman, H.S. (ed.), *Calendar of documents relating to Ireland, 1171–1251* [etc.]. 5 vols, London, 1875–86.

Sweetman, P.D., 'Excavation of medieval "field boundaries" at Clonard, County Meath', *JRSAI*, 108 (1978), 10–22.

Sweetman, P.D., 'Archaeological excavations at Ferns Castle, Co. Wexford', *PRIA*, 79C (1979), 217–45.

Sweetman, P.D., 'Some pottery and clay pipe finds from the Royal Hospital, Kilmainham, Dublin', *DHR*, 35 (1981–2), 71–4.

Sweetman, P.D., 'Archaeological excavations at Shop St., Drogheda', *PRIA*, 84C (1984), 171–224.

Sweetman, P.D., 'The development of Trim Castle in the light of recent research', *Château Gaillard: études de castellologie medievale*, 18 (1998), 223–30.

Sweetman, P.D., *Medieval castles of Ireland*. Cork, 1999.

Sweetman, P.D., *The origin and development of the tower house*. Cork, 2000; repr. in Ludlow and Jameson (eds), *Medieval Ireland* (2004), pp 257–88.

Sweetman, P.D., 'The hall-house in Ireland' in Kenyon and O'Conor (eds), *The medieval castle in Ireland and Wales* (2003), pp 121–32.

Sweetman, P.D., 'Some ringwork castles in County Meath' in Condit and Corlett (eds), *Above and beyond* (2005), pp 393–8.

Sweetman, P.D., 'Woodtown' in *Excavations 2003*, p. 395.

Symonds, Henry, 'The Irish silver coinages of Henry IV', *Numismatic Chronicle*, 5th ser., 1 (1921), 108–25.

Tabor, Raymond, *Traditional woodland crafts*. London, 1994.

Tatton-Brown, Tim, and Dan Miles, 'Salisbury Cathedral', *Current Archaeology*, 188 (2003), 364–9.

Taylor, Christopher, *Village and farmstead: a history of rural settlement in England*. London, 1983.

Taylor, Christopher, *The archaeology of gardens*. Risborough, 1988.

Thacker, Alan (ed.), *Victoria County History of Cheshire, vol. 5, pt 1: the city of Chester*. London, 2003.

Thomas, Avril, 'Financing town walls in medieval Ireland' in Colin Thomas (ed.), *Rural landscapes and communities: essays presented to Desmond McCourt* (Dublin, 1986), pp 65–91.

Thomas, Avril, *The walled towns of Ireland*. 2 vols, Dublin, 1992.

Thompson, J.D.A., *Inventory of British coin hoards, AD600–1500*. London, 1956.

Thorold Rogers, J.E., *A history of agriculture and prices in England*. 7 vols, Oxford, 1866–1902.

Thurgood, J.M., 'The diet and domestic households of the English lay nobility, 1265–1531'. MPhil., University of London, 1982.

Tickell, E.F., 'The Eustace family and their lands in County Kildare, Part III', *JCKAHS*, 13:8 (1960), 364–413.

Tierney, Andrew, 'Pedigrees in stone? Castles, colonialism and Gaelic-Irish identity from the Middle Ages to the Celtic Revival'. MPhil., UCD, 2005.

Tierney, John, 'Woods and woodlands in early medieval Munster' in Monk and Sheehan (eds), *Early medieval Munster* (1998), pp 53–8.

Tierney, John, 'An assessment of the plant remains from Tullykane, Kilmessan, Co. Meath'. Unpublished report, 2001.

Tierney, John, 'A report on the archaeobotanical remains recovered from sites at Old Bawn Road and rere of Main Street, Tallaght, Co. Dublin'. Unpublished report. DEHLG file E000555 [n.d.].

Tierney, John, and Martha Hannon, 'Plant remains' in Hurley and Scully with McCutcheon (eds), *Late Viking-Age and medieval Waterford* (1997), pp 854–93.

Tierney, Michael, 'Excavating feudalism? A medieval moated site at Carrowreagh, Co. Wexford' in Corlett and Potterton (eds), *Rural settlement in medieval Ireland* (2009), pp 189–200.

Tierney, Michael, 'Dublin Road, Naas, Co. Kildare'. Unpublished report. DEHLG file 01E0094 [n.d.].

Tighe, William, *Statistical observations relevant to the county of Kilkenny*. Dublin, 1802.

Titow, J.Z., *English rural society, 1200–1350*. London, 1969.

Titow, J.Z., *Winchester yields: a study in medieval agricultural productivity*. Cambridge, 1972.

Tobin, Redmond, 'Jordanstown (BGE 6/12/1)' in *Excavations 2002*, pp 163–5.

Tobin, Redmond, 'Jordanstown' in Eoin Grogan, Lorna O'Donnell and Penny Johnston (eds), *The Bronze Age landscapes of the pipeline to the West* (Dublin, 2007), pp 221–5.

Toman, Rolf (ed.), *The high Middle Ages in Germany, 1000–1300*. Cologne, 1990.

Trow-Smith, Robert, *A history of British livestock husbandry to 1700*. London, 1957.

Tuck, Anthony, 'Anglo-Irish relations, 1382–1393', *PRIA*, 69C2 (1970), 15–31.

Turrell, S.J., 'The archaeozoology of medieval Dublin and Ireland'. MSc., QUB, 2003.

Turrell, S.J., '32 Cook Street, Dublin' in *Excavations 2004*, pp 116–17.

Turrell, S.J., 'White's Villas, Dalkey' in *Excavations 2004*, p. 106.

Twohig, D.C., 'Anglo-Norman ringwork castles', *Bulletin of the Group for the Study of Irish Historic Settlement*, 5 (1978), 7–9.

Ua Broin, Liam, 'Rathcoole, Co. Dublin and its neighbourhood', *JRSAI*, 73 (1943), 79–97.

Ua Broin, Liam, 'Traditions of Drimnagh, Co. Dublin, and its neighbourhood', *JRSAI*, 73 (1943), 106–15.

Ua Broin, Liam, 'Clondalkin, Co. Dublin, and its neighbourhood: notes on place-names, topography and traditions, &c', *JRSAI*, 74 (1944), 191–218.

Ua Broin, Liam, 'The mountain commons of Saggart', *JRSAI*, 87 (1957), 39–52.

Valante, Mary, 'Dublin's economic relations with hinterland and periphery in the later Viking Age' in Duffy (ed.), *Medieval Dublin I* (2000), pp 69–83.

Valante, Mary, *The Vikings in Ireland: settlement, trade and urbanization*. Dublin, 2008.

Van der Woude, A.M., and Anton Schuurman (eds), *Probate inventories: a new source for the historical study of wealth, material culture and agricultural development*. Wageningen, 1980.

Van der Woude, A.M., Akira Hayami and Jan de Vries (eds), *Urbanization in history: a process of dynamic interactions*. Oxford, 1990.

Veach, C.T., 'Henry II's grant of Meath to Hugh de Lacy in 1172: a reassessment', *RnM*, 18 (2007), 67–94.

Veale, E.M., 'The rabbit in England', *AHS*, 5 (1957), 85–90.

Veale, E.M., *The English fur trade in the later Middle Ages*. Oxford, 1966.

Vicars, Arthur, 'The family of Flatesbury of Ballnasculloge and Johnstown, County Kildare', *JCKAHS*, 4 (1903–5), 87–94.

Vince, A.G., 'Early medieval English pottery in Viking Dublin' in Mac Niocaill and Wallace (eds), *Keimelia* (1988), pp 254–70.

Wadding, Luke, *Annales Minorum seu trium ordinum A.S. Francisco institutorum*. 7 vols, Lyon, 1625–54; new ed., 32 vols, Quarrachi, 1931–64.

Wakeman, W.F., 'Ante-Norman churches in the county of Dublin', *JRSAI*, 22 (1892), 101–6.

Wakeman, W.F., *Catalogue: specimens in the collection of the Royal Irish Academy*. 2 vols, Dublin, 1894.

Wakeman, W.F., 'On a recently discovered pagan sepulchral mound in the grounds of Old Connaught, near Bray, County Dublin', *JRSAI*, 24 (1894), 54–64.

Walker, J.C., *An historical essay on the dress of the ancient and modern Irish.* Dublin, 1788.

Walker, J.C., 'Essay on the rise and progress of gardening in Ireland', *TRIA*, 4 (1799), 3–19.

Walker, Simon, 'Janico Dartasso: chivalry, nationality and the man-at-arms', *History*, 84:273 (Jan. 1999), 31–51.

Wallace, Angela, 'Report on archaeological testing of possible Pale boundary at line of distributor road and sewage linkage, residential development, Woodside, Enniskerry Road, Sandyford, Co. Dublin'. Unpublished report, 2003.

Wallace, Angela, 'Woodside' in *Excavations 2003*, pp 186–7.

Wallace, P.F., 'Dublin's Waterfront at Wood Quay, 900–1317' in Gustav Milne and Brian Hobley (eds), *Waterfront archaeology in Britain and northern Europe.* CBA Research Report, 41 (London, 1981), pp 108–18.

Wallace, P.F., 'The origins of Dublin' in B.G. Scott (ed.), *Studies in early Ireland* (Belfast, 1981), pp 129–43.

Wallace, P.F., 'Carpentry in Ireland, AD900–1300: the Wood Quay evidence' in McGrail (ed.), *Woodworking techniques before AD1500* (1982), pp 263–99.

Wallace, P.F., 'North European pottery imported into Dublin, 1200–1500' in Davey and Hodges (eds), *Ceramics and trade* (1983), pp 275–80.

Wallace, P.F., 'A reappraisal of the archaeological significance of Wood Quay' in Bradley (ed.), *Viking Dublin exposed* (1984), pp 112–33.

Wallace, P.F., 'The survival of wood in tenth- to thirteenth-century Dublin' in André Ginier-Gillet, Marie-Dominique Parchas, Regis Ramiere and Quoc Khoi Tran (eds), *Waterlogged wood study and conservation: proceedings of the second ICOM Waterlogged Wood Group Conference* (Grenoble, 1984), pp 81–7.

Wallace, P.F., 'The archaeology of Anglo-Norman Dublin' in Clarke and Simms (eds), *The comparative history of urban origins in non-Roman Europe* (1985), 2, pp 379–410.

Wallace, P.F., 'The archaeology of Viking Dublin' in Clarke and Simms (eds), *The comparative history of urban origins in non-Roman Europe* (1985), 1, pp 103–45.

Wallace, P.F., 'The economy and commerce of Viking Age Dublin' in Düwel, Jankhun, Siems and Timpe (eds), *Untersuchungen zu Handel und Verkehr der vor- und frühgeschichtlichen Zeit in Mittel-und Nordeuropa IV* (1987), pp 200–45.

Wallace, P.F., 'Archaeology and the emergence of Dublin as the principal town of Ireland' in Bradley (ed.), *Settlement and society in medieval Ireland* (1988), pp 123–60.

Wallace, P.F., 'The archaeological identity of the Hiberno-Norse town', *JRSAI*, 122 (1992), 35–66.

Wallace. P.F., *The Viking-Age buildings of Dublin.* 2 vols, Dublin, 1992.

Wallace, P.F., and Raghnall Ó Floinn (eds), *Treasures of the National Museum of Ireland: Irish antiquities.* Dublin, 2002.

Wallace, P.F., 'A woman of importance in ninth-century Finglas', *AI*, 18:3 (autumn 2004), 7.

Wallace, P.F., 'The archaeology of Ireland's Viking-Age towns' in Ó Cróinín (ed.), *A new history of Ireland: I* (2005), pp 814–41.

Wallace, P.F., 'Wood Quay'. Unpublished report. DEHLG file E000132 [n.d.].

Walsh, Claire, *Archaeological excavations at Patrick, Nicholas and Winetavern Streets, Dublin.* Dingle, 1997.

Walsh, Claire, 'Structural timbers' in Walsh, *Archaeological excavations at Patrick, Nicholas and Winetavern Streets* (1997), pp 189–98.

Walsh, Claire, '123–133 Francis Street, 1–4 Swift's Alley, Dublin' in *Excavations 1997*, pp 44–5.

Walsh, Claire, '17–35 Carman's Hall (odd nos. only)/1–7 Ash Street/33–34 Garden Lane, Dublin' in *Excavations 1998*, pp 46–7.

Walsh, Claire, 'Carman's Hall, Dublin' in *Excavations 1999*, pp 60–1.

Walsh, Claire, 'Newtown link road, St Margaret's' in *Excavations 1999*, p. 92.

Walsh, Claire, 'Archaeological excavations at the abbey of St Thomas the Martyr, Dublin' in Duffy (ed.), *Medieval Dublin I* (2000), pp 185–202.

Walsh, Claire, 'Dublin's southern town defences, tenth to fourteenth centuries: the evidence from Ross Road' in Duffy (ed.), *Medieval Dublin II* (2001), pp 88–127.

Walsh, Claire, 'The Island/Martin's Row, Chapelizod' in *Excavations 2002*, p. 135.

Walsh, Claire, 'Archaeological excavation of the Anglo-Norman waterfront at Strand Street Great, Dublin' in Duffy (ed.), *Medieval Dublin VI* (2005), pp 160–87.

Walsh, Claire, 'Chancery Lane, Dublin' in *Excavations 2003*, p. 125.

Walsh, Claire, 'Eircom Depot, Mill Street, Dublin' in *Excavations 2004*, p. 126.

Walsh, Claire, 'Town Moat, Nicholas St., Dublin 2'. Unpublished report. DEHLG file 91E0016 [n.d.].

Walsh, Claire, 'Back Lane, Dublin'. Unpublished report. DEHLG file 92E0005 [n.d.].

Walsh, Claire, '30–32 Earl St. South, Dublin'. Unpublished report. DEHLG file 95E0041 [n.d.].

Walsh, Claire, 'Archaeological excavation of a development site to the south-east of St Maelruan's, Tallaght, Co. Dublin'. Unpublished report. DEHLG file 96E0188 [n.d.].

Walsh, Claire, '123–133 Francis Street/1–4 Swift's Alley, Dublin'. Unpublished reports. DEHLG files 96E0349 and 97E0129 [n.d.].

Walsh, Claire, '2–5 Meath Market, South Earl Street, Dublin'. Unpublished report. DEHLG file 96E0357 [n.d.].

Walsh, Claire, 'Francis Street'. Unpublished reports. DEHLG files 96E0349 and 97E0129 [n.d.].

Walsh, Claire, 'John Dillon Street, Dublin'. Unpublished report. DEHLG file 98E0158 [n.d.].

Walsh, Claire, '17–35 Carman's Hall (odd nos. only)/1–7 Ash Street/33–34 Garden Lane, Dublin'/ 'Carman's Hall, Dublin'. Unpublished report. DEHLG file 98E0254/99R0002 [n.d.].

Walsh, Claire, 'Newtown Link Road, St Margaret's'. Unpublished report. DEHLG file 99E0028 [n.d.].

Walsh, Claire, 'Turvey Avenue, Donabate'. Unpublished report. DEHLG file 99E0690 [n.d.].

Walsh, Claire, '95–7 Francis Street, Dublin'. Unpublished report. DEHLG file 99E0692 [n.d.].

Walsh, Claire, 'Mark's Alley, Dublin'. Unpublished report. DEHLG file 01E1142 [n.d.].

Walsh, Fintan, and John Harrison, 'Early medieval enclosure at Killickaweeny, Co. Kildare', *AI*, 17:1 (spring 2003), 33–6.

Walsh, Nessa, 'Pre-Romanesque churches in County Dublin and its hinterland: the Golden Ratio' in Duffy (ed.), *Medieval Dublin VIII* (2008), pp 21–35.

Walton, Steve (ed.), *Wind and water in the Middle Ages: fluid technologies from antiquity to the Renaissance*. Tempe, AZ, 2006.

Warhurst, Margaret, *Merseyside county museums: ancient British issues and later coins from English, Irish and Scottish mints to 1279, with associated foreign coins*. London, 1982.

Waterman, D.M., 'Medieval pottery from Dalkey Island' in Liversage, 'Excavations at Dalkey Island' (1968), 55–234.

Waterman, D.M., 'Somersetshire and other foreign building stone in medieval Ireland, *c*.1175–1400', *UJA*, 33 (1970), 63–75.

Watt, J.A., 'John Colton, justiciar of Ireland (1382) and archbishop of Armagh (1383–1404)' in Lydon (ed.), *England and Ireland in the later Middle Ages* (1981), pp 196–213.

Watt, J.A., 'Approaches to the history of fourteenth-century Ireland' in Cosgrove (ed.), *A new history of Ireland: II* (1993), pp 303–13.

Watt. J.A., 'Gaelic polity and cultural identity' in Cosgrove (ed.), *A new history of Ireland: II* (1993), pp 314–51.

Watt, J.A., 'The Anglo-Irish colony under strain, 1327–99' in Cosgrove (ed.), *A new history of Ireland: II* (1993), pp 352–96.

Watt, J.A., J.B. Morrall and F.X. Martin (eds), *Medieval studies presented to Aubrey Gwynn, S.J.* Dublin, 1961.

Webb, J.J., *The guilds of Dublin*. Dublin, 1929.

Webb, J.J., 'Translation of a French metrical history of the deposition of King Richard the Second', *Archaeologia*, 20 (1824), 45, 308–9.

Went, A.E.J., 'Irish fishery weirs II: the Duncannon weir', *JRSAI*, 78 (1948), 1–4.

Went, A.E.J., 'Fisheries of the River Liffey: notes on the Corporation fishery up to the Dissolution of the monasteries', *JRSAI*, 83 (1953), 163–73; repr. in Clarke (ed.), *Medieval Dublin: the living city* (1990), pp 182–91.

Went, A.E.J., 'Fisheries of the River Liffey II: notes on the Corporation fishery from the time of the Dissolution of the monasteries', *JRSAI*, 84 (1954), 41–58.

Westropp, T.J., 'The churches of Dunsany and Skreen, Co. Meath', *JRSAI*, 24 (1894), 222–31.

Westropp, T.J., 'On Irish mottes and early Norman castles', *JRSAI*, 34 (1904), 313–45.

Westropp, T.J., 'Clare Island Survey: history and archaeology', *PRIA*, 31 (1911–15 [1911]), section 1, pt 2, 1–78.

Westropp, T.J., 'Earthwork near Curtlestown, Co. Wicklow', *JRSAI*, 43 (1913), 185–6.

Westropp, T.J., 'The promontory forts and adjoining remains in Leinster: part I, Co. Dublin', *JRSAI*, 52 (1922), 52–76.

White, K.D., *Roman farming*. London, 1970.

White, N.B. (ed.), *The Red Book of Ormond*. Dublin, 1932.

White, N.B., 'The annals of Dudley Loftus', *Analecta Hibernia*, 10–11 (1941), 223–4.

White, N.B. (ed.), *The 'Dignitas Decani' of St Patrick's Cathedral, Dublin*. Dublin, 1957.

Wilde, W.R., *The beauties of the Boyne, and its tributary, the Blackwater*. Dublin, 1849.

Wilde, W.R., *A descriptive catalogue of the antiquities of stone, earthen and vegetable materials* [1857], *Animal materials* [1861] *and gold* [1862], *in the museum of the Royal Irish Academy*. Dublin, 1857, 1861, 1862.

Wilde, W.R., 'On the Scandinavian antiquities lately discovered at Islandbridge, near Dublin', *PRIA*, 10 (1866–9), 13–22.

Wilde, W.R., 'Memoir of Gabriel Beranger and his labours in the cause of Irish art, literature and antiquities from 1760 to 1780', *JRSAI*, 12 (1870–1), 33–64.

Williams, Bernadette, 'The Dominican annals of Dublin' in Duffy (ed.), *Medieval Dublin II* (2001), pp 142–68.

Williams, Bernadette (ed.), *The annals of Ireland by Friar John Clyn*. Dublin, 2007.

Williams, James, 'Coin finds and hoards from Dumfriesshire and Galloway', *Numismatic Chronicle*, 78 (1970), 288–9, 388–9, 442–4, 491–3.

Wilson, C.A., *Food and drink in Britain*. London, 1973.

Wincott Heckett, Elizabeth, 'Textiles, cordage, basketry and raw fibre' in Hurley and Scully with McCutcheon (eds), *Late Viking-Age and medieval Waterford* (1997), pp 743–60.

Witney, K.P., 'The woodland economy of Kent, 1066–1348', *AHS*, 38 (1990), 20–39.

Wood, Herbert, 'The Templars in Ireland', *PRIA*, 26 (1906–7), 327–77.

Wood, Herbert (ed.), *Court book of the liberty of Saint Sepulchre, 1586–1590*. Dublin, 1930.

Wood, Herbert, 'Court book of the liberty of Saint Sepulchre', *JRSAI*, 61 (1931), 202.

Wood, Herbert, and A.E. Langman (eds) and M.C. Griffith (rev.), *Calendar of justiciary rolls, or proceedings in the court of the justiciar of Ireland, I–VII years of Edward II*. Dublin, 1956.

Woolf, Alex, 'Amlaíb Cuarán and the Gael, 941–81' in Duffy (ed.), *Medieval Dublin III* (2002), pp 34–43.

Woolgar, C.M. (ed.), *Household accounts from medieval England*. 2 vols, Oxford, 1992.

Woolgar, C.M., *The great household in late medieval England*. New Haven, CT and London, 1999.

Wren, Joanna, 'Crested ridge tiles from medieval towns in Leinster, 1200–1500AD', MA, UCD, 1987.

Wren, Joanna, 'Roof tiles' in Walsh, *Archaeological excavations at Patrick, Nicholas and Winetavern Streets* (1997), pp 149–52.

Wren, Joanna, 'Roofing tiles and slates' in Halpin, *The port of medieval Dublin* (2000), pp 139–41.

Wren, Joanna, 'Roof tiles' in McMahon, 'Bride Street' (2002), 97–8.

Wren, Joanna, 'Clay building material' in Simpson, 'Dublin's southern frontier under siege: Kindlestown Castle' (2003), pp 353–4.

Wren, Joanna, *Floor-tiles: a guide to the medieval and nineteenth-century floor tiles of Christ Church Cathedral, Dublin*. Dublin, 2003.

Wren, Joanna, 'The roof tiles' in Hayden, 'Arran Quay' (2004), 198–9.

Wren, Joanna, 'Appendix H: medieval and post-medieval roof tiles' in McCutcheon, *Medieval pottery from Wood Quay* (2006), pp 177–95.

Wren, Joanna, 'The roof tiles' in Alan Hayden, *Excavations at the Cornmarket, Dublin*. Forthcoming.

Wren, Joanna, 'The roof tiles' in Ann Lynch and Conleth Manning, *Excavations at Dublin Castle*. Forthcoming.

Wren, Joanna, 'The roof tiles' in Claire Walsh, *Excavations at Hanbury Lane, Dublin*. Forthcoming.

Wren, Joanna, 'The roof tiles' in Linzi Simpson, *Excavations at Temple Bar West (Essex Street), Dublin*. Forthcoming.

Wren, Joanna, 'The roof tiles' in Martin Reid, *Excavations at Meeting House Square, Dublin*. Forthcoming.

Wren, Joanna, 'The roof tiles' in Mary McMahon, *Excavations at the Four Courts, Dublin*. Forthcoming.

Zupko, R.E., *A dictionary of weights and measures for the British Isles: the Middle Ages to the twentieth century*. Philadelphia, 1985.

Glossary

advowson	the right to present a vicar or rector to a church or ecclesiastical benefice
appurtenance	object or right attached to a piece of land, house etc.
arthropathy	joint disease
assart	piece of forest or wasteland brought into arable cultivation
betagh	unfree manorial tenant, almost invariably Irish
black-rents	rents extracted under duress as a form of protection money
brew-house	a building in which the primary activity was brewing beer
caprovine	term used to refer to sheep and goats collectively. The two species are notoriously difficult to tell apart on the basis of skeletal remains alone
carucate	a variable measure of land representing as much as could be tilled with one plough in a year. In medieval Ireland there are documented instances of a carucate comprising 120 acres
collegiate	pertaining to a collegiate church, which was an establishment or college for secular priests
coprolite	fossilised dung
corrodian	lay person who paid to lodge in private accommodation within a monastic precinct. The detailed arrangement for their meals and lodging was called a corrody
crannock	measure of grain that is sometimes stated to be the same as the English quarter. The crannock of wheat contained eight pecks and the crannock of oats sixteen pecks
demesne	that part of a manor comprising the chief residence of the lord and the land farmed by him or on his behalf
distrain	to compel the payment of rents or fines by the seizure and detention of chattels known as distraints
escheats	lands or possessions which revert to the lord or the crown when the holder dies without heirs or is outlawed for treason
estover	the privilege allowed to certain tenants to take from the lord's wood what was required for fuel and general repairs to dwellings and fences
farm	fixed payment for the letting of land, mills, tithes etc. Manorial tenants who lease land by the year are often called farmers
felsite	very fine-grained volcanic/igneous rock composed mostly of feldspar and quartz
feoffees	people who received grants of lands to hold in return for services
fief	land held by a tenant in chief from his lord in return for service which was usually military
fosse	a long narrow trench or excavation, especially in a fortification
galley	large ship propelled by oarsmen and usually used for warfare

garderobe	latrine, usually in a castle
hastivell	an early ripening variety of barley, probably sown in the winter
honour price	under Brehon Law, the price paid in compensation for killing or damaging a person. The higher a person's position in society, the higher their honour price
hundred court	court with jurisdiction over the English territorial division known as the 'hundred'
kame (glacial)	irregularly shaped hill or mound composed of sand, gravel and till that accumulates in a depression on a retreating glacier and is deposited on the land when the glacier melts
leat	an open watercourse conducting water to a mill etc.
littoral	of or on the shore of the sea or a lake; a region lying along a shore
machicolation	opening between supporting corbels for dropping stones etc. on attackers
maslin	a mixed crop of wheat and rye
murage charter	a document that gave permission for tax (on goods traded at urban markets) to be collected in order to raise funds for the construction and maintenance of the town's defences
murrain	unspecific livestock disease
night soil	human faeces
otolith	tiny sensory organs that can be used to identify fish species, and in some cases to determine the age of the fish
pipe rolls	records of the yearly audits made by the exchequer which were rolled into a tight roll resembling a pipe
putlog	small holes to support the ends of logs or timber beams in the walls of buildings, especially in the Middle Ages
relict	an object surviving in its primitive form
scutage	money payment made in lieu of performing military service
seised (of)	in possession of land in a formal feudal sense
shrievalty	the office or term of office of a sheriff or the area administered by a sheriff
stang	variable measure of land which appears from the records to be less than half an acre
stockfish	unsalted fish, especially cod, dried by sun and wind on wooden racks or in special drying houses
suit of court	the duty of a tenant to attend the courts held by the lord of his manor
toponymy	the study of the place-names of a region
tufa	a variety of limestone
turbary	a place where peat is dug
villein	in England, an unfree manorial tenant liable to perform labour services
virgate	variable measure of land which appears from the records to be less than a stang
wether	a castrated adult male sheep

Index